LET'S GO:

GREECE & TURKEY

is the best book for anyone traveling on a budget. Here's why:

■ No other guidebook has as many budget listings.

In Greece & Turkey we list over 4,500 budget travel bargains. We tell you the cheapest way to get around, and where to get an inexpensive and satisfying meal once you've arrived. We give hundreds of money-saving tips that anyone can use, plus invaluable advice on discounts and deals for students, children, families, and senior travelers.

■ Let's Go researchers have to make it on their own.

Our Harvard-Radcliffe researcher-writers travel on budgets as tight as your own—no expense accounts, no free hotel rooms.

■ Let's Go is completely revised each year.

We don't just update the prices, we go back to the place. If a charming café has become an overpriced tourist trap, we'll replace the listing with a new and better one.

■ No other guidebook includes all this:

Honest, engaging coverage of both the cities and the countryside; up-to-the-minute prices, directions, addresses, phone numbers, and opening hours; in-depth essays on local culture, history, and politics; comprehensive listings on transportation between and within regions and cities; straight advice on work and study, budget accommodations, sights, nightlife, and food; detailed city and regional maps; and much more.

■ Let's Go is for anyone who wants to see Greece & Turkey on a budget.

LET'S GO PUBLICATIONS

Let's Go: Alaska & The Pacific Northwest
Let's Go: Britain & Ireland
Let's Go: California
Let's Go: Central America
Let's Go: Eastern Europe
Let's Go: Europe
Let's Go: France
Let's Go: Germany
Let's Go: Greece & Turkey
Let's Go: Ireland
Let's Go: Israel & Egypt
Let's Go: Italy
Let's Go: London
Let's Go: Mexico
Let's Go: New York City
Let's Go: Paris
Let's Go: Rome
Let's Go: Southeast Asia
Let's Go: Spain & Portugal
Let's Go: Switzerland & Austria
Let's Go: USA
Let's Go: Washington, D.C.

Map Guides (coming March 1996)

Let's Go: Boston
Let's Go: London
Let's Go: New York City
Let's Go: Paris
Let's Go: San Francisco
Let's Go: Washington, D.C.

LET'S GO

The Budget Guide to

GREECE & TURKEY 1996

Marios Veletzas Broustas
Editor

Nathaniel Brann Riley
Associate Editor

Cynthia J. Soto
Assistant Editor

MACMILLAN

HELPING LET'S GO

If you want to share your discoveries, suggestions, or corrections, please drop us a line. We read every piece of correspondence, whether a postcard, a 10-page e-mail, or a coconut. All suggestions are passed along to our researcher-writers. Please note that mail received after May 1996 may be too late for the 1997 book, but will be retained for the following edition.

Address mail to:

Let's Go: Greece & Turkey
Let's Go, Inc.
One Story Street
Cambridge, MA 02138
USA

Send e-mail to:

fanmail@letsgo.com
Subject: "Let's Go: Greece & Turkey"

Visit Let's Go at:

http://www.letsgo.com/

In addition to the invaluable travel advice our readers share with us, many are kind enough to offer their services as researchers or editors. Unfortunately, the charter of Let's Go, Inc. enables us to employ only currently enrolled Harvard-Radcliffe students.

Published in Great Britain 1996 by Macmillan Reference Books, a division of Macmillan Publishers Limited, 25 Eccleston Place, London SW1W 9NF and Basingstoke

10 9 8 7 6 5 4 3 2 1

Map revisions pp. 38-39, 68-69, 87, 192, 267, 321, 375, 415, 433, 459, 521, 541 by Let's Go, Inc.

Published in the United States of America by St. Martin's Press, Inc.

ISBN: 0 333 65290 8

Let's Go: Greece & Turkey is written by Let's Go Publications, 1 Story Street, Cambridge, MA 02138, USA.

Printed in the USA on recycled paper with biodegradable soy ink.

About Let's Go

THIRTY-SIX YEARS OF WISDOM

Back in 1960, a few students at Harvard University banded together to produce a 20-page pamphlet offering a collection of tips on budget travel in Europe. This modest, mimeographed packet was offered to passengers as an extra on their student charter flights to Europe. The following year, students traveling to Europe researched the first full-fledged edition of *Let's Go: Europe*, a pocket-sized book featuring irreverent write-ups of sights and a decidedly youthful slant. Throughout the 60s, our guides reflected the times; one section of the 1968 *Let's Go: Europe* discussed "Street Singing in Europe on No Dollars a Day," which we said "has very little to do with music." The 1969 guide to America led off with sound advice on San Francisco's Haight-Ashbury ("dig the scene"). During the 70s and 80s, we gradually added regional and city guides, and expanded coverage into the Middle East, Central America, and Asia.

We've seen a lot in 36 years. *Let's Go: Europe* is now the world's best-selling international guide, translated into seven languages. And our guides are still researched, written, and produced entirely by students who know first-hand how to see the world on the cheap. As the budget travel world expands, so does Let's Go. The first editions of *Let's Go: Central America* and *Let's Go: Southeast Asia* hit the shelves this year, and *Let's Go: India & Nepal* is right on their heels. Our useful new series of map guides combine concise city coverage with vivid fold-out maps. Our new guides bring our total number of titles, with their spirit of adventure and their honesty, accuracy, and editorial integrity, to 28.

HOW WE DO IT

Each guide is completely revised and updated every year by a well-traveled set of 200 students, who work on all aspects of each guide's development. Every winter, we recruit over 110 researchers and 50 editors to write our books anew. After several months of training, Researcher-Writers hit the road for seven weeks of exploration, from Anchorage to Ankara, Estonia to El Salvador, Iceland to Indonesia. Those hired possess a rare combination of budget travel sense, writing ability, stamina, and courage. Train strikes, stolen luggage, food poisoning, and irate tourist officials are all part of a day's work. Editors work from spring to fall, massaging copy written on Himalayan bus rides into witty yet informative prose. A student staff of typesetters, cartographers, publicists, and managers keeps our lively and sophisticated team together. In September, the collected efforts of the summer are delivered to our printer, who turns them into books in record time. And even as you read this, work on next year's editions is well underway.

WHY WE DO IT

At Let's Go, our goal is to give you a great vacation. We don't think of budget travel as the last recourse of the destitute; we believe that it's the only way to travel. Living cheaply and simply brings you closer to the real people and places you've been saving up to visit. Our book will ease your anxieties and answer your questions about the basics—to help you get off the beaten track and explore. Once you learn the ropes, we encourage you to put Let's Go away now and then to strike out on your own. As any seasoned traveler will tell you, the best discoveries are often those you make yourself. When you find something worth sharing, drop us a line. We're Let's Go Publications, One Story Street, Cambridge, MA 02138, USA (e-mail: LetsGo@delphi.com).

HAPPY TRAVELS!

Contents

Maps

Researcher-Writers

Ethel Bonn *Crete, Cyprus, Dodecanese*
Throughout her travels, Eti carried herself with true style and grace. Although she is not a native Greek, she embraced the country's spirit with unusual enthusiasm and sincerity. She never did get that tattoo of Rhodes, but we forgive her because we are sure she picked up a few new *bouzouki* tunes along the way, which she'll share with us. Eti's trek confirmed her love for Crete and she cheerfully discovered the charms of the "other" Mediterranean island. Στην υγεια σου Ετι.

Lisa Cloutier *Ionian Islands, Northeast Aegean Islands, Northern Greece*
When Lisa first landed in Greece, she was armed only with her researcher-writer training manual and and several pairs of floral leggings. But while the crisp mountain air of Northern Greece did not cool her warm personality, her travels enhanced her already remarkable sensitivity and understanding of local cultures. Lisa's insightful copy was as refreshing as a dip in the North Aegean, and her effortless prose as clear as the Macedonian sky. Complementing her peaceful demeanor, Lisa found a new love in these small villages.

Raphael Folsom *Aegean Coast, Black Sea Coast, Mediterranean Coast*
Raph used researching for *Let's Go* as his creative outlet. Eclectic and poetic prose backed up his far-ranging and comprehensive research. His quick and efficient pen raced from İznik to Kars, over hill and dale. Never before has there been an R-W who could present travel writing in such a variety of ways. Would that we could wax romantic about this wight's wonderful work. Wow.

Patrick Heavey *Cappadocia, Cyprus, Eastern Turkey, Mediterranean Coast, İstanbul*
He was featured in the pages of a Turkish fashion magazine and was the object of a cult's affection, but Patrick did not let his newfound fame go to his head. With a critical eye, and a full stomach, Patrick researched every *lokanta,* sweetshop, and gunshop—yes, gunshop—that Turkey has to offer. The bane of every swindling street vendor's existence, Patrick overcame bouts of cholera, dysentery, and the mumps to send back some of the most thorough research this side of the Green Line. Our own Irish icon, St. Patrick discovered paradise on Earth in his Turkish journey.

Tobias Kasper *Athens, Cyclades, Dodecanese, Sporades*
Even Medusa's stare could not prevent Toby from sending us his polished, witty, and insightful copy—although the capricious Greek ferry strikes came pretty close. Toby handled the often wearisome islands with the class of a professional. He uncovered hidden churches and secluded beaches, and pinpointed all the "in" clubs. In four words, Toby was great (all right, that's three but after Toby's effusive Ios copy, we couldn't count either).

Triada Stampas *Ionian Islands, Peloponnese*
Although fearless Triada traveled without inhibition throughout the Peloponnese, her ebullient laughter was never more than a phone call away. Even an earthquake could not shake her indomitable spirit whose warmth and caring enabled her to overcome obstacles that would stifle a lesser person. Instead, Triada always kept her calm and impressed us with her knack for endearing herself to the natives and digging up local lore beyond our wildest imaginations. Her carefully researched copy and entertaining marginalia truly reflected her good-natured resilience.

Acknowledgments

As a book team, we thank Haneen for her superior ME skills and great advice. Sean F. for pinch-MEing, Timur for on-going consulting, the Domestic Room and everyone in the office staff for their support. Thanks also to super-interns Joy and Carlene, and to Eleni Gage and Liz Theran for their advice. Special thanks to Production.

Nat, thanks for being my counterweight; I know the guide has benefited and I'm sure we'll continue to learn from each other. Cindy, after a summer of chatter, you can still smile. Thanks for your unrelenting work and friendship. Domestics, thanks for the laughs; Pat, what would I have done without your e-mail? SoRelle, I'm glad we can share. Jay, thanks for the mental release lunches. Celeste, Jed, Tim, Nadim, Salesfolk, thanks for the summer. V stands for Voutiro. M. Seuozwee. Love and unending gratitude to my three dads, γιαγια, παπου and, of course, μανουλι—**MVB**

Marios, you set an example in work and play, and in the balance between them. Gnothi seauton! Cindy, your constant productivity and enthusiasm inspired. I dedicate the fruits of this summer to Susan Montgomery Riley (Mom); you have always nurtured my interest in cultures and literature. Adam and Jay, you were great apartment-mates. Trina, HRST thanks for all the fun. Y'all inna office, thanks 2!—**NBR**

To Marios and Nat, endless thanks for your warm humor, enthusiasm, and patience. You were an amazing team. SoRelle et Tom (my other half), mercy buttercups for pardoning my French. Domestic Room, thanks for keeping things lively. MB, thanks for the lunches. To "The Gift" and Shabica woman, hummus and tabouli and Boku for being you. Yc-nan, Viv, and the wise ol' man, thanks for an excellent summer. To the block, a big hug. M&D, Ricky, Ling-Ling, love you. Cheers! —**CJS**

Editor	Marios Veletzas Broustas
Associate Editor	Nathaniel Brann Riley
Assistant Editor	Cynthia J. Soto
Managing Editor	Haneen M. Rabie
Publishing Director	Sean Fitzpatrick
Production Manager	Michael L. Cisneros
Associate Production Manager	Eunice C. Park
Cartography Manager	Samuel P. Trumbull
Associate Cartography Manager	Amanda K. Bean
Editorial Manager	Timothy S. Perlstein
Editorial Manager	Haneen M. Rabie
Financial Manager	Katarzyna Drozd
Personnel Manager	Sean K. Desmond
Publicity Manager	Timur Okay Harry Hiçyılmaz
Associate Publicity Manager	Eleni N. Gage
General Manager	Richard Olken
Assistant General Manager	Anne E. Chisholm
Office Coordinator	Jennifer L. Schuberth
Director of Advertising and Sales	Jean C. Anderson
Sales Assistant Manager	Sammy Lai
Sales Representatives	Matthew S. Abramson
	Delphine Gabbay, Godffrey Williams

How To Use This Book

As much as we like to think that we can make it on our own traveling in foreign countries, key bits of advice can make or break a vacation, especially in hassle-prone countries like Greece, Turkey, and Cyprus. Whether a first-time visitor or a veteran traveler, details like hospital phone numbers and candid accommodations listings always come in handy. This year, improved maps, a comprehensive index, and enhanced organization make *Let's Go: Greece and Turkey* more valuable than ever before.

While still in the planning stages of your trip, you may want to look at our new map of archaeological and Byzantine treasures in Greece and Western Turkey. Then, find appealing sights in the index. Or you could page through our regional introductions and read up on the cultures that have shaped the countries you will visit. Then again, you could just flip open the guide and let some interesting tidbit catch your eye. This year, we have included several gray boxes that highlight various aspects of these countries and offer yet another reason for embarking on your vacation today.

Our glossary provides a quick introduction to some basic phrases in Greek and Turkish, and the regional introductions offer important background information on not only customs and culture, but also country-specific conventions that are important to getting around. The Essentials section at the beginning of the guide outlines more general information you'll need before departing.

Destinations are grouped by geographic location to facilitate travel planning. Although extensive information about traveling within and among regions is provided, a useful technique is to use a larger city as a base for daytrips. Our coverage of larger cities is the most exhaustive and, often, services tend to be cheaper. From here you can venture out to some of the smaller towns that lie off the beaten path while still maintaining a high level of comfort and safety.

Within each city, our accommodations, restaurants, clubs, and even sights listings are in the order of what our researchers, in their opinion, have deemed best. We provide detailed prices, hours of operation, street addresses, directions, and phone numbers so that you can plan a detailed itinerary ahead of time. While the capricious nature of schedules in Greece, Turkey, and Cyprus render perfect planning impossible, we provide you with tools to find the information you will need. We wish you safe and happy travels and, without further ado: Let's Go!

A NOTE TO OUR READERS

The information for this book is gathered by Let's Go researchers during the summer months. Each listing is derived from the assigned researcher's opinion based upon his or her visit at a particular time. The opinions are expressed in a candid and forthright manner. Other travelers might disagree. Those traveling at a different time may have different experiences since prices, dates, hours, and conditions are always subject to change. You are urged to check beforehand to avoid inconvenience and surprises. Travel always involves a certain degree of risk, especially in low-cost areas. When traveling, especially on a budget, you should always take particular care to ensure your safety.

ESSENTIALS

Greece, Turkey, and Cyprus are legendary—countries that contain within their cultures, architecture, and even their geography the history of ancient civilizations and mighty empires. Centuries of foreign domination and domestic greatness form a curious juxtaposition that shapes a segue into the modern world.

Tourism is a big business here. Major destinations provide a meta-touristic experience, but seclusion can also be found among ancient ruins, beaches, and remote mountain trails. Greece, Turkey, and Cyprus remain, through it all, relatively refreshing in their innocence.

Plan ahead to get the most out of your vacation, but understand that these countries may not always be accommodating of your itinerary. An astounding amount of travel information is available to best facilitate your trip; stop by your local travel agency or library (or look over the At-Home Resources section, p. 2), and find people who have recently traveled to the places that interest you. A few hours of letter writing and phone calling might yield a ton of pamphlets and maps. Draft a flexible itinerary to give yourself a rough sense of what you want to see.

A note on prices: throughout the guide, we quote prices effective in the summer of 1995. Since inflation and exchange rates fluctuate considerably, be advised that listed prices could rise by an additional 10-30% by 1996. Because inflation in Turkey generally keeps pace with the devaluation of the lira, prices are quoted in U.S. dollars and should be slightly more stable than those in Greece.

PLANNING YOUR TRIP

■■■ WHEN TO GO

Summer is high tourist season in Greece; if you visit between late July and early September, expect to run with large groups. If you feel annoyed by crowds or taxed by the frantic pace of summer travel, consider visiting during off-season (Sept.-May), when inexpensive airfares are easier to obtain and lodging is cheaper. Some facilities and sights may close down, but residents are often more receptive and the weather is far more pleasant. Even during the winter months, some areas continue to be mild. Greece also has winter sports, with ski areas at Parnassos, Mt. Pelion, Metsovo, and elsewhere in northern Greece. But always-changeable ferry schedules become more capricious in winter. Mainland travel is less affected by season.

Climate in Turkey varies substantially. The Mediterranean and Aegean coasts are known for being extremely hot and dry during July and August; in central and eastern Anatolia, winter cold and summer heat are severe. Coastal regions are in general most pleasant and least crowded in the spring and autumn. The Black Sea coast, moderate almost all year, contains areas where rain falls 200 days per year.

Cyprus is at its most attractive from March to mid-June, and from September through November. Summer, especially in Nicosia, can be hot and dry. Troodos, the rainiest part of the island, usually receives snow between January and March. Because temperatures at higher altitudes can drop quickly at night even during summer, if you plan to do extensive camping, be sure to dress warmly

	January	April	July	October
Athens	12°C (54°F)	19°C (66°F)	33°C (91°F)	23°C (73°F)
Thessaloniki	8°C (46°F)	19°C (66°F)	32°C (90°F)	21°C (70°F)
Ankara	0°C (32°F)	11°C (52°F)	23°C (73°F)	13°C (55°F)
Antalya	10°C (50°F)	16°C (61°F)	28°C (82°F)	20°C (68°F)
İstanbul	5°C (41°F)	12°C (54°F)	23°C (73°F)	16°C (61°F)
Trabzon	6°C (43°F)	11°C (52°F)	22°C (72°F)	15°C (59°F)
Cyprus	12°C (54°F)	17°C (63°F)	26°C (79°F)	22°C (72°F)

■■■ AT-HOME RESOURCES

The following organizations and agencies offer a wealth of information. If you don't know where to begin, write a few polite letters. Calling offices directly (or faxing, if you have the means) is always an option and necessary if you're in a rush. Calling usually works best if your questions are general (i.e. "send me stuff on Greece") or exceptionally specific (i.e. "send me updated ferry routes between Cyprus and Rhodes"). Anything in between (i.e. "send me information on museums in İstanbul") is likely to drain your informant's patience.

GOVERNMENT INFORMATION OFFICES

Greek National Tourist Organization (GNTO): In Australia, Third floor, 51-57 Pitt St., Sydney, NSW 2000 (tel. (2) 241 16 63; fax 235 2174). **In Canada,** Head Office, 1300 Bay St., Toronto, Ont. M5R 3K8 (tel. (416) 968-2220; fax 968-6533); 1233 rue de la Montagne, Suite 101, Montréal, Québec, H3G 1Z2 (tel. (514) 871-1535; fax 871-1498). **In Great Britain,** 4 Conduit St., London W1R 0DJ (tel. (171) 734 5997; fax 287 1369). **In U.S.,** Head Office, Olympic Tower, 645 Fifth Ave., 5th Floor, New York, NY 10022 (tel. (212) 421-5777; fax 826-6940); 168 N. Michigan Ave., 6th floor, Chicago, IL 60601 (tel. (312) 782-1084; fax 782-1091); 611 W. Sixth St. #2198, Los Angeles, CA 90017 (tel. (213) 626-6696; fax 489-9744). Provides pamphlets on different regions and tourist literature, including the booklet *General Information About Greece.*

Greek Press and Information Office: In Australia, Suite 103, Stanhill Bldg., 34 Queens Rd., Melbourne 3004 (tel. (3) 867 2737; fax 866 4793). **In Canada,** 80 MacLaren St., Ottawa, Ont. K2P OK6 (tel. (613) 232-6796). **In U.S.,** 601 Fifth Ave., 3rd floor, New York, NY 10017 (tel. (212) 751-8788; fax 752-2056). Provides info on cultural offerings and political & economic developments in Greece.

Turkish Cultural and Information Office: In Australia, Suite 101, 280 George St., Sydney, NSW 2000 (tel. (2) 223 3055; fax 223 3204). **In Canada,** 360 Albert St., Suite 801, Ottawa, Ontario K1R 7X7 (tel. (613) 230-8654; fax 230-3683). **In Great Britain,** First floor, 170-173 Piccadilly, London, W1V 9DD (tel. (71) 355 4207; fax 491 0773). **In U.S.,** Turkish Centre (also Turkish Consulate General), 821 United Nations Plaza, New York, NY 10017 (tel. (212) 687-2194, -5, or -6; fax 599-7568); 1717 Massachusetts Ave. NW, Suite 306, Washington, DC 20036 (tel. (202) 429-9844; fax 429-5649). Other offices are located around the world. Supplies general info and will send you maps and regional brochures.

Cyprus Tourism Organization, P.O. Box 4535, Melkonian Building, 19 Leof. Lemesou, Nicosia, Cyprus (tel. (2) 33 77 15). **In Great Britain,** 213 Regent St., London W1R 8DA (tel. (171) 734 9822; fax 287 6534). **In U.S.,** 13 E. 40th St., New York, NY 10016 (tel. (212) 683-5280; fax 683-5282). Ask for a copy of the comprehensive *Cyprus Travellers Handbook*.

READING UP

Adventurous Traveler Bookstore, P.O. Box 577, Hinesburg, VT 05461 (tel. and fax both 800-282-3963 or 802-482-3546; email books@atbook.com; WWW http://www.gorp.com/atbook.htm). Books and maps.

Bon Voyage!, 2069 W. Bullard Ave., Fresno, CA 93711-1200 (tel. (800) 995-9716; outside U.S. (209) 447-8441); email 70754.3511@compuserve.com). Annual mail order catalog offers an amazing range of products.

Forsyth Travel Library, P.O. Box 2975, Shawnee Mission, KS 66201 (tel. (800) 367-7984). Mail-order w/maps, rail, ferry schedules and *Thomas Cook Timetable*.

Hippocrene Books, Inc., 171 Madison Ave., New York, NY 10016 (tel. (212) 685-4371, orders (718) 454-2366; fax (718) 454-1391). Reference, language guides.

Hunter Publishing, 300 Raritan Center Parkway, Edison, NJ 08818 (908-225-1900; fax 417-0482). Language tapes, maps, and wide selection of travel guides.

Travel Books & Language Center, 4931 Cordell Ave., Bethesda, MD 20814 (tel. (800) 220-2665; fax (301) 951-8546). Atlases, cassettes, wide selection of maps.

Wide World Books and Maps, 1911 N. 45th St., Seattle, WA 98103 (tel. (206) 634-3453; fax 634-0558, email travelbk@nwlink.com). Travel accessories.

GETTING IT ON-LINE

There is a vast amount of information available through the international computer network known as the **Internet.** Some commercial providers, such as America Online, CompuServe, and Prodigy offer sophisticated services like on-line airline reservations. Most universities and many businesses offer students and employees access to the Internet. Commercial gateways provide Internet access to the general public for a monthly fee (usually US$20-30).

One primary means of transmission and discussion of information across the Internet are forums known collectively as Usenet, and individually as **newsgroups.** A basic news-reading program can be accessed on most UNIX systems by typing "rn."

There are various mailing lists that provide messages related to travel, either generally or to a specific area. A good list to start from is the "Travel-L" list. Subscribe by e-mailing "listserv@mv3090.ege.edu.tr". Leave the subject blank; in the body of the message, type "subscribe travel-l <firstname> <lastname>". To receive regular **Greek news** (free), subscribe to "cosmos@panix.com". **Internet Relay Chat** (IRC) allows actual (typed) conversation with users around the world. The number and nature of the "channels" available is more variable than for newsgroups, but you're quite likely to find discussions on travel. Like newsgroups, IRC is virtually unsupervised. From most systems, type "irc" and then type "/help newuser".

Three of the other services available on the Internet are **FTP** (file transfer protocol), **gopher,** and the **World Wide Web** (WWW); each can be used to obtain files and other info. A particularly useful archive is rec-travel at ftp.cc.umanitoba.ca; it includes travelogues and U.S. State Department Advisories. Use your WWW browser to check out the handy CIA World Factbook; point to "http://www.ic.gof/94fact/fb94toc/fb94toc.html". For an archive of **Turkish newspaper summaries** in English, German, or Turkish, type "gopher knidos.cc.metu.edu.tr". These summaries cover every weekday for the past two years, through the past week. Many Internet resources are available through more than one method. The "Student and Budget Travel Resource Guide" lists a wide variety of online travel information. It is available through the WWW at "http://asa.ugl.lib.umich.edu/chdocs/travel/travel-guide.html"; or, send e-mail to "travel-guide@umich.edu".

■■■ PAPERWORK

File all applications weeks or months in advance. The agency might deem your applications inadequate and return them, so leave enough time to resubmit them. Apply off-season (August to December) for speedier service.

PASSPORTS

Citizens of Australia, Canada, Great Britain, Ireland, New Zealand, South Africa, and the U.S. all need valid passports to enter Greece, Turkey, and Cyprus, and to re-enter their own country. Some countries will not allow entrance if the holder's passport will expire in less than six months, and returning to the U.S. with an expired passport may result in a fine. If you plan a long stay, you may want to register your passport with the nearest embassy or consulate; notify them or the local police immediately if your passport is lost or stolen. Your consulate can then issue you a new passport or temporary traveling papers. If you lose your passport in İstanbul, first go to your consulate to get a citizen certificate, then to the tourist police.

Before you leave, as a safeguard, photocopy the page of your passport that contains your photograph and identifying information. (Especially important is your **passport number.**) Also, copy all the pages in your passport that are stamped with visas, and leave a duplicate with a friend. Consulates recommend that you carry an expired passport or an *official* copy of your birth certificate in a separate part of your luggage from other documents. U.S. citizens can request a duplicate birth certificate from the Bureau of Vital Records and Statistics in their region of birth.

Losing your passport can be a nightmare. A replacement may take weeks, and may be valid only for a limited time. Immediately notify the local police and the nearest embassy or consulate of your home government. Provide all the information that you had previously recorded and photocopied and show identification and proof of citizenship. Some consulates issue new passports within two days. In an emergency, ask for immediate temporary traveling papers that will permit you to return to your home country.

Remember, your passport is a public document that belongs to your nation's government. You may have to surrender your passport to a foreign government official; if you don't get it back in a reasonable time, inform the nearest mission, consulate, or embassy of your home country.

Applying for a passport generally involves furnishing a birth certificate, for proof of citizenship, and two identical passport photos.

Australia: You must apply in person at a post office, a passport office, or an Australian diplomatic mission; an appointment may be necessary. A parent may file an application for a child who is under 18. Call toll-free (in Australia) 13 12 32.

Canada: Applications are available at all post offices and most travel agencies. Processing takes approximately five business days for in-person applications and three weeks for mailed ones. For 24-hr. info, call (800) 567-6868 from Canada, 973-3251 from Metro Toronto, or 283-2152 from Montreal; or refer to the booklet *Bon Voyage, But...,* available free of charge from any passport office or from Info-Export (BPTE), External Affairs, Ottawa, Ont., K1A OG2.

Great Britain: Apply in person or by mail to a passport office, located in London, Liverpool, Newport, Peterborough, Glasgow, or Belfast. Forms are also available from main post offices (in Northern Ireland from any local office of the DSS). Processing by mail usually takes 4-6 weeks; the London office offers same-day walk-in rush service. Extensions can be obtained at the nearest British high commission or consulate.

Ireland: Applications available at local Garda stations, or from the Department of Foreign Affairs, Passport Office, Setanta Centre, Molesworth St., Dublin 2 (tel. (1) 671 1633). Express service, available from post offices, has 2-week turn-around.

New Zealand: Application forms must be obtained from your local Link Centre, travel agent, or New Zealand Representative; they must then be completed and mailed to the New Zealand Passport Office, Documents of National Identity Division, Department of Internal Affairs, Box 10-526, Wellington (tel. (04) 474 81 00). Overseas citizens should send the passport application to the nearest embassy, high commission, or consulate that is authorized to issue passports. Standard processing time is 10 working days from receipt of completed application.

South Africa: Applications available at any Department of Home Affairs Office.

United States: Apply at any clerk of court or post office authorized to accept passport applications, or at a U.S. Passport Agency. You must apply in person if this is your first passport, if you're under age 18, or if your current passport is more than 12 years old or was issued before your 18th birthday. For more info, call the U.S. Passport Information's 24-hr. recorded message (tel. (202) 647-0518) which offers general information, agency locations, business hours, etc. For inquiries regarding the processing of your passport, write to: National Passport Center, 31 Rochester Avenue, Portsmouth, NH, 03801 or call (603) 334-0500.

EMBASSIES AND CONSULATES

Greek Embassy: In Australia, 9 Turrana St., Yarralumla, Canberra, ACT 2600 (tel. (6) 273-3158; fax 273-2620). **In Canada,** 80 MacLaren St., Ottawa, Ont. K2P 0K6 (tel. (613) 238-6271; fax 238-5676). **In Great Britain,** 1A Holland Park, London W11 3TP (tel. (171) 229 3850; fax 229 7221). **In Ireland,** One Upper Pembroke St., Dublin 2 (tel. (1) 676-7254; fax 661-8892). **In South Africa,** 995 Pretorius St., Arcadia 0083, Pretoria (tel. (12) 437-352; fax 434-313). **In U.S.,** 2221 Mass. Ave. NW, Washington, DC 20008 (tel. (202) 939-5800; fax 939-5824).

Greek Consulates: In Australia, First floor, 366 King William St., **Adelaide** 5000, S.A. (tel. (8) 211-8066; fax 211 8820); Stanhill House, 34 Queens Road, **Melbourne** 3004, Vic. (tel. (3) 866-4524; fax 866-4933); 20th floor, 15 Castlereagh, **Sydney,** N.S.W. 2000 (tel. (2) 221-2388; fax 221-1423); 16 St. George's Terrace, **Perth,** W.A. 6000 (tel. (9) 325-6608; fax 325-2940). **In Canada,** 1170 Place du Frère André, 3rd floor, **Montréal,** Québec H3B 3C6 (tel. (514) 875-2119; fax 875-8781); 365 Blue St. E, Suite 1800, **Toronto,** Ont. M4W 3L4 (tel. (416) 515-0133; fax 515-0708); 1200 Burrard St., Suite 501, **Vancouver,** B.C. V6Z 2C7 (tel. (604) 681-1381; fax 681-6656). **In U.S.,** 69 East 79th St., **New York,** NY 10021 (tel. (212) 988-5500; fax 734-8492); 650 North St. Clair St., **Chicago,** IL 60611 (tel. (312) 335-3915; fax 335-3958); 2441 Gough St., **San Francisco,** CA 94123 (tel. (415) 775-2102; fax 776-6815); 12424 Wilshire Blvd., Suite 800, **Los Angeles,** CA 90025 (tel. (310) 826-5555; fax 826-8670); 86 Beacon St., **Boston,** MA 02108 (tel. (617) 523-0100; fax 523-0511); Tower Place, Suite 1670, 3340 Peachtree Rd. NE, **Atlanta,** GA 30326 (tel. (404) 261-3313; fax 262-2798); 1360 Post Oak Blvd., Suite 2480, **Houston,** TX 77056 (tel. (713) 840-7522; fax 840-0614); World Trade Center, 2 Canal St., Suite 2318, **New Orleans,** LA 70130 (tel. (504) 523-1167; fax 524-5610). **In New Zealand,** 5-7 Willeston St., 10th floor, P.O. Box 24066, Wellington (tel. (4) 473-7775; fax 473-7441).

Turkish Embassy: In U.S., 1714 Mass. Ave. NW, Washington, DC 20036 (tel. (202) 659-0742). **In Canada,** 197 Wurtemburg St., Ottawa, Ont. K1N 8L9 (tel. (613) 789-4044; fax 230-3683). **In Great Britain,** 43 Belgrave Sq., London SW1 X8PA (tel. (171) 393 0202). **In Ireland,** 11 Clyde Rd. Ballsbridge, Dublin 4 (tel. (1) 668 5240). **In Australia,** 60 Muggaway, Red Hill ACT 2603 (tel. (6) 295 0227; fax 293 6592). **In New Zealand,** 15-17 Murphy St., P.O. Box 12248, Phthorndon-Wellington (tel. (4) 472-1290 or -2; fax 472-1277). **In South Africa,** 1067 Church St., Hatfield 0083 Pretoria (tel. (12) 342 6053), or P.O. Box 56014 Arcadia 0007.

Turkish Consulates: In U.S., 360 N. Michigan Ave. #1405, **Chicago,** IL 60601 (tel. (312) 263-1295); 4801 Wilshire Blvd. #310, **Los Angeles,** CA 90010 (tel. (213) 937-0110); 1990 Post Oak Blvd. #1300, **Houston, TX** 77056 (tel. (713) 622-5849; fax 623-6639.

Cypriot Embassy: In Australia, 30 Beale Crescent, Deakin-Canberra ACT 2600 (tel. (6) 281-0832, -4; fax 281-0860, -901). **In Canada,** Attn: Mr. Michael Paidoussis, Honorary Consul of Cyprus, 2930 Rue Edouard MontPetit, Ste. PH2, Montréal, Québec H3T 1J7 (tel. (514) 735-7233). **In Great Britain,** 93 Park St., London W1Y 4ET (tel. (71) 499 82 72; fax 491 0691). **In U.S.,** 2211 R St. NW, Washington, DC 20008 (tel. (202) 462-5772).

Northern Cyprus Representative Offices: In Canada, 300 John St., Suite 330, **Thornhill,** Ontario L3T 5W4 (tel. (416) 731-1458). **In Great Britain,** 28 Cockspur St., **London** SWIY 5BN (tel. (171) 839 4577; fax 839 5282). **In U.S.,** 821 United Nations Plaza, 6th floor, **New York,** NY 10017 (tel. (212) 687-2350; fax 949-6872); 1667 K St., Suite 690, **Washington,** DC 20006 (tel. (202) 887-6198; fax 467-0685).

VISAS

A visa is an endorsement that a foreign government stamps into a passport; it allows the bearer to stay in that country for a specified purpose and period of time. Citizens of the U.S., Canada, U.K., Ireland, Australia, New Zealand, and South Africa do not need to get a visa ahead of time to visit **Greece;** non-E.U. members will be automatically granted leave for a three-month stay. Apply to stay longer at least 20 days prior to the 3-month expiration date at the **Aliens Bureau,** 173 Alexandras Ave., Athens 11522 (tel. 646 8103, ext. 379), or check with a Greek embassy or consulate. Bona fide tourists with valid passports from Australia, Canada, Great Britain, Ireland, New Zealand, and the U.S. do not need a visa to enter Either Cyprus or Northern Cyprus for stays of up to 90 days. It is suggested that tourists wishing to stay longer leave and then re-enter. Citizens of Australia, Canada, and New Zealand do not need a visa for visits to **Turkey** of up to 3 months. South African nationals, who also do not require a visa, may stay up to one month. Three-month sticker visas are available for cash at ports of entry for citizens of the U.S. ($20), U.K. (£10), and Ireland.

CUSTOMS: ENTERING

Greece Upon entering Greece, you must declare cameras, typewriters, portable radios, and musical instruments. One of each may be brought in duty-free as long as they will be taken with you upon departure. You must also register all currency above $1000, or you may not take it with you when you leave. Duty-free limits include: 10kg of foodstuffs and beverages; 200 cigarettes, 50 cigars, or 250g tobacco; 5 boxes of matches; 2 packs of playing cards; and 1L of alcoholic beverage or 2L of wine. Children under 15 may bring in 5000dr worth of gift articles, everyone else up to 9000dr worth. One shotgun and 200 bullets may also be brought by non-citizens of Greece at least 18 years of age, provided they are declared for personal use; all other weapons and explosives are strictly prohibited. Prescription medications for personal use are the only admissible drugs, and even these may need to be accompanied by the prescription.

Turkey Travelers entering Turkey may bring along: one camera and five rolls of film, one personal stereo and 5 cassettes or compact discs, one video player or slide projector, and no more than 3 musical instruments (harmonica, mandolin, flageolet, flute, guitar, and accordion; no more than one of each kind); 200 cigarettes (or 50 cigars), 200g tobacco (or 50g chewing tobacco), 1kg coffee, 1.5kg instant coffee, 500g tea, 1kg chocolate, 1kg sweets, and five 100cc or seven 70cc bottles of spirits. In addition to these allowances, it is possible to purchase 400 cigarettes, 100 cigars, and 500g pipe tobacco from Turkish duty-free shops on entering the country. Gifts not to exceed 500 DM in value are also admissible duty-free. No sharp instruments or firearms of any sort may be brought in, and under *no circumstances* should you bring any illegal drugs into Turkey (see Drugs, p. 8). To avoid problems when you transport prescription drugs, ensure that the bottles are clearly marked, and carry a copy of the prescription to show the customs officer.

Cyprus Cyprus allows travelers to bring in duty-free not more than 250g tobacco, 1L spirits, ¾L wine, and 0.3L perfume. Other personal effects are permitted, up to a total value of C£50. Travelers importing more than $1000 worth of foreign currency should declare it on form D (NR), especially if they want to take it out of the country later. Illegal drugs, of course, are not to be imported.

CUSTOMS: GOING HOME

Upon returning home, you must declare all articles you acquired abroad and pay a duty on the value of those articles that exceeds the allowance established by your country's customs service. Holding onto **receipts** for purchases made abroad will help establish values when you return. It is absolutely forbidden to export antiques from Turkey, though shopkeepers may try to convince you otherwise. Customs officials may require, even as your plane is boarding for departure, that you produce a signed statement from a Turkish museum curator stating that the item is not an antique. If you purchase anything really old or potentially valuable, have the shopowner draft a signed statement saying that what you bought can be legally exported. Goods purchased at **duty-free shops** abroad are not exempt from duty or sales tax at your point of return; declare these items along with other purchases.

Australia There is no limit to the amount of **Australian** and/or foreign cash that may be brought into or taken out of Australia. However, amounts of A$5000 or more, or equivalent in foreign currency, must be reported. Each traveler over age 18 may bring into Australia 1.125L of liquor and 250 cigarettes or 250g of tobacco products duty/tax free. In addition, a duty/tax free per-person allowance of A$400 (under 18, A$200) is available for other goods intended as gifts. For further information contact the Australian Customs Service, 5 Constitution Ave., Canberra, ACT 2601 (tel. (6) 275-6255; fax 275-6989).

Canada Citizens who remain abroad for at least one week may bring back up to CDN $300 worth of goods duty-free once every calendar year; this amount can not be combined from various trips. Canadian citizens or residents who travel for a period between 48 hours and 6 days can bring back up to CDN$100 worth of goods. You are permitted to ship goods except tobacco and alcohol home under this exemption as long as you declare them when you arrive. Citizens over the legal age may import in-person up to 200 cigarettes, 50 cigars, 400g loose tobacco or tobacco sticks, 1.14L wine or alcohol, and 24 355ml cans/bottles beer; the value of these products is included in the CDN$300. For more info, write to Canadian Customs, 2265 St. Laurent Blvd., Ottawa, Ontario, K1G 4K3 (tel. (613) 993-0534). Or, from within Canada, call (800) 461-9999.

Great Britain When arriving in the U.K. from outside the EU you must declare any goods in excess of the following allowances: (1) 200 cigarettes, or 100 cigarillos, or 50 cigars, or 250 g tobacco; (2)Still table wine, (2 liters); (3) strong liqueurs over 22% volume (1 liter), or fortified or sparkling wine, other liqueurs (2 liters); (4) perfume (60 cc/ml); (5) toilet water (250 cc/ml); and (6) £136 worth of all other goods including gifts and souvenirs. You must be over 17 to import liquor or tobacco. These allowances also apply to duty-free purchases within the EU, except for the last category, other goods, which has an allowance of £71. Goods obtained duty and tax paid for personal use (regulated according to set guide levels) within the EC do not require any further customs duty. For more info, contact Her Majesty's Customs and Excise, Custom House, Nettleton Road, Heathrow Airport, Hounslow, Middlesex, TW6 2LA (tel. (0181) 910-3744; fax (0181) 910-3765).

Ireland Citizens of and visitors to Ireland must declare everything in excess of the following allowances for goods obtained outside the EU or duty and tax free in the EC: (1) 200 cigarettes, or 100 cigarillos, or 50 cigars, or 250g tobacco; (2) 1 liter of alcoholic drinks exceeding 22% vol. or 2 liters of alcoholic drinks not exceeding 22% vol.; (3) two liters of still wine; (4) 50 grams of perfume; (5) toilet water (1/4 liter); (6) IR£34 of other goods per adult traveler (£17 per traveler under 15 years of age). A maximum of 25 liters of beer may be imported as a part of, but not in addition to, the adult allowance. Goods obtained duty and tax paid in another EC country, within certain limits set out for personal use, will not be subject to additional customs duty. Travelers under 17 are not entitled to any allowance for tobacco or alcoholic products. For more information, contact The Revenue Commissioners, Dublin Castle (tel. (01) 679-2777; fax (01) 671-2021) or The Collector of Customs and Excise, The Custom House, Dublin 1.

New Zealand Each citizen may bring home up to NZ$700 worth of goods duty-free if they are intended for personal use or are unsolicited gifts. The concession is 200 cigarettes (1 carton), 250g of tobacco, 50 cigars, or a combination of all three not to exceed 250g. You may also bring in 4.5L of beer or wine and 1.125L of liquor. Only travelers over 17 may bring tobacco or alcoholic beverages into the country. For more information, consult New Zealand Customs Guide for Travelers, available from customs offices, or contact New Zealand Customs, 50 Anzac Avenue, Box 29, Auckland (tel. (09) 377 35 20; fax 309 29 78).

South Africa Each citizen may import duty-free: 400 cigarettes, 50 cigars, 250g tobacco, 2L wine, 1L spirits, 250mL toilet water, 50mL perfume, and other items up to a value of R500. Amounts exceeding this limit but not R10, 000 are dutiable at 20%. Goods acquired abroad and sent to the Republic as unaccompanied baggage do not qualify for any allowances. You may not export or import South African bank notes in excess of R500.

Persons who require specific information or advice concerning customs and excise duties contact: The Commissioner for Customs and Excise, Private Bag X47, Pretoria, 0001. This agency distributes the pamphlet, *South African Customs Information*, for visitors and residents who travel abroad. South Africans in the U.S. should contact: South African Mission to the IMF/World Bank, 3201 New Mexico Ave. #380, NW, Washington, DC 20016 (tel. (202) 364-8320/1; fax 364-6008).

United States Residents returning from abroad must declare all merchandise acquired abroad, including gifts, purchases, articles bought in duty-free shops, and purchases for others. The first $400 worth of merchandise may be entered duty free. To be eligible for this duty-free exemption, articles must be for personal or household use. You may include in your personal exemption: 100 cigars, 200 cigarettes (Cuban tobacco products may only be included if purchased in Cuba), and one liter (33.8 fl. oz.) of alcoholic beverages. (You must be more than 21 years old to bring in alcoholic beverages). This $400 duty-free exemption is good once every 30 days, provided you have been out of the country for at least 48 hours. The next $1000 worth of merchandise will be subject to a flat 10 percent duty rate; beyond that $1400, different duty rates will apply depending upon the type of merchandise or commodity. You must declare all purchases, so it's wise to keep sales slips handy in carry-on luggage. You may mail home bona-fide, unsolicited gifts free of duty if they are worth less than $100. You may not, however, send gifts of alcohol, tobacco, or perfume through the mail. If you are sending a gift into the United States, be sure to mark on the outside of your gift package: the item(s) contained in package, the fact that the contents are unsolicited gifts, and the value of the gift, or of each individual gift if you are enclosing more than one in a single package. If your consolidated gift package, or any single item in it, exceeds the duty-free limit, the U.S. Postal Service will collect customs duties and handling charges in the form of "postage due" stamps. Duty on gifts or other packages mailed from abroad cannot be prepaid. If you are mailing home personal items of American origin, mark clearly on the outside of the wrapping, "American goods returned" in order to avoid paying duty on this package. For more information on what to expect when clearing American customs, get a copy of the booklet "Know Before You Go" from the U.S. Customs Service, Box 7407, Washington, D.C. 20044, or call (202) 927-6724. Somewhat different regulations apply to foreign nationals living in the U.S. These individuals should get a copy of "Customs Hints for Visitors (Nonresidents)."

DRUGS

If you're caught with drugs in Greece or Cyprus, the least you can expect is to be expelled from the country, but remember that your state department can offer little assistance in foreign courts. Possessing drugs in Turkey is an *extremely* serious offense. The safest course while abroad is to *stay away* from drugs and *never* bring drugs across international borders. Should you be imprisoned, consular officers are allowed to visit you, suggest attorneys, and inform family and friends. Their benevolence ends there. As a U.S. State Department bulletin dourly states, you're virtually "on your own" if you become involved, however innocently, in drug trafficking.

Make sure you get a statement and/or prescription from your doctor if you'll be carrying insulin, syringes, or any narcotic drugs abroad. In addition, be aware that **codeine,** a painkiller commonly prescribed by U.S. physicians, is illegal in Greece.

IDENTIFICATION

Always carry at least two forms of ID on your person, including at least one photo ID. A passport combined with a driver's license or birth certificate serves as adequate proof of your identity and citizenship and will help when cashing traveler's checks. Never carry your passport, ticket, identification, money, traveler's checks, insurance, and credit cards together, or you risk being left entirely without ID *or* funds in case of theft or loss. Carry a few extra passport-size photos.

The **International Student Identity Card (ISIC)** is the most widely accepted form of student identification. Flashing this card can garner you discounts on sights, theaters, museums, accommodations, train, ferry, and airplane travel, and other services throughout Greece, Turkey, and Cyprus. In Turkey, the card enables students to visit state-run museums for half-price. Similar discounts can be found in Cyprus. Present the card wherever you go and ask about discounts even when none are advertised. It also provides accident insurance of up to US$2000 with no daily limit. Cardholders have access to a toll-free Traveler's Assistance hotline whose multilingual staff can provide help in medical, legal, and financial emergencies overseas.

Many student travel offices issue ISICs, including Council Travel, Let's Go Travel, and STA Travel in the U.S.; Travel CUTS in Canada; and any of the organizations under the auspices of the International Student Travel Confederation (ISTC) around the world (see p. 29). When you apply for the card, request a copy of the *International Student Identity Card Handbook*, which lists by country some of the available discounts. You can also write to Council for a copy. The card is valid from September to December of the following year. The fee is US$18. Applicants, who must be at least 12 years old, must be degree-seeking students of a secondary or post-secondary school. Because of the proliferation of phony ISICs, many airlines and some other services now require other proof of student identity: have a signed letter from the registrar attesting to your student status and stamped with the school seal, and carry your school ID card. The US$19 **International Teacher Identity Card (ITIC)** offers similar but limited discounts, and medical insurance coverage.

Federation of International Youth Travel Organizations (FIYTO) issues a discount card to travelers who are not students but are under 26. Also known as the **GO25 Card,** this one-year card offers many of the same benefits as the ISIC, and most organizations that sell the ISIC also sell the GO25 Card. A brochure that lists discounts is free when you purchase the card. To apply, bring: (1) proof of birthdate (copy of birth certificate, passport, or valid driver's license); and (2) a passport-sized photo (with your name printed on the back). The fee, which is subject to change in October 1995, is US$16 ($10 without travel insurance), CDN$15, or UK£5. For information, contact Council in the U.S. or FIYTO in Denmark (see p. 29).

HOSTELING ORGANIZATIONS

Hostelling International (HI) is the universal trademark name adopted by the International Youth Hostel Federation (IYHF). The 6,000 official youth hostels worldwide will normally display the new HI logo (a blue triangle) alongside the symbol of one of the 70 national hostel associations. Cyprus has six hostels, Turkey two (in İstanbul and Marmaris). Unfortunately, ongoing negotiations between HI and Greece have suspended the accreditation of Greece's two dozen hostels. For the latest information regarding these hostels, travelers are encouraged to contact the **IYHF Secretariat,** 9 Guessens Road, Welwyn Garden City, Hertfordshire, AL8 6QW, England (tel. (1707) 324170; fax 323980), or the IYHF Athens International Hostel, 16 Victor Hugo St., Athens (tel. (1) 523 4170; fax 523 4015). Despite the name, you need not be a youth; membership is available to all, though youths and the elderly pay a lesser fee. Non-members generally pay $3 extra. Get a membership card before you leave home, as some hostels don't sell them on the spot. One-year HI memberships are available from some travel agencies, including Council Travel, Let's Go Travel, and STA Travel (see p. 29) and from the following organizations:

American Youth Hostels (HI-AYH), 733 15th St., NW, Suite 840, Washington, DC, 20005 (tel. (202) 783-6161; fax 783-6171). Comprised of 38 regional offices which, in addition to licensing hostels (150 in the U.S.), provide local members and visitors with special programs, events, trips, and activities. HI-AYH membership cards cost US$25, under 18 US$10, over 54 US$15, family cards US$35. Membership valid for one year from date of issue. Contact AYH for ISIC, student and charter flights, travel equipment, literature on budget travel, and information on summer positions as a group leader for domestic outings.

Hostelling International—Canada (HI-C), 400-205 Catherine St., Ottawa, Ont. K2P 1C3 (tel. (613) 237-7884; fax 237-7868). One-year membership fee CDN$26.75, under 18 CDN$12.84, two-year CDN$37.45.

Youth Hostels Association of England and Wales (YHA), VHA Adventure Shop, 14 Southampton St., Convent Garden, London WC2E 7HY (tel. (0171) 836 10 36; fax 836 6372). Enrollment fees are UK£9, under 18 UK£3. Children 5-18 enrolled free when a parent joins.

An Óige (Irish Youth Hostel Association), 61 Mountjoy St., Dublin 7 (tel. (1) 830 4555; fax 830 5808). One-year membership IR£7.50, under 18 IR£4, and family IR£7.50 for each adult with children under 16 free.

Youth Hostels Association of Northern Ireland (YHANI), 22-32 Donegall Rd., Belfast BT12 5JN, Northern Ireland (tel. (0232) 31 54 35; fax 43 96 99). Annual memberships UK£7, under 18 UK£3, family UKI£14 for up to 6 children.

Scottish Youth Hostels Association (SYHA), 7 Glebe Crescent, Sterling FK8 2JA (tel. (01786) 45 11 81; fax 45 01 98). Membership UK£6, under 18 UK£2.50.

Australian Youth Hostels Association (AYHA), Level 3, 10 Mallett St., Camperdown, NSW, 2050 (tel. (02) 565 16 99; fax 565 12 35). Fee AUS$40, renewal AUS$24; under 18 fee AUS$12.

Youth Hostels Association of New Zealand (YHANZ), P.O. Box 436, 173 Gloucester St., Christchurch 1 (tel. (03) 379 9970; fax 365 4476). Memberships NZ$24.

Hostel Association of South Africa, P.O. Box 4402, Capetown 8000 (tel. (21) 419 18 53), or 101 Boston House, 46 Strand St., Cape Town 8001. Annual memberships SAR35.

The guides *Budget Accommodations You Can Trust: Europe and the Mediterranean* and *Africa, America, Asia and Oceania*, both US$11, CAN$13, AUS$15, UK£7 are published annually by HI. The former includes affiliated hostels in Greece, Turkey, and Cyprus.

HI operates an International Booking Network (IBN) that allows you to make confirmed reservations at more than 200 hostels around the world. Reservations can be made by visiting any hostel on the IBN and cost US$2-5, payable in the local currency of the country you are booking from. Or call an IBN booking center and use your credit card: Australia (tel. (2) 261 1111), Canada (tel. (800) 663 5777), England (tel. (171) 836 1036), New Zealand (tel. (9) 379 4224), Northern Ireland (tel. (232) 32 47 33), Ireland (tel. (1) 30 17 66), Scotland (tel. (41) 332 3004), and the U.S. (tel. (202) 783-6161). They can be made for up to six consecutive nights and for groups of up to nine people. Cancellations and rebookings can be made up to three days before the date of the reservation. If you book without paying a deposit, make sure you arrive at the hostel by 6pm in order to claim your reservation.

The Internet Guide to Hostelling is a resource for more electronically-oriented travelers. It contains information on hostel locations, news about hostels and hostelling, lists of budget guides, and budget transportation information. On the World Wide Web, use the URL "http://hostels.com/rec-travel/hostels/." Or through gopher, type "gopher hostels.com." FTP is also possible. For more information, email "info@hostels.com."

INTERNATIONAL DRIVER'S LICENSE

Unless you have a valid driver's license from an EU country, you must have an **International Driving Permit** (IDP) to drive in Greece. All foreign motorists, in fact, are encouraged to obtain one. In Cyprus, either an IDP or a six-month **Temporary Driving License** (C£3) is required. Drivers in Turkey must possess an IDP. A valid

driver's license from your home country must always accompany the permit. Even where you don't need an IDP to drive, having one may simplify dealings with non-English-speaking police if you're stranded or in an accident.

IDPs are usually issued in your own country before you depart. U.S. license holders can obtain an International Driving Permit (US$10), valid for one year, at any **American Automobile Association (AAA)** office or by writing to its main office, AAA Florida, Travel Agency Services Department, 1000 AAA Drive (mail stop 28), Heathrow, FL 32746-5080 (tel. (407) 444-4245; fax 444-7823). Canadian license holders can obtain an IDP (CDN$10) through any **Canadian Automobile Association (CAA)** branch office in Canada, or by writing to CAA Ottawa, 2525 Carling Ave., Lincoln Hts., Ottawa, ON K2B 7Z2 (tel. (613) 820-1890). The **Greek Automobile Touring Club (ELPA),** in Athens at both 2-4 Messogion St. (tel. 779 1615) and 6 Amerikis St. (tel. 363 8632), will also issue an IDP upon presentation of a valid driver's license, passport, and one photograph.

Most credit cards cover standard insurance. If you rent, lease, or borrow a car, you will need a **green card,** or **International Insurance Certificate,** to prove that you have liability insurance. Obtain it through the car rental agency; most of them include coverage in their prices. If you lease a car, obtain a green card from the dealer. Some travel agents offer the card, and it may be available at the border. Verify whether your auto insurance applies abroad; even if it does, you will still need a green card to certify this to foreign officials. If you have a collision while in Europe, the accident will show up on your domestic records if you report it to the company.

■■■ MONEY MATTERS

CURRENCY AND EXCHANGE

Before leaving home, exchange US$50 or so for the currency of the country where you are headed. You'll pay a higher exchange rate (and you may have to call your bank ahead to find *drachmae,* Turkish *lira,* or Cypriot pounds), but this will save time and exasperation, especially if you arrive when the banks are closed and you need cash. When exchanging currency, you'll usually lose money due to commissions and high exchange rates; ordinarily exchange in fairly large sums in order to minimize the loss. But you don't want to finish your trip with foreign currency left over, as you will again lose money in exchanging back to your home currency.

Greek *drachmae* are issued in both paper notes (500, 1000, 5000, and 10,000dr) and coins (10, 20, 50, and 100dr). If you're carrying more than US$1000 in cash when you enter Greece, you must declare it upon entry in order to export it legally (this does not apply to traveler's checks). You can bring up to US$445 worth of *drachmae* into Greece. In addition, no more than 20,000 *drachmae* can be taken out of the country when you leave. It is not difficult to exchange money in Greece. Remember that because Greece is a member of the European Union, assorted goods are subject to the **Value-Added Tax (VAT)** of approximately 18%.

The official currency in Turkey is the Turkish *lira* (TL). Coins are divided into 50, 100, 500, and 1000 *lira* pieces, and paper currency comes in denominations of 5000, 10,000, 20,000, 50,000, 100,000, 250,000, and 500,000 *lira* notes. It is hard to get change for bills of 250,000TL or more at museum entrances and cheap restaurants. Once in Turkey, currency can be exchanged almost anywhere, but you get the best rates at banks and exchange bureaus. Turkey has 24-hr. currency exchanges at border crossings, major airports, and train stations; major tourist areas have places to change money on weekends. Even better, commission-free 24-hr. ATM machines are centrally located in the larger cities. Hold on to exchange slips, since you may have to present them when you're re-converting your cash. If you take gifts out of Turkey, you may have to prove that they were bought with legally-exchanged foreign currency. There is no limit to the amount of foreign currency that can be brought into Turkey, but no more than US$5000 in *lira* may be brought into or taken out of the country. If you are coming from Greece, exchange your

money before arriving. The banks that accept *drachmae* exchange them at an absurdly high rate. Value-Added Tax (abbreviated KDV in Turkey) is roughly 15%.

The main unit of currency in Cyprus is the pound (£), which is divided into 100 cents. Coins come in 1, 2, 5, 10, 20, and 50 cent sizes; banknotes in denominations of £1, 5, 10, and 20. Cyprus imposes no limit on the amount of foreign currency that may be imported upon entering the country, but amounts in excess of US$1000 should be declared on Customs form D (NR). No more than £50 in Cypriot currency may be brought into or taken out of the country. Cyprus charges 8% VAT, which quoted prices do not necessarily include.

TRAVELER'S CHECKS

Traveler's checks are one of the safest means of carrying money. Several agencies and many banks sell them, usually for face value plus a 1% commission. American Express and Visa are the most widely recognized. Checks should be ordered well in advance, especially if large sums are being requested. If your checks get lost or stolen, you will be reimbursed by the checks' issuer; be aware that you may need a police report verifying the loss or theft. Inquire about toll-free refund hotlines and the location of refund centers when you purchase your checks. Keep receipts and a record of which checks you've cashed in a separate place from the checks. Leave a photocopy of serial numbers at home. Never countersign checks until you cash them. Always bring your passport with you when you plan to use the checks. Finally, be sure to keep cash for less touristy regions and emergencies.

American Express: Call (800) 221-7282 in the U.S. and Canada; in the U.K. (0800) 52 11 13; in New Zealand (0800) 44 10 68; in Australia (008) 25 19 02). Elsewhere, call U.S. collect (801) 964-6665. The most widely recognized worldwide and the easiest to replace if lost or stolen. Checks can be purchased for a small fee at American Express Travel Service Offices, banks, and American Automobile Association offices (AAA members can buy the checks commission-free). Cardmembers can also purchase checks at American Express Dispensers at Travel Service Offices, at airports, and by ordering them via phone (tel. (800) ORDER-TC (673-3782)). AmEx offices cash their checks commission-free (except where prohibited by national governments), although they often offer slightly worse rates than banks. They also sell Cheques for Two which can be signed by either of two people traveling together. Request AmEx's *Traveler's Companion,* which lists travel office addresses and stolen check hotlines for each European country. Soon, traveler's checks will be available over America OnLine. For more info, call (800) 673-3782, or check ExpressNet on America OnLine.

Barclays Bank: Call (800) 221-2426 in the U.S. and Canada. Sells Visa traveler's checks; a 1-3% commission is charged depending on the bank at which the checks are purchased. When checks are issued, you receive the number to call from outside the U.S. for lost/stolen checks. Barclays cashes Visa checks for free.

Citicorp: Call (800) 645-6556 in the U.S. and Canada; in the U.K. (0171) 982 40 40. Elsewhere, call U.S. collect (813) 623-1709. Sells Citicorp and Citicorp Visa traveler's checks. Commission is 1-2% on check purchases. Citicorp's World Courier Service guarantees worldwide hand-delivery of traveler's checks.

Thomas Cook MasterCard: Call (800) 223-9920 in the U.S. and Canada; in the U.K. call (0800) 62 21 01 or collect (1733) 50 29 95. Elsewhere, call U.S. collect (609) 987-7300. Commission 1-2% for purchases. Buying the checks at a Thomas Cook office may get you lower commissions.

Visa: Call (800) 227-6811 in the U.S.; in the U.K. (0171) 937 80 91. Anywhere else in the world, call the U.S. collect at (212) 858-8500. Sells its traveler's checks by mail; call (800) 235-7366 to order them. Any kind of Visa traveler's checks (Barclays or Citicorp) can be reported lost at the Visa number.

CREDIT CARDS

Credit cards can be either invaluable or a frustrating nuisance—beware ruinous interest rates. Their usefulness varies depending on the country you're in. Major credit cards—**MasterCard** and **Visa** are the most welcomed—instantly extract cash advances of local currency from associated banks and teller machines throughout Greece, Turkey and Cyprus. **American Express** cards also work in some ATMs (for example, in those of AkBank of Turkey), as well as at AmEx offices and major airports. AmEx Cardmembers can enroll in **Express Cash.** For a 2% transaction fee for each withdrawal with a US$2.50 minimum, cardholders may withdraw up to US$1000 in a 7 day period form their bank account or line of credit. To enroll, call (800) 227-4669; outside the U.S., call collect (904) 565-785.

All ATMs require a **Personal Identification Number (PIN),** which credit cards in the U. S. do not usually carry. You must ask AmEx, MasterCard, or Visa to assign you one before you leave; without this PIN, you will be unable to withdraw cash with your credit card abroad. Keep in mind that MasterCard and Visa have different names in Europe ("EuroCard" or "Access" for MasterCard and "Carte Bleue" or "Barclaycard" for Visa). Credit cards prove invaluable in financial emergencies. They also offer an array of other services, from insurance to emergency help—but these depend completely on the issuer.

American Express (tel. (800) 528-4800) has a hefty annual fee (US$55) but offers a number of services. AmEx cardholders can cash personal checks at AmEx offices abroad. Global Assist, a 24-hr. hotline offering information and legal assistance in emergencies, is also available (tel. (800) 554-2639 in U.S. and Canada; from abroad call U.S. collect (301) 214-8228). Cardholders can also take advantage of the American Express Travel Service; benefits include helping change airline, hotel, and car rental reservations, sending mailgrams and international cables, and holding your mail at one of the more than 1700 AmEx offices around the world. **MasterCard** (tel. (800) 999-0454) and **Visa** (tel. (800) 336-8472) are issued in cooperation with individual banks and organizations, and each issuer offers different services.

CASH CARDS

Cash cards—popularly called **ATM cards**—are widespread in Europe. The two international money networks you should know about are **Cirrus** (U.S. tel. (800) 4-CIRRUS (424-7787) and **PLUS** (U.S. tel. (800) 843-7587). Cirrus now has international cash machines in 60 countries, including Greece, Turkey, and Cyprus. It charges $5 to withdraw non-domestically. PLUS is not quite as extensive, only covering 51 countries. Depending on the system that your bank at home uses, you will most likely be able to access your own personal bank account whenever you're in need of funds. Happily, the ATM machines get the same wholesale exchange rate as credit cards, which is generally 5% better than the retail rate most banks use. Unfortunately, there is often a limit on the amount of money you can withdraw per day. Be sure to memorize your PIN code in numeral form, as machines abroad often have no letters on the keys. Also, if your PIN is longer than four digits, be sure to ask your bank whether the first four digits will work, or whether you need a new number

One innovation worth looking into is Visa's **TravelMoney,** which is essentially an ATM card that doesn't require a bank or credit card account. Travelers buy it from a bank by paying whatever they want to have on the card plus a commission of about 2%, The PIN and one-day replacement policy make TravelMoney a convenient and relatively secure way not only to avoid changing money (and the concomitant lousy exchange rates) but also having money sent from home. For more information, call from the U.S. and Canada, (800) 847 2399; from the United Kingdom, (0800) 96 38 33; from France, (05) 90 12 35; from Germany, (0130) 81 09 91; from Italy, (1678) 756 17; from Switzerland, (155) 60 46; from Greece, (00 800) 11 481 03 04; from Mexico, (95 800) 847 23 99; from Japan, (0031) 11 37 94; from other countries, call the U.S. collect, (1 410) 581 9091.

MONEY FROM HOME

One of the easiest ways to get money from home is to bring an **American Express** card. AmEx allows green-card holders to draw cash from their checking accounts at any of its major offices and many of its representatives' offices, up to US$1000 every

21 days (no service charge, no interest). Unless using the AmEx service, avoid cashing checks in foreign currencies; they usually take weeks and a US$30 fee to clear.

Money can also be wired abroad through international money transfer services operated by **Western Union.** In the U.S., call (800) 325-6000 at any time to cable money with your Visa or MasterCard. The money is usually available in the country you're sending it to within an hour, although in some cases this may vary. Rates are US$29 to send US$250, US$40 to send US$500, and US$50 to send US$1000.

In emergencies, U.S. citizens can have money sent via the State Department's **Citizens Emergency Center,** Department of State, 2201 C St. NW, Washington, DC 20520 (tel. (202) 647-5225, after business hours 647-4000). For a fee of US$15, the State Department will forward money within hours to the nearest consular office, which will then disburse it accordingly. The center serves only Americans in the direst of straits abroad and prefers not to send sums greater than US$500. The quickest way to have the money sent is to cable it to the State Department through Western Union or to drop it off at the department itself.

■■■ SAFETY

> Road travel in Turkey is dangerous by European standards (see p. 416). *Let's Go* lists emergency, police, and consulate numbers in every large city.

Tourists are particularly vulnerable to crime because they often carry large amounts of cash and tend to stand out. To avoid such unwanted attention, try to blend in as much as possible, walk with confidence, and check maps at cafés or shops rather than on street corners. Officials, hotel staff, or trustworthy locals can often provide invaluable advice on unsafe areas and what to expect from thieves.

You may consider carrying small whistle to scare off attackers and familiarizing yourself with distress calls in Turkish (*imdat*) or Greek (*astinomia*). An important precaution is to make sure—especially when traveling alone—that someone knows your itinerary. When walking at night, you should turn day-time precautions into mandates. In particular, stay near crowded and well-lit areas and do not attempt to cross through parks, parking lots or any other large, deserted areas. Whenever possible, *Let's Go* warns of unsafe neighborhoods, but only your eyes can tell for sure if you've wandered into one; buildings in disrepair, vacant lots, and general desertedness are all bad signs. A district can change character in the course of a single block. Simply being aware of the flow of people can tell you a great deal about the relative safety of the area. Many notoriously dangerous districts have safe sections; look for children playing, women walking in the open, and other signs of an active community. If you feel uncomfortable, leave as quickly and directly as you can, but don't allow your fear of the new to close off whole worlds to you. Careful, persistent exploration will build confidence and make your stay that much more rewarding.

There is no sure-fire set of precautions that will protect you from all situations you might encounter when you travel. A good self-defense course will give you more concrete ways to react to different types of aggression, but it might cost you more money than your trip. **Model Mugging** (East Coast tel. (617) 232-7900; Midwest (312) 338-4545; West Coast (415) 592-7300), a national organization with offices in several major cities, teaches a very effective, comprehensive course on self-defense. (Course prices range $400-500. Women's and men's courses offered.) Community colleges frequently offer self-defense courses at more affordable prices.

Always wear a seatbelt when driving on Turkish, Greek, or Cypriot roads, which are plagued by hundreds of road accidents each year. Children under 40 lbs. should ride only in a specially-designed carseat, which can be obtained for a small fee from most car rental agencies. If you choose to sleep in your car, be aware that this is one of the most dangerous ways to get your rest—when you lock other people out, you also lock yourself in. Sleeping outside can be even more dangerous—camping is recommended only in official, supervised campsites or in wilderness backcountry.

■■■ SECURITY

Don't put large sums of money in your back pocket. Never count your money in public and carry as little as possible. If you carry a purse, buy a sturdy one with a secure clasp, and carry it crosswise on the side, away from the street with the clasp against you. As far as packs are concerned, buy some small combination padlocks which slip through the two zippers, securing the pack shut. (Even these precautions do not always suffice: moped riders who snatch purses and backpacks sometimes tote knives to cut the straps.) A **money belt** is the best way to carry cash; you can buy one at most camping supply stores or through the Forsyth Travel Library (see p. 3). The best combination of convenience and invulnerability is a nylon, zippered pouch with belt that should sit inside the waist of your pants or skirt. A **neck pouch,** although less accessible, is equally safe. Avoid keeping anything precious in a fanny-pack: your valuables will be highly visible and easy to steal. In city crowds and especially on public transportation, pick-pockets are amazingly deft at their craft. Hold your bags tightly. Also, be alert in public telephone booths. If you must say your calling-card number, do so very quietly; if you punch it in, make sure no one can look over your shoulder. Making **photocopies** of important documents will allow you to recover them in case they are lost or filched. Carry one copy separate from the documents and leave another copy at home. Keep some money separate from the rest to use in an emergency. Label luggage both inside and out.

Among the more colorful aspects of large cities are the **con artists.** Con artists and hustlers often work in groups, and children, unfortunately, are among the most effective at the game. Be aware of certain classics: sob stories that require money, rolls of bills "found" on the street, mustard spilled (or saliva spit) onto your shoulder distracting you for enough time to snatch your bag. Another popular scam in Greece is women who lure male tourists into bars and ask the traveler to buy them highly overpriced drinks (i.e. $50 each) and then back up the bill with some muscle. Be especially alert in these situations. Do not respond or make eye contact, walk quickly away, and keep a solid grip on your belongings.

Be particularly watchful of your belongings on **buses** (for example, carry your backpack in front of you where you can see it), don't check baggage on trains especially if you're switching lines, and don't trust anyone to "watch you bag for a second." **Trains** are notoriously easy spots for thieving. Professionals wait for tourists to fall asleep and then carry off everything they can. When traveling in pairs, sleep in alternating shifts; when alone, use good judgement in selecting a train compartment: never stay in an empty one. Keep important documents and other valuables on your person and try to sleep on top bunks with your luggage stored above you.

Let's Go lists locker availability in hostels and train stations, but you'll need your own padlock. Lockers are useful if you plan on sleeping outdoors or don't want to lug everything with you, but don't store valuables in them. Never leave your belongings unattended; even the most demure-looking hostel (convents included) may be a den of thieves. If you feel unsafe, look for places with either a curfew or a night attendant. Always keep your valuables on your person if you're staying in low-budget hotels where someone else may have a passkey and in dorm-style surroundings.

If you take your **car** on your travels, try not to leave valuable possessions—such as radios or luggage—in it while you're off rambling. Radios are especially tempting. If your tape deck or radio is removable, hide it in the trunk or take it with you. If it isn't, at least keep it concealed. Similarly, hide baggage in the trunk—although savvy thieves can tell if a car is heavily loaded by the way it is settled on its tires. Park your vehicle in a garage or well-traveled area.

■■■ HEALTH

For **medical emergencies** in Greece, dial 166. In Turkey, dial 112 or call your consulate. In southern Cyprus, dial 190.

BEFORE YOU GO

Prepare ahead for minor health problems by packing a compact **first-aid kit**. Some hardware stores carry ready-made kits, but it's easy to assemble your own. Items you might want are bandages, aspirin substitute, mild antiseptic soap or antibiotic cream, a thermometer in a sturdy case, a Swiss Army knife with tweezers, moleskin for blisters, a decongestant, motion sickness remedy, medicine for diarrhea and stomach problems, sunscreen, an antihistamine, insect repellent (the roll-on kind is most convenient), burn ointment, and a soothing lip balm.

Always go prepared with an ample supply of any **medication** you may need while away, as well as a copy of the prescription and/or a statement from your doctor; matching your prescription with a foreign equivalent is not always easy, economical, or safe. Greece and Turkey require few medical preparations; if you're going to remote parts you might want to get **immunizations** against hepatitis A, tetanus, and typhoid. If you expect to be be sexually active, if you will be a health worker, or if you will be visiting remote areas, you should also consider hepatitis B vaccinations.

If you wear **glasses** or **contact lenses,** take an extra prescription with you and make arrangements with someone at home to send you a replacement pair in an emergency. Bring extra solutions, enzyme tablets, and eyedrops—lens solution can be exorbitant when it is available. Remember that traveling does not provide the most sanitary or comfortable conditions for putting in and taking out contact lenses. If you heat-sterilize your contact lenses, you should consider switching temporarily to a chemical system, as your heater will not work properly without a bulky converter, and the availability of equivalent devices in Greece or Turkey is rare.

Any traveler with a medical condition that cannot be easily recognized (i.e. diabetes, epilepsy, heart conditions, allergies to antibiotics) should obtain a **Medic Alert Identification Tag** (US$35 and up) from the Medic Alert Foundation, P.O. Box 1009, Turlock, CA 95381-1009 (tel. (800) 432-5378). In an emergency, their internationally recognized tag indicates the bearer's problem and provides the number of Medic Alert's 24-hr. hotline. Attending medical personnel can call this number to obtain info about the member's medical history. The **American Diabetes Association,** 1660 Duke St., Alexandria, VA 22314 (tel. (800) 232-3472) provides copies of *Travel and Diabetes* and diabetic ID cards with messages in 18 languages. **Global Emergency Medical Services (GEMS)** provides its subscribing travelers with immediate access to an emergency room registered nurse who has on-line access to medical information that you provide, your primary physician, and a network of English-speaking medical providers in 180 countries. For more info, call (800) 860-1111, or write GEMS, 2001 Westside Drive, Suite 120, Alpharetta, GA 30201.

The **United States Centers for Disease Control (CDC),** an excellent source of general health information for travelers, maintains an international travelers' hotline (tel. (404) 332-4559, code 000004), or write directly to the Centers for Disease Control and Prevention, CDC, 1600 Clifton Rd. NE, Atlanta, GA 30333 (tel. (404) 639-3311 to talk to a person). The CDC publishes *Health Information for International Travelers* (US$6), an annual global rundown of disease, immunization, and general health advice, including risks in particular countries. Request the booklet by calling the CDC's hotline, or by writing the Superintendent of Documents, U.S. Government Printing Office, Washington, DC 20402.

For more information, contact the **International Association for Medical Assistance to Travelers (IAMAT).** For no fee, IAMAT offers a membership ID card, a directory of English-speaking doctors around the world who have agreed to treat members for a set fee schedule, and detailed brochures and charts on immunization requirements, various tropical diseases, climate, and sanitation. Contact chapters in the **U.S.,** 417 Center St., Lewiston, NY 14092 (tel. (716) 754-4883); in **Canada,** 1287 St. Clair Avenue West, Toronto, M6E 1B8 (tel. (416) 652-0137; fax (519) 836-3412), or in **New Zealand,** P.O. Box 5049, Christchurch 5.

Reliable **contraception** may be difficult to come by while traveling. Women on the pill should bring enough to allow for loss or extended stays; though it's available over the counter in Greece, Cyprus and Turkey, it might be hard to match the exact formulation. Although **condoms** are easy to find, you might want to stock up on your favorite national brand before you go as availability and quality varies. In Greece ask for *profilaktika* or *kapotes,* in Turkey it's a *preservatif* or a *kilif.*

STAYING HEALTHY ON THE ROAD

When traveling in the warmer months in Greece and Turkey, don't underestimate the dangers of sun and heat, and educate yourself about **heatstroke.** This term refers to a specific ailment that can cause death within a few hours if it is not treated. Heatstroke can begin without direct exposure to the sun; it results from continuous heat stress, lack of fitness, or over-activity following heat exhaustion. In the early stages of heatstroke, sweating stops, body temperature rises, and an intense headache develops, soon followed by mental confusion. Victims should be cooled off immediately with fruit juice or salted water, wet towels, and shade, and given medical attention ASAP. If you're prone to sunburn, apply sun-screen often. If you do get sun-burned, drink even more water than normal.

Heatstroke, food poisoning, bladder infections, diarrhea, exotic flus... all these things *could* strike you during your travels in Greece, Cyprus and Turkey. To protect yourself, be careful about overexposure to the sun. Be especially cautious of food that looks as if it's been standing around. This warning applies to meat products especially; bread products should be safe. Peel your own fruit, and don't eat raw vegetables or other raw foods, especially shellfish or seafood (don't eat mussels in the summer). That warning applies more to rural areas, but you should be careful wherever you go, especially in budget establishments. If you are at all suspicious of the care that has been taken in preparing your food, stick to the well-cooked and still-hot. Cholera, typhoid, and parasites are food-borne. Avoid meat products after extended power outages, as they spoil quickly in the summer heat.

Drink *bottled* water. Drinking unbottled water will probably lead to **diarrhea.** If you do get it, be wary of taking over-the-counter anti-diarrheals; it's not a good idea if your diarrhea is actually a symptom of some other disease. When suffering the tourist's disease, mix up a glass of eight oz. of clean water with ½tsp. of sugar or honey and a pinch of salt. Drink several of these a day, which should prevent dehydration. Eat toast and saltine crackers; drink juice and water. Let things run their course. If after four or five days the symptoms don't go away, or if you develop a fever, you should seek professional medical care. Diarrhea is not all you can get from bad water; typhoid, hepatitis A, and parasites are all water-borne diseases. Two short warnings: If you are bitten by any animal, seek medical attention; and do not swim in small bodies of fresh water; there is a risk for various parasitic infections.

Pharmacies in Greece have a sophisticated staff with more prescribing power than you may be accustomed to. In emergencies you will be given free treatment in state hospitals. The Turkish pharmacy (*eczane*) will have remedies for minor troubles; more serious medical problems should be taken to the *klinik* (private ones tend to be much better than state-run, and are not much more expensive for foreigners, who must pay for care in any case). Pharmacies in Greek and Turkish towns stay open all night on a rotating basis; each should have a sign in the window telling which is on duty that night (the open one is known as the *nöbetçi*). They sell *esem mat,* small rectangles of mosquito repellent to be burned slowly on little heat pads.

Women traveling in unsanitary conditions are vulnerable to **urinary tract and bladder infections,** common bacterial diseases that cause a burning sensation and painful, often frequent urination. Drink water and vitamin C-rich juice. If symptoms persist, see a doctor. Refer to the *Handbook for Women Travellers* by Maggie and Gemma Moss (see p. 25) for more info on women's health.

HIV, AIDS, AND STDS

Be aware of the facts about **HIV,** the human immunodeficiency virus that causes **AIDS,** which cripples the immune system and makes infected people highly susceptible to even minor illnesses. While not everyone who is HIV positive has AIDS, *any person who is HIV positive can transmit this virus* which ultimately leads to death. The World Health Organization estimates that in Europe and Central Asia, there are at least 550,000 HIV+ people and over 500,000 actual cases of AIDS. For more info on AIDS, call the **U.S. Center for Disease Control's 24-hour Hotline** at (800) 342-2437 (TTY (800) 243-7889, Mon-Fri 10am-10pm; Spanish (800) 344-7332, 8am-2am). The **World Health Organization (WHO)** (tel. (202) 861-3200) provides statistical material on AIDS. Write to the WHO, Attn.: Global Program on AIDS, 20 Avenue Appia, 1211 Geneva 27, Switzerland. Council Travel (see p. 29) distributes a free *AIDS and International Travel* brochure containing information on safe sex, HIV testing, hotline numbers, and overseas blood transfusions and injections.

Other diseases (apart from AIDS) are transmitted through sexual contact. You should be relatively safe from STDs if you follow the safe sex guidelines recommended for avoiding HIV. The U.S. Center for Disease Control has an STDs hotline (tel. (800) 227-8922).

■■■ INSURANCE

Beware of buying unnecessary travel coverage—your regular policies may well extend to many travel-related accidents. **Medical insurance** (especially university policies) often cover costs incurred abroad. **Medicare's** foreign travel coverage is valid only in Canada and Mexico. **Canadians** are protected by their home province's health insurance plan for up to 90 days after leaving the country; check with the provincial Ministry of Health or Health Plan Headquarters for details. **Australia** has Reciprocal Health Care Agreements (RHCAs) with several countries; when traveling in these nations Australians are entitled to many of the services that they would receive at home. The Commonwealth Department of Human Services and Health can provide more information. Your **homeowners' insurance** (or your family's coverage) often covers theft during travel. Homeowners are generally covered against loss of travel documents (passport, plane ticket, railpass, etc.) up to $500.

ISIC and **ITIC** provide US$3000 worth of accident and illness insurance and US$100 per day for up to 60 days of hospitalization. The cards also give access to a toll-free Traveler's Assistance hotline (in the U.S. and Canada (800) 626-2427; elsewhere call collect to the U.S. (713) 267-2525) whose multilingual staff can provide help in emergencies overseas. **Council** offers the inexpensive Trip-Safe plan with options covering medical treatment and hospitalization, accidents, baggage loss, and even charter flights missed due to illness; **STA** offers a more expensive, more comprehensive plan. **American Express** cardholders receive automatic car-rental and flight insurance on purchases made with the card (see p. 29).

Remember that insurance companies usually require a copy of the police report for thefts, or evidence of having paid medical expenses (doctor's statements, receipts) before they will honor a claim and may have time limits on filing for reimbursement. Always carry policy numbers and proof of insurance. Check with each carrier for specific restrictions and policies. Most carriers listed have 24-hr. hotlines.

Access America, 6600 West Broad St., P.O. Box 11188, Richmond, VA 23230 (tel. (800) 284-8300; fax (804) 673-1491). Covers trip cancellation, hospital costs, emergency medical evaluation, sickness, and baggage loss. 24-hr. hotline.

ARM Coverage, Inc./Carefree Travel Insurance, 100 Garden City Plaza, P.O. Box 9366, Garden City, NY 11530-9366 (tel. (800) 323-3149 or (516) 294-0220; fax (516) 294-1821). Covers trip delay, medical, baggage loss, bag delay, accidental death and dismemberment, travel supplier insolvency. 24-hr. hotline.

Globalcare Travel Insurance, 220 Broadway, Lynnfield, MA 01940 (tel. (800) 821-2488; fax (617) 592-7720). Complete medical, legal, emergency, and travel-related services. On-the-spot payments and special student programs.

Travel Assistance International, by Worldwide Assistance Services, Inc., 1133 15th St. NW, Suite 400, Washington, DC 20005-2710 (tel. (800) 821-2828 or (202) 828-5894; fax (202) 331-1530). Gives 24-hr. hotline for emergencies and referrals.

Travel Guard International, 1145 Clark St., Stevens Point, WI 54481 (tel. (800) 826-1300 or (715) 345-0505; fax (715) 345-0525). Programs cover trip cancellation and interruption, bankruptcy and financial default, lost luggage, medical, emergency assistance, accidental death. 24-hr. hotline.

Travel Insured International, Inc., 52-S Oakland Ave., P.O. Box 280568, East Hartford, CT 06128-0568 (tel. (800) 243-3174; fax (203) 528-8005). Insurance against accident, baggage loss, sickness, trip cancellation and interruption, travel delay, and default. Covers emergency medical evacuation and flight insurance.

■■■ ALTERNATIVES TO TOURISM

Because most visitors see Greece, Turkey, and Cyprus only through the eyes of a tourist, those who go in order to study or work can expect a particularly unique and rewarding experience. There are several general resource organizations for those interested in alternatives to tourism.

VOLUNTEERING

Volunteer jobs are readily available in Greece, Turkey, and Cyprus. You may receive room and board in exchange for your labor. Opportunities include archaeological digs and community or workcamp projects. The organizations that arrange placement sometimes charge high application fees in addition to the workcamps' charges for room and board. You can sometimes avoid this extra fee by contacting the individual workcamps directly; check with the organization.

Archaeological Institute of America, 656 Beacon Street, Boston, MA 02215-2010 (tel. (617) 353-9361; fax (617) 353-6550) puts out the *Archaeological Fieldwork Opportunities Bulletin* (US$11.00 non-members) which lists over 250 field sites.

Council on International Educational Exchange publishes *Volunteer! The Comprehensive Guide to Voluntary Service in the U.S. and Abroad* (US$13 plus US$1.50 postage). Available from Council Travel offices. Council's **Voluntary Services Department,** 205 E. 42nd St., New York, NY 10017 (tel. (212) 661-1414, ext. 1139). Offers 2-4-week environmental or community service projects in 22 countries around the globe.

Gençtur, 15 Yerebatan Cad., 2nd floor, İstanbul (tel. (212) 520 5274,-5), organizes teenage, group, or international voluntary workcamps in Turkey.

Peace Corps, 1990 K St. NW, Washington, DC 20526 (tel. (800) 424-8580). Volunteers must be U.S. citizens with useful skills willing to make a 2-year commitment.

Volunteers for Peace, 43 Tiffany Rd., Belmont, VT 05730 (tel. (802) 259-2759; fax 259-2922). Complete and up-to-date listings in the annual *International Workcamp Directory* (US$12). Registration fee US$150. Free newsletter.

STUDY

College Year in Athens (tel. (01) 721 8746) runs a two-semester program for undergraduates (usually juniors), which includes travel as well as classroom instruction (in English). The program has two tracks, one in Ancient Greek civilization and one in Mediterranean studies. Scholarship money is available. College Year in Athens also runs two summer programs: a six-week program of academic study and travel, and a three-week immersion in Modern Greek Language.

The **Athens Centre,** Archimidous 48, Athens, Greece 116 36 (tel. (01) 701 2268; fax 701 8603), offers a modern Greek language program. It has semester and quarter programs on Greek civilization in affiliation with U.S. universities. It also offers 4-6 week summer Classics programs, a yearly summer theater program, and a Modern Greek Language program in July on the island of Spetses.

The **Hellenic American Union,** 22 Massalias St., Athens 10680 (tel. (01) 362 9886), offers courses in Modern spoken Greek, studio art, business courses, translation seminar, and Greek literature. An intensive one-month Greek language course is offered in the Cyclades. For a practical education, contact the **Delta School of Technical and Business Studies,** 3 Rethymnou St., Athens 10682 (tel. 822 0083).

More information on educational programs in Greece can be obtained from a Greek Press and Information Office (see p. 2). Your best bet for info on study in Turkey is the education office at the nearest tourist office. You may also enroll in one of several small colleges on Cyprus; contact the Department of Education in Nicosia.

American Field Service (AFS), 3rd Floor, 220 E. 42nd St., New York, NY 10017 (tel. (212) 949-4242; in Springfield, (800) 876-2377). Summer-, semester-, and year-long homestay exchange programs for high school students. Short-term service projects for adults also offered. Financial aid available.

Beaver College Center for Education Abroad, 450 S. Easton Rd., Glenside, PA 19038-3295 (tel. (800) 755-5607; fax (215) 572-2174; e-mail cea@beaver.edu).

This Name Is For The Birds!

Turks are amused by the double meaning of the English word "Turkey." When the professional soccer team of Leeds, England, came to İstanbul to play the local power Galatasaray, their chants exploited this linguistic weakness. The news got into Turkey's press, and thereafter many Turks asked tourists and foreign governments alike to begin using the country's proper Turkish name, *Türkiye.* Clearly, this campaign so far has had underwhelming results. Victory continues to be hampered in English-speaking countries by the convenience of teaching elementary-school geography students that you can "fry Turkey in Greece." Galatasaray, at least, rose to European soccer fame by defeating Leeds

Operates summer-, semester-, and year-long program in Greece. Applicants must have completed three full semesters at an accredited university.

School for International Training, College Semester Abroad Admissions, Kipling Rd., P.O. Box 676, Battleboro, VT 05302 (tel. (800) 336-1616 or (802) 258-3279). Runs semester-long programs featuring cultural orientation, intensive language study, homestay, and field and independent study. Programs cost US$8200-10300.

U.S. Servas Committee, 11 John Street, Suite #407, New York, NY 10038-4009 (tel. (212) 267-0252; fax 267-0292; contact Nori Jaffer-Touré). Homestays.

World Learning, Inc., Summer Abroad, P.O. Box 676, Battleboro, VT 05302 (tel. (800) 345-2929 or (802) 257-7751). 4-6 week-long high school programs in Greece and language-training programs with elective homestays.

WORK

Finding work in Greece, Turkey, and Cyprus is difficult. Job opportunities are scarce and the governments try to restrict employment to citizens and visitors from the EU. Be persistent; the informality of local life will work to your advantage.

For long-term employment in Greece, you must first get a work permit from your employer; permits are available at the **Ministry of Labor,** 40 Pireos St., Athens 10437 (tel. 523 3110). Make all arrangements and negotiations before you leave home.

For **hotel jobs** (bartending, cleaning, etc.) arrive in the spring and early summer to search for work. Most night spots have meager pay. Check the bulletin boards of hostels in Athens and the classified ads in the *Athens News.* Another possibility is to work as a farm laborer. In Greece, the **American Farm School** runs summer work and recreation programs for high school and college students. Write 1133 Broadway, New York, NY 10010 (tel. (212) 463-8434; fax (212) 463-8208), or in Greece, P.O. Box 23, GR-55102, Thessaloniki (tel. 30 (31) 471 803 or 471 825; fax 472 345).

The brightest prospect for working in Turkey is probably **teaching English.** Students with university credentials might fare quite well, but having your credentials verified can take some time. Various organizations in the U.S. will place you in a (low-paying) teaching job, but securing a position will require patience, because teaching English abroad has become enormously popular in the past few years.

The process for obtaining a job in Cyprus is similar. Before you arrive, you must find an employer who can assert that you are particularly suited for your position due to academic interest or experience, and that there are no suitably qualified local employees available in your field.

Central Bureau for Educational Visits and Exchanges, Seymour Mews House, Seymour Mews, London W1H 9PE (tel. (0171) 486 5 01; fax 935 5741). Publishes several guides to work, volunteering and teaching abroad.

Council publishes *Work, Study, Travel Abroad: The Whole World Handbook.* Published by St. Martin's Press (US$14). Write to CIEE—Pubs. Dept., 205 E. 42nd St., New York, NY 10017-5706.

Office of Overseas Schools, A/OS Room 245, SA-29, Dept. of State, Washington, DC 20522-2902 (tel. (703) 875-7800). Teaching jobs abroad.

Surrey Books, 230 E. Ohio St., Chicago, IL 60611 (tel. (800) 326-4430) publishes *How to Get a Job in Europe: The Insider's Guide.* (1995 edition, US$18.)

■■■ WOMEN AND TRAVEL

Women traveling alone are likely to experience harassment and must always take extra precautions. Even groups of two or three women may be bothered. But don't despair. Women have traveled on their own, elegantly and adventurously, for years.

Freelance camping, hitching rides, and swimming, or scuba diving in secluded areas can be *extremely* dangerous. Women will be safer and more comfortable in groups. In Greece, catcalling is frequent, but the extent of the harassment is only verbal and if you do not acknowledge the catcallers, in most cases they will not persist. They may occasionally follow you, but, again, physical harassment is uncommon. The one exception occurs when men greet boats offering women a ride to a distant pension or campsite. These situations may be extremely dangerous and, besides, hawking rooms is *illegal*. Some strategies for combating harassment include wearing a wedding band; both the Greek and Turkish culture are respectful of women who have male authority figures close at hand. Ask women or couples for directions rather than men and keep spare change handy for telephone calls and emergency bus or taxi fares. Leave nighttime activities before closing; you don't want to stumble out into the darkness with a crowd of drunks. Conforming to local standards of dress and behavior can reduce the hassles you encounter. Should you find yourself the object of catcalls or strange propositions, your best response is no response. Avoid prolonged eye contact, except to assert your strength and personhood. To call for help in Greece, hurl **"vo-EE-thee-ah!"**; in Turkey, **"eem-DAHT!"** In Greece and Greek Cyprus, memorize the **emergency police number** (dial 100; in Cyprus, dial 190). Sad to say, a Western woman may want to think twice about **traveling alone in Turkey.** Verbal harassment abounds and even infinitely patient travelers soon lose tolerance for the overwhelmingly officious men. It can be difficult to assess the safety of ostensibly friendly gestures. Often the owner of a pension or hotel will "claim" you once he realizes you're alone. He might ask where you're going, how you're getting there, and other questions about your activities. On the street, pinching, grabbing, and squeezing are not uncommon, but verbal pursuit dwarfs all other forms. The best response to this behavior is to tune out—do not make anything *like* eye contact. To silence a particularly vociferous suitor, shout **"Ayıp"** (Ah-YIHP), or "Shame!" Use the expletive sparingly; Turks take the term seriously. If you find yourself in a threatening situation, threaten to call the authorities. The **emergency police number** is 155. Never hitchhike, and invest in secure accommodations, particularly those with the word "*aile*" (family-style) in their names. Due to the recent proliferation of prostitutes from Eastern Europe, women in some budget establishments may be mistaken for prostitutes.

In much of Turkey, men and women tend to socialize separately. Especially in the smaller towns, men frequent *çay* shops, while the women stay at home. Although women are on the same legal and political footing as men in Turkey, the past is still ingrained in the collective consciousness.

Proper dress is a good idea. In Turkey, stay away from tank tops or short shorts when outside resort areas. In the east, wear long skirts, long-sleeved blouses, and even a head scarf. To avoid offending locals you may wish to cover your knees. In your day bag, carry a rolled-up scarf and a long, light skirt. You can slip these on to go into a mosque or church. Sadly, dress does not help much to put off the irritating men who come on to you in tourist areas; risqué attire, however, can only attract these characters, so avoid it. In Greece, the less touristed the area, the more skin should be covered. Women in Athens should lean toward the conservative.

■■■ OLDER TRAVELERS

Greeks and Turks have a great deal of respect for their elders, so senior citizens should receive a warm welcome. Senior citizens are often offered a variety of discounts and services; **Hostelling International** sells memberships to those over 55 at a reduced rate. Below is a brief list of services that provide additional information:

American Association of Retired People (AARP), 601 E St. NW, Washington, DC 20049 (tel. (202) 434-2277). Members 50 and over receive benefits including the AARP Motoring Plan from Amoco (tel. (800) 334-3300).

Elderhostel, 75 Federal St., 3rd floor, Boston, MA 02110-1941 (tel. (617) 426-7788; fax 426-8351). You must be 55 or over and may bring a spouse of any age. Programs at local universities focus on varied subjects and generally last 1-4 weeks.

Gateway Books, 2023 Clemens Road, Oakland, CA 94602 (tel. (510) 530-0299; fax 530-0497). Publishes *Get Up and Go: A Guide for the Mature Traveler* (US$10.95), and *Adventures Abroad* (US$13) which offer general hints for the budget-conscious senior who is considering a long stay or even retiring abroad.

Pilot Books, 103 Cooper St., Babylon, NY 11702 (tel. (516) 422-2225). Publishes *The International Health Guide for Senior Citizens* (US$5) and *The Senior Citizens' Guide to Budget Travel in Europe* (US$6).

■■■ DISABLED TRAVELERS

Greece, Turkey, and Cyprus are only slowly beginning to respond to the needs of travelers with disabilities. Many cruise ships that sail the Greek islands are equipped to accommodate those with disabilities. Special air transportation is available aboard Olympic Airways to many of the larger islands. Some hotels, train stations, and airports have recently installed facilities for the disabled; however, many of the archaeological sites throughout the region are still not wheelchair-accessible. When making arrangements with airlines or hotels, inform them of your disability; some need time to prepare for your needs.

Useful publications include *Travel for the Disabled*, *Directory of Travel Agencies for the Disabled* and *Wheelchair Vagabond*, **Twin Peaks Press,** P.O. Box 129, Vancouver, WA 98666 (tel. (800) 637-2256; fax (360) 696-3210; US$20). The following organizations can provide further assistance:

Directions Unlimited, 720 N. Bedford Rd., Bedford Hills, NY 10507 (tel. (800) 533-5343; fax (914) 241-0243). Specializes in arranging individual and group vacations, tours, and cruises for those with physical disabilities.

Flying Wheels Travel, P.O. Box 382, 143 W. Bridge St., Owatonne, MN 55060 (tel. (800) 535-6790; fax (507) 451-1685). Arranges international trips for groups or individuals in wheelchairs or with other sorts of limited mobility.

Society for the Advancement of Travel for the Handicapped (SATH), 347 Fifth Ave., Suite 610, New York, NY 10016 (tel. (212) 447-7284; fax ((212) 725-

8253). Publishes quarterly newsletter with trip-planning advice (members free; non-members US$2). Annual membership US$45; students and seniors US$25.

Travel Information Service, Moss Rehabilitation Hospital, 1200 W. Tabor Rd., Philadelphia, PA 19141 (tel. (215) 456-9603). Will refer callers to other agencies.

■■■ BISEXUAL, GAY, AND LESBIAN TRAVELERS

Greeks have a tolerant attitude towards homosexuality. Homosexual sex is legal, though homosexuality as a declared lifestyle is frowned upon. In Turkey, social conservatism and religious dictates keep most activity discreet. If problems arise, plan on authorities to be almost uniformly unsympathetic.

In Greece, Athens in particular offers a variety of gay bars, clubs, and hotels. For further information, consult the **Greek Gay Guide '96,** TΘ 4228, Athens 10210, (tel. (01) 381 5249). Call Mon.-Fri.,7-9pm for an English speaker; the guide is multilingual. The islands of Hydra, Lesbos, Paros, Rhodes, and Mykonos also offer gay and lesbian resorts, hotels, bars, and clubs. Turkey's urban centers do not lack for bars and informal cruising areas (men only), though they may be less obvious. Contact **Lamartin,** c/o İbrahim Eren, Lamartin Cad. 23/6, Tuslim, İstanbul.

Good general resources for gay and lesbian travelers are **Gay's the Word,** 66 Marchmont St., London, WC 1AB, England (tel. 44 (071) 278 76 54), **Giovanni's Room,** 345 S. 12th St., Philadelphia, PA 19107 (tel. (215) 923-2960; fax (215) 923-0813). All bookstores offer mail orders. Useful publications include **Women Going Places** (US$14), a travel and resource guide, emphasizing women-owned enterprises. **Are You Two . . . Together?,** a gay and lesbian guide to some of Europe's hottest spots, lists relevant regional laws (US$18). **Spartacus International Gay Guide** covers most countries of the world. It's available for US$30 from Bruno Gmünder, Postfach 30 13 45, D-1000 Berlin 30, Germany (tel. (030) 25 49 82 00).

■■■ TRAVELING WITH CHILDREN

Greeks and Turks love children. Expect a stream of compliments, advice, and candy. Children often receive substantial discounts on transportation throughout Greece and Turkey, but you shouldn't count on this. A variety of books can prepare you. Try **Travel with Children** (US$11, U.S. postage $1.50), available from Lonely Planet Publications, P.O. Box 617, Hawthorn, Victoria 3122, Australia; in U.S., Embarcadero West, 155 Philbert St., Suite 251, Oakland, CA 94607 (tel. (800) 275-8555; fax (510) 893-8563). **Backpacking With Babies and Small Children** (US$10) is available from Wilderness Press, 2440 Bancroft Way, Berkeley, CA 94704 (tel. (800) 443-7227 or (510) 843-8080).

■■■ DIETARY CONCERNS

The Jewish Travel Guide, which lists synagogues, kosher restaurants, and Jewish institutions in over 80 countries, could help you keep kosher on the road. It's available in the U.K. from Ballantine-Mitchell Publishers, Newbury House 890-900, Eastern Ave., Newbury Park, Ilford, Essex IG2 7HH (tel. (181) 599 8866; fax 599 0984).

Mediterranean cuisine includes tasty **vegetarian** dishes. Vegetarians on Cyprus may be disappointed by the lack of indigenous meatless entrees; in Greece and Turkey, foods such as *fasolia* (beans, *fasülye* in Turkish), *spanakopita* (spinach-filled pastry), and *tyropitakia* (cheese-filled pastry, *börek* in Turkish) are available. In Turkey and Cyprus, *meze* appetizers are plentiful (see Food, p. 425). In summer fresh produce abounds in the outdoor markets; vegetarians find plenty of fresh vegetables, fruits, and interesting cheeses.

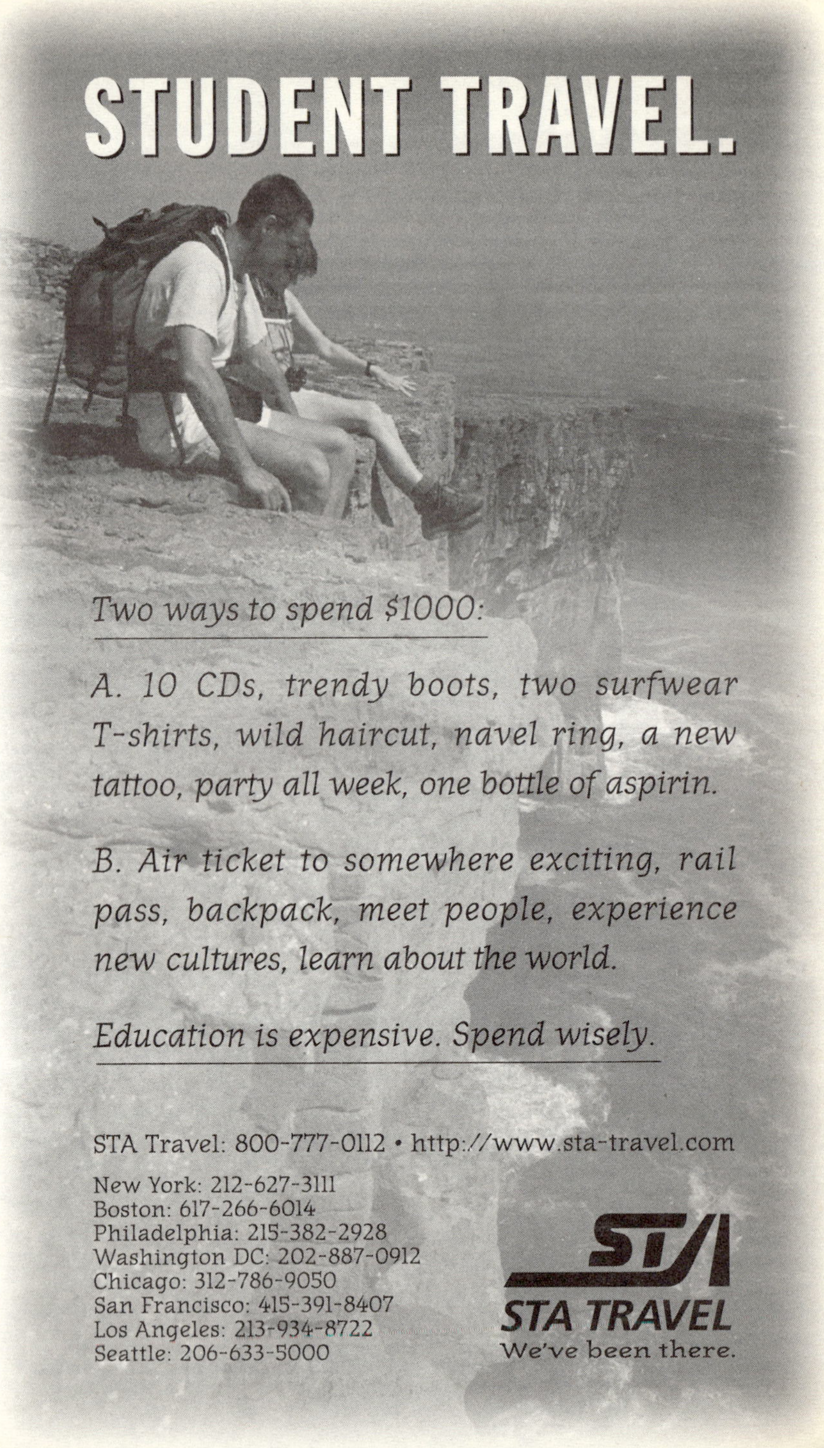
STUDENT TRAVEL.
Two ways to spend $1000:
A. 10 CDs, trendy boots, two surfwear T-shirts, wild haircut, navel ring, a new tattoo, party all week, one bottle of aspirin.
B. Air ticket to somewhere exciting, rail pass, backpack, meet people, experience new cultures, learn about the world.
Education is expensive. Spend wisely.
STA Travel: 800-777-0112 • http://www.sta-travel.com
New York: 212-627-3111
Boston: 617-266-6014
Philadelphia: 215-382-2928
Washington DC: 202-887-0912
Chicago: 312-786-9050
San Francisco: 415-391-8407
Los Angeles: 213-934-8722
Seattle: 206-633-5000
STA TRAVEL
We've been there.

TRAVEL IN THE REGION

BUDGET TRAVEL ORGANIZATIONS

These organizations help with booking flights and acquiring railpasses, student ID cards, and HI memberships.

Campus Travel, 52 Grosvenor Gardens, London SW1W OAG. Supplies student cards, schedules, and other travel products. 37 branches in the U.K. For telephone sales and bookings, in **London** call (0171) 730 3402 for Europe, 730 2101 for North America, and 730 8111 for other destinations worldwide; in **Manchester** (0161) 273 1721; in **Scotland** (0131) 668 3303.

Council on International Educational Exchange (Council), 205 E. 42nd St., New York, NY 10017 (tel. (212) 661-1414). Offers identity cards and a range of publications, among them the magazine *Student Travels* (free) and *The High School Student's Guide to Study, Travel and Adventure Abroad* ($13.95).

Council Travel, (800-2-COUNCIL/226-8624), is a full-service travel agency specializing in student, youth, and budget travel. They offer discount airfares on scheduled airlines, railpasses, hosteling cards, low-cost accommodations, guidebooks (including *Let's Go*), budget tours, travel gear, and international student (ISIC), youth (GO25), and teacher (ITIC) identity cards. Offices in most major U.S. cities and a main office at 205 E. 42nd St., **New York,** NY 10017 (tel (212) 661-1450). Overseas offices include: 28A Poland St. (Oxford Circus), **London,** W1V 3DB (tel. (0171) 437 7767); 22 rue des Pyramides (Metro: Pyramides), 75001 **Paris** (tel. (1) 44 55 55 65); **Nice** (tel. 93 82 23 33); **Munich** (tel. (089) 39 50 22).

CTS Travel, 220 Kensington High St., **London** W8 (tel. (0171) 937 3366 for travel in Europe, 937 3388 for travel worldwide). Specializes in student/youth travel.

Educational Travel Center (ETC), 438 North Frances St., Madison, WI 53703 (tel. (800) 747-5551; fax (608) 256-2042). Flights, HI-AYH cards, Eurail and regional rail passes. Call or write for their free pamphlet *Taking Off.*

Eurolines, 52 Grosvenor Gardens Victoria, London SW1W 0AU (tel. (0158) 240 4511 main office, or (0171) 730 8235 in London). Specializes in coach travel all over Europe, including Turkey.

Federation of International Youth Travel Organization (FIYTO), Bredgade 25H, DK-1260, Copenhagen K, Denmark (tel. (33) 33 96 00; fax 93 96 76). Promotes educational, cultural, and social travel for young people.

International Student Exchange Flights (ISE), 5010 East Shea Blvd., #A104, Scottsdale, AZ 85254 (tel. (602) 951-1177). Offers budget student flights to Europe and Asia, Eurail, HI-AYH memberships, and travel guides. Free catalog.

International Student Travel Confederation, Store Kongensgade 40H, 1264 Copenhagen K, Denmark (tel. (33) 93 93 03; fax (33) 93 73 77). A nonprofit confederation of student travel organizations—not actually a travel service. Sponsors the International Student Identity Card (ISIC).

Let's Go Travel, Harvard Student Agencies, Inc., 53A Church St., Cambridge, MA 02138 (tel. (800) 5-LETS GO (553-8746) or (617) 495-9649). Railpasses, HI-AYH memberships, ISICs, International Teacher ID cards, GO 25 cards, guidebooks (including every *Let's Go*), maps, bargain flights, and a complete line of budget travel gear. All items available by mail; call or write for a catalog.

Rail Europe Inc., 226 Westchester Ave., White Plains, NY 10604 (tel. (800) 438-7245; fax (800) 432-1329). Sells all Eurail products and passes, national railpasses, and point-to-point tickets. Up-to-date information on all rail travel.

Red Bear Tours, 320B Glenferrie Rd., Malvern, Melbourne, Victoria 3144, **Australia** (tel. (039) 824 71 83; fax 822 39 56; toll free (008) 33 70 31). Specializes in independent arrangements for travel to Turkey, Israel, Egypt, and Russia.

STA Travel, 6560 North Scottsdale Rd. #F100, Scottsdale, AZ 85253 (tel. (800) 777-0112 nationwide). Offers discount airfares, railpasses, tours, insurance, and ISICs. In the UK, Priory House, 6 Wrights Lane, **London** W8 6TA (tel. (071) 938 47 11). In Australia, 224 Faraday St., Carlton, **Melbourne,** Vic. 3050 (tel. (03) 347 69 11). In New Zealand, 10 High St., **Auckland** (tel. (09) 309 97 23).

Travel CUTS (Canadian University Travel Services, Ltd.), 187 College St., Toronto, Ont. M5T 1P7 (tel. (416) 798-CUTS (798-2887); fax 979-8167). Offices across Canada. Also, in the **U.K.,** 295-A Regent St., London W1R 7YA (tel. (0171) 637 31 61). Discounted flights; ISIC, GO 25, and HI hostel cards; free *Student Traveller* magazines and info on Student Work Abroad Program (SWAP).

Travel Management International (TMI), Grand Ave., Minneapolis, MN 55409 (tel. (800) 245-3672). Customized trip planning; offers railpasses.

Unitravel, 1177 North Warson Rd., St. Louis, MO 63132 (tel. (800) 325-2222; fax (314) 569-2503). Offers discounted airfares on major scheduled airlines.

University and Student Travel Network (USTN). A national association of university travel agencies. Offers ISICs, GO 25 Cards, and youth hostel cards, STA and Council student tickets, discount airline tickets, rail passes. Member agencies across the U.S., including Berkeley Northside Travel, 1824 Euclid Ave., **Berkeley,** CA 94709 (tel. (510) 843-1000; fax 843-7537; email airfares@ix.netcom.com).

USIT, 19-21 Aston Quay, O'Connell Bridge, Dublin 2 (tel. (01) 679 88 33; fax 677 88 43). Sells ISIC, HI membership cards, and *Let's Go*. Books its own charter flights.

Wasteels, 7041 Grand National Drive #207, Orlando, FL 32819 (tel. (407) 351-2537; in **London** (071) 834 7066). Sells Wasteels BIJ tickets; sold *only* in Europe.

■■■ BY PLANE

Flexibility saves money, especially when faced with the high cost of regularly scheduled direct flights; from North America, an indirect flight through Brussels or Luxembourg may cost considerably less than a direct flight. **Off-season** travelers are faced with less competition for inexpensive seats and benefit from lower fares. **Peak-season** rates are in effect June 1-Sept. 15 and Dec. 10-24. You can save a bundle by carefully arranging your travel dates. Commissions are smaller on budget flights so some travel agents might not be eager to help you search for the cheapest fare. Scan the travel section of the Sunday papers for cheap, albeit erratic, fares. Student travel organizations such as Let's Go Travel, Council, and Travel CUTS offer special deals through ticket consolidators of which regular travel agents may not be aware. In the summer of 1995, New York-Athens round-trip flights cost approximately US$750, and New York-İstanbul round-trip flights cost roughly US$800.

COMMERCIAL AIRLINES

If you decide to use a regular airline, you'll get the greatest reliability and flexibility. Major airlines offer two options for the budget traveler. The first is to fly **stand-by** (without a reservation). Some airlines have begun phasing out standby fares and destinations, and standby tickets are not the budget wonders they once were. You can purchase standby tickets in advance, but you're not guaranteed a seat on any particular flight. The second option is to fly **APEX** (Advance Purchase Excursion Fare), the commercial airlines' lowest regular offer. Specials advertised in newspapers may be cheaper, but have more restrictions and fewer available seats. APEX fares provide you with confirmed reservations and allow "open-jaw" tickets (landing in and returning from different cities). Generally, reservations must be made 7 to 21 days in advance, with 7- to 14-day minimum and up to 90-day maximum stay limits, and hefty cancellation and change penalties. For summer travel, book APEX fares early; by May you will have a hard time getting the departure date you want. **Olympic Airways** (tel. (242) 838-3600) offers a round-trip New York-Athens summer fare of US$1126, 10-30% cheaper in winter. International flights also connect to airports in Crete, Rhodes, and Corfu. **Turkish Airlines' (THY)** fares are exorbitant, but reasonably priced student tickets are sometimes available.

CONSOLIDATORS AND CHARTER FLIGHTS

Ticket consolidators, also known as "bucket shops," resell unsold tickets on commercial and charter airlines. Look for their tiny ads in weekend papers (in the U.S., the Sunday *New York Times* is best), and start calling. In London, the real "bucket shop" center, the Air Travel Advisory Bureau (tel. (0171) 636 50 00) provides a list of consolidators. There is rarely a maximum age or limit on duration of stay; tickets are heavily discounted, and may offer extra flexibility or bypass advance purchase requirements, since you aren't tangled up in airline bureaucracy. But unlike tickets bought through an airline, you won't be able to use your tickets on another flight if you miss yours, and you will have to go back to the consolidator rather than the airline to get a refund. Phone around and pay with a credit card so you can stop payment if you never receive your tickets. Don't be tempted solely by the low prices; find out everything you can about the agency you're considering and get a copy of their refund policy in writing. Also ask about accommodations and car rental discounts; some consolidators have fingers in many pies. Insist on a **receipt** that gives full details about the tickets, refunds, and restrictions, and if they don't want to give you one or generally seem clueless, use a different company. Consult Kelly Monaghan's *Consolidators: Air Travel's Bargain Basement* (US$5, postage US$3.50) from the Intrepid Traveler, P.O. Box 438, New York, NY 10034 for more info.

The theory behind a **charter** is that a tour operator contracts with an airline to fly extra loads of passengers to peak-season destinations. Charter flights fly less frequently than major airlines and have more restrictions, particularly on refunds. They are also almost always fully booked, and schedules and itineraries may change or be cancelled at the last moment (as late as 48 hours before the trip, without a full refund); you'll be better off purchasing a ticket on a regularly scheduled airline. Pay with a credit card if you can; consider purchasing traveler's insurance.

It's best to buy from a major organization that has experience in placing individuals on charter flights. Try **USIT** (tel. (1) 679 8833 in Dublin), **Interworld** (tel. (305) 443-4929), **Rebel** (tel. (800) 227-3235), or Council Travel. The charter companies **Tourlite** (tel. (800) 272-7600) and **Homeric Tours** (tel. (800) 223-5570) offer service to Greece; Tourlite also goes to Turkey. Don't be afraid to call every number for the best deal. Get the company's recent record of delays and cancellations.

HITCHING A RIDE TO EUROPE?!

If budget travel inspires your utmost bravery and patience, **Airhitch,** 2472 Broadway, Suite 200, New York, NY 10025 (tel. (800) 326-2009 or (212) 864-2000) and Santa Monica, CA (tel. (310) 394-0550), will add a certain thrill to the prospects of how you will get to the eastern Mediterranean. Complete flexibility on both sides of the Atlantic is necessary: they may fly you to Athens, or they might land you somewhere else in Europe and leave the rest up to you. Flights cost $169 each way when departing from the Northeast, $269 from the West Coast, and $229 from the Southeast and Midwest. The snag is that you must choose a minimum period of five days in which to travel from a particular region (not a city) and draw up a list of preferred destinations; this procedure must be followed again for the return trip. There are several offices in Europe, so you can wait to register for your return; the main one is in Paris (tel. (1) 47 00 16 30). A similar service is offered by **Air-Tech, Ltd.,** 584 Broadway #1007, New York, N.Y. 10012 (tel. (212) 219-7000; fax 219-0066), 1A York Mansion, Earl Court Rd., London 5W5 9AF, England (tel. (0171) 373 77 96). Air-Tech also arranges courier flights and regular confirmed-reserved flights at discount rates. Be sure to read all the fine print in your agreements with either company. Delays of up to several days have been reported—if you are delayed, you could incur costs that outweigh initial savings. The Better Business Bureau of New York City and *Let's Go* have received complaints about Airhitch; the company has recently changed ownership, but consumers should make careful inquiries. *Let's Go* has received multiple complaints about delays, inaccurate information, and poor service associated with AirTech.

COURIER FLIGHTS

Those who travel light should consider flying to Europe as a **courier.** The company hiring you will use your checked luggage space for freight; you're only allowed to bring carry-ons. Restrictions to watch for: you must be over 18 and have a valid passport; most flights are round-trip only with short fixed-length stays (usually one week); you may not be able to travel with a companion (single tickets only); and most flights are from New York. Round-trip fares to Western Europe from the U.S. range from US$250-400 (during the off-season) to US$400-550 (during the summer). **NOW Voyager,** 74 Varick St. #307, New York, NY 10013 (tel. (212) 431-1616), acts as an agent for many courier flights worldwide primarily from New York. They offer special last-minute deals to such cities as London, Paris, Rome, and Frankfurt for as little as US$200 round-trip plus a US$50 registration fee. Other agents to try are **Halbart Express,** 147-05 176th St., Jamaica, NY 11434 (tel. (718) 656-5000) and **Discount Travel International** (tel. (212) 362-3636).

You can also go directly through courier companies in New York or check your bookstore or library for handbooks such as *Air Courier Bargains* (US$15 plus $3.50 shipping from the Intrepid Traveler, P.O. Box 438, New York, NY 10034). *The Courier Air Travel Handbook* (US$10 plus US$3.50 shipping) explains how to travel as an air courier and contains names, phone numbers, and contact points of courier companies. It can be ordered directly from Bookmasters, Inc., P.O. Box 2039, Mansfield, OH 44905 (tel. (800) 507-2665). A final caveat for the budget conscious: don't get so caught up in seemingly great deals. Always read the fine print; check for restrictions and hidden fees. There are amazingly cheap fares waiting to be unearthed, but you can't get something for nothing.

■■■ BY TRAIN

Greece is served by a number of international train routes that connect Athens, Thessaloniki, and Larissa to most European cities. Count on at least a three-day journey from Trieste or Vienna to Athens. **Turkey** is accessible by rail from points in Europe. Trains are among the cheapest transportation options, but not the most convenient—Eurail is not valid in Turkey. The Turkish rail system is rivaled only by the Greek system as Europe's most antiquated and least efficient.

RAIL PASSES

Eurailpasses are best for those travelers who want to see as much of Europe as possible; to make these passes pay off, you need to make a lot of stops. *The passes must be bought in the United States* or another non-European country, as they are issued only outside of Europe. Passes include unlimited first-class travel and range in cost from US$498 for 15 days to US$1398 for three months. If traveling with a group (2 or more; 3 or more April-September), the **Eurail Saverpass** allows similar unlimited first-class travel in the Eurailpass countries, which exclude Britain and Turkey. These offer slightly discounted per-person rates of US$430 for 15 days, US$550 for 21 days, or US$678 for one month. **Eurail Flexipasses** allow first-class travel for a set number of travel days inside a longer time window; for example, 5 days of travel within a two-month period would cost US$348. Travelers under 26 on their first day of travel are eligible for second-class **Eurail Youthpasses** (ranging from 15 days of travel for US$398 to 2 months for US$768). The **Youth Flexipasses** offer similar discounts: the comparable Flexipass, 5-travel-days inside a two-month window, would cost US$255 with the second-class Youth option. All five passes offer free travel in Greece and 30% discounts on ferries from Brindisi to Patras on Adriatica Lines, or on Hellenic Mediterranean Lines' ferries from Piraeus to Cyprus, Venice, Alexandria, and Turkey (Eurail passes are *not* good for intra-Greece ferries). Keep your validation slip and receipt. Eurailpasses are available from **Eurailpass,** P.O. Box 10383, Stamford, CT 06904; from **Rail Europe, Inc.,** 226 Westchester Ave., White Plains, NY 10604 (U.S. tel. (800) 438-7245; Canadian tel. (800) 361-7245; fax (416) 602-4198), publisher of the free *Europe on Track;* and from most travel agents. Greece and Turkey both have national rail passes as well. When deciding whether to purchase a rail pass for travel primarily in Greece or Turkey, keep in mind that service in these countries is among the slowest in Europe, and individual tickets are among the most affordable. Rail passes in these countries rarely pay for themselves.

RAIL TICKETS

For travelers under 26, **BIJ** tickets, sold under the names **Wasteels, Eurotrain,** and **Route 26,** are a great alternative to railpasses. Available for international trips within Europe as well as most ferry services, they knock 30-45% off regular second-class fares. Tickets are all good for 60 days after purchase and allow an unlimited number of stopovers along the normal direct route of the train journey. Issued for a specific international route between two points, they must be used in the direction and order of the designated route without side- or back-tracking. You must buy BIJ tickets in Europe, at Wasteels or Eurotrain offices (usually in or near train stations). However, detailed information on tickets for international journeys originating in the U.K., France, and Germany is given in the U.S. by **Wasteels Travel,** 7041 Grand National Dr. #207, Orlando, FL 32819 (tel. (407) 351-2537; fax 363-1041). For departure from other countries, tickets can be purchased from European agents or directly at the ticket counter in some nations.

If you board a train that has no available compartment space for a long trip, consider getting off and waiting for the next one—three days in an aisle crowded with travelers and livestock can be a nightmare. *Couchettes,* the economy version of a full sleeping berth, come complete with blankets, sheets, and pillows. If you have any sort of railpass, couchettes are available at an extra charge.

USEFUL RESOURCES

The ultimate reference for planning rail trips is the **Thomas Cook European Timetable** (US$25.95; US$35.95 includes a map of Europe highlighting all train and ferry routes; plus US$4 for postage). This timetable, updated regularly, covers all major and most minor train routes in Europe. In the U.S., order it from **Forsyth Travel Library** (see p. 2). Also look for Lenore Balken's *Camp Europe By Train* (US$15) which covers all aspects of rail travel and includes sections on railpasses, packing, and the specifics of rail travel in each country. The annual *Eurail Guide to Train Travel in the New Europe* (US$15), which gives timetables, instructions, and prices for international train trips, day trips and excursions in Europe, is available in most bookstores; or write to **Houghton Mifflin Co.,** 222 Berkeley St., Boston, MA 02116. Rick Steves' free *Europe Through the Back Door* travel newsletter and catalog, 109 Fourth Ave. N., P.O. Box 2009, Edmonds, WA 98020 (tel. (206) 771-8303; fax 771-0833), provides comprehensive information on railpasses both national and regional. **Hunter Publishing,** 300 Raritan Center Parkway, Edison, NJ 08818 (tel. (908) 225-1900; fax 417-0482) provides a comprehensive catalog of handy rail atlases, travel maps, and guidebooks that might pertain directly to your trip.

■■■ BY BUS

> Road travel in Turkey is dangerous by European standards (see p. 416).

Though European trains and railpasses are extremely popular, the long-distance bus networks of Greece and Turkey are more extensive, efficient, and often more comfortable than train services.

Eurobus, P.O. Box 5220, London W5 1GQ (tel. (0181) 991 5591; fax 991 1442), offers two- or three-month passes for unlimited travel on continental-style coaches with an English-speaking driver and guide. Destinations include major cities throughout continental Europe. Travelers can hop on and off, and move on as often as they wish. The buses also stop door to door at a selection of campsites, hostels, and hotels, and offer on-board video presentation of various regions. Eurobus offers a "supersaver" discount book offering deals throughout Europe. Another option is **Eurolines,** 52 Grosvenor Gardens, Victoria, London SW1W 0AU (tel. (01582) 40 45 11 or (0171) 730 82 35 in London), which specializes in coach travel all over Europe, including Eastern Europe and Russia. **Magic Bus** offers cheap, direct bus service between major cities in Europe, along with competitive airfares. Offices are located at 20 Filellinon St., Syntagma, Athens (tel. (01) 323 7471, -4; fax 322 0219). (Competent, English-speaking staff; open Mon.-Fri. 9am-6pm, Sat. 9am-2pm.)

■■■ FERRY CROSSINGS

Ferry travel is a popular way to get to and travel between Greece, Turkey, and Cyprus. Reservations are recommended for many ferries, especially in high season. Be warned that *ferries run on irregular schedules.* Check in at *least* 2hr. in advance; late boarders may find their seats gone. If you sleep on deck, bring warm clothes and a sleeping bag. Bicycles travel free and motorcycles are transported for an additional charge (check each agency). Don't forget motion sickness medication, toilet paper, and a hand towel. Bring your own food to avoid high prices on board.

Most lines offer **discounts.** Those 26 and under, and ISIC-holders 30 and under, can usually obtain student deck fares for 1000dr less than regular price. A railpass or HI card may entitle you to a small discount on selected routes. Children under 12 pay half-price (those under 2 or 4 ride free, depending on the company). There are group reductions of approximately 10% on one-way and 20% on round-trip tickets (usually 10-person minimum).

The major ports of departure from Italy to Greece are Ancona and Brindisi, on the southeast coast of Italy. Bari, Otranto, and Venice also have a few connections. If coming from the north of Italy, be aware that gassing and theft are not unheard of on the overnight trains from Rome to Brindisi. Some ferry lines offer free deck passage on a space-available basis (you could get bumped by a paying passenger), but all passengers still need to pay the port tax (L10,000, or $6.25, in Brindisi) and, in high season, a supplementary fee of L19,000 ($12). Boats travel primarily to Corfu (10hr.), Igoumenitsa (12hr.), and Patras (20hr.). Prices range L50,000-105,000 ($31-66); in low season L22,000-45,000 ($13-29). For schedules from Greece to Italy, see Patras, Cephalonia, Corfu, or Igoumenitsa.

From Çeşme, Turkey, an Ertürk ferry offers service to Chios (May-June 3-4 per week, July-April 1 per week). Prices are one-way $25, same-day return $30, open round-trip $35. Rhodes is connected by ferry to Marmaris (one-way 10,000dr, round-trip 12,000dr), as well as to Limassol, Cyprus (2 per week, 17hr., 18,500-22,000dr) and Haifa, Israel (2 per week, 36hr., 28,500-33,000dr). These Limassol and Haifa services provide student and youth discounts of 20% year round.

From **Northern Cyprus,** the shortest and cheapest crossing is Taşucu to Girne (Kyrenia) (7hr.). Boats run twice daily in the summer, less frequently in winter, on no set schedule. **Ertürk** and **Fergün** tourism companies sell discounted tickets (see Taşucu for details). You can also cross from Mersin (10hr.).

Hydrofoils (Flying Dolphins) are a tempting mode of traveling. They run more frequently and reliably than ferries at twice their speed, but cost twice as much.

If you're coming from North America and really have travel time to spare, **Ford's Travel Guides,** 19448 Londelius St., Northridge, CA 91324 (tel. (818) 701-7414) lists **freighter companies** that will take passengers worldwide. Ask for their *Freighter Travel Guide and Waterways of the World* (US$15, plus US$2.50 postage if mailed outside the U.S.).

■■■ OTHER CROSSINGS

The Greek government frowns on tourists taking advantage of cheaper fares to Greece for easy access to Turkey, and the information you receive on how to travel between the two countries may be confusing. Contrary to what tourist authorities may lead you to believe, there's no law that prevents crossing the borders. Many travelers make one-day excursions, but you should check into regulations on longer trips. If you fly to Greece on a European charter flight, you can't travel to Turkey.

Athens and İstanbul are connected by Euroways Eurolines bus and by train. If you have a railpass and are traveling from Greece to Turkey, take the train as far as Alexandroupolis, and ride the bus from there. Beware: the 38-hr. ride from Athens will wear out even the most seasoned traveler. The quickest but most expensive option is an Olympic Airways **flight** to İstanbul or other points in Turkey.

Those who **hitch** between Turkey and Greece say that they try to make it to İstanbul in one ride from Alexandroupolis or Thessaloniki; there isn't much traffic, and people are not permitted to walk across the border. *Let's Go* does not recommend hitchhiking. Those who have decided to hitch say they made sure that their driver's car license did not get stamped in their passports (but rather on some other, disposable piece of paper), or they would have needed to produce the car to leave the country. The officials might have suspected that they sold it on the black market.

If you bring your own car into Turkey, you can drive for three months without a *Carnet de Passage,* although the vehicle will be registered on your passport. If you stay longer, you must apply for a *triptique* at the Turkish Touring and Automobile Club. (See p. 3.)

■■■ PACKING

If you don't pack lightly, you will pay with either back problems or in the postage to mail stuff home. The more things you have, the more things you have to lose. The larger your pack, the more cumbersome it is to store safely. Before you leave, pack your bag, strap it on, and walk uphill on hot asphalt for the next three hours. At the slightest sign of heaviness, unpack something. A good general rule is to pack only what you absolutely need, then take half the clothes and twice the money. Leave room for souvenirs and gifts.

Decide whether a backpack, light suitcase, or shoulder bag is most suitable for your travels. If you plan on moving around a lot, a sturdy, internal-frame **backpack** is hard to beat. A small **daypack** is indispensable for flights, sightseeing, and holding your valuables. On short trips, daypacks come in handy for carrying your lunch, camera, canteen, and *Let's Go.*

Bring few, but comfortable, clothes, and keep accessories to a minimum. Choose quick-drying clothes that you can wash in a sink. Loose garments which can be layered are more versatile. It's good to stick to a neutral color scheme; English-language lettering will mark you as a tourist. Dark clothes show dirt less than light ones, though they absorb heat; a small print also hides stains. But a white button-down shirt can be a godsend for both sexes as a cover-up and a reasonably formal piece. Sturdy cotton blend pants or a longish skirt are appropriate in more situations than are jeans, and they dry faster. Women endorse the long skirt as being cooler, looser, and less tourist-looking than pants or shorts. Running shorts, cut-offs, tank tops, and t-shirts brand the tourist. Bare shoulders and bare knees are considered immodest, especially in the countryside. Women, in their day bags, can carry a rolled-up scarf and a long, light skirt. Mosques and other places of worship often refuse admission to visitors who have not bothered to cover up. If you will stray into the north parts of Greece or Turkey, or if you are traveling not in summer, bring raingear and a light jacket or windbreaker.

Appropriate shoes are vital: well-cushioned **sneakers** are good for walking. Lace-up leather shoes with firm grips provide better support and social acceptability than athletic shoes. Leather also feels better on sockless feet (socks and sand don't mix). For your ultimate beach-roaming pleasure, a sturdy pair of sandals are the thing; keep in mind, though, that exposed feet are asking to get lacerated or stung, and cut feet are the bane of the mobile sightseer's trip. If you only want to bring one pair, the best all-around footgear are probably hybrid **sneakers-cum-hiking boots.** A foot powder like talc in your shoes and on your feet can prevent sores, and moleskin is great for blisters. Break in your shoes before you leave home.

You'll probably find the following miscellaneous items valuable: an umbrella, Ziploc bags (for damp clothes, soap, food), a small alarm clock, waterproof matches, sun hat, moleskin, sewing kit, safety pins, sunglasses, electrical tape, earplugs, a personal stereo, Swiss army knife, notebook and pens, plastic water bottle,

Greek and/or Turkish-language phrasebooks, small flashlight, string (makeshift clothesline), towel, and a rubber squash ball (universal plug for sinks without stoppers). Don't forget motion sickness medication for ferry travel. Be sure to consult Security, p. 18, and Health, p. 19, for more items.

Stores in Greece and Turkey stock most **toiletries.** Still, a **cold-water soap** always comes in handy (what could be more *a propos* than all-natural Dr. Bronner's Castile Soap in a mint flavor, sold at camping stores, usable for anything from washing clothes, bathing, and shampooing to brushing your teeth). Pack tampons securely so that they don't fall apart. Don't expect to find your preferred brand of condoms.

Film can be expensive in Greece and Turkey. Despite disclaimers, airport security x-rays can fog film. A lead-lined pouch, sold at camera stores, protects film. Pack it in your carry-on, since airlines use higher-intensity x-rays on checked luggage. **Disposable cameras** eliminate the theft concern and take surprisingly good pictures.

ELECTRICITY

The standard electrical outlet in Greece produces 220 volts AC using the two-pronged plug used in Europe. Although Turkey uses the same plug, be careful and ask the exact voltage, since both 110 volts and 220 volts are used. In Cyprus, 220 volt outlets require either the two or three-pronged outlets used in Africa and Asia. North American appliances are designed for 110 volts AC and the prong won't fit. If you're bringing a beloved electrical appliance, you'll need a converter and a three-pronged adapter, both available in department and hardware stores. Visit a hardware store for an adapter (which changes the shape of the plug) and a converter (which changes the voltage). Don't make the mistake of using only an adapter (unless appliance instructions explicitly state otherwise, as with some portable computers), or you'll melt your radio. To order a converter by mail (about US$20) or to receive their punny pamphlet, *Foreign Electricity is No Deep Dark Secret,* write to Franzus Co., Murtha Industrial Park, P.O. Box 142, Beacon Falls, CT 06403 (tel. (203) 723-6664; fax (203) 723-6666).

■■■ WEIGHTS AND MEASURES

1 centimeter (cm) = 0.39 inches	1 inch = 2.54cm
1 meter (m) = 3.28 feet	1 foot = 0.31m
1 kilometer (km) = 0.62 miles	1 mile = 1.61km
1 gram (g) = 0.04 ounces	1 ounce = 28g
1 kilogram (kg) = 2.2 pounds	1 pound = 0.45kg
1 liter (l) = 0.26 gallons	1 gallon = 3.76l
1 Imperial Gallon (U.K.) = 1.2 gallons	1 gallon = .83 Imperial Gallons
°F = (°C x 1.8) + 32	°C = (°F - 32) x .56

GREECE ΕΛΛΑΣ

US$1 = 224.79dr	**100dr = US$0.44**
CDN$1 = 165.65dr	**100dr = CDN$0.60**
UK£1 = 358.92dr	**100dr = UK£0.28**
IR£1 = 369.67dr	**100dr = IR£0.27**
AUS$1 = 165.67dr	**100dr = AUS$0.60**
NZ$1 = 151.89dr	**100dr = NZ$0.66**
SAR1 = 61.79dr	**100dr = SAR1.62**

Even before Odysseus made his epic voyage across the Mediterranean, Greece was a land for wanderers. The country exhibits an extraordinary range of landscapes and attractions, and even within broad categories (such as beaches, for instance) there are great variations from place to place. Greece's historical ruins are among the world's oldest, and its surprisingly varied topography among the most exquisite. The uniformity of ancient classical aesthetics has given way to an extraordinary mix of popular and ethnic influences and, today, the struggles of the past remain visible in the beauty of present-day Greece.

As far as visitors are concerned, Greece is a country in which utterly hedonistic vacation pleasures and weighty cultural offerings co-exist in a rare successful relationship. Unfortunately, Greece by and large lacks the elaborate vocabulary that afflicts more "sophisticated" national tourist industries. Time here will probably be spent most happily simply soaking up Greece's offerings, natural and constructed, without high expectations for amenities or chi-chi service. Don't allow such expectations to ruin the blissful relaxation you could find while hiking, swimming late at night, eating olives, or visiting a medieval city. All these things, taken together, can be better done in Greece than anywhere else.

ESSENTIALS

■■■ ONCE THERE

TOURIST OFFICES

Tourism in Greece is overseen by two national organizations: the **Greek National Tourist Organization (GNTO)** and the **tourist police** (*touristiki astinomia*). The GNTO can supply general information about sights and accommodations throughout the country. Offices in the U.S. and other countries are listed under tourist offices on p. 2; the main office is at 2 Amerikis St., Athens (tel. (01) 322 3111). Note that the GNTO is known as **EOT** in Greece. The tourist police deal with more local and immediate problems: where to find a room, what the bus schedule is, or what to do when you've lost your passport. They are open long hours and are always willing to help, although their English is often limited. Tourist information for Greece is available in English 24 hr. by calling 171.

Nikis and **Filellinon Streets** in Athens are lined with agencies and organizations geared towards budget and student travelers. We also list similar establishments in different cities in the Orientation and Practical Information section for each region.

BUSINESS HOURS

Most **shops** close on Sundays; only restaurants, cafés, and bakeries remain open. During the week business hours vary, but most places close after 2pm for a siesta and re-open at roughly 6pm. Most **banks** are open Monday through Friday 8am to

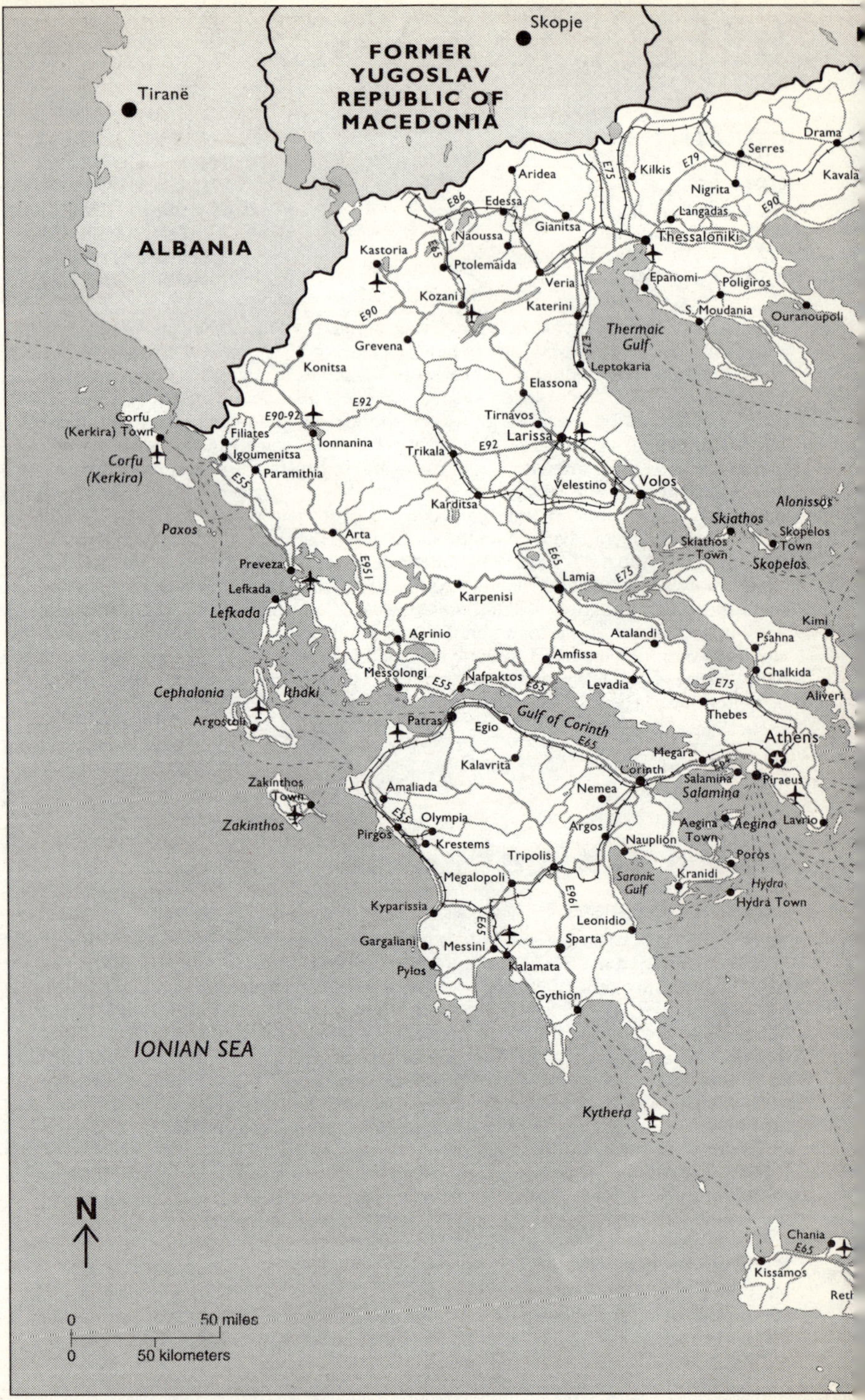
Skopje
FORMER YUGOSLAV REPUBLIC OF MACEDONIA
Tiranë
ALBANIA
Drama
Serres
Kavala
Kilkis
Nigrita
Langadas
Aridea
Edessa
Gianitsa
Naoussa
Thessaloniki
Kastoria
Ptolemaida
Veria
Epanomi
Poligiros
Kozani
Katerini
S. Moudania
Ouranoupoli
Thermaic Gulf
Grevena
Leptokaria
Konitsa
Elassona
Tirnavos
Larissa
Corfu (Kerkira) Town
Filiates
Igoumenitsa
Ionnanina
Paramithia
Trikala
Corfu (Kerkira)
Velestino
Volos
Karditsa
Alonissos
Skiathos
Skopelos Town
Skiathos Town
Skopelos
Paxos
Arta
Preveza
Lamia
Lefkada
Karpenisi
Lefkada
Kimi
Agrinio
Atalandi
Psahna
Amfissa
Chalkida
Messolongi
Nafpaktos
Levadia
Aliveri
Cephalonia
Ithaki
Thebes
Argostoli
Patras
Egio
Gulf of Corinth
Athens
Megara
Kalavrita
Corinth
Salamina
Piraeus
Zakinthos Town
Amaliada
Nemea
Salamina
Zakinthos
Olympia
Argos
Aegina Town
Aegina
Lavrio
Pirgos
Krestems
Nauplion
Poros
Tripolis
Saronic Gulf
Kranidi
Megalopoli
Hydra
Hydra Town
Kyparissia
Leonidio
Gargaliani
Messini
Sparta
Pylos
Kalamata
Gythion
IONIAN SEA
Kythera
N
Chania
Kissamos
0
50 miles
0
50 kilometers

BULGARIA
TURKEY
BLACK SEA
Orestiada
Didimotho
Soufli
Xanthi
Komotini
E85
E90
Alexandroupolis
İstanbul
Sea of Marmara
Limenas
Thassos
Samothraki
Samothraki
Bursa
Limnos
Mirina
Lesvos
Mitlini
TURKEY
Skyros
Skyros Town
AEGEAN SEA
Chios
Chios Town
İzmir
Karystos
Andros
Andros
Tinos
Tinos Town
Kea
Ikaria
Samos
Samos Town
Syros
Kithnos Town
Hermoupolis
Kithnos
Mykonos Town
Mykonos
Delos
Agathonissi
Patmos
Serifos
Leros
Kalymnos Town
Kalymnos
Sifnos
Paros
Naxos
Naxos
Paros
Kos Town
Kos
Milos
Paliegos
Amorgos
Astypalea
Symi
Folegandros
Ios
Nisyros
Rhodes Town
Anafi
Tilos
Thiro (Santorini)
Chalki
Rhodes
SEA OF CRETE
Karpathos
Crete
E75
Iraklion
Agios Nikolaos
Kassos
Sitia
Arkalhori
Timbaki
Mires
Ierapetra
Greece

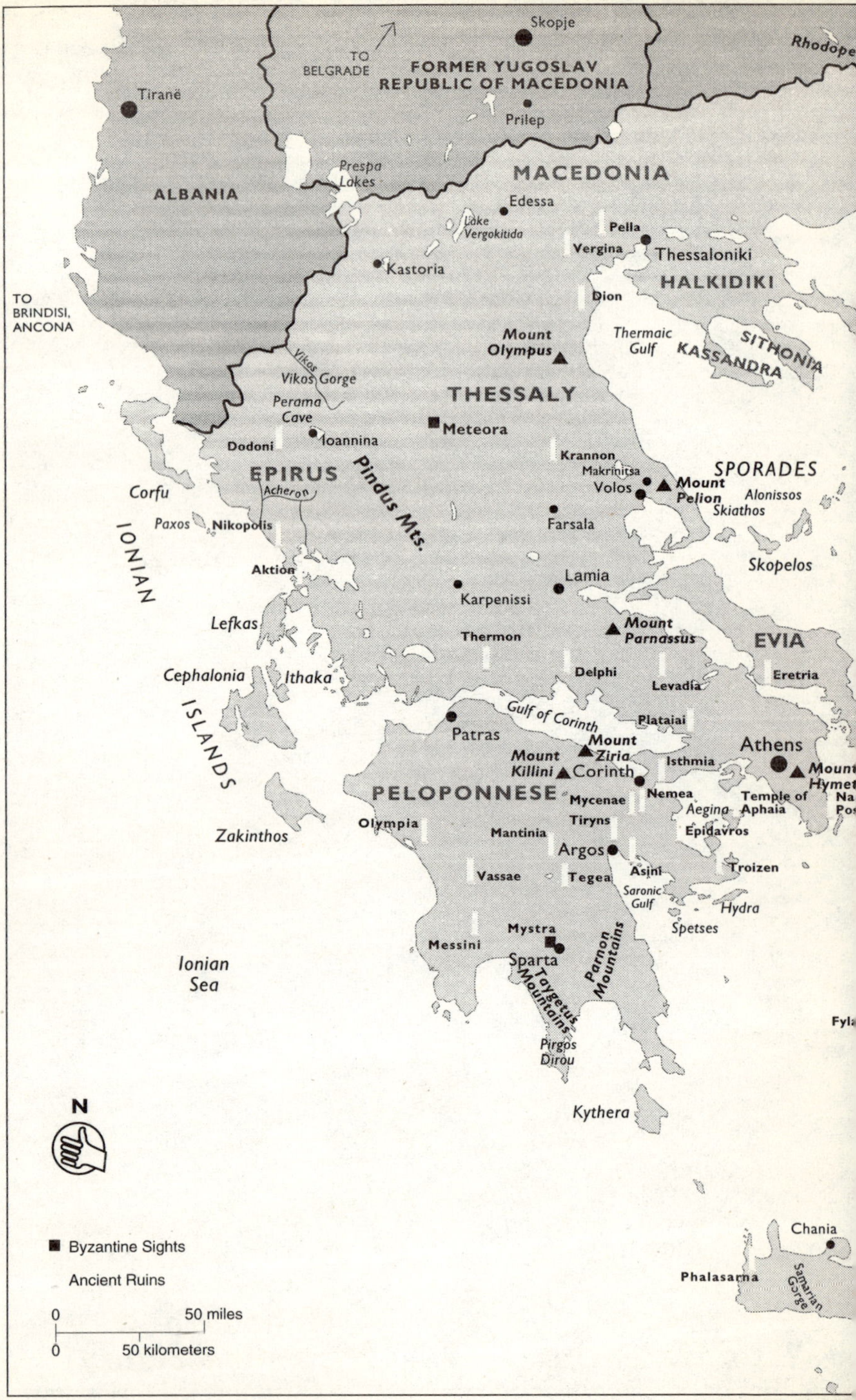
Skopje
TO BELGRADE
FORMER YUGOSLAV REPUBLIC OF MACEDONIA
Rhodope
Tiranë
Prilep
ALBANIA
Prespa Lakes
MACEDONIA
Edessa
Lake Vergokitida
Pella
Vergina
Thessaloniki
Kastoria
HALKIDIKI
TO BRINDISI, ANCONA
Dion
Mount Olympus
Thermaic Gulf
KASSANDRA
SITHONIA
Vikos
Vikos Gorge
THESSALY
Perama Cave
Meteora
Dodoni
Ioannina
Krannon
Makrinitsa
SPORADES
EPIRUS
Acheron
Pindus Mts.
Volos
Mount Pelion
Alonissos
Skiathos
Corfu
Paxos
Nikopolis
Farsala
IONIAN
Skopelos
Aktion
Lamia
Karpenissi
Lefkas
Mount Parnassus
Thermon
EVIA
Cephalonia
Ithaka
Delphi
Eretria
Levadia
ISLANDS
Gulf of Corinth
Patras
Plataiai
Mount Ziria
Athens
Mount Killini
Corinth
Isthmia
Mount Hymet
PELOPONNESE
Mycenae
Nemea
Temple of Aphaia
Aegina
Olympia
Tiryns
Epidavros
Zakinthos
Mantinia
Argos
Troizen
Vassae
Tegea
Asini
Saronic Gulf
Hydra
Spetses
Mystra
Messini
Sparta
Parnon Mountains
Taygetus Mountains
Ionian Sea
Pirgos Dirou
Kythera
N
Chania
Phalasarna
Samarian Gorge
■ Byzantine Sights
Ancient Ruins
0 50 miles
0 50 kilometers

Mts.
BULGARIA
THRACE
TURKEY
Black Sea
Istanbul
Phillippi
Avdyra
Kavala
Alexandroupolis
Sea of Marmara
Thassos
Samothrace
Paleopolis
Bursa
Limnos
Çanakkale
Troy
NORTHEAST AEGEAN ISLANDS
Bergama
TURKEY
Skyros
Lesvos
Aegean Sea
Chios
Nea Moni
İzmir
Mount Ochi
Andros
Ephesus
Samos
Tinos
Ikaria
Heraion
Hierapolis
Kea
Miletus
Kithnos
Mykonos
Syros
Delos
Patmos
Panagia Ekatontapiliani
Leros
Seriphos
Naxos
Kalymnos
Bodrum
Sifnos
Paros
Asclepion
Daylan
CYCLADES
Chozoviotissa
Kos
Knidos
Amorgos
Milos
Ios
Astypalea
DODECANESE
Nisyros
Symi
Colossus
Santorini
Anafi
Tilos
Ancient Thira
Halki
Kamiros
Sea of Crete
Rhodes
Karpathos
TO CYPRUS AND KASTELLORIZO (MEGISTI)
Crete
Iraklion
Kassos
Tylissos
Knossos
Gortina
Phaestos
Hellenic and Byzantine Sights

2pm and 3:30-6pm in some larger cities. Banks offer the best **currency exchange** rate. **Post offices** are generally open Monday through Saturday 7:30am to 2pm. The **OTE,** the Greek phone company, is often open until 7:30pm or later in larger cities. Shops and **pharmacies** are open Monday, Wednesday, and Saturday 8am to 2:30pm and Tuesday, Thursday, and Friday 8am to 1pm and 5 to 8:30pm. There's usually a pharmacy open 24 hr. on a rotating basis; its address should be posted on the doors of all other pharmacies or in the local daily newspapers. **Grocery stores** have longer hours. Government-run **museums** and **archaeological sites** close on Mondays, and have slightly shorter hours from mid-October to mid-May. On holidays, sights often have Sunday opening hours and, in many cases, do not charge admission on these days. All banks and shops close on major holidays. (See Holidays on p. 64 for dates.) In general, travelers from time- and punctuality-obsessed countries should be aware that many establishments in Greece have flexible and variable hours.

EMERGENCIES

In each regional section, under Orientation and Practical Information, we list police telephone numbers. We also list the telephone numbers for ambulances, medical emergency centers, local hospitals, clinics, and pharmacies. Emergency phone numbers, applicable throughout most of Greece and operating 24 hr., include **police** (tel. 100), **first aid** (tel. 166), **fire** (tel. 199), **hospitals** on duty (tel. 106), and **tourist police** (171 in Athens, 922 7777 for the rest of Greece). For **U.S. citizen's emergency aid** call (01) 722 3652 or 729 4301.

■■■ GETTING AROUND

BY PLANE

Olympic Airways, 96-100 Syngrou Ave., 11741 Athens (tel. (01) 929 2111), serves many large cities and islands within Greece. While flying is quickest, it may not be the most convenient or flexible option for travel within Greece; coverage in some remote areas is spotty at best. In the U.S., call the **New York** office, 645 Fifth Avenue, NY 10022 (tel. (800) 223-1226; fax 735-0215). In England, call the **London** office, 11 Conduit St., London WIR OLP (tel. (0171) 409-2400; fax 493-0563). For further flight information within Greece, check the regional Practical Information listings of airports, flight destinations, and prices, or pick up an Olympic Airways Timetable booklet at any Olympic office.

BY BUS

Spending time in Greece invariably means traveling by bus. Service is extensive, frequent in most areas, and fares are cheap. On major highways, buses tend to be more modern and efficient than in the mountainous areas of the Peloponnese or Northern Greece. The **OSE** (see By Train on p. 43) offers limited bus service from a few cities. Unless you're sticking close to train routes, **KTEL** bus service should be sufficient.

Always ask an official about scheduled departures (posted schedules are often outdated, and all services are curtailed significantly on Sat. and Sun.), and try to arrive at least 10min. ahead of time (Greek buses have a habit of leaving early). In major cities, KTEL bus lines have several different stations for different destinations. In villages, a café often serves as the bus station, and you must ask the proprietor for a schedule. Ask the conductor before entering the bus whether it's going to your destination (the signs on the front are often misleading or wrong), and make clear where you want to get off. If the bus passes your stop, stand up and yell *Stasi!* On the road, stand near a *Stasi* (ΣΤΑΣΗ) sign to pick up an intercity bus. KTEL buses are generally green or occasionally orange, while intercity buses are usually blue.

For long-distance rides, generally in Pullmans, you should buy your ticket beforehand in the office. (If you don't, you may have to stand throughout the journey.) For shorter trips, pay the conductor after you have boarded. Some lines offer round-trip fares with a 20% discount. In towns and cities, local buses and trolleys charge roughly 75dr for a ride.

BY TRAIN

In general, Greek trains are not quite as comfortable as the sleek, modern lines in northern Europe, and have more limited service (see Greece Transportation Map). Service to some areas is painfully slow, and lines do not go to the west coast. Trains are not very useful for traveling to remote areas or many archaeological sites, either.

New air-conditioned intercity trains have been put into service on many lines and although they are slightly more expensive and rare, they are worth the price. **Eurail** passes are valid on Greek trains. **Hellenic Railways Organization (OSE)** connects Athens to major Greek cities. For schedules and prices in Greece, dial 145 or 147.

BY CAR

Driving might be the ideal way to tour Greece. There are highways on the mainland, and ferries take you island hopping if you pay a transport fee for the car. Drivers should be comfortable with a standard stick shift, winding mountain roads, reckless drivers (especially in Athens), and the Greek alphabet. Signs in Greek appear roughly 100m before the transliterated versions, which are placed at the turn-offs.

Rentals with unlimited mileage and limited insurance range from 25,000dr in the off-season to 35,000dr in the summer. Gasoline is 200dr per liter—roughly US$5 per gallon. In a full day of touring (300km), Hertz's Subaru 600 (an economy hatchback) will eat up a full tank, translating into 17½ liters and roughly 3500dr. Agencies quote low daily rates, but these prices exclude the 20% tax and Collision Damage Waiver

(CDW) insurance. Without CDW, the driver is responsible for the first 15,000dr worth of damage if theft or accident is not the driver's fault, and the full amount otherwise. CDW insurance (2000dr per day) is strongly recommended.

Read the fine print. Some places quote lower rates but hit you with hidden charges—exorbitant refueling bills if you come back with less than a full tank, 1½-2½dr per kilometer drop-off or special charge, or 100km per day minimum mileage. Most companies won't permit driving the car outside Greece. Hertz and InterRent rent to drivers aged 21, but most other companies only rent to those 23 and older.

The cheapest and largest rental agencies are Just, InterRent, and Retca, with offices in Athens and other mainland cities, as well as on Crete and several of the islands. In Athens, look for **Just,** 43 Syngrou Ave. (tel. 923 8566); **InterRent,** 4 Syngrou Ave. (tel. 921 5788, -9), with other offices in Rhodes, Corfu, and Rethymnon; and **Retca,** 20 Kalisperi St. (tel. 921 4373). Also inexpensive is **Royal Rent A Car,** 44 Amalias Ave. (tel. 324 5366). **Avis, Hertz, Europcar,** and **Budget** operate throughout Greece; their rates are steeper, but service is reliable. It is often cheaper to make arrangements with these companies while still in your home country.

Foreign drivers are required to have an **International Driver's License** and an **International Insurance Certificate** to drive in Greece (see International Driver's License on p. 11). The Automobile and Touring Club of Greece (ELPA), 2-4 Messogion St., Athens 11527 (tel. 779 7401), provides assistance and offers reciprocal membership to foreign auto club members. They also have 24-hr. **emergency road assistance** (tel. 104) and an **info line** (tel. 174; open Mon.-Fri. 7am-3pm).

BY MOPED

Motorbiking is a popular way of touring Greece, especially the islands. Bikes are cheaper than cars and offer more freedom than buses, particularly for visiting remote areas. Plenty of places offer scooters or mopeds for rent, but the quality of bikes, speed of service in case of breakdown, and prices for longer periods varies drastically. Nearly all agencies are open to bargaining. Expect to pay at least 2500dr per day for a 50cc scooter, the cheapest bike able to tackle steep mountain roads. 150cc and 200cc motorbikes cost 20% and 30% more, respectively, and usually require a Greek motorcycle license. Many agencies request your passport as a deposit, but it's wiser to just settle up in advance. If they have your passport and you have an accident or mechanical failure, they may refuse to return it until you pay for repairs. Before renting, ask if the quoted price includes the 20% tax and insurance, or you'll be hit for several hundred unexpected *drachmae.* A word of caution about travel by moped: the majority of tourist-related accidents each year occur on mopeds. Regardless of your experience driving a moped, winding, often poorly maintained mountain roads and reckless drivers make driving a moped hazardous.

BY FERRY (AND HYDROFOIL)

Ferries are the cheapest way to cross the Mediterranean, but be prepared for delays and hassle (see p. 34). Hydrofoils are twice as swift and twice as expensive. Ferry travel is notoriously unreliable. Always confirm your departure times with the tourist or boat office. Don't bother planning an itinerary far in advance. Although boat connections between major islands are frequent during summer, departure times fluctuate from year to year. To get to smaller islands, you often have to change boats several times, and some islands are accessible only a few times per week. Direct connections are less expensive than longer routes (the more stops, the higher the price), but also tend to be less frequent. The English-language weekly newspaper *Athens News* prints summer ferry and Athens bus schedules.

BY FOOT

Let's Go describes hikes and trails in town and city listings; local residents and fellow travelers can suggest even more. Always make sure you have comfortable shoes and a map. Remember that hiking under the hot sun at a high altitude may be more strenuous than you expect. Good sunscreen, a hat, and water are essential. For more information, check out *Greece on Foot,* published by **The Mountaineer Books,** 1011 SW Klickitat Way, Seattle, WA 98134, USA (tel. (800) 553-4453).

BY THUMB

Consider fully the risks involved before you decide to hitchhike. *Let's Go* does not recommend hitching as a means of travel. That said, it's hard to generalize about hitching in Greece. Greeks are not eager to pick up foreigners, and foreign cars are often full of other travelers. Sparsely-populated areas have little or no traffic. Those who do hitchhike write their destination on a sign in both Greek and English letters, and try to hitch from turn-offs rather than long stretches of straight road.

■■■ ACCOMMODATIONS

Relative to the U.S. and elsewhere in Europe, Greece's accommodations remain a bargain. Off-season prices average 20-40% cheaper than during high-season. Prices quoted in the guide are from summer 1995; expect them to rise by 10-20% in 1996.

HOSTELS

Greek youth hostels are an excellent, reasonable alternative to hotels. At the time of publication **Hostelling International (HI)** had yet to reach an agreement with Greek hostels, and they endorse only one hostel in the entire country. Nevertheless, hostels that are not currently endorsed by HI are in most cases still safe and reputable. To obtain an HI membership, please refer to Hosteling Organizations on p. 9.

Greek youth hostels generally have fewer restrictions than those farther north in Europe. Most are open year-round and have midnight or 1am curfews (which are strictly enforced, and may leave you in the streets if you come back too late). In summer, they usually stay open from 6 to 10am and 1pm to midnight (shorter hours in

winter). The larger hostels offer breakfast. Some hostels often have a maximum stay of five days. It's advisable to book in advance in the summer at some of the more popular hostels in Athens, Santorini, or Nauplion.

If you arrive in Greece without an HI card, you can buy an International Guest Card (2600dr), either from the Greek Youth Hostel Association, 4 Dragatsaniou St., seventh floor, Athens (tel. (01) 323 4107; fax (01) 323 7590), or the Athens International Hostel (HI), 16 Victor Hugo St., Athens (tel. 523 1095).

HOTELS

The government oversees the construction and the seemingly random classification of most hotels. Proprietors are permitted to charge 10% extra for stays of less than three nights, and 20% extra overall in high season (July-Sept. 15). In order to get more *drachmae* out of you, they may only offer their most expensive rooms, compel you to buy breakfast, squeeze three people into a hostel-like triple and charge each for a single, or quote a price for a room that includes breakfast and private shower and then charge extra for both.

If proprietors offer a room that seems unreasonably expensive, stress that you don't want luxuries and they may tell you of a cheaper option. Late at night, in off-season, or in a large town, it's a buyer's market. You may consider bargaining. As a security deposit, hotels may ask for your passport and return it when you leave. You can often leave your luggage in the reception area during the afternoon, though check-out is at 11am or noon. Be skeptical about offers to be driven to a pension or hotel. Let the driver show you the destination on a map; it may be miles out of town.

The tourist police are on your side. If a hotel flagrantly violates the prices shown by law at the front desk or on a chart behind each room's front door, or if you think you've been exploited, threaten to report the hotel to the tourist police. The threat alone often resolves "misunderstandings."

- JET SKIS - VOLLEYBALL - BILLIARDS - INNER TUBING - WEIGHT ROOM - BASKETBALL - MOTORCYCLES - MOPEDS -
BOAT EXCURSIONS - SCUBA DIVING - WATERSKIING - BASKETBALL - JET SKIS - VOLLEYBALL - MOTORCYCLES - MOPEDS - FOOZBALL - BILLIARDS - INNER TUBING - CLIFF DIVING - WATERSKIING - BASKETBALL
- CLIFF DIVINGI - FOOZBALL - SCUBA DIVING - INNER TUBING - WEIGHT ROOM - JET SKIS - VOLLEYBALL - BILLIARDS -
WATERSKIING - BASKETBALL - JET SKIS - VOLLEYBALL - MOTORCYCLES - MOPEDS - INNER TUBING - WEIGHT ROOM - FOOZBALL - BILLIARDS - SCUBA DIVING - WATERSKIING - BOAT EXCURSIONS - BASKETBALL
Take a Vacation from Your Vacation ...
Experience
THE Pink Palace
CORFU, GREECE
Recommended by LET'S GO and FROMMERS
The World's Largest Youth Resort
Tel: (661) 53103/53104
ONLY $18 per night*
Breakfast, Dinner & Night Club Included
Pink Palace
Private Rooms
Hot Showers - Laundry Service
Giant Jaccuzi - Dancing til Dawn
Breakfast til Noon - Long Distance Calling
Commission-Free Money Exchange
Get a voucher for ONE NIGHT FREE** when you book your railpass or flight at:
in the United States
Council Travel
CIEE: Council on International Educational Exchange
in Canada
TRAVEL CUTS VOYAGES CAMPUS
*Price in $US at time of printing.
** Based on a minimum stay of 3 nights. Voucher must be stamped by issuing office. One per person per stay.
The Pink Palace accepts:
VISA

One note on Greek toilets: if a trash container is within reach of the toilet, this is where used toilet paper goes. Flushing toilet paper will probably jam the toilet. Many Greek toilets are flushed by pulling a handle that hangs from the ceiling. Also, some hotels may only have pit-toilets; check before accepting a room.

Most D- and E-class hotels start at 3500dr for singles and 5000dr for doubles. A hotel with no singles may still put you in a room by yourself. More info is available from the **Hellenic Chamber of Hotels,** 24 Stadiou St., Athens (tel. 323 7193).

"ROOMS TO LET"

Wherever there are tourists, you'll see private homes with signs offering *dhomatia* ("Rooms to Let"). As you arrive at more popular destinations, proprietors hustling their "Rooms to Let" will greet your boat or bus. Peddling rooms at bus stops or ports is *illegal* according to the tourist police. Generally, you should have a set destination in mind and head there. On occasion the rooms offered to you at the port or bus stop may be cheap. Nonetheless, it is imperative that you make owners pinpoint the exact location of their houses. "Ten minutes away, near the beach," can mean a 45-minute hike from the main town. Most rooms are cheap and perfectly dependable. There may not be locks, towels, or telephones, but there may be warm offers of coffee at night and friendly conversation. Then again, in the more touristed areas, there may be more locks than conversation. Prices here are especially variable, so be sure that you're paying no more than you would at a hotel. If in doubt, ask the tourist police: they'll usually set you up with a room and conduct all the negotiations themselves. Most private rooms operate only in high season, and they're a good option for those arriving without reservations. Sleeping on hotel roofs used to be a cheap option. Now it's illegal. Don't ask, tell, or pursue.

TRADITIONAL SETTLEMENTS

Greece has several traditional villages and buildings which have been preserved and restored by the government in an effort to maintain the country's architectural heritage. The restoration of some Greek villages promises to offer a taste of "small town" Greek life to visitors, and to improve the regional economy. Thus far, more than ten settlements have been converted into guesthouses: Makrinitsa and Vizitsa on Mt. Pelion, Mesta on Chios, Psara Island, Fiscardo on Cephalonia, Kapetanakos in Areopolis, and Papingo-Zagohoria in Epirus. There are 12 reconstructed towers in Vathia (Mani) and an expensive hotel in the Kastro in Monemvassia. Doubles range from 5000 to 10,000dr; the tourist offices can make reservations and provide information. With the EU's new open-door policy, European businesses have been buying and tearing down traditional buildings in order to build modern hotels cheaply. In an effort to preserve traditional architecture, conservation groups have been buying traditional settlements. Cycladic Environments (1-800-719-5260 in the U.S. to reserve) purchases and offers for rent a variety of homes and bungalows (some seen in the 1982 classic film *Summer Lovers*) in Oia on Santorini (see p. 236).

CAMPING

Camping is one of the easiest ways to escape the monotony of barren hotel rooms, hostel regulations, and the other limitations of conventional lodgings. More importantly, it's one of the cheapest ways to spend the night.

In Greece, the GNTO is primarily responsible for campgrounds (see p. 2). **Tourist Guide of Greece,** 137 Patission St., Athens 11251 (tel. 864 1688) has a list of official camping sites. Most of the official GNTO campgrounds have good facilities, including drinking water, lavatories, and electricity. The Hellenic Touring Club also runs a number of campgrounds. In addition, Greece has many campgrounds run by private organizations which may include pools, discos, minimarkets, and the like.

The prices charged at campgrounds depend on the facilities; you'll usually pay roughly 1000dr per person, plus 1000dr per tent. GNTO campgrounds tend to be ritzier and more expensive (up to 1500dr in some places).

On many islands, campers just take to the beaches. Free-lance camping outside campgrounds is illegal, but during July and August, when hotels and pensions are booked solid, illegal camping becomes commonplace. Penalties run the gamut from a stern chastisement to a 50,000dr or higher fine. At peak season when camps are crowded, the police may sometimes ignore sleeping-bagged bodies sprawled in the sand. Those who decide to free-lance camp should make sure to clean up after themselves. Many beaches offer beach huts as well as designated camping sections. We urge you to consider the safety risks inherent in free-lance camping; *Let's Go* does not recommend illegal free-lance camping.

■■■ KEEPING IN TOUCH

Most Greek **post offices** are open Monday through Friday from 7:30am to 2pm, although services (such as mailing parcels) may close early. Some larger offices keep longer hours. To register a letter, ask for *systemeno;* for express, *katepeegon;* for air mail, *aeroporikos*, and write "air mail" on the envelope. A letter or postcard to the U.S. costs 120dr to mail and takes as little as four days or as long as two weeks, sometimes longer from smaller villages.

Even if you have no fixed address while in Greece, you can receive mail through the Greek post office's **Poste Restante** (General Delivery) service. Mark the envelope "HOLD," and address it: "Jane Doe, c/o Poste Restante, Main Post Office, the address of the appropriate office, the postal code, and GREECE (in capital letters)." Write "Air Mail" on the side of the envelope and use a first class stamp. If you are expecting Poste Restante to arrive for you after you leave a town, arrange at the post office to have it forwarded to another Poste Restante address. American Express offices will hold mail for up to thirty days, but often charge a small fee if you aren't a cardholder or don't use their traveler's checks.

Long-distance and collect **phone calls** and telegrams should be placed at the **OTE** (the Greek Telephone Organization) offices. In small villages, offices are usually open Monday through Friday 7:30am to 3pm, in towns 7:30am to 10pm (shorter hours or closed on weekends), and in larger cities 24 hr. If you visit one of the latter in the middle of the night, the door may be locked, but ring and they'll let you in. There's often a long line; try, if at all possible, to call early in the morning. There is no surcharge if you go to an OTE. You can also purchase a phone card from OTE offices or kiosks to make calls from any of the numerous card phones.

To make **direct calls to the U.S. or Canada,** dial 001 and then the area code and number. If you plan on talking for a while, ask the other party to call right back, since rates from the U.S. are cheaper. To make **direct calls from the U.S. to Greece,** dial 011-3, then the city code, then the number. If you call the U.S. collect, you'll be charged the U.S. person-to-person rate; in most cases, you'll still save money over expensive hotel surcharges. To call the U.S. **collect,** dial 008 00 13 11 (AT&T) or 008 00 12 11 (MCI). This method only works on the card phones. To use a **calling card,** dial 008 00 13 11 (AT&T only). An even better option is buying a *telekarta* for 1000dr (and up) at a kiosk or OTE; you can use it at the ubiquitous *kartotilephona* and buy a new one when it runs out. Slide the card into the phone and press "i" on the phones for English language instructions. Remember the time difference.

LIFE AND TIMES

■■■ HISTORY

ANCIENT GREECE

Archaeological evidence places the first settlement of Greece as far back as 6500 BC. Early settlements were established on the mainland near Thessaloniki, on Crete, and, a millennium or so later, on the Cyclades. The first inhabitants of Greece were generally peaceful, pottery-making, agricultural people. Their lack of weapons and fortifications suggests that they lived in relative harmony. They worshiped a fertility goddess and made fat little goddess figurines, thus providing inspiration for New Age craft shops over the centuries. Later on, the dour farmer-poet Hesiod would romanticize this period as the **Golden Age.**

Eventually, competition for trade routes, increased migration, and cultural intermingling led to the development of weapons. Government centered around palaces, built at Knossos, Mycenae, Tyrins, and Argos. The palace at Knossos formed the centerpiece of the **Minoan civilization** that flourished in the second millennium BC, maintaining dominance over trade routes and creating jewelry and whimsical pottery, not to mention the stunning architectural riches that are still visible on Crete. The next major civilization was **Mycenean,** which supplanted its earthy predecessors with a more warlike, aggressively phallocentric society that worshipped male gods. Linear B, a ceremonial script used by the Myceneans, is the forerunner to Greek. The Mycenean era is most famously chronicled in Homer's *Iliad* and *Odyssey.* The origins of Greek mythology can also be traced to this period.

After a 200-year Dark Age, around the 9th century BC, the *polis,* or city-state, became the predominant form of political organization. Despite the relative autonomy of the individual city-states, Hellenic peoples shared a sense of unity and referred to non-Hellenes as *Barbaroi,* a term that connoted foreignness rather than degree of cultural achievement. The **Olympic Games,** were a source of political and athletic pride (See box on p. 127). Seafaring states like Corinth, Megara, and Miletus established colonies as far away as Spain and the Black Sea. Sparta and Athens ultimately emerged as the most powerful of the *polis*. Sparta, relatively defenseless on an agriculturally rich plain, developed an extremely militaristic culture. Children were separated from their parents at the age of seven to begin a military life while unhealthy babies were left to die. By contrast, life was good to Athenians, especially the wealthy. Philosophy, learning, and attempts to institute democracy were the order of the day. Despite an intense rivalry, Sparta and Athens united in defense against the Persian King Darius in the early 5th century BC, winning important victories at Salamis and Platea and saving Greece from foreign domination.

The apex of Athenian civilization, from 480 to 323 BC, is often referred to as the **Classical Age.** In the words of classicist Edith Hamilton, "What was then produced in art and thought has never been surpassed and very rarely equalled, and the stamp of it is on all the art and all the thought of the Western world." Athens grew wealthy from trade and through its command of the Delian League that had been formed as an alliance against the Persians. The cultural achievements of this period provide a heritage which is a source of both satisfaction and frustration for modern Greeks. Athens' glorious Acropolis, including the Parthenon, dates from this period. Playwrights like Sophocles and the boisterous Aristophanes constitute the pinnacle of the intellectual greats that graced Athenian streets.

Sparta's fears about Athenian ambitions culminated during the **Peloponnesian Wars,** which lasted 27 years and ended in a nominal defeat for Athens after its hopeless attack on Syracuse. Athens, nonetheless, maintained its cultural supremacy. Some of Athens' most notable artists (Scopas, Praxiteles), philosophers (Socrates, Plato, Aristotle), and scientists (Hippocrates) flourished during this period.

In the midst of the Peloponnesian War, however, a new political force was gaining strength in **Macedonia.** Between 360 and 320 BC, the Macedonians, under King Philip II, conquered many Greek cities. After establishing a powerful confederacy known as the Hellenic League of Corinth (in 338 BC), Alexander the Great, King Philip's illustrious son, embarked on an historic expedition in 336 BC to crush the extensive empire of the Persians. In only 13 years, Alexander had extended Hellenic rule and influence deep into Africa and as far east as India.

Following Alexander's death, violent conflicts ravaged his empire. During this period, however, Hellenistic culture spread and gained appreciation. In 146 BC, after 50 years of skirmishes and political intrigue, Rome filled the Greek power vacuum. But as fast as Roman legions conquered Greece, Greek culture conquered Rome. By the middle of the 1st century AD, even Nero had a soft spot for Athens, though Alexandria and Antioch surpassed it in reputation. Two hundred years later, after the conversion of the Roman Empire to Christianity and the establishment of the **Byzantine Empire,** the focal point of Hellenic culture shifted from the

Socrates: A Gentleman and a Scholar?

Following in the steps of greats like Socrates may have a meaning altogether different from what you envisioned. Socrates was certainly a great philosopher, and his technique of asking questions to steer his listener into agreeing with him even got the "method" named after him. Since Socrates himself did not write down any of his teachings, all that is known of him comes from the writings of his students, Plato and Xenophon. In *Oeconomicus*, for example, Xenophon portrays Socrates as a man with a keen knowledge of agriculture. Plato's *Symposium* depicts Socrates' scholarly gatherings that were actually drinking parties where Socrates hit on other male members of the Athenian intelligentsia undoubtedly using such witty pick-up lines as, "Is that a Doric column in your toga, or are you just happy to see me?" Perhaps this is why some scholars believe Socrates' wife, Xanthippe, had a quick temper. In one instance, an angry Xanthippe was said to have dumped a chamber pot on his head. The philosopher's only reaction was to comment dryly, "After it thunders, it usually rains." Admirers of the great philosopher might not want to consider repeating his last act. After Socrates was found guilty of corrupting the Athenian youth in 399 BC, he was condemned to death by drinking hemlock.

Peloponnese to Byzantium. Despite this succession of conquerors, however, Greek culture survived, as ruling forces adopted it into their own.

Although Greek culture remained strong following the Frankish conquest of Byzantium in 1204, Greece suffered a more devastating conquest in 1453, when Byzantium, renamed Constantinople after the emperor **Constantine,** fell to the Turks, ushering in four centuries of Ottoman rule. During this time, Greek culture retreated to the private sphere, centering around village life and the Greek Orthodox church, which was tolerated by the Turks.

GREEK INDEPENDENCE

After 400 years of Turkish oppression and numerous false starts, a revolutionary army composed of guerillas from the Peloponnese and the Aegean Islands began battling Turkish armies there in early 1821, eventually declaring independence on March 25. The Greeks followed this success with substantial setbacks due to an outbreak of rivalry between various factions and the intervention of Muhammad Ali, the Ottoman governor of Egypt. Spurred on by the romantic Lord Byron and public sympathy for the Greeks—archaeological treasures from the Classical Age were then on display throughout Europe—European governments intervened. In 1827, at the Battle of Navarino, the navies of Britain, France, and Russia decimated a joint Turkish-Egyptian fleet, releasing the Ottoman grip on Greece.

France, Russia, and Britain, which had finally been persuaded to lend help to the struggle for independence, proceeded to take a controlling role in Greece's future. They drew up borders that limited the new nation to areas with a Hellenic majority, excluding many far-flung Greeks in ethnically diverse areas, as well as the most agriculturally fertile lands of northern Greece. Consequently, Greek politics for the next hundred years or so were driven by the vision of the *Megali Idhea* (Great Idea) of unifying the scattered Greek population into one enlarged, unified state. Reality proved quite different, however.

MODERN HISTORY

Greece's fledgling democracy was thwarted by the assassination of the first elected president, Kapodistrias. After the assassination, the three allied powers intervened once more to create a monarchy. Prince Otho of Bavaria became king. In 1843, the military forced the rather heavy-handed and Germanocentric Otho to agree to a constitution, which he proceeded to ignore. He was finally unseated for good in 1862 and replaced by King George I of Denmark the following year. George I made some half-hearted attempts at land reform and tried to develop Greece's infrastructure, but the country nonetheless remained predominantly agricultural throughout the 19th century, with most capital concentrated in the hands of a few large families.

In 1910, the election of Eleftherios Venizelos as premier inaugurated a period of economic development and geographic expansion. The **Balkan Wars** of 1912-3 enabled Greece to gain Crete and parts of Thessaly and Macedonia. Owing largely to the new king's ties with Germany, Greece remained neutral during much of WWI. Venizelos, however, saw the war as a chance to push Greece's borders forward and at last realize the *Megali Idhea*. He set up his own revolutionary government, which entered the war in 1917. At Versailles, Venizelos pressed Greek claims to Smyrna (İzmir); but insufficient Allied support, Venizelos' defeat in the 1920 elections, and the disastrous Anatolian campaign against Turkey led to a crushing defeat by Atatürk in 1922. Far from gaining additional territory, Greece was forced to agree to an exchange of population with Turkey, resulting in the forced resettlement of millions of Greeks who had been living in Turkish lands.

The next decade or so saw a dizzyingly chaotic succession of monarchy, military rule, and brief intervals of democracy. The Communist Party gained in strength; meanwhile **General Metaxas,** appointed prime minister in 1936, proceeded to develop a form of autocratic rule. Metaxas proved a fervent Greek nationalist, however, and on October 28, 1940, his famous *"Ohi!"* (No) to Mussolini's demand to occupy Greece brought the country into WWII. In 1941 Greece fell to German invaders and for the next four years, Greece was occupied by a group of Axis powers, resulting in widespread starvation, destruction of ancient sites, large-scale executions, and the Nazis' virtual extermination of Greece's Jewish community, which had been among the largest in the Balkans. Resistance was organized by the Communist-led EAM/ELAS, which generally received popular support. Churchill's reluctance to allow a communist movement to ascend to power, however, made for a difficult transition to a post-liberation government, and civil war broke out in 1947. Ultimately, Greece became one of the first arenas of American Cold War military intervention. The U.S. provided vast quantities of aid and numerous military advisers to the Greek government as part of the **Truman Doctrine** to contain the spread of Communism, and the last ELAS guerillas were defeated in 1949. In the next decade and a half, the U.S. maintained heavy involvement in Greek politics, which were dominated by the right-of-center Constantine Karamanlis. Greece at last attained greater stability and a decent rate of economic growth, due in part to U.S. assistance.

Left-wing stirrings continued, however, as did efforts to contain dissent. Karamanlis resigned, to be replaced by centrist Yiorgos Papandreou. The army, feeling threatened by increasing liberalization and political disarray, on April 21, 1967 staged a coup that resulted in rule by a **junta** of colonels for seven years. The junta's Metaxas-style rule included torture, censorship, and arbitrary arrest, but the regime also encouraged foreign investment and continued to enjoy U.S. support. Student demonstrations in Athens were suppressed by martial law in 1973, and a year later, General Ionnidis' attempt to overthrow Cyprus' president provoked a Turkish invasion of Cyprus that ultimately led to the junta's downfall. Karamanlis returned from his self-imposed exile to take charge. As the new prime minister, Karamanlis skillfully orchestrated parliamentary elections and organized a referendum to determine the fate of the government. After the monarchy was defeated by a two-thirds vote, a **constitution** was drawn up in 1975 which established free general elections and a 300-member parliament charged with appointing a ceremonial president. The leader of the majority party in parliament naturally became prime minister. Greece, furthermore, worked to strengthen its memberships in NATO (having joined in 1952), the Council of Europe, and the EU.

Under Prime Minister Andreas Papandreou, the leftist Panhellenic Socialist Movement (PASOK) obtained landslide electoral victories in 1981 and 1985. Papandreou promised a radical break with the past, and initially oversaw the passage of women's rights legislation and advances in civil liberties. But Papandreou also indulged in heavy-handed economic nationalization, and finally imposed austerity measures in exchange for an EEC loan. At the same time, Papandreou's heated anti-NATO rhetoric and his chumminess with Qaddafi and Arafat provoked international alarm. In September, 1988, Papandreou underwent major heart surgery. He tried to run the country while hospitalized, refusing to appoint an interim leader, thus undermining his authority within PASOK. Upon returning to work, Papandreou discovered an embezzlement scandal involving George Koskotas, the chair of the Bank of Crete, which threatened to implicate a number of government officials in corruption and bribery. When Koskotas made allegations against Papandreou himself, the beleaguered Prime Minister eked out only 125 seats in the 300-seat parliament.

In the wake of the scandals, Tzannis Tzannetakis, who was acceptable to both conservatives and leftists, became Prime Minister-designate through a compromise decision of the Communist-rightist coalition. As part of the compromise, the opposing conservative New Democracy (*Nea Demokratia*—ND) and the Communist Party of Greece (*Kommunistiko Komma Ellados*—KKE) forged a short-term alliance to oppose the incumbent socialist leadership. Then in 1990, after three general elections within the space of 10 months, Constantine Mitsotakis of the ND became Prime Minister. Although the ND was only able to obtain 47% of the total vote, the vagaries of Greek electoral law left the party with a slim majority in parliament.

Mitsotakis attempted to lead Greece into the mainstream of European politics and to solve some of the country's festering economic and diplomatic woes. To try to bring Greece's huge debt under control, he imposed a stiff austerity program that limited wage increases, and he began to sell state enterprises that had piled up huge losses. The state agencies, however, provided jobs for large numbers of Greeks who valued the security and undemanding nature of work in the public sector. As a result, he lost the election called suddenly in the fall of 1993 after a group of deputies led by former foreign minister Antonis Samaras bolted from the ND party. Andreas Papandreou returned to power, but this time with a more friendly attitude towards the West, especially the U.S., whose support he continues to court in order to deal with growing problems in the Balkans.

■■■ RELIGION

Worship of gods and goddesses ended after the death of the Roman Emperor Julian. In the post-classical period, Greece saw the rise of cults associated with mysteries such as the Eleusinian and Orphic, in which members enacted rituals associated with the afterlife. Unfortunately, participants swore to keep the rituals secret, so almost all that's known of the mysteries comes from disapproving Christian authors.

The Orthodox Church gained ascendancy following the conversion of Constantine. The Christian faith was officially legitimized by the Edict of Milan, issued by Emperor Licinius in 313 AD, which proclaimed the toleration of Christianity. Constantine's view of the church, however, differed from that of Rome, and in 324 he founded his new capital, the city of Constantinople. Constantine also summoned the first of seven Ecumenical Councils, held in Nicaea, in order to elaborate and unify the content of the faith. During that time religion flourished in ascetic monastic communities such as those on Mount Athos and at Meteora. The schism between East and West occurred, according to some scholars, in 1054 AD when three legates of the Pope came to the Church of the Holy Wisdom (Agia Sophia) in Constantinople and placed a Bull of Excommunication at the altar. During the middle of the 9th century, orthodox missionaries spread Christianity to Slavic peoples in Russia, Serbia, Romania, and Bulgaria. The Patriarch of Constantinople was recognized as the head of an Orthodox Christian "nation." The Ottomans tolerated the Orthodox, but Christians were treated as second-class citizens, and the church's missions were terminated. After the Greek War of Independence, the Church of Greece declared itself officially autocephalous. Today, Greek Orthodoxy is the national religion, although the constitution guarantees freedom of religion. The Church includes the archbishop of Athens, 85 bishops in 77 dioceses, and 7500 parishes. The Patriarch of Constantinople, meanwhile, still presides over Mt. Athos, the Dodecanese, and the Orthodox Church in the rest of Europe, the Americas, Australia, and East Asia.

Like the Roman Church, Orthodoxy insists upon the hierarchical structure of the church, Apostolic succession, the episcopate, and the priesthood. This, however, is where the two churches begin to diverge. Whereas Rome upholds the universal jurisdiction and infallibility of the Pope, Orthodoxy stresses the infallibility of the church as a whole and thus does not have cardinals or a pope. Much of the Orthodox position is based on its exegesis of John 15:26, in which Christ sends the Holy Spirit to man. The Spirit, Orthodox say, proceeds through the Father, while Roman theology says that the Spirit proceeds from the Father and the Son. Orthodox say that the Roman position, which confuses the source of the Trinity and God, ends up being regarded in an abstract sense, not in terms of His personality. Orthodox believe that God is highly personal, that each man can find God by looking within himself. Timothy Ware's *The Orthodox Church* provides a thorough description of both the history of the church and the exegesis behind Orthodox beliefs.

Greek Orthodox priests, who are easily discernible by their long black robes, beards, and cylindrical hats, are closely associated with their parishes and can marry, as most do (higher clergy remain celibate). Celebrations in churches include weddings, baptisms, and celebrations on the feast day of the patron saint.

■■■ LANGUAGE

The language barrier that tourists find upon entering Greece crumbles quickly (less so in the mountainous north and in the Peloponnese). Greeks who work in touristed areas have picked up some English and tourist officials and travel agents are often fluent. Still, try to master some essential Greek phrases. Bring Berlitz's *Greek for Travelers*, or a comparable book that provides key phrases in a clear format.

Be conscious of Greek body language. To indicate a negative, Greeks lift their heads back abruptly while raising their eyebrows. To indicate the affirmative, they emphatically nod once. Greeks wave a hand up and down in a gesture that seems to say "stay there" when they mean "come." Be careful when waving goodbye; keep your fingers loose because gesturing with an open palm and extended fingers may be interpreted as an insult.

Even if you don't know spoken Greek, familiarity with the Greek alphabet is essential. Some road signs, street names, and bus timetables may be transliterated, but many are not. Because Greek is an inflected language, words have different case forms which correspond to their different grammatical functions in sentences. You'll sometimes find three different words for the same name. For a pronunciation guide and a list of useful phrases, consult the glossary at the back of this book.

A note on transliteration: There exists no fully satisfactory system of transliterating one alphabet to the other. Greek letters don't have an exact correspondence with English letters. Like those of the Greek government, *Let's Go's* transliterations are different for each word; the process follows no rigid rules, but is based on historical connotation, local usage, and chance.

■■■ THE ARTS

DECORATIVE ARTS AND ARCHITECTURE

Ancient Greek art can be divided into periods roughly corresponding to historical eras. During the **Bronze Age,** early Greek warrior tribes developed the craft of metalwork. Many sculptures remain from the Minoan and Mycenean civilizations, which emerged in this period. There are plentiful examples of Minoan pottery, many featuring whimsical and colorful sea creatures.

In the **Geometric Period** (900-700 BC), artists developed new techniques and more expressive styles of sculpture and painting. Pottery decoration became more elaborate; jars were completely covered with bands of meanders, zigzags, and identically posed animals and people. Architects of the time created simple structures and designed one-room temples with columned porches and raised altars. Examples of Geometric architecture are concentrated at Olympia.

The **Archaic Period** (700-480 BC) marked the transition from the simplicity of the Geometric Period to the more elaborate and realistic forms of the Classical Period. The cylindrical Doric column and the fluted Ionic column were developed in this period. At the end of the 7th century BC, large-scale standing figural sculptures appeared in sanctuaries. These *kouroi* (feminine, *korē*) evolved into more graceful, simplified figures. The depiction of life and movement became prime concerns in sculpture. Vase painting similarly became more concerned with a realistic portrayal of life. The rigid friezes of marching animals and people of the Geometric Period were replaced with narrative scenes from mythology and, later, with genre scenes. The black figure technique, in which figures were glazed black and details incised into them, gave artists greater precision than before. At the end of the 6th century BC, vase painters adopted the Attic red-figure technique in which the figures were reserved against a black background and the details painted in with a fine brush.

The arts flourished during the **Classical Period** (480-323 BC), as Athens reached the pinnacle of its cultural, military, and economic power under Pericles and his successors. Sculptors such as Praxiteles and Scopas developed the heroic nude form, which idealizes the human body's severe and somber beauty. Praxiteles' statue of Hermes holding the baby Dionysus is housed in the Olympia Museum. Architecture of the Classical period, like Athens' Parthenon, features greater spaciousness, fluidity, and grace than the massive temples of the Archaic Period.

The famous Corinthian column, a fluted column with a multi-leafed top, was first designed during the **Hellenistic Period** (323-first century BC). The Monument of Lysicrates in Athens typifies this architectural design. Several amphitheaters were built at this time, most notably those at Argos and Epidavros, where the acoustics are still so precise more than 2000 years after their construction that a coin dropped on the stage can be heard at the theater's last row. The Romans adopted the Hellenistic style and introduced it to the rest of Europe.

In 395 AD, the Roman Empire split into the Western Empire and the Eastern, or Byzantine, Empire. The Greeks fell under the latter. As the Empire was Christianized by Constantine, Greek artists began to incorporate Christian symbols into their work. During the **Byzantine Period** (500-1200 AD), many churches were built and Christian iconography developed an elaborate repertoire of symbols. Figures of veneration generally appeared in symbolic postures, the most unusual of which is the *anapezousa*, or sleeping Christ, in which the Christ figure is depicted lying down with his eyes open, to express God's vigilance at all times. The most notable examples of Byzantine art include the monasteries built at Osios Loukas, Daphni, Mt. Athos, and Meteora, as well as the churches at Mystra. The churches were built in a cruciform style; a narthex (small chamber) added at one end, and an apse (half dome) at the other. The transept, or crossing, of the two lengths of the church was capped by a domed ceiling. Byzantine artists created beautiful, ornate icons and mosaics to decorate their churches. A mosaic of Christ *Pantocrator* (Creator of All Things) was almost always placed in the dome or apse.

With the liberation of Greece from the Turks in 1821, nationalist sentiment impelled the government to subsidize Greek art. In 1838, the Polytechniou, Greece's first modern art school, was founded. Many artists since have gone abroad to study, and **modern Greek art** has followed the trends and styles of 19th and 20th centuries. Theophilos, Alexis Kontoglou, George Bouzanis, Yiannis Spiropoulos, Sotiris Sorongas and Michael Tombros are among the familiar modern Greek artists.

Greek **folk art** continues to fascinate even the most casual onlooker. Handicrafts include pottery, weaving, metalwork, and woodwork.

LITERATURE

The earliest appearances of the Greek language are Minoan palace record tablets inscribed in duo-syllabic scripts called Linear Script A and B. These treasury records, somewhat uninspiring in content and probably dating from the end of the Bronze Age (roughly 1200 BC), were often preserved, ironically, by being baked hard in the fires that destroyed the palaces themselves. From the 11th to the 8th century BC, the Greeks seem to have been largely illiterate, and it is not until the **Homeric** *Iliad* and *Odyssey* that written material appears. Scholars still question whether the Homeric works were actually composed by the blind bard. While the works show evidence of origin in an oral tradition, it is possible that either Homer or a group of poets worked on the actual hard copy. Columnist Cecil Adams calls Homer "the most famous poet who may or may not have existed." Hesiod, roughly Homer's contemporary, composed *Works and Days*, a farmer's-eye view of life, as well as the *Theogony*, the first systematic account in Greek of the creation of the world and the exploits of the gods. During the 7th century BC, Archilochus of Paros began to write anti-heroic, anti-Homeric elegies, including the oft-imitated fragment in which he expresses no shame at abandoning his shield in battle to save his own life. On the island of Lesvos, during the 5th century BC, the gifted lyric poet Sappho and her contemporary, Alcaeus, sang of love and the beauty of nature. Pindar (518-438 BC), acclaimed by the ancients as the greatest of lyric poets, wrote Olympic odes commissioned by nobles to commemorate athletic victories.

Literature flourished in the **Classical Period.** Aeschylus, Sophocles, and Euripides developed ritualistic dramas and staged innovative tragedies, while Aristophanes produced raucous comedies (see Theater on p. 59). Orators like Gorgias practiced rhetoric, and the sophists taught methods of philosophical dialogue. Herodotus, the so-called "Father of History," captured the monumental battles and personalities of the Greco-Persian conflict in the *Persian Wars,* while Thucydides immortalized the Athenian conflict with Sparta in his *Peloponnesian War.* Callimachus (c. 305-240 BC) wrote Alexandrian elegies, of which only fragments remain. His influence, however, was to be felt during the Alexandrian revival in Rome, when neoteric poets like Catullus took his warning *mega biblion, mega kakon* (Long book, big bore) to heart. Callimachus was also the first poet to write in the vision genre, a poetic topos that holds an important place in the literature of the Middle Ages. His pupil, Apollonius of Rhodes, wrote the epic *Argonautica,* chronicling the legendary voyage of Jason and the Argonauts.

During the **Byzantine Era,** religious poetry flourished, though not necessarily to the exclusion of secular works. Photios (c. 820-893 AD), who was twice appointed Patriarch of Constantinople, admired the "pagan" works of Homer and encouraged their study. Photios himself wrote several important works, including the massive *Biblioteca,* a Byzantine cross between the *Encyclopaedia Britannica* and *Reader's Digest.* Later, under the Franks (1204-1460), Greeks developed the pseudo-historical romance, including the *Life of Alexander;* and personal love poems, such as the *Erotopaegnia* (Love Games). Klephts (Bandits) composed stirring folk ballads in the 16th century, when they weren't raiding Turkish installations. Byzantine heritage survived in revolt against Roman Catholic and Turkish propaganda, manifesting itself during the Period of **Religious Humanism** (1600-69).

The Ionian School (beginning with the revolution in 1821), saw the rise of Andreas Kalvos (1796-1869) and Dionysios Solomos (1798-1857). Kalvos' lyrical poetry, known for powerful tributes to freedom, earned him high esteem among modern poets. Solomos is often called the "national poet of Greece," and it was his *Hymn to Liberty* that became the Greek national anthem. During the second half of the 19th century, revolutionary hero John Makriyiannis (1797-1864) wrote his vivid *Memoirs,* considered a masterpiece of Greek literature. The 20th century has seen the emergence of a great many poets, including Angelos Sikelianos, Constantine P. Cavafy, and Kostas Varnales. Cavafy, who won the Nobel Prize in 1963, has had a wide-ranging influence, attracting the attention of writers such as E.M. Forster and W.H. Auden. Also among modern greats are Kostas Karyotakes and the lyricist Nikos Karvounes, who was the first to translate Walt Whitman's works into Greek. Greece produced a wide variety of poetry in the 20th century. While George Seferis' poems evoke the legacy of the past, the mystical, erotic works of 1979 Nobel laureate Odysseus Elytis celebrate nature. Yiannis Ritsos blends revolutionary and mythological symbolism. Stratis Haviaris' *When The Tree Sings* depicts WWII through the eyes of a young boy. Perhaps the best known modern Greek author is Nikos Kazantzakis. His many works include *Odyssey,* a modern sequel to the Homeric epic, *Report to Greco, Zorba the Greek* (1946), and *The Last Temptation of Christ* (1951), of which the latter two were adapted for the cinema.

The landscape of Greece has also inspired some of the most inventive travel writing by English-speaking authors, such as Edward Lear's lively journals of his years in Greece, Henry Miller's classic *The Colossus of Maroussi,* and the varied works of Lawrence and Gerald Durrell, who lived in a house still visible on Corfu.

CLASSICAL MYTHOLOGY

Greek mythology is second only to the Bible in its influence on the Western imagination. Greek myths were passed from generation to generation, region to region, and gradually embellished, interpreted to reflect local concerns. The anthropomorphic gods and goddesses lived as immortal beings with divine power. Yet often tired of the tedium of divinity, they descended to earth to intervene romantically, mischievously, or combatively in human affairs, often disguised as animals or humans.

Traditionally, there are 14 major deities: Zeus, king of gods; his wife Hera, who watches over child-bearing and marriage; Poseidon, god of the sea; Hephaestus, god of smiths and fire; Aphrodite, goddess of love and beauty; Ares, god of war; Athena, goddess of wisdom; Apollo, god of light and music; Artemis, goddess of the hunt; Hermes, the messenger god and patron of thieves and tricksters; Hades, lord of the underworld; Demeter, goddess of the harvest; Dionysus, god of wine; and Hestia, goddess of the hearth.

In addition to the 14 gods, many humans and minor deities figured prominently in Greek mythology. The three Fates—Atropos, Clotho, and Lachesis—spun, measured, and snipped the threads of humans' lives; the Furies, also optimistically called *Eumenides,* or "kindly ones," punished evildoers; and the nine Muses brought inspiration to poets, artists, and musicians. Dryads and Naiads inhabited trees and streams; nymphs cavorted in the fields; Satyrs, or goat-men with long beards and tails, frolicked with Maenads in the holy groves; a good time was had by all. Humans had their place in mythology as well, though not always willingly; the talented weaver Arachne, because she dared compete with Athena, was turned into a spider, lending her name to taxonomy; Tantalus was condemned to stand in a pool in Tartarus, forever tormented by hunger and thirst and surrounded by food and water just beyond his grasp; and Europa was ravished by Zeus disguised as a bull.

The extramarital exploits of Zeus are even more infamous than those of less powerful but equally randy minor deities. Zeus was a sexual gymnast, ready and willing to bed down with just about anyone, as long as his baleful wife Hera wasn't looking. Zeus' mortal lovers, however, were not always willing or easily accessible: Danae, imprisoned in a tower by her father, was impregnated by Zeus in the form of a golden shower; Ganymede, a Trojan shepherd, was snatched up from earth to be the cup-bearer of the gods. Worse still for mortals, Hera, powerless to injure her husband directly, would lavish her vengeance on the object of his lust. Io was turned into a cow and chased by an enormous gadfly; Leto, pregnant with Artemis and Apollo, was forbidden to rest on solid ground until the itinerant island of Delos lent its shore for her to give birth upon; Callisto, who got off relatively easy, was changed into a bear. Semele, one of Zeus' voluntary cohorts, dissolved into ash when—at her request—he appeared to her in his full Olympian brilliance. The overarching lesson of stories involving Zeus and sex seems to be that mortals never win.

An accompanying book of mythology might inspire your Greek travels. Both Edith Hamilton's and Bullfinch's *Mythology* are eminently readable. Another excellent choice is Ovid's *Metamorphoses,* a principal source for our knowledge of mythology. Keep in mind that the 1st-century BC-1st-century AD Roman poet uses the gods' Latin names (Jupiter for Zeus, Venus for Aphrodite, etc.).

THEATER

The earliest forms of drama are said to have developed in the 5th century BC from goat songs (*tragodoi*) related to the cult of the god Dionysus. Wealthy patrons would sponsor public festivals in his honor; contests were held in open-air theaters and choruses of masked men would sing and dance. According to legend, drama was born when young Thespis, an Athenian, stepped out of the chorus to give a brief soliloquy (he was, of course, the first thespian).

One of the great tragedians, **Aeschylus** (525-456 BC) perfected this new art form by adding a second actor and having the two actors each play several characters. His famous works include the perplexing *Prometheus Bound,* and the *Oresteia,* a trilogy about Agamemnon's ill-fated return home from the Trojan war and its aftermath; **Sophocles** (496-406 BC) created the famous *Oedipus* trilogy; and **Euripides** (485-406 BC) wrote *Medea* and *The Bacchae.* "Old Comedy," a bawdy, slapstick medium, arose in the late 5th century. The greatest playwright of this genre was **Aristophanes** (450-385 BC), who wrote *The Clouds, Lysistrata,* and *The Frogs.* Unfortunately, only 11 of his 40 plays survive. **Menander,** the father of "New Comedy," wrote more mannered comedies, love stories (usually involving lovers star-crossed through cases of mistaken identity, kidnapping, etc.) with happy endings. This set the tone for later writers (hello, Shakespeare). Greek theater did not end with the Classical era; particularly on Crete, drama continues as a vital art form.

The **Athens Festival,** held from June to September, features Classical drama at the ancient **Theater of Herod Atticus** located below the Acropolis. The festival also includes concerts, opera, choruses, ballet, and modern dance. Ancient plays are staged from July to September at the **Epidavros Festival,** 78km from Athens. A language barrier won't detract from the ominous choreography of the chorus, which, in Aeschylus' time, made "boys die of fright and women have miscarriages." Tickets and programs for the theater series at both festivals are available two weeks in advance at the Athens Festival Box Office, 4 Stadiou St., inside the arcade. The same office sells tickets for a number of other smaller theaters and festivals. The **Philippi, Thassos,** and **Dodoni Festivals** all feature performances of classical drama in ancient theaters. The **Lycabettos Theater,** on Lycabettos Hill in Athens, hosts a variety of artistic events from mid-June to late August, and the **Lyric Theater,** known as the *Lyriki Skini,* presents operatic plays at 59 Akadimias St., Athens.

MUSIC AND DANCE

Musical instruments date from the Bronze Age on Crete, reinforcing scholars' belief that early poetry was often sung or chanted. As drama evolved, choruses played a major role in Greek plays. Before the 5th century BC, the Greeks had no system of musical notation, yet they managed to develop a theory of harmonics.

Throughout the Byzantine era, folk music and dances assumed regional traits: the South emphasized tragic and mourning dances, the North produced war and rural harvest dances, and religious and burial dances were performed on Crete. These regional influences are still evident. For example, pontic-influenced dances like *kotsari* are danced only in the north, while islands have their own dances called *nisiotiko*. Nonetheless, dances have become somewhat more standardized. *Tsamiko* and *kalamatiano,* for example, are now danced throughout the country.

Today, it's common to see a wide circle of locals and tourists, hands joined, dancing to the tunes of *bouzouki,* clarinets, and lyre in some regions. The leader of the dance performs the fancy footwork, winding around a white handkerchief and twirling around in circles, sometimes throwing in a few backward somersaults. Don't hesitate to join in; the dance steps for the followers are repetitive—you'll learn quickly. Just stamp your feet, yell *Opa,* and have fun.

To see authentic Greek dancing, check out the **Dora Stratou Folk Dance Theatre,** which performs at the open-air theater at Philopappus Theatre and on 8 Scholion St., both in Athens, at 10pm from May through September. From June through

Cries From the Underground

Much of Greek lyric song is romantic and poetic, but at the end of the 19th century a new style of music began to develop on Turkey's western coast that would unsettle these classical notions. *Rembetika* was popularized in Greek cities by convicts who embraced the lustful strains of the music and lamented about smoking hashish and life on the run. During the exchange of populations with Turkey in the 1920s, the music was invigorated by the scores of refugees who lived in shantytowns on the outskirts of major Greek cities. This music that had been voice of the underground emerged, in its mature state, as the cry of the underclass. *Rembetika,* the music of Smyrna cafés and Greek jails, is still played on the *bouzouki* and *baglama* and features lyrics such as these from the *Little Old Monk (1929).* For more info consult Holst's *Road to Rembetika.*

I'll become a little old monk and wear a monkish habit
And I'll carry a string of beads, sweetheart, just to please you.
Your lips tell me one thing... and your friends tell me another.
I'd rather be stabbed twice...than hear the words you're saying.
I fixed myself up as a monk, stayed in a monastery.
Then I fell into your hands, nagging bitch,
And got myself unfrocked.

October, in the old city of Rhodes, the **Nelly Dimoglou Troupe** features dances from northern and central Greece and the Dodecanese. The Athens and Epidavros Festivals (see Theater on p. 59) also include dancing. Greek dancing is particularly enjoyable at one of the many village or church festivals held throughout the summer in various parts of Greece. Generally, the festival is held surrounding the dates which the church's patron saint celebrates. Check the Entertainment listings in major cities for additional information and ask tourist officials about local festivals.

A grittier, more urban variety of music that developed in the 1930s, *rembetika* uses traditional Greek instruments to sing about drugs, prison, and general alienation. *Rembetika* became popular again in the 1970s but is played only in a few clubs today. Greek popular music continues to evolve, incorporating influences from *rembetika* as well as gypsy and traditional folk music.

■■■ FOOD AND DRINK

Greek food is simple and healthy. Recent medical studies have highlighted the Greek diet as a good model for healthy eating: its reliance upon unsaturated olive oil and vegetables has led to few heart attacks in a fairly sedentary population.

A Greek restaurant is known as a *taverna* or *estiatorio,* while a grill is a *psistaria.* Before ordering, see what others are eating. If you don't know the word for what you want, point. Most places have a few fixed-price dishes available anytime; make sure they have your dish before you sit down. Waiters will ask you if you want salad, appetizers, the works, so be careful not to wind up with mountains of food (Greek portions tend to be large). Don't be surprised if there is an extra charge for the tablecloth and bread, often listed on the menu as the *couvert.* Service is always included in the check, but it is customary to leave a few *drachma* as an extra tip.

Breakfast can be bread, *tiropita* (cheese pie), or a pastry with *marmelada* (jam) or *meli* (honey). A particular breakfast favorite among Greeks is *patsa* (a soup made of calf or lamb tripe), served only in the early morning and particularly soothing to a travel-weary stomach. Lunch is eaten between noon and 3pm. The evening meal is a leisurely affair served late by American standards, usually after 8 or 9pm, and as late as 11pm to 1am during the summer in the larger cities. Greek restaurants divide food into two categories—*magiremeno,* meaning cooked, or *tis oras* (of the hour), indicating grilled meat. The former is generally cheaper. *Tis oras* includes grilled *moschari* (veal), *arni* (lamb), or *kotopoulo* (chicken), served with *patates* (french fries), *rizi* (rice), or *fasolia* (beans). Popular *magiremeno* dishes include *mousaka* (chopped meat and eggplant covered with a rich cream *béchamel*), *pastitsio* (a lasagna-like dish of thick noodles with *béchamel*), *yemista* (tomatoes and peppers stuffed with rice or meat), *dolmadhes* (grape leaves stuffed with rice and minced meat, and *youvarelakia* (meatballs covered with egg and lemon sauce). Fried zucchini, stuffed eggplant, *tzatziki* (spicy cucumber and yogurt salad), and/or *horta* (greens—either beet or leeks—served with oil and lemon) accompany meals at most *taverna.* Feel free to order these vegetables as the main dish. Vegetarians might also try *spanakopita* (spinach-filled pastry) or *tiropita* (cheese pie in a similar flaky crust). *Briam*—potatoes and other vegetables cooked in oil—is another delicious possibility. Seafood is as readily available as you'd expect in a such an ocean-begotten nation, but more expensive than you'd think. Don't leave without trying fresh octopus (*chtopodi*) marinated in olive oil and oregano. Don't miss the *taramosalata* (dip made with caviar).

You can hardly avoid *souvlaki,* a large skewer of steak, generally pork or lamb. A *souvlaki pita,* appropriately known as "the budget food of the masses," consists of a pita crammed full of skewered meat and fillings (only roughly 250dr). *Gyros* also abound in street vendor fast-food stands. *Bifteki* are a more tender, spicy version of hamburgers; you are usually served two as well as fries. For a healthy staple at a *taverna,* try a *choriatiki,* a "Greek" salad containing olives, tomatoes, onions, cucumbers, and hefty chunks of feta cheese. (Ask for it *horees ladhi* if you don't want it swimming in olive oil.) Usually accompanied by a basket of bread and a glass of water, these salads make inexpensive and satisfying meals.

Visit an *agora* (market) to stock up on the fruit available all summer. Greek fruit has few preservatives and, thus, is tastier than most fruits found in Western Europe or the United States. The fresh figs available in late August and September (*seeka*) are delicious. After dinner, Greeks enjoy *karpouzi* (watermelon) or *peponi* (canteloupe). You should also try the freshly made yogurt (*yiaourti*), a thicker, fattier version of what most Americans are used to, with honey and melon mixed in. Sample indigenous cheeses like *feta* and *kaseri,* a yellow semi-soft cheese.

Greek pastries are delectable and available at *zacharoplastia,* or sweet shops. *Baklava*, a honey-rich, filo-dough pastry filled with chopped nuts, beats all the rest (usually 400dr); try *galaktobouriko,* a custard-filled dough; *kareedhopita,* a walnut cake; *melomakaron,* honey-nut cookies; *kataïfi,* strands of angel hair wrapped around nuts and cinnamon; *koulouria,* shortbread cookies; or *kourabiedhes,* powdered sugar-coated almond cookies. Also try the fruit and cream laden *tartes*. Remember that *pasta,* in both Greek and Turkish, means pastry, not noodles.

Greek coffee is the most popular beverage. Like Turkish coffee, it's strong, sweet, and has a sludge-like consistency. Ask for *gliko* for sweet, *metrio* for medium, and *sketo* or *pikro* for a bitter, sugarless cup. Greek (*elliniko*) coffee is usually served with a glass of water. American-style coffee (called *Nescafé*), usually instant, is also available. If you ask for *café frappe,* you'll get a tall glass of frothy iced coffee.

A favorite Greek snack is *ouzo* with *mezedhes,* tidbits of cheese, sausage, and octopus. *Ouzo* is a distilled spirit to which anise is added, lending it a licorice taste. *Ouzo* is drunk mostly in the islands, while potent *Raki* and *Tsipouro*, a grain-alcohol moonshine, are popular on the mainland and on Crete.

One of the great arts in Greece is wine-making, and every region has its own specialty. Long ago, the Greeks discovered that when wine is stored in pine-pitch-sealed goatskins, it develops a fresh, sappy flavor. After much deduction, they discovered that adding pine resin in varying amounts during fermentation achieves the same result. The resulting wine became known as *retsina.* Resinated wines now come in three varieties: white, rosé, and red (*kokkineli*). White *retsina* is generally cheaper than beer. To try homemade wine ask for *doppio* (local) or *spitiko* (house) *krasi*. There are also a number of non-resinated wines, including sweet (*gliko*), and semi-sweet (*imigliko*). Try the white wines of the northern Peloponnese: Rotonda, Demestika, and Santa Helena are dry. Achaïa-Clauss and Cambas Vintners are good wines. As an after-dinner aperitif, Greeks imbibe Metaxa brandy or *ouzo*.

A good place to taste various Greek wines is at a local wine festival, where you can drink all the wine you want for a flat admission fee. The wine festival in Alexandroupolis runs from early July to mid-August. On Crete, the festival in Rethymnon is held in July, while the one at the village of Dafnes (near Iraklion) runs in mid-July.

■■■ THE MEDIA

A decade ago much of Greek media was state-owned and thus was a propaganda tool for the government. In recent years, private organizations have bought media outlets, making the media a prisoner of the free market instead. Many Greek language **newspapers** are still sensationalistic—more akin to New York Newsday than to USA Today (which, by the way, is sold at major tourist hubs). A few reputable papers are *Eleftherotipia, Kathimerini* (daily) and *Bēma* (published every Sun.). Unlike their newsprint counterparts, glossy Greek **magazines** are worthwhile. *Diabazo* and *Anti* are more scholarly journals; *Clique* caters to the teeny-bopper crowd; and *Taxydromos* is a more sophisticated glamour magazine. American and British magazines like *Vogue* and *Cosmopolitan* also circulate (in Greek). The most noticeable change in Greek media has been in the **television** industry. Whereas ERT1 and 2 were the original stations, both state-owned, private channels like Mega Channel and ANT-1 have brought high-tech production and, of course, more wacky American sit-coms to the Greek viewing public. *Let's Go* does not recommend the morning talk shows, which make Oprah seem interesting. Greek radio plays a wide range of music in large cities, but in the remote locales, you'll only be able to tune in that loud Greek-pop that bus drivers insist on playing at full blasts during long trips.

■■■ SPORTS

Sports fanatics may be quick to associate Greek sports lore with the country's ancient "sound mind, sound body" fascination with athletics. Indeed, present-day Greece is still governed by its fascination with sport. Although everything from handball to water polo is popular, soccer and basketball are the country's games of choice. Of the several Greek A-League **soccer** teams, three stand out in the hearts and apparel of Greek sports fans: *Olympiakos* (red), *Panathinaikos* (green) and AEK (yellow). Even the least devout of sports fans wear their favorite team's colors that, for some, are revered on a level well beyond religion. Although British hoodlums don't frequent soccer matches in Greece, the experience is significantly more rowdy than an afternoon at an American baseball game. Call the Soccer Federation, 11 N. Saripolou St., Athens (tel. 824-5125). **Basketball** is the country's newfound passion. The primary teams are the same as in soccer, but unlike the soccer league, Greek basketball is one of the premier European leagues. It has featured such foreign NBA stars as Roy Tarpley, Dino Radja and Walter Berry. During this upcoming season, Dominique Wilkins will be playing for the Greek team *Panathinaikos,* which has reached Europe's version of the Final Four each of the past two years. *Olimpiakos* is another basketball powerhouse. For more information, contact the Basketball Federation, 11 N. Saripolou St., Athens (tel. 824 4125). For **golfing,** there are 18-hole courses in Athens, Rhodes, Corfu, and Porto Carras on Halkidiki. Call the Glyfada Golf Course and Club in Athens, near the airport (tel. 894 6875). **Tennis** has also gained great popularity among Greeks, especially with the success of native son Pete Sampras. There are public tennis clubs throughout the country. In Athens, call Agios Kosmas at 923-2872. **Watersports** are what most sports enthusiasts who visit Greece dream about. Windsurfing, water skiing, sailing, and other sea sports can be found at most popular beaches. For windsurfing info, call the Hellenic Wind-Surfing Association at 7 Filellinon St. in Athens (tel. 323 0068). For info on sailing, contact the Sailing Federation at 15A Xenofontos St. in Athens (tel. 323 5560). **Scuba diving** is forbidden in all Greek waters. It is allowed only under supervised conditions in Chalkidiki, Mykonos, Corfu, Cephalonia and Zakynthos. For information, contact the Union of Owners of Diving Centers, 67 Zea Port, Piraeus (tel. 922 9532). Surprisingly, **skiing** has become increasingly popular among Greeks, and ski resorts can be found throughout the country. Contact the Greek Skiing and Alpine Federation, 7 Karageorgi Servias St., Athens (tel. 323 4555). For info on **mountain climbing** and **hiking,** call the Greek Touring Club at 12 Politechniou St. in Athens (tel. 524 8600).

Falling Star Lands in Athens

The "Human Highlight Film" is bringing his highwire act to Athens. While NBA star Dominique Wilkins no longer appears on NBA courts, his stature is more than enough for fans of the Athens' *Panathinaikos* team. Wilkins, a member of the original Dream Team, left the Boston Celtics last summer after the team refused to grant him a loan that had been stipulated in his contract. Wilkins will join ex-Celtic Stojko Vrankovic on the perennial powerhouse that has finished in Europe's final four the past two years. Incidentally, *Panathinaikos*, like the Celtics, wear green uniforms and have the three-leaf clover as their symbol. Wilkins signed a two-year deal worth $7 million. By the way, Wilkins also gets a house and two Mercedes. Not bad for an aging star, who can now relive some of his past Boston glories. Wilkins, a sure bet for the NBA hall of fame, led the league in scoring for several years while playing for Atlanta and is likely to do the same in Athens.

■■■ THIS YEAR'S NEWS

During the past year, PASOK has begun to settle several problems which threatened the stability of the political climate. In January, 1995, charges that Mitsotakis was involved in political corruption were dropped. One month later, the government agreed to support Costis Stefanopoulos to succeed Karamanlis as president. Stefanopoulos, a former member of the New Democracy (ND) party, a short-lived breakaway party, was chosen as a compromise candidate. The narrow election of Stefanopoulos avoided national elections at a time when PASOK and ND are questioning their own leadership. PASOK now has the opportunity to pursue a contractionary hard *drachma* policy that will reduce the public deficit. Before the next election, scheduled for November, 1997, party members must also settle internal differences. The aging Papandreou is under criticism from his own party because he has been unwilling to resign from his post as party head. The ND party also has an opportunity to resolve its own internal divisions before the next election.

An important current issue is the influx of Albanians fleeing their country; they walk over mountains, swim to Corfu, or ride boats into Greece. Albanians were initially welcomed, but outbreaks of crime in Greece and anger at the growing persecution of ethnic Greeks living in Albania turned popular opinion against the refugees, and deportation is now common, though many flee again days later. Relations between Albania and Greece have been greatly improved in recent months and talks seem to be leading towards a friendship treaty which includes provisions on the Greek minority in Albania and the Albanian migrants in Greece.

The question of Macedonia remains a contentious issue among many Greeks, particularly in the North. In April, 1992, a former province of Yugoslavia declared itself the independent Republic of Macedonia. Many Greeks felt an important part of their history and cultural identity had been usurped and were outraged. Ancient Macedonia, home to Alexander the Great, was probably a Hellenic civilization, not Slavic. (Slavs moved into the Balkan peninsula until the 6th century AD.) The slogan "Macedonia is Greece 3000 years" now adorns everything from bumper stickers to ferry tickets in Greece. In February, the European Court of Justice began considering the Commissions's suit against Greece over its trade embargo on the Former Yugoslav Republic of Macedonia. Greece and the EU now seem willing to compromise.

■■■ HOLIDAYS

The Greek penchant for celebrations is infectious, and visitors are welcomed and swept up in the festivities. Many towns honor their patron saint with special festivals. Businesses shut down for the day, and there is usually live music and Greek dancing in front of the local church. The following list of festivals includes holidays of the Greek Orthodox Church and traditional festivals celebrated in rural and agricultural areas. Note: the dates for some religious holidays change annually. Check dates and additional information on festivals, artistic events, and religious fairs at tourist offices or the local police.

Jan. 1: Feast of St. Basil. Carrying on a Byzantine tradition, Greeks cut a New Year's sweet bread called *Vassilopita,* baked with a coin inside. The person who gets the slice with the coin is that year's lucky person.

Jan. 6: Epiphany. Celebrated in the West as the day the Magi appeared in Bethlehem to greet the baby Jesus, in the Eastern church Epiphany is recognized as the day Jesus was baptized by St. John. In Greece, *kallikantzaroi* (goblins) appear between Christmas and Epiphany. Village bonfires scare them away. At Epiphany, waters are blessed and evil spirits leave the earth. A cross is thrown into harbors all around Greece and the young men who fetch the cross are considered blessed.

Jan. 8: Gynaecocracy (St. Domenica's Day/Midwife day). Women of child-bearing age bring gifts to the midwife. In the villages of Komotini, Xanthi, Kilkis, and Serres, women gather in the cafés, while men look after the households; the men are allowed to join their wives in celebrations after dusk.

Feb. 1-Feb. 23: Carnival. Three weeks of feasting and dancing before the Lenten fast begins on Feb 24. Notable celebrations occur in Patras and Cephalonia.

March 25: Greek Independence Day. Commemorates the 1821 struggle against the Turkish Ottoman Empire. Also a religious holiday, the Feast of the Annunciation, when the angel Gabriel told Mary of the Incarnation.

April 12: Good Friday. People carry lit candles in a procession through town or around the church in one of the most moving liturgies in the Greek church.

April 14: Easter. The most holy day in the Greek calendar. After a midnight mass that is followed by a meal, celebrations on Easter Sunday typically include feasting on spit-roasted lamb and red-dyed hard-boiled eggs, followed by dancing.

April 23: St. George's Day. Celebration in honor of the dragon-slaying knight. Festivities at Limnos, Chania include horse races, wrestling matches, and dances.

May 1: Labor Day. Also Feast of the Flowers. Wreaths of flowers hung outside people's doors. The odd Communist demonstration.

May 21: Anastenaria. Also called **Feast of St. Constantine and St. Eleni.** Celebrations include fire dancing and walking on burning charcoal. Celebrated in Agia Eleni, Thessaloniki, and Veria.

Early-mid June: The Day of the Holy Spirit. This national religious holiday takes place 40-50 days after Easter and is celebrated differently in each region.

June 3: Pentecost.

Late June-early July: Navy Week. Fishers' and sailors' festivals at various coastal towns. On Volos, a re-enactment of the journey of the Argonauts is staged.

Aug.: Epirotika Festival, in Ioannina; **Olympus Festival,** in Katerini; **Hippokrateia Festival,** on Kos. All three feature artistic exhibits and performances.

Aug. 15: Feast of the Assumption of the Virgin Mary. Celebration throughout Greece, particularly on Tinos, in honor of Mary's ascent to Heaven.

Sept. 8: The Virgin's Birthday. In some villages an auction is held to determine who will carry the Virgin's Icon. The money is used to provide a village feast.

Sept. 14: Exaltation of the Cross. In villages, the altar cross is venerated and paraded through the town, while children sing hymns.

Oct. 26: Feast of St. Demetrius. Celebrated with particular enthusiasm in Salonika. The feast coincides with the opening of new wine, so there is heavy drinking.

Oct. 28: National Anniversary of Greek Independence. Called "*Obi* Day" in honor of Metaxas's famous "*Obi*" (No) to Mussolini.

Dec. 24-25: Christmas. As part of the festivities, children traditionally make the rounds singing *kalanda* (Christmas carols).

Athens ΑΘΗΝΑ

A city of six-million-plus, Athens sits unsettled in the shadow of its history beneath the Acropolis, the most poignant reminder of its former greatness. But although its bright destiny has been thwarted by war, and then expansion, Athens perseveres. Visitors harboring mental images of togas and philosophers may be disappointed because Athens is a 20th-century city in every sense of the word: it is crowded, modern, and polluted. The Neoclassical mansions that graced the city's streets only thirty years ago have been replaced by white monolith towers that can accommodate Athens' growing population. The Plaka neighborhood in the city center remains the only remnant of Athens' recent grandeur.

Unlike many of its European neighbors, Athens must struggle to regain the acceptance of its people. Column-bound temples stand as proud reminders of the faith of the ancient Athenians, but modernity cannot rest on teetering ruins: the city needs a subway, a manageable telephone system, and efficient living. In recent years Greece has begun to drag itself towards the Age of Efficiency, but Athens cannot help but be reminded of its history.

In the city center, Byzantine churches, situated beside ancient ruins, stand amid Neoclassical cafés and modern vendors. The incessant roar and exhaust of engines from buses, cars and motorcycles stifles the air. Recently, the government has taken steps to revitalize the city and, last year, reduced the amount of traffic in the city's center in hopes of kindling memories of Athens' more ethereal past. The Acropolis and the area around it, including Plaka and Monastiraki, are majestic, and the city offers countless other pleasant neighborhoods.

If the touristed areas of Athens get to be too much, seek refuge in one of the many squares where the city's authentic lifestyle, as interesting and varied as the ancients in the Agora, is on display. Trendy hotspots like Kalithea or seaside *tavernas* in Piraeus reveal the wealth of Athens' present even as its past looks on.

HISTORY

A competition between Poseidon and Athena determined how Athens would be named. The gods of Olympus decreed that whoever gave the city the most useful gift would become its patron god. Poseidon struck the rock of the Acropolis with his trident and salt water came gushing forth. The populace was awestruck, but Athena's more practical gift, an olive tree, won her the right to rule.

Historically, Athens became a town of note in the 16th century BC. Around the 8th century BC, the city became the artistic center of Greece, conspicuous for its pottery. It unified with Attica at about the same time, but the best was yet to come. After dramatic victories over the Persians at Marathon and Salamis in the 5th century BC, Athens enjoyed a 70-year Golden Age, reaching its apogee under the patronage of Pericles. Iktinos and Kallikrates designed the Parthenon; Aeschylus, Sophocles, and Euripides wrote tragic masterpieces, and Aristophanes penned ribald comedies. Early historians, Herodotus in particular, challenged the assumption that gods, not human beings, govern history. Hippocrates, with a similar confidence in human autonomy (and anatomy), developed the study of medicine.

The bloody and drawn-out campaigns of the Peloponnesian War (431-404 BC) between Athens and Sparta heralded the demise of Periclean Athens. Political power in Greece then shifted north to the court of Philip of Macedon and his son Alexander the Great. Through the late 5th and 4th centuries BC, however, Athens remained important as a cultural center, producing three of the most influential western philosophers, Socrates, Plato, and Aristotle, as well as the great orator Demosthenes. But by the 2nd century BC, the ravenous Roman Empire had feasted on Athens and drained the city of its zest. By the time the Byzantine Empire split off from the foundering remains of the Roman Empire (285 AD), Athens was no more than an overtaxed backwater specializing in Neoplatonism. The city remained the center of Greek education with elaborate institutes of learning, but the city's status (as well as its buildings) lapsed into ruin when Justinian banned the teaching of philosophy in 529 AD.

Around 1000, Basil II, the Holy Roman Emperor, visited Athens. After praying to the Virgin Mary in the Parthenon, Basil ordered craftsmen to restore Athens to its former glory. Under successive conquerors—the Franks in 1205, the Catalans in 1311, and the Accajioli merchant family in 1387—Athens underwent a resurgence. Although many hailed the introduction of Muslim Ottoman rule in 1456 as a great deliverance, Athens remained in cultural hibernation until 1834, when it was proclaimed the capital of the new, independent Greece. Modern Athens, with its squares, wide boulevards, and tranquil National Garden, embodies plans drawn up by German architects under the direction of the Bavarian King Otho, who was awarded the newly created kingdom of Greece in the late 19th century.

In the 20th century, Athens has grown exponentially in population and industry, for two reasons. First, in 1923, the establishment of the Republic of Turkey led to a Turkish-Greek exchange of populations, which produced a mighty burden for the burgeoning city. Second, as with all industrial cities, Athens attracted workers from destitute regions of Greece. The past century has seen the population explode from 169 families to more than half the population of Greece—six million people. In an attempt to counteract noise and pollution, the transit authority now bans cars from a number of streets in the historic Plaka district and limits driver access downtown on alternate days. The subway, still under construction, should also eliminate much of the traffic, noise, and smog but, for now, it only adds to the confusion. Zeus' thunderbolt now shakes down acid rain, and longtime residents rue the infamous *nephos* (smog cloud) that settles in a most sinister fashion over Athens in summer.

ORIENTATION AND PRACTICAL INFORMATION

Coming from either airport, the bus stops at **Syntagma** (Constitution) **Square** (C4). The center of modern Athens, this bustling plaza is packed with overpriced outdoor cafés (including a Hellenic McDonald's), luxury hotels, and flashy banks. A pale yellow Neoclassical building, formerly the royal palace and now home to the Greek Parliament, gazes over the toe-nipping traffic of Syntagma. The square is a good spot to begin your tour of the city. The **Greek National Tourist Office,** the **post office,** the **American Express office, transportation terminals,** and a number of **travel agencies** and **banks** surround the square. **Filellinon Street** and **Nikis Street,** parallel thoroughfares which head out from Syntagma towards Plaka (B5), contain many of the city's budget travel offices, cheap hotels, and dance clubs. Unfortunately, Syntagma is currently being torn up for the subway; cranes and dirt will detract from the square's charm for at least another year.

In front of the Parliament, facing Syntagma Sq., is the **Tomb of the Unknown Warrior** (C5). The **Zappeion** (C5-D5), an exhibition hall, rests in the tranquil **National Garden,** bordering the south side of the Parliament. Continue east to the heavily guarded **President's House** (D5) and **Athens Stadium** (D6; constructed in 1896 for the first modern Olympiad). **Hadrian's Arch** (C6) and the **Olympeion** stand just south of the Garden in full view of the city's crowning glory, the **Acropolis** (A5-B5). On the north side of Syntagma, the city's embassies, consulates, and premier hospital (Evangelismos) congregate on broad **Vasilissis Sofias.** The Benaki, Byzantine, and War Museums, and the National Gallery cluster on this avenue (D4-E4). The affluent and chic **Kolonaki** (D4) district is bordered by Vasilissis Sofias, in the shadow of Lycabettos Hill.

Northwest of Syntagma, **Omonia Square** (B2), actually a circle, is the site of the city's operational central subway station from which trains run to Monastiraki (A4; 3min.) and Piraeus (20min.), among other destinations. Inexpensive shops for food, clothing, and jewelry abound, but with the influx of refugees in recent years, this Times Square-esque area has become increasingly unsafe; however, there are many cheap lodgings here. Mind your own business and try to be inconspicuous. Don't

A
B
C
1
2
3
4
5
6
Iliou
K. Paleologou
Aristotelous
To National Archaeological Museum
Tossitsa
EXARHIA
Methonis
Mezonos
VATHIS SQUARE
Stournara
Solomou
Favierou
Kapodistriou
Kaningos
Tzortz
Botassi
Soultani
Eressou
Victor Ougo
Sokratous
Tritis Septemvriou
Halkokondili
Veranzerou
KARAISKAKI SQUARE
Karolou
OSE
OMONIA
KANINGOS SQUARE
A. Metaxa
Valtetsiou
Arahovis
Akominatou
Koumoundourou
National Theatre
Satovriandou
Themistokleous
Agiou Konstandinou
Deligianni
To Train Station
Leonidou
Bus #051
Zinonos
Menandrou
OMONIA SQUARE
Gamvetta
E. Benaki
Messolongiou
Zoodohou Pigis
Keramikou
Kolonou
Agissilaou
P. Tsaldari
Sokratous
Fidiou
Mavromichali
Didotou
Har. Trikoupi
Navarinou
Em. Banaki
Athinas
Geraniou
Santaroza
Arsaki
Opera House
Solonos
Main Tourist Office
Theater Museum
Eleftheriou Venizelou (Panepistimiou)
Ipokratous
Sofokleous
Pesmazoglou
Akadimias
Massalias
ELEFTHERIAS SQUARE
To Kerameikos Museum
Evripidou
University
Omirou
Sina
Dragatsaniou
Aristofanous
Agiou Dimitriou
Aiolou
KLAFTHMONOS SQUARE
Sari
Praxitelous
Stadiou
Athinas
Kolokotroni
OTE
Tourist Office
Voukourestiou
To Thissio
Ermou
Perikleous
Leka
MONASTIRAKI
Kapnikarea
American Express
Theseion (Temple of Hephaestus)
Ifestou
SYNTAGMA
Mitropoleos
Ermou
Olympic Airways
Agora
Mitropoli Cathedral
Agia Eleftheria
Tourist Office
Mitropoleos
Stoa of Attalos Museum
Aiolou
Adrianou
Apolonos
OSE
Tomb of Unknown
Voulis
Xenofontos
Greek Folk Musical Instruments Museum
Kiristou
Lissiou
Nikis
Agii Apostoli
Nikodimou
Filellinon
Agia Triada
PLAKA
Greek Folk Museum
Metamorphosis
Kidathineon
Adrianou
Areopagus
Acropolis
Amalias
Jewish Museum
Parthenon
Theatre of Dionysus
Beulé Gate
Hadrian's Arch
Vasilissis Olgas
Dionissiou Areopag
Rovertou Galli
Kariatidon
Makrigianui
PHILOPAPPOU
Mitseon
Temple of the Olympian Ze
Andrea Singrou

D
E
F
Athens Central City
Alexandras
Armatolon Klefton
Gerodimou
Paligenessias
Daskalogiani
Nikotsara
Laskareos
Vatatzi
Komninon
Vasiliou Voulgaroktonou
Ipokratous
Asklipiou
Apokafkon
Sinessiou kirinis
Grigoriou Theologou
Fanarioton
Sarantapichou
Em. Benaki
Metsovou
Zoodohou Pigis
Har. Trikoupi
Mavromichali
Tsimiski
Methonis
Ipokratous
Asklipiou
Nik. Ouranou
Dafnonomili
Ag. Issidorou
Doxapatri
Part. Fotiou
Sarantapichou
Lycavittos Theatre
Lycavittos Hill
Konlari
Mela
Tim Filimonos
Agios Georgios
Sina
Herssonos
Statha
Dimaki
Athineon Efivon
Dimoharous
Dinokratous
To Athens Concert Hall
Eleftherias Park
Rongakou
Str Sindesmou
Fokilidou
Anagnostopoulou
Tsakalof
Skoufa
Solonos
Aristipou
Kleomenous
Dinokratous
Marasli
Aristodimou
Anapiron Polemou
Xenokratous
Souidias
Spefsipou
Patriarhou Ioakim
Genadiou
Iassiou
Monis Petraki
Ravine
Alopekis
Marasli
Papadiamantopoulou
Sissini
Iridanou
LONAKI
Kanari
Irodotou
Loukianou
Ploutahou
Ipsilandou
Hatzigianni Mexi
Vendiri
Alios
Benaki Museum
Museum of Cycladic & Ancient Greek Art
Ipsilandou
National Gallery
Vasilissis Sofias
Parliament
RIGILIS SQUARE
Vasilissis Sofias
War Museum of Greece
Byzantine Museum
Vasileos Konstaninou
Michalakopoulou
Vrassida
Orminiou
Iona Dragoumi
Singrou Park
Mourouzi
Niriidon
Alkimahou
Andinoros
Kritonos
Efroniou
Dioharous
Likiou
Rigilis
Rizari
Sp. Merkouri
Vas. Georiou B
Presidential Residence
Vas. Georgiou B
Vas. Alexandrou
Zappeion Exhibition Halls
Irodou Atikou
Aminda
Arhelaou
Ergotimou
Ifontos
Drakondos
Amassias
Issiodou
Fokianou
Arktinou
Pafsania
Elanikou
Theagenous
Erifilis
Formionos
Vasileos Konstaninou
Arianou
Fedrou
Stravonos
Thironos
Agras
Eratosthenous
Ironos
Aristoxenou
Pangratiou Park
Sp. Merkouri
Pratinou
Astidamandos
Aristarhou
Zindodotou
Ieronos
Egiptou
Kononos
Athens Stadium
Agras
PLASTIRA SQUARE
Eftihidou
Ymittou
Ymittou
Damareos
N

travel alone at night. Two parallel avenues connect Syntagma Sq. to Omonia Sq. (Panepistimiou and Stadiou). The **university** (C3) and **library** are on Panepistimiou St., halfway between Syntagma and Omonia. North on Patission St., which intersects the two avenues just before Omonia, is the **National Archaeological Museum.** Both train stations, **Larissis** and **Peloponnese,** are on Konstantinoupoleos St. northeast of **Karaiskaki Square** (A1), and can be reached on foot ½hr. along Deligiani St.

Just west of Syntagma (follow Ermou St. or Metropoleos St.), **Aiolou Street** and **Athinas Street,** running between Omonia and the Acropolis, are lined with shops and department stores where wares spill out onto the sidewalk. Along Athinas St., midway between Omonia and **Monastiraki** (A4; Athens' garment district), between Evripidou and Sofokleous St. (A3-B3), is the **food market.** Here, the **Athens Flea Market,** the city's "new *agora*" (marketplace) surrounds the old one. South of here towards the Acropolis lies **Plaka,** the oldest section of the city, now brimming with shops, restaurants, and hotels. South of the Acropolis and neighboring Philopappou Hill (A6; towards Athens' port, Piraeus) is the **Koukaki** section, a relatively calm residential area, and **Koukaki Square,** which contains an open produce market as well as the Olympic Airways headquarters. **Singrou** (B6) divides this area from the **Kinossargous** section. To get to Koukaki from Syntagma, walk down Amalias (which becomes Singrou beyond Hadrian's Arch) and turn right; for Kinossargous, turn left at Singrou. Singrou continues straight down to the water, where it meets **Possidonis,** which contains numerous beaches, good clubs, and access to the airports. **Vouliagmenis** also heads south from below Plaka, leading to Glyfada and more nightlife.

Make use of the two quality **maps** available at the tourist office: the city one is clear and includes bus and trolley routes, and a more detailed street plan graces the pages of *Greece-Athens-Attica* magazine. Athenian geography mystifies newcomers and natives alike; if you lose your bearings, ask for directions back to the well-lit Syntagma, or look for a cab. The Acropolis provides a useful reference point. In contests between pedestrians and motorists, Athenian drivers always take the right of way; be alert when crossing the street; drivers rarely pause for pedestrians. Be aware that Athenian streets often have multiple spellings or names. Lysikrateus is also Lisicratous or Lissi Kratous; Aiolou is also known as Eolou and Eolu; Victoriou Ougo is Victor Hugo. Panepistimiou St. is also commonly called Eleftheriou Venizelou.

Several publications list general information about Athens. Pick up a copy of the tourist office's *This Week in Athens,* which gives addresses, hours, and phone numbers for nightclubs, theaters, sights, museums, libraries, restaurants, airlines, churches, and more. News and movie/restaurant/exhibit listings appear daily in Athens' English-language newspaper, the *Athens News* (200dr). The *Weekly Greek News* (250dr) and *Greece's Weekly* focus more on Greek politics and some international news. The monthly *Athenian* magazine features stories about Greek culture.

In summer, businesses are generally open Mon. and Wed. from 8:30am to 3pm; Tues., Thurs., and Fri. from 8am to 2pm and from 5:30 to 8:30pm; and Sat. from 8am to 3pm. High-season officially runs from mid-June to mid-September.

Tourist Office: Information window at the **National Bank of Greece,** 2 Karageorgi Servias, Syntagma Sq. (C5; tel. 322 2545). Bus and ferry schedules and prices; lists of museums, embassies, and banks; colorful brochures on travel throughout Greece. Ask for the detailed Athens map if you plan to stay. Open Mon.-Fri. 8am-2pm and 3:30-8pm, Sat. 9am-2pm. There is an office in the **East Terminal** of the airport (tel. 961 2722). Open Mon.-Fri. 8am-10pm, Sat. 10am-5pm; off-season Mon.-Fri. 9am-6pm, Sat. 10am-5pm. The **central office** is at 2 Amerikis St. off Stadiou St. (C3; tel. 322 3111). Open Mon.-Fri. 8:30am-2:30pm.

Tourist Police: (tel. 171). English spoken; open 24 hr., 365 days a year; helpful.

Police: (tel. 100). Not likely to speak English.

Main Post Office: 100 Aiolou St., Omonia Sq. (B2; tel. 321 6023). **Postal Code:** 10200. **Syntagma Sq.,** on the corner of Mitropolis (tel. 322 6253). **Postal Code:** 10300. **60 Mitropoleos,** a few blocks from Syntagma Sq. (tel. 321 8143). Poste Restante holds mail for one month. (All open Mon.-Fri. 7:30am-8pm, Sat. 7:30am-2pm, Sun. 9am-1:30pm.) **Parcel post** for sending packages abroad at **29 Kou-**

moundourou (A1-A2; tel. 524 9359; open same hours as above), and **4 Stadiou,** in arcade (tel. 322 8940). Open Mon.-Fri. 9:30am-2pm.

OTE: 15 Stadiou St. (C4; 24 hr.). Offices at Omonia Sq. (at the end of Stadiou St.), and 50 Athinas St. are both open Mon.-Fri. 7am-10pm. The Omonia office doesn't cater to tourist needs; try 15 Stadiou St. to converse in English. Make overseas collect calls from any of these offices. For info on overseas calls, dial 161 or 162; for directory assistance in Athens call 131; outside Athens, 132. You can make local calls at the OTE or at many of the street-side kiosks that have telephones on their side-window ledges (10dr). Most **phone booths** in the city operate by convenient telephone cards that can be purchased for 1300, 6000, or 11,5000dr at OTE offices and some kiosks. Push the "i" button on the phones for English-language instructions. Calls are terminated when credit runs out. Visit the OTE for more details. For telephone info call 134; for complaints 135; for a domestic operator speaking English 151 or 152. **Telephone Code:** 01.

The Hellenic Chamber of Hotels: In the National Bank of Greece next to the tourist office (C4; tel. 323 7193). Provides information and reservations for A, B, and C class hotels throughout Greece and some less expensive ones in Athens. All reservations require a cash deposit. Open Mon.-Thurs. 8:30am-2:30pm, Fri. 8:30am-1:30pm, Sat. 9am-1pm. An early visit is a crowdless visit.

Tourist Agencies: For **ISIC/FIYTO** purchases, see Identification on p. 9. In Athens, the ISIC can be bought for 2400dr at either **USIT Youth Student Travel,** 3 Filellinon St. (tel. 324 1884; fax 322 5974; open Mon.-Fri. 9am-5pm, Sat. 10am-2pm), or **I.S.Y.T.S.L.T.D.,** 11 Nikis St., 2nd floor (tel. 322 1267; fax 322 1531; open Mon.-Fri. 9am-5pm, Sat. 9am-1pm). The latter sells FIYTO cards as well. Travel agencies along Nikis and Filellinon St. off Syntagma Sq. offer student discounts on international plane and train travel. There are *no* discounts for foreign students on domestic travel in Greece. **Magic Travel Agency** (or **Magic Bus**), 20 Filellinon St. (tel. 323 7471, -4; fax 322 0219), stands out. Extremely competent, English-speaking staff. Open Mon.-Fri. 9am-6pm, Sat. 9am-2pm. **Consolas Travel,** 100 Aiolou St., (tel. 325 4931; fax 321 0907). Next to the post office, offers reliable advice and often hires travelers. They have a second office on 18 Filellinon St (tel. 323 2812). Talk to Mr. Consolas about his new project, a traveler's co-op on Gavdos, an island south of Crete. Generally, it is best to shop around and look for specials at the agencies, which are all near one another. Bus and train travel to faraway destinations is both lengthy and arduous; consider traveling by plane instead. Student international flights are particularly affordable, and spending the extra cash will spare you body cramps associated with narrow seats, long hours, and winding roads.

Greek Youth Hostel Association: 4 Dragatsaniou St., 7th floor (B3; tel. 323 4107; fax 323 7590), elevators on right as you enter arcade. Lists hostels in Greece and sells HI cards for 2600dr (passport, photo ID required). Open Mon.-Fri. 9am-2pm.

Embassies: Australia, 37 D. Soutsou St. (tel. 644 7303). Open Mon.-Fri. 8:30am-12:30pm. **Canada,** 4 Ioannou Genadiou St. (tel. 725 4011). Open Mon.-Fri. 7:30am-3:15pm, consular section Mon.-Fri. 9am-noon. **German,** 3 Dimitriou St. (tel. 728 5111). Open 9am-noon. **Great Britain,** 1 Ploutarchou St. (tel. 723 6211), at Ypsilantou St. Open for visas Mon.-Fri. 8am-1pm. Visas granted for all Commonwealth countries. **Ireland,** 7 Vas. Konstantinou Ave. (tel. 723 2771). Open Mon.-Fri. 9am-3pm. **South Africa,** 60 Kifissias St. (tel. 680 6645). Open Mon.-Fri. 8am-1pm. **Turkey,** 8 Vas. Georgiou B. St. (tel. 724 5915). Comprehensive listing of embassies available at the tourist office. **U.S.,** 91 Vasilissis Sofias (tel. 721 2951; fax 725 3025). Open Mon.-Fri. 8:30am-5pm. Visas can be obtained 8am-noon. Bring one photo.

Banks: National Bank of Greece, 2 Karageorgi Servias St., Syntagma Sq. (tel. 322 2738, -7). Open Mon.-Thurs. 8am-2pm and 3:30-6:30pm, Fri. 8am-1:30pm and 3-6:30pm, Sat. 9am-3pm, Sun. 9am-1pm. AmEx, the post office, some hotels, and other banks (list available at tourist office) **exchange currency.** Expect commissions of 5% on average. Most banks close at 2pm on weekdays and are closed on weekends. Currency exchange at the airport is available 24 hr., but fee is high.

American Express: 2 Ermou St., P.O. Box 3325, above McDonald's in Syntagma Sq. (tel. 324 4975, -9). Air-conditioned and filled with Americans, the office cashes traveler's checks with *no commission,* runs a travel agency, holds mail for one month, and provides special services for cardholders. Open Mon.-Fri. 8:30am-4pm, Sat. 8:30am-1:30pm; (only travel and mail service on Sat.).

Flights: East Terminal, foreign airlines and some charters; **West Terminal,** Olympic Airways domestic and international service; **New Charter Terminal,** most charters. From Athens, take the double-decker Express bus #090 and #091 from either Syntagma Sq., in front of the Bank of Macedonia/Kenny Rogers, or Stadiou St. near Omonia Sq. (#090 serves all three terminals, while #091 only goes to East and West). Buses run roughly every ½hr., 6am-9pm, 160dr; every 40min., 9pm-11:30am, 160dr; and every hr. on the half-hour, 11:30am-5:30am, 200dr. From airport to Athens, look to your left after exiting customs for the blue and yellow express buses (160-200dr). A taxi costs 1500-2000dr, with an extra charge for luggage. Beware of drivers who rig the meters. Drivers may be unwilling to pick up travelers laden with luggage and might also make you share a cab. Express buses and cabs may be your most reliable travel option. Plane fare to İstanbul 31,000dr (Thai Airlines tickets to İstanbul tend to be cheaper and more convenient.)

Trains: Larissis Train Station serves northern Greece (Thessaloniki 3500dr). Take yellow trolley bus #1 from El. Venizelou (also called Panepistimiou St.) in Syntagma (every 10min., 5am-midnight, 75dr). **Peloponnese Railroad Station** (tel. 513 1601), is in a Victorian-style building with a silver roof. From Larissis, exit to your right and go over the bridge, or catch blue bus #057 from El. Venizelou (every 15min., 5:30am-11:30pm, 75dr). Serves Patras (1600dr) and elsewhere in the Peloponnese. Also has OSE buses to Bulgaria, Germany, Italy, and Turkey. For more information, call **Hellenic Railways (OSE),** (tel. 524 0601, -45).

Subway: One-line system running from Piraeus harbor to Kifissia in north Athens with stops at Monastiraki, Omonia, and Victoria, among others. Runs every 10min., 5am-midnight, 75-100dr. Buy tickets in stations, punch ticket with orange machine before entering, and hang on to stub until exiting. Inspectors randomly check trains, and passengers without tickets are fined 1500dr. Athens remains in the process of constructing a more extensive subway system. The project has been moving slowly, hampered by financial difficulties and archaeological finds; don't expect completion until at least 1999.

Buses: For Athens and its suburbs, buses are blue and are designated by 3-digit numbers. Fare 75dr. Convenient for travel across the city, they are also ideal for daytrips to places like Daphni and Kesariani. For longer trips, take the orange or green buses. There are two main blue bus terminals, **Terminal A,** 100 Kifissou St. (tel. 514 8856), and **Terminal B,** 260 Liossion St. (tel. 831 7059). Terminal A serves most of Greece, including the Peloponnese and northern Greece, and can be reached by blue bus #051, caught at the corner of Zinonos and Menandrou near Omonia Sq. (every 10min. 5am-11:30pm, 75dr). Be forewarned: the "tourist info" booth at Terminal A is a privately-run agency; don't let them dissuade you from visiting the hotel you are interested in and don't get duped into buying useless "vouchers." Terminal B (Mavromateon stop, at one corner of Areos park) serves some destinations in central Greece and Evia including Delphi, Meteora, and Kimi. It can be reached by blue bus #024, caught at El. Venizelou (Panepistimiou St.; every 20min., 5am-midnight, 75dr). Note that the number of the bus may be displayed either above the windshield or on a sticker in the windshield near the front door. Bus stops list the numbers of the buses they serve. Buy a ticket at a kiosk from a station vendor and stamp it yourself at the orange machine on board. Kiosks only sell tickets for Athens and its suburbs; if you're heading farther afield, get to the station 1hr. before the departure time. Beware: bus strikes are frequent, but not all companies strike at once. Note that if you don't stamp your bus, trolley, or subway ticket (even when it seems nobody is there to make you pay) and hold onto it, you may get caught by police in a spot-check and fined 1500dr for not paying for the 75dr ticket.

Trolleys: Yellow, crowded, and sporting 1- or 2-digit numbers. Fare 75dr. Trolleys no longer accept money. Buy a ticket (or book of 10) ahead of time at a kiosk. Frequent service; convenient for short hops within the city. Tourist office map of Athens shows most trolley routes.

Taxis: The meter starts ticking at 200dr, with an additional 58dr per km within city limits (be forewarned—the rates double between midnight and 5am). 113dr per km in the suburbs. For trips from the airport, there is a 300dr surcharge, and from bus and railway terminals 160dr (plus another 55dr for each piece of luggage over 10kg). Hail your taxi, shouting your destination. Empty taxis are rare. It is common to ride with other passengers going in the same direction. For an extra 300dr, call a radio taxi (Ikaros, tel. 513 2240; Hermes, tel. 411 5200; and Kosmos, tel. 420 0042). A full list of radio taxis appears in the *Athens News.* Pay what the meter shows, rounded up to the next 50dr, but be wary of drivers who tinker with their meters. Get in the cab and *then* tell the driver where you're going—otherwise the driver might refuse if your destination is inconvenient. Most drivers don't speak English so have your destination written down (in Greek if possible).

Ferries: Most dock at **Piraeus.** From here they go to all Greek island groups except the Sporades (which leave from Ag. Konstantinos or Volos) and the Ionian Islands (which leave from Patras in the Peloponnese). Some popular destinations from Piraeus (all fares one-way) are Santorini (10hr., 4250dr), Mykonos (6hr., 3450dr), Ios (9hr., 4250dr), Aegina (1½hr., 950dr), Paros (5-6hr., 3150dr), Rhodes (17hr., 6700dr). International departures to Haifa, Alexandria, and Limassol also leave from Piraeus. (Contact **Port Authority of Piraeus** at tel. 426 6000.) From Athens to Piraeus, take the subway to the last stop, or take green bus #40 from Vasileos Konstandinou across from the Public Theater (every 10min., 75dr). To reach Syntagma (in Athens) from Piraeus, walk left (facing inland) along the waterfront to Roosevelt St., take the subway to Monastiraki (75dr), turn right up Ermou St., and walk 5min. Boats also leave from **Rafina,** a port suburb east of Athens, to Andros, Tinos, and Mykonos (see also Piraeus, p. 86 and Rafina, p. 90). To Kea or Kithnos, take a ferry (1600-2450dr) from **Lavrio** (see p. 89). The orange bus to Lavrio leaves from Mavromateon St. near Areos Park (take bus or taxi from Syntagma) for 700dr. Always check ferry schedules at the tourist office or in the *Athens News* just prior to departure, with the Port Authority of Piraeus (tel. 426 6000) or any travel agency. Schedules change frequently without notice. Buy tickets at travel agencies in Athens or Piraeus. Ferry info is in any Greek-language newspaper or dial 143 for a Greek-recorded timetable (call day before or morning of departure).

Flying Dolphins: Hydrofoils speed above water between islands and from some ports, serving the Argosaronic, Sporades, and Cyclades groups. **Ceres' Flying Dolphins** (tel. 428 0001) and **Ilios Lines' Dolphins** (tel. 322 5139) are the two main companies. Hydrofoils, roughly twice as expensive and twice as fast, leave from **Zea Port** near Piraeus, Agios Konstantinos, and Volos. The tourist office and travel agencies can also provide guidance and info.

Car Rental: Places abound on Singrou Ave., all charging 12,000-13,000dr for a small car with 100km mileage. Most require drivers to be 23 or older and to have driven for at least a year.

Luggage Storage: At the airport 100m outside on your right as you exit baggage claim and customs; look for the yellow 'lockers' sign. 700dr per piece per day. 24 hr. Keep your ticket stub to reclaim; pay when you collect. After midnight you pay for an extra day. Several offices on Nikis and Filellinon St., including **Pacific Ltd.,** 26 Nikis St. (tel. 323 6851 or 324 1007). Per piece: 300dr per day, 700dr per week, 2000dr per month. Open Mon.-Sat. 7am-8pm, Sun. 7am-2pm. Many hotels have free, or at least inexpensive, luggage storage; ask the manager.

Laundromats: The Greek word for laundry is *plinitirio,* but most places have signs saying "Laundry." Self-serve laundromats include one at **10 Angelou Geronta St.** in Plaka, and also at **9 Psaron St.** (tel. 522 2856) and **41 Kolokinthous and Leonidou St.** (tel. 522 6233), near the train stations. Expect to pay roughly 2000dr per load for wash, dry, and detergent.

Libraries: In the **Hellenic American Union,** 22 Massalias St., behind the university (tel. 362 9886; fax 363 3174), there is an **American Library** on the 4th floor (open Mon. and Wed. 9am-4pm, Tues. and Thurs.-Fri. 9am-2:30pm and 5-8:30pm, Sat. 9am-3pm) and a **Greek Library** with English books on Greece on the 7th floor (open Mon. and Fri. 10am-5pm, Tues. and Thurs. 9am-1pm and 5-8pm, Wed. 1-8pm). **British Council Library,** Kolonaki Sq. (tel. 363 3215), has English reading material and sponsors cultural events. (Open Mon.-Fri. 9:30am-1pm.)

International Bookstores: Eleftheroudakis Book Store, 4 Nikis St. (tel. 322 9388). Air-conditioned and shiny, this bookstore is a true pleasure. Greek, English, French, and German books, classical and recent literature, many travel guides, including *Let's Go.* Open Mon.-Fri. 9am-8:30pm, Sat. 9am-3pm. **Pantelides Books,** 11 Amerikis St. (tel. 362 3673). A small store overflowing with books on social sciences, dictionaries, best-sellers, children's books, and sci-fi novels; best philosophy/critical theory selection in town. Open Mon. and Wed. 8am-4pm, Tues. and Thurs.-Fri. 9am-2:30pm and 5-8:30pm, Sat. 9am-3pm. **Compendium Bookshop,** 28 Nikis St. (tel. 322 1248). Popular and large used book selection. Best selection of *Let's Go* around. Open Mon.-Wed. 8:30am-3:30pm, Tues. and Thurs.-Fri. 8:30am-8:30pm, Sat. 9am-3pm.

Hospitals: Public State Hospital (*Geniko Kratiko Nosokomio*), 154 Mesogion (tel. 779 1806, -7; fax 770 5980); **Hegia,** 4 Erithrou Stavrou (tel. 682 7904; fax 684 5089), is a top-notch private hospital in Marousi. Closer to the center of Athens, try the state hospital at 72 Vas. Sofias (tel. 722 0811, -2), and at 80 Vas. Sofias (tel. 777 0501; fax 777 6321). Near Kolonaki is a public hospital at 45-47 Evangelismou (tel. 722 0101; fax 729 1808). In Greek, "hospital" is *Nosokomio*.

Pharmacies: Identifiable by a Byzantine-style red or green cross hanging into the street. The daily *Athens News* (200dr) lists each day's emergency pharmacies and their hours in its Useful Information section.

Emergencies: For **doctors** (2pm-7am), call 105; for an **ambulance** call 166, and for **poison control,** dial 779 3777. The **National AIDS Center** can be reached at 644 4906. The daily emergency hospitals are listed in the *Athens News.* Tourists can receive free emergency health care.

Medical Emergency: Dial 166.

Red Cross First Aid Center: #21, 3 Septemvriou St. (tel. 150 or 522 5555). Three blocks north of Omonia Sq., on the left. 24 hr. English spoken.

ACCOMMODATIONS

Since most budget hotels are located in crowded and noisy sections, be sure to ask for a room that faces away from the street. Some balconies, however, offer stunning views of Athens. If you are planning to stay fewer than three nights, a hotel owner can legally add a 10% surcharge to your bill. Hotel owners used to allow guests to sleep on the roof for a small fee when the rooms are full. Although the practice is still in effect at some hotels, it is *illegal.*

Many hotel hawkers meet trains at the station. Most distribute pamphlets with maps for decent places near the station, some of which are listed here. Others, however, have been known to lure tourists into fleabags miles from anywhere and then charge exorbitant rates. Have the hawker point out the place on a large map of the city and set a firm price, in writing if possible, *before* leaving the station. Men arriving by bus from the airport should be aware of "friendly barkeepers" who may direct you to brothels rather than budget hotels. Do not sleep in the parks, even as a last resort. Camping anywhere in Athens is illegal, and extremely unsafe besides. Some hotels offer breakfast for roughly 1000dr. While this is convenient, you can visit a bakery and buy milk or juice for significantly less.

Note that the prices quoted below are from mid-1995, and are expected to increase in the next year. In 1996, expect a 10-20% rise from the prices in these listings. Prices are 20-40% less in the off-season (September through May).

Plaka-Syntagma Area

Most of the city's cheap hotels cluster in this central and busy part of town, and this really is the best place to stay—safest, quietest, most convenient, and best for people-watching. Follow in Lord Byron's footsteps and sleep under the majestic classical temples. Because of the area's popularity, most of these places are crowded in high season—make a reservation; it's worth it.

Hotel Tempi, 29 Aiolou St. (tel. 321 3175; fax 325 4179). From Syntagma Sq., follow Ermou St. and take a right on Aiolou (also spelled Eolu and Eolou). Airy rooms, many with Parthenon views. A gracious couple oversees the hotel. Paperback book exchange. Singles 4200dr, w/bath 5000dr; doubles 5800dr, w/bath 6800dr; triples 7500dr, w/bath 9000dr. 24-hr. hot water. Laundry service 1000dr.

Thisseos Inn, 10 Thisseos St. (tel. 324 5960). From Syntagma Sq., take Karageorgi Servias (which becomes Perikleous), and Thisseos St. is on the right. Increasingly popular with students who want to stay near Syntagma's attractions but far from its noise. Very quiet at night. TV in reception area, communal kitchen, common showers (hot 24 hr.). Curfew 2am. Dorm beds 2000dr, doubles 4500dr.

Student-Travelers Inn, 16 Kidathineon (tel. 324 4808). In the middle of one of Plaka's busiest streets, this hotel targets backpackers. A little pricier than some, its convenient locale, friendly owner, great staff, courtyard café, and hardwood floors make it worthwhile. 24-hr. hot showers. Curfew 1:30am. Singles 5000dr, doubles 7000dr, triples 9000dr, quads 11,000dr. Breakfast 800-1000dr.

Hotel Phaedra, 16 Herefondos St. (tel. 322 7795). From Hadrian's Arch on Vas. Sofias, walk 1 block up Lysikrateous St. to the intersection with Herefondos. Next to a small park and Byzantine Church. Many rooms have balconies with Acropolis views. Check-out noon. Singles 5500dr, doubles 7000dr, triples 9000dr, quads 10,000dr. Breakfast 1300dr.

Hotel Festos, 18 Filellinon St. (tel. 323 2455). Although the facilities are a bit run-down, this is a festive and fun place; reservation often needed. Bar with daily happy hour and nightly movies. Wide range of food served (compared to other places anyway). Check-out 9am. Curfew 2am. Dorm bed 2000dr, doubles 7000dr, triples 10,500dr, quads 12,000dr. Hot showers morning and evening only.

Hotel Amazon, 19 Mitropoleos (tel. 323 4002). Nice, clean rooms fairly close to Syntagma Square. Singles 6500dr, doubles 8000dr, triples 9400dr.

Acropolis House, 6 Kodrou St. (tel. 322 2344, -6241). Turn left off Mitropoleos onto Voulis and follow it to the end, at the base of a small hill. A truly elegant (and crowded) hotel. Reservations are a must. Centrally located, thus noisy both morning and night. Check-out noon. Singles 7500dr, w/bath 9000dr; doubles 9000dr, w/bath 10,500dr; triples w/bath 14,000dr.

Monastiraki-Thission Area

Near the central food market and the central tourist market, this neighborhood has an ever-increasing, never-ceasing noise problem. But it's also near the Acropolis and the subway, practically on top of the Agora site, and home to some bargains.

Pella Inn, 104 Ermou St. (tel. 325 0598, -2229; fax 325 0598), is a 10-min. walk down Ermou from Syntagma Sq., 2 blocks from the Monastiraki subway station (entrance on Karaiskaki St.). In a noisy part of town, but popular and lively. Most balconied rooms have a tremendous view of the Acropolis. Lounge and snack bar with eye-opening yellow and red furniture. Singles 5000-7000dr, w/bath 9000dr; doubles 7000-9000dr, w/bath 9000dr; triples 10,000dr. Breakfast 1230dr. Free luggage storage.

Railway Station Area

This overcrowded business and residential center is too far away from Syntagma for week-long stays, but ideal for a stopover because of its proximity to trains, buses, and (via the Victoria or Omonia subway stop), Piraeus. Be careful getting around the Omonia Sq. area: carry your wallet in your front pocket and try to move in groups. Most places listed here are large, popular, lively, and generally cheaper than those farther south. Most hotels have bars that serve breakfast, snacks, and drinks. Victoria is quite alive at night, and not at all tourist-infested.

Athens International Hostel (HI), 16 Victor Hugo St. (tel. 523 4170; fax 523 4015). From Omonia Sq., walk down Third September St., take a left on Veranzerou; it will become Victor Hugo after crossing Marni St. The only HI-affiliated youth hostel in Greece. HI membership required (2600dr at hostel; get photo from nearby booth), although you can buy nightly passes for 500dr. All beds 2000dr per person per night, including sheets and breakfast. Reservations recommended, especially if you want a double (which also includes sheets and breakfast). Rooms closed 10am-2pm for cleaning.

Youth Hostel Annabel, 28 Koumoundourou St. at Veranzerou (tel. 524 5834). From Omonia Square, follow Agiou Konstandinou, and Koumoundourou is on the right. Run by friendly New Zealanders, this independent hostel is extremely popular with English-speaking tourists and *Let's Go* users (who get a 10% discount). Travel services and a bar. Check-out 11am. No curfew. Singles 3500dr; doubles 4500dr, w/bath 5000dr; triples 6500dr, w/bath 7000dr. Free 24-hr. showers. Breakfast 700-1000dr. Free luggage storage.

Hostel Aphrodite, 12 Einardou St. (tel. 881 0589 or 883 9249; fax 822 0732). From the subway stop at Victoria Sq., follow Heiden for four blocks, take a right on Michail Voda, and a left two blocks later onto Einardou. From the train station, follow Filadelfias until Michail Voda. Nestled in a quiet (and safe) residential neighborhood, the rooms here are pleasant and clean. Although a bit far from Syntagma, easy access to both the train station and Victoria Sq. and the proximity of good food make this an enjoyable place to stay. Friendly basement bar, travel services (ask about the 20-day island pass which allows travel between Piraeus, Paros, Naxos, Ios, and Santorini for 9500dr). Dorm beds 1500dr, doubles 5000dr, triples 6600dr, quads 8000dr. Breakfast 800-1000dr.

Hotel Appia, 21 Menandrou St. (tel. 524 5155, -4561; fax 524 3552). From Omonia Sq., follow Tsaldari St. to Menandrou St. Newly renovated and painted in 1994, this modern hotel caters more to families than to backpacking students. Telephones, ceiling fans, and radios in all rooms. Air-conditioned lobby. Check-out noon. Singles 3000dr, w/bath 4500dr; doubles 5500dr, w/bath 7500dr; triples 6500dr. 24-hr. hot water. Breakfast 700dr (8-10am). Reservations strongly encouraged for July-Sept.

Hotel Arta, 12 Nikitara St. (tel. 362 7753). From Syntagma or Omonia, take Stadiou to Benaki, turn left, and take the third left on Nikitara. Modern hotel, endearing non-English speaking reception. Immaculate rooms with desks, phones, and A/C. Singles 5000dr, w/bath 6000dr; doubles 6000dr, w/bath 7000dr; triples 7500dr, w/bath 9000dr; breakfast 900dr. Free luggage storage. Reception always open.

Hotel Vienna, 20 Pireos St. (tel. 524 9143). From Omonia Sq. follow Tsaldari, which is the same street as Pireos. Like Appia, more family-oriented and expensive than student hostels. Clean bedrooms with telephones. 24-hr. bar and TV room. Check-out noon. Single w/bath 5000dr, double w/bath 7000dr, triples 8600dr, breakfast 600dr.

Hostel Argo, 25 Victor Hugo St. (tel. 522 5939; fax 864 1693). Down the street from the official hostel. Endearing, English-speaking staff. Quiet and relaxing with a TV in the lobby. Hot showers am and pm. Check-out noon. No curfew. Singles 3700dr; doubles 5000dr, w/bath 6000dr; triples 6600dr, w/bath 7500dr; quads 8000dr; breakfast 500dr; laundry 1500dr. Free luggage storage.

South of the Acropolis

These rooms are in relatively quiet residential areas. To the west, Koukaki and Veikou present 15-20-min. uphill hikes to the Acropolis or Syntagma Sq. To the east, Pangrati, a ½-hr. walk from Syntagma, can be easily reached by trolley.

Youth Hostel #5 Pangrati, 75 Damareos St., Pangrati (tel. 751 9530; fax 751 0616). Take trolley #2 or #11 from Syntagma Sq. to Filolaou or walk through the National Garden, down Eratosthenous St. to Plastira Sq., and down Frinis St. until Damareos is on the right. There is no sign for the hostel on the street; there is only the number 75, and a black and grey door. Out of the way, but very lively and social, with many young guests and an English-speaking owner. No curfew, but quiet after 11pm. Singles 3500dr, doubles 4500-5000dr, dorm beds 1500dr. Hot shower 50dr. Breakfast 450-650dr. Kitchen use 150dr per person. Sheets 100dr, pillowcases 100dr, blankets 50dr. Laundry 700dr. Key deposit 300dr.

Marble House Pension, 35 Zini St., Koukaki (tel. 923 4058 or 922 6461). From south side of Acropolis, follow Erechthiou St. until it ends and turn left onto Veikou, which will intersect Zinni. Set back from the street in a foliage-covered building in a quiet corner. Popular for extended stays. Singles 5000dr, w/bath

6000dr; doubles 7000dr, w/bath 8000dr; triples 8000dr; breakfast 900dr. Weekly and monthly rates also available.

Art Gallery Hotel, 5 Erechthiou St., Veikou (tel. 923 8372). From south side of Acropolis, Erechthiou stretches directly towards this pension. Bathrooms, ceiling fans, and telephones in all rooms. Lounge and bar on 4th floor. Geared toward an older clientele. Singles 6800dr, doubles 8200dr.

Hotel Greca, 48 Singrou St., Veikou (tel. 921 5262 or 923 3229; fax 360 1438). A family-oriented hotel on a busy, noisy avenue. Check-out 11am. Doubles 6000dr, w/bath 8000dr; triples 9000dr, w/bath 12,000dr. Luggage storage 300dr per piece per day.

FOOD

Athens offers a mélange of stands, open-air cafés, outdoor sidestreet *tavernas* and intriguing dim restaurants frequented by grizzled Greek men. Athens' culinary claim to fame is cheap and plentiful street food. *Souvlaki* (220-300dr), either on a *kalamaki* (skewer) or wrapped in *pita,* is the Greek alternative to fast food. A *tost,* a grilled sandwich of variable ingredients (normally ham and cheese) for 250-500dr is another option. Locally brewed beer (Amstel and Heineken, also known as "Green Beer") runs roughly 200dr per bottle. *Tiropita* (hot cheese pie), and *spanakopita* (hot spinach pie) go for around 250dr. Ice cream is sold at almost every kiosk. A *koulouri,* a donut-shaped, sesame-coated roll, makes a quick breakfast for 50-100dr.

By far the most popular place for tourists to eat is Plaka. Don't venture here for taste or price; it's people-watching which makes a meal here memorable. You'll find many interesting places up and down Adrianou and Kidatheneon St. Once seated at the establishment of your choice, relax: Greek restaurants are not known for their speedy service. Women should know that Plaka is a popular spot for *kamakia* (literally, "harpoons") who enjoy making catcalls at women as they walk by. Sometimes they may even follow you, but keep walking and ignore them; in most cases, harassment is only verbal. Most places in Plaka serve early or all day, but outside these touristed quarters few restaurants open before 8pm. Restaurants tend to be deserted at 6pm, near-empty before 10pm, and crowded from 11pm to 1am.

Plaka-Syntagma

For do-it-yourself meals, various **minimarkets** on Nikis St. and in Plaka sell basic groceries. The Thisseos Inn in particular offers noteworthy kitchen facilities.

Eden Vegetarian Restaurant, 12 Lissiou (tel. 324 8858). On the corner of Minissikleous on the west side of Plaka. Airy and secluded. Popular with both herbivores and omnivores. Tofu-meat in dishes like *mousaka* and lasagna (both 800dr). Entrees 1100-1600dr. Crusty, tasty bread included.

Zorbas, 15 Lissiou (tel. 322 6188), right across the street from Eden, is one of the cheapest places around. Entrees 1100-2800dr, most under 1500dr. Try the lamb Zorbas (1500dr) or the pumpkin balls (600dr).

Possidon Restaurant, 35 Kapnikareas St., at the corner of Adrianou (tel. 322 3822). Very large and popular. Boasts a wide array of hot and cold appetizers and entrees (1300-3800dr). Pasta dishes 1000-1500dr. Outdoor tables with cushiony seats. Visa and MasterCard accepted.

Blue Velvet, 3 Nikis St. (tel. 323 4971). Mexican fast food joint run by a Californian. Take-out and delivery available. Burritos 580-680dr, tacos 580-780dr.

T. Stamatopoulos, 26 Lissiou St. (tel. 322 8722). Near the Eden Restaurant. Overflowing with lush, green plants and featuring live music in the summer, this makes a very festive place to dine. Entrees 1750-2950dr. Veal special 1850dr.

Michiko, 27 Kidathineon St. (tel. 322 0980). Nirvana for some: eat sushi (prepared at your table by a Japanese chef, 1500-4800dr) in a red Japanese garden with lanterns and delicately arching bridges. *Sukiyaki* 5000dr, teriyaki chicken 2950dr.

To Gerani, 14 Tripodon St. (tel. 324 7605). From Kidatheneon, one of Plaka's busiest strips, Tripodon is a side street. In a quiet niche with a wonderful balcony, To Gerani is more affordable than most, but be forewarned—they don't make many dishes each night, so be sure to ask what's available before chomping into the bread. Two or three small entrees make a good meal (800dr each).

Thanasis, 69 Mitropoleos St. (tel. 324 4705), a meat-eater's delight with tasty *souvlaki* dinner (1100dr).

To Xani, 138 Adrianou St., in the heart of Plaka. Standard fare, but has a quiet back garden. Entrees 1500-3000dr. Fixed meals 2100-2400dr.

Golden Flower, 30 Nikis St. (tel. 323 0113). Tired of Greek food? A well-maintained Chinese place. Vegetable dishes 1100-1200dr, chow mein 1800-2250dr.

Byzantio, 18 Kidathineon St. (tel. 322 7368). In a small square, strategically located on one of Plaka's main pedestrian alleys. *Souvlaki* dinner 1600-2200dr.

For better (and cheaper) food, wander outside Plaka. Again, the listings below are but a small sampling.

Taverna Ayli, 21 Proussis (tel. 882 2155). A few blocks from the train station, near Hotel Aphrodite. Excellent food served in a pleasant garden. Most entrees 1000dr.

La Meloise, 35 Thoukididou St. (tel. 983 6156), Kalamaki, is worth a stop on the way to the airport bars or Glyfada. Excellent crepes whipped up by a French chef; both sweet (20 varieties, from 550dr) and salty (30 varieties, from 800dr). Italian ice cream 250dr per scoop. Beer 400-800dr. Open 10am-3am.

Restaurant of Konstantinos Athanasias Velly, Varnava Sq., Plastira. Take trolley #2, 4, 11, or 12 to Plastira Sq., walk 3 blocks up Proklou St. to Varnava Sq. At the square's far right corner, in a small white house with flowers in front. A real treat: small, authentic, delicious, cheap. No English spoken, but you can point. Tomato salad 350dr, *keftedes* (Greek meatballs) 700dr.

To Meltemi, 26 Zinni St. (tel. 924 7606), Koukaki. Near the Marble House Pension. Menu changes daily at this authentic *taverna.* Medium-sized variety plate 1300dr.

Giamas, 38 Zaimi St., behind the National Museum. Artsy, all-Athenian clientele drops by for friendly, cheap eats. Try the baked fish, if available. Good alternative to the café in front of the museum.

For an after-dinner treat, there are tons of sweetshops in Plaka, many virtually indistinguishable from their neighbors. *Baklava* tends to go for 250-400dr, ice cream 150-300dr per scoop. **Lalaggis,** 13 Speusippou St. in Kolonaki, is an above average sweetshop in the heart of the city (*baklava* 250dr). Check out their branch in Pagrati, at 29 Empedokleous St. **Artos & Zoe,** 73 Ermou St, has lots of yummy cookies and breads (*tiropita* 200dr). **Floca** is a chain, but tends to be better than average.

ENTERTAINMENT

Visitors to Athens often restrict themselves to the familiar Plaka and Monastiraki neighborhoods. Nights in Athens, however, can best be enjoyed by venturing beyond the heavily touristed areas to one of the city's clubs, theaters, or bars. Don't be fooled into thinking that nights here are full of hokey Greek dancing and dish-throwing. On the contrary, Athenian nightlife is varied and diverse enough to please highbrow, chic sophisticates; down and dirty backpackers; as well as members of the elite who have not gotten their fill of intellectual stimulation during the day. Nightlife is very different in the off-season when many outdoor spots close, but there should be plenty to do throughout the year.

During the summer months, young and hip Athenians head to the numerous seaside clubs in **Glyfada** (past the airport) and on **Possidonos Ave.** The most beautiful of these are right on the beach, with calming ocean views to help cool off the frenzied interiors. Take your pick of clubs with a sit-down, mill-around crowd, or choose more dance-oriented discos. Either way, the music is usually American or British from 11pm or midnight until 2 or 3am, when either Greek music is played, or a Greek singer takes center stage amidst clouds of hurled flowers. Put on your best clubbing outfit because many of these clubs will not admit anyone in shorts. Covers range 1000-2000dr, and drinks are often ridiculously priced (beers run 1000-2000dr, cocktails 1500-3000dr). This is the place for the best people-watching.

Nearby, off the water, on Vouliagmenis St., are the best bars. Some good hotspots include **La Playa, Must, Bouzios, Mercedes, Zephyros,** and **Wild Rose.** There are several other popular hangouts near the airport, including the aptly named **Aerodromio** disco. Since you probably won't want to head out to any of these until after the buses have stopped running, expect to pay 1500-2500dr each way for a taxi from Plaka. Be careful of cabbies trying to rip you off—either fix a price beforehand or keep a close eye on the meter.

To quiet hungry stomachs, ask your taxi driver to take you to the **meat market** on Athinas St., between Syntagma and Omonias, where popular early-morning restaurants replace the meat market (3-7am). Simply go into the kitchens and point away; *patsa* soup is an especially stomach-calming favorite.

If you're determined to stay around **Plaka,** there are several forgettable bars and clubs near Nikis and Filellinon. Be prepared to rub shoulders with other tourists or Athenians trying to pick up foreigners. More popular (and less expensive) options include simply hanging out and people-watching or drinking the balmy summer nights away at the bars run by several of the hotels (the Student Travelers Inn and Festos Hotel have two of the best).

Needless to say, plenty of other parts of town have good clubs. Try venturing to the posh **Kolonaki** district, on the way to Lycabettos. Although the Gucci shoes in the chic shop windows might cost more than your whole vacation, a coffee or beer at any of the outdoor *tavernas* will not blow your budget. While in the area, dig **Jazz Club 1920,** 10 Ploutarchou St. (tel. 721 0533), just up from the British Embassy. (Open nightly 10:15pm-1:15am for jazz, blues, latin, and rock.) In **Kifissia,** a hip residential area north of Athens, there are many slick *tavernas* and discos. Here you'll find the **Divina,** 2 Argiropoulou (tel. 801 5884), where you can boogie in air-conditioned comfort, and the **Follie Café,** known for its acid jazz, though it may be closed in the summer. For **gay** (primarily male) **clubs,** try **Lembessi St.** off Singrou. Many of the clubs here tend not to be too friendly to itinerant heterosexuals.

Back in Plaka, **Cinema Paris,** at 22 Kidatheneon, shows recent films at an outdoor theater (two shows per evening, 1500dr). Try to attend the late show since traffic noise and lingering dusk tend to mar the early one. Sit near the front to hear the already hushed film over intruding *bouzouki* music. Check the *Athens News* or a Greek paper for full movie listings. Most cost 1000-1500dr and are concentrated on Stadiou, Panepistimiou, and Patission St.

The **Athens Festival** runs annually from June until September, featuring classical theater groups performing in the **Odeon of Herodes Atticus.** Performances are also staged in **Lycabettos Theater** at the top of Lycabettos Hill, and in Epidavros (see p. 119). The Greek Orchestra performs during this festival, as do visiting groups, which have ranged from the Bolshoi to B.B. King; from the Alvin Ailey Dance Company to classical Greek dramas; and from Pavarotti to the Talking Heads. The **Festival Office** (tel. 322 1459, -3111; ext. 240) is in the arcade at 4 Stadiou St. Student tickets are generally affordable (1500-2500dr; open Mon.-Fri. 8:30am-2pm and 5-7pm, Sat. 8:30am-2pm, Sun. 10am-1pm). The **Athens Box Office of the National Theater** (tel. (01) 522 3242) is at the corner of Agiou Konstandinou and Menandrou St. Tickets cost 3000-4500dr, 2000dr for students.

If you've had enough to drink, the hokey **Sound and Light Show** (which depicts the Parthenon over the centuries) on Pnyx Hill (opposite the Acropolis) can be quite entertaining, though you'll leave unsure whether the title refers to the program or the click and flash of cameras saving tourists thousands of words (tel. 322 1459; after 2pm 922 6210; April-Oct. shows daily in English at 9pm; in French Wed.-Thurs. and Sat.-Mon. 10:10pm; in German Thurs.-Fri. 10pm; admission 1200dr, students 600dr.) Nearby in Dora Stratou Theatre on Philopappou Hill, **Greek dancers** kick and holler to live music on an open-air stage, celebrating traditions from all regions of the country. (For information, call 324 4395 between 9am and 1:30pm; from 7:30pm on, call 921 4650. Shows May-Sept. nightly 10:15pm, with an additional show Wed. and Sun. 8:15pm; tickets 1700-2000dr.)

Athens' two principal markets attract everyone from bargain-hunters to inveterate browsers. The **Athens Flea Market,** adjacent to Monastiraki Sq., has a festive, bazaar-like atmosphere and offers a potpourri of second-hand junk, costly antiques, and everything in between. Although parts of it have become overtouristed, there is still the occasional treasure to be found, and lots of neo-hippies to watch besides. The market is open daily (8am-2pm), and Sunday is the grand bazaar when the flea market overflows the square and Fillis Athinas St. A huge indoor-outdoor **food market** lines the sides of Athinas St. between Evripidou and Sofokleous St. A sight, to be sure, the **meat market** is huge, but not for vegetarians or the faint of heart. Skinned rabbits with cottontails still on, livers, and kidneys hang throughout. There are also less visually challenging foods, such as fruits, vegetables, breads, and cheeses. It's open the same hours as regular food stores, but Athenian restaurateurs go early and purchase the choice meat and fish. Restaurants in the meat market are open at night.

Greek Shadow Puppet Theater

As children gather earnestly around the screen of fine white material stretched across a frame, a bell rings and the shadow puppet theater begins. *Karaghiozis*, a poor, long-armed, balding hunchback appears dressed in rags, often without shoes. Always hungry and lacking money, he survives by his cunning: impersonating Turkish *hodjas*, politicians, or Hercules during his journey to the underworld. Shadow puppet theater first appeared in Java, China and India, from which it spread to Turkey. The Turkish version, *Karagöz* (Black Eye), was popularized in Greece following the exchange of populations. The tales, which were passed down orally, often involve *Karaghiozis* trying to get rich and are peppered with slapstick humor. In its finest form, performances are accompanied by a small band and conducted by one or two puppeteers, who often mimic ten different voices, and interject poignant social commentary and contemporary satire that is sophisticated enough for adults. Despite the rise of cinema and television, *Karaghiozis* remains popular among the young and the young at heart. Performances are rare and staged in Greek, but worthwhile.

SIGHTS

Acropolis

The **Acropolis** (A5-B5), or "high city," with its strategic position overlooking the Aegean Sea and Attic Plains, has served as both a military fortress and religious center. The heights afford an expansive view of Athens and the Aegean. Without a doubt, the Acropolis, particularly the Parthenon, is Athens' highlight. Today, the hilltop's remarkable ruins grace otherwise rubble-strewn grounds. Ongoing renovations require that steel scaffolding cling to the ancient marble columns.

In the 13th century BC, wealthy landowners overthrew the monarchy in Athens who had ruled the city safely from their fortress in the Acropolis. The new rulers, the *Aristoi* (excellent ones), shifted the center of their government away from the Acropolis, ruling the *polis* (city-state) from the lower foothills of the city. The Acropolis, far from being abandoned, was then used as a shrine to two aspects of the goddess Athena: Athena Polias, goddess of crops and fertility, and Athena Pallas, military guardian of the city. Following the Greek custom of putting money under the protection of a deity, the Acropolis also housed the city treasury.

In 507 BC, the tyrannical *Aristoi* were overthrown and Athens began its successful experiment with democracy. In 490 BC, Athenians began constructing a temple on the Acropolis. When the Persians sacked the temple ten years later, the Greeks threw the violated religious objects off the side of the Acropolis and buried the litter (now unearthed and displayed in the Acropolis Museum).

In response to the Persian threat, Aegean rulers formed the Delian League. Pericles appropriated part of the taxes paid by the league to beautify Athens. Among his projects were the temples of the Acropolis, the Temple of Hephaestus in the *agora,* and the Temple of Poseidon at Sounion. These developments slowed during the Peloponnesian War (431-404 BC), but by then the Athenians were committed to Pericles' plans, and construction sputtered along throughout the war and after his death in 429 BC. Four of the buildings erected at that time still stand today: the Parthenon, the Propylaea, the Temple of Athena Nike, and the Erechtheum. Their construction has had an unrivaled influence on Western architecture.

Through the Hellenistic and Roman periods, the function of the Acropolis altered as often as it changed hands. The Byzantines converted it into a Christian place of worship. In a typical example of Christianity appropriating older 'pagan' symbols, the Parthenon became the Church of St. Sophia ("Sophia," like "Athena," means wisdom). In 1205 AD, when Athens was liberated from the Byzantines by Frankish crusaders, the Acropolis once again became a fortress, serving as palace and headquarters for the Dukes de la Roche. The political situation settled down, and the Parthenon was then transformed into a Catholic church (Notre Dame d'Athènes). In the 15th century, Turks turned the Parthenon into a mosque and the Erechtheum into the Turkish commander's harem.

Tragedy befell the Acropolis during the Venetian siege in 1687, when a Turkish supply of gunpowder stored in the Parthenon was hit by a shell and exploded, destroying many sculptures. In 1822, the Greeks finally regained the Acropolis. Apart from a six-year occupation by the Ottoman Turks from 1827 to 1833 and a brief Nazi occupation in WWII, the Acropolis has been in Greek hands ever since.

The ramp that led to the Acropolis in classical times no longer exists. Today's visitors make the 10-min. climb to the ticket-window, enter through the crumbling **Beulé Gate** (added by the Romans and named after the French archaeologist who unearthed it), and continue through the **Propylaea,** the ancient entrance. Unfortunately, the site is not wheelchair-accessible. The marble can be slippery, so be careful if you are wearing shoes that have seen better days. Don't wear heels.

The Propylaea became famous for its ambitious multi-level design, although the entrance itself, begun by Mnesicles between 437 and 432 BC, was never completed. In Roman times, the structure extended as far as 80m below the Beulé Gate. At the cliff's edge, the tiny **Temple of Athena Nike** was built during a respite from the Peloponnesian War, the so-called Peace of Nikias (421-415 BC). Known as the "jewel of Greek architecture," this temple with eight miniature Ionic columns once housed a winged statue of the goddess. One day, in a paranoid frenzy, the Athenians feared that their deity (and peace) would flee the city, so they clipped Athena's wings. Below the temple are the remains of the 5m-thick **Cyclopean wall,** which once surrounded the whole of the Acropolis.

The **Erechtheum,** to the left of the Parthenon as you face it, was completed in 406 BC, just prior to Athens' defeat by Sparta. Lighter than the Parthenon, the Erechtheum is a unique two-level structure that housed a number of cults, including those of Athena, Poseidon, and the snake-bodied hero Erechtheus. The east porch, with its six Ionic columns, was dedicated to Athena Polias and sheltered an olive wood statue of her. On the south side of the Erechtheum, facing the Parthenon, are the **Caryatids,** six columns sculpted in the shape of women. Their artful tunics, which seem to flow into fluted columns towards the base, are plaster replicas. The originals were moved to the Acropolis Museum to protect them from air pollution.

Looming over the hillside, the **Parthenon,** or "Virgin's Apartment," keeps vigil over Athens and its world. Designed by the architects Iktinos and Kallikrates, the Parthenon was the first building completed under Pericles' plan to revive the city. It once housed the legendary gold and ivory statue of Athena Parthena sculpted by Phidias. The temple intentionally features many almost imperceptible irregularities; the Doric columns bulge in the middle and the stylobate (pedestal) of the building bows slightly upward in order to compensate for the optical illusion in which straight lines, viewed from a distance, appear to bend. Originally made entirely of marble except for a long-since-vanished wooden roof, the building's stone ruins attest to both the durability of the structure and the elegance of the Classical age.

Metopes around the sides of the Parthenon portray various victories of the forces of order over disorder. On the far right of the south side, the only side which has not been defaced, the Lapiths battle the Centaurs (Centauromachy); on the east the Olympian gods triumph over the giants (Gigantomachy); the north depicts a faintly visible victory of the Greeks over the Trojans; and on the west, one can vaguely make out the triumph of the Greeks over the Amazons (Amazonomachy). A better-preserved frieze in bas-relief around the interior walls shows the Panathenaic procession in Athena's honor. To avoid massive crowds and the broiling midday sun, visit early in the morning. Cold drinks are hard to come by; bring bottled water to avoid the overpriced refreshment stand at the entrance (soda 800dr). You can reach the entrance, which is on the west side of the Acropolis (tel. 321 0219), from Areopagitou St. south of the Acropolis, or by walking uphill from Plaka. Follow the spray-painted signs at intervals in the narrow passageway. (Open daily 8am-6:30pm; winter 8:30am-4:30pm; admission 2000dr, students 1000dr with ISIC. Free on Sun. and holidays. 1000dr charge for a video camera.)

The **Acropolis Museum** (tel. 323 6665), footsteps away from the Parthenon, contains a superb collection of sculptures, including five of the Caryatids of the Erechtheum (the sixth, stolen, now resides in the British Museum). Most of the treasures housed here date from the transition period from Archaic to Classical Greek art (550-400 BC). You can trace this development in the faces of the statues, from the stylized, entranced faces and static poses of Archaic sculpture—seen in the famous *Moschophoros* (calf-bearer)—to the more familiar, naturalistic (though idealized) figures of Classical art. Only a few pieces from the Parthenon are here—Lord Elgin helped himself to the rest, and they are now in the British Museum. The collection is nonetheless impressive. (Museum open Mon. 11am-6:30pm, Tues.-Fri. 8am-6:30pm, Sat.-Sun. 8:30am-2:30pm; admission included in Acropolis ticket. Cameras w/flash allowed, but no posing next to the objects.) From the southwest corner of the Acropolis, you can look down on the reconstructed **Odeon of Herodes Atticus,** a functioning theater dating from the Roman Period, c. 160 AD. Nearby are the ruins of the Classical Greek **Theater of Dionysus** (tel. 322 4625; entrance on Dionissiou Areopagitou St.), the **Asclepion,** and the **Stoa of Eumenes II.** The Theater of Dionysus dates from the 4th century BC. (Open daily 8:30am-2:30pm; admission to all three 400dr, students 200dr.)

Near The Acropolis

The **Athenian Agora** (A4), at the foot of the Acropolis, was the administrative center and marketplace of Athens from the 6th century BC through the late Roman Period (5th-6th centuries AD). The decline of the Agora paralleled the decline of Athens, as barbarian attacks buffeted both the city and the square from 267 BC to 580 AD. It was in the Agora and on the **Pnyx** (the low hill and meeting place of the assembly, 1km to the south) that Athenian democracy was born and flourished. Socrates frequented the Agora, as did Aristotle, Demosthenes, Xenophon, and St. Paul. According to Plato, Socrates' preliminary hearing was held at the **Stoa Basileios** (Royal Promenade), which has been recently excavated and lies to the left as you cross the subway tracks upon leaving the Agora.

The sprawling archaeological site features three remarkable constructions. The **Temple of Hephaestus** (A4), on a hill in the northwest corner, is the best-preserved Classical temple in Greece. Built around 440 BC, it is especially notable for its friezes which depict the labors of Hercules and the adventures of Thisseos. The ruins of the **Odeon of Agrippa** (concert hall), built for the son-in-law of the Emperor Augustus, stand in the center of the Agora. In 150 AD the roof collapsed, and the Odeon was rebuilt as a lecture hall at half its former size. The actors' dressing room was made into a porch supported by colossal statues (the ruins of 3 of these statues remain to guard the site). To the south, the elongated **Stoa of Attalos** (A4), a multi-purpose building for shops, shelter, and informal gatherings, was rebuilt with new materials between 1953 and 1956 and now houses the **Agora Museum** (tel. 321 0185). The original structure, built in the second century BC, was given to Athens by Attalos II,

King of Pergamon, in gratitude for the education he had received in the city. The museum contains a number of relics from the site and offers a cool sanctuary from the sweltering summer sun. (Agora and museum open Tues.-Sun. 8:30am-3pm; admission to both 800dr, students 400dr.) There are several entrances to the Agora, including one at the edge of Monastiraki, one on Thission Sq. and one on Adrianou St. You can reach the Acropolis from here by exiting the south side of the Agora (follow the path uphill) and then turning right. The most commonly used gate is the one near the Acropolis entrance (turn right as you leave the Acropolis).

Northwest of the Agora, on the other side of the tracks at Thission Station, 148 Ermou St., is **Kerameikos.** This is the site of the 40m-wide boulevard that ran from the Agora, through the Diplyon gate, and 1½km to the sanctuary of Akademos, where Plato founded his Academy in the 4th century BC. Public tombs for state leaders, famous authors, and battle victims were constructed along this road. Worshipers began the annual Panathenaean procession to the Acropolis at the Diplyon Gate, one of the two gates excavated at this site. The sacred road to Eleusis, traversed during the annual Eleusian processions, ran through the Sacred Gate, the second gate on the site. Family tombs adorn either side of the Sacred Road outside the gate. A **museum** on the site (tel. 346 3552) exhibits finds from recent digs as well as an excellent pottery collection. (Site and museum open Tues.-Sun. 8:30am-3pm; admission to both 400dr, students 200dr.)

The **Temple of Olympian Zeus** (C6) also deserves a visit. Fifteen majestic columns are all that remain of the largest temple ever built in Greece. Started in the 6th century BC, the temple was completed 600 years later by the Roman emperor Hadrian. Nowadays, the Corinthian columns stand in the middle of downtown Athens, below the National Garden. The remains of a Roman bath, tiles and all, can also be seen here (Vas. Olgas and Amalias Ave.; tel. 922 6330; open Tues.-Sun. 8:30am-3pm; admission 500dr, students 300dr). Next to the Temple is **Hadrian's Arch** (C6), which was built in the 2nd century BC to mark the boundary between the ancient city of Thisseos and the new city built by Hadrian.

MUSEUMS

The **National Archaeological Museum,** 44 Patission St. (B1; tel. 821 7717), is well worth delaying your jaunt to the islands. Take trolley #2, 4, 5, 9, 11, 15, or 18 from the uphill side of Syntagma or trolley #3 or 13 on the north side of Vasilissis Sofias. Pieces that would be the prizes of lesser collections seem almost unremarkable amidst the general magnificence. Expect to spend a long time here.

Among the museum's exhibits (all labeled in English as well as in Greek) are finds from Heinrich Schliemann's digs at Mycenae, including the golden "Mask of Agamemnon" (which is, in fact, the death mask of a king who lived at least three centuries earlier than the legendary Agamemnon). Also displayed are samples of Bronze Age jewelry and pottery from Mycenae and other sites in the Peloponnese.

Don't leave without viewing the *kouroi,* or standing males (rooms 7, 8, 9, 11, and 13). They are displayed chronologically, allowing you to see the evolution of this form. Minoan frescoes (one flight up) are intriguing; excavated from the town of Akrotiri on Santorini, these painted treasures were buried during a volcanic eruption around 1500 BC. The frescoes present a unique glimpse of life in the Bronze Age. The bronze statue of Poseidon in Room 15 is eerily life-like. With its hollowed-out eye sockets, it is genuinely impressive, as are the bronze sculptures in general. The comic mask of a slave from Diplyon (room 30), made during the 2nd century BC, adds irony to the exhibits—with a wide, toothless grin and crazy eyes, the face seems amused by the starkly stoic statues which surround it. Also worth viewing is the extensive vase collection (on the same floor as the frescoes). (Museum open Mon. 12:30-7pm, Tues.-Fri. 8am-7pm, Sat.-Sun. and holidays 8:30am-3pm; admission 2000dr, students 1000dr; free Sun. and holidays; no flash photography.)

Opened in 1986, the **Goulandris Museum of Cycladic and Ancient Greek Art,** 4 Neophytou Douka St. (D4; tel. 722 8321), near Kolonaki, has a stunningly displayed collection in a modern building with A/C. Cycladic art is best known for its minimalist marble statues of female figures. The sculptures' beauty verifies that art was an important aspect of ancient Cycladic societies. Allow yourself to be lured to the bronze jewelry from Skyros as well as to the collection of Greek vases and statues from 2000 BC to the 4th century AD. (Open Mon., Wed.-Fri. 10am-4pm, Sat. 10am-3pm; admission 400dr, students 200dr.)

The **Benaki Museum,** at the corner of Koumbari and Vasilissis Sofias (D4; tel. 361 1617), houses a diverse collection of treasures in a beautiful Neoclassical building which was once the residence of philanthropist Anthony Benaki. The museum displays Bronze Age Greek relics, Byzantine icons, gold jewelry of the 5th century BC, textiles and costumes from the islands, and relics from the War of Independence. It also explores the influence of neighboring cultures on Greece by juxtaposing Islamic, Arabic, and Coptic artwork with Greek. Unfortunately, the Benaki will be closed until at least summer 1996.

Inside an elegant Florentine building with serene courtyards, the **Byzantine Museum,** 22 Vasilissis Sofias (E4; tel. 723 1570), has an excellent and extensive collection of Christian art from the 4th-19th centuries. The collection includes early Byzantine sculptures, an icon collection that contains works from the entire Byzantine period, and a reconstructed early Christian basilica. There are also a number of superb reliefs done in bronze, silver, and gold. One wing of the building features an array of well-preserved frescoes and mosaics. The exhibits are poorly labeled, however, so consider buying a catalog (600-800dr) before you visit. (Open Tues.-Sun. 8:30am-3pm; admission 500dr.)

Next door to the Byzantine Museum is the **War Museum** (E4; tel. 729 0543). This museum traces the history of Greek armaments from Neolithic eras, through the 5th-century BC Persian invasion and the expeditions of Alexander the Great, to the submachine guns of the modern era. The primary emphasis, however, is on the modern Greek arsenal. (Open Tues.-Sun. 9am-2pm; free.)

The **National Gallery** (Alexander Soutzos Museum) is set back from Vasilissis Sofias at 50 Vasileos Konstandinou (F4; tel. 721 7643). The museum exhibits Greek artists' works, supplemented by periodic international displays. The permanent collection includes some outstanding works by El Greco. The drawings, black-and-white photographs, and sculpture gardens are also impressive. Consult *This Week in Athens* or call the museum for information on current exhibits. (Open Mon. and Wed.-Sat. 9am-3pm, Sun. 10am-2pm; free.) At the **Theater Museum,** 50 Akadimis St. (tel. 362 9430), behind the university, you can view costumes, models, photographic paraphernalia, and dressing rooms. (Open Mon.-Fri. 9am-3pm, Sun. 10am-1pm; admission 300dr.) In Plaka, the **Greek Folk Art Museum,** 17 Kidatheneon St. (tel. 322 9031), exhibits *laiki techni* (popular art) from all over Greece, including embroidered textiles, costumes, and puppets. Ornamental ecclesiastical silverwork and household pottery are also on exhibit. Don't miss the groovy wall paintings by folk artist Theophilos Hadzimichail. (Open Tues.-Sun. 10am-2pm; admission 500dr, students 300dr; cameras 500dr.) The **Greek Popular Musical Instruments Museum** (B4; tel. 325 0198) has an exquisite, interactive display of an array of musical instruments used in the 18th, 19th and 20th centuries. (Open Mon.-Fri. 8:30am-7pm.)

On the south side of the Acropolis, just off Dionysiou Areopagiotou St., you can satiate your lust for gold at the **Ilias Lalounis Jewelry Museum** (B6). This private museum houses over 3000 designs created by Lalounis, as well as collections displaying the history of jewelry in Greece from ancient to modern times, including a workshop where visitors can observe jewelry-making different techniques. (Open Mon. and Thurs.-Sun. 9am-4pm, Wed. 9am-9pm; admission 800dr, students 500dr.)

The **Jewish Museum,** 36 Leoforos Amalias, third floor (C5; tel. 323 1577), is in a 19th-century building with a United Nations flag. An impressive collection of textiles, religious artifacts, and documents traces the roots of the Greek Jewish communities dating from the Hellenistic period. The museum also contains the reconstructed Synagogue of Patras. (Open Sun.-Fri. 9am-1pm; free.)

Byzantine sanctuaries, like their Classical counterparts, have been incorporated into the urban landscape. Traffic on Ermou St. must go around **Kapnikaria Church,** which has been stranded in the middle of the street, one block beyond Aiolou St. Walking down Mitropoleos from Syntagma, you may also notice a tiny church on the corner of Pentelis St., around which a modern building has been constructed. Other Byzantine churches in Athens include the **Agia Apostoli** (A5), at the east edge of the Agora; **Metamorphosis,** in Plaka near Pritaniou St.; **Agia Triada,** on Filellinon St., a few blocks from Syntagma; and **Agios Eleftherios,** next to the **Mitropoli Cathedral** (B4), on Mitropoleos St. Peek in for a respite from the day's heat. Most of these churches are open in the morning and for services, and require proper dress: skirts for women, long pants for men, and long-sleeved shirts for everyone.

Athens is far more than a conglomeration of ancient ruins, museums, and street-hawkers—the city offers dramatic views, charming byways, and cool foliage. Long before recorded time, the Greeks invented the evening stroll (*volta*). Today's place to ramble is along the romantic walkways of Plaka. The streets, strung with white lights and replete with restaurants and cafés, are ideal for an evening's promenade. Bustling Plaka represents a rejuvenation of the historic area. In the past few years, the government has curbed the violence, prostitution, and general decay that once plagued this section of the city and created a renovated, lively, pleasant neighborhood. Be sure to also venture uphill off the main drags through the shoulder-width streets of an anachronistic residential area.

The **Chapel of St. George** (E4), on top of rocky **Lycabettos Hill,** offers a beautiful view of the city. Burn off dinner by walking up, or take the funicular (130dr, 220dr round-trip) to the top—the station is a healthy hike at the end of Ploutarchou St. (Chapel open Wed. and Sat.-Sun. 8:45am-12:15am, Thurs. 10:30am-12:15am, Mon.-Tues. and Fri. 9:30am-12:15am.) The Acropolis, bathed in an amber glow, offers a magical nighttime perspective on Athens. While the café is expensive and the area is not as safe as it used to be, the Acropolis view makes a visit to Lycabettos a transcendent experience. Up here, with the sprawling body of concrete a mere blur below and the traffic no more than a low murmur, the breezes are refreshing and the aura of the city inspiring. Afternoons are less crowded than evenings.

The cool, pleasant **National Garden** (open sunrise to sunset), adjacent to Syntagma Square, is a great escape from the noise, heat, and frantic pace of Athens. Walk along its tranquil paths and visit the duck pond and poor excuse for a zoo. Women should avoid strolling alone here.

When you're passing through Syntagma Sq., don't miss the changing of the guard in front of the **Parliament** building (C4-D4). Every hour on the hour two sets of enormously tall *evzones* (guards) slowly wind up like toy soldiers, kick their heels about, and fall backwards into symmetrical little guardhouses on either side of the **Tomb of the Unknown Warrior** (C4). Unlike their British equivalents, *evzones* occasionally wink and even smile at tourists. Their jovial manner is as delightful as their attire—pom-pom-laden clogs, short pleated skirts (*foustanela*), and pony tail-tasseled hats. Every Sunday at 10:45am, the ceremony occurs with the full troop of guards, a band, and even greater pomp than usual.

NEAR ATHENS

■■■ KESARIANI AND DAPHNI

If you're worn down by Athens's insane congestion, visit the **Monastery of Kesariani** (tel. 723 6619) for serenity and salvation. Located near the top of **Mt. Hymettus,** the site was originally a temple to Dimitra, goddess of agriculture and nature. In the Roman period (200-300 AD), another temple was erected in its place, employing the architectural techniques of the day. The structure's stones were used in the 14th century to build the existing monastery. The 17th-century frescoes (painted by Ioannis Ypatios) and the sacred atmosphere are splendid. Come alone or with a spiritual friend; tour buses are likely to whirl you through too quickly.

To reach Kesariani take blue **bus** #224 from the ΚΗΠΟΣ stop two blocks up Vas. Sofias from Syntagma Sq. (every 15min., 20min., 75dr). Get off at the last stop, follow the left-hand road uphill and, when you reach the overpass, bear right under it, staying to the right through two forks. A few minutes farther up the road, it splits, the right going up the mountain, the left coming down from it. Once again, stick to the right. Roughly a 5-min. jaunt farther uphill, just as the road bends left, two branches spring from the right side. Ignore the barred one on the right, and take the stone-embedded path right up to the monastery. The entire walk takes 40-50 min., so be sure to bring lots of water. If you drain your water bottles, a 15-min. walk up the main road leads to a small store and a drinkable fountain. For a fabulous view overlooking Athens all the way to the sea, keep walking on the road for 15 more min. past the store. Numerous hiking trails meander away from the road throughout the area. The Monastery makes a wonderful spot for a picnic. (Monastery open Tues.-Sun. 8:30am-3pm; admission 800dr, students 400dr.)

Built on the site of the ancient Temple of Daphnios Apollo and surrounded by a high fortified wall is the **Monastery of Daphni** (tel. 581 1558), a peaceful retreat 10km west of Athens, along the Ancient Sacred Way. Cool breezes sweep the area, and the 11th-century structure is pock-marked with birds' nests. The monastery has served as both an army camp and a lunatic asylum, which may explain the pronounced scowl on Christ's face as he stares down from the masterful mosaic dome. (Open daily 8:30am-3pm; admission 800dr, students 400dr, no charge for video, no flash cameras allowed.) **Camping Daphni** (tel. 581 1563) is halfway down the road to the monastery. (Reception open 7am-10pm; check-out 2pm; 1000dr per person, 2000dr per small tent, 3200dr per large tent; prices w/shower.)

To reach Daphni from Athens, take bus #860 or 880 from the **El. Venizelou St.** complex in front of the National Library, University, and Academy of Arts. From Piraeus port, take #804, 805, or 845 (every 15min., 6am-11:30pm, 35min., 75dr). From the bus stop, cross the highway and go down the road towards the monastery.

■■■ PIRAEUS ΠΕΙΡΑΙΑΣ

The natural harbor of Piraeus has been Athens's port since the early 5th century BC, when Themistokles began fortifying Piraeus, then an island, as a base for the growing Athenian fleet. In approximately 450 BC, Pericles added the Long Walls from Athens to Piraeus, bridging the land masses. Though the opening scenes of both Kazantzakis' *Zorba the Greek* and Plato's *Republic* depict Piraeus as a charming port town, these days Piraeus has lost that loving feeling: it's dirty and smoggy, with endless stores vending cheap tourist trinkets and "aged" pastries glistening with grease. Use Piraeus only as the point of departure to most of the Greek isles. To get here, take the subway (75dr) from Monastiraki, Omonia, or any other station, to the last stop in the Piraeus direction, or take green bus #40 from Filellinon St., just off Syntagma Sq. (75dr). Get off at the Public Theater (Demotikon Theatron) and head right, toward the port. Either way, the trip takes roughly 20 min. from downtown Athens. Long-distance trains for Patras and the Peloponnese leave daily from the station on Akti Kalimassioti. Long-distance trains for northern Greece (Larissis) leave daily from the station on Ag. Dimitriou across the harbor.

ORIENTATION AND PRACTICAL INFORMATION

Ferries ply the waters from Piraeus to nearly all Greek islands except the Sporades and Ionian groups. There's a small but invaluable map of Piraeus on the back of the Athens map available at the tourist office in Syntagma Sq. Most of the boats and ticket agencies are on two streets, **Akti Possidonos** and **Akti Miaouli.** The subway deposits you at the top of Akti Possidonos; facing the water, head left. It merges with Akti Miaouli at **Themistokleos Square,** where you arrive if you walk down **Vas. Georgiou** (from the bus stop at **Korai Square.** Themistokleos Square is also the

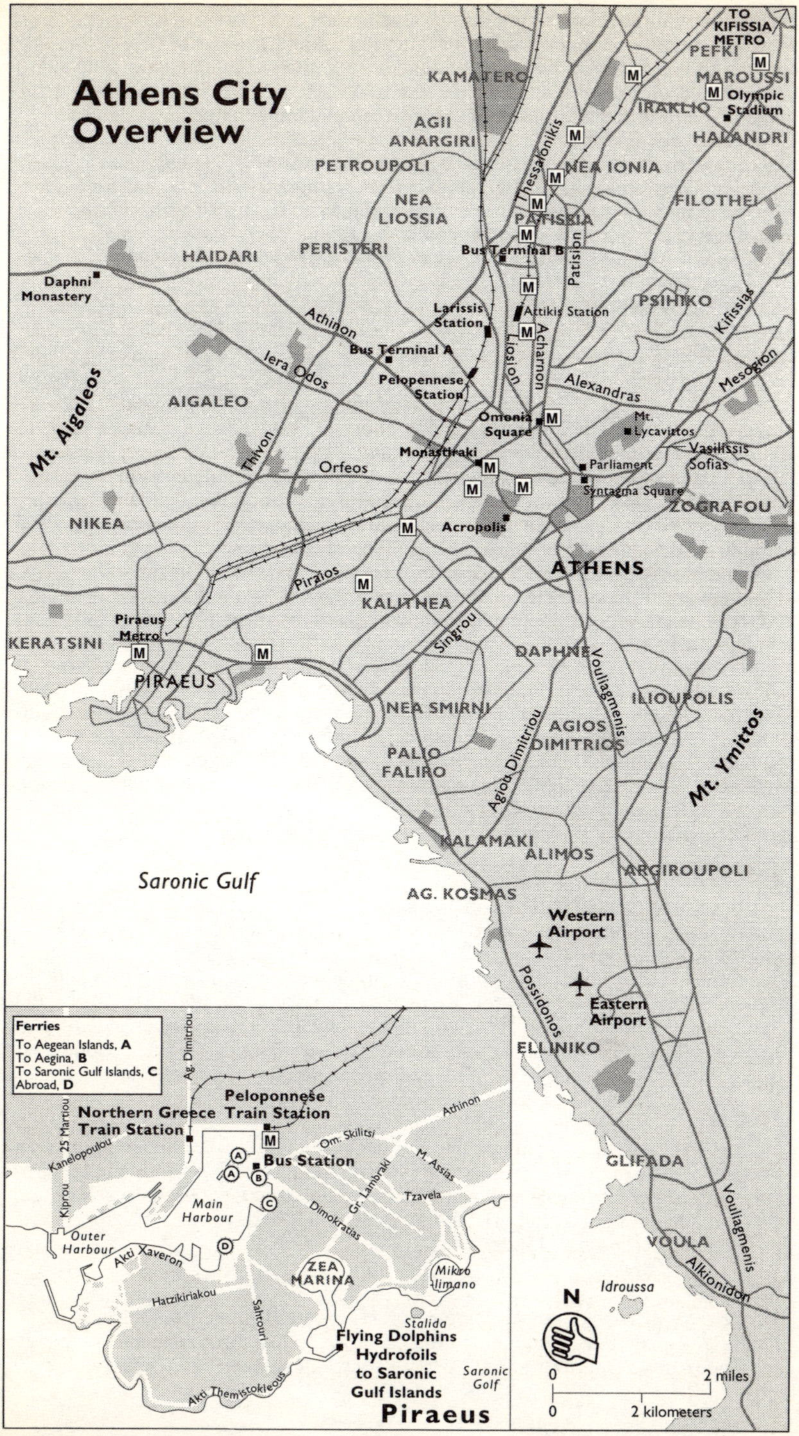
Athens City Overview
TO KIFISSIA METRO
PEFKI
MAROUSSI
Olympic Stadium
IRAKLIO
HALANDRI
KAMATERO
AGII ANARGIRI
PETROUPOLI
NEA IONIA
Thessalonikis
NEA LIOSSIA
PATISSIA
FILOTHEI
HAIDARI
PERISTERI
Bus Terminal B
Patision
Daphni Monastery
Larissis Station
Attikis Station
PSIHIKO
Kifissias
Athinon
Bus Terminal A
Iera Odos
Peloponnese Station
Liosion
Acharnon
Alexandras
Mesogion
Mt. Aigaleos
AIGALEO
Omonia Square
Mt. Lycavittos
Thivon
Monastiraki
Parliament
Vasilissis Sofias
Orfeos
Syntagma Square
ZOGRAFOU
NIKEA
Acropolis
ATHENS
Piraios
KALITHEA
Piraeus Metro
KERATSINI
Singrou
DAPHNE
PIRAEUS
Vouliagmenis
ILIOUPOLIS
NEA SMIRNI
AGIOS DIMITRIOS
Agiou Dimitriou
PALIO FALIRO
Mt. Ymittos
KALAMAKI
ALIMOS
ARGIROUPOLI
Saronic Gulf
AG. KOSMAS
Western Airport
Possidonos
Eastern Airport
ELLINIKO
GLIFADA
VOULA
Vouliagmenis
Alkionidon
Idroussa
N
0 2 miles
0 2 kilometers
Ferries
To Aegean Islands, A
To Aegina, B
To Saronic Gulf Islands, C
Abroad, D
Ag. Dimitriou
25 Martiou
Peloponnese Train Station
Northern Greece Train Station
Athinon
Om. Skilitsi
Kanelopoulou
Bus Station
M. Assias
Gr. Lambraki
Kiprou
Main Harbour
Tzavela
Dimokratias
Outer Harbour
Akti Xaveron
ZEA MARINA
Mikro limano
Hatzikiriakou
Sahtouri
Stalida
Flying Dolphins Hydrofoils to Saronic Gulf Islands
Saronic Golf
Akti Themistokleous
Piraeus

departure point for boats to the Saronic Gulf Islands and **hydrofoils** to Aegina (6 per day, 40 min.) There are no student discounts on domestic travel in Greece, but discounts on international fares can be found (one-way boat to Haifa, Israel 25,000dr). The larger ferries dock at Akti Miaouli; international ferries are at the end toward the Customs House. Small ferries depart from Akti Possidonos.

Post Office: On Tsamadou St., on the right off Antistasseos St., one block inland from Themistokleos Sq. The subway station offers travelers several amenities, including another, smaller **post office** (open Mon.-Fri. 7:30am-2pm) to the right of the Akti Possidonos doors. **Postal code:** 18501.

OTE: On Akti Possidonos, between Gounari and Antistasseos (open 7:15am-1pm). **Telephone Code:** 01.

Tourist Agency: Kentriko (tel. 412 1181 or 412 1172; fax 413 3193), in the subway station, with a large-lettered sign. Although the office deals mainly in steamer bookings, the clerk, Mr. Takis, offers extremely helpful advice—between phone calls—on where to find your boat in the glut of vessels in the port, and luggage storage (300dr). Inquire about their special 20-day unlimited island-hopping packages, available after June 15 (9000dr). (Open 5:30am-9pm.)

Banks: It is harder to avoid banks than to find them in this town; both the **National Bank** and the **Commercial Bank** have offices along the waterfront, and there is a **Citibank** with **ATMs** at 47-49 Akti Miaouli (tel. 417 2153). These all **change money,** as does the **Thomas Cook,** one block down Akti Possidonos from the subway, and the numerous other exchange agencies which litter the port. (Banks open Mon.-Thurs. 8am-2pm, Fri. 8am-1:30pm.)

International Bookstore: Telstar Booksellers, 57 Akti Miaouli (tel. 429 3618), offers an impressive array of magazines in English, French and Arabic, and a small selection of paperbacks and some stationery supplies. Open Mon.-Sat. 7:30am-8pm.

On the opposite side of the peninsula is the port of **Zea.** Hydrofoils depart from here to the other Saronic Gulf islands and to Kea and Kithnos. Along the water and under the sidewalk at Zea are a **port police** office (tel. 452 5315), a **post office** (open Mon.-Fri. 7:30am-2pm), and a **tourist office** (tel. 413 5716; open Mon.-Fri. 7:30am-3pm; look for the EOT sign). Private boats dock in the harbor on the left (facing the water); hydrofoils await on the right. To get to Zea, walk away from the water on any of the roads off Akti Miaouli; it takes roughly 10 min. to get there.

ACCOMMODATIONS

For those unfortunate enough to be marooned by ferry schedules, your best bet is to head away from the water, toward where the hotels will at least be safe. **Hotel Phidias,** 189 Koundouriotou St. (tel. 429 6480), is close to Zea on a sidestreet off Boumboulinas, which itself springs from Akti Miaouli. (Singles 6000dr, doubles 8000dr, triples 9500dr; all w/bath.) **Hotel Glaros,** 4 Char. Trikoupi St. (tel. 451 5421 or 453 7887; fax 453 7889), on a street which runs away from the lower part of Akti Miaouli, offers cheap rates. (Singles 4500dr, w/bath 5500dr; doubles 6500dr, w/bath 7500dr.) Don't sleep in the dirty and dangerous park at Themistokleos Sq.

FOOD

Inexpensive fast-food restaurants line the dock, offering mediocre fare at uniform prices. To find a good, cheap meal, the best approach is to do it yourself at the **grocery store** (located downstairs), one block up Antistasseos St. The bakery **Europa,** 166-168 Koundouriotou (tel. 412 0961), near Hotel Phidias, offers cheap, mouth-watering treats (*baklava* 150dr).

SIGHTS

The prize possession of the **Archaeological Museum,** 31 Char. Trikoupi St. (tel. 452 1598), is the ancient "Piraeus Kouros," a large hollow bronze statue with outstretched arms. (Open Tues.-Sun. 8:30am-3pm. Admission 500dr, seniors over 60

400dr, students 300dr, European students free. No charge for video, no flash allowed.) A small collection, but a cultural break from the grim outdoors. Near the museum is the 2nd-century BC **Hellenistic theater.** Farther south at Zea, facing the harbor and underneath the sidewalk on Akti Themistokleous, is the **Maritime Museum** (tel. 451 6822), which traces the history of the Greek navy using detailed ship models. The courtyard is home port to torpedo tubes, naval weapons, and anchors. (Open Tues.-Fri. 9am-2pm, Sat.-Sun. 9am-1pm; admission 400dr.)

■■■ THE PETALION GULF COAST

CAPE SOUNION

Local legend has it that off the coast of Cape Sounion lie the remains of fabled **Atlantis,** which sank into the sea millennia ago. The **Temple of Poseidon** (tel. 39 363) still stands on a promontory high above the coast. The sublime view of the azure Aegean makes a visit here a spiritual experience—even for lapsed Poseidon worshippers. The original temple was constructed around 600 BC, destroyed by the Persians in a 480 BC temper-tantrum, and rebuilt by Pericles in 440 BC. The 16 remaining Doric columns still suggest the graceful symmetry of the original temple. Scattered remains of the **Temple of Athena Sounias,** the patron goddess of Athens, litter the lower hill. Sunrise is the ideal time to view the temples. If you sleep in, try to visit before early afternoon (when the tour buses funnel in), or around sunset (after they've drained out). Pack a lunch and bypass the pricey cafeteria. (Site open daily 10am-sunset; admission 800dr, students 400dr, European students free.) Last bus to Athens departs according to hour of sunset; check the schedule at the bus station upon arrival. From a cliff adjacent to the temple, watch the sun's orange glow illuminate the temple columns and sink beyond the rocky coast.

To reach the ocean, follow one of the many paths from the inland side of the temple. The agile and adventurous can negotiate the cliff on the ocean side. Chaotic with vacationing families, the **beaches** along the 70km Apollo Coast between Piraeus and Cape Sounion have a crowded carnival atmosphere, especially on summer weekends. Some are owned by hotels, which charge a 150dr admission fee, but towns usually have free public beaches as well, and some seaside stretches along the bus route remain almost empty. The driver will let you off almost anywhere.

There isn't much else to Cape Sounion. On the road leading from the bus stop to the center of town, there is a **National Bank** (tel. 19 500; open Mon.-Thurs. 8:30am-2pm, Fri. 8:30am-1:30pm).

Two buses travel the 70km road to Cape Sounion. One goes along the coast and stops at all points on the **Apollo Coast,** leaving every hour on the half hour (6:30am-6:30pm) from the 14 Mavromateon St. stop in the square just below Areos Park in Athens. You can meet the bus 10min. later on Filellinon St. at Xenofontos St., but all the seats will probably be filled (2¼hr., 1000dr). The other bus, following a much less scenic inland route, leaves from Areos Park (every hr. on the hr., 6am-6pm, 2¼hr., 1000dr). Every hour, buses head from Cape Sounion to the port of **Lavrio** (20min., 200dr). **Ferries** go from Lavrio to Kea (1½hr., 1800dr) and Kithnos (2hr., 2000dr). For for tickets call 26 777.

If you want to spend the night to see the temples or if you miss the last bus to the ferry at Lavrio accommodations can be found at **Aegaeon Hotel** (tel. 39 200; fax 37 234) located 5 min. from the bus stop toward the temples (if you plan to stay, get off the bus at the main stop rather than up at the temples). It is hard to miss the large concrete building down by the beach on the right. (Singles 11,200dr, doubles 16,000dr, all w/baths.) The two restaurants on the road down to the hotel, as well as the one in it, offer similar, decently-priced meals. For those seeking the great outdoors experience, **Camping Sounion Beach** (tel. 39 358 or 39 718) is located 5km toward Lavrio, conveniently at a bus stop. (900dr per person, 600dr per small tent, 1000dr per large tent, all including showers.) The **Belle Epoque Hotel** (tel. 27 130 or 26 059) has reasonably-priced rooms. (Singles 5000dr, doubles 10,000dr, triples

15,000dr. Full breakfast 1500dr.) To find it, walk a very short distance from the bus stop away from both the port and the center of town. In the middle of the town is a well-stocked **supermarket** (tel. 23 879; 24 hr). **Telephone Code:** 0292.

RAFINA

For the purposes of most travelers in Greece, Rafina might as well be named "Little Piraeus." Situated across from its larger twin on the Attic Peninsula, Rafina shares many of Piraeus' "qualities:" noise, dirt, high prices, and little entertainment. Nonetheless, Rafina is more pleasant on the eyes, ears, and lungs than its counterpart.

The **port police** (tel. 22 888), in a small booth near the dock, have up-to-date information but don't speak English very well. For information and ferry tickets, try one of the English-speaking offices along the waterfront. The offices clearly display which tickets they sell. **Strintzis Lines, Gatsos Lines, Agoudimos Lines** and **Ventouris Ferries** operate various ferries, while **Ilios Lines** and **Hermes Lines** operate hydrofoils. Following the ramp up from the waterfront will bring you to Plastira Sq. Facing the square with the water at your back, the **post office** stands two streets to the right on Eleftheriou Venizelou (open Mon.-Fri. 7:30am-2pm); the **OTE** is across the street on the far side of the square (open Mon.-Fri. 7:30am2:30pm). The **Commercial bank,** on the far left corner (open Mon.-Thurs. 8am-2pm, Fri. 8am-1:30pm), and the **Ionian Bank,** located two blocks farther inland, offer **currency exchange. Pharmacies** are all around, particularly on Kyprion Atoniston. Taxis line up right in front of the square. **Postal Code:** 19009; **Telephone Code:** 0294.

Rafina is accessible by frequent **buses** from 29 Mavromateon St., two blocks up along Areos Park in Athens (every 30min. 5:45am-10:30pm, 1hr., 380dr). **Ferries** sail to Karystos in Evia (2-3 per day, 2hr., 1424dr), Marmari in Evia (3-4 per day, 1½hr., 914dr), Andros (2 per day, 2hr., 1968dr), Tinos (2 per day, 4hr., 2741dr), Mykonos (2 per day, 5hr., 3276dr), and 1 per week to Paros (3276dr) and Naxos (3500dr). **Hydrofoils** sail to Andros (2 per day, 1hr., 4121dr), Tinos (2 per day, 2hr., 6168dr), Mykonos (2 per day, 2½hr., 7333dr). There is a weekly hydrofoil to the Cyclades and other island groups. For info call the **Port Authority of Rafina** (tel. 22 300).

Be prepared to pay heartily for the dubious pleasure of spending a night in Rafina. **Hotel Korali** (tel. 22 477), in Plastira Sq., offers cramped but clean rooms with shared baths (singles 5090dr, doubles 7270dr, triples 10,179dr). If you have money to burn, **Hotel Aura's** (tel. 22 780, -3; fax 23 320) similar rooms are immeasurably enhanced by ocean views (make sure to ask for rooms facing the water). Visible from the port, this enormous concrete building can be reached by heading left at the top of the ramp leading away from the boats. (Singles 10,130dr, doubles 15,533dr. 10% surcharge for stays shorter than three nights.) Those who wish to **camp** can head to the beach of **Kokkino Limanaki** (tel. 31 603, -4), 1.2km from the port (1500dr per person or tent, shower included).

For a small harbor town, Rafina has a plethora of cafés, cafeterias, and *tavernas,* but none are particularly appealing or inexpensive. A trip to one of the several **grocery stores** around Plastira Sq. and the post office is more likely to satisfy.

MARATHON

In 490 BC, when the Athenians defeated the Persians at the bloody battle of Marathon, the messenger Pheidippides ran 42km (26mi) to Athens to announce the victory, and then collapsed dead from exhaustion. Today, international marathons (*sans* fatal collapse) commemorate this act. Runners trace Pheidippides' route twice annually, in April and October.

Beautiful **Lake Marathon,** with its huge marble dam, rests 8km past the otherwise uninspiring town. Until WWII, the lake was Athens's sole source of water. At **Ramnous,** 15km to the northeast, are the ruins of the Temples of Nemesis, goddess of retribution, and Themis, goddess of custom, law, and justice.

On the coast near Marathon, **Schinias** to the north and **Timvos Marathonas** to the south are popular beaches. Thick pine trees prick the long and sandy stretch at Schinias. Both beaches are too congested for comfort on the weekend, but they're relatively empty midweek. Many people camp at Schinias since the trees offer good protection, but the mosquitoes are thirsty and mean. *Let's Go* does not recommend illegal freelance camping.

The **bus** for Marathon leaves from 29 Mavromateon St. by Areos Park in Athens (every ½hr., 5:30am-7pm, 1hr., 700dr). Ask the driver to let you off at the sign for the museum ("Mouseion and Marathonas"). Follow the signs and don't despair; the museum is 2km farther (roughly a 30-min. walk) at the end of the paved road. To reach the Marathon Tomb or the nearby beach, walk 1½km back toward Athens. Lake Marathon, Amphiareion, and Ramnous are accessible by automobile only.

■■■ DELPHI ΔΕΛΦΟΙ

Zeus sent forth two eagles from opposite ends of the earth in hopes of discovering the world's center. The birds impaled each other with their beaks above Delphi and fell to the ground where the *omphalos* (navel stone) still marks the spot of their ill-fated rendezvous. The birds' landing also marked the sight of the Oracle of Apollo, where troubled denizens of the ancient world flocked in the 2nd millennium BC to seek *Pythia's* profound, if cryptic, advice.

If modern Delphi is the center of anything, it's of the tour-bus circuit. Basically a one-oracle, two-street town, Delphi is a package-tour planner's fantasy. The town's two main streets are lined with semi-identical hotels, restaurants, and gift shops, making tourism here comfortable, if a bit pre-packaged. Even package tour groups, however, cannot spoil the town's spectacular ruins and gorgeous views.

Orientation and Practical Information The **tourist office** (tel. 82 900), in the town hall on Pavlou St., with entrances on both Pavlou and Apollonos, gives helpful tips about the area and can supply some hotel and camping rates (open Mon.-Fri. 7:30am-2:30pm). If the office is closed, check the front window for posted museum, site, and bus schedules. On the second floor of 46 Apollonos St. on the left, up the hill from the bus station, are the **tourist police** (tel. 82 220, -2; open daily 9am-2pm, but someone's there 24 hr.). The **post office** (tel. 82 376; open Mon.-Sat. 7:30am-2pm, Sun. 9am-12:30pm) and the **National Bank of Greece** (open Mon.-Fri. 8am-2pm, 6-7:30pm) are on Pavlou St. Both change money, as does the bank machine outside the National Bank, which accepts Mastercard. Farther down Pavlou is the **OTE** (open Mon.-Sat. 7:30am-3:10pm, Sun. 9am-2pm). At the foot of Pavlou St. across from Hotel Pythi, are free **public toilets** and the **taxi stand** (tel. 52 000). **Postal Code:** 33054; **Telephone Code:** 0265.

Buses leave Athens for Delphi from the station at 260 Liossion St. (tel. (01) 831 7096; 5 per day, 3hr., 2400dr). Take blue bus #024 from Amalias Ave. at the entrance to the National Garden or El. Venizelou (Panepistimiou) by Syntagma Sq. to get to the station (½hr., 75dr). Buy your ticket at the booth labelled ΔΕΛΦΙΟΣ. Try to arrive early to avoid long lines. Also, note that often you may have to take the Amphissa bus, which stops at Delphi. With a railpass, take a train to Levadia and, from there, buses head to Delphi (600dr). From Delphi buses leave for Thessaloniki via Volos, Larissa, and Katerini (5 per week, 6hr., 5500dr), Patras (1-2 per day, 3hr., 1950dr), Lamia (2-4 per day, 2hr., 1450dr), Nafpaktos (3-4 per day, 2½hr., 1700dr), Amphissa (6 per day, ½hr., 300dr), Itea (6 per day, ½hr., 300dr), and Galaxidi (3 per day, 50min., 550dr). At the bus station/café (tel. 82 317; open daily 8am-10pm) most of the staff speak English and will help decipher intricate bus schedules.

Accommodations In a town packed with shiny, expensive hotels that cater to the rich and beautiful, the **youth hostel,** 29 Apollonos St. (tel. 82 268) at the crest of the hill is a reprieve. The manager, a gregarious New Zealander, offers excellent advice about exploring the region. Unfortunately, the back rooms, which have balconies with exceptional views, are directly above Taverna Vlachos, which stays busy late (midnight-1am) in the summer. (Doubles 6000dr, dorm beds 1500dr, sheets and blanket 200dr; hot water 6-8pm; curfew 11pm; check-out 10am; open

March-Nov.) If the hostel thing isn't for you, check out **Pension Odysseus** (tel. 82 235), on Filellinon, parallel to and below Pavlou. The view is slightly marred by unsightly telephone lines, but the rooms are clean and there is a very pleasant vine-covered patio. (Singles 4500dr, doubles 6000dr, triples 7500dr.) Other accommodations are charted on the town map to the left of the café/bus station. Closest to the station, the immaculate **Hotel Athina,** 51 Pavlou St. (tel. 82 239), provides balconied rooms with marvelous views of the Gulf of Corinth. (Singles 3500dr; doubles 4000dr, w/bath 5000dr; triples 6500dr, w/bath 7500dr; check-out 11am.) The pleasant **Hotel Pan,** 53 Pavlou St. (tel. 82 294; fax 82 320), shares the view, and has an airy breakfast room. (Singles 5000dr, doubles 7000dr, triples 8000dr.) The same nice management presides over **Hotel Pythia,** 3 Pavlou St. (tel. 82 328), across and down the street. (Singles 5000dr, doubles 7000dr, triples 8000dr; all with bath.) The nearest campsite is **Apollo Camping** (tel. 82 762, -50; fax 82 639), 1.5km down from the bus station. **Delphi Camping** (tel. 82 363) and **Chrissa Camping** (tel. 82 050) are 4 and 10km farther down the road. All cater more to package groups, but charge 1000dr per person, 500dr per tent, and have pools.

Food And Entertainment Almost all of Delphi's *tavernas* have terraces that overlook the mountains and the Gulf of Corinth. Sitting in any of them feels a little like being Mr. Rourke on Fantasy Island; you'll keep expecting Tattoo to come scampering out of the kitchen with a floral lei and some more *tzatziki*. There are two good, inexpensive restaurants close to the youth hostel. **Taverna Vlachos** (tel. 82 448), underneath the hostel, is just about the cheapest and most popular place around. The Greek salad (700dr) reminds one of just how good olive oil can taste, while the speedy, polite service might make you forget that you're in Greece (fixed menus 1300-2100dr). A few doors down, **Taverna Lekaria** (tel. 82 864) offers the same gorgeous view and dishes like stuffed tomatoes (1100dr). **Markets** can be found along Apollonos and Pavlou St. For the best fresh breads and pastries in town, venture uphill off Apollonos St. past the left of the church and follow signs to the **bakery** (tel. 82 045) on the right (open 5am-10pm).

The only place to shake a leg after dark is **Club No Name,** on Pavlou St., where you can mingle with Delphi's youth for a 500dr cover, sipping 500dr beers or 1000dr cocktails. Better yet, if your timing is lucky, there is a **Festival of Ancient Greek Drama** put on by the **European Cultural Center of Delphi** (tel. 82 731, -92; fax 82 733). The Center, which is open daily 9am-2pm, also has temporary international art exhibitions. To find it, walk down the Amphissa/Itea road and follow the signs back uphill. Delphi is home to several other summer festivals, so ask around and keep a sharp eye out for posters when you arrive.

SIGHTS

The ancient Greek gods expressed their wishes to humans through oracles. Politically, **Delphi's oracle** was supreme: leaders throughout the Mediterranean sought its infallible advice. Whenever a Greek city won a battle, its leader would erect a dedicatory offering to the oracle. As a result, the entrance to the sanctuary was cluttered with monuments from all over Greece.

To the ancients, a temple was only complete with striking natural surroundings. Resting near the foot of Mt. Parnassos, the Oracle's site is flanked by a towering cliff on one side and the ominous 600m-deep Pleistos ravine on the other. Legend claims that Apollo slew the monster Python, which had presided over Delphi. But the snake, an earth-spirit, continued to speak to postulants through an intermediary, an elderly woman known as the *Pythia,* who could be seen only by specially elected priests. Sitting directly over the *omphalos,* the *Pythia* inhaled the vapors wafting up from the chasm below, and then chanted deliriously. Her incoherent mutterings were "versified" by the priests, who would announce her prophecies to the waiting public. The Delphic Oracle remained important among Greeks from the 7th century BC until after the Christianization of the Roman Empire.

The main body of structures, known as the **Sanctuary of Apollo,** lies 300m east of town on the road to Athens (follow the highway and take the paved path on your left to the ruins and museum). **Maps** of a first-century BC reconstruction of the site are available in the shops in town, or at the kiosk across from the bus station, for 300dr. A map aids the understanding of the ancient site but is not needed for orientation. The "Delphi" brochure, free at the tourist info office, has a smaller map. The half dozen English language **guidebooks** available at the museum (1500-2500dr) are far from indispensable for the ruins, where most signs are in English, but they come in handy in the museum, where Greek and French are *de rigeur*.

Now as then, the **Temple of Apollo** is the prime attraction. The building burned in 548 BC, and the 373 BC reconstruction was shattered by an earthquake. What stands today are the remains of a second united effort at reconstruction. This is where oracular priests would announce the *Pythia's* verdicts. The huge walls were once inscribed with famous maxims of Greek philosophers. Also notable at the site are the theater and the stadium. Scamper up the hills past tour groups to the stadium, sit and relax, then meander down the mountain at your leisure, pitying the tour groups huffing and puffing their way up. Some shameless individuals pick a group to follow and mooch info off their loquacious guide. (Site open Mon.-Fri. 7:30am-7:30pm, Sat.-Sun. 8:30am-3pm; off-season Mon.-Fri. 7:30am-5:30pm, Sat.-Sun. 8:30am-3pm; admission 1200dr, students 600dr.) Be sure to visit Delphi's **Archaeological Museum** (tel. 82 312), located just before the Pythian Sanctuary along the path from town. It contains at least two indisputable masterpieces of ancient Greek art: the frieze of the Siphnian Treasury and the Charioteer of Delphi. (Open Mon. noon-6:30pm, Tues.-Fri. 7:30am-7:30pm, Sat.-Sun. 8:30am-3pm; admission 1200dr, students 600dr.)

The unfenced ruins of the **Temple of Pronaia Athena** are roughly 200m past the main set of ruins heading away from town. (Entrance on your right just past the "exit" sign.) On your way, you'll pass the **Castelian Spring** on your left, where pilgrims cleansed themselves both physically and spiritually before calling upon the oracle. Drinking from the spring is said to give you the gift of eloquence (are you listening Dan Quayle?). To your right is the millennia-old **Gymnasium.** The three remaining Doric columns of the circular 4th-century **Tholos** at Athena's sanctuary are the most photographed of Delphi's ruins. Although scholars have inferred from ancient texts that the *Tholos* was an important part of the Delphic complex, no one now knows exactly what function it served. Next to the *Tholos* lies the **Treasury of Marseilles;** this gift from the citizens of ancient France attests to the extent of the oracle's prestige. (Ruins always open; free.)

■ NEAR DELPHI

LEVADIA

For die-hard oracle fans who want a second opinion, the **Oracle of Trophonios** is on a cliff which overlooks Levadia (ancient Lebadea). The site once attracted pilgrims on their way to Delphi. In the 14th century, Frankish Crusaders built a castle over the site of the oracle, now a 15-min. walk from town. It is the best-preserved castle in the area. From the bus station, turn right, and walk uphill to the square, and go right again onto Venizelou St. At the end of the street take a right, then a left at the church. The oracle once stood at the stream; the castle ruins are 200m farther.

Buses to Athens (2hr.) via Thebes (45min.) leave hourly from 6am to 8pm (1900dr). Levadia is also accessible by train from Athens, but the station is 5km from town, and the buses in town have a penchant for waiting for more than one train and then dropping travelers off 10min. away from the bus stop to Delphi and Osios Loukas (with no directions in sight, of course). If the scarcity of bus connections compels you to spend the night in Levadia, the **Hotel Erkina** (tel. (0201) 28 227), on the first right off Venizelou, has rooms (singles 3000dr, doubles 5000dr). You will probably prefer to push on to Delphi or Athens for the night.

OSIOS LOUKAS

Although it is toilsome to reach, **Osios Loukas** is worth the trouble. This pastoral and inspiring spot may instill in you pangs of longing for the monkhood. More than 1700m above sea-level, the stone monastery complex contains magnificent mosaics and affords tremendous views. Dress modestly (no shorts or bare shoulders, no pants for women); makeshift coverings are available at the gate.

To allow for transportation difficulties, give Osios Loukas a full day. There's one daily **bus** which leaves Levadia at 1:40pm (45min., 480dr) and stops in Distomo along the way. In Athens, take blue bus #024 from Amalias St. or El. Venizelou to the Liossion St. Bus Station (every 20min., ½hr., 75dr) and buy a ticket to Levadia (hourly 6am-8pm, 2hr., 1900dr). Six buses per day leave from Delphi (700dr). If you can't make it to Levadia for the 1:40 bus, take one of the frequent Delphi-Athens buses and ask the driver to let you off at the crossroads for Distomo; the turnoff is easy to miss (460dr). From there, it's a 3km walk to Distomo, where you can get a taxi. The 9km trip to the monastery costs 1000-2000dr. The bus from Distomo arrives at 1:40, and at 2pm the monastery closes for the afternoon. Don't despair; relax and spend a pleasant 1½hr. in the charming courtyard (catch up on your post-card-writing). The monastery re-opens at 4pm, and the gift shop is open all day. From Levadia, the bus to Distomo takes ½hr. (190dr).

Getting out of Ossios Loukas may also be problematic. Travelers used to mooch lifts from commercial tour **buses,** but they're increasingly wary of police and thus reluctant to let people bum rides. The bus station in Distomo is a joke—buses, when they come, only go to Levadia. The best bet to anywhere else is to share yet another **taxi** (4000dr). All this means that your afternoon of birds, breezes, and mosaics may wind up being rather pricey, but a taxi can save you grief.

The **post office,** where you can change money, is down the hill near the bus stop (open Mon.-Fri. 7:30am-2pm). The **OTE** is a few buildings down the road (open Mon.-Fri. 7:30am-3pm). Call the **police** at 22 100 and for **medical emegergency** dial 22 791. **Telephone Code:** 0267.

If you're stranded in Distomo, there are two hotels up the hill to the right of the main intersection. The first you'll come to is **Hotel America** (tel. 22 079, -82; singles 3000dr, doubles 6000dr). **Koutiaris Hotel** (tel. 22 268), near Hotel America, offers slightly larger rooms (singles 4400dr, doubles 5600dr). Eating options are sparse; a *souvlaki* joint, **Corner,** is up the main road on the left. **Odysseus** (tel. 22 616) is on 10th Iouniou 1944 St., 400m past the bus stop. (Open Mon.-Sat. 7am-2am.) There are several **supermarkets** and **pharmacies** in town.

Kill some time (you'll need to) at the **archaeological museum,** up the road to Osios Loukas. (Open Mon.-Fri. 8am-6pm, Sat.-Sun. 9:30am-3pm.) Ask to be let into the locked half in order to see a few cool mosaics. The main building in the Osios Loukas complex, the arresting **Church of St. Luke** is dedicated to a local hermit, known for his powers of healing and prophecy. According to locals, when Luke died in his cell in 953 AD, a myrrh tree sprouted from the cold floor. The entrance to the 10th-century church is adorned with Byzantine mosaics, most notably a face-less Doubting Thomas inserting his finger in Christ's wound. The most beautiful mosaics, the Nativity, Presentation at the Temple, and Baptism, are tucked into the squinches that support the dome. Although not as famous as the ones in the upper church, the 11th-century frescoes that cover most of the **crypt's** interior are every bit as gorgeous; flashlight needed for best viewing. Don't miss the saintly frescoes removed from their original homes and now displayed in a building at the very back of the complex, off the courtyard behind the churches. The oldest part of the monastery is the 10th-century **Church of St. Mary** adjoining the larger church. Despite Osios Loukas' indoor attractions, the flowers, birds, and encompassing mountains outside the monastery (tel. (0267) 22 797) are most enthralling. (Open daily 8am-2pm and 4-7pm; admission 800dr, students 400dr.)

ARACHOVA

Stacked onto the slopes below Mt. Parnassos, the village of Arachova, 10km east of Delphi, revels in its own relaxed atmosphere in the summer and caters to skiers in winter. This is a perfect place to collapse after you've spent the day fighting the crowds at Delphi. Grandparently villagers sit in the town's central plaza, many wrapped in Arachova's intricate handwoven shawls. The area's culinary distinctions are its amber honey and tasty *saganaki,* fried cheese. You can even buy a take-home variety. Arachova's most important incarnation, however, is as a ski resort. The main street oozes with *souvlaki* and souvenirs. The sweaters, woven rugs, and coonskin-type hats that you'll find here befit the town's popularity in winter.

The **tourist office** (tel. 31 630, -92), in the first of the town's three squares (coming from Delphi) on the west end, is aimed at the ski crowd and may close during summer months. Next door, the **post office** changes money. (Open Mon.-Fri. 7:30am-2pm.) Directly across the square from the post office is the **OTE.** (Open Mon.-Sat. 7:30am-3:10pm.) The **bank** is on the main street, 50m west of the bus station. (Open Mon.-Fri. 8:30am-1pm.) The **police** are across from the bus station, on the second floor (tel. 31 133). Farther east, past the third square, is a **pharmacy** (tel. 31 186). **Postal Code:** 32004; **Telephone Code:** 0267.

Roughly 5 **buses** per day run between Athens and Delphi, stopping in Arachova, while an additional 8 make the run from Arachova to Delphi (20min., 160dr). All buses to Delphi go to Itea (2hr., 550dr) and two continue from Itea to Galaxidi (15min., 150dr). A pink and white "Celena" sign identifies the bus station (tel. 31 790), which doubles as a café and winter restaurant. Eleni, the helpful heptilingual owner, will assist you with bus timetables and accommodations.

On the east side of town, near the square, are several hotels, pensions, and "Rooms to Let," including **The Apollon** (tel. 31 073), the **Women's Agricultural Tourist Cooperative Office** which rents rooms, and **Pension Nostas** (tel. 31 385). Each offers doubles for 10,000-15,000dr (off season 5000-8000dr). Ask at the "Celena" bus station café for rooms around town. The closest **campground** is west of Delphi (see p. 91). Moderately priced *tavernas* include **Liakoura** (tel. 31 783), next to the OTE (*saganaki* 900dr, *souvlaki* 1250), and **Laka** below the police station (greek salad 1000dr, *saganaki* 500dr).

Apollo and the Muses now share their abode with ski buffs on **Mt. Parnassos.** The mountain (2700m) is one of the most accessible. If you're interested in hiking up in summer, take a taxi to the **Mt. Parnassos Ski Center,** 27km northwest of Arachova. From the ski center it's a steep 2km climb up to the summit, where vultures glower overhead. The ski season on Mt. Parnassos runs roughly from December 1 to May 1. There are 14 lifts, and tickets average 3000-5000dr per day; rentals are 1500-3500dr per day. To stay in the area, try Delphi or Arachova, but you'll have to pay 7000-8000dr for the round-trip cab, since the taxi lobby won't allow public buses to run to the ski center (taxi tel. 31 566). Alternatively, make a daytrip from Athens (bus leaves 6am, 3hr., round-trip 2500dr). For info on skiing, find Mr. Kostas Koutras at his **ski shop** (tel. 31 841, -767) on the first left coming from Delphi.

ITEA

A quiet escape from Delphi, this semi-industrial town offers only a rocky beach and the long waterfront boardwalk lined with cafés and *tavernas.* Enjoy the view in the afternoon when the construction has silenced and the sun glints on the water. The beach east of town is equipped with outdoor showers. A cleaner and more solitary beach is **Kira Beach,** 2km from town. The **post office** is along the beach near the bus stop. (Open Mon.-Fri. 7:30am-8pm, Sat. 7:30am-2pm.) A **bank** is across the street. (Open Mon.-Thurs. 8am-2pm, Fri. 8am-1:30pm.) Itea has the only **motorbike rental** shop in the Delphi area; inquire at the **tourist shop** Tsonos (tel. 33 717). It's past the post office 100m to the left of the bus station (small bikes 2500-4000dr per day). Frequent **buses** run from Delphi to Itea (11 per day, 6:30am-8:20pm, 1hr., 300dr). The last bus back to Delphi from Itea is at 5:45pm; a **taxi** (tel. 32 200) is a good option for late returns (1200-2500dr according to the number of passengers).

It's a 5-6hr. walk uphill to Delphi. If for some reason you want to stay here, try the **Hotel Galini** (tel. 32 278, -323), on the waterfront street Akti Possidonos. (Singles w/bath 5500dr, doubles w/bath 7500dr.) Or continue to walk, with the water on your right, down the street to **Hotel Akti** (tel. 32 015, -257), which is cheaper but not quite as clean. (Singles 3000dr, doubles 4000dr, triples 5000dr.) Moderate cuisine for moderate prices can be found along the waterfront. The **Dolphin II Restaurant,** on the water as you walk away from town, has superb seafood, as do most of the restaurants along Akti Possidonos and the beach.

GALAXIDI

Seventeen kilometers from Itea, Galaxidi, across the harbor, is home to better beaches. The name of this seafaring town, a coagulation of *gala* (milk) and *xidhi* (vinegar), reflects the bittersweet experiences of a seaman's wife. These days in Galaxidi, there's no need for wives to wring their hands—they can find their husbands floating their boats at one of the town's cafés. A wealthy town visited primarily by boaters, Galaxidi emulates the rhythms of the sea—a deep repose rippled with activity and a tide of visitors.

The bus drops off at one end of Nik. Mama, the main street in the town center that leads down to the waterfront and harbor. Though Galaxidi is pretty sleepy most of the year, things get hectic here just before Easter. If you happen to be here on Mardi Gras, be sure that you're not wearing your Sunday best—wild food fights break out, with colorful pies being the weapon of choice. There are also more sedate pleasures, such as watching the town's children Greek dance in traditional costume. Galaxidi's **post office** is at the end of Nik. Mama (open Mon.-Fri. 7:30am-2pm). For indigestion and other mild post-party traumas, head to the **pharmacy** at 15 Nik. Mama. The **OTE** is down the first right from the bus stop off Nik. Mama (open Mon.-Fri. 7:30am-3:10pm). **Postal Code:** 33052; **Telephone Code:** 0265.

The cheapest place to stay is **Galaxidi Camping** (tel. 41 530), 2km from town. Freelance campers say there are plenty of beach spots, especially beyond the pine forest, but *Let's Go* does not recommend illegal freelance camping. In town, on Nik. Mama St., is **Hotel Poseidon,** blessed with a friendly manager (tel. 41 426; singles 3000dr, doubles 6000dr.) **Pension Votsalo** (tel. 41 788, -542) is a little bit hard to find, but offers some of the cheaper rooms in town (doubles 7000dr, w/A/C 8000dr). Walk down the street opposite the bus stop until you reach the water and then continue along the right-hand waterfront; look for the sign up the second street heading inland. At the other end of town, several blocks down the last right off Nik. Mama before the water, **Hotel Galaxidi** (tel. 41 850; fax 41 026) has nice rooms w/A/C. (Singles 6000dr, doubles 10,000dr, triples 12,000dr.) In August or any summer weekend, expect the prices to be roughly 20% higher than listed. There are also a few "Rooms to Let"; ask at the bus station/*taverna* or other restaurants, or keep your eyes peeled for the ubiquitous signs.

It doesn't take much to figure out that fish is the local specialty. The main waterfront (turn left at the end of Nik. Mama) is lined with fish *taverna,* most of which serve a variety of species for 3000-10,000dr per kilo. If fish isn't your cup of tea, try the flower-embraced patio of **Restaurant Dervenis,** a block down the first right off Nik. Mama from the bus stop (*mousaka* 1000dr). But perhaps the best deal is a trip to either of the supermarkets on Nik. Mama, and then a swing through **To Konaki,** an excellent **sweet shop** next to the supermarket closest to the bus stop (scoop of ice cream 150dr, special soupy almond concoction 1800dr per kilo).

For wonderful swimming, head to the forest side of the harbor (over the "bridge" as you walk down Nik. Mama past Restaurant Steki), and walk all the way around. Small islands float offshore, and flooded caves overhang scant beaches. Rouse yourself from the beach to visit the nautical **Museum of Galaxidi** (tel. 41 086). Make a left off Nik. Mama opposite the Galaxidi Supermarket, walk a few blocks, and then turn right as you see the small church on your left. (Open Mon.-Tues. 9:30am-1:30pm, Wed.-Fri. 9:30am-2:30pm; admission 100dr.) The **Church of St. Nicholas,** near the museum, houses many fine mosaics. The 13th-century **Monastery of**

Transfiguration, with sublime 1000-year-old wood carvings and an encompassing view of town, is 6km from Galaxidi.

Many travelers continue from Galaxidi to **Nafpaktos,** close to the mouth of the Gulf and to the ferry crossing for the Peloponnese at **Antirion.** The **bus** to Nafpaktos runs out of Delphi, and stops in Galaxidi (2½hr. from Delphi, 2hr. from Galaxidi). If you stay, try the **Aegli** (tel. (0634) 27 271; singles 3500dr, doubles 6000dr).

■■■ THEBES (THIVA) ΘΗΒΑ

Thebes once ranked among the most powerful cities of ancient Greece. Its location gave it control over the strategic routes connecting the Peloponnese and Attica with northern Greece; its fertile soil cinched the town's prosperity. But the town is most famous as the setting for the story of Oedipus. Modern Thebes can't compete with its racy past. Razed by Alexander the Great in the 4th century BC, it has never recovered. It is a noisy, inelegant town, with little to see besides the museum. How interesting you find it depends entirely on whether you get an evocative kick from being at the scene of supposed mythical misdeeds.

Orientation and Practical Information The **OTE** is in the center of town (open Mon.-Fri. 7:30am-10pm). The **post office** is near the top of Epaminon street (open Mon.-Fri. 7:30am-2pm) and Thebes' new **bus station** is on Kiprou St., perpendicular to Epaminon. Follow signs to the town center for all other amenities. Bus service is frequent to Levadia (460dr) and the terminal at 260 Liossion St. in Athens (every hr., 1300dr). To travel to Chalkis, take the frequent Athens bus to the Skimatari stop (½hr., 400dr). Across the street, the Athens-Chalkis bus runs every ½hr. (10min, 300dr). For a **taxi,** call 29 788. **Postal Code:** 32200; **Telephone Code:** 0262.

Accommodations If you are obliged to spend the night here, the **Hotel Niovi,** 63 Epaminon St. (tel. 29 888), is your best bet. (Singles 4200dr, w/bath 5000dr; doubles 5500dr, w/bath 6500dr.) The more luxurious **Hotel Meletiou** (tel. 27 333) is across the street (singles 6000dr, doubles 9000dr; all w/bath). In the evening the many *tavernas* that line Epaminon and Pindari streets provide lively R&R for the neighboring military base.

Sights Follow Epaminon St. downhill, take a right, and on your left will be the **Archaeological Museum.** Be sure to see the Mycenaean *larnakes,* clay coffins adorned with paintings of funerary rites, mosaics, and reliefs. The guidebook is particularly informative. (Open Tues.-Sun. 8:30am-3pm; admission 400dr, students 200dr.) The scanty remains of the **House of Kadmos,** a Mycenaean palace dating from the 14th century BC, are visible from Pindarou St. Underneath the modern town of Thebes are an extensive Mycenaean **palace** and **acropolis.** Historians and archaeologists begrudge Thebes' every new building, fearing construction may endanger what little remains of the great Mycenaean civilization.

■■■ EVIA (EUBOEA) ΕΥΒΟΙΑ

Wrenched from the mainland by an ancient earthquake (or perhaps by Poseidon's trident), Evia grazes the coastline north of Athens. The second-largest island in Greece (after Crete), Evia was, in ancient times, a major trading center and maritime power. Although nowadays the local tourist committee likes to highlight Evia as a Greek island with frequent bus service from the mainland, it seems more like a part of Central Greece. Travelers may pass over the short wooden swingbridge at Chalkis and barely notice it. What *is* noticeable about Evia is its central mountain range choked with chestnuts and pines—paradise for hikers. Though several beaches are sprinkled around the coast of Evia, it has yet to be infested with too many swanky resorts. Few islanders speak English, but many speak German or French.

CHALKIDA (CHALKIS)

Bus travelers through Evia will almost inevitably encounter the suffocating port town of Chalkida. But spending time here may be not be as uneventful as you think. Aristotle was desperate because of his inability to comprehend what still may be the most interesting thing about Chalkida, the bizarre tidal flow through the straits between Evia and the mainland. Aristotle threw himself in the nearby Evia strait in a fit of anguish; please refrain from following in his footsplashes. Contemporary scientists can't fully explain why the water changes direction at the narrowest point between the two land masses—up to 6 times daily during full and near moons (1-4 times daily for the rest of the month).

The English-speaking **tourist police** (tel. 22 100) are located two flights above the police station at 32 El. Venizelou; they can help with bus schedules. (Open Mon.-Fri. 8am-2pm.) The **post office** is on Karamourzouni St., the second left off El. Venizelou as you walk uphill from the water. (Open Mon.-Fri. 7:30am-2pm.) The **OTE** is located on Papiadaiou St.—walk up El. Venizelou four full blocks from the water (two blocks after the park with the fountain), then make a left on Papiadaiou, continuing over for one block. (Open Mon.-Sat. 8am-7:30pm.) You can **change money** closer to the water at the **National Bank** (open Mon.-Thurs. 8am-2pm, Fri. 8am-1:30pm). The bus station in the center of town, at the top of the road that crosses the bridge, is a likely spot for the modern visitor to despair. A **bus** from Liossion Station in Athens goes to Chalkida (every ½hr., 1½hr., 1100dr); the **train** runs nearly as frequently from the Larissa station (18 per day, 2hr., 880dr). Arrival by train leaves you on the mainland; just cross the bridge to the island and the busier section of Chalkida. Roughly 5 blocks to the left of the bridge is El. Venizelou St., running uphill. If you get off at the bus depot, look for Papanastasiou, a wide, busy street, and turn right; walk down one block to El. Venizelou St. **Flying dolphins** now leave from the dock to the right of the bridge as you face the mainland. Purchase tickets to Limni, Aedipsos, and the Sporades at the shack on the waterfront just in line with the dock (tel. 21 521, -621). For **taxis,** dial 24 411. **Postal Code:** 34100; **Telephone Code:** 0221.

If you must spend the night, try **Hotel Kentrikon,** (tel. 22 375) on Ageli Gobiou St. near the square on the Evia side of the bridge. (Singles 5000dr, doubles 6000dr.) The true budget traveler must prefer to brave the rooms at **Hotel Kymata** (tel. 21 317), on the waterfront street on the left side of the square (facing the water). At least the rooms have high ceilings. (Singles 3000dr, doubles 4000dr.) This town is littered with overpriced food on the water, so you're better off roaming back streets. If you're bored while waiting for some transportation out of Chalkida, the **Archaeological Museum** (tel. 76 131), on El. Venizelou, has a decent collection. (Open Tues.-Sun. 8:30am-3pm; admission 500dr, students 300dr.)

ERETRIA

Modern-day Eretria rests languidly on the coast, still free from an overabundance of tourists. First inhabited between the 15th and 17th centuries BC, permanent occupation began in the 8th or 9th century BC. The town rivalled ancient Chalkis as the most important city on the island, its importance stemming from its convenient location for trade between Greece (and later Italy) and the Near East. In the 3rd century BC, Menedimos, the town's most famous son and a disciple of Plato's, founded a school of philosophy here. The Roman era saw a decline in Eretria's fortunes, and the town was only sporadically occupied from the 1st century AD onwards. More recently, the town's easy access from Chalkida (½hr. by bus) and from Oropos on the mainland (½hr. by ferry) has led to a moderate resurgence. It is one of the larger towns on the coast south of Chalkida.

Orientation and Practical Information The first, and more convenient, of the two bus stops, is at the lower end of the main commercial street, Menedimos. A little farther along, the same road leads to the **National Bank,** which **changes money** (open Mon.-Thurs. 8am-1:30pm, Fri. 8am-1pm). Two blocks up is the intersection with the town's other main road, Archaiou Theatrou. There is a map of town here, helpfully labelled in English and Greek. A left turn here brings you to the **post office** (open Mon.-Fri. 7:30am-8pm, Sat. 8:30am-2pm), which changes money, and at the end of the street, the Archaeological Museum, an extensive area of low-lying ruins, and the scant remains of the ancient theater. A right at the main intersection leads to the **OTE** (open Mon.-Fri. 8am-3pm), a few blocks down on the right, and then to a small square where the town's past and future meet—fenced ruins are overlooked by the bright lights and whizzing bumper cars of an amusement park. Continuing straight ahead, you'll find one wing of the town's waterfront, lined with *tavernas* and, eventually, the town's few hotels. A right down the other waterfront road yields more *tavernas* and the ferry dock for boats to Oropos. Eretria is accessible by **bus** from Chalkida because everything heading south to Karystos, Kimi, or Amarinthos swings through here (roughly every ½hr., 30min., 320dr). There is also a **ferry** from Oropos on the mainland (every ½hr. 5am-9pm and hourly until 11:45pm, 30min., 270dr). **Taxis** can be found by the water or by calling 62 500. **Postal Code:** 34008; **Telephone Code:** 0221.

Accommodations There are few places to stay in Eretria, and the hotels are mostly on the exorbitant side, catering to package tours. **Pension Diamanto** (tel. 62 214) has rooms w/bath and A/C above the Babylon Café, along the waterfront stretch of Archaiou Theatrou St. (doubles 8000dr, triples 10,000dr). Farther down the same street, turn left at the sign and walk 200m inland for the beautiful modern apartments (all w/kitchen, fridge, and bath) of the **Eretria Sun Rise Hotel** (tel. 60 004; fax 60 648). Sadly enough for the budget traveler, this hotel is one of the better deals in town. (Doubles 11,000dr, triples 14,000dr.) Ask at *tavernas* for rooms.

Food and Entertainment Your culinary needs (and wallets) are best served by avoiding the waterfront places and heading inland. The nameless *taverna* near the post office has stuffed tomatoes for 600dr. After dinner, life centers around the waterfront. For dessert, try the large **sweet shop** on Archaiou Theatrou St. (ice cream 100dr per scoop); for some nightlife, pick the crowd and ambience you like best; most places serve beer for 500dr, cocktails for 1000dr.

Sights Still, the best reason to come to Eretria is its history. The **Archaeological Museum** (tel. 62 206) is at the inland end of Archaiou Theatrou St. It's not the biggest collection around, but there are some quality pieces, such as a gorgeous terra cotta Gorgun's head from the 4th century BC, and the mysteriously six-fingered Centaur of Lefkandi, which dates from 750-900 BC. (Open Tues.-Sun. 8:30am-3pm; admission 500dr, students 300dr.) Beyond the museum is a large excavated area of the old city. Although there is nothing particularly spectacular here, it's kind of cool to simply wander in (there is no gate to the fence which surrounds the site) and let your imagination roam. The ancient theater is behind the excavations, but it is less well-preserved and the entrance is barred by a fence. Far more amazing than either of these is the creatively-named **House with the Mosaics.** You must find someone at the museum to bring you to the site (300m away) and unlock it, but it's definitely worth it. The four mosaics in two separate rooms are among the best preserved and most ancient (4th century BC) of all Greek mosaics. Because of their age and importance, they are enclosed in a room which visitors can't enter without special permission, but the glass walls afford a good view. The Swiss School of Archaeology in Greece has put out a brochure (in Greek, English, French, and German) which explains the history of the house (available from the museum for 1000dr). There are no set hours when the House is open or closed, but since the key must be obtained from the Archaeological Museum, it is *de facto* open Tues.-Sun. 8:30am-3pm (free).

KARYSTOS

Surrounded by mountains and flanked by two long sandy beaches, Karystos, which takes its name from the son of the centaur Chiron, is easygoing despite being the largest town in South Evia. Pointed round straw umbrellas, like the mushrooms in *Fantasia,* dot the sands that extend in either direction from the port. Although it's not likely to be the next Mykonos, this town has promise.

Orientation and Practical Information The bus stops one block above the main square, next to the **National Bank** (open Mon.-Thurs. 8am-2pm, Fri. 8am-1:30pm); look for the KTEL sign above a restaurant roasting chickens in the window. To find the **police station** (tel. 22 252), turn into the small alley past the bank and climb the stairs. The **OTE** (open daily 7:30am-3pm) is on Amerikis, the next cross-street beyond the square, across from the bright blue-domed Church of St. Nicholas. To reach the **post office** from the OTE, turn left on Amerikis and then take the first right past the playgrounds; you'll see the round yellow sign (open Mon.-Fri. 7:30am-2pm). **Buses** from Karystos travel twice daily to Chalkis (4hr., 1700dr) and Stira (1¼hr., 500dr), and thrice daily to the slightly crowded resort town of Marmari (30min., 250dr). Two **ferries** per day head to Rafina (2hr., 1400dr) and Marmari (1½hr., 800dr). In Karystos, ferry tickets are sold at the tourist office of **South Evia Tours** (tel. 24 277; fax 22 461), on the left of the square as you face the water (open 8am-10pm). **Flying dolphins** go thrice weekly to the Cyclades islands of Andros (4512dr), Tinos (8068dr), and Mykonos (9768dr). **Taxis** (tel. 22 200) queue in the square. **Postal Code:** 34001; **Telephone Code:** 0224.

Accommodations The **tourist office,** on the left-hand side of the square (facing the waterfront) helps find rooms and decipher ferry schedules. Look for "Rooms to Let" signs at restaurants on the dock. **George and Bill Kolobaris,** 42 Sahtouri St. (tel. 22 071), offer cozy rooms and boundless hospitality. George may pick you up on his motorbike and sing to you on the way to his pension. (Doubles 5000dr; includes hot water and use of kitchen.) A left turn at the waterfront leads to the cheap, if unenthralling, rooms of the **Hironia Hotel** (tel. 22 238 or 23 973; singles 4000dr, doubles 6000dr). Carry on along the waterfront (200m) to the more luxurious rooms of **Hotel Karystion** (tel. 22 391; fax 22 727). The proprietor, the amiable Charis Mitros, is the president of the local Tourist Association and a good source of info about the area; he also speaks fluent English. (Doubles w/bath and breakfast 10,000dr for the pleasing views, 9000dr if you want your balcony facing the town.)

Food and Entertainment The octopi lined up and drying in the sun give fair warning of the town's favorite food. Find incomparable food and prices at **Kabontoros,** one block inland on Parodos Sachtouri St., the alleyway a half block right of the main square. (Sautéed green beans in olive oil with a side sauce of puréed garlic, 800dr.) If you want to try somewhere else, walk past the touristy crowds in the *tavernas* and pizzerias lining the waterfront to the very end of the strip (on the far right facing the water) until you come to the all-Greek crowd at **Kalamia** (tel. 22 223; stuffed tomatoes 650dr). If you're not stuffed after your meal, skip down the alleyway off Parodos Sachtouri St. to the water and find **Tsimis' sweet shop.**

Various seaside pubs and cafés are popular day and night. **Archipelagos,** on the beach at the right edge of town, offers beer for 500dr. The view and heady sea air here may tempt you to linger. For serious dancing, head to the **Barbados Disco** (tel. 24 119), 3km from town towards the mountains. The 1300dr cover includes your first drink. A cab will run 500dr, probably more after midnight.

Sights To inspect the interior of the coastal **Fort of Bourtzi,** which dates from the Crusades, ask at the tourist office. (Fort open for 2hr. in the morning, July-Aug., Mon. and Wed.-Fri.) Otherwise, peek into one of the holes at the back of the fort (from which boiling oil was poured on attackers) to imagine life in the 1100s. If you're lucky, you may catch a summer student theatrical production inside. There is a **Folklore Museum** on Sachtouri St., the first street parallel to the waterfront, several blocks to the right of the main square, opposite the ruins of a **Temple of**

Apollo. At the other end of town, past the fort, an **Archaeological Museum** should be open by 1996, in the waterfront building which houses the library.

If you have a free morning, explore the villages north of Karystos. Follow Aiolou St., one block east of the square, out of town; continue straight at the crossroads toward **Palio Chora,** a village that dawdles among lemon and olive groves. For a more strenuous walk, turn right at the crossroads outside Karystos and go towards the village of **Mili.** The road ascends sharply and follows a clear stream to the village, where water flows from the mouths of three lions in a small roadside fountain. From Mili, a 20-min. hike up the hill on the left and across the stone bridge leads to **Kokkino Kastro** (the Red Castle), a 13th-century Venetian castle named for the blood that was spilled there during the war between the Greeks and the Turks. The village of **Agia Triada** is also worth a trek; take a left at the crossroads and walk to this shady valley that features two small, rustic churches under gnarled trees.

For more extensive hiking, climb Evia's second-highest mountain, **Mt. Ochi** (1398m), where Zeus and Hera supposedly fell in love. It's located in the heart of the placid south area. The stone refuge hut on the mountain is a 3-4-hr. hike from Karystos. Some claim that the refuge, made of unmortared stone blocks during the Pelasgian Period, was a temple to Hera; others believe it was a signal tower. The ruin is known as the "dragon's house," and it's allegedly haunted.

KIMI

With an abundance of foliage and cool, tangy sea breezes, Kimi offers a refreshing respite from the parched Greek summer. Dubbed "the balcony of the Aegean" because of its perch 250m over the water, Kimi was once a major harbor renowned for its fishing, figs, and fine wine. But 30 years ago, disease destroyed all the vineyards and the population dropped from 30,000 to 10,000.

Orientation and Practical Information Kimi has two main parts: Kimi Town, built atop a hill, overlooks its port Paralia Kimi, on the waterfront 4km away. To reach the main square of Kimi Town from the bus station, make a right as you exit the station and turn left up the steep hill. At the crest of the hill is the main drag; a right from here leads to a plaza around the town church. Across from the church is the **National Bank** (open Mon.-Thurs. 8am-2pm, Fri. 8am-1:30pm), and one block above the church is the **post office** (open Mon.-Fri. 7:30am-2pm). The **OTE** is one block below the church on the right. (Open Mon.-Fri. 7:30am-3:10pm.) The **police** (tel. 22 555) are two blocks behind the church, but it's easiest to reach them by continuing straight on the road up from the bus station, following it as it bends downhill and to the right. Entrance to the yellow building is on the downhill side (24 hr.). The road leading down to Paralia Kimi begins at the corner, just before the post office, also where the bus stops. The Georgios Papanicolaou **hospital/clinic** (tel. 22 322), which houses Kimi's **health center** (tel. 23 252, -3), is located 3km from the station. To get there, head north from the station, make a right on the first main road, and follow it uphill until you reach the hospital. Although most buses stop at Paralia Kimi, some linger first at the bus depot in Kimi Town. To get to the beach/port from town, wait at the station or the stop by the post office on the main square. **Buses** run to Kimi directly from 260 Liossion St. in Athens (6 per day, 3½hr., 2400dr) and from Chalkis (8 per day, 2¼hr., 1350dr). From Karystos, take the bus to Lepoura for a magnificent tour of the mountainside (2 per day, 2½hr., 1000dr) and transfer from Lepoura to Kimi (3 per day, 1hr., 550dr). For further info, call Kimi's bus station at 22 257. Buses negotiate the 52 twisting turns to Paralia Kimi and back 3 times daily (180dr). The 5km downhill walk affords glorious views, but keep an eye out for traffic. Two agents in Paralia Kimi sell **ferry** tickets. To the left of the road descending from Kimi Town, next to the Sosco gas station, is the agent for ferries (tel. 22 601) to Skopelos (4hr., 4102dr) and Alonissos (3hr., 3780dr). In July and August, the ferry runs twice a week. To the right of the road descending from Kimi Town, in the blue and white striped building 75m down, is the agent for **Likomedes** (tel. 22 020, -522; open 8:30am-1:30pm and 5-9pm). This vessel serves Skyros exclusively (2-3 per day,

2hr., 1820dr). Buy tickets at the small shack on the dock. **Flying dolphins,** handled by the agent 20m up the road to Kimi, go to Skiathos (9330dr), Skopelos (8391dr), Alonissos (7797dr), Marmaris (13,239dr), Skyros (4002dr), and Ag. Ioannis on the mainland (9955dr). A **taxi** (tel. 23 666 in Kimi Town, 23 255 in Paralia Kimi) costs roughly 700dr between the two. Buses returning to Chalkis or Athens leave Paralia Kimi 10min. before their scheduled departure from Kimi Town. **Postal Code:** 34003; **Telephone Code:** 0222.

Accommodations Because there is no public transportation to the north coast's beaches (and because the *meltems* wind batters it in July and August), Kimi is more popular as a jumping off point to the Sporadic Islands than as a place to spend much time. Hotel proprietors are well aware of this, so prices are high. In Paralia Kimi, the hydrofoil agent (tel. 23 722), 20m up the road to Kimi Town, has modern rooms (doubles w/bath 7000dr). **Hotel Beis** (tel. 22 604), at the left of the waterfront facing the water, has many more rooms (doubles w/bath 8000dr).

Food Restaurants and cafés line the harbor at Paralia Kimi. On the south side of the waterfront, you'll find decent meals at **To Aigaio** (spaghetti with meat sauce 850dr). For a quick and inexpensive meal in Kimi Town, go past the post office to **Pikantiki Restaurant** (spaghetti 600dr). Otherwise, you'll have to find sustenance at *souvlaki* stands, or the **supermarket** (which has a good deli counter) down the main road past the OTE. You'll find fresh produce on the street behind the church.

Sights A small whitewashed seafarer's chapel and the ruins of a windmill are poised on the hill behind town. A climb to either affords tremendous views of Kimi and the sea. On the east side of the same mountain, 5km from Kimi, is the 700-year-old, majestically situated **Monastery of the Savior.** When pirates landed at Kimi in the late 18th and 19th centuries, signals calling for aid were sent from the **Venetian Castle** above the monastery and passed along to other castles. Voyeurs might enjoy the **Folklore Museum** (tel. 22 011) on the road descending to Paralia Kimi. They have a collection of traditional women's undergarments (we've come a long way, baby!) and an exhibit dedicated to Kimi's most famous son—**Georgios Papanicolaou,** inventor of the Pap smear. (Open daily 10am-1pm and 6-8:30pm; admission 400dr.) A 10-min. walk to the left (facing the water) from the ferry landing in Paralia Kimi leads to a public beach where you can perfect your island tan before traveling.

LIMNI

According to legend, Zeus married Hera in Limni. An infelicitous earthquake destroyed the wedding temple long ago, but today, Limni, a lively port town, nonetheless has much to offer. Activity centers on the long waterfront stretch that looks on rickety, bobbing rowboats and neon windsurfers. Adjacent to a rocky beach and connected by bus and hydrofoil to surrounding towns, Limni makes a pleasant base for exploring Northern Evia. As tourists are few and transient, there are only a few hotels, so call for reservations, especially on weekends.

Buses drop off at the center of the waterfront, next to the **bank.** (Open Mon.-Thurs. 8am-2pm, Fri. 8am-1:30pm.) The **post office** (open Mon.-Fri. 7:30am-2pm) is in the little square just off the waterfront, up the street from the bank. On the same street past the square on the left is the **flying dolphin agency** (a man in a pastry shop; tel. 31 254). To find the **OTE,** walk down to the far left of the waterfront, walk uphill two blocks, and look for the blue sign. (Open Mon.-Fri. 7:30am-3:10pm.) **Postal Code:** 34005; **Telephone Code:** 0227.

Buses run from Chalkis to Limni (4 per day, 2hr., 1200dr). There is also bus service to Aedipsos (½hr., 400dr) with connections to Istea (½hr., 260dr) and Pefki (15min., 140dr). **Flying dolphins** run from Chalkis to Limni and continue on to Aedipsos (3 per day). Others run from Agios Konstantinos (4 per day) and the Sporadic islands. All have extra connections in high season.

If you plan your stay in advance, make reservations at the **Plaza Hotel** (tel. 31 235), whose lovable rooms are filled with antiques (doubles 6500dr). A larger, more impersonal option is **Hotel Limni** (tel. 31 378, -16). The clean, spacious rooms have private baths. (Open Mar.-Nov. and for special occasions off-season; doubles 7000dr; breakfast 600dr.) Both are on the waterfront.

Nights are cool in Limni, but most people still choose to dine by the water. Go for a slow stroll (*volta*) before you munch on something in a waterfront *taverna, ouzerie,* or sweetshop. Kicklines of severed octopus legs and other exotic catches hanging on racks by the tables signal fresh seafood. You can find clear-water bathing on a rocky beach just past the far right-hand end of the waterfront.

AEDIPSOS

The village of Aedipsos, 30km northwest of Limni, is one of the largest resorts in Evia. Praised by Herodotus, Aristotle, and Aristophanes for its healing sulphurous waters, Aedipsos attracts older tourists who suffer from arthritis and rheumatism, but is worth a daytrip for anyone who wishes to enjoy the hot springs' relaxing vibes. Aedipsos is also an attractive town in itself; with a café-lined waterfront shaded by trees, it has a more rustic feeling than most resort towns. Locals advise that you swim no longer than ½hr., as hours of bathing will leave you in a therapeutic stupor. The bus drops off in a small square at Ermou St., from which you will be able to see the waterfront. The **hot springs** are in a large complex on a road heading inland from the left end of the waterfront (facing the water) 200m past the post office. A variety of specialized pools and equipment is available. If you prefer a more scenic spot to swelter, walk through the park across the street and go down to the beach where the hot springs flow to the sea.

The **tourist police** on the first floor of 3 Oceanidon St. (tel. 22 456) might be of some help. Facing the water from the town square, take a right onto Ermou St., then your first left. The **OTE** is hidden behind a black gate and a garden in the square (open Mon.-Fri. 7:30am-3pm). The **post office** (open 6:30am-12:30pm and 5-6:30pm), which exchanges money, is on 25th Martiou, a left (facing the water) turn away from the water at the left end of the waterfront (open Mon.-Fri. 7:30am-8pm). **Buses** run between Athens and Aedipsos (3 per day, 3¼hr., 2200dr) and between Aedipsos and Limni (30min., 400dr). **Flying dolphins** connect Aedipsos with Limni, Chalkida, and the Sporades. The hydrofoil agent can be found in the center of the waterfront (tel. 23 760). There are plenty of hotels in Aedipsos. **Hotel Aigli** (tel. 22 215) on the waterfront corner of Ermou, has some of the more affordable rooms (doubles 7500dr). Otherwise, especially in the high season, try the cheaper "Rooms to Let" along Ermou St. and 25th Martiou St. (doubles 5000-8000dr).

Peloponnese ΠΕΛΟΠΟΝΝΗΣΟΣ

Separated from the rest of the mainland by the Corinth Canal, the Peloponnese is a fertile hand-shaped plain that unites human achievement and natural beauty. The ancient theater at Epidavros, the shell of a medieval city at Mystra, Agamemnon's palace at Mycenae, and the site of the first Olympic games, Olympia, are impressive architectural and artistic masterpieces. Beyond these massive ruins, however, the Peloponnese's rocky mountains conceal undeveloped sandy beaches and wondrous mountain villages such as Dimitsana and Stemnitsa.

CORINTHIA AND ARGOLIS ΚΟΡΙΝΘΙΑ ΚΑΙ ΑΡΓΟΛΙΔΑ

Argos—a grotesque beast covered with 100 unblinking eyes—once stalked vast stretches of the north Peloponnese, subduing unruly satyrs and burly bulls. Today's Argolis and Corinthia hold impressive monuments produced during the Peloponnese's 3,500-year-history. In summer, try to visit the sites at Mycenae, Corinth, Tiryns, and Epidavros early in the day, before tour groups arrive and the heat soars. Nauplion is a good place to base yourself as you visit the nearby ruins.

■■■ NEW CORINTH ΚΟΡΙΝΘΟΣ

New Corinth sits squat and square across from the Gulf of Corinth just west of the Corinth Canal. Not to be confused with its ancient predecessor, Corinth's dusty, noisy, industrial façade manages to retain some charm. The city boasts an attractive park in the center of town, a relaxing waterfront, and a cosmopolitan atmosphere. The victim of serious earthquakes in 1858, 1928, and most recently in 1986, Corinth now issues building permits for only the most shatterproof structures, which makes the city secure, albeit uninspiring. Tourist police warn that women should not walk alone in poorly lit areas after midnight.

ORIENTATION AND PRACTICAL INFORMATION

You'll find everything you need near the park. The main drag, **Ethnikis Antistasis Street,** borders the park and runs to the sea. **Ermou Street** runs parallel to Ethnikis Antistasis and bounds the park on the other side. **Kolokotroni Street** runs along the city's eastern side, parallel to Ethnikis Antistasis. The station for **buses to Athens** and the vicinity lies at the corner of Ermou and Koliatsou on the park. The other **bus station,** serving the rest of the Peloponnese, is one block past the park at Aratou and Ethnikis Antistasis. To reach the main park from the train station, walk ½ block up Demokratias, turn right on Dimaskinou, then left on Ermou several blocks later.

Police: 51 Ermou St. (tel. 22 143). Faces the park, near the bus station. Open 24 hr. but travelers may be better off dealing with the English-speaking **tourist police** housed in same building (tel. 23 282; open daily 7:30am-10pm).

Post Office: (tel. 22 015), on Adimantou St., which borders the park on the end farthest from the water. Open Mon.-Fri. 7:30am-2pm. **Postal Code:** 20100.

OTE: 32 Kolokotroni St. (tel. 22 111). Open daily 7am-10pm; collect calls Mon.-Fri. 7am-10pm. **Telephone Code:** 0741.

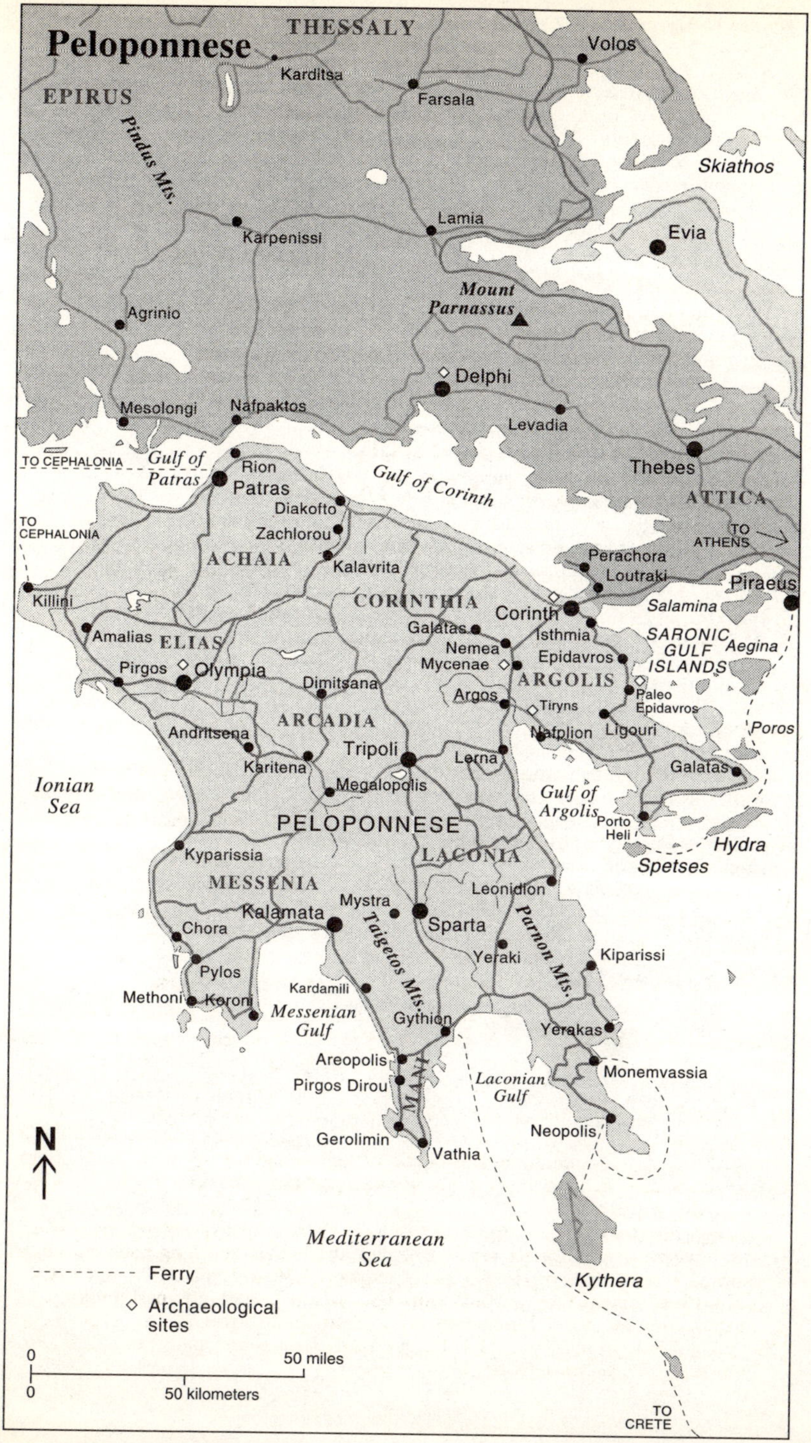
Peloponnese
THESSALY
EPIRUS
Pindus Mts.
Karditsa
Farsala
Volos
Skiathos
Karpenissi
Lamia
Evia
Mount Parnassus
Agrinio
Delphi
Mesolongi
Nafpaktos
Levadia
Thebes
ATTICA
TO CEPHALONIA
Gulf of Patras
Rion
Patras
Gulf of Corinth
Diakofto
Zachlorou
TO CEPHALONIA
ACHAIA
Kalavrita
TO ATHENS
Perachora
Loutraki
Piraeus
Killini
CORINTHIA
Corinth
Salamina
Amalias
ELIAS
Galatas
Isthmia
SARONIC GULF ISLANDS
Aegina
Nemea
Mycenae
Epidavros
Pirgos
Olympia
ARGOLIS
Dimitsana
Argos
Tiryns
Paleo Epidavros
ARCADIA
Nafplion
Ligouri
Poros
Andritsena
Tripoli
Karitena
Lerna
Galatas
Ionian Sea
Megalopolis
Gulf of Argolis
Porto Heli
PELOPONNESE
Hydra
Kyparissia
LACONIA
Spetses
MESSENIA
Leonidion
Mystra
Kalamata
Sparta
Chora
Parnon Mts.
Taigetos Mts.
Yeraki
Kiparissi
Pylos
Kardamili
Methoni
Koroni
Messenian Gulf
Gythion
Yerakas
Areopolis
MANI
Monemvassia
Laconian Gulf
Pirgos Dirou
Neopolis
Gerolimin
Vathia
N
Mediterranean Sea
Kythera
Ferry
Archaeological sites
0
50 miles
0
50 kilometers
TO CRETE

Banks: National Bank, 7 Ethnikis Anastisis St. (tel. 24 149), on the corner of the first block in from the water offers **currency exchange.** Open Mon.-Thurs. 8am-2pm, Fri. 8am-1:30pm. Other banks scattered in the area.

Trains: Demokratias St. (tel. 22 522). Trains run to Athens (14 per day, 2hr., 800dr) via Isthmia. Two major train lines serve the Peloponnese: one along the northern coast from Corinth to Pirgos and south to Kyparissia; the other south from Corinth to Tripolis and Kalamata. Almost all major coastal cities in the Peloponnese can be reached by train from Corinth. Trains go to Patras (9 per day, 8am-8pm, 2hr., 980dr), Pirgos (5 per day, 8am-7pm, 4hr., 1640dr), Olympia (4 per day, 5hr., 1780dr), Argos (5 per day, 1hr., 510dr), Tripolis (3 per day, 2hr., 900dr), Kalamata (3 per day, 5½hr., 1640dr), Lefktro (3 per day, 3hr., 1140dr), Kyparissia (4 per day, 5hr., 2050dr), and Kalavryta (6 per day, 1½hr., 900dr). Express trains can cost 400-1000dr extra. 25% off for round-trips. **Luggage storage** costs 250dr per piece per day. Trains from Athens to Patras may be full, so be prepared to wait or take the bus.

Buses: Ermou and Koliatsou Station (tel. 25 645). Buses run until 10:10pm. Buses to Ancient Corinth (every hr., 6am-9pm, 20min., 175dr), Athens (every ½hr., 5:30am-9:30pm, 1¼hr., 1250dr), Loutraki (every ½hr., 6am-10pm, 20min., 220dr), Isthmia (5 per day, 20min., 175dr), and Nemea (7 per day, 1hr., 650dr). **Ethnikis Antistasis and Aratou Station** (tel. 24 403) runs a bus to Mycenae (hourly, 1hr., 600dr), Argos (hourly, 1½hr., 750dr), and Nauplion (2hr., 950dr); it leaves at 7:15am and every hr. 8:30am-9:30pm. Note that the bus to Mycenae drops passengers at Fichtia, a 1½-km walk from the site (see Mycenae below). To catch a bus to Sparta and other southern locations on the Peloponnese, take the Loutraki bus to the Corinth Canal and pick up buses coming from Athens to Sparta (7 per day), Kalamata (10 per day), Koroni, and Tripoli.

Taxis: (tel. 24 844 or 26 900). Along the park side of Ethnikis Antistasis St.

Car Rental: Gregoris Lagos, 42 Ethnikis Antistasis St. (tel. 22 617). Across the street from the moped rental. Prices start at 6500dr per day up to 100km, 50dr per additional km. Minimum age 21. Open daily 8am-1pm, 4:30-9pm.

Moped Rental: Liberopoulos, 27 Ethnikis St. (tel. 72 937 or 21 847). Past the park, heading inland. Mopeds 3500-4000dr per day, 17,000dr per week. Open daily 8am-1:30pm, 5-9pm.

Laundromat: 49 Adimantou St. (tel. 22 247). Across from OTE and 77 Koliatsou St. Walk through the park and head toward the water. Cheaper rates if you don't want clothes ironed, so specify.

Public Toilets: Across from the park on Ethnikis Anastasis St. Avoid these like the plague, which they may well house. But if you've gotta go, they're free.

Pharmacy: 27 Ethnikis Anastasis St. (tel. 24 213). Open Mon. and Wed. 8am-2pm, Tues. and Thurs.-Fri. 8am-2pm and 5-9pm. Many others on Koliatsou St.

Hospital: Athinaion St. (tel. 25 711). Inland past the train station, bear left. 24 hr.

ACCOMMODATIONS

Most hotels in Corinth are clustered near the waterfront and the railroad station, conveniently located near the ancient sites.

Ephira Hotel, 52 Ethnikis Antistasis St. (tel. 24 021). Two blocks inland from the park. Spacious rooms, ceiling fans, private baths, daily maid service. Singles 6000dr, doubles 8000dr, triples 9500dr. Continental breakfast 1000dr.

Hotel Acti, 3 Ethnikis Antistasis St. (tel. 23 337). Near the waterfront. Tiny, tidy rooms. Singles 3500dr, doubles 5000dr.

Blue Dolphin Campground (tel. 25 766) is 3km from Ancient Corinth, right on the beach. 1050dr per person, small tent 750dr, large tent 850dr, 600dr per car, electricity 600dr.

Camping Korinth Beach (tel. 27 969 or 29 057), down the road from the Blue Dolphin Campground. 700dr per person, 500dr per tent. To get to either campground, take the bus to Ancient Corinth and get out at the bottom of the hill.

FOOD AND ENTERTAINMENT

Fast food joints and pizza places crowd the waterfront and the sidewalks near the park. **Kentriko,** on Ethnikis Anistasis St., is extremely popular among the locals (*gyro* 280dr). In the center of the waterfront is the **Hambo** (club sandwich and fries 650dr). If atmosphere is what you crave, try **Kanita,** a lively *taverna* frequented by travelers. (Greek salads 700dr, entrees 850-1500dr.)

Summer weekends are filled with music, dance, and car races along the harbor front. There's a well-stocked **supermarket** (open Mon.-Fri. 8am-1:30pm, 5-9pm) at 57 Adimantou St. near the bus stations.

SIGHTS

If you spend the day in town rather than at the ruins, you may want to amble on out to the **Folklore Museum,** housed in a modern white building next to the waterfront at the end of Ermou St. (open daily 8am-1pm; free). The **Apollon cinema** on Koliatsou St. shows films of all genres, from *101 Dalmatians* to *Eat Drink Man Woman*. The town **beaches** to the west are rocky, seaweed-strewn, and crowded, and while the water is clean, the beaches themselves are cluttered with litter. Or littered with clutter. Whichever it is, they're messy.

■■■ ANCIENT CORINTH

Strategically based on both the Corinthian and Saronic Gulfs, the ancient city was a powerful commercial and maritime center and one of the most influential cities in ancient Greece. Corinth, which was allied with Sparta, reached the apex of its power in the 5th century BC, but the increase in Athenian naval power led to an inevitable clash. The conflict became the chief cause of the Peloponnesian War, from which the Corinthians, with Sparta, emerged victorious. Nonetheless, Ancient Corinth was greatly weakened and Sparta alone became the leading Greek city. Eventually the city was conquered by the Romans, who exterminated the city's population in 146 BC. Corinth remained deserted and its treasures were sold in the Roman markets until Julius Caesar repopulated the city as a colony in 44 BC. Much to the dismay of St. Paul, who preached here in 51 AD, this decadent band of Corinthians raged on, worshipping Aphrodite.

Orientation And Practical Information Enveloping ruins that have seen eons pass, the village of Ancient Corinth offers the peace and serenity that its modern counterpart lacks. The passage of time here slows to a trickle, and days languish endlessly. **Taxis** will take you up for the steep price of 1200dr. **Buses** travel from Modern Corinth to Ancient Corinth at the mountain's base every hour, returning every ½hr. (½hr., 175dr). The **post office** (open 7:30am-2pm), along the road to Modern Corinth, offers **currency exchange. Telephone Code:** 0741.

Accommodations Anceint Corinth's pensions are a great alternative to the bustling hotels in the new city. At **Rooms Marinos** (tel. 31 209 or 31 180) Papa Spiros and Mama Elisabeth run a peerless, extended-family-style establishment with a huge yard where their three screaming, perpetually happy grandchildren play. They serve excellent home-cooked meals in enormous portions, complete with Mama's own honey-laden desserts. Rooms have been recently renovated. To get here, go right at the fork behind the bus stop (away from the entrance to the ruins), walk along Sisyphos St., and turn right, uphill, at the sign for Argos. Singles 5000dr, doubles 8500dr, triples 11,500dr (breakfast included). **Shadow Rooms** (tel. 31 481) and its downstairs *taverna,* near the end of the village towards the highway is a wonderful place to spend the night. The new pale pink rooms are sparkling clean and have private bathrooms with shower (singles 4500dr, doubles 7500dr, triples 9000dr). Four km above the city, the Acrocorinth is open around the clock. Some bring sleeping bags and spend the night, but *Let's Go* does not recommend it.

Food The *taverna*, near Shadow Rooms, has breakfast for 1000dr; lunch and dinner entrees cost 700-2500dr. At the site, you can eat at the **Acrocorinthos Restaurant,** (tel. 31 503 or 31 099) ledged on top of the mountain. (Open daily 9am-10pm; *souvlaki* 1350dr, *mousaka* 100dr.) **O Tassos** (tel. 31 225) is a delightful *taverna* on the road to modern Corinth (superb *mousaka* 900dr), after the post office.

Sights The remains of the ancient city stand near the base of the Acrocorinth. This is where the **Ministry of Culture Archaeological Museum** (tel. 31 207) and **archaeological site** are located. Columns, metopes, and pediments, apparently spread by a whimsical Fury, lie in fascinating chaos in the museum's courtyard. Facing the museum, the Corinthian columns on your left are the façade of a Roman shrine. Pick up Nikos Papahatzis' guidebook, *Ancient Corinth*, at the museum entrance if you missed it at the ticket counter (1700dr). The museum, erected in memory of Ed Alonzo Small ("a scholar who delighted in the culture of Hellas"), houses a wonderful collection of statues, Byzantine glass and pottery, well-preserved mosaics, and tiny clay figurines. Its collections of sarcophagi (one with a skeleton under glass) and headless statues in the green, open-air courtyard are impressive and eerie. The **Asclepion Room** off the inner courtyard displays a collection of votive offerings from the sick to the god of medicine: misshapen phalluses, sore ears, and wart-afflicted hands.

As you exit the museum, to your left stands the archaeological site including the remains of the 6th-century BC **Temple of Apollo.** Behind the museum is the **Fountain of Glauke,** named after Jason's second wife who drowned herself while trying to douse the flames that sprouted from an enchanted shirt given to her by the vengeance-minded Medea, Jason's first wife. In the middle of the row of central shops, you'll see the **bema** on the right, a dais from which the Romans made announcements and official proclamations; it was later converted into a Greek, then Catholic church. Ahead is the **Julian Basilica.** To the left a broad stone stair descends into the **Peirene Fountain.** This is where the Ancients say winged Pegasus was drinking when he was captured by Bellerophon. Crawl into the tunnels behind the fountain for a cool, if somewhat damp, break. Just past the fountain is the **Perivolos of Apollo,** an open-air court surrounded by partially restored columns. Near the Perivolos is the **public latrine.** These were only for men, the most outgoing of whom used to sit next to each other and chat. (Site and museum open daily 8am-7pm, Sept.-June 8:45am-3pm; admission to both 1200dr, students 600dr; free on Sun.)

Built on the lower of the Acrocorinth's twin peaks, the **fortress** has foundations dating back to ancient times. The upper summit originally held a **Temple to Aphrodite,** which was served by 1000 "sacred courtesans" who initiated free-wheeling disciples into the "mysteries of love." The breezy and surprisingly intact remains are a medievalist's fantasy. Relatively tourist-free, the fortress contains acres of towers, mosques, gates, and walls. From atop this mountain on a clear day, you can see far enough to verify your mapmaker's rendition of the northeast Peloponnese and the Corinthian and Saronic Gulfs. Until roughly 20 years ago you could see all the way to the Acropolis of Athens; now you can see the pollution in between.

In early July, Ancient Corinth celebrates Agioi Anargyroi, its most important **summer festival,** commemorating the physicians Saint Kosmos and Saint Damian.

■ NEAR CORINTH

ISTHMIA

Ancient Greek jocks used to gather in Isthmia and Nemea to compete in the Pan-Hellenic Games, drink beer, and slap each other's backsides. Pindar preserves the memory of these games in his odes honoring the victors. Take the bus from Corinth heading toward Isthmia, and ask to be let out at the **museum,** a green building up and on the right of the road from the bus stop. The carefully diagramed exhibits display finds from the Temple of Poseidon and the sites of the Isthmean games. Of particular interest are the glass *opus sectile* (mosaic panels), discovered at nearby

Kenchreai which managed to survive the earthquake of 375 AD. They depict plants, birds, humans, and the city's ancient harbors. The entrance to the ruins lies to the right of the museum. All that remains of the **Temple of Poseidon** is its despoiled foundation. The **theater** is below and farther to the right of the temple. **Cult caves,** where many people enjoyed dinner and entertainment during the Archaic Period, lie above the theater. (Museum and site open Tues.-Sat. 8:45am-7pm, off season 8:45am-3pm, Sun. 9:30am-2:30pm, closed holidays.) **Telephone Code:** 0741.

NEMEA

Pausanias wrote in the 2nd-century AD edition of *Let's Go: Nemea*, "Here is a temple of Nemean Zeus worth seeing although the roof has fallen in and the cult statue is missing." Were he to visit it today, he might be peeved that the temple has dwindled to three columns. The walkway takes you past a wall built around a glass-encased grave, complete with skeleton. Don't miss the well-preserved **baths.** The **stadium** is 500m down the road to Corinth. The well-organized **museum** on the site (tel. (0746) 22 739) has excellent explanatory notes in English, some artifacts, and several reconstructions of the site. (Museum and site open Tues.-Sun. 8:30am-7pm. Off-season Tues.-Sat. 8:30am-3pm. Admission 500dr, students 300dr.) The ruins of Ancient Nemea are 4km from Modern Nemea, so if you are coming by bus from Corinth, ask to be let off at the ancient site (1hr., 650dr). **Telephone Code:** 0746.

LOUTRAKI

The name, oddly enough, may seem familiar. Much of the bottled water (½liter, 70dr) you'll be clutching during your travels gushes from Loutraki's sweet wells, but Loutraki hardly springs to mind as an ideal Mediterranean vacation spot. A clean, friendly, non-touristy little city, Loutraki rests across the crescent-shaped bay from Corinth, a 20-min. bus ride (220dr). If you're visiting Corinth, you might want to stop by and tap the source of the town's allure. Stroll along the white stone boardwalk that flanks the body-blanketed beach, shadowed by the **Yerania Mountains** that rise abruptly above the city. The main street is El. Venizelou, which runs parallel to the water, curves at the port, and becomes Georgiou Lekka St.

Orientation and Practical Information To get to Loutraki from Isthmia, cross the canal bridge; the bus stop is next to a railroad station sign. Stay on the bus until the last stop, a triangular road island where El. Venizelou St. meets Periandou and Eth. Antistasis. **Buses** (tel. 22 262) from Loutraki go to Athens (8 per day; 6am-7:30pm; 1250dr, 2000dr roundtrip), Corinth (every ½ hr., 5:30am-10:30pm, 20min., 220dr), Perachora (9 per day, 6am-8pm, 20min., 175dr), and Vouliagmeni (July-Aug. only; departs10am, returns 1pm, 45min., 680dr).

From the bus station, walk down **El. Venizelou Street,** with the water to your left, and you'll reach the **post office** at #4 28th Octovriou St., one block down to the right (open Mon.-Fri. 7:30am-2pm). The **OTE** is at 10 El. Venizelou. (Open Mon.-Fri. 7:30am-3:10pm.) **Police** keep the peace across the street from the OTE (on 2nd floor; tel. 63 000 or 22 258). English-speaking **tourist police** (tel. 65 678) respond to the needs of travelers. (Open daily 9am-9pm.) To get to the **National Bank,** 25 Martiou Square, bear left where the road forks (open Mon.-Thurs. 8:30am-2pm, Fri. 8:30am-1:30pm). Day boat excursions are available at the dock past the park. **Albona Cruises** goes to Lake Vouliagmeni (the "Blue Lake"; Tues.-Thurs., 2200dr). Cruises down the Corinth Canal leave Sundays at 10am and Thursdays at 5pm (3950dr). For **moped rentals,** make a right at the post office and turn at the second corner on the left to reach **Andreas** (tel. 23 812; Vespas 4000-5200dr, bikes 1000dr). Follow E. Venizelou St. (which changes to G. Lekka St.) toward the mountains. Periandrou St., the first side street on the right across from the bus station's road island, is home to **Laundry Self-Service** (tel. 63 854; open Mon.-Tues. 8:30am-1:30pm, Wed.-Sat. 8:30am-1pm and 6-9pm; wash 1200dr, wash and dry 1600dr, ironing on request). On the left, the densely congregated trees guard a **public fountain** that spouts Loutraki water; fill your bottle. For the **health center,** dial 63 444.

There is a **pharmacy** (tel. 21 787), at 21 El. Venizelou, and a movie theater opposite the tennis courts (summer only). **Postal Code:** 20300; **Telephone Code:** 0744.

Accommodations There are only a few budget hotels in Loutraki. One of these, the **Hotel Brettagne** at 28 G. Lekka St. (tel. 22 349), has a kindly, semi-English-speaking manager. Rooms and baths sparkle, and every floor has a refrigerator. (Singles 3800dr, doubles 5800dr, triples 7500dr.) To find **Pension Marko** (tel. 63 542), go left from the bus station (facing the water) and take your second right onto L. Kalsoni St. Marko. They offer singles for 6000dr and doubles for 8000dr, all with balcony and bath/shower. **Camping** is at Lake Vouliagmeni, accessible by bus.

Food and Entertainment There are plenty of places to eat on the waterfront and on El. Venizelou St. If you're going out at night, take a taxi—the trendiest Loutraki night-spots are 3 to 4km away from town. The **Aphroditi** (tel. 21 002) always draws crowds. Popular in-town discos include **Biblos** and **Club Bazaar,** both on El. Venizelou St.

Sights The majority of Greek tourists go to Loutraki for the healing waters. Whirlpool baths and hydromassage are offered at the **Hydrotherapy Thermal Spa** (tel. 22 215) at 26 G. Lekka St. These will cure "rheumoatoarthritic, spondycarthritic" and "chronic gynecological diseases," or so the bilingual sign printed on the door promises. (Open Mon.-Sat. 8am-1pm.)

XILOKASTRO

In the traditional scurry between Athens and the ferry drop-off in Patras, tourists usually ignore the windswept north coast of the Peloponnese. Greek vacationers alone enjoy this string of resorts lining the shore between Corinth and Patras. The expansive beach and ivory-tinted boardwalk of Xilokastro are marvelous for meandering. **Mt. Ziria** (2600m), the Peloponnese's second-highest peak, looms above. Ask the **police** about the 3¼-hr. climb up Mt. Ziria. To get to police the station, walk one block on Athomporto St. away from the water. The beach and most of the hotels are east of the square.

Buses (tel. 22 218) run to Athens (every hr. until 8:40pm, 1¼hr., 1850dr). If you're coming from Corinth, catch the bus at the canal or ask at the station about buses which stop at Xilokastro on their way to other destinations. The bus that runs along the new highway drops you on the side of the road (2km above town), while local buses go directly into town. **Trains** to Kalamata (2100dr), Corinth (320dr), and Athens (1550dr) stop here, but rail service isn't as reliable as the buses. The **train station** (tel. 22 297) is on D. Mousoura St. From the bus station, the **post office** is one block down Leoforis Tsaldari St. with the water to your left. (Open Mon.-Fri. 7:30am-2pm.) The next block has a **pharmacy** and leads to the main square, with banks and some good *souvlaki* joints. **Postal Code:** 20400; **Telephone Code:** 0743.

The **Hotel Periandos** (tel. 22 272) provides cozy rooms. Walk east along the waterfront and turn inland after the Hotel Fadira. Singles 6500dr, doubles 7500dr, triples 6500dr. The coast between Xilokastro and the town of Kiato to the east vaunts splendid beaches. The beach to Corinth is a continuing chain of campsites. Among them are **Camping Akrata** (tel. (0696) 31 378 or 31 067; 920dr per person, 520dr per car, small tent 630dr, large tent 730dr, electricity 400dr); and **Camping Lemon Beach** (tel. (0696) 31 639, 950dr per person, 500dr per car, small tent 850dr, large tent 1000dr).

■■■ MYCENAE ΜΥΚΗΝΕΣ

No city figured more prominently, or morbidly, in Greek mythology than Mycenae. The city was allegedly founded by Perseus, who slew Medusa, the snake-haired gorgon whose looks could kill. Eventually the Mycenaeans chose Atreus, whose family was immortalized by Aeschylus in the Oresteia trilogy, as their ruler. But out of hatred for his brother, Thyestes, Atreus murdered his nieces and nephews (Thyestes' sons and daughters) and served them to their dad for dinner. This culinary *faux pas* provoked the wrath of the gods; they upheld the curse that Thyestes had pronounced on Atreus and his progeny. When Atreus' son Agamemnon returned after ten years at the Trojan War, he was met by his bitter wife Clytemnestra, her lover Aegisthus, and Aegisthus' lethal dagger. Agamemnon's son Orestes later avenged the murder of his father by slaying his mother, but was then haunted by the Furies, who tormented those who killed their family members. Athena finally pardoned Orestes and lifted the curse from the House of Atreus.

Mycenae's hazy origins, its interactions with other Near Eastern civilizations, and its subsequent decline have long beguiled historians. The site was settled as early as 2700 BC by tribes from the Cyclades who were colonizing the mainland. Clay tablets written in Linear B, an early form of Greek, were found at Pylos and Knossos and serve as a record of the Mycenaeans' well-developed bureaucratic system of account-keeping. Mycenae flourished financially after the fall of Knossos around 1400 BC, and Mycenaean culture spread as far as Cyprus, Syria, and Sicily. Mycenae was probably destroyed by Dorian tribes from the north led by disgruntled rivals of the House of Atreus, imprisoning the Furies under faraway Athens.

The well-preserved ruins of ancient Mycenae, which include an extensive fortress and remarkable treasures, now in Athens, found in beehive tombs, are among the most celebrated archaeological discoveries in modern history. In summer, mobs stampede to the famed Lion's Gate and Tomb of Agamemnon. Visit early in the morning or late in the afternoon to avoid becoming part of them. Although most travelers make Mycenae a daytrip from Athens, Argos, or Nauplion, you can spend the night in the adjacent modern village, where restaurateurs across the street from each other will vie for your attention in one of several languages.

ORIENTATION AND PRACTICAL INFORMATION

The only direct **buses** to Mycenae are from Nauplion (3 per day at 10am, noon, and 1:30pm; 40min.; 460dr) and Argos (6 per day, 30min., 240dr). A bus from Athens (15 per day, 2½hr., 1750dr) stops at Fichtia, 1½km away. Three buses make the return trip from Nauplion at 11am, 1pm, and 3pm. Stops are in the town of Mycenae (up the street from the Iphigenia Restaurant) and at the site (a 20-min. uphill walk from the town). Buses and **trains** (5 per day) run from Athens via Corinth to Fichtia. There is another bus stop by the intersection near the train station. Although the town has no banks, the **post office** (open Mon.-Fri. 8am-10pm, Sat. 8am-3pm) at the site handles **currency exchange. Telephone Code:** 0751.

ACCOMMODATIONS

Mycenae has few inexpensive accommodations. If campgrounds aren't your thing, seek out private rooms; look for signs on the side streets.

Belle Helene Hotel (tel. 66 225). Serves as a bus stop on the main road. It has clean, spacious rooms with carpeting, but there is some noise from the restaurant downstairs. Heinrich Schliemann stayed here while excavating the site, as did lyrical beatnik Allen Ginsberg, who came in 1961 lacking the money to eat. While in Mycenae, Ginsberg composed a poem about his stay in the hotel's register. The register display on the wall also claims that Virginia Woolf and Claude Debussy slept here (but not in the same bed). Doubles 5000dr, triples 7000dr. Singles negotiable.

The Hotel Klitemnistra (tel. 76 451) is also on the main road, closer to the ruins. It features enormous rooms, 24-hr. hot water, and a restaurant downstairs. Singles 4000dr, doubles 7000dr, triples 8500dr, breakfast included.

Camping Atreus (tel. 76 221), at the bottom of the hill on the side of town farther from the ruins. The more luxurious of the area camping sites, Atreus offers a TV room, kitchen, and a cafeteria/bar. 850dr per person, 400dr per tent. Hot showers and electricity included.

Camping Mycenae (tel. 76 247 or 76 121) is in the middle of town, closer to the ruins. The surrounding orange and lemon groves lend the camping their wondrous fragrance. There is also a bar/restaurant and a kitchen, where the gracious owner prepares inexpensive homemade food. 750-850dr per person, 400-500dr per tent. Hot showers included.

FOOD

Most of the restaurants in town prey on tourists willing to pay, but a few pleasant, cheap places survive. **Restaurant/Taverna Micinaiko,** next to the youth hostel, has nice folks and tasty food. They offer a 15-20% student discount. Prices are marked in high season; otherwise, ask. (Greek salad 700dr, chicken 950dr, *mousaka* 900dr.) **Menelaos,** next door to Taverna Micinaiko, has a shady porch to dine on and interesting wall murals, especially *en route* to the restroom. (Retsina 400dr per ½kg, Greek salad 750dr, *mousaka* 1000dr.) Students receive a 10% discount. **Aristidis O Dikeos** (tel. 76 258) across the street has a pleasant proprietor whose taverna is easily distinguished by its flower-filled porch. (Greek salads 700dr; *dolmadakia, or* stuffed vine leaves, 900dr).

SIGHTS

The excavated site of Ancient Mycenae extends over a large tract of rough terrain tucked between Mt. Agios Elias to the north and Mt. Zara to the south. The site is enclosed by 13m-high, 10m-thick monstrous walls called "Cyclopean" by ancient Greeks. The ancients believed that Perseus and his descendant who founded the city could only have lifted the stones with the help of the Cyclops, one-eyed giants with superhuman strength. Although modern historians scoff at monsters (and probably can't see Mr. Snuffleupagus either), they have no better explanations of how the stones were moved. The bulk of the ruins standing today date from 1280 BC, when the city was the center of the far-flung Mycenaean civilization.

German businessman, classics scholar, and amateur archaeologist Heinrich Schliemann uncovered Mycenae in 1874, having located the site by following clues in the writings of Homer and later Greek tragedians, who had placed the House of Atreus in the vicinity. Schliemann began digging just inside the citadel walls at the spot where several ancient authors indicated the royal graves would have been located. Discovering 15 skeletons "literally covered with gold and jewels," most of which he gave to his new sixteen-year-old Greek wife, Schliemann believed he had unearthed the skeletons of Agamemnon and his followers and sent a telegram to the Greek king that read: "Have gazed on face of Agamemnon." Less romantic archaeologists, however, have dated the tombs to four centuries before the Trojan War. One skull, sporting a golden death mask still referred to as "The Mask of Agamemnon," is now exhibited in the National Archaeological Museum in Athens.

Before visiting the site, consider obtaining a map and flashlight. The book by S. E. Iakovidis, covering both Mycenae and Epidavros, includes a map and is well worth the 2000dr. For a more scholarly approach, try the book by George E. Mylonas, director of the excavation (1700dr). If you plan to go to many sites in the Peloponnese, or want information on other ruins, buy the large guide, *The Peloponnese,* by E. Karpodini-Dimitriadi (2800dr). All are available at the entrance to the sight in Greek, English, German, and French.

The bus will take you to the end of the asphalt road; the ruins are on your right. Down the hill in the lower parking lot area is the largest of the *tholos* (beehive) tombs, the so-called **Tomb of Agamemnon,** in the Treasury of Atreus. As you walk into the tholos, look up; the lintel stone weighs 120 tons. To the right on the walk up to the main site are pathways to two often overlooked *tholoi*, the **tomb of Aegistheus** and the more interesting **tomb of Clytemnestra.** Bring a flashlight; the *tholoi* are dark inside. The gate and the **Cyclopean Walls** of the upper citadel date from the 13th century BC. The imposing **Lion's Gate,** with two lionesses carved in relief above the lintel, is the portal into ancient Mycenae. These lionesses were symbols of the house of Atreus, and their heads (now missing) had eyes of precious gems. Schliemann found most of his artifacts (now on display in Athens) in **Grave Circle A.** These 16th-century BC shaft graves were originally located outside the city walls, but the city grew and now they rest to the right of the entrance. The **barracks** are up the stairs to your left immediately after the gate. The exterior path from the postern gate to the barracks has rewarding views and breezes.

The ruins on the hillside are the remnants of various homes, businesses, and shrines. The **palace** and the **royal apartments** are at the highest part of the citadel on the right. The open spaces here include guard rooms, private areas, and more extensive public rooms. Look for the **megaron,** or royal chamber, it has a round hearth surrounded by the bases of four pillars (note the pillar bases). To the left of the citadel sit the remaining stones of a Hellenistic **Temple of Athena.** At the far end of the city, between the palace and the **postern gate,** is the underground cistern used as refuge in times of siege. Be careful—the steps are worn and slippery.

Follow the asphalt road 150m back toward the town of Mycenae to the **Treasury of Atreus,** the largest and most impressive *tholos*. The tomb of Agamemnon can be reached through a 40-m passage cut into the hillside. The famous tomb was found empty, but is believed to have held valuable goods that were spirited away by thieves. A new museum is being built on the site, with hopes of housing treasures by 1996 currently in the National Gallery. (Site open Mon.-Fri. 8am-7pm, Oct.-March 8am-5pm; admission to citadel and Tomb of Agamemnon 1500dr, students 800dr, free on Sun. Keep your ticket or you'll pay twice.)

■■■ ARGOS ΑΡΓΟΣ

A busy and modern city, Argos is larger and less picturesque than nearby Nauplion, from which most travelers choose to visit Argos' archaeological sites. Because this makes for few overnight sightseers, Argos can seem poorly equipped for tourism at times. Argos itself is pleasant enough, with an inviting central square dominated by the grand **Church of St. Peter** and some appealing café-studded side streets. The square provides refuge from the city's heat and confusion. The entire city has a fabulous view of the Venetian fortress of Larissa on the hill.

ORIENTATION AND PRACTICAL INFORMATION

The four streets that form the sides of the central square in Argos correspond roughly to the four points of the compass. Surrounding the large and beautiful Church of Saint Peter, they are the principal avenues of the city. Visible from the square is **Larissa Hill,** topped by the Venetian **citadel** of the same name. Larissa borders the city on the west. **Vasilios Georgiou B** is parallel to the citadel. Opposite this street on the east side is **Danaou St.** The north edge is **Vasilios Konstantinou,** and the south side is **Vas. Olgas St.**

Police: 10 Agelou Bobou St. (tel. 67 222). From the northeast corner of the square, follow Corinth St. and turn right on Agelou Bobou. English spoken. 24 hr.

Post Office: 16 Danaou St. (tel. 68 066). Past the southern end of the square. Open Mon.-Fri. 7:30am-2pm. **Postal Code:** 21200.

OTE: 8 Nikitara St. (tel. 67 599). North of the park. Open daily 7am-10pm. **Telephone Code:** 0751.

Banks: National Bank (tel. 68 211), on the eastern side of the square offers **currency exchange,** 1 block behind Danaou St. and the park. Open Mon.-Thurs. 8am-2pm, Fri. 8am-1:30pm. There are other banks around the square area.

Trains: The train station (tel. 67 212) is 1km south of the main square. To get to the main square from the station, take a right on Nauplion St. and bear left on Vas. Sofias at the 5-way intersection. Five trains per day go to: Athens (3hr., 1700dr); Corinth (1hr., 510dr); Tripolis (1hr., 590dr); Kalamata (3½hr., 1280dr); Mycenae (10min., 105dr); and Nemea (45min., 210dr). Discounted round-trip tickets.

Buses: There are two bus stations. The first is a few doors down from the **Athinon Station,** on Vas. Georgiou B., near the corner of Vas. Olgas St. (look for the Arcadia café). Buses go to Athens (every hr. 5:30am-8:30pm, 2½hr., 1900dr), Nauplion (every ½hr., 5:30am-8:30pm, ½hr., 200dr), Nemea (2 per day, 1hr., 460dr), Mycenae (4 per day, 25min., 240dr), and Prosimni (2 per day, 30min., 240dr). The **Arcadia-Laconia Station** is at 24 Pheithonos St. (tel. (0752) 22 094). Follow Vas. Olgas St. 2 streets past the museum, and turn left. Walk down several blocks, past the Agricultural Bank. Buses leave from here for Tripolis (8:30am, 11:30am, 2:30pm, and 5pm; 1hr.; 900dr). From Tripolis you can make connections to Sparta, Olympia, Andritsena, Gythion and Monemvassia.

Hospital: (tel. 24 455), on Corinth St., opposite St. Nicholas Church.

ACCOMMODATIONS

Argos has few overnight visitors, hence few accommodations. Since the sights can be seen in half a day, it's possible to make Argos a daytrip from Nauplion, or, if you want to camp, from Tolo or Mycenae.

Hotel Apollon, 13 Papaflessa St. (tel. 61 182 or 68 065). Take Nikitara off the square, turn left at the red and yellow café, then turn right immediately into the nearby alley—it's on the left. Follow the signs. Large, tidy rooms. Singles 3200dr, w/ bath 3700dr; doubles 4700dr, w/ bath 6000dr; triples 6700dr, w/ bath 7700dr.

Hotel Theoxenia, 31 Tsokri St. (tel. 67 808). Follow Vas. Konstantinou to the left (west) for about 150m until you see the arches on the left. Theoxenia is the hotel closest to the Argos ruins and right across from the market place. Standard rooms. Singles 3900dr, doubles 6100dr, triples 8300dr.

Hotel Mycenae (tel. 68 754 or 68 332), in the main square across from the church. Offers nice rooms and great location in what is undoubtedly the prettiest part of Argos. Singles 4200dr, doubles 7500dr. All rooms with private bath.

FOOD

Restaurants on the square or behind the bank offer standard, overpriced fare, but one nice place is **Restaurant Aglee** (tel. 67 266) in the northwest corner of the square (omelettes 700dr, pizza 1250dr). You can stock up at the **supermarket** on Vas. Sofias St., off the northwest corner of the square, or at the **bakery** near the Arcadia-Laconia bus stop. For a fast food fix, there's an **Igloo** (ice cream franchise) opposite St. Peter's church.

SIGHTS

According to Homer, Argos was the kingdom of the hero Diomedes and claimed the allegiance of Mycenae's powerful king Agamemnon. Invading Dorians captured Argos in the 12th century BC, around the same time as the fall of Mycenae, and then used it as their base for controlling the Argolid Peninsula. Through the 7th century BC, Argos remained the most powerful state in the Peloponnese, and even defeated its rival Sparta. By the 5th century BC, however, it was no match for the invincible Spartan war machine. In the famous battle of 494 BC, Kleomenes and the Spartans nearly defeated Argos but failed to penetrate the city walls.

In medieval times, Franks, Venetians, and Turks captured and ruled Argos in turn. They each had a hand in creating the **Fortress of Larissa,** a splendid architectural hodgepodge which includes Classical and Byzantine elements. Getting to the fortress is a hike. You can walk along Vas. Konstantinou St. for roughly 1hr. or climb the foot path from the ruins of the ancient theater. The ruins, which lie among overgrown weeds, are mainly of interest to avid scholars of bees or architecture—particularly those endowed with cars. Archaeologists had hoped to uncover a large part of the ancient city of Argos, but most of it lies under the modern town. The principal **excavations** have occurred on the city's western fringe; digs are currently going on there and in different areas throughout the town. To get to the site, walk past the post office and turn right and walk to the end of Theatron St.

With a seating capacity of 20,000, the ancient **theater** was the largest in the Greek world when it was built in the 4th century BC. Though not as well preserved as its more famous counterpart in Epidavros, it is striking nonetheless. Next to the theater are the **Roman baths.** Segments of wall give a good impression of the original magnitude of these ancient social centers. The **Roman Odeon** (indoor theater) is here; as is the **agora,** with blue-and-white mosaics still in place. Past the Odeon are the remains of a smaller theater. (All sites open Tues.-Sun. 8:30am-3pm. Free.)

Hera was the patron deity of the Argives and the temple of her cult, the **Argive Heraion,** is a short bus ride north of Argos. (Take the Prosimni bus, 200dr.) The complex contains, among other things, a pair of temples, a *stoa,* and baths. At **Prosimni,** several km northeast of Argos and past the Heraion, archaeology aficionados will delight in a series of prehistoric graves. A few km east of Agias Trias lie the remains of the city of **Dendra,** where tombs yielded the completely preserved suit of bronze armor now on exhibit in the Nauplion museum.

The small but superb **museum** (tel. 68 819), west off the main square on Vas. Olgas St., has a collection of Mycenaean and pre-Mycenaean pottery, some of which dates back as far as 3000 BC. Among the exhibits are outstanding 5th-century Roman mosaics, an intriguing array of headless Roman figures displayed as if in conversation, and a full suit of Mycenaean armor. (Open Tues.-Sun. 8:30am-7pm; off-season 8:30am-3pm; admission 300dr, students 200dr.)

■■■ NAUPLION (NAFPLIO) ΝΑΥΠΛΙΟ

The small city of Old Nauplion is a soothing antidote to the hustle of Corinth and the hordes of sun-worshippers on the islands. Venetian architecture, shady squares, and hillside stairways that foil noisy mopeds make Old Nauplion a perfect base for daytrips into the Peloponnese and nearby ruins. In contrast, New Nauplion is unattractive—its design kindles thoughts of an on-going construction site. Visible remnants of Nauplion's illustrious past include the "dreaded" Palamidi, a Venetian fortress in which Turks imprisoned the national hero Kolokotronis before the Revolutionary War of 1821, and the Bourtzi, a floating Venetian stronghold that once housed retired executioners, but now caters to people of a more benign sort—tourists who explore the island and partake of the refreshments at the snack bar atop its fortress.

Nauplion has suffered from chronic instability. Before the Venetians built it on swamp land in the 15th century, the city (named for Poseidon's son Nauplius) was made solely of the hilltop fortresses. It passed from the Venetians to the Turks and back again. In 1821, it served as headquarters for the revolutionary government, and the capital of independent Greece (1829-1834). John Kapodistrias, the president of Greece, was assassinated in St. Spyridon Church. (The bullet hole is still visible in the church walls; the assassins hid behind the fountain across the street.) Recent years held less calamity for the city, and, under the watchful eyes of its surrounding fortresses, Nauplion seems content to while away a few more centuries in serenity.

ORIENTATION AND PRACTICAL INFORMATION

The bus terminal, on **Singrou Street,** sits near the base of the Palamidi fortress, which caps the hill to the right facing inland. To reach **Bouboulinas Street,** the waterfront promenade, just walk right (facing the bus station) down Singrou to the harbor. The area behind Bouboulinas and Singrou is the old part of town, with many shops and *tavernas.* If you arrive by water, Bouboulinas St. will be directly before you, across the parking lot and parallel to the dock.

There are three other principal streets, all of which run off Singrou Street parallel to Bouboulinas. Moving inland, the first is **Amalias,** a chief shopping street. The second, **Vasileos Konstandinou,** ends in **Syntagma Square** (Platia Syntagmatos), which has *tavernas,* the bookstore, the bank, the museum, and at night, scores of aspiring soccer stars. The third street is **Plapouta,** which becomes **Staikopoulou** in the vicinity of Syntagma Sq. Here you'll find more good restaurants. Across Singrou St., Plapouta becomes **25th Martiou,** the largest avenue in town. This side of Singrou St.—everything behind the statue of Kapodistrias—is the new part of town.

Tourist Office: (tel. 24 444). Facing the Palamidi fortress, go left, and the office will be past the road to the fortress on the right, across the street from the OTE.

English-speaking office provides free pamphlets and maps and change money when banks are closed. Open daily 9am-2pm and 4-9pm.

Tourist Police: (tel. 28 131). Past the tourist office, it's the building right under the Palamidi, on the second floor. English-speaking police are very helpful and cheerfully provide pamphlets and info. 24 hr.

Police: (tel. 22 458). On Praitelous St., a 15-min. hike along 25th Martiou St. from the bus station—follow the signs. The location keeps most travelers away; if you show up, you'll get attention. Open 24 hr. for drug busts, murders, and other felonies; **security police** (tel. 27 776), in the same building, concern themselves with robberies and other less glamorous crimes.

Post Office: (tel. 24 230 or 24 231). The large yellow building on the corner of Sidiras Merarchias and Singrou St., 1 block from the bus station toward the harbor. Open Mon.-Fri. 7:30am-2pm. **Postal Code:** 21100.

OTE: 25th Martiou St. at Arvantias (tel. 22 139, 22 121 or 25 899). In yet another yellow building across Kapodistrias Square. Open daily 7am-10pm. **Telephone Code:** 0752.

Banks: The **National Bank** in Syntagma Sq. (tel. 28 355) is open Mon.-Thurs. 8am-2pm, Fri. 8am-1:30pm. Other banks in Syngtama Sq. and on Amalias St. charge 500-700dr commission for **currency exchange.**

Ferries: There are no regular ferries out of Nauplion or Tolo. The Pegasus, an expensive cruise ship, offers day tours and leaves every Wed. and Fri. from Tolo. Cruise tickets to the Saronic Gulf islands range from 4000-7000dr. For tickets or reservations, consult **Staikos Tours,** 50 Bouboulinas St. (tel. 27 950 or 22 444), on the left of the waterfront. (Open daily 8:30am-3:30pm, 6-10pm. More convenient is the **flying dolphin** which operates in July and Aug. A dolphin leaves for Piraeus Tues.-Sun. at 7:15am (4hr., 5089dr), stopping in Spetses (1hr., 2236dr); Ermione (1¼hr., 2355dr); Hydra (2hr., 2452dr); Poros (2½hr., 3344dr); and Aegina (3hr., 4417dr). From Spetses you can make further connections. Staikos also arranges for **plane** and **train** travel.

Buses: (tel. 27 323). Singrou St., off Kapodistrias Square. Buses go to Athens (every hr. 5am-8pm, 3hr., 2100dr), stopping at Argos (30min., 200dr) and Corinth (2hr. 950dr); Mycenae (3 per day, 40min., 460dr); Epidavros (4 per day, 1hr., 460dr); Tolo (hourly, 7am-8:30pm, 20min., 200dr); Kranidi (3 per day, 2hr., 1200dr); Galatas (5:45am and 2pm, 2hr., 1300dr); and Ligouri (every 2hr., 5:30am-7:30pm, 1hr., 460dr).

Taxis: (tel. 27 393 or 23 600) congregate on Singrou St. across from the bus station. The trick is to get a driver who operates out of the destination you desire; they charge less if they're returning. Taxi to Palamidi fortress 700dr.

Bike/Moped Rental: Motomania (tel. 21 407), on Navarino St.; take Konstantinou St. towards New Nauplion and Navrinou is on your left. Mopeds 3500dr per day. Open daily 8am-9pm.

English Bookstore: Odyssey (tel. 23 430), Syntagma Sq. Pick up Penguin Classics for light summer reading. Tour books, newspapers, magazines and dictionaries also available. Open daily 8am-10pm; off-season Mon.-Sat. 9am-1pm, Sun. 5-9pm.

Town Hall: (tel. 24 444), near the hydrofoil landing. Changes money and offers information. Open 9am-1pm and 5-9pm.

Medical Emergency: Call the tourist police or visit **Nauplion Hospital** (tel. 27 309). Walk down 25th Martiou St. and turn left onto Kolokotroni St., which eventually becomes Asklipiou St.

ACCOMMODATIONS

Prices have risen in the old part of town, but it's still the cheapest, most pleasant district. Check the streets at the east end of town (below Dioscuri Hotel) for rooms. In off-season, prices are 20-40% less.

Youth Hostel (tel. 27 754), Neon Vyzantion St., at Argonafton, a 15-20min. hike from the bus stop. Renovated during the summer of 1989. Run by a friendly couple and their daughter. Dimitrios will wake you at 8am as he strolls through the corridor playing *Que Sera, Sera* on his accordion. On nights of the Epidavros festival (weekends in July and August), buses drop people off at the hostel, and the curfew is 1am. Bedrooms closed 10am-5pm. Curfew 11pm. 1000dr per person. Breakfast 500dr. Home-cooked dinner 1000dr.

Eleni's Rooms, on the far right of Old Nauplion just below the Xenia hotel. Take the second to last street on your left; it's the first door on your right. Doubles and triples 7000dr, some with full kitchen, some with verandas. Call Hotel Byron (tel. 22 351) to reserve, but be clear because a double at the Hotel Byron will set you back 12,000dr.

Hotel Epidavros, (tel. 27 541) on Ipsiladou St., 1 block below Amalias and 4 blocks up from Bouboulinas. Divided into two parts, hotel and pension. The hotel, described by the owner as a "family" kind of place, is clean and roomy. Singles 7000dr, doubles 9000dr. All rooms have private bath.

Hotel Argolis (tel. 27 721), in the new town, on the Argos road right before the turn-off for the youth hostel. Noisy but comfortable bedrooms. Doubles 6000dr, triples 7200dr.

Hotel ERA (HPA in Greek), 9 Vas. Georgiou B St. (tel. 28 184). Off Bouboulinas St. in the new part of town. Clean, airy rooms. Doubles 6000dr, triples 7500dr. Off-season doubles 2300dr, triples 3000dr.

FOOD AND ENTERTAINMENT

Restaurants, *tavernas,* and fast-food joints are interspersed throughout the town but concentrated in certain areas on the waterfront and in Syntagma Square. These tend to be overpriced and overcrowded. **Ellas** (tel. 27 278), in Syntagma, is the cheapest (entrees 950-1250dr) and boasts an international clientele including Marcello Mastroianni (ask to see the pictures). Better dining options are a street above the square on Plapouta-Staikopoulou. **Taverna Basiles** (tel. 25 334), behind the National Bank of Greece, is the cream of the crop. Their specialty, rabbit in onions (1200dr), will delight even the most avid Beatrix Potter fan. **Zorba's Tavern** to the left has similar prices and offerings as its neighbors but is especially popular among locals (*mousaka* 900dr). **The Old Mansion** (tel. 22 449) on Ipsalidou St. is one of the treasures hidden in Nauplion's back streets. Its specialty is veal in cream sauce (1350dr), with vegetarian options like vine leaves (850dr) as well. **Taverna Kakanarakis,** parallel to the Old Mansion, two blocks closer to the water on Vas. Olga St. Head into the kitchen to pick and choose. (Chicken 1200dr.)

Nauplion's discos have all relocated to **Tolo** (15min. and 1400dr by taxi; see Tolo on p. 118). Most of the action in town now happens at after-dinner ice cream joints. Dessert shops crawl with lascivious teenagers, but the **Igloo** (an ice cream chain), 100m out of the lower left corner of Syntagma Sq., is especially popular. If you're desperate to dance, there's the **Disco Troll,** 2km out of town (400dr taxi). If all play and no work has made you regress, head to the **Luna Park** (permanent carnival) at the right end of the harbor and re-live your childhood under the neon lights. Or take a **minicruise** of the harbor (they run until 7pm), and tour around the Bourtzi. Small *caïques* leave from the end of the dock (500dr round-trip).

SIGHTS

A stroll through the streets of Nauplion is more edifying than a slide show in Architecture 101. Everywhere you look there is impressive contrast from the building styles from various periods. An amazing example is the 18th-century **Palamidi fortress** (tel. 28 036), property first of Venice, then of Turkey, now of Greece. The roughly 999 grueling steps that once provided the only access to the fort have been superseded by a 3km road. Taxis cost 700dr each way, or you can attack the road by foot. If you opt for the steps, bring water and climb in the morning. At the top, you can walk around the intricate, well-preserved walls. The views of the town, gulf, and much of the Argolid are spectacular. The steps begin on Arvanitias St., across the park from the bus station. A snack bar on site opens at 9:30am and serves fresh juices. The lion steles that adorn some of the lower citadel's walls are Venetian. Years ago, there were eight working cisterns at the site and you can still tour the cool interiors of the two remaining underground reservoirs. (Open Mon.-Fri. 8am-

6:30pm, Sat.-Sun. 8:30am-3pm. Off-season Mon.-Fri. 8:45am-2:30pm, Sun. 8:45am-2pm; admission 800dr, students 400dr.)

The walls of the **Acronauplion** were fortified by three successive generations of conquerors: Greeks, Franks, and Venetians. Approach the fortress either by the road near the back parking lot or by the tunnel that runs into the hill from Zigomala St., where you can take the Xenia Hotel elevator. The views of the Palimidi, the Gulf, and Old Nauplio are fantastic.

Ludwig I, King of Bavaria, had the huge Bavarian Lion carved out of a monstrous rock as a memorial after seeing many of his men die in an epidemic in 1833-34. Today, a small park sits in front of it. Instead of turning right onto Praxitelous St. to go to the tourist police, make a left onto Mikh. Iatrou St. and walk 200m.

Nauplion's **Folk Art Museum** (tel. 28 379), winner of the 1981 European Museum of the Year Award, comprehensively displays the styles and weaving techniques of ancient, medieval, and 18th-century Greek clothing. (Enter on Ipsiladou St. off Sofroni.) The exhibits here are superb and include encyclopedic explanations in English. (Open Wed.-Mon. 9am-2:30pm. Closed in Feb. Admission 400dr, students 200dr.) The **Military Museum,** one block above the Folk Art Museum, has artifacts, paintings, and high-quality black and white photographs from the burning of Smyrna, the population exchanges of the 1920s, and WWII. (Open Wed.-Mon. 10am-1pm; free.) The **archaeological museum** (tel. 27 502), in a Venetian mansion on Syntagma Sq., has a small but esteemed collection of pottery and sympathetic-looking idols, as well as a perfectly preserved Mycenaean suit of bronze armor. (Open Wed.-Mon. 8:30am-3pm; admission 400dr.) Across from the bus station, near the statue of Kapodistrias, there's a playground in a large, peaceful park; the **carnival** is at the right end of the waterfront.

■ NEAR NAUPLION

Several kilometers south of town, crowded **Tolo** and **Asini** have long, sandy beaches. Northwest from Asini are the remains of the 3rd millennium ancient Asini. The ruins include the walls of an acropolis and remains from several other buildings. **Karathona Beach** (ΚΑΡΑΘΟΝΑ) is accessible by foot: follow the road which curves around the left-hand side of the Palamidi. There's also a footpath from the parking lot between the Palamidi and the end of Polizoidou St. It runs along the water from the left. The 45-min. walk conceals three quiet, rocky coves. Karathona beach is nothing special, just a thin strip of sand in the middle of nowhere.

Four kilometers northwest of Nauplion on the road to Argos lie the Mycenaean ruins of **Tiryns** (or Tirintha), birthplace of Hercules. Perched atop a 25m-high hill, Tiryns (tel. 22 657), the finest prehistoric site outside of Mycenae was impregnable during ancient times. That is, until it was captured by the Argives and destroyed in the 5th century BC. Parts of the stronghold date as far back as 2600 BC, but most of what remains was built 1000 years later, in the Mycenaean era. The massive walls surrounding the site indicate the immensity of the original fortifications. Standing 8m in height and width, the walls were called "Cyclopean" by ancients who believed only a Cyclops could have lifted stones to build them. They reach a width of 20m on the eastern and southern slopes of ancient acropolis. Inside these structures lurk vaulted galleries. The palace's frescoes are on display in the National Archaeological Museum in Athens. One huge limestone block, the floor of the bathroom, remains. The site is easily reached by the Argos bus from Nauplion (every 30min., 175dr). (Open daily 8am-6:30pm; admission 400dr, students 200dr.)

TOLO (ΤΟΛΟ)

Tolo exists mainly to provide what nearby Nauplion and the archaeological sites lack; a spectacular sandy beach and tons of discos. That's it—no culture, art, or architecture; just beach, booze and boogying. Party on.

Orientation and Practical Information The town is long and thin, arranged around the main street, **Bouboulinas.** After roughly 700m (water on your left), the street curves sharply and becomes **Sekeri St.** Shortly after, the town peters out. There is a **Commercial Bank** on Sekeri St. past the curve (open Mon.-Fri. 8am-1pm). Nearby is the **post office** (open Mon.-Sat. 7:30am-2pm). The **police station** (tel. 59 202) is at the end of town closest to Nauplion; go right at the meat market and take the first set of stairs on your left. The **OTE** is farther down Sekeri St.; turn right at the blue OTE sign and walk up the hill (open Mon.-Sat. 7:30am-3:10pm).

Buses go from Nauplion every hour on the half-hour, passing through (and, if requested stopping in) Asini and Drepano (1:30am-9:30pm, 200dr). **Hydrofoils** run in July and August to Spetses (1½hr., 2235dr), Hydra (2hr., 2450dr), Aegina (3½hr., 4420dr), and Piraeus (4hr., 4724dr), with another line going to Monemvassia (3½hr., 3959dr), and Kythera (8203dr). An expensive **tour boat,** the Pegasus, leaves on Wednesday and Friday on a Poros-Hydra-Spetses cruise (4700dr, round-trip 7000dr). For reservations or tickets contact **Tolon Tours** (tel. 59 686, open daily 9am-2pm and 5-10pm), on Bouboulinas St. They will also arrange for **bicycle rental** in Drepano at 2500dr per day. For **moped rental** try Moto-Rent (tel. 21 407) on the beach close to Nauplion (small moped 3500dr per day, large moped 4500dr per day). **Postal Code:** 21056; **Telephone Code:** 0752.

Accommodations Most of Tolo's hotels are along Bouboulinas or Sekeri St., where private rooms and campsites abound. Some places to try are: the **Hotel Christina** (tel. 59 001), at the edge of town, close to Nauplion. Paul, the friendly, English-speaking manager will do everything he can to keep you happy and satisfied, including money exchange and renting mopeds. Simple rooms, some with balconies and oceanfront views. Doubles 8000dr, triples 9500dr, quads 11,500dr. Reservations recommended. **Rooms Mari,** 31 Bouboulinas St. (tel. 59 006, -522). Snazzily decorated black-and-white rooms right above the beach (singles 67500dr, doubles 8500dr). **Arcadia Rooms** (tel. 59 551), at 25 Bouboulinas St., has singles for 6500dr, doubles for 8000dr, and triples for 9600dr) To camp, try **Sunset Camping** (tel. 59 566; 1200dr per person, 600dr per car, small tent 900dr, large tent 11,000dr); or **Camping Xeni** (tel. 59 133), on a large stretch of beach (1000dr per person, 600-800dr per tent). Nearby **Asini** also has camping, but prices are higher.

Food and Entertainment There are several *tavernas* along Bouboulinas and Sekeri St., with prices at the high end of reasonable. One of the cheaper places is **Restaurant Koronis** (spaghetti 800dr). **Taverna Marina** is a typical family-style *taverna* with entrees averaging 1250dr. A large **supermarket** is on Sekeri St.

Tolo's discos are legendary for miles around. There are three right after the curve in the road: **Gorilla** (1000dr cover and first drink), **Rainbow** (500dr cover), and the brand new **Europower** (no cover). For daytime entertainment, try the beach (the closer to Nauplion the better). There are umbrellas (700dr), kayaks (600dr per day), jet skis (5000dr per hr.), pedal boats (1200dr per hr.) and windsurfing equipment (2000dr per hr.) for rent, as well as loquacious rental personnel.

■■■ EPIDAVROS ΕΠΙΔΑΥΡΟΣ

Henry Miller claimed that amidst Epidavros' powerful serenity he heard the pounding "great heart of the world." It's easy to see why; the theater at Epidavros is acoustically impeccable. From the top of its graceful, perfectly preserved 55 tiers of seats, you can hear a *drachma* drop onstage. Even with the midday din of eager tourists and busloads of schoolchildren singing hymns and folksongs, Epidavros, surrounded by pine groves, is endowed with a sense of peacefulness that relaxes frenzied tourists. You'll leave with a serene feeling, in the site's healing tradition.

Try to visit Epidavros on a Friday or Saturday night from late June to mid-August when the **National Theater of Greece** and visiting companies perform plays from the classical Greek canon (Euripides, Sophocles, Aristophanes, etc.). Performances are at 9pm, and tickets can be purchased at the theater four hours before showtime. Also buy tickets in advance in Athens at the **Athens Festival Box Office** (tel. (01) 322 1459; see p. 78). In Nauplion, buy tickets at **Bourtzi Tours** (tel. 21 249), next to the bus station, 4 Singrou St. For performances by the National Theater of Greece, tickets are also available at the **Athens Box Office of the National Theater** (tel. (01) 522 3242; see p. 78). Tickets cost 3000-4500dr, 2000dr for students. The rule which prohibits children under six is strictly enforced. All performances are in Greek, so bring your favorite translation.**Telephone Code:** 0753.

Unless you're going to Epidavros for the theater, make the small town a daytrip from Nauplion, Athens, Corinth, or a Saronic Gulf Island, since it has few accommodations. Bypass the Xenia, the expensive hotel near the site, and head for cheap lodgings in touristy **Ligouri,** 4km from Epidavros. The **Hotel Alkion** (tel. 22 002; fax 22 552) is just past the turn-off for Epidavros and has A/C, hot water, and a restaurant open for all three meals. (Singles 4900dr, doubles 7000dr, triples 8000dr.) If you're in Ligouri for a meal, visit the **Restaurant Oasis** (tel. 22 062), the first place on the road from Nauplion. Here Greeks outnumber tourists, and the owners imbue the place with a festive spirit; it's the favorite summer hangout of actors from Epidavros (pork chops 1200dr). To get to Ligouri, take a taxi (800dr). Some hitchhike the 4km between the theater and Ligouri. A **bus** from Nauplion leaves 3 times per day, and drops off near two campgrounds at **Paleo Epidavros,** 15km from the site. On nights of performances, additional **KTEL** buses make a round-trip to Epidavros, leaving Nauplion at 7:30pm (925dr). **Telephone Code:** 0753.

The theater is a grand structure, built in the early 4th century BC to accommodate 6000 people. In the 2nd century BC, additional tiers were added for a total capacity of roughly 14,000. Despite severe earthquakes that destroyed much of the sanctuary in 522 and 551 AD, the theater was miraculously saved; it is considered the best-preserved of all Greek theaters. Note the restored Corinthian columns which support the entrances. Performances were staged here until the 4th century AD. A pine grove surrounding the theater hides it from the entrance path.

While the other key sites in the Argolid (Mycenae, Nauplion, and Tiryns) were built as fortified cities, the small state of Epidavros was designed as a sanctuary for healing. Its ruins, the remains of hospital rooms and sick wards, attest to the blurred boundaries between medicine, magic, and religion common in antiquity. From its founding in the 6th century BC, Epidavros was dedicated to gods of medicine—first Maleatas, then Apollo, and finally Apollo's son Asclepius.

The **museum** is on the way from the theater to the ruins. The first room includes painted decorations from the ruins and huge stones containing inscriptions of hymns to Apollo and Asclepius, and accounts of repairs to the temple. Prominently featured are a number of lamps, votive offerings, surgical instruments including dagger-like scalpels, and a stunning selection of original statues. The second room houses copies of offerings from the cured (the originals are in the National Archaeology Museum in Athens). You'll find sculpture fragments from the temples of Asclepius and Artemis, a reconstruction of the *tholos* floor in the third room, and a spectacular Corinthian column collection. (Theater, site, and museum open Tues.-Sat. 7:30am-7pm, Nov.-Apr. 7:30am-5pm; admission 1500dr, students 800dr; free admission (to the theater only) on Sun. Hold onto ticket stub for the museum.)

The ruins of the Sanctuary of Asclepius are extensive and can be confusing. Walking from the museum, you will first come across the **Gymnaseum** on your right, which contains the remains of an **odeon** built by the Romans. On your left are the remains of the **stadium.** In front and to the left are the ruins of the **Temple to Asclepius** and the famous **tholos,** thought to have been designed by Polykleitos, the same architect as the theater. The *tholos* contains a maze, the purpose of which is unknown. Farther from the theater lie the ruins of the extensive baths built by the Romans before Sulla destroyed and looted the site in 89 BC.

ELIAS AND ACHAÏA ΗΛΕΙΑΣ ΚΑΙ ΑΧΑΙΑ

In the rural provinces of Elias and Achaïa, tomatoes ripen beneath a blazing sun as beachgoers redden to a similar hue. The area between Pyrgos and Patras, the capitals of Elias and Achaïa, is a vegetable farmer's dream. Corn fields, rimmed with golden-sand beaches, are studded with ancient, Frankish, and Venetian ruins. The locals call these regions of the Peloponnese "tame" as opposed to the "wild" landscape in other parts of Greece. The current tranquility of the Northwest Peloponnese hides centuries of diverse cultural influence. The Achaïans from the Argolid were the first settlers of Achaïa, and in 280 BC the Achaïan Confederacy was created. In 146 BC the region fell to the Romans, in 1205 AD it was captured by the Franks, in 1460 it became Turkish property, and from 1687 to 1715 it was a Venetian colony. Ruins from each of these periods stand to this day. In 1828 Achaïa was liberated, and it has remained Greek ever since.

■■■ PATRAS ΠΑΤΡΑΣ

Mountains encircle the east and west edges of this noisy harbor town. The older, more sedate streets encompassing the castle look down on a homogeneity of high-rises that languish under a shroud of smog. Every day thousands of people pass through this lively city, the third largest in Greece, as they shuttle between destinations all over the Peloponnese, the Ionian islands, and Italy. If you must stay, however, you'll find a decent amount of diversion, especially if you visit during Carnival (mid-January to Ash Wednesday), when the city breaks out into one huge party.

ORIENTATION AND PRACTICAL INFORMATION

If you're coming from Athens by car, choose between the **New National Road,** an expressway running inland along the Gulf of Corinth, and the slower, more scenic **Old National Road,** which hugs the coast. Those coming from the north can take a ferry from **Antirio,** in central Greece, across to **Rio** on the Peloponnese (4 per hr., 7am-11pm, ½hr., 270dr, 1720dr per car), and hop on bus #6 from Rio to the station, four blocks uphill from the main station, at Kanakari and Aratou St. (½hr., 130dr).

If you're arriving by boat from Brindisi or any of the Ionian islands, turn right as you leave customs onto **Iroon Polytechniou Street** to get to the center of town. From the bus station to the train station, the road curves and its name changes to **Othonos Amalias Street.** Just past the train station is the large **Trion Simahon Square,** with palm trees, cafés, kiosks, and a large floral clock.

Tourist Office: (tel. 65 33 58). Outside customs, on the waterfront just before Iroon Polytechniou. Multilingual, helpful staff gives free maps and brochures, and helps with accommodations. Check here for complete consular information and bus and boat timetables, since each company supplies information only for its own services. Open Mon.-Sat. 7:30am-9pm, Sun. 2:30-9pm.

Tourist Police: (tel. 22 09 02). New office at the customs pier, offers same services as tourist office. Friendly and multilingual. Lots of pamphlets. Open 7am-11pm.

Post Office: Mezonos Enzieni St. (tel. 27 77 59, -46 42). Walk 2 blocks towards the bus station from customs and make a left onto Zaïmi—it's 3 blocks up on the left. Open Mon.-Fri. 8am-8pm. Also a **mobile post office** just outside customs. Open whenever the ferries come in. **Postal Code:** 26001.

OTE: At customs. Open daily 7am-9pm. For collect international calls, go to the OTE at Trion Simahon Sq. Open Mon.-Fri. 7:20am-3pm, Sat.-Sun. 7:30am-1pm. Also west of town at the corner of Kanakari and Gounari St., up from the waterfront. **Telephone Code:** 061.

Consulates: British, 2 Votsi St. (tel. 27 73 29), corner of Othonos Amalias St.

Banks: National Bank of Greece (tel. 22 56 56), Trion Simahon Sq., on the waterfront, just past the train station. Open Mon.-Thurs. 8am-2pm and 6-7:30pm, Fri.

8am-1:30pm and 6-8:30pm, Sat.-Sun. 11am-1pm and 6-8:30pm. Also at customs daily 7-10am and noon-8pm, and at the mobile post office just outside.

American Express: Handled by **Albatros Travel,** 48 Othonos Amalias St. (tel. 22 01 26). Full travel services; holds mail for cardholders. No cash advances. Open 8am-2pm and 5-11pm.

Trains: Station (tel. 27 36 94) on Othonos Amalias St., 5 blocks to the right down the waterfront from customs. To: Athens (9 per day, 2580dr) via Corinth (1470dr), Kalamata (2 per day, 6hr., 1500dr), and Pyrgos (8 per day until 8:30pm, 2hr., 820dr), transfer here for Olympia. Expect delays and a shortage of seats, especially on the trains to Athens. Even if you have a railpass, reserve a seat at the ticket window before taking a train.

Buses: KTEL (tel. 62 38 86, -7), 3½ blocks to the right, down the waterfront from customs, on Ag. Andreas. To Athens (every hr. until 9:30pm, 4hr., 3030dr), Killini (summer only, 8am and 2:45pm, 1½hr., 1100dr), Kalamata (2 per day, 4hr., 3400dr), Pyrgos (11 per day, 1500dr), Tripolis (2 per day, 4hr., 2600dr), Ioannina (4 per day, 3650dr), Thessaloniki (3 per day, 7000dr), Kalavrita (3 per day, 1300dr), and Egion (every hr., 7am-10pm, 600dr). Buses to Lefkas leave from the intersection of Favierou and Konstantinoupoleos St., several blocks up from customs. **OSE** buses leave from the train station for Athens and Methoni. Some ferry companies also run their own buses with A/C to Athens (2500dr).

Ferries: From Patras, boats reach Cephalonia, Ithaki, and Corfu, in addition to Italy's Brindisi, Bari, and Ancona. Most boats depart at night; check-in is 2hr. before departure. For ferries to Brindisi or the Ionian Islands, show up at customs at the main terminal; ferries to Bari and Ancona leave from a pier 1km to the west. Ticket prices fluctuate tremendously. In general, expect a discount if you are less than 26, a student, or on a railpass and going to Brindisi. In high season, it's a good idea to make telephone reservations with a travel agent. The waterfront is coated with travel agencies all selling **ferry tickets** for roughly the same prices: Cephalonia and Ithaki 2800dr (usually 1 boat per day), Brindisi 9000dr, 8250dr with a student card, roughly 5000dr with a railpass. Italy-bound ferries stop over at Corfu. For tickets to Italy try **Mediterranean Star,** 34 Othonas Amalias St. (tel. 27 02 61, -18 28). Open daily 9am-9:30pm. For tickets to Cephalonia and Ithaki try **Strintzis Tours,** 14 Othonas Amalias St. (tel. 66 26 02). Open daily 9am-9pm.

Luggage Storage: 250dr per day; closes at 8pm. Ask at "Dafni" Travel, 5 Othonos Amalias St. (tel. 42 70 29) for InterRail information or at the tourist police.

Laundromat: at Zaïmi and Korinthou, up 4 blocks from the waterfront. Wash and dry 1500dr. Open Mon.-Sat. 9am-9pm.

International Bookstore: Romios Librarie, behind the bus station on Kapsali. Also keep an eye on the streetside kiosks. Open daily 8am-9pm.

Hospital: Open on alternate days, **Ag. Andreas** (tel. 22 38 12) is 3-4km up Gounari and **Rio Hospital of Patras University** (tel. 99 91 11) is 5km away. The **Red Cross Emergency Station** (tel. 150), at Karoloua and Ag. Dionysiou St., several blocks from customs, dispenses first aid. For an ambulance, dial 166.

ACCOMMODATIONS

Cheap accommodations are threaded through the tangle of buildings on Ag. Andreas St., one block up and parallel to the waterfront. The tourist police has listings of hotels and pensions. C and D class listings are cheapest.

Youth Hostel, 68 Iroon Polytechniou St. (tel. 65 21 52). From the ferry, turn left and walk 1½km. This turn-of-the-century mansion sat empty for 40 years after it was used as a German officers' headquarters in WWII. It's a bit cramped (8 beds per room), but has a convenient location and harbor view. No curfew. Check-out 10:30am. Bed 1500dr, sheets 100dr; metered telephone for calls.

Pension Nikos, 3 Patreos St. (tel. 62 37 57), off the waterfront. Friendly owner, negotiable prices. Single 3500dr; double 5000dr, w/bath 6000dr.

Hotel Hellas, 14 Ag. Nikolaou (tel. 27 33 52). Large, clean rooms and a huge hall bathtub in an ancient building. Singles 2500dr, doubles 6000dr, triples 7200dr.

Hotel Parthenon, 25 Ermou St. (tel. 27 34 21), off Ag. Andreas. Big rooms fill this old building. Singles 4300dr, doubles 6200dr, triples 7100dr.

Kavouri Camping (tel. 42 21 45), 2km east of town, next to the Patras swimming pool. Crowded, but cheap. Take bus #1 from in front of Ag. Dionysios Church; walk up Norman St. 1 block and turn left. Person 650dr, car 480dr, small tent 300dr, large tent 700dr.

Rio Camping (tel. 99 15 85), 8km east of Patras. Person 750dr, car 520dr, small tent 480dr, large tent 850dr.

Rio Mare (tel. 99 22 63), near Rio Camping. Person 1000dr, car 640dr, small tent 700dr, large tent 890dr. Simply grand.

FOOD AND ENTERTAINMENT

A great, nameless fish *taverna* lies past the youth hostel on the water. It's run by the local fishermen's club, so everything's guaranteed to be fresh, and their prices are the cheapest on the water (entrees 400-1100dr). If you happen to be in Patras on July 15, stop here for the annual **sardine festival.** There's live entertainment (if you can call it that), and the fried sardines, beer, and wine are all free, courtesy of those wacky fishermen. Stop by the new **Europa center** (tel. 43 48 01), at the corner of Othonos Amalias and Karolou, east past the KTEL bus station. This bright pink establishment caters to all the needs of a traveler: tickets to Italy, tourist info, a café and restaurant, stores, a disco, and clean toilets. (Open daily 6:30am-3am.) There are decent fast food places near Trion Simahon Sq. The best *souvlaki* grills are past Georgiou Sq. along Korinthou St. A **fruit stand** is on the corner of Ermou and Ag. Andreas, and another sits under a canopy at the corner of Aratou and Korinthou, up a few blocks from the water. **Bakeries** begin to pop up on the corner of Karolou and Ag. Dionysiou, and at the youth hostel on Kourou St. Friendly, family-run restaurants cling close to the **castle.** Dried fruits and nuts, yogurt, and ice cream entice from little shops near the square with the botanical clock, while on Iroon Polytechniou, to the beach, there are many good, cheap **tavernas** (entrees 550-1000dr, salads 300dr). The best and most affordable fish *tavernas* cluster on Othonos Amalias.

SIGHTS

The largest Orthodox cathedral in Greece, **Agios Andreas,** is dedicated to St. Andrew, who lived and died in Patras. As he felt himself unworthy to die on the same kind of cross as Jesus, St. Andrew was martyred by crucifixion on an X-shaped version. A little more than 10 years ago, the Catholic Church in Rome presented the Bishop of Patras with the saint's head, which is enshrined in an ornate gold and silver reliquary in the church, next to magnificently colored frescoes, a tremendous wooden carved chandelier, and an icon of Christ. To the right of the cathedral is the old church of St. Andrew, which houses a small **well** said to have been built by the saint himself. It can be reached by a doorway to the right of the church, and legend has it that whomever drinks from this well will return to Patras again. (Open to tourists 9am-dusk. Dress modestly; photography and videotaping prohibited.) To get here, follow the water to the west end of town, roughly 1½km from the port.

The Venetian **castle** and surrounding park dominate the city. This 13th-century fortress was built on the ruins of the ancient acropolis, once the site of the temple of the Panachaïan Athena. Parts of the walls are still intact, and the view from the surviving battlements is calming. To get here, follow Ag. Nikolaou St. inland from town; you'll see the daunting staircase up ahead. (Open Tues.-Sat. 8:30am-5pm, Sun. 8:30am-3pm.) **Taxis** also make the trek here (tel. 22 28 29). Up from Vas. Georgiou Sq., the **Ancient Odeum** has been preserved; the Patras Festival brings a series of performances here. (Closed Mon.) Work out your aggressions at the local Luna Park carnival's **bumper-car rink,** Athinon and Ag. Sofias St., one block up and four blocks left from customs (500dr for 15min., open in the evenings from 7pm onwards). The **Archaeological Museum,** 42 Mezonos (tel. 27 50 70), next to Olgas Sq. at the corner of Mezonos St. and Aratou, exhibits vases, statues, and other archaeological finds labeled with bilingual plaques. (Open Tues.-Sun. 8:30am-3pm; free.)

A scenic traipse leads to **Achaïa Clauss winery,** 9km southeast of town. Its German founder, Baron von Clauss, was dazed with lust for a woman named Daphne.

Upon her death, he took his blackest grapes and made a sweet wine in her honor, called *Mavrodaphne,* "Black Daphne." (Tours 9am-7:30pm; off-season 9am-5pm; free.) Bus #7 (20min., 185dr) from the intersection of Kolokotroni and Kanakari St.

The **carnival season** in Patras begins around January 17 every year and lasts until Ash Wednesday. The locals describe *karnavali* as an indefinable energy that sweeps through town. There are feasts and parties every night, with people of all ages dancing in the streets. Patras' bash is rumored to be the best carnival in Greece.

■ NEAR PATRAS

A 1-hr. train ride east from Patras leads to **Diakofto.** From here, take the tiny rack-railway train and marvel at the glorious landscape (480dr). Midway to Kalavrita the train stops in Zachlorou to allow hikers and donkey renters to climb to **Mega Spilaeou.** As the train ambles up the mountainous range, a waterfall bubbles through the rocks alongside the train tracks. If you arrive hours before the next train, catch the **bus** to Kalavrita on the sidewalk in front of the pharmacy and hotel (1020dr). The folks at the newspaper shop down the street have schedule info. The bus trip, which winds through cherry orchards and tiny mountain villages, will take your breath away. The village of **Kalavrita,** at the end of the line, is also a popular **ski resort,** and is famous for its plane trees, charming homes, and tranquil atmosphere. A Venetian fortress, "the castle of Orea," stands outside town. From the train station, follow Ag. Alexiou St. up into the town—after four blocks the **OTE** is at the corner of Ag. Alexiou and Kommenou St. (Open Mon.-Sat. 7:30am-10pm.) The **police** (tel. 23 333; open 24 hr.) are three blocks beyond the OTE, off Ag. Alexiou at 7 Fotina St. The main square is across from the large church a few blocks up from the train station. The **post office** is on the square. (Open Mon.-Fri. 7:30am-2pm.) There's a **bank** on 25th Martiou, which leads to the main square. The **Hotel Paradissos** (tel. 22 210, -303), on Kallimani St., offers pleasant rooms w/ clean bath. (Singles 5000dr, doubles 7000dr.) Down the street close to the main square, **Hotel Maria** (tel. 22 296) offers impressive rooms w/ bath. (Doubles 8500dr.) **Buses** leave from the station at the end of Kallimani St. **Postal Code:** 25001; **Telephone Code:** 0692.

The famous monastery of **Mega Spilaeou** is 9km away. The bus from Diakofto goes near the monastery (1km away), or take a taxi (3800dr round-trip; the driver will wait ½hr.). A monk will greet you and give you a guided tour through the museum and church. The extensive museum collection includes an intricate 350-year-old cross and an icon of the Theotokos (Mother of God), said to have been made by St. Luke. Built in 362, the monastery is 1000m above sea level.

Five **trains** per day leave Kalavrita, stopping at Zachlorou, close to the monastery, on their way to Diakofto. Trains leave from here for Patras (last train at 6:45pm, 280dr) and Athens (last train at 7:41pm, 950dr).

■■■ KILLINI ΚΥΛΛΗΝΗ

Most travelers come to Killini simply to catch the ferries to Zakinthos and Cephalonia. If you're stuck here for any length of time, hunker down at Killini's broad, sandy beach. The few tourists—mostly Greek, French, and Italian—who come here neither spoil the town's uncommercial air nor rush its leisurely tempo.

Orientation and Practical Information The path to town from the dock leads to the **police** (tel. 92 202). The **port police** (tel. 92 211; open 24 hr.) are on the dock. From the police station, walk a few blocks along the water on your left to reach the **OTE,** inside a tiny corner store. (Open summer daily 8am-1pm and 5-10pm.) The **post office** is a few blocks farther down, on a side street leading inland. (Open 7:30am-2pm.) **Buses** travel to Killini from Pyrgos (3 per day until 2:35pm, 1hr., 800dr) and Patras (2 per day, 1½hr., 1160dr). If you miss the bus from Patras, take the bus to Lehena (10 per day, 1½hr., 600dr); from there, buses continue to Killini (11:20am and 2:45pm, 20min., 110dr). **Taxis** also go from Lehena to Killini

(1500-1800dr). A daily bus to Athens leaves Killini at 9:30am. **Ferries** sail from Killini to Zakinthos (7 per day, 1½hr., 1040dr), and Cephalonia (2 per day, 3hr., 2360dr). Buy boat tickets on the dock. **Postal Code:** 27068; **Telephone Code:** 0623.

Accommodations The cheapest rooms in Killini are "Rooms to Let" along Glaretzas St., one block above the beach and parallel to the water. The **Glaretzas Hotel** (tel. 92 397) has light, fresh rooms with Scandinavian-revival decor. (Singles w/bath 5000dr, doubles w/bath 8500dr.)

Sights Twenty km from Killini are the Frankish **Chlemoutsi Castle** and the mineral springs of **Loutra Killinis,** a well-manicured resort with a long beach. Getting to either is difficult unless you have your own transportation or are willing to pay for a taxi (1200dr to the castle, 3000dr to Loutra). From the square, buses leave for Loutra (6 per day, 140dr), and drop off at either the turn-off to the castle, the mineral springs, or the camping area, **Camping Killinis** (tel. 96 259), close to the sea with a market and hot showers (person 1080dr, car 650dr, small tent 720dr, large tent 900dr, electricity 490dr). Three buses per day leave Loutra for the castle.

Nearby is **Karitena,** the village pictured on the 5000dr bill. The birthplace of Kolokotronis, Karitena has ruins of a Frankish castle and a 13th-century church to St. Nicholas. It's tiny, but its beauty may entice you to stay; **Stamata Kondopoulos** (tel. 31 206) has rooms across from the post office (singles 2500dr, doubles 4200dr).

■■■ OLYMPIA ΟΛΥΜΠΙΑ

Were it not for the ruins of the site of the ancient Olympic games, modern Olympia would be a pleasant little town with absolutely no reason for tourists to set foot in it. As it stands, Olympia is as multicultural as the games that it gave rise to: walk the streets and hear English, Greek, French, German, Italian, and Japanese—and that's just from the restaurateurs.

ORIENTATION AND PRACTICAL INFORMATION

Modern Olympia essentially consists of a 1km main street, **Kondili Avenue.** The bus will drop you off next to the ruins across from tourist information. Head out of town and left for a 5-min. walk to the ruins and the new museum. On the other side of town, towards Pirgos, sports enthusiasts will appreciate the **Museum of the Olympic Games** (tel. 22 544), which houses ancient sports paraphernalia. Located on Angerinou St., it's two blocks uphill from Kondili Ave. (Open Mon.-Sat. 8am-3:30pm, Sun. 9am-4:30pm; admission 500dr, students free.) The tourist shops all open late (10:30am) and close late (11pm). Since the town caters mainly to tourists, most restaurants open at 8am and close after 1am.

Tourist Office: (tel. 23 100). Kondili Ave., on the east side of town, towards the ruins. *Beaucoup de* helpful information. Open in summer daily 8am-10pm.
Police: 1 Em. Kountsa St. (tel. 22 100). Open 9am-9pm, but someone's there 24 hr.
Post Office: On a nameless, uphill side street just past the tourist information center. Open Mon.-Fri. 7:30am-2pm. **Postal Code:** 27065.
OTE: Kondili Ave., past the post office. Open Mon.-Fri. 7:30am-3:10pm. **Telephone Code:** 0624.
Bank: National Bank, on Kondili Ave., offers **currency exchange.** Open Mon.-Thurs. 8am-2pm, Fri. 8am-1:30pm.
Buses: The bus stops directly across from the tourist information shack, which has an up-to-date schedule posted outside. Buses go to Pirgos (15 per day, 6:30am-9:45pm, 40min., 320dr), and Tripolis (3 per day, 2 on Sun., 3½hr., 2000dr). Change at Pirgos for other points in the western Peloponnese. Schedules for Pirgos are available at the tourist information center.
English Bookstore: Galerie Orpheas, Kondili Ave., on the east end of town. Carries a good selection of guidebooks and translations of classics. Open 8am-11pm.
Hospital: tel. 22 222. Olympia uses Pirgos' hospital.

ACCOMMODATIONS

If all you want is a cheap place to crash, head for the youth hostel. Otherwise, choose from dozens of cheap hotels, most of which offer private baths, balconies, and modern rooms. Private rooms in Olympia are surprisingly uncrowded. Prices vary but hover around 5000dr per double. They are 20-40% less in off-season.

Youth Hostel, 18 Kondili Ave. (tel. 22 580). Narrow bunks in plain rooms. Checkout 10am. 1300dr per day, membership not needed for one-night stay, no curfew.

Hotel Hermes, Kondili Ave. (tel. 22 577). At the end of town, just before the entrance for Camping Olympia. Singles 4000dr, doubles 5500dr. Show your *Let's Go* to receive prices quoted here.

Pension Possidon (tel. 22 567), offers clean rooms (take a left at the National Bank and go uphill two blocks, doubles 6000dr).

"Rooms to Let": Ask at the **Anesti Restaurant** (tel. 22 644), Avgerinou St., for new rooms w/bath, hot water, and balconies (doubles 5000dr). Or, inquire at the **Ambrosia Restaurant** (tel. 22 916). The Spiliopoulou family rents nice rooms. Doubles 5000dr. Mention *Let's Go* and get a 10% discount.

Camping Diana (tel. 22 314) is the most convenient, located next to the sports museum. Offers a small, clean pool, hot water, and breakfast (700dr). Person 1300dr, car 800dr, small tent 850dr, large tent 1000dr, electricity 600dr.

Camping Olympia (tel. 22 745), 1km west on the road to Pirgos, has a slightly larger pool and shady sites. Person 1150dr, car 630dr, small tent 760dr, large tent 880dr, electricity 630dr, pool 500dr.

Camping Alfios (tel. 22 950, -1), 1km trek uphill from the western edge of town. The most luxurious, has a pool with diving board, café, and minimarket. Person 1150dr, car 700dr, small tent 750dr, large tent 900dr, electricity 600dr.

FOOD

Most restaurants and *tavernas* are visible on Kondili Ave. **Taverna Praxitelis** (tel. 23 570), next to the police, is friendly and affordable (entrees 1000-2500dr). In the center of town near the taxi stand, **Ambrosia** (tel. 22 916) offers tasty meals (entrees 800-1250dr) and a 10% discount to *Let's Go* users. The **Stronka** pastry shop, on the road to the Museum of Olympic Games, serves superb yogurt with honey (400dr). Generally avoid restaurants with a large seating capacity; these fill up with noisy bus tours and often have mediocre food. For night life, there's **Zorba's, Calypso,** and **Stadium.** All are cheesy, cheerful, and easy to find.

■ ANCIENT OLYMPIA

This legendary site between the Kladeo and Alphios Rivers was not a city, but an event. Here, the leaders of rival city states shed their armor and congregated in peace to enjoy the Olympic games and make offerings to the gods.Only game officials were permitted in the sacred town of Olympia. The center of town was reserved for the **Altis,** a walled enclosure or sacred grove of Zeus. On the far east side were the **stadium** and the **echo stoa,** which was said to have had a seven-fold echo. Facilities for both administrators and participants comprised the remaining three sides of the Altis. Over the centuries, council houses and treasuries were added to the site. In addition, victors often built monuments to the gods here.

The site's dimensions remain impressive, although the ruins are not particularly well-preserved. The setting is also striking for its natural beauty and tranquility. Few sections are cordoned off and you can walk or climb on the colossal remains of the Temple of Zeus. A guide and map are vital, as the ruins are poorly marked. Two thorough guides are available at the site: the red *Olympia* by Spiros Photinos (1500dr); and the blue *Guide to the Museum and Sanctuary* by A. and N. Yalouris (2200dr). The thigh-high remains of the **Gymnasium,** dating from the 2nd century BC, lie inside the main gate. To the left as you enter is the **Prytaneion,** with its sacred hearth. Past the Gymnasium stand the re-erected columns of the **Palaestra.** This building was the wrestling school, a place for athletes to practice and dress and philosophers to ruminate. The next group of buildings includes the **workshop of Phidias,** the famous artist (supposedly the creator of the ivory and gold statue of Athena for the Parthenon) who was commissioned to produce a sculpture for the site. His tools, terra-cotta molds, and a cup bearing his name turned up during excavations. Farther on is the huge **Leonidaion,** the former lodgings of game officials.

The gigantic **Temple of Zeus** dominated the entire complex. Parts of the original mosaic floor can still be seen on the temple base. The nave of the temple once housed Phidias's 13m ivory and gold statue of Zeus on his throne, reckoned by the Greeks to be one of the seven wonders of the ancient world. Emperor Theodosius ordered that the gold and ivory statue be brought to Constantinople, where it was destroyed by fire in 475 AD.

On the north edge of the Altis are the dignified remains of the **Temple of Hera.** Built in the 7th century BC, it is the oldest and most well-preserved building on the site, as well as the oldest Doric temple in Greece. Originally built for both Zeus and Hera, it was devoted solely to the goddess when Zeus moved to separate quarters in the south. The temple testifies to the ancient worship of female deities, fecundity, and mother earth. The **Olympic flame** is still lit here, then borne to the site of the modern games by the necessary vehicles, runners, school children, Hell's Angels, and anyone else wishing to join the panoply.

The archway on the east end of the Altis leads to the **stadium.** As originally constructed, the arena's artificial banks could accommodate 40,000 spectators. The **judges' stand** is still in place, as are the starting and finishing lines. Beyond the stadium flows the Alphios River, said to run underground all the way to Sicily, information which Hercules once found handy when he had to clean the Augean stables. (Tel. 22 517; site open Mon.-Fri. 7:30am-7pm, Sat.-Sun. 8:30am-3pm; admission 1200dr, students 600dr.) Public bathrooms and water fountains are inside the site.

The gleaming **New Museum** (tel. 22 742), across the street from the site, is set among marble pavilions and tree-lined avenues. It houses a large collection of well-displayed statues, including the Baby Dionysus attributed to the 4th-century BC sculptor Praxiteles, and a number of figurines including the **Little Man with the Big Erection** pictured on postcards throughout the country. It also contains two impressive constructions made of surviving pieces of the pediments of the Temple of Zeus, and miniature reconstructions of the site as it might have appeared in antiquity. (Open Mon. 12:30-7pm, Tues.-Fri. 8am-7pm, Sat.-Sun. 8:30am-3pm; admission 1200dr, students 600dr; cameras w/flash 500dr; video cameras 1000dr.)

Spirit of '76

Olympia has always been a place of worship. Initially, shrines were built here to honor an assortment of gods, like Zeus or Michael Jordan. In later years, the Olympiad celebrated men's physical form and athletic achievements. But only recently have the games included such physically challenging sports as rhythmic gymnastics and ballroom dancing. Women (except for the Priestess of Demeter) were not invited to participate in or attend the games, and were especially forbidden from entering the locker rooms. In fact, they were hurled off a cliff if they were caught entering the Olympic assembly (at least according to Pausanias, the Peloponnesian travel writer of the 2nd century AD). Beginning in 776 BC, young male jocks from all over Greece (and later Rome) would gather in Olympia for the quadrennial festival of Olympian Zeus, and the athletic competition and drinking games that accompanied it. The games began as a simple footrace and wrestling match, but gradually expanded to a five-day extravaganza, including six different kinds of races, boxing, wrestling, and the pentathlon (wrestling, discus toss, javelin throw, long jump, and one-stadium-length race). The games themselves commanded respect. Under normal circumstances, Greek cities perpetually battled each other, but warring subsided when the Olympic Truce was declared. The truce was violated only twice during the history of the games.

ARCADIA ΑΡΚΑΔΙΑ

Poets since Theocritus have fancied Arcadia as the archetypal scene of pastoral pleasure. Gods, too, appreciated the area: Pan and Dionysus chose this lush, mountain-ringed land as the site for their gleeful dances. Rural serenity can still be found in the hidden bays, deep green vegetation, dramatic mountains, and vast fir forests. Elsewhere, as in the bustling metropolis of Tripolis, the modern era has brought a rumble of buses and cargo to the fields where satyrs once cavorted.

■■■ TRIPOLIS ΤΡΙΠΟΛΗ

Tripolis is the transportation hub of Arcadia. Its crowded sidewalks and perilous streets, negotiated by motorists who demonstrate their driving prowess by narrowly missing pedestrians, can initially be dismaying. Buses to the wonderful mountain villages are infrequent, and travelers may have to spend the night. If you stay, don't despair; Tripolis has beautiful squares with cafés, churches, trees, and a tourist-free atmosphere. It'll cost you, though; many wealthy Greeks living abroad return to their Arcadian homeland for the summer months and are willing to pay through the nose for the privilege of staying here; unfortunately, you'll have to as well.

ORIENTATION AND PRACTICAL INFORMATION

The distinctive character of each of Tripolis' attractive squares is often lost on the weary traveler. Seeming uniformity can lead to profound disorientation. Most buses arrive at the Arcadia bus station in the big rotary, **Kolokotronis Square,** marked by the Arcadia Hotel and the statue of Kolokotronis. Five blocks down Georgion St., the unmarked street next to the Arcadia on the left leads to **Agiou Vasiliou,** an even larger square marked by the Church of Agios Vasilios. The bus station, OTE, police station, tourist office, and post office are on side streets off this square, with the police located on the airy and attractive **Petrinou Square,** marked by the large Neoclassical Maliaropoulio theater. Buses to the south and to Patras leave from the KTEL Messinia Café across from the train station. To get into the center of town from the train station, walk up Lagopati St. (directly in front of the station) and take a left on Venizelou St.; you'll arrive at Kolokotronis Square. A dense, disorienting map is on the wall in the Galaxy Hotel on Agiou Vasiliou Square.

Tourist Office: (tel. 23 18 44). In the town hall down Ethnikis Antistasis St. (look for the flag and the colored glass windows). This new office provides maps, books, and information on Arcadia in English. Open 8am-12:30pm.

Police: (tel. 22 24 11 or 23 18 44). Ethnikis Antistasis St., off the right-hand side of Ag. Vasiliou Sq. across from the theater—go to the 2nd floor. 24 hr.

Post Office: (tel. 22 54 29). Plapouta St., past the coffee shops (corner of Ag. Vasiliou Sq.), near Galaxias Hotel. Open Mon.-Fri. 7:30am-2pm. **Postal Code:** 22100.

OTE: #29 28th Octovriou St. (tel. 22 63 99). From Ag. Vasiliou Sq., take Eth. Antistasis St. (on the right) and bear left immediately on 28 Octovriou St. Open 24 hr. **Telephone Code:** 071.

Bank: National Bank, on Ethnikis Antistasis, 1 block from Ag. Vasiliou Sq. (tel. 22 54 89 or 24 29 53), offers **currency exchange.** Open Mon.-Thurs. 8am-2pm, Fri. 8am-1:30pm. There are many other banks throughout the city.

Trains: The **train station** (tel. 24 12 13) is 1km west of Kolokotronis Sq. Go through the bus station and turn right; the train station is at the end of the street. Trains go northeast to Athens (3 per day, 4hr., 1500dr), Corinth (2½hr., 900dr), and Argos (1½hr., 590dr); and southwest to Kalamata (3 per day, 3hr., 840dr).

Buses: Arcadias Station (tel. 22 25 60) sends buses to Athens (13 per day, 2hr., 2400dr), Dimitsana (8:30am and 6:15pm, 1½hr., 1000dr), Pirgos (8:30am and 6:15pm, 4hr., 2250dr), Andritsena (11:45am and 9:45pm, 1hr., 1250dr), and Megalopolis (9 per day, 4:45am-9:45pm, 30min., 550dr). **Blue buses** leave from the kiosk at Platia Areus for Tegea and Mantinea (every hr., 15min., 190dr). Buses go from the **KTEL Messinia and Laconia** bus depot (tel. 24 20 86) across from the train station to Kalamata (3 per day, 1300dr), Pylos (2 per day, 1950dr), Sparta (12 per day, 6:30am-9pm, 1hr., 850dr), or Patras (6am and 2:30pm, 3½hr., 2550dr).

English Bookstore: On Ag. Vasiliou Sq. Sells newspapers and magazines.

Hospital: Dial 166 for emergency or medical assistance.

ACCOMMODATIONS

Tripolis is better suited for the numerous conventions in town than it is for budget travelers. **Hotel Ikinouria** (tel. 24 10 01) has small rooms, but it's the cheapest (doubles 4350dr). From Kolokotronis Sq., walk down Greg. Lambraki St., the road to Sparta (also known as Ligouriou St.); it's a block past the fruit stand/toilet paper merchant on the left. **Hotel Alex,** 26 Vas. Georgios St. between Kolokotronis Sq. and Ag. Vasiliou Sq. (tel. 22 34 65), offers standard rooms in varying shades of puce. It's near the bus station, but the nonstop roar from the traffic below will make Tripolis seem like the city that never sleeps; or, rather, the city that won't let *you* sleep. (Singles 4000dr, w/bath 5500dr; doubles 6600dr, w/bath 8000dr.) Camping near or around Tripolis is non-existent. There are no official campsites and unofficial camping is prohibited by the local authorities. If possible, don't spend the night.

FOOD AND ENTERTAINMENT

Most *tavernas* and restaurants in Tripolis border the three main squares. Try **To Konaki,** an agreeable restaurant off Ag. Vasiliou Sq. on Petropoulou St. Clean, with attentive service and piquant *tzaziki* (250dr) or scrumptious *saganaki* (650dr; opens for dinner around 9pm).

The summer entertainment in Tripolis is at the cultural events 400m from Ag. Vasiliou Sq. and at nearby villages. Posters advertise dance groups, theatrical performances, and choirs. Also, keep an eye out for "ΙΕΡΑ ΠΑΝΗΓΥΡΙΣ" signs, advertising festivals in small villages. The most excitement is in the squares, where residents hang out and cultural groups sometimes perform. During Easter the town's bishop roasts a lamb in one of the squares, and all attendants eat for free. Other impromptu events of a more secular nature (dancing and drinking) take place nightly.

SIGHTS

The new **Archaeological Museum** (tel. 24 21 48), is on Evangelistrias St., in a yellow flower-bedecked building. From Kolokotronis Sq. to Ag. Vasiliou Sq., take the first left and turn left again. It's packed with pottery from the Paleokastro tombs; look for a giant *amphora* flanking the entrance. (Open Tues.-Sun. 8:30am-3pm; admission 500dr, students 400dr.) The large blue **Church of Agios Vasilios** is in the square of the same name. (Open to visitors 9am-dusk except during services.) Note the shops underneath the church, a great place to buy religious art.

Traveling companies and local performance groups stage shows in the attractive **Maliaropoulio Theater,** which dominates Petrinou Sq. All are in Greek; if you're interested, ask at the tourist office (tickets 1000-4000dr).

■■■ ANDRITSENA ΑΝΔΡΙΤΣΑΙΝΑ

Andritsena is falling apart, but that's what makes it lovable. A haphazard tumble of red-roofed old houses and shops with faded, speckled façades sprawls endearingly along a mountainside. Tourists are rare, despite the nearby temple at Vassae. Andritsena is a good base from which to visit Vassae; otherwise, there are more picturesque villages that are easier to reach and have more amenities.

In town, the **police** (tel. 22 209) are near the Shell station (24 hr). The **post office** (open Mon.-Fri. 7:30am-2pm) and **National Bank** (open Mon.-Thurs. 8am-2pm, Fri. 8am-1:30pm) are next to the Shell station in the square. The **OTE** is off the main street, near the church. (Open Mon.-Fri. 7:30am-3pm.) For the **clinic,** dial 22 210, -1. **Postal Code:** 27061; **Telephone Code:** 0626.

Andritsena is 1½hr. west of **Megalopolis** and the same distance east of Pirgos. **Buses** leave from the Café Apollon in the main square (Greek coffee 150dr). Buses to Athens (8:30am and 2pm, 1½hr., 950dr) also stop in Argos (2200dr), Tripolis (3 hr., 1250dr), and Karitena (390dr). Buses also go to Pirgos (8am and 2pm), where they make connections for the rest of the Western Peloponnese.

There are only two options for slumber in town: **Hotel Pan** (tel. 22 213), next to the Shell station (ask here if no one is at the desk), which offers largish doubles with private bath for 5000dr; and the modern **Hotel Theoxenia** (tel. 22 219) at the other end of town (singles 8000dr, doubles 11,000dr). If you yearn passionately for touristy activity, visit the little **folk museum** with its bizarre collection of bric-a-brac and well-displayed costumes. (Open daily 11am-1pm; admission 300dr, students 200dr.)

■ NEAR ANDRITSENA: VASSAE

Rising on the slopes of Mt. Kotilion, the **Temple of Epicurus Apollo** was built in tribute to Apollo for saving the people of Phygalia from a plague. Iktinos, the architect who built the monument in 420 BC, later earned a fat fee by designing the Parthenon. The extant columns are thought to be the first of the Corinthian design.

Vassae remains sacred and solitary. The approach from Andritsena slithers up along cliffs for 14km, snaking between smooth rock pinnacles. At last the temple appears, pillar fragments littering its ancient **agora.** Though grand, the temple is now veiled by a canopy and entombed by scaffolding to protect it from acid rain. Those who hitchhike get to Vassae (there is no bus) by waiting at the turn-off just outside Andritsena on the road to Pirgos. Some travelers wait around the center of town outside a café and flag down cars with foreign license plates. You can also share a **taxi** from Andritsena (roughly 3000dr round-trip). Make it clear from the start that this is a group rate; some drivers may charge per person. Or you could walk back to town (3½hr. over the hills).

■■■ DIMITSANA AND STEMNITSA ΔΗΜΗΤΣΑΝΑ ΚΑΙ ΣΤΕΜΝΙΤΣΑ

West of Tripolis, the little villages of Dimitsana and Stemnitsa make good bases for hiking, walking, or just slowing down to enjoy the villages' natural beauty. This area is known as the "Switzerland of Greece" for its green mountains and chalet-like houses. The atmosphere, however, is far from Swiss; in Dimitsana and Stemnitsa, travelers can still discover the charms of traditional village life. The Erimanthos, Menalo, and Oligirtos mountain ranges separate the old settlements of the west Peloponnese from the beach resorts of the east. The timeless mountains are ancient and gnarled, and lush vegetation clings to all but the highest summits. When making treks into the mountains, don't be fooled by Greece's daytime heat; mountain towns get unbelievably chilly after twilight.

In **Dimitsana** the bus deposits you on Labardopoulou St. next to the **post office** (tel. 31 234; open Mon.-Fri. 7:30am-2pm), and a café which doubles as a **taxi stand.** Uphill from the café is **Pesonton Sq.** The **police** are up around the corner from the post office. To get to the **museum** and **library** (open 8am-1pm), follow the main street from the bus station and ascend the stairs before the main square (marked by a yellow sign). The town has been an educational center for more than 300 years; these two institutions commemorate its scholarly achievements. The **icon museum** (tel. 31 465), in the alley to the right of the *souvlaki* café, is also worth a look. (Open Sat.-Tues. and Thurs. 9:30am-1:30pm.) Continuing on, you'll reach the **OTE,** 402 Labardopoulou St. (tel. 31 599; open Mon.-Fri. 8:20am-2pm). The **National Bank** (tel. 31 210, -503) is at #406 just past the OTE. (Open Mon.-Thurs. 8am-2pm, Fri. 8am-1:30pm.) **Postal Code:** 22007; **Telephone Code:** 0795.

Buses run from Tripolis to Dimitsana (daily at 1pm, 1½hr., 800dr) and from Dimitsana to Tripolis (daily at 6am and 11am). There are additional buses leaving for Tripolis, Pirgos, and Olympia from nearby **Karkalou,** on the main highway, a 20-min.

(800-1000dr) taxi ride away. Remember to leave time for connections, as there are only two taxis in town. Ask the police or in the cafés for details.

There's one hotel in town, the pretty but pricey **Hotel Dimitsana** (tel. 31 518, -9), on the road to Stemnitsa (singles 7500dr, doubles 12,000dr), all with breakfast. Another option is a delightful, appliance-filled room at **O Tholos Restaurant,** with bath and television (7000dr, w/kitchenette 8000dr).

From Dimitsana, hike 11km along the road through perfumed wildflowers (or shell out 100dr for a cab) to **Stemnitsa,** a perfect honeymoon location with beautiful homes, sun-dappled squares, and lovely restaurants. Completing the fantasy is a gorgeous hotel on the main road, **Hotel Triokolonion** (tel. 81 297; singles 5500dr, doubles 7800dr, private bath and breakfast). The **post office** (tel. 81 280) is behind the church in the square (open 7:30am-2pm). The square hosts a kiosk with telephone, outdoor cafés, and *tavernas.* Try **Café Psigoporio** for sumptuous salad (600dr) and their special lamb chops. **Postal Code:** 22024; **Telephone Code:** 0795.

Off the road from Dimitsana to Stemnitsa are several monasteries, some built right into the mountain face. One of these is the **Monastery of Ag. Ioannis Prodromos,** 12km from Dimitsana. The road goes from asphalt to dirt, and finally becomes a footpath on the mountain. Here you can see the icons painted on the bare stone walls and monastic cells almost defying gravity as they hang off the mountain. Inhabited by only twelve monks. (Open dawn-dusk to modestly dressed visitors; free, though a small donation is expected.)

MESSENIA ΜΕΣΣΗΝΙΑ

Messenia refreshes travelers as an oasis of abundance in the arid Peloponnese. Olives, figs, and grapes spring from the rich soil on the region's rocky coastline, which remains largely tourist-free. Most Messenians live at the head of the gulf, around sprawling Kalamata, a convenient town from which to tour Mani's west coast. More alluring is the somnolent port town of Pylos, strategically located for bus, moped, and car travel to Koroni, Methoni, and the beaches of the south.

■■■ KALAMATA ΚΑΛΑΜΑΤΑ

Kalamata, the second-largest city in the Peloponnese after Patras, flourishes as a port and beach resort. Although Kalamata's past is not immediately evident, it was here that the Greek War of Independence of 1821 began. On March 23, two days before the official start of the war, a group of Kalamatans, impatient for the end of Turkish rule, overtook the sleeping Turks in a massacre that is commemorated each year with a reenactment of the Greek victory, parades, and traditional dancing.

ORIENTATION AND PRACTICAL INFORMATION

Kalamata's busiest areas form an "L," with the bus station and outdoor market at the top of the "L." The vertical stem is formed by the main thoroughfare, **Aristomenous Street,** which runs through vast **Georgiou Square,** site of most of the city's amenities, before it becomes **Fillelinon St.** At the corner of the "L" is the Levi's factory and the port; **Navarinou Street** runs along the waterfront to form the horizontal leg.

Kalamata is large and spread-out—the bus station is 3km from the beach—but has an efficient public transportation system. **Bus** #1 (150dr anywhere along the line; every hr. 8am-10pm) takes you anywhere you want to go. Catch buses at one of the blue *stasis* signs. Buses begin their route at **23rd Martiou Square.** To get there, follow Artemidos St., three bridges from the bus station and three blocks to the left. Then cross the third bridge off Artemidos and turn right onto **Aristomenous St. Taxis** from the bus station to the waterfront cost 550dr.

Tourist Police: 46 Aristomenos St. (tel. 23 187), in the same building with the **police** (tel. 100). English-speaking tourist police are on the 2nd floor. Open daily 7:30am-9:30pm, but the regular police will help at any time. **Port police** (tel. 22 218) on the harbor past the Levi's factory.

Post Office: 4 Iatropolou St. (tel. 22 810). Near the south end of Georgiou Sq. Another branch on the waterfront at the port past the Levi's factory. Both are open Mon.-Fri. 7:30am-2pm. **Postal Code:** 24100.

OTE: Georgiou Sq., opposite the National Bank. Open 7:30am-10pm. **Telephone Code:** 0721.

Banks: National Bank of Greece, on Aristomenous St., off the north end of Georgiou Sq. and on the waterfront on Akrita St. Offers **currency exchange.** Open Mon.-Thurs. 8am-2pm, Fri. 8am-1:30pm. Cirrus accepted. Other banks in the city.

Flights: To Athens daily at 7:15pm (45min.; 12,900dr; children younger than 12, 5000dr). **Olympic Airways,** 17 Sideromikou Stathmou St. (tel. 22 376), just before train station. Open 8am-4pm. Taxis to the airport cost 1500dr. Inquire at the KTEL station for airport-bound buses; schedules erratic.

Trains: (tel. 23 904). Station at the end of Sideromikou Stathmou St. Turn right on Frantzi St. at the end of Georgiou Sq., and walk a few blocks. Cheaper and slower than buses. Head to Athens (4 per day, 5:30am-3:40pm, 7hr., 2160dr) via Tripolis (2½hr., 840dr). Trains also go to Argos (4hr., 1280dr), Corinth (5¼hr., 1640dr), Kyparissia (2hr., 590dr), Pirgos (3¼hr., 860dr), Patras (5½hr., 1500dr), and Olympia (1100dr).

Buses: (tel. 22 851). Information 7am-2pm. Travel to Athens (8 per day, 10:30am-10:30pm, 5hr., 3500dr) via Megalopolis (900dr). Also to Tripolis (1300dr), Argos (1750dr), and Corinth (2900dr). Patras (2 per day, 4hr., 3350dr) via Pirgos (2hr., 1900dr), Sparta (2 per day, 800dr) via Artemisia (410dr), Mavromati (2 per day, 410dr), and Koroni (5-7 per day, 1½hr., 620dr). Some buses continue to Methoni (1½hr., 900dr) and Finikountas (2hr., 1100dr). For Areopolis and Gythion, go via Itilo (2hr., 1100dr), where you'll change buses immediately. The bus from Itilo goes to Areopolis (15min., 200dr) and then Gythion (½hr., 40dr).

City Buses: Depart from the bus depot near 23 Martiou Sq. Take the #1 here for the waterfront or camping areas (150dr; open 8am-10pm).

Moped Rental: Bastakos Motor Bikes, 190 Faron St. (tel. 26 638). Mopeds 3200dr per day, bicycles 1600dr. Or **Alpha Rental** (tel. 93 423), on Vironos St. Mopeds 3500dr per day, bicycles 1500dr per day. Both are near the waterfront.

Taxi Service: (tel. 21 112). To the campsites from the city costs roughly 500dr.

Road Help: (tel. 104; 24 hr.), to reach the auto club ΕΛΠΑ (Greece's AAA).

Pharmacy: Many line Aristomenous St. Most open daily 8am-2pm, Tues. and Thurs.-Fri. also 5:30-9pm. For 24-hr. pharmacy information dial 100.

Hospital: Athinou St. (tel. 85 203).

Medical Emergency: Call 25 555.

ACCOMMODATIONS

Most of Kalamata's hotels are along the waterfront. Accommodations abound but "Rooms to Let" are uncommon here.

Hotel Nevada, 9 Santa Rosa (tel. 82 429). Take bus #1 and get off as soon as it turns left along the water. The walls of these clean rooms are layered with a bizarre hodgepodge of posters. Tons, and we mean *tons,* of potted plants—you'll spot them a block away. Singles 3400dr, doubles 4900dr, triples 6790dr.

Avra, 10 Santa Rosa (tel. 82 759), across the street. Clean and comfortable rooms. Chirping birds in the lobby. Doubles 6000dr, triples 7000dr.

Hotel Plaza (tel. 82 590), on Navarinou St., is the place for anyone determined to stay on the waterfront. Stay on the #1 bus until you see the sign. Doubles have gorgeous seaside view. Singles 6500dr, doubles 9100dr, triples 10,800dr.

Camping Patista (tel. 29 525), 2km east along the water. Take bus #1 to the waterfront Mobil gas station and walk 100m. It's on the left, off a driveway. (550dr per person, 500dr per car, small tent 750dr, large tent 900dr, electricity 500dr.) The hotel here rents rooms of varying size and quality (starting at 2000dr). Often has maintenance and fruit-picking work available to campers.

Camping Maria's Sea and Sun (tel. 41 060). Luxurious as far as campsites go, and farther east. 1150dr per person, 650dr per car, small tent 790dr, large tent 915dr, electricity 350dr, hot showers included. Take bus #1.

FOOD AND ENTERTAINMENT

Before leaving town, sample the famous Kalamata olives and figs. Stop by the collection of edibles at the **New Market,** just across the bridge from the bus station. The best sit-down meals can be found at the string of restaurants along the waterfront. Try **Routsis Restaurant,** on the water opposite the Plaza Hotel, for good, cheap food (spaghetti 600dr). Its neighbor to the left, **Korali,** serves hearty, inexpensive meals (*mousaka* 950dr, *souvlaki* 150dr). Closer to the port is **Poikilia** (entrees average 1200dr). In general, restaurants nearer the harbor are more expensive.

At night, head to Georgiou Square or to the real nightlife on the waterfront. Kalamata's newest disco, **Palladium,** costs a fortune (cover 1200dr, includes one drink), but more moderately priced clubs surround it on the water. The most popular bar for under-30s is **Biraria,** on the waterfront near the corner of the "L." Other bars cluster enviously around it.

SIGHTS

Only a few sights remain in Kalamata. The **Castle of the Villehardouins,** which crowns a hill above the old city, has proven remarkably indestructible. Built by the Franks in 1208, it was blown up by the Turks in 1685 and restored by the Venetians a decade later. It even remained relatively unscathed by the 1986 earthquake. Today the castle houses an open-air theater, which hosts "Cultural Summer of Kalamata" in July and August with everything from jazz and rock to classical Greek drama. (Ticket prices depend on the event, and start at 500dr.) To get to the gates from 23 Martiou Square, walk up Ipapandis St. past the church on the right side, and take your first left. At the foot of the castle is the **Convent of St. Constantine and Helen,** where nuns sell their linen and lacework at bargain prices. At the far end of the site is the **Byzantine Church** where a doe-eyed Virgin Mary icon was found, giving the city its name, which means "good eyes." (Open 8am-dusk; free.) The remains of a Byzantine church molder at the far edge of the site; scramble up for a sublime view. (Open 8am-dusk; free.) At 221 Faron St., off the waterfront, Kalamata's **School of Fine Arts** exhibits work by Greek artists. (Open daily 9am-1pm and 6-10pm.) Kalamata also supports two professional theaters and cinemas. Ask the **tourist police** for information on events in the **Pantazopoulion Cultural Center** on Aristomenon St. Local archaeological finds are exhibited in the nearby **Benaki Museum,** while folk art, crafts, and icons are on display at the **Folk Art Museum.**

Kalamata has been trying, with considerable success, to clean up its beaches. They are less crowded and less spoiled as you proceed eastward. The water here is the warmest in Greece. With large shady trees, cafés, a performance area, and a duck pond, the **Train Park** (at the end of Aristomenous St., on the waterfront) extends several blocks towards Georgiou Square. The main attraction is a simulated train station, life-size and open for exploration.

■ NEAR KALAMATA

For more antiquities, take the bus from Kalamata to **Mavromati** (Mon.-Sat.) to the well-preserved remains of **ancient Messene** (not to be confused with modern Messini) on Mt. Ithomi. The striking 4th-century BC wall epitomizes the period's defensive architecture. An **agora, theater,** and **Temple to Artemis** also remain. Continue up the road to the fallen doorpost of the colossal **Arcadian Gate,** designed by Epaminondas, the architect of Megalopolis. Also nearby is the 16th-century **Monastery of the Vourkano,** with some outstanding frescoes. The only difficulty with this trip is the timing. If you want more than 15min. at the site, catch the morning bus and return on the post-Petralona leg of the evening bus, or take a taxi (4500dr).

The road from Koroni to Kalamata hugs the east coast of the Messenian peninsula. Between Harokopi and the coastal town of **Petalidio (Phone Code:** 0722) is a long chain of beaches. **Koroni** is a pleasant fishing village with a beautiful long sand beach and a castle of its very own. Unfortunately, it connects by bus only to Kalamata, making it difficult to reach. Pleasant **Koroni Camping** (tel. (0725) 22 119; 800dr per person, 600dr per car, small tent 650dr, big tent 950dr) has **watersports.**

■■■ TAYGETUS MOUNTAINS

South of Kalamata, the bus to Areopolis winds through the Taygetus mountains, which soar to 2630m at their highest point. The alluring grey peaks of Mani loom behind olive-covered hillsides. The first major bus stop comes at the coastal village of **Kardamili.** The town is a popular beach resort, so there are many "Rooms to Let," but call ahead in the summer (expect to pay 3000-5000dr for doubles). In the center of town hospitable **Joanna Stefania** (tel. 73 242) rents spotless doubles with balconies and a communal kitchen (6600dr, w/bath 8000dr). Look for the sign above **Gelateria** (which serves delicious exotic ice cream; 2 scoops 300dr). On the Kalamata side of town, rooms are near a gorgeous white pebble beach. Follow the blue signs to **Camping Melitsina** (tel. 73 461; 1050dr per person, 700dr per car, small tent 790dr, large tent 950dr, electricity 600dr). On the other end of town, follow the red and white "Rooms to Let" signs right after the post office and a cobblestone path. Here you'll find **Olivia Koumanakou's** tidy pension with a communal kitchen (tel. 73 326; singles 5500dr, doubles 7000dr). For inspired food, try the family-run **Taverna Kiki,** on the waterfront below the village. There is a **supermarket** and **bakery** near the square. Kardamili's **police station** is on the main road across from the church; farther towards Itilo is the **post office** (open Mon.-Fri. 7:30am-2:30pm). Following the road from Kardamili to Itilo, you will find several coves with pebble **beaches. Telephone Code:** 0721.

If you're bound for Areopolis, change buses in the village of **Itilo** immediately upon arrival—the bus leaves promptly. This peaceful town is riveted on the fully frescoed **Monastery of Dekoulo** and the 17th-century Turkish fortress poised on a neighboring hill. The entertainment quarter consists of two cafés off the small square and a reasonably priced restaurant. The bus continues 3km down to the magnificently situated **Neo Itilo.** At the heart of an enormous natural bay encircled by monumental barren mountains, the town's white pebble beach is ideal for swimming. For a room, try the **Hotel Itilo** (tel. (0733) 51 300). From Neo Itilo, the road winds uphill, affording a view of **Limani,** the old harbor of Areopolis, with its sprinkling of fishing boats. The tiny port is home to the Mavromichaeli **Castle of Potrombei.** From here, buses continue to Areopolis. The bad roads and reckless drivers make this ride as much fun as putting your stomach through the spin cycle.

■■■ PYLOS ΠΥΛΟΣ

Pylos' shady square and tile houses framed by bobbing flowers are typical enough for a port town. But the sharp rock face of Sfakteria Island is a peculiarity that gives Pylos a defiant appearance in addition to a protected harbor. The town, also known as Navarino, is renowned for the 1827 sea battle which gave Greece its independence. As Turkish forces, reinforced by the Egyptian fleet, battered the coast, the English, French, and Russian fleets arrived at Navarino and saved the beleaguered Greeks. Pylos now espouses a warm, carefree attitude; a glance at its waterfront's inviting turquoise waters, filled by dozens of sunbathers, is enough to convince anyone that this is a place of endless summer daze.

Orientation and Practical Information The **police** (tel. 22 316; 24 hr.) are located on the second floor of a building on the left side of the waterfront (facing the water). Continue around that turn to reach the **port police** (tel. 22 225). The

post office (tel. 22 247) is on Nileos St., uphill to the left (facing the water) from the bus station (open Mon.-Fri. 8am-2pm). To get to the **OTE,** pass the post office and take your first left; it is on the right of the square, 2 blocks uphill. (Open Mon.-Fri. 7:30am-3:10pm.) A **National Bank of Greece** is also on the waterfront. (Open Mon.-Thurs. 8am-2pm, Fri. 8am-1:30pm.) The **hospital** phone number is 22 315. **Postal Code:** 24001; **Telephone Code:** 0723.

Buses (tel. 22 230) leave regularly for Kalamata (9 per day, Mon.-Sat. 6:35am-9pm, Sun. 6 per day, 9am-9pm, 1¼hr., 750dr), Athens (daily at 9am, 7hr., 4000dr), and Finikountas (Mon.-Sat. 4 per day, 2 on Sun., 45min., 360dr), via Methoni (15min., 175dr). No buses travel directly to Koroni, but you can go to Finikountas and take the 5pm bus from there to Koroni. Buses also leave for Kyparissia (Mon.-Sat. at 7, 9, 11am, and 1:35pm; Sun. at 11am, 2hr., 900dr), all stopping at Nestor's Palace (30min., 300dr) and Chora (35min., 300dr). For moped rental, try **Venus Rent-A-Car** (tel. 22 393, -12; open 8:30am-1pm and 6-9pm; mopeds 2500-4800dr per day).

Accommodations There are several "Rooms to Let" signs as the bus descends the hill. In general, expect to pay 3500-5000dr for singles, 4500-7000dr for doubles, and 5000-8000dr for triples. Try the clean and simple rooms of **Anna Panoskalsi** (tel. 22 935), up the hill from the far right of the harbor. Go up a flight of stairs just past the new Hotel Koralis, and follow the sign for rooms (singles 4000dr, doubles 6000dr). **Navarino Beach Camping** (tel. 22 761) lies 6km north at Yialova Beach. (Person 1250dr, small tent 750dr, large tent 950dr, electricity 600dr.)

Sights **Fortresses** guard both sides of Pylos' harbor. **Neokastro,** which stands guard on the south, is easily accessible from the town: walk up the road for Methoni and turn right at the sign. The well-preserved walls enclose a church (originally a mosque), a citadel, a building flanked by detritus from the Battle of Navarino, and a brand-new **archaeological museum.** (Open Tues.-Sun. 8:30am-3pm.) The **Paleokastro,** north of Pylos, is harder to reach. Drive to Petrochori and proceed south with caution—the road is poor, though clearly marked. The overgrown weeds around the castle are home to hundreds of snakes and lizards.

Pylos' tiny **museum,** 1½ blocks up Fillelinon St. on the left side of the square, houses finds from Hellenistic and Mycenaean tombs. (Open Tues.-Sun. 8:30am-3pm; admission 400dr, students 200dr; free on Sun.) To see **Sfakteria** up close, you can take a **boat tour** from the port. The hour jaunt around the island stops at various monuments to the allied sailors of the Battle of Navarino and shows off a sunken Turkish ship. Boat captains often try to organize groups for tours (roughly 10 people). Inquire at the small booth on the waterfront or at the neighboring coffee bar under the police station, where the captains often rest.

■ NEAR PYLOS

While the *Odyssey* only vaguely mentions the location of the Palace of Nestor, and Homer describes three places called Pylos, the American archaeologists who dug at Pylos are confident that their excavations have uncovered the actual palace where Nestor, Odysseus' bud, met with Telemachus. Besides pieces of wall and a remarkably well-preserved ancient bathtub, though, the ruins are not much to speak of. The University of Cincinnati's scholarly guide (500dr) is available at the entrance to the site. (Open Mon.-Sat. 8:45am-3pm, Sun. 9:30am-2:30pm; admission 400dr, students 200dr; free on Sun.) Buses from Pylos and Kyparissia stop outside the site.

KYPARISSIA

Kyparissia, guarded by a mountain fortress, is a conundrum: a place that looks like a city but has the friendliness of a quiet mountain town. It serves mainly as a transportation hub, though. Since the train tracks end here, from where buses continue north or south, a stop is almost inevitable. On the square, there is a **National Bank** (open Mon.-Thurs. 8am-2pm, Fri. 8am-1:30pm) and **post office** (open Mon.-Fri.

7:30am-2pm). The **OTE** is just off the uphill right corner (open Mon.-Fri. 7:30am-10pm, Sat.-Sun. 9am-2pm and 5-10pm). The **police** (tel. 22 333, -500) are farther up the street; for the **port police,** dial 22 128.

Trains go to Kalamata (4 per day, 2hr., 590dr) and Athens (5 per day, 8hr., 2560dr); four of these go via Tripolis (2½hr., 860dr), and five go via Pirgos (1½hr., 540dr) and Patras (3½hr., 1140dr). To get to Kyparissia's fortress, walk one block from the train station; at the five-way intersection take the second sharpest right. **Buses** leave for Athens (daily 8:45, 11am, 3, and 9:15pm; 5hr.; 3700dr) via Tripolis (1450dr) and Corinth (2550dr); Patras (daily 9am and 3pm, 2½hr., 2350dr); Chora (3 per day, 600dr); Pirgos (4 per day 8am-3:30pm, 1½hr., 900dr); and Pylos (3 per day, 2hr., 900dr). **Postal Code:** 24500; **Telephone Code:** 0761.

Hotel Vassilikon, 7 Alexopoulou St. (tel. 22 655), has singles for 5000dr, doubles for 6000dr. **Inn Trifilia** (tel. 22 066), 25th Martiou St., charges 4800dr for humble but well-kept doubles with shared balconies. The purple and white **Hotel Tsolaridis Beach** (tel. 22 145, -389), near the beach, is a conspicuous treasure. Rooms are large and so clean they're sanitary (singles 5000dr, doubles 7000dr, special family rates available.) Posh **Camping Kyparissia** (tel. 23 491), at the far right of the waterfront, has ping pong, a restaurant/bar/minimarket, and a washing machine (900dr). (Person 950dr, car 540dr, small tent 700dr, large tent 1000dr, electricity 500dr.) It's conveniently located near **Sunset Bar** for late-night debauchery.

■■■ METHONI ΜΕΘΩΝΗ

With its hibiscus-lined streets, Methoni is a refreshing reprieve for the weary traveler. Peer through the flowering trees at the spectacular 13th-century fortress along the beach. Forever "the Camelot of Greece," Methoni was once offered by Agamemnon to Achilles to cheer the sulking warrior. Cervantes was so taken with the place that he churned out romances even while imprisoned under Turkish guard.

The town's two main streets form a "Y" at the billiard hall where the Pylos-Finikountas buses stop. Shops are on the upper fork to the right; the beach and fortress are at the end of the lower street, down to the left. The **police** (tel. 31 203) are on a side street off the left fork near the beach. Past the sign on the left fork is the **post office** (open Mon.-Fri. 7:30am-2pm). The **OTE** (open Mon.-Fri. 7:30am-3:10pm) is on the next parallel street to the left. The **National Bank of Greece** is 40m down the right fork (open Mon.-Thurs. 8am-2pm, Fri. 8am-1:30pm). **Buses** go to Kalamata (4 per day, 1½hr., 900dr) via Pylos (15min., 175dr). Four per day travel to Finikountas (30min., 180dr). Two doors from the OTE, buses leave for Athens via Pylos, Kyparissia, Pirgos, and Patras. Ask at the police station or the general store for info. You can contact the **medical clinic** at 31 456. **Postal Code:** 24006; **Telephone Code:** 0723.

Hotel Alex and **Hotel Giota** (tel. 31 290, -1), both behind the OTE, run by the Pavlogiannis family, offer clean rooms in the town's beachside square (singles 6000dr, doubles 8000dr; breakfast 800dr). **Camping Methoni** (tel. 31 228) is crowded but next to the sea (person 1050dr, small tent 600dr, large tent 850dr). Generally, rooms are cheaper farther from the beach. **Hotel Finikas** (tel. 31 390), on the same street as the post office, offers small, recently renovated, homey rooms (singles 7000dr, doubles 10,000dr, triples 12,000dr).

A visit to the southwest Peloponnese should include a trip to Methoni's **Venetian fortress,** a 13th-century mini-city. The **Bourzi,** a small tower built by the Turks to fortify the shore, sits halfway around the wall over the sea. Venture into the fortified walls, cisterns, parapets, and vaulted passages if only to see the birds in the corners of the ceiling. (Fortress open daily 8am-7pm, Sun. 8am-6pm; free.)

■ NEAR METHONI: FINIKOUNTAS ΦΟΙΝΙΚΟΥΝΤΑΣ

Halfway between Methoni and Koroni, Finikountas, a colorful fishing village, coaxes visitors to join tranquil summer activities, like basking in sunshine, swimming in clear blue seawater, and watching colorful *caïques* glide across the surface. For swimming, take the time to go to **Paradise Beach,** the less-crowded cove beyond the rock jetty to the east. If you do stay, change money in advance; Finikountas has neither a bank nor a post office. The **Supermarket Phoenix** sells postage stamps and houses an **OTE** (open daily 7am-1pm and 5-9pm). **Buses** stop across from the Hotel Finikounta and head to Kalamata (3 per day Mon.-Sat., Sun. 3pm; 2hr.; 950dr) via Methoni (½hr., 180dr) and Pylos (45min., 220dr). Buses also go to Kalamata via Harokopio (at 7:30am and 4:30pm, 1½hr., 950dr). **Telephone Code:** 0723.

Look for "Rooms to Let" signs along the waterfront or on the road from Koroni as you enter town. Most restaurateurs either rent rooms or know people who do. **Moudakis Restaurant** (tel. 71 224), to the right of the KMoil gas station (facing the water), has singles for 3700dr, doubles 7000dr. Rooms away from the water are slightly cheaper. Finikountas has two campgrounds. **Camping Ammos** (tel. 71 262) is 2km east of town (person 1100dr, car 660dr, small tent 660dr, large tent 800dr, electricity 540dr). **Camping Anemomylos** (tel. 71 360) is 1km to the west (950dr per person, 750dr per car, small tent 650dr, large tent 810dr, electricity 600dr).

LACONIA ΛΑΚΩΝΙΑ

In the 10th century BC, a tribe of Doric warriors from the north invaded the southwest Peloponnese, drove out its Mycenaean inhabitants, and executed any stragglers unlucky enough to get in their way. Famed mainly for slaughtering their enemies, the region's new masters also distinguished themselves by their curt speech. While their northern counterparts argued in long, flowery rhetoric, Laconians often dispatched their opponents with a single, caustically witty phrase. Thus, those antipathetic to prolix epideictica accordingly received the appellation of the people so disposed—in short, the reticent became "laconic." The Ancient Laconian qualities are still manifest throughout the area, especially in the barren peninsula. Although Laconia boasts three of the Peloponnese's most popular sites—Mani's Pirgos Dirou caves, Sparta's nearby Byzantine ruins of Mystra, and Monemvassia's "rock"—the region remains low key; even its tourist industry is far less businesslike than on the islands or in Athens. Laconia's friendly villages are a welcome break from the urban atmosphere of other, more touristed areas.

■■■ SPARTA ΣΠΑΡΤΗ

The Spartans are portrayed as the bad guys of the classical world—totalitarian warmongers who insisted on pestering the civilized Athenian democrats. These stereotypes, however simplistic, hold true; Sparta's reputation for brutal, no-nonsense militarism is well-deserved. Around 700 BC, after Sparta barely subdued a revolt of the Messenians, the leader Lycurgus instituted reforms that transformed Sparta, body and soul, into a war machine. For the next 350 years, it dominated the entire central Peloponnese with its invincible armies and austere discipline. Outside of war, Sparta contributed little to Greek history; no philosophy, poetry, art, or architecture ever truly flourished here. Weary of further Athenian expansion, Sparta attacked its rival, beginning the 28-year-long Peloponnesian War. After triumphing in 404 BC, it emerged as the supreme military power in the Hellenic world. The Spartans reveled in their power, not even bothering to build walls around their city. Ultimately, only the combined effects of earthquakes, depopulation, and the resistance of its neighbors broke Sparta's hegemony.

A young Spartan's training for a life of war began early, even before conception. Lycurgus believed two fit parents produced stronger offspring, so he ordered all Spartan women to undergo the same rigorous training endured by men. Furthermore, newlyweds were permitted only an occasional tryst on the theory that the heightened desire of the parents would produce more robust children. If they weren't winnowed out as weak or deformed, boys began a severe regimen of training under the auspices of an adult Spartan. The young were forced to walk barefoot to toughen their feet and wore only a simple piece of clothing in both summer and winter to expose them to drastic weather changes. The Spartan creed dictated that young men be guarded against temptations of any kind; strict laws forbidding everything from drinking to pederasty governed Spartans' actions. Moreover, young Spartans were given the plainest and simplest foods for fear that rich delicacies would stunt their growth. (One visitor to Sparta, upon sampling the fare, allegedly quipped, "Now I know why they do not fear death.")

Fortunately, modern Sparta hardly resembles a fascist boot camp. With its nightly roar of mopeds and its monotonous, modern architecture, the city is, ironically, culturally similar to Athens (though it's much smaller and quieter). The fruit trees that line the city's busiest streets lend it an almost endearing quirkiness, but Sparta is very much a city that goes about its own business; little effort is taken to win people over to this town's charms. Still, Sparta is the best and most convenient base from which to explore the Byzantine ruins of Mystra, only 6km away.

ORIENTATION AND PRACTICAL INFORMATION

Sparta's two main streets, **Paleologou** and **Lykourgou,** laced with orange, lime, and palm trees, intersect in the center of town. To get to the center from the bus station, walk left on Paleologou for two blocks. The town square is one block to the right of the intersection on Lykourgou, and all of the necessary amenities are nearby on these two streets. The ruins are on the north edge of town, behind you at the end of Paleologou St. Sparta is laid out in an appropriately no-frills grid.

Tourist Office: (tel. 24 852). To the left of the town hall in the square. The English-speaking staff helps with bus schedules, hotels, and information. Map 400dr. Open daily 8am-12:30pm.

Police: 8 Hilonos St. (tel. 26 229). From the intersection, turn left on Lykourgou St. away from the square. The police are on a side street to the right, past the museum. Helpful, earnest, English-speaking **tourist police** (tel. 20 492; open daily 8am-3pm and 7-9pm) are housed in the same building.

Post Office: (tel. 26 565). Past the OTE on Kleombrotou St., 1 block up from the intersection off Paleologou St. Open Mon.-Fri. 7:30am-2pm. **Postal Code:** 23100.

OTE: 11 Kleombrotou St. (tel. 23 799). Open daily 7am-9:40pm. **Telephone Code:** 0731.

Banks: National Bank (tel. 22 997), on the corner of Dioskouron and Paleologou St., 3 blocks down from the intersection, offers **currency exchange.** Open Mon.-Thurs. 8am-2pm, Fri. 8am-1:30pm. Other banks line Paleologou; take your pick.

Buses: (tel. 26 441). Vrasidou St. off Paleologou, 2 blocks from the main intersection. Buses go to Athens (9 per day, 6:30am-8pm, 5hr., 3050dr), via Corinth (4hr., 1950dr) and sometimes Tripolis (3 per day, 1¼hr., 850dr). Buses also head to Neapolis (2-4 per day, 4hr., 2100dr), Monemvassia (2-3 per day, 2½hr., 1500dr; change buses in Molai), Pirgos Dirou and the caves (daily, 2¼ hr., 1200dr) via Areopolis (2hr., 1000dr; change buses in Gythion), Kalamata (2 per day, 2hr., 800dr), Tripolis (3 per day, 1¼hr., 850dr), Gerolimenas (daily, 3hr., 1550dr), and Gythion (5 per day, 1hr., 650dr). For buses to Mystra, there's a bus station at the corner of Leonidou and Kythonigou 2 blocks past the town hall; follow signs (approximately every 1½hr., 6:50am-8:20pm, 175dr). The schedule is variable; you may want to call the tourist office to check.

Pharmacies: 117 Paleologou St. (tel. 27 212). Open daily 8am-2pm and 5:30-9pm. Three other pharmacies on Paleologou St. and many more throughout the city.

Hospital: Nosokomeio St. (Hospital St.) onto Meilonus. (tel. 28 671, -5). 24 hr.

Police Emergency: Dial 100.

ACCOMMODATIONS

Something of Ancient Sparta must still linger in the modern city, for a stay at one of the town's more inexpensive hotels is certainly a character-building experience.

Rooms are sparse and small; in these "Spartan" rooms, luxury is for the weak. The cheapest place to stay is the **Hotel Panellinion** (tel. 28 031), just past the Lykourgou intersection, with minimalist rooms with balconies almost large enough to stand on (singles 4000dr, doubles 6000dr). Or try **Hotel Cecil** (tel. 24 980), 5 blocks north on the corner of Paleologou St. and Thermopilion St. The traffic roars audibly, but the rooms are unsullied. They'll give you free maps and other Sparta info (singles 4000dr, doubles 6000dr; hot showers). A more luxurious place is the **Hotel Laconia** (tel. 28 951, -2), on Paleologou St. between the bus station and the center of town (singles 6000dr, doubles 9000dr). Near Mystra is the new **Camping Castle View** (tel. 99 303), with pool, wonderful modern showers and toilets, a minimarket, and amiable owners (800dr per person, 550dr per car, small tent 400dr, large tent 600dr, electricity 550dr). To get to the campground, take the regular Mystra bus and ask the conductor to let you off at the site.

FOOD AND ENTERTAINMENT

Sparta's few restaurants serve expensive fast food. For a reasonably priced meal under the fluorescent lights of **Dhiethnes,** head to the far right of the main square facing the row of cafés (entrees 1400dr). A good grill (tel. 27 350) is across from the Hotel Cecil on Paleologou St. (entrees 900dr). Several blocks up from the post office, past Paleologou St., on Kleombrotou St., the sidewalks are crowded with fruit and vegetable stands.

At night, bop 2½km down the road towards Gythion to the **Aithrio Disco.** The **Imago,** a hip, artsy bar, is in the alley behind the town hall and offers a gay-friendly atmosphere (open 10pm-3am).

SIGHTS

There is almost nothing left of Ancient Sparta to clue us in to the people who lived there. Then again, maybe this lack of ruins is the most telling clue of all. At the north end of Paleologou St. stands an enormous **statue of Leonidas,** the famous warrior and king of the Spartans. The Spartans built a large pseudo-tomb for their leader, who fell at the Battle of Thermopylae in 480 BC, in hopeful anticipation of his remains, which were never found. The tomb lies in the middle of a grove that is now a public park, to the left of the ancient ruins. The ruins themselves lie to the north of the modern city (facing the statue of Leonidas, bear left). Modern visitors are apt to be disappointed if they expect to find a southern counterpart to the Parthenon. On the other hand, there is a refreshing absence of postcard-sellers and beer stands. The ruins (1km from the main square at the north edge of the modern city) consist of the outlines of one of the largest theaters of ancient Greece and some fragments of the acropolis. Three miles away are three remaining platforms of the **shrine to Menelaus and Helen,** history's most sought-after babe. The remains of the Spartans' **shrine to Apollo** are on the road to Gythion. A short walk east on the banks of the Eurotas River leads to the **sanctuary of Artemis Orthia.** Spartan youths had to prove their courage here by unflinchingly enduring public floggings. Headless statues beckon you to enter the **archaeological museum** (tel. 28 575), through its beautiful, well-kept park from Lykourgou St. (on the opposite side of Paleologou from the square). The collection includes spooky votive masks used in ritual dances at the sanctuary of Artemis Orthia, the famous head and shoulders of the statue of Leonidas (490-480 AD), and a bronze boar which bristles in the room to the left of the entrance. (Open Tues.-Sat. 8:30am-3pm, Sun. 9:30am-2:30pm; closed weekends Oct.-May; admission 500dr, students 300dr; free on Sun.) For modern art, visit the **Coumantarios Art Gallery,** 123 Paleologou St. (tel. 26 557; English not spoken). The permanent collection of 19th-century French and Dutch paintings is impressive. On the second floor are temporary exhibits of work by modern Greek artists (open Tues.-Sat. 9am-3pm, Sun. 10am-2pm; free).

For an evening excursion from Sparta, share a cab to the village of **Parolis,** 2km from Mystra. There you can sit in a *taverna* and watch the nearby waterfalls. Two kilometers farther is the village of **Tripi,** which has larger waterfalls, some of which run right under the excellent and affordable grill-restaurant **Exochiko Kentro** (tel. 98 314). Down the road past the restaurant is the **cave of Kiades,** where ancient Spartans tossed their sickly or deformed babies.

■ NEAR SPARTA: MYSTRA ΜΥΣΤΡΑ

The extraordinary medieval ruins of Mystra stand 6km west of Sparta. Overflowing with Byzantine churches and castle ruins, this site reveals the splendor of Byzantium's final flourish. In the late 14th century, Mystra, prospering from a lucrative silk industry, became an intellectual center. Many free thinkers, unhappy under the control of repressive feudal lords and clergy, surged into town and set up schools, tying Mystra to the Florentine humanist movement. Philosophers and students wandered the intricate network of paths that weaves the city together and that today renders sightseeing a complex affair. Try tracing a path around several key sites on the three tiers that correspond to the sectors for the commoners, the nobility, and the royalty (in ascending order, naturally). Fortunately, Mystra is one of the better-labeled sites in Greece. Enter through the main gate; the complexity will be easier to handle.

Don't miss the **Metropolis of St. Demetrios** in the lower tier, with its sanctuary and museum of architectural fragments. Wander on to the two churches of the monastery of **Vrontochion, St. Theodori,** and the frescoes of the **Aphentiko** (or Hodegetria). On the same tier is the **Pantanassa,** a convent with a beautifully ornamented façade and a multitude of frescoes, not to mention a miracle-working Virgin Mary icon. Finally, at the extreme left of the lower tier, the **Church of Perivleptos** is perhaps Mystra's most stunning relic—every inch of the church is bathed in exquisitely detailed paintings of religious scenes and figures, most of which had their eyes gouged out by invading Turks (you can still see the holes). Climb up to the **castle,** the fortress that was Mystra's first building (the town developed downward), built by the crusader Guillaume de Villehardouin in 1249 AD. The castle is closer than it looks—you can get there in roughly 1hr. walking from the main gate.

There are water taps inside the entrance through the main gate, at the Metropolis and at Pantanassa, but it's a good idea to bring your own water to combat Mystra's murderous heat. Also, wear tough shoes; many of the paths are rocky and slippery. You'll enjoy Mystra more with a guidebook—buy one with a map at the entrance kiosk (700-2500dr). Even a cursory inspection of the site requires at least 3hr., including the long climb to the summit. Be forewarned: it's been years since bathrooms at the site were in working condition. (Site open daily 8am-9pm. Spring and fall hours 8am-5pm; winter 8:30am-3pm; admission 1200dr, students 600dr; free on Sun.) In summer, try to be at the site by 8am, since the sun becomes unbearable as early as 10am. If you arrive by bus from Sparta, get off at the sign for the Xenis restaurant, with the ruins on your left. Continue up the road, past the bend to the main gate; the site is 1½km beyond the town of Mystra. Aside from campsites, accommodations at Mystra are pricey; visit from Sparta.

■■■ GYTHION ΓΥΘΕΙΟ

Situated on the east coast of Mani and connected by ferry with Kythera and Crete, Gythion, a lively port town, is an ideal place to station oneself while touring the bleakly dramatic territory of Mani. A ½-hr. bus trip will bring you to Areopolis, the haunting fortified town which historically served as Mani's center. A concrete causeway connects Gythion to the tiny island of **Marathonisi,** where Paris and Helen consummated their ill-fated love. Modern Gythion boasts beautiful sand and stone beaches, picturesque houses, and friendly, affable people.

ORIENTATION AND PRACTICAL INFORMATION

The bus stop is on the north side of the waterfront, near the town's amenities and cheaper stores. Small **Mavromichali Square** is in the middle of the waterfront near the quay. The harbor road continues to the right and south, where it eventually meets the causeway to Marathonisi.

Police: (tel. 22 271, -100). On the waterfront, 500m before the bus station.
Port Police: (tel. 22 262). Before the causeway, past Mavromichali Sq.
Post Office: Ermou St. Open Mon.-Fri. 7:30am-2pm. **Postal Code:** 23200.
OTE: At the corner of Herakles and Kapsali St. Open Mon.-Fri. 7:30am-2:30pm. **Telephone Code:** 0733.
Tourist Agency: Theodore V. Rozakis (tel. 22 650, -207), on the waterfront near the square. Provides information and tickets. Open daily 7am-11pm.
Banks: The **National Bank,** just beyond the bus stop towards the water. Offers **currency exchange.** Open Mon.-Thurs. 8am-2pm, Fri. 8am-1:30pm. There are other banks in the same area.
Buses: Station (tel. 22 228) is on the north end of the waterfront. Buses head to Athens (6 per day, 7:30am-3:45pm, 3700dr) via Sparta (1hr., 650dr); Kalamata via Sparta (2 per day, 650dr) or via Itilo (2 per day, 600dr); Monemvassia (daily, 2hr., 1200dr); Gerolimenas (2 per day, 2hr., 900dr) via Areopolis (½hr., 400dr), Pirgos Dirou, and the caves. Buses also go to the campgrounds (including Meltemi, Gythion Beach, and Mani) south of town (6am, 10:15am, 1pm, and 7pm; 175dr).
Ferries: Depart from the quay to the right of Mavromichali Sq. and run to Kythera (daily, 1100dr) and Crete (Wed. and Sat., 4000dr).
Flying Dolphins: More frequent than ferries. For tickets or info contact **Olympia Travel** on the waterfront (open daily 9am-11pm; tel. 24 501 or 22 996).
Taxis: Call 23 400.
Moped Rental: Moto Mani (tel. 22 853), on the waterfront near the causeway. Mopeds 3500dr per day; reduced prices for longer rentals and 100km allowance per day free. Open daily 9am-9pm.
Health Clinic: (tel. 22 001, -2, or -3). Along the right side of the waterfront.

ACCOMMODATIONS

Bypass Gythion's expensive hotels by staying in "Rooms to Let" or at one of the four nearby campgrounds. **Xenia Karlafti's** (tel. 22 719) rooms are in a house enclosed by a black railing, near the port police. The rooms are spacious and clean, and the gracious manager provides a breakfast area, washing machine, and clothesline for her guests (doubles 5000dr, triples 6000dr). Just behind the OTE at **Herakli #22** (tel. 22 915), you'll find spacious rooms with groovy large balconies and international magazines. The owner, a Greek Canadian, is only around to rent rooms June-Aug. (doubles 4000dr). Try **Koutsouri Rooms** (tel. 22 321). From Mavromichali Square, go up Tzanaki Gregoraki, turn right at the clock tower; the rooms are just past the bakery on your left. This sweet family will invite you to join them, their dog Boopie, and their amorous turtles in the garden as they watch TV. (Singles 4000dr, doubles 5000dr, triples 6000dr. Suites w/kitchen 7000dr.) The most luxurious campgrounds are **Meltemi** (tel. 22 833; 950dr per person, 550dr per car, tent 850dr, electricity 550dr) and **Gytheio Bay Campgrounds** (tel. 22 522; 1100dr per person, 600dr per car, small tent 700dr, large tent 800dr, electricity 700dr). Also try **Mani Beach** (tel. 23 450; 920dr per person, 520dr per car, small tent 600dr, large tent 900dr, electricity 500dr). The campgrounds are south of town and accessible by bus.

FOOD AND ENTERTAINMENT

For a reprieve from the restaurants along the waterfront and the grocery stores around the main square which charge exorbitant prices, head to **Kosta's,** a non-touristy establishment across from the public beach near the bus station (chicken in sauce 900dr). The **Cork Room** (tel. 22 122), also on the waterfront, serves cheap and delicious food (lemon roast pork 1000dr, spaghetti 550dr), while a decently-priced place in the square is **Poulikakis** (chicken and spaghetti 950dr). **Supermarkets** are along Vas. Georgiou St. As you walk along the waterfront towards the bus station, bear left at the fork for Vas. Georgiou. There is a fruit and produce **open-air market** every Tuesday and Friday morning (4:30am-noon) between Herakles and

Archaia Theatrou St. The **bakery** up from Super Cycle Moto to the right has delightful cheese pie (200dr). This area also offers some cheap *souvlaki* joints (200-280dr). The small parks near the bus station or on the island are a short walk away and are perfect, cool spots for picnics.

If you're drained from the sun, revitalize at **Disco Ferrari** on Selinitsa beach (1500dr cover w/first drink), or **Spider Disco** 3km down the road to the Acropolis.

SIGHTS

The ancient **theater** of Gythion, tucked away in a corner, has endured the centuries remarkably well. Note the differences between the seats for dignitaries in front and the simpler seats farther back. To get there, walk down Herakles St. from the bus station, go to Ermou St. and then right onto Archaiou Theatrou St. to its end. If you arrive in the early evening, join the local soldiers getting their nightly pep talk here. **Paliatzoures antique shop** (tel. 22 944, -806), on the waterfront at #25 Vas. Pavlou, is the last of its kind in the entire Peloponnese, selling old Greek farming tools, household implements, and even some trade tools from the Orthodox Church. (Open daily 10:30am-2pm and 6-11:30pm.)

There is a **public beach** just north of the bus station, but the best beaches are north and south of town. Three kilometers to the south is the long, sandy beach of **Mavrovouni,** with a high surf and a number of surfer bars (mixed drinks 900-1000dr, beer 500dr). Three kilometers north is rocky **Selinitsa,** which has earned accolades from the European Union for its clean water. This beach is at its prettiest beneath the Lakonis bungalows. Neither beach is accessible by bus; ride a moped or take a taxi (500dr). Farther north than Selinitsa (½km past the bungalows) is a sandy beach which houses the remains of an abandoned drug-runner's ship.

For daytime entertainment, across the causeway on **Marathonisi Island** is the newly-opened **Maniot Museum,** housed in the island's Tzanetaki tower (named after the family who owned the private island before donating it to the national tourist board). The museum, which houses Maniot crafts, is near the site of Helen and Paris' ill-received tryst. (Open daily 9am-5pm; admission 600dr, students 300dr.) When traveling from Gythion to Areopolis, keep your eyes peeled for the Frankish **Castle of Pasava** on the right (roughly 10km down the road). It's possible to tour the ruin. Farther along, the **Castle of Kelefa** looks out to sea.

MANI MANH

Mani is a minimalist's dream. The sparsely-settled territory stoically circles the cinnamon-brown Taygetus Mountains, set off by the neighboring sea. Plants and towering buildings add muted greys and greens to the stark landscape. The houses nestled along the countryside are familial fortresses, with tiny lookout windows to the outer-world, that are an uneasy reminder of Mani's turbulent, at times violent, past.

Mani's residents broke off from Sparta during the Roman Period and founded the League of Laconians. They resisted foreign rule ferociously, thereby gaining the name "Maniotes" (from the Greek *mania* or fury). Old Mani is best characterized as the Greek version of *The Godfather's* Sicily—vendettas, organized crime, the works. Ultimately, the Maniots' obstinacy paid off, as even today Maniotes boast that not a single Turk has set foot on Mani soil. In the Revolution of 1821, Maniot women joined in the struggle for independence by driving Turkish forces back to sea at the points of their farming sickles. Today, Maniot culture has softened considerably, and although they revel in their historical ferocity, the inhabitants make excellent hosts to wandering tourists seeking beautiful beaches and views.

■■■ AREOPOLIS ΑΡΕΟΠΟΛΗ

In spring and autumn, this clifftop village attracts artists seeking inspiration from its austere scenery. Summer brings tourists in search of respite from Gythion or a place to stay the night *en route* to the Glyfatha Lake Caves to the south. In Areopolis, sit under the stars in contented reverie and listen to the occasional snorts of farm animals, or join the locals in the central plaza, which may feel a lot like home.

Orientation and Practical Information The **police** (tel. 51 309), down a little street off the square and opposite the bus station, speak very little English. Kapetan Matapan St., off the square, is home to the **post office** (open Mon.-Fri. 8am-1:30pm). To get to the **National Bank** (Mon.-Fri. 9am-noon; only open Tues. and Thurs. in off-season), walk down Kapetan Matapan St., turn right at the first small church, and continue up the street; it is before the Hotel Mani. The bus station and the post office will **change money** and traveler's checks for a hefty fee. In case of emergency, call the **hospital** at 51 259. **Postal code:** 23062. **Telephone Code:** 0733.

The **bus stop** is on one side of the square, located in the restaurant Nicola's Corner. Three buses per day (tel. 51 229) make the trip from Kalamata to Itilo (2hr., 1100dr), with connections to Areopolis. Buses from Areopolis go to Kalamata (3 per day, 1500dr) via Itilo (½hr., 400dr), and Sparta (4 per day, 700dr), stopping in Gythion (4 per day, 30min., 200dr). Two buses per day go to the Glyfatha Lake Caves near Pirgos Dirou (11am, return at 12:45pm; 1pm, return 2:45pm, 175dr), stopping in the town (175dr), where connections can be made to Vathia (660dr) and Gerolimenas (660dr). Hitching to the caves is easy and even encouraged by locals, who might help you find a ride; regardless, we don't recommend it.

Accommodations If you spend the night here, try to find a room in the old town, which best evokes Mani's intriguing, turbulent past. Great rooms in a traditional Maniot tower are available at **Tsimova** (tel. 51 301), off Kapetan Matapan St., to the left behind the church. Supposedly, Kolokotronis slept here. Proprietor George Versakos has an impressive antique gun collection that is officially considered a "private military museum." (Singles 4000dr, doubles 6000dr, breakfast 500dr.) If you don't mind a much bleaker room (snazzed up by leopard-pattern furniture), George will rent you lodgings across the street (4000dr for 2-3 people). The cheapest rooms in town are off Kapetan Matapan St. above the **Xanthi Restaurant** (tel. 51 205, 2500dr per person).

Food For dinner, try either of the neighboring restaurants on the right side of the town square. **Tsimova** serves mostly grilled food (*kalamari* 900dr), while **Nicola's Corner** cooks traditional dishes. Both are good places to sit and sip tasty Greek coffee (150dr). For swimming, locals leave town and head down and left to the port town of Limeni, a short but steep walk away.

Mani's Honey Makes Money

Peddlers at roadside honey stands take their business—one of the region's most revered traditions—seriously. Honey-making is so serious, in fact, that an off-the-cuff statement that the honey for sale is not *natural* may be taken as a personal affront. The bees that produce Maniot honey, you will no doubt be told, only pollinate wildflowers, giving the honey a pleasantly light, *natural* taste and odor. Persistence in challenging the honey's source will meet with a passionate diatribe about honey-making: the honey is collected in beehive cubes which contain small honeycomb boards. The boards are collected by well-protected—but nonetheless fearless—bee collectors who place ten boards at a time into a large, metal centrifuge. The liquid honey is separated from the semi-solid wax and, after sitting in a vat for days to let the oils rise to the top, *pure* honey is siphoned out of the bottom. Of course you could skip the lecture and just buy the sweet, thick, *natural* Maniot honey (2000-2200dr per kilo).

■■■ PIRGOS DIROU AND GLYFATHA LAKE CAVE

With its subterranean river, the **Glyfatha Cave** (also known as Spilia Dirou or Pirgos Dirou), is one of Greece's most splendid natural attractions. The boat ride through the cave is 1.2km and lasts roughly ½hr. Originally discovered at the end of the 19th century and opened to the public in 1971 (a new section was found in 1983), the cave is believed to be 70km long and may extend all the way to Sparta. Vermilion and white stalagmites slice through the water, which is 30m deep in places and squiggling with eels. Bats, among the other happy denizens of the caves, fly around the maroon stalactites. Don't miss "Poseidon's Foot," a striking formation that looks like a giant foot hanging in the air. Since some guides speak only Greek, buy the small book available in English from the store near the entrance (1000dr). After the boat trip, walk through more of the caves at your own pace. The caves are 4km away from town, accessible by bus, and an easy trip from Gythion by moped. Many hitchhike, especially in summer when hordes of tourists accompany them. (Open June-Sept. 8am-6pm; off-season 9am-4:30pm; admission 2300dr and expect to wait an hour.) If too many people beat you there, you may not get in after 4pm. The beach at the site is free, and there's a cafeteria. (For information, call 52 222, -3.)

PIRGOS DIROU

South along the road from Areopolis is the village of **Pirgos Dirou.** Although far less interesting than Areopolis, the village is closer to the cave. It's possible to walk here from Areopolis (follow the signs at the other end of town from the road, 5km). Roughly ½km before Pirgos Dirou town, **Yiannis Kolokouris** (tel. 52 204, -40) rents petite, clean rooms above his restaurant (doubles 5000dr, triples 7000dr). **Panorama** (tel. 52 280) offers rooms 1km from the caves (doubles 6500dr). "Rooms to Let" signs dot the road from town to the grottoes. In town, the **Hotel Diros** (tel. 52 306, -440) has clean rooms (singles 8000dr, doubles 9000dr). Right at the town turn-off to the caves, there is a **post office** (tel. 52 249; open Mon.-Fri. 7:30am-2pm), and **Baker's Supermarket** (tel. 52 255) lies farther along the road towards the caves (open 7am-10pm). A particularly good option is **Greek Kitchen and Bar,** near the south end of town; they have some free camping space. **Telephone Code:** 0733.

Near Pirgos Dirou

South of the caves, Mani sheds its tourist-brochure gloss. Here lies the Mani of bandits and blood feuds, where camouflaged tower houses peer wearily from the rocky terrain and Byzantine barrel-vaulted churches complement the landscape. There are no gas stations in the south or east of Mani; be sure to ask about locations ahead of time. Just 2km from Pirgos Dirou is a turn-off for **Harouda** and the church of **Taxiarchis** (another 2km away). This church, decorated with blue and green ceramic plates and intricately patterned masonry, is situated in a mesmerizingly calm olive grove; climb to the church terrace for the view. (Open until sunset.) Parallel to the main road, a side street passes a series of hillside villages, including **Vamvaka** and **Mina,** each with tower houses and small churches. To rejoin the main road, turn downhill at any of the extremely rocky junctures. Two sumptuous swimming coves are off the main road near **Mezapos,** which also has a 12th-century church. Continuing south, you'll eventually touch water at the craggy port of **Gerolimenas** (Old Port), once called home by bloodthirsty pirates. Try the **Hotel Akrotenaritis** (tel. 54 205), farther from town (doubles 4800dr, w/bath 5400dr), or the **Akrogiali** (tel. 54 204), on the far right of the harbor (doubles 6000dr, w/bath 8000dr; A/C included). A few nice **beaches** lie beyond town, to the southeast. Two **buses** leave daily for Athens via Areopolis and Gythion (6:45am and 5pm).

On Mon., Wed., and Fri., buses continue to Vathia from Gerolimenas. Only 20 or so people live year-round in **Vathia,** a photogenic medley of mountains, crumbling fortresses, and deserted towers. The government is trying to revive the town by enticing travelers to stay in one of 14 restored tower houses. Call 54 229 for info.

■■■ MONEMVASSIA ΜΟΝΕΜΒΑΣΙΑ

The ancient Byzantine city of Monemvassia juts out from a rocky island. Seen from the west, the island appears uninhabited, and from the mainland only a small *taverna* and gas station are perceptible; a short walk east along the sea, however, reveals sloping fortified walls and a staircase that climbs the sheer 350m promontory. At the mountain's summit is the **citadel,** fortified by the Venetians in the 16th century. The town, equally reinforced, rests below. Monemvassia was first conquered in 1248 AD by Guillaume de Villehardouin, and in the hands of the Franks it functioned as a stopover for crusaders headed east. In later years it was captured by the Turks, the Pope, and finally the Venetians.

Today, one must pass through a small, covered gateway to enter Monemvassia's town (hence the name, meaning one-way). Entering old Monemvassia gives visitors an eerie Twilight Zone-like feeling of having crossed a gateway into another time. The narrow streets are a medieval delight to explore, full of mysterious stairways and jasmine-filled courtyards. Visible immediately, a sinuous path lined with helical staircases serves as the "main street" and leads to shops and restaurants. Continue past the small strip of tourist traps to reach the **town square.** Facing the ocean, the **Christos Elkomenos** (Christ in Chains) church is on the left. On your right is a church that has been made into a mosque. Follow the labyrinthine walkways and stairs to visit the island's myriad churches. The **Agia Sofia,** a Byzantine church modeled after the famous monastery at Daphni, presides on the edge of the ruins. Some of the original frescoes were restored 30 years ago.

A narrow causeway connects the island to the mainland and the modern town of Monemvassia, which is splattered with hotels, restaurants, and gift shops. Thus, the medieval village still retains its original character, a fact made even more astounding when you remember the asphalt road that led you here. Only its small main street is filled with souvenir shops, trendy cafés, and restaurants—serenity dominates elsewhere. This antique town, miraculously uncrowded, has unsullied pebble beaches to the east and west on the mainland.

Orientation and Practical Information In modern Monemvassia, **23rd Iouliou St.,** the principal thoroughfare, runs along the waterfront straight up to the causeway that leads to the island. Across from the bus station is the **National Bank** (tel. 61 201; open June-Sept. Mon.-Fri. 9am-1:30pm; Oct.-May only Tues. and Thurs.), and next door, the **post office** (tel. 61 231; open Mon.-Fri. 7:30am-2pm). On 28th Octovriou St., which runs off 23rd Iouliou St., just past the bus station, is the **police station** (tel. 61 210), in a house with a brown wooden door. (Official hours 8am-8pm, but someone is always there.) The police have some rooms listings. The **OTE** (tel. 61 399; open Mon.-Fri. 7:30am-3pm) is uphill bearing left from the bus station. Helpful **Malvasia Travel** (tel. 61 752) is near the bus station and opposite the post office (open 7am-2:15pm and 5:30-9:30pm). Ask the manager about currency exchange and **moped rental** (4000dr per day, plus gas). **English language books** and newspapers are available at **Lekakis Supermarket** (bear left at the fork past the post office; open daily 7am-11pm). **Postal Code:** 23070; **Telephone Code:** 0732.

The **bus station** (tel. 61 752) is on 23rd Iouliou St., in the Malvasia travel agency opposite the post office. Buses for all destinations either connect or stop in Molai (no direct routes). The only exception is the express to Athens (daily, 5hr., 3250dr). Buses leave (2-4 per day) for Sparta (2½hr., 1500dr), Tripolis (3½hr., 2300dr), Corinth (4½hr., 3380dr), and Athens (6½-7hr., 4350dr) via Molai (½hr., 380dr). Daily buses connect from Molai to Gythion, leaving Monemvassia at 11:15am (1½hr., 1200dr). **Ferries** leave twice a week for Kyparissa (1½hr., 8640dr), Piraeus (6hr., 3600dr), Neapolis (1290dr), Kythera (2260dr), and Crete (3050dr). In the summer, **flying dolphins** go to Kythera (1hr., 4700dr) and Neapolis (Mon.-Thurs. at 12:55pm, Sat. at 11:45am, 4700dr). The hydrofoil leaves daily at 2pm for Piraeus (4hr., 7000dr) with many stops on the islands (including Spetses, Hydra, and Kythera). An express leaves for Piraeus (6 per week, 3hr., 7000dr), stopping only at

Spetses and Portoheli. Schedules change frequently; check at the ticket office (tel. 61 219), next to the Mobil station on the island side of the causeway.

Accommodations There are three accommodations options in Monemvassia. The first option is in the medieval village on the island, but accommodations here are scarce and fail to meet even the loosest definition of budget. Still, it's an amazing place to stay; for a treat call **Malavasia Hotel** (tel. 61 323), with singles for 10,000dr and doubles at 12,000dr. A more affordable choice is to pitch a tent at **Camping Paradise** (tel. 61 123), 3½km along the water on the mainland (800dr per person, 550dr per car, small tent 600dr, large tent 750dr, electricity 400dr). Finally, "Rooms to Let" signs adorn many houses along 23rd Iouliou St., right on the water (doubles 5000-7000dr). On Spartis St., near the bank and the post office, the **Hotel Akrogiali** (tel. 61 360), wearing a sign bearing the owner's name, S. Sofos, is about the cheapest hotel in the modern town (singles 4000dr, doubles 6000dr). The **Hotel Aktaion** (tel. 61 234), on 23rd Iouliou St. near the causeway, is more expensive but has clean, modern rooms with balconies, bug screens, and reading lamps (singles 6000dr, doubles 7000dr). Prices are 20-40% less in the off-season.

Food Meals on the island are expensive. For fairly-priced fare, try **Matoula** (tel. 61 660) and eat under the gnarled fig tree in the pleasant garden (entrees average 1300dr). If you stay on the mainland, avoid the "tourist-strip" and grab some food at **Taverna Nikola,** on the main road (stuffed tomatoes 750dr, chicken 900dr). Cheapest of all is *souvlaki* or *gyros* (both 270dr) at **Fotis Souvlaki,** a small strip of tables all decked out in red along the waterfront, or other *souvlaki/gyros* joints in town.

■ NEAR MONEMVASSIA

NEAPOLIS

The cute 'n' cozy port town of **Neapolis** is a good starting point for trips to Kythera or Crete. Quiet and friendly, this town is also a nice place to linger. The **police** (tel. 22 111), which double as **tourist police** (though they may be less helpful in the latter role), are on Ag. Triados St., which is to the right of the square. Turn the corner from the police station and, at the next corner, you'll come to the **post office** (open Mon.-Fri. 7:30am-2pm). The **OTE** (open Mon.-Fri. 7:30am-3:10pm) is roughly 200m up Spartis St., at the left end of town (facing inland). The **National Bank of Greece,** 160 Akti Boion St. (open Mon.-Thurs. 8am-2pm, Fri. 8am-1:30pm), offers **currency exchange. Telephone Code:** 0734.

Four **buses** per day travel to Athens (7hr., 5150dr), stopping *en route* at Molai (1¼hr., 1000dr), Sparta (3hr., 2100dr), Tripolis (4½hr., 2900dr), and Corinth (6hr., 4000dr). Tickets can be purchased from the tiny **KTEL office** (tel. 23 222) just past the upper right-hand corner of the square (facing inland) in the center of town. **Ferries** leave daily for Kythera, Crete, and Elafonisos. The **Miras Ferries** office at #154 Akti Boion St. (the waterfront road) sells ferry and **flying dolphin tickets.**

"Rooms to Let" in town are roughly 3000-5000dr for a single, and 4000-7000dr for a double. *Tavernas,* grills, and fast food joints line the waterfront.

KYTHERA ΚΥΘΗΡΑ

Myth holds that Zeus threw Chronus' severed genitalia into the ocean where Kythera came to be, and later Aphrodite sprang from the surrounding waters. Kythera, reclining just to the south of the Peloponnesian cities of Monemvassia, Neapolis, and Gythion, is an isolated and lovely spot. The land's tranquil mountainous landscape harbors a collection of evergreens and flowering shrubs, secluded villages, and sandy beaches. Although not really connected to any group of islands, Kythera has slid under Piraeus's administration.

Although the government has attempted to promote tourism by putting up new road signs and the like, this is not a destination set up for the budget traveler. Kythera is perfect for those who wish to get away from it all for two weeks (although those seeking *complete* isolation head to the nearby island of **Antikythera,** wired for electricity only six years ago). The rest of us struggle with 2am ferry drop-offs, infrequent or non-existent bus connections, and a scarcity of budget accommodations. But whatever your means of travel, Kythera rewards with serenity, beautiful landscapes, azure water, and relaxed, welcoming inhabitants.

Ferries dock in Kythera at either the west port, **Agia Pelagia,** or the newer port of **Diakofti,** designed to eventually take the role of Kythera's main port. The island's main road runs between Agia Pelagia and **Kapsali,** lively port towns whose harbor is frequented by yachtsmen, with smaller villages connected by subsidiary roads. Besides the port towns, this road passes through **Potamos, Livadi,** and **Kythera** (Chora)—Kythera's larger inland towns. It's best to station yourself on the southern half of the island, closer to the moped rentals, "Rooms to Let," restaurants, and shops. Kapsali has hopping nightlife; Chora has fabulous views and some of life's necessities (such as a bank); and the inland town of Livadi has the cheapest rooms.

Orientation and Practical Information Agia Pelagia's **tourist office** (tel. 33 815) is open to greet all who anchor at their port (except for those unfortunate enough to be arriving on the 2am ferry). They provide maps and help locate rooms in town. **Post offices** exist in Chora (tel. 31 274) and Potamos (tel. 31 228); each is located in its respective town square. (Open Mon.-Fri. 8am-2pm and Sun. 8am-2pm.) **Police** are located in Chora (tel. 31 206), past the road leading out of town to the castle, and in Potamos (tel. 33 222). To get to the **OTE** in Chora (tel. 31 212) go up the stairs next to the square's travel agent (look for the sign) and follow the path to the street behind the square. (Open Mon.-Fri. 7:30am-3:10pm.) There are **National Banks** in Chora (tel. 31 209, -218) and Potamos (33 209, -350), each in its town's main square. The island's **hospital** is in Potamos (tel. 33 325, -203; open 24 hr.), and all doctors speak English. **Postal Code:** 80200; **Telephone Code:** 0735.

Olympic Airways (tel. 33 297) offers **flights** to Athens (daily 1 and 4:20pm, 13,600dr). Cost conscious travelers should opt for one of the two **ferries** that leave from Agia Pelagia on the northeast tip of the island. The "Martha" heads 5 times per week to Neapolis (1hr., 1550dr) and Gythion (3hr., 950dr), while the "Theseus" leaves 3 times per week for Crete (4hr., 3350dr) and Piraeus (9hr., 4700dr). Ferry schedules are posted all over the island, but are subject to change. Check with any **Miras Ferries** office. In Agia Pelagia, consult **Conomas Travel** (tel. 33 490, -890); in Kapsali, **Pateros Nikitas** (tel. 31 301); and in Chora, **Rama Travel** (tel. 31 561). The **port police** (tel. 31 222 in Kapsali, 33 280 in Agia Pelagia) can give you complete info about all sailings. **Flying Dolphins** whisk you from Piraeus to Kythera in mid-afternoon (the ferry usually arrives at 2 or 3am). Hydrofoils leave 5 times per week for Piraeus (5hr., 11,350dr), Aegina (4½hr., 9900dr), Poros (8900dr), Hydra (8850dr), Neapolis (2300dr), Monemvassia (4700dr), Spetses (3hr., 8200dr), and Portoheli (8200dr). **Taxis** can be found in Livadia (tel. 31 160, -860), Chora (tel. 31 320, -196), and Potamos (tel. 31 480). In Kapsali, look outside Panayopolis Moto-Rent for Antonis Stathis' blue Datsun (tel. 31 640). A taxi from Chora or Kapsali to the airport should cost 2800-3000dr; from Agia Pelagia to Chora or Kapsali should run roughly 3500dr. The taxis have meters, but bargain for a flat rate beforehand.

Buses are unfortunately lacking. One shuttles between Agia Pelagia and Kapsali in July and August (4 per day), stopping at villages on request. Locals and tourist agencies know the schedule. **Mopeds** are a much easier way to get around; with outlets on the waterfront in Kapsali (tel. 31 789), Agia Pelagia (33 194), Tsikalaria (tel. 31 551), and one in the square at Kythera, **Panayiotis Rent** is the most convenient rental option (open Mar. 1-Nov. 14). Offices **rent cars** at 8500dr per day.

Accommodations Chora Town has few budget accommodations, and most are booked weeks in advance, especially in August. **Pension Ketty** (tel. 31 318) lets tastefully furnished rooms. Look for the signs near the phone booth across from the bank. (Doubles 8000dr; less in off-season.) Near the bakery, **Mr. Lourandou** (tel. 31 106) rents clean rooms (singles 5500dr, doubles 7000dr, triples 9600dr). Or stay at swanky **Castello Rooms** (tel. 31 069), in the castle-like building to the left of the post office (follow signs; doubles 8000dr, w/kitchen 10,000; studios for 4 people w/ kitchen 13,500dr). It may be easier to find somewhere to crash in Livadi.

Kapsali has a few rooms to rent with the added attraction of being right on the beach, near the ballyhoo of the partying crowds. Look for signs on the street behind the waterfront. **Mr. and Mrs. Megaloudi** (tel. 31 340) have pleasant doubles on the waterfront (9500dr with bath and refrigerator). Sheltered in a conifer forest, a beautiful **campground** (tel. 31 580) lies 300m from Kapsali up the road to Kythera (700dr per person, small tent 700dr, large tent 950dr; open June 15-Sept. 15). People arriving by ferry in the middle of the night sometimes freelance camp on the beach and head for the campground in the morning.

Food and Entertainment Most waterfront restaurants in Kapsali and Agia Pelagia are overpriced, but **Artema** on the water in Kapsali is fair (spaghetti 750dr). For inexpensive Greek food with a twist, head inland and try **Toxotis Restaurant** in Livadi, one of the best on the island. In Kythera, try **Zorba's,** located on the main street, downhill from the square (chicken 700dr, open for dinner only). For dessert, Livadi's bakery has tasty treats.

For a small island, Kythera has quite a few bars with pricey drinks (1000-1500dr). In Chora, try **Merrato,** down the street from Zorba's. In Kapsali, there's the **Yachting Club, Bikini Red, Corto-Maltese,** and the new **Barbarosa Music Bar.**

Sights Kythera is selective in exposing its secrets. Start your brave exploration with a climb to the **castle** in Chora. The summit, dappled with the ruins of old churches and buildings, offers an intoxicating view of Kapsali's double harbor. The **Archaeological Museum,** with Mycenaean and Venetian finds, is just out of town, past the turn-off into Chora on the road to Livadi. (Open Tues.-Fri. 8:30am-2pm, Sun. 9:30am-1pm; free.) A visit to the cave of **Agia Sofia Milopotamou** takes an afternoon and would make Indiana Jones intensely envious. You'll have to bike down treacherous rocky roads, hike up a cliff, and crawl around in small clammy spaces. Wear sturdy shoes; the passage is dark and slippery. A few feet from the entrance to the grotto are several beautiful frescoes. (Open July-Sept. Mon., Wed., and Sat. 4-8pm; admission w/tour 500dr. Double-check times with the police; hours change.) If you go to the square in Milopotamou at 4pm, the guide will lead you to the cave on the partially paved road in your car or motorbike. If you arrive later, follow the signs out of town. For a much smaller but more spiritual cave, go to **Feloti.** Take the first left onto a dirt road just past the turn-off to Chora. When you reach the coast, park your moped and follow the path to the left until you see a little white steeple poking out of the rock; just in front of it is the entrance to the cave. People swim off the rocks near the cave or from the small pebble beach to the right. Tiny **Potamos,** 20km north of Kapsali on the main road, has a spectacular Sunday morning market. Kythera is renowned for its honey (jars 1800-2200dr).

Kythera is full of beautiful **beaches.** The one in Kapsali is the most convenient; the water's clean and there's a beautiful cove to the right accessible by a strong swimmer or an average pedal boat renter. Locals say that the island's three superior beaches are Fryiamos, Melidoni, and Kaladi. Secluded **Fryiamos** beach is easily reached by car or by moped. It's possible to walk from the road. Leave your moped at the fork near Kalamos and proceed uphill for a long hike; the left path leads to Fryiamos. Alternatively, try **Melidoni** on the southwest coast. When you're leaving Livadi, turn left at the fork, and continue until you reach Drimona. Enter the town and follow signs to Agios Kosmas. Pass the church on the left and plunge down the treacherous, sandy road. **Kaladi** is between the villages of Paleopoli and Arlemona. The town beach in Kapsali, while rocky, is clean and clear and full of bathers, dramatic rock formations, and, occasionally, dramatic bathers in formation.

Northern Greece

Northern Greece seldom finds its way onto postcards, but not for lack of beauty. Robust and pretension-free, the region waits to be discovered by adventurous travelers seeking refuge from swarming hotel owners and fast-talking salespeople. Greece's forgotten half is graced with goat-paths on pine-filled mountains that lead to some of the country's most precious Byzantine treasures, graceful springs, and breathtaking mountaintop vistas. Waving green trees, lush vegetation, and endless farmland in intricate patchworks of cultivated fields, as well as fruit and olive groves, characterize this gorgeous region of hidden treasures.

THESSALY ΘΕΣΣΑΛΙΑ

Outside its charmless industrialized urban centers, Thessaly's villages conceal some of the best nature trails in Greece. To the west of the cultivated Thessalian plain, the monasteries of Meteora cling to towering gray pinnacles. The rocky crags of Mt. Olympus, throne of the pantheon of Greek gods, watch over Aegean beaches with stark majesty. To the southeast, traditional mountain hamlets on Mt. Pelion lie scattered among forests, apple orchards, and grapevines that reach out to the sea.

VOLOS ΒΟΛΟΣ

Not exactly picturesque, but endowed with the quieter charms of a city with a small-town feel, Volos serves as a convenient base for the region. The city has pleasant streets, some surprising architecture, and numerous tiny alley thoroughfares. Alongside the waterfront, the resort-like east part of town is conducive to nighttime strolls. Despite Volos' bland reputation, time spent exploring won't be wasted.

ORIENTATION AND PRACTICAL INFORMATION

The bus station (tel. 33 254) is located at the end of Gr. Lambraki St. away from town, an easy 10-min. walk from town and the waterfront: the main road leading from the bus station to town runs past the train station and the tourist office and onto Dimitriados St., from which intersecting roads lead to various hotels.

Tourist Office: (tel. 23 500 or 36 233). On the waterfront in Riga Fereou Sq. Eager to provide more information than you could possibly need. List of hotels posted after closing. Open Mon.-Fri. 7am-2:30pm and daily 5-7pm in July and Aug.

Tourist Police: #179 18th Octovriou St. (tel. 27 094). The street was recently renamed; locals still call it "Alexandras St." Provides assistance in English when the tourist office is closed. Open daily 7am-2:30pm, but bang on the door anytime. **Police:** (tel. 26 121). 24 hr.

Post Office: On P. Mela St., off 18th Octovriou St. Open Mon.-Fri. 8am-8pm. **Postal Code:** 38001 for public offices or 38334 for street addresses.

OTE: Corner of Eleftheriou Venizelou and Sokratous St., across from the covered fruit and vegetable market. Open 24 hr. **Telephone Code:** 0421.

Trains: The train station (tel. 28 555 or 24 056) is 1 block west of the tourist office (coming from town, turn right at the kiosk past the tourist office). Must change in Larissa (15 per day, 1hr., 510dr) for Athens or Thessaloniki, unless you catch the daily super-express train to Athens (4hr., 5020dr). Otherwise to Athens (9 per day, 5hr., 2620dr), Thessaloniki (8 per day, 4hr., 1640dr), and Kalambaka (4 per day, 4hr., 1110dr). Only the express train has air-conditioning.

Buses: Buses travel daily to Athens (10 per day, 5hr., 4300dr), Thessaloniki (5 per day, 3¼hr., 2900dr), Larissa (12 per day, 1hr., 900dr), Portaria (10 per day, 45min., 190dr), Makrinitsa (10 per day, 50min., 240dr), Zagoria (4 per day, 2hr., 700dr), Horefto (2 per day, 2¼hr., 800dr), Afissos (5 per day, 45min., 318dr), Platania (3 per day, 2hr., 900dr), Drakia (2 per day, 50min., 260dr), and Ag. Ioannis (2 per day, 2½hr., 1050dr).

Ferries: 3-4 boats daily to Skiathos (3hr., 2303dr), Skopelos (4½hr., 2822dr), and Alonissos (5hr., 3182dr). Fewer on weekends.

Flying Dolphins: Hydrofoils run with equal frequency at twice the price to Skiathos (1¼hr., 4640dr), Skopelos (2hr., 6006dr), Alonissos (3hr., 6911dr), and Glossa (2658dr). Inquire at the agencies lining the waterfront.

Car Rental: Theofanidis Hellas, 79 Iasonos St. (tel. 32 360), 1 block parallel to the waterfront. 10,000dr for a Fiat Panda.

English Bookstore: Bookstop, 163 Alexandrias St. (tel. 22 924), behind Ag. Nikolaos church. Open Wed.-Fri. and Sun. 8:30am-1:30pm and 5:30-9pm, Mon.-Tues. and Sat. 8:30am-1:30pm.

ACCOMMODATIONS

If you're stranded, head downtown near the waterfront to unchic but cheap hotels.

Hotel Akropolis, 47 Korai St. (tel. 25 984). A favorite among young travelers. The manager rents spacious, clean rooms and provides valuable information in English and German. Singles 3000dr, doubles 4000dr, triples 6000dr. Closed in winter.

Hotel Iolkos, 37 Dimitriados St. (tel. 23 416). Once catered to diplomats and statesmen, but now caters to the likes of us. Singles 3300dr, doubles 4400dr.

Hotel Iasson (Jason), 1 P. Melo St. (tel. 26 075). Bare, well-scrubbed rooms that have recently been renovated. Singles 5000dr, doubles 7000dr, triples 9000dr.

Hotel Philipos, 9 Solones St. (tel. 37 607). Provides comfortable rooms with fans, private baths, TV, and a telephone—at a price. Singles 7711dr, doubles 10,796dr, triples 12,955dr.

FOOD AND ENTERTAINMENT

Cafés and *tavernas* drench the waterfront like oil on a Greek salad. Sailors feast on grilled octopus at the inexpensive **Ouzerie Nautilia,** 1 Argonafton, just before Riga Fereou Sq. (most entrees 1200dr; open daily 6am-2am). Try the **Ouzerie Iolikos** on the waterfront by the first ferry offices. They cater to serious seafood aficionados in a family-style environment—a little insect repellent, however, might help you linger longer than the mosquitoes (octopus salad 1100dr, stuffed peppers 800dr). **Athenaiki Taverna** (tel. 23 054), on Venizelou St., serves heaping portions of roast chicken (760dr) and other staples under colorful murals (open daily 7am-11pm).

Between midnight and sunrise, the *tavernas* and *ouzerie* along the waterfront overflow with people slouched in chairs, absorbing alcohol. For even more slothful entertainment, laze in one of the two **movie theaters** along the promenade (one is open-air with movies in English). In late July and August, Volos hosts a festival in Riga Fereou Park, featuring concerts, dances, and special exhibits.

SIGHTS

Volos' **Archaeological Museum,** 1 Athonassaki (tel. 25 285), displays finds from the latter part of the Paleolithic Era to the Roman period (including an engrossing exhibit of small clay figurines from the Neolithic era). The museum is set in a verdant floral garden in the east part of town and is well worth the ½-hr. walk from the waterfront. (Open Tues.-Sun. 8:30am-3pm; admission 400dr, students 200dr, cameras w/flash 600dr, free w/o flash.) Inquire here or at the tourist office for information on the nearby archaeological sites at **Dimini** and **Seskio** (free).

■■■ MOUNT PELION PENINSULA
ΟΡΟΣ ΠΗΛΙΟ

In mythology, the rugged Pelion Peninsula was home to centaurs—half-man, half-horse creatures—and to Chiron, their mentor. Legend proclaims that Chiron, a physician, chose Pelion as a stomping ground because it contained more than 1700 medicinal herbs. The diversity of plant life in the region stems from a cool, moist climate, a feature appreciated today by sun-weary tourists. Pelion's tortuous terrain once helped protect it from invasion; while the rest of Greece strained under Turkish rule, the peninsula fanned Greek nationalism. Steep slopes now form a barrier to hypertourism, resulting in fewer visitors than they deserve.

MAKRINITSA

Winding up the twisting road from Volos to beautiful Makrinitsa, you'll transcend noise and smog, but not souvenir stands. The stone houses and cobblestone streets of this ancient village clutch the hillside overlooking Volos and the Aegean. Hiking trails weave past mountain springs, goat-begotten hills, and age-old monasteries. Presiding over the town square, tiny **Agios Yiannis** monastery has nifty samples of wood carving. Walk 1km along the trail uphill from the parking lot to austere **Agios Gerasimos,** with a clock tower and resident peacock. Continue to the 17th-century **Monastery of Sourvias,** a ½-hr. stroll away. (All open 7am-1pm and 3-8pm. Women must wear a dress or trousers; men may wear long shorts.)

Makrinitsa has been designated a traditional settlement by the Greek National Tourist Organization so staying here will cost an arm and a leg. Either splurge on one of the town's posh pensions or make Markrinitsa a daytrip. **Pension Archontiko Diomides** (tel. 99 430), uphill from the Galini Restaurant (look for the sign), has beautiful rooms with whitewashed interiors, wood carvings, and patios. (Singles 7500dr, doubles 8500dr w/bath, triples 9500dr, quads 10,000dr.) The **Hotel Achil-**

les (tel. 99 177), just before the square, offers bright, modern rooms with sea views. (Doubles 10,000dr, triples 12,000dr.) Have breakfast (1000dr) in the "taxidermist's-heaven-decor" café. We're talking birds, ducks, foxes, and cowskins on the walls. For a slightly less expensive, equally pleasant option, try the **anonymous pension** on the main road before the main square; look for the grapevine in the yard after the first series of stores. Clean, large, old-style rooms (doubles 6500dr, w/bath 7500dr; triples 9000dr). **O Theophilos** (tel. 99 435), on the path through the square, offers doubles with wooden beds and fireplaces (singles 8000dr, doubles 12,000dr).

The **Pantheon** (tel. 99 143), in the square, serves local specialties on a vast cliff-hanging terrace (open daily 9am-midnight). Makrinitsa has paltry practical conveniences. To change money go to nearby Portaria. There's no post office; the kiosk sells stamps, and letters must be left in the mailbox. **Telephone Code:** 0421.

AROUND THE PELION PENINSULA

There are two ways to explore the villages around Volos: either across the peninsula and along the road high above the Aegean coast, or along the coast of Pagassitikos Bay. The former is more agreeable, since the inland areas, Aegean coastline, and far ends of the peninsula are more alluring and less crowded than along Pagassitikos Bay from Volos and Agria to Afissos. There are no large hotels here, but small establishments and numerous "Rooms to Let" fill the vacuum (doubles average 5000dr).

Buses from Volos serve most of the 24 major villages (4-5 per day; see p. 150), but buses between smaller towns are scarce. To explore the peninsula in a short period of time, rent a car or motorbike in Volos. Streets have dangerous, winding curves and hairpin turns; drive with caution.

If you opt for the Aegean route, the first place of interest after Makrinitsa is the ski town of **Chania,** 26km from Volos. The precipitous **ski slopes,** 2km off the main road, are served by chair lift and T-bar (open Jan. to mid-March). The **Youth Hostel Mt. Pelion** (tel. (0421) 24 290) serves as a base for hikes in the hills and treks to the beach. (1000dr per person; open July-Aug.)

The road forks 14km east of Chania. Turn north for **Zagora,** the largest of Pelion's villages. It's a pretty town, with old vine-webbed stone homes and cheap "Rooms to Let." Better yet, continue downhill through the orchards of "the green" (the east part of the peninsula) to the fine sands hugging the Aegean at the town of **Horefto,** 8km from Zagora. The sea here is incredible hues of blue and green. On the far side of town is the sardinically-packed **Campground Horefto** (tel. 22 180; person 900dr, tent 950dr; open May-Sept.). Though it's small, it has lots of leafy trees—plus it's practically on top of the crashing waves. An even better alternative is **Andy's** pension (tel. 22 447), run by a warmhearted, older couple who offer sunny, spotless rooms with the Aegean as a front yard. (Doubles 3850dr, w/bath 5400dr; hot showers 250dr.) The **Hotel Votsala** (tel. 22 001) on the right end of the waterfront, has glorious sylvan views and large, private baths (singles 6000dr, doubles 7000dr, triples 8300dr).**Telephone Code:** 0426.

Eight kilometers east of Horefto is **Pouri,** "The Balcony of the Aegean," which, at 400m, offers a view all the way to Halkidiki. For roughly 500dr, a local fisherman will take you to one of the nearby sea caves. Two **buses** per day connect Volos with Zagora (2hr., 700dr), and Horefto (2¼hr., 800dr). Pouri's **Telephone Code:** 0426.

From Zagora, follow the right-hand fork through cherry and apple orchards into the picturesque hamlets of **Anilio** and **Makrirahi.** This stretch makes a great hike. Ten km from Makrirahi is the turn-off for **Agios Ioannis,** a beautiful but pricey beach resort. The **Hotel Anesis** (tel. 31 323) is typical of what you'll find here (singles 8000dr, doubles 9200dr; showers included). On the far side of the footbridge, at the south end of the beach, many travelers freelance camp. **To Akrogiali** serves cheap local specialties (open daily 8am-midnight). **Telephone Code:** 0422.

The path over the footbridge, up the hill at the end of town, leads to secluded **Damouhari Cove,** with two small pebble beaches, the ruins of a Venetian castle, and an olive grove (45-min. walk from town). **Buses** run to Ag. Ioannis from Volos (2 per day, 2hr., 1050dr). The road heads south, then forks to **Kissos,** the highest village on the east slope, which has the 18th-century **Basilica of Agia Marina** and private rooms. Stop by **Tsangarada,** 5km farther, to visit the local landmark, a 1000-year-old plane tree with a 4.5m circumference. **Milopotamos,** an exceptional pint-sized beach near the cliffs, is 8km away. Morning **buses** come regularly in July and August. Two *tavernas* serve the beach, and a few rooms rest 1km up the hill.

The alternate route from Volos along Pagassitikos Bay leads first to **Agria,** a resort town with seafood *tavernas* whose patrons dine late into the night. Two campgrounds in olive groves around **Gatzea** make this part of the coast a satisfactory stopover. **Camping Hellas** (tel. 22 267) is crowded, but on a sandy beach (person 1000dr, small tent 650dr, large tent 800dr, trailer 1200dr). **Camping Marina** (tel. 22 277) is emptier and better-tended, with a rock beach (person 950dr, tent 900dr). Heading inland at Kala Nera, you'll come to two rustic highland villages. From the cool plaza of the first, **Milies,** look down to the bay below or visit well-preserved frescoes in the **Church of the Taxiarches** (dress appropriately; donation appreciated). Consider skipping the kitschy town museum; for cheese in a more palatable form, try *tyropsomo* (cheese bread), a local specialty. Three kilometers north and uphill from Milies, the town of **Vizitsa** lies in sedate splendor with a café and a few rooms. The tourist office is restoring some mansions in this village, but it remains more solitary than Makrinitsa. **Buses** run from Volos to Milies (6 per day, 1hr., 400dr) and Vizitsa (1hr., 450dr). **Telephone Code:** 0423.

■■■ METEORA ΜΕΤΕΩΡΑ

The mysterious black rock formations of Meteora rise majestically above the surrounding Thessalian plain. According to one theory, the rocks are large salt deposits from a primordial sea. Whatever their origin, the spectacle of the formations would be worth visiting even if they didn't hold 24 Byzantine monasteries with beautiful frescoes and astonishing views. Six of the 24 are still inhabited by religious orders and are open to the public. Although the site is one of the most popular in Northern Greece, the monasteries themselves offer an experience both dazzling and serene.

In the 9th century AD, hermits and ascetics began occupying the pinnacles and crevices of Meteora, where they built a church dedicated to the Virgin. As religious persecution at the hands of Serbian invaders increased in the 12th century, Christians flocked to take refuge on the summits of these impenetrable columns of rock. In 1356, the region's first official monastic community was founded. In the late Byzantine Period, when the Turks ruled Greece, Meteora became a bastion of Christian faith, eventually growing into a powerful community of 24 monasteries, each embellished by the finest artists. The communities' wealth, however, turned out to be their downfall. Quarrels over riches led to neglect and deterioration during the 16th century. But all was not lost; some of the monasteries **(Grand Meteoron, Varlaam, Agia Triada,** and **Agios Nikolaos)** are active to this day, while **Agios Stephanos** and **Agia Barbara** (Roussanou) now serve as convents.

ORIENTATION AND PRACTICAL INFORMATION

Buses travel from the main square in Kalambaka to the Grand Meteoron (2 per day, 1 per day in winter, 20min., 175dr). Flag down the bus at any of the blue *stasis* signs along its route or go to the bus station. The bus may stop at the different monasteries along the way to Grand Meteoron: don't be too hasty to get off since it's best to begin your walking tour from the Grand Meteoron, the uppermost monastery, and to visit the others in succession as you make your descent back to town. Five kilometers from Kalambaka lies the scenic hamlet of **Kastraki,** which is more restful, less crowded and closer to Meteora than Kalambaka.

At least a full day is needed to see the monasteries, although it may be more rewarding to spend more time visiting only a few in order to get a feeling for the monastic lifestyle. Grand Meteoron and Varlaam are the largest and cater to tourists; the others are more intimate. Modest dress (pants for men, skirts for women) is strictly enforced. Visitors should cover their shoulders and men with long hair should wrap it in a bun (as do the monks). Unflattering cover-ups are available for rental at monastery entrances. Photography and video filming inside the monasteries are absolutely forbidden. The monasteries have staggered closing days, but all are open Saturday, Sunday, and Wednesday during the summer. (Open 9am-1pm and 3:20-6pm, but most stay open until visitors have left; admission to each 400dr.)

ACCOMMODATIONS

Centrally located **Camping Vrachos** (tel. 22 293) has an algae-free pool (person 800dr, tent 500dr). **Camping Meteora Garden** (tel. 22 727; fax 23 115) lounges a deceptively-far 500m out of Kastraki on the Ioannina-Kalambaka highway, but has modern facilities and a sparkling pool (person 900dr, tent 600dr). Look for the new bungalows and a miniature golf course. The **Hotel Kastraki** (tel. 22 286) is conveniently located on the road to Meteora and has rooms even your mother would consider clean (singles 5000dr, doubles 6000dr).

THE MONASTERIES

The Monastery of the Transfiguration (Metamorphosis), known as the **Grand Meteoron,** is the oldest and largest. Built on the most massive of the occupied stone columns, the complex looms 500m above the Thessalian plain. Founded by Athanasius, a monk from Mt. Athos, the monastery rose in the hagio-hierarchy when John Uresis, grandson of the Serbian prince Stephen, retired here in 1388.

The Grand Meteoron's central feature is the 16th-century **Church of the Transfiguration,** with brilliant frescoes of the Roman persecution of the Christians in its narthex. Directly across is a chamber filled with carefully stacked skulls and bones, the remains of past monks. (Grand Meteoron, open every day except Tues.)

Three hundred km down the road from the Grand Meteoron stands the **Varlaam Monastery,** the second largest monastery on Meteora. Built in 1517, the monastery's crowning glory is its chapel's 16th-century frescoes, including a particularly disturbing depiction of the Apocalypse. Varlaam also has an extensive net and pulley system, which shows how earlier visitors were pulled up (every day but Fri.).

Visible from most of the valley, **Agia Barbara** (also called Roussanou) is the most spectacularly situated and frequently photographed monastery. Originally founded in the 14th century, Agia Barbara was abandoned in the early 1980s due to deterioration of its walls, which were built directly into the rock formation. Seven years ago, a small group of nuns moved in and worked to restore it; parts are still under scaffolding. Smaller and less visited than Varlaam and Grand Meteoron, it features a lovely little church completely covered in frescoes. Nun-made lace is available for sale. (Open daily during the summer, but closed Wed. off-season.)

Versatile **Agios Stephanos,** at the road's end, was founded as a hermitage, became a monastery in the 14th century, and is now a convent. Stephanos is cleaner, lighter, and more spacious than Grand Meteoron and Varlaam. Of its two churches, only the more modern **Agios Charalambos,** built in 1798, is open. Although small, the museum displays artifacts of intricate detail (closed Mon.).

Highway to Heaven (Sort of)

The first ascetics scaled the sheer cliff faces by wedging timbers into the rock crevices, thereby constructing small platforms, traces of which can still be seen. After the monasteries were completed, visitors usually arrived by means of extremely long rope ladders, but when these were pulled up, the summit became virtually inaccessible. Visitors who were either too weak or too timid to climb with the ladders were hoisted up in free-swinging rope nets. The half-hour ascent, during which the rope could be heard slowly unwinding, no doubt fostered profound faith in God. Motorized winches have since replaced monk-powered, rope-spool cranes, and today only provisions, not pilgrims, are elevated. In 1922, steps were carved into the rocks and bridges built between the pillars, so even the vertigo-prone would feel secure.

The Monastery of **Agia Triada** (Holy Trinity) lies 3km down the road towards the main intersection. Movie buffs will recognize it from the James Bond flick *For Your Eyes Only.* Looming above Kalambaka, the peak of Agia Triada gives a soul-searing view of the town 1320m below and the snow-capped Pindos Mountains in the distance. The monk Dometius built the monastery in 1476, but the wall paintings were added 200 years later. Gardens fill areas between the buildings. A 3km footpath to the right of the entrance to Agia Triada leads to Kalambaka (closed Thurs.).

Back down the road, past the main intersection and only 2½km before Kastraki, rests the Monastery of **Agios Nikolaos,** also called **Anapafsa.** Built in 1388 and expanded in 1628, its highlight is the fresco work painted by the 16th-century Cretan master Theophanes. Visitors are admitted only in small groups, so wait in the entrance at the top of the steps for the door to open. (Open daily.)

■ NEAR METEORA: KALAMBAKA ΚΑΛΑΜΠΑΚΑ

Once famous for its architecture, Kalambaka lost most buildings of importance to the occupying Nazis' brand of urban renewal. Today, the town caters to international tourists visiting Meteora.

Orientation and Practical Information Kalambaka has two main squares. The first, two blocks up from the **bus station,** is the town's central transit hub, where **taxis** congregate, and from which all major thoroughfares radiate. The second, a few blocks to the right facing Meteora, has mostly shops and restaurants. The non-English-speaking but amiable **police,** 10 Hagipetrou St. (tel. 22 109), will help travelers find rooms (office open 9am-9pm; officer on duty 24 hr). To get there from the bus station, walk one block uphill and take your first right. Facing the square is an **Ionian Bank** (open Mon.-Thurs. 8am-2pm, Fri. 8am-1:30pm). Down Ioanninon St. (if you can't find the street sign, look for the traffic signs for Ioannina and Grevena, located at the top of the street), are the **OTE** (open Mon.-Fri. 7:30am-3:10pm) and the **post office** (open Mon.-Fri. 7:30am-2pm) diagonally across from each other. By way of Trikalon St. (Road to Trikala), you'll come to Riga Fereou Sq., which, according to locals, is the town's "real" square because it boasts a pleasant, leafy park. Facing the park is a **National Bank** (open Mon.-Thurs. 8am-2pm, Fri. 8:30am-1:30pm). Beyond the park, Trikalon St. transforms into an all-out nightlife scene: bars, discos, neon, and a hopping crowd. There are **international bookstores** on both of the town's main squares, but **Inter-Press** (tel. 23 575; open 8am-11pm), farthest from the bus station on the corner, has the best selection of English-language books and foreign newspapers. A **health center** (tel. 22 222 or 24 111) is located 1km from town (open 24 hr.). **Postal Code:** 42200; **Telephone Code:** 0432.

Trains depart from the station on the main "highway" behind the bus station and off to the left (when coming downhill from the bus station). They go to Athens (6 per day, 5hr., 2500dr), Thessaloniki (4 per day, 4hr., 2050dr), Alexandroupolis (3 per day), Livadia (6 per day), and Volos (4 per day); A/C express trains cost 4500dr (2 for Athens and 1 for Thessaloniki daily). When going to Athens, be sure to change trains in Paleofrasis. **Buses** travel from Kalambaka to Meteora (2 per day, 9am and 1:20pm, 20min., 175dr). Take the early bus so you have time to hike around visiting the monasteries, which are open only 9am-1pm and 3:30-5pm. Most people walk (6km downhill) back to Kalambaka, visiting monasteries along the way. Buses also go to Volos (4 per day, 2450dr); Ioannina (1900dr) via Metsovo (3 per day, 1100dr); and Athens via Trikala and Lamia (6 per day, 4450dr).

Accommodations Private rooms abound, but it's illegal for owners to solicit at the bus or railway stations, and police warn against renting from those who do. **Koka Roka** (tel. 24 554) warrants the 550m or so walk up from the bus station. You'll thank yourself wholeheartedly for making the effort. Cozy, traditional, and utterly delightful. (Singles 3000dr, w/bath 4000dr; doubles 6000dr, w/bath 7000dr; triples 7500dr. Prices negotiable for longer stays.) From the bus station, walk 2 blocks up to the central square and turn right onto Vlachava St., just below the Hotel Aeolic Star. Koka Roka is at the top of Vlachava, roughly 2min. beyond the Byzantine Church, at the beginning of the footpath to the Agia Triada Monastery. You might want to call from the station to check on room availability—and besides, Arthur, the English-speaking son of the proprietor, just might give you a ride up on his motorcycle. Also worth considering is the friendly **Hotel Aeolic Star** (tel. 22 325), with spotless rooms. (Singles 4000dr, w/bath 5000dr; doubles 5500dr, w/bath 8000dr; triples 7000dr, w/bath 9000dr.) They're located straight up from the bus station at the top of the central square. The **Hotel Astoria,** 93 G. Kondilli St. (tel. 22 213), across from the train station, has dark, modern rooms. (Singles 4000dr, doubles 5000dr.) There are seven **campgrounds** near Kalambaka, three of which are in **Kastraki,** closer to Meteora.

Food For a hearty meat dish (manly grunt here; the region is known for its meat), head to **Nikos Tavern** (tel. 22 138), across from the bookstore (entrees 1500dr). **Restaurant Panellinio,** in the central square, has tasty and satisfying vegetarian entrees (800dr), and also opens early for breakfast. **Restaurant Aitineio,** on Trikalon St., just before the park, provides a pleasant terrace amidst traditional *bouzouki* music. A broad range of traditional dishes graces the menu (entrees 1200dr). The open-air *taverna* at **Koka Roka** rewards wayfarers from the monasteries (and anyone else) with delicious homemade specialties (entrees 1000dr). **Droutkas,** a sweet shop and bar on Trikalon St., beyond the park and opposite the Shell station, is one of Kalambaka's most popular hangouts. Also try **Rompos,** just before the Hotel Aeolic Star, at the corner of Vlachava St. There are several **markets;** the largest is uphill past Hotel Astoria (open daily 7am-2:30pm and 5-9pm). Kalambaka holds a 3-day **wine festival** with traditional dancing and **free wine** in late August. In late July there's also the town **panēgiri,** the celebration of the town's patron saint.

Sights Kalambaka's foremost sight is the Byzantine **Church of the Dormition of the Virgin.** Follow the signs, ubiquitous around the central square, and after several blocks you'll spy the graceful bell tower of the old church, haloed by a stork's nest. Built in the 11th century on the ruins of a 5th-century basilica, the main structure was remodeled in 1573. Unfortunately, the interior frescoes, painted by the Cretan monk Neophytos, have been badly blackened by centuries of candle flames and incense. George Dailianas is the church tour guide (when he's not planting trees), and is particularly fond of practicing his already adept English with visitors. Modest dress preferred. (Open daily 9am-2pm; admission 300dr.)

■■■ METSOVO ΜΕΤΣΟΒΟ

Although officially designated a "traditional settlement" by the Greek National Tourist Organization, Metsovo has nonetheless fallen prey to commercialization. All of the buildings have been spruced up and painted, and many original slate roofs have been replaced by maintenance-free tile. A subsistence-agriculture-and-petty-commerce economy has been replaced with a booming trade in postcards and handmade wooden trinkets. Despite its pre-packaged feel, or perhaps because of it, this snug little mountain hamlet, perched just below the 1850m Katara Pass, is delightful. Metsovo succeeds because it manages to reveal small village charms while remaining upscale and comradely for visitors. Native Metsovians are descendants of the *Vlachi,* a people once believed to have migrated from Romania, but now surmised to have been Greeks trained by the Romans to guard the Egnatia Highway connecting Constantinople with the Adriatic. The *Vlachi* language is so heavily influenced by Latin that it was used to communicate with the Italians during WWII. Today, it survives only on Metsovo's cobblestone streets. When you visit, bring a light sweater—the hilly area can be cool at night.

Orientation and Practical Information Under an outdoor café in the square is a huge map of the town, which lists (in English) all hotels, sights, monasteries, restaurants, the town's two discos, and the town's "sanitary station" (for **medical emergencies**). In the square there is a **National Bank** (open Mon.-Thurs. 8am-2pm, Fri. 8am-1:30pm). The bank to the right of the newsstand has a 24-hr. **ATM.** To reach the **OTE** (open daily 7:30am-3:10pm), cut through the courtyard in front of the bank, then turn left and wind around to the right. The municipal **police** (tel. 41 183, -9) are on the right past the courtyard (office hr. 8am-2pm and 4-6pm but open 24 hr.). The police chief speaks English. Up the main road from the square at the fork is the **post office** (open Mon.-Fri. 7:30am-2pm). **Telephone Code:** 0656.

From the little shed in the square, **buses** go to Ioannina (4 per day, 900dr) and Trikala via Kalambaka (3 per day, 1500dr). Buses to Thessaloniki stop at the main highway above town (6 per day, about 3000dr). For schedule info, go to the café across the main street from the bus stop shed.

Accommodations Unblemished, inviting rooms fill the "1st hotel in Metsovo" and indubitably the best bargain, **Hotel Athens** (tel. 41 725), down the hill from the main square (singles 5000dr, doubles 6000dr). Denise, the owner's daughter, speaks enchanting English and is a wealth of good-natured info about the town. Sample the homemade specialties from their peaceful, parkside restaurant (vegetarians rejoice!). If rooms are full, owners direct you to the nearby **Hotel Filoxenia** (tel. 41 806). Rooms here have quite a view (doubles 8000dr). The **Tsanaka** family offers traditional, clean rooms on the street past the newsstand and the OTE. (Doubles w/ TV, kitchen, and bath 8000dr; triples 9000dr.) They have pamphlets about Metsovo, with listings of local hotels. The **Hotel Acropolis** (tel. 41 672) is up near the highway (doubles 9300dr, triples 10,500dr). In the mysterious words of the tourist brochure: "Enjoy and relax. In Metsovo even sleeping is an oxygenated pleasure!"

Food and Entertainment Venture up the main road (way up) and turn left at the corner past **To Spitiko,** with specialties like boiled goat (950dr) and homemade *trahanas* (semolina soup 350dr). Climb the steep, narrow walk-turned-steps immediately to your right and press on until you hear the refreshing gurgle of water from within the plateau-like residential square. Look for the sign and balconies. Invent your own delightful walk back down into town.

Sights A wonderful example of Metsovite living during earlier decades is the **Tossizza Museum,** housed in a stone and timber Epirot mansion on the left up the main road (look for the sign opposite the Shell station). It's full of *Vlachi*-handcrafted furniture and clothing, suggestive of how Metsovite families spent long winters cooped up in their homes. The upper floor was Vangeli Averof's apartment when he was a diplomat. Wait at the door until the guide appears (roughly every ½hr.; open daily except Thurs. 8:30am-1pm and 4-6pm; admission 300dr.) The **art gallery** off the main square is a treat. (Open daily except Tues. 9am-1:30pm and 5-7:30pm; winter 9am-1:30pm and 4-6pm; admission 300dr, students 200dr.)

Gracing the central square is a statue of Michalis Tossizza, a native who found fame and fortune in Romania and shared his luck (i.e. money) with Athens and Metsovo, building stadiums and museums (including the Tossizza museum). Signs near the square lead to Ag. Nikolaos Monastery and its 14th-century chapel. Minutes from the main road heading out of town towards the Katara Pass, hike over alpine meadows amid the Pindos Mountains. A small ski lift operates in winter above the town.

EVRITANIA ΕΥΡΥΤΑΝΙΑ

At the end of every goat path in Evritania's pine-capped mountains lies a fragrant feast, the kind of place adventuresome nature-lovers adore. Rare, first-time visitors to this region, in which roads were only carved out in the late sixties by the army (seeking out leftist guerrillas) and paved in the mid-eighties, discover untouched mountainsides and serene villages that still mirror life as it was forty years ago. Only recently, with the establishment of a **ski resort,** has the region turned its attention to tourism, but the fledgling industry has not yet affected the culture or prices. Not surprisingly, in a region where chickens outnumber cars, Evritania is considered to have the purest environment in all of Europe, the fourth cleanest in the world—your body knows. Close your eyes. Breathe in. Contain yourself if you can.

■■■ KARPENISI ΚΑΡΠΕΝΗΣΙ

Karpenisi, the capital of Evritania, attracts its fair share of visitors each year: nature lovers who explore the mountains and rivers, and skiers, particularly, who take advantage of the city's proximity to the Velouchi ski center, 12km away. For this reason, Karpenisi is a comfortable destination, with numerous hotels and cozy *tavernas,* and honest-to-goodness hospitality that is wholesomely refreshing.

Karpenisi confers almost inexplicable invigoration upon unsuspecting visitors. Established in Byzantine times, 11th-12th century A.D., the city is set along the northwest slope of Mt. Velouchi, highest of the Timfristos Mountains, within a panoply of crisp forests of fir and chestnut, driving rivers, and ethereal blue-green lakes sweetened by the cool mountain climate. Despite its tranquil setting, Karpenisi has weathered a history of devastations—by Turks, Albanians, and Germans—and today, small and uncluttered, bearing modern façades, the city is not much to look at. But it's a fine place to look from, with an understatedness that helps you appreciate the surroundings all the more, for the true graces of Karpenisi are triumphant.

Orientation and Practical Information Karpenisi is a city that is almost impossible to get lost in—straightforward, compact, and imminently "readable." Since it is spread along a slope, you can find almost everything within a 5-min. walking radius from the square. The main road leading down from the bus station forks at the square. To reach the **post office** (tel. 22 342), take the downhill road behind the square (cornered by the National Bank) and make your first left onto Ag. Nikolaou after you pass the big yellow supermarket to your right (open Mon.-Fri. 7am-3pm). The **OTE** (open 7am-10pm) and the **police station** (tel. 22 233 or 25 100; 24 hr.) are in close succession along the road forking off to the right. Next door, to the left of the OTE, on Georgiou Tsitsara, is an **Agricultural Bank of Greece** (open Mon.-Thurs. 8am-2pm, Fri. 8am-1:30pm). Edging the square is a **National Bank** (open Mon.-Thurs. 8am-2pm, Fri. 8am-1:30pm) and the local **taxi stand** (tel. 22 666). The bus station is just uphill from the square on the main road. **Buses** run to Athens (2-3 per day, 5-6hr., 3950dr), Lamia (4 per day, 1150dr), Agrinio (2 per day, 1700dr), and the villages of Proussou (daily, 500dr), Mikro Horio (1-2 per day, 220dr), and Megalo Horio (1-2 per day, 220dr). 1-2 buses per day also run to surrounding villages like Frangista and Viniani with prices ranging 500-1000dr. In the square fronting the cafés is the **Town Hall,** where you can satisfy your quest for tourist/travel information during work week business hours. Diagonally across the street from the Agricultural Bank, after Maxim's Café, at 2 Georgiou Tsitsara, is the Karpenisi chapter of the **Greek Mountaineering Club (EOS),** which may be able to field your questions concerning mountaineering in the Timfristos Mountains. For the **hospital,** call 22 315. **Postal Code:** 36100; **Telephone Code:** 0237.

Accommodations Karpenisi has no shortage of good-quality hotels, mainly because people flock here in the winter for the nearby Velouchi Ski Center, which can only accommodate 50 people. The skiing season runs from November through March. **Hotel Galini,** 3 R. Ferou (tel. 22 930), on a quiet street close to the square and the *tavernas,* has cozy pleasant rooms w/baths. Make your first right after the Agricultural Bank. Friendly family atmosphere makes up for marginal English (singles 4406dr, doubles 8812dr). Another friendly and relatively inexpensive option is the rustic **Anessis Hotel,** 50 Zinopoulou (tel. 22 840), on the outskirts of town but within walking distance of the square. Follow the road that forks left from the top of the square, past Hotel Elvetia; Anessis will be on your right. English-speaking staff has ski info (singles 5000dr, doubles 8000dr). **Hotel Mt. Blanc** (tel. 22 322), just past the OTE on the way to the police station, is a spacious hotel with an outdoor terrace (singles 6000dr, doubles 8800dr, 3-person family suites 15,800dr).

Food and Entertainment After you've had one meal—even just a drink—at the **Taverna Klymataria** (tel. 22 230) on Kosma Aitolou, you might not want to try any place else. Light and cheerful, with a cozy fireplace, Byzantine-style woodwork, and a small bar, the *taverna* is a sure bet for a pleasant meal. They offer seasonal specialties, classic grill, vegetarian options, special home wine, and live traditional Greek music Friday and Saturday nights (full meals 1500dr). The amicable owner, Fotis, speaks excellent English and Italian, and will endear the wise with thoughtful conversation. They're located a few blocks down from the Agricultural Bank, named after the tree growing out front. (Open "all day" summer, weekends and festivals, and "evenings only" during off-season.) **Taverna Panorama** (tel. 25 976), down the street from Hotel Galini, doesn't exactly have a panoramic view, but offers a broad (relatively panoramic) menu and outdoor dining. The menu, also in English, includes vegetarian options (eggplant salad 400dr, full meals 1500dr). Friendly and accommodating. (Open daily 10am-3am.) The **sweetshop** of Georgos Kitsios and Co. (tel. 24 082), just opposite the square at 13 Zinopoulou (look for the pink-and-white sign), has probably the best selection of sweets in Karpenisi, and some of the best *baklava* you may ever taste (loads of walnuts and not too sweet). (Open daily 8am-11pm.) **Café T&T** next door has drinks (open daily 6am-3am). If you're looking for a good loaf of bread, the **bakery** of Dedoussis Perikes, 36 Athanasiou Karpenisioti (tel. 22 288), next to the yellow supermarket on the way to the post office, has all kinds of breads, pies, cookies, and a happy, heart-warming, home-baked aroma (open daily 7am-9pm). While in town, ask around about **local fairs** that are held throughout the summer. They feature live Greek music, and tasty lamb.

■ NEAR KARPENISI

The villages surrounding Karpenisi quickly make up for the city's lack of splendor. While they vary vastly in size and location, each of the stone-house villages offers remarkable authenticity and hospitality. **Megalo** and **Mikro Horio** ("large" and "small" village) are fine examples of Evritania's hamlets closer to Karpenisi. Farther along this same road is the monastery of **Proussos** (33km from Karpenisi; look for road signs). Perched on the edge of a cliff overlooking a sea of pine trees and an oddly-placed clocktower, the monastery houses some fine Byzantine art and treats visitors to sweet *loukoumi* and Greek coffee. The other major road out of town, which heads to **Agrinio,** passes through the picture-perfect villages **Anatoliki** (East) and **Ditiki** (West) **Frangista.** An immediately appealing place, Anatoliki Frangista is filled with historical buildings and churches, gorgeous wildflowers, black-clad shepherds, and renegade goats. For lodging head to Ditiki Frangista. Also stop by for a quick cup of coffee at lovely **Sotira,** a café next to running springs 2km from Anatoliki Frangista, which is also home to a historic Byzantine church.

EPIRUS ΗΠΕΙΡΟΣ

Epirus is among the least-touristed regions in Greece. It is also among the most beautiful, featuring stark mountains, gorgeous wildflowers, and lush forests. It is in Epirus that traditional mountain villages, inhabited by black-clad women and staff-holding shepherds, can still be found. The region spent 482 years under Ottoman rule and holds ancient ruins, Roman artifacts, and Turkish mosques in close proximity to one another. Epirus is also home to the best mountain climbing, hunting, and hiking in Greece. Although the picturesque town and resplendent beaches of Parga see their share of visitors, the mountains and timeless villages of Zagoria near the Vikos-Aoos National Park remain undisturbed. If you came to Greece in search of traditional, isolated settings, do your roaming in this region.

■■■ IGOUMENITSA ΗΓΟΥΜΕΝΙΤΣΑ

Igoumenitsa may be your first stop on the Greek mainland (boats from Brindisi and Corfu stop here), and if you begin exploring the country here, you'll be in good company; that's what Lord Byron did in 1809. Igoumenitsa is the consummate transportation hub, linking northern Greece, the Ionian Islands, and foreign destinations. There are no you-haven't-lived-until-you've-seen-them sights, sprawling beaches, or trendy clubs, but if you spend a night here, you'll contentedly stroll along what is actually a lovely waterfront. If you're bored, count the number of times you've looked at your ferry ticket until you fall asleep.

Orientation and Practical Information The staff of the **tourist office** (tel. 22 227), on the waterfront in the customs complex (look for the building labelled "BANK"), is knowledgeable and helpful; (open daily 7am-2:30pm). **Tourist police** (tel. 22 222) and **municipal police** (tel. 22 100), both in the station across from the Corfu harbor, do not speak English. The **OTE** (open daily 7am-8pm) and **post office** (open Mon.-Sat. 7:30am-2pm) are in the same building on Evangelistrias St., which runs inland to connect the waterfront to Kyprou St., leading to the bus station. To get here from the station, turn left, away from the piney knoll. Three **banks,** including the **National Bank,** line the waterfront (open Mon.-Thurs. 8am-2pm, Fri. 8am-1:30pm). When they're closed, most ferry agencies change money (open until roughly 9pm). Banks and **ATM** machines along the waterfront are set up for exchanging money into various international currencies.

Buses leave for Ioannina (10 per day, 2½hr., 1500dr), Thessaloniki (daily, 8hr., 6450dr), Athens (4 per day, 8½hr., 6900dr), Parga (4 per day, 1hr., 900dr), and Preveza (2 per day, 3hr., 1700dr). To reach the port from the bus station (tel. 22 309; only 2 blocks inland), turn right (towards the pine-covered hill) as you emerge from the station, and then right again. At the waterfront, turn left. Igoumenitsa has three ports, which you'll come to in succession. The "old port" mostly sends boats to Italy; the "Corfu" port, 1km farther, serves its namesake (buy your tickets in the yellow kiosk in the parking lot) and houses the police. Beyond the "Corfu" port is the "new port," which sends both to Italy and Corfu. **Ferries** go to Corfu hourly (4:30am-10pm, 2hr., 836dr). For tickets to Italy or the former Yugoslavia, shop around at the many waterfront agencies. "Budget" carriers vary from year to year, and some have student rates. Try to make reservations early. If you're simply in search of info, ask more than one agency; no single answer is sure to be accurate. Also, check charges for a stopover in Corfu. Igoumenitsa's primary ferry agencies sell tickets for most shipping lines: **Jardolinija** (tel. 22 871); **R-Line** (tel. 23 970); **Anek** (tel. 22 104); and **Fragline** (tel. 22 958). **Adriatica** (tel. 22 952) and **Hellenic Mediterranean (HML)** (tel. 22 780) are the only two lines that accept Eurail and Inter-Rail passes. Destinations include Brindisi (9 per day, 10hr., deck 5000dr), Ancona (daily, 23hr., deck approx. 16,600dr, off-season 14,600), Venice (daily, 6:15am, deck 15,800dr), Otranto (weekly but not guaranteed year-round, 10hr., 3000-4000dr), and Bari (2 per day, deck 6500dr, students 5500dr). Prices do not include port dues (1500dr in Greece, 4000 lire in Italy). Most boats depart before noon; arrive early or plan to spend the night. The **hospital** (tel. (0664) 22 204) is 20km away in Filiates; for **emergencies** call 24 420. **Postal Code:** 46100; **Telephone Code:** 0665.

Accommodations The nondescript **Rhodos Hotel** (tel. 22 248), which features the alliterative sign "Rent Rooms Rodos," offers bland but clean singles

(4000dr), doubles (5500dr), and triples (7500dr). From the bus station, continue along the road towards the piney knoll—you'll reach the hotel in less than a minute. **Orepano Beach Camping** (tel. 24 442) is nearby (person 600dr, tent 700dr).

Food Pick up **groceries** at the stores in the seaward corners of Demarkiou Sq., or head to **Martini's Taverna,** on the street connecting the waterfront and the bus station, for traditional Greek food at great prices (stuffed tomatoes and salad 950dr). **The Bakery Alexiou Spiridon** (tel. 24 617), just off the waterfront at 3 El. Venizelou St. on your way to the ports, offers a pleasing, family-style array of baked goods and sweets, including nutritious and hard-to-find whole grain and special diet sugar-free breads (open 5am-11pm). Look for the Ionian Bank at the waterfront corner or try to catch the subtle white "Bakery" placard hanging a few storefronts inland.

■■■ PARGA ΠΑΡΓΑ

Parga is invigoratingly different from Preveza and Igoumenitsa, its bland coastal neighbors. Snug within an arc of green mountains, the town is sheltered from the sea by a row of rocky islets and rests in coves of stunning, sand-and-turquoise beaches. Compact and relatively uncrowded (except in August when it oozes with Italians), Parga offers visitors an effervescent nightlife and friendly atmosphere. The narrow streets, whitewashed or Neoclassical houses, and harbor views create a romantic mood that seems to have infected even the pink pastel supermarket.

Orientation and Practical Information To reach the bus station from the port, head to the northwest corner of the waterfront (with the ocean behind you). Continue one block inland. Here you'll find the **National Bank of Greece.** (Open Mon.-Thurs. 8am-2pm, Fri. 8am-1:30pm.) Turn right and proceed up the street, passing the crimson **OTE** (open Mon.-Sat. 7:30am-10:30pm, Sun. 9am-2pm and 5-10pm). Parga has a herd of unofficial tourist offices: **Kanaris Travel** (tel. 31 039) and **Charitos Travel** (tel. 31 900) on the waterfront; **West Travel** (tel. 31 233; fax 31 348) and **Bettina Travel** (tel. 31 203) a half-block inland. Each helps find rooms, rents mopeds, and arranges daytrips. (Open Mon.-Sat. 9am-2pm and 6-9:30pm.) They also sell **ferry tickets** to Paxos and Antipaxos (daily, 4000dr round-trip, 3000dr round-trip for just Paxos), and Corfu Town (Fri., 8000dr). The bus station (tel. 31 218) is a 2-min. walk up Bagka St., under the Snack Bar Pizza Grill sign. **Buses** connect Parga with Preveza (5-6 per day, fewer on weekends, 2hr., 1100dr), Igoumenitsa (3-4 per day, 1hr., 900dr), Athens (4 per day, 9½hr., 6350dr), and Thessaloniki (daily, 7450dr). The **post office** (tel. 31 295; open Mon.-Fri. 7:30am-2pm) and **police station** (tel. 31 222) are next door. The **port police** can be reached at 31 227, the **fire station** at 31 199. **Postal Code:** 48060; **Telephone Code:** 0684.

Accommodations Although the number of vacationers in Parga increases each year, the number of new rooms grows even faster. Hotels in Parga are expensive; check out the rooms extolled by folks who greet incoming buses, or try off the beaten track, at the south end of the town and the top of the hill. Better yet, head to one of the tourist offices. Singles are scarce but can be found for 5000dr, 6000dr w/bath; doubles are roughly 7000dr, 8000dr w/bath; triples are rare and cost 20% more than doubles. Tourist agencies suggest that large groups call ahead. The **Pension Axis** (tel. 31 090), up the road to the left of the church (turn left at the bakery), offers tidy rooms in a mom-and-pop atmosphere. (Doubles 6600dr, triples 7500dr.) Another option is **Parga Camping** (tel. 31 161, -797), 1km north along the road, complete with a private road to the beach, a market, a budget restaurant, and spacious campsites among the silver-leafed olive trees (open April-Oct.; person 900dr, small tent 650dr, 750dr). **Valtos Camping** (tel. 31 287), located on "the big beach" behind the castle, is also popular and has similar rates.

Food Head 500m inland from the entrance to the Venetian fortress to the **Restaurant Panorama** (tel. 32 447; open 9am-midnight) and try the *mousaka* (1200dr) while enjoying the view of the bay and beaches. The restaurant will pay for your taxi to their establishment. At the **Caravel Café,** right as you head towards the ferry dock, you can sip *café frappe* (350dr) before your ferry leaves. The waterfront, sedate by day, is thronged with amblers during the nightly stroll, 8-9pm.

Sights The **Venetian fortress,** the largest in the area, dominates the town. It was constructed by the Normans, but the Venetians controlled it from 1401 to 1797. Today the structure seems a mere shell beneath the shade of majestic pines. But in the afternoon heat, it's a luscious spot for a picnic or a snooze. Follow the steps from the harbor up the hill, only 5min. from the water. (Open daily 7am-10pm; free.) Subdued green floodlighting creates a tasteful backdrop for a waterfront dinner or walks on the pier. Three min. down and behind the castle to **Valtos Beach,** a voluptuous crescent of fine pebbles and clear water. All beaches around Parga are steeply shelved; roughly 6m out from shore, the bottom plunges. The town beach pales in comparison to Valtos, but is clean and relaxing. The islets 100m offshore, home to a small, postcard-worthy church, are a short swim or pedalboat ride away.

A popular daytrip from Parga is the boat trek up the ancient **Styx** (Acheron), the mythical pathway to the underworld. The trip takes 45min. by boat from Parga to the mouth of the river; the boat then meanders for a ½hr. up the river, between reeds and phlegmatic terrapins. As Dante could attest, all good journeys to the underworld require capable guides. Unlike Dante, we have to pay for ours (daily trips depart at 10am, 2200dr). Ask at the waterfront kiosk, which sells boat tickets to Valtos Beach (every 20min. 9am-11:30pm, 250dr one-way, 400dr round-trip) and excursion tickets to the outlying smaller beaches (1200dr). Near Parga, accessible only by car or taxi (3500-4500dr), is **Necromonteion,** the Oracle of the Dead. The Necromonteion's main subterranean chamber, cool and dimly lit, seems convincing as a threshold to another world. On rare occasions travel agencies organize trips—ask around. (Open 8am-3pm; admission 400dr.)

■■■ IOANNINA ΙΩΑΝΝΙΝΑ

With its Eastern flavor, staid castle walls, idyllic lake island, and racy, if troubled, past, Ioannina is much more than a mere transportation hub. It is Epirus' largest city, the capital of the region, and, curiously, the town with the most marked Turkish influence in all of Greece. Founded by Emperor Justinian in 527 AD, Ioannina has suffered under a colorful succession of petty autocrats. The town was invaded by Normans in 1082, conquered by Turks in 1430, and finally taken by Greek armies in 1913. Ioannina's most notorious foreign ruler, however, was Ali Pasha, Turkish governor of Epirus just before the Greek Revolution. Ali attempted to secede from the Ottoman empire and create an independent kingdom. His exploits became infamous as he combed the region amassing a harem of hundreds of young women (and men) to serve as concubines. Those who resisted, like virtuous Kiria Efrosini, were thrown into the lake. Efrosini, her faithful maid, dove in after her.

ORIENTATION AND PRACTICAL INFORMATION

Ioannina's main bus station is between **Zossimadon** and **Sina Street.** To get to the smaller station, amble down **28 Octovriou Street,** cross **Demokratiou Square,** and proceed roughly four blocks on **Vizeniou Street.** Ioannina's main street runs northwest from the tourist office first as Demokratiou Sq., next as **Averof Street,** then as **Georgiou Street,** leading to the Old Town, castle, and harbor. The city of Ioannina is built around a large lake with an **island** in the middle. To reach the dock, walk straight down Averof St., past the bank to the left of the walls.

Tourist Office: (tel. 25 086). To reach this English- and German-speaking office, take the road to the left of the Agricultural Bank, rotate right at the grass triangle, and walk past Hotel Palladion to Octovriou St. Take a right at the main junction and the tourist office will be 200m along on the right in Botsari Sq. Pick up the free tourist booklet with its excellent map. The congenial staff sometimes lets you store luggage. Open Mon.-Fri. 7:30am-2:30pm and 5-8pm, Sat. 9am-2pm.

Police: (tel. 26 326). On Octovriou St. near the OTE and the post office.

Post Office: On Octovriou St. Open Mon.-Fri. 7:30am-8pm, Sat. 7:30am-2pm. **Postal Codes:** 45221 and 45444.

OTE: On Octovriou St. Open 6am-midnight. **Telephone Code:** 0651.

Hellenic Mountaineering Club: 2 Despotatou Ipirou (tel. 22 13 80). An excellent source of info on mountain trips for the outlying region. Open Mon.-Fri. 7:30-9pm. See Vikos Gorge and Zagoria Villages on p. 165.

Banks: The **National Bank** is on Averof near the tourist office; saunter towards the waterfront. Open Mon.-Fri. 8am-2pm, Fri. 8am-1:30pm.

Flights: Leave for Athens (1 per day, more on Fri., 17,000dr) and Thessaloniki (1 per day except Tues., 10,700dr). The **Olympic Airways** office (tel. 26 518) sits across from the tourist office. Open Mon.-Fri. 8am-3:45pm.

Buses: Leave from the main terminal for Athens (12 per day, 8hr., 6000dr), Igoumenitsa (up to 9 per day, 2½hr., 1500dr), Metsovo (6 per day, 3hr., 900dr), and Thessaloniki via Larissa (5 per day, 7hr., 5000dr) and Konitsa (daily, 959dr). Check the schedule; changes are common. The other station's buses go to Preveza (8 per day, 2hr., 1500dr) and Dodoni (2 per day Mon.-Wed. and Fri., 320dr).

Laundromat: 86 Napoleon Zerva St., a 5-min. walk from the tourist office. Wash 850dr, dry 100dr per 10min. Open Mon.-Fri. 8:30am-3pm and 5:30-9:30pm, Sat. 8:30am-2:30pm.

Hospital: (tel. 26 292), 5km from the center of town.

ACCOMMODATIONS

Rooms in Ioannina are generally comfortable but lacking in character. Motels cluster around the main bus station (these can be a bit grimy) and in the roads off Averof St.

Hotel Egnatia, 20 Dagli-Aravadinou St. (tel. 25 667 or 24 886), one block from the main bus station. Pricey, but convenient if you're stranded at night and have to catch an early bus. Singles w/bath 7986dr, doubles 11,016dr.

Hotel Tourist, 18 Koletti St. (tel. 26 443 or 25 070). Conveniently close to the bus station and Averof St., has clean, simple rooms with shared baths. Singles 4000dr; doubles 6000dr, w/bath 9000dr; triples w/bath 10,500dr.

Hotel Metropolis (tel. 25 507 or 26 207), at the corner of Averof and Kristali St., is noisy but less expensive. Singles 3000dr, doubles 6000dr, triples 7000dr.

Camping Limnopoula (tel. 25 265 or 26 319). Along the lake, 1km from the city center (walk along A. Papandreou St.). Open May-Oct. Person 800dr, tent 500dr.

FOOD AND ENTERTAINMENT

Several unpretentious, reasonably priced restaurants are on Georgiou St. in the Old Town. **Restaurant HBH,** 4 Georgiou St. (tel. 73 155), serves up astounding portions at astonishing prices (heaping plate of rice, giant beans, and aubergine 700dr). Across the street, the **Restaurant Pantheon** (tel. 26 414), run by affable English-speaker Saras Elias, has quick service and a varied menu (entrees from 800dr; open 7am-midnight). For a hearty meal at a low, low price, try **Nick's Grill** on Averof (*gyros* 230dr, fries 250dr). At the south end of the central park (follow signs to the Archaeological Museum) is the more costly **Restaurant Litharitsa** (tel. 20 043 or 23 085), a cafeteria offering a standard omelette-and-burger menu (1300-1500dr) from an outdoor terrace with a dramatic view of the lake and surrounding mountains. The structure, dating from Ali Pasha's heyday, together with its setting, make for a nice beverage break (open daily 6pm-1am). Take along your favorite book for a relaxing read at the popular and atmospheric **Diethnis Café and Sweetshop,** on Averof St. across from the park, a few storefronts down from 28 Octovriou. All manner of coffees, ice creams, Greek sweets, and exotic pastries (open daily 7am-2am). **Sweetshop Nousias,** at 1 Karamanli St., where Karamanli meets Averof by the old town, offers a varied selection of sweet treats and baked delights. (Open daily 9am-

11pm.) In the evenings, teens frolic along Averof and cruise the harborfront, where women sell Turkish delight (*loukoumi*), and gypsies sell roast corn.

SIGHTS

Ali Pasha fans get their fix at the island's **Ali Pasha Museum** on the site of Ag. Nikolaos monastery, where Ali Pasha once sought refuge (to no avail) from the assailing Sultan's forces. The diminutive museum displays his costumes and those of his mistress, and shows how he lived and where he died. He was shot through the floorboards of his apartments and posthumously and ceremoniously beheaded on the stone steps. (Open daily 9am-10pm; admission 100dr.) Also interesting is the island's car-free village. In its pine-forested interior, cunning chickens wander among whitewashed houses, elaborate gardens, small shops, and winding paths that lead to gates of curiously silent **monasteries. Boats** leave for the unnamed scenic island (every ½hr., 7am-midnight, 15min., 180dr; winter every hour, 7am-10pm), home to several wonderful *tavernas* and the cheapest silver in all of Greece.

There's plenty to see on the mainland. Just above the harbor are the massive stone walls of the **Castle of Ioannina,** built near the time of the city's founding and reinforced in the 11th and 14th centuries. Today, they divide the old and modern parts of the city. Among the old buildings, the streets of the old city hold a **synagogue** built in 1790, a testament to the city's once-large Jewish population. At the north tip of the walls reposes **Ali Pasha's tomb.** To see skateboarding, motorbike stunts, and lots of commemorative statues, head to the city **park** on your right (facing the harbor past a large café halfway down Averof Street).

There's a heavy museum scene in Ioannina. The modern **Archaeological Museum** (tel. 33 357) has a slowly gestating collection featuring minute stone tablets etched with political, romantic, and cosmological questions that Roman emperors asked of the oracle at Dodoni from the 6th to the 3rd century BC, translated for your convenience. The museum also houses paintings by 19th-century Greeks, mostly portraits, though you'll also find a few fun fish paintings. The museum is in a park off Averof St., below the clock tower. (Open Mon. noon-6pm, Tues.-Fri. 8am-6pm, Sat.-Sun. 8:30am-3pm; admission 400dr, free on Sun. and holidays.) The **Municipal Museum** (tel. 26 356) resides in the **Asian Aga Mosque,** called the *Tzami* by natives, a splendid 18th-century reminder of Turkey's 500-year ascendancy in the province. Once the home of Ali Pasha, it relates the history of Ioannina's old Jewish and Muslim inhabitants. The mosque sits at the edge of the old town, reflected in the lake next to Skilosofou St. (Open Mon.-Fri. 8am-8pm; admission 500dr, students 300dr.) Nearby is the **Archaeological Site of the Inner Acropolis,** which, in addition to its fine views of lake and city, has particularly interesting broad stone tunnels that are fun to explore (off to the right when you enter the site). (Open Tues.-Sun. 7am-10pm.) Also on-site is a **Byzantine Museum,** featuring some large, wood-carved iconostases and a **Silverworks Museum,** with beautiful and delicate examples of silvercraft. (Both museums open Tues.-Sun. 8:30am-3pm; admission 500dr, students 300dr, seniors 400dr.) The **Folklore Museum** (tel. 20 515), off Pargis Sq. (follow the signs), concerns itself mainly with beautiful Asian-inspired costumes and old tools. (Open Mon. 5:30-8pm, Wed. 10am-1pm.)

The cave at **Perama** is not to be missed. Its caverns are cool (15-20°C), enchanting, and accessible. The cave is roughly 5km northeast of Ioannina on the Metsovo highway and can be reached by local bus #8, which you can catch behind the park across from 28 Octovriou (every ½hr., 260dr round-trip). The 45-min. guided tour of the grottoes takes you past astounding, backlit stalagmite and stalactite formations with imaginative names. (Open daily 8am-8pm; admission 1000dr, students 500dr.) Wax figure and Classics buffs will enjoy the **Vrelli wax museum,** which has the world's only **full-body wax statue of Socrates** (unique but unimpressive). The museum is 13km from Ioannina towards the unenthralling village of **Mouzakai.** (Open 8:30am-7:30pm; free.) Take bus #2 (8 per day, ½hr., 250dr); it stays at the site for 20-25min. while you watch the statues come to life before your very eyes.

Off the highway between Ioannina and Igoumenitsa, and accessible by bus, is the village of **Lia,** immortalized by Nicholas Gage's 1983 book *Eleni.* An immediately appealing place, Lia is filled with historical buildings, gorgeous wildflowers, black-clad shepherds, and renegade goats. **Telephone Code:** 0664. Bus service twice weekly from Ioannina, daily from Igoumenitsa, and twice weekly from Athens.

■■■ VIKOS GORGE AND ZAGORIA ΒΙΚΟΣ ΚΑΙ ΖΑΓΟΡΙΑ

This spectacular combination of dramatic scenery, Dali-esque rock formations, and gray-stone villages inexplicably fails to attract more than a handful of adventurous travelers. From the 15th to the 17th centuries, the mountain villages of the Vikos area, northeast of Ioannina, formed a political and economic confederation recognized by the ruling Turks. Unique architecture and fierce regional pride emerged from the confederation's prosperity. In 1973, the Vikos Gorge and the intersecting Aoos River and canyon were declared a national park. More recently, the GNTO labeled the majestic stone villages "traditional settlements."

MONODENDRI

While most people come to Vikos to hike and mountain-climb, there's also plenty for the less adventurous. When driving to the village of Monodendri, the gorge is straight up. Admire the view—it's like a miniature Grand Canyon with no pollution, commercialism, or honeymooners. Feel free to unlatch the door of the always-unlocked **monastery of Agia Paraskevi.** Built in 1412, the monastery is a good example of architecture blending with its surrounding natural area (in this case the impressive gray mountains and monoliths). If you catch the Monodendri bus, walk down from the bus stop to the main square marked by a playground, church, and **Kikitsa's Restaurant,** home of her famous *alevropita,* a cheese pie large enough for 4 people (2300dr). This is the place to ask for rooms. Three people offer accommodations. (Doubles average 6000dr.) Just outside Kikitsa's is a store (open daily 10am-4pm) selling handmade embroidery made by abandoned or poverty-stricken children and Greek-Albanian refugees at the nearby **Rizarios handiwork school.**

Since bus service is almost as forbidding as the gorge itself, and hitching almost impossible, getting here without a car can be problematic. The most frequent connections drop you off in Konitsa, near the north end of the national park (5:15am-6:45pm, 3-7 per day, 950dr). The same bus that leaves Ioannina at 5:30am stops in the villages of Monodendri (1½hr.), Papingo, Aristi, Kipi, and Tsepelovo (Mon.-Fri.). It makes a return trip from Monodendri at 4:30pm. The schedules are in a constant state of flux; check the chalkboards in the Ioannina station for details. On weekends, buses run less frequently, or in many cases not at all.

HIKING THE GORGE

Monodendri is also the best place to start a journey through the gorge. In Ioannina, drop by the Mountaineering Club and pick up the self-explanatory flyer *Vikos-Aoos National Park.* The club office has rough contour sketches of part of the area; you can photocopy these across the street. Bring provisions and camping gear. There are few hotels (though you may be able to arrange to rent a room) and only a couple of small *tavernas.* Fill several canteens from the well in the town center (or bring bottled water) before setting off into the gorge—there's no more water until the Klima Spring, a 4½-hr. hike from Papingo, and even that dries up in hot weather. Entering the gorge from Monodendri puts you at its south end. **Vikos** village, a 4½-hr. hike away, is located near **Aristi** and **Papingo.** Papingo gives you access to another gateway into the gorge. To get there, take the 5km road (not 2km, as the sign asserts) from Vikos. In the shadow of towering columns of rock, the stone-and-slate village of Papingo, another traditional settlement, radiates the charm of traditional village life. "Rooms to Let" are your best bet for lodging (2500-3000dr per person). The **mountaineering club** in the center of town is more helpful, but has wildly erratic office hours loosely based on the traditional 8am-1pm and 4-6pm schedule. Buses from Ioannina to Papingo (2 per day Mon. and Thurs.-Fri., 500dr) continue on to the even smaller village of **Mikro Papingo,** site of the trail head and the welcoming pension, **Agnanti's Rooms** (tel. 41 123; doubles 7000dr).

From here, the trail ascends **Mount Astraka** (2436m) and then it is a 6-hr. hike to **Gamila Park** on the summit. About halfway up you'll encounter the main hut, maintained by the mountaineering club in Papingo. The hut is a good deal for groups—it costs 10,000dr for up to eight people, plus 1500dr per each additional person. Continue northeast over the **Koutsometros Range** into the **Aoos River Gorge. Mount Gamila** (2478m) looms on your right, and Konitsa is far left, past the gorge's end. You can also head to **Provatina (sheep) cave,** roughly 4hr. from Megalo Papingo, and majestic **Drakolimni Lake** (4½hr. away). The **Despina** and **Leonidos** refuges offer superb views. From these, hike to the broad summit of Mt. Gamila. The tourist office discourages women from hiking alone.

Far below, **Konitsa** offers a convenient base to begin your trek in the opposite direction, with supermarkets, hotels, and a choice of *tavernas.* Leaving Konitsa, follow the road down to the bridge over River Aoos. A 1-hr. hike along the footpath leads to a monastery. Another 4-hr. hike leads to the Gamila shelter. In Konitsa's square cluster the **bus station, post office** (open Mon.-Fri. 7:30am-2pm), two **banks** (open Mon.-Thurs. 8am-2pm, Fri. 8am-1:30pm), and a few hotels. The **police** (tel. 22 202) are down the hill, on the main road (24 hr.).

■■■ DODONI ΔΩΔΟΝΙ

Ancient Dodoni rests at the foot of a mountain 21km south of Ioannina. Though the oracle at Delphi is better known, Dodoni is mentioned by name in the *Iliad,* the *Odyssey,* and in Herodotus' writing. It is here that Ulysses came for absolution after killing Penelope's suitors. The site has been a religious center for almost 4000 years, playing host to successive waves of mother-earth worshippers, tree worshippers, Zeus worshippers, and garden-variety Christians. Around 800 BC, the site became an oracle dedicated to Zeus, who, while courting a nearby cypress tree, was believed to have resided here as the roots of a giant oak. The Helloi interpreted the rustling of the huge oak's leaves as Zeus' advice, and the Argonauts, according to legend, had wood from the tree made into a ship keel, endowing the vessel with the ability to speak in times of need. A temple was built sometime around 500 BC, then destroyed along with the oak tree by the Romans in 167 BC. The last vestiges of the old religion were further subverted by the Christians, who built a basilica on the site (its remains are still visible) in an attempt to diminish pagan influences by incorporating them into Christianity.

The central attraction at Dodoni is a restored 3rd-century **amphitheater** that originally seated 18,000 but was reconstructed by the Romans for gladiator games. In the first week of August, the theater hosts a festival of classical drama. The remains of the oracle and foundations of several buildings, including a temple to Aphrodite and a hall for pilgrims, await next to the theater. A small oak has been thoughtfully replanted in the middle of the ruins of Zeus' sanctuary. (Open Mon.-Fri. 8am-7pm, Sat.-Sun. 8:30am-3pm; admission 400dr, students 200dr.)

The peaceful village of Dodoni, next to the ruins, is reached by **buses** from Bizanious St. in Ioannina (Mon.-Wed. and Fri. 2 per day, 320dr). The buses return almost immediately after reaching Dodoni, but you may be able to sweet-talk your way onto a tour bus heading back to Ioannina. Groups may take a taxi (3000dr). Decide on a price before going; taxis will usually wait for ½hr.

MACEDONIA ΜΑΚΕΔΟΝΙΑ

Once the stomping ground of Alexander the Great, Macedonia, now the largest Greek province, retains its proud tradition. Thessaloniki, the focal point of Northern Greece, has emerged as a worthy competitor to Athens in fashion and nightlife. The countryside conceals the Lake District's natural splendor and the excavations at Pella, Dion, and Vergina pay homage to the region's past. Men may find a trip to the monastic community of Mt. Athos the highlight of their trip (the peninsula is closed to women). Macedonian pride is visible throughout this region of deep green foliage and red-roofed houses similar to those found in Eastern Europe. Don't confuse terrain with culture: as evinced by the controversy over the naming of *that* ex-Yugoslavian province, *this* Macedonia is determinedly Hellenic.

■■■ KASTORIA AND THE LAKE DISTRICT ΚΑΣΤΟΡΙΑ ΚΑΙ ΠΕΡΙΦΕΡΕΙΑ ΤΗΣ ΛΙΜΝΗΣ

Kastoria, Florina, and Pella, tucked against the borders of Albania and the former Yugoslavia, are rarely visited by tourists. Despite the lack of interest, the natural setting is stunning, the villages attractive and unassuming, and the absence of sputtering buses refreshing. English-speaking residents are about as scarce as goats' wings here, but immerse yourself in your surroundings by trying out your Greek.

The city of **Kastoria** (named after Kastor, one of Zeus' sons) originally rested securely on an island in Lake Kastoria. Around the 10th century AD, the townspeople began dumping garbage into the lake to build a causeway to the shore. Today, the bulk of the city is squeezed onto this narrow isthmus, and the island proper is nearly deserted. Kastoria, reminiscent of Switzerland, rests on the edge of a group of mountains separated by a lake. Savor the beauty of the lake all you want, but don't even think about taking a dip—the town recently stopped dumping raw sewage into the water, but the biological clean-up process is still years from completion.

Orientation and Practical Information In the indefinite interim before Kastoria opens up its new **tourist offices,** seek out info on the first floor of the town hall (tel. 27 312; open Mon.-Fri. 7am-2:30pm), where English-speaking assistants in the mayor's office provide maps and answer questions. There are no tourist police, but the kindly **municipal police** (tel. 83 333), located behind the bus station on Gramou St., are somewhat familiar with English. The **National Bank** is on the mainland at 11 Noembriou St., which you can pick up from Gramou, bearing left as you head northeast uphill. (Open Mon.-Thurs. 8am-2pm, Fri. 8am-1:30pm.) They have a 24-hr. **ATM** which accepts Mastercard or Cirrus. The **post office** is along the lakefront road, Megalou Alexandrou Ave., around the bend from the bus station. They also conduct exchange. (Open daily 7:30am-2pm.) The **OTE** is uphill, midway between Davaki Sq. and Dexamenis Sq., at 33 Ag. Athanasiou St. (open daily 7am-10pm). **Flights** to Athens daily except Thurs. (7800dr). Olympic Airways office on the waterfront (tel. 22 275 or 23 125) is open Mon.-Fri. 8:30am-4pm. To get to the airport, 12km out of town in Argos, take a taxi (1400dr). Kastoria's main bus terminal (tel. 83 455) is on 3 Septemvriou, one block inland from the lake. **Buses** run to Thessaloniki (6 per day, 4½hr., 3100dr), Edessa (6 per day, 1750dr), Athens (2 per day, 8050dr), Kozani (5 per day, 1450dr), Veria (daily, 2100dr). To reach Florina or Kalambaka, multiple bus connections are required. The kind bus station staff will help you figure it all out. **Taxis** (tel. 82 100, -200) are available 24 hr. They converge near the bus station. To contact the **hospital,** call 28 341, -2, or -3. **Postal Code:** 52100; **Telephone Code:** 0467.

Accommodations **Hotel Acropolis** (tel. 83 737, -587), located one block behind the bus station at 14 Gramou St., is one of the best bargains in Kastoria. Opt for a higher floor to secure a view of the lake. (Singles 4250dr, w/bath 4835dr; doubles 4860dr, w/bath 6500dr; triples 5835dr, w/bath 7800dr). Neighboring **Hotel Anesis,** 10 Gramou St. (tel. 83 908, -9; fax 83 768), is a slightly fancier option (singles 7800dr, doubles 10,000dr, triples 12,000dr, all w/bath and TV). **Hotel Kastoria** (tel. 85 508) is 1km to the right (facing the water) of the bus station on the waterfront road. Spacious, neat rooms are free of tacky decoration. (Singles 6000dr, doubles 7000dr, triples 10,000dr, quads 12,000dr; breakfast 800dr.) Professional, English-speaking **Europa Hotel,** 12 Ag. Athanasiou St. (tel. 23 826, -7; fax 25 154), on the main road out of Davaki Sq., running towards Dexamenis Sq., offers spacious rooms w/bath and TV. (Singles 8400dr, doubles 10,400dr, triples 13,100dr; breakfast 1100dr.) You can **camp** by Mavriotissa for roughly 1000dr per person if you get permission from the priest.

Sights Along with its voluminous fur production (some 5000 garments per day), Kastoria is renowned for its churches—40 Byzantine and 36 post-Byzantine edifices scattered throughout the city—with elaborate masonry and exquisite decoration. In most churches, though, the saints' eyes have been gouged out. Greeks explain that occupying Turkish soldiers desecrated the images, while Turks claim that faithful pilgrims collected the eyes as talismans. Regardless, the tiny Byzantine **Panagia Koumblelidhiki** (open 9am-2pm and 6-9pm), in the center of town, and the **Church Mavriotissa** (open 9am-10pm), 3km out of town, house particularly spectacular frescoes which, unfortunately, are marred by modern graffiti. To visit Mavriotissa, stroll out of town past the hospital and towards the island. The priest who lives there conducts a tour (in Greek or German) and opens the churches generally between 9am and 10pm. To be certain of getting in, however, and to facilitate your visit to any other church, make your first stop the **Byzantine Museum** (tel. 26 781), off Mitropoleos St., in Dexamenis Sq., at Kastoria's center. At the museum arrange for a guide to open the churches for you. Take the time to appreciate the superb icons on display, among the finest in the region. (Open daily except Mon., 8am-2:30pm; free.)

AROUND THE LAKE DISTRICT

One kilometer out of town stands **Mount Psalida,** where, legend has it, Alexander the Average resolved to become Alexander the Great by conquering the world. Bounded by the Yugoslavian and Albanian borders and Kastoria, the tranquil **Lake District** is an area of dense wilderness and swimmable lakes. **Florina,** accessible from Edessa and Thessaloniki, makes a good base from which to explore the area. **Trains** run from Thessaloniki (5 per day, 4hr., 1370dr) and Edessa (2-3 per day, 2 hr., 720dr). **Buses** connect from Thessaloniki (6 per day, 3½hr., 3000dr) and Edessa (6 per day, 2hr., 1200dr). For the Florina bus station, call 22 430. Florina has little to offer tourists apart from its location, a fragrant market area, and the **Hotel Ellenis** (tel. 22 671) in the town center. (Singles 5000dr, doubles 8000dr, triples 9000dr.) The Alpine Club runs a large refuge near the village of **Pissoderi** on Mt. Verna. **Postal Code:** 53100; **Telephone Code:** 0385.

■■■ EDESSA ΕΔΕΣΣΑ

Greek vacationers love Edessa because it contains the country's only waterfalls. Perched securely on top of a steep, formerly fortified butte on the foothills of Mt. Vermion, the city was given the name of "Edessa" (meaning "the waters") by the occupying Bulgarian army. The town ends on the brink of a ravine, where the numerous streams flowing under Edessa's arched stone bridges cascade into an abyss, plummeting more than 25m to the verdant valley floor. Frankly, though, it's not quite as magnificent as it sounds; concrete viewing balconies, overgrown weeds, and danger signs along the water's edge domesticate the experience. But, if

Edessa's main attraction is not as spectacular as it tries to be, the town's temperate climate, aromatic flowers, petite parks, and water-bound walkways—adorned with benches, fountains, and outdoor cafés—make for fanciful strolls.

Orientation and Practical Information Hotels and the town center await at the top of Pavlou Mela, where the road meets the intersection of Egnatia and Democratias St. You can reach Democratias St. by following 18th Octovriou. For **tourist info,** call 24 330 (daily 7:30am-2pm). If you're in dire need of information, turn right at 20 Democratias (walking away from the bus station) and look for the **police station** (tel. 23 333; 24 hr.), at the corner of Filippou and Iroon Polytechniou. Edessa's **post office** on Democratias St., one block from the *agora,* exchanges money for a piratical commission. (Open Mon.-Fri. 7:30am-2pm.) The **OTE** is a blue and white building facing the Byzantine clock tower on Ag. Dimitrios. The **National Bank of Greece,** 1 Demikratou St., is surrounded by an iron fence on the corner of 2 Arch. Penteleiminos. (Open Mon.-Thurs. 8am-2pm, Fri. 8am-1:30pm.) The main bus station (tel. 23 511) is at the corner of Pavlou Mela and Filippou St. **Buses** run to Athens (5 per day, 8hr., 7300dr), Thessaloniki (15 per day, 2hr., 1300dr), and Veria (6 per day, 1hr., 750dr). A second depot, marked by a bus sign, is located at a family-run sandwich shop and grill just up the block at Pavlou Mela and Egnatia (look for "KTEL" painted on the window). Buses go to Kastoria (5 per day, 2hr., 1700dr) and Florina (6 per day, 2hr., 1200dr). The train station (tel. 23 510) is at the end of 18th Octovriou St. **Trains** run to Florina (2-3 per day, 2hr., 720dr), Thessaloniki via Veria and Naoussa (9 per day, 2hr., 840dr), Kozani (4 per day, 820dr), and once daily to Athens, either directly (7000dr) or via Plati (3640dr). Take the train rather than the bus—the view is nicer and the fares are cheaper. **Taxis** (tel. 23 392 or 22 904) congregate on 18th Octovriou St., near the bank. **Telephone Code:** 0381.

Accommodations The **Hotel Alfa,** a "C" class hotel, has clean rooms with TV and bath (singles 6000dr, doubles 10,500dr). Next door, the **Hotel Pella,** 30 Egnatia St. (tel. 23 541), two blocks up O. Mela from the bus depot and across the square, has rooms with bath (singles 7104dr, doubles 9083dr).

Food and Entertainment Edessa has no shortage of cheese pies and rotisserie chicken. The fish tavern **Boulgouri,** near 18th Octovriou on the way to the train station, provides a pleasant atmosphere for a fish dinner (1200dr). A good way to appreciate the town is to walk west up Monasteriou St. (behind Egnatia and to the right of the **Byzantine Clock Tower**), to the **Byzantine Bridge,** under which flows the main rivulet that eventually splits off to form the many streams flowing through town. Many unpretentious cafés reside here, facing a quiet park.

Sights Since all streams flow roughly west to east, follow any watercourse walkway back to town. To reach Edessa's largest waterfall, **Katarrakton,** keep to the stream farthest to your left (with your back to the bridge.) As the stream forks, pursue the branch to your left. The roar of surging cascades and the vision of bustling souvenir stands will herald your arrival. Enthusiasts should continue down the path at the bottom of Katarrakton into the valley to see the three more sizable falls near the hydroelectric plant or stroll into the waterfall's none too impressive cave (50dr). Almost all the cliff-side terraces spanning the east rim of town offer beautiful panoramic vistas of the agricultural plain below. You will be able to spot a large, red-tiled building complex—a convent—and the adjacent pillared ruins of the ancient town, worth the hike down to explore more closely. Below the town to the east lie the 4th-century BC **ruins** of the ancient city which were unearthed in 1968; follow the signpost on the road to Thessaloniki. Among the remains are towers, walls, and a gate. Until the discovery of the ruins at Vergina, Edessa was thought to be ancient **Aigai,** the capital of Macedonia. Except for a few small churches, the only other tourist attraction is a small **Archaeological Museum** in the Mosque on Stratou St. at the edge of town. The museum was closed in summer, 1995.

■■■ VERGINA ΒΕΡΓΙΝΑ

The discovery of the ancient ruins of Vergina, 13km southeast of Veria was an archaeological watershed. In 1977 and 1978, Manolis Andronikos discovered the remains of royal tombs and a large palace that date from 350 to 325 BC. No one is really sure who these deceased royals were, but their tombs display such superb artistry that some scholars believe that these could have belonged only to the royal Macedonian family of King Philip II, father of Alexander the Great. The dig turned up some fabulous treasures, now on display in Thessaloniki's Archaeological Museum (see p. 176). If Philip II were buried here, that would suggest that Vergina, and not Edessa, was the site of the ancient Macedonian capital of **Aigai,** where members of the royal family were buried.

A superb, modern complex encloses the tombs; but the scattered rubble, unfortunately, is poorly labeled and makes little sense to the dilettante. Buy a book about the site. A good selection of books on Vergina as well as other sites is available at the café/souvenir stand across the street from the tombs. The site office farther up the hill, at the entrance to the palace ruins, sells books but has a limited selection.

To reach the sites from the bus stop, simply mind the signs and follow the road out of the village. A pleasant 10 to 15-min. walk will find you at the gateway to **The Royal Tombs.** Inside, archaeologists found a gold chest that contained the cremated remains of some royal personage. A little farther uphill are the open ruins of the 3rd-century **Palace of Palatitsa** (tel. (031) 92 394). Look for the exquisite mosaic floor on the south wing of the ruins. (Open Tues.-Sun. 8:30am-7pm; admission 500dr, students 300dr, seniors 400dr). **Buses** run from Thessaloniki to Veria, 74km away (every ½hr., 2hr., 1100dr), and from Edessa to Veria (9 per day, 750dr). From Veria, take the "Alexandria" bus and get off at Vergina (7 per day, 15min., 240dr).

■■■ THESSALONIKI ΘΕΣΣΑΛΟΝΙΚΗ

Cosmopolitan Thessaloniki encircles its harbor and waterfront promenade with assurance. Wealthy, youthful, energetic, in proud display of sophisticated shops, cafés, and myriad tree-lined avenues, modern Thessaloniki will reward visitors with a rich experience. The city is at its best at the close-cornered markets that fringe popular squares, heralding thick-walled ruins and Roman monuments. Its well-trafficked thoroughfares, lined with modern high rises, continue to accommodate splendid, if time-weary, mansions, and are surreptitiously punctuated with small, concealed churches. The old city's quiet, winding, castlebound streets surprise the wayfarer with their residential charms and panoramic views. Few foreigners make it this far north, but those who do discover a pleasant anomaly: a Greek urban center that shows off its history without being overshadowed by it.

The capital of Macedonia and the second largest city in Greece, Thessaloniki is teeming with Byzantine churches and Roman ruins, and offers one of the best archaeological museums in Greece. On the crossroads of important trade routes, Thessaloniki has flourished since its founding in 315 BC by Cassander, brother-in-law of Alexander the Great. Named for Cassander's wife, ancient Salonika prospered after the Roman conquest of Greece. Being the only port on the Via Egnatia (the ancient east-west highway) no doubt helped, and the city's cultural influence led Paul the Apostle, in the 1st century AD, to write two epistles to disciples of the churches he founded here (I and II Thessalonians). While Athens was in the throes of a cultural slump, Thessaloniki usurped its position as the most important Greek city in the Byzantine Empire. After the 10th century, missionary followers of the brothers Methodius and Cyril (inventors of the Cyrillic alphabet) exerted their wide-ranging influence from headquarters here. In the early 20th century, the city's population, which included Slavs, Albanians, and a vast Jewish community, was more characteristically Balkan than Hellenic; more homogeneous today, the city nonetheless continues to project cultural vigor.

ORIENTATION AND PRACTICAL INFORMATION

Thessaloniki's gridded street plan, laid out by a French architect, greatly simplifies transit. The three main streets—Nikis, Tsimiski, and Egnatia—run parallel to the waterfront. The cheapest hotels are on **Egnatia,** banks and the post office on **Tsimiski,** and nondescript office buildings on **Nikis.** The main shopping street is **Ermou,** between Tsimiski and Egnatia. **Aristotelous** intersects all three at right angles to form **Aristotelous Square** on the waterfront, where the tourist office, train office, and airport bus terminal are located. The railway station is west of the square along Monastiriou St.; the main park, fairgrounds, and university are east of the downtown area. The **Lefkos Pirgos** (White Tower), the symbol of Thessaloniki, stages a solitary, if transcendent, game of chess over the harborfront. **Navarinou Square,** whose centerpiece of Roman ruins is intriguing in itself, incorporates old and new in a captivating meeting ground for Thessaloniki's youth. Roughly 15 blocks inland, north of **Athinas Street** and flanked by ancient castle walls, wind the streets of the **old town.** A marvelous place for morning or evening strolls, here you'll find a welcome degree of tranquility, panoramic views, and inexpensive *taverna*.

Tourist Office: Off Aristotelous Sq. at #8 (tel. 27 18 88 or 22 29 35), 1 block from the water. Take any tram on Egnatia to Aristotelous Sq. The Michael Jordan of tourist offices. Has city maps, hotel listings, and train, bus, and boat schedules. Ask about events, especially the **International Trade Fair,** the **Film and Song Festival,** held annually in Sept., and the **Dimitria Cultural Festival,** held in Oct. Open Mon.-Fri. 8am-8pm, Sat. 8:30am-2pm. Also at the **port** (tel. 59 35 78) near the Olympic Airways office and the **airport** (tel. 42 50 11, ext. 215).

Tourist Police: 10 Egnatia St. (tel. 45 32 23). Less helpful than the tourist office. English and German spoken. Open 24 hr., or so they say.

Main Post Office: 45 Tsimiski St., midway between Agia Sophias St. and Aristotelous St. Open Mon.-Sat. 7:30am-8pm. **Postal Code:** 54101.

OTE: 27 Karolou Diehl St., at the corner of Ermou, 1 block east of Aristotelous. Open Mon.-Sat. 24 hr. **Telephone Code:** 031.

Banks: National Bank of Greece, 11 Tsimiski St. Open for **currency exchange** Mon.-Fri. 8am-2pm and 6-8pm, Sat. 8am-2pm, Sun. 9:30am-12:15pm. 24-hr. **ATM** takes Mastercard and Cirrus; many Visa-accepting ATMs scattered elsewhere. Smaller banks charge slightly higher commission. **Citibank,** 21 Tsimiski St. (tel. 54 624, regular hr.) can handle sophisticated international banking needs.

American Express: Northern Greece representative at **Memphis Travel,** 23 Nikis St. (tel. 22 27 96), on the waterfront. Open Mon.-Fri. 9am-1pm.

Consulates: U.S., 59 Nikis St. (tel. 24 29 05), on the waterfront west of the White Tower. Men can pick up a form letter here requesting permission to enter Mt. Athos (women are forbidden there; see Mt. Athos on p. 182). Open Tues.-Thurs. 9am-noon. **Britain,** 8 Venizelou St. (tel. 27 80 06). Also for other EC countries (open Mon.-Fri. 8am-3pm). **France,** 8 Mikenzi St. (tel. 24 40 30), across from the church of Ag. Sofia (open daily 9am-1pm). **Bulgaria** (tel. 82 92 10); **Cyprus** (tel. 26 06 11); **Italy** (tel. 83 00 55); **Turkey** (tel. 20 99 64).

Ministry of Northern Greece: (tel. 26 43 21), on the corner of Ag. Dikitiriou St. and Venizelou. After obtaining form letters from the U.S. consulate, men wishing to visit Mt. Athos must obtain permits here. Open Mon.-Fri. 10:30am-2pm.

Flights: Airport (tel. 47 39 77), 16km from town. Take bus #78 (110dr) or a taxi (about 1800dr). **Olympic Airways Office,** 3 Koundouriotou St. (tel. 23 02 40). Flights to Athens (7 per day, 19,400dr), Limnos (daily, 13,000dr), Lesvos (1 per week, depart 6am, 18,800dr), Crete (daily, 27,600dr), Rhodes (2 per week, 29,800dr), and Ioannina (daily except Tues., 10,000dr). Olympic Airlines flights also connect Thessaloniki with major European cities and Larnaka in Cyprus. Open Mon.-Sat. 8am-3:30pm, open for phone reservations only Mon.-Fri. 3:30-8pm. Lufthansa, British Airways, and charter companies also fly into Thessaloniki.

Trains: Main Terminal (tel. 51 75 17), Monastiriou St., in the western part of the city. Take any bus down Egnatia St. (75dr). Trains to Athens via Larissa (10 per day, 8hr., 3440dr), Edessa (8 per day, 2hr., 840dr), Florina (5 per day, 4hr., 1370dr), Alexandroupolis (5 per day, 8hr., 3000dr), İstanbul (2 per day, 23hr.,

Thessaloniki
1 Acropolis
2 Tower of Trigoniou
3 Forest Theater
4 Cemetery
5 University
6 International Trade Fairgrounds
7 OTE Tower
8 Archaeological Museum
9 Vlatades Monastery
10 Oslos David
11 Alatza Imaret
12 Ayios Nikolaos Orphanos
13 Rotunda
14 Arch of Galerius
15 Ayios Panteleimon
16 Transfiguration
17 State Theater of Northern Greece
18 Garden Theater
19 Vassiliko Theatro
20 White Tower
21 Octagon Building
22 Ayia Sophia
23 Profitis Ilias
24 Ayios Dimitrios
25 Roman Forum
26 Plateia Dikasterion Terminal
27 Cifte Hamam
28 Panayia Chalkeon
29 Olympic Terminal
30 Train Station
31 Municipal Market
Urban Bus Terminal
PLATIA DIKITIRIOU
PLATIA DIKASTIRION
GK. Railway Station
PLATIA ARISTOTELOU
PLATIA ELEFTHERIAS
PLATIA VARDARI
Zografou
Dimadou Vlatadon
Agiou Dimitriou
Ag. Sofias
Egnatia
Ermou
Tsimiski
El. Venizelou
I. Dragoumi
Aristotelous
Langada
Monastiriou
26 Oktovriou
Dodekanissou
Salaminos
Politehniou
Kassandrou
Olimbiados
Athinas
Churchil (Dikitiriou)
Filipou
Ioustinianou
Klafthmonos
Eptapirgiou
Stavrou Voutira
Nav. Koundourioti

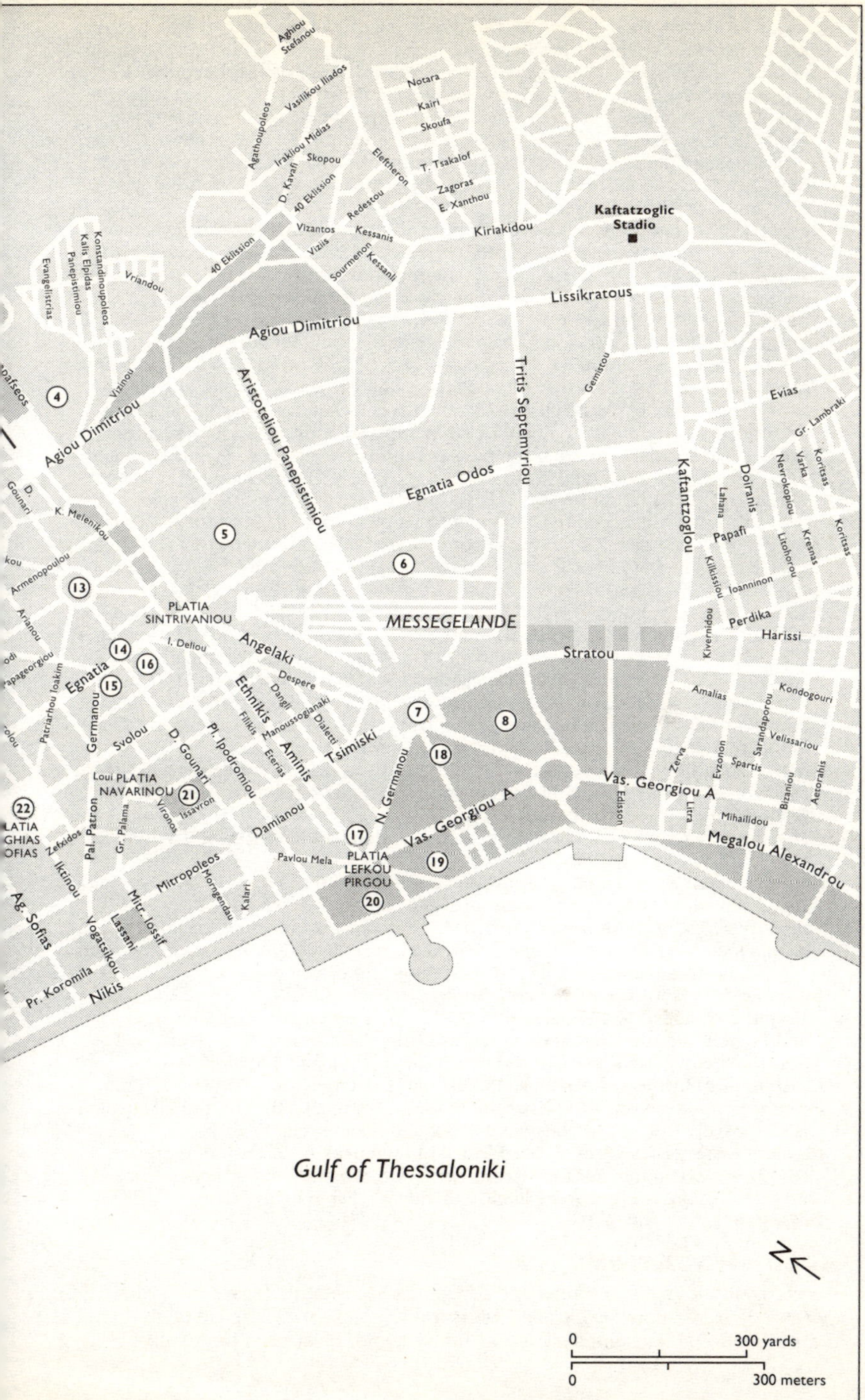
Aghiou Stefanou
Vasilikou Iliados
Agathoupoleos
Irakliou Midias
Skopou
D. Kavafi
40 Eklission
Notara
Kairi
Skoufa
T. Tsakalof
Zagoras
E. Xanthou
Eleftheron
Redestou
Vizantos
Kessanis
Vizis
Sourmenon
Kessanli
Kiriakidou
Kaftatzoglic Stadio
Konstandinoupoleos
Kalis Elpidas
Panepistimiou
Evangelistrias
Vriandou
Lissikratous
Agiou Dimitriou
Vizinou
Aristoteliou Panepistimiou
Tritis Septemvriou
Gemistou
Evias
Gr. Lambraki
Koritsas
Varka
Nevrokopiou
Doiranis
Lahana
Kaftantzoglou
Egnatia Odos
D. Gounari
K. Melenikou
Armenopoulou
Papafi
Litohorou
Kresnas
Kilkissiou
Ioanninon
PLATIA SINTRIVANIOU
MESSEGELANDE
Kivernidou
Perdika
Harissi
Arianou
I. Deliou
Angelaki
Stratou
Egnatia
Patriarhou Ioakim
Despere
Dangli
Ethnikis
Amalias
Kondogouri
Germanou
Svolou
D. Gounari
Pl. Ipodromiou
Filikis
Manoussoglanaki
Dialetti
Eterias
Aminis
Tsimiski
Velissariou
Sarandaporou
Zerva
Evzonon
Spartis
Aeorahis
Loui PLATIA NAVARINOU
N. Germanou
Vas. Georgiou A
Vas. Georgiou A
Edisson
Litra
Mihailidou
Bizaniou
Issavron
Vironos
Damianou
PLATIA AGHIAS SOFIAS
Zefxidou
Pal. Patron
Gr. Palama
Pavlou Mela
PLATIA LEFKOU PIRGOU
Megalou Alexandrou
Iktinou
Mitropoleos
Morngendau
Kalari
Ag. Sofias
Vogatsikou
Lassani
Mitr. Iossif
Pr. Koromila
Nikis
Gulf of Thessaloniki
N
0
300 yards
0
300 meters

about 11,800dr), Sofia (1 per day, 9hr., 10,000dr). You can also catch trains from Athens headed for the Czech Republic (leaves 7am, 24hr., 37,000dr), Germany (leaves 7:20am, 26hr., 25,000dr), Hungary, Poland, and parts of the former USSR. Buy tickets at the station or at **State Railway Offices (OSE),** 18 Aristotelous St. (tel. 27 63 82). Open Tues.-Fri. 8am-8:30pm, Mon. and Sat. 8am-3pm. From here, trains head to Athens (18 per day, 3440dr), Kalambaka (10 per day, 2050dr), Volos (13 per day, 1640dr), Edessa (2 per day, 840dr), Alexandroupolis (2 per day, 2990dr), and all other stations on the mainland. Comprehensive, legible schedule is available in Greek.

Buses: The privately run **KTEL** bus company operates out of stations scattered throughout the city, each generally servicing a different area. While printed schedules and price lists are virtually nonexistent, departure times are posted above ticket counters. The depot directly across from the railway station runs buses to Athens (10 per day, 7½hr., 6800dr). To the left of this terminal is a KTEL station with buses heading to Trikala (6 per day, 3½hr., 3000dr). Behind the Athens bus depot sits another KTEL station (tel. 52 72 65 or 52 82 81), with buses leaving daily at 10am for Preveza and Parga (6500dr). The nearby KTEL (tel. 52 21 61) on the corner of Anagenniseous St. and I. Venizelou has departures for Florina (6 per day, 3½hr., 3000dr). From **22 Anagenniseous St.,** a few blocks closer to the waterfront and away from the railway station, buses run to Edessa (every hr. 6am-7pm, 2hr., 1300dr) and Volos (4 per day, 3hr., 3000dr). From **2 N. Kazantzaki St.** (tel. 52 21 62) buses leave for Kastoria (5 per day, 4hr., 3100dr). For transport to the Halkidiki peninsula take the #10 bus (75dr) from the main railroad station or along Egnatia St. to the depot on the east side of town at **68 Karakassi St.** (tel. 92 44 44, -5). (See Halkidiki, p. 181.) Call 142 for Greek language info.

City Buses: 75dr, 150dr to the beaches for swimming (bus #69 leaves every 15min., 45min. ride).

Ferries: 3 departures per week in summer for Lesvos (13hr., 6650dr), Limnos (7hr., 3900dr), and Chios (18hr., 6500dr). On Mon., Wed., and Fri. boats leave for Paros (6980dr), Santorini (7100dr), Skiathos (3650dr), and Iraklion (8110dr). Buy tickets at **Nomikos Lines,** 8 Kountourioti St. (tel. 52 45 44 or 51 30 05); take your first left after Nikis becomes Kountourioti St. along the waterfront. Open Mon.-Fri. 8:30am-8:30pm and Sat. 8:30am-2:30pm.

Flying Dolphins: Hydrofoils travel daily (Sept.-June 4 per week) to Skiathos (3½hr.), Skopelos (4½hr.), and Alonissos (5hr.). Fares average roughly 10,000dr. Buy hydrofoil tickets at **Crete Air Travel,** 1 Dragoumi St. (tel. 54 74 07 or 53 43 76), directly across from the main port. Open Mon.-Fri. 8am-4pm and 5-9pm, Sat. 8am-4pm, Sun. noon-5pm.

Laundromats: Bianca, 3 L. Antoniadou St. (tel. 20 96 02). From the Arch of Galerius, go inland up the median boulevard, and turn right at the KousKous Café. It's directly across from the small church. 1400dr per load includes wash, dry, and soap. Open Mon.-Fri. 8am-2:30pm. **Mimoza 2** (tel. 24 00 53), located at 56 Olimbou St., north of Egnatia St., does dry cleaning and pressing.

International Bookstore: Molcho Books, 10 Tsimiski St. (tel. 27 52 71), across from the National Bank. Founded in 1888. Offers extensive selections in English and French. International newspapers available daily. Open Mon., Wed., and Sat. 8:30am-2:50pm, Tues. and Thurs.-Fri. 8:30am-2:20pm and 5-8:30pm.

Camping Equipment: Petridhis, 43 Vas. Irakliou. Open Mon.-Fri. 8am-2:30pm.

Hospital: Ippokration, 49 Konstantinoupoleos (tel. 83 79 20). This public hospital is supposedly the best in Thessaloniki. Some doctors speak English.

Medical Emergency: Red Cross First Aid Hospital, 6 Kountourioti St. (tel. 53 05 30), located at the entrance to the main port. Provides minor medical care in a no-frills fashion. Bring a Greek-English dictionary. Services are free.

Emergency: Call 100 or 166.

ACCOMMODATIONS

Hotels await along the western end of Egnatia St., roughly between Vardari Sq. (500m east of the train station) and Dikastirion Sq. Prices rise 20% in Sept. during the international fair. Single women should avoid, or at least buddy-up before accepting offers for, cheap rooms touted by English-speaking tourist information impersonators at the train station.

Hotel Argo, 11 Egnatia St. (tel. 51 97 70). Old rooms, but the best bargain in town. Don't be surprised if classical music greets you at the door. Singles 4000dr, w/bath 5000dr; doubles 5000dr, w/bath 6500dr; triples 6000dr, w/bath 8000dr.

Hotel Atlas, 40 Egnatia St. (tel. 53 70 46 or 51 00 38; fax 54 35 07). Sort of modern; thoroughly spotless. Some rooms have TVs. Singles 4500dr; doubles 6500dr, w/bath 8000dr. Add 20% for extra bed.

Hotel Akropole, 4 Tantolidou St. (tel. 53 61 70). Near Dimokratias Sq.; off Egnatia. Clean rooms, but tacky decor. Singles 4500dr, doubles 6500dr, triples 7600dr.

Hotel Aegean, 19 Egnatia St. (tel. 52 29 21). Blandly Mike Brady-designed hotel from the 70s, but bright and cheery. Singles 7000dr, w/bath 8750dr; doubles 9500dr, w/bath 11,300dr; triples 11,600dr, w/bath 13,500dr.

Hotel Kastoria (tel. 53 62 80), at the conjunction of Egnatia St. and L. Sofou St. Corner location means cacophony in stereo. Tidy, dark rooms with clean baths. Singles 4000dr, doubles 5000dr, triples 6500dr.

Hotel Tourist, 21 Mitropoleos (tel. 27 63 35). Centrally located (one block from Aristotelous Sq.) on a pleasant, tree-lined street near the waterfront, this generically named hotel has an interesting ambience, with 14-ft. ceilings, cavernous hallways, and an old-fashioned salon and elevator. Singles 7500dr, w/bath 8500dr; doubles 10,800dr, w/bath 12,960dr; triples 14,500dr, w/bath 15,000dr.

Youth Hostel, 44 Alex. Svolou St. (also called Nikolaou St.; tel. 22 59 46). If you're desperate for a cheap place, take tram #8, 10, 11, or 31 on Egnatia and get off at the Arch of Galerius. Go towards the water and turn left 2 blocks later onto Svolou. On a noisy street. Obviously communal baths. Reception open all day. Bathrooms closed 11am-6pm. Showers 6-10pm only (free). 11pm curfew recently relaxed—try to be in by midnight. Check-out 11am.

Camping: Take city bus #72 to **Agia Triada** for **Thermaikos Beach Campground** (tel. (0392) 51 352). Supermarket, showers, beach. 950dr per person, 800dr per tent. **Asprovalta** (tel. (0397) 22 249), 80m outside of the city towards Kavala, has similar facilities. 850dr per person, 600dr per tent.

FOOD AND ENTERTAINMENT

Thessaloniki's downtown is flecked by inexpensive self-service foodlets and shops. Lively and full of bargains, the *agora* (marketplace) is bounded on four sides by Irakliou, Egnatia, Aristotelous, and Venizelou St. To stock up on fruits, vegetables, bread, and groceries, visit the open-air markets of Vati Kioutou St. just off Aristotelous. The restaurants along the seaside serve standard fare at near-identical prices. Explore the old town for inexpensive, family-oriented *tavernas*.

The Brothers, in Navarino Sq., offers traditional Greek meals and an exceptional potato salad. Roughly 1700dr per person. Open daily noon-midnight.

Milos, 2km west of the city center. A mellow, artsy assortment of bars, *taverna,* and a newsstand on the grassy grounds of an old mill. Milos is one of the most popular gathering points for locals. It often features art exhibits and performers, including American jazz musicians and German acrobats. Cocktails 1400dr. No cover, but there may be a charge for concerts (1500-3500dr). Take bus #31 (75dr) or a taxi (roughly 350dr from the train station, or 550dr from Aristotelous Sq).

Ta Spata, 28 Aristotelous (tel. 23 19 66), offers a wide selection of tasty, inexpensive entrees (1500dr). Crowded with Greeks and tourists. Open 11am-midnight.

Canoniero, 130 Epta Pirgiou, is in Kastra, just outside the walls. Splendid view of Thessaloniki by night and even better pizza. Open daily 10am-3am.

New Ilisia, 17 Leontos Sofou St. (tel. 53 69 96), a neighborhood restaurant and grill located off Egnatia St., serves traditional Greek food in an unpretentious setting. Entrees around 1200dr. Open daily 8:30am-2am.

Taste of China (tel. 27 66 65), on Vyros St. off Navarinou Sq., fronting the ruins. Chinese chef flames up fresh, tasty meals to order (vegetable chop suey 950dr).

Sweet Shops: Poxani, 7 Venizelou St. (tel. 22 35 25), just inland from the corner of Venizelou and Tsimiski St., a few blocks west of Aristotelous Sq. Fanciful treats and even sweeter staff (open 7am-10pm). Also try **Titania,** 22 Karolou Dienl St. (tel. 27 98 79), just inland from Tsimiski and a half block down from the OTE. Surprising array of sweet-scented cookies inside.

ENTERTAINMENT

Thessaloniki's nightlife used to be centered around bars, but has lately become café-centric. Cafés abound; try the **Journal** across from the Agia Sophia. The king of all café-hangouts for bohemian locals, however, is Milos. On weekend evenings, mingle with Greeks along **Plaza Dhimitrio Gounari.** Fashion-conscious couples promenade from the waterfront to the Arch of Galerius. Others mellow out with a cup of coffee in the park and at **Navarinou Square,** one block west of D. Gounari. Lesbian and gay revelers head to **Taboo** on Kastritsiou St., one block from Egnatia. Turn toward the water on Mitropolitou Genadiou and take your first left.

People frolic in the cobblestone streets of the **Kastra** (old city) until unimaginably late hours, when the *bouzouki* music and Greek dancing finally ceases. To get there, take bus #22 or 23 from Eleftherias Sq. on the waterfront, or walk. Bus #5 or 6 will carry you to American-style dance clubs in **Kalamaria** (pronounced ka-la-mar-YA), by the sea. In summer, weekend nightlife centers in the suburb of **Nea Krinis.** Take bus #5 from Aristotelous Sq., or pick it up on Mitropoleos St. to get to the **Amusement Park** in Salminan.

At Thessaloniki's **movie theaters** you can see vaguely recent American releases—both art-house and Hollywood—in the company of hip young Salonicans. **Natali Cinema,** 3 Vassilissis Olgas (tel. 82 94 57), on the waterfront, 5min. past the White Tower heading away from the city center, shows open-air movies in summer. (Shows nightly at 9 and 11pm; admission 1500dr.)

SIGHTS

If you have time for only one stop in the city, head to the superlative **Archaeological Museum** (tel. 83 05 38 or 83 10 37), which spotlights a collection of Macedonian treasures, like delicate gold foil crowns and wreaths, figurines, and gold *larnakes* (burial caskets) which once contained the cremated royal family of Vergina. (Open Mon. 12:30-7pm, Tues.-Fri. 8am-7pm, Sat.-Sun. 8:30am-3pm; reduced hours in winter; admission 1500dr, seniors 1100dr, students 800dr. Take bus #3 from the railway station to Hanth Sq.) The **International Fairgrounds,** next to the museum, hold a variety of festivals in Sept. and Oct. (for info call 23 92 21).

On the other side of the park on the waterfront looms the **Lefkos Pirgos** (tel. 26 78 32), all that remains of a Venetian seawall. Formerly known as the Bloody Tower because an elite corps of soldiers was massacred within it, the structure was painted white to obliterate the gruesome memories. The tower, which houses a fascinating museum of early Christian and Byzantine art, presents a slide show every hour. (Same hours as archaeological museum; admission 800dr.) The extensive ruins of the **Eptapirgion Walls,** erected during the reign of Theodosius the Great, stretch along the north edge of the old city. Take bus #22 or 23 from Eleftherias Sq. on the waterfront. Eleftherias Sq. is also where bus #5, 33, and 39 leave for the **Ethnology and Popular Art (Folklore) Museum,** 68 Vas. Olgas St. (tel. 83 05 91), which houses traditional costumes. (Open Fri.-Wed. 9:30am-2pm; free.)

The celebrated **Arch of Galerius** stands at the end of Egnatia St., at the corner of Gounari St. (under renovation and covered with scaffolding in 1995). Next to it and closed for reconstruction is the **Rotunda,** which started out as an emperor's mausoleum, but was renamed **Agios Georgios** by Constantine the Great. For further historical pursuits, head north of Dikastirion Sq. to the Roman ruins between Filippou and Olibou St. The ruins, which include a somewhat hyper-restored theater, are still being excavated. The crux of the remains of the **Palace of Galerius,** near Navarino Sq., is the well-preserved octagonal hall.

Over the centuries, most of the churches in this region were damaged or destroyed by recurring earthquakes. The few lucky survivors, such as **Agios Dimitrios** (tel. 27 00 08), **Panagia Halkeon** (tel. 27 29 10; on the corner of Egnatia and

Aristotelous St.), and **Agios Nikolaos Orfanos** (tel. 21 44 97; 20 Iradotou St.) all feature brilliant mosaic work and frescoes from the late Byzantine era.

Another noteworthy example of Byzantine art in Thessaloniki is the splendid 9th-century mosaic of the Ascension in the dome of the **Agia Sophia** (tel. 27 05 23), in the park of the same name at the corner of Ermou and Agia Sophias St. The church, modeled after the Ayasofya in İstanbul, has extraordinary iconography with a particularly stunning dome. More mosaics decorate the **Panagia Ahiropitos** (tel. 27 28 20), two blocks farther north at 56 Agia Sophias St. (Churches open approximately 7:30am-noon and 5-10:30pm; closed for morning services Sun. and holidays.) You can also visit the beautiful **Old Synagogue** at 35 Sigrou St. (tel. 52 49 68). The temple is no longer in use, but the caretaker at the **Jewish Community Center,** 24 Tsimiski St., will let you in.

■ NEAR THESSALONIKI

PANORAMA

Atop Mt. Hortiatis, this site has a name that says it all. Unfortunately, most of the sheds for viewing the valley and the city of Thessaloniki have been usurped by private residences. Because of the cool, soothing weather at the summit, the suburban village is a popular destination for summer excursions, and it's possible to find cafés that offer impressive views out to the Aegean nestled among pines. Make the 10km trip by bus #57 or 58 from Dikastirion Sq. (every ½hr., 20min., 75dr), at the corner of Mitropolitou Genadou and Ioustinianou St. Bus #61 goes to the village of **Hortiatis,** perched on the side of the mountain 10km past Panorama.

Perea, Agia Triada, and **Nea Mihaniona** are as full of bikinied urbanites as you'd expect for beaches accessible by bus from Greece's second-largest population center. From Dikastirion Sq., bus #72 goes to Perea, Agia Triada, and to Nea Mihaniona (every 10min., 45min., 150dr). Agia Triada has **Epanomis** (tel. 41 378), one of the best campgrounds in northern Greece. The water is somewhat fetid; for less bacterial swimming, head to the Halkidiki peninsula (see p. 181).

PELLA

The ruins of ancient Pella, discovered by a farmer in 1957, prove a rewarding daytrip. Pella, 38km west of Thessaloniki, served as a port in ancient times, when the surrounding plain was covered with water from the Thermaïko Gulf. Around 400 BC, King Archelaus opted to build his palace there, and Pella became a great cultural center, the largest city in Macedonia. Pella was the first capital of a united Greece during Philip II's reign; his son, Alexander the Great, used the city as the starting point for his lifelong mission to unify the world under Macedonian rule. On the other side of the highway, the small but impressive **Pella Museum** (tel. (0382) 31 278 or 31 160), contains the exquisite mosaics "Dionysus Riding a Panther" and "The Lion Hunt." With their skillful use of chiaroscuro and foreshortening, these are the earliest-known mosaics that attempt to convey three-dimensionality. (Museum and ruins both open Mon. 12:30-7pm, Tues.-Sat. 8am-7pm, Wed. 8am-8pm, Sun. 8:30am-5pm; admission to both 400dr.)

Buses to Pella depart from the 22 Anagenniseos depot near the train station in Thessaloniki (every ½hr., 550dr). Walk down Octovriou St. past the courthouse and turn right onto Anagenniseos St. The KTEL is on the corner of Damonos St. Pella takes roughly 1hr. to see and 2½hr. total with round-trip transportation; the museums alone make the trip worthwhile. Buses to Thessaloniki (2-3 per hr.) pass the site, which is right on the main highway. To go between Pella and Vergina, change buses at the *taverna* in **Halkidona,** 3km east of Pella.

■■■ MOUNT OLYMPUS ΟΛΥΜΠΟΣ

The charm of Olympus does not lie in its natural beauty; nor its physical magnitude; the beauty of Olympus is spiritual, it is divine . . .

—Boissonade

Rising from the coastal plain 90km southwest of Thessaloniki, Mt. Olympus so impressed the seafaring ancient Greeks that they exalted it as a suitable home for gods. First climbed in 1913, Olympus has been harnessed by a network of well-maintained hiking trails that make the summit accessible to anyone with sturdy legs. The zenith rewards visitors with incomparable views and ethereal blue skies, particularly in June and September, when the air is clearest.

Mt. Olympus is buried in six or more feet of snow each winter, so the unofficial climbing season lasts only from May to October. If you make the ascent between May and September, you'll need no special equipment besides sturdy shoes (hiking in sandals is discouraged), sunglasses, serious sunscreen, a hat, and water. If you plan on climbing the upper regions, you may need a waterproof windbreaker, an extra shirt, and gloves. Water purification tablets might come in handy. You can rush through the climb in one day, but plan on a two- or three-day trip to fully enjoy the wilderness. Consider staying overnight in one of the refuges or camping on the mountain. In either case, bring warm clothes and leave your pack in Litohoro.

LITOHORO

The gateway to Olympus is the small village of **Litohoro.** Surprisingly, given its proximity to the mountain, the friendly town is relatively free of souvenirs and other tourist accoutrements. Near the bus station, on the main street, is the official **tourist office** (tel. 83 100; open only mid-June-Sept. daily 9am-2:30pm and 3:30-9pm). They offer free maps of the area. Litohoro's **National Bank** (tel. 81 025) resides in the main square (open Mon.-Thurs. 8am-2pm, Fri. 8am-1:30pm) with the **post office** (open Mon.-Fri. 7:30am-2pm). The **OTE** is across from pieces of a playground undergoing construction, on the main street (open Mon.-Sat. 7:30am-3:10pm). **Postal Code:** 60200; **Telephone Code:** 0352.

Trains (tel. 61 211) stop at the Litohoro station on the line between Thessaloniki and Volos (from Athens 7 per day, 7hr.), but since the station is close to the beach and several km from town, you must catch the Katerini-Litohoro bus on the main road 150m from the station. **Buses** (tel. 81 271) from the KTEL station opposite the church in the main square travel from Litohoro to Thessaloniki and back, via Katerini (up to 12 per day, 2hr., 1350dr), Katerini (every hr., 316dr), Larissa via Katerini (8 per day, 1300dr), and Athens (3 per day, 6000dr).

Near the bus station in Litohoro, down the main street on your right, are the offices of Greece's two alpine clubs: the **EOS Greek Mountaineering Club** (tel. 81 944; open only in summer, Mon.-Fri. 9am-12:30pm and 6:30-8:30pm, Sat.-Sun. 9am-noon) and the **SEO Mountaineering Club of Greece,** located past the taxi stand and the Ereto Restaurant, at the far end of the parking lot (tel. 82 300; open Tues., Thurs., and Sat. 7:30am-9:30pm).

SEO's Main Refuge is the highest in the Balkans and offers a glorious view of the mountain, the valley, and Thessaloniki (2760m; open July-Aug.), but **EOS's Refuge A** (open June-Sept.) is closer to the end of the road, thus more accessible by car. Both refuges have running water and cost roughly 1700dr per night; less for club members. Be advised that the refuges fill up Friday and Saturday nights. Try to make your reservations through the club offices, or at the Youth Hostel. EOS owns three other refuges on Mt. Olympus that are locked on weekdays; keys are available at the EOS office. Both clubs provide maps and information about the mountain, maintain the trails, and organize emergency rescues. Litohoro has a **health center** with emergency facilities (tel. 22 222).

Most youthful climbers stay at the small **Youth Hostel** (tel. 81 311 or 82 176) and vie for the two shower/bathrooms at once. Follow signs 200m up the hill from the

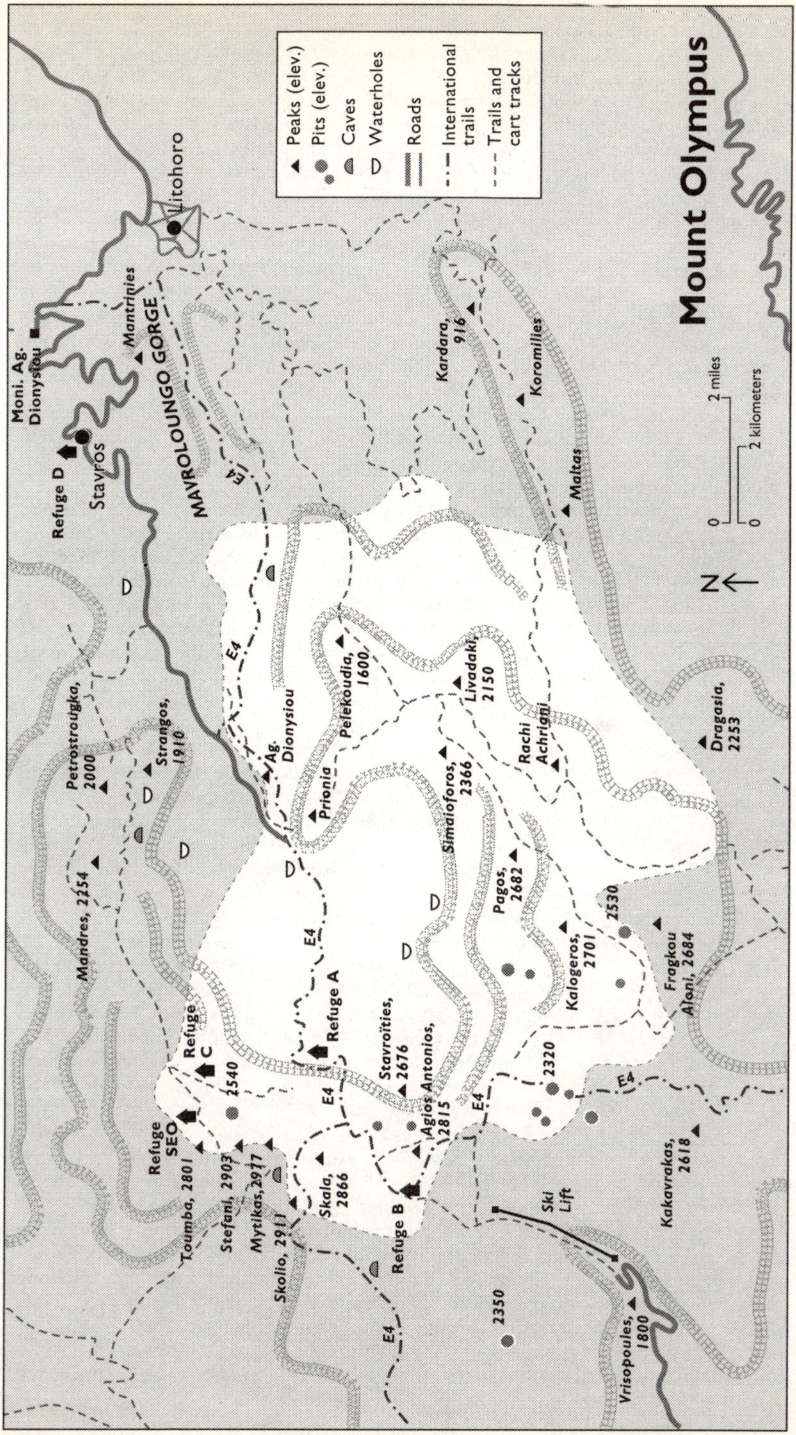
Mount Olympus
Peaks (elev.)
Pits (elev.)
Caves
Waterholes
Roads
International trails
Trails and cart tracks
0 2 miles
0 2 kilometers
N
Litohoro
Moni. Ag. Dionysiou
Mantrinies
MAVROLOUNGO GORGE
Refuge D
Stavros
E4
Kardara, 916
Koromilies
Maltas
Petrostrougka, 2000
Strangos, 1910
Ag. Dionysiou
Pelekoudia, 1600
Livadaki, 2150
Prionia
Simaiaforos, 2366
Rachi Achrigni
Dragasia, 2253
Mandres, 2254
Pagos, 2682
2530
Refuge C
Refuge A
Kalogeros, 2701
Fragkou Aloni, 2684
2540
Stavroïties, 2676
Refuge SEO
Agios Antonios, 2815
2320
Toumba, 2801
Stefani, 2903
Mytikas, 2917
Skala, 2866
Skolio, 2911
Refuge B
Ski Lift
Kakavrakas, 2618
2350
Vrisopoules, 1800

square. The hostel is closed each day 2-6pm, has check-out at 9am and a curfew of 11pm. The reception is open 9am-2pm and 6-11pm. Guests can drop off their luggage (450dr) and use the kitchen (200dr). Singles, doubles, and dormitory beds all cost the same per person (1400dr). Road and topographical maps are for sale, and hiking boots, day packs, mountain clothing, mopeds, and bicycles are available for rental. Constantine, the proprietor, is extremely knowledgeable about the mountains and trails, and has amassed a wealth of information about the many additional (and very worthwhile) sites and activities of interest around Litohoro. You won't find such information anywhere else in Litohoro, and it's available only to hostelers. The hostel is open year-round and phone reservations are accepted. The pleasant **Hotel Aphroditi** (tel. 81 415 or 83 071) is located on the road to the youth hostel. Many of the comfortable rooms offer stunning views of the mountain. (Singles 7711dr, doubles 8262dr, triples 9914dr.) Four **campgrounds** squeeze between the railroad and the beach, 5km out of town across the highway. **Do not freelance camp** on the north side of the road connecting the town and the highway: this is a training ground for the armored units of the Greek army.

The popular **Olympus Café** is in the main square. (Entrees 900dr. Open noon-midnight.) From the northwest corner of the main square, follow the road uphill 5min. and turn left to reach **Taverna Pazari,** which is plagued by noisy traffic, but offers good *kalamari* or red snapper (entrees roughly 1100dr).

Mount Olympus has eight peaks: **Kalogeros** (2701m), **Toumba** (2785m), **Profitis Ilias** (2786m), and **Antonius** (2815m) are dwarfed by the thrones of **Skala** (2866m), **Skolio** (2911m), **Stefani** (also called the Throne of Zeus, 2909m), and **Mytikas** (or the Pantheon, 2917m). There are two approaches to the peaks from Litohoro, and they can be accomplished as a cycle, taking two nights in the mountains, instead of one. To reach the beginning of both trails, take the road that winds upward just before the square in Litohoro. There is no bus service between the trails and the village, so it's best to find a group at the hostel to share a taxi (5000dr to Prionia). Those who hitch usually start early, since most climbers drive up in the morning. Hiking alongside the Enipeas River from Litohoro to Prionia is another option; the 18km trail is good but difficult. It begins past the town cemetery and Restaurant Mili in the upper part of Litohoro. At the fork in the trail, follow the yellow diamond marker uphill on the left side of the **Mavrolungo Gorge.** This exhausting path takes you up and down hills for 4hr., but traverses astonishing scenery. Note the cave where Agios Dionysios, Litohoro's patron saint, lived in the 16th century. You will also pass the charred shell of a monastery that gave refuge to Greek partisans during WWII until the Nazis burned it. If you decide not to hike through the gorge, walk to Prionia along the asphalt road (which becomes an unpaved path).

At **Diastavrosi,** just 14km from Litohoro, the first trail slopes up to the right of the road. This route offers impressive views of the Aegean, the Macedonian plain to the north, and the smog layer over Thessaloniki far below. You can find water in two places along this trail: at the turn-off between Barba and Spilia (1½hr. from the trail head), marked on the trail, and at the spring at Strangos. It's a long haul (5-6hr.) from the start of the trail to the **SEO refuge,** "Giosos Apostolides," where you can seek shelter (1700dr). Ample blankets are provided; hot meals served throughout the day. Bottles of water cost 200dr. At 2760m (only 157m from the summit of Olympus), this shelter is less frequented than its counterpart Refuge A, below, and offers a magnificent view of the Stefani peak at sunrise. Just as exhilarating is the lunar landscape overlooking the **Plateau of the Muses,** named after the mythical sisters who inspired creativity. From here, the summit is a painless 1½hr. away.

Mytikas is the highest (2917m) and most-climbed peak of Olympus. From Refuge A, take the path uphill and follow the red marks along mountain meadows strewn with indigo wildflowers. The last leg of the ascent to Mytikas is usually made by one of two routes. If you take the fork in the path at Refuge A, you'll see the peak **Skala** (2866m) to your left and the SEO Refuge to your right. From Skala, there is a sinuous descent a bit before the ascent to Mytikas. This trail to Mytikas, prone to rock slides and avalanches, is considered dangerous. It's not a good idea to lug a large pack along this route. Many trails are appropriate only for experienced hikers in excellent physical condition, particularly the rockslide-plagued **Locki.** If you return to Skala, it's a relatively easy walk to **Skolio,** the second highest peak (2911m) and the best point for viewing the sheer western face of Olympus. From Refuge A, you can go directly to Skolio, taking the path left from that to Skala.

HALKIDIKI ΧΑΛΚΙΔΙΚΗ

Three-pronged like Poseidon's trident, the Halkidiki peninsula advances southward into the Aegean, yielding spectacular scenery and some of the finest sandy beaches in Greece. On the eastern prong is **Mount Athos,** the largest enduring monastic community in Western society, which earns the region its title, the Monastic Republic of Mt. Athos ("athos" means "holy"). **Kassandra** on the western leg contains ritzy resort towns for the upper crust. Sandwiched between them is **Sithonia,** whose largely unspoiled interior is ringed with gorgeous, if crowded, beaches.

Attempting to use public transportation on Halkidiki can be quite a challenge. Frequent buses run between the 68 Karakassi St. station in Thessaloniki (tel. (031) 92 44 44; see p. 174) and the three peninsulas, but bus service does not accommodate travelers wishing to hop from peninsula to peninsula; you may have to return to Thessaloniki in order to catch a bus to another peninsula.

■■■ SITHONIA ΣΙΘΩΝΙΑ

Although it withstood the barrage longer than its western neighbor, Sithonia has recently been seduced by visitors sporting BMWs and fistfuls of *drachmae.* The area has since plunged head first into the sordid world of beachside villas and plastic souvenirs. On the more isolated beaches to the south, a measure of tranquility persists. Incidentally, the south is not serviced by public transportation. Sithonia is popular as a weekend beach and nature retreat from hot Thessaloniki. There are two back-road routes through Sithonia: west via Nea Marmaras, and east via Vourvourou. Travel is more flexible going west, since **buses** travel to Nea Marmaras (6 per day, 3hr., 2050dr) and continue around the peninsula to Sarti (5 per day, 3½hr., roughly 3000dr). Buses run directly from Thessaloniki to Vourvourou (3 per day, 3hr., roughly 2000dr). Another option is to take a bus to Agios Nikolas at the neck of the peninsula (3 per day, 3hr., roughly 1800dr), and work your way down from there.

Nea Marmaras' tourist police (tel. (0371) 23 496) are in an unmarked house on the first street parallel to the highway (open daily 8:30am-2:30pm and 8:30-10pm; English not spoken). The town **post office** is in the second square, near the Restaurant Giorg #3 (open Mon.-Fri. 7:30am-2pm). To reach the **OTE** from the bus stop, walk to the bottom left corner of the square, then hike up the street for about 2min. (open 7:30am-midnight). The **National Bank** is on the main street (open Mon.-Thurs. 8am-2pm, Fri. 8am-1:30pm). **Telephone Code:** 0375; **Postal Code:** 63801.

Before arriving at Nea Marmaras (also called Marmaras), you'll pass the beach at **Agios Ioannis,** where some stake tents. Numerous signs for official campgrounds line the roads. Nea Marmaras is a small upscale vacation spot with jewelry stores and stylish bars. Rooms here are expensive (doubles from 8000dr). The English-speaking staff at **Doucas Tours** (tel. (0375) 71 959), near the bus stop, recommend rooms. (Open daily 7:30am-2pm and 5:30-9:30pm.) **Albatros Rooms To Let** (tel. 71 003, -738), located on Themistokli St., has spacious, modern, clean rooms with kitchenettes, large balconies, and comfortable beds (doubles 7000dr). On the beach, **Camping Marmaras** (tel. 71 901) is 1km back and clearly marked by road signs. (Person 1000dr, tent 900dr; open June-Sept.)

Nea Marmaras enjoys an elite reputation largely due to the **Porto Carras** hotel complex situated just across the bay. This jet-set amusement park contains restaurants, boutiques, beaches, an open-air cinema, and a new casino, **Casino Magic.**

Although doubles start at 30,000dr, all rooms are fully booked in summer. Ferries shuttle between Restaurant Giorg #3 and Propondis in Marmaras to Porto Carras (every ½hr., 15min., 250dr). The 25-min. walk around the coast is free.

The best dinner option is the moderately priced seafood (1200dr) at **Dionysios Tavern** (open 9am-midnight). The **Cool Bar** (tel. 71 829) on the waterfront in the town's second square is, surprisingly enough, just that. Chic young Greeks converge here on summer nights (open 9pm-2:30am.) The **bus** around the peninsula to Sarti (5 per day, 1hr., 580dr) passes by the most deserted, desirable turf on Sithonia. After climbing the road 5km south of Porto Carras, you'll see a beach near **Agia Kiriaki,** with a small reef and an outlying island. It's a long, hard climb down from here.

■■■ MOUNT ATHOS ΑΓΙΟΝ ΩΡΟΣ

The monasteries on Mount Athos (*Agion Oros*) have been the standard-bearers of asceticism for more than a millennium. Today, the easternmost peninsula of Halkidiki is an autonomous state comprising 20 Eastern Orthodox monasteries and countless *skites,* or hamlets, with some 1400 monks. The absence of development has helped to preserve the peninsula's luxuriant foliage. This dense tangle of green, especially present on the eastern side, provides cover for snakes, bats, and myriad insects. Only the jagged marble peak of Mt. Athos itself, soaring 2033m above the encircling waves of the Aegean, is exposed. Against the background of this lush landscape, the monks of Mount Athos isolate themselves from the outside world in an attempt to transcend material pleasures and live a truly spiritual life. The community on Mount Athos has been structured to varying degrees since 883, when Basil I issued an imperial charter to Athos preventing local military officials from interfering with the monks. An edict of the Emperor Constantine from 1060, enforced to this day, forbids women—and female animals—from setting foot on the peninsula.

HISTORY

According to legend, the Christian history of Mt. Athos began when the Virgin Mary, on a sea trip from Ephesus to visit Lazarus in Kitium on Cyprus, was thrown off course by a tempest and led by divine sign to the Athonite coast. The peninsula, known then as Akte, was a notorious center of paganism, but the moment Mary's foot graced its soil, the false idols all smashed to bits in proclamation of their own worthlessness. Mary then declared Athos her holy garden, forbidden to all other women for eternity, and blessed the land before sailing back to Jaffa.

Following centuries of occupation by Christian hermits and ascetics, the oldest monastery (**Megisti Lavra**) was established in 963 AD by Athanasius, a rich man's son turned monk. Under the protection of Byzantine emperors, the building of monasteries flourished until, at its zenith in the 15th century, Mt. Athos harbored 40 monasteries and some 20,000 monks. When Constantinople fell to Turkish armies in 1453, the monastic community prudently surrendered, thus remaining unplundered and relatively autonomous. In 1926, a decree of the Greek government made Mt. Athos officially part of Greece while allowing it to retain an autonomous theocratic government. Due to gradual attrition and the diminishing influx of young novices, Mt. Athos' eminence slowly declined until the 1950s, when it became a prime target of greedy real estate developers. In recent decades, however, *Agion Oros* has been miraculously rejuvenated, and hundreds of young men, inspired to take their vows, have donned the black robes and hat of Orthodox monasticism. Now more than 1400 monks live alone in *skites* or inhabit the 20 monasteries.

Athos contains unsurpassed wealth in Paleologian and Late Byzantine art, manuscripts, treasure, and architecture. Each monastery also houses *lipsana,* remains of dead saints which only Orthodox Christian men are allowed to see. Especially impressive is the hand of Mary Magdalene, who bathed Jesus, which remains (skin intact) in **Simonos Petra** as warm as a living hand.

The most impressive part of the Athos experience, however, is not the material treasure, but the monks themselves, who offer their stories and advice along with

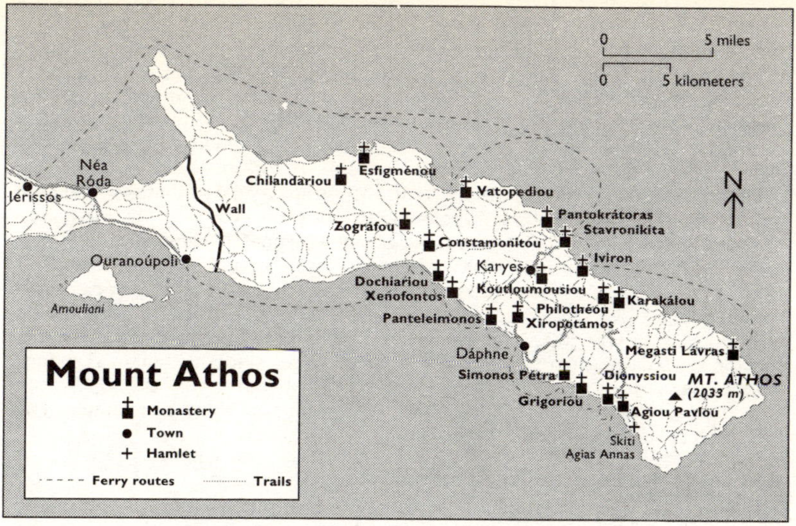

complimentary *loukoumi* and coffee or *raki.* Most visitors to Athos, both Greek and foreign, find the brotherhood comforting and discover astounding internal peace of mind, regardless of their religion. A trip to Athos is not merely a visit to monasteries, and should not be approached as such, but is an attempt to understand the ascetic way of life. Pilgrims who plan to rush through too many monasteries quickly change their minds once on the mountain. Theoretically, tourists are not allowed on the mountain—only pilgrims—and, in some cases, non-Orthodox travelers may feel uncomfortable, although they are generally welcomed.

Any visit to Athos will be greatly enhanced by reading beforehand about the art, history, and legends of the individual monasteries. *Athos the Holy Mountain,* by Sydney Loch, a book with the same title by Philip Sherrard (1985), and *Mount Athos,* by Norwich, Sitwell, and Costa, are highly informative.

ORIENTATION AND PRACTICAL INFORMATION

When visiting Mt. Athos, keep in mind that guests from "the outside world" inherently conflict with the spiritual goals of the monastic life. The monks, however, have an old tradition of hospitality. Hone your awareness and sensitivity. Some rules include no photographing icons or wall-paintings and no swimming.

Those without a permit can view the monasteries by boat. A **day cruise** from Thessaloniki costs 8000dr. From Ouranoupolis, tours (roughly 3½hr.) cost 3000dr. Contact **Doucas Travel,** 8 Venizelou St., Thessaloniki (tel. (031) 26 99 84) or try **Avdimiotis Theophilos** in Ouranoupolis (tel. (0337) 51 207, -244).

Permits

A special entrance permit, issued only to adult males, is required in order to visit Mt. Athos. To get this, first get a letter of recommendation from your embassy or consulate (tell them you are a student interested in theology, history, architecture, or Byzantine art); a letter from your university stating your academic interest in Mt. Athos could be helpful. Deliver this letter to the **Ministry of Northern Greece,** at room 218 Pl. Dikitirou, Thessaloniki (tel. (031) 27 00 92; open Mon.-Fri. 8am-2pm). A separate permit is required for photographing the art in the monasteries. Citizens of countries with consulates in Thessaloniki can conduct the entire process there; U.S. and British consulates can give you the form letter in very little time. If you rush from there to the Ministry, you might be given your permit on the same day. They might insist that underage visitors be accompanied by someone older than 21, though the Ministry can waive this restriction. Because only 10 foreigners per day are admitted to Mt. Athos, the summer months are always booked well in advance. Either wait for a cancellation or write a letter to the Ministry of Northern Greece at least a month in advance to secure a reservation. If you can show proof that you are Orthodox (baptism papers, a letter from your bishop, etc.), you may be allowed to be the day's eleventh visitor. For reservations, call the Agion Oros office in Thessaloniki at (031) 33 31 81.

Visitor's passes, or *diamonitiria,* to Mt. Athos are issued in Ouranoupoli (see below). Non-Greeks must bring permission papers from Athens or Thessaloniki to the office located up the hill, just past the gas station your left. Generally, this needs to be done 15 days in advance in order to obtain the faux-parchment pass with your name on it. A regular (non-Greek) permit is good for four days. Getting it extended means going to Karyes, where your extension request will almost certainly be rejected. Permits cost 5000dr for foreigners, 3000dr for Greeks (who are allowed to stay for seven days); students (with ISIC) 3000dr, Greek students 1000dr. You must strictly observe the date of arrival on your permit. If you arrive a day late, you will be turned away. Don't forget to bring your passport, or you won't be admitted. The tourist office in Thessaloniki has more info.

Getting There and Accommodations

Permit in hand, arrive in Halkidiki the night before your entry date into Athos. The standard approach to Athos is via Ouranoupoli, by boat to Daphni, then bus to the capital city of Karyes. **Buses** for Ouranoupoli leave from Thessaloniki's Halkidiki station (tel. 92 44 44), located at 68 Karakassi St. (3-7 per day, 3hr., 2850dr). A bus for Thessaloniki will be waiting immediately after your arrival from the mountain.

Ouranoupoli is a beach resort favored by Germans, quiet in the off-season. Stay here overnight to catch the morning ferry to Daphni. Tickets may be purchased on board. One inexpensive hotel in Ouranoupoli is the no-frills **Hotel Akrogiali** (tel. 71 201), on the waterfront (singles 4000dr, doubles 7500dr, triples 9000dr). **Hotel Athos** (tel. 71 368), above the supermarket one block from the bus stop, is also an option, with clean baths, marble floors, and spacious balconies (singles 6000dr, doubles 9000dr, triples 9000dr, quads 11,000dr). Search and you can find private rooms for less (roughly 3000dr with bargaining). One good pension option is the **Pension Aliki** (tel. 71 235, -145), located on your first left before Hotel Akrogiali. Rooms are clean, with private baths and refrigerators, and the owners will hold your bags while you visit the holy mountain (singles 4000dr, doubles 6000dr, triples 7500dr). **Postal Code:** 63075; **Telephone Code:** 0377.

Since you'll be doing a lot of hiking on Mt. Athos, arrange to leave your belongings behind in Ouranoupoli (preferably at the place you've stayed), and carry just a daypack and a water bottle. Be sure to bring long pants, as the monks forbid visitors to wear shorts. Meals at monastery refectories are hearty: bread and cheese, beans, sometimes fish or noodles. The meals are eaten in silence while a priest reads from the Bible. As no lunch is served and hiking will make you hungry, it doesn't hurt to stock up on snacks. During fasting periods, guests are fed normal rations.

Two **ferries** serve the Mt. Athos peninsula: one from Ouranoupoli to Daphni (operating year-round, 10am, 750dr), and one, on the other side of the peninsula, from Ierissos to Monastery Iviron. The ferry from Ierissos operates very seldom, however, so ask around. In winter, the first bus from Thessaloniki to Ouranoupoli (6am) arrives in time for the ferry. In order to catch the early one in the summer, arrive the night before (last bus 6:30pm). Both trips take roughly 2hr. (750dr). The Ierissos ferry continues all the way to Monastery Megisti Lavras; if you're impatient or unable to walk, you can catch this ferry to go monastery-hopping (for a few hundred *drachmae*) once you have your final permit.

Arrive at the port at roughly 9am and look for the stand where officials will issue your final permit. From Daphni you can take the bus to the capital city of Karyes, which has an **OTE** to the right of the Athonite Holy Council building and two inexpensive hotels (1500dr per person). You may also take a smaller boat to the monasteries or *skites* on the west side of the peninsula (150-350dr). Boats generally leave soon after arrival, and operate on a whimsical, non-specific schedule. They usually are supposed to go to Levra, but often stop short (roughly 3hr.). Some monks may approach you in Daphni and say that the boat to Lavra will not leave. They may offer to make the trip on a *caïque* for 20,000dr. Don't get swindled; even monks can lie.

Remember that walking is an integral part of the Athos experience. Before you leave Karyes, pick up the brown *Mount Athos Touristic Map,* which includes a pamphlet offering general information (500dr). For greater detail about Mt. Athos, pick up one of the well-illustrated guidebooks (2500dr).

Accommodations and **food** in the monasteries are free, but you are entitled to a one-night stay only, unless you receive permission for an extension from the *archontari* (guest-master). The gates close at sunset; you *must* reach the monastery before this time or you will not be permitted to enter. Allow plenty of time to get to the monasteries. Paths are narrow, overgrown with vegetation, and poorly marked; furthermore, the ones on the map might unexpectedly fork in four different directions, or not exist at all. It's a good idea to keep to the roads or seaside paths and to travel in groups. Another good strategy is to follow the telephone poles that run between monasteries. Even if you are turned down for lodging at a monastery, you will be offered a cup of Greek coffee and *loukoumi* for your efforts.

MONASTERIES OF THE MOUNTAIN

Each of the 20 monasteries has a distinct character. **Megisti Lavra,** the largest, is imposing and fortress-like; the monks tend to be old and conservative. **Iviron** is delightfully dilapidated, full of relics and icons. The gas lighting gives the guest house an air of mystery. Along with moated-and-turreted **Vatopedi,** these two are the most frequently visited of the cloisters. While beautiful and well worth seeing, they can be aptly referred to as the "museum monasteries;" try to visit some of the smaller and more remote spots as well.

At one time, there were nearly equal numbers of Greek and Slavic monks at Athos, but the Russian Revolution cut off the supply of funds and novices at its source, and today only three Slavic monasteries remain. The Russian **Panteleimonous,** the Bulgarian **Zografou,** and the Serbian **Xilandariou** contrast with the monasteries on the rest of the peninsula. Elsewhere on Mt. Athos, **Ag. Dionisiou** has foreboding, dark iconography. **Philoteou,** embedded in a plush forest, is the only monastery with a grassy courtyard and is known for being relatively liberal.

The most complete experience at Mt. Athos involves developing an understanding and appreciation of the monastic way of life. Always address monks by their title, *Pateras,* and instead of goodbye say *evlogite* (Bless us, Father). Although most monks are Greek, the Athos renaissance has drawn neophytes from the U.S., Canada, Germany, France, England, and elsewhere. Many young monks are university-educated, and some speak English reasonably well. When you arrive at a monastery, ask the *Archontari* if it's possible to speak with someone.

Life on Mt. Athos befuddles the outsider. Meatless meals are eaten in silence. Men cover their bodies completely at all times and male animals are castrated. Novices learn to repeat the Prayer of the Heart with each breath: inhaling they recite, "Lord Jesus Christ," and, exhaling, "Have mercy on me, a sinner," until prayer becomes reflex, uniting mind and heart. All monasteries follow their own time system: midnight is marked by the setting of the sun, placing the island ahead of secular time.

Climb Mt. Athos for a day or two of invigorating hiking crowned by an august view. The approach is by path from the skitic community of **Agia Anna.** A 5-hr. climb will take you to the **Church of the Panagia,** dedicated to the Virgin Mary, which has beds for an overnight stay. The summit is another hour away. You might want to stay overnight at Panagia to watch the sun rise.

■■■ KAVALA ΚΑΒΑΛΑ

The modern port city of Kavala, a tobacco town and a bastion of communism in the 1930s, reversed both its preferred commodity and political orientation after the end of WWII. Today, having born the brunt of Greco-Turkish conflict and Bulgarian occupation, Kavala remains a trading center. A bustling city with tree-lined avenues, stretching from the seaside up the slopes of Mt. Simvolo, Kavala is well-organized and relatively smog-free. Buried beneath the new city is the 3000 BC city of Neapolis. Paul the Apostle later came here to preach and dubbed the city Christoupolis. Although modernized, Kavala retains something of a traditional appeal, as congested avenues give way to fruit vendors and flower markets, particularly around Kavala's charming old section, the **Panagia District** (Virgin Mary).

ORIENTATION AND PRACTICAL INFORMATION

The city's main draw, the Panagia District sits east of the port on its own peninsula, hemmed in by ancient walls and under the shadow of the dominating Byzantine fortress. Just outside these walls is the main square, **Eleftherias Square,** from which Kavala's two major commercial streets, **Eleftheriou Venizelou** and **Erithrou Stavrou,** extend westward. **Vassileos Pavlou** runs along the waterfront near the Thassos ferry dock. Parallel to it, one block inland is Erithrou Stavrou, two blocks inland Eleftheriou Venizelou. The Panagia district is directly behind the Aegean ferry dock. The entrance is near **Doxis Square.**

Tourist Office: On its own little traffic island at the corner of Eleftherias Sq., one block inland from the main port (tel. 22 24 25, -87 62, or 23 16 53). They have city maps and a list of hotels, arrange inexpensive accommodations, and help with international travel. Open Mon.-Fri. 7am-2:30pm.

Tourist Police: Ground floor of police station (tel. 22 29 05). Open daily 7:30am-2:30pm.

Port Police: (tel. 22 37 16). On second floor of the OTE building. Open 24 hr.

Police Station: 119 Omonias St. (tel. 22 29 05). Four blocks north of the port. Open 24 hr. Emergency tel. 100.

Post Office: (tel. 83 33 30). Main branch at K. Mitropoliteou St., on the corner of Erithrou Stavrou, one block north of the bus station. Will **exchange currency.** Open Mon.-Fri. 7:30am-8pm. **Postal Code:** 65110.

OTE: (tel. 22 30 99). West of the main port at the corner of Ethnikis Andistassis and Averof St., across from the Thassos ferry. Open daily 7am-midnight. **Telephone Code:** 051.

Banks: The **National Bank of Greece** is on the corner of Omonias and Paulo Mela St., one block north of the GNTO. Open Mon.-Thurs. 8am-2pm, Fri. 8am-1:30pm. A 24-hr. cash machine is available for Mastercard or Cirrus cardholders. The **Commercial Bank,** 17 Eleftherias Venizelou across from the tourist office, is open the same hours and has a 24-hr. **ATM** that accepts Visa.

Flights: Olympic Airways (tel. 22 36 22), across from Thassos ferry dock, on the corner of Ethnikis Aristasis and Kavalas Hris. Tickets to Athens (daily at 8:10pm and Tues., Thurs., and Sat. at 8:10am; 1hr.; 15,800dr) and transit destinations available. Public buses to airport run 2hr. before scheduled airplane departures (½hr., 500dr), and from airport to Kavala center immediately following flight arrivals. Office open Mon.-Fri. 8am-3:30pm.

Trains: There is no train station in Kavala, but catch a bus (every 20min., 40min., 680dr) to the train station in Drama (tel. (0521) 32 444), and from there the 5pm daily to İstanbul (7hr., 6300dr) or one of 6 daily trains to Alexandroupolis. Otherwise, take a bus to Xanthi (every ½hr., 1 hr.) and hop on the 8pm train to İstanbul (12hr.). For further information on rail service and tickets, ferry tickets, and international bus service to İstanbul (daily except Thurs., leaves at 5am) and Sofia, Bulgaria (Thurs. and Sat., leaves at 8am), contact **Alkion Tourist Office** (tel. 23 10 96; fax 83 62 51), Venizelou 24. Open Mon.-Fri. 8:30am-2pm and 5-8pm, Sat. 8:30am-1pm.

Buses: (tel. 22 35 93). At the corner of Filkis Eterias and K. Mitropolitou St., a block from Vassileos Pavlou St. and the waterfront, around the corner from the OTE. Buses to Thessaloniki (hourly 6am-8:15pm, 2½hr., 2200dr), Drama (every 20min., 40min., 680dr), and Xanthi, numerous small villages, beaches to the west (take bus to Iraklitsa, every 20-30min., 20 min., 220dr), and Athens (3 per day, 10hr., 8500dr, A/C). Contact the **KTEL Office** near the post office (tel. 22 33 22; open daily 5am-8:30pm) or the Alkion agency. For bus service to Alexandroupolis (5 per day, 2400dr), you must go to the **Dore Café,** on Erithrou Stavrou St., beyond the Oceanis Hotel. They handle tickets and post departure times. The bus stops directly across the street from them; snack and wait.

Ferries: For tickets and information, contact **Nikos Milades** (tel. 22 64 17), in the corner of the main port beneath the castle. Open daily 8:30am-1:30pm and 5:30-8:30pm. Ferries go to Limnos (4 per week, 5hr., 3100dr), Lesvos (2 per week, 12hr., 5100dr), Samos (1 per week, 20hr., 7250dr), Chios (2 per week, 15hr., 6000dr), Patmos (1 per week, 8620dr), Sigri (1 per week, 4050dr), Ag. Efstraitos (3 per week, 3100dr), and Piraeus (1 per week, 25hr., 7000dr). During July and Aug., ferries shuttle to Samothraki (5 per week, 4hr., 2350dr). Contact **Arsinoi Travel,** 16 K. Dimitriou (tel. 83 56 71) for more info. Open daily 8am-9pm.

Flying Dolphins: Hydrofoils connect Kavala with nearby Thassos (10 per day, 40min., 1400dr), Alexandroupolis (2 per week, 2hr., 10,250dr), Lesvos (3 per week, 4hr., 9800dr), and Limnos (1 per week, 2hr., 6250dr). For tickets and schedule information, head for the well-marked booths near the hydrofoil dock, opposite the OTE.

Taxis: Congregate in Eleftherias Sq. (tel. 22 44 36 or 22 36 60). Open 24 hr.

Hospital: 113 Amerikanikou Erithrou Stavrou (tel. 22 85 17 or 22 45 55). Open 24 hr. Call 166 in case of emergency.

ACCOMMODATIONS

Rooms that are simultaneously attractive, clean, *and* inexpensive are tough to find in Kavala. There are several pensions and budget hotels clustered around Eleftherias Square. Rooms come easier on weekends, when crowds flock to Thassos.

George Alvanos, 35 Anthemiou St. (tel. 22 84 12, -17 81). A 10-15min. walk from the center. Follow Poulidou St. into Old Town, bear left at Mehmet Ali St., then left onto Anthemiou. A homey establishment with spotless shared bathrooms and access to a kitchen. Proprietors speak only Greek, though their English-speaking children may be around. Singles 3000dr, doubles 4000dr. Kitchen 600dr. 10% discount with a copy of *Let's Go* Oct.-May only. Call ahead; it fills quickly.

Hotel Panorama, 26 Venizelou St. (tel. 22 42 05). Clean rooms, professional staff, and a good location just one block from the waterfront. Singles 5000dr, w/bath 6000dr; doubles 7000dr, w/bath 8000dr.

Camping Irini (tel. 22 97 85, -76). Take the #2 or #3 bus east or walk 2km along the coast from the port. The campground closest to town. Tent 600dr. Car and tent 1450dr. Mobile home 1500dr. Electricity 500dr. As the number of people or length of stay increases, prices are reduced.

FOOD AND ENTERTAINMENT

Dining in Kavala may not be like savoring a crepe on the French Riviera—or in Athens for that matter—but it offers quality Greek food at reasonable prices. **Mihalakis,** 1 Kassanarou St. (tel. 22 11 85), three blocks inland from the post office, is in a quiet courtyard away from waterfront pedestrian traffic. Delicious grilled chicken and *kleftiko* (1450dr). (Open daily 7:30pm-whenever.) **Panos Zafeira,** 20 K. Dimitriou St. (tel. 22 79 78), is situated on the waterfront (*mousaka* 800dr; open 9am-midnight). Also try **Milano Spaghetti** (tel. 83 85 08), across from the Thassos ferry dock and next to the OTE. (A variety of Italian dishes for 900-1800dr; open daily 9am-midnight.) **Verona Pizza Grill** (tel. 83 54 00), at the Thassos ferry dock and around the corner from the OTE, is one among many cafés, but a good place to sit while waiting for your ferry. (Meals roughly 1750dr per person; open daily 10am-1am.) For the queen of Kavala's **sweet shops,** find your way to **Kypseli** at 6 P. Mela St. From the tourist office, walk inland one block and turn left onto the pedestrian alley. Two blocks down is P. Mela St. Behold the pink awnings to your left. (Open daily 8am-10pm.) If you desire true gluttony, head to **Patisserie Menlae.**

During summer, bars in the center of Kavala empty out at 11pm, when locals head to beachside discos. In **Palio** (roughly 7km on the way to Iraklitsa) are **La Fer** and **Oceanis.** Taxis cost roughly 1200dr from the center of Kavala. These are upscale clubs with open courtyards and no cover; drinks run roughly 1200dr each. Both alternate house music with Greek tunes. In Iraklitsa, **Enjoy** rocks in a garden courtyard until 2am. The Greek program starts at 3am, with mellow bellydance-type music. If you're homesick, visit **Apollo Cinema** (tel. 22 34 03) on Venizelou St., one block inland from the waterfront. American films are screened nightly at 8:15pm and 10pm (1500dr, students 1000dr).

SIGHTS

The sprawling, 13th-century **Byzantine Castle's** (tel. 83 86 02) turreted walls dominate the city; saunter atop them for a city view. Refreshments are available. (Open daily 10am-7pm; free. A guard often gives tours; tipping is polite.) A small **amphitheater** is set up for occasional evening music and cultural performances. For scheduled events, ask the guard or at the refreshment stand. During the **Eleftheria Festival** (freedom festival) in June, students celebrate Kavala's liberation from the Turks by performing dances at the castle. Visitors are welcome to join in.

The 400-year-long Ottoman domination of northern Greece left its mark on the city. The **İmaret** (Ottoman soup kitchen for the poor), the largest Muslim building in western Europe, is now a trendy bistro. On the corner of Pavlidou and Mehmet Ali St. stands the **House of Muhammad Ali.** Born here in 1769, Ali was the self-appointed ruler of Egypt who reportedly floated like a butterfly but could sting like a bee. (Ring for the caretaker; tip 100dr.)

You just can't overlook the colossal 16th-century **Kamares Aqueduct** at the north edge of the old town, near Nikotsara Sq. Süleyman the Magnificent had the graceful, double-tiered structure built to transport water from mountain springs above the city. Hitchcock would have been proud: large flocks of birds call the aqueduct home. On the other side of town, overlooking the water, the **Archaeological Museum** (tel. 22 23 35) on Erithrou Stavrou St. contains such treasures as polychrome busts of goddesses from Amphipolis and a Hellenistic dolphin mosaic from Abdera. (Museum open Tues.-Sat. 8:30am-3pm, Sun. 9:30am-2:30pm; admission 500dr, students 300dr, seniors 400dr.) Kavala has a small **folk art museum** (tel. 22 27 06; open daily 8:30am-2:30pm; free, but a donation is tacitly requested).

■ NEAR KAVALA

Several sandy **beaches** west of Kavala are accessible by intercity bus. The closest is just outside the city of **Kalamitsa.** At **Batis,** 3km outside of Kavala, is a **GNTO campground** (tel. 24 30 51), which you might mistake for a parking lot. (920dr per person, 1150dr per large tent, 700dr per small tent, 550dr for kids, 1200dr per mobile home, 300dr to swim.) There's a supermarket and snack bar. Every ½hr., blue bus #8 treks to Batis from Kavala. Hourly buses to Iraklitsa stop at Batis (120dr). For car rentals, **Budget Rent-a-Car** (tel. 22 87 82) is at 35 Venizelou (cars 12,000dr per day; open Mon.-Fri. 8am-1pm). **Philippi,** roughly 15km north of Kavala, lies in ruins. Philip II of Macedonia founded the city to protect Thassian gold miners from Thracian attacks. Modestly enough, he named the city after himself—his son later followed suit in Egypt. Crucial battles of the Roman civil war dogged the city in 42 BC, when Marc Antony's soldiers defeated the army of Brutus and Cassius.

In 50 AD, missionaries Paul and Silas arrived from Anatolia to preach Christianity, and the first European Christian, Lydia, was baptized here. The **Cell of Paul** is the apostle's own budget accommodation. Shut the door and peek at the Roman **latrines;** most of the 42 marble seats are intact, but the lids have all been left up. (Site open Tues.-Sun. 8am-7pm, admission 300dr. Call 51 64 70 for more info.)

The entrance on the other side of the highway leads up to the **acropolis.** On summer weekends, classical drama is performed; it's worth attending even if it's all Greek to you. Ask at the theater or the Kavala GNTO for details. (Tickets 2000-2500dr. Site open daily sunrise-sunset; admission 200dr, students 100dr.) There's a **museum** nearby (tel. 51 62 51; open Tues.-Sun. 9am-3pm, admission 300dr, students free.) A **bus** to Philippi leaves every 20min. (50min., 600dr). Tell the driver you're going to the archaeological site, and not the village. Otherwise, you'll end up in the boonies. The bus back to Kavala stops down the road from the site.

THRACE ΘΡΑΚΗ

For centuries, Thrace has served as the meeting place for the diverse cultures of Turkey and Greece. Separated from Turkish Thrace by the Evros River, Thrace, which is Greece's northernmost province, serves as both a political and cultural gateway between the two countries. Ruled by the Ottomans until 1922, the region still bears evidence of Turkish influence in the small Turkish and Armenian communities scattered throughout it. In general, however, Thrace is now as Greek as the blue and white gate at its border. Its complex political history is mirrored in its chaotic landscape—a tangle of rivers, arable land, swamps, and lonely rolling hills.

■■■ ALEXANDROUPOLIS ΑΛΕΞΑΝΔΡΟΥΠΟΛΗ

Traveling through Thrace inevitably means a stop at the modern city of Alexandroupolis, which lies on the main west-to-east highway and is accessible by rail. This mellow, if somewhat seedy, port city is packed in the summer with overland travelers and Greek vacationers. Accommodations in July and August are scarce, so calculate your boat and train connections to avoid an overnight layover.

Especially in summer, Alexandroupolis is not the ideal departure point for Turkey. Trains are hot, slow, and crowded; most buses to Turkey originate in Thessaloniki and become tourist-laden by the time they reach Alexandroupolis. If you *must* get to **Turkey** from here, take a train (daily at 10:50pm, at least 9hr., 4500dr) or bus (9:30am, 8½hr., 4500dr) to **İstanbul.** Both depart from the train station, where you can buy tickets. People hitching make a trilingual sign asking for a ride across the border—you can't cross on foot. Count on a 1-hr. delay in Turkish customs.

ORIENTATION AND PRACTICAL INFORMATION

The **ferry dock** and **train station** (tel. 26 395, open 6:30am-11:30pm) are virtually neighbors along the waterfront, south of Platia Eleftherias. The intercity **bus station** is 5 blocks inland, and slightly west. Facing the water, a right turn from the train station will take you to the active center of the waterfront.

Tourist Office: (tel. 24 998). On the main boulevard, Leoforos Demokratias (two streets inland from the police), inside the city's theater. English-speaking staff provides information on cheap rooms and travel. Open Mon.-Fri. 8am-2:30pm.

Police: Just before the lighthouse (built in 1880) is Karaiskaki St., running inland. There, is the police station, 6 Karaiskaki (tel. 37 424, open 24 hr.), which has a **tourist info** desk (open Mon.-Fri. 8am-2pm). The **port police** (tel. 26 468) are on the waterfront, two blocks before the lighthouse, at the corner of Botsari (24 hr.).

Post Office: (tel. 23 122). Along the waterfront, past Karaiskaki St. Open 7:30am-2pm. **Postal Code:** 68100.

OTE: (tel. 26 199). Around the corner from the MTO, on the corner of Ioakim Kaviri and Venizelou St. Open 24 hr. **Telephone Code:** 0551.

Banks: The **National Bank** is on L. Demokratous St., east of the buses. Cash 24 hr. with Mastercard or Cirrus card. The **Commercial Bank,** one block east (left facing the water), gives Visa advances during bank hours. Both open Mon.-Thurs. 8am-2pm, Fri. 8am-1:30pm.

Flights: Olympic Airways (tel. 26 361, -207; office open Mon.-Sat. 8am-4pm), 4 Ellis St. (roughly 400m west, left facing inland, turn right at the waterfront) flies daily to Athens (40min., 16,000dr). There are no buses to the airport.

Trains: To Thessaloniki (3 per day, 8hr., 3000dr). An air-conditioned express train speeds there daily at 7:05am (4hr., 4500dr).

Buses: There's no direct **bus** to Thessaloniki, but you may be able to get there by first taking a bus to Kavala (7 per day, 2½hr., 2200dr). Buses go to Xanthi (6 per day, 1600dr) and Komotini (12 per day, 900dr).

Ferries: There is no direct ferry to Kavala. Ferries run to Samothraki (1-2 per day, 2½hr., 1800dr). One per week heads to Limnos (4hr., 2600dr). Contact **Arsinoi Shipping** (tel. 26 721, 22 215; open daily 7am-9pm) or **Saos Tours** (tel. 26 721; open daily 8am-2:30pm and 5-8pm) for tickets and info; they are next to each other, in from the waterfront on Kyprou St., opposite the entrance to the docks.

Flying Dolphins: On the corner of Ionos Dragoumi and Venizelou, one block left from the OTE (facing inland), **Kikon Tours** (tel. 32 398; fax 34 755). Hydrofoils run 3 per week to Lesvos, with varying stops (all tickets 9200dr). Dolphins head to Kavala (2 per week, 2hr., 7200dr) and Limnos (1 per week, 2hr., 5000dr).

Taxis (tel. 27 200, 28 484, or 27 700) run 24 hr.

Hospital: (tel. 25 772; 24 hr.), on Dimitras St.

ACCOMMODATIONS

Inexpensive accommodations are hard to come by. Look for "Rooms to Let" signs along the street leading inland from the train station. The waterfront area is pleasant.

Hotel Majestic (tel. 26 444), in Eleftherias Sq., visible from the train station. Rooms are old, but clean, and the owners are friendly. On the average, singles run roughly 3650dr, doubles 5700dr. Prices somewhat variable.

Hotel Mitropolis (tel. 26 443 or 33 808), on the corner of Emporiou and Athan. From Platia Eleftherias turn left onto Emporiou and walk down several blocks (to the left facing inland). The rooms are immaculate, with baths, radio, and phone. Doubles 9000, triples 12,000dr; less in off-season.

Hotel Erika (tel. 34 115), around the corner from Hotel Majestic, on the waterfront. Rooms w/TV, fridge. Singles 8100dr, doubles 11,800dr, triples 13,500dr.

Camping Alexandroupolis (tel. 28 735) is conveniently located 3km northwest of Alexandroupolis, off L. Demokratias St. A bus runs hourly to Hili or Makri. The campground is on the beach and has clean facilities. 1500dr per person, tent 450dr, sleeping bag 350dr; less in off-season.

FOOD AND ENTERTAINMENT

On Kyprou St. (200m left of rail station facing inland) are restaurants and *ouzerie* with decent, cheap food (spaghetti and Greek salad, 1200dr). Fish *tavernas* cluster 100m left of the rails (facing inland) on a small street parallel to the water. A popular and congenial feasting ground is the **Ouzerie Mynos** opposite the post office on the waterfront, unmistakable for its Hollandesque windmill, and unforgettable for the sweet, permeating scent of olive oil and freshly baked bread.

The waterfront is jammed with cafés. A young, upscale crowd congregates on Nikis Fotas St., perpendicular to the water, at the intersection with the post office. Nightly strolls along the waterfront are popular among locals.

SIGHTS

Pay your respects to the 18th-century icon of a limber Christ whose legs form a heart at the excellent Neoclassical **Ecclesiastic Art Museum,** next to the Cathedral of St. Nicholas, two blocks inland from the bank. Go to the nearby church of Ag. Nikolas and ask a priest to let you in. A polite donation of 100-200dr is expected (open 10am-midnight). Daily **excursions** to Feres, the Evros Delta, Kipi Soufli, Didimothio, Metaxaedes, and the hills of Dadia depart from the KTEL office.

Crete KPHTH

In middle of the sable sea there lies An isle call'd Crete, a ravisher of eyes, Fruitful, and mann'd with many an infinite store; Where ninety cities crown the famous shore, Mix'd with all-languag'd men.

—*Homer,* Odyssey

There's a Greek saying that the Cretan's first loyalty is to the island and second to the country. Indeed, some of Crete's rugged individualism—that treats even Greeks as foreigners—still exists; simply look to the long-mustached men who sit by the harbor polishing their high black boots. Like the island, they are hospitable, but prefer to keep their distance, staid and stoic.

Crete's history combines trauma, glory, and mediocrity. This island, which was inhabited as far back as 6000 BC (Neolithic Period), was supposedly both the birthplace of Zeus and the home of the man-eating Minotaur, who dwelled at Knossos. Crete's golden days began when the Minoans arrived from Asia Minor around 2800 BC. These inhabitants dwelled in caves and open settlements. Among the artifacts found from this time are stone and bone tools and female figurines signifying a savvy cult of the Mother Goddess. This period lasted until 3000 BC and the ascendancy of the renowned **Minoan civilization.**

Minoans, from Asia Minor and from a colony on Akrotiri, Santorini, established a civilization now known for its sophisticated art and architecture. In 1700 BC an earthquake devastated the island. The Minoans subsequently began rebuilding vast, elaborate villas and palaces. Following the reconstruction and revival, Crete entered glorious days. Prosperity from newly established trade with other countries lasted until 1450 BC, when an unknown catastrophe—either invading Myceneans or more natural disasters (possibly the eruption of Santorini)—destroyed the island's cities once again. Only Knossos, which was apparently ruled by Myceneans, survived.

After this second obliteration, Crete became less influential in world affairs, but continued to be a nexus for the cultural *avant-garde.* By the 8th century BC, Dorians were occupying the island, and jewelry-making, sculpture, and pottery thrived.The Roman conquest in 67 BC found the island increasingly unstable, with aristocratic families dominant and intercity warfare frequent. In the Medieval and Modern periods, Crete was ruled in succession by the Byzantine, Arab, Genoese, Venetian, and Turkish empires, and in 1898, the island became an English protectorate. Finally, after the Balkan War of 1913, Crete joined the Republic of Greece.

For more background on Crete, read Adam Hopkins's witty anecdotal history, *Crete: Its Past, Present, and People;* Dilys Powell's archaeologically inclined *Villa Ariadne;* or Michael Herzfeld's anthropological account of the Cretans, *History of the Past: A Cretan Town.*

GETTING THERE

Olympic Airways has cheap, fast, domestic **flights** from Athens to Sitia on the east, Iraklion in the center, and Chania on the west. Most flights take less than an hour. Check out the practical information listings in your destination city.

Most travelers arrive in Crete by **ferry.** The island has frequent connections during summer, but boats often fall behind schedule. The larger a boat, the more frequently it runs, and the more dependable its schedule. All prices listed are for deck-class accommodations. Boats run to Iraklion, Chania, Kastelli, and Agios Nikolaos. There are **international ferry** connections to Ancona in Italy, Çeşme in Turkey, Limassol on Cyprus, and Haifa, Israel. For Egypt, change boats in Cyprus. From April to October, the *Vergina* leaves Haifa, Israel on Sundays and travels to Cyprus, Rhodes, Iraklion, and Piraeus; deck-class costs roughly 20,000dr between any two ports. Those heading to Italy must go to Piraeus and change boats.

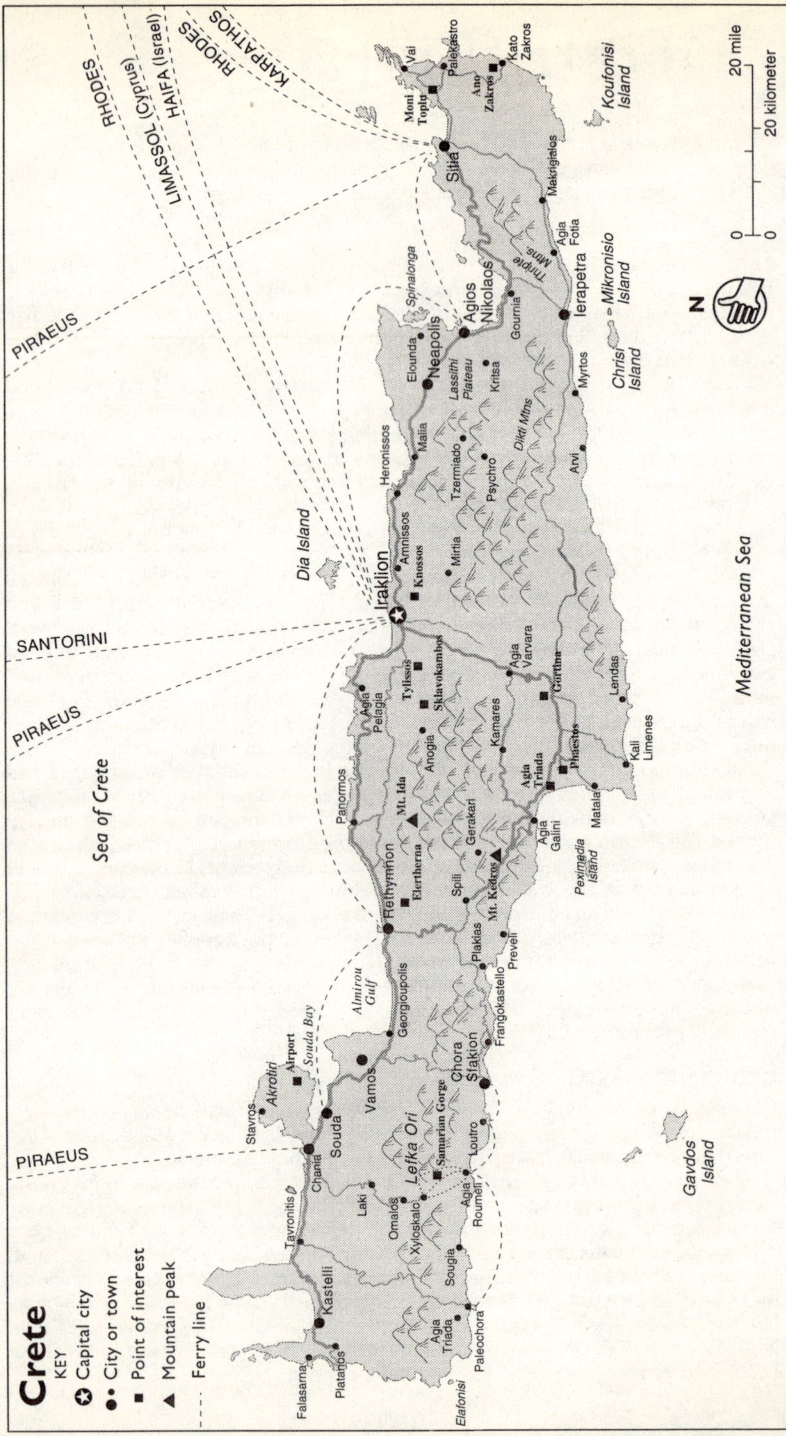
Crete
KEY
Capital city
City or town
Point of interest
Mountain peak
Ferry line
PIRAEUS
SANTORINI
PIRAEUS
RHODES
LIMASSOL (Cyprus)
HAIFA (Israel)
RHODES
KARPATHOS
PIRAEUS
Sea of Crete
Dia Island
Mediterranean Sea
Falasarna
Platanos
Kastelli
Tavronitis
Chania
Stavros
Akrotiri
Airport
Souda Bay
Souda
Vamos
Almirou Gulf
Georgioupolis
Rethymnon
Panormos
Agia Pelagia
Iraklion
Amnissos
Knossos
Heronissos
Malia
Elounda
Neapolis
Spinalonga
Agios Nikolaos
Sitia
Moni Toplu
Vai
Palekastro
Ano Zakros
Kato Zakros
Koufonisi Island
Makrigialos
Agia Fotia
Thripte Mtns
Ierapetra
Mikronisio Island
Chrisi Island
Myrtos
Arvi
Gournia
Kritsa
Lassithi Plateau
Dikti Mtns
Psychro
Tzermiado
Mirtia
Agia Varvara
Gortina
Lendas
Kali Limenes
Phaestos
Agia Triada
Matala
Agia Galini
Kamares
Tylissos
Sklavokambos
Anogia
Mt. Ida
Gerakari
Eleftherna
Spili
Mt. Kedros
Paximadia Island
Plakias
Preveli
Frangokastello
Chora Sfakion
Loutro
Agia Roumeli
Samarian Gorge
Lefka Ori
Laki
Omalos
Xyloskalo
Sougia
Agia Triada
Paleochora
Elafonisi
Gavdos Island
N
0 20 mile
0 20 kilometer

CENTRAL CRETE

■■■ IRAKLION (HERAKLION) ΗΡΑΚΛΕΙΟ

Iraklion, Crete's metropolis and the fifth largest city in Greece, has stumbled in recent years as developers have crammed concrete hotels within the old city's Venetian walls. The city has many of the vices and few of the virtues of urban life, but there are worse things than being stranded here for a day. Take in the magnificent ruins at Knossos, the impressive archaeological museum, perhaps even the tomb of Nikos Kazantzakis—but then take the first bus out.

Iraklion's slick bars and discos help visitors dull their senses and save the city from utter dreariness. If you're rambling through Crete in summer, you'll probably meet throngs of people headed for Iraklion to help with the mid-August grape harvest; ask at the tourist office for harvest work.

ORIENTATION AND PRACTICAL INFORMATION

Though Iraklion spreads for miles, almost everything important lies within the circle formed by Dikeosinis Ave., Handakos St., Doukos Bofor Ave., and the waterfront. The city centers are **Venizelou Square,** known to tourists as **Lion Fountain Square,** where Handakos St. meets Dikeosinis and 25th Augustou Ave. in the center of town, and **Eleftherias Square,** at the intersection of Doukos Bofor and Dikeosinis Ave. in the east side of the old city.

Tourist Office: 1 Xanthoudidou St. (tel. 22 82 03 or 24 46 62). Opposite the Archaeological Museum in Eleftherias Sq. Free city maps, lists of hotels, message-board for travelers, bus schedules, and some boat schedules (check times with the boat company). English-speaking staff is helpful but overworked. Ask here about harvest jobs. Open Mon.-Fri. 8am-2:30pm.

Tourist Police: 10 Dikeosinis St. (tel. 28 31 90 or 28 96 14), one block from 25th Augustou Ave. and Dikeosinis intersection. Open daily 7am-11pm. Provides general tourist info similar to tourist office. **Police:** Same location as the tourist police. Less informed, but willing to help 24 hr. One station services the east side of town (tel. 28 45 89 or 24 34 66); another station in the same building takes care of the west (tel. 28 26 77 or 28 22 43). **Port Police** (tel. 22 60 73).

Post Office: The main office is off Gianani St. Open Mon.-Fri. 7:30am-8pm. **Branch office** in El Greco Park. Open Mon.-Fri. 8:30am-3pm. **Postal Code:** 71001.

OTE: 10 Minotavrou St. Follow signs down Minotavrou near El Greco Park. Telephones, telegrams, and telex. Open daily 7am-11pm. **Branch office** in Eleftherias Sq. Open Mon.-Fri. 8am-11pm; Nov.-Feb. 1-9pm. **Telephone Code:** 081.

Tourist Agencies: Shop around amongst the hordes of agencies on 25th Augustou Ave. Two agencies for air, boat, and bus tickets are **Prince Travel,** #30 25th Augustou Ave. (tel. 28 27 03, -6; open Mon.-Fri. 9am-2:30pm and 5-7:30pm, Sat. 9am-2pm) and **Kavi Club Student Travel,** 2 Papa Alexandrou St. (tel. 22 11 66; open Mon.-Sat. 8am-8:30pm, Sun. 6-8:30pm), near the tourist office.

Banks: The banks on 25th Augustou Ave. are open Mon.-Thurs. 8am-2pm, Fri. 8am-1:30pm. The **National Bank,** 25th Augustou Ave., just beyond CaRavel (open Mon.-Thurs. 8am-2pm, Fri. 8am-1:30pm.) Gift shops in Venizelou Sq. **exchange currency** after hours at slightly lower rates. Many tourist agencies exchange currency at bank rates and remain open until 9pm.

American Express Office: Recently moved to 13 Arkoleontos St., near Lion Fountain Sq. (tel. 34 25 01, -2). Handles client mail and arranges for cardholders to cash checks at local banks. Open Mon.-Fri. 8am-5pm, Sat. 8am-2pm, Sun. 10am-1pm.

Flights: Olympic Airways, 42 Eleftherias Sq. (tel. 22 91 91). Open Mon.-Fri. 8am-3pm. The Stratones city bus #1 goes from Eleftherias Sq. to within 50m of the airport (6am-11pm, every 10min., 170dr). Flights leave for Athens (6 per day, 45min., 19,200dr), Mykonos (1 per week, ½hr., 18,000dr), Rhodes (4 per week,

½hr., 19,000dr), Thessaloniki (5 per week, 1hr., 27,600dr), Santorini (3 per week, ½hr., 13,400dr), and Corfu via Athens (3 per day, 2hr., 18,000dr). **Air Greece** offers less frequent but less expensive, service to Iraklion; for info, call their office in Athens, 20 Syntagma, (tel. (01) 325 5011).

Buses: There are several **KTEL** bus terminals, so match the station to your destination. **Terminal A** (tel. 24 50 17, -9), between the old city walls and the harbor near the waterfront, serves Ag. Nikolaos (22-24 per day until 9pm, 1½hr., 1150dr), Lassithi (1-2 per day, 2hr., 1150dr), Hersonissos (every ½hr., 45min., 460dr), Malia (every ½hr. 6:30am-10pm, 1hr., 600dr), Sitia (5 per day until 4pm, 3¼hr., 2350dr), Ierapetra (7 per day until 5:30pm, 2½hr., 1700dr), Archanes (13 per day, 6 on Sun., ½hr., 280dr), Ag. Pelagia (5 per day, 45min., 500dr). **Terminal B** (tel. 25 59 65), outside the Chania Gate of the old city walls, runs buses to Phaestos (9-10 per day, 1½hr., 1050dr), Ag. Galini (6-7 per day, 2¼hr., 1250dr), Matala (5-7 per day, 2hr., 1250dr), Lentas (1 per day Mon.-Fri., 3hr., 1300dr), Anogia (5 per day, 2 on Sun., 1hr., 600dr), and Fodele (2 per day Mon.-Fri., 1hr., 550dr). The **Chania/Rethymnon Terminal** (tel. 22 17 65) is near the waterfront. Walk down 25th Augustou Ave. to the waterfront, turn left, and look for the Xenia Hotel after a few blocks—it's at the top of the courtyard to your left. To Chania (14 per day, 2150dr) and Rethymnon (17 per day, 1½hr., 1250dr). The bus company publishes handy little schedules available at main stations and the tourist office, but they are subject to change.

Ferries: Boat offices on 25th Augustou Ave. Most open daily 9am-9pm. Boats leave for Athens (2 per day, 12hr., 5450dr), Santorini (5 per week, 4hr., 2570dr), Paros (5 per week, 8½hr., 4498dr), Naxos (1 per week, 7hr., 4498dr), Mykonos (2 per week, 9hr., 4807dr), Rhodes (2 per week, 12hr., 5657dr), and Thessaloniki (3 per week, 11hr., 8976dr).

Taxis: Radio Taxi of Iraklion (tel. 21 01 02, -46; 24 hr.) Take a taxi from Iraklion to Ag. Pelagia or Hersonissos for 3500dr. Farther destinations will cost you (Rethymnon 9000dr, Ierapetra 12,000dr, Chania 15,500dr).

Car Rental: Rental car companies are scattered along 25th Augustou Ave. Shop around. Make the owners compete for your business by quoting prices from their neighbors. For advance reservations, call **Budget Rent-a-Car,** 25th Augustou Ave. in Iraklion (open daily 8:30am-10pm) or their central office in Athens (tel. (01) 922 4444). **CaRavel** at #39 25th Augustou Ave. (tel. 24 53 45, -50; fax 22 03 62) offers cars to anyone more than 19 years old. Prices average 9000dr per day. A copy of *Let's Go* will get you free insurance or 40% discount on any car. Car delivered free from airport. Open daily 7am-10pm.

Moped Rental: Iraklion's rates are among the highest in Crete. Cheap rentals line Handakos St., El Greco Park, and 25th Augustou Ave., but prices fluctuate significantly. Check if the quoted price includes the 20% tax and insurance. Also ask what the bike insurance covers. 50cc bikes 3500dr per day, tax and third-party liability insurance included. **Nikos Rent-a-Vespa** (tel. 22 64 25), 16 Doukos Bofor St., across from Marin Hotel. Open daily 8am-8:30pm.

Luggage Storage: #48 25th Augustou Ave. (tel. 28 17 50), opposite the National Bank. 500dr per day per piece. Open 7am-11pm.

Laundromat: Washsalon, 18 Handakos St. (tel. 28 08 58; fax 28 44 42). Wash 1000dr, dry 1300dr. Self-service. Also provides luggage storage (250dr, w/locker 350dr). Open daily.

Public Toilets: El Greco Park. Open 7am-9pm. 30dr. Also in the public gardens near Eleftherias Sq.

Library: Vikelaia Municipal Library (tel. 24 65 50, -2), in Venizelou Sq. Limited number of books in English, on the second floor. Open Mon.-Fri. 8am-3pm.

Bookstores: 6 Dedalou St. has a wide variety. Newsstands in Eleftherias Sq. sell foreign newspapers like the *International Herald Tribune* as well as paperbacks. Open 8am-10pm. The bookstore at the base of Chandakos St. near the water (tel. 28 96 05) has a huge selection of Penguin classics, and is run by the English-language book wholesaler for Crete and the Middle East who also runs **Planet Bookstore,** (tel. 28 15 58), a 5-floor mega-store on the corner of Hortatson and Kidonias St. Open Mon.-Fri. 8:30am-2pm and 5:30-8:30pm, Sat. 8:30am-noon.

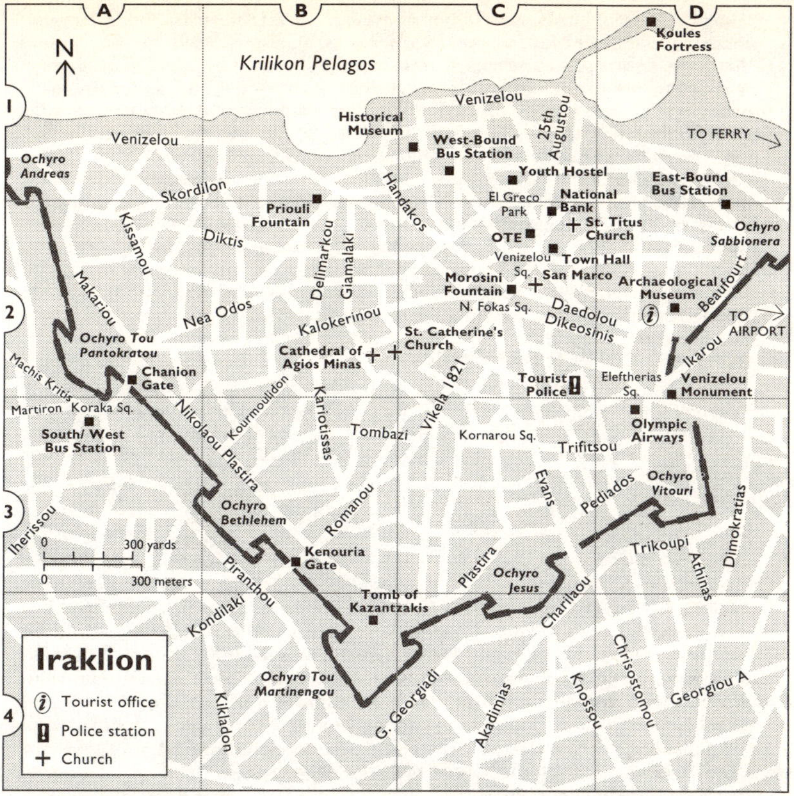

Pharmacy: On Koroneou, off of 25th Augustou Ave. (tel. 22 46 08). One is always open 24 hr.; its name and address is posted on the door of every pharmacy. All are marked by a red cross.

Hospital: Venizelou St. (tel. 23 95 02 or 26 93 73), on the road to Knossos. Take bus #2 (20min.). Also **Panepistimiako Hospital** (tel. 26 91 11 or 26 94 62). One open 24 hr. each day; schedule rotates.

ACCOMMODATIONS

Iraklion has a bunch of cheap hotels and hostels, most near Handakos St., at the center of town. Others are on Evans and 1866 St., near the market. If you arrive late at night and take a taxi, be aware that some taxi drivers get commissions from hotels.

The "**Rooms to Let" Association** (ΦΙΛΟΞΕΝΙΑ; tel. 22 92 52), run by a conglomerate of hotel owners, is not a great resource for places to stay in Iraklion, but is a godsend for advance bookings in Hersonissos, Malia, and resorts in eastern Crete. Good luck finding the small office at Kornarou Sq. Phone calls often suffice; some English spoken. (Open 9:30am-1pm.)

Youth Hostel, 5 Cyronos St. (tel. 28 62 81 or 22 29 47), off 25th Augustou Ave. Standard hostel rooms; cool and quiet. Curfew midnight. 1000dr per person; larger rooms for families and couples. Luggage storage 300dr; 24-hr. hot water; check-out 10am, open for late arrivals. Café-bar breakfast 350dr, beer 350dr.

Hotel Rea, Kalimeraki St. (tel. 22 36 38 or 24 21 89). Walking toward the harbor, turn right off Handakos St., 2 blocks above the waterfront. Clean, airy rooms, with pleasing pastel trim. Doubles 5000dr, w/bath 6000dr; triples 6500dr, w/bath

7500dr; dorm-like quads 8000dr; hot showers included. Breakfast 750dr. Luggage storage free. Reduced rate on rent-a-car services. Manager speaks English.

Hellas Rent Rooms, 24 Handakos St. (tel. 28 08 58; fax 28 44 42), but as of summer 1996 at the site of the old youth hostel. Newly renovated, but under the same owner as the former hostel. Dorm beds 1400dr; doubles 4000dr.

Rent a Room Vergina, 32 Chortason St. (tel. 24 27 39). Walking toward the harbor, turn right off Handakos onto Kidonias, take your first left on Hortason, and walk down 2 blocks; its on the right. Clean, homey rooms. Washtubs and clotheslines. High ceilings, new furniture. Free luggage storage. Check-out noon; deposit necessary with advance reservations. Doubles 5000dr, triples 7000dr.

Kretan Sun, #10 1866 St. (tel. 24 37 94). Bare, tidy rooms. Some are huge. Directly above the open-air market—noisy in the mornings, and the entrance can disappear among market stalls. Singles 4000dr, doubles 5000dr, triples 6500dr, quads 7500dr. Check-out 11am; free luggage storage.

FOOD AND ENTERTAINMENT

Around the Morosini Fountain, near El Greco Park, and in Eleftherias Sq. are ritzy cafés perfect for lounging. Take a left off 1866 St., one block from Venizelou Sq., to reach tiny Theodosaki St. Though not the most upscale place in town to dine, it's certainly colorful, with 10 *tavernas* serving Greek fare jammed side by side. The cheapest dishes go for roughly 650dr and the portions are impressive. If there's no menu, fix the price before you sit. For more elegant dining, try any of the *taverna*s on shop-and-boutique-lined Daedolou St. *Souvlaki* joints abound on 25th Augustou Ave. **Thraka** is the most fun thanks to Plato Kallergon, the jovial owner. Try the *souvlaki* with bread crust (350dr). To find the one spot where young Iraklionites take refuge from the whirlwind of summer tourists, walk on to Daedalou St. from the Lion Fountain Sq. and take a left onto the first side street you see. In an instant, the mad shopping bustle will dim, and you will find yourself among the tranquil backgammon pieces and the lazy steam of coffee cups. (Open Mon.-Sat. 9:30am-1am, Sun. 6pm-1am.) The manager of the **Minos Restaurant,** on Daedalou St., will personally guide you to have a look in the kitchen (swordfish 1900dr).

During the day, the best show in town is the open-air **market** on 1866 St., which starts near Venizelou Sq. Both sides of the boisterous, aromatic, narrow street are lined with stalls piled high with sweets, spices, fresh fruits, vegetables, cheeses, and meat in glass cases. The huge cauldrons of yogurt sold here far eclipse the filtered, pasteurized brands found elsewhere (700dr per kg). (Market open Mon. and Wed. 8:30am-2:30pm, Tues. and Thurs.-Fri. 8:30am-2:30pm and 5-8:30pm, Sat. 7am-2:30pm.) To satisfy a sweet craving, try one of the two **sweet shops** in Lion Fountain Sq. who sell *bougatsa,* a cheese or cream-filled phyllo pastry. (Open 6am-11pm.)

Iraklion natives are the first to point out that the "in" places change rapidly, so ask around. If you're feeling energized after your archaeological excursions, you could head to **Factory,** formerly Athina, which plays rave and disco on Thurs.-Sat. nights. For Greek music, head to **Café Aman. Disco Trapeza** sports a young crowd. Schedules for Iraklion's **movie theaters** are posted next to the tourist police office. The **Galaxia** (tel. 23 42 72) is an outdoor cinema open June-Sept. Shows are listed in Eleftherias Sq., next to the Astoria Hotel. (Daily show times 8:30 and 10:30pm; admission 1300dr.) For an evening of free sociological entertainment, join Greeks and tourists at Venizelou Sq., where Iraklion's annual **summer festival** (mid-June to mid-Sept.) combines cultural events such as concerts, theater, ballet, and folk dancing. Get a schedule from the tourist office, or call 28 22 21 for info.

SIGHTS

Iraklion's capital attraction is its superb **Archaeological Museum,** one of the finest in Greece, off Eleftherias Sq. (tel. 22 60 92). Exhibits are organized chronologically from the Neolithic period to Roman times. The museum's most outstanding feature is the **Hall of the Minoan Frescoes.** An illustrated guide available at the Museum's gift stand is well worth the 1500dr; otherwise you'll have to see the frescoes *sans* historical insights. The frescoes depict ancient Minoan life: ladies in blue offering libations, blue monkeys frolicking in the palatial gardens, and costumed Minoans forming a ritualized procession against an impressionistic mountain landscape. (Open Mon. 12:30-7pm, Tues.-Sun. 8am-7pm; admission 1500dr, students 800dr; free on Sun.) Iraklion also has a **Historical Museum** (tel. 28 32 19), on the corner of Grevenon and Kalokerianou, two blocks from the Xenia Hotel. Unlike the crowded Archaeological Museum, this museum is undervisited. Its eclectic collection includes frescoes, Turkish gravestones, finely woven tapestries, photographs from the WWII German invasion and the only **El Greco** on Crete—strange, considering that El Greco, or Theotokopoulos, was a native Cretan. The museum also features a reconstruction of Kazantzakis' library. (Open Mon.-Sat. 9am-2pm; admission 800dr.)

The austere **Tomb of Kazantzakis** has views of Iraklion, the sea, and the Mountain of Zeus to the east. To get there, either walk along the top of the Venetian walls to Martinengo Bastion at the south corner of the city, or go down Evans St. until you reach the walls and the bastion. Because of his heterodox beliefs, Kazantzakis, the author of *The Last Temptation of Christ,* was denied a place in a Christian cemetery and was buried here without the full rites of the Orthodox Church. True aficionados can visit the **Kazantzakis Museum,** in the nearby village of Varvari. The carefully presented exhibit includes many of the author's original manuscripts, as well as photographs of his theatrical productions. A slide show (in English) provides historical background. A bus from Station A takes you to Mirtia (22km from Iraklion), only a short walk from the museum. For schedules, inquire at the station, or call 24 50 17, -9. (Open Mon.-Sat. 9am-4pm; admission 400dr.)

Several interesting churches hide in the modern maze of city streets. Built in 1735 in Agia Ekaterinis Sq., the **Cathedral of Agios Minas** features six icons by the Cretan master Damaskinos (tel. 28 24 02; 24 hr.). **St. Catherine's Church** (tel. 24 21 11), also in the square, served as the first Greek university after the fall of Constantinople in 1453. (Open Mon., Wed., and Sat. 10am-1pm, Tues. and Thurs.-Fri. 10am-1pm and 4-6pm; admission 400dr.) **St. Titus Church,** 25th Augustou Ave., is a Turkish mosque converted into a Christian church. The **Armenian Church** at 16 Kalokerianou St. (tel. 24 43 37), dates back to 1666; its Israeli-born priest gives free tours of the grounds. **Agios Mattheos,** a 10-min. walk on Markopoulou St. from Agia Ekaterinis Sq., has several excellent icons. Ask the priest behind the church for the key.

As you scamper around, take note of the various monuments built during the long Venetian occupation of Iraklion. The most popular is the 17th-century circular **Morosini Fountain** in Lion Fountain Sq., graced with marble lions. Several others deserve a visit: the reconstructed **Venetian Loggia,** Lion Fountain Sq.; the 13th-century **Basilica of St. Mark,** 25th Augustou Ave., now an exhibition hall; the **Venetian Arsenal,** off Kountouriotou Sq., near the waterfront; **Koules Fortress** (tel. 24 62 11), which guards the old harbor (open Mon.-Sat. 8am-6pm, Sun. 10am-3pm; admission 500dr); and the impressive 15th-century **Venetian walls** that encircle the city.

It's El Greco to Me

Though he made his name at the Spanish court, Domenikos Theotocopoulos (1541-1614) clung to his Greek heritage throughout his artistic career. Born at Iraklion (then under Venetian rule) the Cretan artist incorporated his early Byzantine training with the teachings of the Venetian and Roman schools, where he trained with masters like Titian, Raphael, and Michelangelo. El Greco, as he came to be known, was a master of Mannerism, a style of painting that places internal emotions above nature and the ancients. El Greco's reputation was built on his portraits and religious imagery that featured rigid figures filled with surprising emotion. His best-known work, *The Burial of the Count Orgaz*, staged a historical event in the contemporary world, a tradition in Western painting that echoes throughout the history of art. Although El Greco moved to Toledo, Spain, in 1576, the Spanish subjects and contexts of his work never eclipsed his feeling that he was a stranger in that land—and throughout his career, El Greco would continue to sign his paintings in Greek.

■ NEAR IRAKLION

Iraklion is an ideal base for exploring Central Crete. Many archaeological sites, including the great Minoan complex at Knossos and lesser Minoan finds at Malia, Tylissos, and Arhanes, are within a half-day's excursion from the city.

KNOSSOS

Knossos is undoubtedly the most famous archaeological site in Crete; few visitors escape the island without at least a token visit. Myth claims that when King Minos of Crete refused to sacrifice a fine white bull to Poseidon, the sea-god drove both Pasiphaë, Minos' queen, and the bull mad with lust. Their passion spawned the Minotaur, who stalked through the labyrinth and required 14 well-cooked Athenian youths per year. Finally Theseus, Prince of Athens, entered the maze and slew the monster with the aid of Ariadne, Minos' daughter, and Daedalus, the master architect who designed the labyrinth. Theseus had intended to take Ariadne back to Athens to marry her (or so he said—the cad), but at the bidding of Dionysus, he abandoned her on the island of Naxos. When Minos discovered that Daedalus had helped Theseus escape, he imprisoned both the architect and his son, Icarus. Daedalus built them both wings of feathers and wax and off they flew. Hubristic Icarus, however, soared too close to the sun, melting his waxen wings and fell into the Aegean near the modern island Ikaria. Mary Renault's novel *The King Must Die* is a compelling account of the story, as is Ovid's *Metamorphoses.*

During the first millennium BC, Cretans were ridiculed for imagining that they sprang from such illustrious forebears as the Minoans. Time, however, has proven the Cretans right. Arthur Evans, one of Heinrich "Troy" Schliemann's British cronies, purchased the hill and spent the next 43 years and his entire fortune excavating it. His thorough work showed that from 1700 BC to 1400 BC, Knossos was indeed an important city that stood at the center of the first great European civilization.

Dr. Evans creatively, though in many instances inaccurately, restored large portions of the palace to what he believed were their original configurations, based on evidence unearthed during the excavations. Walls, window casements, stairways, and columns were reconstructed in reinforced concrete, and copies of the magnificent frescoes were mounted in place of the originals (now in Iraklion's Archaeological Museum). In some cases restorations prevented the walls from falling down as the excavations continued, but Evans' reconstruction crossed the boundaries of preservation and reflected his own interpretation. While purists feel that the complex at Knossos is an outrage, it is impressive nonetheless.

Plans are currently in the works for making the site more comprehensible to the untrained eye. By the summer of 1996, signs should label structures, and marked paths should prevent oblivious wanderers from destroying the palace's walls. The extended series of magazines (storage rooms with large clay jars) give the palace its labyrinthine architecture and are its claim to fame. The large open space in the middle of the site, imaginatively named the Central Court, was quite possibly an arena for bull-leaping (a Minoan rites of passage ceremony). The **Throne Room,** to the left of the Central Court, enshrines the original throne. A wooden replica is in an adjacent room for your very own Kodak moment. The throne faces a frustratingly enigmatic structure known as a lustral basin (a deep square area possibly used for religious purposes). Note the elaborate drainage system, occasional mason marks on the cut-stone architecture, and the I-shaped cement bumps on the ground where doors ingeniously slid into the walls and let in, or kept out, the sunlight. Don't miss the Queen's Bathroom—over 3000 years ago that lucky girl could flush her own toilet. Finally, gaze upon the Royal Road in the complex's northwest sector.

For general reference, check out *Knossos and the Iraklion Museum,* by Costis Davaris (1500dr) and *Knossos: The Minoan Civilization,* by Sosso Logadiou-Platonos (1200dr), both on sale at the site. Even more helpful and enlightening is an English-speaking tour guide (roughly 1500dr for a 1-hr. tour). Make sure that the guide is official and has the required papers, or he could be spouting nonsense. The ruins (tel. 23 19 40) are open daily 8am-7pm. (Admission 1500dr, students 800dr; free on Sun.) Take bus #2, which stops along 25th Augustou Ave.—look for the signposts on the west side of the street. (Daily 7am-10:30pm every 20min., 170dr.) You can also take a bus from Bus Station A in Iraklion.

TYLISSOS, FODELE, AND GORTINIA

Although Knossos is secure in its status as the most popular site on Crete, it cannot lay claim to being the oldest. At **Tylissos,** 14km southwest of Iraklion, archaeologists have unearthed a Minoan city dating back to 2000 BC. Unlike Knossos, the ruins at Tylissos remain relatively unaltered. (Open daily 8:30am-3pm; admission 400dr.) Buses for Tylissos leave from Terminal B every 15min. (25min., 400dr). Halfway between Tylissos and Anogia are the remains of the Minoan villas at **Sklavokambos.**

Also accessible from Iraklion is **Fodele,** a village full of orange trees and famous as the home of **El Greco** (see box on p. 197.) For info on buses to Anogia and Fodele, see p. 194.The first stop of historical interest on the road south, **Gortina** contains the ruins of the Greco-Roman city, Gortyn. In 67 BC, when ancient Gortyn fell to the Romans, the city was designated the capital of the island. Most of the remaining ruins here are from the Roman occupation, including the **Roman Odeon** (music hall). One of the few remains from the Hellenistic city, the Law Code tablets, are the most important extant source of information regarding pre-Hellenistic Greek law. They are written in a Dorian dialect of Greek and date from roughly 450 BC when the city thrived under Greek control. The stones were so handsomely cut that the Romans used them as building materials for the odeon.

The site of ancient **Gortyn,** en route to Phaestos, is on your right as you come from Iraklion. The first thing you'll see is the bird-inhabited 7th-century **Basilica of Saint Titus.** The odeon is behind the church. The site also has a hall with 14 sculpted figures and a mammoth statue of a soldier. (Site open daily 8:30am-3pm. Admission 400dr, students 200dr.) To get to Gortyn, take one of the many **buses** that go to Matala or Phaestos. See those towns for schedule details.

PHAESTOS AND AGIOS IOANNIS

Imperiously situated on a plateau with a magnificent view of the surrounding mountains, the palace at Phaestos (tel. (0892) 91 315) housed powerful Minoan royalty. At the turn of the century, Halbherr began excavations here and unearthed two palaces. The first was destroyed by the earthquake that decimated Crete around 1700 BC; the second was probably leveled in a mysterious catastrophe in 1450 BC. Surprisingly enough, a final excavation in 1952 came upon traces of two even older palaces. Since the excavations, minor reconstruction work has been done on the walls, chambers, and cisterns. Built according to the standard Minoan blueprint, the complex included a great central court, from which extended the private royal quarters, servants' quarters, storerooms, and chambers for state occasions. The grand staircase is still intact. Phaestos may be a disappointment to those not well-versed in Minoan archaeology because it's difficult to visualize what the palace looked like in its heyday. The incredible artifacts from Phaestos in the Iraklion museum alone make a visit to the site worthwhile. (Open daily 8am-6pm; admission 1200dr.)

A 10-min. walk down the twisting road to Matala leads to the tiny rural village of Agios Ioannis. A few hundred meters farther down the road in the cemetery is the **Church of Agios Parlos,** which merits the short walk. Parts of the church are thought to be pre-Christian and the restored frescoes date from the early 14th century AD. **Buses** from Phaestos go to Iraklion (5 per day, 1½hr., 1150dr), Matala (2 per day, 20min., 200dr), and Agia Galini (3 per day, 25min., 200dr).

■■■ MATALA ΜΑΤΑΛΑ

LSD, psychedelic colors, and groovy music once filled the caves, strewn along Matala's sloping seaside cliffs. Anyone who visited Matala 20 years ago is likely to muster only intoxicated memories of a more hallucinogenic trip. Before you pack your rolling papers, be aware that hardly anything of these hedonistic fiestas remains, and Matala is now a resort town for vacationing families. Along the beach are huge, pale cliffs with three tiers of caves that have been inhabited since Neolithic times. The cliffs fortifying the inlet terrace form inviting platforms from which to survey the sea.

Orientation and Practical Information Matala has three main streets: one on the water, one behind it, and one that intersects both. On the first you'll find cafés, restaurants, souvenir stands, and a covered market; on the second, the bus station, motorbike rental agencies, and stores. At Matala's square, these two join the hotel-and-pension-lined road to Phaestos.

Several motorbike rental places, all in the main square, handle currency exchange at close to bank rates—try **Festos Rent-A-Car** (tel. 42 372 or 42 723; open 9am-10pm), **Monzo Bikes** (tel. 42 586 or 42 757; open 9am-11pm), and **Motor Manos** (tel. 42 359; open 8am-11pm). These shops also serve as informal tourist offices, and provide info on hotels and beaches. Monzo and Manos rent **mopeds** for 3000dr per day (insurance included), with reduced prices for longer rentals. The **OTE,** in the beach parking lot, resembles a small prison. (Open Mon.-Sat. 8am-11pm, Sun. 9am-2pm and 5-10pm.) The **laundromat,** across from the campground, up a small asphalt road, in an unmarked white building, charges 1000dr per wash, 400dr for drying. (Open daily 9am-1pm and 3-7pm.) The **post office** is near the entrance to the beach parking lot. (Open Mon.-Fri. 8:30am-2pm.) In summer, **buses** go to Iraklion (5-7 per day, 2hr., 1250dr), Phaestos (7 per day, 20min., 450dr), and Agia Galini (1-4 per day change at Phaestos, 45min., 650dr). The town's **police station** (tel. 42 168) is behind the bakery on the second inland road. The **hospital** and **pharmacy** are in Mires, 17km northeast. In an emergency, call 23 312 and a doctor or dentist will drive to Matala. **Public toilets** are located in the main square next to Monzo Bikes. **Postal Code:** 70200; **Telephone Code** Is 0892.

Accommodations Matala has more than a dozen hotels and pensions, but bargains are scarce. Singles cost as much as doubles and rarely drop below 3000dr in the summer. German and British developers often pack the town with tour groups, but there are lots of "Rooms to Let" on the road forking off the main road 750m out of town. It may be a good idea to make Matala a daytrip. Cheaper accommodations are available in Matala's surrounding villages, but don't try to sleep on the main beach or in the nearby caves—it's illegal and police occasionally raid them. Your best bet in town is **Rent Rooms Dimitri's** (tel. 23 726, 22 718, or 24 510; fax 42 740). From the town center, walk out of town 200m, turn right onto the winding road at the blue Dimitri's Villa sign, then follow the path around. Dimitri's has immaculate, shiny rooms with private bath, balconies, and hot water. He offers complimentary drinks for all guests, maid service, and will even secure reservations for equally fantastic rooms in Plakias and Agia Galini at the prices listed for his pension. *Let's Go* users receive exchange without commission, 600dr breakfast and 25% discount on rented bikes too. (Singles 2500dr, doubles 3300dr, triples 4000dr.) Another fine option is **Pension Matala View** (tel. 42 114). Turn right opposite the Zafira Hotel, near the main square. They have tidy, good-sized bedrooms with baths and balconies. (Singles 3500dr, doubles 5000dr, triples 6000dr.) **Pension Jannis** (tel. 42 784), a 10-min. walk past Tsirterakis on the road to Phaestos (ask at the Xenophon Hotel) has doubles for 4000dr. Spacious **Matala Camping** (tel. 42 720 or 42 340), on your right in the town center, has showers. (Person 950dr, tent 650dr, car 600dr.) Other places in town fill quickly, so start searching early.

Food and Entertainment The restaurants along the waterfront are hard to tell apart. One thing is for sure—you pay for the view. Better food, as usual, is farther from the mainstream hangouts. **Nassos,** near the waterfront, offers good *souvlaki-pitas*, and **Antonio's Taverna,** near the turn-off for Dimitri's Rooms, has tasty chicken. There are a number of inexpensive minimarkets and bakeries in town as well. Nightlife in Matala means drinking, dancing, and gazing at the ocean until dawn. **Giorgos, Kahlua,** and **Rock** on the waterfront are a safe bet.

Sights Matala's main attraction is its three tiers of **caves** next to the beach. Hike along them to find a private spot. Sit in its cool, dim interior and spy on the beach action below while reflecting on the cave's possible previous occupants: flower children, Nazis searching for British submarines, and long ago, Roman corpses.

Matala has more than its share of great beaches. Past the crashing waves, enjoy the dim outline of Paximadia Island. Hundreds of people crammed around you will also admire the view. For an equally good shore and more secluded caves, join **nude bathers** on **Red Beach,** 20min. down the path behind the church. Comparatively shut off, with a small community of freelance summer residents and a lone *taverna,* **Kommos Beach** is a 5km walk from Matala. Archaeologists are currently excavating a Minoan site that overlooks the sea, arguably the bluest in Crete. The presence of the site guarantees that the coast will remain undeveloped. The bus from Iraklion will let you off roughly ½km from the beach (bus schedule posted by the station in Matala). Bring water; the ½km hike down is long and dusty.

■ NEAR MATALA: AGIA GALINI (ΑΓΙΑ ΓΑΛΗΝΗ)

Agia Galini, a once-tranquil fishing village west of Matala on the southwest coast, has become a pleasant resort town with glitzy hotels, discos, and bars. Friendly locals make up for the busloads of people you could have met at home.

Orientation and Practical Information Agia Galini is perched on a hill—no matter where you are in town, just head down to reach the sea. The **post office** (open Mon.-Fri. 8am-2pm) is below the bus station on the left. The **OTE** is at the bottom of the hill on the harbor in high season and uphill from the harbor off-season (open daily 7:30am-10pm; off-season 7:30am-3pm). The extremely helpful **OPSIS tourist agency** (tel. 74 056) is across the street from the post office. They speak fluent German, French, Dutch, and English. They also rent cars (8000-11,000dr). (Open daily 8:30am-1pm and 5-10pm.) **Public toilets** are next to the OTE, as well as the **police** (tel. 91 210; 24 hr.), and the **port police** (tel. 91 206; 24 hr.). Several agents rent bikes, both in the upper and lower level of town. Try **Biggis Bikes** (tel. 91 142), near the post office. (Open 8:30am-6:30pm; automatic 80cc mopeds 3500dr, 150cc Vespa scooters 4000dr, insurance included.) Farther down from the post office, toward the harbor and on the left is a **pharmacy** (tel. 91 168; open 10am-2pm, 6-10pm). A **doctor** is located a few doors down from the OPSIS office, toward the harbor (tel. 91 091; open Mon.-Fri. 10am-1:30pm and 7-8pm, Sat. noon-1pm and 7-8pm, Sun. 7-8pm). Facing the harbor, turn left at Biggis and then turn right onto **Vas. Ioannis Street,** Agia Galini's main drag. **Candia Tours** (tel. 91 278; fax 91 174; open daily 9am-1pm and 5-9pm; closed off-season) and a **bookstore** called "Book Shop/Leather" (open daily 9am-11pm) are both on this street. The **health center** (tel. 91 111) is in the police station. (Open Mon.-Fri. 9am-2pm and 5:30-8:30pm; winter 9:30am-1:30pm.) **Postal Code:** 74056; **Telephone Code:** 0832.

Accommodations The pensions along the upper tier of Agia Galini are cheaper than the hotels in the center of town. **Hotel Manos** (tel. 91 394), 25m from the bus stop, has attractively-furnished rooms with wide, comfortable beds and grapevine-entwined shared balconies. (Doubles w/bath 5000dr.) About halfway up the main road or up the steps from the harbor (take a right on the tier before the Hotel Daedalus) is **Hotel Acteon** (tel. 91 208), which has decent, large rooms. Ask for the middle floor—it's high enough for a view of the water, but too low for the glorious panorama of the parking lot. (Doubles 4000dr, triples 5000dr; prices negotiable in early season; reserve 2 weeks in advance.) Next door is the **Hotel Mirago** (tel. 91 140, -494), with clean, bright rooms. (Doubles 4000dr, triples 5000dr.) **Camping Agia Galini** is at the turn-off 3km before town on the road from Iraklion.

From the harbor, follow the beachfront 500m and look for the sign. Walk across the tilted footbridge to the end of the beach, and then walk another 150m. The grounds have gravel tent sites shaded by olive and carob trees. Beware of the dogs. At the end of the beachfront, rent paddle boats (1500dr per hr.).

Food and Entertainment Agia Galini is smothered by restaurants, bars, and discos, which have similar prices (beer 500dr). Agia Galini's specialty is the roof-garden bar/restaurant; most serve dinner (meals 2500dr, *gyros* 300dr).

WESTERN CRETE

While Crete's eastern half has been home to burgeoning tourism for years, Western Crete has remained quieter and more rustic. In the west, beaches are less-populated and much of the scenery remains undisturbed. Chania's café-lined yet tranquil port, the stunning Samaria Gorge, and the sandy beaches of Paleochora all encourage travelers to heed the prophetic words of the Village People and "Go West."

■■■ RETHYMNON ΡΕΘΥΜΝΟ

The Turkish and Venetian influences that pervade the cities of northern Crete are best appreciated in Rethymnon's harbor. Arabic inscriptions lace the walls of its narrow, arched streets, minarets highlight the old city's skyline, and an imposing Venetian fortress guards the harbor's west end. On any given day, even the most energetic travelers may inexplicably find themselves waking up just in time for the afternoon *siesta,* wandering aimlessly at sunset, and lounging until the wee hours of the next morning in a café by the ocean.

ORIENTATION AND PRACTICAL INFORMATION

To get to **Arkadiou Street** and the waterfront from the bus station, turn right down Demokratias St. to the Venizelou monument, cross **Kountouriotou Street,** and walk down **Varda Kallergi Street.** You'll find everything you need in the rough triangle formed by Arkadiou, **Antistassios,** and **Gerakari Street,** but get the tourist office's free map anyway.

Tourist Office: (tel. 29 148). Down by the waterfront, west of the Old City. Efficient staff provide free maps, bus and ferry schedules, museum hours, and a list of all-night pharmacies. They also suggest daytrips and publicize local events. Open Mon.-Fri. 8am-2pm.

Tourist Police: Iroon Polytechniou St. (tel. 28 156; fax 53 450). Three blocks south of fortress. Services similar to tourist office. Open Mon.-Fri. 7am-10pm.

Police: (tel. 25 247). Located in Iroon Square. 24 hr.

Association of Rooms to Let: 2 Petichaki St. (tel. 29 503). The English-speaking staff on the second floor of Nileas Tours represents the association, which can hook you up with one of 7000 beds in the Rethymnon prefecture.

Post Office: Moatsou St., near the public gardens. Open Mon.-Fri. 7:30am-8pm, Sat. 7:30am-2pm. Caravan office, on the beach, open Mon.-Fri. 8am-8pm, Sat. 8am-2pm. **Postal Code:** 74100.

OTE: 28 Kountouriotou St. Open Mon.-Sat. 7am-midnight, Sun. 8am-11pm; Nov.-April 7am-10pm. **Telephone Code:** 0831.

Banks: Bank of Crete, at the intersection of Kountouriotou and Varda Kallergi, near the bus station offers **currency exchange.** Open Mon.-Thurs. 8am-2pm, Fri. 8am-1:30pm. Many banks are marked on the tourist office map. The **National Bank** is on Kountouriotou St. (open Mon.-Thurs. 8am-2pm, Fri. 8am-1:30pm).

Flights: (tel. 24 333 or 22 257), on Koumoundourou St., near the National Bank (open Mon.-Fri. 8am-8pm, Sat. 8am-3:30pm).

Buses: KTEL station (tel. 22 212, -659), facing each other on opposite corners of Demokratias and Moatsou, 1 block inland from the Venizelou monument on Kountouriotou. To Iraklion (17 per day, 1½hr., 1250dr), Chania (16 per day, 1hr., 1200dr), Agia Galini (4 per day, 2hr., 1000dr), Plakias (6 per day, 1hr., 800dr).

Taxi: (tel. 22 316, 24 316, or 28 316). 24 hr.

Moped Rental: Motor Stavros, 14 Paleologou St. (tel. 22 858). 80cc motorcycles 5000dr, insurance and taxes included. Bikes 1200dr. Prices negotiable. (Open daily 9am-9pm.) **Fahrrad Rent-a-Vespa,** 15 Kountouriotou St., across from the OTE. Mountain bikes 2500dr. Others center around the Venizelou Monument.

Laundromat: 45 Tombasi St. (tel. 22 011), next to the youth hostel. Wash 1500dr. Dry 500dr. Open Mon.-Sat. 7:30am-9pm. Drop-off service.

International Bookstore: International Press, Petichaki St. (tel. 51 673 or 24 111), near the water. Open daily, 9am-11pm. **Spontidaki Toula,** 43 Touliou St. (tel. 20 307). Buys and sells used books in many languages.

Hospital: Trantalidou St. (tel. 27 814), in the southwest corner of town. 24 hr.

ACCOMMODATIONS

Arkadiou St. and the harbor, near the fortress and the Venetian port, are lined with hotels and "Rooms to Let." Most are spacious, sparsely decorated, and expensive. The **Association of Rooms to Let** headquarters on Petichaki St., a block from the harbor, will tell you what's available. Prices are 20-40% less in off-season.

Youth Hostel, 41-45 Tombasi St. (tel. 22 848). Ramshackle but friendly, and crammed in summer. Reception open 8am-noon and 5-9pm; no curfew. Bar. 1000dr per person; breakfast 400dr. Hot showers in summer 8-10am and 5-8pm.

Olga's Pension, 57 Souliou St. (tel. 29 851). On a nicely restored street off Ethnikis Antistaseos. George, the jovial proprietor who is reminiscent of Santa Claus, keeps a continual garden party going. Cheery decor in the comfortable rooms. Note the trippy mosaic made of coins on your way up the front stairs. Homemade *raki* at the terrarium. Singles 4000dr, doubles 5500dr, triples 6000dr, quads 6500dr. All w/bath included. Please don't pull on George's beard.

Vrisinas, 10 Chereti St. (tel. 26 092), off Arkadiou St. Centrally located, but still tranquil. Top-notch rooms. Doubles 4000dr, triples 5500dr.

Hotel Paradisos, 35 Igoum Gavril St. (tel. 22 419). From the bus station, walk down to the Venizelou monument and turn left on Kountouriotou St., which becomes Igoum Gavril. Clean, quiet, nondescript rooms and a spacious shower and bath. Singles 2900dr, doubles 3900dr, triples 4500dr; hot showers 400dr.

Elizabeth Camping (tel. 28 694), 3km east of town at the beginning of the old road to Iraklion. Tent pitches on shaded grass. The staff lends camping and kitchen supplies. Self-service *taverna* 9am-11pm. Person 1000dr, tent 800dr, car 800dr; free parking next to reception. Open May-Oct.

Arkadia Camping (tel. 28 825, 29 927), 500m beyond Elizabeth. Gravel pitches. Self-serve *taverna* 7am-11pm, and store 8am-9pm. Currency exchange, moped rentals. Person 800dr, tent 500dr, small car 350dr, large car 600dr. **Buses** run from the Rethymnon station to both campsites (100dr). If you're arriving from Iraklion, ask the driver to let you off at one of the sites.

FOOD AND ENTERTAINMENT

Rethymnon has plenty of *souvlaki* (150dr) stands scattered throughout the city. There's also an **open-air market** on weekdays next to the park, between Moatsou and Kountouriotou St. Generic seafood restaurants line the old harbor. For reliable if overpriced meals, visit the restaurants on the old Venetian harbor. For a special meal, seek out **Alana's,** 11 Salaminos (tel. 27 737), on a quiet side-street. The roomy courtyard, attentive service, and Venetian fountain create a romantic setting. (Open daily 6pm-1am; menu for 2 including aperitif, fish, salad, and wine 7000dr.) If you have access to a car or feel like taking a long walk, join the locals at **Zizi's Taverna,** 4km east of town in Platanes, on the old road to Iraklion.

The bar scene at Rethymnon centers around Petichaki St. and Nearchou St. near the west end of the harbor. The happening **Rockafé Bar** on Petichaki St. and the

Fortezza Disco Bar (tel. 21 493) at 14 Nearchou St. bookend several Greek *bouzouki* places. Both have pricey 1000dr beers. On the other side of the beach, the outdoor **Dolphin Disco** sports a pool (beer 500dr).

SIGHTS

Rethymnon has been occupied nearly continuously since the late Minoan period. At its cultural and economic apex in the 4th century BC, it was overrun by Myceneans. During the Fourth Crusade, the Franks sold the island to the Venetians for 520 pounds of silver. The latter fortified Rethymnon, which was crucial to their chain of trading outposts. The Ottomans took the city in 1646, enlarging it and incorporating Turkish designs into the extant Venetian buildings. For enlightening background, read *Rethymnon: A Guide to the Town,* by A. Malagari and H. Stratidakis (800dr).

Rethymnon's **Archaeological Museum** is adjacent to the fortress. Once inside, you'll feel like you've wandered into the storeroom of an absentminded archaeologist: headless statues lean on walls behind rows of figurines, and Minoan sarcophagi lie next to Roman coins. (Open Tues.-Sun. 8:30am-3pm; admission 500dr.)

At some point during your visit make a pilgrimage to the enormous **Venetian Fortezza,** dating from around 1580. The walls of the citadel are in excellent condition, but most of the buildings inside the fortress were destroyed by Turks in the 17th century, and even more bit the dust three centuries later during WWII. (Open daily 8:30am-7:30pm; admission 300dr.) The city's **Renaissance Festival,** featuring theater, concerts, and exhibits, is held in the fortress in July and August.

Rethymnon's Turkish legacy is evident in the city's Islamic structures: the **Neratzes Minaret,** on Antistassios St.; the **Nerdjes Mosque,** one block farther, which was formerly a Franciscan church; the **Kara Pasha Mosque,** on Arkadiou St., near Iroon Sq.; and the **Valides Minaret,** which presides over **Porta Megali** gate at the beginning of Antistassios St. in 3 Martiou Sq.

Rethymnon's annual **Wine Festival,** during the first week in August, is a crowded all-you-can-drink fest which costs only 500dr. (Bring your own carafe—souvenir glasses are expensive.) A local dance troupe performs early in the evening; later on it's a free-for-all. Every odd year, an exhibition of Cretan handicrafts coincides with the wine festival. The work is worth a look, but you can usually find better prices at local artisans' shops in each major town. Rethymnon's own craft shops cluster around Arkadiou, Antistassios, and Gerakari Street. The **Herb Shop,** 58 Souliou St., stocks folk remedies and herbs exclusive to Crete, for emergency aromatherapy.

Cretans who sought refuge in the Early Byzantine **Arkadi monastery** in 1866, 23km from Rethymnon, blew themselves up rather than surrender to the Turks. The monastery, now in ruins, also has a museum (200dr).

■■■ CHANIA XANIA

Chania survived an attack from Germany's best paratroopers during WWII and, earlier, endured occupation by the Minoans, Turks, Venetians, and Egyptians. Nonetheless, Chania (pop. 70,000) today is a vibrant town of tall, skinny, four-story Venetian structures. Chania was the capital of Crete until 1971, when the title was passed to Iraklion. With its thriving nightlife and chaotic history, however, Chania is still regarded by many islanders as the spiritual capital of the island. Meander through the winding streets (an architectural pastiche of styles from different occupations), absorb the folk music from streetside cafés, or while the day away gazing at the old Venetian Harbor. No matter how tourist-oriented the waterfront cafés become, they don't mar the beauty of the harbor, silhouetted at sunset by Turkish domes. It's no longer the capital, but Chania remains for many their favorite city in Crete.

ORIENTATION AND PRACTICAL INFORMATION

From the bus station, walk right on Kidonias St. for two blocks and turn left onto Platia 1866; going north, the road becomes Halidon St. and leads to the old **harbor,** the setting for much of Chania's nightlife. To lighten the load while looking for a room, leave your bags at the bus station (storage open 6am-8pm; 100dr per bag). Ferries dock in the nearby port, **Souda.** A bus from Souda drops off at Chania's Municipal Market (10min., 240dr). Facing the market, turn left and walk two blocks west on Gianari St., then right onto Halidon. Even with maps from the tourist office, finding your way around the city is no cinch. Luckily, Chania isn't too large so you can't stay lost for long. Chania's business district is mostly contained within the area across from the market, around the intersection of **Gianari Street** and **Tzanakaki Street.**

Tourist Office: 1st floor of the Megaro Pantheon, Platia 1866 (tel./fax 92 624), behind the Greek Agricultural Bank. Provides info on flights, ferries, buses, hotels, and package tours, and offers free maps. Open Mon.-Fri. 7:30am-2:30pm.

Tourist Police: 44 Karaiskaki St. (tel. 71 111), by the central bus station. Gives directions in English. Open daily 7:30am-8pm. **Port Police:** (tel. 98 888).

Post Office: 3 Tzanakaki St. Open Mon.-Fri. 7:30am-8pm. **Postal Code:** 73100.

OTE: 5 Tzanakaki St. Exceptionally efficient. Open daily 6am-midnight; off-season 7am-11pm. Telex and telegram Mon.-Fri. only. **Telephone Code:** 0821.

Association of Rooms to Let: Unikreta travel agency, 18 Isodion St. (tel. 43 601). Facing inland, a block left of harbor center. Open daily 10am-1pm, 6-8pm.

Banks: Credit Bank, 106 Halidon St., near Platia 1866. Open Mon.-Thurs. 8am-2pm, Fri. 8am-1:30pm, Sat. 9am-noon for **exchange** (Sat. is summer only). **National Bank** on the corner of Nikiforou and Foka St. Open Mon.-Thurs. 8am-2pm, Fri. 8am-1:30pm.

Flights: Olympic Airways, 88 Tzanakaki St. (tel. 57 701), near the public garden. Buses for the airport leave from the main office on Tzanakaki 1½hr. before each flight. Ticket issuance Mon.-Fri. 8am-3:15pm. Phone reservations Mon.-Fri. 7am-8pm, Sat. 8am-4pm. Flights to Athens (3 per week, 18,500dr).

Buses: Central bus station, on the corner of Kidonias and Kelaidi St. (tel. 93 052, -306). Bus schedules change often; go to tourist office for an updated schedule. To Paleochora (4 per day), Chora Sfakion (3 per day), Kastelli (13 buses per day), and Samaria (4 buses per day).

Ferries: ANEK Office, Venizelou Sq. near the National Bank of Greece. The *Kriti* and the *Aptera* go to Piraeus (7pm, tourist-class 5700dr, deck-class 3950dr). Bring food and warm clothing; the trip takes 11hr., and it's chilly at night.

Moped Rental: Cluster on Halidon St. Automatic mopeds at 3500dr per day; 90cc models at 4500dr, and 250cc at 6000dr. **Olympic Rent-a-Car,** 74 Halidon St. (tel. 94 915; fax 88 025), rents **cars** (8000dr per day); 10-25% discount for *Let's Go* users. Open 8am-10pm.

Laundromat: (tel. 52 494), located next to Hotel Fidias. Wash 800dr, dry 700dr. Soap free. Open daily 8am-10pm.

Hospital: Corner of Dragoumi and Kapodistriou St. (tel. 43 811). East part of town. Out-patient clinic open Mon.-Sat. 12:30-2pm and 6-9pm, Sun. 8am-9pm. For **emergencies,** call 22 222.

ACCOMMODATIONS

In the old town, most of the inexpensive pensions overlook the harbor, a convenient but noisy area. Small hotels sprout from the beaches on the west coast, but expect to lay out the cash for the brown sand of **Nea Kydonia** and **Agia Marina.** Tourist officials and police oblige with info, but don't give recommendations. Some people freelance camp on the east side. Be wary of the eclectic bunch of locals at the bus station who illegally try to entice newcomers to stay in their private rooms. A much better choice is the Association of Rooms to Let. Tell them what you want in a room and they'll give you a list of addresses and phone numbers.

Meltemi Pension, 2 Agelou St. (tel. 40 192). At the very end of the west side of the harbor, next to the Naval Museum. This cozy townhouse has camera-ready vistas and a library of foreign books. Singles 3000dr, doubles 7000dr.

Eygenia Rooms II (tel. 94 357). Left up Agelou from Meltemi Café at the end of the harbor. Private showers, common kitchen. Doubles 7000dr, w/bath 8000dr.

Hotel Fidias, 6 Sarpaki St. (tel. 52 494). From Halidon St., turn right at the cathedral on Athinagora St., which becomes Sarpaki St. With poster-coated walls and linoleum floors, the lodgings look like clean dorm rooms. Run by a Greek actor-turned-hotel-owner. Hot showers, TV, international calls. Singles 2500dr, doubles 3500dr; dorm triples 1600dr per person.

Rooms for Rent No. 47, 47 Kandanolou (tel. 53 243 or 93 210), on Kastelli Hill. Turn left off Kanevaro as you come from the harbor. Look for enormous sign on the left. Family-run pension has sunny balconies with stunning views of the open sea. Rooms with basins. Doubles 6000dr, triples 8000dr.

Camping Chania (tel. 31 138), is roughly 2½km from town. Take the Kalamaki bus from Platia 1866 (100dr). Bordered by flowers and shaded by olive trees. *Taverna* and minimarket. Person 1000dr, small tent 760dr. Open Mar.-Oct.

FOOD AND ENTERTAINMENT

Many cafés cater to a non-touristy crowd. When you get off the bus, head to the inconspicuous **Yordanni's** (tel. 44 710) at 18 N. Plastira, the insider's place for *bougatsa,* a phyllo pie filled with white, salty Cretan cheese (350dr). Yordanni's is Yorgasmic! For an intimate dinner, try **Tamam,** Zabeliou 49 (tel. 96 080), which features super veal with mushrooms (950dr) as well as vegetarian alternatives. One block off the waterfront, at 2 Moshon, try **Sultana's Home Cuisine** (tel. 97 218), housed in a Venetian palace built in the 15th century (spaghetti w/ octopus 1500dr, *mousaka* 1000dr, baklava 600dr). Another picturesque setting is the **Tholos** restaurant at 36 Agion Delta (tel. 46 725). Dine on seafood risotto in a romantically aging building. For fabulous Greek specialties, try **Karnago** (tel. 53 366). Walk east on the harbor, towards the dock, where the private boats are kept. There'll be a plaza on your right; turn right, and the restaurant is directly ahead. Past Karnago on the harbor, **Dinos** is famed all over Crete for its outstanding seafood.

Late at night, Chania's normally sluggish bloodstream heats up considerably. The **Plaza Disco** right on the harbor is definitely the place to be. The pricey 1500dr cover includes your first drink. Make it count—after that, beers are 1000dr (shots, 500dr). Tiny **Fagotto Bar,** 16 Agelou (tel. 57 487), has hot jazz until late at night. The **Praxis Café,** 3 Skufon St. (off Zambeliou on the west side of the harbor), is a grotto-like bar with tables outside. Around 1am, the crowds move to the discos. Try **Club "Street,"** next to the Amphora Restaurant on the harbor; **Kirkis,** on the west waterfront; and **Nemesis,** off the east side of the harbor.

SIGHTS

Kastelli Hill, the area north of Kanevaro St., is studded with reminders of Chania's past. Remnants of Ancient Kydonia's Bronze-Age prosperity are evident at the **Late Minoan House** (circa 1450 BC), on the corner of Kandanoleu and Kanevaro St. Unfortunately, the site is fenced off. In the Middle Ages, Venetian occupiers enriched the city's architecture, but much of their artistry was destroyed in WWII. Chania has many empty frames of Venetian houses open to the sky and intermingled with modern structures. With their melange of Turkish and Venetian buildings, the waterfront alleys reflect the city's varied history. The former Chania Tourist Office at the harbor's east end inhabits a converted mosque that dates back to the arrival of Turks in 1645. Pass through several archways on Moshon St. to reach the **Venetian Chapel,** decorated with Latin inscriptions and Turkish graffiti. Young Greeks mellow out in the **Municipal Gardens,** once the property of a Turkish *muezzin* (prayer caller). The leafy grounds also harbor a small zoo. Beyond the gardens to the east, turn left onto **Sfakianaki,** a 19th-century neighborhood with the **Historical Museum and Archives,** 20 Sfakianaki St. (tel. 22 606).

The **Venetian Inner Harbor** is a thriving social scene and an architectural relic that retains its original breakwater and Venetian arsenal. The Venetian **lighthouse** was restored by the Egyptians during their occupation of Crete in the late 1830s. Enter at the east end of the harbor. On the opposite side of the main harbor, the **Naval Museum** (tel. 55 301) exhibits nautical pictures, models, pieces of boats, and seashells. (Open daily 10am-4pm; admission 400dr, students 200dr.) The **Archaeological Museum** (tel. 80 334), on Halidon St. opposite the cathedral, displays Cretan artifacts. Once a Venetian monastery, it also served as the Mosque of Yusuf Pasha. (Open Tues.-Fri. 8am-3pm; admission 500dr, students 200dr.)

■ NEAR CHANIA: SAMARIA GORGE

The most popular excursion from Chania is the 5-hr. hike down the formidable 16km (10mi) Samaria Gorge, Europe's longest. Worn away by millions of years of river runoff, the White Mountains' pass retains its allure despite being mobbed by visitors and spotted with tourists' litter. Bird watchers can glimpse the rare bearded vulture; horticulturists can admire the wildflowers and shrubs which peek out from sheer rock walls; goat lovers can spot the nimble *agrimi,* a wild Cretan species in one of its few remaining natural habitats. The Samaria Gorge is an exceedingly beautiful hike. Follow Chania Forest Protection Service's rules to keep it that way.

The 44km, 1½-hr. bus ride from Chania to **Xyloskalo,** at the start of the trail, enjoys spectacular scenery. Passing between cliff walls up to 300m high, the path, only 3m wide at some points, winds down along a riverbed that runs nearly dry in the summer. Parts of the hike are shaded by clumps of pine trees, goats, or the towering walls of the gorge itself. The hike ends in the small town of Agia Roumeli on the south coast. From there a boat sails to Loutro and Chora Sfakion, where you can catch a bus back to Chania. Experienced hikers and masochists can hike from Agia Roumeli to Chora Sfakion (10hr.) along one of the most outstanding coastlines in the country (see Southwest Coast, p. 209). The bus to Chania from Chora Sfakion passes through the village of **Vrises,** where there are doubles to let (4000dr). The downhill hike favored by most people (from Xyloskalo in the Omalos Plain to Agia Roumeli) takes 4-6hr. A less-traveled path ascends Mt. Gingilos to the west.

Whichever route you choose, bring plenty of water and trail snacks, and wear good walking shoes. The Gorge is dry and dusty in summer, and the stones on the path become slippery. Furthermore, the altitude often makes the top of the gorge cold and rainy. If you get tired on the hike, don't worry; you can always take the donkey-taxis which patrol the trail. If you want to see only the dramatic tail of the gorge, start from Agia Roumeli. The path to the trail begins just behind Rooms Livikon. From the quay, walk straight to the rear of the village. Known as "Samaria the Lazy Way," the 2-hr. climb to the north takes you to the gorge's dramatic and narrow pass, the "Iron Gates." The gorge is open May 1-Oct. 15, and sometimes until Oct. 30; during the winter and spring, the river goes back to work cutting its trail through the rock. Flash floods in the winter have claimed many lives. During the open months, passage is officially allowed through the gorge between 6am and 4pm (admission 1000dr). For gorge info, call the **Chania Forest Service** (tel. 22 287) or pick up an info sheet at the tourist office.

Pricey accommodations for the night before the hike are available at the **Tourist Pavilion** (tel. 63 269) in Xyloskalo. Limited reservations can be placed with the Chania tourist office. Five kilometers north of Xyloskalo, **Omalos** has cheap lodgings and food at **Drakoulaki's Restaurant** (tel. (0821) 67 269; doubles 4000dr, triples 5000dr). On the plain of Omalos, take a left onto a dirt road for the 1½-hr. trek to the Spartan **Kallergis refuge huts.** From there, hikers can make a day's climb to the summit of **Pakhnes** or **Mount Ida** (2456m), where Zeus was raised from babyhood. Call the **Greek Alpine Club** (tel. 24 647) in Chania for info.

Buses for Omalos and Xyloskalo leave Chania 4 times per day. When you ask to buy a ticket to Omalos, the ticket office at the bus station will sell you a round-trip ticket from Chania to Omalos and from Chora Sfakion to Chania (1900dr); if you don't plan to return to Chania by bus via Chora Sfakion, ask for a one-way ticket. Since Agia Roumeli is connected by boat to Chora Sfakion, you can make the complete round-trip from Chania in one day, leaving on either of the morning buses. Taking the earliest bus will ensure cooler weather and less company for the hike. Alternatively, plan a leisurely hike and spend the night in a coastal town.

A hot and dusty hike beyond the official exit from the gorge leads to **Agia Roumeli,** a seedy oasis for tired and thirsty hikers. Those 3km aren't entirely terrible, though—think of it as a goat photo-op. Finally you arrive in Agia Roumeli proper, a town with little to show but its beach. The black pebbles are unbearably hot, but the water is refreshing. The town itself exists mainly to sell food, souvenirs, and lodgings for tired, susceptible hikers. If you do stay, you can sleep at **Hotel Livikon,** on the inland end of town. (Singles 4000dr, doubles 5000dr, triples 6000dr.)

■■■ PALEOCHORA ΠΑΛΕΟΧΩΡΑ

Once a refuge for the embattled rear guard of the 1960s counterculture, Paleochora is the only stop for some devotees. Just 77km from Chania, Paleochora has all the elements of a retreat where you'd gratefully languish: a wide, sandy beach with a shady grove and a stunning backdrop of Cretan mountains, one main street with necessities and *tavernas,* and a harbor lined with reasonably priced pensions.

Orientation and Practical Information Paleochora is on a small peninsula. Running north-south through the town center is **Venizelou Street,** the main thoroughfare. It crosses **Kentekaki Street,** which leads west to the beach and east to the harbor. **Buses** to Chania (3 per day, 2hr., 1150dr) stop at this intersection.

The **tourist office** (tel. 41 507; open daily Wed.-Mon., 10am-1pm and 6-9pm) is on Venizelou St., as is a **bank** (open Mon.-Thurs. 8am-2pm, Fri. 8am-1:30pm), and the **OTE** (open Mon.-Sat. 7:30am-11pm, Sun. 3:20-11pm). The **police station** (tel. 41 111) is on Kentekaki, near the quay; **port police** can be reached at 41 214. The **post office** (open Mon.-Fri. 7:30am-2pm) is on the beach next to the Galaxy Café. The **Association of Rooms to Let** (open daily 9am-noon and 5-10pm) is based at Paleochora Travel on Venizelou St. (tel. 41 223). **Paleochora Travel** (tel. 41 589, -250; fax 41 250) can be very helpful (open daily 9am-1pm and 4-10pm). From Paleochora, 1-2 **ferries** per day leave for Elafonisi (1hr., 1140dr), Sougia (30min., 850dr), Ag. Roumeli (1hr., 1900dr), Ch. Sfakion (3hr., 3200dr), Loutro (2¾hr., 2600dr), and Gavdos Island (3½hr., 2800dr). Package deals to Samaria Gorge are also available, which include bus, guide, boat from Ag. Roumeli back to Paleochora, and admission to the site (7000dr). For a taxi, call **Paleochora Taxi Office** (tel. 41 128, -061). The **medical center** sits down the road from Interkreta Travel (from the office, make a right onto the cross street). Look for the sign with the blue cross. (Open Mon.-Fri. mornings until 2pm.) The **pharmacy** is on Venizelou St. (tel. 41 498; open Mon.-Sat. 8:30am-2pm and 5:30-11pm). **Postal Code:** 73001; **Telephone Code:** 0823.

Accommodations Walk along the road closest to the harbor to find small hotels. Stop by Café Alaloom, adjacent to the OTE, to book a room at **Savas Rooms** (tel. 41 075; studios 6000dr), on the outskirts of Paleochora. **Rooms Oriental Bay** (tel. 41 322) is a picturesque alternative: it's right on Rocky Beach as you enter the town (doubles 7000dr, triples 8000dr). **Camping Paleochora** (tel. 41 120), rests 1½km east of town. (Person 600dr, tent 400, moped rental 200; hot showers and a *taverna.* Open Mar.-Oct.) To reach the campground, walk north on Venizelou (away from the harbor), turn right opposite the gas station, and take your second left on the last paved road before the beach. From there it's 1km to the site.

Food and Entertainment Downstairs from Rooms Oriental Bay you'll find drinks and a relaxing meal on the waterfront (beer 350dr, mixed drinks 800dr; delicious lamb chops 1100dr). There are several markets in the center of the town, on Venizelou St. *Tavernas* line the road and have similar menus. **Paleochora Club,** near the camping, is the town's open-air disco (open noon-4am; beer 500dr).

AROUND THE AREA

Six kilometers above Paleochora lies the peaceful town of **Azogizes,** which affords a lovely view of the promontory and the sea. Here you'll find the 13th-century caves of the 99 Holy Fathers and a museum featuring relics of the Turkish occupation dating from 1770. Farther inland, the frescoed churches of Kakodiki date back to the 14th century. These mountain villages can be approached by taking the bus toward Chania. Boats run twice weekly (3hr., 2800dr) to the nearly deserted island of **Gavdos,** the southernmost point of Europe.

The difficult but satisfying journey to miraculous **Elafonissi,** a small uninhabited island at the southwest corner of Crete, must be made on foot. No boats make the crossing, but at low tide the ocean is so shallow that you can wade out to the island. A recent influx of tourists has left this retreat strewn with litter, but the authorities are increasing their efforts to keep it clean. Stock up on provisions ahead of time in Kefali and Vathi; the residents of nearby **Moni Chrisoskalitissis** can provide water and lodgings. **Buses** run daily from Kastelli as far as Chrisoskalitissis (9:30am and 2:30pm, 900dr). From there, a 5km hike leads to a pinkish-white beach. Alternatively, hook up with excursions leaving from Paleochora or Chania.

■■■ SOUTHWEST COAST

Between Agia Roumeli and Chora Sfakion, Loutro reclines in a tiny cove which yawns into the Libyan Sea. Loutro holds the distinction of being the only town in Crete where, in an effort to shield the area from the bad influence of the rest of Europe, topless sunbathing is prohibited. Surrounded by the ocean on one side and austere mountains on the other, the prawn-sized village can be reached only by boat. Because of the logistical difficulties, Loutro is a quiet respite from the south coast and worth seeing for its sheer seclusion. The beach here is rocky, but not entirely uncomfortable. **Ferry** service connects Loutro with Chora Sfakion (4 per day, 390dr) and Ag. Roumeli (3 per day, 620dr).

There are rooms to rent along the cove and, since it takes roughly 4min. to see all of Loutro, it's easy to check them out. Singles are rare but you may be able to bargain with a proprietor. On the west end of the cove, **Vangeli and Giorgo's** rents doubles. Next door, is Loutro's nameless **Hotel,** which also has rooms. East of the kiosk, **Manousos** has similar offerings.

CHORA SFAKION

The scenic town of Chora Sfakion lacks the intimacy of Loutro or Paleochora, but serves as the transportation hub of the south coast. The town's pebbly cove and fishing fleet look tempting from afar, but up close you see that the beach is littered with trash. Chora Sfakion's one strong point, but also its downfall, is that it has frequent bus connections. Since Chora Sfakion lacks the dusty heat that pervades Agia Roumeli, it's an adequate resting spot after the Samaria Gorge hike. The **post office** (open Mon.-Sat. 7:30am-2pm) is next to Sfakia Tours on the waterfront. The **OTE** (open Mon.-Fri. 7:30am-3:15pm) is on the road leading away from town, near where buses leave. The **supermarket** is also on the street behind the harbor; stock up here if you plan a tour of more remote beaches. The **police station** (tel. 91 205; 24 hr.) and **port police** (tel. 91 292) is on the corner of the waterfront near the **bus station** (usually staffed in the hour before a bus departure) and a travel office, **Sfakia Tours** (tel./fax 91 130; open daily 8am-10pm; mopeds 4500dr per day). **Postal Code:** 73001; **Telephone Code:** 0825.

Buses from Chora Sfakion go to Plakias (2 per day, 1¼hr., 800dr) and then to Rethymnon (4 per day, 1½hr., 1200dr) to meet the ferry. At the same time, a bus leaves for Agia Galini (2 per day, 2hr., 1850dr) or Anapolis (4 per day, 30min., 250dr). To get to Iraklion from Chora Sfakion, change buses at Rethymnon. Four buses per day go to Chania (2hr., 1200dr), but be sure to ask the exact time of departure at the station. If your ferry is late, don't worry—the buses wait for the boats arrive. **Boats** from Chora Sfakion travel to Ag. Roumeli (5 per day, 1¼hr.). Most of these routes stop in Loutro. These run only from April to Oct.; in winter, reach Loutro by foot or fishing boat. Always check boat schedules with the ticket office (tel. 91 221). (Chora Sfakion-Gavdos Sat.-Sun. 9am, returning 5pm.) **Caïques** to Sweetwater Beach run twice daily.

There are plenty of inexpensive accommodations here. The cool, grotto-like **Hotel Xenia** (tel. 91 202) has spacious, immaculate rooms. (Singles 6000dr, doubles 8000dr, triples 10,000dr.) **Lefka Ori** (tel. 91 209), on the waterfront, rents singles for 5000dr and doubles with small, dark bathrooms for 6000-10,000dr. **Rooms Samaria** (tel. 91 261), on the east end of the back street, is large and cool, with wrought-iron balconies, but can get buggy. (Open March-Nov.; doubles w/terrace and bath 6000dr; triples 8000dr.)

EASTERN CRETE

The road east from Malia and Hersonissos leads to less frequented, more rewarding territories. The endlessly winding main highway joining Malia and Hersonissos to Agios Nikolaos, Ierapetra, and Sitia is spectacular; it grips the side of the mountains, ascending and descending deep valleys. Its destinations are equally worthwhile: white villages with small green gardens, olive plains and astonishingly blue sea. The area is well-served by buses, making it cheap and amenable to exploration.

■■■ HERSONISSOS ΧΕΡΣΟΝΗΣΟΣ

This port town, 26km east of Iraklion, is free of ancient sites, monasteries, or Cretan village culture. More than 40 bars, discos, and nightclubs cluster in a 500m radius, and the beach is never far away. If you're bored with Iraklion's nightlife, just hop on the bus; you probably don't have to know the Greek words for vodka and orange juice here, considering it's about as Greek as Las Vegas.

ORIENTATION AND PRACTICAL INFORMATION

There is one main road in Hersonissos, **Eleftheriou Venizelou,** with offices, markets, and discos. Perpendicular streets lead to the beach and other parts of town.

Tourist Police: 4 Minoas St. (tel. 22 222, -100), toward the beach in the police station. Some info on Hersonissos. Limited English spoken. Open daily 9am-10pm.
Post Office: 2 Eleftherias St., perpendicular to El. Venizelou. Follow the signs. Open Mon.-Fri. 7:30am-2pm. **Postal Code:** 70014.
OTE: Behind the town hall on Eleftherias St., down El. Venizelou from the post office. Open Mon.-Fri. 8am-2pm. **Telephone Code:** 0897.
Tourist Agencies: Zakros Tours on El. Venizelou (tel./fax 24 715). Open daily 8am-10pm. **Mareland Travel** at 16 Saniudaki St. (tel. 24 424, -6), up the street from the police station. Open daily 8:30am-midnight. Both rent cars, sell boat tickets, exchange money, and have maps.
Banks: There are several banks on El. Venizelou that change money, including the **National Bank** on the east end of the road. Open Mon.-Thurs. 8:30am-2pm, Fri. 8am-1:30pm. The tourist offices also exchange money.
Buses: There are several bus stops in Hersonissos but no central bus station. Buses run east and west every ½hr. Service to Iraklion (45min., 460dr), and from Iraklion via Hersonissos to Malia (1hr., 600dr), Agios Nikolaos (1½hr., 1150dr), Sitia (3¼hr., 2350dr), and Ierapetra (2½hr., 1600dr).
Car and Motorbike Rental: There are several agencies on El. Venizelou.
Taxi: Station (tel. 23 723, 22 098) on the west end of El. Venizelou near the Hard Rock Café. 24 hr.
Laundromat: 188 El Venizelou St. (tel. 23 608). Wash and dry 2200dr.
Public Toilets: Across from Zakros tour office, on El. Venizelou St.
Pharmacies: Several on El. Venizelou. Get off the bus at the first stop in Hersonissos from Iraklion, cross the street, and after 2 or 3 blocks, a pharmacy will be on

your left (tel. 22 473). Open Mon.-Fri. 8am-3pm and 8-11pm. Consult the signs on the doors of any to find one open after hours.

Medical Emergency: Dr. Babis Kokodrulis (tel. 22 063; fax 21 987) has a medical office at El. Venizelou St., opposite the bus stop from Iraklion, before the pharmacy. (Open daily 9am-1pm and 5-10pm.) For emergencies, call his home (22 836) or his mobile phone ((094) 51 71 70). There is also the **Hersonissos Health Center,** 19 El. Venizelou (tel. 25 141), near the Hard Rock Café. 24 hr.

ACCOMMODATIONS

Hersonissos' digs can be pricey and hard to come by. Tour companies book a majority of the rooms for the entire season. Before arriving, consult Iraklion's **"Rooms to Let Association"** (see Iraklion, on p. 195).

Youth Hostel, Plaka-Drapanos (tel. 23 282). Cheap beds and fun owners. No curfew. Roughly a mile from town toward Iraklion; get directions or ask the bus driver to let you off there (1500dr per person).

Selena Pension, 13 Marogaki St. (tel. 22 412), just off Main St. Follow the signs, toward waterfront. Family-run, on a quiet small street. Immaculate modern rooms with private bath. Doubles 7000dr.

Camping: Camping Hersonissos, Anisara (tel. 22 902). Take a bus or walk 3km toward Iraklion; on right. Restaurant, minimarket, bar, hot water. Person 900dr, tent 550dr. **Camping Caravan,** Limenas (tel. 22 025). Walk or take bus 2km east toward Agios Nikolaos until the Nora Hotel, then another 300m. English spoken. Person 1100dr; tent 800dr. Open March-Oct.

FOOD AND ENTERTAINMENT

The Hersonissos waterfront sports the usual assortment of restaurants serving "traditional Greek food." For less commotion try **Selena Restaurant,** beneath Selena Pension (Greek salad 500dr, *tzatziki* 400dr). **Taverna Kavouri** (tel. 21 161) is a thoroughly enjoyable escape from the commercialized waterfront (walking toward Iraklion, turn right onto Irinis kai Filias St. near the Hard Rock Café, and walk around the bend). 15 tables rest under grapevines and among hanging fishing equipment from more physically industrious days. No menu; just go into kitchen and point at whatever looks appealing (such as the chicken for 1500dr). Opens at 6pm.

For daytime entertainment, the **Lychnostatis** (tel. 23 660) open air museum exhibits Cretan houses, and offers windmill, ceramic, and weaving workshops as well as the *in vivo* opportunity to tread grapes or bake pumpkin pie. (Roughly 1km toward Agios Nikolaos. Open Tues.-Sun. 9:30am-2pm for visit and 3 daily guided tours, 2250dr.) Nightlife in Heronissos is "jammin'" as Greeks like to say. The bars and discos that line Main St. and the Paraliakos offer every kind of atmosphere, music, and drink imaginable. Try the **Black Cactus, Quarto** (tel. 23 590; open daily 9pm-6am), and **Prince** (tel. 23 029; open 10:30pm-5am), all on Main St. As the night progresses, hit the bars on Paraliakos and on the waterfront (beer 300dr). The dance floors of **Disco 99** (open 9pm-4:30am) or **La Luna** (tel. 22 014; open 10:30pm-5am), are hipper than your average Greek disco, with a young crowd and murals to complete any evening of hedonism. During the day, most people wake up around noon and head to the beaches to rest up for another night out on the town.

■■■ MALIA ΜΑΛΙΑ

Once hospitable, Malia has been increasingly encroached upon by self-aggrandizing hotels whose neon signs welcome guests in five tongues. The number of advertisements in languages other than Greek is matched only by the number of sandwich boards displaying kitschy photographs of food. Nonetheless, the palatial Minoan site at Malia merits a visit. Make Malia a daytrip or, if you must stay, head straight for Malia's old village, away from the bustling waterfront. It's worth searching out the few remaining peaceful rooms in this mostly unremarkable beach resort.

Orientation and Practical Information The main road from Iraklion (Eleftheriou Venizelou) should satisfy most practical needs, while the path down to the beach, with the discos and watering holes, panders to the primal. The **post office** is off the main street toward Iraklion (look for the sign), behind the church. (Open Mon.-Fri. 7:30am-2pm.) The **National Bank** is just off the main road. Bear left at the first street past the road to the beach. (Open Mon.-Thurs. 8am-2pm, Fri. 8am-1:30pm.) The **OTE** is in the old village; follow signs from 25th Martiou, at the Bimbo Café. (Open Mon.-Fri. 7:30am-3pm.) **Buses** connect Malia with Iraklion via Hersonissos (every ½hr. until 10pm, 1hr., 600dr), Agios Nikolaos (25 per day, ½hr., 550dr), and Lassithi (8:45am, returning at 2pm, 1½hr., 900dr). **Taxis** (tel. 31 777; 24 hr.) idle at the intersection of the main road and the beach path. There's a **laundromat** (tel. 31 709, -61) next to the Malia Holidays Hotel. (Open Mon.-Sat. 9am-8pm; wash and dry 2300dr.) If you require medical assistance, Dr. Tsagari Georgia (tel. 31 529) has a **medical office** on the main road, next to the bus stop, above the market. In case of emergency, call him at home (tel. 31 880), or on his mobile phone (tel. (094) 52 51 42). The **pharmacy** (tel. 31 332) is next to his office (open Mon.-Sat. 9am-10pm, Sun. on rotating basis). **Postal Code:** 70002; **Telephone Code:** 0897.

Accommodations Finding reasonably priced rooms in Malia is a challenge. Unmarked private homes are your best bet. Otherwise, look for the cluster of pensions and "Rooms to Let" in the old village (which you can vaguely wander into off 25th Martiou St.). Walking away from town, after the point where the bus drops you off on the main road, make a right onto 25th Martiou St. to reach **Pension Aspasia** (tel. 31 290), with large, clean, balconied rooms and common baths. (Doubles 6000dr, triples 8000dr.) Or try **Pension Menios,** #2 25th Martiou St. (tel. 31 361), near the corner of the main road. It has new, immaculate rooms and wood furnishings. (Doubles 6000dr, triples 7500dr. Small balconies and private baths.)

Food and Entertainment Eating in Malia is cheap compared with the rest of Crete. Places on the waterfront road serve an English breakfast for 600dr. Many restaurants offer special combination dinners: salad, a main course (typically *mousaka,* lasagna, or chicken), and coffee or *metaxa* brandy, all for 1500dr.

Predictably, the waterfront is the center of Malia's nightlife. Start the mini-pub crawl at the **Picadilly Pub** with a cheap brew (burp!). Brits hang out in Malia's only all-night pub, **Gallia** (burp! burp!) on the road to Iraklion, 15min. past the Mobil Station. Also try **Cloud 9, George's Dancing Bar,** and the **London Pub** (burp!). **Flash Flash** is the flashiest of all. **Aria** is the largest disco in Crete.

Sights The **Minoan Palace** at Malia (tel. 31 597), one of the three great cities of Minoan Crete, lacks the labyrinthine architecture and magnificent interior decoration of Knossos and Phaestos, but is still imposing. First built around 1900 BC, the palace was destroyed in 1650 BC, rebuilt on an even more impressive scale, but then destroyed again around 1450 BC. Notice the **Hall of Columns** on the north side of the large central courtyard, incomprehensibly named for the six columns supporting the roof. The *loggia,* the raised chamber on the west side, was used for state ceremonies. West of the *loggia* are the palace's living quarters and archives. Northwest of the *loggia* and main site slumbers the **Hypostyle Crypt** that may have been a social center for Malia's intelligentsia. Follow the road to Agios Nikolaos 3km to the east and turn left toward the sea, or walk along the beach and then 1km through the fields. (Open Tues.-Sun. 8:30am-3pm; admission 800dr, Sun. free.)

■■■ AGIOS NIKOLAOS ΑΓ. ΝΙΚΟΛΑΟΣ

Overgrown Agios Nikolaos is an appealing mix of humility and pretension. Good ol' St. Nick still retains some of the facets of a low-key fishing village, but has moved closer to the out-of-control mood of a nouveau chic resort town. The town's visitors include beach-obsessed patrons, one-stop holiday-makers, and hikers on their way to more obscure destinations. There are few bargains in Agios Nikolaos or in its satellite beach towns, but the town's intense nightlife, its diverse selection of intriguingly glamourous tourists, and its remnants of indigenous Cretan culture make Agios Nikolaos a lively concoction—a place that's fun without the sense of having been used up and spit out by tourists.

ORIENTATION AND PRACTICAL INFORMATION

It's easy to get around Ag. Nikolaos—the center of town is actually a small peninsula, with beaches on three sides and most services, hotels, restaurants, and discos in the center. If you've just gotten off the bus, walk to the end of the block (with the terminal on your right), and take the first right. Follow **Venizelou Street** to the monument, where it leads into **Roussou Koundourou,** which heads downhill to the harbor. The tourist office is to the left, across the bridge. Don't confuse the overly nepotistic streets: R. Koundourou, I. Koundourou, and S. Koundourou St.

Tourist Office: 22 S. Koundourou St. (tel. 22 357). At the bridge between the lake and the port. Knowledgeable staff finds rooms. Messages, currency exchange, bus and boat schedules, and a free brochure with town map and practical info. Open Apr.-Oct. daily 8:30am-9:30pm.

Police: (tel. 22 321). Cops share the **Tourist Police** building (tel. 26 900). Follow 28th Octovriou St. past Venizelou Sq. until it becomes G. Kontoghianni St. After a good 10-min. walk, it will be on the right-hand side of the street.

Post Office: #9 28th Octovriou St. (tel. 22 276). Open Mon.-Fri. 7:30am-8pm, Sat. 7:30am-2pm. **Postal Code:** 72100.

OTE: (tel. 28 099). Corner of 25th Martiou and K. Sfakianaki St. 3 blocks east of the lake. Open 6am-midnight; Nov.-May 6am-10:30pm. **Telephone Code:** 0841.

Banks: National Bank of Greece (tel. 28 855), at the top of R. Koundourou St., near Venizelou Sq. Open for exchange Mon.-Thurs. 8am-2pm, Fri. 8am-1:30pm.

Flights: Olympic Airways (tel. 22 033), is on Plastira St. overlooking the lake. Open Mon.-Fri. 9am-4pm. Closest airports are at Iraklion and Sitia.

Buses: (tel. 22 234). Atlandithos Sq., the opposite side of town from the harbor. To Iraklion via Malia (24 per day, 1½hr., 1150dr), Lassithi (2 per day, 2½hr., 1550dr), Ierapetra (8 per day, 1hr., 600dr), Sitia (6 per day, 1½hr., 1200dr), and Kritsa (12 per day, 15min., 180dr). Buses to Elounda (15 per day, 20min., 180dr) and Plaka (6 per day, 40min., 280dr) leave from the stop opposite the tourist office.

Ferries: Massaros, 29 R. Koundourou St. (tel. 22 267). Air and ferry tickets for departures from Ag. Nikolaos and Crete. Open Mon.-Sat. 9am-3pm and 6-9pm, Sun. 10am-3pm. For ferries to Piraeus, the Greek Islands, Cyprus, and Israel, cross the street to **Nostos Tours** (tel. 22 819). Open daily 8am-9:30pm.

Car Rental: Economy Car Hire, 15 S. Koundourou St. (tel. 28 988); also an office at 5 K. Sfakianaki St. Fiat Panda 24,000dr for 3 days, unlimited mileage, and insurance included. Also rents motorbikes.

Motorbike Rental: Adonis, on S. Koundourou, near the Perikleous St. intersection, rents 50cc mopeds for 3000dr, 100cc for 4000dr, insurance included. (Open daily 8am-8pm.) There are lots of agencies—shop around and bargain.

International Bookstores: Anna Karteri, 5 R. Koundourou St. (tel. 22 272). Huge selection of English books, as well as German and French. Open Mon.-Fri. 8am-10pm, Sat. 8am-2pm.

Pharmacy: At the top of R. Koundourou St. Open Mon.-Fri. 8am-2pm and 5:30-9:30pm. Check on doors for lists of those open on weekends.

Hospital: Paleologou St. (tel. 25 221), at the north end of town. From the lake, walk up Paleologou St., 1 block past the museum.

ACCOMMODATIONS

As a result of Agios Nikolaos' popularity, many of the better hotels are booked months in advance by European tour groups, and the few cheap places in town have a slow turnover rate. Neighboring tourist beach resorts, and even pensions, have been similarly affected. If you plan a long stay in town, arrive early in the day or make reservations. Prices 20-40% less in off-season.

Argiro Pension, 1 Solonos St. (tel. 28 707). From the tourist office, walk up 25th Martiou and turn left onto Manousogianaki. After four blocks, go right onto Solonos. Unsullied, cool rooms in a huge, stately old house with a serene, jasmine-scented garden and a kind owner, Koula, who provides a fridge for guests. Quiet, yet close to town. Doubles 4500dr.

The Green House, 15 Modatsou St. (tel. 22 025). From the tourist office, turn left onto R. Koundourou, left again onto Iroon Polytechniou, and right onto Modatsou. Relax in the shady, tangled garden. If you're lucky, you'll get homemade Italian ice from the multilingual proprietors. Doubles 4000dr.

Christodoulakis Pension, 7 Stratigou Koraka St. (tel. 22 525). Spotless rooms, kitchen facilities, and friendly proprietors. Singles 3000dr, doubles 5000dr.

Pension Perla, 4 Salaminos St. (tel. 23 379). Big rooms, some with balconies and ocean views. Comfortable TV lounge. Singles (negotiable) 3500dr, doubles 7200dr, triples 9000dr; breakfast 750dr. Owner also manages **Pension Adonis.**

FOOD AND ENTERTAINMENT

Restaurants are expensive here. If you don't mind relaxed service, go to **Stelio's,** at the bridge, for a dazzling harborside view and excellent *tzatziki* (500dr). Next door, at the **Actaion,** fish dishes start at 1200dr. (Open 10am-11pm.) The **New Kow Loon Chinese Restaurant,** 1 Pasifais St. (tel. 23 891), serves decent cuisine. (Open daily noon-3pm and 7pm-1am.) The **Embassy Indian and European Cuisine,** 5 I. Kondilaki St. (tel. 24 775), near the taxi stand, offers a huge variety of vegetarian and side dishes at reasonable prices (vegetable *samosa* 800dr, nan bread 450dr). It also offers meat lasagna (1500dr) and shepherd's pie (1300dr) for that European carnivore in you. (Open daily 6pm-2am.) For a sensational view of the sun setting over the harbor, have a long drink at the **Mediterraneo Terrace Bar,** near the building with the huge "Lipstick Bar" sign. This sophisticated oasis also offers dinner (at a king's ransom), but stick to the drink and blend into the atmosphere.

For nightlife, stroll around the harbor on I. Koundourou St., or walk up 25th Martiou St. The **Tequila Bar** and the **Sorrento Bar** on the waterfront, are good places to warm up before hitting the dance floors. (Beer 500dr.) **Charlie Chan's** nightclub is farther down on the waterfront (beer 500dr, mixed drinks 700dr during happy hour 11pm-2am). **Sixties,** on R. Koundourou, has nostalgic tunes and friendly bartenders.

SIGHTS

According to legend, Artemis and Athena bathed at the "bottomless" lake, **Xepatomeni,** near the tourist office (it is actually 64m deep). In 1867, the regional governor dug a canal linking the lake with the sea, creating a perpetual flushing mechanism. Three beaches are within easy walking distance of the main harbor. With minimal effort, you can sunbathe on the concrete piers which jut out from S. Koundourou St. To reach a better spot, catch an hourly bus headed to Ierapetra or Sitia and get off at **Almiros Beach,** 2km east of Agios Nikolaos. The sandy beach at **Kalo Chorio,** 10km farther along the same road, is less crowded. Get off the bus headed for either Sitia or Ierapetra at the Kavos Taverna (tell the driver to stop).

For more cerebral pursuits, visit one of Ag. Nikolaos' two museums, or see if anything's playing at the theater on M. Sfakianaki St. The **Archaeological Museum** (tel. 24 943), just outside the center of town, a few blocks down the road from Iraklion, houses a modest collection of Minoan artifacts. (Open Tues.-Sun. 8:30am-3pm; admission 500dr.) The **Folk Art Museum,** in the tourist office's building, displays tapestries and embroidered clothes. (Open Sun.-Fri. 10am-1:30pm and 6-930pm; admission 200dr; free on Sun.) To shop for inexpensive clothes, visit the weekly **market** on Ethnikis Antistassios St., next to the lake. (Open Wed. 7am-noon.)

■ NEAR AGIOS NIKOLAOS: KRITSA

Although it is only 9km from upscale Agios Nikolaos, the hilltop village of Kritsa seems worlds apart. Every balcony and rooftop is trimmed with vines and ripening fruit; under their shade, women weave blankets and embroider blouses. Many of the homemade crafts are embarrassingly cheap. Be choosy when buying, however, because, even here, some items are imported from Taiwan. The unloading buses of tourists are an unfortunate reminder of your proximity to Agios Nikolaos, but the buses come only for a short time; nightfall restores serenity to the town.

The **post office** is above the square to the right. (Open Mon.-Sat. 7:30am-2pm, Sun. 9am-1:30pm.) An **international phone** is in Koutoulakis Snack Bar in the square. (Open 7am-9pm.) **Buses** run hourly between Agios Nikolaos and Kritsa (15 per day, 30min., 170dr). In summer, afternoon buses to Kritsa fill up quickly; arrive early. **Postal Code:** 72051; **Telephone Code:** 0841.

The archaeological site of **Gournia-Minoan Palace** is located 1.9km from Agios Nikolaos. Take the bus heading to Ierapetra or Sitia—ask the driver to stop there. (Open Tues.-Sun. 9am-3pm; admission 800dr.) One kilometer before Kritsa on the road from Agios Nikolaos, Crete's Byzantine treasure, the **Panagia Kera,** honors the Dormition of the Virgin. The interior of the domed church is adorned with a patchwork of smoky 14th-century paintings in the central nave, and 15th-century Byzantine frescoes in the adjoining wings. (Open Mon.-Sat. 9am-3pm, Sun. 9am-2pm; admission 350dr, students 250dr; free on Sun.)

■■■ IERAPETRA ΙΕΡΑΠΕΤΡΑ

Ierapetra aims for the glitz and the neon glamour of resort towns, but it hasn't quite mastered the technique. Instead, Ierapetra sits in tourism's rare *purgatorio:* it teeters between the cosmopolitan and the rural. Its inhabitants are simple and hospitable, hoping to draw visitors to nearby unspoiled beaches and villages. But Ierapetra has not managed to attract the masses of visitors it craves.

Ierapetra's star attraction is its remote island, **Chrisi,** eight nautical miles from the mainland. One small ferry goes there at 10:30am and returns at 5pm (4500dr). Free from stores, and crowds, Chrisi is completely flat, adorned by green pine, and surrounded by transparent green sea. Pack a lunch and bring water; you won't even find a small market, though there is a lone *taverna* located near the dock

Orientation and Practical Information Most of Ierapetra's services are on the streets parallel to the waterfront. The **police station** (tel. 22 560) is on the waterfront, a few blocks before Eleftherias Sq. (24 hr.) The **port police** (tel. 22 294) are near the excursion boat port. The **National Bank,** in Eleftherias Sq., is across the street from Ierapetra Express. (Open Mon.-Thurs. 8am-2pm, Fri. 8am-1:30pm.) In Kothri Sq., five blocks west of the bus station toward the port, is the **post office,** 3 Stilianou Hota St. (Open Mon.-Fri. 7:30am-2pm.) The **OTE** is at 25 Koraka St., three blocks from the water. (Open Mon.-Fri. 7:30am-10pm.) **Tourist agencies** on the street parallel to the water distribute free city maps. A helpful source of info is the **Ierapetra Express office,** 24 Eleftherias Sq. (tel. 28 673 or 22 411; open Mon.-Sat. 8am-2pm and 5-9pm, Sun. 8:30am-1pm and 5-9pm.) **Olympic Airways** (tel. 22 444) is on Plaka Venizelou. (Open Mon.-Fri. 8:30am-1:30pm and 6-8:30pm, Sat. 8:30am-1:30pm.) The **bus station** (tel. 28 237) is on Losthenous St. To get to the waterfront from there, head past the palm tree and you'll see signs for the beach. **Taxis** line up in Venizelou Sq. and by the bus station. Rentals in Ierapetra are expensive; for daytrips, try **Galaxie Moto** (tel. 25 374), 18 Metaxaki St. (50cc bikes 3000dr per day, 80cc 5000dr; open 8am-9pm). **Europlan,** 39 M. Kothri St. (tel. 26 771), rents cars (25,000dr, 3 days, unlimited km). The **hospital** (tel. 22 488) is left off Losthenous St., towards Agios Nikolaos. The town has several **pharmacies,** including one in Eleftherias Sq. (tel. 22 236). (Open Mon.-Fri. 8am-2pm and 5:30-9pm.) Check notice posted on door for a weekend pharmacy. **Postal Code:** 72200; **Telephone Code:** 0842.

Accommodations Try **Cretan Villa,** 16 Lakerda St. (tel. 28 522). Look for signs at the bus station. The drab exterior of the 200-year-old building hides a cool garden surrounded by beautiful, high-ceilinged rooms. The owner, a University of Missouri alum, speaks fluent English. The rooms are a bit pricey, but worth your while. (Singles 5000dr, doubles 7000dr; all-you-can-eat breakfast 1000dr.) **Pension Diagoras** (tel. 23 898, -218), 1 Kyvra St., is above café-bar Diagoras on the waterfront. These are immaculate rooms with balconies. (Singles 4000dr; doubles 6000dr.) Two neighboring campgrounds, **Ierapetra** (tel. 61 351) and the new **Koutsounari** (tel. 61 213), 9km away on the coastal road to Sitia, both charge 1000dr per person, 800dr per tent. Each has a restaurant, bar, and beach. Take the bus to Sitia via Makri Gialo (7 per day) and ask to be let off at the campgrounds.

Food Nearly all of Ierapetra's restaurants lie on the waterfront and feature identical prices (*mousaka* 830dr). Among the generic, touristy *tavernas,* the **Cafe Ouzerie Sympathy** is exceptional in all senses. No pictures of food; just the open-air grill and tantalizing aroma of broiling octopus (1200dr). Don't miss the lobsters, yanked from the sea at your request. (Open 9am-2pm and 5-10pm.) Most of the town's shops and stores stand one block from the waterfront on Kountourioti St.

Sights There are loads of historical sights in Ierapetra; unfortunately, most are closed. Locals laud **Napoleon's House,** in the old town, where the French commander supposedly spent the night on June 26, 1798, en route to Egypt to battle the Mamluks. The restored **Venetian fortress** (*Kales*), at the extreme south end of the old harbor, was begun in the early 13th century and now slowly crumbles into the sea (closed). Also in the old town is a **mosque** and an **Ottoman fountain,** built near the end of the 19th century. Ierapetra's **Archaeological Museum,** on the waterfront, has a small collection of Minoan and classical artifacts from the south coast. (Open Tues.-Sat. 9am-3pm; admission 400dr, students 200dr.) Nightlife in Ierapetra is low-key. There are a few bars (**Bar Alexander** attracts mostly locals and plays good Greek music) and one disco, **Zanadu,** on the lively waterfront.

■■■ SITIA ΣΗΤΕΙΑ

A scenic drive on coastal and mountain roads from Agios Nikolaos leads to Sitia, a sleepy fishing and port town. The wave of tourism that has engulfed the coast from Iraklion to Agios Nikolaos slows to a trickle before Sitia. Use Sitia as your base for exploring Crete's east coast, including Vai, the Toplou Monastery, and Kato Zakros.

ORIENTATION AND PRACTICAL INFORMATION

To get to the center of the waterfront from the bus station, head for the sign for Vai and Kato Zakros, then bear left. Dimokritou and Venizelou intersect with the waterfront at the square where you will find a small palm-treed traffic island, Sitia's restaurant strip, and several kiosks.

Tourist Police: 24 Mykonos St. (tel. 24 200). From the square walk straight and take your second left. After 1½ blocks, it will be on your left. Open 7:30am-2:30pm. **Police:** (tel. 22 266, -59). Same location. 24 hr.

Post Office: Main branch, 2 Ethnikis Antistasis St. (tel. 22 283). From the bus station, walk south and follow the road around to the right. Open Mon.-Fri. 7:30am-2pm. **Postal Code:** 72300.

OTE: 22 Capitan Sifis St. Go to the main square on the waterfront, turn inland at the National Bank, and walk uphill 2 blocks. Open Mon.-Sat. 7:30am-10pm. **Telephone Code:** 0843.

Banks: National Bank of Greece, in Venizelou Sq. opposite the statue of a soldier encircled by palm trees, offers **currency exchange.** Open Mon.-Thurs. 8am-2pm, Fri. 8am-1:30pm.

Flights: Go to Karpathos (1½hr., 7600dr), Kassos (1hr., 7600dr) and Rhodes via Karpathos (16,200dr plus 3000dr airport tax). There are also flights to Athens (3 per week, 21,000dr). **Olympic Airways,** 56 Eleftheriou Venizelou St. (tel. 22 270), is off the main square to the east. Open Mon.-Sat. 8am-1:30pm and 5-9pm. No buses to airport. Taxis cost 400dr for the 1km uphill ride.

Buses: 4 Karamo St. (tel. 22 272), on the east end of the waterfront. To Agios Nikolaos (6 per day, 1½hr., 1200dr), Iraklion (5 per day, 3¼hr., 2350dr), Ierapetra (5 per day, 1½hr., 1000dr), Vai (3-4 per day, 1hr., 480dr), and Kato Zakros (2 per day, 1hr., 850dr).

Ferries: The *Kornaros* travels weekly to Kassos (4hr., 2300dr) and Karpathos (5hr., 2300dr) and 3 per week to Piraeus (16-17hr., 4880dr) via Agios Nikolaos (1½hr., 1323dr) and Milos (7-8hr., 2788dr). **Porto Belis Travel,** 3 Karamanli St. (tel. 22 370), near the bus station, provides ferry and rooms info, airplane tickets, car and moped rentals, and currency exchange. Open daily 8:30am-9pm. Reduced hours in off-season.

Taxi: (tel. 22 893). Congregate in Venizelou Sq.

Car Rental: Sitia Rent-a-Car, 4-6 Itanou (tel. 23 770, -030), first left walking towards town from bus station. Fiat Panda 8500dr per day, 30dr per km over 100km. Open daily 9am-1pm and 3-9pm.

Moped Rental: Petras (tel. 24 849), on Ithanou up the block from Sitia Rent-a-Car. Vespa 80-100cc for 1800-4500dr. Open 8am-8pm.

Pharmacies: Many on streets behind waterfront. Go straight from the square up 1½ blocks, on the left. Open Mon. and Wed. 8am-1:30pm, Tues. and Thurs.-Fri. 8am-1:30pm and 5:30-8:30pm. Check signs posted on front doors for pharmacy open on weekends.

Hospital: 28 Capitan Sifis St. (tel. 24 311), at the corner of Arkadiou. 24 hr.

ACCOMMODATIONS

It is difficult to find rooms in July and Aug., but during mid-Aug., when the Sultana Festival is held, it is nearly impossible. Off-season prices are 20-40% less. The youth hostel is friendly and informal, but for more privacy, head for the two areas in Sitia where you'll find budget rooms—along the main road up to the hostel, and in the back streets at the west end of the waterfront, especially Kornarou and Kondilaki St.

Youth Hostel, 4 Therissou St. (tel. 22 693). From the bus station, take a left on Ithanou (after road bends it becomes Papanastasiou), follow until the BP gas station, where road becomes Therissou, and uphill another 100m on the left. There's a kitchen and an outdoor garden. Only 50 beds, but you may be able to sleep on the veranda or the floor. Calm and clean under new management. Reception open 9am-1pm and 6-9pm; if no one is around, find a bed and register later. Hot water all day. Open year-round. 1200dr per person.

Venus "Rooms to Let," 60 Kondilaki St. (tel. 24 307). Walk uphill from the OTE and take your first right. Green courtyard, sunny rooms with balconies, and kitchen facilities. A true bargain. Clean shared baths. Tiny singles 3500dr, doubles 4500dr, triples 7000dr. Friendly owner speaks English, German, and French.

"Rooms to Let" Apostolis, 27 Kazantazis St. (tel. 22 993 or 28 172). Clean, pleasant rooms with private baths. Large balcony with shaded tables and potted plants. Wash basin and lines. Doubles 6000dr, triples 8000dr. Reservations suggested.

FOOD AND ENTERTAINMENT

Sitia's restaurants specialize in fresh fish and lobster. **Zorba's** (tel. 22 689), on the west side of the harbor, has a variety of good, moderately priced entrees (*mousaka* 800dr). **Taverna Panorama** (tel. 25 160) in neighboring Agia Fotia on the road to Paliokastro and Vai, serves home-cooked traditional Cretan dishes. The menu varies daily, but specialties include octopus cooked in red wine and tomato sauce, fresh fish, and grape leaves. It is usually only open for dinner, but call ahead. The *taverna* is run by a kindly couple, out of their own kitchen. Fountalidou St., off N. Katzanakis St., has numerous fruit shops and small markets.

During the middle of August, Sitia hosts the **Sultana Festival,** which features unlimited wine, dancing, and music for roughly 2000dr. Nightlife is not Sitia's strong point, but one exception is the **Planetarium Disco,** mountainside, 2km west of 2nd pier on a sweeping balcony. The 1500dr cover includes first drink. (Open 1am-sunrise.) **De Sitia Peris** is a "garden bar" in Sitia—walk past all of the *tavernas* on the harbor—it's near the end. 1000dr cover includes first drink. (Open 10pm-4am.)

SIGHTS

Life in Sitia centers around the waterfront. Much of the old quarter is terraced along the hillside on the west part of the city. The **fortress** at the hilltop provides a view of the town and the city's bay. The town's **beach,** extending, 3km east of Sitia toward Petra, is next to the road. Its distant end is usually empty.

The **Archaeological Museum** (tel. 23 917) houses a small collection from nearby sights. Take a left on Ithanou. When you come to the sign for Iraklion, take a left on the road to Ierapetra. Be sure to note the Late Minoan Paliokastro Kouros statuette, perhaps one of the very first representations of Zeus. (Open Tues.-Sun. 8:30am-3pm; admission 500dr, students 300dr, free on Sun.) The **Folklore Museum,** 13 Therissou St. (tel. 22 861), is on the road to Iraklion roughly 50m before the youth hostel. This is a new address; old signs may direct you the wrong way. There are underfrequented displays of 19th-century tapestries, beddings, icons, and various contraptions. (Open Mon.-Fri. 9:30am-3pm, Sat. 9:30am-3pm; admission 300dr.)

■ NEAR SITIA

Toplou's monks, under siege by pirates and Turks for centuries, carefully armed their **monastery**. Their efforts went for naught in 1471, when the entire complex fell to the Turks who destroyed it. The rebuilt structure now contains a number of relics, including the 2nd-century BC inscription of a treaty between the Cretan cities of Itanos and Ierapetra and the province of Magnesia in Asia Minor, and elaborate icons by the 18th-century master Ioannis Kournaros. Dress appropriately (pants for men, long skirts for women). The monks lend clothes if need be. **Buses** do not go to the monastery; get off the Vai bus 12km outside Sitia at the *Moni Toplou* turnoff, and walk the last 3km. Drivers follow the road east from Sitia along the coast and turn at the junction. (Open daily 9am-1pm and 2-6pm; admission 400dr.)

Not long ago, tourists headed east to the sylvan palm beach at **Vai** for refuge from Sitia's crowds. Today, several buses roll into this outpost every day, depositing tourists eager to ponder Europe's only natural palm forest. Legend has it that the forest is the legacy of the Arabs who conquered Crete in the 9th century. It's worth battling the mobs for your gorgeous piece of beach. A restaurant and café serve the beach, but there are no accommodations. (Park open 7am-9pm; free.) Most travelers visit Vai via the crowded public bus from Sitia. Buses leave Sitia and stop at Paliokastro en route to Vai (4 per day; 1hr.; Sitia-Vai 440dr, Paliokastro-Vai 180dr).

Camping is forbidden in the park itself, but many people unfurl sleeping bags in the cove to the south of the palm beach. If sandy pajamas and the possibility of arrest don't appeal to you, rent a room in quiet Paliokastro, a town 8km back toward Sitia. Whenever you start to long for hoards of people, cheesy umbrella-shaded drink tables, and the aroma of cocoa butter, head for Vai. A **tourist office** and **currency exchange** center is located in the parking lot (open daily 11am-6pm; closed Nov.-Mar.). A tourist shop and refreshment stand are located by the palm tree-studded entrance. When the *au naturel* method of beaching becomes passé, check out the **watersports** on the far end of the beach. (Jet skis 5000dr for 15min., water skis 4000dr for 10min., banana boats 2500dr per person for 15min. or 2000dr per person when you come with your gang, para-diving 8000dr for 10min., and pedal boats 2000dr per hour.) There is also a **scuba diving center** (tel. (0843) 71 548). At the Vai tourist shop, inquire about the nearby **Open Air Banana Plantations and Sub-Tropical Cultivations** (tel. (0843) 61 353). An old sea captain gives tours in German, English, French, and Greek. (Open Apr.-Oct. 8am-8pm; admission 800dr, group rate 600dr.) Just beyond Vai, **Itanos Beach** is much more mellow and secluded. Do the Minoan thing and explore the beachside archaeological site.

PALIOKASTRO

This lazy, dreamy village is the perfect place to use as a base for exploring eastern Crete. Its majestic beaches and serene landscape make up for the virtual lack of anything else to do. If you're into olive trees, bring a camera.

Orientation and Practical Information Paliokastro's square contains all necessities in just a few buildings. The **police** (tel. 61 222) stand guard, ready for action, above the tourist souvenir shop. Unexpectedly, the village's most brilliant resource is the **OTE** (tel. 61 225). The diligent staff exchanges money, sells stamps, hands out free maps, suggests area excursions, and helps tourists find rooms. Incidentally, they also have two metered phones and sell phone cards. (Open daily 9am-10pm; Nov.-Mar. 9am-1pm and 5-8:30pm.) One phone card machine is located in the square behind the fountain, the other is across the street from Kastri Pizza, where the only road in town forks off to the left. **Buses** run from Sitia to Paliokastro (3-4 per day, ½hr., 350dr) and continue on to Vai (1hr., 480dr). A taxi from Sitia costs 2500dr. The **Hotel Hellas** (tel. 61 240) rents **motorbikes,** and, not surprisingly, **Lion Cars** (tel. 61 482) rents cars. A cheese and meat shop, two small fruit and food stores, and a bakery are behind the Hotel Hellas, near the church. **Postal Code:** 72300; **Telephone Code:** 0843.

Accommodations **Yiannis Perrakis,** a kind-hearted Greek and German-speaking villager, and his wife run one of the loveliest pensions in town (tel. 61 310). When you get off the bus, follow the road which forks to the right. Look for greenhouse-enclosed banana trees on your right; the pension is up the gravel path on the left. Lemon trees and magenta flowers invite you to immaculate, bright, beautiful rooms. (Singles 2500dr, doubles 4000dr, triples 4500dr; prices lower off-season.) Alternatively, the **Thalia Hotel** (tel. 61 448, -217) is equally clean and pleasant. From the square, go past the church and *gyro* stand. The pension will be on your right. (Doubles 5500dr, triples 6600dr; breakfast 750dr; closed off-season.)

Food and Entertainment A handful of *tavernas* cluster in Paliokastro's tiny square. The **Hotel Hellas** serves standard Greek food. A **sweet shop** is next to the bus stop, near the Hotel Itanos. Locals know that the best music and atmosphere can be found at the **Enigma Bar.** From the square, follow the left fork of the road on the way to Vai. A young, chic Euro-crowd frequents the **Design Bar,** a glittery disco replete with pink exterior, strobe lights, and shimmery fountain. Paliokastro, and neighboring Agathia, are divine places to try *raki,* the indigenous moonshine of Crete. Sip it slowly; it comes in thimble-sized glasses for a reason.

Sights If you've got a beach fetish, you've come to the right place. For sizzling and swimming in the immediate area, orient yourself around **Kastri Hill** (the mysteriously sloping land mass by the sea). A 25-min. walk (although only enchanting for the first 5min.) through a labyrinthine path of silvery olive groves leads to either **Kouremenos Beach** (on the left side of Kastri) or **Chiona Beach** (on the right). Kouremenos is the site of the **Nathalie Simon (French) Windsurfing Club.** Eastern Crete kicks up quite a wind at times, and conditions are said to be great during the summer. For priority reservations, contact the Paris office (tel. (33-1) 46 56 79 79; fax 46 56 51 55). Otherwise, wait until you get there and inquire at the OTE (560francs for 10hrs., 80francs for 1hr., 1½hr. lesson 175F). Chiona Beach has its advantages as well: two stellar *tavernas* await you after a long hard day at the beach.

Alas, when that twinge of cerebral guilt strikes, stop by the archaeological site of **Roussolakos,** near Chiona Beach. Three series of excavations, begun in 1902, continue to this day. Follow the well-marked signs posted throughout the "seven buildings" of the site, which dates to 3000-2000 BC. Make sure to notice the **Minoan Hall** (Polytheon), the well-planned architecture, and the site of the discovery of the Paliokastro Kouros and sealstone. If you just can't get enough of this stuff, hike to the top of Petsofas and commune with the gods of the **Minoan peak sanctuary.**

Cyclades ΚΥΚΛΑΔΕΣ

"Happy is the man, I thought, who, before dying, has the good fortune to sail the Aegean Sea."

—Nikos Kazantzakis

Chances are, when people speak longingly of the Greek islands, they're talking about the Cyclades. Whatever your idea of the Aegean—winding cobblestone streets and whitewashed houses, *ouzo* sipped seaside during warm sunsets, inebriated revelry—you can find it here. The islands can be grouped into three broad categories. Although each has quiet villages and untouched spots, Mykonos, Santorini, and Ios are known to all as the party islands and are the most heavily touristed. Of these three, Mykonos is the most chic and most expensive; Santorini runs a close second in sophistication (and price), but also offers an impressive history and some of the most spectacular views in all of Greece. Ios can be summed up in four words: American frat party run amok (all right, that was five words, but after a week on Ios you won't be able to count either). Paros, Naxos, and Amorgos are also popular, but are less frantic and more pristine. Syros, Tinos, Andros, Kea, Kithnos, Serifos, Sifnos, and Milos get few foreign visitors, and are primarily dependent on Greeks tourists. If you visit during the winter, you may be the only foreigner on some of these islands. (Be forewarned that tourist amenities on many of these islands, especially accommodations, are open April through October only).

MYKONOS ΜΥΚΟΝΟΣ

Mykonos has been an object of envy and desire ever since the 18th century, when pirates vied for the right to lounge on the island's long, blonde beaches. Mykonos today is chic and sleek, playing host to sophisticated revelers who retain a strong sense of history and culture. Temptation abounds on this island, where gold-filled shop windows and pricey restaurants aimed at a wealthier crowd nonetheless capture the imagination of those who can least afford it. After several years of decline, Mykonos' gay scene has begun to regain the acclaim which made it the hottest spot for gays in the Mediterranean. A word of caution: don't pester Petros the Pelican, the island's mascot. According to one popular tale, Petros was killed several years ago when a couple of tourists tried to procreate with him. The story is not true, but please let Petros find his own mate. After all, besides the obvious difficulties of forming a truly meaningful relationship with a pelican, he bites.

■■■ MYKONOS TOWN

If you stay in Mykonos long enough, chances are you will spend at least one drunken evening lost in Mykonos Town's maze of endless, winding alleys lined with indistinguishable whitewashed buildings. These labyrinthine streets, closed to motor traffic, were created to disconcert and disorient pirates. Despite the influx of tourists, the town has resisted large hotel complexes. Fishing boats in the harbor, basket-laden donkeys, drag queens, high-fashion models, and Petros the Pelican help preserve the town's authentic charm. Nonetheless, Mykonos is unmistakably a tourist town. Depending on your degree of homesickness, you will either exult or grieve over the availability of cheeseburgers, milkshakes, fish and chips, Chinese food, and "English breakfasts." Don't come to Mykonos to experience unadulterated Greek culture; come instead to witness an unstoppable world of Dionysian delight.

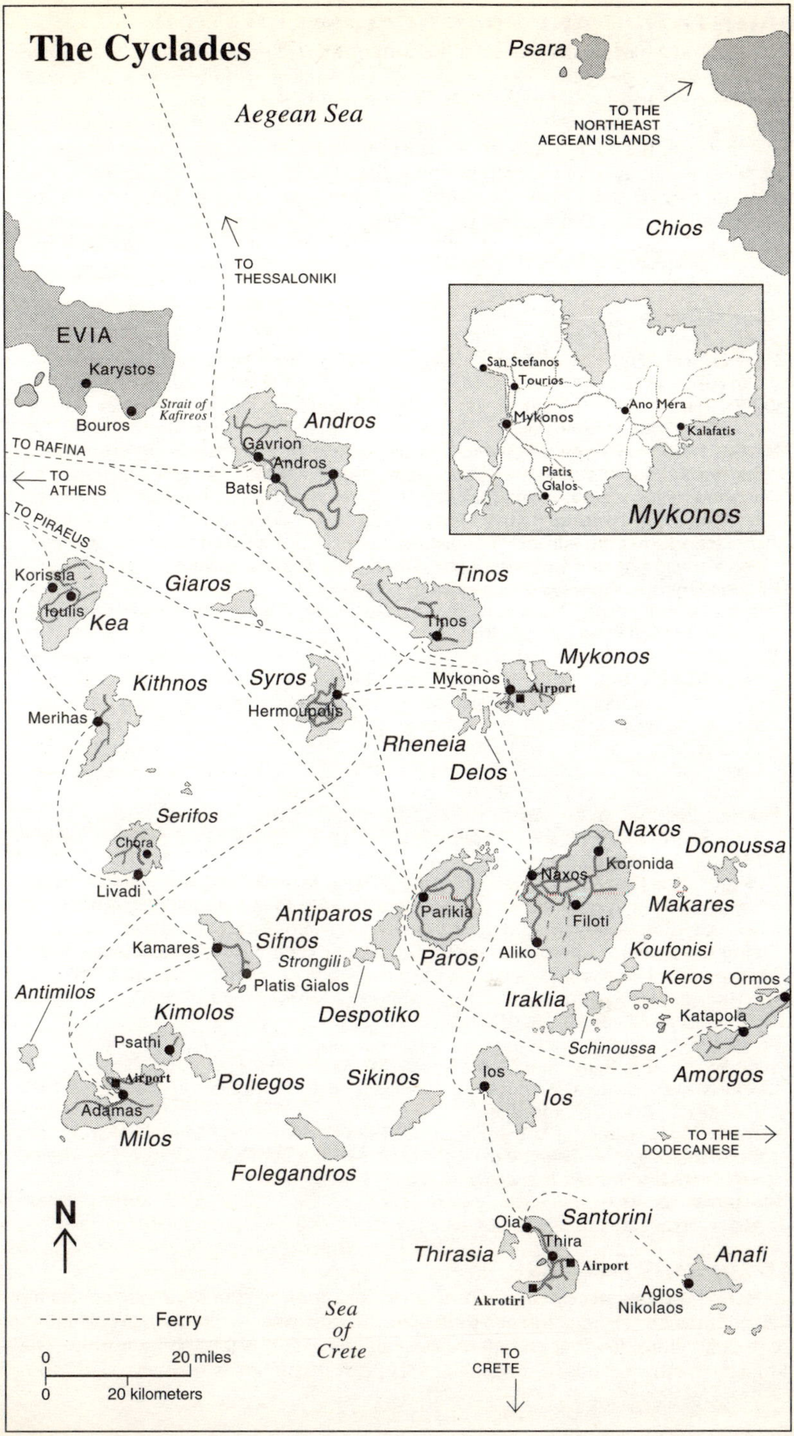
The Cyclades
Aegean Sea
Psara
TO THE NORTHEAST AEGEAN ISLANDS
Chios
TO THESSALONIKI
EVIA
Karystos
Bouros
Strait of Kafireos
Andros
Gavrion
Andros
Batsi
TO RAFINA
TO ATHENS
TO PIRAEUS
Korissia
Ioulis
Kea
Giaros
Tinos
Tinos
Mykonos
Mykonos
Airport
Syros
Hermoupolis
Kithnos
Merihas
Rheneia
Delos
Serifos
Chora
Livadi
Naxos
Naxos
Koronida
Donoussa
Makares
Filoti
Aliko
Parikia
Paros
Antiparos
Sifnos
Kamares
Strongili
Platis Gialos
Despotiko
Koufonisi
Keros
Ormos
Katapola
Iraklia
Schinoussa
Amorgos
Antimilos
Kimolos
Psathi
Airport
Poliegos
Adamas
Milos
Sikinos
Ios
Ios
Folegandros
TO THE DODECANESE
Santorini
Oia
Thira
Airport
Akrotiri
Thirasia
Anafi
Agios Nikolaos
N
Ferry
0 20 miles
0 20 kilometers
Sea of Crete
TO CRETE
San Stefanos
Tourios
Mykonos
Ano Mera
Kalafatis
Platis Gialos
Mykonos

ORIENTATION AND PRACTICAL INFORMATION

Boats dock at a pier on the far left of the waterfront (facing inland). One road leads along the water past the town beach to **Taxi Square** and the center of town. Another road heads uphill to the **"North Station"** bus depot, then wraps around Mykonos Town to the **"South Station"** on the opposite side. Everything you need or want is near the waterfront—banks, travel agencies, shops, cafés, *tavernas,* bars, and discos—but much of the real shopping, fine dining, and partying goes on in the infamous narrow, winding back streets (especially Matogianni, Kalogera, Mitropoleas, and Enoplon Dinameon). On the right side is another pier for excursion boats. Past the pier is a series of churches, the lovely part of town called **Little Venice,** and a small hill with a line of five windmills.

Tourist Police: (tel. 22 482). In an office at the ferry landing. Open daily 8am-3pm and 7-9pm. For town police, call 22 235. 24 hr.

Post Office: (tel. 22 238). Two blocks to the left (facing inland), on the waterfront. **Currency exchange.** Open Mon.-Fri. 7:30am-2pm. **Postal Code:** 84600.

OTE: (tel. 22 499). Far left of the waterfront, uphill from the ferry dock. Open Mon.-Fri. 7:30am-midnight, Sat.-Sun. 8:30am-11pm. **Telephone Code:** 0289.

Banks: National Bank of Greece, in the center of the waterfront, offers **currency exchange.** Open Mon.-Thurs. 8am-2pm, Fri. 8am-1:30pm; exchange window open Mon.-Thurs. 8am-2pm and 6:30-9pm, Fri. 8am-1:30pm and 6:30-9pm, Sat.-Sun. 10am-1pm and 5:30-8:30pm.

American Express: (tel. 22 422). Left of the bank inside **Delia Travel Ltd.** Full AmEx travel services for cardholders. Open daily 8:30am-9:45pm.

Flights: Olympic Airways flies to Athens (5-10 per day, 45min., 17,400dr). Take a taxi (1000dr) from Mykonos Town. The main Olympic Airways Office is perched uphill from the bus stop.

Buses: Two stations. **"North Station,"** uphill from the ferry dock, serves Ag. Stefanos beach (16 per day), Ano Mera and Kalafatis (8 per day), Elia Beach (6 per day), and Kalo Livadi beach (2 per day). **"South Station,"** uphill from the windmills at the opposite edge of town, serves Plati Yalos beach (every ½hr.), Paradise Beach (every ½hr.), Ornos Beach (21 per day), and Ag. Ioannis (20 per day). All fares 175dr. Detailed schedules are posted at each station. The last buses to and from the beaches (in July and Aug. only) are around 3-4am.

Ferries: Boats sail frequently to Tinos (2-4 per day, 45min., 1265dr), Paros (1-3 per day, 2hr., 1545dr), Naxos (1-2 per day, 3hr., 1360dr), Syros (1-2 per day, 2½hr., 1335dr), Andros (1-3 per day, 3½hr., 2475dr), Santorini (1-3 per day, 6½hr., 2830dr), Ios (1-2 per day, 4hr., 2665dr), Piraeus (1-2 per day, 6hr., 3650dr), and Iraklion (3 per week, 4660dr). Ferries travel daily to Milos (3872dr) and Sifnos (2712dr) and weekly to Amorgos (2300dr) and Samos (3000dr).

Flying Dolphins: Hydrofoils are faster but more expensive and less reliable. They serve the other Cyclades—Paros (3135dr), Tinos (2514dr), Santorini (6282dr), Syros (2665dr), Andros (5490dr), Naxos (2723dr), Ios (5920dr), Amorgos (5920dr), and Rafina (7400dr).

Moped Rentals: Agencies surround both bus stops. 1500-5000dr (depending on model) per day. Some rent Jeeps as well (10,000-16,000dr per day).

Laundromat: Quite a few around, especially near North Station. Expect to pay 2500dr for wash, dry, and soap.

International Bookstore: International Press, follow signs from waterfront; in the small square opposite Pierro's. Eclectic assortment of books, newspapers, and difficult-to-find American magazines. Open 9am-2pm and 6-11pm.

Hospital: (tel. 23 994, -6). 1km east of Mykonos Town. Take the bus to Ano Mara (8 per day, 160dr) or a taxi (600dr).

ACCOMMODATIONS

Hotels on Mykonos are *expensive.* Period. No bargains here. But rooms are generally well-maintained, clean, and sure to provide an all-around satisfying stay. Luckily there is an alternative: accommodations-hawking here is a full-blown industry. While most other islands feature subtle whispers and offers for "Rooms to Let," the mob of "representatives" at the port in Mykonos are armed with slick photo-montages and shuttle vans with the engines running. You may see the competition lower prices before your eyes. If you're daunted by this display, bear right coming off the boat; you can't miss the line of numbered offices—1 for hotels (tel. 24 540), 2 for "Rooms to Let" (tel. 24 860), and 3 for camping (tel. 23 567). These provide info on availability, location, and prices, and will telephone proprietors on your behalf. You may miss out on the best deals if you dilly-dally getting off the boat or bother to consult the office. In high season especially, empty rooms fill up fast. Also, beware of hotel owners who say their rooms are "on the beach"—they are often miles away from town. Freelance camping is illegal.

Mykonos has more visitors than just about any other island, so in high season, without a reservation, you may have to spend a night camping or in a private room before you'll find a vacancy in one of the hotels. Prices are 20-40% less in off-season.

Chez Maria Pension, 30 N. Kalogera St. (tel. 22 480). From the waterfront, turn inland next to Sea & Sky Travel Agency onto Natogianni St., then right onto Kalogera after a few blocks. Cheaper than most, Chez Maria offers clean, traditionally decorated rooms. Doubles 10,000dr, triples 15,000dr.

Hotel Phillippi, 32 N. Kalogera St. (tel. 22 294), next to Chez Maria. Friendly owners, gorgeous gardens, and spacious rooms. Doubles 12,000dr, triples 16,500dr.

Hotel Apollon (tel. 23 271 or 22 223), on the water. The oldest hotel in town, in a traditional house with many rooms overlooking the harbor. Singles 8650dr, doubles 12,974dr, triples 16,218dr.

Hotel Karboni/Matogianni (tel. 22 217), on Matogianni St. inland from the waterfront. Clean and standard. Doubles 12,000dr, triples 14,500dr.

Hotel Maria, 18 Kalogera St. (tel. 24 212). In an alley off Kalogera next to the sweet-smelling bakery (apple pie 250dr). Don't confuse it with Chez Maria or the nearby Marios Hotel. Air-conditioning. Run by Petros, a former soccer star. Doubles 13,000dr, w/bath 16,000dr; triples 18,000dr.

Paradise Beach Camping (tel. 22 852, -129; fax 24 350), located at a beach 6km from the village. Take a bus here (350dr round-trip). Situated directly on one of the island's most popular beaches. Even though it's quite large, it often feels crowded and is something of a design nightmare. But if you want to party all day and night, this is the place to be. Paradise has boutiques, bungalows, a disco, and beach volleyball. 1500dr per person, 800dr per tent.

Mykonos Camping (tel. 25 915, -916; fax 24 578), near Paradise Beach, is smaller, quieter, cleaner, and more scenic. Same amenities as Paradise Beach (see above). 1500dr per person, 800dr per tent.

FOOD

On Mykonos, overpriced, self-consciously trendy food is the rule, but several cheap, good places can be found nonetheless.

Niko's Taverna (tel. 24 320), in a cluster of restaurants inland from the excursion boat docks. A hoppin' place for traditional Greek cuisine. Baked *kalamari* and cheese 1000dr. Mussels with tomato and cheese 1000dr. Open daily noon-1am.

Chez Maria, in the Chez Maria Pension. A wonderful place for a fancy meal. The service is up to foreign standards. Chicken w/cream sauce and lemons 2300dr.

Eden Restaurant (tel. 22 855), is buried past the end of Kalogera, but fortunately there are plenty of signs. This (along with Chez Maria Pension) is a great place to come for a special occasion. Dine on the house specialty, Vine Grower's Lamb (2900dr), beside a shimmering swimming pool.

Ta Kiouria (tel. 22 866), opposite Niko's. Some interesting specials. Veal *souvlaki* 1500dr. *Saganaki* 700dr.

Paraportiani Taverna (tel. 23 531), next to Ta Kiouria. Smaller portions but a tad more sedate. Stuffed tomatoes 900dr, lamb with okra 1400dr.

La Mexicana (tel. 24 194), on Matogianni, offers an alternative to the standard fare. Food cooked up by Joe, of San Antonio, Texas. Cheese enchiladas 1650dr.

Taverna Antonini (tel. 22 319), in lively, convenient Taxi Sq. (the open plaza on the waterfront). *Mousaka* 1100dr. Chicken kebab 1500dr.

Alexi's, at the back of Taxi Sq., below the Piano Bar. Since 1970—the oldest greasy spoon in Mykonos. *Souvlaki-pita* 300dr, hamburger 500dr. 24 hr.

The Donut Factory, at the intersection of Mitropoleos, Ipirou, and Enoplon Dinameon St., roughly 3 blocks down from South Station. Delightful doughnuts (250-300dr), fresh fruit juices (500-600dr), and banana fritters (400dr).

Snowstorm, around the corner from the Donut Factory, has scrumptious homemade ice cream (1 scoop 250-300dr) and ice cream cocktails (800-1300dr).

Mediterranean Delights (formerly Yatagan), has some of the islands' most spectacular sweets. Treat yourself to a piece of chocolate *baklava* (450dr).

ENTERTAINMENT

There are too many bars and discos to list in full, so here are some favorites. Few have cover charges, but drinks are so expensive that you'll forget you got in free.

Skandinavian Bar, near Niko's Taverna and the waterfront. This perennially packed party complex sprawls over 2 buildings and a patio. Early evening mellowness becomes madness 'round midnight. *Everyone* will pass through. Open nightly 7:30pm-3am, Sat. 'til 4am. Beer 500-700dr. Cocktails (try the Suffering Bastard, Sex on the Beach, or Impatient Virgin) 1100dr.

Windmill Disco, near Skandinavian Bar. Very popular spot in a refurbished windmill; go crazy by the indoor palm tree. Greek music 9-11pm, then jam to the wild sounds of disco. Beer 500dr, cocktails 1000dr. No cover.

Pierro's, on Matogianni St. Mainly gay, but comfortable for all with open minds. Best dancing on the island, loud music; the crowd spills out into the square. Shares building with the not-so-**Irish Bar Stavros.** Beer 1000dr, cocktails 2000dr.

Nepheli-Blue Bar, upstairs from Pierro's; a popular gay hangout. Beer 1000dr, cocktails 1400-1600dr. Next door, **Icaros** has a similar atmosphere.

Montparnasse, on Agion Anargyron St. in the Little Venice district. Step into a Toulouse-Lautrec; have a cocktail by the bay window overlooking the water while being serenaded with classical music. Serene and sophisticated. Wine 800dr, cocktails 1600-1800dr.

Caprice Bar, on the water in Little Venice. Popular and crowded, with a fresh fruit motif befitting a waterfront bar—beware the sea spray, matey.

Uno, at the inland end of Matogianni, tends to be quite crowded. Beers 1000dr, cocktails 2000dr.

The Yacht Club, right at the ferry dock, on the south side of the waterfront. An all-night café where the island goes to recuperate. A motley mixture of tired tourists and hung-over Greeks. Beer 400-500dr. 24 hr.

The Hard Rock Café (tel. 24 913). The apocalypse must be upon us. Dubbed the "Acropolis of Rock," this café is modeled after the American classic. From noon to 4am, free pink buses depart every ½hr. from the ferry dock. Sort of fun, if only for the purpose of shaking your head in disbelief. A dizzying meld of Hollywood and Greece. Friday at midnight, every woman who jumps in the pool for the "Ladies' Swimming Competition" receives a free bottle of champagne. Contrast this with Mt. Athos (see p. 182). Cheeseburgers 1350dr. Open daily noon-4am.

SIGHTS

The prime daytime activities on Mykonos are shopping and perfecting that tan. **Galatis,** left of Taxi Sq. (facing town), has lovely handwoven sweaters (from 10,000dr). Note the list of signatures of famous people, like Jackie O., who shopped here. (Open April-Oct. daily 9am-10pm.) **O Liondis,** 55 Matogianni St., sells individually-crafted leather sandals from 3500dr. **Vienoula's,** around the corner, has handmade jackets and sweaters (from 5000dr). Mykonos is also famous for gold, silver, ceramics, and watercolors, but you may have to settle for a more inexpensive t-shirt (1500dr). Occasionally, however, you can find gold earrings for under 10,000dr.

To pretend that people come here to experience cultural enrichment or indigenous Greek life verges on the ridiculous. Nevertheless, the **Archaeological**

Museum, on the uphill paved road between the ferry dock and the center of town, has a 7th-century BC *pithos* (large earthenware vessel) with relief scenes from the Trojan War, and a bronze *kouros.* (Open Tues.-Sun. 8:30am-3pm; admission 400dr, students 200dr.) The **Aegean Maritime Museum,** around the corner from the inland end of Matogiannis, next to Vienoula's, contains ship models, rare ancient coins with nautical subjects, and navigational instruments. (Open daily April-Oct. 10:30am-1pm and 6:30-9pm; admission 200dr, students 100dr.) The **Folklore Museum** is in the nearly 300-year-old house of a former sea-captain, at the north edge of town, inland from the excursion boat docks. The lovely collection is open at convenient hours for beach-goers. (Open April-Oct. Mon.-Sat. 5:30-8:30pm, Sun. 6:30-8:30pm; free.) Next door is the **Paraportiani.** This cluster of white churches, probably the most famous of Mykonos' sights, sits below five stoic windmills.

You will inevitably find yourself on the beach. Nearest to town, after the unexceptional town beach, is **Megali Ammos,** a 1km walk past the windmills on the southwest corner of the harbor. **St. Stefanos Beach** is not spectacular, but very convenient (16 buses run from "North Station" inland from the ferry dock every day 8:15am-2am, 10min., 140dr). Crowded **Psarou Beach** is also close to town. The **nudist beaches,** full of gay men (though anyone is welcome), are unquestionably the best on the island and can be reached by catching a bus (175dr) to **Plati Yialos** (not bad in its own right), and taking a *caïque* from there. **Buses** leave every ½hr. 9am-midnight from "South Station" roughly 250m up the hill along the street that runs behind the windmills. (Look for painted signs pointing to "buses for Plati Yialos.") From Plati Yialos, *caïques* go to **Paradise Beach,** officially called Kalamopodi (270dr), and **Super Paradise Beach** (340dr). Paradise Beach can also be reached by the 7km strip of road connecting it to town. A large, more secluded **nude beach** is **Elia** (430dr). From the same bus stop, buses also run hourly to the beach at Ormos.

If you can bear to abandon the beaches, visit **Ano Mera,** the island's only other village, 7km away. The main item of interest is the 18th-century Tourliani monastery, featuring an ornate, 16th-century marble tower covered with folk carvings. Buses travel from "North Station" eight times daily.

DELOS ΔΗΛΟΣ

The sacred heart of the Cyclades, Delos holds the famous Temple of Apollo, built to commemorate the birthplace of Apollo and his twin sister Artemis. After Zeus impregnated Leto, he cast her out, fearing his wife Hera's wrath. Leto searched desperately for a place to give birth and at last came across this rocky island bobbing in the sea. She declared that the child would stay forever at his birthplace, casting light upon the riches all around. At her word, the island stopped drifting, and Leto, reassured, decided to stay. Upon her son's birth, the island was bathed in radiance; its name, A-delos (meaning invisible) was changed to Delos because it could now be clearly seen. Immensely grateful, Leto promised to make the island the seat of Apollo's worship. The presence of the sanctuary made Delos a religious center. Thus Delos, despite its small size, became the hub of the Cyclades.

The mortal history of the island has not been as charmed. Delos had long been a religious and commercial focus for the Cyclades when the Ionians dedicated it to the cult of Leto in the 10th century BC. By the 7th century BC, Delos had become the political and trade center of the Aegean League of Islands. Three centuries of struggle for hegemony between the Delians and the Athenians ensued. During these years, the Athenians ordered at least two "purifications" of the island, the latter, in 426 BC, decreeing that no one should give birth or die on its sacred grounds. Delians who violated the edict were banished to nearby Rheneia. The Athenians later instituted the quadrennial Delian Games, which they always dominated.

After Sparta's defeat of Athens in the Peloponnesian War (403 BC), Delos enjoyed independence and wealth. Sweet prosperity soured, however, during the Roman occupation in the 2nd century BC. The island subsequently became the slave-trading center of Greece, where the transfers of as many as 10,000 slaves occurred daily. By the 2nd century AD, after successive sackings, the island was left virtually uninhabited apart from a few odd pirates. Today, its only residents are legions of leaping lizards and members of the French School of Archaeology, which has been excavating ruins here since 1873.

A map to the extensive site is highly recommended, whether you choose to follow the tour detailed below, tag along with a guided tour, or improvise. For more background information, a readable source is *Delos: Monuments and Museum,* by Photini Zaphiropoulou, which includes a map (1500dr, available at the entrance and at the museum or at tourist shops in Mykonos). If you visit Delos unprepared, you may feel overwhelmed by the multitude of ruins.

Occupying almost an entire square mile of this very small island, the archaeological site is neatly sectioned off into the central part of the city, including the Temple of Apollo and the Agora; the outlying parts of the ancient city; Mt. Kythnos; and the theater quarter. While it takes several days to explore the ruins completely, you can see the highlights in three hours or less. Most of your fellow ferry passengers will follow a similar route when they disembark; reverse the route if you want some privacy. Bring a water bottle; the cafeteria on site is pretty expensive.

From the dock, head straight to the **Agora of the Competaliasts,** where Roman guilds built their shrines. Nearby are several parallel **stoas,** the most impressive of which were built by Philip of Macedon. This line of altars, pillars, and statue bases (you can still see the statues' prints) forms the western border of the **Sacred Way.** Follow this road to the **Temple of Apollo,** with its immense, partly hollow hexagonal pedestal that once sustained the weight of the 8m-tall marble statue of the god of light. The famous, skinny **Delian Lions,** a gift of the people of Naxos to the holy island, lie 50m to the north. In the 7th century BC, nine marble lions were placed in a row on a terrace facing the sacred lake; only five remain here—a sixth, pirated by the Venetians, guards the entrance to the arsenal in Venice.

Proceed up the small crest left of the lions, to the creatively named **House of the Hill.** Because the building was dug deep into the earth, this archetypal Roman house is still substantially intact. Downhill lies the **House of the Lake,** with a well-preserved mosaic decorating its atrium and the desiccated **Sacred Lake.** A lone palm tree keeps watch over the surrounding shrubbery. Next to the cafeteria, the **museum** contains an assortment of archaeological finds from the island; unfortunately the best sculpture from the site is in Athens. (Delos museum open Tues.-Sun. 9am-2:30pm.) From there, hike up the path on **Mt. Kythnos** (where Zeus watched the birth of Apollo) and you'll pass several temples dedicated to the Egyptian gods. The elegant bust in the **Temple of Isis** depicts the sun. The 120m hill affords a marvelous view of the ruins and islands. The **Grotto of Hercules** is on the way down. Its immense building blocks seem to date it to Mycenaean times, though some experts suggest it is a Hellenistic imitation of Mycenaean architecture.

At the base of the hill, go towards the water to the **House of the Dolphins** and the **House of the Masks,** which contains the renowned mosaic *Dionysus Riding a Panther.* Continue on to the **ancient theater,** which has a rather sophisticated cistern (as cisterns go), **Dexamene,** with nine arched compartments. Also try to explore the **House of the Trident,** graced by a mosaic of a dolphin twisted around a trident; the **House of Dionysus,** containing another mosaic of Dionysus and a panther pal; and the **House of Cleopatra.** The famous statue of Cleopatra and Dioscourides is sequestered in the museum; a plaster copy takes its place on the site. (Ruins open Tues.-Sun. 9am-2:30pm; admission 1200dr, students 600dr.)

GETTING THERE

Delos is most accessible as a daytrip from Mykonos. **Boats** leave from the dock on the waterfront near town (not the dock for large ferries) Tues.-Sun. roughly every 30-45min. 8:30am-3pm (1500dr round-trip). Most will let you explore the site for 3hr. Each boat line has several return trips in the afternoon, so you have some flexibility about how much time you spend exploring. Tickets are available at many tourist offices along the waterfront and in town or can be bought at the dock. If you're apt to get seasick, ask at travel agencies to find out which excursion boats are the largest and most stable. Other nearby islands (especially Tinos, Naxos, and Paros) offer joint trips to Mykonos and Delos, but often allow less time to explore the ruins.

IOS ΙΟΣ

If you're not drunk by the time you get here, you will be by the time you leave. On Ios, beers go down and clothes come off faster than you can say *Opa*. Think spring break in Florida with a backdrop of whitewashed buildings and people speaking English with European accents. It has everything your mother warned you about: people swilling wine from the bottle at 3pm, wishing you slobbery "good evenings"; drinking games all day along the beach; condoms scattered on dirt roads; men and women dancing naked in bars (of which Ios had 113 at last count); and more. There is zilch to do in Ios but sleep late, sunbathe in the afternoon, and join the drunken cavorting by night. Make the pilgrimage to this mecca of the young and the restless only if you're prepared for hangovers, the occasional groping hand, and the lustful stares of the inebriated. Men, women, dogs, and cats alike often come to Ios looking for sex, so be prepared for some rather crude propositions. In the spirit of *Spinal Tap's* musical genius Nigel Tufnell, this place goes to eleven.

ORIENTATION AND PRACTICAL INFORMATION

Ios is simple. The good life centers around 3 locations, each about 20min. apart along the island's paved road. The **port** is at one end of the road; the **village,** the focus of nocturnal activity, sits directly above it on the hill; and gorgeous, crowded **Mylopotas beach** rests over the hill on the other side of the village. Buses shuttle from port to village to beach and back roughly every 20min. (8am-midnight, 180dr).

Ferries from Ios go to Piraeus (2-4 per day, 7-10hr., 4650dr), Naxos (5 per day, 2hr., 2140dr), Santorini (6 per day, 1hr., 1430dr), Paros (5 per day, 2½hr., 2440dr), Mykonos (3 per day, 5hr., 2780dr), Syros (1-2 per day, 5hr., 3120dr), Crete (6 per week, 3960dr), and less frequently to smaller Cycladic islands. **Flying Dolphins** serve Rafina (7784dr), Santorini (2744dr), Paros (4968dr), Naxos (4300dr), Mykonos (6028dr), Syros (6783dr), Andros (7754dr), and Tinos (6649dr). There are 4 round-trip excursions per week to Sikinos (2000dr) and Folegandros (3000dr).

The port where the boat lets you off is not the heart of the Dionysian oblivion, but a colorful, breezy harbor with cheesy yet pleasant restaurants, an abundance of ferry agents, and an overtaxed beach. **Acteon Travel** (tel. 91 343, -318, or -002; fax 91 088) has offices all over the island, an English-speaking staff, free luggage storage, and a full-service **American Express** office. The main office is by the bus stop in the port. (Open 8am-midnight and occasionally later for incoming ferries.) To find serious drinking, climb the infamous "donkey steps" to the right of the paved road, which lead to the village; the strenuous ascent assures that the rooms along the stairs are the last to fill up. Otherwise, join the rest of the visitors who cram themselves into the bus that shuffles between the ferry landing and the village (160dr). Bus service stops for the night at midnight. When ferries dock after buses have stopped, some travelers have been known to climb up the stairs instead of taking the main road into town. This is generally a bad idea, though, particularly for women, who have been assaulted there after dark. You can always crash portside at the cute 'n' crowded **Camping Ios** (tel. 91 329; person 1200dr, tent rental 1000dr).

■■■ IOS VILLAGE

Miraculously, Ios Village has not become as trashed as its visitors. If you arrive in the morning, you'll peer skeptically at the cluster of whitewashed houses that look too innocuous to be Party Central. As you approach, however, the sheer density of bars with storefront advertising gimmicks, the occasional dried sidewalk vomit, and the odd comatose carouser will be assurance enough that you got off at the right port.

ORIENTATION AND PRACTICAL INFORMATION

You can do most of your "serious" business within 5 minutes by foot from the village bus stop on the paved road opposite the large, blue-domed church. The **Tourist Information Center** (tel./fax 91 118), immediately adjacent to the bus stop, sells ferry and hydrofoil tickets, provides currency exchange, helps with accommodations, and offers free luggage storage and safety deposit boxes. (Open 7:30am-noon.) Behind the helpful tourist office are the English-speaking **police** (tel. 91 222; 24 hr.), and the **port police** (tel. 91 264) are at the far end of the harbor next to Camping Ios. The **post office** (tel. 91 235; open Mon.-Fri. 7:30am-2pm) is buried in the old village between the main road and the road with many bars; look for signs. The **OTE** (tel. 91 399) is a few minutes out of the village along a path starting from the main paved road after Sweet Irish Dream. Look for signs. (Open daily 8am-10pm.) Next to the main church is the **National Bank** (open Mon.-Thurs. 8am-2pm, Fri. 8am-1:30pm). The village branch of **Acteon Travel** is just up the road from the bus stop. Funky cartoon maps and English info booklets are available free at most travel agencies in the village and port. If you aspire to see more than the beach and village, you can rent a moped (2800dr and up) or a jeep (20,000dr, driver included), but motor travel is prohibited on bad roads marked on the island map. Otherwise, public transport suffices. Two streets up in the densely packed village is the town square, off which you can find those oh-so-needed **public toilets.** The **Medical Center** (tel. 91 227), full of travelers patching up wounds from drunken mishaps, is near the police station (open daily 9:30am-1:30pm and 6-9:30pm). For **emergencies,** call (0934) 20 200, 24 hr. A **pharmacy** (tel. 91 562) is on the bar-infested street in the old village. (Open Mon.-Sat. 9am-2pm and 5-10pm.) There is a **supermarket** in the complex with Acteon Travel. **Postal Code:** 84001; **Telephone Code** is 0286.

ACCOMMODATIONS

In an uncharacteristically civil step for an island famous for its insanity, Ios has outlawed the dock hawks who seem to meet every other ferry in Greece with offers for rooms-to-let. Coming off the boat, on your left is the **Community Tourist Office** (tel. 91 028 for info and reservations), a booth generally staffed by helpful English speakers who will call the proprietors of rooms anywhere in Ios and arrange to have them come and pick you up for free. As with all the islands, hotel owners must pay to be listed with the community, so if they tell you that a place in *Let's Go* doesn't exist, simply walk down the road and Acteon Travel will phone for you. Open for all incoming boats. Depending on season, prices for (scarce) singles range 2000-6000dr, w/bath 3000-7000dr; doubles 2500-7000dr, w/bath 3000-10,000dr; triples 4500-9000dr, w/bath 5000-12,000dr. There may be cheaper rooms in the village, but it is easiest and safest to trust the reliable Community Office.

Pension Markos (tel. 91 059; fax 91 060). From the bus stop, take the right (uphill) just before the supermarket. It's on another side street to the left, with a sign visible from the street uphill. Friendly, lively, clean, popular, and not too noisy. Bar serves breakfast (600dr) all day, plus pizza, sandwiches, and drinks. Probably the best option in the cluster behind the bus stop (if not on Ios); make a reservation a few days in advance. Doubles 7000dr, triples 10,000dr.

Francesco's (tel. 91 223). From the top of the "donkey steps," walk up the path to the small square next to the church and National Bank, take the uphill steps in the left corner of the square, and then your first left. Recently renovated with a spectacular view of the water and a popular/rowdy bar. Francesco is a true character and will do his best to see you enjoying yourself on Ios. Doubles 6000dr, w/bath 8000dr; triples 6000dr, w/bath 9000dr. Reservations encouraged.

Hotel Petradi (tel. 91 510), equidistant from the village and the beach on the main road. Every room has a balcony with a romantic ocean view. Large, pleasant patio. Quiet at night. Doubles 8000dr, triples 9000dr. Restaurant/bar downstairs.

Kolitsani View (tel. 91 061). Follow the path past the OTE and look for the white archway. Approximately 5min. from the village's action, a quieter collection of rooms with a family atmosphere. "Kolitsani" is the name of a small beach accessible only by foot between the port and main beach. Expansive view of beaches and Santorini (on a clear day). Doubles 7000dr, w/bath 9000dr; triples 9000dr, w/ bath 13,000dr.

Pension Panorama (tel. 91 592, -186). A bit of a hike uphill on a path below the village. The view makes up for the hike for those who won't be stumbling home blind drunk. Doubles 9000dr, triples 12,000dr. English breakfast 1000dr.

Far Out Camping (tel. 92 301, -2; fax 91 560) at the far end of Mylopotas beach, is the hippest, most luxurious choice. Club Med at 1000dr per night, with a restaurant, bar, minimarket, basketball, volleyball, swimming pool, showers, launderette, live music, and "happenings" during summer. 1000dr per person, doubles 5000dr, triples 6000dr. Tent rental 200dr. Open April-Sept.

Camping Stars (tel. 91 302), on Mylopotas beach, is quieter and less crowded than Far Out. Person 1150dr, tent 600dr, doubles 9000dr. Open June-Sept.

Camping Mylopota Beach (tel. 91 554), also on Mylopotas beach, offers a lower-octane version of Far Out. 800dr per person, 400dr per tent.

Camping Ios (tel. 91 329) at the port is ideal for late-night arrivals. 1200dr per person, tent rental 1000dr. Open June-Sept.

FOOD

Interspersed among the omnipresent bars and discos in Ios village are several good, reasonably priced restaurants. You can't beat **Pithari** near the National Bank for Greek specialties (veal with tomato sauce and potatoes 1200dr, *souvlaki* 1200dr). **The Nest,** uphill off the main street, also serves authentic Greek cuisine at affordable prices (chicken with tomato sauce 800dr, fried *kalamari* 850dr). There are countless cheap, greasy *gyro* joints near the bars just waiting to serve starving revelers. Ready for some variety after having eaten at Far Out Camping for the past week? Mylopotas Beach actually offers two quality international restaurants. **Harmony,** on the right at the bottom of the footpath leading to the beach from the village, offers Mexican food and has a large number of daytime activities and games for those bored of lounging on the beaches (burritos 1600dr). Just down the slope is **Delfini,** with an enormous menu of Thai food (stir-fried vegetables with basil and garlic 1400dr). True gourmands might want to make their ways to **Polydoros,** 2km north of the port on Koubara Beach, for what's reputed to be the island's best food.

ENTERTAINMENT

Of Ios' alleged 113 bars, at least 90% are packed into the initially unassuming old village area. Some of the larger and louder hang-outs can be found along the main paved road. Smaller bars line the main pedestrian street in the village, which could be intimate if it weren't for the loud music and continuous traffic of increasingly wasted amusement-seekers passing in (and out). Some bars offer happy hours early in the evening, but the real drinking doesn't begin until at least 11pm. From then on, the drunken mob shuffles to the ever-popular Irish pubs ('cause, you know, IOS means Irish Over Seas) and rattling discos. You won't have problems finding cheap beer (300-400dr); the places listed here tend to be slightly more expensive, but there's always a good reason—either they're the best, or they fit a particular niche.

Sweet Irish Dream, a large building down towards the "donkey steps." Everyone ends up here, but the cheaper option is to loosen up elsewhere before hitting here after 2am to dance on a few tables. Beer 500-600dr. Cocktails 700-800dr.

The Slammer Bar, just uphill from the Main Square/Meeting Place in the Village. Its specialty: tequila slammers, a shot glass filled with tequila, Tia Maria, and Sprite, slammed on the bar (600dr). Always packed.

Kalimera, lower down off the main strip. Perhaps the classiest bar, playing jazz, acid jazz, and reggae. Beers 500-800dr. Cocktails 1000-1200dr.

Dubliner, across the street from Sweet Irish Dream, with a pub-like wooden section and a jamming disco section. Heats up later, but also a nice place to sit earlier in the evening. Beer 400-500dr. Cocktails 600dr.

Scorpion Disco, outside of town on the way to the beach. A dance emporium. 800dr cover includes first drink.

Sports Bar, close to the main square. Popular among the big, burly, ass-slapping crowd. Live satellite feeds for international sporting events. Often live music as well. Beer 450-700dr. Cocktails 700-1000dr.

Pegasus, near the Sports Bar; loud rock. Beer 500-600dr. Cocktails 600-1000dr.

Blue Note, popular with Americans, Scandinavians, and those staying at Francesco's. Beers 400-500dr.

BEACHES

With the exception of a solitary monastery, some castle ruins, and a modest pile of rubble at the north tip of the island reputed to be **Homer's tomb** (but what pile of rocks isn't?), the **beaches** are the place to be on Ios. Most head for **Mylopotas Beach** on foot (roughly 20min. downhill) or by frequent bus service from the port or village (8am-1am, 180dr). The beach, like the town, is a bastion of bacchanalia. The outer reaches offer a modicum of privacy. The farther you go, the fewer clothes you'll see (or wear). **Watersports:** windsurf (2000dr per hour), waterski (3000dr per hour), or snorkel (800dr per hour), but for Pete's sake, put some clothes on first.

Of course, there are prettier and less crowded beaches on Ios. Excursions leave daily for the **nude beach** at beautiful **Manganari Bay,** stopping at the monastery (11am, return 6pm; 2000dr). Nudist, secluded **Psathi** on the eastern coast is a 7km walk along donkey tracks. Several times per week, an excursion goes to Psathi, stopping at the castle ruins (11am, return 6pm; 2000dr). Other nudist beaches include **Koubara** (2km walk north from the port) and **Ag. Theodoti** near Psathi.

SANTORINI (THIRA) ΣΑΝΤΟΡΗΝΗ, ΘΗΡΑ

Santorini is the diamond at the end of this string of pearls. Plunging cliffs, burning black-sand beaches, and deeply scarred hills make its landscape as dramatic as the cataclysm that created it. Even those with no interest in Santorini's intriguing past will find ample delights in its present: long stretches of beach, tiny cliffside towns, and spectacular landscapes forged by centuries of volcanic activity. Santorini's whitewashed homes are strewn against a cliffside, its ridges rising sharply out of the Aegean. The black beaches—stark against cobalt waters—and the boiling fields of pumice are unique in their beauty among the Greek islands.

HISTORY OF THE ISLAND

From approximately 2000 BC to 1628 BC, one of the most advanced societies in ancient Greece flourished on this isle (then called Thira). Then in 1628 BC, a massive volcanic eruption buried every sign of civilization beneath tons of lava and pumice. In the centuries since, fact and fiction have mingled, leading some to identify Santorini as Plato's lost continent of Atlantis. More serious historical speculation has convinced many scholars that the eruption on Santorini triggered a tidal wave large enough to account for the destruction of several Minoan sites in Crete.

In 1967, Prof. Spyridon Marinatos, an advocate of the latter theory, resumed excavations on the Akrotiri site. The Greek School later unearthed a town, preserved virtually intact, like Pompeii in Italy, beneath layers of volcanic pumice. Its paved streets are lined with multi-story houses, with wood-framed doors and windows.

Modern Santorini is really only the eastern crescent of what was once a circular island, originally called "Strongili," or round. The explosion in 1628 BC left a crust of volcanic ash overstretching the hollow center of the island. When the crust caved in, water filled the resulting *caldera* (basin) that is now Santorini's harbor. The two islands to the west, **Thirasia** and **Aspronisi,** appear to be separate, but are in fact a continuation of the rim of the original island. Approaching Santorini from the north, you will first see Thirasia, which has two small villages. Closer to Santorini are two extraterrestrial rock formations that rise out of the water, Nea Kameni and Palea Kameni. You can climb Nea Kameni, the larger of the two, still an active volcano.

ORIENTATION AND PRACTICAL INFORMATION

Since Santorini is the final stop for many **ferries** in the Cyclades and also frequently a stop for some Crete-bound ferries, it is easily accessible, but also densely crowded. Your boat will dock at one of the ports: **Athinios** is the most important and has frequent buses (at least 20 per day, ½hr., 280dr) to Thira (the main town) and to Perissa Beach. Hostel-bound travelers can board the free shuttle bus to either Thira Youth Hostel or Perissa Youth Hostel. It is also possible to get free rides from the pension proprietors who swarm the port. At the old port of **Thira,** you'll be confronted by a 587-step footpath leading up the cliff to the town above (a difficult 20min. climb). The cable car on the left departs every 20min., 6:40am-midnight, and costs 700dr, or for the same price you could hire a mule. Boats occasionally dock at **Oia,** on the northern cape of the island.

From Santorini, **ferries** depart for Piraeus (3-6 per day, 10hr., 4650dr), Ios (6-10 per day, 1½hr., 1430dr), Paros (8-10 per day, 5hr., 2634dr), Naxos (6-8 per day, 4hr., 2400dr), Mykonos (3-5 per day, 7hr., 2940dr), Crete (1-3 per day, 8hr., 2540dr), Syros (1-2 per day, 6hr., 3284dr), Rhodes (2 per week, 16hr., 6183dr), Sikinos (6 per week, 1757dr), Folegandros (5 per week, 1737dr), Anafi (3 per week, 1757dr), Milos (3 per week, 2500dr). Three ferries per week head to Sifnos, Serifos, and Kithos (2634dr), 2 per week to Kassos (3782dr), Karpathos (4495dr), and Thessaloniki (7800dr), and 1 per week to Skiathos (6932dr), Skiros (6286dr), and Amorgos (4434dr). **Flying Dolphins** serve Rafina (9212dr) and major islands: Ios (2743dr), Paros (5712dr), Naxos (4852dr), Mykonos (6394dr), Syros (7150dr), Tinos (7118dr), and Amorgos (4434dr). **Olympic Airways** has **flights** from Santorini to Athens (6-8 per day, 17,800dr), Mykonos (1-2 per day, 12,800dr), Crete (1 per day, 13,400dr), Rhodes (1 per day, 18,000dr), and Thessaloniki (3 per week, 25,000dr), although fare increases are expected.

Renting a moped may be the ideal way to travel around the island, especially since the roads are well-paved. During the summer, however, Santorini becomes densely crowded and moped dealers rent bikes to just about anyone. Inexperienced riders, poor bikes, and carefree drivers create danger. If you choose to ride, make sure you're satisfied with the bike's quality and be cautious. Travel by foot or bus (Santorini's service is excellent) may be a better option. The least painful (but least adventurous) choice is a half- (3000dr) or full-day (3500dr) bus tour. **Kamari Tours** (tel. 31 390 or 31 455), with offices all over, is expensive but reputable. Visit other agencies and ask about student discounts. There is a severe **water shortage** on Santorini; fresh water accounts for most of the price of rooms on the island.

■■■ THIRA TOWN

The center of activity on the island is the capital city, **Thira** (Fira), which in Greek means "wild island." Some say that the harbor below the town plunges into a bottomless abyss which leads to the door between heaven and hell. Stepping off the bus from the port, you may conclude that hell is actually on this side of the door. First-time visitors have been known to wonder aloud if they disembarked on the wrong island when confronted with the mess of glitzy shops, whizzing mopeds, and hordes of tourists. Fortunately, the ugly roadside strip is only one aspect of this multi-faceted town. Thira is perched on a cliff and the short walk to the town's western edge, the *caldera,* reveals a stunning view of the harbor, Santorini's coastline, and the neighboring islands and volcano, making it a popular site for weddings and honeymoons. Thira's expensive cafés, trendy shops, and jewelry stores line the back streets. On the east side, the island's characteristic barrel-vaulted houses spread out on more secure footing, their quiet tree-canopied streets trailing off into the surrounding countryside. Although the town is overrun with tourists in summer, nothing can destroy the pleasure of wandering among the narrow cobbled streets, inspecting the craft shops, and arriving at the western edge of town in time to watch the sun bathe the harbor in a magenta glow.

ORIENTATION AND PRACTICAL INFORMATION

It's easiest to navigate about Thira if you envision the city divided into three parts, each running north-south. Facing the street with the bus station behind you, begin by heading left (north), and walk uphill to **Theotokopoulou Square,** which is full of travel agencies, banks, and restaurants galore. At the fork in the road, the street on the right is **25th Martiou Street,** the main paved road leading from the square north towards Oia. It is home to both of Thira's youth hostels (look for signs) as well as other accommodations. This is the first part; during the day, it is the most crowded. The second part houses Thira's back streets that are lined with jewelry stores, sweet shops and, by night, many of the best bars and discos. To get here, head up from the left branch north of the bus stop to 25th Martiou and turn on to any westbound street. Farther west is the third part, the *caldera,* where expensive restaurants and art galleries are overshadowed only by the spectacular view.

Tourist Police: (tel. 22 649). On the main road south of the bus depot. Open 24 hr. They share a building with the **police.**

Port Police: On the main road (tel. 22 239), north of Theotokopoulou Sq.

Post Office: 25th Martiou St. (tel. 22 624), between the square and the bus stop. Open Mon.-Fri. 8am-2pm. **Postal Code:** 84700.

OTE: 100m north of the square on the road to Oia. Open Mon.-Fri. 8am-2:30pm, Sat. 7:30am-midnight, Sun. 9am-midnight. **Telephone Code:** 0286.

Tourist Agencies: Dozens surround Theotokopoulou Sq., with ferry tickets, currency exchange, some student discounts, room finding, excursion booking, and luggage storage. **Pelikan Travel** (tel. 22 220 or 23 667), on the northwestern corner of the square, has particularly efficient and courteous service. **Luggage storage** 300dr per day. Open daily 8am-11pm, or later if the island's busy.

Banks: National Bank of Greece, on the avenue that branches off from the main road south from the square, offers **currency exchange.** Open Mon.-Thurs. 8am-2pm, Fri. 8am-1:30pm. The nearby **Agricultural Bank** and **Commercial Bank** also change money and have the same hours.

American Express: In the office of **X-Ray Kilo Travel and Shipping Agency** (tel. 23 401, -083), in the square. All AmEx services. Open daily 8am-11pm.

Flights: Olympic Airways (tel. 22 493, -793). From the bus depot, go downhill on the main road, take your first left, then a right. Reservations suggested 1-2 weeks in advance. Standby tickets possible (arrive 2hr. before take-off). Office open Mon.-Fri. 8:30am-4pm.

Buses: Travel to Perissa (25 per day, ½hr., 300dr), Kamari (40 per day, 20min., 175dr), Akrotiri (15 per day, ½hr., 280dr), Athinios (10 per day, 15min., 280dr), Oia (25 per day, ½hr., 220dr), and the airport (12 per day, ½hr., 175dr).

Taxis: Call 22 555.

Moped and Car Rental: Mopeds 2000-3500dr. Cars start at 10,000dr, less in off-season. Most places cluster downhill from Theotokopoulou Sq. Check bikes before renting; dealers may rent lemons. Some travel agencies also rent cars.

Laundromat: Penguine (tel. 22 092, -492), north of the square on the left. Wash 1000dr. Dry 800dr. Soap 200dr. Open daily 8:30am-3pm and 5-9pm.

Public Toilets: 25th Martiou St., down and across the street from the bus depot.

International Bookstore: International Press (tel. 22 942), at the top of the plaza between Theotokopoulou Sq. and the cliff (look for signs). International papers and magazines. Beach-reading books. Open daily 8:30am-10pm.

Pharmacy: Down from the main square (tel. 23 444; open daily 8:30am-10:30pm).

Medical Center: (tel. 22 238, -7). The first left off the main road down from the bus depot. Routine cases and free physicals 9am-2pm. Emergencies 24 hr.

ACCOMMODATIONS

Santorini certainly does not lack accommodations, but in summer the pensions and hotels are almost all booked by noon. The cheapest options, and your best bet if you arrive late, are the youth hostels in Thira: two at Perissa Beach and one at Oia (see Southern Santorini, p. 234, and Northern Santorini, p. 236). You can start hunting early the next morning for other lodgings, if you wish. Thira is centrally located, but there are good accommodations in private homes all over the island, so don't hesitate to branch out. The settlement of **Karterados** 2km south of Thira provides many options. Private doubles in outlying towns run as low as 2500dr. Head for **Karterados, Messaria, Pyrgos, Emborio,** or any of the small inland towns along the main bus routes. Some hawkers at the port misrepresent their rooms, so be clear about where you are going and what you are getting.

In Thira, doubles run roughly 5000-6000dr in high season. Prices listed below are for peak season; rates decrease by as much as 50% off-season. Many naturalists opt to **camp** at Perissa Beach or Kamari Beach on Southern Santorini.

Thira Youth Hostel (tel. 22 387), on the left roughly 300m north of the square, set back 25m from the road to Oia. Without a doubt the nicest hostel in Thira. Clean, quiet, and livable dorm rooms, a few even quieter "small dormitories," and pension-quality private rooms with baths. Dorm rooms either mixed gender or women-only. Snack bar, breakfast served. Dorms 1300dr, small dorms 1600dr, private rooms 3000dr per person. Hot showers 24 hr., but bring your own toilet paper. Free transportation to Perissa and Athinios. Reception open 8am-2pm and 5-10pm. No curfew but owner enforces quiet after 11pm. Check-out noon.

Kontohori Youth Hostel (tel. 22 722, -3), down a slope roughly 400m north of the square. Look for signs. Popular among the crowd working or staying for long spells on Santorini, but still not the most soothing place to spend time. Single-sex dorm beds. Snack bar, breakfast served. Reception open 24 hr. No curfew. Check-out noon. Dorms 1800dr, doubles 4500dr, roof 1500dr. Hot showers 4-9pm only.

Kamares Youth Hostel (tel. 24 472), north of the square with a turn-off before Kontohori hostel; just above Thira Hostel. Single-sex dorm rooms. Beds on canopied roof are best deal. Roof snack bar. Reception open 8am-1pm and 5-9pm. No curfew. Check-out noon. Dorms 1300dr, roof 1100dr. Hot showers 5-9pm only.

Pension Andreas (tel. 22 588 or 23 562), one of a line of new, clean, affordable, and nearly identical pensions lining the road to Santorini Camping. Doubles 5000-8000dr. Triples 7500-10,000dr. Equally pleasing and with similar prices are **Pension Petros** (tel. 22 573) and **Pension Soula** (tel. 23 473, -787, -753).

Villa Litsa, 25th Martiou St. (tel. 22 267). North of the square. Go up the green Astroturf stairs. Large, slightly ornate rooms with baths. Every 3 rooms share a kitchen. On a noisy street. Doubles 9000dr. Triples 12,000dr. Open June-Sept.

Santorini Camping (tel. 22 944, 25 062 or 25 064; fax 25 065). Follow the blue signs leading east of the square inland. Attractive camping area with swimming pool available (700dr for non-campers, including the first drink). Check-out noon. 1400dr per person, 900dr per tent. Hot showers 5-9pm. Café, bar, and minimarket. Reception open 8am-midnight.

FOOD AND ENTERTAINMENT

Escape from the bustle at **Nikolas Taverna,** on a side street a few blocks above Pelikan Travel (take a right at the Hotel TATAKH). This traditional *taverna,* with a posted menu only in Greek, is frequented almost exclusively by locals and serves delectable beef stew with noodles (1300dr) and stuffed tomatoes (750dr). On the *caldera* overlooking the water, **Restaurant Niki (NIKH)** (*kalamari* 1000dr, *saganati* 450dr) and the **Volcano Restaurant** (stuffed grape leaves 700dr) serve relatively inexpensive food. For a touch of elegance, try **Meridiana,** which features perhaps the best view in Thira (liqueur and chocolate mousse 1500dr), or **Alexandria's,** at the far left of the *caldera* below Hotel Atlantis (meal-sized appetizers 1900dr, the fantastic ancient Turkish dessert *künefe* 1500dr, see p. 428). Lighter, cheaper fare abounds as well, especially around the square (gyros 300-350dr).

Slightly higher on the main road is **The Roasters,** a good cheap restaurant with a special appeal for vegetarians (daily vegetarian plate 750dr, *dolmades* 480dr). The **Blue Note** bar is home to **Mama's Breakfast Café,** where the ebullient owner—famous for pinching customers' cheeks and proclaiming "Mama loves you babies,"—serves breakfast 7am-1pm (500-900dr). **Sweet shops** litter the windy streets between the main road and the *caldera,* but tend to have uniform fare at uniformly high prices (*baklava* 350-400dr). Those with a real sweet tooth will want to check out the candy store **Popori,** near Restaurant Niki (3200dr per kilo). For the cheapest water around, head down the hill past the bus station until you spot the sign touting **Santo Wines/Supermarket/Coop.** Not only is water inexpensive (85dr for a 1.5L bottle!) and food cheap, but there is also a variety of household products.

Thira's nightlife is deservedly well-known, ranging from hot, packed clubs that rival Ios to mellow jazz bars. **Tropical,** high up on the *caldera,* is usually hopping, and is run by a sweet California girl who knows how to mix drinks (beer 500-600dr, cocktails 1000dr). The **Blue Note,** down on the Oia road, also tends to be packed and even has a free pool table (beer 400-700dr, pitchers 2200dr). **Tithora Club** is built into a 14th-century cave on the east side of the road to Oia, and is great for those who prefer hard, loud rock (beer 500-700dr). To experience the watering-hole atmosphere of **Two Brothers,** take a left at Hotel Tataki (beer 500-600dr). The **Kira Thira Jazz Club,** a bohemian refuge with live jazz (beer, sangria 800dr) is on the same street as Nikolas Tavern. Later at night, discos take over for some of the most intense, slickest dancing in Greece. Two of the most popular are the **Koo Club** and **Enigma.** Most crank on into the wee hours and charge ridiculously high covers (1000-3000dr, with drinks priced to match).

SIGHTS

Thira's **Archaeological Museum** (tel. 22 217), near the cable cars, holds an impressive collection of vases, mostly from the site of ancient Thira. Keep climbing upward in the winding alleys and follow the signs. (Open Tues.-Sun. 8:30am-3pm. Admission 800dr, students 400dr; free on Sun. if unaccompanied by a guide.) The private **Museum Megaro Gyzi,** near Kamares Hostel, has an engrossing collection of old maps, engravings, and photographs of Santorini and other islands. (Open Mon.-Sat. 10:30am-1:30pm and 5-8pm, Sun. 10:30am-4:30pm. Admission 400dr, students 200dr, free on Sun.) In July and August, the museum hosts several classical music concerts and temporary art exhibitions.

■■■ SOUTHERN SANTORINI

AKROTIRI

The archaeological site in **Akrotiri,** where extensive excavations are still underway, bewilders novices. (Open Tues.-Sun. 8:30am-3pm. Admission 1200dr, students 600dr; free on Sun.) Breeze through quickly on your own, buy a book (1000dr), or tag along with a guided tour. Bus tours (3000-3500dr) are coupled with a visit to Profitias Ilias Monastery and a local wine-tasting.

Prof. Marinatos found the paved streets of Akrotiri lined with houses connected by a sophisticated central drainage system. Each house had at least one room lined with frescoes, some among the most magnificent in Greece. Along with pottery and stone vases unearthed at Akrotiri, the frescoes are on loan to the National Archaeological Museum in Athens pending completion of the new museum at Santorini. Archaeologists found no bones in Akrotiri; the fate of the people remains a mystery. Since only heavy objects, and no valuables, were found, a common theory is that everyone escaped before the eruption. Fifteen buses per day run here (280dr).

Five minutes from the sight is **Red Beach,** named for the reddish rock formations on the coast. Akrotiri is not a convenient place to stay (and it's really dusty), but if you must, there is a "youth hostel" in the basement of a restaurant on the dirt road from the site to the Red Beach (2000dr per night).

BEACHES

Santorini's two most frequented black-sand **beaches** are **Perissa** and **Kamari** on the southeast coast. Perissa, the farther of the pair, is more popular with students and offers two youth hostels, camping, and a casual nightlife. Bring along a straw mat and sandals; the black sand sizzles in the sun. The water here, as elsewhere on the island, is brisk and clear with a slippery rock and seaweed bottom.

Perissa

The **Perissa Youth Hostel** (tel. 81 639), 400m along the road leading out of town, has a sociable bar/snack bar and a swimming pool. (Reception open 8:30am-2pm and 4-10pm. No curfew. Dorm beds 2500dr, private rooms 4000dr. Sheets 200dr. Continental breakfast 500dr. Hot salt-water showers 24 hr. Kitchen facilities.) Up and across the street, independent **Youth Hostel Anna** competes with new, clean women's and mixed dorms, and a connected restaurant. (Reception open 8:30am-2pm and 4-10pm. No curfew. Dorm beds 1800dr. Hot showers 8-11am and 4-7pm). Enormous **Perissa Camping** (tel. 81 343) is adjacent to the beach. (Check-out 1pm. 900dr per person, 550dr per tent.) Rooms in private homes (you'll meet the proprietors at the dock) offer more privacy. (Doubles 5000-7000.) At night, taste the delicious calzones, pizza, and pasta at **Bella Italiana** near the end of the main road (hot pepper and onion calzone 1150dr) and, if so inclined, prowl the main road for bars and discos. **Dave's Place** (beer 400dr, cocktails 600dr) and the **Beer Garden** (beer 300dr and up, cocktails 600dr) are two affordable and friendly choices near the hostels. Roughly 25 buses per day travel from Thira to Perissa, stopping in Pyrgos.

Kamari

Kamari Beach is closer to Thira and more popular with well-to-do tourists. Roughly 40 buses per day (175dr) travel from Thira, and there's a rocky **shuttle boat** ride between Kamari and Perissa as well (every ½hr., 10am-4pm, 700dr). The long beach is covered in umbrellas and lined with pricey hotels, cafés, and travel agencies. Double rooms range 5000-20,000dr. Contact **Kamari Tours** (tel. 31 390) or stop in the office on the waterfront for aid and advice. The **Hotel Golden Sun** (tel. 31 301), on the road inland from the beach at the **Yellow Donkey Disco,** has clean rooms with balconies (12,000dr). The budget traveler may fare best at **Kamari Camping** (tel. 31 453), 1km inland along the main road out of town. (1300dr per person, 700dr per tent; open June-Sept.). The winery **Canava Roussos** (tel. 31 954, -278), 1km from the campsite, offers wine tasting (100dr per glass; open 10am-8pm). A summer **folklore festival** is held June 15-Sept. 15 (Fri.-Sun., 8pm-midnight). Entrance fee of 3000dr covers the first bottle of wine.

Monolithos

Those who prefer sandier beaches might want to check out **Monolithos Beach.** More popular with locals than with tourists, this smallish beach is easily accessible due to its proximity to the airport (15 buses per day, 175dr). This is definitely not a place to stay, but if you want a bite to eat, fish *taverna* Skaramagas is the least expensive on the strip (*kalamari* 1000dr, Greek salad 600dr).

PYRGOS AND ANCIENT THIRA

Buses to Perissa stop in lofty **Pyrgos,** which is surrounded by medieval walls. A Venetian fortress from the 14th-16th centuries, the town then came under Turkish rule until 1828. The village's 25 blue- and green-domed churches dot the horizon. The **Profitis Ilias Monastery,** roughly a 1-hr. hike up the mountain from Pyrgos, lugubriously shares its site with a radar station. On July 20, the monastery hosts the **Festival of Profitis Ilias.** From Profitias Ilias, it's approximately a 1-hr. hike to the ruins of ancient **Thira.** The ancient theater, church, and forum of the island's old capital are still visible, though less spectacular than the Akrotiri excavations. (Open Tues.-Sun. 9am-3pm; free.)

The southern end of the island has a few villages where you can spend the night. Cheerful, whitewashed **Emborio,** some 3km inland from Perissa, has frequent bus connections to the beach and to Thira.

■■■ NORTHERN SANTORINI

OIA

Oia (pronounced EE-ah), an intricate cliffside town on the northwest tip of the island, famous for its dazzling sunsets, is a fascinating mixture of devastation and renewal. The 1956 earthquake leveled this small town on the island's rocky north point. Its present 600 inhabitants have carved new dwellings into the cliffside among the shattered ruins of the old. Although the budget traveler will not thrive long in Oia, an afternoon visit affords enough time to wander the cobbled streets; window-shop at exquisite jewelry, craft, and embroidery shops; and peruse the menus of elegant, expensive restaurants before the riveting descent of the sun. A 20-min. climb down 252 stone stairs at the end of the main road brings you to rocky **Ammoudia** beach, with a few boats moored in a startlingly deep swimming lagoon. **Buses** run from Thira to Oia (25 per day, ½hr., 220dr) and a few **ferries** dock at Oia before continuing to Thira or Athinios—check when you buy your ticket.

If you opt to stay in Oia (and boy, is it tempting), you'll probably cross paths with Manolis or Markos Karvounis. Their family runs Youth Hostel Oia, the Karvounis Tours travel agency, and the Neptune restaurant. The **Youth Hostel Oia** (tel. 71 465; fax 71 291) is the classiest of Santorini's youth hostels, with a superb view from the roof terrace and a bar open for breakfast or evening drinks. (Dorm beds 3000dr, includes breakfast.) When it's full below, the roof is available (1700dr including breakfast. Hot water 24 hr. Wheelchair accessible.) Contact **Karvounis Tours** (tel. 71 290, -2; fax 71 291). Another fascinating, but somewhat expensive, option is renting a 400- to 600-year-old **cave house** from **Cycladic Environments,** an American firm dedicated to preserving local architecture. For reservations in the U.S. call (800) 719-5260; prices range from 8000dr per person. As of summer 1995, the cheapest ones went for roughly 24,000dr for three people. Modern rooms range 4500-9000dr for doubles. Oia prides itself on being an escape from the rest of the world and is a popular site for honeymoons and weddings (contact Karvounis Tours for wedding information). This atmosphere makes it difficult to find short-term accommodations—most proprietors expect a stay of at least 5 days.

Likewise, dining will cost you. Along the main road, **Thalami** under the octopus sign has *mousaka* for 1000dr and mussels for 1400dr. The Karvounis' **Neptune,** sophisticated yet casual, offers stuffed tomatoes for 900dr, *kalamari* for 1000dr. **Restaurant Lotza** is ideal for lunch with a view (omelettes 900dr, curried chicken 1500dr) and **Melissa's** rooftop terrace has live jazz piano nightly from 10pm (glass of wine 1000dr). For cheap fare, try **Café Greco** with *gyros* in pita for 350dr.

The bus route between Thira and Oia passes through the tiny, quiet-as-a-whisper town of **Imerovigli.** Ask the driver to let you off if you want to explore. Imerovigli's sunset view is said to rival that of Oia and Thira, and the town hosts fewer members of the camera-toting set.

■■■ THIRASIA AND SURROUNDING ISLANDS

Santorini's unspoiled junior partner Thirasia (pop. 300) is worthy of a detour. Built along the island's upper ridge, the villages of **Manolas** and **Potamos** have spine-tingling views of Santorini's western coast. Thirasia has been virtually untouched by contemporary society, and a visit here will be a refreshing change from the Cycladic crowds. The only way to reach Manolas is to climb the rocky stairs (roughly ½hr.) or take a donkey (400dr). If you walk, do so when the sun is low—profuse perspiration permeates midday excursion. As you reach the top, you'll find a *taverna* on your left and a minimarket on the right. Farther down on the right is another *taverna,* with a breezy roof terrace. Manolas has no hotels, but you can ask a donkey-owner at the dock to direct you to private rooms.

Excursions to Thirasia are often coupled with trips to the volcanic crater and hot springs and sometimes Oia as well. Tours can be found at the various travel agencies (1000-4000dr). Trips to the volcano and hot springs, as inexpensive as 1500dr round trip, can be wonderfully convivial. Be forewarned that to get to the hot sulphur springs, you'll have to swim through cold water first; to get to the volcano's crater, you'll have to hike uphill for ½hr.

PAROS ΠΑΡΟΣ

The geographical center of the islands, Paros offers a taste of almost every aspect of life in the Cyclades. To enjoy such variety, however, you'll have to skimp somewhat on quality. Paros' interior is less idyllic, its villages less picturesque, and its beaches not quite as luscious as those of nearby Naxos. Its nightlife, although quite lively and festive, is not as raucous as on Ios or as chic as on Mykonos. Its history and cultural heritage can't quite compare to Santorini's. Still, this jack-of-all-trades of an island can offer a diversity of options not found on other islands and thus has remained one of the most popular of Cycladic destinations year after year. Paros is also a convenient base for excursions to other islands. In summer, pensions fill up quickly. If you can't find accommodations in any of the main coastal towns, try one of the small villages linked to the port town of Paroikia by bus, any of the island's secluded beaches, or even Antiparos. There are also several official campsites on the island.

■■■ PAROIKIA

Paroikia's flower-filled streets wind beneath archways, past two-story whitewashed houses, historic basilica, and windmills. The town, which occupies the site of the ancient city, makes for pleasant walks. The road leading from the waterfront to the town is the island's commercial center.

ORIENTATION AND PRACTICAL INFORMATION

From the ferry, most restaurants, hotels, and offices lie to the left (facing inland). Straight ahead, past the windmill and the tourist offices, is the main square, behind which a whitewashed labyrinth brims with shops and cafés. To the far right around the bend, a host of bars, the island's party district, await. Starting around September 10, foreigners can earn measly wages during the two-week grape harvest.

Tourist Office: (tel. 24 555 or 24 456). To the right of the windmill, facing inland, the Hostelier's Association of Paros lists prices of hotels, finds "Rooms to Let" and provides general tourist info. As usual, hotels must pay to be listed here, so don't be dismayed if they tell you the place you're looking for doesn't exist.

Police: (tel. 23 333). Across the square behind the OTE, on the 2nd floor above the photo shops. 24hr. **Tourist police** (tel. 61 673) are in the same building. Open 9am-3:30pm. **Port Police** (tel. 21 240) are off the waterfront, past the bus station. Information about all sailings. 24hr.

Post Office: On the north side of the waterfront, 2 blocks past the bus stop. Open Mon.-Fri. 7:30am-2pm. **Postal Code:** 84400.

OTE: One block south of the windmill (its back borders the main square). Open Mon.-Sat. 7:30am-10pm. **Telephone Code:** 0284.

Tourist Agency: The **General Travel Agency** (tel. 24 415, -6; fax 24 417) across the street has up-to-the-minute ferry, hydrofoil, and airplane schedules. Open 9am-3pm. The first street heading inland to the left of the windmill (just before the church) is also lined with travel agencies.

Banks: National Bank of Greece (tel. 24 543). From the windmill, head into the pedestrian square—it's at the far corner in the fortress-like building. Open Mon.-Thurs. 8am-2pm, Fri. 8am-1:30pm; **currency exchange** also Sat. 10am-1pm.

Flights: Olympic Airways (tel. 21 582, -43), on Propona St., the street bordered on its left by the garden with the small blue-and-white church which leads inland to the main church. Open Mon.-Fri. 8am-3pm. They send 6 flights per day to Athens (16,000dr). All the latest transportation info is in the windows and sidewalk displays of the plethora of travel agencies around the windmill and ferrydock. Take a taxi to the airport (2000dr), or catch the bus to Aliki (240dr).

Buses: (tel. 21 395, -133). Complete schedule posted in the shack a few blocks to the left of the windmill (facing inland). Buses run to Naoussa (20-30 per day, 15min., 200dr), Lefkes (14 per day, 25min., 220dr), Pounda (10-20 per day, 15min., 170dr), Aliki and the airport (15 per day, ½hr., 250dr), Piso Livadi (15-20 per day, 40min., 350dr), Chrisi Akti (15-20 per day, 50min., 450dr), Drios (15-20 per day, 1hr., 450dr), and the Valley of the Butterflies (15 per day, 10min., 170dr).

Ferries: Sail to Piraeus (3-9 per day, 5-6hr., 3320dr), Naxos (5-9 per day, 1hr., 1254dr), Ios (3-8 per day, 2½hr., 2293dr), Santorini (4-9 per day, 3½hr., 2490dr), Mykonos (1-4 per day, 2hr., 1515dr), Syros (1-2 per day, 1½hr., 1310dr), Amorgos (daily, 3hr., 2390dr), Rhodes (daily, 16hr., 6253dr), Crete (6 per week, 8hr., 4320dr), Thessaloniki (3 per week, 10hr., 7010dr), Sifnos (5 per week, 2hr., 1930dr), Samos (5 per week, 6hr., 3573dr), and Ikaria (5 per week, 4hr., 2230dr). There are also less frequent connections to nearly every other island: Astypalea, Kos, Karpathos, Kassos, Kalymnos, Patmos, Andros, Tinos, Folegandros, Milos, Anafi, Skiathos, Asyros, and so many more. **Excursion boats** head to Mykonos/Delos (8000dr), Naxos (4000dr), Santorini (9000dr), Sifnos (6000dr), and Amorgos (8000dr). Ask at travel agencies for info.

Flying Dolphins: Catamarans and hydrofoils speed to Santorini (1-4 per day, 5600dr), Mykonos (1-4 per day, 3100dr), Ios (1-3 per day, 5000dr), Naxos (1-2 per day, 2160dr), Syros (1-3 per day, 2670dr), and Rafina (7 per week, 6615dr).

Luggage Storage: The cheapest tend to be at the travel agencies (300dr per day).

Laundromat: For full- or self-service, turn right at Travel Service Irelena (past the bus station on the harbor) and walk 50m. Machines in the back of a souvenir shop. Wash 1200dr. Wash, dry, and soap 1800dr. Open 8:30am-10:30pm. For self-service, go inland at the Memphis Café, opposite the bus station. Wash 950dr, dry 600dr. Open daily 9am-2pm and 6-9pm.

Public Toilets: Beside the small blue 'n' white church north of the windmill. 50dr.

English Bookstore: M.K. Bizas (International Press) (tel. 21 247), past the National Bank; head straight and it's on your right. Large selection of English books. Open daily 9am-10:30pm.

Pharmacy: (tel. 22 223). Next to the self-service laundromat. Open daily 8:30am-1:30pm and 5:30-8:30pm. Others abound, particularly in the old town.

Medical Clinic: (tel. 24 410). Across the street from the toilets. Free physicals. Open Mon.- Fri. 9am-2pm and 6-9pm. Open for emergencies 24hr.

ACCOMMODATIONS

Many hotels and "Rooms to Let" are near the waterfront and in the old town, but a slew of new, fairly cheap pensions and boarding houses have opened up behind the town beach. The dock hawks often offer good deals. Just make sure it's not too far from the town center. In high season, scarce singles cost roughly 4000dr, doubles 6000dr, and triples 8000dr. You may have to consider Naoussa, Piso Livadi, or Antiparos. During the off-season, rooms are 20-40% cheaper than the prices listed.

Festos Pension (tel. 21 635), sister to its swinging namesake in Athens. Turn right on the street before the waterfront church. Follow this travel-agency-lined street to the very end, past the large church on the left. Turn right and look for the sign on the left. Very friendly English-speaking reception, a hangout spot, and cheap breakfast. 5000dr per person. Laundry 1200dr. Reservations recommended.

Hotel Dina (tel. 21 325), past the National Bank near the end of "Market" street. An upscale pension; serene, immaculate, and cordial, with a pleasant garden. Doubles 10,500dr. Triples 13,000dr. Reservations preferred.

Jane's Place (tel. 21 338, -928), run by Jane and Argiris Apostolopoulous, is in the old town behind the bar Pebbles. If you're coming from the island side (Market Street), it's past the May Tay Restaurant on the right, towards the water. Doubles 6000dr, triples 7500dr. Most of the tidy rooms have private baths.

Parasporos Camping (tel. 22 268 or 21 100), 1500m south of the port with frequent shuttle bus service—if you're lucky you'll get the wildly painted yellow bus (900dr per person, 500dr per tent). Includes market, showers, laundry, kitchen.

Koula Camping (tel. 22 081, -082), 400m north of town on the beach. Amenities include market, showers, laundry, kitchen. Person 1000dr, tent 500dr.

FOOD

Restaurants are everywhere—in the old town, on the waterfront, and behind the town beach. As usual, the more authentic places tend to be away from the water. Inland, many *tavernas* have pleasant gardens. Many are similar, so examine the crowd and the food, and decide which appeals to you most.

L'Italiano, left of the waterfront. Sick of Italian food cooked by Greeks? Head here for the real stuff. Excellent *gnocchi* with bleu cheese and zucchini 1300dr.

Happy Green Cow, a block farther inland off the main square. Good vegetarian food in a psychedelic setting. *Falafel* 500dr, *soya gyros* 800dr.

To Tamarisko, near Mimikos Rooms—follow the signs. Lush flower garden, romantic setting. Meatballs 1200dr, pork "Tamarisko" 1600dr.

Levantes (tel. 23 613), near Hotel Dina on the "Market" street beyond the National Bank. Middle Eastern and Greek delicacies. Tabouli 600dr, hummus 500dr.

Apollon, past Levantes. A pricey but very nice *taverna* with seating in a garden. *Mousaka* 1500dr, *kalamari* 1450dr.

Nick's Hamburgers, next to Corfo Leon. Paros' first hamburger joint, established 1977. 100% beef. Nikburger 430dr. Nikfeast (2 burgers, chips, and salad) 890dr.

ENTERTAINMENT

Almost all of Paros' nightspots are along the waterfront south of the windmill. On any given night, throngs of foreigners congregate on the strip, sit in circles around *ouzo* bottles, and sing drunken songs. On the far end of the ferry dock, just before the small white bridge, are hangouts for English-speakers.

Irish Bar Stavros has a rambunctious crowd; the bartenders and the clientele periodically dance on the bar. The bar is bathed in Irish memorabilia and includes an incongruously sedate garden (beer 500dr, cocktails 1000dr).

The Slammer Bar/7 Muses Disco, specializes in tequila slammers for 400dr—there are posted instructions for the uninitiated.

The Paros Experience. Two mind-boggling party complexes round out any night out on Paros. The larger of the two, at the far end of the strip of bars, contains under one roof **The Dubliner, Down Under, Cactus Shots Bar,** and the **Hard Rock Club.** Sit around or dance to any of the four tunes blaring simultaneously (beer 600-700dr, cocktails 1000dr). A little closer to town is the other boozing megaplex, containing **The Londoner, Tequila Bar,** and **Sodoma Dance Club** (beer 600-700dr, cocktails 1000dr).

Aroma's Café, for when you get hungry, or when everything has closed. Head down the road inland for a slice of pizza (300dr). Open 24hr.

Saloon D'Or, the oldest bar on a waterfront strip closer to town. Tempting drink specials; try the fruit cocktail. Also try **Pebbles** near the Saloon D'Or.

Evinos, perched above the buildings; escape the streetside din with jazz and classical music pushing into the wee hours. Beer 500-600dr, cocktails 1000-2000dr.

SIGHTS

Anyone with a fondness for Byzantine architecture will be enraptured by the **Panagia Ekatontapiliani** (the Church of Our Lady of 100 Gates), an imposing 6th-century edifice that houses three separate adjacent churches, cloisters, and a large peaceful courtyard resplendent with pear and orange trees. Only 10 of the 100 doors are immediately obvious—don't waste your time counting. The main structure is the mammoth **Church of the Assumption,** with three tremendous chandeliers. **Church of St. Nikolas** (the oldest of the three) flanks this central structure to the north as does the **baptistry** to the south. To reach the church, walk inland from the public garden. (Open daily 8am-1pm and 4-9pm.) Behind the church, next to the schoolyard, is the **Archaeological Museum,** which includes a 5th-century BC statue of Wingless Nike and a piece of the Parian Chronicle. (Open Tues.-Sun. 8:30am-2:30pm; admission 500dr, students 300dr, Sun. free.)

Just 10km south of town is the cool, spring-fed **Valley of the Butterflies** (Petaloudes), home to an enormous spawning swarm of brown-and-white-striped butterflies. These amazing creatures cover the foliage, blending into their surroundings until they expose their bright red underwings in flight. In June the butterflies converge on this lepidopterous metropolis to mate. You can visit by taking the bus from Paroikia that goes to Aliki (15 per day, 10min., 170dr). Ask to be let off at the butterflies *(petaloudes).* From there, follow the signs up the steep winding road 2km to the entrance. You can also take a tour from one of the various travel agents (2500dr), although it would be a shame to be whisked through here too quickly. (Open Mon.-Sat. 9am-8pm, Sun. 9am-1pm and 4-8pm; admission 230dr.)

■■■ NAOUSSA

Naoussa is a pleasant alternative to Paroikia. It is a natural harbor, cradled on both sides by long, sandy arms in the shape of crab claws. Naoussa has long been a popular port. Ancient Persians, Greeks, Romans, medieval Venetians, Saracens, Turks, and Russians have all anchored at the harbor. The tradition continues today as visitors the world over converge on Naoussa's magnificent beaches and dizzying array of accommodations, restaurants, and shops. Although much of the town has been usurped by this current influx, a stroll along the harbor proves that beneath its tourist-friendly exterior, Naoussa remains, at heart, a traditional Greek fishing village.

Orientation and Practical Information From the bus stop, face the water and cross the small bridge on the left. The road leads to the **police** (tel. 51 202; 24hr.) on the right and to the **OTE** (tel. 51 200; open Mon.-Sat. 7:30am-11pm, Sun. 8am-11pm) on the left. On the right side of the same bridge is a **pharmacy.** (Open Mon.-Sat. 8:30am-2pm and 5:30-9:30pm, Sun. 10am-1pm and 6-8:30pm.) Farther to the right near the water are the **National Bank of Greece** (open Mon.-Thurs. 8:30am-2pm, Fri. 8:45am-1:30pm) and **public toilets.** If you get off the bus and face inland, the commercial street to your left has English books from Shakespeare to Danielle Steele at the **General Bookstore.** Walking along the street roughly 400m (passing by the blue-domed church), you'll find the **post office** (tel. 51 495; open Mon.-Fri. 7:30am-2pm, Sat. 8am-2:30pm) on the right just past the Santa Maria turnoff. **Postal Code:** 84401; **Telephone Code:** 0284.

From Paroikia, roughly 30 buses a day make the 15-min. trip to Naoussa (200dr). On the water, across from the bus stop in Naoussa, a blue booth sells round-trip tickets for small boats going to beaches at Kolibithres (365dr), Monastiri (450dr), Laggeri (625dr), and Santa Maria (970dr). There are also bus connections to Santa Maria (6 per day), Ampelas (2 per day), Piso Livadi (13 per day), Drios (13 per day), Aliki (5 per day), Petaloudes (5 per day), and back to Paroikia (40 per day).

Accommodations For a small town, Naoussa offers many hotels and "Rooms to Let." In off-season, prices decrease by 20-40%. **Pension Hora** (tel. 51 011), at the top of the stairs just past the OTE, has clean rooms with balconies and refrigerators. (Doubles 12,700dr.) Right next to the bus stop, **Hotel Aliprantis** (tel. 51 571, -648) is convenient. (Doubles 12,500dr.) English-speaking Katerina at **Simitzi Tours** (tel. 51 113; fax 51 761; 8:30am-midnight in high season), opposite the bus stop, rents studios with kitchens (for 2-4 people, 6000-20,000dr depending on season and number of people). "Rooms to Let" cost roughly 5000-10,000dr for doubles 6000-

12,000dr for triples. There are two campsites near Naoussa. Two kilometers back towards Paroikia awaits **Camping Naoussa** (tel. 51 595; person 1100dr, tent 900dr), and 4km toward Santa Maria beach lies the new **Camping Surfing Beach** (tel. 51 013 or 52 491; fax 51 937; person 1200dr, tent 600dr).

Food and Entertainment Restaurants offering Greek and international cuisine line the inland street in front of the church and cluster near the harbor by the National Bank. **Diamantis,** behind the church, is an excellent choice for Greek fare (swordfish *souvlaki* 1100dr, stuffed tomatoes 850dr). **Zorba's,** with eye-catching pink tablecloths and blue chairs, is in front of the church (four-cheese tortellini 1350dr, *pastitsio* 950dr; open 24hr.; Visa accepted).

Surprisingly, there's a lack of casual bars in Naoussa. After dinner, try your luck swatting mosquitoes at the outdoor **movie theater** next to Diamantis (shows nightly at 10pm). On the first Sunday in July, cruise around Naoussa's harbor and feast on free fish and wine as you watch traditional dancing at the **Wine and Fish Festival.** On August 23, festivities commemorate a naval victory over the Turks.

■■■ AROUND PAROS ISLAND

Cutting through the center of the island towards the east coast, you'll reach **Marathi,** 5km from Paroikia. The marble quarries that made Paros famous in ancient times are nearby. Still considered to be among the finest in the world, Parian marble is translucent up to 3mm thick, one-third the opacity of most other marble. The quarries are now idle (they're also difficult to find).

Lefkes, 5km from Marathi, was the largest village on the island in the 19th century when Parians moved inland to escape the pirates swashbuckling off the coast. Now a quiet village of 400 inhabitants, its classic Cycladic architecture makes it the prettiest town in Paros' interior. Road meets sea at **Piso Livadi,** 11km from Lefkes. If you're not into Paroikia's nightlife, Piso Livadi can be a fine place to while away your hours on Paros. **Perantinos Travel & Tourism** (tel./fax 41 135), across from the bus stop, provides info on rooms around town as well as an international phone. (Open 9am-10pm.) Doubles range from 5000-10,000dr, depending on season and quality. Up the street from the bus stop toward Paroikia are two straightforward, clean, hotels: **Hotel Piso Livadi** (tel. 41 309; doubles 5000dr, w/bath 8000dr; triples 6000dr, w/bath 9500dr) and **Londos Hotel** (tel. 41 218; doubles 10,000dr). Serene **Camping Captain Kafkis** (tel. 41 479) is roughly 1km back along the same road (person 920dr, small tent 630dr, large tent 730dr).

South of Piso Livadi is unimpressive Loagas beach; 3km farther ranges **Christi Akti,** "Golden Beach." It's one of the largest and best beaches on Paros. **Drios,** the next beach south, is quieter, rockier, and more secluded. The decadent seek rooms here so they can roll out of bed and immediately run naked into the sea.

Public buses run from Paroikia to **Pounda** (25 per day, 15min., 170dr) and **Aliki** (15 per day, 40min., 250dr) on Paros' west coast, home of pleasant, remote beaches. From Pounda, 30 boats per day cross to **Antiparos** (10min., 150dr). There are also boats from Paroikia's harbor to **Krios, Martselo, Kaminia,** and **Agios Fokas** beaches (every 15min., 9:30am-7pm), all of which are relatively calm and secluded.

■ NEAR PAROS: ANTIPAROS

Like Piso Livadi on mainland Paros, Antiparos is a quiet, easygoing alternative to Paroikia and Naoussa. Those uninterested, or unable, to find rooms on Paros take refuge here. Literally "opposite Paros," Antiparos is so close to its neighbor that, according to local lore, travelers once signaled the ferryman on Paros by opening the door of a chapel on Antiparos. Its proximity and unique underground caves also make Antiparos a popular daytrip. From Paroikia, take a direct boat (12 per day, 45min., 410dr each way), or one of the 25 daily buses to Pounda (15min., 170dr) followed by one of 30 daily boats to Antiparos (10min., 150dr each way).

Orientation and Practical Information Most of this small island is undeveloped—virtually all of its 700 inhabitants live in the town at which the ferry docks, and there's no bus service (except to the stalactite caves). At the harbor you'll find a few waterfront restaurants and several hotels and pensions. Tourist shops, *tavernas,* and bakeries line the street leading from the dock to the center of town, where a cluster of funky pubs and bars have opened up. The center has a wide-open plaza with cafés under shady trees. Go through the stone archway to the right of the square to reach the **Castle of Antiparos,** a village built in the 1440s.

Oliaros Tours (tel. 61 231; fax 61 496) on the waterfront next to the National Bank, assists with finding rooms (doubles roughly 9000dr) and has boat and bus schedules. It also has an international telephone and currency exchange. The **National Bank** next door is open only during high season (Mon.-Fri. 9:45am-1pm). The **post office** is on the left side of the street leading from the waterfront to the square (open Mon.-Fri. 7:30am-noon). Past the post office the road bends left and passes the diminutive **OTE,** which will be on your right just before the road opens into the main square (open Mon.-Fri. 8:30am-12:30pm and 5-10:30pm). Closer to the water on the same street as the post office are the self-service **laundry** (wash, dry, and soap 2000dr; open 10am-2pm and 5-8pm) and an **English bookstore** (tel. 61 255). Behind the unobtrusive wooden sign hides a stupendous collection of new and used books, both meaty and cheesy, in English, French, German, Greek, Italian, and Dutch (500-1500dr). (Open 10am-4pm and 7pm-midnight.) The number for the **police** is 61 202, for a **doctor** 61 219. **Postal Code:** 84007; **Telephone Code:** 0284.

Accommodations Rooms are easy to find. The **Mantalena Hotel** (tel. 61 206), to the right of the dock (facing inland), has clean rooms with private baths and balconies. (Doubles 8000dr.) On the road to Camping Antiparos, the **Theologos Hotel** (tel. 61 244) offers beautiful, sunny rooms with private refrigerators and gleaming bathrooms (doubles 8000dr). Pleasant, cheap (6000dr) rooms lie inland to the left of the harbor (facing town). **Camping Antiparos** (tel. 61 221) is 800m northwest of town on Ag. Yiannis Theologos Beach (person 900dr, tent 200dr).

Food and Entertainment Some excellent restaurants include **Taverna Klimataria** (take a left down the alley next to the bookstore), under blazing pink azalea bushes (*kalamari* 1000dr, Greek salad 800dr) and **O Spyros** next to the National Bank on the waterfront (*kalamari* w/pasta 800dr). The inland main square is jam-packed with rock 'n' roll bars and watering holes, as Antiparos follows the lead of its neighbors. Choose your favorite ambience from among **Time Pub, Clown Pub, The Doors,** and many more. Beers run 400-700dr.

Sights Antiparos' main attraction are its cool, wet stalactite caves at the south end of the island. Names of the caves' famous visitors are written on the walls with their years of entry (alongside some of their less famous 20th-century counterparts who took it upon themselves to leave a mark). Some of the stalactites were broken off by Russian naval officers in the 18th century and "donated" to a St. Petersburg museum while still more were destroyed by Italians during WWII. Despite the graffiti and history of theft, the caves, plunging 100m down into the earth, retain their beauty. Ask a ticket taker about the various stories associated with the caves: how Queen Amalia lost her earrings in 1840 or how a team of French archaeologists spent Christmas, 1673, inside. **Excursion buses** run from Antiparos' port every morning hour (20min., 1000dr round-trip). (Caves open 10:15am-4:45pm; 400dr.)

NAXOS ΝΑΞΟΣ

Alluring interior villages and tranquil beaches draw a crowd of old and young alike to the Cyclades' largest and most fertile island. Naxos' rocky promontories, squat windmills, and demure villages tucked between rolling hills are still illuminated by one of the sky's brightest stars. Natural wealth has made the island one of the richest of the Cyclades, a fact which becomes apparent on a short walk through town of Naxos. The island's independence of foreign money is a refreshing change.

Naxos has one of the most colorful Cycladic histories: Parians, Cretans, Ionians, Athenians, Macedonians, Egyptians, Rhodians, Romans, Byzantines, Venetians, Turks, and Russians all ruled the island in succession. The island's strongest historical link, however, is shrouded in myth. After Ariadne, the daughter of King Minos of Crete, saved Theseus from her father's labyrinth, the young prince fled with her to Naxos. After they had spent the night there, Theseus, who said he was going to wash his hair, abandoned her. Even mythical princes are only after one thing. Ariadne wept at finding herself alone on the shore, but her despair was soon remedied. Along came Dionysus who, on his way, had quite an adventure. Captured by pirates, he immobilized the ship's sails with spontaneously growing vines and turned the malevolent buccaneers into serpents and himself into a lion. Arriving on Naxos, Dionysus married Ariadne. When she died, the god put her bridal wreath among the stars where the Corona Borealis shines today.

■■■ NAXOS TOWN

Naxos Town can be roughly divided into two sections: the old, historic, mesmerizing half and the newer, practical, altogether uninteresting half. The latter includes the buildings on the far side of town near Agios Georgios beach and the whole waterfront façade. Old Naxos lies behind the waterfront shops, on the hill leading up to Venetian castle. As you wander through the tangled streets of old Naxos Town, you may feel as though you jumped into a painting. The ancient wooden porticoes and glimpses of the brilliant blue sea enhance the charm; flowers and trellised plants engulf the old homes of the castle, and colorful markets whirl with activity.

ORIENTATION AND PRACTICAL INFORMATION

All ferries and hydrofoils dock in Naxos Town. Maps can only get you so far; streets are poorly labeled and tend to zig and zag. The first street back from the waterfront, running parallel to the sea, is **Nikodemos.** Behind lies **Old Market Street.,** the easiest entrance into the labyrinthine heart of town, which wraps itself around the castle. The arrows painted by hotel and restaurant owners may orient you best.

Tourist Office: (tel. 24 358, -525; fax 25 200) after hours, on the waterfront opposite the ferry dock and bus depot. If you need it, they have it: advice on hotels and rooms-to-let; booking service for Naxos and all of Greece; bus, ferry, and hydrofoil schedules; currency exchange; international telephone; luggage storage (300dr); safety deposit boxes (300dr); and *Let's Go* guides for rent. In case of emergency or extreme frazzlement, ask for Despina; she speaks fluent English. They buy and sell used books. Open daily 8:30am-10pm.

Police: (tel. 22 100 or 23 280). Turn onto paved inland street, bear right; the police station is on the left. Open 24 hr.

Port Police: Nikodemos St. (tel. 22 300), above Zas Travel on the waterfront. Entrance around back. Open 24 hr.

Post Office: Walk down the waterfront (water on your right), left after Hotel Hermes, and take your first right. Open Mon.-Fri. 7:30am-2pm. **Postal Code:** 84300.

OTE: Next to the Hotel Hermes and opposite the bank, at the south end of the harbor. Sept.-June open Mon.-Fri. 7:30am-3:30pm; July-Aug. Mon.-Sat. 7:30am-10pm, Sun. 9am-10pm. **Telephone Code:** 0285.

Bank: The **National Bank of Greece** offers **currency exchange.** Walk down the waterfront with the water on your right; the bank is on the southern end. Open Mon.-Thurs. 8am-2pm, Fri. 8am-1:30pm. Several other banks line the waterfront.

Tourist Agency: CIAO Travel (tel. 23 933; fax 28 495). Friendly, helpful office with cheap luggage storage (200dr), a public telephone, **currency exchange,** accommodation and ticket info, and moped rental. Open daily 8am-midnight.

Flights: Two Olympic Airways flights per day to Athens (18,500dr). Call **Naxos Tours** (tel. 22 095) for information and tickets.

Buses: The depot is directly in front of the ferry dock. Schedules are posted both at the Tourist Information Center and the **bus station** across the street and a little to the left (facing inland) from the depot. Arrive ½hr. early; buses tend to be packed, especially the ones to Filoti (6 per day, 300dr) and Apollonas (5 per day, 2hr., 850dr). Buses also run to Agia Anna beach (21 per day, 15min., 220dr) via Agios Prokopios beach, Chalki (6 per day, ½hr., 280dr), Apiranthos (5 per day, 1hr., 440dr), and Pyrgaki beach (3 per day, 1hr., 320dr).

Ferries: Travel to Piraeus (3-5 per day, 7hr., 3708dr), Paros (3-5 per day, 1hr., 1221dr), Ios (6 per day, 1½hr., 1957dr), Santorini (6 per day, 3hr., 2217dr), Mykonos (2-3 per day, 2hr., 1326dr), Syros (2 per day, 2½hr., 1808dr), Amorgos (daily, 3½hr., 2020dr), and Crete (954dr). Ferries also depart from here to numerous smaller Cycladic islands, and occasionally to the Dodecanese islands and Crete. Ferries to Iraklia, Schinoussa, Koufonisi, and Donoussa (daily at 3pm, 1½hr., 1067dr).

Flying Dolphins: There are hydrofoils to Rafina (6746dr), Mykonos (2655dr), Ios (4120dr), Santorini (4672dr), Paros (2497dr), Andros (5347dr), Iraklion (2380dr), and Amorgos (4244dr).

Taxis: Call 22 444, or walk a little way down the waterfront where they gather.

Motorbike Rental: Theoharis (tel. 23 498), in the same office as CIAO Travel. Bikes run 3000-4000dr per day. Open daily 8am-midnight.

Laundromat: Vesta Pro-Wash (tel. 23 316), before the post office. Wash 1000dr. Dry 800dr. Luggage storage (300dr). Open Mon.-Sat. 9:30am-1:30pm and 5-9pm.

Public Toilets and Showers: Behind Toast Time on Nikodemos St. Turn left after Zas Travel. Toilets 100dr, showers 600dr. Open daily 8am-2pm and 5-11pm.

English Bookstore: Vrakas, look for the signs on the waterfront street and the storefront reading "gold-silver used books." In the back of a jewelry shop, Vrakas buys and sells used books (200-1800dr) and has amassed a strange collection (sort of like a library tag sale) over the years.

Pharmacy: several along the waterfront, each with posted hours and directions to a pharmacy open 24 hr.

Health Center: (tel. 23 333 or 22 661) on the edge of town on the road to the villages. Has 14 doctors (some English-speaking) and can access helicopter service to Athens in emergencies. 24 hr.

ACCOMMODATIONS

In late July and August on Naxos, most hotels fill to capacity. At other times of the year, expect to pay 20-50% less. People who meet the boat charge roughly 4000-4500dr for singles, 5000-8000dr for doubles, and 7000-10,000dr for triples. A plethora of inexpensive rooms can be found by pursuing the trail of rooms-to-let signs in old Naxos Town, among the most pleasant settings.

Anna Legaki's Rooms (tel. 22 837), take the first left before the post office and look for the sign on the right. Although the rooms aren't huge and are in the less desirable, newer part of town, Anna and her family's hospitality more than make up for it. Doubles 5000dr, triples 7000dr. Includes breakfast.

Hotel Panorama (tel. 24 404), in Old Naxos near Hotel Dionysos (follow red-hand signs pointing the way). Clean and welcoming, especially suited to families. Very proud of the—you guessed it—panoramic view of the harbor and town. Doubles 8000dr, triples 10,000dr. Breakfast 750dr.

Hotel Anixis (tel. 22 112), also next to Hotel Dionysos. Sparkling and verdant. Doubles 9000dr, triples 11,000dr. Breakfast 700dr.

Hotel Chateau Zevgoli (tel. 22 993), follow the light blue signs in old Naxos. The nighttime haunt of Despina, goddess of the tourist office. Bedside dried flowers, potpourri in the bathrooms, nurturing owners—your mother would be glad you're staying here even if it stretches your budget. Doubles 16,000-18,000dr, triples 19,000-21,500dr.

Hotel Dionysos (tel. 22 331), in old Naxos. Follow the signs. Essentially a youth hostel and accordingly cheap; a bit run down (lots o' mosquitoes and other beasties), but social. Stay if you're desperate for lodging. Check-out noon. Dorm beds 2500dr, doubles 5000dr, roof 2000dr.

Naxos Camping (tel. 23 500, -501), the closest to town. 1.5km by foot along St. George's beach. Swimming pool. 1000dr per person, 630dr per tent. 10% discount to *Let's Go* readers.

Maragas Camping (tel. 24 552 or 25 204; fax 24 552). Farthest away but also the nicest and virtually on the beach. 1400dr per person, 750dr per tent. Shuttle bus service waits at the ferry-docks, or take the frequent buses to Ag. Anna beach.

Camping Apollon (tel. 24 113, -8). Located between the two beaches. Swimming pool, private rooms. 1000dr per person, 200dr per tent, dorm beds 1500dr.

FOOD AND ENTERTAINMENT

Located on or near the waterfront, many of Naxos' restaurants flaunt polished appearances and multi-lingual menus. Restaurants in the maze of Old Naxos are generally more scenic and more likely to have authentic, tasty food. Picnicking is a down-to-earth alternative. Inquire at the shops about the famous local wines, liqueurs, and cheeses. The two markets on the waterfront are the most convenient, but the **Cold Market** is cheaper and has better fruits and vegetables.

Christo's Grill, one street back from the waterfront near the dock, is a meat eater's heaven. (Chicken 800dr.) **Koutouki,** high up in the old city, is one of the hungry traveler's best pit stops in town. All portions are big and entrees come with mixed vegetables, french fries, and rice. (*Souvlaki* 1300dr, stuffed peppers 1300dr.) **Apolafsi** (Delight), on the second floor on the water, has good quality Greek "apolafsi" (veal, smoked pork, 1300dr; veal with pasta 1000dr). **Nikos,** above the Commercial bank on the waterfront, is a large, popular restaurant. (Naxos cheese 600dr, fried meatballs 1000dr.) Naxos also abounds with lighter fare—crepes, omelettes, *tost*, pastries, and the like. **Rendez-Vous** (PANTEBOY) on the waterfront prides itself on hot, delicious, gooey *loukoumades* (honey pastries) for 500dr. Farther down, **Aktaion** competes for the sweet-toothed crowd (chocolate pastry 450dr).

Naxos' nightlife isn't as frenetic as that of some of the other islands. Many people stroll the main promenade before heading to a bar. Bars offer happy hours in the earlier part of the evening (8-11pm) with drinks at half-price. For those who must boogie, there are a few nearby discos as well (usually open at 11pm). Popular bars include: **The Jam,** behind the OTE, with loud music and (allegedly) 2002 different cocktails (1000-1500dr each), **Mike's Bar,** across the street, decorated with Dali posters all over (draft beer 300-700dr), and **Musique Café,** a popular hangout on the waterfront all day long (beer 600-800dr, cocktails 1000-1200dr). Two lively discos are the **Ocean Club,** behind the National Bank with the latest in Euro dance music (beer 800-1000dr), and **Asteria Disco,** 5min. from town on Ag. Georgios beach with music ranging from Guns 'n' Roses to the Village People (beer 700dr).

SIGHTS

While in Naxos Town, walk around the old **Venetian Castle,** a series of mansions inhabited by descendants of the original Frankish and Venetian nobility. Up from the Hotel Pantheon, The Castle and The Loom merit a visit for folk art merchandise. The engrossing **Archaeological Museum** is in a house where Nikos Kazantzakis, author of *Last Temptation of Christ* and *Zorba the Greek,* once studied. The museum contains beautiful Cycladic artifacts, as well as vases, sculpture, jewels, and implements found in Mycenaean and Geometric chamber tombs. (Open Tues.-Sun. 8:30am-3pm; admission 500dr, students 300dr, free on Sun. and holidays.)

From the waterfront, you can see the white chapel of *Myrditiotissa* floating serenely in the harbor on its man-made islet. Nearby is the **Portara,** an intriguing marble archway on the hilltop near the port. According to myth, this was where Ariadne lost Theseus and found Dionysus; later, it was the site of Ariadne's palace. Excavation has debunked this romantic reasoning—in fact, the archway, along with the platform and some columns, is merely detritus from yet another temple to Apollo. Today it makes an excellent spot for a banana liqueur and *baklava* picnic.

■■■ AROUND NAXOS ISLAND

Those who leave having seen only Naxos Town will have missed the island's true beauty. The expansive interior of Naxos, the largest of the Cyclades, is decorated with rolling hills, staggering rock formations, craftily terraced hillsides, expansive olive groves, tranquil white villages, countless churches, and herds of sheep and goats. The ideal way to appreciate the landscape is on foot. Villages are situated so that food and shelter are available at convenient intervals and many are connected by footpaths. Away from the tourist hustle of Naxos Town and the beaches, the local Greeks are extremely cordial and gracious—don't be surprised to receive a hearty "yia sou" as you cross paths with a friendly shepherd.

Mopeds can be ideal for reaching the popular beaches south of town and some nearby inland sites and villages. Much of the island, however, is mountainous and roads are not in the best condition; several people die each year on Naxos' more rocky, tortuous roads. Many travelers opt instead to take a morning bus to **Apollonas** (Apollon) (2hr., 850dr), a small fishing village on the northern tip of the island. From Apollonas, you can slowly make your way back to Naxos alternating between bus and foot, stopping in towns like Korouida, Koronos, Apiranthos, Filoti, and Chalki. On the initial bus trip to Apollonas, examine the exhilarating scenery and note which areas you may want to investigate further on the way back.

The first hour of the ride from Naxos Town to Chalki takes you through cultivated mountainsides rich with olive trees, churches, and wildflowers that sprout each spring and summer. Before Chalki, there's a turn-off for **Ano Sangri,** an isolated town of winding flagstone streets 1km west of the road. You can get off the bus at the turn-off and walk, or trek the entire way from Naxos Town (roughly 1½hr.).

Chalki, a placid village surrounded by Venetian towers, marks the beginning of the magnificent **Tragea**—an enormous, tremendously still Arcadian olive grove. Stop in at the **Panagia Protothonis,** the parish church of Chalki, right across from the bus stop. Restoration work there has uncovered wall paintings from the 11th through 13th centuries. If the church is closed, the priest can let you in.

If you have a motorbike or car, an alternate route takes you from Naxos Town through Melanes to **Flerio,** where one of the magnificent **kouroi** of Naxos sleeps in a woman's garden. *Kouroi,* larger-than-life, Egyptian-influenced sculptures of male figures, were first made in Greece in the 7th century BC. This one was probably abandoned in its marble quarry because it broke before completion. Its owner runs a small *kafeneion* in the garden. From Flerio, backtrack and follow a road which passes through a trio of charming villages built in a river valley—**Kato Potamia, Mesi Potamia,** and **Ano Potamia**—before reaching Chalki. A map is essential.

Soon after leaving Chalki you'll reach **Filoti,** a village where the Tragea ends and the road climbs the flanks of Mt. Zas. These slopes offer superb views extending all the way to Poros and the sea beyond. Serious hikers might want to check out the **Cave of Zeus,** most easily accessible from Filoti. Legend has it that this is the spot where the king of gods was raised by an eagle (from which he received the power of hurling thunderbolts). This 150m deep cave is a good 1½-hr. trek uphill from Filoti. Determined mythologists, or those simply looking for a good hike with some excellent views, should wear sturdy footwear, bring water and a flashlight, and should not come alone (last year it took a helicopter search crew a week to find a man who fell and injured himself here). If this excursion sounds appealing, head up the road to Apiranthos for roughly 20-30min. until a dirt road branches off on the right. Follow this road to its end (passing through a gate on the way), just before a clearing with a drinkable **spring water fountain.** From there, keep going on, staying on the left (uphill) whenever possible. Look for red marks on stones, but don't expect any signs. Forty-five minutes more should bring you past some rather difficult terrain to a second potable fountain, just below the mouth of the cave. The grotto itself is large, cool, and rather slimy, but quite interesting to explore.

A 15-min. bus ride from Filoti brings you to the small town of **Apiranthos,** which houses the **Michael Bardani Museum** in a white building on the right side of the main street. The museum contains many remnants of Cycladic artifacts. Also in Apiranthos are a modest **folk art museum** and a **Geology Museum.** All three are "officially" open only early in the day (8am-2pm). The museums lack posted hours, and the villagers won't necessarily open the doors for you. Many homes in Apiranthos are 300-400 years old, and lie in the shadows of the two castles which dominate the town (closed to the public). The mountain views from the edges of the town are stunning, and locals are cordial to the few tourists who come this way. From Apiranthos through **Koronos** and **Koronida,** a 1-hr. drive away, the road snakes through interior mountain ranges. The terraced landscape, laden with fruit and olive trees, plunges dramatically into the valleys below.

One of the most famous *kouroi* of Naxos lies a short walk from the harbor at **Apollonas.** At 10½m long, this *kouros* is more massive, if less finely sculpted, than the one in Flerio, and is also incomplete. From the Apollonas bus stop, walk back along the main road uphill until you come to the fork in the road. Take a sharp right (onto the fork the bus did not take coming into town) and walk up until you see the stairs at the "ΠΡΟΣ ΚΟΥΡΟ" sign. It's roughly a 20-min. walk.

On your return trip from Apollonas to Chalki, you might want to get off the bus at Filoti (roughly 2km away) and walk through the **Tragea.** Footpaths off the main road will lead you into the dense grove. It is easy to get delightfully lost wandering among the scattered churches and tranquil scenery of the Tragea. Head west to return to the main road. A map is more than helpful here. Would-be hikers might pick up a copy of *Walking Tours on Naxos* by Christian Ucke, an exceedingly informative book available from the Tourist Office in both English and German.

The most remote, uncrowded **beaches** and clearest waters are the farthest from town. Near town, the long sandy stretches of **Agios Georgios, Agios Prokopios, Agia Anna,** and **Plaka** are crammed with sunbathers and unsightly modern buildings. All traces of authentic Greek culture are obliterated along these beaches, which are lined with hotels, rooms-to-let, bars, *tavernas,* discos, and *creperies.* As you move away from town; younger, more beautiful, and less clothed bathers begin to take over. By Agia Anna, you'll probably encounter **nude sunbathers.** Why not join them? The beaches at **Mikri Vigla, Kastraki, Aliko,** and **Pyrgaki** are also accessible by bus from Naxos Town. Here desert meets sea; scrub pines, prickly pear, and century plants grow on the dunes behind you, shooing you towards the water.

AMORGOS ΑΜΟΡΓΟΣ

Amorgos' stunning cliffside monastery, scattered churches, and assorted beaches offer a welcome respite from the throngs of tourists on other islands. Although the island's popularity has increased since the filming of *The Big Blue* here in 1988, Amorgos is still the place to come for a lazy, restful couple of days. Ferry connections are relatively infrequent and generally stop at Amorgos' two ports in succession—**Aegiali** in the northeast and the larger **Katapola** in the southwest. Be sure to disembark at your desired port; transportation between the two is rare.

■■■ KATAPOLA

Katapola, the island's central port, is an idyllic village with windmills, whitewashed houses, and narrow streets in the shadow of the remnants of a Venetian castle. It is small, quiet, and free of the bustle of many other port towns in the Cyclades.

Orientation and Practical Information Near the ferry dock is a **tourist office** labeled "ΠΡΑΚΤΟΡΕΙΟ" (tel. 71 278), home to helpful info, currency exchange, an international telephone, and some ferry and hydrofoil tickets. (Open daily 8:30am-2pm and 5-11pm.) If they don't sell the ticket you want, they'll tell you where to buy it. Since there's no post office or OTE in Katapola, inquire here about stamps and phone cards. The **port police** (tel. 71 259; 24 hr.) are on the right along the road to the **pharmacy** (tel. 71 400; open Sun.-Fri. 9am-2pm and 6:30-9:30pm, Sat. 10:30am-1pm and 6:30-9pm); both are on a side street heading inland from the main square. **Public toilets** are at the beginning of the rocky town beach across the street from **Rent-A-Bike Thomas** (tel. 71 007), where a helpful English-speaker charges 2500-3000dr per day for a moped. Call a **taxi** at 71 255. **Postal Code:** 84008; **Telephone Code:** 0285.

Depending on the season, 2 -3 **buses** per day (1hr., 400dr) connect the two towns along a bumpy dirt road, stopping at Chora along the way (15min. from Katapola, 45min. from Aegiali). Since the bus is tiny, arrive early to secure a seat. An occasional ferry (2-3 per week) runs from Katapola to Aegiali in the morning, returning in the afternoon or evening. Contact one of the several tourist offices in either town for more detailed schedules on both the bus and ferry. From Amorgos (both ports), **ferries** sail to Piraeus (2-4 per week, 8-13hr., 3940dr), Naxos (1-2 per day, 4-7hr., 2015dr), Paros (1-2 per day, 2357dr), Mykonos (3 per week, 2600dr), Tinos (3 per week, 2600dr), and Syros (3 per week, 2530dr). **Hydrofoils** head 2-4 times per week to Rafina (8000dr), Naxos (4244dr), Paros (5300dr), Santorini (4250dr), Ios (4004dr), Mykonos (5800dr), Syros (7370dr), Tinos (5800dr), and Andros (5683dr). Ferry and hydrofoil schedules are chaotic. Ask a travel agent for help.

Accommodations There are tons of appealing pensions and "Rooms to Let;" it's probably best to walk straight past the dock hawks who swoop down upon you. As is standard practice, prices for accommodations during the off-season are lower by 20-40%. To find the overflowing garden, soothing view, and free kitchen facilities at **Dimitri's Place** (tel. 71 309), walk along the harbor with the water on your left and take a right just before the small bridge. From there, look for the adorable Dimitri's P(a)lace sign. (Doubles 5000dr, w/bath 8000dr.) Also in a lovely garden setting is **Pension Anna** (tel. 71 218); follow the signs on the inland road behind the small square with Pension Amorgos. To get here, go to the left and double back higher up. (Doubles 6000dr, studios w/kitchens 10,000dr.) Closer to the water and not as lovely are **Pension Amorgos** (tel. 71 013, -121), with blue trimmed rooms (doubles 6000dr, w/bath and kitchen 7000dr) and **Katapola "Rooms to Let"** on the waterfront near Rent-A-Bike Thomas. (Doubles w/bath 7000dr.) Cheapest of all, pleasant **Amorgos Camping** is a short walk from town; cross the small bridge on the quay; follow the signs. (Person 750dr, tent 500dr; breakfast 500dr.)

Food The waterfront is lined with *tavernas* and cafés. **Akrogiali,** on the corner of the waterfront plaza, is a bit pricey, but the Greek salads (780dr) are huge and every meal includes a complimentary glass of wine. **The Corner** serves standard fare (*pastitsio* 800dr). For a change of pace, try the creperie down the street from the port police and pharmacy (cheese, ham, and tomato crepe 900dr).

■■■ AROUND THE ISLAND

Katapola literally means "below the town." In this case, the town above is **Chora,** also known as Amorgos, 6km from the harbor along the island's only significant paved road. Less convenient as a base for your stay, Chora is nonetheless a restful and ravishing option. Sights include a 14th-century Venetian **fortress,** a row of retired windmills precariously perched on the mountain ledge above town, simple churches, and a handful of craft shops. Roughly 9 buses per day travel from Katapola (15min., 160dr), the famous monastery, and Agia Anna beach. Chora is home to Amorgos' only **post office** (tel. 71 250) past the small square on the uphill end of town (open Mon.-Fri. 7:30am-2pm), and its main **OTE** (tel. 71 399), at the very top of the town near the stairs leading down the other face of the mountain to the monastery. (Open Mon.-Fri. 7:30am-3pm.) There is a **police station** (tel. 71 210) here, down a bit and to the left (facing uphill) of the post office, but they're not all that helpful. (Open 8am-2pm.) If you spend the night, look for "Rooms to Let" signs throughout the town's narrow streets or ask at *tavernas*. Near the bus stop, look for signs to **Pension Panorama** or **Pension Illias** (tel. 71 277). Both offer clean, stark rooms. (Doubles 7000dr.) Several *tavernas* and cafés are tucked in the meandering streets. Wander until you find **Kastanis** for hearty fare and occasional live Greek music. (*Mousaka* 950dr.) **Liotrivi,** below the bus station, offers *kalamari* and stuffed tomatoes for 900dr each.

A trip to Amorgos is incomplete without a visit to the **Chozoviotissa** monastery. Walk ½hr. down a path of steps and loose rocks or trave; 5min. by bus from Chora to the beginning of a steep 1km path to the 11th-century whitewashed edifice. The monastery is built so flawlessly onto the sheer face of a cliff that it appears to have grown there. Legend has it that attempts to build the monastery on the shore were twice thwarted by divine intervention before the workers discovered their bag of tools mysteriously hanging from the cliff, causing them to interpret the omen as advice on where to recommence construction. The monastery is undoubtedly one of the most exhilarating visual spectacles in all of Greece. If you complete the hike up between 8am and 2pm (also 5-7pm in the summer), the monks may reward you with free cold water, Greek liqueur, and sweets. Contrary to the sign posted at the base of the climb, spare clothing is available at the entrance, but it is more respectful for men to wear long pants, women dresses or long skirts; no bare shoulders.

TINOS ΤΗΝΟΣ

Tinos has been a place of religious significance for Greeks since the War of Independence, when a nun named Pelagia, guided by a vision, found a miracle-working icon of the Virgin and Christ buried in an underground church. The **Icon of the Annunciation,** also known as the *Megalochari* (Great Joy) or *Panagia Evangelistria,* is one of the most sacred relics of the Orthodox church. Each year on the Feasts of the Annunciation (March 25th) and the Assumption (August 15th), thousands of pilgrims crowd the island to pray at the icon.

Although the icon is its primary attraction, Tinos has played home to some of Greece's most prominent artists and offers 100 other churches, 15 natural beaches, 10 museums, a rustic interior, and a more authentic view of Greece than most Cycladic isles. Much of the island's beauty lies in Tinos' countryside, punctuated by beautiful **dovecote towers** that play home to countless pigeons.

■■■ TINOS TOWN

Tinos Town is unmistakably a place of religious worship. Even sellers of tacky Greek souvenirs sell cheap, imitation icons here. The town is clean and generally calm except for the yearly fortnight when it overflows with pilgrims. This port rose to international prominence on August 15, 1940, when an Italian submarine torpedoed the Greek cruiser "Elli," which was docked in the harbor for the holiday. The attack came two months before Mussolini declared war.

Orientation and Practical Information All boats dock in Tinos Town. From the dock, walk left to the center of town where you can't miss **Leoforos Megalochares,** a wide avenue leading uphill to the Neoclassical façade of the **Panayia Evangelistria** church. Running parallel to Leoforos Megalochares up to the church, **Evangelistrias Street** (nicknamed Bazaar St. by the locals), overflows with religious trinkets. There are no tourist police, but the **police** (tel. 22 100), 5min. out of town on the road to Kionia, can help. The **post office** is on the far right end of the waterfront, behind the small square with the war monument (open Mon.-Fri. 7:30am-2pm). A few blocks up on the right is the **OTE** (open Mon.-Fri. 7:30am-3:10pm). A smaller OTE is at the harbor, in the white building by the water (open daily in summer 8am-11pm). The **National Bank of Greece** is on the waterfront across from the bus depot. (Open Mon.-Thurs. 8am-2pm, Fri. 8am-1:30pm.) **Public toilets** are at the opposite end of the waterfront near Dolphin Sq., behind the Hotel Lito. Tucked into a row of *tavernas* next to Hotel Lito on the left-hand side of the waterfront is an overgrown newsstand with the latest English-language **pulp fiction** (tel. 22 581; open daily 8am-11pm). **Postal Code:** 84200; **Telephone Code:** 0283.

Buses (tel. 22 440) leave from the station a few storefronts left of the National Bank. They depart 2-7 times daily for the villages of Pyrgos (600dr), Panormos (650dr), Kalloni (470dr), Steni (250dr), Skalados (320dr), Kionia (170dr), and Porto (170dr). A schedule is posted in the station window. For a **taxi,** dial 22 470 or inquire at the blue booth to the right of the waterfront (6am-2am). Renting a **moped** is probably the best way to see Tinos, but take special care on the narrow, gravel mountain roads. Both the yellow and red paths on the town map are pretty bad; be cautious. Try **Vidalis,** 16 Zanaki Alavanou St. (tel. 23 400), which leads off the right side of the waterfront (facing inland), or **Jason's** (tel. 22 583), just before Alavanou St., on the waterfront (50cc bike 1500dr per day at both).

Tinos can be reached by frequent ferries and hydrofoils from both Piraeus and Rafina near Athens, as well as Mykonos, Syros, and Andros. **Ferries** from Tinos travel to Mykonos (2-4 per day, 40min., 1200dr), Andros (2-3 per day, 2hr., 1645dr), Syros (1-2 per day, 40min., 850dr), Piraeus (1-2 per day, 5½hr., 3585dr), and Rafina (2-4 per day, 4hr., 2740dr). During high season, there is also weekly service to Paros (3065dr), Naxos (3550dr), Santorini (7000dr), and Ios (6500dr). **Flying Dolphins** serve essentially the same destinations (except Piraeus), Mykonos (2450dr), Andros (3420dr), Rafina (6170dr), Paros (3065dr), Naxos (3550dr), Santorini (7000dr). There is also a daily **excursion boat** to Mykonos and Delos (9am-6pm, 4000dr).

Accommodations Tinos has plenty of accommodations, except at festival time (Eastern Orthodox Easter week and occasionally on July and August weekends, when Athenians flock here). Most hotels are expensive, so try your bargaining skills with the crowd of smiling faces holding "Rooms to Let" signs when you disembark. If the hustlers are too much, head to **Lucas Apergis'** fine rooms (tel. 23 964, -231), take a left onto Zanaki Alavanou St. just before the post office, then the second left after the garden with the little boy fountain, and a final left at the top of the street, where you'll see signs. (Doubles 5000dr, triples 6000dr; both w/bath.) On the far right side of the waterfront, in a traditional house with green shutters and a balcony overlooking the harbor, **Giannis** (tel. 22 515) offers airy rooms with kitchen and laundry facilities, and a lovely flower garden sitting area. (Doubles 5000dr, triples 7500dr.) As ferries unload, look for Anna, a blond Dutch woman who rents **Anna's Rooms.** If you miss her or want any info on the island, look for her at the bar Zorbias, on the water behind Hotel Lito, around the bend, to the left of the harbor. A clearly-marked 10-min. walk to the right-hand side of town, well-kept **Tinos Camping** (tel. 22 344, -548), has kitchen and laundry facilities, showers, bungalows, a bar-restaurant-café, and animals wandering the tents. (Person 1000dr, tent 700dr.)

Food and Entertainment The most reasonably priced food in Tinos Town is not found in the restaurants in the main square. Take the first right off Evangelistras St. and pass the other restaurants until you come to **Pigadi** (tel. 24 240; *mousaka* 900dr). The second left off Megalochores leads to **Peristeriones** (tel. 23 425); try the house specialty, vegetable fritters (550dr). **Meskltes** is a pastry shop, and 2 doors farther to the left, a restaurant/pizzeria. After having pizza made in a traditional oven (1500-3700dr), spaghetti (14 varieties, from 1000dr), or a calzone, top off your meal with a sweet cheese pie (250dr). There is a branch of the sweet shop at the base of Evangelistras St., across from a *gyros* joint (*gyros* pita 300dr). Most of the town's bars are on the water to the left of the harbor, behind Hotel Lito. **Sivylla,** close to the port but one block inland, plays Greek and American dance music and becomes jam-packed on weekends (beer 800dr, cocktails 1200dr). There's one disco past the Hotel Lito, but in general, wander the strip until the music and crowd strike your fancy; prices are pretty similar (beer 500-800dr, cocktails 1000-1500dr).

Sights In 1822, Sister Pelagia, a Tiniote nun, had a vision in which the Virgin Mary instructed her to find an icon buried at the site of an ancient church, destroyed in the 10th century by pirates. A year later, the icon was housed, amid great rejoicing, in the **Panagia Evangelistria,** where it resides to this day. To the faithful, the find is evidence of the power and presence of the Holy Virgin. The relic reputedly has curing powers and is almost entirely covered with gold, diamonds, and jewels left at the church by people wishing to thank the Holy Mother for their good health. Countless *tamata*—beautifully crafted plaques praising the Virgin for healing the body part depicted—have won the Panayia the title of "Lourdes of the Aegean." The church contains more candles than Methusaleh's birthday cake.

The most devout pilgrims make the journey up Leoforos Megalochares (the wide road rising from the sea to the church) on their knees to show their reverence. Others light offertory candles (100-1000dr donation depending on candle size). In a chapel below the marble entrance stairs flows the **Well of Sanctification**—a natural spring discovered during excavations—from which the faithful fill their jugs for drinking or carrying as talismans. The spring was said to have been dry until the icon was unearthed; since then it has flowed continuously. On March 25 and August 15, flocks of devout pilgrims arrive at the church. There are lodgings and facilities, but on August 15, Tinos Town is so crowded that the nearly 30,000 visitors sleep *everywhere*—along the dock, on the sidewalks, and even in the church itself—almost sinking the island under their weight. The next day, after making the 10km walk to the convent of Kechrovouni in a procession led by the icon, the masses depart on dozens of ferries specially chartered for the fête. No one will stop you here, but try to come modestly attired (long sleeves and pants or skirts, no bare shoulders) and be respectful of the Orthodox worshipers—remember, your sightseeing is a serious and moving religious event for them. Don't miss the oil painting of a weeping Mary Magdalene contemplating the crown of thorns in the gallery opposite the church entrance. A free English information booklet full of history, colorful reports of miracles, and explanations of holidays, is available at the second floor to the right of the sanctum. (Open daily 7am-10pm; free.) Tinos is also famed for its art. After you visit the Panayia, drop by the church complex's art and archaeological museums, featuring works by native Tiniotes. (Open same hours as church; free.)

Tinos' **Archaeological Museum,** on Leoforos Megalochares across and uphill from the OTE, contains artifacts from Poseidon's sanctuary at Kionia, a 1st-century BC sundial, and a few vases from Xombourgo. (Open Tues.-Sun. 8:30am-3pm; admission 500dr, students 300dr.) At **Kionia,** explore the ruins of the 4th-century BC temple of Poseidon and Amphitrite, then sit by the sea at the steadily touristed **Tinos** or **Stavros Beaches,** both near town. If you stay late at Stavros, enjoy the locally-acclaimed **Chroma Bar/Homa Club. Agios Fokas,** a closer and equally crowded beach, is a short walk east (on the opposite side) of Tinos Town.

■■■ AROUND THE ISLAND

To get to spectacular **Kardianis** beach, take the Pyrgos bus to Kardiani and travel down the winding street from the main road. Exploration of rustic Tinos will reward adventurers with secluded beaches and wonderful views of the fecund Tinos countryside. The 1000 **dovecots** dotting the landscape have become the island's symbol. Built in medieval times, these small white buildings have intricate geometric latticework where birds roost. Stop by the picturesque town of **Pyrgos,** 33km northwest of Tinos Town (buses 3 times daily, 1hr., 600dr). With an impressive marble quarry, Pyrgos has always been home to Tinos' artists and sculptors, including Giannouli Chalepas, whose "Sleeping Daughter" graces Athens' central graveyard. Two km northeast of Pyrgos, Panormos Bay has a small beach and three *tavernas.* Be careful not to get stranded in the village—there are no night buses on Tinos and taxis are hard to find.

If you have wheels, investigate the delightful villages that encircle **Mount Exobourgo,** 14km north of Tinos Town, and the precipitous site of the Venetian Fortress, **Xombourgo.** After withstanding 11 assaults, this 13th-century citadel, then the island's capital, fell to the Turks in 1715. It was the very last territorial gain of the Ottoman Empire. Climb the mountain from the east foothill (near the village of Xinara or Loutra), and indulge in the resplendent panorama.

SYROS ΣΥΡΟΣ

Syros' rise as a commercial power began when the Phoenicians used the island as a major sea port. Venetian control of the island, which began in the 13th century, solidified Syros' title as the trading capital of the Cyclades. The large Catholic population here has its origins in this era, and the privileges accorded Catholics under the subsequent Turkish rule guaranteed that Syros would keep its high status. Many of the grand buildings in Hermoupolis date from this period, when rich merchants built luxurious mansions and erected numerous monuments. But all good things must come to an end, and the advent of steam-powered ships coupled with the rise of Piraeus sent Syros into a nosedive. During the last twenty years Syros has managed to recover, primarily on the back of a ship-building industry which now keeps the island busy year-round and assures that it will not have to prostrate itself before the God of Tourism. Nevertheless, there are usually a fair number of non-natives at any given time: tourists seek to improve their tans on the beaches on the south and west coasts; business people visit the island, which has managed to establish itself as an administrative center for the Cyclades; and Athenians jet in for the weekends.

■■■ HERMOUPOLIS ΕΡΜΟΥΠΟΛΙΣ

With a Greek Orthodox church on one hill and a Catholic church on the other, Hermoupolis, the spiritually sated "city of Hermes" (god of commerce), rests serenely on its natural harbor. Despite its decline as a major port, the city remains the shipping center of the Cyclades. Elegant Miaouli Sq. and the 19th-century mansions in Dellagrazia let us peek at Hermoupolis' opulent past and explain its former nicknames: the "Manchester of Greece" and "little Milan."

Orientation and Practical Information The center of activity in Hermoupolis is Miaouli Sq., two blocks up El. Venizelou St. from the center of the harbor. You can't miss the palatial town hall and large marble plaza. The **police** (tel. 22 620) and the **tourist police** (tel. 22 610) are opposite town hall on A. Singrou, a small, alley-like street. The **post office** (tel. 22 596) is roughly 40m down the second right off El. Venizelou, heading to the square from the port. (Open Mon.-Fri. 7:30am-2pm.) The **OTE** (tel. 22 799) is on the right side of the square as you face the town hall. (Open 6am-midnight.) In Syros, **Gaviotis Tours** (tel. 86 244), near the ferry dock and across from the bus depot, provides posted schedules and prices and sells tickets for ferries, hydrofoils, and flights. (Open 9am-10pm.) The **National Bank** on Kosti Kalomenopoulou St. (easy for you to say), in an elegant building two blocks to the right of the square (facing inland), offers **currency exchange.** (Open Mon.-Thurs. 8am-2pm, Fri. 8am-1:30pm.) Follow Geor. Souri St. out of the square and turn right at the smaller square. **Taxis** can be called at 86 222 or caught in front of town hall. In case of medical emergency, call the **hospital** at 22 555. **Postal Code:** 84100; **Telephone Code:** 0281.

Flights head to Athens (2-3 daily, 13,700dr). **Buses** (tel. 22 575) leave from the depot near the ferry dock and travel regularly to Galissas and nearby beaches (18 per day), Kini (6 per day), and Ano Syros (3 per day). A current schedule is posted next to the buses. From Syros, **ferries** head from the right of the harbor (facing the water) to Piraeus (1-4 per day, 4½hr., 3300dr), Tinos (2-3 per day, 40min., 910dr), Mykonos (2-3 per day, 1½hr., 1400dr), Andros (2 per week, 2030dr), Paros (1-2 per day, 1½hr., 1300dr), Naxos (1-2 per day, 2½hr., 1950dr), Ios (daily, 4hr., 3000dr),

Santorini (daily, 5hr., 3200dr), Rhodes (2 per week, 5300dr), Kos (2 per week, 5050dr), and several of the smaller Cycladic islands. **Flying Dolphins,** departing from across the ferry docks (on the left, facing the water), speed to Rafina (6200dr), Tinos (2250dr), Mykonos (2650dr), Andros (3400dr), Santorini (7050dr), Ios (6650dr).

Accommodations Hermoupolis has plenty of cheap rooms. Off-season prices are generally cheaper by roughly 20-40%. At the ferry dock is a large map with names and phone numbers of hotels. For a friendly, affordable option with a pleasant garden, try **Pension Venetiko,** 2 Em. Riodi (tel. 81 686 or 28 596), roughly two blocks from the lower right corner of the main square (facing inland). (Doubles 6000dr.) For a dose of luxury, head to **Ariadni "Rooms to Let"** (tel. 81 307 or 80 245) on Nik. Fillini St. near the ferry dock (look for signs). Ariadni prides itself on a class "A" rating, and deservedly so. The rooms are spotless and radiant. You may feel incongruous in grimy backpacker clothes. (Doubles 10,000dr, triples 12,000dr.) Another option is **Kastro Rooms,** 12 Kalomnopoulou St. (tel. 28 064), on the same street as the National Bank. (Doubles 9000dr, triples 12,000dr.) Rooms are borderline luxurious and feature some of the few shower curtains you'll find in Greece.

Food and Entertainment For a traditional Greek dinner, hike to the **Tempelis** *taverna,* just below the Orthodox church. From Miaouli, climb up the long staircase behind the town hall just to the left of the clock tower until you come to Athan. Diakou, a paved road going downhill to the left. Turn left on this street, then right on Anastaseos; the restaurant is on the left. The owner doesn't speak English, but the menu is bilingual and you can always point and smile. Another true *taverna* experience awaits at **Folia,** which can be reached by heading up the main road leading from the top right corner of the main square. Stay to the left of St. Nicholas and keep going up, even after the road turns to stairs. Look for the sign on the left and take this street (Xenofontos). After roughly 50m, take a right and head uphill to the restaurant. (Chicken *souvlaki* 1100dr, pigeon 1050dr; they also have great *baklava.*) If your ferry arrives in Syros late at night and you're famished, head straight to **Elysee,** on the far right-hand edge of the harbor (chicken *souvlaki* 1200dr). For friendly, family-run service and good food, go to **Mavrikaki** on the left side of the harbor (facing inland). (Greek salad 800dr, *gyros* to go 240dr.) To satisfy that sugar craving, try **Melissa** on the first right of El. Venizelou, or **Kechaglas** on the waterfront corner of the same street (*baklava* 300dr).

At night, both the waterfront and Miaouli Sq. buzz with activity. On any given night you can hear loud techno at **Corto Bar** on the waterfront, the Violent Femmes at **Café Palladium** next to town hall, Tracy Chapman at **Cotton Club** on the waterfront, and Top 40 pop at **Highway Bar** on the waterfront. At these places and the boisterous **Pyramidia** in Miaouli Sq., beer costs 500dr, drinks 1000-1200dr.

Sights Make the ascent to **Ano Syros,** a medieval Venetian settlement that is still home to Syros' Catholics. To get there, go up the steps behind Miaouli Sq. or take the bus from the waterfront. The **Archaeological Museum,** just off Miaouli Sq., to the left of the Town Hall under the campanile, has a small collection of Cycladic art. (Open Tues.-Sun. 8:30am-3pm; free.) At the **Church of the Assumption (Kimisis Theotokou),** on St. Proiou St., view a painting created in 1562 at age 20 by famed Greek artist **El Greco.** This painting's discovery on Syros helped confirm the painter's Greek origin, dispelling inaccurate theories that he was Spanish.

■■■ AROUND THE ISLAND

Galissas, a village to the west of Hermoupolis, has a busy beach. Climb past the chapel of Agia Pakou on the left side (facing the water), to discover **Armeos Beach**—tiny, beautiful, and **nudist.** Be forewarned that there are those who make the hike merely to ogle at the tiny, beautiful nude people. Women sunbathing alone may feel uncomfortable; bring a liberated, naked male friend. There is a dizzying collection of "Rooms to Let" signs at the bus stop. The rooms at **George's Restaurant** (tel. 42 066), up the main inland street from the bus stop, are decorated with hand-woven tapestries (doubles 6000dr, triples 8000dr). **Angela's "Rooms to Let"** (tel. 42 855, -9), behind the mini-golf, has large, immaculate rooms surrounded by a spacious outdoor garden (doubles 10,000dr, triples 13,000dr; private bath included). Angela also has fully stocked apartments which are suitable for up to four people (12,000dr). Also try **Tony's "Rooms to Let"** (tel. 42 482), at the end of the same street in the village (doubles 5000dr, triples 6000dr). Near Galissas beach are two **campgrounds, Yianna** (tel. 42 418) and **Two Hearts** (tel. 42 052), representatives from which may greet you at the dock with shuttle buses. Yianna is more sequestered and offers a *taverna,* minimarket, hot showers, kitchen, laundry, safe-deposit boxes, and a nightly disco from 9pm to 2pm (person 1000dr, tent 500dr). Follow the signs from the bus stop. Two Hearts has two red hearts on its signs and advertises itself as a romantic campsite. It offers a restaurant and minimarket, but no tunnel of love, alas. (Person 1200dr, tent 630dr, two-person cabin 3000dr.)

Galissas beach has most amenities imaginable—a moderately priced *taverna* on the beach affiliated with the Dolphin Bay Hotel, a less expensive self-service restaurant next door, mini-golf (next to Galissas Tours; open 7pm-1am), a few English-language books at the Golden Corner, and even video games in the café/bar next to Galissas Tours. Although Americans laugh at the name, the **Green Dollars Bar** contributes to the playful scene with not only darts and backgammon, but a life-size chessboard in a small courtyard (draft and bottled beer 300-400dr, drinks 900dr). If you exhaust the offerings at Galissas beach, **Galissas Tours** (tel. 42 801; fax 42 802; open 9:30am-2:30pm and 5-10pm), lets you make phone calls, change money, buy ferry tickets, rent mopeds (3500dr) or cars (from 11,000dr), or take excursions around the island by boat (2500dr to St. Stephanos Fisherman's Grotto).

From Hermoupolis roughly 18 buses per day travel to Galissas, alternating between a direct 15-min. route and a 45-min. route that stops in other villages first (200dr). In Hermoupolis, buses leave from the depot near the ferry dock and a current schedule is posted near the buses. Farther south along the coast are the beaches at **Poseidonia, Finikas, Angathopes,** and **Komito,** all connected by bus to Hermoupolis. The beach resort of **Vari** is most popular with families and package tour groups. North of Galissas is the tiny fishing village of **Kini.**

ANDROS ΑΝΔΡΟΣ

Tiers of straw fields, ranges of imposing rock, and stretches of low-lying green and purple growth are partitioned by a network of streams and stone walls, lying like a spider's web fallen on the face of Andros' hillside. Winding above splendid scattered beaches, the hour drive from the ferry landing at **Gavrio** to **Andros Town** is magnificent. The ruins sprinkled across the Andrian hills memorialize the island's checkered history of Ionian, Spartan, Venetian, and Turkish occupation. Despite this tumultuous past, Andros today is one of the most peaceful of the Cyclades.

■■■ GAVRIO

Crowned by the three-domed Church of Saint Nikolas, the dusty port town of Gavrio has little else to offer tourists. Most visitors stay overnight to catch an early ferry, but you can also use Gavrio as a base to explore some of the best stretches of smooth sand between the port and the popular tourist beach town of Batsi.

The **tourist office** (tel. 21 466; fax 71 571) is across the street from the bus stop, up a short flight of stairs (open 8:30am-2:30pm). Good **maps** are available at tourist shops (250dr). The **police** (tel. 71 220) are to the right on a road parallel to the waterfront, up the steps opposite the bus stop. The building is unmarked, so look for the faded silver plaque (24 hr.). The **OTE** stands one block to the right of Hotel

Galaxy, on a side street in a building with green shutters (open Mon.-Sat. 7:30am-10pm, Sun. 9am-2pm and 5-10pm). The **post office** is two blocks farther on the waterfront (open Mon.-Fri. 7:30am-2pm). As you face the water, the **Agricultural Bank** is on the corner at the left-hand end of the waterfront façade. (Open for **currency exchange** Mon.-Thurs. 9am-2pm, Fri. 9am-1:30pm.) A **pharmacy** is located in the right-center of the waterfront (tel. 71 329; open daily 8:30am-2pm and 5:30-10:30pm). For medical emergencies call the **hospital** at 22 222. **Postal Code:** 84501; **Telephone Code:** 0282.

To get to Andros Town, take one of the **buses** from the depot next to the ferry dock (5-7 per day, 1hr., 630dr). The same bus passes through Batsi (from Gavrio 15min., 170dr; from Andros Town 45min., 500dr). From Andros, **ferries** sail to Athens' minor port, Rafina (2-5 per day, 2hr., 2000dr). They also head to Tinos (2-4 per day, 2hr., 1640dr), Mykonos (1-3 per day, 2½hr., 2400dr), Syros (3 per week, 1600dr), Paros (2 per week, 2150dr), and Naxos (4 per week, 2370dr). Ferries run weekly to Thessaloniki (6360dr), Crete (5380dr), and Skyros (3090dr). **Flying Dolphins** zip to Tinos (daily, 3419dr), Mykonos (daily, 5418dr), Paros (4 per week, 4618dr), Naxos (4 per week, 5347dr), Ios (2 per week, 7038dr), and Santorini (2 per week, 7038dr). Hydrofoils travel weekly to Sifnos and Seriphos (6800dr). They also speed to the resort town of Batsi (1 per day, 4121dr). A **taxi** to Andros Town costs 3500dr. The **EKO station** (tel. 71 231; open 7am-10pm), next to the supermarket at the right edge of the waterfront (3000dr per day), and **George's Moto** (tel. 71 003) at the right edge of the waterfront have **moped rental** (3500dr per day).

Most accommodations are designed for longer term visits and family groups, but simple rooming arrangements and camping are also available. A fine bet for staying a night in Gavrio is **Camping Andros** (tel. 71 444), which has its own restaurant, minimarket, showers, and pool. From the OTE, there are signs to guide your 5 to 10-min. walk (1000dr per person, 600dr per tent). At the center of the waterfront, **Hotel Galaxias** (tel. 71 005, -228) is the only hotel in town (doubles 7500dr), with rather standard, somewhat boring rooms. Look for "Rooms to Let" signs.

Fix your own meals with goodies from the **supermarket** on the right end of the waterfront (facing inland). **Galaxias,** in the same building as the hotel and **San Remo,** next to the post office, have Greek dishes and pastas for similar prices (stuffed tomatoes 900dr). Make the 1-hr. hike northwest to take in the magnificent views from **Agios Petros,** a stunning 19m tower dating from the Hellenistic period.

■ NEAR GAVRIO: BATSI

Batsi is undisputed as the tourist capital of Andros. It is easier to find accommodations here than in either Gavrio or Andros Town. Though accommodations may be more plentiful here, they also tend to be pricey. Expect to pay 8000-10,000dr for a double at one of the beachfront hotels. Look for "Rooms to Let" signs or inquire at souvenir or tourist shops. There is a **mobile post office** just one block inland from the water, conveniently located for beachgoers writing postcards. (Open Mon.-Fri. 7:30am-2pm.) There is also a **National Bank** branch up the road to Andros Town; it is near the first bus stop. On a street parallel to the main road, accessible from the stairs just past the National Bank, is **Dolphin Hellas Travel** (tel. 41 185; fax 41 719). Run by an English woman, the office is quite helpful. (Open 9:30am-1:30pm and 6-9pm.) On the road to Andros Town are the ruins of the ancient capital, **Paleopolis,** where remains of a theater and a stadium still stand. Roughly 2km southeast of Palaeokastro is the **Bay of Korthion,** with some of the finest swimming spots on Andros. North of Korthion are the remnants of the **Castle of the Old Woman.** At this site in the 16th century, Turks slaughtered Venetians.

■■■ ANDROS TOWN (CHORA)

A sophisticated village with striking Neoclassical architecture, **Andros Town** makes a worthwhile destination for island-hopping travelers. Built on a narrow peninsula, this town begins high above the water and gently slopes downhill to meet the sea on a windswept promontory. The benefice of the wealthy local Goulandris family has built two amazing museums in town.

Orientation and Practical Information At the far inland end of the main street, next to a playground, is the **police station** (tel. 22 300; 24 hr.). Towards the water, the **post office** (where you can change money; open Mon.-Fri. 7:30am-2pm) resides next to an open, airy square where **taxis** (tel. 22 171) queue. The **OTE** is across from the central square on the left (open Mon.-Fri. 7:30am-3pm). The **National Bank of Greece** is on the left farther down, on the way to the water (open Mon.-Thurs. 8am-2pm, Fri. 8am-1:30pm). **Pharmacies** are along this route. **Rent-A-Bike Aris** (tel. 24 381) is located on the section of the main road to Gavrio open to traffic (mopeds 3500dr per day). **Postal Code:** 84500; **Telephone Code:** 0282.

The **bus station** is coupled with a friendly restaurant just to the right of the section of the town's main street that is closed off to traffic. A full schedule is posted in the outdoor waiting area. Walk down the stairs next to the high blue domes of the church to find the town's center.

Accommodations Rooms tend to be both hard-to-find and expensive. **Hotel Egli** (tel. 22 303), fills up quickly; reservations are a good idea (doubles 10,000dr, triples 12,000dr). The expansive, expensive **Hotel Xenia** (tel. 22 270) abides down to the left (facing the water) from the main street, where the beach meets the upward slope (doubles 10,000dr, triples 12,000dr). Otherwise, look for "Rooms to Let;" the numerous places on the beach get cheaper farther from the main drag. In high season, expect doubles to go for 5000-10,000dr.

Sights Following the main street downhill leads to a small square with outdoor cafés and a marble fountain. On the left is the **Archaeological Museum** (tel. 23 664), which has an excellent display on the Geometric village of Zagora and many later (through Byzantine) marble relics, including a deservedly famous 2m-high statue of the messenger god Hermes. (Open Mon. and Wed.-Sat. 10am-2pm and 6-8pm, Sun. 10am-2pm, evenings summer only; admission 500dr, students 300dr.) Down the steps to the left of the square is the **Museum of Modern Art** (tel. 22 650), which prominently displays works by 20th-century Greek sculptor Michael Tombros. The weird, vibrating noises from downstairs are not a mechanical failure but the clatter of the electromagnetic "pieces" of the artist Takis. Don't miss the enormous temporary exhibition space across the street a little farther downhill. (Admission 1000dr, students 500dr, under 12 or over 65 free; one admission fee for both museums.) Continuing straight through the square, through the white archway you'll find the free **Maritime Museum of Andros** (open Mon. and Wed.-Sat. 10am-1pm and 6-8pm, Sun. 10am-1pm), something of a let-down after the splendor of the first two museums. Proceed farther for a view of the crumbling walls of an off-island Venetian turret. After trekking around town, walk down the steps to the right of the square to a golden, sandy beach. Take a dip and wash those cares away.

MILOS ΜΗΛΟΣ

For an island associated with such celebrated artistic achievements as the Venus de Milo, Thucydides's *Melian Dialogue,* and the *film-bête Milo & Otis,* Milos leaves a lot to be desired. It retains its small-town atmosphere, unequipped for mass tourism. The island's volcanic landscapes and charming alleyways make a brief visit worthwhile, but there is not much else to see. The mineral-rich island has always prospered from the production of obsidian, sulphur, and porcelain, but after Milos refused to join the Athenian League during the Peloponnesian War, Athens executed the men and enslaved the women and children. Milos eventually recovered and reached the height of its artistic achievement in Roman and Early Christian times. Since then, Milos has flourished as a cosmopolitan mining center.

ADAMAS

Milos is derived from the Greek word for apple, so it seems quite appropriate that its main town be called "Adam"as. Unfortunately, the port is no Garden of Eden. Nonetheless, **Adamas** makes for convenient ferry and bus connections.

Orientation and Practical Information Across from the dock, the extremely competent **tourist information office** (tel. 22 445) has posted maps and ferry and bus timetables. They can equip you with complete lists and maps of all the rooms and hotels on the island. (Open 10:15am-4:15pm and 5:15pm-midnight.) One good travel agency is **Milos Travel** (tel. 22 000, -200; fax 22 688), on the waterfront. The English-speaking staff sells most ferry tickets. (Open daily 9am-10pm.) The **post office** (open Mon.-Fri. 7:30am-2pm), **bank** (open Mon.-Thurs. 8am-2pm, Fri. 8am-1:30pm), and **port police** (tel. 22 100; up steps to left of travel agency; 24 hr.) are all along the waterfront. The **bus stop** and **taxi stand** (tel. for both 22 219) are in a busy area on the waterfront. Taxis are available 24 hr. A complete bus schedule (roughly 180dr) and a list of fixed taxi fares are posted. The **Olympic Airways** office is on 25th Martiou St. (tel. 22 380; open Mon.-Fri. 8am-3:30pm). The **pharmacy** is one block from the bus stop on 25th Martiou St. (tel./fax 22 178; open Mon.-Sat. 8am-2pm and 6-10pm). You can rent a **moped** from the dealer on the waterfront (2500dr per day). **Postal Code:** 84801 in Adamas, 84800 elsewhere; **Telephone Code:** 0287.

There are 3 daily Olympic Airways **flights** between Milos and Athens (12,600dr). From Milos, **ferries** follow a twisted and complex, yet well-posted, schedule. The destinations are Piraeus (1-3 per day, 8hr., 3650dr), Sifnos (1-3 per day, 1½hr., 1350dr), Serifos (Sun.-Thurs. 1-3 per day, 3hr., 1350dr), Kithnos (Sun.-Thurs. 1-3 per day, 2150dr), Kimolos (4 per week, 1280dr), Folegandros (4 per week, 1280dr), Sikinos (4 per week, 2400dr), Santorini (4 per week, 2500dr), Ios (2 per week, 2500dr), and 1 per week to Kassos (5150dr), Karpathos (6100dr), Rhodes (7800dr), and Nauplion (3476dr). Ferries also head to the Cretan ports of Iraklion (3 per week, 4025dr), Agios Nikolaos (1 per week, 3580dr), and Sitia (1 per week, 3580dr).

Accommodations The prices of even the cheapest accommodations in Adamas will appall the frugal traveler. Your best bet is to roam the streets and ask at *tavernas* for private rooms. Trekking down the beach away from the dock and exploring side streets away from the waterfront are most likely to yield satisfying results, although it may be necessary to venture to Plaka or Pollonia to find a vacancy in the peak summer months. With persistence and tough bargaining, doubles can be found for 4000-7000dr, triples 5000-9000dr. It is possible to camp on a secluded beach, although camping is illegal, and there are no campsites on Milos. *Let's Go* does not recommend freelance camping on Milos. For clean, quiet rooms and a vine-colored garden bar, stay at the **Semiramis** (tel. 22 118), off 25th Martiou, two blocks from the waterfront. (Doubles 10,000dr, triples 13,000dr; reserve 2 weeks in advance; prices lower in off-season.)

Food The waiters at the two neighboring restaurants on the corner of the waterfront are understandably brusque with English-speaking customers in summer, but the food is superb. Try the veal with spaghetti (1100dr) or the broad beans (700dr) at **Kinigos** (around the first bend on the waterfront). **Floisvos,** before the bend in the waterfront, doesn't look like much, but offers superb cheap food, like chicken with tomatoes (850dr). For an elegant dinner, ask for a table on the water at **Trapatseli's Restaurant,** a 5-min. walk on the road to Achivadolimni Beach (octopus in vinegar and olive oil 1100dr).

AROUND THE ISLAND

Six winding km from Adamas, the timeworn town of **Plaka** rests upon the mountaintops. You can conduct postal business at the bus stop (follow the path leading left to the end; open Mon-Fri. 7:30am-2pm). The Milos **police** (tel. 21 378) are in the square off the bus stop. (Open 24 hr.) The **health center** (tel. 22 700) can be found on the road from Adamas to Tripiti; ask the bus driver to let you off there. The terrace of the **Church of Panagia the Korfiatissa** leans into a view of verdant countryside, blue ocean, and red islets a god's arm's length away. Next door, the town's **Folk Museum** (tel. 21 620) has an eerie display of mannequins. (Open Tues.-Sat. 10am-1pm and 6-8pm, Sun. 10am-1pm. Admission 400dr, students 200dr.) Near the bus stop, on the road to Tripiti, the **Archaeological Museum** (tel. 21 292) houses artifacts unearthed at Fylakopi, including the mesmerizing "Lady of Fylakopi." (Open Tues.-Sun. 8:30am-3pm. Admission 400dr, students 200dr.) For a truly spectacular view, head upwards until you reach the monastery **Panagia Thalassitra** at the top of the old castle. The 15-min. walk from the bus stop is more than worth it: from the summit, the island is visible, spread out far below like a child's board game.

South of Plaka, outside the small town of **Tripiti,** several more sights wield archaeological clout. The **catacombs,** hewn into the cliff face, are the oldest site of Christian worship in Greece. (Open Mon.-Tues. and Thurs.-Sat. 9am-2pm; free.) Archaeological finds in the ancient city on the hillside above the catacombs represent three periods of Greek history. You can still see part of the stone wall built by the Dorians between 1100 and 800 BC. A plaque marks the spot where the **Venus de Milo** was buried around 320 BC; she now resides in the Louvre. The well-preserved theater dating from the Roman occupation offers a riveting ocean view.

Pollonia, to the northeast, is a quiet fishing town with a pleasant beach. Boats run between Pollonia and the tiny island of **Kimolos** (2-3 per day, 1200dr). Kimolos Town and the port of Psathi are perfect places to unwind. Few tourists venture here. Archaeology buffs will want to scramble among the ruins of **Filakopi,** 3km from Pollonia towards Adamos, where British excavations unearthed 3500-year-old frescoes of flying fish and lilies (now exhibited in the National Museum in Athens). About 6km west of Pollonia is **Papafragas,** where gangling rock formations surround a pool of clear blue water. Take the bus from Adamas; ask the driver to stop at Papafragas. Buses run frequently from Adamas to Plaka and Tripiti (every ½hr., 180dr) and Pollonia (every 45min., 330dr).

There are several **beaches** with exceptional seascapes on Milos. Most are on the eastern half of the island, inaccessible by bus. Rent a moped and head for beautiful **Firiplaka** (a 45min. moped ride). Other beaches of renown on the southeast coast are **Paleochori** and **Kiriaki** (6 buses per day from Adamas, 250dr), and, northwest of Plaka, secluded **Plathiena.** 7 daily buses from Adamas jaunt to the more densely populated **Achivadolimni Beach.** On the southern coast, **Provatas** (8km from Adamas) is an ideal spot for a swim. A daily boat travels to quiet **Emporio Beach;** ask for Captain Nicholas at the small pier in Adamas (round-trip 900dr). The excursion boat which travels around the island daily is an excellent way to see all the beaches, slivers of fishing villages, and the lava formations of **Glaronissia** and **Kleftiko** that are otherwise not accessible by road (boat departs 9am, returns 6pm; 3000dr).

SIFNOS ΣΙΦΝΟΣ

In ancient times, Sifnos was renowned for the plethora of gold, silver and copper in its mines. Legend has it that each year the islanders, in order to placate Apollo, would send a solid-gold dancer (usually performing to the tune of *Rah Rah Rasputin*) to Delphi. One year, the locals decided to substitute a gold-plated egg. As a result of this insult, Apollo sank the Sifnian mines under the sea and cursed the land with infertility. Barrenness claims most of Sifnos's western half, where boats dock. A short bus ride brings you to whitewashed villages sprinkled across the terraced walls of Sifnos's eastern, better half. This side of Sifnos is affluent, with olive grove-gorged hillsides plunging down to rock caves and calm beaches. Tourism is more easygoing here than on most islands, but accommodations are limited, and simply not available in July and August. During high season your best bets are private rooms from affable residents, camping, or making reservations several months in advance.

■■■ KAMARES

Boats dock at Kamares, a magnificent harbor fortified by formidable brown cliffs which stand in fierce contrast to the gentle emerald sea. Here you can secure a room, swim, dine, and meander into the shops featuring ornate **pottery** molded by local craftspeople; look for KEPAMIKO signs throughout the village.

Orientation and Practical Information Just opposite the ferry dock, the **Village Community of Apollonia Sifnos Tourist Information Office** (tel. 31 977) can answer all queries—in English. They also find rooms and decipher boat and bus schedules (200dr). (Open 9:30am-10pm or until the last ferry arrives.) The **port police** (tel. 31 617; 24 hr.) next door have sea travel information. A visit to the **Aegean Thesaurus Travel Agency** (tel. 31 145 or 32 190), located just inland from the dock, almost always pays off. The friendly, English-speaking staff **exchanges currency,** finds accommodations, stores luggage, and sells maps (300dr). (Open daily 9:30am-10pm, or until the last ferry arrives.)

From Sifnos, **ferries** head to Piraeus (1-4 per day, 6hr., 3500dr), Milos (1-3 per day, 1½hr., 1350dr), Kimolos (1-3 per day except Sun., 1¼hr., 1300dr), Serifos (1-3 per day except Fri., 1hr., 1000dr), Kithnos (1-3 per day except Fri., 2½hr., 1800dr), Folegandros (2-4 per week, 45min., 1020dr), Sikinos (2-4 per week, 2½hr., 1650dr), Santorini (2-3 per week, 4hr., 2500dr), and 1 per week to Crete (4000dr), Rhodes (8500dr), Syros (1670dr), Tinos (1326dr), Kassos (5075dr), Karpathos (5075dr), Diafani (5075dr), and Chalki (8500dr). Ferries travel to Paros, Mykonos, Naxos, Tinos, and Syros only in high season. There is **hydrofoil** service twice weekly to Paros (4000dr), Mykonos (6000dr), Tinos (6000dr), Andros (6550dr), and Rafina (6700dr)—more expensive during high season. From Kamares, buses leave for Apollonia at least every hour from 7:30am to midnight (200dr).

Accommodations During the high season, you are unlikely to find a budget hotel room; try private rooms, either by following "Room to Let" signs or by asking at one of the many waterfront *taverna*. Off-season prices are roughly 1000-2000dr lower. (Doubles 6500-8500dr, triples 8000-11,000dr.) In Kamares, **Hotel Stavros** (tel. 32 383 or 31 641; fax 31 709) has pleasant rooms, many with panoramic views of the harbor's beach. (Doubles 9000dr, triples 11,000dr, rooms w/bath). Freelance camping on Sifnos is illegal, but **Maki's Camping** (tel. 32 366) lies across the road from the beach in Kamares (1000dr per person). Other campsites in more secluded parts of the island include calm, clean **Platis Yialos Camping** (tel. 31 786), with a restaurant and minimarket, beautifully set amid olive trees and stone walls, a 10-min. walk inland from the Yialos Square bus stop. (800dr per person; opens in July.)

Food Kamares is home to numerous *taverna*. Each offers food of roughly the same quality and price, but many have seaside seating. Chick peas are a local specialty found in fried balls and on Sundays only in a soup called *revithada* (700dr); it gets polished off early; try it for lunch to be sure to get some. There are also several **groceries** and **bakeries,** which sell the local almond cookie delicacy, *amigdaloto*.

■■■ APOLLONIA

Apollonia, the island's capital, serves as the central hub for travel around the island. Buses to Kamares (175dr) stop in the square in front of the post office, while those heading to outlying villages and beaches like **Kastro** (175dr) and **Plati Yialos** (230dr) stop around the corner near the Hotel Anthousa. Buses run to all 3 locales at least once every 1½hr.

Orientation and Practical Information To the left past the square and up a set of shop-lined steps is the Apollonia branch of **Aegean Thesaurus** (tel. 32 190 or 31 145; open daily 9:30am-10pm). Your source for **currency exchange,** luggage storage, room finding, and comprehensive bus and ferry schedules for 500dr. The square itself holds the **post office** (open Mon.-Fri. 7:30am-2pm, Sat. 8am-2:30pm), the **National Bank** (tel. 31 237; open Mon.-Thurs. 8am-2pm, Fri. 8am-1:30pm) and a **pharmacy** (tel. 31 047; open 9am-1pm and 6:30-11pm). The **police station** (tel. 31 210) is off the main square on a side street next to the museum. For **first aid,** call 31 315. **Postal Code:** 84003; **Telephone Code:** 0284.

Accommodations During the summer, vacancies in Apollonia are rare. Here, too, your best bet is to look for pensions that cost roughly the same as those in Kamares. Prices are generally lower in the off-season. The **Hotel Sofia** (tel. 31 238), just off the square, is nifty. (Doubles 9000dr, triples 11,000dr. Private baths. Reservations should be made a month in advance.) The **Hotel Anthoussa** (tel. 31 431 or 32 207), framed by flowered trees and located above the pastry shop, has more luxurious accommodations with daily cleaning service. (Doubles 11,000dr, triples 14,000dr; reservations needed several months in advance.)

Food Restaurants are excellent and not as expensive as their beautiful exteriors might suggest. The better *tavernas* are along the path across from the police. The restaurant at the Sifnos hotel is good (meatballs 1100dr). *Revithia* are served here with olive oil and lemon, cooked over a low fire all night in special ovens at Artemonos. (Roughly 800dr at your friendly *taverna.* Go early—it's gone by dinner.)

Sights The **Museum of Popular Art** in the square features beautiful hand-woven laces, traditional dress, local pottery (still a primary industry), and several unusual paintings. (Open daily 9:30am-1:30pm and 6-8pm, but you must call 31 341 to set up an appointment. Admission 200dr.)

■■■ AROUND THE ISLAND

Travel in Sifnos is easy with the map available at any kiosk (300dr). Pack some picnic treats in Apollonia to nibble as you go through adjacent hillside Cycladic villages. The quiet but expansive white village of **Artemonas,** to the north, has many fine mansions built by refugees from Alexandria, and boasts a magnificent view. A few km to the east, the enchanting **castle,** fitted like a skull-cap atop a rocky dome (heading out to sea), amply rewards its visitors. Climbing to the top of the island's fortified former capital through its twisted whitewashed streets, you'll find a tiny **archaeological museum.** (Open Tues.-Sun. 9am-3pm; free.) The solitary seaside chapel is arresting. There are no hotels, but ask around for rooms. You can swim at the pebble beach to the right (facing the water) or walk left at the base of the hill to the monastery of **Panagia Poulati.** The smooth rock alcove below reputedly offers the best swimming on the island.

Casual **Faros,** to the south, has several popular beaches. Farther east, **Fasolou,** the island's only **nude beach,** is tucked away beneath promontories. Continue west along the rocky hillside path past a dilapidated mine to reach a better beach at **Apokofto.** You can also reach Apokofto by getting off the bus to Platis Yialos at the Chrysopigi stop. At the far end of this bay, you'll see the striking **Panagia Chrysopigi.** A bridge connects this 17th-century monastery's rocky islet to the mainland. People swim from the flat rocks at the end of the islet. The monastery (tel. 31 482) has rooms to let (doubles 4000dr); make reservations about two months in advance. Forty days after Easter, the two-day festival of Analipsos is celebrated at

Chrysopigi. Up the path from Chrysopigi, **Vassilis Restaurant** offers food with a view; roast chicken (1000dr) or veal in a clay bowl (1100dr). To go to Chrysopigi, take the bus to Platis Yialos and ask the driver to let you off; it is a 20-min. walk.

Platis Yialos, the longest, most popular beach on the island, is accessible by bus from Apollonia every hour from 9am to 10pm. **Excursion boats** go to the beach and **fishing** destination of **Hersonissos** (Mon.-Tues. and Thurs.-Sat., 1200dr round-trip). To admire icons and an awe-inspiring view, ask to be let off 3km before the normal stop at **Panagia tou Vounou.** (Monastery accommodations: doubles 4000dr, triples 8000dr, w/bath.)

SERIFOS ΣΕΡΙΦΟΣ

As the daytime boat docks in the port town of Livadia, your first vision of Serifos is of the chocolate-brown hills and the ghostly white capital (Chora) gripping a mountain peak. Mythology claims that on this rocky isle, Perseus, the son of Zeus and Danae (who was immortalized by Harry Hamlin in the seminal cinematic tour-de-force *Clash of the Titans*), turned King Polidectis and his servants into stone by showing them Medusa's head; hence the stark, still, barren terrain. Even the main waterfront strip is a dirt road. With bus service running only between its port and capital, this mysterious island challenges the adventurer, but still keeps to itself.

■■■ LIVADIA

All boats dock in friendly, albeit non-descript Livadia. Don't be dismayed by the row of hokey bars playing American classic rock on the waterfront road; the island has much more than Livadia's uninspired exterior.

ORIENTATION AND PRACTICAL INFORMATION

An island map which lists useful telephone numbers is available at kiosks (250dr).

Tourist Office: (tel. 51 479, -107; fax 51 547). At the end of the dock, up the stairs, and to the left of the small shack that used to be the OTE. Open daily 8:30am-2:30pm.

Port Police: (tel. 51 470). Located next to the tourist office. **Police** (tel. 51 300) in same building. Both 24 hr.

Telephone Code: 0281. **Postal Code:** 84005.

Ventouris Sea Lines: (tel. 51 115). Farther along the waterfront, clustered around the bus stop and market. Sells ferry tickets. Open 9:30am-1:30pm and 6:30-10pm.

Serifos Travel Agency: (tel. 51 241). Behind the market. Offers hydrofoil and ferry tickets not sold at the other office. Along with Ventouris, your best source for English-language information on convoluted boat schedules. Same hours as Ventouris; it is safest to visit either office close to scheduled departure times.

Ferries: Serifos can be reached by regular ferries from Piraeus and other Western Cyclades as well as occasional boats from Paros, Syros, Ios, and Santorini. From Serifos, ferries travel to Piraeus (1-3 per day, 4hr., 2900dr), Kithnos (1-2 per day except Fri., 1½hr., 1740dr), Sifnos (1-3 per day, 45min., 980dr), Milos (1-2 per day, 2hr., 1335dr), Kimolos (1 per day, 2hr., 1335dr), Folegrandros (2 per week, 3hr., 1000dr), Sikinos (2 per week, 5hr., 2400dr), Ios (2 per week, 5½hr., 2500dr), Santorini (1 per week, 6½hr., 2500dr), Paros (2 per week after July 1, 1600dr), Syros (1 per week, 1280dr).

Flying Dolphins: High-speed connections to Rafina (5800dr) and weekly trips to Paros (1hr., 4000dr) and Mykonos (1½hr., 5000dr).

Taxis: Call 51 226, -435.

Pharmacy: (tel. 51 482, -205). Near the market and travel agency. Open Mon.-Fri. 9am-2pm and 6-9pm, Sat. 10am-2pm.

Hospital: Call 51 202.

ACCOMMODATIONS

On Serifos, don't expect people to aggressively offer rooms at the port. Instead look for pensions on the waterfront, on the street parallel to the waterfront road, and on the road that bears left from the Milos Express office heading toward the campgrounds (doubles starting at 6500-7000dr). Arrive early or call the tourist police a few days in advance for information about reservations in private rooms. Freelance camping on the beaches is tempting, but illegal. Prices are roughly 2500-4000dr less in the off-season. Prices are 2000-4000dr less in off-season.

Hotel Serifos Beach (tel. 51 209, -468), set back a block from the beach, but easy to find by virtue of its large blue sign on the main waterfront road. Fairly old building offers great rates and many rooms. Doubles 7500dr, triples 9000dr.

Hotel Albatross (tel. 51 148), farther down the beach, also offers decent rates. Doubles 9000dr, triples 11,000dr.

Pension, two doors past the Albatross. Doubles 8000dr, triples 9000dr.

Coralli Camping (tel. 51 500; fax 51 073), at the far end of the beach, is a 10-min. jaunt from the harbor. Take the inland road to the right of the dock, follow it up, and turn left onto the winding way through behind Livadakia Beach. The campsite, bedecked with flowers, has a bar, restaurant, minimarket, and laundry facilities. Camping 1000dr per person, 200dr per small tent, 400dr per large tent; open May-Oct. Private rooms here: doubles 8500dr, triples w/bath 10,000dr.

FOOD AND ENTERTAINMENT

For an adventurous, memorable meal, saunter to the very end of the town beach (all the way to the right facing inland) and look left for scattered tables, mismatched chairs, loose chickens, ducks, donkeys, sheep, inchworms, and other representatives of the animal kingdom. The restaurant has no sign, but ask for **Sklavani's** if you need directions. Preparations take time, but you'll be rewarded with fresh vegetables and fish at incredibly low prices (eggplant 350dr, fish 600dr). Dinner is served from 7pm and the barnyard ambience is unforgettable. For a pleasant meal along the waterfront, try **Stamadis. Vitamin C,** near the dock, offers delicious *tost* (950dr) and refreshing fresh-squeezed orange juice (600dr). You can get fresh fruit at the **Marinos** market on the waterfront, past the main stretch of *tavernas* and shops. (Open daily 8am-2pm and 4:30-10pm.)

■■■ AROUND THE ISLAND

Not surprisingly, the beaches here are a prime attraction. A 2-hr. walk past Livadakia Beach leads one to the adjoining sandy havens of **Koutalas, Ganema,** and **Vaya Beach. Psili Ammos,** perhaps the island's best, is a 45-min. walk past Livadakia Beach in the other direction. **Karavi,** over the hill from Livadakia Beach, away from Livadi Harbor, is a popular **nudist beach,** although not everyone on it is nude.

The northern part of the island promises small traditional villages, scattered churches, several monasteries, and traces of ruins. The rest of the island is fairly inaccessible without a car or moped, a map, and excellent driving skills. For **moped rental,** call **Blue Bird** (tel. 51 511; 3000dr). By car or moped, visit the **Monastery of the Taxiarchs,** 10km beyond Chora towards the village of Galini. Built in 1400 AD on a site where a Cypriot icon mysteriously appeared (and returns whenever removed), the monastery houses an Egyptian lantern and several Russian relics in addition to the enigmatic icon. Try to visit close to sunset in order to meet the lone monk who has lived there for 20 years. It is unadvisable for female travelers to visit alone. Lucky visitors may be treated to coffee and cherries.

CHORA

Chora, the island's capital, is perched 5km above Livadia on a mountaintop. The town tumbles downhill like a Cubist's attempt at urban planning, producing an unusual, intricate aesthetic. Pick your way through alleys and underpasses up to the top of the eerie, quiet town. Three postcard-worthy white churches rise out of the ruins of the old *kastro* (fortress) which dates back to the Roman occupation of Greece, and gives an eagle-eye view of the southeastern hills of the isle and the surrounding sea. Scattered fertile patches stream down the mountain. **Buses** from the center of the waterfront in Livadia stop first in Chora (6 per day in Sept. and June, 18 per day in July and Aug., no service during *siesta*; 175dr) near the **post office** (open Mon.-Fri. 7:30am-2pm). Change your money here or at a travel agent; there's no bank on Serifos. The second bus stop is at the top of the hill in the café-laden square.

To find rooms-to-let in Chora, follow the high paved road from the bus stop away from town, past the windmills. On the right, you'll spot palatial rooms with startling views (tel. 51 510); look for red "Rooms To Let" signs (doubles 8000dr). Or head down until you come to **Aranemia** (tel. 51 717) on the second-highest road, 200m on the right past the "Rooms to Let" sign. (Doubles 8500dr, triples 7800dr.) Both have nice rooms with gorgeous views. Reservations for both pensions should be made a month in advance. Most *tavernas* and all discos are in Livadi; buses stop running at 11pm, stays in Chora are only for those seeking a secluded existence.

The **Archaeological Museum** lurks inside the beautiful, incongruous, faded orange Neoclassical town hall in the central *platia*, up the stairs to the right of the Upper Chora bus stop. (Open Tues.-Sun. 8:30am-noon.) The easily-missed entrance is through a green door on the right side of the building.

ΚΕΑ TZIA KEA

Kea is criss-crossed with gray stone fences that snake through the island's plentiful fruit orchards, archaeological remains, windmills, and rocky coves. The ruins of the recently excavated site on the picturesque peninsula of Ayia Irini suggest an image of the ancient city: a thriving commercial center with temples, aqueducts, and fortress walls. Kea is the birthplace of the 5th- and 6th-century BC poets Bacchylides and Simonides, the latter of whom is renowned for his epigram praising Athenian bravery in the Battle of Marathon. Kea is also infamous for its classical counterpart to the Kevorkian suicide machine: citizens toasted their 70th birthdays with a cup of hemlock. Although many bars have long since stopped serving hemlock, visitors may still exalt in the pleasure of feasting on *pasteli,* a confection made with sesame seeds and the golden thyme honey that pours forth from the hills.

The island's proximity to Athens makes it a popular weekend getaway for Athenians, so it's best to visit on weekdays, when accommodations are not in great demand and beaches are deserted.

ORIENTATION AND PRACTICAL INFORMATION

Boats dock in the relatively quiet but congenial harbor of **Korissia.** From the left of the dock, a strip of gift shops and cafeterias stretches along the waterfront. One of the first shops you will see is the **Stegadi** shop, which doubles as a hydrofoil agency and **tourist information office** (tel. 21 435). The **police** (tel. 21 100) are located at the end of the strip just where the road curves to the left around the beach. The **OTE** (tel. 22 399, open Mon.-Fri. 7:30am-3:10pm) is in a stucco white square alongside the tiny beach parking lot.

Nestled 5km uphill is the island's capital, **Chora,** or ancient **Ioulis.** The **post office,** to the left of the bus stop, is open Mon.-Fri. 8:30am-2pm. To the right of the bus stop is the **pharmacy** (tel. 22 277; open Mon.-Tues. and Thurs.-Fri. 8am-2pm and 6-9pm, Wed. and Sat.-Sun. 9am-2pm). The **bank** (tel. 22 350, -063), which also serves as a convenience store and **first aid** station, is located farther into town. (Open Mon.-Thurs. 8am-2pm, Fri. 8am-1:30pm.) **Postal Code:** 84002. **Telephone Code:** 0288.

To reach Kea from Athens, take the **ferry** from Lavrion (2-5 per day, 1½hr., 1600dr) or the hydrofoil from Zea in Piraeus (1 per day in high season, 4400dr) or from Kithnos (1-2 per day, 2520dr). There are no regular ferries between Kea and other islands, nor are there ferries to or from Piraeus. Though a ferry departure from Lavrion is the cheaper option, getting there entails a 1½-hour bus ride: take the bus from 14 Mavro Mateou St. in Lavrion (800dr).

Ask at Stegadi or at the police station for the season's bus schedule. Buses connect each town at least twice per day. Buses run to Voukari and Otzias from Korissia (80dr), and from Chora (250dr). They also go to Poiessa (220dr from Korissia, 160dr from Chora). It's worth traveling from Chora to Poiessa just for the spectacular view. You may opt to rent a moped at Korissia (roughly 4000dr per day).

ACCOMMODATIONS

Rooms to rent in Korissia lie along the waterfront, where the boats dock and behind the town beach, but they fill quickly in July and August. **Hotel Korissia** (tel. 21 484, -355) has clean, pleasant rooms and a very helpful proprietor, Mr. Takis Andronikos. (Sept.-June singles 6000dr, doubles 8000dr; July-Aug. singles 8000dr, doubles 10,000dr.) **Hotel Karthea** (tel. 21 204, -417; fax 21 417) has several clean rooms. (Singles 8650dr, doubles 10,380dr.) Not surprisingly given the wonderful views, rooms are hard to find in Chora, especially in July and August. Try **Hotel Ioulis Kea** (tel. 22 177) for good rates (singles 5500dr, doubles 7800dr; add 500dr for bath).

SIGHTS

Beaches with clear emerald waters lie north of Korissia; a single road follows the shore, along which many homes double as private rooms. **Yialiskari,** 1km to the north, is a small, clean, sandy beach. **Vourkari,** 2km away, is a fishing town with colorful sailboats in its harbor. There are several picturesque but generally expensive fish restaurants on the waterfront. The capital houses a small **Archaeological Museum** (free; open Tues.-Sun. 8:30am-3pm), but ancient Ioulis's glory is best evoked by the enormous **Lion of Kea,** embedded in stone 1km east of Chora. The **Kea Kouros,** a life-sized statue of a young male sculpted in pre-classical archaic style, was discovered at the nearby site of ancient Korissia in 1930, but now resides at the National Archaeological Museum in Athens. The peninsula of **Ayia Irini,** across the bay from Korissia, contains remnants of settlements that seem modest to the layman, but actually constitute one of the most important archaeological sites in the Cyclades. Excavated by American archaeologists since the 1960s, Ayia Irini is a 2500 BC settlement that traded with the Minoan and Mycenaean civilizations. The city reached its zenith between 1600 and 1450 BC, but was sparsely settled thereafter. (Open Mon.-Sat. 9am-3pm.)

The road cuts inland at a highway sign and continues 3km to the quiet bay of **Otzias.** If the 10 or 15 people on the beach are too many for you, rent a paddle boat (1000dr per hr.) and find your own sandy shore in the bay. For other **sea adventures,** try waterskiing (3500dr per hr.) or a banana-shaped vessel tugged by a power boat that may land you fortuitously in Kea's waters (1000dr per hr.). The 5½km, uphill country path after Otzias leads to the **Monastery of Panagia Kastriani** (tel. 31 348), where rooms for a pious overnight may be available. A popular beach lies south of Korissia at the site of another ancient city, **Poiessa,** whose name, which means "green" in ancient Greek, appropriately describes the ubiquitous cherry and orange *perivolia* (orchards). Freelance camping on most beaches is prohibited. In late July, Kea celebrates a festival called **Ta Simoneida** in honor of its great ancient poet. The event features dancing, theater, sports, and a bazaar.

KITHNOS ΚΥΘΝΟΣ

Travelers rarely make it to Kithnos, lending the island a curiously quiet air, even in mid-summer. Secluded beaches and gorgeous views from chalky mountaintops are disturbed only by Athenians returning to their vacation homes for weekend getaways during the summer months.

■■■ MERICHAS

Boats dock in the small port of **Merichas,** which is lined with private boats belonging to the island's fishermen. The **tourist office** (tel. 32 250), practically on the dock, provides maps, information on the island, and boat schedules, but has limited hours (open July-Aug; 11am-1pm and 5-8pm). The best time to find ferry lines open is up to an hour before departure. The **port police** (tel. 32 290) can be contacted for information on all sailings during other hours. Just off the dock area behind the information shack is the **Milos Express** ferry office (tel. 32 104, -248), another source for ferry information as well as **motorbike** rental (4000dr). (Open 9am-1pm and 5-9pm, although there is often someone here all day long.) Next door, beneath a canopy of green grapevines, sits the **pharmacy** (tel. 32 240; open Mon.-Fri. 8:30am-1:30pm and 6-8:30pm, Sat. 10am-1pm). Further along the waterfront are the **Ventouris Sea Lines** office (tel. 32 242; open 9am-2pm and 5-9pm), with more ferry tickets, and the representative of the **National Bank of Greece** (tel. 32 345) in a store that doubles as a minimarket and hydrofoil agent. (Open 8am-3pm.) It is easiest to find **taxis** simply by heading to the central town square, although calling 31 272 may also produce results.

From Kithnos, **ferries** voyage to Piraeus (1-3 per day, 3hr. tour, 2600dr), Serifos (1-3 per day, 1½hr., 1740dr), Sifnos (1-3 per day, 2½hr., 1780dr), Milos (1-3 per day, 4½hr., 2140dr), Kimolos (1-2 per day except Sunday, 4½, 2000dr), Santorini (2 per week, 6hr., 2490dr), Syros (weekly, 1900dr). There are also one to two **flying dolphins** each day to Zea port in Piraeus (5430dr) via Kea (2370dr), and once per week a ferry sails to Lavrion near Athens (2020dr). Hydrofoils go to Piraeus (5800dr), Kea (2520dr), and Lavrion (2000dr).

Private rooms are readily available in Merichas; you're likely to be approached upon arrival (doubles 5000dr, negotiable). An especially nice one is the aptly named **Panorama** (tel. 32 184; located to the left of the Milos Express office, up towering white steps). It has palatial rooms that overlook the harbor, all with kitchenette and bath. (Doubles 8000dr, triples 10,000dr. Reservations suggested for July and August.) "Room to Let" signs abound here, but if you are having no luck, try one of the following numbers: 32 069, -105, -370, -273.

■■■ AROUND THE ISLAND

Like almost everything in Kithnos, the **bus** schedule is incredibly seasonal. During the peak months of July and August, 6 buses per day run from Merichas to Driopida (200dr) and Kanala (300dr), and 5 per day to Chora (200dr) and Loutra (300dr), but during the rest of the year frequencies drop to thrice and twice daily (at best). From the bus stop in **Chora** (Kithnos Town), follow the footpath past the circular red sign prohibiting cars to the **post office** (open Mon.-Fri. 7:30am-noon). If you take a right before the post office and the small square, you'll double back to the **OTE** (open Mon.-Fri. 7:30am-2pm) and the **police** (tel. 31 201; open 24 hr.). There are also several *tavernas* and minimarkets in Chora to satisfy your hunger. **Taxis** are available in Chora or by calling 31 272 or 31 280. In case of **medical emergency,** call a doctor at 31 202 in Chora or 32 234 in Driopida. Near Chora, on the road from Merichas is **Kalva,** the island's premier disco (open nightly 11pm-4am). Kithnos's **telephone code** is 0281; its **postal code** is 84006.

Loutra, the village inlet resting down winding roads from Chora, is named for its hot springs, which reputedly can cure rheumatism and gynecological problems. **Kithnos Bay Hotel** (tel. 31 218, -441) is pricey but offers new, attractively furnished, air-conditioned rooms with balconies and baths. (Doubles 13,200dr. All w/bath; continental breakfast included.) Rooms also adorn quiet, sandy beaches in **Kanala.** Try calling 32 377 and a van will take you there (doubles 8000dr).

Dodecanese ΔΩΔΕΚΑΝΗΣΙΑ

The Dodecanese have managed through their unique past to amass one of the most unusual, but also the most compelling, collections of culture and architecture in the Mediterranean basin. After being settled by Dorians in ancient times, the region was captured in 1309 by the Knights of the Order of St. John, who remained there until the island fell to the Turks in 1512. During the Ottoman occupation, locals formed schools to preserve the indigenous culture; but although they played a key role in organizing the 1821 Greek revolution, the Dodecanese would not join the new nation for a century. In that time, the island group was subject to Italian control and then, during WWII, was occupied by the Germans. The effects of history are clearly seen in this motley collection of islands, where inspired landscapes are dotted with classical ruins, grand Italian buildings, and restored medieval homes. Today, the Dodecanese, and Rhodes in particular, endure tourism of frenzied proportions, which is minimized only by the islands' distance from the mainland.

RHODES (RODOS), ΡΟΔΟΣ

Rhodes is the undisputed tourist capital of the Dodecanese. While the resort towns suffer from the maladies brought on by crowds and commercialism, most of the island remains uncrowded and serene. Sandy beaches stretch along the east coast, jagged cliffs skirt the west, and green mountainscapes fill the interior, where villagers continue their centuries-old traditions. At Kamiros, Ialyssos, and Lindos is the clearest evidence of the island's classical past, while medieval fortresses rivaling those of France and Spain slumber in Rhodes, Lindos, and Monolithos. Although modern hotels dominate city skylines and all the major shopping streets and New Town beaches are crowded, soothing strolls are still possible in smaller villages and along the cobblestone streets of the Old Town.

■■■ CITY OF RHODES ΡΟΔΟΣ

Led by the prosperous cities Ialyssos, Lindos, and Kamiros during the 7th century BC, the island of Rhodes began to flourish as a major trading center. In 408 BC, near the end of the Peloponnesian Wars, the three city-states united and founded the city of Rhodes to serve as the island's capital. Determined to create a city which would reflect the prestige and prosperity of the new state, civic leaders hired Hippodamos from Miletus, the I.M. Pei of his day. Rhodes' exceptional harbor and fine architecture made it one of the ancient world's most beautiful cities.

Always putting commerce ahead of politics, Hellenistic culture flourished in Rhodes during the next centuries. Alliances with Rome during the Carthaginian Wars helped secure Rhodes' independence until, in 42 BC, Cassius plundered the city as punishment for its residents' having backed his rivals. The island fell to the Goths in 269 AD; but 28 years later, the Byzantine Empire consummated its political and cultural control over the island. Over the centuries, Crusaders, Ottoman Turks, and Italians ruled in succession; Greece finally wrested control of the island from the Germans after WWII.

Although Lindos is the one city on the island which has been continuously populated since ancient times, the city of Rhodes has always been the source of the island's vitality. Though dominated by the legacy of the Knights of St. John and

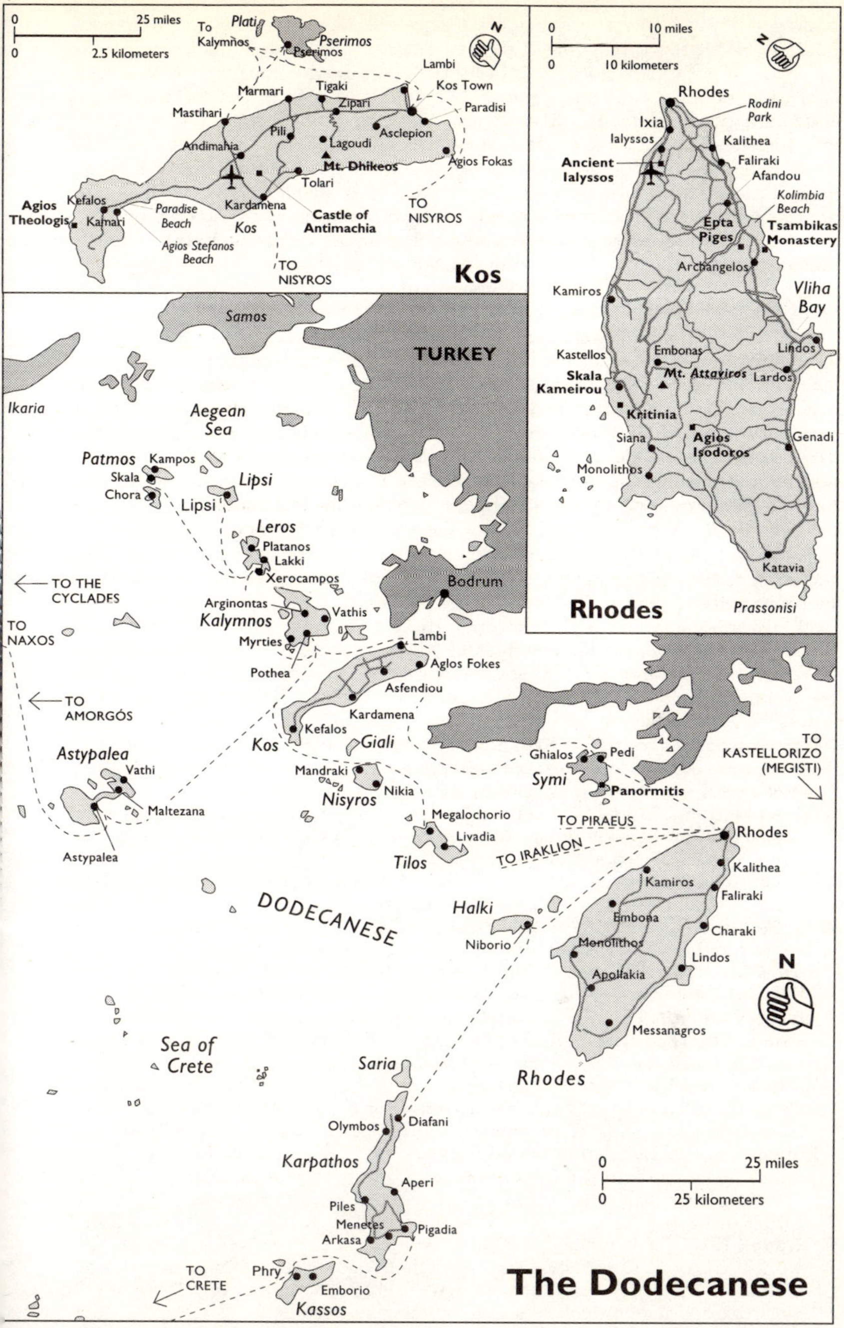
Kos
0
25 miles
0
2.5 kilometers
To Kalymnos
Plati
Pserimos
Pserimos
Lambi
Kos Town
Paradisi
Marmari
Tigaki
Zipari
Mastihari
Pili
Asclepion
Lagoudi
Andimahia
Mt. Dhikeos
Agios Fokas
Tolari
Agios Theologis
Kefalos
Kamari
Paradise Beach
Kardamena
Castle of Antimachia
TO NISYROS
Kos
Agios Stefanos Beach
TO NISYROS
Rhodes
0
10 miles
0
10 kilometers
Rhodes
Rodini Park
Ixia
Ialyssos
Kalithea
Ancient Ialyssos
Faliraki
Afandou
Kolimbia Beach
Epta Piges
Tsambikas Monastery
Archangelos
Kamiros
Vliha Bay
Kastellos
Embonas
Lindos
Skala Kameirou
Mt. Attaviros
Lardos
Kritinia
Siana
Agios Isodoros
Genadi
Monolithos
Katavia
Prassonisi
Samos
TURKEY
Ikaria
Aegean Sea
Patmos
Kampos
Skala
Chora
Lipsi
Lipsi
Leros
Platanos
Lakki
Xerocampos
TO THE CYCLADES
Bodrum
Arginontas
Kalymnos
Vathis
TO NAXOS
Myrties
Lambi
Pothea
Aglos Fokes
Asfendiou
TO AMORGÓS
Kardamena
Kefalos
Kos
Giali
Astypalea
Vathi
Maltezana
Astypalea
Mandraki
Nikia
Nisyros
Ghialos
Pedi
Symi
Panormitis
TO KASTELLORIZO (MEGISTI)
Megalochorio
Livadia
Tilos
TO PIRAEUS
TO IRAKLION
Rhodes
Kalithea
Kamiros
Faliraki
DODECANESE
Halki
Embona
Charaki
Niborio
Monolithos
Lindos
Apollakia
N
Messanagros
Sea of Crete
Saria
Rhodes
Olymbos
Diafani
Karpathos
0
25 miles
0
25 kilometers
Aperi
Piles
Menetes
Pigadia
Arkasa
TO CRETE
Phry
Emborio
Kassos
The Dodecanese

reminded of this by a vast impregnable fortress, Rhodes retains vestiges from each period of occupation, including Turkish mosques and Italian restaurants.

Today, Rhodes takes good care of its visitors. The city is packed with typical Greek island tourist amenities—leather belts and bags, t-shirts, hotels, bars, discos, and international newsstands. The atypical, however, is what strikes visitors—medieval turrets and archways, decaying mosques and minarets, palm trees, and live snake exhibitions. If you go to the city of Rhodes to see historical sights, it amply rewards; but if you hope for an isolated beach spot, you'll have better luck elsewhere on the island. The main beach to the west of the city is always crowded.

Pick up a free copy of the *Rodos News* at many travel agencies and hotels; it includes helpful info about the city and island.

ORIENTATION AND PRACTICAL INFORMATION

The city is divided into two districts: the **New Town,** stretching to the north and west, and the **Old Town,** below it, encapsulated within the medieval fortress walls. There are three adjacent harbors. Most boat traffic uses the **Mandraki,** the New Town's waterfront. Private yachts, hydrofoils, and excursion boats dock here. International and most domestic ferries use the **Commercial Harbor** outside the Old Town; **Acandia,** the harbor below it, provides a port for cargo ships. Beaches are located north beyond the Mandraki and along the city's west coast. **Rimini Square,** beneath the fortress turrets at the junction between the Old and New Towns, has the city's tourist office, both bus stations, and a taxi stand. To get here from the Mandraki, walk to the base of the vase-shaped Mandraki and head one block inland along the park on the New Town side. To get to **Symi Square,** which leads south to **Museum Square,** follow the city wall on the side of the park opposite Rimini Square back towards the water and go through the gate into the Old Town. **Sokratou Street,** the major thoroughfare in the Old Town, runs east-west a few blocks south of Museum Square and is your yellow brick road when searching for lodgings. The tourist office's map is a great help.

City of Rhodes Tourist Office: Rimini Sq. (tel. 35 945). Multilingual staff helps with bus, boat, and excursion schedules; accommodations; and currency exchange. Free city maps available. Open daily 8am-9pm.

Greek National Tourist Office: (tel. 23 255, -655). At the corner of Makariou and Papagou St. in the New Town. Walk up Papagou several blocks from Rimini Sq. Open Mon.-Fri. 7:30am-3pm.

Police: (tel. 23 294). On Ethelondon Dodekanission St., 1 block behind the post office. Lost and found. Open 24 hr. The **tourist police** (tel. 27 423 or 23 329) are located at Museum Sq. in the Old Town. The **port police** (tel. 22 220 or 28 888) are just to the left of the post office. Complete boat schedules.

Post Office: Main branch on the Mandraki (tel. 22 212). Message board. Open Mon.-Fri. 7am-8pm. Parcel service 7:30am-2pm. (Poste Restante window takes a lengthy lunch hour.) Also a **mobile branch** (on wheels), in the Old Town on Orfeos, near the Palace of the Grand Masters. From Museum Sq., head down Ipoton. Open Mon.-Fri. 7:30am-2pm. **Postal Code:** 85100.

OTE: 91 Amerikis St. (tel. 24 499), corner of 25th Martiou St. in the New Town. Open daily 6am-11pm. **Telephone Code:** for the northern half of the island 0241, below Kolymbia on the east 0244, below Kalavarda on the west 0246.

Budget Travel: Castellania Travel Service (tel. 75 860, -2; fax 75 861), in Hippocrates Sq. at the intersection of Sokratous and Aristotelous in the Old Town. Unbeatable English information and tickets for travel throughout Rhodes, the Dodecanese, Greece, and the rest of the world. Low prices on **international travel. ISIC cards** issued (2600dr), free luggage storage, ambient music, the works. Ask for Christos. Open 8am-midnight in the summer, 8am-1pm and 4-8pm off-season. **Triton Holidays** (tel. 21 690), 9 Plastira St. in the New Town, is also well-regarded and particularly useful for incoming visitors.

Banks: Ionian and Popular Bank, 4 Symi Sq. (tel. 27 434) in the Old Town offer **currency exchange.** Open Mon.-Thurs. 8am-2pm, Fri. 8am-1:30pm. Cash on Visa available at **National Bank of Greece,** Kyprou Sq. (tel. 27 031), in the New

Town. Open Mon.-Thurs. 8am-2pm, Fri. 8am-1:30pm. Exchange only Mon.-Fri. 3-8pm, Sat. 9am-1pm, Sun. 9am-noon. 24-hr. **ATM.** Many other banks in the New Town; few in the Old Town.

American Express: c/o Rhodos Tours Ltd., 23 Ammohostou St., P.O. Box 252, (tel. 24 022). Open Mon.-Fri. 8:30am-1pm and 5-8pm, Sat. 8:30am-1:30pm.

Flights: Olympic Airways, 9 Ierou Lohou St. (tel. 24 571), near the central OTE. Open Mon.-Sat. 7:30am-4pm; 4-9pm call 24 555 or 92 839. The **airport** (tel. 92 981) is on the west coast, 17km from town, near the city of Paradisi. Public buses run almost every hr. (7am-midnight; 280dr). Arrive at least 1hr. before scheduled departure. Domestic flights to Rhodes are usually booked at least two weeks in advance. Flights soar to Athens (3-4 per day, 23,000dr), Kos (3 per week, 12,000dr), Karpathos (1-2 per day, 11,800dr), Kassos (3 per week, 11,800dr), Crete (4 per week, 19,000dr), Santorini (3-4 per week starting in April, 18,000dr), and Mykonos (3 per week starting in June, 18,000dr). Off-season departures are less frequent and subject to change; all plane fares include taxes. There are **international flights** to Rome and Larnaka. Most flights to northern Europe are group charters, but you may be able to snag an empty seat at a reasonable price—ask at travel agencies.

Ferries: Rhodes is the most accessible island by ferry in the Dodecanese. There is a direct daily ferry to Piraeus (14hr., 7000dr), and indirect ferries via Kos (3000dr), Kalymnos (3600dr), Leros (4060dr), and Patmos (4640dr). Twice per week, a ferry takes the long route to Piraeus via Karpathos (3330dr), Kassos (3900dr), Crete (5445dr), Santorini (5437dr), Paros (5585dr), and Naxos (5050dr). Another weekly ferry sets sail for Piraeus, Chalkis, Karpathos, Kassos, Crete, Santorini, Milos, Sifnos, Serifos, and Kifnos. **International ferries** head to Limassol, Cyprus (2 per week, 17hr., 18,500dr during low season) and Haifa, Israel (2 per week, 36hr., 28,500dr during low season). During high season (June 12-Sept. 10), expect a 15% increase in prices. Student and youth fare (20% discount) available year round for Limassol and Haifa. Shop around to avoid getting ripped off. There are daily trips by ferry and hydrofoil to Marmaris, Turkey. Prices vary, and round-trips may be cheaper than one-way tickets at some agencies. (Ferry roughly 10,000dr one-way, 12,000dr round-trip; hydrofoil faster, with roughly the same prices.) The night before leaving for Turkey, you must leave your passport at the travel agency and arrange to pick it up before leaving the next day.

Flying Dolphins: Hydrofoil service connects Rhodes with the Northeast Aegean islands, Turkey, and the Dodecanese. Schedules here vary from day to day and should be checked at travel agencies (Symi 2675dr, Tilos 4589dr, Nisyros 5327dr, Kos 6665dr, Kalymnos 8055dr, Astypalea 8550dr, Samos 12,036dr, Patmos 10,338dr, and Leros 9076dr). Round-trip excursions run daily to Symi (3500dr) and Kos (10,000dr). For more information call 20 971.

Buses: East served by KTEL. Lindos (13 per day, 800dr), Faliraki (22 per day, 250dr), Archangelos (13 per day, 450dr), Kolimbia Beach (7 per day, 450dr), Afandou (15 per day, 300dr), and others—consult schedules at bus station, Rhodes tourist information office, DNTO, or *Rodos News,* or call 27 706 or 24 268 for current details. **West** served by RODA, Paradissi Airport (10 per day, 250dr), Ancient Kamiros (2-3 per day, 800dr), Monolithos (2 per day, 1050dr), Petaloudes (2 per day, 700dr), and others—consult printed schedules, or call 26 300. Stations lie on opposite sides of Papagou St. at Rimini Sq.

Taxis: In Rimini Sq. (tel. 27 666). Radio taxis also available (tel. 64 712, -34). 24 hr.

Moped Rental: In the city of Rhodes or in Faliraki. Prices vary depending on the season. Off-season, mopeds go for 2000dr; but be prepared to pay as much as 4000dr in summer. Ask for proof that the bike is covered by third-party insurance. Making the circuit of the island in one day is impossible: the island's size is deceptive, and roads in the south are primitive.

Bike Rental: Mike's Motor Club, 23 I. Kazouli St. in the New Town (tel. 37 420). Mountain bikes 1000dr. Open daily 8am-8pm. Cobblestones in the Old Town and maniacal drivers in the New Town make roads here generally unsafe for cyclists.

Laundromat: #32 28th Octovriou St. (tel. 33 320), between Dragoumi and Fanouraki in the New Town. Wash 900dr, dry 200dr per 20min., soap 200dr. Open Mon.-Fri. 4:30-8pm, Sat. 9am-5pm. Self-service. In the Old Town, try **Hobby**

Laundry, 31 Platonos St. (tel. 21 872), near Kavo D'Oro restaurant. Wash 1150-1400dr, dry 450-500dr. Open daily 8am-8:30pm.

Public Toilets: Strategic locations include Rimini Sq., the new market, and in the Old Town at Orfeos St. and at Sokratous St.; but bring your own toilet paper.

Libraries: Catholic Academy Library, 7 Dragoumi St. (tel. 20 254), off Diakou in the New Town. English books on the island's history and a few novels. Open Mon.-Tues. and Thurs.-Fri. 9am-2:30pm, Wed. 9am-2:30pm and 5:30-8pm. The library in the **Municipal Cultural Centre,** Rodiaki Epavli-King's Garden (tel. 37 144), has an English section. Open Mon.-Fri. 7:30am-2:30pm and 6-9pm, Sat. 8am-noon. The **Municipal Library** (tel. 24 448) located at 1 Aristotelous St. in the Old Town. Open Mon.-Tues. and Thurs.-Fri. 9am-2pm, Wed. 9am-2pm and 5-7:30pm.

English Bookstore: Small collection of English books available at **Kostas Tomaras Bookstore,** 5-7 Soph. Venizelou St. in New Town (tel. 32 055). Open Mon.-Fri. 8am-1pm and 5-9pm, Sat. 8am-2pm.

Consulates: The Voice of America, just past Sigouru St. (tel. 24 731), southeast of the city. Equipped to handle consular matters, especially in an emergency. Open Mon.-Fri. 8am-4:30pm. A **British** Vice-Consul is available Mon.-Sat. 8am-2pm through **Lloyd's Travel Bureau,** #23 25th Martiou St. (tel. 27 306, -247). The **Turkish** Consulate, 10 Iroon Polytechniou St. (tel. 23 362 or 24 603), helps with travel to Turkey. Open Mon.-Fri. 8am-1pm.

Hospital: (tel. 22 222 or 25 555), Erithrou Stavrou St. off El. Venizelou. Open for emergencies 24 hr. Visitor's clinic open daily 5-9pm.

Road Emergencies: Dial 104.

Medical Emergencies: Dial 100.

ACCOMMODATIONS

Old Town

Pensions are scattered about the narrow pebbled paths of the Old Town, the preferred resting place for most travelers. Winding streets are inconsistently named; bite the bullet and buy a map, even if doing so brands "tourist" across your forehead. Off-season prices run roughly 20-40% cheaper than in summer.

Pension Sofia, 27 Aristofanous St. (tel. 36 181 or 30 990), in Harritou Sq. From Sokratous St., turn onto Apellou St. south, pass the Sydney Hotel and Kavo D'Oro restaurant, and cross the parking lot to the right—look for a sign. Family-run, clean, and bright. Rooms have private baths. The balcony abounds with plums, jasmine, and basil. Doubles 6000dr, triples 7000dr.

Hotel Andreas, 28 Omirou St. (tel. 34 156; fax 74 285). Just off Omirou; follow the signs. Many rooms have nifty loftbeds, and the terraced bar with dangling vines affords an excellent view of the city. Doubles 7000dr, triples 10,000dr. Breakfast 900dr; laundry 1000dr.

Minos Pension, 5 Omirou St. (tel. 31 813). Immaculate rooms with clean common baths. Narrow spiral staircase leads to a sprawling balcony with a view. Doubles 8000dr, triples 10,000dr.

Hotel Spot, 21 Perikleous St. (tel. 34 737). Newly renovated rooms w/bath gleam like polished teeth. Doubles 8500dr.

Pension Apollo, 28C Omirou St. (tel. 32 003 or 35 064), next to Hotel Andreas. One of the most affordable, yet still clean, choices around. Doubles 5000dr.

Sydney Hotel, 41 Apellou St. (tel. 25 965). Across from Kavo D'Oro. Wood-paneled rooms w/bath. Doubles 9000dr, triples 11,000dr.

Hotel Stathis (Steve Kefalas' Pension), 60 Omirou St. (tel. 24 357). Gracious Steve spent 20 years in the Montreal hotel business before returning to his homeland. French and English spoken. At night the music from the nearby folk dance theater will either delight or irritate you. Noon check-out. Dorm beds 2000dr, doubles 6000dr. Breakfast 500dr, laundry 950dr.

New Town

The New Town, with its large apartment buildings and commercialized atmosphere, seems rather charmless; however, it is near the closest swimmable beach and has ample nightlife. Expensive hotels, generally occupied by lemmings on package tours, overshadow the coast. Affordable pensions can be found along the narrow streets of Rodiou, Dilberaki, Kathopouli, and Amarandou. Information about New Town pensions is available at the City Tourist Office.

Hotel Capitol, 65-67 Dilberaki St. (tel. 62 016 or 74 154). Spacious rooms in a house once inhabited by the mayor of Rhodes. On a quiet street away from the bars and discos. Private showers in all rooms. Singles 7000dr, doubles 12,000dr, triples 15,000dr, quads 17,000dr. Breakfast included.

Sotiras Studios, in Sotiras, 6km from Rhodes Town. Brand new with full kitchens. Inquire at Castellania Travel for details (75 860, -2; fax 75 861). Doubles 8000dr, quads 12,000dr.

FOOD AND ENTERTAINMENT

The Old Town's squares and alleyways are lined with *tavernas* (entrees 1000-1500dr). For better, cheaper food, avoid crowded, shop-lined thoroughfares. The family-run **Kavo D'oro** (tel. 36 181) has delicious meals and fabulous Greek music in a quiet, shady corner. Try the *papoutsaki* (stuffed eggplant, 1000dr), or the tasty *gemista* (stuffed tomatoes, 950dr). Otherwise, the Old Town's restaurants tend to be uniformly touristy and expensive; at least most of them accept credit cards. The New Town is infested with fast food places with similar prices. (*Tost* 400dr, hamburgers 500dr.) From Hippocrates Sq., go south on Pithagora, turn right at Platonos, left at a small square into a larger one, and behold **Aigaion** (tel. 36 228) on the right. Quiet, new, welcoming, and home to culinary pleasures (grilled octopus 1200dr, *saganaki* shrimp 1400dr). Fruit vendors cluster in the New Market. A deli across the street from the city tourist office in Rimini Sq. has a large selection of meats and cheese. Believe it or not, there's also a place to buy health food: **Paneri Health Foods,** 1 L. Fanouraki (tel. 35 877) has grains, herbs, pasta, vitamins, skin care products—even Birkenstocks. (Open Mon.-Fri. 9am-2pm and 5-9pm, Sat. 9am-2pm.)

The **Folk Dance Theater** (tel. 29 085), well signposted on Andronikou St. in the Old Town, stages hokey performances during the summer that feature dances and songs from all over Greece. (Shows May-Oct. Mon.-Fri. at 9:15pm; admission 2800dr, students 1500dr.) Evening **Sound and Light Shows** at the palace give an account of the Turkish siege of the city during the Crusader occupation. Although it sounds enthralling, don't expect to see much. The entrance is on Papagou St. in Rimini Sq. (English shows Mon.-Tues. at 9:15pm, Wed. and Fri.-Sat. at 10:15pm, Thurs. at 11:15pm; admission 1000dr, students 600dr.) **St. Francis Church** (tel. 23 605), at the intersection of Dimokratias and Filellinon St., echoes with organ recitals Wed. nights at 9pm. Once or twice a month, performances are given at the **ancient theater** near Monte Smith; check with the tourist office. The **National Theatre** (tel. 29 678), off the Mandraki next to the town hall, stages occasional winter productions. Watch a new flick or a subtitled classic at the **Rodon,** near the National Theatre. (Daily shows at 8:30 and 10:30pm; admission 800dr.)

According to the effusive *Rodos News,* Rhodes has more discos per capita than London, Paris, New York, or Berlin. The New Town is definitely the scene: most places start shaking around 11pm and don't fizzle out until 3am. Crowds of tourists, mostly young Brits, flock to the clubs near the intersection of Diakou and Venizelou and along Orfanidou. Prices vary by season but tend to be virtually identical from bar to bar. Don't be surprised by pricey covers at dance clubs during high season. Keep an eye out for street hawkers handing out free entrance cards. The **1960s Bar, Luka's,** and the **Underground** (with a huge London Underground sign) line Diakou, while the **Down Under Aussie Bar, Flanagan's Irish Bar,** and the **Hard Rock Café** are popular international watering holes on Orfanidou St., on the west edge of New Town. **Bar Berlin** (tel. 32 250) on Orfanidou and **Valentino's** (tel 34 070) off Apellou St. in the Old Town are two **gay bars.** The best disco in town is **Amazon (La Scala),** full of fountains, tropical waterfalls, garden pools, and a light show straight out of LaserFloyd. La Scala is one of a cluster of discos near the beach to the west outside of town. To get there from the Old Town, take Voriou Ipirou St. from near Amboise Gate—the clubs are just after the intersection with Kennedy St. Closer discos include **Zig Zag** and **Zoo Club** on Diakou. For true class, try Rhodos' tribute to Elvis, **Presley's** on Dragoumi St. in the New Town, or **Grand Master's Inn,** 64 Sokratous St. in the Old Town, where two knights in armor greet guests from the balcony.

SIGHTS

Rhodes' most famous sight can no longer be seen. The **Colossus of Rhodes,** a 35m bronze statue of Helios, the island's patron deity, was one of the seven wonders of the ancient world. Work commenced in 302 BC by Chares of Lindos. Legend has it that it stood astride the harbor—highly improbable, though you'll see various pictures to the contrary. An earthquake toppled it just 65 years after it was built. Bronze deer (one *sans* antlers) mark the spot in the harbor where it allegedly stood.

The Old Town: The Castello

Replacing Hellenistic structures (most of which had survived intact for centuries until the knights' arrival) with their own array of castles and fortresses, medieval knights left an enduring mark on the city. The best place to begin exploring the Old Town is **Symi Sq.,** inside the gates at the base of the Mandraki, the main passages between the Old and New Towns and the waterfront. To the right with your back to the arch is the **Municipal Art Gallery,** housing paintings by local artists. (Open Tues.-Sat. 8am-2pm; admission 500dr.) Behind the Temple stands the **Inn of Auvergne,** built in 1507, with a staircase attached to the façade in the Aegean style.

Past Symi Sq. is **Argykastron Square,** with a relocated Byzantine fountain in the center. Set back on the right of the square is the 14th-century **Palace of Armeria,** now the **Archaeological Institute.** With its small windows and lumbering Gothic architecture, this structure resembles a fortress. Connected to the palace is the **Museum of Decorative Arts,** which houses Dodecanese costumes, carved sea chests, and ceramic plates. (Open Tues.-Sun. 8:30am-3pm; admission 600dr, students 300dr.) After the low archway is **Museum Square** On the left is the **Church of St. Mary,** a.k.a. the Church of the Virgin of the Castle. The Knights of St. John transformed this structure, originally an 11th-century Byzantine work, into a Gothic cathedral. Most of the rich interior frescoes were obliterated by the Turks as they transformed the building into the Enderoum Mosque. The Italians made the mosque into a church, which has since retired in schizophrenic dotage to a quiet existence as a museum featuring icons from all over the island. (Open Tues.-Sun. 8:30am-3pm; admission 600dr, students 300dr.) The **Inn of the Tongue of England** stands beyond the church. Built in 1919, the stately Inn is a copy of the original 1493 structure. Dominating the other side of the square with its beautiful halls and courtyards, the former **Hospital of the Knights** now houses the **Archaeological Museum.** Most of the island's archaeological treasures are located here. Note the small but exquisite *Aphrodite Bathing* from the first century BC, the 4th-century Apollo, and the poignant collection of Classical and Hellenistic gravestones. (Open Tues.-Sun. 8am-7pm; admission 800dr, EC students 300dr, other students 400dr, free on Sun.)

The wide cobblestone street (Ipoton St.) that slopes uphill next to the museum is the most austere street in the Old Town. More than 500 years ago, the **Avenue of the Knights** was the main boulevard of the inner city, where most of the Knights lived. The Order of the Knights of St. John of Jerusalem consisted of seven different religious orders, called "tongues" since each spoke a different language. Their Inns, now government offices, are not open to tourists. Because each tongue was responsible for guarding one segment of the city wall, parts of the wall are labeled "England" or "France" on the map. Though their order was officially dedicated to healing, the Knights were primarily warriors; and even these elegant residences bear a curious resemblance to fortresses.

At the top of the street is a second archway leading to Kleovoulou Sq.; to the right sits the pride of the city, the **Palace of the Knights of St. John.** Also called the Palace of the Grand Masters, it boasts 300 rooms, moats, drawbridges, huge watch towers, and colossal battlements. The structure survived the long Turkish siege of 1522, only to be devastated in 1856 by the explosion of 300-year-old ammunition left forgotten in a depot across the street. The Italians undertook the task of rebuilding the castle at the beginning of this century. Quixotically determined to outdo even the industrious Knights, they restored the citadel and embellished many of the floors with famous Hellenistic mosaics taken from the island of Kos. In the early part of this century, the Italians used the palace as a seat of their government, where notables such as Victor Emmanuel III and Mussolini were entertained. The interior decoration was completed only a few months before the start of WWII, however, so the Italians had little chance to savor the fruits of their megalomaniacal effort. Don't miss the coins, illuminated manuscripts, icons, and sculptures, including the *Aeneid*-inspired depiction of boy-eating snakes. Bring the kids. (Palace open Tues.-Sun. 8am-7pm; admission 1200dr, students 600dr.) You can walk on the city walls (Tues. and Sat. 2:45-3pm; admission 1200dr, students 600dr).

Ancient remains are found mainly outside this area. Several blocks west of the south end of the Old Town off Diagoridon, a **stadium,** a small **theater,** and a **Temple of Apollo** have been partially reconstructed on the hill near Monte Smith. The stadium and theater are quite well preserved, but the temple, to put it graciously, is an irreparable ruin. The few standing columns can be seen from the ferry; they're just before the last stretch of hotels. (Open 24 hr.; free.) The only other pre-Roman site, the ruined 3rd-century BC **Temple of Aphrodite,** survives incongruously amid the modern traffic and medieval surroundings.

The Old Town: The Chora

To experience a different era of the city's history, turn right into Kleovoulou Sq. after the palace. After passing under several arches, turn left onto Orfeos St., better known as the **Plane Tree Walk.** The large **clock tower** on the left marked the edges of the wall that separated the knights' quarters from the rest of the city. The setup was identical during the Ottoman Era, but the boundaries changed: the Old Town as a whole became a ghetto of Turks and Jews, while the Christian Greeks lived outside its walls. For 600dr, you can climb the tower and take in the view; they'll give you a free drink for your trouble (open 9am-11pm). Just one block from the clock tower stands the **Mosque of Süleyman.** The original mosque on this site was built immediately after Sultan Süleyman the Magnificent captured Rhodes in 1522. The present one, an early 19th-century construction, has red-painted plaster walls, a garden, and a stone minaret, making it a good landmark in the Old Town and the best-kept symbol of a time Rhodians would rather forget. (Closed to the public.)

Across the street from the mosque is the **Turkish library,** built in 1794, full of 15th- and 16th-century Persian and Arabic manuscripts, including Qur'ans with extraordinarily intricate calligraphy. (Closed to the public.) The other Turkish buildings and monuments in the Old Town are in various states of picturesque decay.

Leading downhill from the Mosque of Süleyman is the main shopping strip, **Sokratous Street.** Because fur can be imported to Rhodes duty-free, outlets are inescapable here. Continuing east along Aristotelous St., you'll reach **Martyron Evreon Square** (Square of the Jewish Martyrs) in the heart of the old Jewish Quarter. In 1943, 2000 Jews were taken from this square to Nazi concentration camps; only 50 survived. A little way down Dossiadou St., where it becomes Simiou St., stands the **synagogue,** restored by the survivors after the war. Oriental rugs cover the stone mosaic floor, and "eternal lamps" hang in front of the curtained arc. Around the walk, plaques commemorate those lost in the war. To see the synagogue's interior, ask Lucia, who lives above, to contact the caretaker Mr. Soviano at 16 Polytechniou St. (tel. 27 344). Services are held Fri. at 5pm; modest dress.

At the threshold between the Old Town and the New Town at Eleftherias Gate near Symi Sq., don't miss the small herd of deer kept in the city's moat. More than 800 years ago, deer were imported to alleviate a serious snake problem. Apparently, the deer took perverse pleasure in impaling the snakes with their hooves and antlers; Rhodians have been grateful ever since. Now indicative of a more general sense of protection, the deer statues in Mandraki's harbor have become the city's symbol.

The New Town and Mandraki

Italian architecture dominates this modern business district. Mussolini-inspired buildings of massive, multicolored stone preside over wide Eleftherias St. The Bank of Greece, the town hall, the post office, and the National Theater are the more imposing structures on the far side of the street. Directly opposite, along the waterfront, is the majestic **Governor's Palace** and a cathedral built by the Italians in 1925. The cathedral replicates St. John's Church, which was leveled in an 1856 explosion.

Named after Süleyman's admiral who died while trying to capture Rhodes from the Knights of St. John in 1522, the **Mosque of Mourad Reis** is an important remnant of the Turkish presence. The small, domed building inside is his mausoleum.

Three **windmills** (no longer functional) stand halfway along the harbor's pier. The **Fortress of St. Nicholas** at the end of the pier was built in 1464 and guarded the harbor until the end of WWII. (Generally closed to the public.) An **aquarium** is at the north tip of the island. (Open daily 9am-9pm; admission 600dr, students 300dr.)

■■■ EASTERN RHODES

Excursion boats trace the beach-filled coast from Rhodes to Lindos, leaving in the morning and returning in the afternoon. They make several stops, often including Faliraki. Schedules and prices are posted at their dock along the lower end of the Mandraki: most cost roughly 3500dr round-trip. **Waterhoppers** (tel. 20 971) offers **scuba diving** excursions to Kalithea (10,500dr; non-diving passengers 5000dr; children under 6 free; snorkeling free). Certificates available (5-day course 75,000dr).

Beyond the city, the landscape slowly subsides into countryside. **Rodini Park** is a forested area with streams, trails, a restaurant, and some animals left from the time when Rodini was a zoo. Ten kilometers south of town lies **Kalithea,** site of a deserted spa that once bathed leisure-class Europeans. Pebble mosaic walkways guide visitors past chipped pink columns and the central bath, whose roof has cutout stars still showing traces of blue. For food there is only the meager snack bar at the beach cove, nearby Koskinou (2km inland) or Faliraki, or the city of Rhodes. **Buses** to Faliraki run 22 times daily (250dr); to Lindos run 13 times daily (800dr).

FALIRAKI

The popular resort Faliraki is 5km farther south from Kalithea. Its sandy beach and rocking nightlife make Faliraki Rhodes' equivalent of Malia (see p. 211). Like its Cretan counterpart, Faliraki bears more resemblance to a New Jersey boardwalk than to a Greek town, but at least it has a nice beach. Across the bus stop, on the right side of the main road connecting the beach to the Rhodes-Lindos highway, is the **first aid station** (tel. 85 555) located in a white building. (Open daily 8am-6pm.) Call the **hospital** (tel. 25 555) in Rhodes for medical service during other hours. Faliraki's **pharmacy** is on the main road (open Mon.-Sat. 9am-10pm, Sun. 9:30am-1pm and 4:30-10pm). The **taxi stand** is across from the first aid station. **Buses** run between Rhodes City and Faliraki (24 per day, 8:30am-11pm, 230dr). Buses from Faliraki to Lindos run from the stop at the intersection of the Rhodes-Lindos highway and the road to Faliraki beach (10 per day, 550dr).

There's an official **campsite** (tel. 85 516, -358) off the main road 1½km before Faliraki; ask the bus driver to let you off. Facilities include TV, disco-bar, market, and swimming pool. (1150dr per person, 500dr per tent; hot showers included.) Otherwise, accommodations in Faliraki are hard to come by during the peak season because most establishments rent their rooms to British tour package companies. Faliraki is best seen as a daytrip from Rhodes City. Food here isn't cheap, but there are a couple of fast food places.

During the day, the beach teems with sunbathers. On the north side of the beach enjoy **Mike's Windsurfing.** As night falls, the volume rises at all bars on the main street. **Chaplin's** is incongruously noisy with Friday afternoon karaoke competitions. **Bianco** offers pool and pinball, while **Jamaica Bar** recreates a tropical Caribbean atmosphere. Disco names and locations change frequently, but don't worry: you'll have more trouble avoiding Faliraki's nightlife than finding it.

Eleven km farther south, just before Kolymbia, a road to the right leads to a dirt road 3km away, which continues to **Epta Piges** (Seven Springs). The nature walks in this area are wonderful, but most people trek no farther than the inexpensive restaurant next to the main stream. (Springs open 24 hr.; free.) There's no direct bus service; ask any Lindos/Archangelos bus driver to let you off at the appropriate intersection. Continue inland past Epta Piges to visit the Byzantine **Church of Agios Nikolaos Fountoucli,** 3km past Eleousa, which has 13th- and 15th-century frescoes. **Buses** stop at Eleousa (3 per day) on the way to Rhodes. Villagers in **Arthipoli,** 4km away, rent rooms. Otherwise, take a moped; scarce traffic makes hitching difficult.

A worthwhile stop if you're exploring by moped or car is the **Tsambikas Monastery,** a Byzantine cloister atop Mt. Tsambikas. The asphalt ends at the Tsambikas Beach turn-off, but the road ahead takes you most of the way. You'll have to walk the last kilometer. **Kolymbia** and **Tsambikas** beaches are sandy and peaceful. **Buses** run from Rhodes to Kolymbia (10 per day) and return 11 times per day (400dr). From Lindos to Kolymbia 3 buses run daily and 1 returns the next morning (450dr). Buses leave for Rhodes from Tsambikas at 9am and return at 3 and 4pm (450dr).

Roughly 10km farther down the road from Tsambikas (15km north of Lindos), take the turn-off to **Charaki,** where you can swim next to a hill topped by the crumbling **Castle of Feracios,** built by the Knights of St. John. Quite a few rooms and several restaurants line the beach. **Buses** to Charaki leave from Rhodes (Rimini Sq.) at 10am and 1pm and return at 7:45am, 3:20, and 6:10pm (550dr).

LINDOS

With beautiful whitewashed houses clustered beneath a soaring castle-capped acropolis, Lindos is the most picturesque member of the Rhodos family. Vines and flowers overhang narrow streets, and pebble mosaics carpet courtyards and line doorways. The town's charms, however, are no secret. In summer, Lindos' packed streets make the city of Rhodes resemble a ghost town—and inflated prices match the demographics. Lindos is also notoriously hot and short of accommodations in the summer, making it a place to visit outside of high season if possible. **Buses** run to Lindos leave from Rimini Sq. in Rhodes. **Excursion boats** from Rhodes depart at 9am and return at 5pm, sometimes stopping at other points on the coast.

Orientation and Practical Information Lindos is a pedestrian-only city. All traffic stops at Eleftherias Sq. From there, **Acropolis Street,** the main avenue, leads through the eastern part of town and up to the well-signposted acropolis. **Apostolous Pavlou,** the second main street, runs perpendicular to Acropolis St., west from the Church of the Assumption Madonna, whose stone belfry (covered with scaffolding) rises above the middle of town. No other streets are named. Houses are distinguished only by number, and those change periodically.

The **tourist office** (tel. 31 288), in Eleftherias Sq. (where buses stop), helps with accommodations, maintains a **currency exchange,** and provides maps and transportation information. Their useless glossy brochure about Lindos costs 300dr. (Open 9am-10pm.) **Pallas Travel** (tel. 31 494; fax 31 595), 100m east of the church, has an equally useless brochure for free. They also hold mail, arrange babysitting services, and offer various excursions (open 9am-10pm). Other travel offices line Apostolous Pavlou St. The **National Bank** is on Apostolous Pavlou (open Mon.-Thurs. 9am-2pm, Fri. 9am-1:30pm, Sat. 9am-1pm). The **post office** (open Mon.-Fri. 8am-2pm), and **pharmacy** (tel. 31 294; open Mon.-Sat. 9am-9:30pm, Sun. 9am-3pm) are up the hill to the right of the donkey stand. Most of the town's other services are near Acropolis St. Sheila Markiou, an expatriate Bostonian, runs a superb **lending library** (tel. 31 456, -43) of more than 7000 English, Italian, German, French and Greek books (100dr per day w/1500dr deposit; used books 300-1200dr). Walk to Pallas Travel and bear right where the road forks; the library is just up and to the left (open daily 9am-8pm). Borrow a used book to read while you do your **laundry** at Sheila's service, next to the library (1000dr per 10-lb. load). The **medical clinic** (tel. 31 224) is behind the church. (Open daily 9am-1:30pm and 6-8pm.) For **medical emergencies** after hours call the **doctor** at home (tel. 31 527), or the **health center** in Archandelos (tel. 22 400). There are **public toilets** across from the information office near the taxi/bus station (100dr). The **police** (tel. 31 223) are at 521 Vas. Pavlou (open Mon.-Fri. 8am-3pm; emergencies 24 hr.). **Postal Code:** 85107; **Telephone Code:** 0244.

Accommodations In July and August, Lindos is best seen as a daytrip; lodgings, even in the tiniest spots, are hogged by European package tours. Off-season lodgings are easier to find and cost a fraction of summer prices. During the summer, arrive early in the morning before the tour buses rumble in, and ask the tour companies' offices if they have any empty rooms. The few free agents rent doubles for 5000-7000dr in high season; singles are difficult to find. For a good place to start looking, bear left downhill at the Commercial Bank near the bus stop. This road leads down to the beach and is packed with pensions and private rooms. **Pension Electra** (tel. 31 266) at #66 offers a garden, terrace, and clean rooms. (Doubles 9000dr, w/bath 13,000dr.) Less expensive rooms await in more remote corners. Inquire at Restaurant Stefany's on 230 Acropolis St. about rooms in **Pension Venus,** which has a classy stone archway at the entrance and simple doubles (10,000dr).

Food and Entertainment Eating on a budget in Lindros poses a challenge: restaurant prices range from expensive to exorbitant. The only cheap alternatives are *souvlaki-pita* bars, creperies, or grocery stores on the two main streets. "Snack bar" shops serve the best option in Lindos: a bowl of homemade yogurt with honey and fresh fruit (500-700dr). Try Greek food with a Cypriot twist at the **Cyprus Taverna** (tel. 31 539). The rooftop tables below the acropolis provide a chance to brood over the ruins (*kleftiko* 1350dr, *hummus* 450dr). Lindos' nightlife is loud and fervent. Most people visit the town's bars until the music ends at midnight; they then head to the discos on the other side of the main square. Indulge in cheap booze right under the acropolis at **Lindos By Night** (tel. 31 463; open daily 7pm-3am; pints of beer 500dr, cocktails 700dr).

Sights Lindos' premier attraction, the ancient **acropolis,** stands amidst scaffolding at the top of sheer cliffs 125m above town. The impenetrable walls of a Crusader fortress further enclose the caged structure. Excavations of the site by the Danish Archaeological School between 1902 and 1912 yielded everything from 5000-year-old Neolithic tools to a plaque, inscribed by a priest of Athena in 99 BC, listing the dignitaries who visited Athena's Temple—Hercules, Helen of Troy, Menelaus, Alexander the Great, and the King of Persia. The winding path up to the acropolis is veiled in lace tablecloths sold by local women; the cobwebbed pall makes for a surreal ascent. Right before the final incline, don't miss the fabulous ancient Greek warship (*trireme*), carved into the cliffside as a symbol of Lindos' inextricable ties with the sea. The 13th-century **crusader castle** looms over the entrance to the site. As you leave the castle, make a U-turn to your left to reach the imposing **Doric Stoa** (arcade) whose 13 restored columns dominate the entire level. The arcade, built in approximately 200 BC at the height of Rhodes's glory, originally consisted of 42 columns laid out in the shape of the Greek letter "Π." The large stone blocks arranged against the back wall originally served as bases for bronze statues which have long since been melted down.

At the top of the steps, the **Temple of the Lindian Athena** comes into view. According to myth, a temple was built here as early as 1510 BC. All that remains today are parts of the temple built by the tyrant Cleoboulos in the 6th century BC. Once a tremendously important religious site, it's now one of the few ancient temples with inner walls still fairly intact; colonnades flank both sides. Donkey rides to

Travel Gear

Supreme Convertible back-pack/carry-on suitcase with innovative hideaway suspension and parallel stay internal frame. Includes leather trim, lumbar support pad, torso and waist adjustments, and a dual pocket detachable daypack. Waterproof Cordura nylon, lifetime guarantee. 4400 cubic inches, 14" x 26" x 14". Black, Hunter, or Navy. *As seen on cover in Hunter.* $175

Backpack/Suitcase Hideaway suspension with an internal frame turns this backpack into a carry-on suitcase. Detachable daypack makes it three bags in one. Lightweight and versatile, Waterproof Cordura nylon, lifetime guarantee. 3750 cubic inches, 14" x 24" x 11". Black, Hunter, or Navy. *As seen on cover in Navy.* $130

Padded Toiletry Kit Large padded main compartment to protect contents. Mesh lid pocket with metal hook to hang kit on a towel rod or bathroom hook. Features two separate small outside pockets and detachable mirror. 9" x 4 3/4" x 4 1/4". Black, Evergreen, or Blue. *As seen on cover in Blue.* $20

Departure Pouch Great for travel or everyday use. Features a multitude of inside pockets to store passport, tickets, and monies. Includes see-thru mesh pocket, pen slots, and gusseted compartment. Can be worn over shoulder, around neck, or cinched around the waist. 6" x 12". Black, Evergreen, or Blue. *As seen on cover in Black.* $16

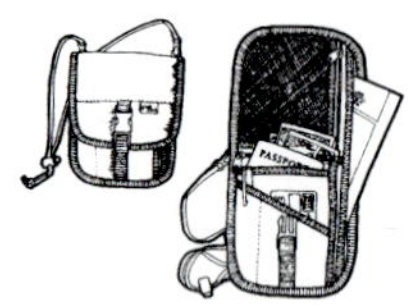

Padded Travel Pouch Main zipper compartment is padded to protect a compact camera or mini binoculars. Carries as a belt pouch, or use 1" strap to convert into waist or shoulder pack. Front flap is secured by a quick release closure. 6" x 9" x 3". Black, Evergreen, or Blue. *As seen on cover in Evergreen.* $26

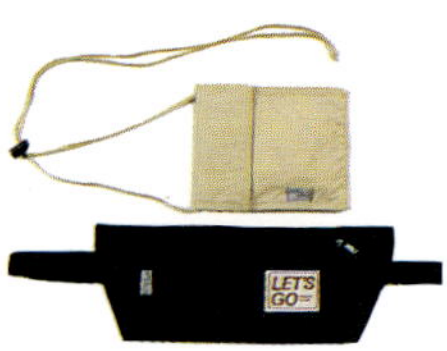

Undercover Neckpouch Ripstop nylon with a soft Cambrelle back. Three pockets. 5 1/4" x 6 1/2". Lifetime guarantee. Black or Tan. $9.95

Undercover Waistpouch Ripstop nylon with a soft Cambrelle back. Two pockets. 4 3/4" x 12" with adjustable waistband. Lifetime guarantee. Black or Tan. $9.95

*Prices and availability of products are subject to change.

Discounted Airfares

Available on international flights all over the world. Domestic fares too! For prices and reservations, call 1-800-5-LETS GO.

1996 International ID Cards

Provides discounts on accommodations, airfares, tourist attractions, rental cars and more! Also includes basic accident and medical insurance. Instructions for ordering are located on the next page, at top of order form.

International Student ID Card (ISIC)....................$18
International Teacher ID Card (ITIC)....................$19
International Youth ID Card (GO25)................$18

Hostelling Essentials

1996-97 Hostelling Membership: Often required at international hostels. Cardholders usually receive first preference and discounts. Must have a U.S. address to apply.

Adult (ages 18-55)..$25
Youth (under 18)..$10
Senior and Family memberships also available.Please call.

Sleepsack: Required at all hostels. Two thin sheets sewn together (78" x 30") with 18" pillow pocket. Durable poly/cotton. Washable, folds into pouch size..$13.95

1996 International Youth Hostel Guide (IYHG): Contains essential information about the 4000 hostels located in Europe and the Mediterranean. $10.95

Travel Guides

Let's Go Travel Guides: The bible of the budget traveler! All 22 titles available.

Europe • USA & Canada...............................$18.99

Regional & Country Guides (please specify)....$16.99

Alaska & The Pacific Northwest • Austria & Switzerland • Britain & Ireland • California & Hawaii • Central America • Eastern Europe • France • Germany • Greece & Turkey • Ireland • Israel & Egypt • Italy • Mexico • Southeast Asia • Spain & Portugal

City Guides (please specify).........................$15.99

London • New York City • Paris • Rome • Washington, DC.

Let's Go Map Guides: New item for 1996! Includes fold-out maps and up to 40 pages of text!

City Maps (please specify) $7.95

Boston • London • New York City • Paris • San Francisco • Washington, DC

Eurail Passes

The most convenient and affordable way to travel in Europe. Save up to 70% off the cost of individual tickets.

Prices listed are 1995 prices. 1996 prices were not available at time of publishing; prices are expected to increase 5% to 6% and are subject to change. Please call before ordering to verify prices.

Eurailpass (First Class): Unlimited train travel for a specified duration of time. Accepted in 17 countries.

15 days...$498
21 days...$648
1 month...$798
2 months...$1098
3 months...$1398

Eurail Flexipass (First Class): Individual travel days that can be used at your convenience within a two month period.

Any 5 days in 2 months..............................$348
Any 10 days in 2 months............................$560
Any 15 days in 2 months............................$740

Eurail Youthpass (Second Class): The same advantages of the Eurailpass but for those travelers who will be under 26 years old by the first date of the travel on the train.

15 days...$398
1 month...$578
2 months...$1078

Eurail Youth Flexipass (Second Class): The convenience of the Eurail Flexipass but for those travelers who will be under 26 years old by the first date of the travel on the train.

Any 5 days in 2 months..............................$225
Any 10 days in 2 months............................$398
Any 15 days in 2 months............................$540

Europass: Offers the option of purchasing travel days within a two month period for 3, 4, or 5 country combinations for the following countries: France • Germany • Italy • Spain • Switzerland. Associate countries can also be added. Call for more details.

Regional and Country Passes and Point-to-Point Tickets also available. Call for more details.

1-800-5-LETS GO

Order Form

Please print or type. Incomplete applications will not be processed.

International Student/Teacher Identity Card (ISIC/ITIC) (ages 12 and up) enclose:

1. Proof of status (letter from registrar or administrator, proof of tuition payment, or copy of student/faculty ID card. FULL-TIME only.)
2. One picture (1 1/2" x 2") signed on the reverse side.
3. Proof of birthdate (copy of passport, birth certificate, or driver's license).

GO25 card (ages 12-25) enclose:

1. Proof of birthdate (copy of passport, birth certificate, or driver's license).
2. One picture (1 1/2" x 2") signed on the reverse side.

Last Name | First Name | Date of Birth

Street | *We do not ship to P.O. Boxes.*

City | State | Zip Code

Phone (very important!) | Citizenship (Country)

School/College | Date of Travel

Description, Size	Color	Quantity	Unit Price	Total Price

Shipping & Handling

Domestic

If order totals ....add
up to $30.00.......................$4
$30.01-100.00....................$6
over $100.00......................$8
add additional $5 for AK & HI

International

via Federal Express............$30

Total Merchandise Price	
Shipping and Handling (See box at left)	
Add $10 for Rush, $20 for Overnight	
MA Residents (Add 5% sales tax on gear & books)	
Total	
From which Let's Go Guide are you ordering?	

Master Card/Visa/Amex Order

cardholder name ______
card number ______
expiration date ______

Allow 2-3 weeks for delivery. Rush orders guaranteed within one week of our receipt.

Make check or money order payable to:

Let's Go Travel

53A Church Street • Cambridge, MA 02138 • USA

1-800-5-LETS GO

the acropolis are a rip-off (850dr each way); the walk isn't too strenuous. (Acropolis open Tues.-Sun. 8:30am-3pm; admission 1200dr, students 600dr; free on Sun.)

The graceful stone bell tower projecting from the middle of town belongs to the **Church of the Assumption Madonna,** rebuilt by the Knights of St. John circa 1489. Brightly colored 18th-century frescoes, retouched by the Italians in 1927, illuminate the interior. (Open daily 9am-1pm and 3-5pm; modest dress required.) At the southwest foot of the acropolis are the remains of the **ancient theater.** The **Voukopion** is on the north side of the rock face, visible from the donkey path. This cave, which the Dorians transformed into a sanctuary for Athena, is believed to date from the 9th century BC and was supposedly used for special sacrifices that could be performed only outside the acropolis.

■■■ WESTERN RHODES

A string of high-rise hotels abuts the 8km stretch of sand west of Rhodes. The west end of this luxury hotel district is the town of modern **Ialyssos** (Trianda). The hotels were built in the late 60s and early 70s under Greece's military dictatorship. Along with Lindos and Kamiros, Ancient Ialyssos, 5km inland near the town of **Filerimos,** was once one of the three great cities on the island. The ruins are rather meager. Most impressive are the 4th-century BC Doric fountain ornamented with four lion heads, the adjacent monastery, and the Church of Our Lady of Filerimos (actually four conjoined chapels). The church and monastery stand on the site of a 3rd-century BC temple to Athena and Zeus Polias. On the stone floor just inside the doorway of the room to the left rests a remnant of the original Byzantine structure: a fish (the symbol of Christ) carved into one of the red stones. The path past the chapel leads to the ruins of a Byzantine castle. (Site open Tues.-Sun. 8:30am-3pm; admission 400dr, students 200dr; free on Sun.)

Unfortunately, there is no easily negotiable road to Filerimos. Taxis from Rimini Sq. will make the round-trip (3000dr). Aside from a moped, the only other alternative is the bus from Rhodes to modern Ialyssos (6 times per day, last bus at 10:55pm; 220dr), but the bus stops 5km before the town. Taxis will cost 1500dr.

Sandy cliffs line the coast south of Filerimos. Nearby, two religious festivals take place on the road to Kamiros. At **Kremasti,** 12km outside Rhodes, locals celebrate the *Panagia* (the name-day of the Virgin Mary) for nine days beginning August 14. The **Monastery of Agios Soulas,** 18km on the inland road at **Kalavarda,** hosts a grand name-day festival for its patron saint on July 28-29. In between, only tiny villages animate the coast, and the beaches are mediocre. **Buses** to Kremasti from Rhodes are the same as those running to Ialyssos (8 per day, last bus at 10:30pm; 230dr). Buses run to Kalavarda from Rhodes 2 times per day (6:30, 7pm; return 5:45am, 7:30pm; 380dr). The **telephone code** changes to 0246 for the southwest.

An interesting excursion, often done as a daytrip, is **Petaloudes,** a valley roughly 25km from the city. Also known as the Valley of the Butterflies, it is famous for its lepidopterous metropolis in July and August. On off-days you'll find more befuddled tourists here than butterflies and more spoony couples than singles. Nevertheless, the valley is charming, with small waterfalls, pools, and wooden bridges. (Open daily mid-June-Aug. 9am-6pm; admission 250dr.) Roughly 1km down the road is the 18th-century monastery of the **Panagia Kalopetra. Buses** from Rhodes travel here (Mon.-Fri. 9:30, 11am; return 10:10, 11:45am, 2:30pm; 700dr). Petaloudes is accessible from the coastal road 3km after Paradisi. Take the turn-off to Kalamonas, and the valley is 9km farther.

Ancient Kamiros, 35km from the city of Rhodes, was a prosperous city surrounded by farmland in the 6th and 5th centuries BC. Stone houses, the reservoir cisterns, fallen pillars of temples, and the main cobblestone street have survived, leaving a life-size blueprint of a small ancient city. The site's view of the Aegean and neighboring valleys is striking. (Site open Tues.-Sun. 8:30am-3pm; admission 400dr, students 200dr; free on Sun.) Two buses per day come from Rhodes (40min., 700dr). 15km beyond Ancient Kamiros, **Kamiros Skala** has a few *tavernas* and a boat launch. Boats leave daily for Chalki (1000dr); inquire at the tourist office in Rhodes. To get here take the Monolithos bus (see below).

Beyond Kamiros Skala at Kritinia, there is a turn for **Embona,** a village renowned for its dancing and traditional costumes. In Embona a large group of squat, modern houses sits in contrast to the lush vegetation and the rocky slopes of Mt. Atavyros, the tallest mountain on the island (1215m). Despite its uncomely mask, the town conducts a thriving tourist trade on summer evenings. South of Kamiros Skala, both coastal and mountain roads traverse high ridges, affording views of Alimnia and Tragousa and other small islands off the coast on the way to Monolithos. A small **castle** on the cliffs by the sea rests near the quiet mountainside village of **Kritinia.**

Monolithos (single rock), on the island's southwest tip, is tiny, barely more than a collection of scattered houses. The **Castle of Monolithos,** 2km west, is well worth the trip. In ruins, the fortress sits at the summit of a 160-m rock pillar, and visitors can walk inside (24 hr.; free). To get here, follow the only western road out of town. Despite its uninspired name, the **"Restaurant-Bar Greek Food,"** at the top of the road, has decent entrees. Two buses leave Rhodes daily for Monolithos via Embona and Ag. Isidoros (depart at 1:15pm, return at 6:15am the next day, 2½hr., 1100dr).

■■■ SOUTHERN RHODES

In the south, the island assumes an entirely different character. Here in farm and goat-herding country, grassy yellow flatlands slope gradually into hills studded with low-lying shrubs. **Buses** to Lardos leave daily (3 per day, 800dr). Tues., Thurs., and Sat., buses travel to Asklipio (900dr), Katavia (1200dr), and Messanagros (1100dr).

Beaches at rotund **Lardos** (10km south of Lindos), **Kiotari** (18km south), and **Katavia** (24km south) are as sleepy as their towns. **Genadi,** 22km south of Lindos, has rooms to let. The road on the southeast is preferable; southwest routes are unpaved.

For isolation, take the dirt road (you may need a jeep) to the **lighthouse** at **Akro Prassonisi,** on the island's south tip. The couple living there rarely gets visitors in summer; in winter they get none, as the sea covers the isthmus. Rustic **Skiadhi Monastery,** halfway up a hill on a steep alternate road between Apollakia and Messanagros, is an unsurpassed photo opportunity. To get to the monastery from **Apollakia,** take the dirt road 4km to Katavia and turn left onto the well-marked monastery turn-off (manageable on a motorbike). Follow the dirt road past pumpkin patches and wheat fields for several km. Apollakia has a few cheap pensions and restaurants.

It is simple to orient yourself in **Lardos.** There is one *plateia*, and not much else in town. **Lardos Holiday Tours** can supply some information (open Mon.-Sat. 9am-1pm and 5-9pm). You can **exchange currency** here Mon.-Sat. 10am-1pm and 5-9pm. Alternatively, a **mobile bank bus** stops in the square Mon.-Wed. and Fri. at 10:30am. The *plateia* also has a **Teo Rent a Car** (tel. 43 390 or 44 095) and a **pharmacy** (open 9am-1pm, 5-11pm). The postman sets up shop every Mon., Wed., and Fri. at 10am for roughly 1hr. in the medical office. Surprisingly, the **medical office** also houses a doctor, who keeps hours Mon.-Thurs. 9:30am-1pm and Fri. noon-1pm (tel. 44 347; **emergency** 44 097). The nearest **police** stand guard in neighboring **Gennadi** (tel. 43 222), 14km from town. **Telephone Code:** 0244.

From Lardos, you can visit the **Convent of Ipsanis** (5km outside of Lardos) or the **Monastery of Tharri** in neighboring **Laerma** (12km outside of Lardos).

KOS ΚΩΣ

While it is not commonly recognized for its contributions, Kos' past is as varied and rich as that of other notable Greek islands. Its residents have dabbled in the fields of medicine, literature, religion, and politics, and Kos is known as the home of Hippocrates, father of medical science, whose 2400-year-old oath is still taken by doctors. In ancient times, the island was respected both as a major trading power and as the sacred land of Asclepius, god of healing. The home of poets Theocritus and Philetas, it reached its prime as a literary center under the Ptolemies. At that time, its population neared 160,000 (compared to today's 20,000). Several hundred years later, Kos served as an episcopal seat for the Byzantine Empire. It was also occupied by pirates and various predatory naval forces. The Knights of St. John appropriated Kos in 1315, transforming it into one of their outposts. From then on, its history has been akin to that of the other Dodecanese islands: first the Turks took over Kos, and then, in the 20th century, the Italians, Germans, and British.

Belying its complex and intriguing past, Kos today drowns in a flood of package tours and, in many places, poses as a full-fledged resort. The ancient ruins of Kos Town are surrounded by loud bars; lengths of sandy beaches in the south hold mammoth hotels. If this scene sounds irksome, take advantage of lower off-season prices; or seek out the island's quieter beaches and pristine mountain villages.

■■■ KOS TOWN

In Kos Town, minarets from Turkish mosques stand alongside grand Italian mansions and the massive walls of a Crusader's fortress. Brilliantly colored flowers and date palms embellish the streets, squares, and ancient monuments. The town is an archaeological repository of archaic, classical, Hellenistic, and Roman ruins. Unfortunately, it's also one of the most expensive places in the Dodecanese. Package tour agents have made contracts with many of the cheapest pensions, leaving very few rooms for independent travelers. Despite this, the remarkable combination of ancient, medieval, and modern styles make Kos a very pleasant city in which to wander, especially early in the morning, before the tours and the heat set in.

ORIENTATION AND PRACTICAL INFORMATION

As your ferry pulls into the harbor of Kos Town, you'll see only the colossal walls of the Castle of the Knights of St. John. Don't be alarmed; if you walk left from the harbor (facing inland), the stately trees which frame the **Avenue of Palms** (also called Finikon Street) will assure you that you're not in Alcatraz. Continuing along the waterfront past the Palms leads to **Vas. Georgios** and the rocky beach alongside it. Turn right onto the Avenue of Palms and follow it to the next corner of the fortress and you'll come upon **Akti Kountouriotou,** another waterfront street that wraps around the lightbulb-shaped harbor. The city bus station, boats to Turkey, travel agencies, restaurants, and Kos' thriving nightlife can all be found here. With the water on your right, the left after Tsaldari St. is **Megalou Alexandrou,** which heads inland to **Palaiologou Square,** the ruins of ancient Kos Town, and eventually the inland villages. Continuing along the waterfront, you'll come across the dolphin fountain and, eventually, the popular sandy beach north of town.

Tourist Office: (tel. 28 724 or 24 460), one block below the Agora on Vas. Georgious. The tourist office has free, exceedingly helpful maps of the city, which kiosks and newsstands sell for 250dr. (Open 9am-3pm.)

Police: (tel. 22 222, -801, or -100). On Akti Miaouli St. in the large Italian building next to the castle. Some English spoken. Open 24hr. **Tourist Police** (tel. 22 444) in the same building. Open 7:30am-2pm. **Port Police** (tel. 26 594), past the City Bus stop on Akti Kountouriotou.

Post Office: 14 Venizelou St. (tel. 22 250). Follow the signs from Vas. Pavlou, which lead past Eleftherias Sq. and the fruit market. Open Mon.-Fri. 7:30am-2pm, Sat. 8am-2pm, Sun. 9am-1:30pm. **Postal Code:** 85300.

OTE: (tel. 22 259). Around the corner from the post office, at the corner of L. Virona and Xanthou. Open Mon.-Sat. 7:30am-2:30pm. The easiest and most noise-free place to make international calls on Kos. **Telephone Code:** 0242.

Banks: National Bank of Greece (tel. 28 517), in back of the Archaeological Museum, one block inland from the water on A.P. Ioannidi, with a 24-hr. **ATM** that accepts Mastercard and Cirrus. (Open Mon.-Thurs. 8am-2pm, Fri. 8am-1:45pm.) **Commercial Bank,** 7 Vas. Pavlou (tel. 28 525; head inland from the

City Bus station), advances money on Visa (open Mon.-Thurs. 8am-2pm, Fri. 8am-1:45pm). After hours, change money at the travel agencies along the waterfront.

Tourist Agencies: Like so many islands, no one agency in Kos has comprehensive boat information. Two large ferry companies (DANE and GA) and two hydrofoil lines (Ilio and Dodecanese) frequently serve Kos and its neighbors. **Travel Agency Koulias** (tel. 27 311, -7; fax 21 517), on the ground floor of the waterfront building with the DANE SEA LINE sign, sells DANE and Dodecanese hydrofoil tickets, offers printed schedules, and exchanges currency (open 8am-10:30pm). Your best bet, especially if you're trying to do anything vaguely complex (like get to the Cyclades), is to wander into the numerous agencies clustered where Vas. Pavlou meets the harbor until your questions are answered.

Flights: Head to Athens (2-3 per day, 18,600dr) and Rhodes (3 per day, 9000dr). **Olympic Airways,** 22 Vas. Pavlou St. (tel. 28 331, -2). Open Mon.-Fri. 8am-3:30pm. (On weekends, call 51 567 for info.) Olympic runs a bus from Kos Town to the airport 2-4 times per day (1000dr); schedule posted in their front window. Or ask to be let off near the airport by either the Kardamena or Kefalos buses. Taxis from Kos Town to the airport run roughly 3000dr.

Buses: (tel. 22 292). Leave from Kleopatras St. near the inland end of Pavlou St. to Tigaki (12 per day, ½hr., 200dr), Marmari (12 per day, 35min., 220dr), Asfendiou-Zia (3 per day, 40min., 220dr), Pyli (5 per day, ½hr., 220dr), Mastihari (4 per day, 45min., 380dr), Antimachia (6 per day, 40min., 310dr), Kardamena (6 per day, 45min., 380dr), and Kefalos (6 per day, 550dr). Full schedule posted by the stop.

City Buses: (tel. 26 276). Leave from 7 Akti Kountouriotou on the water. Fares 150-200dr, to Agios Fokas (50 per day, 15min., 230dr), Nea Halicarnassus (Lampi) (34 per day, 230dr), Marmaroto (7 per day, 150dr), and Asclepion (16 per day, 15min., 150dr). Schedules available at the station.

Ferries: Sail to Piraeus (1-4 per day, 11-15hr., 6331dr), Rhodes (2-4 per day, 4hr., 3025dr), Kalymnos (1-2 per day except Sun., 1¼hr., 1354dr), Leros (1-2 per day except Sun., 2½hr., 1945dr), Patmos (1-2 per day except Sun., 4hr., 2427dr), Astypalea (0-1 per week, 2389dr), and Karpathos (0-1 per week, 8hr., 2957dr). Ferries travel weekly to Thessaloniki (17hr., 10,457dr), Paros (3419dr), Naxos (3467dr), Syros (5486dr), Nisyros (1339dr), Tilos (1404dr), Symi (2208dr), and Kastelorizo (2789dr). Greek **boats** leave for Bodrum, Turkey (near ancient Halicarnassus), in the morning (12,000dr round-trip); Turkish boats leave in the afternoon (roughly 12,000dr one-way). You'll have to pay a Turkish port tax (roughly US$10). Since travel is international, it's not regulated by the Greek government; shop around and ask for student discounts.

Flying Dolphins: Hydrofoils zoom to Rhodes (2 per day, 6665dr), Kalymnos (1-2 per day, 2700dr), Leros (1-2 per day, 3000dr), Patmos (1-2 per day, 5300dr), Samos (6 per week, 5900dr), Symi (4 per week, 4700dr), Lipsi (4 per week, 2700dr), Nisyros (3 per week, 2764dr), Tilos (weekly, 2800dr), Agathonisi (2 per week, 5600dr), Ikaria (weekly, 2900dr), and Fourni (2 per week, 6900dr).

Taxis: (tel. 23 333, -4). Stand near the inland end of the Avenue of Palms.

Car/Moped/Bike rentals: Outlets abound, but if you can't find any, try a travel agent. Cars 9000dr and up. Mopeds 2500-4500dr. Bikes 400-1000dr.

Laundromat: 124 Alikarnassou St., turn off Megalou Alexandrou on either Pindou or Kyprou St. and walk two blocks. Wash, dry, and soap 1400dr. Open Mon.-Fri. 8:30am-1:30pm and 5-9:30pm, Sat. 8:30am-4pm.

Public Toilets: On the Avenue of the Palms, almost directly below the bridge from the Plane Tree to the Castle. Free.

Hospital: On Mitropoleas St., between El. Venizelou and Hippocrates (Ippokratous). **Emergency** tel. 22 300 (24hr.); information tel. 28 013. There are several **pharmacies.** Generally open Mon.-Tues. and Thurs.-Fri. 8:30am-1:30pm and 5-9pm, Wed. and Sat. 8:30am-2pm; check doors for info on off-hours pharmacy.

ACCOMMODATIONS

During July and August, hotel vacancies are rare, so start your room search early. Inexpensive places are mostly on the right side of town (facing inland). If your boat docks in the middle of the night, rent a room from one of the people who meet the boat. Otherwise, it's best to seek out your own room. Camping on the beach or in the park along the Avenue of Palms is not allowed. Prices are generally 20-40% lower during the off-season.

Pension Alexis, 9 Irodotou St. (tel. 28 798, 25 594, or 29 351). Take your first right off Meg. Alexandrou; it's on the back left corner of the first intersection. International ambience and a jasmine-vined patio. Alexis may be the most hospitable proprietor you'll come across. If his rooms are full, he'll put you up with a mattress and sheets on the patio (1200dr) or give you a deal at his elegant **Hotel Afendoulis** (tel. 25 321) in the ritzier part of town (doubles w/bath 7000dr). Balconied, wood-floored rooms and bath. Guest books dating back to 1979 document the many visitors who stayed here. Prices flexible, especially if you're carrying *Let's Go*. Doubles 5500dr, triples 9000dr, breakfast 600dr.

Pension Nitsa, 47 Averof St. (tel. 25 810), near the beach north of town. New, super-clean rooms, all with private baths and kitchenettes. Doubles 8000dr.

Hotel Hara (tel. 22 500), on Chalkonos St. near Arseniou St., 1 block inland from the water in the southeast part of town. Quiet area and homey rooms. Private phones; baths, towels, and soap provided. Doubles 8500dr, triples 9800dr.

Kos Camping (tel. 23 910, -275), in Psalidi, 2.5km out of town. Inconvenient, unless you've got a moped (which they rent) or really want to avoid Kos Town. Kitchen and laundry facilities, minimarket, bar, restaurant, and motorbike rental. 1500dr per person includes tent.

FOOD AND ENTERTAINMENT

As a rule, avoid the bombast of the waterfront and head inland for more authentic and less expensive Greek food. **Taverna Theodoros,** 22 Pindou St., the fourth right off Meg. Alexandrou, has relaxing ambience and delicious dishes (stuffed tomatoes 800dr). Across the street, **Taverna Barba George** serves a luscious chicken *souvlaki* wrapped in bacon and smothered with melted cheese (1350dr). Kos Town has several Chinese restaurants, including two, **Shanghai** and **Peking,** near Hotel Hara (chicken w/mushrooms and bamboo shoots 1400dr). On the same street is **Taj Mahal,** an Indian restaurant (mixed vegetables 700dr, chicken w/spinach 1190dr). Those looking for something sweet to cap off an evening would do well to head to **To Epekial,** a block from the museum (*baklava* 300dr). Near Pension Alexis is a sweet shop/bakery. The fruit and vegetable **market** in Eleftherias Sq. on Vas. Pavlou St. is inside a large yellow building with a depiction of grapes over the doors. Jars of thyme-flavored Kos honey (½kg 1000dr) are genuinely mouth-watering. (Open Mon.-Fri. 7am-9pm, Sat. 7am-6pm, Sun. 10am-2pm.)

At night, Kos Town hosts a romping party. Its crowded bar scene is concentrated alongside the agora on Nafklirou St. in the south and by the beach on Porfiriou St. to the north. In the agora, loud music, flashing lights, and narrow streets make for an especially congested night; despite being the pricier of the two areas, it's already crowded by 11pm and keeps rocking into the wee hours. Join the masses at **Forum, Bar 33,** and **Charisma Club** (beer 700dr, cocktails 1500dr at each). The bars by the beach are only slightly less crazed; try **Pub Cuckoo's Nest** or **Crazy Horse Saloon** for 500dr beers (often accompanied by free shots). The beach is also home to two of Kos' fashion-conscious discos, **Heaven** and **Kahlua.** Both charge 2000dr covers (including first drink) and may look down on backpackers' road-worn wardrobe.

SIGHTS

The 15th-century **Castle of the Knights of St. John** was reinforced with elaborate double walls and inner moats during the 16th century in response to Turkish raids. To enter the castle, cross a bridge from the Plane Tree. The Order of St. John on Kos was originally dedicated to nursing and healing the sick, though you'd never know it from the size of the fortifications. (Open Tues.-Sun. 8:30am-3pm; admission 800dr, students 400dr; free on Sun.)

Before crossing the bridge, between the Avenue of the Palms and the ruins of the agora you'll see the gigantic **Plane Tree of Hippocrates,** allegedly planted by the great physician 2400 years ago. (The tree, with a 12m diameter, is actually 500 years old.) Nonetheless, Hippocrates is said to have taught pupils and written books under its foliage. A spring next to the tree leads to an ancient sarcophagus that the Turks used as a cistern for the nearby variegated **Hadji Hassan Mosque.** Behind the tree, the monumental former **Town Hall,** originally the Italian Governor's Palace, now houses police, justice, and governmental offices. The most impressive Turkish structure is the **Defterdar Mosque** in Eleftherias Sq. A few blocks away, on Diakou St., is the abandoned **Synagogue of Kos,** in use until WWII. For a sample of Byzantine architecture, visit the city's **Greek Orthodox Cathedral** on the corner of Korai and Agios Nikolaou St. To observe yet another cultural influence on the island, check out the many fanciful mansions in the vicinity built during the Italian occupation; one of these is now the Platanos Restaurant.

The **Archaeological Museum** (tel. 28 326), down Nafklirou St. alongside the ruins of the ancient agora to Eleftherias Sq., features the celebrated statue of Hippocrates found at the Odeon of Kos. A magnificent 2nd-century AD Roman mosaic in the central courtyard depicts Hippocrates and a colleague entertaining the god Asclepios. (Open Tues.-Sun. 8:30am-3pm; admission 800dr, students 400dr; free on Sun.)

The field of ruins bounded by Nafklirou St., Hippocrates St., and the waterfront is the **agora.** Here stand the remains of a **Temple of Aphrodite,** as well as the 2nd-century **Temple of Hercules.** (Agora open 24hr.; free.) The other expansive site, whose structures date from the 3rd century AD, is more impressive. Two short stairways descend to the ruins from Grigoriou St., which runs along the south edge of town; any of the main roads intersect it roughly 1km from the sea. The site itself is bordered by two Roman roads—the **Cardo,** meaning "axis," which runs perpendicular to Grigoriou St., and the **Decumana,** meaning "broadest," which parallels Grigoriou and intersects Cardo to form a corner. An ancient gymnasium, a swimming pool from the Roman period, and an early Christian basilica built on the ruins of a Roman bath all loll nearby. At the end of the Decumana, the 3rd-century AD **House of Europa,** protected under a modern wooden shelter, contains a striking mosaic floor depicting Europa's abduction by a bullish Zeus. (24hr.; free.)

Down Grigoriou to the left (facing the Odeum, a small ancient theater on the opposite side of Grigoriou from the site), near Pavlou, stands the **Casa Romana,** uncovered by an Italian archaeologist in 1933. This 3rd-century AD structure concealed the ruins of an even more striking Hellenistic mansion two centuries older, with relics of man-eating creatures. (Open Tues.-Sun. 8:30am-3pm; admission 500dr, students 300dr; free on Sun.) Across the street from the Casa Romana are the meager ruins of a **Temple of Dionysus.**

The town of Kos has a narrow, crowded strip of **beach** running southeast of town. The beach running north of town is far nicer and has **watersport** rentals. Continue walking west roughly 4km, to **Lampi Beach,** a sandy, quiet point at the northernmost tip of the island. Several splendid beaches are a little farther from Town. Shady **Tigaki,** 10km west of Kos, is popular. Rooms are nearby (doubles from 5000dr). Be prepared for "snug" bus rides to Kos Town (12 per day, ½hr., 200dr).

■■■ THE ASCLEPION

The Asclepion, an ancient sanctuary dedicated to the god of healing, lies 4km west of Kos Town. In the 5th century BC, Hippocrates opened the world's first medical school here and encouraged the development of a precise and systematic science of medicine. Combining early priestly techniques with his own, Hippocrates made Kos the foremost medical center in ancient Greece.

Most of the ruins at the Asclepion actually date from the 3rd century BC. The complex was constructed on five levels terraced into a hill overlooking Kos Town and the Aegean. Remains of the ancient buildings are plentiful, and if you can ignore the swarms of tourists, it's easy to envision the structures as they once stood. A forest of cypress and pine trees, sacred in ancient times, adjoins the site. No one was allowed to give birth or die in this area. The 2nd-century AD Roman baths lie inside the site.

Stroll past the *natatio* (pool), the *tepidarium* (room of intermediate temperature), and finally the *caldarium* (sweating room).

The most interesting remains at Asclepion are in the three central terraced planes, called **andirons.** These contain the **School of Medicine,** statues of deities, and a figure of the god Pan, the mythical half-goat, half-human. Climb the 30 steps to the second andiron to see the best preserved remains of the Asclepion; the elegant, slender, white columns of the **Temple of Apollo** from the 2nd century BC, and the 4th-century BC **Minor Temple of Asclepios.** The 60-step climb to the third andiron leads to the forest-ensconced remains of the **Main Temple of Asclepios** and affords a view of the whole site, Kos Town, and the Turkish coast.

Buses go to the Asclepion in the summer (16 per day, 150dr). The site is also easy to reach by bike or moped. (Follow the sign off the main road west and continue as straight as possible.) Taxis to the site should cost roughly 500dr. (Site open June-Sept. Tues.-Sun. 8:30am-3pm; admission 800dr, students 400dr; free on Sun.)

■■■ CENTRAL KOS

The impact of package tours seeking "traditional Greek villages" is beginning to wear on the villages south of Kos Town. Where fertile fields once yielded quantities of tomatoes and olives, tourism is now the main crop. Nevertheless, this area makes wonderful terrain for day-long excursions by bike or moped, especially because the island has many paved roads. It is possible to go from Kos to Mastihari and then up to Pyli and Zia entirely on back roads.

For those who prefer the bus, the main road leads first to the modern village of **Zipari,** which includes the ruins of the early **Christian Basilica of St. Paul,** 11km southwest of Kos Town. From there, a twisting road slowly winds through the green foothills of the Dikeos Mountains to **Asfendiou,** which consists of five small settlements, of which **Lagoudi** is the prettiest. It's easy to hike for hours and not encounter a soul. Buses from Kos go to Asfendiou-Zia (3 per day, 40min., 220dr).

Continuing south from Lagoudi, the road narrows to a mule path and the hills become even less cultivated. A mere 8km farther (although a good spell of it is uphill) you'll come to the compact ruins of old Pyli—well-preserved 14th-century frescoes in a Byzantine church built within the walls of a Byzantine castle. Buses go to Pyli from Kos (3-4 per day, ½hr., 220dr). From Pyli, a twisting, pothole-plagued paved road (rough on mopeds) climbs over the hills and descends into Kardamena.

One kilometer before Antimachia on the main road, to the left, is the turn-off for the **Castle of Antimachia.** Yet another legacy of the Knights of St. John, the fortress sits majestically on an isolated hilltop. Mastihari and Kardamena are the two resorts of central Kos. Both offer grand beaches, streets with few cars, and places to eat fresh food. **Mastihari,** north of Antimachia, is quiet, cozy, and popular among families. If you wish to make this more than a daytrip, try **Hotel Arant** (tel. 51 167; fax 51 168), equidistant from the bus stop and the beach (doubles 7000dr) or try any of the many pensions and rooms available along the beach. (Doubles 8000dr.) **For You Tourist Services** (tel. 51 149, -520), a block from the bus, helps find rooms. **Boats** go to Kalymnos from Mastihari (3 per day, 810dr). Three to four **buses** per day leave Kos for Mastihari (45min., 380dr). **Kardamena,** 5km south of Antimachia, is a garish Euro-package-tour plastic village. It's difficult to find a room, but you won't want to stay anyway. The **Community Tourist Office** (tel. 91 139) at the bus stop, which masquerades as a main square, helps with accommodations. (Doubles from 5000dr, a few triples from 7000dr; open summer 10am-10pm.)

■■■ SOUTHERN KOS

Rolling hills, ravines, and occasional cow pastures cover southern Kos. **Kefalos,** Kos' capital in ancient times and the only town of any real substance on the south half of the island, is neither overcrowded nor terribly interesting. The best beach in all of Kos stretches on the southeast shore of the island along the main road before Kefalos. The continuous sands are broken up into many beaches, depending on where you enter. **Paradise** beach has a small bus stop and, therefore, the greatest crowds. For more open space, try **Magic** beach or **Camel** beach north of Paradise. Closer to Kefalos, where the road descends to sea level, **Ag. Stefanos** beach has been appropriated by Club Med. For those who can't afford Club Med, there are numerous pensions and "Rooms to Let" along the main road. In Kamari, the next beachfront town past Ag. Stefanos, the **Hotel Maria** (tel. 71 308) rents bright doubles with baths for 6000dr. Three to six buses per day (1hr., 550dr) travel as far as Kefalos. Ask the driver to let you out at any of the beaches on the way.

KALYMNOS ΚΑΛΥΜΝΟΣ

Kalymnos has always been famous for its sponge-diving industry. In years past, most men would depart for five or six months to dive for sponges in the south waters of the Libyan Sea, off the coast of North Africa—a solution to the problem of earning a living while living on a large, barren rock. Today, the squishy amorphous yellow lumps lurk everywhere (warehouses, tourist kiosks, restaurant display-cases) hearkening back to the island's glory days as the sponge capital of the world.

Unfortunately, the sponges are dying off, and Kalymnos' former staple industry is now in decline. The island's economy has been partially resuscitated by an influx of tourists on its western beaches. But perhaps because it refuses to give in to tourism, Kalymnos feels more traditionally Greek than most of its neighbors. Most of the island's development clings to the coast, leaving the interior mysteriously barren. The rugged mountains, cascading into wide beaches and blue-green water, more than compensate for this island's lack of ruins. Most tap water on the island is salty.

■■■ POTHEA

During the Italian occupation at the turn of the century, many locals painted their houses blue, Greece's national color, to antagonize the Italians. Pink and green buildings have since infiltrated Pothea's neighborhoods and, although slightly grayed, this relatively large town (pop. 10,000) remains more variegated than its white Aegean counterparts. Unfortunately, its rainbow architecture is Pothea's only endearing characteristic; most tourists head straight for the beach towns on the west coast of the island.

ORIENTATION AND PRACTICAL INFORMATION

Ferries unload at the far left end of the port (facing inland). The road leading from the dock bends around the waterfront until it runs into the large, cream-colored, Italian municipal building and then a church and town hall. A narrow shop-lined street, **Eleftherias** heads one way inland at this point, leading to **Kyprou Square** which is home to the post office, OTE, police, and taxis. The waterfront road continues past Town Hall, but there is little of interest besides several fruit stands. The second most important avenue, **Venizelou** intersects Eleftherias at the end of the harbor near the Agios Christos church. Continue on this road to reach the west part of the island. Follow the harbor promenade past the police station, to join up with the road leading to Vathis. Most streets in Pothea remain unnamed, but it's easy enough to trace the landmarks.

Tourist Office: (tel. 29 310). Along the waterfront, in a small shack in the shadow of the Olympic Hotel. The office resembles a toolshed. English-speaking help with rooms, transportation, and sights. Bus schedules, xeroxed maps of island and town. Open Mon.-Thurs. 8am-7pm, Fri. 8am-3:30pm, Sat.-Sun. 10am-1pm.

Police: (tel. 22 100). A block beyond the port police, away from the water from the back left corner of the inland square. 24hr. The **port police** (tel. 29 304 or 24 444), are in the yellow building across from the customs house, at the end of the ferry dock. Updated ferry information (in Greek). 24hr.

Post Office: (tel. 28 340). From the inland square, bear right and go 1 block inland. Open Mon.-Fri. 7:30am-2pm. Also has currency exchange. **Postal Code:** 85200.

OTE: (tel 29 599). Past the post office on the right. Open Mon.-Fri. 7:30am-3pm. **Telephone Code:** 0243.

Bank: National Bank of Greece (tel. 29 794), on the waterfront, advances cash on Mastercard and Visa and offers **currency exchange.** Both open Mon.-Thurs. 8am-2pm, Fri. 8am-1:30pm.

Tourist Agencies: Sadly, there's no one agency to satisfy all your tourist needs—especially if you're looking at boat schedules. **Magos Travel** (tel. 28 777, -652), on the waterfront near the port police, sells hydrofoil tickets and some ferry tickets (open 8:30am-9pm). The **Kamiros Office** (tel. 28 651), near the Olympic Hotel, sells more ferry tickets, but between Magos and Kamiros, you still can't find all tickets (open 9am-1pm and 5:30-9pm). If neither suits your needs, look at the posted schedules in offices between the two.

Flights: Olympic Airways (tel. 29 265 or 28 903). There's no airport, but the office is open for reservations. Take the first left past the National Bank; it's 50m on the left, around the bends. Open Mon.-Fri. 8:30am-1:30pm and 5-8pm.

Buses: Every hour on the hour 7am-10pm, buses leave for Kastelli (50min.) via Chora (10min.), Panormos (15min.), Myrties (20min.), and Massouri (25min.). Fares 100-250dr. Five buses go to Vilhadia, 2 to Emborio, 4 to Vathis, 3 to Argos, and 2 to Plati Gialos. Buses to towns in the west leave from the town hall in the center of the harbor. Buses to Vathis from the northeast corner of the waterfront.

Ferries: Sail to Piraeus (2 per day, 13hr., 4974dr), Leros (1-3 per day, 1hr., 1404dr), Patmos (1-3 per day, 3hr., 1994dr), Kos (1-3 per day, 1½hr., 1350dr), Rhodes (1-3 per day, 6hr., 3606dr), Astypalea (2 per week, 3hr., 2200dr), Lipsi (3 per week, 1968dr), Tilos (4 per week, 1968dr), Symi (2 per week, 2600dr), Nisyros (4 per week, 1515dr), Paros (1 per week, 3151dr), Naxos (2 per week, 2947dr), Mykonos (1 per week, 3852dr), and Tinos (1 per week, 4068dr). There are daily **excursions** from Kalymnos to the small island of **Pserimos** between Kalymnos and Kos (round-trip 1500dr), home to superior beaches and a few *tavernas*. Check travel agency windows for other excursions. There is also a small boat that runs between Kalymnos and Mastihari on Kos 3 times per day (800dr).

Flying Dolphins: To Kos (2 per day, 2708dr), Leros (daily, 2898dr), Patmos (daily, 4147dr), Lipsi (4 per week, 3635dr), Ikaria (2 per week, 5531dr), Fourni (2 per week, 6078dr), Agathonisi (weekly, 5450dr), and Samos (daily, 5808dr).

Taxis: (tel. 24 222 or 29 555). Congregate in Kyprou Sq.

Car/Moped Rental: Try any of the various agencies. Cars from 9000dr, mopeds from 2000dr.

Pharmacy: One of many is near the intersection of Eleftherias and Venizelou (tel. 29 338; open Mon.-Tues. and Thurs.-Fri. 9am-1pm and 5:30-8:30pm, Wed. 9am-2pm). For weekend or after-hours pharmaceutical relief, consult posted signs in windows of closed pharmacies, or contact the police.

Hospital: (tel. 28 851). On the road to Chora, 10km from Pothea. 24hr.

ACCOMMODATIONS

Securing a room in Pothea is hassle-free; pension owners await even late-night ferries and the tourist office shack is helpful. For true hospitality, head inland from the waterfront at the National Bank, take the first left, follow the bends, and look for signs to the Panorama Hotel. When the road splits at the embankment wall, go right: the first white house on the right is **"Rooms to Let" Katerina** (tel. 22 186). Katerina rents large, spotless rooms with tile floors, communal bath and kitchen facilities, and a cacti-strewn terrace overlooking the town and harbor. Family members or guests can help you communicate. (Doubles 4000dr, triples 5000dr.) On the way to Katerina's, turn right instead of left at the Astor Sponge Factory, to find the hospitable **Greek House** (tel. 29 559), which has pristine rooms w/bath. (Doubles 5000dr.)

FOOD

Clustered tightly on Pothea's harbor is the typical array of café/bars and modest *tavernas.* Try the **Navtikos Omilos Restaurant** (tel. 29 239), isolated at the end of the harbor (facing inland, all the way on the left). Depending on the season, you'll be treated to either front row seats to the lights and crowds of the town's amusement park (open June-July) or you'll enjoy a quiet meal looking out on the water. In any event, the food is inexpensive (spaghetti *neapolitana* 490dr, Greek salad 500dr).

SIGHTS

Learn first-hand about the island's historic **sponge industry.** On the waterfront near the port police is the sponge shop of **Nikolas Gourlas.** Mr. Gourlas speaks English and will be happy to show you around the factory where sponges are cleaned and chemically treated. (Sponge mementos from 500dr.) The original sponge factories stretch along the east end of the harbor on the road to Vathis. From Venizelou St., follow the blue signs to the **Museum of Kalymnos,** housed in the former mansion of Nikolaos Vouvalis, a turn-of-the-century sponge baron from Kalymnos. Visiting the museum means following an employee to each of the four open rooms where they unlock the door, let you in, and wait for you to finish looking. The most interesting feature of the house is the sumptuously decorated parlor, where portraits and animal skins hint at the life-style of wealthy Kalymnosites. (Open Tues.-Sun. 10am-2pm; free.) The hilltop **Monastery of Agion Pantes** overlooks the town. Visitors can enter at the gate on the right side; the first chapel on your left contains the bones of a canonized church official in an elaborate sarcophagus. The view from up here is sublime: you can see all the way to Telendos Island. (Always open; free.)

From the customs house, take the roads to the left to reach the beach at **Therma,** 2km away. Arthritic patients make pilgrimages to the sanitarium here to wade in its **sulphur mineral baths.** (Doctor's permission required to bathe. Those without medical problems won't want to con a prescription; the baths have a strong phosphorous odor.) The main beach is crowded; a short walk around the bend leads to a quiet swimming spot. Farther west from Therma (backtrack towards Pothea and then head slightly north) is the tranquil beach at **Vlichadia** (6km from Pothea).

■■■ WESTERN COAST

Kalymnos has two main roads: one runs northwest out of Pothea, the other northeast. A few kilometers along the northwest road a side road to the left leads up to a crumbling fortress of the Knights of St. John, also called **Chrissocherias Castle.** Hidden in its remains are a number of little chapels, open to view. Painted sections of wall or floor indicate where privateers dug holes to search for buried treasure. The **Pera Castle,** a fortress from the Byzantine epoch, looms north of Chrissocherias across the valley. This structure, originally Byzantine, was enlarged and fortified by the Knights. Nine tiny white churches are scattered throughout the ruins and maintained by elderly Chorian women. Directly opposite lies the small village of **Argos**—once the ancient city of Argiens, now a suburb of Pothea. Both the Pera Kastro and Argos overlook the town of **Chora,** once Kalymnos' capital but now little more than another of Pothea's tentacles.

One kilometer or so beyond Chora, just after the road begins to descend into Panormos, a few white steps by the side of the road lead to the shell of the **Church of Christ of Jerusalem,** a Byzantine church built by the Emperor Arcadius to thank God for sparing him in a storm at sea. The stone blocks with carved inscriptions are from a 4th-century BC temple to Apollo that stood on the same site. By incorporating and subordinating these architectural elements, the church came to be viewed as a symbolic victory over paganism. (Always open; free.) At Panormos, the road branches. One offshoot goes to **Kantouni,** where the beach is clogged with litter. An antidote to this frenetic scene is the **Kantouni Beach Hotel/Pool Bar,** a relaxed pool bar on the waterfront that's open to the public. Also on the waterfront, the

Rock and Blues Pub and the **Domus Bar** bump and grind late into the evening. Another road from Panormos leads, after 2km, to the sandy and less crowded beach of **Plati Gialos.** Stay at **Pension Plati Gialos** (tel. 22 014), perched on the cliff with a memorable view of the coastline. (Doubles 6000dr.) Both the gray-sand beach at **Myrties,** 7km up the coast, and the pebbly one at **Massouri,** the next town up, can be alarmingly full. Both towns offer a few budget accommodations. Try the **Rinio Pension** (tel. 22 726), between Myrties and Massouri. (Peaceful doubles w/bath and kitchenette 6000dr.) Nearby, **Niki's Pension** (tel. 47 201) makes a fine place to stay. The sign on the main road leads up stairs and over rough terrain to the most scenic rooms in Massouri; private baths and breakfast are included. (Doubles 5000dr, triples 7000dr; reservations recommended.) Massouri, the center of the island's nightlife, entertains with the great pubs **Flamingo, No Name,** and **Smile.**

Myrties' finest attraction, a short boat ride (every ½hr., 15min., 200dr) out of town, is the tiny, rocky islet of **Telendos,** severed from Kalymnos by an earthquake in 554 AD. A city occupied the faultline where the island cracked—traces of it have been found on the ocean floor, but the rift is invisible on the surface. The Roman ruins on Telendos are modest at best, but a few small, secluded beaches fringe the island. (Turn right from the ferry dock for the best beaches.) Past the beaches to the right is the **Byzantine Monastery of St. Constantine.** (Open only for liturgy.) Accommodations in Telendos fill only for a couple of weeks in August. Most pensions charge 3000-5000dr for a double; prices are generally lower during the off-season. **Uncle George's Pension** (tel. 47 502), near the docks, has an excellent restaurant and clean rooms. (Doubles w/bath 4000dr.) Inquire at the restaurant **Ailena** for similar rooms a little closer to the beaches. (Doubles 3000dr.) Farther along toward the beaches is another option, **Galanomatis** (tel. 47 401; doubles 4000dr). Before leaving Myrties, look back at Telendos to see a woman's profile along the left-hand side of the mountain. According to residents, she's mourning her lost husband as she looks forlornly out to sea.

Back on Kalymnos, the emptiest beach stretches out at **Arginontas,** at the end of a long, narrow inlet. Both roads to the beach rise dramatically along cliffs that plunge into turquoise water. Though not the cleanest place on the island, **Vanzanelis'** (tel. 47 389), at Arginontas Beach, has a *taverna* and doubles w/bath for 8000dr. Two buses from Pothea venture this far (250dr). The last village on the west side, **Emborio,** is unruffled and remote. **Harry's Restaurant** (tel. 47 434), 20m from the beach, provides good food and beds. (Doubles 9000dr.) The **Restaurant Themis** (tel. 47 277), the white building with blue trim facing the beach, has nice doubles with a stately balcony (5000dr). It too has private baths. A small boat makes an **excursion** from Myrties to Emborio daily at 10am (1500dr).

Although most of Kalymnos supports only grass and wildflowers, the valley at Vathis (6km northeast of Pothea) is a rich potpourri of mandarins, limes, and grapevines. The valley starts at the village of **Rina.** There's no beach here (swim off the pier), but the exquisite scenery and lack of tourists compensate for the lack of sand. On the north side of the inlet is **Daskaleios,** a stalagmite cave you can swim to. In Rina, stay at the **Hotel Galini** (tel. 31 241; doubles w/bath and balcony 6000dr). The three *tavernas* on the tiny waterfront also rent rooms.

In the tiny hamlet of **Ellinotourkobiblio** resides a lone monk, Nat "Π" Rilopoulos, who has lived in a deserted cave for nearly a century, according to University of Liverpool scholar Cynthia Sotiropoulos. A monument has been erected to the pious monk and overlooks the babbling brook of St. Marios the oft-forgotten. A visit here is sure to surprise as the cave has a nasty habit of disappearing.

PATMOS ΠΑΤΜΟΣ

One of Greece's most sacred islands—signs at the port warn that nudism and other "indecent" behavior will not be tolerated—Patmos' historical and religious significance is evident. In ancient times, the people of Patmos worshiped Artemis, goddess of the hunt, who was said to have raised the island from the sea. Orestes built a grand temple to Artemis after seeking refuge on Patmos from the Furies who were pursuing him for murdering his mother, Clytemnestra.

While he was in exile from Ephesus, St. John established a Christian colony here and purportedly wrote the Book of Revelations in a grotto overlooking the main town. In the 4th century AD, when the Christian faith spread with the Byzantine Empire, a basilica replaced the razed Temple of Artemis. In the 11th century, the fortified Monastery of St. John was constructed on a hill that surveys the entire island. The monastery, protected first by the Byzantines, then by the Roman Pope, and finally by the Turks, still stands today. Until recent centuries, only monks inhabited the island, but news of its austere rocky mountains and serene beaches eventually spread. Patmos today is lively and sophisticated, and thus far has managed to successfully strike a delicate balance between today's popularity and a solemn past.

■■■ SKALA

Built along a graceful arc of coastline, Skala gives only a hint of the diversity of the island's terrain. Patmos' port and central city, Skala was not developed until the 19th century, when fear of pirates subsided and people could live safely by the water. The main administrative buildings, which now house the post office and customs house, were constructed during Italian occupation (1912-1943). Today, whitewashed churches are camouflaged among the village buildings, but Skala also offers more secular features of the island: lively cafés, bars, *tavernas,* and shops.

ORIENTATION AND PRACTICAL INFORMATION

Skala's amenities are all within a block or two of the waterfront. Small ferries dock opposite the line of cafés and restaurants, while larger vessels park in front of the interloping Italian building that houses the police and post office. The building borders the main square, where banks are located. Skala is on a narrow part of the island; if you walk away from the water, you'll be on the other side in 10 minutes.

Tourist Office: (tel. 31 666). Around the corner from the post office, off the main square. Maps, brochures, bus schedules, info on all ferries, and help with accommodations. Ask for the free and chipper *Patmos Summertime* guide, which includes maps of Skala and the island. Open Mon.-Sat. 9am-1pm and 6-8:30pm.

Police: (tel. 31 100, -303), in the large Italian building by the main square. **Port Police** (tel. 31 231), to the left of the ferry dock, facing inland; next to the "Welcome" snack bar. Friendly info on ferries. 24hr., but knock forcefully if it's late.

Post Office: (tel. 31 316). On the main square, next to the police. Open Mon.-Fri. 7:30am-2pm. **Postal Code:** 85500.

OTE: Follow the signs in the main square; walk inland on the shop-lined thoroughfare roughly 150m. Open 7:30am-9:45pm. The café-bar at the boat dock has an international telephone. **Telephone Code:** 0247.

Banks: National Bank of Greece in the square (tel. 31 123, -774, or -591). Cash advances on Mastercard and **currency exchange.** Open Mon.-Thurs. 8am-2pm, Fri. 8am-1:30pm. Also exchange at the **post office** and **Apollon Agency.**

Tourist Agencies: All over the waterfront, but each offers info only on those ferry lines for which they sell tickets. Consult the tourist office or the port police for complete schedules and then ask where to buy your particular ticket. **Apollon Tourist and Shipping Agency** (tel. 31 356, -4; fax 31 819) is the not-so-helpful local agent for **Olympic Airways.** (Open 8:30am-8:30pm.)

Buses: Stop in front of police station. From Skala, 12 per day go to Chora (10min.), 8 to Grikou (10min.), and 4 to Kampos (15min.). All fares 170dr. There are frequent returns to Skala and service between Chora and Grikou. Consult schedule posted at bus stop or tourist office.

Ferries: Daily service to Piraeus (10hr., 5339dr), Leros (1½hr., 1330dr), Kalymnos (2½hr., 1938dr), Kos (4hr., 2382dr), and Rhodes (10hr., 4639dr). Boats also run to Lipsi (4 per week, 1040dr), Samos (6 per week, 2130dr). Ferries run twice weekly to Ikaria (1576dr), Fourni (1718dr), Naxos (2426dr), Paros (2600dr), and Agathonisi (1515dr), and once a week to Lesvos (4004dr), Limnos (5810dr), Thessaloniki (9729dr), Mykonos (2600dr), Syros (2820dr), Nisyros (2463dr), and Tilos (2755dr). Private **excursion boats** go to Lipsi (daily, 1500dr one-way, 2200dr round-trip), Samos (4 per week, 3500dr one-way), Kos (4 per week, 4000dr one-way) and weekly to Samos and Kuşadası, Turkey (6000dr, 9500dr round-trip; plus 7000dr in Greek and Turkish port taxes).

Flying Dolphins: Two per day to Leros (2740dr), Kalymnos (1938dr), Kos (5374dr), Agathonisi (3225dr), and Lipsi (2500dr). Also to Samos (2-3 per day, 3345dr), Ikaria (daily, 3350dr), Fourni (3 per week, 2790dr), and Chios (6 per week, 6946dr).

Taxis: (tel. 31 225). Congregate in the main square 24hr. in summer, but difficult to catch in the *après*-disco flurry or from 3-6:30am. Taxis to Chora 700-1000dr.

Car Rental: Patmos Rent-a-Car (tel. 32 203). Also near tourist office (leave the office, turn left; the sign is up the steps). Open daily 8:30am-9pm. 9000dr and up.

Moped Rental: Express Moto (tel. 32 088). Exit the tourist office, turn left, and make the first right. Open daily 8am-8pm. Mopeds from 2000dr per day. **Theo and Georgio** (tel. 32 066), on the street parallel to the waterfront, near the intersection of the two, rents mopeds from 2500dr and bikes for 1000dr.

Luggage Storage: Free in the Welcome Cafeteria next to the ferry dock. Low security (your bag sits in a corner of the restaurant unguarded).

Laundromat: Just Like Home, on the waterfront road towards Meloi and Kampos. 2000dr per 5kg load (wash, dry, and soap). Open Mon.-Tues. and Thurs.-Fri. 8:30am-1pm and 4-8pm, Wed. and Sat. 8:30am-1pm.

International Bookstore: International Press (tel. 31 427), behind the Pantelis Restaurant; look for the signs. International newspapers, magazines, and a small collection of English books. Open daily 8am-9:30pm.

Pharmacy: (tel. 31 500), behind Apollon Travel, on the first street parallel to the waterfront. Open Mon.-Tues. and Thurs.-Fri. 8:30am-1:30pm and 5:30-9pm, Wed. and Sat. 8:30am-1:30pm and 7-9pm, Sun. 11am-12:30pm and 6:30-9pm. Call 31 500 or 32 262 for after-hours emergencies.

Hospital: (tel. 31 211), 1½km up the road to Chora. Open 8am-2pm. In an emergency, call the police, who know doctors' schedules and will contact them.

ACCOMMODATIONS

In summer, Skala's hotels are often full, but finding a room in a pension or private home is usually easy. Even boats arriving at 1am are greeted by a battalion of locals offering rooms. (Average prices: singles 4000dr, doubles 6000dr.) Off-season prices are generally lower by 20-40%. To find a room, walk left from the ferry dock and right onto Vas. Georgiou St. Roughly 50m on the left, after Pizza Zacharo, across from the basketball court, is a "Rooms to Let" sign. **Maria Paschalidis** (tel. 32 152 or 31 347) runs a jubilant pension with spotless rooms, permeated by the fragrance of jasmine and roses. (Doubles 5000dr, triples 7500dr.) Between Maria's rooms and Pizza Zacharo, above a Tae Kwon Do school, is **Pension Sofia** (tel. 31 501, -876). Knock on the second floor or ask next door on the right for the immaculate rooms. Little English spoken, but tons of hospitality (doubles 5500dr, breakfast 500dr). Closer to town is **Hotel Rodos** (tel. 31 371; follow the side street next to Pantelis past the international press) with quiet, simple, clean rooms and chickens in the field below. (Doubles 7000dr.) Many rooms can be found on Vas. Georgiou St. and on the street that leads to the OTE. Two kilometers northeast of Skala, the excellent **Flower Camping** at **Meloi** (tel. 31 821) has a minimarket and a popular café/restaurant. Follow the waterfront road all the way to the right, facing inland: look for signs. (Person 1200dr, tent 400dr; tent rental available.)

FOOD AND ENTERTAINMENT

Several seafood restaurants with pricey fish entrees line the waterfront. For better and more reasonably priced fare, head for the locally-acclaimed **Grigoris,** across from the bus stop, at the corner of the road to Chora (swordfish *souvlaki* 1200dr).

Pantelis (tel. 31 230) has inexpensive, delicious vegetable dishes (okra 700dr; omelette with potatoes and feta cheese 700dr). It is behind the central strip of cafés, on the street parallel to the waterfront. **Augerinos,** on the road to the OTE, has excellent take-out *souvlaki-pita* (350dr). There are several **groceries** clustered around the main square, as well as numerous **sweet shops,** where you can try the Patmian dessert *pouggia,* a ball of honey and nuts (almonds, walnuts, or peanuts) covered in dough and sometimes smothered in powdered sugar (220-300dr). The cheapest ice cream around can be found at a pastry shop right near Maria's and Sofia's (one large scoop 130dr). As befits such a sacred island, the nightlife here tends to be rather tame, more centered on promenading or casually sipping drinks than on rowdy carousing. One of the most popular hang-outs is **Arion,** a café next to Apollon Travel (beers 500-850dr, cocktails 1200dr). Sit outside or dance inside **Meltemi Bar** at the far left of the harbor facing the water. (Beer 500dr, cocktails 1500dr.) **Café Evelyn** next door offers cheaper beer but less ambience (beer 350-550dr).

■■■ CHORA

From almost any part of Patmos, you can see the white houses of Chora and the majestic, gray walls of the nearby Monastery of St. John the Theologian above. Roam Chora's labyrinthine streets, snug in the shelter of the monastery, and view the Patmos shoreline and the outlying archipelago.

Orientation and Practical Information Because of the convoluted layout of the town and the dearth of street names, it's impossible to give precise directions. The map of Patmos available at kiosks and tourist shops comes with a sketchy illustration of town. Take care of business before arriving; a few phonecard telephones and a mailbox at the bottom of the hill are the only links between Chora and the outside world. **Buses** travel to Chora from Skala (12 per day, 15min., 120dr). The bus drops off at the top of the hill outside the town; this is also the point of departure for buses from Chora to Grikou. A taxi here from Skala costs roughly 1000dr. If you decide to walk (4km and steep), the steps to Chora will be quicker and safer than the main road.

Accommodations There are no pensions in Chora, and few places rent rooms; more than likely, you'll be offered entire houses, or at least studios, complete with kitchens and private baths (starting at 8000dr). If you can afford the prices and want to stay in this picturesque village, talk to the tourist office in Skala, which can arrange a place, or ask at a *taverna* in Chora (Vangelis is the most likely). Also try calling one of the people listed below and arrange to meet them somewhere in the village. (Most don't speak English.) Try **Apostolidi Agelike** (tel. 31 675; studios from 8000dr), **Markos Farmakakis** (tel. 32 114; apartments from 9000dr), or **Maria Dalari** (tel. 31 616; houses from 11,000dr).

Food and Entertainment A very popular restaurant in Chora is **Vangelis,** which has a pleasant garden and an affordable menu (*mousaka* 800dr). Head towards the monastery and follow the signs. **To Pantheon,** near the bus stop, has less ambience, but offers fried zucchini and eggplant w/garlic sauce for 700dr. (Opens for dinner at 9pm.) Near Vangelis, **Café Stoa** knows its drinks (beer 500dr).

Sights The turreted walls and imposing gateway of the **Monastery of St. John the Theologian** make it look more like a fortress than a place of worship. St. Christodoulos founded the monastery in 1088, nearly 1000 years after St. John's celebrated stay on the island. Pragmatic considerations proved more important than aesthetics, as the proximity of Muslim Turkey made the monastery a constant target of pirate raids. The memorial to St. John was transformed into a citadel with battlements and watchtowers. The monastery has 10 chapels because church law forbade hearing mass twice daily in the same one.

As you enter the courtyard, notice the 17th-century frescoes to the left that portray stories from *The Miracles and Travels of St. John the Evangelist,* written by John's disciple Prochoros. To the upper right, a fresco portrays St. John's miraculous duel with a local priest of Apollo named Kynops. When the saint threw Kynops into the water at Skala, the heathen was turned into stone. The rock is still in the harbor—ask any local to point out the unfortunate heretic's corpse.

Continue to the **Chapel of the Virgin Mary,** covered with original 12th-century frescoes. In 1956, tremors revealed these frescoes underneath the 17th-century ones currently exhibited. The **treasury** (admission 500dr) safeguards jewels, icons, ornamented stoles donated by Catherine the Great of Russia, a 6th-century copy of St. Mark's Gospel, an 8th-century Book of Job, and silver plates, goblets, and crucifixes. The **Chapel of the Holy Christodoulos** holds the remains of the monastery's illustrious founder. Shortly after Christodoulos' death, many visitors attempted to appropriate his saintliness by carrying away his remains, so the monks built a marble sarcophagus and covered it with a heavy, silver reliquary.

In the summer, try not to visit the monastery at midday, when it becomes crammed with tourists and hollering tour guides. If you come in off-season, one of the monastery's 20 monks (there were once 1700) may volunteer to show you around (tel. 31 398; monastery and treasure museum open Mon., Wed., and Fri. 8am-1:30pm, Tues. and Thurs. 8am-1pm and 4-5:30pm, Sat. 8am-1pm and 4-6pm, Sun. 10am-noon and 4-6pm. Dress appropriately—no shorts or bare shoulders. If necessary, wrap a towel or shawl around legs or shoulders; free).

Half-way uphill on the winding road that connects Chora and Skala (2km from each) is a turn-off for another monastery, the **Apocalypsis,** a large, white complex of interconnected buildings. Most people come here to see the **Sacred Grotto of the Revelation,** adjacent to the Church of St. Anne. In this cave, St. John dictated the *Book of Revelation,* the last book of the New Testament, after hearing the voice of God proclaim "Now write what you see, what is to take place hereafter." (Rev. 1:19). According to legend, when God spoke to St. John, he cleft the ceiling of the cave with a three-pronged crack representing the Holy Trinity. Silver plating marks the spot where St. John presumably slept (tel. 31 234; Apocalypsis open same hours as Monastery of St. John; dress appropriately; free).

■■■ AROUND PATMOS ISLAND

Grikou has a relatively empty sand beach with watersport rentals (paddleboats 1500dr per hr.), a few hotels, and a couple of restaurants. Only 5km southwest of Skala, and 5km west of Chora, the town is visited by several buses daily from both (170dr). At the south, quiet end of the beach, **O Flisvos** (tel. 31 380, -961) rents doubles (5000dr) above a shaded *taverna* overlooking the bay. At the north end (left, facing the water) of Grikou is a smaller cove not visible from the bay (watch the thistles prone to attack exposed skin). Mopeds can continue 2km south to the secluded Plaki beach, where the road degenerates. Only 3km west from Plaki is **Psili Ammos,** the best beach on the island. Try hiking to it, but get directions first. An easier route is by **excursion** boat from Skala (daily 10am, returning at 4pm, 1200dr). .

ASTYPALEA ΑΣΤΥΠΑΛΙΑ

Few travelers venture to butterfly-shaped Astypalea, the westernmost of the Dodecanese islands—everyone else doesn't know what they're missing. This quiet, unobtrusive island with vaguely Cycladic architecture and a colorful port, strewn with fishing nets, retains the conveniences of its larger neighbors. Farther inland, the jagged hills and secluded orange and lemon groves merit leisurely exploration.

Orientation and Practical Information Ferries land at the town of **Astypalea.** Surrounded by tawny hills, the town itself is a hillside conglomeration of cubical dwellings. Just before the town's small beach, the **police** (tel. 61 207) and **port police** (tel. 61 206) share a building. (Both open daily 8am-7pm.) The **OTE** (tel. 61 212, -5) is at the foot of the Paradissos Hotel (open Mon.-Fri. 7:30am-2pm). M. Karakosta, in the store under the Aegean hotel, is an agent of the **National Bank of Greece** (open Mon.-Thurs. 8am-2pm, Fri. 8am-1:30pm). For transportation questions, try the **travel agency** (tel. 61 224; open Mon.-Fri. 9am-1pm). The **post office/currency exchange** (tel. 61 223; open Mon.-Fri. 7:30am-2pm) and several **supermarkets** (open daily 9am-1pm and 5-9pm) are all in this older section of town. In case of medical emergency, call the clinic at 61 222. **Postal Code:** 85900; **Telephone Code:** 0243. **Ferries** arrive in Astypalea sporadically. Boats travel to Piraeus (4 per week, 10-18hr., 5341dr), Kalymnos (2 per week, 3hr., 2200dr), Kos (2 per week, 3½hr., 4500dr), Paros (3 per week, 3000dr), Naxos (2900dr), Santorini (1 per week, 2500dr), and Amorgos (1 per week, 2500dr). As always, ferry schedules change frequently; check with the port police or the travel agency. Ferries do not leave Astypalea every day, so you may be stuck here for a few days.

Accommodations Rooms on the island fill up fast in August and July, but the available ones are cheap (singles 5000dr, doubles 7000dr, triples 8000dr). Ask the travel agency for help. Also try the **Hotel Aegean** (tel. 61 236) and the **Hotel de France** (tel. 61 259). **Camping Astypalea** (tel. 61 338) is 2½km east of town near Marmari; follow signs or take a bus towards Maltezana (person 900dr, tent 600dr).

Sights At the top of the hill, a striking row of windmills leads to the **castle,** a ramshackle Byzantine structure shedding segments of walls and windows. From here there is a clear view of the island and its flock of tributary islets. A 20-min. walk west (over the hill) from town will bring you to the sandy beach, **Livadia.** The pleasant beach is pestered with tents and children during July and August, but on the beach of **Tzanaki,** a 20-min. hike along the coast to the southwest, **nude bathers** do their thing. **Ag. Konstantinos** beach is served by a dirt road (1½-hr. hike from Livadia).

In the other direction from Astypalea Town, the quiet fishing villages of **Maltezana** and **Analipsi** occupy the narrow isthmus. Home to some largely intact Roman mosaics, peaceful Maltezana is accessible by bus (2 per day, 120dr). The narrow natural harbor at **Vathi** is subdivided into Exo Vathi (outside) and Esa Vathi (inside). In the winter when the winds are too strong for boats to dock at Astypalea, the ferries go to the bay at **Ag. Andreas.** The lovely beach here is accessible by road. Another rocky road leads to the **Ag. Ioannis Monastery,** majestically balanced atop a hill.

KARPATHOS ΚΑΡΠΑΘΟΣ

Karpathos is what every island strives to become; it is genuinely friendly, with a charming port town, a number of truly interesting villages, and some of the most beautiful, non-touristed beaches in Greece. The remoteness of this 42km island anchored halfway between Rhodes and Crete, as well as sparse ferry schedules, guarantee its serenity. Karpathians embody Greece's famed hospitality; cheerful greetings from strangers are common. In the mountains, residents preserve tradition, but Karpathos Town (officially "Ta Pigadia") straddles the crucial line between quaint and cosmopolitan. Many Karpathians live part-time in the U.S., infusing the island with American dollars. As a result, Karpathos is one of the wealthiest islands in Greece, and is comfortable for English-speakers, while remaining inexpensive.

War and conquest characterize Karpathos' history. Karpathians fought with Sparta in the Peloponnesian War in 431 BC and lost their independence to Rhodes in 400 BC. In 42 BC the island fell to Rome; in 395 AD Byzantium annexed it. A few centuries later, Karpathos was ruled by the Arabs, followed by the Genovese pirate

Moresco, the Venetians, and the Ottoman Turks. Turkish rule ended only when the Italians conquered the island during WWI; the Germans relieved them in WWII. In 1948, after 654 years of foreign conquest, Karpathos finally became part of Greece.

■■■ KARPATHOS TOWN

Karpathos Town used to be referred to as Ta Pigadia, meaning "the wells." Before that, the town was called Possi, for "Poseidon Polis," but many objected to this name, which also meant "drinking about." Today, Karpathos Town is the island's administrative and transportation center.

ORIENTATION AND PRACTICAL INFORMATION

The best way to orient yourself in Karpathos Town is to bear in mind the Greek free spirit. The streets and square are not named, but don't fret. There are only two main roads: one runs along the water and is lined with *tavernas*, cafés, pharmacies, and the National Bank; the other, approximately one block inland, runs somewhat parallel to the first and contains the post office, bakery, and a plethora of signs for various guest houses. If the Chevy Chase in you still insists on buying a map, make sure it is up to date. The best places to purchase accurate town maps are **Karpathos and Possi Travel Agencies** (400-500dr). Maps of the area in tourist shops are often old and will serve to confuse rather than assist.

Police: (tel. 22 222, -18). At the corner of Ethn. Anistassis St., next to the post office. They don't speak much English, but try valiantly to help you. Open 24 hr.

Post Office: Take the uphill road right of the bus station. Open Mon.-Fri. 8am-1:30pm. **Postal Code:** 85700.

OTE: Walk past the post office, then take a left uphill. Open Mon.-Fri. 7:30am-3pm. **Telephone Code:** 0245.

Travel Offices: Karpathos Travel (tel. 22 754, -148; fax 22 754). On Dimokratia St. between the bus station and waterfront, has complete bus information and most boat schedules. The staff arranges accommodations, rents cars (32,000dr for 3 days, insurance and tax included), and exchanges currency. The office sells tickets for excursions to the villages of Lefkos, Diafani, and Olymbos. (Open Mon.-Sat. 8am-1pm and 5:30-8:30pm, Sun. 9-11am and 6:30-8:30pm.) Both Karpathos and **Possi Travel** (tel. 22 235; fax 22 252), around the corner on the waterfront on Apodimon Karpathion St., sell maps for 500dr. (Open Mon.-Sat. 8am-1pm and 5:30-8:30pm, Sun. 9am-noon and 6-8pm.) Possi also offers all travel services.

Banks: National Bank, across the street, to the left of Possi Travel, offers **currency exchange.** Open Mon.-Thurs. 8am-2pm, Fri. 8am-1:30pm. Visa and Mastercard **ATM** outside.

Flights: Olympic Airways office (tel. 22 150, -057; open Mon.-Fri. 8am-3pm) is on the street parallel to the water, one block back. There are three nonstop **flights** per week to Athens (24,700dr), but you can go via Rhodes (4 per day, 24,600dr). There are also flights to Kassos (4 per week, 5800dr tax) and to Sitia, Crete (1 per week, 10,600dr).

Ferries: On Wed., a ferry heads for the other Dodecanese Islands, Crete, Santorini, Paros, and Piraeus (Wed. and Sat.). Boats also chug to Rhodes (4½hr., 3350dr), Kassos (1½hr., 1300dr) and Iraklion (Wed. and Sat., 6hr., 3350dr).

Buses: One block up Dimokratia St. from the center of town. Serves most of the island's villages (300-1000dr); check the schedule at Karpathos Travel or call Manolis at 22 192 for more bus info.

Taxis: (tel. 22 705; 24 hr.). Go to all the villages and are as cheap as the bus when split between four or more people (roughly 2000dr to nearby villages). Taxi prices, regulated by the government, are posted in Karpathos Travel and at the taxi station on Dimokratia St.

Moped/Car Rental: On the same street as the post office, but farther down the road leading out of town, **Gatoulis Motorbikes** (tel. 22 747) rents excellent 50cc automatics (3200dr per day). Cars 12,000dr per day plus tax. Open daily 8am-2pm and 5-9pm.

International Bookstore: John Pavlakos (tel. 22 389), next to Possi Travel, has writing supplies and guidebooks. Open Mon.-Sat. 9am-2pm and 5:30-11pm.

Pharmacies: There are three **pharmacies** in town, all near the water. Open Mon.-Fri. 8am-1pm and 5:30-8:30pm. Check notices on door for other pharmacies.

Medical Assistance: Contact the **Health Center** (tel. 22 228), a large white building 100m past Platia 5 October, on N.K. Matheou St. After 2pm, go directly to the center (don't call) and ring bell for emergency. No English spoken. 9am-2:30pm.

ACCOMMODATIONS

Freelance camping, though illegal, transpires mostly undisturbed on the town beach to the north. Room prices are roughly 1000-2000dr less in off-season.

Mertonas Studios (tel. 22 622 or 23 079), located 2 blocks to the left and uphill of the bus station, facing inland. In what may be the best deal in town, Eva Angelos rents gorgeous, furnished studios with fully stocked kitchens, luxurious private baths, and maid service that would make Mr. Clean weep with joy (doubles 6000dr). Reading her guests' fortunes in coffee grounds is Eva's specialty. She also offers her studios in the winter for 50,000dr per month for a double w/o utilities.

Avra Hotel (tel. 22 388), from the waterfront, take the second right off Dimokratia St.; it's one block ahead on the right. Doubles 6000dr, triples 7000dr.

Harry's Rooms to Rent (tel. 22 188), just up the hill and to the left from the Avra. Modern, clean rooms with balcony. Singles 2400dr, doubles 3500dr.

Rooms to Rent Konaki (tel. 22 908), 100m past the Avra Hotel on the right, is immaculate and pleasant, with private baths and a spacious, homey reception area, albeit without English-speakers. Doubles 5000dr, triples 6000dr.

FOOD AND ENTERTAINMENT

Restaurants are scattered along the waterfront where Karpathians come for their nightly stroll. To meet beachgoer demands, newer *tavernas* are poking up just north of town on Limiadis St. They get more touristy farther down the waterfront. Most offer complete meals for a pricey 1800dr. **O Costas,** near the pier, is authentic and tasty (*kalamari* 950dr). Around the harbor, **Land and Sea** (tel. 22 007) grills tasty chicken breasts with rice, peas and potatoes (1600dr). **Anemoroussa,** specializing in Italian fare, has delicious pasta dishes (1300dr), served on a breezy patio above the waterfront. **Café Anapsyktirion** (tel. 22 309), behind the church and opposite the fruit stands, is frequented by a young, hip crowd. **Karpathos Kafenio** (tel. 23 160) is another inexpensive alternative (croissant 300dr, pastries 550dr). The town's sweetshop **Bee-Hive** (tel. 22 530) is up the block from Karpathos travel. Most of the town's several **minimarkets** are on the same road as Karpathos Travel. The most acclaimed artist on Karpathos, **Minas Vlahos** displays his works at his Art Center next to the mayor's office. Just follow the tranquil vibes of Enya radiating from his studio. Hand-made cards 500dr. (Open Mon.-Sat. 9am-1pm and 5-9pm.)

Nightlife converges around the waterfront's north end. **La Mirage,** a romantic spot hovering high above the harbor, plays live Greek music (beer 450dr). Along the waterfront, the popular **Eros Bar** provides a scenic balcony and cozy tables on which to drink your *drachmae* away.

■■■ SOUTHERN KARPATHOS

The rest of southern Karpathos is known for its stone farmhouses, tiny isolated chapels, and tendon-tearing views over terraced hillsides to the sea. On August 6, the towns of Menetes, Aperi, and Othos hold lively church festivals.

On a branch of the road south out of Karpathos Town are the hillside towns of **Menetes** and **Arkasa.** Menetes' huge church sprouts from the terraced houses below; its marble pillars were salvaged from the ruins of an early Christian basilica. In the house in front of the church there should be a woman who has a key. Ask at **Manolis Kafeneion** (tel. 81 356) for a key to the tiny **folk art museum** (free). In Arkasa, the remains of five parallel Cyclopean walls divide the peninsula southwest of town. **Buses** from Ta Pigadia leave for Arkasa (1-2 per day, 20min., 600dr); check the schedule for afternoon return times. **Taxis** from Ta Pigadia cost roughly 2000dr.

The island's only other paved road leads north and then west out of Karpathos Town into lush hiking country. Freelance campers can be found on a small beach cove close to the sandy shore of Agios Nikolaos. Follow the road from Arkasa to Agios Nikolaos, a 5-min. walk from Anna's boarding house. **Aperi** became the island's capital in medieval times when Arab raids forced the Karpathians to abandon their coastal town. Today it remains the island's bishopric, its spiritual capital. The church here contains the *Panagia* (Virgin Mary) icon revered throughout Karpathos. Legend has it that long ago a monk was chopping wood when blood suddenly spurted from one of the logs. The perplexed monk recognized the log as an icon of the Virgin Mary, and although the object disappeared several times, it always reappeared in an old church in Aperi. The monk understood that the Panagia wished to stay in that spot, and in 1886 a bishop's church was built. (The church is open to visitors 8-11am, when overseer is present.) Buses go to Aperi (600dr).

Two outstanding beaches are on the coast near Aperi. At **Ahata Beach,** a spring refreshes bathers and campers. A boat stops at this quiet, secluded beach twice a week en route to Diafani; inquire at Karpathos Travel.

Farther north on the coast, **Lefkos** is toilsome to reach but has a fabulous beach, perfect for tuning out distractions. A stout cave with pillars supporting the ceiling is a 10-min. walk up the hill to the north. **Buses** travel Mon., Wed., and Sat. at 9:30am from Karpathos Town to Lefkos and Mesochori (1½hr., 1000dr). Taxis cost 6000dr. **Soundias Pension** (tel. 71 203) has clean beach doubles with bath and balcony (5000dr). Next door, 10 min. on foot from the cave, **Nikos Pediaditis** (tel. 71 222) runs a small *taverna* within a terrace trellised with geraniums and oleanders. **Michalis,** above the beachfront pensions, serves delicious fish anytime.

Amopi Beach, 8km south of Karpathos Town towards the airport, has clean golden sand and is the most crowded beach on the island. Two **buses** per day travel to the beach from Karpathos Town (20min., 700dr). For the illusion of seclusion, check out the several kilometers of relatively unpopulated beach that stretch south below Amopi. If the fierce wind kicks up an infamous Amopi dust storm, move one cove south to the pebbly beach and enjoy the breeze.

■■■ NORTHERN KARPATHOS

There are no good roads which connect the rural north and commercial south of Karpathos. Whatever modernization might have infested this beautiful, arid region was stalled by a 1983 fire which devastated most of the Aleppo Pine Forests between Spoa and Olymbos. Daily **excursion boats** from Karpathos Town are the most reliable and scenic means of transport. Karpathos Travel offers boat-and-bus trips to Diafani (2hr. each way; 4500dr includes round-trip bus to Olymbos). Twice per week a boat journeys to the dazzling white beach of **Apela,** and to the island of **Saria** north of Karpathos (from Diafani 1hr., round-trip 2000dr). Here you can visit **Palatia,** a deserted village halfway up the east coast with peculiar, cone-roofed houses built by Syrian pirates in the 7th-9th centuries. Don't get stranded here; the village has few inhabitants and no water.

DIAFANI

Staying in languorous Diafani (transparent) allows you to stick close to the beaches and the harbor of North Karpathos. If exploring quaint Olymbos is your goal, however, take the first bus out of Diafani and absorb Olymbos at your leisure (2 per day, 350dr). Diafani has nothing more to offer than overpriced *tavernas* and a sleepy port. **Orphanos Travel and Shipping Agents** (tel. 51 410; fax 51 316), on the dock to the right of the *tavernas,* offers **exchange services,** room info, and ferry and excursion tickets. Ask about free boat trips to local beaches (open daily 8am-10pm). There's no bank in Diafani. A telecard **phone** is in front of the travel agency. The

police station (tel. 51 213) is in the center of town (24 hr.). There's a **post box,** but the postman only rings 3 times per week.

Hotel Nikos (tel. 51 410, -289; fax 51 316), one block behind the waterfront to the left, has comfortable cool rooms with private bath. (Singles 4500dr, doubles 5000dr, triples 7500dr; breakfast included.) The **Golden Beach Hotel** (tel. 51 215), on the center of the waterfront, has standard rooms, narrow beds, and a view of the harbor, and also offers travel services. (Singles 2500dr, doubles 4000dr.) The **Mayflower Hotel** (tel. 51 315) has standard rooms w/o baths (doubles 3000dr; breakfast 1000dr) and an adjacent *taverna.* From Diafani, take the signposted ½hr. walk north through the Pefka pine forest to **Vananda,** a beach shingled with flat stones. Nearby, the **Minas Taverna** (tel. 51 288) lets rooms starting at 2500dr per person, and a **campsite** (tel. 51 288) offers shaded pitches starting at 700dr per person.

OLYMBOS

Olymbos is traditional, though no single word can convey the thoroughness of its isolation and insularity. Ethnologists and linguists have lauded the region's preservation of its centuries-old customs; several words in the local dialect date to 1000 BC. The radiant long-sleeved white shirts and flowered aprons worn by women—a striking contrast to their weathered skin—vivify the gray, windswept village. From the flat base of the village, tireless women carry sacks of produce on their heads step by step to *their* houses, which, according to the village's matriarchal tradition, their *daughters* will inherit. Plaster-sculpted nymphs, angels, eagles, and Venetian lions decorate the exteriors of traditional homes. Two working windmills overlook the cliffs on the west side of the village—here the women of Olymbos grind flour for bread, which they bake in huge stone ovens smoldering under the hillside. Meanwhile, the men idly play backgammon or musical instruments in the coffeehouses.

The **folk museum,** adjacent one of the windmills (pick your way up the narrow village path), offers a free glimpse of a 19th-century Karpathian home, with tools, adornments, and overpriced souvenirs outside. While you're there, check out the windmills. If someone is present, you can brave the tiny ladder inside and watch one whirl behind the scenes.

If you're willing to bound over stone walls, visit the oldest chapel on Karpathos, **Agia Triada,** one of two adjacent stone chapels easily visible from the town above (look down to the right of the bus stop for earthy red arched roofs). The frescoes inside are 13th- or 14th-century "aniconic" geometric paintings of birds and fish.

Pension Olymbos (tel. 51 252), around to the left of the bus stop near the start of the village, rents old-style rooms with hand-carved beds. (Doubles 3500dr, w/ bath 5000dr.) Anna and Michalis also serve home-cooked food in the adjacent *taverna.* Melodious Michalis may serenade lucky visitors with his lyre. *Pastitsio* and *mousaka,* both 1800dr, are worth every *drachma*. **Hotel Aphrodite** (tel. 51 307, -454), in the town center just before the museum, has modern, attractive rooms with private baths and a good view (doubles 5000dr). Inquire at Parthenonas Restaurant in the town center; ask for Nikolaos, who speaks New York-accented English. **Michalis Restaurant** (tel. 51 304), just across from the bus stop, rents spacious, immaculate rooms with private baths and balconies that overlook winding stone roads. (Doubles 5000-6000dr; breakfast included.) **Posidon Pension** (tel. 51 297) serves up bare doubles (3000dr) w/ external baths. Newer rooms with private baths are available in the large white pension to the right of the bus stop (doubles 4000dr); inquire at the Posidon Restaurant. One of the few men whom you'll see laboring in Olymbos is the cobbler **Nichokis Kanakis,** who makes the red and tan leather boots that are standard footwear in the village. At 45,000dr per pair, though, these boots were not made for walking.

To travel between Olymbos and Diafani, you can take a taxi (2000dr for 5 people) or the small bus that leaves Diafani daily (when the boat from Karpathos Town arrives) and Olymbos daily (20min., 350dr). The dusty 2-3-hr. hike along a valley floor is another alternative, if you've got the time and energy

SYMI ΣΥΜΗ

The mountainous island of Symi is a small but dramatic showpiece of the Dodecanese. The famous Panormitis Monastery rests in a remote spot at the island's south end, while the historic port of Ghialos adorns the north tip. Monasteries were the only dwellings on these steep, barren shores until commercial growth in the 19th century led to the construction of the port. During this period, shipbuilding, sponge diving, fishing, and commercial trade flourished, while the Symiots received concessions from the Sultans. Ships made in Symi still have a reputation for being easily handled and quick. Ghialos is one of the loveliest ports in Greece: islands dot the ocean corridor to the town, and pastel houses ring the waterfront. Despite Symi's charms, backpackers may meet with a cool reception. The island's livelihood depends on the whims of wealthy Italian visitors, and if you're not prepared to spend lots of money, you may have to clamor for attention.

The Greek government declared the port of Symi a historic site in 1971. Many Neoclassical houses here date from the 19th century. Around town, the abandoned buildings attest to the depletion of the island's population from 20,000, at the peak of its sponge-fishing industry to 2500 today. Symi is fighting its way back from this recession, but remains comparatively poor. The entire island seems to anticipate the docking of excursion boats. The waterfront, unbearably hot in summer, can also be unbearably frenetic when boats arrive. The evenings are more peaceful, as island residents linger in the *tavernas* and drink; few tourists stay here overnight. The island's interior is calm and fragrant: Symi still cultivates its own spices, and many more grow wild in the hills.

Orientation and Practical Information As you disembark at the Ghialos clock tower (on the right side of town facing inland), the **post office** is next door down the quay (open Mon.-Fri. 7:30am-2pm). The **police** (tel. 71 111) are next to the clock tower. You can exchange money at the **National Bank,** straight ahead and to the right after the footbridge where the harbor bends left, or the **Ionian Bank** closer to the water (both open Mon.-Thurs. 8am-2pm, Fri. 8am-1:30pm). Head inland along the left-hand side of the park in the middle of the harbor and follow the signs from the Naraida restaurant to the **OTE** (open Mon.-Fri. 8:30am-3pm). Behind the Ionian Bank, **Symi Tours** (tel. 71 307) sells hydrofoil tickets and exchanges money (open 8am-2pm and 5:30-10pm). For ferry tickets, go between the bank and Symi Tours, take a right, then a quick left, and head to the shipping agency sign outside a textile shop (tel. 71 254; open Mon.-Fri. 8am-1pm and 5-9pm). **Taxis** (tel. 72 180) congregate on the east waterfront past the Ionian Bank. The **Symi Bus,** actually a van, leaves from a stop a short distance farther up along the waterfront (hourly, 150dr). Free **public toilets** are located to the left of O Meraklis Restaurant down an alleyway. There is a **pharmacy** (tel. 71 888) on the east side of the harbor (open 9am-3pm and 5-9pm). For emergency **medical assistance,** call the doctor at 71 316. **Postal Code:** 85600; **Telephone Code:** 0241.

Most of Symi's visitors come on daily **excursion boats** from Rhodes, which visit the Panormitis Monastery and Ghialos (3500dr round-trip), and if you're trying to do anything else, be prepared for confusing schedules and sporadic departures. Almost everything leaving Symi goes through Rhodes anyway, so in case of extreme trouble, you can always hop on an excursion boat heading back there (1750dr one-way). Twice a week, **ferries** pass through Symi on the way to Piraeus (6020dr), Kos (1916dr), and Kalymnos (2400dr), stopping once a week at Tilos (1417dr) and Nisyros (1900dr). Also twice weekly, **flying dolphins** head to Rhodes (2736dr), Kos (4675dr), and Kalymnos (6901dr) and once a week to Samos (10,600dr).

Accommodations Although most travelers don't spend the night, enough do that the usual herd of rooms proprietors await ferries and hydrofoils. **"Rooms to Let" Aigli** (tel. 71 392), on a side street parallel to the east waterfront, rents clean, high-ceilinged rooms with spacious common baths and a small shared balcony (refrigerators available; doubles 7000dr). **Helena "Rooms to Let"** (tel. 71 931), opposite the Ionian Bank, is another reliable option (doubles 7000dr). **Hotel Kokona** (tel. 71 451), farther inland to the left of an old church tower, at the back of a small plaza off to the right past Meraklis, is also reliable (doubles 8500dr).

Food and Entertainment Despite the influx of excursion boats, restaurant prices have not yet gone sky high. *Mousaka* averages roughly 800dr, *dolmades* 600dr. Waterfront restaurants are expensive, so the farther you walk from the ferry landing the better. Check out the plaque above **Les Caterinettes Restaurant:** this is the house where the Italians signed the agreement surrendering the Dodecanese to the Allied Powers on May 8, 1945 (stuffed eggplant 980dr). **Meraklis,** a block back from Symi Tours, specializes in luscious stuffed tomatoes (850dr). Other excellent dinner options are **George's Restaurant** and **Restaurant Panorama,** both at the top of the steps to the upper part of the village. Sit on a veranda overlooking the harbor below. (Greek salad 600dr, *kalamari* 1000dr.)

For 700dr cocktails between 8 and 9pm or friendly conversation all night long, visit the **Jean and Tonic Pub** up the hill from George's. Jean, a British vacationer who loved Symi so much that she never went home, has been running her bar for ten years now, and can help with accommodations. **Pat's Bar** in the harbor (run by Jean's sister) satisfies your alcohol yearnings (cocktails 600dr 7:30-8:30pm). To cool off back in the port, try **Igloo** ice cream, inland from the waterfront.

SIGHTS

Panormitis Monastery, the grand Monastery of the Archangel Michael the Panormitis, friend of travelers, looms at the center of a remarkable horseshoe-shaped harbor in the south part of the island. The monastery was founded at the spot where a local woman chanced upon an icon of Michael. Although it was brought to Ghialos, the icon kept returning to Panormitis. The palatial white buildings of the monastery, dominated by an elegant turn-of-the-century bell tower in the center, have been a popular stopover for Dodecanese sailors in years past. Within the monastery complex are a restaurant, a small food store, a library, "Rooms to Let," and a little museum featuring a bizarre collection of reliquaries and stuffed sea creatures (Museum open only when excursion boats and buses dock.) The small monastery church houses an exceptional wooden altar screen. The famous icon is known throughout the Dodecanese for its wish-granting powers, and tokens in the museum represent supplicants' requests. No regular buses run to the monastery, but tour buses from Ghialos run roughly 4 times per week (1hr.), and an excursion boat from Ghialos heads here as well. All excursion boats from Rhodes stop here.

The only other site worth visiting at the port is the small **Naval Museum,** at the back of the main waterfront strip. (Open daily 10:30am-3pm; admission 250dr, students free.) A steep 20-30min. hike ends at Chorio, the section of town fortified against pirate raids. Several sets of stairs lead up from the east side of the waterfront. The shadiest and most straightforward is the one farthest along the water, quite close to the road bending upwards. Follow the road at the top of the stairs and you'll see signs for the **museum,** which houses classical and Byzantine pieces as well as island costumes and utensils. (Open Tues.-Sun. 10am-2pm; free.) Signs lead through a maze of streets to the ruins of the old **castle.**

Nos Beach, a 10-min. walk from Ghialos (head north along the waterfront, past the shipyard), is tiny, but is the closest beach to the port; a small *taverna*/disco lingers nearby. The beach at **Emborio,** 45min. past Nos, is mediocre, but the views along the way make the walk worthwhile. **Pedi,** a short distance by bus, boasts radiant sands and water; there you can stay at the **Hotel Gallini.** Symi's tiny coves shelter a few excellent beaches accessible only by boat (daily, 1600dr) at **Ag. Marina, Nanou,** and **Marathounda** on the east side of the island. Boats also go to **Sesklia Island** just south of Symi (round-trip 4000dr). Excursion boats follow no set schedule; in the morning, they all line up with destinations and prices posted.

Ionian Islands
ΝΗΣΙΑ ΤΟΥ ΙΟΝΙΟΥ

The Ionian Islands have shared an historic fate apart from the rest of Greece. Situated on the country's western edge, the islands escaped Turkish occupation, and were instead overrun by the Venetians, the British, the French, and the Russians. The Ionians' uninvited visitors, milder and more concerned with development than the Turks, left a lasting cultural, commercial, and architectural imprint. Despite being governed as a British protectorate until 1864 and occupied by Italian forces during WWII, the islands are comparatively wealthy. They also retain an international flavor; where else in Greece can you find pick-up games of cricket? Historical ties make the islands a favorite among Brits and Italians, and they also see the usual ferry-hopping backpackers who make the short trip over from Italy.

CORFU (KERKYRA) ΚΕΡΚΥΡΑ

Corfu has been renowned for its lush beauty ever since its first visitor, Odysseus, washed ashore. At various times the property of Franks, Venetians, and the French, Corfu's most noticeable foreign influence comes from the British. Traditionally a favorite haunt of European royalty and aristocrats, Corfu is the most eclectically international Ionian island. Only here do British palaces sit on an esplanade modeled after the rue de Rivoli in Paris next to the shuttered alleyways of an ersatz Venice. Not to mention the international cricket matches and Asiatic Museum of Art.

CORFU TOWN

Corfu Town is the logical base for touring the island; all ferries and most buses originate here. At the New Port, a barrage of tourist officers proffering scooters, ferry tickets, and rooms greets arrivals. Apart from this melee, Corfu's two fortresses hulk over the waterfront, still guarding the Old Town. Quieter and more dignified, the narrow lanes near the Spianada (esplanade) and near Sanrocco Sq. present a charming mix of Byzantine, Venetian, and Greek architecture. Despite the numerous souvenir shops and the preponderance of English-speakers, the Old Town retains much of Corfu's traditional character, with its narrow streets, pastel and white Neoclassical buildings, brilliant pink flowers, and stray cats.

ORIENTATION AND PRACTICAL INFORMATION

Familiarize yourself with the Theotokos family. Four of Corfu's main streets are named after members of this clan; you may pass from **N. Theotoki Street** to **M. Theotoki Street** to **G. Theotoki Street** to **I. Theotoki Street** without even realizing it. Use a map (available at kiosks and the Lyroudis bookstore for roughly 300dr; keep in mind that the tourist office has moved 2 blocks west since the map was issued) and you'll be fine. Better yet, get lost in the **historic center** and bask in Neoclassical splendor. On the north coast of town are the **New Port,** which serves boats to Patras and the international ferries, and the **Old Port,** where boats leave for Paxos and Igoumenitsa. The New Fortress, behind which sits Corfu's long-distance **bus station,** separates the two ports. The Old Fortress and the **Spianada,** an esplanade ringed by chic cafés, dominate the east shore. From the Old Port, to get to the Spianada, the center of the action and home to a helpful info booth, follow the waterfront road (which changes names repeatedly) with the water on your left around the bend of the peninsula, where it turns inland to become I. Kapodistriou St.—*voilà* Espianada. From the New Port, apply the same strategy, or turn inland onto Napoleontos St., then left onto I. Theotoki. This leads you past **Sanrocco Square,** the city-bus terminus, and on to **Georgiou Theotoki Street** and the Old Town. The Old Town, a beautiful, befuddling maze of alleyways, is at the center.

National Tourist Office: (tel. 37 520). At Rizospaston Voulefton and Iak. Folila, near the post office and police station. The building is marked, but climb upstairs to the second floor to find the office. Friendly, multilingual staff has all the info you could hope for. (Open Mon.-Fri. 8:30am-1:30pm.) After 2:30pm and Sat.-Sun., go to the municipal office. (Open Mon.-Sat. 9am-9pm, Sun. 9am-3pm.) Since the publication of the map, the office has moved 2 blocks west. A tourist office kiosk in Sanrocco Sq. provides similar services. Open daily 9am-9pm.

Municipal Tourist Offices: (tel. 58 509 or 42 601). On the Spianada, one across from Customs, and one inside Customs (at the port). The office on the Spianada has a multilingual electronic info screen attachment on the side. Look for the green "i" symbol. Open April-Oct. Mon.-Sat. 9am-9pm, Sun. 9am-3pm. Very helpful bilingual staffers dispense pamphlets, bus schedules, and general information.

Tourist Police: (tel. 30 265). In New Fortress Sq. Open 7am-9:30pm.

Post Office: 19 Livadi Ave. (tel. 39 604). Open Mon.-Fri. 8am-8pm for stamps and Poste Restante, for all else 7:30am-2:30pm. **Postal Code:** 49100.

OTE: Main office, 9 Mantzarou St., off A. Theotoki St. Open daily 8am-midnight. Smaller offices at Kapodistriou St., on the Esplanade and in mobile white buildings at both Old and New ports. Open daily 7:30am-10:40pm. **Telephone Code:** 0661 for Corfu Town, 0662 for South Corfu, 0663 for North Corfu.

Room-Finding Services: Tourist agencies along Arseniou St. from the Old Port to the Old Fortress and along Stratigou St. by the New Port find rooms in pensions. Many operate without commission and have direct pipelines to cheap lodgings of which the tourist police are unaware. Most open 8:30am-1:30pm and 5:30-9pm. Singles from 3000dr, doubles from 4000dr, triples from 5000dr; add 1000-1500dr for private bath. Prices usually negotiable for longer stays. Consider asking at the tourist police for rooms or calling "the Association of Owners of Private Rooms and Apts. in Corfu" (tel. 26 133; fax 72 560), in the heart of the old town. The organization is still in its formative stages—best to call before seeking them out.

British Vice Consul: 1 Menekratous (tel. 30 055 or 37 995), down the street from the post office. Open Mon.-Fri. 8am-2pm. Call 39 211 in an emergency.

Banks: 4 banks on G. Theotoki St., near where it narrows and becomes Voulgareos, including the **National Bank.** Most open Mon.-Thurs. 8am-2pm, Fri. 8am-1:30pm. Some have additional hours July-Aug. 4-6pm or 5:30-7:30pm and Sat. 8:30am-1pm. **Barclay's Bank** in Sanrocco Sq. (tel. 46 121), open Mon.-Thurs. 8am-2pm, Fri. 8am-1:30pm. Try the currency exchange window at the **airport** (open when planes arrive or depart). Though always obliging, most hotels and tourist agencies near the Old Port charge 20% commission. The tourist office booths also change money at the National Bank rate.

American Express: Representative is **Greek Skies Travel,** 20a Kapodistriou St., P.O. Box 24 (tel. 30 883 or 32 469), at the south end of the Spianada. Holds mail and cashes AmEx Traveler's Cheques. Open Mon.-Fri. 8am-noon and 5:30-8:30pm, Sat. 8am-noon.

Flights: 20 Kapodistriou St. (tel. 38 694, -5, or -6; airport 30 180), on the Spianada. Free buses from the airport. A taxi ride takes only 5min. and is the only way to get to the airport unless your hotel or tour group has buses. (Before getting in, agree on a fare of roughly 1500dr.) To Athens (3-4 per day, 50min., 19,100dr including 1100dr tax) and Thessaloniki (3 per week, 19,100dr). A new airline, **Air Greece,** is starting up service between Corfu and Athens. Only 4 flights per week (Mon.-Tues. and Fri.-Sat.) but 3000dr cheaper. Contact **Chalikipoulos Travel,** 5 Arseniou St. (tel. 24 023 or 30 626; fax 37 079 or call Air Greece at 33 410). Book 2-3 days ahead, 1 day ahead off-season.

Buses: KTEL (long-distance), behind the New Port on Avraniou St. (tel. 30 627 or 39 985). Pick up a handy timetable available at the station or from tourist agencies. Schedules for the main KTEL line are also posted on a billboard outside the

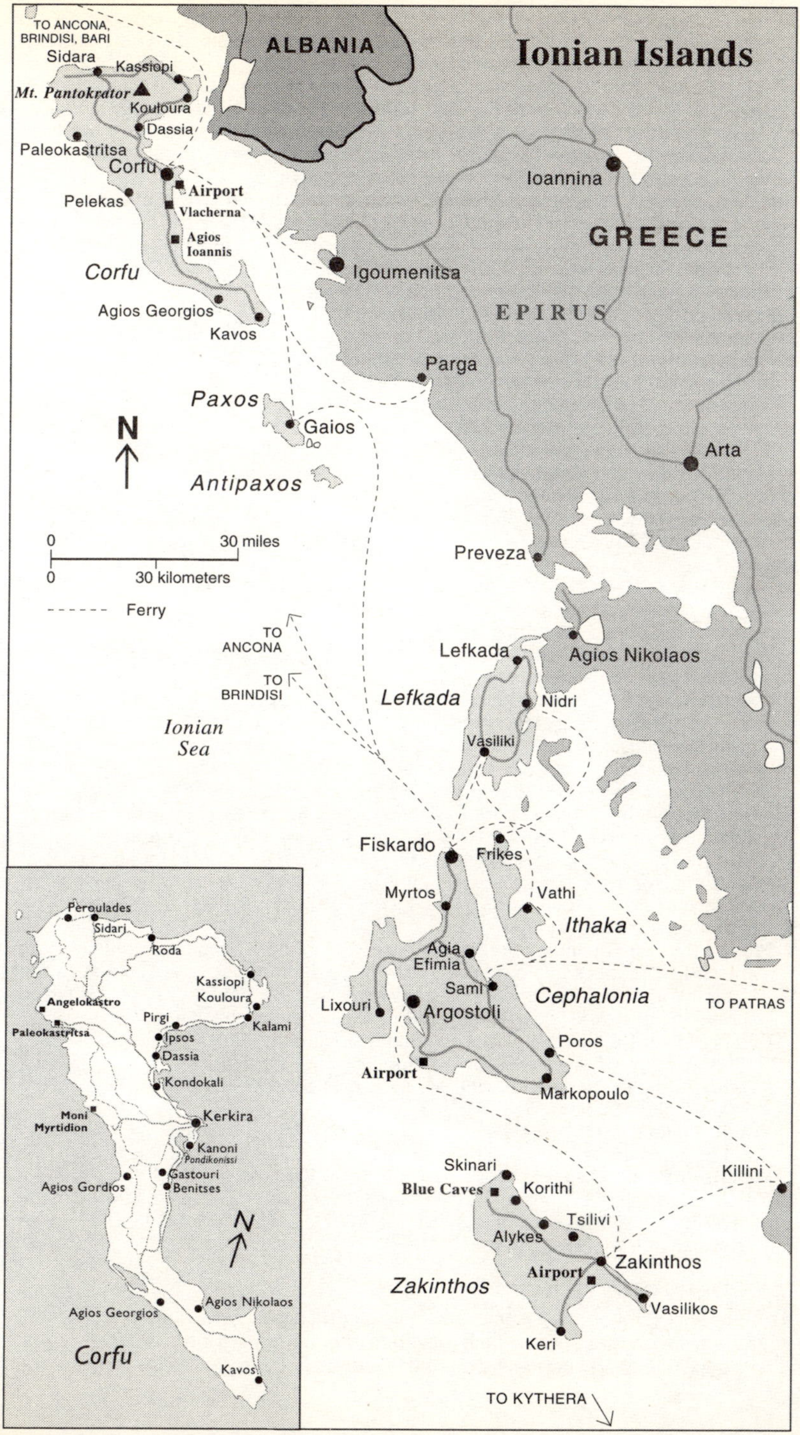
Ionian Islands
ALBANIA
GREECE
EPIRUS
TO ANCONA, BRINDISI, BARI
Sidara
Kassiopi
Mt. Pantokrator
Kouloura
Dassia
Paleokastritsa
Corfu
Airport
Pelekas
Vlacherna
Agios Ioannis
Corfu
Agios Georgios
Kavos
Ioannina
Igoumenitsa
Parga
Paxos
Gaios
Antipaxos
Arta
N
0
30 miles
0
30 kilometers
Ferry
Preveza
TO ANCONA
TO BRINDISI
Lefkada
Agios Nikolaos
Lefkada
Nidri
Ionian Sea
Vasiliki
Fiskardo
Frikes
Myrtos
Vathi
Ithaka
Agia Efimia
Sami
Cephalonia
TO PATRAS
Lixouri
Argostoli
Poros
Airport
Markopoulo
Skinari
Killini
Blue Caves
Korithi
Tsilivi
Alykes
Zakinthos
Airport
Zakinthos
Vasilikos
Keri
TO KYTHERA
Peroulades
Sidari
Roda
Kassiopi
Kouloura
Angelokastro
Paleokastritsa
Pirgi
Kalami
Ipsos
Dassia
Kondokali
Moni Myrtidion
Kerkira
Kanoni
Pondikonissi
Gastouri
Agios Gordios
Benitses
N
Agios Nikolaos
Agios Georgios
Corfu
Kavos

new office behind Corfu Town's New Fortress, from which the green KTEL buses leave. Other (blue) buses, including those to Kontokali (the youth hostel), leave from Sanrocco Sq.—schedules are printed on the signs. To Paleokastritsa (11 per day, 45min., 360dr), Glyfada Beach (9 per day, 45min., 260dr), Kavos (12 per day, 650dr), Kassiopi (9 per day, 500dr), Sidari (11 per day, 480dr), Ag. Gordios (7 per day, 220dr), Athens (2 per day, 6250dr), and Thessaloniki (1 per day, 6600dr). Buses run less frequently on Sun. Buy tickets for Corfu destinations on the bus, all others in the office. Open daily 5:30am-8pm.

City Buses: #10 to Achilleon from Sanrocco Sq. and the Old Town in front of the Hotel Constantinoupolis (6 per day), #6 to Benitses (13 per day), #7 to Dassia (every ½hr. 7am-10pm), #8 to Triklino (10 per day), #11 to Pelekas (9 per day). Schedule distributed at the gray info booths and the youth hostel. Fares for city buses average 110-155dr. Less frequent service on Sun.

Ferries: Book a day early in high season, especially to Italy—even deck class sells out. Agents for the various shipping companies line Xen. Stratigou St., opposite the New Port. Prices vary little among agents, although occasional discounts are offered. Try **Fragline** to Brindisi (Mon.-Fri. at 9am, 8hr., 4000dr), and Patras (2 per day, 10-11hr., 6000dr). **Adriatica** and **Hellenic Mediterranean** recognize Eurail and Inter-rail passes. Ferries also sail for Ancona (1 per day, 22hr., 14,400dr), Bari (3-4 per week, 6000dr), and other Italian ports of call. Ferries to Igoumenitsa run hourly (840dr). To Paxos, you have a choice of ferry (1 per day, Mon.-Tues. and Thurs.-Sat., roughly 2500dr) or catamaran (1 per day, 3273dr). When traveling to foreign ports find out if the port tax is included in the price of your ticket. Ferry agencies, open all day in high season, follow regular store hours off-season (Mon., Wed., and Sat. 8am-2pm; Tues., Thurs., and Fri. 8am-1:30pm and 5-8pm); always open at ferry departures. For changes and updates on ferry schedules, contact the **port police** (tel. 38 425) in the customs house along the port, or the **port authorities** (tel. 32 655 or 40 002).

Taxis: At the Old Port, the Spianada, Sanrocco Square, and G. Theotoki St. For **Radio Taxis,** call 33 811 or 41 333.

Car Rental: A Fiat Panda goes for 10,000-12,000dr, plus 10-20dr per additional km, with 100km free. Make sure quoted prices include the 20% tax. Third-party insurance is usually included. You must have a current driver's license or international permit to rent cars. Full collision insurance costs roughly 1500dr per day. Roads are deserted during siesta (2-5pm). Agencies along Xen. Stratigou all rent for roughly 10,000dr per day. **Hertz** and **Interrent/Europcar** are more expensive. International car rental at **Greek Skies,** 20 Kapodistriou St. (tel. 33 410). Reasonable replacement service for breakdowns at no extra charge. Min. age 21-23; for more expensive cars, min. age 25 with credit card. Full payment in advance or major credit card required. Open Mon.-Fri. 8:30am-1:30pm and 5:30-8:30pm, Sat. 8:30am-1:30pm.

Moped Rental: The most popular way to see the island is by moped. Rental places abound; you shouldn't pay more than 3000-4000dr per day. Make sure the brakes work. You're responsible for any damage to the vehicle, but the rental fee should include third-party liability and property damage insurance.

Luggage Storage: Several places on Avrami St., directly across from the New Port. 250dr per day. Check access times before leaving your bags.

Laundromat: I. Theotoki St. (tel. 35 304), near Sanrocco Sq. Wash 1200dr, dry 400dr. Open 9am-9pm.

Public Toilets: On the harbor at the Old Port, on the Spianada near the bandstand, and in Sanrocco Sq. Those on the Spianada are wheelchair accessible.

Hospital: Corfu General Hospital, Polithroni Kostanda (tel. 45 811, -2, or -3; emergency room 25 400). For a list of foreign language-speaking doctors, call the Medical Association of Corfu at 39 615 or 46 023, or call the tourist office. For an **ambulance,** call 39 403 or 166.

ACCOMMODATIONS

Decent, reasonably priced rooms are available in Corfu. Some hotel managers fill their rooms with camp beds which they then offer as dorms for the price of singles. True singles are nearly impossible to find. Hotels near the water fill up first, and the effectiveness of bargaining diminishes later in the day. Fortunately, prices drop roughly 1000dr per person in off-season, and longer stays are often discounted at small pensions. Consider finding a room in a base town and taking advantage of Corfu's extensive bus service for daytrips around the island. Freelance camping is practically impossible and indubitably illegal.

Youth Hostel Kontokali (tel. 91 202), 4½km north on the main road from the port on the edge of Kontokali Village. Take the #7 Dassia bus from Sanrocco Sq. or across from the Hotel Constantinoupolis near the Old Port (every ½hr. until 10pm, 20min., 155dr). Taxi will cost roughly 1500dr. The cheapest place to stay on Corfu (1500dr per person). No curfew. Location not central, but bus service is accessible. Near a mediocre beach and a not-so-groovin' disco. Large supermarket nearby, restaurant and pool in hostel. Reception open 8am-12:30pm and 5-8pm.

Hotel Acropolis, 3 Zavitsanou St. (tel. 23 936 or 39 569; fax 23 937), fronting the old port and fairgrounds. Big old building, but rooms are clean; management somewhat indifferent but friendly. 5000dr per person.

Hotel Evropi (tel. 39 304). From the New Port where the boats to Italy dock, look across the street for the fork in the road and bear left, looking for the red signs. Conveniently located, liveable rooms with a tacky feel. Singles 4500dr; doubles 5500dr, w/bath 7000dr; triples 7500dr, w/bath 9000dr.

Camping: Corfu has 15 official campsites, and prices are strictly regulated by the local government. All campsites here charge roughly 1000dr per person, 700dr per small tent, 850dr per large tent, and 850dr per car. Rates should be 100dr less in the off-season. Confirm rates with the tourist office and be sure to pick up the brochure printed by the camping owners association of Corfu, which includes a map outlining the location of each campsite and a table of useful info, including postal codes, phone numbers, owners' names, amenities, and distances to town and beaches. Close to Corfu Town are **Kondolaki Camping** (tel. 91 202), next to the youth hostel and **Dionysus Camping Village** (tel. 91 147; fax 91 760).

FOOD

The premier restaurant areas are at the two ends of N. Theotoki St., near the Spianada and by the Old Port. Lunch is served outdoors until 3pm, dinner until 11pm. Because nearly all the restaurants in town are strictly regulated by the tourist police, the prices are fair but the cuisine monotonous. For cheap do-it-yourself fare, go to the daily open-air **market** on Dessila St., near the base of the New Fortress. Some stalls stay open all afternoon, but arrive around 7:30am for the best selection of goodies. The **Supermarket Spilias,** 13 Solomou St. near the bus station (open Mon., Wed., and Sat. 8:30am-1:45pm; Tues. and Thurs.-Fri. 8am-1:30pm and 5:30-8:30pm) and the **Supermarket Koskinas,** in Sanrocco Sq. (open Mon.-Fri. 8am-2pm), have a more than adequate supply of materials to fix a snack.

Nautikon, 150 N. Theotoki (tel. 30 009). Near the Old Port. Large and friendly. Appetizing food, some English spoken, and 50 years of experience. The delicious *mousaka* (1100dr) will impress even palates tired of this Greek standard. (Most entrees 1300-1500dr.) Open April-Oct. daily noon-midnight.

Pizza Pete, 19 Arseniou St. (tel. 22 301). On the waterfront halfway between the Spianada and the Old Port. New owners Yiannis and Takis, former waiters at Pete's, carry on the 15-year-old tradition of fine dining. Great grub (entrees 1300-1900dr). Try the "Pete special" pizza (1400dr). Open April-Oct. 10am-3am.

Restaurant Bellissimo, 2 Kyriaki (tel. 41 112), off of N. Theotoki. Coming from the Spianada, turn left onto the narrow alleyway to Kyriaki. In a charming gardened enclave of its own. Nicely priced (*kalamari* 800dr, *sofrita* 1100dr).

Taka Taka, up the hill from the National Bank on Voulangeos St. *Gyros pita*—cheapest meal in town (200dr)—but you might need 3-4 to fill your belly. ½L of Heineken 250dr. Open daily 7pm-1am.

Pallada, near the green-bus station. The view isn't much to speak of, but the food is good, Greek, and cheap. Entrees 800-1200dr.

Cavalieri Hotel, Root Garden Restaurant, on I. Kapodistriou at the top of the hill from the Espianada. The view is everything. Go at night. Pricey but fun (espresso 600dr, spaghetti with shellfish sauce 1500dr). Open daily 6:30pm-1am.

Sweet Shops: Bakery-hopping can best be done along Philarmonikis, as most sweet shops in the old town are along this road which runs parallel to the Spianada, one block inland. To get you started, try **Bella Piazza,** 8 Philarmonikis, which offers an enticing array of traditional sweets and breads. From N. Theotoki heading inland, turn right onto Philarmonikis. The shop is roughly 3 storefronts down. (Open 7:30am-9pm.)

ENTERTAINMENT

In the evening, parade up and down the Spianada and its adjacent park. It's perky until early morning. But don't get too carried away—cafés along the Spianada charge three times more than cafés in less popular locations. Wander off the main catwalk into the streets of the Old Town. You might catch the dulcet tones of Corfu's seven music schools practicing simultaneously. The **Pallas Cinema** on A. Theotoki St. near Sanrocco Sq. and the open-air cinema on Marasli St. often screen English language films (1500dr). The annual **Corfu Festival** in August and September features an international selection of ballet and orchestral music. The best times to visit Corfu, however, are during Carnival and Easter week, when Corfu's inhabitants practice the unique local tradition of smashing pottery to celebrate the Resurrection. Check at the tourist office for details.

The east coast of Corfu is awash with **nightclubs,** which cater mainly to British package tours. To the south, in Benitses and Kavos, the dancing can sometimes turn to fighting. There's less trouble in the resort towns of Gouvia, Dassia, and Ipsos north of Corfu Town, but you might find yourself forgetting you are in Greece. For bars and clubs that are both safe and authentically Greek, head north of Corfu town past the Old Port along the port road. **Eidolo** plays only Greek music, while **Sax,** a favorite with the locals, is a classy, somewhat costly bar in a converted stable. The **Coca** club is great for dancing.

SIGHTS

Built by the Venetians in the late 14th century, the **Palio Frourio** (Old Fortress), east of the Spianada, was thought to be impregnable. In 1864, however, the British blew it up before leaving Corfu to the Greeks. It was renovated for the European Socialist Party Leaders' Conference in 1993, and is now open to the public. On the grounds is the **Church of St. George,** harmoniously adapted to accommodate museum displays, including absolutely exquisite mosaics. The church's evocative interior is further enhanced by the echoing tones of a Byzantine choir (tapes on sale from 1400dr). Multimedia meets the surreal in the building opposite the church, in whose centuried chambers glow visions of "Byzantium," choreographed austerely across multiple video screens in utter silence. (Site open Tues.-Fri. 8am-7pm, Sat.-Sun. and holidays 8:30am-3pm; admission 800dr, students 400dr.)

At the north end of the Spianada stands the **Palace of St. Michael and St. George.** Unmistakably British, the palace was built as the residence of the Lord High Commissioner. Facing a cricket green where local clubs and visitors from abroad play matches during summer, the building now houses the **Museum of Asiatic Art,** an extensive collection of Japanese, Chinese, and Indian wood carvings, silk screens, porcelain figures, and mosaics from the Byzantine basilica in Paleopolis (closed for renovation in 1995). The **Archaeological Museum,** 1 Vraila St., on the waterfront south of the Spianada, contains relics of the island's Mycenaean and Classical past; a highly advanced civilization flourished here. An intimidating—but smiling—Gorgon sculpture glowers over the collection, which includes a hoard of ancient coins from different regions. (Open Tues.-Sat. and holidays 8:30am-3pm, Sun. 9:30am-2:30pm; admission 800dr, seniors 600dr, children and students with ID free; Sun. free.)

Corfu's two most famous churches are the **Church of St. Jason and Sosipater,** and the **Church of St. Spyridon.** The former is a 12th-century Byzantine stone structure located in a fishing neighborhood on the way to Mon Repos Beach (continue past the Archaeological Museum along the waterfront), with a dazzling array of silver and gold ornaments, medieval paintings, an impressive ceiling mural, and gorgeous Byzantine icons. The church was once covered entirely by murals of saints, but the islanders painted them to prevent their decimation by the Turks. The Church of St. Spyridon, named for the island's patron saint, was built in 1590 (take Ag. Spyridon off the Spianada and the church is on your left; another entrance on the other side). Although St. Spyridon had been dead since the 4th century AD, he is said to have appeared in 1716 and shattered the morale of the invading Turks. Following outbreaks of plague in the 17th century, residents of Corfu began parading the silver reliquary containing the remains of the saint around town every Palm Sunday and on the first Sunday of November. Each year he is given a new pair of slippers to replace the old pair he wears out wandering the island doing good deeds. In the right light, if you lift the gold cover, you can still see his oddly disconcerting grin beneath a black shroud behind the glass. St. Spyridon holds a traditional Greek Festival, with music and dancing, on July 13. Both churches are open until 7pm.

North of N. Theotoki near the Spianada is the Ionian Bank Building, which houses a **museum of paper currency.** (Open Mon.-Sat. 9am-1pm; free.) Behind the Old Port lies the old **Jewish Quarter** of town. The **synagogue,** on Velissariou St., served a growing Jewish community from its construction in 1537 until 1940, when 5000 Jews were gathered on the Spianada to be sent to Auschwitz. For fans of Cousteau-like exploration, the confused **shell museum,** 7 Solomou St. (tel. 42 900), in the old town, has a biological lab-style collection of fetuses and stuffed birds and snakes. Also, lots of shells. (Open 9:30am-7pm; admission 400dr, students 200dr.) The 375-year-old **New Fortress,** above the ferry ports, affects panoramic views of Corfu Town, and is a nice place for a sun-drenched picnic. The fortress houses a small gallery of etchings, maps, and watercolors with nautical motifs, and contains an additional museum exhibit of reproductions and noteworthy items from other museums around Greece. There is also a dimly lit and cavernous café serving up espresso (350dr), beer (350dr), and snacks—a unique and memorable way to experience the richly atmospheric fortress chambers. The New Fortress is also a site for occasional open-air concerts. (Open daily 9am-9pm; admission 400dr.)

Corfu's most recently opened sight is the **Mon Repos Estate,** which the British government gave to the Greek royal family in 1864. Since the royals' exile in 1967, the lovely Neoclassical palace has fallen into disrepair, and large gardens filled with rare trees have become overgrown. In 1992 the mayor of Corfu opened the grounds to the public, stating that since a temple to Artemis rests on the area, the land, like any site of archaeological significance, belongs to the Greek people. Former king Constantine, in exile in London, is currently suing for possession. (Site open until 6pm; free.) Be sure to make the haunting, tree-lined walk if you can; the site may not be open for long, and it isn't often that you get to see Doric temples in people's backyards. Just before the large, gated entrance to the Estate is the entrance to the **monastery of St. Efthimeaus.** (Open 8am-1pm and 5-8pm.) On the opposite side of the road is the **Archaeological Site of Paleopolis Roman Baths,** closed to the public but visible through the fence. Be careful crossing the street.

■■■ SOUTHERN CORFU

Some 6km south of Corfu Town, the islet of **Vlacherna,** home to a tiny white **church** and parallel to the famous postcard island of Pondikonissi, connects to the main island via a causeway: take bus #2 (Kanoni) from the Spianada and ask the driver to let you off near Vlacherna (every ½hr. until 10pm, 230dr).

Nearby stands **Achillion Palace,** 9km south of the port of Corfu in the village of **Gastouri.** Eccentric and ostentatious, it was commissioned by Empress Elizabeth of Austria as a summer residence in honor of Achilles and Thetis. The Empress' Achilles fetish may be due to the death of her favorite son, whom she felt resembled the god. Kaiser Wilhelm II of Germany whiled away his summers here, until WWI diverted his attention. The gardens and view are especially cinematic: the 1981 James Bond flick *For Your Eyes Only* was filmed here. (Open daily 9am-4pm; admission 700dr, children 350dr.) While in the area, do what most don't—leave the palace for long enough to explore the intriguing village of Gastouri. Take bus #10 from Sanrocco Sq. (6 per day, every 3hr., ½hr., 155dr). The arriving buses also make return trips. Fewer buses on weekends and holidays.

Farther south is the rowdy little tourist/fishing village of **Benitses,** where you can see the remains of a Roman bathhouse and a 3rd-century AD Roman villa. Bus #6 runs to Benitses from Sanrocco Sq. (every hr., 30min., 250dr). At the lively waterfront bars and discos, shoot pool, watch videos, or cruise. At night, be forewarned that the brawling and dancing at some of the bars can get out of control. Most have happy hours and infamous all-you-can-drink specials. You might as well have stayed at home and gone to a frat party. The **Museum of the Sea** offers hung-over revelers a soothing way to pass the time (open Tues.-Sat. 10am-7pm).

Shallow but clear and pleasant, **Kavos Beach** lies at the south tip of the island, 47km from Corfu Town. Buses leave from behind the New Fortress (roughly every hr. 5am-7:30pm, 650dr). On the southwest coast stretches the gorgeous, sandy beach at **Agios Georgios** (2 buses per day from behind the New Fortress, 1hr., 480dr). The nearby, attractive **Vitalades Beach** is one of Corfu's few deserted spots.

■■■ NORTHERN CORFU

Tacky come-ons to tourists scar the first 20km of the coastline north of Corfu Town. The resort towns of **Dassia, Ipsos,** and **Pirgi** consist of a long chain of hotels, discos, and boutiques. Official campsites are plentiful in this area: Dassia has **Karda Camping** (tel. 93 595) Ipsos has **Ideal Camping** (tel. 93 243) and **Corfu Camping Ipsos** (tel 93 579), while Pirgi has **Paradissos Camping** (tel. 93 558). These campsites cost 1000dr per person, 700dr per small tent, 850dr per large tent, and 850dr per car. All have markets on the premises and include hot showers. For nightlife, head to any of these towns; for less spoiled country, venture farther north.

The Kassiopi **bus** serves this coast. It leaves from the bus station and stops at every hamlet along the way (9 per day, Sun. 2 per day, 1¼hr., 500dr). Past Pirgi, the road begins to wind below steep cliffs. **Mt. Pantokrator,** on your left, towers 1000m above, and the cliffs on the right loom dramatic as Albania comes into view across the straits. After passing through Nissaki and Gimari, you'll reach **Kouloura,** 28km north of Corfu, with its Venetian manor-house, pebbled beach, marina, and matchless *taverna.* The right fork to **Kalami** meanders down to a sandier beach where there are "Rooms to Let" (July-Aug. doubles roughly 8000dr). Author Lawrence Durrell lived in Corfu with his family, including his wacky brother Gerald, in the 1930s. His small white house can still be seen (from the outside, at least). Buy the brothers' Corfu-inspired books (Lawrence's *Prospero's Cell* and Gerald's *My Family and Other Animals*) in Lyroudi's bookstore. Rooms are available for rent in both towns. The walk to Kalami or Kouloura from the main road takes roughly 15min.

Kassiopi, 36km north of Corfu and just 2km across the sea from the Albanian port of Sarande (see box on p. 308), is over-commercialized and caters mostly to English couples with young children. The white-rock beaches are clean but overcrowded. Greeks still warn that if you swim too far into Albanian waters you may be shot on sight; perhaps an exaggeration, but don't push your luck. For a thrill, try parasailing. For salamanders, overgrown weeds, and barbed wire, trek over to the 9th-century **fortress** which the Venetians destroyed in 1836, overlooking the beach. The **Panagia Kassiotropi Church** is where the Virgin Mary reportedly emerged from an icon and restored a blinded boy's sight. Doubting town officials were convinced because the boy's new eyes were blue instead of their original brown. **Travel agencies** on the main street help find rooms. Expect to pay 8000dr for doubles and 10,000dr for triples. There are no singles in Kassiopi. The innkeepers here, accustomed to package tourists, deplore one-night stays and often charge a premium for them. The preponderance of English-speaking tourists makes it seem like Britain, only warmer.

Northwest from Kassiopi on the main road, the quieter beach resorts of **Roda Chanin** and **Sidari** provide excellent camping and sandy beaches enveloped by cliffs. Sidari is particularly spectacular, especially the stretch of picture-perfect coves and beguiling sea caves along the shore towards Peroulades. A 5th-century BC temple has been found here as well. Try **Roda Beach Camping** (tel. 63 209) or buy supplies at the market here. Catch a sunset at **Peroulades;** by road, the 3km walk there takes you past farms and fruit trees. The bus to Sidari leaves from behind the New Fortress (11 per day, 480dr). In Sidari, hire a motorboat for a daytrip to the tiny islands of **Othoni, Erikoussa,** and **Mathraki** (1hr., roughly 1500dr), inhabited exclusively by fishers, farmers, and their crops. For more info, inquire at **Sellos Travel** (tel. 31 239). Each of these islands is picturesque and quiet. There are no hotels available, only a few rooms. Sidari has eight C-class hotels with "budget" prices. Affordable hotels in Roda include the **Milton** (tel. 93 295) and the **Silva Beach Hotel** (tel. 93 134). **Telephone Code:** 0663.

To wander even farther off the main trail, explore the mountain villages in the north of the island, each with gorgeous views, a couple of *tavernas*, and a few foreign visitors. A bus from Kassiopi occasionally runs to the village of **Loutses,** passing the little hamlet of **Perithia,** near Mt. Pantokrator. Moped travel allows you to revel in the rugged scenery. The gas station nearest Paleokastritsa is 15km back toward Corfu Town on the main road.

■■■ WESTERN CORFU

Swimming on Corfu's west coast is like being trapped inside an all-blue kaleidoscope. The **Paleokastritsa** (Old Castle) **beach** rests among some of the loveliest scenery in Greece, with six small coves and sea caves casting shadows over shades of blue; this also makes Paleokastritsa's beautiful beach the coldest on the island. Renting a pedal boat is the best way to visit the caves (1500dr per hr.). The 13th-century fort of **Angelokastro** sits above the town, while a natural balcony, **Bella Vista,** rests halfway up. Jutting out over the sea is the bright white **Panagia Theotokos Monastery** with a collection of Byzantine icons, gorgeous views, and the skeleton of a sea monster, no kidding. (Open April-Oct. daily 7am-1pm and 3-7pm.) Come as early as possible; by mid-morning it is a mess of cameras and tour buses. **Buses** run to Paleokastritsa from behind the New Fortress (11 per day, 45min., 360dr). Travelers willing to hunt can find affordable lodgings: wander up the footpath to Lakones and comb the olive groves for inexpensive pensions (5000-7000dr), or check out **Hotel Apollon** (tel. (0663) 41 211), whose large, clean rooms offer a splendid view of the beach. (Doubles 7000dr; breakfast 1000dr.) **Il Pirate** restaurant offers good food for slightly less predatory prices than its neighbors (pasta entrees 800-1300dr). There is a **market** on your right as you come into town.

South of Paleokastritsa is **Pelekas,** an excellent base town in the west with some of the island's best beaches. Kaiser Wilhelm II used to watch the sun set over the Ionian Sea from a small hill outside town. **Agatha's Travel Service** (tel. 94 283, -602) on the main street in town, to the left of the church, rents mopeds (3000dr per day) and can help find rooms. (Open 8:30am-2am.) Doubles start at 4000dr.

The western exposure and elevation of Pelekas make it ideal for watching sunsets over whitewashed villages in the hillsides. **Pelekas Beach,** a ½-hr. downhill walk from town, attracts a large number of backpackers. The beach is popular with freelance campers, as accommodations are nonexistent. Although freelance camping is illegal, police don't generally hassle sleepers. Don't attempt to make the harrowing, hairpin journey by moped. Bus #11 runs to Pelekas Town from Sanrocco Sq. (9 per day, ½hr., 230dr). **Glyfada Beach,** 5km up the coast from Pelekas Town, is served directly by the Glyfada bus from behind the New Fortress (hourly, ½hr., 260dr). It is far more touristed, but still clean and picturesque. Both beaches, crisply bracketed by scrubby cliffs, are remarkably shallow. Single women, watch out for smooth-talking Greek *kamakia* (literally, "harpoons") who cruise Glyfada, occasionally making a move. *Kamakia* make their living getting foreigners to pick them up and support them for a few days. They even have a union. Just ignore them.

A little north of Glyfada and accessible via dirt path off the main Pelekas road lie the isolated beaches of **Moni Myrtidon** and **Myrtiotissa,** extolled by Lawrence Durrell as the most beautiful beaches in the world. They're sandy, clean, and green. A section of sand at Myrtiotissa is the island's unofficial **nude beach.** Everything here is very casual, although once in a while the local monks from the Monastery of Our Lady of the Myrtles complain to the police, who reluctantly bring offending nudists to court. Above these beaches in the olive trees is the small restaurant **Myrtiotissa.** You can camp here for free and use the bathroom if you buy breakfast (850dr) and clean your site when you're done camping.

Agios Gordios, accessible by bus (7 per day, 45min., 220dr), with its steep cliffs and impressive rock formations, is the setting for the **Pink Palace** (tel. (0661) 53 024, -103, -104; fax 53 025). Run by Greek "Dr." George, his sister Magda, and an energetic crew of Aussies, Brits, Canadians, and Swedes, this resort has legendary status among English-speaking beach revelers and late-night-drinking-party-aficionados. An eternal pink *ouzo* circle for some, the Pink Palace also attracts substantial crowds of road-weary young travelers who celebrate their "vacation from vacation" by extending their stays (longer stays receive certain discounts) and taking advantage of opportunities to do everything from innertubing, jet skiing, and parasailing...to cliff diving and bungy jumping. Many of these activities—particularly, oh, say, cliff diving—are unsafe. Also available to guests are basketball and volleyball courts (with organized tournaments), bus excursions, laundry services, long-distance AT&T service, money exchange, and free safety deposit. Oh, and don't forget the weekly toga parties. The Pink Palace spans from road to beachfront and includes 13 buildings which can house up to 700 people. They won't turn anyone away, but reservations are accepted and a call will get you a free ride from port to palace. Rooms vary in size, quality, and location (4300dr per person, terrace cots 3300dr; price includes all-you-can-eat breakfast, dinner, towels, shower, and nightclub).

Daytrip to Albania

Improved relations between Greece and Albania have made Albania's Ionian coast accessible to tourists in Greece. One of the more popular and easily accessible spots for a daytrip is the Greek settlement of **Butrint,** Albania one of archaeology's better-kept secrets. Layer upon layer of civilization, from as early as the 6th century BC to the 19th AD, has left its mark on the small site. Very little effort has been made to maintain Butrint, now overgrown and deserted, for today's visitors. Not every ruin is labeled, and the rest are described cursorily in Albanian. But this is part of Butrint's appeal. Wandering around, it is easy to imagine discovering these treasures for the first time. In Butrint, no one will tell you to climb out of that 2nd-century well when you feel like playing Indiana Jones. (Ruins open 8am-sunset; admission 150 lekë, or $2.)

The best way to reach Butrint is by **taxi** from Sarande (45min.). It costs roughly 1000 lekë ($11) round-trip, including the wait while you tour around the site. There may also be a morning bus. A 1-min. ride in the ferry stationed across from the entrance to the ruins takes you to an **island.** There stands a 19th-century triangular **fortress** built by the Turks. Check it out before leaving. Two **ferries** per day leave from Corfu to Sarande (1½hr., 3000 lekë, or $34).

ZAKINTHOS ΖΑΚΥΝΘΟΣ

Most visitors to Zakinthos come to admire the island's gorgeous beaches. While the east makes the trip worthwhile, the less popular Vrachionas mountains on the west fringe and the flower-filled villages in the interior conceal some deserted beaches and quiet towns. Sunbathers share sand at Gerakas Beach with the *Caretta caretta* turtles, who consider the coast to be prime real estate. If you tire of vying for elbow-room, however, seek solitude in the fragrant pink-blossomed interior or in the west.

■■■ ZAKINTHOS TOWN

Tidy Zakinthos Town welcomes visitors to the east coast of the island with arcaded streets and whitewashed buildings. After an earthquake destroyed it in 1953, locals renovated the city to its former state, making an effort to stay true to the Venetian architecture in certain areas like the spacious Solomou Sq. to the right of the boat landing. It's a pretty town, but with all the other opportunities available, you may want to blow this joint and head for the more remote beaches.

ORIENTATION AND PRACTICAL INFORMATION

As you disembark from the ferry, you'll see the stately **Solomou Square,** lined with palm trees and pastel buildings. Along the waterfront, **Lombardou Street** and the boardwalk beckon with *gelateria* and tourist gift stores. The first street parallel to Lombardou away from the water is **Filita Street,** home to the bus station; behind it are **Foskolou, Alex. Roma** (the main shopping street), and **Tertseti,** in that order. Behind Solomou Sq., **Vasileos Georgiou B** leads quickly to **Agiou Markou Square.**

Police: (tel. 22 200). Lombardou and Fra. Tzoulati St., 5 blocks along the waterfront from Solomou Sq. 24 hr. Laid-back **tourist police** (tel. 27 367) speak English, answer questions, and can help find accommodations. Open 8am-10pm or later.

Post Office: (tel. 42 418). On Tertseti and Skirou Gouskou St. **Exchanges currency.** Open Mon.-Fri. 7:30am-8pm. **Postal Code:** 29100.

OTE: 2 Vasileos Georgiou B, between the two squares. Open daily 7am-10pm. **Telephone Code:** 0695.

Banks: National Bank of Greece, El. Venizelou St., near Solomou Sq., next to the town hall. **Currency exchange.** Open Mon.-Thurs. 8am-2pm, Fri. 8am-1:30pm.

Flights: Flights to Athens (2 per day, off-season 1 per day, 45min., 16,300dr). **Olympic Airways,** 16 Alex. Roma St. (tel. 28 611 or 42 617). Open Mon.-Fri. 8am-4pm. The **airport** (tel. 28 322) is 6km south near Laganas.

Buses: 42 Filita St. (tel. 22 255), on the corner of Eleftheriou St. (6 blocks along the water from Solomou Sq., then 1 block back). Long-distance buses piggyback on the ferry to Patras (3 per day, 3hr., 1175dr) and then to Athens (4 per day, 6hr., 4035dr). Schedules for local service posted outside the bus station. A more complete list is available at the info window here. Buses run to Volimes (3 per day, 420dr), Vasiliko (Porto Roma) and Geraka (2 per day, ½hr., 250dr), Alykes (4 per day, ½hr., 250dr), Argasi (7 per day, 175dr), Tsilivi (9 per day, 175dr), and Laganas (12 per day, 175dr). Buses run less frequently Sat.-Sun., and the schedule changes often, so ask for the updated schedule at the desk.

Ferries: Arrive at Zakinthos Town port from Killini on the Peloponnese (4-6 per day, 1½hr., 1050dr). Also from Ag. Nikolaos to Pesado in Cephalonia (2 per day, 1½hr., 805dr). Tickets available at the **boat agencies** along the waterfront. For more info call the port police (tel. 22 417). Some agencies run a bus to the north of the island for the Cephalonia ferry (departing from Skinari and Ag. Nikolaos).

Flying Dolphins: Run to Argostoli on Cephalonia (2 per day, 45min., 5200dr), Ithaka (2 per day, 1½hr., 6085dr), and Lefkada (2 per day, 2¼hr., 7375dr).

Taxis: Vasileos Georgiou B (tel. 28 655). Also Solomou Sq. (tel. 23 628).

Car Rental: Hertz, 38 Lombardou St. (tel. 45 706), on the waterfront. Cars from 15,100dr per day and 72dr per km. Many moped places also rent cars. Must be 21. Open 8am-1:30pm and 5:30-9pm.

Moped Rental: Try **Stamatis Rental,** near the customs building on Lombardou St. (tel. 23 673). Mopeds 2500dr per day, bicycles 600dr. Open 8:30am-9pm.

Laundromat: To Magiko, 71 Foskolou St. Dry cleaning, too. Open Mon. and Thurs.-Fri. 8am-1:30pm and 5:30-9pm, Tues.-Wed. and Sat. 8am-2pm.

Hospital: (tel. 22 515, -514), above the city center. Open 24 hr.

ACCOMMODATIONS

Most people stay outside Zakinthos Town, near the beaches. Signs for "Rooms to Let" plaster every road on the island, and several excellent campgrounds dot the shore (see Around the Island, below). If you find a place outside town, don't worry—buses are frequent and taxis inexpensive on the main roads.

Rooms in Zakinthos Town are expensive and scarce in July and August. If you're stuck in town for a night try the **Ionion Hotel,** 18 Alex. Roma (tel. 42 511), which offers clean rooms with big balconies (singles 3000dr, doubles 5000dr). For "Rooms to Let" near town, call **Fotis Giatras** (tel. 23 392; no English spoken). Located 2km from a popular beach. (Singles 5500dr, doubles 8500dr; moped rental 2200dr per day). Taxis from town to Giatras' place cost roughly 820dr.

FOOD

The restaurants clustered in Ag. Markou Sq. are a tad overpriced, but a *souvlaki-pita* or a *tiropita* will set you back a mere 250dr. At the corner of Rizospaston and Ignatiou, **To Tavernaki** serves wonderful veal with potatoes (1100dr). There's a well-stocked **market** on Lombardou St. between the gas stations (open daily 8am-2pm and 6-8pm), and another one block back on Filita. Day or night, head to the café-bar **Platia San Marco,** which dominates the square. They play loud, groovy English disco music, and have a diverse clientele. (Mixed drinks 800-1200dr.) On your way home from the Venetian castle, you can stop at the **House of Latas** (tel. 26 178) and listen to their quartet sing Greek folk songs and local *cantadas.* (Open 8pm-2am; large swordfish with vegetables 1350dr.)

SIGHTS

Zakinthos is famous for its **Church of Agios Dionysios** (named not for the ancient Greek god, but in honor of St. Denis, the island's patron saint). Located roughly 10 blocks east on the waterfront, the church displays a silver chest which holds the saint's relics. Dress code strictly enforced. In Solomou Sq., the **Byzantine Museum** (tel. 42 714) houses icons from the "Ionian School," a distinctive local hybrid of Byzantine, Renaissance styles and other religious eras. (Open Tues.-Sun. 8:30am-2:30pm; admission 800dr, students 400dr; free on Sun.) Above the town is the **Venetian Castle** where Solomos wrote the words to the Greek national anthem. The castle affords a neat view of the town. (Open 8am-7pm; free.)

■■■ AROUND THE ISLAND

The terrain and beaches on Zakinthos will easily lure you away from the otherwise pleasant port town. It's possible to see the entire island, including the inaccessible western cliffs, by boat (leave daily at 9am from Zakinthos Town; 8hr.; 7500dr, lunch included). Local tourist offices also offer a bus tour of the entire island on Thursdays (3500dr). Boats make excursions to the blue caves, turtle beach, and "Smuggler's Wreck." Inquire at the tourist police or agencies. To explore independently, tour the island by moped (there's at least one rental place at each beach) or bus. Because the island is developing rapidly, many new roads won't appear on maps, but the most recent map available is the yellow Zakinthos map found at kiosks (350dr).

The beaches at **Laganas,** 10km south, have been mangled by large hotels, souvenir stands, and mobs of tourists. If you must stay, try **Laganas Camping** (tel. 51 708, -585), which maintains a pool (person 1350dr, car 800dr, small tent 730dr, large tent 1100dr). The white-sanded **Tsilivi Beach** remains one of the best beaches on the island, but unfortunately, many other people also realize this. **Tsilivi Camping** (tel. 44 754), also called Zante Camping, is Zakinthos' only campsite located on a beach; it has a cafeteria and minimarket (person 1120dr, car 930dr, small tent 850dr, large tent 1080dr, 10% discount for *Let's Go* users). From Zakinthos Town, walk to the beach along the asphalt road skirting the shore. **Planos,** just inland, has plenty of rooms. **Buses** run from Zakinthos Town to the beach (5 per day, 165dr).

Unscathed beaches carpet the peninsula extending out to the town of **Vasilikos,** 16km from Zakinthos Town, and are most plentiful near **Porto Roma.** Signs for "Rooms to Let" coat the road to Vasilikos, especially near **Agios Nikolaos Beach.** On the other side of Vasilikos, facing Laganas Bay, lies **Gerakas Beach.** Daily **buses** leave Zakinthos Town for Vasilikos (2 per day, 250dr).

It is a 5-min. walk from Gerakas to **Turtle Bay.** For 9 million years, the 100-150kg. mothers-to-be of the *Caretta caretta* species of sea turtle have returned from Africa to these beaches to deposit their eggs safely in the softest sand in Greece. Once in danger of becoming hotel property in the early 80s, the area is now a protected site. The *Caretta caretta*, commonly known as a Loggerhead turtle, only lays her eggs at night, when no humans are allowed on the beach. But if you visit during the day, you might get lucky and see a pregnant 150-kg turtle splashing towards you. Concern for the turtles' environment may prompt you to swim elsewhere.

Alykes, 16km from Zakinthos Town, is more pleasant and less crowded than its counterparts in the south. Filled with romantic restaurants and fringed with soft, clean sand beaches, Alykes gets somewhat crowded, although less so than the other resort towns. For spacious, clean, balconied doubles with bath (5000dr), ask at **Montes Restaurant** (or Jimmy's Place; tel. 83 101, -2), off the main drag. The **Apollo Restaurant,** on the edge of town, has fantastic chicken *souvlaki* (850dr). For a post-feast party, head to **Disco Dream** (beer 450dr).

The residents of the sprawling old village of **Volimes** specialize in needlepoint and crochet. Bring cash because this is the perfect opportunity to get a cheap, colorful rug, or other non-tacky presents (no credit cards accepted). One kilometer east up the hill in the upper part of the village (Ano Volimes), the **Women's Agricultural Tourist Cooperative** in the main square finds rooms with a local family. If the office is closed, inquire about "Rooms to Let" at the *pantopoleion* (grocery store) opposite, or the **police** (tel. 31 204) next door. Crumbling medieval bell towers and abandoned windmills dot the lower part of the village.

At the extreme north tip of Zakinthos is the tiny village of **Korithi,** locally known as Agios Nikolaos, from where the ferry to Cephalonia departs. Special buses occasionally come out to meet the ferry (ask at the bus station in Zakinthos Town). Here you can embark on a visit to the beautiful **blue caves,** seen only from the water. A 1-hr. motorboat excursion from the beach costs roughly 1000dr per person; you can also rent canoes and other small craft on the tiny beach.

Turtles turtles

The largest turtle in the world, second only to the leatherback, **Loggerheads** (*Caretta caretta*) are a species of marine turtle that roam the Atlantic, Caribbean, and Mediterranean seas, nesting every spring and summer on coastal lands from Britain to Argentina and Africa, often after strenuous migrations. Their name comes from their massive heads, crowned with looming and soulful brown eyes; their disproportionate skull does not, as one might hope, house a brain of equal size, but rather accommodates an extremely powerful jaw-closing muscles, handy for the turtles' primarily carnivorous diet. Loggerhead turtles weigh 100-150kg and grow to an adult size of 1m. Their smooth, elongated carapace, or upper shell, is covered with red and brown markings, as is their thick, leathery skin. Females tirelessly deposit roughly 100 eggs in each clutch 3-4 times per nesting season, every 14-17 days. After August, hapless hatchlings can be seen frantically scurrying to their watery homes.

Humans are a major threat to this endangered species. The bright lights of tourism and the commercial development of beaches and nearby towns is rapidly depriving *Caretta caretta* of their nesting habitats—not only in the Ionian Islands and the Aegean and Mediterranean coasts of Turkey (see p. 491), but also on American Atlantic coasts as well. Preservation of the nesting beaches can ensure that Greek natives and visitors alike will be able to appreciate these peaceful animals for years to come.

LEFKADA (LEFKAS) ΛΕΥΚΑΔΑ

Separated from Greece by a 50m canal, Lefkada resembles mainland Greece shrunken and transmuted into a floating resort. Although Lefkada has some of the least spoiled beaches in Greece, the atmosphere in town is less than enthralling. The hospitality of Lefkada's inhabitants swells the farther away from the congested northeast edge of the island you travel. According to Thucydides, Lefkada (Greek for white rock) was part of the mainland until 427 BC, when inhabitants dug a canal. The modern bridge, which connects Lefkada to the mainland, has only recently replaced the archaic chain-operated ferry built by Emperor Augustus.

■■■ LEFKADA TOWN

Lefkada Town, directly across from the mainland, is untouristed and humid, with some picturesque streets and squares. Overall, however, the town seems a poor, dusty copy of upscale Greek resort towns.

Orientation and Practical Information There is no tourist office, but the **tourist police** (tel. 26 450; open7am-10pm), a few blocks to the right of Lefkada Town's bus station (facing the water), offer handy brochures, and will call around for rooms. The tourist police are in the same building as the **police station,** 30 Iroon Politechniou (tel. 22 346; 24 hr.). The **post office** is at 1 Stratigou Melas St. (open Mon.-Fri. 7:30am-2:30pm; English spoken). For the **OTE,** turn right off Stratigou Melas to Pataneromenis St., head back towards the beginning of town, and look for the tower. (Open daily 7am-10pm.) English-speaking travel agents provide similar services as the tourist office. Turn left from the bus station and follow the road around to the westerly side of Lefkada Town's waterfront. The first pedestrian-like alleyway, running inland, becomes **Dörpfeld Street,** the main street, lined with tourist services. (Wilhelm Dörpfeld was the archaeologist who unsuccessfully tried to identify Lefkada as Homer's Ithaka.) For budget travel try **Lefkada Travel** (tel. 22 430) on Dörpfeld St., **Melas Travel** (tel. 22 538, -905) or **St. Maura Travel** (tel./fax 25 119). All travel agencies are open normal business hours (8am-2:30pm and 6-8pm), sometimes longer in high season. The **Agricultural Bank** stands opposite the Hotel Patras off the same street, on the inside corner of Antistasis Sq. (Open Mon.-Thurs. 8am-2pm, Fri. 8am-1pm.) From the bus station (tel. 22 364) on the waterfront, **buses** cross the canal to Athens (5 per day, 5½hr., 5100dr) and Aktion (4 per day, 300dr). To reach Preveza, take the ferry from Aktion across the mouth of Amvrakikos Bay (every 20min., 15min., 80dr). The 21km journey by taxi costs 2500-4000dr. The **local island buses** run to Nidri (16 per day, ½hr., 240dr), Agios Nikitas (5 per day, 20min., 200dr), Poros (2 per day, 45min., 380dr), and Vasiliki (4 per day, 1hr., 550dr). Be sure to pick up a bus schedule brochure at the station (or from tour offices) detailing additional transit routes and indicating return times. **Ferries** link Lefkada with Ithaka and Cephalonia to the south. From Vasiliki in Lefkada, ferries make the run to Fiskardo on Cephalonia (2-3 per day, 1hr., 935dr), then to Ithaka (1¾hr., 985dr) and on to Sami on Cephalonia (2½hr., 1700dr). From Nidri in Lefkada, ferries sail to Cephalonia and Frikes on Ithaka (3 per day, 935dr). For Vasiliki ferry info call 31 555; for Nidri 92 427. Travel offices have info and sell tickets. Lefkada may well be **excursion boat** paradise. Excursion boats **Nidri Star** and **Vassiliki Star,** bearing their home port namesakes, run daily day-long cruises to Cephalonia, Ithaka, and Skorpios (9am departure, roughly 3500dr). Excursion boats also shuttle beach devotees to Lefkada's numerous cloistered beaches, including the famously beautiful **Porto Katsiki,** inaccessible by bus. Some also stop at the cave of **Papanikoli.** Inquire at waterfront kiosks or travel offices, or try to read the hard-to-miss signs aboard the little boats. **Postal Code:** 31100; **Telephone Code:** 0645.

Accommodations The charming and clean **Hotel To Byzantino** (tel. 22 629) is at the end of Dörpfeld St. next to the harbor (singles 4135dr, doubles 7600dr, triples 9420dr). Look for the "Hoivendar Hotel" sign. Farther up the street in the corner of the main square, **Hotel Patras** (tel. 22 359) offers cozy, clean rooms overlooking the cafés (singles 6000dr, doubles 8500dr, triples 10,000dr). Also try asking a travel company for rooms (doubles from 6500dr, triples from 8000dr).

Food A jolly owner makes for a good time at the popular **Taverna Pyrofani** in a whitewashed building roughly two blocks from the water on Dörpfeld (entrees 900-1200dr; open daily noon-midnight). Also try **Regentos,** off the main square on Verrioti St.; follow the signs to the self-proclaimed cosmic tavern. (*Mousaka* 700dr, grilled meats 1000dr; open daily 7:30pm-2am.)

Frolic through the famous **Folklore Festival,** now in its 33rd year, in the first and third weeks of August. (Details from Lefkada Travel; tickets roughly 500dr.) Also look for the **folklore museum** signs to the right of the main square. The small museum offers a taste of old Lefkada. (Open Mon.-Fri. 10am-1pm and 7-10pm; admission 500dr.) Groove over to the bizarre **Phonograph Museum** (open Mon.-Fri. 9am-1pm and 6-11pm), past the square to the left; inquire at the meat market for access. The **Archaeological Museum,** 1km down the road to Ag. Nikitas, is tiny and worthwhile for only the most dedicated, since the majority of Lefkada's treasures are in Athens or in Ioannina. (Open 9am-12:30pm and 6-8pm; admission 500dr.)

■■■ AROUND THE ISLAND

While Lefkada Town has no sandy beaches, the north half of the west coast offers miles of deserted white pebbles and clear water. Rent a moped at **Santa's Rentals** (tel. 25 250), or one of the other places to the right of Dörpfeld St. on the water port (3000dr per day), and follow the signs for Kathisma. The best stretch lies north of **Agios Nikitas.** Buses leave from Lefkada Town for Ag. Nikitas (6 per day, 200dr). The road there leads to the monastery **Moni Faneromenis** (tel. 22 275), with a sweeping view of the ocean and one resident monk (monastery open 7am-10pm; free). Follow the footpath through the woods for a pick-up game of basketball with the students at the monastery school. Michael Jordan look out.

Nidri, a strip of garish tourist agencies and tacky cafés, ensnares unwary travelers solely because it's the last stop of the otherwise delightful Frikes-Nidri ferry. The waterfront, flush with pleasure boats, boasts a handsome view of the dappled coves of numerous small islands. The **post office** (open Mon.-Fri. 7:30am-2pm) and **OTE** (open Mon.-Fri. 8:30am-12:30pm and 5:30-9:30pm) are on the main street, occasionally referred to as Center St. Many stores and tour offices display signs indicating telephone access for local and international calls on their premises. **Buses** from Nidri go to Lefkada (15 per day, ½hr., 240dr), Vlino (16 per day, 150dr) and Vasiliki (5 per day, 300dr). "Rooms to Let" are scattered along the main and virtually only street, parallel to the waterfront. In July and August, when the entire island slumps under the burgeoning weight of tourists, rooms are always full, and prices inevitably high (doubles from 7000dr). The self-explanatory **Beautiful View** pension (tel. 92 361), along the main street to the left from the ferry, offers doubles for 6000dr. On the road from Nidri to Lefkada rests **Camping Episkopos** (tel. 23 043 or 71 388; person 850dr, car 500dr, small tent 600dr, large tent 700dr). To escape the pervasive manufactured appeal of Nidri, climb the 5km to **Neochori** at dusk. Three kilometers south is the tiny village of **Vliho,** accessible by bus from Lefkada (9 per day, 150dr), with a striking church (proper dress required) in an idyllic setting of wildflowers and cypress trees. **Thesimi Camping** (tel. 95 374), on the road from Nidri to Vliho, has rates similar to Camping Episkopos.

Vasiliki, at the south tip of Lefkada Island, with white pebbled beaches and cafés drawn straight up to the water's edge, bears charms both tranquil and invigorating. **Buses:** 5 per day from Lefkada, 550dr; 5 per day from Nidri, 300dr. Smaller and currently less touristed than Nidri, Vasiliki is becoming increasingly popular with the young international watersports crowd. Rated among the world's finest **windsurfing** resorts, "the 3rd best in Europe," Vasiliki is usually graced with consistent gentle winds in the morning, which rise to steady force-five gales in the afternoon, to tempt and tease novices and experts alike. The **Vasiliki Club** (tel. 31 588), on the beach in front of the campground, offers board rentals (3500dr per hr., 8000dr per morning, 10,000dr per afternoon) and instruction (6500dr includes tuition, simulator practice, and 1hr. board rental; open 10am "until the wind stops;" rescue boats on call until everyone's safely ashore).

The main road running inland from the waterfront winds past the **post office** (open Mon.-Fri. 8am-2pm). Also along this road, before the post office, is **Samba Tours** (tel. 31 520, -555; fax 31 522), an all-purpose tour office willing to "help and advise by fax or phone" (open daily 8:30am-11pm). The **police** (tel. 31 218; 24 hr.) are a short distance inland along the road cornered at the waterfront by the Alexander the Great Restaurant. From Vasiliki, 2-3 **ferries** per day run to Fiskardo, Cephalonia (1hr., 935dr), Ithaki (1¾hr., 985dr), and Sami (2½hr., 1700dr). Inquire at the kiosk next to the pier. To contact the **health center,** call 31 065. **Postal Code:** 31082; **Telephone Code:** 0645.

Rooms are plentiful and signs easy to spot, particularly along the road leading uphill from the bus stop (on the waterfront and along the main post road beyond the post office). The popular **Vasiliki Beach Camping** (tel. 31 308, -457; fax 31 458) boasts superlative amenities and rests a hop, skip, and a jump away from the beach. Head for the beach and make a right on the road running inland just before the Windsurfing Club Center #1 (person 1450dr, children 1000dr, under 4 free; small tent 1050dr, large tent 1500dr, cars 1000dr, trailers 1600dr). The **Galaxy Market** (tel. 31 221), around the corner at the back side of the ferry dock, lets tidy, simple rooms (singles 6000dr, doubles 7000dr). The **Vasiliki Bay Hotel** (tel. 23 567 or 31 667; fax 22 131), one of two upscale hotels in town, is located off the road running inland from the Alexander the Great Restaurant, around the corner from the **Blue Garden Chinese Restaurant** (dinner only). (Singles 12,000dr, doubles 17,000dr, triples 20,500dr, all with private bath.)

Full meals can be inexpensive and well-prepared in Vasiliki, even in the waterfront cafés and eateries. Most have similar menus and prices, so choose your haunt according to what aspect of sun and sea seems most appealing. Give the **Alexander the Great Restaurant** a try; it is on the waterfront on the way to the beach (mixed salad 500dr—with fresh parsley; fried kalamari 600dr—with a touch of thyme). **Zeus' Bar,** on the waterfront, a haven for the high-spirited, serves up drinks to soothe the salt- and sun-weary (particularly refreshing is the orange juice and soda water, in a tall glass, 300dr; open daily morning to late night). For a morning treat or for bus journey snack provisions, try the **bakery** above the bus stop. Scoop into their big barrels of tasty sweet rolls (molasses and a taste of caraway 50dr).

At the southernmost tip of the island there's a **lighthouse** built on the site of the Temple of Lefkas Apollo. Worshipers exorcised evil with an annual sacrifice here. The victim, usually a criminal or a mentally ill person thought to be possessed, was thrown into the sea from the cliffs. Live birds were tied to the victim's arms and legs for amusement as well as aerodynamic advantages. It was from these 70m cliffs that the ancient poet Sappho leapt to her death when Phaon rejected her. The cliff, called **"Sappho's Leap,"** is known in Lefkada as Kavos tis Kiras (Cape of the Lady).

ITHAKA (ITHAKI) ΙΘΑΚΗ

The legendary home of Odysseus, Ithaka boasts an impressive reputation and a mild geography. Sparse seaside villages and unspoiled coves encircle the mountains where Penelope waited faithfully for her husband. Vathi, the main town, is a pastel harbor with stunning architecture and not much else. Ithaka offers little to do, but it's a wonderful place for doing little.

■■■ VATHI

Vathi is the main port and largest town on the island. Ferries to Ithaka dock here or at **Piso Aetos,** a deserted harbor at the foot of a mountain that is a 10-min. ride to the left of Vathi (taxis cost 1500-2000dr). The casual town curves around the edge of a long, natural harbor (the largest such harbor in all of Greece) and is almost completely circumscribed by mountains. In the evening, the town's cats, children, and scooters crowd around the right-hand side of the waterfront with equal disregard for passers-by. Art galleries, craft stores, and souvenir shops control the waterfront, which sprawls at the far right-hand corner of the horseshoe as you face the town.

Orientation and Practical Information The **post office** is on the main square (open Mon.-Fri. 8am-1:30pm). The **OTE** (open Mon.-Sat. 7:30am-3:10pm) sits on the water. The **Marlines** office, located opposite the ferry landing, keeps somewhat irregular hours, but is open when boats come in. One block in from the corner of the harbor near Polyctor Tours is the **National Bank of Greece** (open Mon.-Fri. 8am-2pm). Getting to Ithaka will be easier for you than it was for Odysseus (although with the capriciousness of Greek ferry schedules, you never know); the web of **ferries** around the Ionian islands enmeshes Ithaka. Boats run between Frikes on Ithaka to Nidri on Lefkada (2 per day, 2½hr., 960dr). From Vathi there are ferries to Agia Efimia on Cephalonia (4pm, 1hr., 970dr), Sami on Cephalonia (7am, 1hr., 960dr), and Astakos on the mainland (11am, 2hr., 1296dr). There are also boats from Piso Ateos to Sami (7am, 2 and 8:30pm, 500dr), and to Brindisi in Italy (3-4 per week, 12-14hr., 15,500dr, no student discounts). Be sure to check boat schedules at your port of departure. **Flying Dolphins** run one per day, with stops at Zakinthos (6000dr), Cephalonia (2040dr), Patras (6120dr), and Lefkada (2445dr). **Delas Tours** (tel. 33 103, -15) sell hydrofoil tickets. Most **moped rental** places charge roughly 3000dr per day. Try your luck at **Moto-Rent** (tel. 32 035) near Lazarus Tours. You can also rent small motorboats (where the little boats dock) for 8000dr. For a **taxi,** call 33 030. The **bookstores** (tel. 33 204 for the one on the left, tel. 32 413 for the one on the right) on either side of the bank sell English-language reading material ranging from Homer to *Beverly Hills 90210* fan magazines. The **hospital** can be reached at 32 222, the **police** at 32 205, the **port police** at 32 909, and the **pharmacy** at 32 251. **Postal Code:** 28300; **Telephone Code:** 0674.

Accommodations Helpful, friendly **Lazarus Tours** (tel. 32 587), open 9am-10pm, rents the cheapest rooms (doubles w/bath 6000dr). Farther from the ferry landing, **Polyctor Tours** (tel. 33 120, open 8am-10pm) also helps find rooms starting at 8000dr for a double w/bath (50% student discount in June and Sept.). The chunky **Hotel Mentor** (tel. 32 433, -292) is next to the OTE. This hotel's high prices (singles 8550dr, doubles 11,5300dr, triples 16,800dr; breakfast included) are flexible, and, unfortunately, the lowest in town. Your best bet is a private room. The average peak season room price in Vathi is roughly 7000dr per night, although there are a few rooms with shared baths starting as low as 4000dr. Freelance **camping** on the beach under the eucalyptus trees or any place else outside is generally tolerated, provided that campers clean up after themselves.

Food Restaurants tend to be expensive. To save a few *drachmae* on food, try **Fast Food,** at the side of the harbor away from the ferry landing. The fare is better than the name suggests. In the center of town, one block back from the water and across from the scooter rental place, is **Taverna To Trexantiri** (tel. 33 066), popular among locals (entrees average 1100dr).

Sights The **Vathi Archaeological Museum** is small but free (open Mon.-Fri. 9am-3:30pm). Those with poetic imaginations may want to make the 45-min. climb up to the **Cave of the Nymphs,** where Odysseus hid the treasure the Phoenicians bestowed upon him. To get here, walk around the harbor with the water on your right, and follow the signs. Peerless views of Vathi unfold during the climb. Bring a flashlight. (Admission 200dr.) It's a 2-hr. hike southeast up a well-marked but rocky road to the Homeric **Arethousa Fountain,** along a steep mountain path through pear orchards. In summer, the fountain is dry. To find the path to the fountain, follow Evmeou St. up the hill until it turns to dirt, and look for signs. Spend an afternoon sifting through the multicolored stones of the beach at **Piso Aetos Bay,** 15km from town. Ask at Polyctor Tours about the **Greek Theater Festival** (late August) and the popular **Music Festival** (early July; Greek folk and modern music) which take place in Vathi. There is a **Wine Festival** in Perahori on the last Sunday of July.

■■■ AROUND ITHAKA ISLAND

An excursion from Vathi transports to scenic, remote villages scattered across Ithaka's rocky coast. The island's one **bus** runs north from Vathi, passing through the villages of Lefki, Stavros, Platrithiai, Frikes, and Kioni. Leaving Vathi at 6:30am and 10:40am, it arrives in Kioni 1hr. later (300dr). The stunning road skirts both sides of the isthmus, and offers superlative views of the strait of Ithaka and Cephalonia on the west, and of the coastline on the east. Check the times of return buses before setting out; taxis from Kioni to Vathi cost roughly 3800dr.

Stavros, the highest point on the island, merits a visit for its mountaintop location, if not its lone sight. The schoolmaster's wife has a key to a small museum at the alleged site of **Odysseus' Palace,** recommended for fanatical Homerists; a small tip is expected. Homer described this site as the place from which three different waters could be seen. Still visible from this point are the Bays of Frikes, Aphales, and Polis.

CEPHALONIA ΚΕΦΑΛΛΩΝΙΑ

The east and west coasts of arid Cephalonia are generally steep and rocky, and the inland areas are forbiddingly mountainous. In contrast to many of the other Ionian islands which have been home to vacationers since Roman times, Cephalonia, with its rugged countryside, has remained relatively tourist-free despite its beautiful, sandy beaches, easy bus connections, friendly people, and charming towns. In this century, Cephalonia has endured a plucky but troubled history. When the Germans invaded in 1943, 9000 Italian soldiers occupying the island mutinied and resisted their Nazi "allies" for seven days. Only 33 Italians survived. Ten years later, a disastrous earthquake forced the island to rebuild. Because of this, only Fiskardo, which was relatively undamaged, retains the pastel Neoclassical look associated with the Ionian islands. Nonetheless, Cephalonia's coasts and inland cities, which are home to unique flora, are the perfect place for a relaxed vacation.

■■■ ARGOSTOLI

The capital of Cephalonia, Argostoli is a busy, noisy town whose palm-tree-lined streets are regularly jammed with traffic. Argostoli hosts an international **singing festival** in late August.

ORIENTATION AND PRACTICAL INFORMATION

Tourist Office: (tel. 22 248, -466). At the port. Gives free maps and offers candid advice on accommodations, restaurants, and beaches in the area. Also has a list of "Rooms to Let." Open Mon.-Fri. 8am-10pm.

Tourist Police: 52 Metaxa St. (tel. 22 200), right of the bus station. Little English spoken. 24 hr.

Post Office: (tel. 23 173). Walk two blocks inland from the port to D. Konstantinou, the town's main street, and turn right. Open Mon.-Fri. 7:30am-2pm. **Postal Code:** 28100.

OTE: Uphill edge of the square (open 7am-11:30pm). Telephone Code: 0671.

Banks: Sprinkled along the waterfront and Konstantinou St. (open Mon.-Thurs. 8am-2pm, Fri. 8am-1:30pm); note that the National Bank does not have currency exchange.

Flights: The **Olympic Airways** office occupies 7 R. Vergoti St. (tel. 28 808, -81). Olympic flies to Athens at least once per day (14,100dr).

Buses: The bus station (tel. 22 281) is on the waterfront. (Open 7am-8pm.) Buses head to Skala (Mon.-Sat. 4 per day, 550dr, Sun. 10am), Poros (4 per day, 1¾hr., 650dr), Fiskardo (2 per day, 1½hr., 750dr), Sami (4 per day, 360dr), Assos (2 per day, 1¼hr., 550dr), Ag. Gerasimos (3 per day, 9:30am-2pm, 220dr), and Kourkoumelata (4 per day, 7:15am-1:45pm, 180dr). There are also buses which piggyback on the ferry to Athens (7:45am and 1:30pm). Buses to Argostoli meet most of the **ferries** arriving in Sami (5 per day, 45min., 360dr). The road winds around hairpin curves, treating passengers to glorious mountain vistas, screaming engines, and high blood pressure.

Ferries: Unlike most islands, Cephalonia has several ports for different destinations. Buses connect Argostoli to other ports. From **Sami,** boats sail to Ithaka (daily at 4pm, 1hr., 960dr) and Patras (daily 8:45am, 2800dr). This is also the place to catch boats to Italy. Boats to Brindisi leave daily at 8:30am (14,700dr). Boats also leave for Bari (daily at 3pm, 15,950dr). From **Agia Efimia,** service links Cephalonia with Astakos on the mainland (2 per day, 9:15am and 5:30pm, 3½hr., 1700dr) and Ithaka (daily at 9:15am, 2400dr). From **Argostoli** boats go to Killini on the mainland (daily at 9am, 2360dr), and several boats shuttle to nearby Lixouri. Ferries also leave **Fiskardo** for Lefkada (daily 9:30am, 3:45 and 6pm, 1hr., 900dr). From **Pesada** you can get to Zakinthos (daily 7:45am and 5:30pm, 1hr., 830dr), and from **Poros** there are more boats to Killini (daily at 9:15am, 3:30 and 7:30pm, 1600dr). Check current times with travel agencies.

Car and Moped Rental: Myrtos Rent-a-Car (tel. 24 230 or 25 023). On the waterfront. Rents cars starting at 12,500dr per day (open 8:30am-1pm and 7-9:30pm). Mopeds options abound; try **Safe Moto** on the waterfront towards the bridge (2500-3500dr per day).

International Bookstore: Two blocks down from the post office, across from the church, **Petratos Bookstore** is stuffed with foreign newspapers and magazines. Open Mon.-Sat. 8am-1pm and 5-9pm, Sun. 8am-noon; reduced hours in winter.

ACCOMMODATIONS

Cheap rooms are rather scarce in Argostoli. The **Hotel Parthenon** (tel. 22 246), a spiffy white building on a small side street left of the post office, offers sunny balconies and doubles at cheap prices (singles 3000dr, doubles 5500dr). The **Argostoli Beach Campground** (tel. 23 487), 1½km from town, is a convenient option (open April-Oct., person 1400dr, car 935dr, small tent 800dr, large tent 1250dr).

FOOD

Restaurants by the water are pricey. A wallet- and palate-friendly choice is **Restaurant Anonymus** (tel. 22 403), 100m left of the bus station (entrees 880-1100dr). Another fun place is **Restaurant Hellenic,** 8 Ag. Gerasimos (tel. 23 529), one block inland from the port police; excellent service (entrees 800-1500dr).

SIGHTS

From Petratos Bookstore, go one block farther; you'll hit the square and the **Argostolian Archaeological Museum** (open Tues.-Sun. 8:30am-3:30pm, 400dr). From the museum, turn right onto R. Vergoti St. and continue two blocks to reach Corgialenios Library, which houses the **Historical and Folk Museum** (tel. 28 835). This museum is crammed with household belongings from the 19th century. Argostoli's French coffee cups, English top hats, and antique dolls all create a picture of confident luxury. Best of all are the photographs of Argostoli during the last century, including shots of the damage from the devastating 1953 earthquake and the ensuing reconstruction. (Open Mon.-Sat. 8:30am-2:30pm; admission 400dr.)

■ NEAR ARGOSTOLI

The Venetian **Castle of St. George,** 9km southeast of Argostoli, rests on a hill overlooking the village of Travliata. Chug along the road to Skala and turn right when the road splits. **Buses** travel to the site (3 per day, 10min., 135dr). From the battlements, admire the panorama that inspired Lord Byron. (Open Tues.-Sun. 8:30am-3pm; free.) To swim at **Lassi,** one of the island's best sandy beaches, follow the road leading from the town to the airport. There are several options for exploring more of the island. Boats leave regularly for **Lixouri,** in the center of the west peninsula (every hr., 30min., 220dr). Once home to the satiric poet Lascaratos, Lixouri offers miles of practically tourist-free coastline. Rent **mopeds** at several places in Lixouri; **buses** run to several smaller villages in the area.

A few beaches and interesting towns dot the island south of Argostoli. One of the best beaches is at **Ormos Lourda,** in the middle of the south coast; closer to Argostoli is **Platis Gialos** (7 buses per day, 30min., 150dr). Here visit one of Byron's adopted towns (though his house no longer exists) at **Metaxata,** or see **Kourkoumelata,** a village completely restored by a Greek tycoon after the 1953 earthquake. If you decide to stay, check out the comfortable **Hotel Kourkoumi** (tel. 41 645), which offers doubles w/baths and breakfast for 6000dr. A many-layered *tholos* tomb found in the village of **Dargoti** is thought to be Odysseus' grave, supporting the theory that Homer's Ithaka was really modern-day Cephalonia. **Poros,** on the southeast coast, is a modern coastal town with a beach; "Rooms to Let" are everywhere. Buses run from Argostoli (4 per day, 1½hr., 650dr).

On the night of August 15, the nearby village of **Omala** hosts a festival and a vigil in the saint's church. East of Argostoli is the monastery **Agios Gerasimos,** in which a monk's preserved corpse lies in state; the town goes wild on the saint's namedays (Oct. 20 and Aug. 16). Contact the tourist office for more info. Omala has an excellent **Archaeological Museum** (tel. 28 300; open 8:30am-3:30pm).

By far the best beach on the island is the pebble-and-sand beach at **Scala.** The town itself is prohibitively expensive (7000dr for plain singles), but the beach to the right of the rocks is heavenly. Three buses per day come from Argostoli; the latest returns at 5pm. If you must stay, ask at **Scalini Tours** for rooms, and catch a bite at the **Sun Rise Restaurant** (beef stew 850dr).

■■■ SAMI

A small town on a harbor surrounded by lush green hills, Sami stays quiet during the day, offering an ethereal small pebble beach. By night the town waxes romantic to the glimmer of lighted ships in the harbor.

Orientation and Practical Information The blue and white Hotel Kyma, two blocks from the ferry landing, dominates Sami's main square. I. Metaxa St., which bears right as you face the hotel, leads to the **post office** (open Mon.-Fri. 7:30am-2pm). The **OTE** (open Mon.-Fri. 7:30am-3:10pm) is opposite the cathedral, near the **police station** (open 24 hr.). There is no official tourist office, but the police may be able to answer your questions. The **Marketou Travel/Strintzis Line Office,** on the waterfront just to the left of the ferry landing in Sami (tel. 22 055 or 23 021), is also very helpful. You can **exchange money** at the **bank** on Sami's waterfront (open Mon.-Fri. 8am-2pm) or at most of the travel agencies. **Postal Code:** 28080; **Telephone Code:** 0674.

Accommodations Lodgings in Sami cost 20-40% less off-season. Try the **Hotel Kyma** (tel. 22 064) in the town square. Many of the clean rooms offer spectacular views and cool breezes. (Singles 4500dr, doubles 9000dr.) The **Hotel Melissani** (tel. 22 464), several blocks back from the water on the left side of town as you face inland, offers lovely views of the harbor and surrounding hills. (Singles 7700dr, doubles 9695dr.) The rooms above the **Riviera Restaurant** (tel. 22 246) on the waterfront go quickly in summer. (Doubles w/bath 5500dr.) **Karavomilos Beach Camping** (tel. 22 480) is just off the beach, 700m to your right while facing inland. The affable management offers laundry facilities and a minimarket (person 1350dr, car 960dr, small tent 910dr, large tent 1430dr).

Sights The caves of **Melissani** and **Drograti,** two sites near Sami, impress both troglodytes and surface-dwellers. Melissani, the more impressive of the two, can be reached by foot from Sami (30min.). Follow I. Metaxa and turn right at the sign for **Agia Efimia,** then follow the signs past the village of Karavomilos. At the lake, guides punt around the two large caverns flooded with sparkling water, studded with lichen-covered stalactites and squirming with eels and fish. For best viewing, go when the sun is high. (Open until nightfall; admission 950dr; a polite 50dr tip is expected.) To reach Drograti, 4km from Sami, head inland on the road to Argostoli and follow the signs. (Open until nightfall; admission 750dr.) Just 10km north of Sami at the other end of the bay is the pretty harbor town of Ag. Efimia (2 buses per day from Sami, 10:15am and 4pm, 360-550dr).

■■■ AROUND CEPHALONIA

Cliffs plunge into the sea along the coastal road north from Argostoli or Sami to Fiskardo. The beaches of **Agia Kyriaki** and **Myrtos** on this road are generally serene. Signposts on the main road after the hamlet of Divarata advertise Myrtos, but swim cautiously there; the undertow can be powerful and sudden. Roughly 4km up the road are the fragrant gardens of **Assos,** joined by a narrow isthmus to an island with a Venetian fortress. A daily bus from Argostoli departs at 2pm, returning the next day at 6:45am (550dr); the ½-hr. walk from the main road is challenging.

The road north ends at **Fiskardo,** the only town on the island left undamaged by the 1953 earthquake and thus the only remaining example of 18th- and 19th-century Cephalonian architecture. Once called Panoramos, Fiskardo was magnanimously renamed after Robert Guiscard, a Norman, who died here in 1085 while attempting to conquer the town. A ruined Norman church visible from the harbor is believed to predate Robert by some 800 years. Alongside the dilapidated old Venetian lighthouse, pine-sheltered campsites await. Rooms are expensive (doubles 7000-10,000dr), but the cheapest are on the road out of town past the bakery and left. The **Panoramos** is Fiskardo's most accessible hotel (tel. 51 340; doubles w/bath 13,000dr). Restaurants line the harbor and are fairly expensive. The **Restaurant Fiskardo,** along the harbor, serves the tasty local specialty *kreatopita* (meat pie). (Open noon-midnight.) Fiskardo's beach is unbeatable: it lies ½km out of town on the road back to Argostoli and offers flat rocks for sunbathing. One **bus** per day arrives from Sami (1hr., 550dr). Two buses arrive daily from Argostoli (1½hr., 750dr), and there's a daily ferry connecting Sami and Fiskardo.

On August 15, an unusual and spooky festival in the village of **Markopoulo** in the southeast corner of the island celebrates the Assumption of the Blessed Virgin Mary. Celebrants hold an all-night church liturgy. According to legend, during the service hundreds of small harmless snakes with black crosses on their heads appear and slither over the icons.

Northeast Aegean Islands ΒΟΡΕΙΟΑΝΑΤΟΛΙΚΑ ΝΗΣΙΑ ΤΟΥ ΑΙΓΑΙΟΥ

After centuries of resisting the Ottoman Empire, the Northeast Aegean Islands have learned how to stay closely guarded. Though pirates and Ottomans no longer pose a threat, many of the islands continue to isolate themselves from an influx of tourism in hopes of preserving their traditional Greek atmosphere. In the North Aegean, intricate, rocky coastlines enclose thickly wooded mountains and bland port towns that give way to unspoiled villages and secluded beaches. Located only a few miles off the Turkish border, the islands have a sizable military presence and the large numbers of young soldiers may prove intimidating for single women. Less well traversed than any other archipelago, these islands remain both tranquil and resplendent. If you've been imagining undiluted Greek culture without the complicating intrusion of foreign influence, you may well find it here.

CHIOS ΧΙΟΣ

When the mythical hunter Orion drove all the wild beasts off Chios, grand pine, cypress and mastic trees sprouted on the vast mountainsides. Since antiquity, Chios has cultivated and exported mastic (*masticha,* a bitter-sweet, gummy resin used in varnishes, cosmetic creams, chewing gum, floor waxes, and many color television sets). Long both a military base and a center of Greek shipping, Chios has only recently been opened to the tourist industry, and the island remains pleasantly indifferent to the vagaries of foreigners. Chios' striking volcanic beaches, strewn with rounded black stones, and medieval villages are not easily accessible from the more popular Cyclades. While an increasing number of Northern Europeans visit the island, most of the tourists it attracts are Greeks and Greek-Americans visiting with their Chiotian families.

Sakız Adası (Mastic Island), as Chios is known in Turkish, has endured numerous invasions and catastrophes brought on by its prime location. The reputed birthplace of both Homer and Christopher Columbus, Chios has been successively under Venetian, Genoese, Turkish, and Greek rule since 1204. In 1822, a failed Greek rebellion against the Turks, who had ruled since 1566, led to the slaughter of more than 25,000 Greeks. The massacre drew European attention and sympathy to the Greek fight for independence, inspiring Lord Byron to join the struggle in which he eventually died. In 1881, a major earthquake brought more destruction to Chios. Foreign rule continued until Chios was reunited with Greece in 1912 after the Balkan Wars.

CHIOS TOWN

Chios Town is home to many sailors (identifiable by their red license plates), and several wealthy ship owners (identifiable by their fancy cars). Ravaged by German

TO KAVALA
TO ALEXANDROUPOLIS
Limenas
Neos Prinos
Theologos
Thassos
Kamariotisa
Therma
Samothrace
Alonia
Samothrace
Dardanelles
Gökçeada
Çanakkale
TO THESSALONIKI
Plaka
Sardai
Panagia
Bozcaada
Myrina
Moudros
Thanos
TURKEY
Limnos
Aegean Sea
TO KIMI
Molyvos
Mitilini Channel
Mandamados
Ayvalik
Eressos
Mitilini
Mesotopos
Agiassos
Lesvos
Plomari
Psara
Marmara
Andipsara
Limnos
Strait
Chios
Chios Town
Chios
Mesta
Çesme
GREECE
Pirgi
Emborios
Samos Town
Kokari
Karlovàssi
Pythagorion
TO PIRAEUS
Samos
Evdilos
Armenistis
Agios Kirikas
Ikaria
Fourni
Northeast Aegean Islands
N
0
50 miles
0
50 kilometers

troops during WWII, the unadorned waterfront, with its modern Athenian-style skyline, turns an indifferent face to the newcomer. Though it is packed with numerous restaurants, clubs, and cafés, as well as the requisite ferry offices and businesses, the waterfront, like the rest of Chios Town, endures tumultuous automotive frenzy.

ORIENTATION AND PRACTICAL INFORMATION

Most information and services, buses, and taxis are around **Vounakio Square,** the social center of town, which is located one to two blocks inland from the middle of the waterfront. Most points of interest around the island are accessible only from Chios Town, the source from which all transit routes radiate. Avoid the hassle of noisy traffic by understanding the city's rhythms. Catch a mid-afternoon snooze, or wait again until after 2am, when traffic dies down. Every night the waterfront closes itself off to traffic, cafés pack, and the promenade begins, offering pleasant respite from the clamor that roars after the midday shutdown. Between 9pm and 1am, this is the place to be.

Tourist Office: 18 Kanari St. (tel. 44 389). Turn off the *limani* (waterfront) onto Kanari St., towards the square. They'll be almost immediately to your left (look for the "i" sign, the official "information" designation). In addition to providing voluminous brochures, the friendly, attentive staff can give lists of accommodations, change money, and answer questions.

Port Police: (tel. 44 434). Friendly, located in the white building at the far corner of the northern side of the harbor. Open 24 hr.

Post Office: (tel. 23 407). Just after the Olympic Airways waterfront office, follow Omirou St. Open Mon.-Fri., 7:30am-2pm. **Postal Code:** 82100.

OTE: (tel. 23 599). Across from the tourist office. Open Mon.-Sat. 7am-11pm, Sun. 8am-10pm. **Telephone Code:** 0271.

Tourist Agencies: Your best friend on the island might just be found in **Hatzelenis "tourist office"** (tel. 26 743). To find them, when facing the water, turn left and walk down to the white building at the northern elbow of the harbor. Find rooms anywhere on the island, explains the ins and outs of Chios' chaos and *kleos* (glory), and makes travel arrangements, including daily trips to Turkey. They also have nifty old postcards at nifty old prices (50dr), and sell maps of Chios (300dr). Open daily 7am-1pm and 6-9pm, and usually when boats arrive (often late at night).

Banks: Several banks which offer **currency exchange** are located in the vicinity of the OTE and are open Mon.-Thurs. 8am-2pm, Fri. 8am-1:30pm. The **Ionian Bank** is at 16 Kanari, across from the tourist office (also open Sat. 9am-1pm). The **National, Commercial,** and Ionian banks have **ATMs.**

Flights: Olympic Airways (tel. 23 998; open Mon.-Fri. 8am-4pm). On the waterfront near the corner of Psychari St. Flies to Athens (4-6 per day, 13,000dr), Lesvos (2 per week, 6400dr), and Thessaloniki (2 per week, 21,000dr). The air schedule is much more convenient than the ferry schedule, which seems specially designed to deprive passengers of sleep.

Ferries: Travel to Piraeus (1 per day, 9hr., 4204dr), Lesvos (6 per week, 3hr., 2832dr, leaves at 4am), Samos (1-2 per week, 3hr., 2209dr), Patmos (2 per week, 7hr., 3449dr), Thessaloniki (1 per week, 18hr., 7152dr, leaves at 4am), and Kavala (1 per week, 16hr., 6072dr). Ferries reach Ikaria via Samos and Limnos via Kavala. There are also excursions to Çeşme on the Turkish coast (1-2 per day; off-season 2-4 per week; 40min.; 8000dr, round-trip 12,000dr, 4000dr port tax not included). The price of these trips may vary according to the boat company; compare prices at different agencies.

Flying Dolphins: Speed to Samos and Lesvos 3 times per week, but cost twice the ferry rate.

Buses: (tel. 27 507). Leave from both sides of Vounakio Sq., right off the public gardens. Blue buses (tel. 22 079), on the right side of the square on Dimokratias St., are for travel within the immediate vicinity of Chios Town (9km). Frequent trips to Karfas, Vrondados, and Karies. Green buses (tel 27 507), to the left of the square at 13 Vlatarias St. behind the Omeros cultural center, serve the rest of the island. Buses leave for Mesta (3 per day, 700dr), Pyrgi (5 per day, 500dr), Kalamoti (4 per day, 500dr), Elata (3 per day, 500dr), Didima (2 per day, 320dr), Ag. Giorgis (5 per day, 240dr), Litni (2 per day, 500dr), Karmadilla (3 per day, 600dr), Lagada (3 per day, 320dr), Kambia (2 per day, 850dr), Komi (2 per day, 600dr), Emborio (2 per day, 600dr), and Limni Meston (3 per day, 800dr). Summer schedules are posted in the window. Remember to note times for return trips.

Taxis: (tel. 41 111; 24 hr.). Stop at the main square.

Car Rental: Cars available for 9000-10,000dr per day. Insurance extra.

Moped Rental: Several similar stores rent for 3000dr per day.

Laundromat: Mr. Quick Laundry, on Rodokaki St. Open Mon.-Fri. 8am-2pm and 6-10pm. Full service only, 1700dr.

Hospital: (tel. 44 306 or 44 301) 2km north of Chios towards Vrondados; 24 hr.

Pharmacies: Chios Town has more than 20. Open Mon. and Thurs.-Fri. 8am-2pm and 5-8pm, Tues.-Wed. 8am-2pm. Check the notices on all pharmacy doors to find which are open on weekends.

ACCOMMODATIONS

Most of Chios Town's accommodations are located in converted neoclassical mansions with creaky wooden staircases and high ceilings. In high season, when rooms are scarce, it's better to let a tourist agency call around for you. Expect to pay 4000dr and up. Most cheap pensions cluster at the south end of the waterfront.

Chios Rooms, on the waterfront, past the turn-off to Pension Giannis, is managed by the Hatzelenis office. Filth-free, high-ceilinged singles 3500dr during low season; doubles 6000dr, w/bath 7000dr. Inquire first at the **Hatzelenis tourist office** (tel. 27 295).

Rooms Alex (tel. 26 054), located near the Archaeological Museum, is a particularly good option for first-time visitors. Alex, a retired ship captain, is knowledgeable and speaks four different languages. Rooms are clean and comfortable. Alex will meet you at the pier if you make reservations, and occasionally help you cook a meal if you provide the food. Doubles 5000dr, w/bath 6000dr.

Artemis Rooms, 3 N. Vamva St., (tel. 25 011), two blocks up from the waterfront and down the road from the cathedral, offers homey, clean rooms (doubles starting at 3500dr) and kitchen facilities on a noisy, but convenient street.

Pelineon Rooms (tel. 41 361 or 24 585; fax 29 761). Run by business-keen George Psoras. Doubles w/ bath 4000-7000dr.

Chios Camping (tel. 74 111), on the beach at Agios Isidoros, 14km north of Chios Town. Has its own rocky beach (950dr per person). Open July-Sept. Unofficial camping is prevalent but illegal.

FOOD AND ENTERTAINMENT

Myriad vendors hawk their milk, cheese, meat, bread, and produce around Vounakio Sq. Good restaurants are harder to find, but you can get a nice light lunch of stuffed (vegetarian) vine leaves for 750dr at the **Dolphin Taverna** on the waterfront. For captivating service and a tasty, fresh meal, try the **"To Meatemi" Greek Tavern Restaurant,** sandwiched among the numerous waterfront cafés. Look for the beige-and-brown striped interior and the "homemade spesialities" sign out front (1300dr for a spesial meal). If you don't mind a longish stroll, the **Hotzas Taverna** (tel. 23 117), in a traditional house on 74 Stef Tsouris St., serves delicious and inexpensive fresh food. Follow Vamva St. inland from the waterfront to the Bank of Crete, turn left, bear right at the first fork, and keep walking. The **Two Brothers Taverna** (tel. 21 313), 36 Livanou St., one block inland from the waterfront, has yummy vegetarian pizza. (Full meals average 1450dr. Open daily noon-4pm and 8pm-midnight.) For 250 dr., you can lunch on the fresh *spanakopita* (spinach pie) available early in the day in the numerous **pastry shops** around Vounakio Sq. and along Rodokanaki St. **Café Everest,** on Rodokanaki St. close to the cathedral, offers a pleasant retreat from the late afternoon uproar. Relaxed prices for coffees and pastries make it a real treat.

For a nightcap, head out of town on Livanou St. past the grungy local beach, and you will come to several **discos** packed with Chiotians, foreigners, and Greek soldiers catching a little R&R. One way to judge a place's popularity is to count the number of motorcycles out front.

SIGHTS

The town has several relics of its past, as well as an active shopping district centered on Vounakio Sq. The walls of the **Byzantine Kastro,** a castle reconstructed by the Genoese, enclose the narrow streets of the **Old Town.** Inside the main gate off the square, across from the taxis, is a tiny and peaceful **Byzantine Exhibition** (tel. 22 819; open Tues.-Sun. 9am-3pm; free). The **Turkish Mosque,** on Vournakio Sq. (look for the stripe), has conveniently metamorphosed into a museum that displays various finds from the archaeological site at Emborio. (Open Tues.-Sun. 8am-1:30pm; free.) The town's **Archaeological Museum,** 5 Micalon St. (tel. 44 239), 4 blocks inland on the far south of the waterfront, has an unenthralling collection of ceramics, bronze artifacts, sculptures, and coins. (Open Mon. and Wed.-Sat. 8:45am-3pm, Sun. 9:30am-2:30pm; admission 200dr, students 100dr.) Try to visit the **Folklore Museum** on the first floor of the **Korais Library** (open Mon.-Thurs. 8am-2pm, Fri. 8am-2pm and 5-7:30pm, Sat. 8am-12:30pm), adjacent to the **Mitropolis**. If you're up for a walk with a worthwhile destination, venture to the **Faros Museum,** displaying relics from Asia Minor. Ask the tour office to show you directions on a map. The popular sandy beach of **Karfas,** victim of Chios' latest burst of development, is only 6km south of Chios Town. The rocky beaches of **Vrondados** and **Daskalopetra,** 9km north of town, are also nearby. Take a blue bus from Vournakio Sq.

The impressive **Nea Moni** (New Monastery), built in the 11th century, is cradled by the pine-covered mountains 16km west of Chios Town. Long ago, an icon of the Virgin Mary miraculously appeared to three hermits who promptly founded the monastery with the aid of an exiled emperor. Over the centuries, the monastery complex was rebuilt and enlarged. Although rather run-down, it remains one of the most important Byzantine monuments in the world. Like the rest of Chios, the monastery's peaceful exterior belies its tragic past. Thousands of monks living here were killed in the 1822 Turkish massacre; the modest chapel to the left of the church contains a chilling display of the victims' skulls and bones. Though an earthquake in 1881 destroyed much of the complex itself, most of it has been carefully restored and the interior is pleasantly chaotic. The 11th-century mosaics in the inner narthex are worth a look. Even their state of partial decrepitude can't hide the original artistry. (Open daily dawn-1pm and 4-8pm; free.) Several kilometers past Nea Moni on the paved road is the **Monastery Of Trion Pateron** (Three Fathers), which commemorates the three ascetic hermits who founded Nea Moni. 15km west of Nea Moni is **Anavatos,** staggeringly beautiful but—again—with a tragic past. The women and children of the village's 400 families threw themselves off the precipitous cliffs of this "Greek Masada" after their failed attempt to withstand the Turkish invasion in 1822. Check with the bus station (green bus) for excursion packages to both sites (1-2 per week, 1500dr round-trip.) If you miss the bus, you can take one of the more frequent buses to Karies (6 per day, 15min., 220dr), and walk the remaining 6km up the steep hillside to Nea Moni. Taxi drivers may agree to drive you to the site, wait a half hour, and bring you back. Assemble a group of fellow sightseers, since you'll pay by the carload. From Karies, a taxi-tour of Nea Moni and Anavatos costs 6000dr (decide on a fare before leaving for the monastery). The road is hilly but well-paved until Nea Moni, where it deteriorates into an uneven, rocky path, passable by car and motorcycle, but very rough on mopeds.

■■■ SOUTHERN CHIOS

PIRGI

The villages in the southern half of the island, called *Mastichochoria,* are home to Chios's famous resin, produced by squat mastic or lentisk trees. The main "mastic village" is Pirgi, 25km from Chios and high in the hills. This unique town is a maze of alleys lined by traditional homes. Bear right at the fork in the road and walk into town past the first seven or eight houses. You'll see the English-speaking Chios headquarters of the **Women's Agricultural Tourist Collective** (tel. 72 496), which arranges rooms in private farmhouses in Armolia, Pirgi, Olymbi, and Mesta. The female farmers, symbolized by the *melissa* (bee), will show you around their farms if you so choose. It's best but not absolutely necessary to make reservations a few weeks in advance, or at least to call before actually arriving in Pirgi, especially in July and August. (Office open Mon.-Sat. 8am-2:30pm; singles 3600dr, doubles 5500dr, triples 6000dr; some rooms have private baths; breakfast 600dr, afternoon meals 2000dr.) You can also make your own arrangements for "Rooms to Let" with village proprietors; look for rooms-to-rent signs scattered about town. Walking into Platia Georgiou M. Theotoka, where the police are located, turn right and continue 100m, following signs for **Rent Rooms Nikos** (tel. 72 425). Nikos has immaculate rooms, some with private baths, that include shared kitchen facilities and are surrounded by the mastic countryside (doubles 4500dr and up). A mobile **National Bank** comes to Pirgi Mon. and Thurs. noon-1:30pm. The **Commercial Bank** drops by Wed. and Fri. 10-11am. The **post office** is in the main square, Despoti Germ. Theotoka. (Open Mon.-Fri. 9am-12:30pm.) Taking a left from this square onto Mich. Kolika St., you'll find the one-room **OTE** (open daily, roughly 9:30am-1pm and 4-10pm). In Georgiou M. Theotoka Sq. are the **pharmacy** (tel. 72 444; open Mon.-Fri. 9am-2pm and 5-8pm; call during off-hours in an emergency) and the **police** (tel. 72 222; 24 hr.). **Marianne Rent Motor** (tel. 72 488; open daily 8am-9pm) rents **mopeds** (2500dr) and **bikes** (1000dr), and runs a little shop where you can snack, **change money,** and learn about the village (located just up the road from the bus stop). There are plenty of pleasant cafés and restaurants as you meander through the village alleys and square.

Just northeast of the square is the 14th-century **Agioi Apostoloi** church, a replica of the Nea Moni. Every inch of its walls and ceiling is covered with 16th-century frescoes and paintings created by a Cretan iconography school. The caretaker must unlock the front gate for you; ask for Michalis Vassilis at 27 Mix. Kolika St., directly across from the OTE. (Open Mon.-Fri. 9am-3:30pm; 100dr donation is expected.)

One kilometer back along the road to Chios and 5km south is the beach of **Emborio.** Don't pass up the chance to swim here. Its light brown volcanic cliffs are a striking contrast to the black stones and deep blue water below. The bus from Chios Town or Pirgi drops you off at the harbor. Follow the only road to the right (facing the water), and walk up and then down the hill to find the first beach. Up the steps to the right, there's a smaller, less crowded shore. Bring extra sunscreen since the

Craftsmen With a Fork and a Dream

For romantics who would prefer goat-tending in a traditional village to life in the big city, Pirgi offers this charm, while at the same time blinding visitors with a dazzling spectacle. Although it is built in the twisting alleyways of a medieval castle, Pirgi is more recognizable for its *ksista*, the unique geometric patterns that coat walls of every house in the village. Instead of whitewashing homes as is common in the Cyclades, Pirgian craftsmen first coat each house with a paint made from the gray stone beach at Emborio. The houses are then whitewashed and, while the paint is still wet, the craftsmen form geometric patterns with a fork, creating the village's trademark design. After both coats of color have dried, artists paint colorful designs on some parts of the wall, adding splendid color to the black-and-white geometric designs.

black stones absorb merciless rays, and wear sandals to protect your feet from the sharp stones. No-camping rule is strictly enforced.

MESTA

Ten kilometers west of Pirgi is the anachronistic village of Mesta, where buildings are entirely connected by arched medieval stone. During the Genoese occupation, the town was constructed as a sheltered maze to stave off pirates. Buses stop on the main road outside the city walls. From here, follow the *kentro* signs through labyrinthine alleys to the main courtyard, Platia Taxiarchou.

The **Women's Agricultural Tourist Collective** (tel. 72 496) arranges rooms in Mesta. Around the square, ask for Despina who enthusiastically answers all sorts of questions about the village and the Women's Collective. Also usually in the square from 7am to 7pm, jovial Dimitris Pippides (tel. 76 319) speaks flawless English and books tastefully restored **rooms** in old houses. (Doubles 6500dr, houses also available.) There's no post office in Mesta, but the **postman** comes around 11am to pick up mail. Once weekly or so a **doctor** and a **dentist** make appearances in the village; arrivals are announced publicly in the square. The **National Bank** comes to Mesta (Mon. and Thurs. 2pm-2:30pm), as does the **Commercial Bank** (Fri. 9:30-10am). Both banks will **exchange money. Taxis** are available 24 hr. (tel. 76 236). The town's two **cafés** and one restaurant, **Mesaionas** (tel. 76 050), in the courtyard, serve specialties like beef with onions and Mesta's sweet red wine (900-1100dr).

Six towers once punctuated the town's fortified walls. In 1850, the main tower was demolished to make room for the **Neos Taxiarchi,** the fourth-largest church in Greece, built entirely by volunteer laborers. This *ecklesia,* in the main Platia Taxiarchon, is extremely ornate; Russian chandeliers and gold incense burners dangle from its ceiling and a four-tiered Russian iconostasis separates the altar from the vestibule. The Neos Taxiarchi replaced the nearby **Paleos Taxiarchi,** which dates from 1200 AD. Follow the road past the GNTO, and then take a right after exiting the stone village. It's the building immediately on the right. The caretaker must open both churches. Ask around in the square for him, but keep in mind that he's known to take afternoon siestas; if you want to be sure to see the churches, arrive in Mesta in the morning. A 100dr donation to the church is expected.

■■■ NORTHERN CHIOS

Always the poorer—and less-visited—region, the north half of Chios is the silent partner of the *Mastichochoria*. **Voriochora** (North Town) was left even more destitute by the 1981 fire, but its beaches and quaint villages remain tranquil and inviting. Since few foreigners visit, it may be difficult to find a place to stay. The best way to appreciate this part of the island is to travel by moped. Roughly 5km outside Chios town, just past Vrondados, the beach of **Daskalopetra** (teaching rock), is where Homer supposedly held class. After Daskalopetra, the main roads wind northwest along the coast past Marmaron to **Nagos** (30km away), which features a gray stone beach. **Volissos** (40km west), Homer's legendary birthplace, is crowned by a Byzantine fort and girdled by stone houses. On July 22, the island gathers in Volissos for a festival honoring **St. Marcela,** protector of the island and of the mastic trees, who proclaimed that mastic trees would grow only on Chios. St. Marcela was killed by her father, a Turk, but when flowers sprouted from her grave she was recognized as a saint. Some say that during the festival the sea turns red, boils and miracles occur.

A few kilometers south of Volissos, a long beach stretches out along the four-house village of **Limnia.** Green **buses** run to Kardamila (about 6 per day, 750dr) and Volissos (2 per week, 750dr). If you visit **Inousses,** the little islet northeast of Chios, you will probably be among the few, the proud, the ten-or-so tourists on the island. The marvelous beaches here are completely deserted; during the afternoon *siesta* you can meander the streets with only stray cats for company. Wealthy ship-owners are responsible for the private yachts, Mercedes Benzes, and luxurious villas that line the coast. A daily ferry leaves Chios Town for Inousses and the fishing village

Lagada (1hr., 1000dr). Less frequent *caïques* travel to the Inousses as well (2500dr round trip). **Telephone Code:** 0272.

LESVOS (LESBOS) ΛΕΣΒΟΣ

It seems odd for Lesvos' seemingly barren, volcanic landscape to have nurtured one of the richest cultural legacies in the Aegean. After all, Lesvos does not immediately strike visitors as an island that was once home to the musician Terpander, the poet Arion, the writer Aesop, and most notably the 7th-century BC poet Sappho. The main tourist haunts in particular seem to indicate that Lesvos' greatness is merely part of its fabled past. Yet even in this century, Lesvos has given rise to the Nobel Prize winning poet Odysseus Elytis, the Neoprimitive artist Theophilos, art publisher Tériade, and the family of 1988 U.S. Presidential candidate Michael Dukakis.

Until recently, the island (often called Mitilini after its principal city) was relatively remote, cultivating its offbeat character (it's known for horse breeding, serious *ouzo* drinking, and leftist politics). Although Lesvos' major towns now host a growing number of foreign visitors, tourism has not reached Cycladean proportions. Most travelers to the sparsely populated island stay for months at a time, exploring the many historical sites and uncovering the island's truly variegated landscape: tall pines, cornfields, and taffy-trunked olive trees that rise from the scruffy hillsides.

Legend has it that the population of Lesvos, Greece's third largest island, was once entirely female. This notion may owe its origin to the Athenian assembly's 428 BC decision to punish the recalcitrant residents of Mitilini by executing all adult males on the island. After some debate, however, the decision was repealed. For hundreds of years, Mitilini flourished as a cultural center. Its inhabitants would have been astonished to know that later generations would consider 5th-century Athens, not Mitilini, to be the zenith of Greek civilization. The island's Philosophical Academy, where Epicurus and Aristotle taught, brought it particular fame.

■■■ MITILINI

Mitilini, the central port city and capital of Lesvos, can be picturesque from a distance. It is a yawning harbor adorned with yachts, colorful fishing boats, and an encircling weave of red-tiled dwellings, modern high-rises, and Neoclassical mansions standing in shoulder to shoulder ascent up the Amali mountains. The city sits under the shadow of the decaying Gattelusi castle, and is accented by the prominent dome of Agios Therapon, the city's hallmark. Yet a closer look proves Mitilini kinetic, crowded, crumbling—her once grand Neoclassical mansions too expensive to restore, illegal to tear down—in a regrettable state of decay.

ORIENTATION AND PRACTICAL INFORMATION

The city spreads chaotically along the waterfront, **Pavlou Koudoutrioti,** and **Ermou Street,** which runs parallel one block inland. The most interesting quadrant of town is the old market, which advances inland from the waterfront, below the castle and to the right of the church. It's easy to get lost among the market's knotted streets and cobbled ways so conducive to adventure. For those tired of pristine shops, an assortment of flea markets, produce stands, and neighborhood stores is a welcome change. Here you can shop free of tacky key chain peddlers and take in the aroma of the nearby fish market.

Tourist Police: (tel. 22 776). From the ferry, head left towards the interior harbor and main waterfront road. The official "passport control building" at the corner of the pier houses the tourist police. Enter by the back side, which doubles as a **tourist office.** They speak English, help find rooms, offer free brochures, and make a good first stop upon arrival by ferry. Open daily 7am-10pm.

Port Police: 27 Votsani St. (tel. 28 888, -27). In the same building with the **police,** a few blocks south of the port on the waterfront.

Post Office: (tel. 28 823). On Vourhazon St. near the intercity bus station. **Exchanges currency.** Signs pointing the way to the post office are behind the park (which has public toilets), near the taxi stand. Open Mon.-Sat. 7:30am-2pm **Postal code:** 81100.

OTE: (tel. 28 299). Two doors up the road from the post office. Open daily 7am-10pm. **Telephone code:** 0251.

Banks: Several banks line Pavlou Koudoutrioti along the waterfront (open Mon.-Thurs. 8am-2pm, Fri. 8am-1:30pm). The **Credit Bank** at the center of the waterfront has an **ATM** that accepts Visa and American Express.

Flights: To Athens (3 per day, 14,800dr), Limnos (daily, 12,400dr), Thessaloniki (daily, 18,600dr), and Chios (6400dr). Take a blue bus to the airport (300dr) 3km south of Mitilini. You can also reach the airport by taking the **Olympic Airways bus** (400dr) from the main office, 44 Kavetsou Ave. (tel. 28 659, -60; open Mon.-Fri. 8am-3pm, Sat.-Sun. 7am-3pm for phone reservations). Check with any ticket agent for times and locations. Book flights roughly a week in advance.

Buses: (tel. 28 725). **Green buses** leave from the intercity bus station (tel. 28 873) and service destinations all around the island. The station is behind and adjacent to Ag. Irinis park, on a diagonal 1½ blocks in from the south edge of the harbor. During the summer, buses from Mitilini go to Molyvos (4-5 per day, 2hr., 1100dr), Sigri (2-3 per day, 1650dr), Vatera (2-3 per day, 100dr), Agiassos (2-3 per day, 460dr), Skala Eressos (2-3 per day, 3hr., 1600dr), and Plomari (4-5 per day, 1¼hr., 750dr, last return 4pm). Buses reduced on weekends.

City Buses: Blue buses, based on the waterfront, service local routes around Mitilini, including Loutropoli.

Ferries: Connect Lesvos to the Northeast Aegean and beyond. **NEL Lines,** 47 Pavlou Koudoutrioti St. (tel. 22 220), located along the first stretch of waterfront 3 blocks from the pier, runs a relative monopoly over Lesvos ferry transit, and is the only place to buy ferry tickets. Open Mon.-Fri. 7am-9pm, Sat.-Sun. 7am-2pm. During the summer, ferries travel to Piraeus (1-3 per day, 13hr., 5277dr), Chios (1-2 per day, 3½hr., 2751dr), Limnos (5 per week, 6hr., 3057dr), Kavala (2 per week, 12 hr., 5094dr), Thessaloniki (2 per week, 12-13hr., 6996dr) and Ayvalık, Turkey (2 per day, 1hr., 14,000dr).

Flying Dolphins: Contact **Dimakis Tours** (tel. 20 716 or 27 865), a few storefronts before the ferry office. Hydrofoils speed 3 times per week to Plomari, Alexandroupolis, Kavala, Limnos, and Chios. Twice as fast, but also twice as expensive.

Moped/Car Rental: To explore this large island, you may prefer to rent a **moped** (4000dr per day) or **car** (8500dr per day) at one of numerous rental stores.

Laundry: On El. Venizelou, next to the bus station and across from the supermarket; wash 900dr, dry 600. Open Mon.-Fri. 8:30am-1:30pm and 5:30-9pm.

Hospital: (tel. 43 777). Southwest of the city on E. Vostani; open 24 hr.

Emergency: Dial 166.

ACCOMMODATIONS

Dhomatia IREN, 41 Komminaki St., (tel. 22 787). One block inland, on the left-hand corner of Imvrou St. and Komninaki St. From the ferry landing, walk along the first stretch of waterfront, just past the Flying Dolphin and Superfast Ferry offices, and turn down Imvrou. IREN, on a quiet street, has cool, commodious rooms, a house dog named Ralph, and 24-hr. hot water. Vassili, a personable professional photographer, touts his "Bed and Breakfast" as "a house that can be a home for you," and will let you use his kitchen. St. Doubles 4000dr.

Hotel Anna-Lena (tel. 21 494), located along the tourist café-laden avenue on the south waterfront. Offers clean, simple rooms with baths. Inquire at their waterfront *taverna,* Fanari, prominently signposted near the corner of Pavlou Koudoutrioti and the string of waterfront cafés. Doubles 5000dr.

Pension Petrakis (tel. 41 779 or 24 134), is cheap and livable, a good choice for travelers running out of money but who want a central location. Look for the three-story building and yellow signs for "Moto Petraki and Hotel," across from the local (blue) bus station on the waterfront. The owners manage a host of pensions in and around Mitilini; if you're stuck for a room, they may be able to help. Singles 2800dr, doubles 3500dr, triples 4500dr.

FOOD

Cafés and *taverna* abound along the waterfront. Locals tend to dine to the north, tourists to the south, although not exclusively. For a full-fledged, fresh fried fish feast, you might consider the more touristed **tavernas** on the southern waterfront, if for no other reason than to enjoy your meal in a traffic- and congestion-free environment. Elsewhere, cheese pies, charmless croissants, and *gyros* abound. A better option is stuffed vine leaves (800dr), mmm, mmm good and available at local *taverna*. For breakfast with the locals, saunter behind the local bus station onto Limnou St. and take the first right onto Thasou St. You'll see them, they'll see you—expect a few stares, and real Greek coffee. For a sweet fix you won't soon forget, head up Alkaiou St., which runs inland from the waterfront a few blocks north of the park. Two nice little **sweetshops** cluster together within the street's first tiny little block. At the edge of the block, look up (and to your left): the dome of Agios Therapon rises into the sky like the most splendid confectionery.

SIGHTS

The ubiquitous signs in Mitilini helpfully egg on tourists to the various sights. The **Archaeological Museum,** 7 Argiri Eftalioti St. (tel. 28 032), has an impressive, beautifully displayed collection of the island's historical finds. All pieces are labeled and accompanied by thorough descriptions of the archaeological sites' roles in Lesvian history. The artifacts include Mycenaean, protogeometric, and archaic pottery; Classical and Hellenistic vases and sculpture; and remnants from the Temple at Fressos. Make sure to visit the second, smaller building hiding behind the main museum quarters; it contains ancient tablets of rare Aeolian type along with several statues. (Open Tues.-Sun. 8:30am-3pm; admission 450dr, students free.) If you have a spare hour in Mitilini, visit the enormous, late 19th-century **Church of St. Therapon,** on Ermou St., whose dome seems to betray Western influence. The church towers over the fish market's daily catch—sardines, octopi, and occasionally small sharks. (Open 9am-7pm; free.) Behind the church is the **Museum of Byzantine Art** (tel. 28 916; open Mon.-Sat. 9am-1pm; admission 300dr). By the tall clock tower at the south end of the harbor is the impressive **Church of Ag. Theodoros.** The church contains the bones and skull of its patron saint, who was killed by the Turks. From the ferry dock, all roads leading uphill will take you to the **Gattelusi castle** (tel. 27 970). Surrounded by redolent pines above the town, the *kastro* protects its purview over Mitilini and across to Turkey. It was originally constructed by Emperor Justinian on the site of a Byzantine castle, but has since been repaired by the Genoese, the Turks, and the Greeks. The walls contain leftovers from each epoch, and are capped by a telephone cable, the 20th century's contribution. The castle is named for Francesco Gattelusi, who received Lesvos as dowry in 1355 after he married the daughter of the Byzantine Emperor. Subsequently, the castle has been overrun by Turks and Greeks (open Tues.-Sun. 8:30am-3pm; free). The highest point on the north side of Mitilini town is the 3rd-century BC **ancient theater,** built during Hellenistic times. Here 15,000 spectators attended performances with acoustics as perfect as Epidavros'. In fact, the theater was so impressive that it gave Pompey the idea to build the first stone theater in Rome. The theater and castle are currently being excavated. (Open Tues.-Sun. 8:30am-3pm; free.)

■ NEAR MITILINI

The pleasant and pebbly GNTO **beach,** north of the main pier beneath the castle attracts hordes in the summer (open daily 8am-8pm; admission 150dr). **Neapolis Beach,** a 5km bus ride south, is also jammed. For a peaceful, deserted stretch of sand, persevere and head 13km south of Mitilini to the beach at **Agios Ermogenis.**

It's slightly more touristy, but there are also fewer people. A taxi costs 3000-4000dr if the driver agrees to go; most don't like to because the dirt road ruins their cars.

Only 4km south of Mitilini along the same route (El Venizelou), the tiny, unassuming village of **Varia** surprises wayfarers with the worthwhile **Theophilos Museum** (tel. 41 644), which features the work of the famous Neoprimitivist Greek painter Theophilos Hadzimichali (open Tues.-Sun. 8am-2pm and 5-8pm; admission 350dr). Next door is the **Musée Tériade.** Tériade, a native of Lesvos whose real name is Stratis Eleftheriadis, rose to fame as the foremost publisher of graphic art in Paris during much of the 20th century. The museum displays an excellent collection of Picasso, Miró, Leger, Chagall, and Matisse lithographs. (Open Tues.-Sun. 9am-2pm and 5-8pm; admission 350dr.) **Buses** to Varia depart from the waterfront depot (tel. 28 725; every ½hr., 15min., 210dr).

Follow Naumahias Elis (running along Mitilini's north port) 4km north, then head 2km west to prance amid a well-preserved Roman aqueduct at **Moria. Buses** to Moria run every ½hr. from the waterfront (230dr).

■■■ NORTHERN LESVOS

MOLYVOS (MITHIMNA)

On the island's north tip, Molyvos is the Lesvos's most visited spot after Mitilini. Also an artist colony, the town conveys an almost picture-perfect charm: stone houses, topped with red tiles and neatly cornered with multi-colored shutters, stack up intricately into a castle-peaked hill. Exploring the cobbled weave of alleys is a fine afternoon adventure, likely to reward with magnificent terraced vistas of the Aegean and of Turkey. The **Genoese fortress** is striking in the evening light; walk up during the day for a view of the coastline and a closer look at the wildflowers growing in the ruins. Upon your descent, take your first left to enter the small **church** with the brown gate. The soul-penetrating eye above the altar will make even the most unrepentant hedonist squirm. But if you still feel like basking decadently in the sun, avoid the crowded beach in town; instead, try the pebble beach of **Eftalou,** 5km north of Molyvos (bus 200dr).

Orientation and Practical Information Just up from the bus stop (bear left at the fork), on Poseidonos St., is the municipal **tourist office** (tel. 71 347), which keeps sporadic hours, but is usually open when buses arrive. They have free brochures and find rooms. Next door is a **National Bank** (open Mon.-Thurs. 8am-2pm, Fri. 8am-1:30pm). At the top of the hill, the road forks; bear right and you will come to the **main post office** (tel. 71 246; open Mon.-Fri. 7:30am-2pm), which also changes money. There is also a **mobile post office** on the main traffic highway (summer Mon.-Fri. 8am-2pm). The steeply ascending cobbled road to the right of the tourist office is the town's main market thoroughfare. Although this is a typical tourist row with restaurants and glitzy shops, the street's leafy grapevines and fragrant flowers form a soothing tunnel of cool air. Nearby is **Akti Rentals** (tel. 71 997), which rents **motorbikes** (3000dr), **cars** (8500dr), and **jeeps** (14,000dr). (Open daily 9am-1:30pm, 5:30-9:30pm.) Bear left from the fork to reach the local **laundry.** (Wash 1100dr, dry 600dr, regardless of full or self-service; ask about rates per item; open daily 9am-3pm and 5-10pm.) On the first uphill stretch is a **pharmacy** (tel. 71 903) and an official **medical office.** Across from the main post office is a thickly shaded, cave-like café, the local haunt for morning coffee. At the corner, you'll find signs with arrows to significant sights such as the town hall, public library, and **archaeological museum** (open Tues.-Sun. 8:30am-3pm), and the **police station** (tel. 71 222). Special **taxi phones** (just pick one up and dial the number posted) are just about everywhere, especially along the "traffic route," as are regular phone booths. **Postal Code:** 81108. **Telephone Code:** 0253.

Accommodations Rooms in **private homes** are the least costly housing options. Avoid the condominium-style hotels close to the beach. Let the tourist office call around for you, or even help you sort through the offers made by locals greeting you at the bus stop. If the tourist office is closed, take heart: on nearly every turn in Molyvos' cobbled intricacy are "Rooms to Let" signs in traditional homes, at whatever altitude you decide to perch. During peak season, rooms can get expensive: the same room that cost 4000dr in June may cost 7500dr in July and August. Particularly welcoming are the cool, high-ceilinged rooms let by **Eleni Vourgoutsi** (tel. 71 065; doubles w/bath 4000dr). Heed the first rooms sign you come to, on the right, up the cobbled market street just past the tourist office. Farther up the road, visible off a side street to the right, is **Nassos Guest House** (tel. 71 022), which offers 8 rooms, some with bath (doubles from 5000dr). If no one is in, inquire at Nassos Restaurant. **Camping Mithyma** (tel. 71 169, -079) is 1km east of town; follow the road to the right of the bus station. The campsite is comfortable, with hot water and a refrigerator, but quite a hike from town (900dr per person, tent 900dr).

Food From the beach head into any of the numerous beachfront cafés, but the *tavernas* with decks cantilevered out above the main road are particularly nice. The **Taverna Sansibaba,** near the OTE, offers live Greek music Tuesday and Thursday nights, and has a pleasant terrace shaded by large plane trees, overlooking the Aegean. **Gato's,** farther up, also makes the farthest reach out from the cliffside, offering unparalleled views and fashionable fare.

Sights The rugged road north out of Molyvos heads to **Eftalou** (5km northeast), home to a long stretch of secluded **beaches,** many lying beneath towering rocky cliffs. To reach these beaches, walk through a small white building containing a **thermal bath** not much bigger than a jacuzzi (free). Walk 15min. to the south of Molyvos along the coastal road for the tiny but breathtakingly beautiful **Avlaki Beach,** nestled in a secluded cove. Over the hill where the main road curves left is a gate leading to a narrow dirt path. Hike down this steep, winding route to the beach and enter the gates of paradise. Molyvos also has an **archaeological museum** and regular exhibitions by local artists in the town hall.

■■■ SOUTHERN LESVOS

PLOMARI

In 1841, after an arson demolished the village of Megalochori, people resettled in the Turkish-inhabited region 12km south, now modern **Plomari,** the island's second-largest city. From its earliest days, this southern coastal town has manifested a split personality: it is at once a no-holds-barred resort town (with discos, cheery *tavernas,* and all the other accoutrements of package tour groups) as well as an all-out fishing village, with people mending their nets on the pier and nailing octopi to telephone poles to dry in the sun. The overall effect, aided and abetted by Plomari's large *ouzo* industry, is cheerful and relaxing. The local product is far better than the bottled industrial variety. Try a sample at the **Barbayanni Ouzo Factory** (tel. 32 741; open Mon.-Fri. 8am-7pm, Sat. 8am-3:30pm), roughly 2km east towards Ag. Isodoros on the way to Plomari. An annual week-long **Ouzo Festival** is held in late August and features song, dance, drunken tourists, and of course free *ouzo*. Large groups may receive a free tour. Throughout the summer, Plomari hosts several religious celebrations and cultural events. The **Festival of Benjamin** commemorates the revolutionary leader of the 1821 war against the Turks with dancing and theatrical presentations in Greek (one week in late June).

Orientation and Practical Information Manolis Stefanis at **Plomari Travel** on Lesviou St. (tel. 32 946) has information about everything from accommodations to excursions. To get to Plomari Travel from the **Commercial Bank** at the end of the square, turn right into **B. Lesviou Sq.,** and then take your first right up Lesviou St. The **bank** is also in the square. (Open Mon.-Thurs. 8am-2pm, Fri. 8am-1:30pm.) The **OTE** (tel. 32 399; open daily 7:30am-10pm) and the **post office** (tel. 32 241; open Mon.-Fri. 8am-2pm) reside in Plomari's main square. **Postal Code:** 81200; **Telephone Code:** 0252.

Buses go to Plomari (3-5 per day, 750dr) and Agiassos (5 per day, 460dr). The road hugs the **Bay of Geras,** offering eye-dilating views of both the coast and the interior, and passes through the charming villages of **Paleokipos** and **Pappados.**

Sights Beaches appear intermittently around Plomari. To reach rocky **Arnovdeli Beach,** turn onto Ag. Nikolaou Rd. and follow the signs; it's roughly a 15-min. walk south of town. If you continue straight on Ag. Nikolaou, you'll come to **Agios Nikolaos,** a church sparkling with icons spanning 400 years. If you aren't into stone-infested coasts, the best beaches for you (and loads of other people) are at **Agios Isodoros,** 3km east of town along the main road.

Fifteen km north of Plomari, the village of **Agiassos,** on the slopes of Lesvos's Mt. Olympus, remains an active center for ceramic crafts. An Orthodox church here, even more exuberantly decorated than others, contains an icon of the Virgin Mary made by St. Lucas, originally destined for Constantinople in 330 AD. When the priest transporting it heard that war was being talked about, he feared for the icon's safety and deposited it in the church. Every year on August 15, Agiassos hosts *Panagia,* the grand celebration in honor of the Virgin Mary. The village also boasts an **Ecclesiastical Museum,** with Byzantine religious works (ask church officials and priests in town about the exhibit), a **Folk Museum** run by the town and featuring traditional costumes, and a **library** with some English books.

■■■ WESTERN LESVOS

SKALA ERESSOS

Determined sunbathers congregate at **Skala Eressos** (known as "Skala"), located at the opposite end of Lesvos from Mitilini. Skala's 1½km **beach** has won the EU's "Blue Banner" award for cleanliness. Its western half is one of the few legal **nude beaches** on the island. Skala's companion village of **Eressos,** 3½km inland, the poet **Sappho's birthplace,** is a gathering place for lesbians during the summer. Both villages are unaffected by hyper-tourism and have reputations as havens for relaxed, tolerant travelers. To get to the west from Mitilini, take a **bus** (Mon.-Fri. 1-3 per day, 2¾hr., 1600dr). Renting a car or motorbike is more convenient—if you can manage the 95km roller-coaster-like ride.

Orientation and Practical Information **Eressos Travel** (tel. 53 076, -7; fax 53 576), one block northwest of the main square, hosts a **currency exchange,** a private kiosk for international and local telephone calls, excursion information, car and motorbike rental information, and accommodation arrangements (open daily 9am-10pm; reduced hours during off-season). There are **post offices** in Skala Eressos (off the main square; open daily 7:30am-2pm) and Eressos (tel. 53 227; open Mon.-Fri. 7:30am-2pm). The **OTE** (tel. 53 399; open Mon.-Fri. 7:30am-2:30pm) is located in Eressos along with the **police station** (tel. 53 222). **Snapi Travel** on the water has info on rooms, car and moped rentals, and excursions. (Open Sat.-Thurs. 10am-noon and 6-10pm, Fri. 10am-noon.) **Postal Code:** 81105; **Telephone Code:** 0253.

Accommodations Ask at **Eressos Travel** about the **Eressos House,** which has sparkling double rooms with private bathrooms and shared refrigerator (6000dr). **Rooms to Let Maritsa Padermou** (tel. 53 267) has spotless, breezy doubles (5700dr) and triples (7000dr), all with private baths and shared refrigerator. **Pension Krinelos** (tel. 53 246) has new, beautifully furnished rooms with private baths and an airy terrace, including a bookcase stocked with forsaken books visitors left behind. (Singles 5200dr, doubles 6500dr, triples 7800dr.) Both Padermou and Krinelos are located in a quiet field 100m from the sea; facing the water, they are to the right and back of the beach parking lot. Ask around for private rooms (doubles 5500dr, triples 6600dr, studios 7000dr) or sacrifice privacy by **camping** on the beach six blocks west of the town's center. Tassos Kokkas at **Exersis Travel** (tel. 53 044) provides help in procuring rooms.

Food Surrounded by new-fangled outdoor cafés and a serene view of the Aegean Sea, the stone-layered square of **Anthis and Evristhenous** is a hot spot for Skala's young international visitors. Restaurants with bamboo-covered wooden piers sit right at the beach and serve up elegant sunset views of **Sappho's Profile** along the western mountains. The **Gorgona** (open June-Oct. daily noon-4pm and 6pm-midnight) has ample portions of authentic Greek cuisine at moderate prices. Adjacent to the Gorgona is the rocky-façaded **Sympathy Café and Pub,** which attracts many Germans. (Open May-Oct. daily 10am-3am.) At the end of the walkway is the **Bennetts' International and Vegetarian Restaurant** (tel 53 624; open mid-April to mid-Oct. daily 9:30am-4pm and 6-11pm). Run by Max and Jackie Bennett, a British couple, the restaurant has lots of meatless options. Prices are reasonable and you'll lick the platter clean. The café/bar **Filoxenia** (tel. 53 131), across the street from Eressos Travel, is a popular breakfast spot with a rooftop terrace. It offers whole wheat pancakes (500dr) and cocktails (800-1000dr). (Open daily 10am-1pm and 5pm-3am.) Nick and Linda, the amiable Canadian couple who used to run Filoxenia, have many interesting stories about Skala Eressos. They live here all year; ask around for their new address. They also rent new **mountain bikes.** On Kountouriotou St. (facing the water, turn right from Eressos Travel and walk 50m), there is an **open-air cinema** that shows movies in English (with Greek subtitles). Shows (500dr) start at 9:30pm.

Sights The early Christian basilica of **Agios Andreas,** three blocks north of the beach, once housed 5th-century mosaics, which can now be found in Mitilini's Archaeological Museum. (Basilica open 8am-2pm.) Greek Orthodox services are held here on Sundays (7-10am). Behind the church is the **Skala Museum** (tel. 53 352), with displays of 5th- and 6th-century vases, sculptured tombstones, inscriptions in the Aeolian dialect, and an anchor of a Turkish frigate from the Greek War of Independence in 1821. (Open Tues.-Sun. 8am-3pm; free.) In the museum yard is the tomb of St. Andrew. The uphill road leading east is the pilgrimage route for travelers going to the remains of **Sappho's Home** in Eressos. At dusk, the view from the hill is transcendent. The river, just west of Skala's center, serves as habitat to many rare and exotic birds. (Peak **birdwatching** season here is early April-mid-June.) Farther inland at **Antissa** are the **petrified trees** of Lesvos, preserved by volcanic activity at least 700 thousand years ago in one of only two such forests in the world (the other is on the Arizona-New Mexico border in the U.S.). Roughly 200 plant and animal fossils make up the "forest" which requires a 1½hr. walk (open daily 8:30am-4pm; free). From Mitilini town, take the bus to Sigri and walk or ride the 8km to the forest. From Skala, rent a moped or car, or check at Eressos Travel about tours.

SAMOS ΣΑΜΟΣ

With its sultry landscape and engrossing architectural remains, Samos is perhaps the most beautiful and certainly the most touristed island in the Northeast Aegean. The island draws an older, more sedate crowd, and is quieter than the more popular spots in the Cyclades and the Dodecanese. Still, its largest cities—Samos Town, Pythagorion, and Kokkari—and its nearly-tropical deep green terrain are packed in July and August.

The wealthiest of the Aegean islands, Samos was home to many notable Greek architects, sculptors, poets, philosophers, and scientists. Samos' illustrious citizenry has included Epicurus, the moral philosopher; Aesop, the author of fables; and Aristarchus, the astronomer who argued that the sun was the center of the universe nearly 1800 years before Copernicus. The island's most beloved native son, however, is the ancient philosopher Pythagoras, whose visage has been adopted as the symbol of Samos.

Many people come to Samos simply to make the short hop over to **Kuşadası** for the nearby ruins of **Ephesus** on the Turkish coast. The archaeological site is the most extensive and possibly the most evocative remnant of ancient Hellenic civilization. Founded around 1100 BC, Ephesus rapidly blossomed into the largest metropolis in Asia Minor (See Ephesus on page 472).

■■■ SAMOS TOWN

With its wide white sidewalks, colorful fishing boats, and picturesque red-roofed houses nestled in the mountainside, Samos Town is among the Northeast Aegean's more attractive ports. While the waterfront is a snarl of tourist shops and cafés, the street one block inland is pleasant, and the garden-laced residential lanes farther back are more representative of local life.

ORIENTATION AND PRACTICAL INFORMATION

Samos Town unfurls from north to south around a crescent-shaped waterfront. **Pythagoras Square,** easily identifiable by its four large palm trees, hosts banks, cafés, and taxis.

Tourist Office: (tel. 28 530, -82) Follow signs from the waterfront, on a side street one block before Pythagoras Sq. The helpful staff helps find accommodations. Open July-Aug. Mon.-Sat. 9am-1pm and 6-8:30pm.

Port Police: (tel. 27 318). At the end of the ferry dock.

Post Office: (tel. 27 304). One block up from the waterfront behind the Hotel Xenia; turn at the immense palm tree and walk through the municipal gardens (open Mon.-Fri. 7:30am-2pm). **Postal Code:** 83100.

OTE: Next to the post office. Open daily 7am-10pm. **Telephone Code:** 0273.

Tourist Agencies: Almost all travel agencies along the waterfront (to the right of Samos Tours) speak English and offer assistance in finding rooms. **Samos Tours** (tel. 27 715), at the end of the ferry dock, is well-staffed and provides information on everything from museum hours to accommodations. Free luggage storage. Open daily 6am-midnight and usually whenever a boat arrives. **ITSA Travel** (tel. 23 605; fax 27 955), right next door, offers similar services. Free luggage storage. Open daily 6am-2:30pm and 5pm-midnight.

Flights: Olympic Airways (tel. 27 237; open Mon.-Fri. 8am-4pm) offers daily flights to Athens (50min., 14,800dr). There are also bi-weekly flights to Chios, Lesvos, Mykonos, and Kos. Samos' **airport** (tel. 61 219) is 4km out of Pythagorion and can be reached by taxi from Samos Town (4000dr).

Ferries: Run regularly between Samos Town and Piraeus in summer (daily, 12hr., 4824dr), stopping at Ikaria (2-3hr.). To Naxos and Paros (at least 4 per week, 3540dr), Chios (3 per week, 2300dr), Ikaria (1690dr), Fourni (1320dr), Karlovassi (905dr), Kavala (7230dr), Lesvos (3400dr), Limnos (5790dr), and Patmos (2560dr). During the summer, ferries also travel to the Cyclades, Syros, and Mykonos (once weekly, 3300dr). From Mykonos, boats run every half hour to Tinos. Ferries to Kuşadası, Turkey leave from Samos Town (daily at 8am and 5pm) and Pythagorion (3 per week). About half as many boats make the crossing off-season. A boat ride to Kuşadası costs about 6000dr (with slight discount for a round-trip ticket). You'll be charged a Turkish port tax of 3000dr or US$10. You'll also be charged a 4000dr Greek port tax. It is preferable to pay the Turkish tax in dollars. If you stay overnight in Turkey and leave from Kuşadası, you'll have to pay the tax again. The 5000dr tours of Ephesus are not worth it. Remember to give the travel agent your passport the day before you intend to sail.

Flying Dolphins: Trips from both Samos Town and Pythagorion to Patmos, Kos, Rhodes, Leros, Kalymnos, Ikaria, Fourni, Chios, Lipsi, and Agathonissi. Expect to pay double the ferry fare and to reach your destination in half the time.
Taxi Stand: (tel. 28 404), Pythagoras Sq.
Motorbike Rental: Probably the best way to see the island and the only way to get around the more mountainous and remote western end (800-5000dr per day).
Laundromat: Near Georgiou's Taverna. Wash 800dr, dry 600dr, soap 150dr. Open daily 8am-11pm. There's a **dry cleaner** next door.
Public Toilets: Lurk to the left of the entrance to the municipal gardens.
Buses: (tel. 27 262). To get to the station, follow the waterfront past Pythagoras Sq., turn left at Europe Rent A Car onto Lekati St., and walk one block. The bus schedule is posted here, but you can also pick up a copy at most tour offices. Fares range from 175dr to 1400dr. Weekdays, buses travel to Tsamadou (9 per day), Karlovassi (6 per day), Votsalakia (1 per day), Drakei (1 per day), Pagondas (2 per day), Heraion (3 per day), Ammos (2 per day), Pythagorion (9 per day), Chora (6 per day), Mitilini (5 per day), and Vourliotes (2 per day). Fewer buses run on Sat. and Sun.
Hospital: (tel. 27 407 or 27 426). To the left of the ferry dock (facing inland).

ACCOMMODATIONS

There are not nearly enough rooms to go around on Samos; finding one can be a wearying process. If the following are full, try the pensions around the Ionia.

Pension Ionia, 5 Manoli Kalomiri St. (tel. 28 782). To get there, turn right at the end of the ferry dock, take a left onto E. Stamatiadou St. before the Hotel Aiolis on the waterfront, and then take the second left onto Manoli Kalomiri St. Three buildings of inexpensive, attractive rooms. Friendly Mr. Zavitsanou will give you a cot in the garden if rooms are full. Singles 3000dr, doubles 4000dr. 24hr.-hot showers.
Hotel Artemis, (tel. 27 792), on Pythagoras Sq. Run by the affable, English-speaking Mr. Kostas, who offers clean rooms, helpful service, and directions to a few good restaurants. Doubles 4000 dr, w/bath 5000dr.
Pension Trova, 26 Kalomiris St. (tel. 27 759). Up the road just to the left of Pension Ionia, or, from the waterfront, take Thiseos St. up two blocks to Kalomiri St., continue uphill, and look for signs. Run by the utterly delightful Maria Trova. Gracious rooms and rooftop balconies overlook town and port. Singles start at 2000dr, doubles w/ bath 4000dr.

FOOD AND ENTERTAINMENT

Bask in the soft sea air and feast on well-prepared traditional Greek cuisine. **Georgiou's Taverna,** behind the Hotel Aeolis to the left of Pythagoras Sq. (facing inland) is a better deal than the waterfront tourist spots. Dishes are well-prepared and service is friendly (open daily 11am-11pm). **Taverna Ouzeria Diodia** resides at the waterfront edge of a little alley (look for the blue sign with the fish cartoon). To get there, saunter down the waterfront past Lefkadi St., the bus station, and the police station. Serves a great Greek meal. **Sweet shops** abound in Samos, particularly along the pedestrian road parallel to the waterfront, one block in. **Mascot** is an especially good choice, with outdoor seating along the cobbled walk.

SIGHTS

The **Byzantine Museum** (tel. 27 312), one block back from the ferry pier, behind the cathedral, is housed in the former residence of the prince of Samos. It holds a reliquary with a cast of St. George's footprint. (Open Mon., Wed., and Fri. 9am-1pm; 100dr.) Finds from local digs, including an impressive 5m-tall Kouros from 575 BC, have made their way to the recently re-opened, award-winning **archaeological museum** (tel. 27 469), next to the post office. (Open daily 8:30am-3pm; admission 800dr, students 400dr.) Nearby, the lilliputian but lovely **municipal gardens** (free) contain caged monkeys and birds, 200 varieties of flowers, and a little café.

■■■ PYTHAGORION

Boats from Patmos and points south arrive in Pythagorion, the former capital of Samos. The town's numerous archaeological sites, quaint side streets, and proximity to some of the island's nicest beaches make it a worthwhile destination, especially for travelers who are only spending a few days on Samos.

Orientation and Practical Information Fourteen kilometers south of Samos Town, Pythagorion is served by convenient, hourly buses (240dr, only 5 per day off-season). The **bus stop** is on the main street, which runs perpendicular to the waterfront. The English-speaking **tourist office** (tel. 61 022) is in a pink building, halfway between the bus stop and the water (open April-Oct. Mon.-Fri. 9am-1pm and 6-9pm, Sat.-Sun. 10am-2pm). On the same street, there is a **bank** (open Mon.-Fri. 8:30am-2pm), and **post office** (open Mon.-Fri. 7:30am-1:30pm). Next door are the **tourist police** (tel. 61 100). The **OTE** (open Mon.-Fri. 8am-1pm, 5-9pm) is on the waterfront to the left of the intersection with the main street (facing inland). The **port police** (tel. 61 225) are at the other end of the waterfront.

Pensions are overpriced and congested in summer (doubles 5000-7000dr). Most are on either side of the main street, a block or two inland. Hotels line the waterfront and the main street (6000-12,000dr).

Sights The ancient city of Pythagorion, at one time the island's capital, thrived during the second half of the 6th century BC under the reign of Polykrates the Tyrant. According to Herodotus, Polykrates undertook the three most daring engineering projects in the Hellenic world, all of them in and around Pythagorion. One of the most impressive is the **Tunnel of Eupalinos** (tel. 61 400), 1.5km up the hill to the north of town, which diverted water from a natural spring to the city below. About 1.3km long, it is in remarkably good condition, though only about 50m are open to visitors. (Open Tues.-Sun. 9am-2pm. 500dr, students 300dr, senior citizens 400dr, free on Sundays.) Polykrates's second feat was the 40m-deep **harbor mole** (rock pier), on which the modern pier now rests.

Polykrates's *magnum opus* stood 5km west of Pythagorion, toward Ireon. The goddess Hera had been worshipped on Samos for seven centuries when Polykrates decided to enlarge her temple. Supported by 134 columns, the **Temple of Hera** (tel. 95 277), erected in 530 BC, was 118m long and 58m wide, and one of the seven wonders of the ancient world. Damaged by fire in 525 BC, it was never completely reconstructed, perhaps because in 522 BC Polykrates himself was damaged and never reconstructed. With the help of the map near the entrance (labeled in German), you can see how various incarnations of the temple were cantilevered atop one another. (Open Tues.-Sun. 8:30am-3pm; 800dr, students 400dr, free on Sun.)

There are 3 buses per day from Samos and Pythagorion to the site. You can also stroll along the beach from Pythagorion; the Ireon is waterfront property with a back gate leading right onto the beach. If you can't enter through the gate, continue along the beach past two houses, where a path brings you inland to the main road and main entrance. This inland path runs close to the route of the ancient Iera Odos (Sacred Way) from Pythagorion to the temple.

On the south side of town rest the ruins of the **Castle of Lycurgus,** built during the beginning of the last century by Lycurgus, a native of Samos and a leader in the Greek War of Independence. The **Church of the Transfiguration,** built within the ruined walls, is a pale blue variation on classical Orthodox architecture and interior decoration. (Free, but a small donation to the church is appreciated.)

Blocks of column, wall, and entablature are strewn throughout Pythagorion like Lincoln Logs after a floorquake, and the presentation in the small **Archaeological Museum** (tel. 61 400) is no different. In fact, only a little over half of the collection fits into the building; assorted ruins are scattered on the sidewalk in front. (Open Tues.-Thurs. 9am-2pm, Fri.-Sun noon-2pm; free.)

■■■ NORTHERN SAMOS

KOKKARI

Built on a peninsula 10km west of Samos Town, the village of Kokkari deserves a spot on your Samos itinerary. White pebble beaches and clear waters almost completely encompass the village. Along the main road (to your right when facing the church and bus stop) is the **Agricultural Bank of Greece** (Mon.-Fri. 9am-1pm, summer hours), and in the main square is the **Commercial Bank** (Mon.-Fri. 9am-2pm). A mobile, yellow **post office** (Mon.-Fri. noon-2pm) sits off the main road along the street just to the right of the shop where the bus lets you off. At this shop and other souvenir stores, you can **change money** after hours. Up to 9 daily **buses** leave Samos Town for Kokkari (200dr) on the Samos-Tsamadou line. A bus schedule is posted on the blue sign in front of the church. Farther down the road is a shack-like **OTE** (open Mon.-Sat. 4-11pm, Sun. 6-11pm). The **tourist office** (tel. 92 333) is down the road across from the OTE (open daily 9am-1pm, 5-10pm). **Rental stores** are open 8:30am-10pm. Cars rent for 9000dr per day (including insurance) and mopeds start at 2000dr. The town's few **pharmacies** are open 9am-1:30pm and 6-9:30pm during the week, and 10:30am-1pm on weekends. The local **doctor's office** (tel. 92 203) is located on Waterfront St. (Open Mon.-Fri. 9am-2pm, Tues., Wed., and Fri. 5-9pm.) After hours, if you need **medical assistance,** try calling 69 935 or ask the townsfolk for the doctor's home number.

Kokkari has become increasingly popular over the past few years, particularly among German tourists. German is at least as widely spoken among the locals as is English. You will find numerous rooms for rent, especially along the waterfront, but they can smell a bit fishy and are often noisy in the evening. **Hotel Elena** (tel. 92 164) has pleasant rooms on a quiet, beautiful little side street, run by a cheerful German-speaking older couple. Take the same route you would to get to the post office mobile. Just before the **laundromat** (wash 800dr, dry 600dr, soap 150dr), turn right onto a little side street. Look for the sign. (Doubles w/bath from 4000dr.)

NORTHERN COAST

The northern coast of Samos, particularly the stretch between Kokkari and Karlovassi, has a few deserted pebble beaches tucked away in little coves that are occasionally whipped by strong winds. Most of the coast is easily accessible from the road to Karlovassi, and the drive or the bus ride is worthwhile for the scenery alone.

Lemonakia Beach, 1km west of Kokkari and next to Tsamadou, and the wide white beach just west of **Avlakia,** are both alluring. You can trek into the mountains from the village of **Platanakia,** near **Ag. Konstandinos,** in the "valley of the nightingales." The valley is famous for its lush greenery, tall trees, and the thousands of birds that wake up to chorus in the mountain valley after midnight. The best time to hear them is at 3am. The best time for hiking is May through June and especially September, when the grapes from nearby vineyards are harvested and sweeten the air. Locals expect the village of Platanakia to become a major tourist desination in about five years. **Buses** from Kokkari cost 175dr. The 16th-century monastery **Moni Vrontianis** rests near the village of **Vourliotes,** 5km south of Avlakia.

Karlovassi, Samos's western port, is an unattractive city cluttered by towering hotels and empty modern buildings. But since the bus stops here and many ferries dock here before continuing to Samos Town, you might use Karlovassi as a base for excursions to western Samos. Doubles start at 3000dr. The **OTE** (open Mon.-Fri. 7:30am-10pm) and the **post office** (open Mon.-Fri. 8am-2pm) are neighbors on Agios Nikolaos St., near the square. Head down toward the ocean (with the hostel on your left) to the popular beach of **Limani.**

■■■ WESTERN SAMOS

Speckled with tiny villages and manicured fields, Western Samos is best explored by moped, though bus service from Karlovassi is adequate (2 per day, 950dr). The village of **Platanos,** planted 500m above the Aegean, offers an exquisite view of both sides of the island. **Mr. Menegas** (tel. 33 229) runs a cheap restaurant and hotel right on the main square (doubles 3500dr).

Marathokampos, 7km southwest of Platanos, is uncrowded and probably the easiest place on the island to find rooms (doubles 4500dr). A couple of km west of this peaceful coastal hamlet stretches the spacious beach at **Votsalakia;** another km farther is an even better beach at **Psili Ammos.** Two buses per day serve these beaches from Karlovassi. From Psili Ammos, the unpaved road continues clockwise beneath **Mount Kerkis** (1440m), winding around the island's western end in a harrowing passage overlooking dramatic mountain vistas.

IKARIA IKAPIA

Ikaria is associated with one of the best known—and most exhaustively plumbed—Greek myths. Daedalus fashioned wings for his son Icarus to use when escaping from Crete. Intoxicated with his newly acquired power, Icarus soared too close to the sun, melted his waxen wings, and plunged to his death near Ikaria's coast. In spite of the island's mythological fame, however, Ikaria's tourist industry is decidedly low profile. The notoriously idiosyncratic Ikarians have successfully resisted development; now visitors, mostly Greek, come for the promise of healing offered by Ikaria's medicinal springs, renowned for their radioactivity and chemical composition. At one time, Ikaria was known for its thriving apricots, but locals got tired of "shaking the trees" to harvest the fruits. Now Turkey has the Ikarian apricot trees.

Ikaria is split by a rocky mountain chain. The deceptively sparse landscape boasts up to 2500 species of plants, mostly herbs, which give subtle color and fragrance to the island. Large patches of Ikarian forest, devastated by a 1993 fire, are slowly returning to life. Most villages cling to the winding, windy coastline. The two main port towns, the larger **Agios Kirikos** to the north and **Evdilos** to the south, are located on opposite faces of the island. The mountains are separated by long, treacherous distances, and locals maintain themselves in relative isolation. Ancient Greek is still spoken. Some villages, notably **Agios Christos,** have built reputations for their nocturnal habits, drawing heat from the Greek government, which wishes to standardize business hours. Stores, including pharmacies, are open only in the mornings and evenings, often until 2am. Most of Ikaria appears subliminally affected by this: expect quiet, lazy days and lively, late nights.

■■■ SOUTHERN IKARIA

AGIOS KIRIKOS

Unassuming and congenial, Agios Kirikos is filled with white-washed houses; and its waterfront is lined with small cafés where the locals congregate. As Ikaria's main port, Agios Kirikos is the most convenient place from which to coordinate travel. Although the town's pier is marked by a large sculpture of Icarus plummeting to the ground, getting here has become considerably easier and safer since Icarus' time. Coming off the ferry, walk up the pier and onto the main waterfront road. A right turn will take you to the town square.

Orientation and Practical Information On the way to the town square from the ferry dock, you will pass the **Sine Rex,** the town's **movie theater,** and **Ikariada Travel** (tel. 23 322 or 22 277; fax 23 708), which offers friendly, English-speaking service and can arrange room or vehicle rental. They have offices in Therma, Evdilos, Armenistis, and Fourni. Open daily 8am-9:30pm. **Dolihi Tours** (tel. 23 230 or 71 240), located on the corner of the waterfront road just beyond the cafés, also sells tickets, distributes tourist information, and can help arrange lodging in Ag. Kirikos, Armenistis, and other towns. (Open daily 8am-1pm and 6-10pm, off-season 8am-1pm.) The **port police** (tel. 22 207) and **tourist police** (tel. 22 222; open daily 8am-2pm) share a building; climb the steps to the left of Dolihi Tours and continue up the road. There is a **hospital** nearby (tel. 22 330). Agios Kirkiros has two pharmacies. The island's only two **banks** are in Ag. Kirikos, in the square near the cafés and ferry offices. Open Mon.-Fri. 8am-2pm. After hours, tour offices and big hotels offer **currency exchange.** No credit cards are accepted on the island. About 100m up the street to the right of the National Bank is the **post office** (tel. 22 222; follow the sign; open Mon.-Fri. 8am-2pm), and the **OTE** (tel. 22 399; open Mon.-Fri. 7:30am-3pm). **Postal Code:** 83300; **Telephone Code:** 0275.

Ikaria's new **airport,** opened in June, 1995, will offer service to Athens (2 per week, 1hr, 15,000dr). The airport is located on the northeast tip of the island, near Fanari Beach. Ikaria is on the regular **ferry line** (off-season 3 per week) from Piraeus to Samos via Paros. Ikaria is 3hr. west of Samos Town (1700dr) and 9hr. from Piraeus (3464dr). Boats alternate stops at Evdilos on the north coast and Agios Kirikos, arriving at either location at about 2 or 3am. It can be difficult to find a hotel on your first night, so know the port where you will be arriving and call ahead if possible. From Agios Kirikos, boats also voyage to Patmos (3hr., 2500dr), Paros (4hr., 2000dr), Mykonos and Tinos (3hr., 2000dr). **Flying dolphins** leave from Ag. Kirikos regularly. They go to Samos (45 min., 3500dr), Patmos (45 min., 3500dr), Chios (1½hr., 6200dr), and Fourni (30 min., 2200dr). Places on the waterfront, and in Evdilos and Armenistis, rent **mopeds** (3000dr per day). **Vega** (tel 23 637; open daily 8am-9:30pm), on the waterfront near Ikariada Travel, rents motorbikes (3000dr; insurance 1000dr), cars (8000dr; insurance 2000dr), and jeeps (10,000dr; insurance 3000dr). Gas stations are open Mon-Sat 8am-2:30pm and 5-8pm, Sun. 8am-1pm.

Accommodations Climb the stairs to the left of Dolihi and take your first left, just before the police station, to reach the new **Hotel Kastro** (tel. 23 480). Comfortable, modern rooms overlook the harbor (starting around 6000dr, can peak to 10,000dr in July and August). To reach **Hotel Akti** (tel. 22 694), climb the same stairs to the left of Dolihi but take your first right into a tiny, short, seemingly private alley and climb the steps. Follow the new signs. Hotel Akti has a decidedly Greek appeal, enhanced by a plant-filled courtyard overlooking the Aegean Sea. Singles 4500dr, doubles w/bath 6500dr, triples 7500dr. On the way to Hotel Akti you'll pass the **Hotel O'Karras** (tel. 22 494), which offers pink rooms with firm beds and spacious baths. Singles 2500dr, w/bath 3500dr; doubles 4000dr, w/bath, 4500dr.

Food and Entertainment The **T'Adelfia Taverna,** the town's most established full-scale restaurant, offers summer "Greek nights" with music (entrees from 700dr; open 9am-2am). New restaurants are opening up near the local **clubs**, outside the square beyond the pier. For a quick meal, head to the inexpensive waterfront takeouts. There are a few rock **beaches** just west of the ferry dock, but if you continue past the tourist police to the east of town, you can clamber down to the sandy beaches and crystal blue water at the coves.

■■■ NORTHERN IKARIA

EVDILOS

Heading north from Ag. Kirikos, the tiny road to Evdilos offers breathtaking views of the coast as it snakes along sheer cliffs through the florid hill country. From the island's eastern heights you can see Samos, Patmos, and the Fourni Archipelago, but taking pictures near the military base is forbidden. On the way to Evdilos, the road passes a few tiny villages and beaches, many of which offer services and accommodation. **Bus** service is unreliable and tourist routes operate only in July and August. The schedule reported by the tourist police is often inaccurate. **Taxis** may be your best bet, so buddy up to cut costs (Ag. Kirikos to Evdilos 6000dr; Ag. Kirikos to Armenistis 7000dr; Armenistis to Evdilos 2000dr).

Evdilos, the island's minor port town, features red-tiled roofs against a background of lesser hills, with trees, terraces, and grasses. The town overlooks a cove with a sandy beach. The **post office, OTE,** and **pharmacy** keep hours similar to the offices in Ag. Kirikos. There is one **health clinic** (tel. 31 228), numerous restaurants, and rooms to let. Proprietors descend upon those stepping off the ferry from Piraeus. The beaches near Kampos, 500m west of town, induce euphoria.

ARMENISTIS

Armenistis, 58km from Ag. Kirikos, considered by some the "Greek Mexico" because of its relaxing environment, is the most touristed Ikarian haven. Its two sandy beaches are particularly popular. Life here, as elsewhere on Ikaria, sleeps away the day and dances away the night. **Hotel Pashala** (tel. 71 302) is comfortable, with cheap, clean rooms and a pleasant restaurant. Doubles 3500dr, but expect to pay more in July and August. Call ahead if possible. It's located along the same road as the *tavernas*, which offer traditional Greek cuisine. **Restaurant Simbioso** is well-liked, offers numerous vegetarian options, and has mouth-watering homemade cakes for breakfast. The popular **Livadi Camping** (tel. 41 349), on the beach roughly 300m before town, charges 500dr per person. If the crowding at Armenistis overwhelms you, the mountain villages of **Christos Rachon** (near the Monastery of Evangelistrias), **Frantato,** and **Dafni** provide calming alternatives.

THASSOS ΘΑΣΟΣ

Thassos's imposing, dark green mountain side differs strikingly from the chalky dry cliffs on many Greek islands. Villages, archaeological sights, and beaches are all engulfed in plush foliage on Thassos, which is nicknamed "Green Island." Despite suffering devastating fires in 1985 and 1993, the once-charred forests are slowly reviving. With its still-abundant vegetation, pine-forested coastal drives, and abundant bee-keeping and jam-making, Thassos remains an island of natural riches.

Since antiquity, the island has thrived on the gifts given to it by Hades, the god of wealth. Thassos cut loose from the Delian League of Athens in 411 BC, only to be recaptured by the Athenians 22 years later. Nonetheless, the island maintained a veneer of wealth and independence. During Roman times, builders from all over the world sought Thassosian marble, and its gold mines made Thassos one of the richest members of the Delian League. The island was the birthplace of Timoxenos, an athlete credited with some 1400 victories, and the home of Hippocrates for three years. During medieval times, marauding pirates and Ottoman invaders prompted the population to desert the city and hide out in the interior of the island. The Turks and then Egyptians controlled the island until it was retaken by the Greeks in 1912.

■■■ LIMENAS (THASSOS TOWN)

Built atop the foundations of the ancient city of the same name, Limenas has become the island's capital and tourist center. Accordingly, this lively albeit dusty port is more crowded and more expensive than the rest of the island.

ORIENTATION AND PRACTICAL INFORMATION

The only street sign you'll ever see is **19th Octovriou Street,** the main way one block from and parallel to the waterfront. Unless you enjoy wandering, buy a street map (250dr) at a kiosk or tourist shop, or get excellent directions. For assistance, consult the large blue sign across from the Mobil station, which lists the names and phone numbers of area hotels, pensions, and campgrounds.

Tourist Police: (tel. 23 111). Affable and English-speaking, but they may not be able to provide all the information you need. Open Mon.-Fri. 8am-2pm. The **port police** (tel. 22 106) are in a small gray building at the center of the waterfront.
Post Office: Head inland from Thassos Tours and turn right at the first corner (you can see it from that corner). Open Mon.-Fri. 7:30am-2pm. **Postal Code:** 64004.
OTE: On the main street behind the post office. Open Mon.-Fri. 7:30am-3:10pm. **Telephone Code:** 0593.
Tourist Agency: Thassos Tours (tel. 22 546 or 23 225; fax 23 005; open daily 9am-10pm). Continue up the waterfront road from the port police toward the old port (now used only for small boats), until you see their blue awning. Here Evangelos, the director, will provide candid advice and honest deals on everything from accommodations and car rentals to ferry tickets and special excursions.
Bank: National Bank of Greece, near the main square (open Mon.-Thurs. 8am-2pm, Fri. 8am-1:30pm) has an automated 24-hr. cash exchange machine and an **ATM** that accepts Mastercard and Cirrus.
Buses: Station (tel. 22 162; open 7:30am-8:15pm) to the right of the ferry landing, next to the "Mobil" sign. Buses head west across the island to easily accessible Limenaria, stopping en route at Skala Prinos (10 per day, 20min., 310dr), Panayia (12 per day, 15min., 175dr), and Skala Potamia (12 per day, 50min., 180dr). Other buses trek to Potos and Pefkari (10 per day, 1¼hr., 750dr), Aliki Beach (3 per day, 1hr., 1100dr), and Theologos (5 per day, 1½hr., 950dr). Ask at the tourist police or the bus office for schedules. Because bus service is erratic, leave several hours leeway to catch the last boat off the island.
Ferries: Run from Limenas to Keramoti (10 per day, 30min., 280dr), Kavala (2 per day, 1¼hr., 550dr), and from Prinos to Kavala (1 per day at 6am, 1½hr., 550dr). Be sure to note from which port, Limenas or Prinos, your boat leaves. If it leaves from **Prinos,** you can easily get there from Kavala. Contact **Theagenis Tours** (tel. 71 538; fax 71 888), directly up the street from the ferry landing, who are proficient in English and very helpful, with information on buses between Kavala and Prinos as well as the usual tourist agency services and vehicle rentals. To continue on to other islands of the Northeast Aegean, you must first return to Kavala for ferry connections.
Flying Dolphins: Hydrofoils zip between Thassos's main port of Limenas and nearby Kavala (7 per day, 40min., 1400dr). Schedules are posted near the pier, and docked boats indicate upcoming departure times from signs on board.
Moped/Car Rental: Nine agencies rent motorbikes, but one of the better ones is **Thassos Tours** (2000dr per day). They also rent cars (12,000dr per day, including tax, insurance, and 100km).
Hospital: (tel. 22 222; in Prino, 71 100). Near the OTE. Open 24 hr.

ACCOMMODATIONS

Accommodations are a free-for-all on Thassos, especially on the weekends when Greeks flock to the island from nearby Kavala and Thessaloniki. Consequently, prices may bear little relation to the official rates set by the government. Roughly 100m to the left of the Thassos-Kavala hydrofoil dock, behind the **Marina Restaurant,** sit several reasonably priced pensions. A listing of hotels, pensions, and campgrounds (with phone numbers and class ratings) is posted in front of the bus stop.

Giorgos Raxos (tel. 22 778), has a great bargain with his unnamed pension. Although there's no sign, you can't miss the distinctive, to say the least, green-tiled house. Rooms are spacious and clean. Doubles 4000dr, triples 5000dr.
Hotel Dionisos (tel. 22 198), down a small side street off the main road to the right of Gregory's Art (facing inland). Sparkling rooms in a central but quiet location. Singles 7000dr, doubles 7500dr, triples 8500dr.
Pension Philipus (tel. 23 076, -513), is run by a friendly woman who maintains 15 gracious rooms, all with bath and access to kitchens. With the post office at your

left, continue along the road, past the dry cleaners, and follow the bend in the road. The pension is on the left with a blue "Philip" sign. Doubles 7500dr.

Villa Edem (tel. 23 096), a 5-10-min. walk from the center of town, will nevertheless reward the sojourner with a choice of studios with fully equipped kitchens and balconies, or rooms w/breakfast for 7000-8000dr. All with modern showers and very hot water. True garden setting and a likeable owner, Dimitrius.

Camping Ioannidis, (tel. 71 477, -377). For the hardy traveler. Take the bus (310dr) to this campsite, 13km west of Limenas on the road to Skala Prinos (850dr per person, tent 850dr). Tell the bus driver you are going to the campsite.

FOOD

For a yummy snack head to the ever-popular **Appetitio,** near Gregory's Art, and order a cheese- or cream-filled pie, *bougatsa* (300dr). For a more filling meal, **Selianos** taverna (tel. 23 214), 200m inland past the port, serves *kolikomezedhes* (zucchini burgers, 700dr) and *octopomezedhes* (octopus; 800dr). It's worth the trip. For a hearty, traditional Greek meal, walk up to Prinos and at the crossing look past the supermarket for **Toxotis** (open 1pm-1am), a local favorite. **Platonakia,** on the waterfront near the old port, serves pricey, but delicious meals (1800dr).

SIGHTS

In addition to impressive remains of buildings and walls dating from the 6th and 5th centuries BC, the island flaunts a 4th-century BC Greek **theater,** built on the remains of the acropolis of ancient Thassos. The ruins are easy to find; turn right behind the old port and continue to a three-pronged fork in the road beyond a recessed ruin—the middle path leads to the theater. Unfortunately, the classical dramas usually staged here in the summer have been suspended due to renovations. The archaeological sites are free and always open. The **Thassos Museum** (tel. 22 180), near the old port, contains mosaic floors and sculptures found on the site, including a colossal 6th-century BC marble statue of Apollo with a ram draped around his shoulders. (Open Tues.-Fri. 8am-7pm, Sat.-Sun. 8am-3pm; admission 500dr, EU students 200dr, older travelers 400dr.) Next to the museum is a large **agora** (same hours, free).

■■■ EAST COAST

Buses travel from Limenas to Limenaria (8 per day, 700dr), stopping 10km south in the villages of **Panagia** and **Potamia** (1500-1550dr). Three km apart, both villages overlook Ormos Potamias, a gorgeous, sandy cove. The aromas of grilled goat meat and syrup-saturated walnuts greet you as you approach Panayia, which retains its traditions despite a minor tourist influx. Potamia houses a small **Folk Museum,** tucked under the shadow of the town church, featuring traditional costumes and outdated agricultural tools (open Mon. and Wed.-Sun. 8:30am-3pm). Both villages have private rooms; Panayia also has an inexpensive hotel, the **Helvetia** (tel. 61 231), at the north entrance to town (doubles start at 5000dr).

The golden beach of **Chrisi Ammoudia** stretches endlessly 6km east of Panayia. Farther south, Potamia's beach is capacious, but less attractive. (Those who choose to camp may be able to use the water tap at the entrance to the olive grove, roughly 1km from the beach towards Potamia.) The twin coves of **Aliki** (11km south of Kinira) hide the most tranquil beaches on the island. The northernmost one, sheltered by foliage, is often isolated; undress at your own risk. The south beach cove, formed as sand shifted over a Roman marble quarry, shelters slabs of bleached white rock and crevices ideal for snorkeling. The main beach in between gets more crowded, but it's good for grabbing a meal at one of the seaside *tavernas.* Towel off and trudge to the monastery of **Archaegelon,** a simple, whitewashed church with stone floors and colorful icons. (Open daily 8:30am-8pm; cover-up clothing provided for visitors; 200dr donation expected.)

■■■ WEST COAST

No longer the capital of the island as it was in Turkish times, **Limenaria** has a small waterfront that is home to numerous cafés, *tavernas,* and shops. Even though inexorable daily buses haul in tourists from Limenas (700dr), finding a private room amidst Limenaria's Turkish houses is not difficult (doubles start at 5000dr). Facing inland, the **post office** and **national bank** are to the right of the harbor. The **police** are on the waterfront; they're friendly but don't speak English. Exemplary beaches are at **Pefkari** and **Potos,** 4km away. Seven buses per day run from Limenas to Potos (750dr). **Pefkari Camping** (tel. 51 190), 1km north of Potos, runs an outstanding campground (750dr per person; 950dr per tent; 950dr per car; electricity 1000dr).

SAMOTHRAKI (SAMOTHRACE) ΣΑΜΟΘΡΑΚΗ

Samothraki first welcomed Greek colonists in the 7th century BC. The island soon achieved fame as a religious center specializing in the worship of the *libiri,* twin gods who helped infertile women bear children. At the **Sanctuary of the Megaloi Theoi** (Great Gods), Philip of Macedon met his wife Olympius. This meeting is said to have led to **Alexander's conception.** The starkly beautiful island, now home to 999 churches but fewer than 3000 people, draws the occasional hardy adventurer. Fegari, the highest peak in the Aegean (1670m above sea level), rises out of this stony, oblong isle. According to Homer, it is from this summit that Poseidon cheered for warriors at the Trojan War.

■■■ KAMARIOTISA

The waterfront of Kamariotisa, Samothraki's port, is surrounded by modest houses, and though the town has ample tourist venues, these are pleasantly free of neon-lit restaurants blasting bad Euro-techno.

Orientation and Practical Information The **port police** (tel. 41 305; 24 hr.) are on the waterfront facing inland two blocks left of the ferry dock; look for the Greek flag. The **police** (tel. 41 303, -203) are situated at the top of the hill in front of the ruins of the castle. Their office is open daily 7:30am-2:30pm; ring the bell after 2:30pm and someone will answer. The castle (24 hr., free) rests above the panorama of the rising, wooded cliffs. On the road stretching inland, just across from the **National Bank** (which is on the waterfront and open in July and Aug. solely for **currency exchange** Mon.-Fri. 8am-2pm), is the **pharmacy** (tel. 41 581; open Mon.-Fri. 9am-1:30pm and 6:30-8:30pm, Sat. 11am-1pm). Just up the road on the left from the pharmacy is a **minimarket** and **OTE.** (Open daily 8am-1pm and 4-10pm.) A 10-min. jaunt up the quiet hillside's main street, characterized by red-tiled houses and chickens dodging the occasional passing automobile, brings you to another **OTE** (tel. 41 212; open 7:30am-3:10pm) and the **post office** (tel. 41 244; open Mon.-Fri. 7am-2pm), as well as the **Agricultural Bank of Greece** (open Mon.-Fri. 8am-2pm). **Postal Code:** 68002; **Telephone Code:** 0551.

Ferries connect Samothraki with Alexandroupolis (1-3 per day, 2½hr., 2200dr), Limnos (1 per week, 3½hr., 2350dr), and Kavala (3-4 per week, 4hr., 2810dr). Saos Tours and **Arsinoi Shipping,** in Samothraki (tel. 41 565) and Alexandroupolis (tel. 26 721), can help with tickets and information. In summer, **buses** run frequently from the ferry dock to Chora (10-12 per day, 180dr), Therma (10-12 per day, 340dr), Alonia (180dr), Psira Potomos (340dr), Lacoma (220dr), Profitis Ilias (4 per day, 340dr), Paleopolis (180dr), Kariotis (220dr), and the campsites (400dr). All island bus rides last less than a ½hr. and cost 320dr or less. Bus info and ferry tickets can be obtained along the waterfront at **Saos Tours** (tel. 41 505). **Taxis** await customers near the bus stop (tel. 41 341) between 8am and 1am. **Moped rental** is available at the unnamed garage opposite the ferry dock (tel. 41 511; open daily 8:30am-9pm; 4000dr per day). Car rentals are available at Saos Tours (12,000dr per day).

Accommodations The English-speaking Saos Tours, your all-purpose tourist agency, can brief you on the room situation. Doubles without bath average 5500dr, with bath as much as 8000dr. Friendly, family-run **Vasiliki Karoyiannis** (tel. 41 165) has clean rooms with shared baths (doubles 5000dr, triples 5500dr). Hang a right just past the National Bank at the restaurant/rooms sign to get there. The restaurant below has delicious, fresh *loukoumades* (Greek honey doughnuts, 500dr). Roughly 100m farther to the right (facing inland) are the well-maintained rooms of **Maria Mamougiorti** (tel. 41 315), who speaks German. Look for the blue-and-white "rent rooms" sign high above on the building. (Doubles 5600dr, triples 6300dr.)

Food and Entertainment Along the waterfront are several fish tavernas, which serve only one fish or meat dish each day. For pasta or vegetarian fare, try the smaller ouzerie. The restaurant beneath **Mrs. Karoyiannis'** pension has delicious authentic Greek meals, served on tables scattered along a quiet side street (entrees 950dr). The nightlife, which congregates in Kamariotisa, may not lastingly relieve your ennui, but you can try the several café-bars on the waterfront: **Bloody Mary, Diva, Big Blue,** and **Cocktail.** One km west (left facing the water) are the dance clubs **Disco Rebel** and **Music Hall Apropto** (drinks 1200dr; no cover).

Sights Just 7km east of Kamariotisa is **Paleopolis** (Old City), with the ruins of the Megaloi Theoi. Dedicated to Axieros (Demeter, the goddess of the harvest and of fertility), and a mumbling hubbub of other deities as well, the Megaloi Theoi witnessed the initiations of both the Spartan King Lysander and the historian Herodotus. Ruins of the theater, temenos, and palace remain. (Site open Tues.-Sun. 9am-3pm; admission 450dr, students 250dr.) The worthwhile **Paleopolis Museum,** next to the ruins, houses local artifacts including gargantuan entablatures from the Rotunda Arsinoe and the Hieron, and a cast of the Nike of Samothrace. Sign the guest book if you think the original Nike, now in the Louvre, should be returned to Samothraki. (Museum open Tues.-Sun. 9am-3pm; admission 450dr, students 250dr.)

■■■ AROUND THE ISLAND

The road northeast from the main port of Kamariotisa treads the coast to **Paleopolis** (7km) and **Therma** (or Loutra, 6km farther). **Chora** (sometimes called Samothraki), the island's capital, is roughly 6km from the inland port; **Lacoma** lies 9km south.

THERMA

Next to the bus stop in Paleopolis are private rooms; inquire at Saos Tours. Six km east of Paleopolis is arguably the most beautiful part of the island, **Therma,** named for its therapeutic water and **thermal baths** (open daily 8-11am and 5-7pm). When you get off the bus, the baths are in the white buildings on the right. The town, 200m uphill from an uncrowded, stony beach, is nestled in a lush forest full of ferns and fruit-laden trees. Ask around for the sweet *prousti,* which is made only on Samothraki. Rooms are plentiful, but things get dicey in late June, when journalists swarm the island for their annual convention.

Tasoula Parselia (tel. 98 318) has bright, airy rooms with bath and shared kitchens. (Doubles 8300dr, triples 9000dr.) To get to this pension in the midst of shady woods, follow the main street leading inland from the bus stop—it's at the top of the hill, roughly 100m away, on the right. **Anna Chaila** (tel. 98 235) has older, clean rooms with bath. From the bus stop, follow the road that bears left, then look for the signs—it's next to the OTE agency and the Anna Chaila *taverna.* (Doubles 6000dr, triples 7000dr.) If you don't mind walking downstairs to shower, **Alexan-**

dra Hatzistephanou (tel. 98 272), across from Parselia Tasoula's, has simple, clean rooms, shared bath, and refrigerator (doubles 5700dr). There are two **campsites** several kilometers east of Therma, before Fonias. The **GNTO** facility (tel. 98 229) is 690dr per person, 460dr per tent, and 575dr per car.

GRIA VATHRA

In Gria Vathra, a 15-min. walk south from Therma, are the island's waterfalls; if you can manage the dirt paths, look for the unique blue, butterfly-like insects. These waterfalls are a nature-lover's delight. Swimming in the ponds beneath the waterfalls can be a chilling thrill, as it gets very cold even in the hottest months. If you head past Therma several km you'll come to a good beach at **Fonias,** and continuing east another 16km to the eastern side of the island, you'll find another at **Akr. Kipos.** The island's best beach, **Pahia Ammos,** is on the central-south part of Samothraki, accessible only by car or moped. Several km east of Pahia Ammos, there's an exquisite beach at **Vatos** (find a private boat to sail you there; 50,000dr per trip; boats hold 20-25 people). For a dazzling view of the Aegean, head to **Profitis Ilias** and gaze at the majestic scenery while sampling some of the island's famed fat-free roast lamb.

LIMNOS ΛΗΜΝΟΣ

It is said on Limnos that when one insensitive clod made a dirty joke about Aphrodite, the goddess put a curse on the island, causing the women to kill the men. Only the king, helped by his daughter, escaped. Upon arrival, the Argonauts found grieving widows; shortly thereafter, the repopulation of the island was underway.

Situated strategically as a potential "cork" for the Black Sea, and as a buffer between Turkey and the rest of Greece. Her scruffy hills, filled with the bleating of goats, shoulder vast expanses of golden grassed meadows. Knuckled ridges of volcanic handiwork and fantastic rock formations fall away to long, unspoiled stretches of smooth, sandybeaches. Modern by most standards, this eighth largest of the Greek islands remains one of the Northeast Aegean's best-kept secrets.

■■■ MYRINA

The island's capital and primary port, Myrina is a charming, well-proportioned fishing village keenly aware of its beauty. The skyline, made strange by volcanic configurations, is dominated by an impressive Genoese-Turkish fortress which is illuminated at 10pm each night (along with the church across the harbor). Against the star-studded sky, its turreted tower achieves almost ethereal definition.

Orientation and Practical Information The harborfront fashions a plaza around which are numerous *taverna,* the ferry and tour agencies, and a few oldish hotels. **Kyda St.,** the main road leading inland, takes you past a variety of shops and into the town's central square, recognizable by its many **taxi stands** (tel. 23 033 or 22 348). The **OTE** (tel. 22 299; open Mon.-Sat. 7:30am-10pm, Sun. 8am-1pm and 5-10pm) and a **National Bank of Greece** (open Mon.-Thurs. 8am-2pm, Fri. 8am-1:30pm), which has an **ATM,** are in the square. One block farther along Kyda St. is Garofalidi St., where you will find the **post office** (tel. 22 462; open Mon.-Fri. 7:30am-2pm) and a self-service **laundry** (tel. 24 392; open daily 8:30am-2pm and 5-9:30pm; 1700dr per kilo). The **police** (tel. 22 200) are a few blocks past the post office and the **hospital** (tel. 22 222) is to the left of Garofalidi St., on the street farthest from the waterfront. The **bus station** (tel. 22 464) is located in El Venizelou Sq., the second square you come across as you continue up Kyda St., past Garofalidi St. Buses are few and do not go to most towns (open Mon.-Fri. 8am-2:15pm, Sat. 8am-noon). The best way to see Limno is by renting a **bicycle** (1000dr), **moped** (2500dr), **car** (8000dr), or **jeep** (9000dr); insurance extra. **Express Rental office**

(tel. 23 830; fax 23 494), at the far corner of the waterfront in Myrina, below the Kastro, rents all four. **Postal code:** 84100. **Telephone Code:** 0254.

For Olympic Airways **flights** (tel. 22 078) to Athens (3-4 per day, 12,800dr), Thessaloniki (1 per day, 13,000dr), or Mitilini (1 per day, 12,600dr), **Praulis Travel** (tel. 22 471 or 24 617; fax 22 471), located in Myrina's port square, can provide information. Buses to the **airport** (tel. 31 204) cost roughly 1150dr. **Ferries** depart from the side of the port opposite the castle, a short hike from the port square. In high-season, ferries run to Kavala (4 per week, 6hr., 3091dr), Lesvos (4 per week, 6hr., 3021dr), Thessaloniki (2 per week, 7hr., 4151dr), Chios (1 per week, 4642dr), Rafina (4 per week, 4647dr), Agios Efstratios (3 per week, 1571dr), Piraeus (3 per week, 5166dr), Samos (1 per week, 5789dr), and Patmos (1 per week, 5952dr). Contact **Nicos Vayakos' Tourist and Travel Agency** (tel. 22 460 ; fax 22 900) in Mirina's port square. **Flying Dolphins** leave from the opposite side of the port, beneath the castle; they speed once per week to Kavala (7250dr); Chios (10,100dr); Mitilini, Lesvos (6700dr); and Plomari, Lesvos (8600dr).

Accommodations and Food Those arriving by ferry in July and August will be met by locals offering private rooms. Try the **Hotel Aktaion,** on the harborfront below the castle. The pristine rooms have sinks, refrigerators, and balconies overlooking the colorful fishing boats. (Singles 4500dr; doubles 8000dr, w/bath 9000dr; triples 10,500dr.) For expansive rooms with a kitchenette go to the **Apollo Pavilion** (tel. 23 712), near the police station on Garofalidi St. (doubles 9500dr, triples 10,600dr). A multitude of fresh fish *taverna* line the harborfront. For dinner, try one with ample view of the castle, so you can watch the lights go on. For breakfast, try **La Luna Café,** on the harborfront next to the Express Rental shop.

■■■ AROUND LIMNOS ISLAND

The home of the legendary smith Hephaestus (who gave Prometheus fire), Limnos inspires the imagination with a landscape as simple as it is enthralling. Beaches are numerous and varied enough to suit any personality. Explore the areas beyond the port town, specked with clusters of small stone houses, fields of hay, and almond groves—you may be the only traveler. There are three major archaeological sites around the island: **Ephestia, Kaverio,** and **Poliochini,** the earliest Neolithic city in the Eastern Mediterranean, which antedates even Troy I. **Poliochini** was the site of seven cities from 5000 BC to 1500 BC. **Petrides** (tel. 22 039), on the main shopping road, is one of two travel agencies offering tours to all three sites (2 per week, 3000dr). Visit the **archaeological museum** (tel. 22 990) on the beachfront of Myrina (open Tues.-Sun. 8:30am-3pm; admission 500dr, students 300dr; Sun. free).

Sporades ΣΠΟΡΑΔΕΣ

The jagged coasts and thickly forested interiors of the Sporades (Scattered Ones) were first colonized by Cretans, who cultivated olives and grapes on the scattered islands until Athenians took over in the 5th century BC. The residue of ancient structures on these islands attests to the 2nd century BC Roman presence and the Venetians' 13th century rule. The Venetians were forced out by the Turks, who controlled the islands until 1821, when the Sporades became Greek.

Lush islands of fragrant pines, luxurious beaches, and abundant fruit orchards, the Sporades of today offer travelers (mostly Germans, Norwegians, and Brits), a smorgasbord of earthly delights. Although word has gotten out about the Sporades, and the islands' fledgling tourist facilities are quickly maturing, there are spots on this small archipelago that remain relatively quiet and inexpensive.

SKIATHOS ΣΚΙΑΘΟΣ

Secondary to the other Sporades in natural beauty, Skiathos has tried to compensate by hosting the group's largest social scene. In terms of the number of visitors, the strategy has been a success, but most islanders agree that Skiathos is now too expensive. Although it lacks the sophistication and charming architecture of that other notorious pelagic playboy, Mykonos, Skiathos certainly rivals Mykonos in cost. Since the traditional culture has been pretty much obliterated, the only recourse may be to read about it. Fortunately, Skiathos was home to the wonderful short story writer Alexandros Papadiamantis (1851-1911), and this is one of the few places where his books can be found in English translation.

SKIATHOS TOWN

Skiathos Town has weathered the deluge of foreign tourists far better than much of the coastline. The cobblestone streets of the commercial section are packed with loitering tourists and expensive stores, but in the residential neighborhoods, balconies burst with white gardenia blossoms and magenta bougainvillea, while grapevines overhang shady, undisturbed terraces. Skiathos Town is known as *the* place to party in the Sporades—the slew of nightclubs and discos rhumbas until at least 4am.

ORIENTATION AND PRACTICAL INFORMATION

Disembarking from the ferry or hydrofoil, you'll see a long waterfront, lined with travel agencies, *taverna,* and various bike and car rental dealers. The waterfront strip is intersected by **Papadiamanti Street,** the main drag. Traveling inland, Papadiamanti is intersected by Pandra St. at the National Bank of Greece, and by **Evangelistra Street,** farther inland at the post office. Parallel and to the left of Papadiamanti, but not sprouting until Pandra, is **Politechniou Street,** home to a string of decent bars. On the far right of the waterfront, still facing inland, a road winds up to the airport and several beaches. On the far left, along a harbor perpendicular to the main waterfront, is a row of fishing boats that charter daily excursions. Frequent bus service links Skiathos Town with Koukounaries beach and points in between, leaving from close to the road out of town. A mediocre map is available at all kiosks (300dr).

Tourist Police: (tel. 23 172). On the right side of Papadiamanti St., inland past the OTE. Some English spoken. Ask for the thick *Summer in Skiathos* brochure. (Open 8am-9pm.) **Police** (tel. 21 121) are across the street. (24 hr.)

Post Office: (tel. 22 011). Papadiamanti St. at Evangelistria St. Open Mon.-Fri. 7:30am-2pm. **Postal Code:** 37002.

OTE: (tel. 22 135). Papadiamanti St., one block inland from the post office, in an ugly white building. Open Mon.-Fri. 7:30am-10pm. **Telephone Code:** 0427.

Banks: National Bank of Greece, midway up Papadiamanti St., on the left side, offers **currency exchange.** Open Mon.-Thurs. 8am-2pm and 7-9pm, Fri. 8am-1:30pm and 7-9pm, Sun. 9am-noon. Lines are excruciatingly long and slow during July and Aug. Cash enough money to tide you over *before* you arrive in Skiathos.

American Express: (tel. 21 463, -4). Papadiamanti St., on the left before the post office, in the travel agency of Mare Nostrum Holidays. All tourist services, including excursions around the island (4200dr per full day). Open Mon.-Sat. 8am-2pm and 5-10:30pm, Sun. 9:30am-1pm and 5-10:30pm.

Flights: (tel. 22 376). Five flights daily to Athens (50min., 14,800dr). **Olympic Airways Office** (tel. 22 229, -049) midway up Papadiamanti St. Call 24 hr. prior to take-off to confirm flight. Open Mon.-Fri. 8am-4pm. Take a taxi to travel between airport and harbor (1000dr).

Buses: From the bus stop shack at the far right end of the wharf (facing inland), along the island's main road, ending at Koukounaries beach (every 15-20min., 7:15am-1am, 240dr).

Ferries: Nomikos/Goutos Lines (tel. 22 209), in the middle of the waterfront; open daily 7am-11pm. Ferries travel to Skiathos most frequently from Agios Konstantinos, Volos, Skopelos, and Alonissos. From Athens, take the daily bus from the station at 260 Liossion St. (hourly, 6:15am-9:30pm, 2½hr., 2450dr) to Agios Konstantinos, and then the **ferry** from there at noon or 1pm (3½hr., 3000dr). From Volos, 1-3 boats sail daily (3hr., 2300dr). All ferries usually continue on to Skopelos and Alonissos. Ferries run from Skiathos to Skopelos (4-5 per day, 1½hr., 1300dr) and Alonissos (2-4 per day, 2hr., 1450dr). To get to the Pelion Peninsula, catch one of the **excursion boats** leaving the fishing village of Platania at either 8am or 9am, returning from Koukounaries Beach on Skiathos at 5pm (1500dr).

Flying Dolphins: (tel. 22 018). At center of waterfront. Open daily 7:30am-9:30pm. Hydrofoils travel to Agios Konstantinos (3-4 per day, 1¼hr., 5302dr), Skopelos (9-11 per day, 35min., 1815dr), Volos (5-6 per day, 1¼hr., 4629dr), Alonissos (8-9 per day, 1hr. 5min., 2346dr), Platania (1-2 per day, 25min., 2569dr), and Thessaloniki (1 per day, 3¼hr., 10,011dr).

Taxis: (tel. 21 460). Queue along the waterfront; prices are posted on the shack.

Moped Rental: Numerous interchangeable places along the waterfront and road heading to the beaches. Bikes from 2500dr per day.

Laundromat: Miele (tel. 22 341). Make a right off Papadiamanti at the National Bank. Wash 1500dr, dry 500dr per 15min., iron 500dr per ½hr. Open daily 8am-11pm. Detergent and required 500dr tokens available at the grocery store across the street (open daily 8am-2pm and 5-11pm).

English Bookstore: Skalino (tel. 23 647). Make a left on Evangelistra St. and it's on your right. Some English-language material, including Papadiamantis' books.

Pharmacy: (tel. 22 988). On the right side of Papadiamanti St., just past the post office. Open daily 8:30am-1:30pm and 5:30-10:30pm.

Medical Emergency and Hospital: (tel. 22 040, -222), on the "Acropolis" hill behind Skiathos Town. 24 hr.—after 1pm, emergencies only.

ACCOMMODATIONS

Finding rooms in July and Aug., when most Greeks vacation, can be difficult. Usually visitors make reservations before they arrive. Singles are almost impossible to come by in the high season, while doubles often cost 10,000dr. "Rooms to Let" are your best bet; some proprietors offer facilities such as a refrigerators and space on the roof to dry clothes. Signs abound and hordes await ferry and hydrofoil arrivals, but if you're stuck, try the **Office of "Rooms to Let"** (tel. 23 852 or 22 990), right on the dock (open 8:30am-11:30pm). Try Evangelistra St. or the streets parallel to it.

Pension Danaos (tel. 22 834), on a left-hand side street off Papadiamanti two blocks inland from the post office, is cheaper than most (doubles 10,000dr).

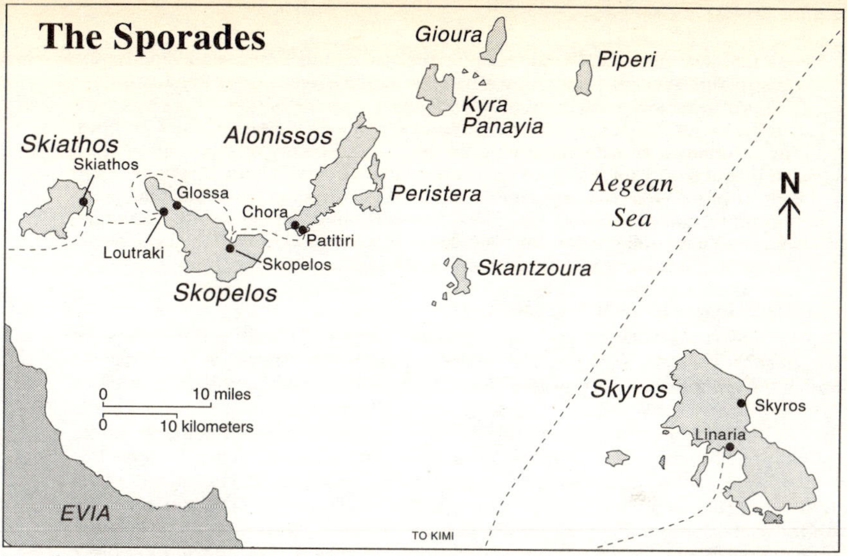
The Sporades
Gioura
Piperi
Kyra
Panayia
Alonissos
Skiathos
Skiathos
Glossa
Chora
Peristera
Aegean
Sea
N
Loutraki
Patitiri
Skopelos
Skantzoura
Skopelos
0 10 miles
0 10 kilometers
Skyros
Skyros
Linaria
EVIA
TO KIMI

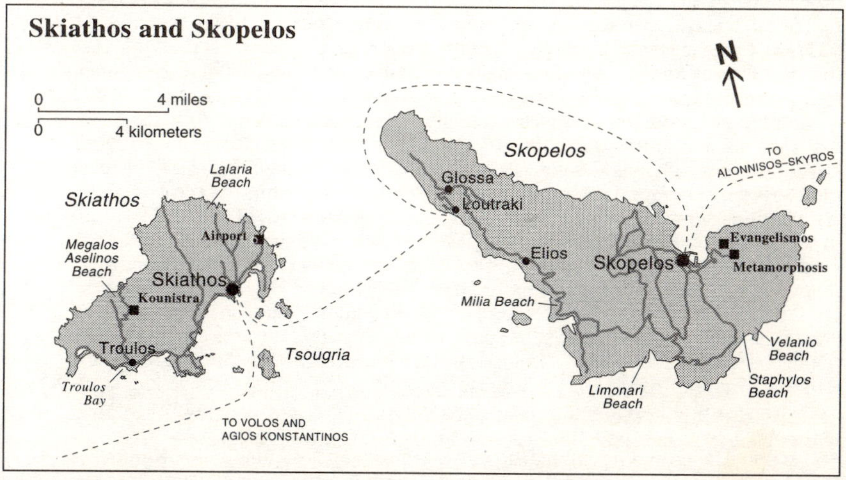
Skiathos and Skopelos
N
0 4 miles
0 4 kilometers
Skopelos
TO
ALONNISOS–SKYROS
Glossa
Loutraki
Lalaria
Beach
Skiathos
Airport
Megalos
Aselinos
Beach
Skiathos
Kounistra
Elios
Skopelos
Evangelismos
Metamorphosis
Milia Beach
Troulos
Tsougria
Velanio
Beach
Troulos
Bay
Limonari
Beach
Staphylos
Beach
TO VOLOS AND
AGIOS KONSTANTINOS

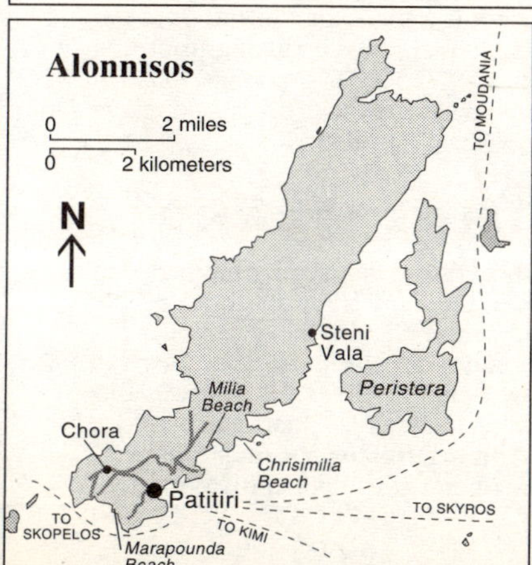
Alonnisos
TO MOUDANIA
0 2 miles
0 2 kilometers
N
Steni
Vala
Peristera
Milia
Beach
Chora
Chrisimilia
Beach
Patitiri
TO SKYROS
TO
SKOPELOS
TO KIMI
Marapounda
Beach

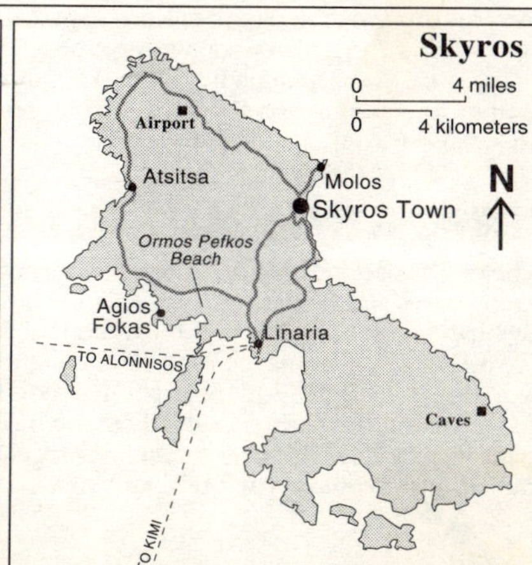
Skyros
0 4 miles
0 4 kilometers
Airport
Atsitsa
Molos
Skyros Town
N
Ormos Pefkos
Beach
Agios
Fokas
Linaria
TO ALONNISOS
Caves
TO KIMI

Pension Galini (tel. 22 258), on a side street parallel to Evangelistra (follow the signs to the Taverna Ilias). You can take dance classes from Zana (doubles 10,000dr; ask about student discounts).

Camping Aselinos (tel. 49 312), located near one of the island's nicer beaches, offers a *taverna,* a palm canopy on the beach, and plenty of shady spots. It's a pain to reach on your own, but they run frequent buses (20min., 250dr); inquire at either of the two waterfront info booths (14,000dr per person, including tent).

Camping Koukounaries (tel. 49 250), on the bus route, between stops 19 and 20, has a restaurant, minimarket, and wooded campground 1km from the beach (person 1400dr, small tent 800dr, large tent 1000dr).

FOOD AND ENTERTAINMENT

Dining in Skiathos is bound to be an expensive affair. The cheapest option is to hit the *gyros/tiropita* stands which line Papadiamanti and the waterfront or to forage in any of the numerous **supermarkets** (there is also a good baker across from Pension Danaos). There are also many overpriced Greek *taverna* to try. **Dionissos** on Pandra St. is a little cheaper than most and has an enormous menu (four-cheese risotto 1200dr, fixed menus 1900-3500dr). **Aura,** a small meat-lovers' haven, is squinched between large shops on the steps leading uphill on the left end (facing inland) of the waterfront (chicken 950dr). Otherwise, you can shell out lots of money for some pretty good international cuisine. On the waterfront, **Kalypso** (tel. 23 051) offers upscale Italian fare (pastas 1400-2000dr). Uphill and slightly inland from the other end of the harbor (past Aura) is a multinational cluster. **Garden of the East** (tel. 21 627) has Chinese vegetarian dishes for 900-1000dr; **Le Bistrot** (tel. 21 627), across the street, does Italian, including snails in a spicy sauce for 1500dr. **Chez Julien** rounds out the trio with French food such as oven-baked scallop shells for 1200dr.

Nightlife here runs the gamut from mellow waterfront *taverna* to hellbent all-night discos. For more sophisticated decor, however, you'll pay up to a 1000dr cover charge which includes your first drink. Generally, Evangelistras and Polytechniou streets are home to most pubs and simple discos. For larger, tropical, chic discos with delusions of grandeur, walk along the waterfront east of town. Most close in the off-season. **Kalypso,** the classiest place in town, is on the water above the restaurant of the same name; the door is on the street parallel to the waterfront road. Enjoy the bartender George's pleasant conversation as you sip his well-mixed concoctions. Classical music grooves until 'round midnight, when an eclectic mix of jazz, reggae, New Age, and African takes over in a gay-friendly atmosphere. (Beers 600dr, cocktails 1200-1400dr.) The last of the waterfront discos, **BBC,** has the best dancing and features rave and other fast-paced music. (Beer 1000dr, cocktails 1800dr.) **Admiral Benbow** may be Polytechniou's most eccentric pub. Brits Mick and Elaine play oldies, rock, blues, and soul and serve imported beers and ciders for 500-700dr. The crowd resembles the music—mostly oldies but goodies. **Kentavros Bar,** Mitrop. Ananiou St., parallel to Papadiamanti, is a short jaunt inland from the waterfront. This groovy bar with space to boogie plays music ranging from Eric Clapton to jazz. (Open nightly from 9:30pm; beer and wine 500dr, drinks 1000dr.) **Remezzo** is popular on the strip. If you call trading bumps with sweaty strangers "dancing," then this is the place for you. (Beer 800dr, cocktails 1500dr.)

■■■ AROUND SKIATHOS ISLAND

The north coast of Skiathos, accessible only by boat or by hiking paths, has secluded sandy coves and is relatively peaceful. In contrast, the south shore, easily accessible by bus, car, or moped, is very crowded, but the sand is fine and the water clear.

The island's main paved road runs along the south coast from Skiathos Town to Koukounaries. Unsightly resort hotels dominate the beaches. A **bus** travels this route leaving the harbor in Skiathos Town (every 15-20min., 7:15am-1am, 240dr), with stops at many beaches, including **Megali Ammos, Nostos, Vromolimnos, Platanias,** and **Troulos.** The bus route and the road end at the pine grove beach of

Koukounaries, where swaying branches shelter clear turquoise water and fine white sand. Water-skiing and wind-surfing schools and sailboat, canoe, and pedal boat cartels all converge on these pristine shores. A short walk away is the curved yellow **Banana Beach,** slightly less populated than the others. To get there from Koukounaries, take the paved road to the left of the bus stop, follow it to the bend, and make a right on the uphill dirt road. At the top, take the worn path through the gate on the left. A quick scamper over the next hill leads to interestingly-named **Little Banana Beach,** a **nude beach** full of unpeeled bathers. The beach is especially popular with (but not exclusively for) gay men.

Just east of Troulos a road turns off for **Asselinos,** a beach and campground on the north edge of Skiathos. From the main road, it is a 45- to 60-min. walk to **Megalos Asselinos** beach, home to a *taverna*, campsite, and good snorkeling. You can reach it by car, troika, moped, rollerblades, inflatable armadillo, or a long walk from Troulos. Alternatively, take the high road which forks after 2km—the right branch leads uphill to **Panagia Kounistra,** a small monastery with a grape arbor and a *taverna* within its walls. To the right of Megalos Asselinos is **Micros Asselinos.** The latter is the more secluded of the two, though neither is crowded, except at lunchtime when excursion boats stop at Megalos Asselinos. Getting to Asselinos Town is a bit easier—buses leave until 10pm from **Asselinos Tours** (tel. 21 095 or 49 394) on the waterfront for the 20-min., 250dr trip.

West along the coast past Lalaria Beach are the ruins of the medieval walled **castle** (a 2-hr. walk on a path from Skiathos Town). The Greeks built the castle during the 16th century to take refuge from marauding pirates. When independence dawned in the 19th century, they abandoned this headland and began work on what has blossomed into present-day Skiathos. Two churches are all that remain of the ancient community. The **Church of the Nativity** is most intriguing, with fine icons and some frescoes. Daily excursion boats leave from the long strip at the far left side (facing inland) of Skiathos' harbor for Lalaria, on a tour of the caves and castle (2500-4000dr round-trip). Buy a ticket on the boat; departure is between 9 and 11am, return 4pm. For a full day of swimming, hop on one of the boats that leave for the small island of **Tsougria** (hourly, 10am-5pm, round-trip 1200dr). Boats also leave the harbor each morning for a full-day excursion to Skopelos and Alonissos (4200dr).

SKOPELOS ΣΚΟΠΕΛΟΣ

The looming cliffs rising from the coastline gave this island its name, Steep Rock From The Sea. Tempering the mountains' starkness, acres of pine, olive, and plum trees blanket the hills. Originally a Cretan colony ruled by King Staphylos, strategic Skopelos has been occupied by Persians, Spartans, Athenians, Romans, Franks, Venetians, and Turks. It was conquered in 1538 by the illustrious Turkish admiral Khayr El-Din Barbarossa (Red Beard), who put the entire population to death. Today, Skopelos' own culture dominates and the island has managed to keep tourism within sane limits. Women practice their traditional occupations of weaving and embroidery, and wear the distinctive Skopelan *morko*—a silk shirt, short velvet jacket with flowing sleeves, and a kerchief, all finely hand-embroidered. Only the harbor area of Skopelos Town has been transformed to suit foreign expectations.

■■■ SKOPELOS TOWN

Except for the front line of tourist offices and *tavernas* curving around the horseshoe waterfront, Skopelos Town is a complex and delightful cobblestone maze stacked up against a hillside. Even the tourist shops are examples of true handiwork. The tightly packed architecture in Skopelos Town is a jumble of Venetian, Byzantine, Macedonian, and Neoclassical styles, visible in 123 of the island's 360 churches that are in Skopelos town. The roofs here are made of overlapping slate tiles, and weigh roughly 10 tons on average. Expensive to build and maintain, they are gradually being replaced by red ceramic tiles. For a view of this vividly-colored settlement, climb to the top of the castle walls on the north side of town.

ORIENTATION AND PRACTICAL INFORMATION

Boats dock at the small jetty on the left tip of the horseshoe as you look seaward. Tourist agencies and scattered *tavernas* line the waterfront. Behind the crowded eateries, one block from the Commercial Bank, **Galatsaniou Street,** darts upward, a fashionable path rich with trinkets and goodies. Buses depart from the right edge of town, facing the water; an inland square directly opposite the stop is affectionately known to locals as "Souvlaki Square" for its cheap eats. On the right leg of the horseshoe, the lush pine hillside hides three monasteries.

Police: (tel. 22 235). Behind the National Bank. Open Mon.-Fri. 7am-2:30pm.

Post Office: At the top of the horseshoe where the block of *tavernas* ends and the bus stop area begins, take the first right inland, make a sharp left before you enter the small inland square (look for the sign to your left), then your first right, then your first left (then shake it all about and do the hokey-pokey). Or just follow the clear signs. Open Mon.-Fri. 7:30am-2pm. **Postal Code:** 37003.

OTE: Take Galatsaniou St. from the waterfront for 50m. Open Mon.-Sat. 7:30am-10pm, Sun. 9am-2pm and 5-10pm. **Telephone Code:** 0424.

Tourist Agencies: Several on the waterfront. Most exchange currency, rent mopeds and/or cars, and sell ferry and/or hydrofoil tickets. None is especially helpful in locating rooms around the island, although **Thalpos'** (tel. 22 947, 23 466; fax 23 057) English-speaking staff offers helpful general advice from an office on the second floor near the middle of the waterfront (open daily 9am-3pm and 6-10:30pm). Most agencies are open from around 8 or 9am to 10:30 or 11:30pm, with some taking a late afternoon siesta.

Banks: National Bank of Greece, on the left leg of the horseshoe waterfront. Open Mon.-Thurs. 8am-2pm, Fri. 8am-1:30pm. It has an **ATM** which accepts Mastercard and Visa. **Commercial Bank,** at the center of the waterfront. Open Mon.-Thurs. 8am-2pm, Fri. 8am-1:30pm.

Buses: At the parking lot area behind the beach at the left edge of town facing inland. To Stafilos and Agnotas beaches (22 per day, 175dr each way), Panormos (16 per day, 320dr), Milia beaches (16 per day, 400dr), Elios swamp (8 per day, 420dr), and Glossa Town (8 per day, 600dr).

Ferries: At least 2 boats per day come from Volos and Agios Konstantinos. A daily bus from Athens runs to Agios Konstantinos (hourly 6:15am-9:30pm, 2450dr); from there the ferry to Skopelos is 3480dr, from Volos 2820dr. Ferries from Skopelos travel to Skiathos (1½hr., 1280dr), Alonissos (½hr., 950dr), and Kimi (2 per week, 4hr., 4100dr). The ferry to Alonissos leaves in the evening and returns in the morning, so you'll have to spend two nights there to stay a full day. Alternatively, you can take an **excursion boat** from Skopelos (1hr., 2000dr).

Flying Dolphins: Zoom from Skopelos to Agios Konstantinos (1-2 per day, 2hr., 7065dr), Volos (3-5 per day, 6005dr), Skiathos (8-10 per day, 45min., 1815dr), Alonissos (1-4 per day, 20min., 1464dr), and less frequently to Thessaloniki (11,205dr), Kimi (8391dr), and Chalkida (9357dr). Most ferries and hydrofoils also stop at **Loutraki,** the port for the north town of **Glossa** on Skopelos.

Taxis: (tel. 23 240). At the center of the waterfront amid the block of tavernas. Taxis stick around in the square approximately 7am-2am.

Moped Rental: Throughout town. A cheap one is **Motorbike for Rent/Horizon** (tel. 23 279). Make a left on the street heading diagonally away from the inland square and walk by the bars. 1500-2000dr per day.

Laundromat: Several around town, including one near Greca's Crêperie and a second inland past the National Bank. Wash (including soap) 1800-2400dr; dry 1100dr; ironing services available. Open 9am-2pm and 5:30-9:30pm.

Pharmacy: (tel. 22 252). Across from the OTE. Open Mon.-Fri. 9am-2pm and 5:30-11pm. Also on the waterfront. Open Mon-Sat. 9am-2pm and 5pm-midnight, Sun. 10:30am-2pm and 6pm-midnight.

Medical Center: (tel. 22 222). Follow the left-hand road inland from Souvlaki Square until it dead-ends, then turn right and you'll shortly see it on the right. Open Mon.-Fri. 8:30am-1:30pm for free walk-ins, 24 hr. for emergencies.

ACCOMMODATIONS

If you don't get scooped up by hustlers, the cheapest accommodations can be found by wandering through the narrow labyrinthine streets behind the waterfront and looking for "Rooms to Let" signs or asking locals. If you prefer a larger, more anonymous hotel, try **Hotel Georgios L.** (tel. 22 308), on the far right of the waterfront, facing inland (doubles 7000dr). Oddly enough, there are no campgrounds on Skopelos and while *Let's Go* does not recommend illegal, freelance camping, many pitch tents nearby and between Milia and Elias beaches.

FOOD AND ENTERTAINMENT

Skopelos is blessed with quite a few tasty, affordable dining options; as usual, the waterfront is not the place to find them. Locals are unanimous in their praise of **Perivoli** (tel. 23 758), on the right a short distance farther inland from the Souvlaki Square. The culinary delights here (Greek with an international inflection) are well known, so reservations are a good idea for high season weekends (pasta with a 3-cheese and cream sauce 1200dr, seafood risotto 1600dr). **Greca's Crêperie,** on a side street leading right from the same square, is the most authentic of the numerous creperies, with delicious fare prepared by a Parisienne (salty or sweet crepes 800-1200dr). After dinner, polish off your appetite at **Wine & Honey,** inland from the Commerical Bank, with scrumptious Turkish and Greek sweets (cookies 2000-3200dr per kilo). They also have a large selection of limited-edition Greek wines.

Although the nightlife on Skopelos doesn't compare with neighboring Skiathos, there are still plenty of places to boogie. The most popular tourist bars are **Glaros** and **La Costa** on the waterfront (both have beers for 800dr, cocktails 1600dr). Locals are more likely to sit and people-watch at the **Mediterranean Bar,** on the water farther out of town than the previous two (beer 500dr, cocktails 1300dr); **Plefsis** (a.k.a. **Vrachos** because of its perch on the large ledge which juts into the waterfront road), with beer 1000dr, cocktails 1500dr; or **Apo Kata,** on the street heading out of town (a sharp left) from Souvlaki Square (beer 800dr, cocktails 1500dr). You can also dance at the last of these, but the best disco in town is **Kirki**—follow the signs on the road to Staphylos (turn left after Hotel Amalia if the signs are mysteriously invisible). The cover is 1500dr (includes first drink), beer 1000dr, and cocktails 1300dr, but this is the place to dance, although it doesn't usually get to its best before 2am. For something different, try either of the two live Greek music places. **Xarama,** on the far side of the ruined castle on the hill on the north part of town (facing inland), is expensive but has a beautiful view and rocks in the summer (cover 1500dr, beer 1500dr, cocktails 2000dr). **Meitani,** across town across from Apo Kata, is a bit tamer, but still fun (cover 1500dr, cocktails 2000dr).

■■■ AROUND SKOPELOS ISLAND

Mt. Palouki, which faces the town across the water, conceals three **monasteries.** Two paved roads leave the town from the bus depot on the right end of the waterfront. To get to the monasteries, follow the left road, which circles the harbor, ascends the mountain, and becomes a dirt road 600m past the Hotel Aegean. At the next fork, two signs will point the way to the monasteries (½hr. by foot from town). **Evangelismos,** clinging to the rocks across from Skopelos Town, hails from the 18th century, but its enormous gold-plated altar screen from Constantinople is 400 years older. Take the left-hand fork up the hot and winding mountain road (a 45min. walk). Start early in the morning before the heat and bugs intensify. (Monastery open daily 8am-1pm and 5-8pm.) If you are a dedicated monastophile or a masochistic hiker, descend back to the fork and climb to the **Monastery of Metamorphosis,** standing amid pines on a breezy knoll. The little chapel, set in a flowery courtyard, dates from the 16th century. (A 1½-hr. walk from the fork; open daily 8am-1pm and 5-8pm.) **Prodromou** is visible from Metamorphosis, on the next ridge. Once a monastery, this refuge is now a cloister dedicated to St. John the Baptist and inhabited by nuns. (A 2-hr. walk from the fork, open daily 8am-1pm and 5-8pm.) All three monasteries provide bell-bottoms and long-sleeved smocks for men and women to meet the dress requirement. They are moped-accessible to experts or fools. Several tourist offices offer expensive **excursions** to the monasteries. (High season only, Wed. 10am-noon, 4000dr; book in advance.)

Beaches line the coast south of Skopelos up to Loutraki. The main one, **Staphylos Beach,** is long, sandy, and very crowded. Archaeologists discovered the tomb of the ancient Cretan general Staphylos on a hillside near here, as well as a gold-plated sword dating from the 15th century BC (now in the Volos museum). A better option is **Velanio Beach,** accessible by the ridge at the east edge of Staphylos. Advertised as the only legal **nude beach** on Skopelos, it is considerably less crowded and less cluttered with plastic pails and their screaming, toddling owners. The inhibited bather need not fear—about half of the beach-goers elect to keep their bottom piece on. Farther along the paved road is **Agnotas,** a pleasant harbor good for a seaside picnic or *taverna*-prepared meal (locals recommend the *taverna* Takonis). The beach is small, crowded, plagued by sea urchins, and too close to the boats, but there's a *caïque* that shuttles every ½hr. to uncrowded **Limnonari Beach** (500dr round-trip).

For a superb hike, take the bus to Glossa and walk the dirt track across the island to the **Monastery of Agios Ioannis,** clinging to a boulder above the ocean. (Take the main road east from Glossa and turn left on the first dirt road to Steki Taverna; after that it's clear sailing.) At the road's end a path drops to the sea, and stone steps, cut in the escarpment, lead up to the monastery. There is a cistern of potable water in the rock. Allow at least a 4-hr. round-trip to visit Agios Ioannis, and bring at least a liter of water per person. Most of the road is navigable on motorbike.

Eight buses run daily as far as Glossa, with many more stopping at the intervening beaches (see schedule on p. 352). For those who don't want to venture far from Skopelos Town, the cliff-bound beach of **Sares** is accessible by **boat** (400dr).

ALONISSOS ΑΛΟΝΝΗΣΟΣ

Alonissos is—to make the inevitable pun—the most isolated and, with only 1700 inhabitants, the least populated of the Sporades. Its story is also one of the saddest in the tumultuous post-war history of Greece. In 1950, Alonissos' once-lucrative vineyards were annihilated, and much of Alonissos' male population was forced to take up construction work in Athens. By 1965, just as the island had recovered some measure of prosperity through farming and fishing, an earthquake struck, shaking down the harbor of Patitiri and the capital town of Alonissos on the hill above. The dictatorship then began a housing development in the port town of Patitiri, and forced all but nine Alonissians to leave their town.

As a result of this devastation, Alonissos lacks polished beauty, but it is one of the friendliest and least touristed islands in Greece. The beaches are magnificent, and the mountains maintain a pristine, almost icy, emptiness. Old Alonissos has a delightful charm and views to die for. If the sedate, unruffled atmosphere here suits you, you may be tempted to stay a while, but come soon—architects and real estate agents are already setting up shop.

■■■ PATITIRI

All boats dock at Patitiri, for all intents and purposes the only town on the island. As your boat glides toward the port, you'll see whitewashed Old Alonissos clutching the slopes of the hill. Patitiri, a city of concrete buildings and interchangeable restaurants, is neither the best nor the subtlest introduction to Alonissos. Unassuming during most of the year, Patitiri attracts the usual jumble of island-hoppers in the summer, as well as an assortment of travelers using this city as a home base.

Orientation and Practical Information From the docks, there are two main parallel streets, **Pelasgon** on the left and **Ikion Dolophon** on the right. To locate the **police** (tel. 65 205), follow the "bakery" sign on the right 20m up Pelasgon. The station is across from the bakery on the slope above the avenue (24 hr.). The **post office** is 100m up Ikion Dolophon St. (open Mon.-Fri. 7:30am-2pm). The **OTE,** on the right corner of the waterfront as you face inland, is in the tile-roofed building, although by 1996 it might have moved to a new building near the **hospital** (tel. 65 208), 600m up Ikion Dolophon, on the right on the way up to Old Alonissos (OTE open July-Aug. Mon.-Sat. 7:30am-3:10pm, Sun. 9am-2pm.) In the middle of the waterfront are the two friendliest and most fluent travel agencies. **Ikos Travel** (tel. 65 320, -648) is run by the amiable, English-speaking Mr. and Mrs. Athanassiou, who find rooms, change money, buy Flying Dolphin tickets, and book excursions (open 9am-10:30pm). **Alonissos Travel** (tel. 65 188; fax 65 511), just to the left, offers similar services (open 9am-10pm in July and August 8am-11pm). The equally friendly English-speaking staff at the **Flying Dolphin offices** is also nearby. The **National Bank of Greece** (open daily 8am-10pm) is 30m up Ikion Dolophon St. Almost all boats to the Sporades, whether from Agios Konstantinos or from Volos, stop at Alonissos. **Ferries** come from Athens via Agios Konstantinos (5½hr., 3850dr) and Volos (5hr., 3180dr). They also travel here frequently from Skiathos (2hr., 1500dr), Skopelos (½hr., 950dr), Kimi (2 per week, 3hr., 3780dr), and Thessaloniki (1 per week, 5730dr). **Flying dolphins** zip between Alonissos and Agios Konstantinos (2½hr., 7415dr), Volos (2½hr., 6710dr), Skopelos (15min., 1470dr), Skiathos (1hr., 2350dr), Skyros (1hr., 4400dr), Kimi (2½hr., 7770dr), and Thessaloniki (11,200dr). A **pharmacy** (tel. 65 540) is located 50m up Ikion Dolophon St., on the left. (Open daily 9am-1pm and 6-8:30pm.) **Taxis** wait at the foot of the jetty on the waterfront (tel. 65 573, -425). Most moped rentals are clustered on Pelasgon St.—shop around. **Orpheus Laundry** rests 150m up Pelagson Ave., just before the gas station on the left. (Open Mon.-Sat. 9am–12:30pm. Wash 1400dr, dry 1200dr, soap 300dr.) Near the laundry, **Rent-A-Bike** (tel. 65 371) rents Yamaha bikes (50cc 2500dr per day, 80cc 3000dr). **Rent-A-Boat** on the right of the waterfront rents two-person boats (800dr per day), ideal for reaching distant beaches. The bus, leaving from the foot of the jetty, travels between Patitiri and Old Alonissos 3-4 times per day (200dr one-way). Ikos Travel displays timetables. **Postal Code:** 37005; **Telephone Code:** 0424.

Accommodations Upon arriving on Alonissos, you will be accosted by room-renting locals offering the best deal in town. Prices are negotiable and vary, according to season, from 1000 to 5000dr per person. There is a pension (tel. 65 451) near the laundromat which has nice, new rooms (doubles 5000dr) as well as slightly older ones (doubles 4000dr). If a new world order takes over and you are not approached, the **Office of "Rooms to Let"** (tel. 65 577), in a brown shack in the center of the waterfront, will be able to help. (Open 9am-10pm.) Also look for signs advertising rooms on the two inland streets perpendicular to the waterfront. Covered with stones the size of baseballs, the town beach by the port is unsuitable for sleeping. **Dimakis Pension** (tel. 65 294), is 20m up Pelasgon Ave.; inquire at Boutique Mary. (Doubles 4000dr, w/bath 5000dr.) **Café Pleiades** (tel. 65 636), uphill just before the bakery, rents rooms with views of the village and the harbor. (Doubles 4500, apartments for 3 people 7500dr). Guests are entitled to a 10% discount on breakfast at the café. For camping head to **Camping Rocks** (tel. 65 410), a partially uphill, 1km hike following the signs (on Pelasgon. This, the only easily accessible official campsite, is acceptable only if you plan on going to sleep after 3:30am when the disco finally stops blaring (person 1500dr,w/tent).

Food and Entertainment At the waterfront *tavernas,* dine under canvas or a canopy of leaves while watching the water lap the docks. The absence of aquatic amusement is about the only thing which distinguishes restaurants on either of the inland roads from the waterfront places, but prices are universally expensive. For an after dinner drink, pick your favorite ambience from among waterfront watering holes such as **Pub Dennis, Pub Nefeli,** and **Pub IX Muses,** which all offer beers for roughly 600dr, cocktails for 1200dr, and serve a variety of dessert. Later, try **Disco 4x4** just up Pelasgon, perhaps most notable for a colorful array of weekend contests and games (beers 1000dr, cocktails 1500dr).

THE OLD TOWN (CHORA)

A trip to the island is not complete without a visit to Old Alonissos. Set high on the hill to ward off pirate attacks, this rebuilt Chora (Old Town) stands out amidst the craggy rock. Although you could never tell from the outside, intriguing, tourist-free Old Alonissos is an international village, full of expatriates and lined with the abodes of absentee home-owners. The island's only **bus** runs between Chora and Patitiri hourly 9am-3pm and 7-11pm (10min., 200dr). A schedule is posted on the sidewalk in front of Ikos Travel, where the bus picks you up. A **taxi** will give you a ride for roughly 2000dr round-trip, which can be split by four people. A walk to the town, however, affords glorious views of the countryside. Start on Pelasgon and follow the main road uphill. At forks, either follow signs to Chora or take the uphill choice. **Maps** (500dr) can help. Make sure to bring at least a liter of water per person with you—the parching walk from Patitiri takes roughly 1hr. On its hill, the town is quiet, breezy, and cool. Old Alonissos' 12th-century **Christ Church** is one of the few churches in the Greek islands where men and women are segregated during services. To gain entrance, you'll have to speak to Papa Gregorias, village priest and local legend. Women may feel more comfortable here in groups. The fabulous views and quaint atmosphere make this an ideal dinner or drinks destination. Check out the sunset while sampling Celeste's authentic Italian cuisine at **Nappo;** follow signs to the right of the main street (pastas 1000-1500dr, pizzas 1200-1800dr). The almond sweets at **Kaphereas** may be the best on the island; the breathtaking view midway on the main street, alone is worth a visit.

■■■ AROUND ALONISSOS ISLAND

Only the south end of the island is inhabited, leaving the mountainous central and north sections cloaked by pristine pine forests. Since the island's roads are unpaved and there is little public transportation, yer own two feet are the best means of transportation and exploration on Alonissos. The dirt roads are passable by motorbike as far north as Diasello, about three-fourths of the way to the north tip. Motorbikes can be rented from both inland-leading streets of Patitiri (2000-3000dr per day—shop around). The tourist agencies sell good maps (500dr).

A ½-hr. downhill walk south leads to any of four beaches: **Marapouda, Vithizma, Megalo Mourta,** or **Mikro Mourta,** sheltered beneath steep pine-clad slopes on the tip of the island. Alternatively, take an **excursion boat** from Patitiri (boats leave in the morning as they fill, round-trip 1200dr). During the 4th century BC, Alonissos was known as "Ikos," and Tsoukalia was the site of the island's pottery workshops. Many of the shards discovered at Tsoukalia are marked *Ikion,* "product of Ikos."

In the other direction, *caïques* (800dr) bring you up the coast to **Milia** and **Chrisi Milia**—considered by some to be the outstanding beaches of Alonissos—and **Kokkinokastro,** where the ancient acropolis of Ikos has been inundated by the sea. For an additional several hundred *drachmae* you can continue to **Steni Vala** or **Kalamakia,** or farther still to **Agios Dimitrios,** a long, sweeping, semi-circular beach.

■■■ NEARBY ISLANDS

For a negotiable 3000-4000dr per person, you'll find that Alonissos is the place from which to visit some of the smaller members of the Sporades by **charter boat.** The only inhabitants of lovely **Skantzoura,** to the east, are shepherds, their amiable sheep, and one lone monk. Another jaunt takes you to **Gioura,** home of the cyclops Polyphemos, where Odysseus and his crew nearly met their end. Several islands claim this distinction, but Gioura, with its large cavern complete with thousands of stalagmites, best fits the Homeric description. The cavern, however, is temporarily closed. There's a mesmerizing seaward view from atop the steep cliff. Gioura is home to herds of brown goats, with black crosses covering their spines and shoulderblades, who have been a protected species in the national park of Gioura since 1930. **Kira Panagia,** the largest of the small islands, has a charming monastery, and several fine snorkeling spots. The distant island of **Piperi** is a **wildlife sanctuary;** waterfowl and a large abbey of monk seals make their homes there. Officials discourage visits by nonspecialists, but ask at the tourist office in Athens for the requisite permit. Given this exception, **excursion** boats run to all the islands.

SKYROS ΣΚΥΡΟΣ

Rolling purple hills nibbled at by goats, groves of fragrant pines, sandy beaches, and gnarled cliffs form the spectacular backdrop for daily life on Skyros. The island's idiosyncratic culture remains strong; throughout the entanglement of sidestreets, women embroider and weave rugs while men fashion sandals, ceramics, and intricately hand-carved wooden furniture.

By far the quietest island of the Sporades, Skyros is the largest and most isolated as well. Unfortunately, increasing tourism is beginning to spoil the island's charm. Where rooms once offered glimpses of distinctively Skyrian domestic life, many "Rooms to Let" have now succumbed to the generic (and surely cheaper) mode of a stark white bed in a white room. But this new brand of uniformity is by no means pervasive; Skyros has a quirkier, more private side also well worth discovering.

■■■ SKYROS TOWN

Crowned by a Venetian castle, Skyros Town spills down from this rocky summit away from the sea. The town's offbeat architectural layout is the result of several pirate invasions. As a safety measure, houses were built on the cliffside facing inland. As you approach by bus, there is no sign of the town until you actually enter it. Skyros Town's steep and narrow paths make for a *de facto* ban on cars. What confounded pirates then may confuse you now; make sure to get clear directions to wherever you're going.

ORIENTATION AND PRACTICAL INFORMATION

Boats to Skyros dock at quiet **Linaria,** where a bus for Skyros Town, and perhaps one for Molos on the beach, will be waiting (180dr). Be sure to hurry to the bus once you get off the ferry, or you'll be stuck. Ask the drivers their destinations, as buses may be marked somewhat counterintuitively (e.g., "Topikon" (The Place), for the town and "Skyros" for the beach). A **taxi** ride to Skyros runs 1500dr. The bus drops off just outside this maze-like town. Continue along the bus' aborted path to the town's **central square** and you'll be on the main drag, **Agoras Street.** Again, like the town, this strip of restaurants, travel agencies, and tourist shops is completely hidden. Follow Agoras to its end on the opposite side of town and you will arrive at an **open square,** overlooking Molos and the sea, in the center of which stands the bronze statue of the uncharacteristically **nude English poet** Rupert Brooke. From this square a path leads down to Molos. Once downhill, the road leads to a little church. Turn right and you'll reach Molos Beach. Turn left and you'll have a long inland walk to several hotels. Ask for directions; Agoras St. twists and winds confusingly. Once off the main drag, you'll spend the afternoon reorienting yourself.

Police: (tel. 91 274). Follow the street across from Skyros Travel to the end, then take a right. It's the white building with light blue gates and trim.

Post Office: Make the first right as you walk from the bus stop to the central square (tel. 91 208). Changes money and cashes traveler's checks. Open Mon.-Fri. 7:30am-2pm. **Postal Code:** 34007.

OTE: From the bus stop, turn around and walk back out of town—it stands 50m on the right, under the blue awning (tel. 91 599). Open Mon.-Fri. 7:30am-3:10pm. **Telephone Code:** 0222.

Budget Travel Offices: Skyros Travel (tel. 91 123, -600), on Agoras St., is the agent for Flying Dolphins and Olympic Airways. Organizes boat trips to the south (6000dr) and cheaper bus trips (600-1000dr), helps locate lodgings, and sells island maps (400dr) that are better than those sold on the street. Open 9:15am-2:15pm and 6:30-11pm. A few steps downhill on Agoras, the **Flying Dolphin Office** (tel. 92 152) has hydrofoil info and maps. Open 9am-2pm and 7-11pm.

Banks: National Bank of Greece (tel. 91 802), up from the bus stop, on the left before the central square. Open Mon.-Thurs. 8am-2pm, Fri. 8am-1:30pm.

Flights: 10km from Skyros Town on the north tip of the island (tel. 91 660). Accessible by foot or taxi. One flight Mon., Wed., Fri. to Athens (13,800dr).

Buses: From Linaria to Skyros Town, Skyros Town to Molos, and Linaria to Molos (plus returns), each roughly 6 times per day, each 180dr.

Ferries: To get to Skyros, first travel by bus from Athens to Kimi on Evia (6 per day, 3½hr., 2400dr). June 15-Sept. 15 ferries from Kimi's port area, Paralia Kimi, travel twice per day to Skyros (2hr., 1820dr). There is no ferry service to the other Sporades, but tickets may be bought in Linaria for the weekly routes to Tinos (3730dr), Mykonos (4377dr), Paros (4593dr), Santorini (7180dr), Crete (7188dr), and Thessaloniki (5890dr).

Flying Dolphins: To Alonissos (4396dr), Skopelos (4581dr), Skiathos (5803dr), Kimi (4102dr), Marmaris (8514dr), and Volos (10,187dr) 6 times per week.

Taxis: (tel. 91 666). Queue at central square, not to be confused with Rupert's square, which is at the far edge of town.

Medical Center: (tel. 92 222). Clinic with two doctors located at the edge of the village, 400m from the bus stop.

ACCOMMODATIONS

There are "Rooms to Let" in tiny Linaria. For most of your stay, however, you will probably want to base yourself in Skyros Town, because it has more creature comforts. One of the highlights of staying in Skyros is seeing the interior of a Skyrian house. Rooms are embellished with an assortment of family heirlooms: crockery, copperware, dolls, icons, portraits, and hand-carved furniture from all over the world. Initially, only aristocratic families possessed these precious items. By the late 19th century, though, as the upper class moved to Athens and began to sell off their possessions cheaply, members of the lower class began to decorate their homes as well. Reinforced with heavy cross-beams and thatched with local "bamboo," the ceilings of these homes are also artistic masterpieces. Unfortunately, you're not likely to see any of this if you're snatched up by someone whose business is renting rooms; you'll have better luck with the casual offer from a local. Try wandering through the back streets of Skyros Town or along the dirt roads by Molos beach. Expect singles in high season to be 3000-4000dr, doubles 4000-8000dr.

For something more organized, check out beautiful, marble-floored **rooms** (tel. 91 459) below the National Bank of Greece in Skyros Town. Blooming plants surround the entrance, the lobby is clean and comfortably furnished, and showers are hot and have good water pressure. (Doubles 7000dr.) If your primary goal in visiting Skyros is to soak up the sun, you can stay a bit closer to the beach. At the end of the marble steps leading down from the **naked poet statue** awaits a house with blue railings (tel. 91 386) and **rooms** with balconies. (Doubles 7000dr.) Next door is a **campground** (tel. 92 458) in a pleasant, if dry, field. There is a restaurant and a minimarket but few other amenities (i.e., no hot water). (Person 1250dr w/tent.) On the road to the right past the campground, leading to the beach, is **Pension Galini** (tel. 91 379), which offers clean rooms (singles 5000dr, doubles 6000dr).

FOOD AND ENTERTAINMENT

As always, small, half-hidden *tavernas* may offer better deals and better food than their more flashy, better-situated counterparts. **Sisyfos** (tel. 91 505), on Agoras St. 50m past the bus stop, caters to both vegetarians and carnivores. (Vegetarian stuffed tomatoes 900dr, *mousaka* 990dr.) **Kabanera** (tel. 91 240) lies tucked away in the maze of Skyros Town. Walk up Agoras St. until you come upon the first **fish taverna** sign and follow it and its successors. (*Kalamari* 950dr, *pastitsio* 8050dr.) For quick, cheap eats, try the **souvlaki-pita/gyros stand** in the central square (*gyros* 250dr).

There is also a collection of *tavernas* on the beach, at the end of Molos away from Skyros Town. The very last in the row, **Milos** (tel. 91 378), reputedly has the best lobster with pasta (8000dr per kilo), a specialty of the island. Closer to town, **Taverna Thomas** (tel. 91 942, -03) has numerous vegetarian specialties (croquettes 700dr, eggplant imam 900dr). Skyros, like the rest of the Sporades, produces much of the pine resin that flavors *retsina* in the country's largest distilleries; its own brand of kegged *retsina* is among Greece's finest. Particularly good is *Kokkinelli* (rosé)—ask for it *apo to vareli* (from the barrel).

Most bars open at 9 or 10pm and close at 2 or 3am, and since most of them form a line on Agoras St., walking casually up the street until you find your preferred atmosphere may be best. You'll come across **Rodon,** with large multicolored balls hanging from the ceiling (beer 600dr, cocktails 1200dr); the **Renaissance Pub** in the central square with a roof garden (beer 500-600dr); **Apocalypsis** on the far side of the main square with a big-screen TV and dancing (beer 700dr); and **Kalypso** farther uphill to the right when Agoras St. turns deceptively left (beer 600dr, cocktails 1200dr). Cheaper drinks can be found at *tavernas* or take-out food places along Agoras. The late-night scene is rather tame. The only disco is **Skyropoula,** at the bottom of the steps. Heading down to the **naked Rupert Brooke statue,** turn right at the sign (although the steps are the quickest way down from the town, the road is much better when it is lit at night). Starting down this road to Molos, head right where you'd go left for the beach, and you'll come to it.

SIGHTS

A variety of **myths** draw their inspiration from Skyros. Legend has it that the Athenian king Theseus met his end when he was unceremoniously dumped off this cliff by Skyros' King Lykomedes, with whom he had hoped to find asylum. The warrior Achilles spent much of his youth here. To prevent his enlistment to fight in the Trojan War, his mother dressed him up as a girl. But when Achilles couldn't resist buying a sword from Odysseus, the well-worn traveler called his bluff. Skyros was also the home of Atalanta, the princess who refused to marry anyone who could not defeat her in a foot-race. Her suitor Melanion (or Hippomenes) slowed her down, winning the race by throwing three golden apples in her path.

Perched atop Skyros Town are the **Monastery of St. George** and the **Castle of Licomidus.** Check out the monastery's 11th-century fresco of St. George. The castle, meanwhile, is generally believed to be Venetian, but evidence now indicates that the Venetians cheated, simply renovating an earlier Byzantine fortification. The reclining marble lion set into the stone wall above the castle's entrance dates from the 4th century BC, when Athenians taunted Skyrians with this symbol of Attic ascendancy. On the southeast side of the castle peak lie the remains of an aqueduct whose main shaft was once used as a prison. To get there, make the steep hike uphill from anywhere on Agoras St. As you climb to the fortress, you'll be surrounded by dancing doves, leaping lizards, and striking scenery. The view at the top is spectacular. (Open daily March-Aug. 7am-10pm, Sept.-Feb. 7:30am-6pm; free.)

Take Agoras St. to the tip of town; you'll find a plaza circumscribing the bronze statue of **naked English poet** Rupert Brooke, who died of fever here en route to Gallipoli during the disastrous Dardanelles campaign of WWI. The poet's tomb, constructed near a bay in south Skyros, is the island's only modern claim to fame. On the statue's right side, down the marble stairs (also leading to the beach), is the **Archaeological Museum** (tel. 91 327; open Tues.-Sun. 8:30am-3pm; admission

500dr, students 300dr.) Down the steps and to the left of the **naked Brooke statue,** the fascinating **Faltaits Museum** (tel. 91 232) has a superior folk art collection. The building and its contents were given to Skyros by Manos Faltaits, a descendant of one of Skyros' 20 families, who governed locally from the 13th century until the 1820s. The museum has a superb collection of local embroidery, carved furniture, pottery, costumes, and copperware, as well as rare books and relics from the island's annual carnival. It also runs a **theater** and **music festival** from the last week of July to the last week of August; inquire at the museum or the affiliated shop on Agoras St. (Open daily 10am-1pm and 5:30-8pm. Guided tour in English; free.)

If you are on Skyros 40 days before Easter, you'll witness the **Skyrian Carnival,** a part religious, part folk satire festival. A *geros* (an old man dressed in a goat mask and costume clanging some 80 sheep bells attached to his waist) leads a *korela* (a young man dressed in Skyrian women's clothes but wearing a goat mask) and a *frangos* (a mocking figure dressed as a 17th-century European man with one large bell), on a wild, raucous dance through the town to the Monastery of St. George. The ritual, commemorating a legendary land-use dispute between shepherds and farmers, is unique to Skyros and possibly the occasional adventurous fraternity.

The pleasant beach below the town stretches along the coast through the villages of Magazia and Molos, and continues around the point. Crowded and crawling with children in July and August, it's undeniably convenient: just a 15-min. walk down the stone steps from the **naked Rupert Brooke** statue. By car or moped, turn left coming into Skyros Town just after the bus stop at the sign for Magazia and Molos. There you'll find multiple water toys (waterskis, paddleboats, sailboards, etc.) for rent. Ten minutes south of the town beach is the local **nudist beach**—ironically named *Tou papa to homa* (The Sands of The Priest)—which is cleaner and less crowded than the town beach, and naturally, has lots more naked people (not including bronze, **naked Brooke**). The regular public buses which run from Linaria to Skyros Town also stop midway at the crowded **Ormos Mealos** beach.

■■■ AROUND SKYROS ISLAND

Skyros is roughly 5km wide at its narrowest point, and 35km long, but most of the island is inaccessible. You can explore it by car, motorbike, or by one of the organized bus or boat trips. If you rent a motorbike, a map is essential (available for 400dr from Skyros Travel). Several roads have been paved recently, so travel is now easier and safer. Once home to a company of nymphs, **Nifi Beach,** on the south side of Skyros, is beautiful and deserted, with a natural spring. The rest of the south part of the island is scenically barren, with dirt paths leading to the beaches. The most interesting sites here are accessible only by boat. The sea caves at **Spiliés** were once a pirate grotto, and one of the largest pirate centers in the Aegean was **Despot's Island.** During the Turkish occupation, merchant and war ships used this natural port as a shelter from storms; in WWI, the British commandeered it as a naval base.

In the barren interior of the south region live the Skyrian *Pikermic*—ponies related to the Shetlands. In recent centuries, the population of Skyrian ponies grew large, but starvation decimated the herds, and less than 100 of the animals remain.

The north part of the island, optimistically named *Meroi* (tame), is hilly, covered with pine trees, and scarcely cultivated. Going north from Skyros Town, turn right for the beach at the little white chapel of **Agia Ekaterina.** If you continue straight and take a left on the road to the airport (marked with a highway sign), the road will take you high into the hills, and then dip down to cross a long valley. When you reach the top of the island, you'll come to a crossroad. Straight ahead lie two very pleasant beaches and the **airport.** The road continues around the west side of the island to the beach at **Kalogrias** and then the beautiful **Atsitsa Beach,** where rocks and pines are mirrored in the water. A *taverna* here lets rooms, and there's camping on the beach. The **Atsitsa Center,** a holistic health and fitness joint, operates on the beach, so don't be surprised if mantras and a sense of peace emanate from the sands. Transcendental meditation isn't exactly a part of most Skyrians' lives. Yet.

Saronic Gulf Islands ΤΑ ΝΗΣΙΑ ΤΟΥ ΣΑΡΩΝΙΚΟΥ

Diverse, captivating landscapes and proximity to Athens have made the Saronic Gulf Islands an enduringly popular destination. Narrow alleys and walkways barely separate houses that lead up to mountainous interiors decorated with ancient temples and tranquil monasteries. Many of the islands' beaches are pebbly, but the surrounding plush green hills make them some of Greece's most scenic swimming spots.

Despite geographic proximity, each island retains its own distinct character. Poros' magnificent lemon grove, Aegina's temple of Aphaia, Spetses' pine-filled forest and Hydra's fashionable waterfront attract countless Athenians seeking weekend getaways. The Saronic Gulf Islands' popularity also makes them among the most expensive in Greece, and freelance camping is illegal. Since the islands can be unbearably crowded on the weekends, try to visit during the week and find a pension or private room.

AEGINA ΑΙΓΙΝΑ

Aegina's whitewashed buildings, narrow streets, horses in brightly-colored tassels, and aqua-hued water seem like they have been produced in a Disney studio. Unfortunately for those seeking solitude, Aegina is an easy day trip for Athenians; on weekends, half the city makes its way there. Try to avoid spending too much time in Aegina town, whose bustle is reminiscent of the traffic in Athens. Instead, you may want to head for the purple and white sands of Agia Marina and Marathon. In recent years, even Agia Marina has begun to attract more tourists. Nevertheless, the beaches alone make Aegina worth the trip.

In ancient times, relations between Aegina and Athens were hardly chummy. The little island made up for its size with spunk and initiative, resisting Athenian encroachment. The island produced the first Greek coins—the silver "tortoises" which gained great financial leverage throughout the Greek world—and at pan-Hellenic games, Aegina's sprinters zoomed past the competition. With the onset of the Persian War in 491 BC, the Aeginetans sided first with Xerxes' army, to the ire of the besieged Athenians. In 480 BC at Salamis—the greatest of all Greek sea battles—they returned to the Greek side and won the praise of the Delphic Oracle as the swiftest navy on the seas. Island life flourished and Aegina's inhabitants built the magnificent Temple of Aphaia during the next 30 years. But they suffered the misfortunes of having taken the wrong side in the Athenian-Spartan clash and were thoroughly trounced by Athens in 459 BC. By 431, Athens had displaced Aegina's population with Athenian colonists. Sparta restored the native population to the island in 405 BC.

To get to Aegina from Athens, take green bus #40 from almost anywhere in Athens and get off at the Public Theater (*Demotikon Theatron*) in Piraeus (½hr., 75dr). From there, you can see the pier where ferries leave for Aegina. Alternatively, take the subway (75dr) to the stop at Piraeus and walk the few blocks to the ferry.

■■■ AEGINA TOWN

Most likely you will disembark in the port of **Aegina Town,** the central point of departure for buses around the island. For the best beaches you will probably want to head elsewhere. Some ferries go directly to **Agia Marina** (on the opposite coast). If the ferry drops you off there, walk uphill to the main road, turn left, and hop on the bus to Aegina Town (every 50min. from Agia Marina, ½hr., 300dr).

ORIENTATION AND PRACTICAL INFORMATION

There are two main piers on the harbor. Hydrofoils leave from the smaller one, ferries from the larger one around the corner.

Tourist Police: (tel. 22 100) Offices are two blocks up Leonardou Lada St. English-speaking. Open 24 hr.

Port Police: (tel. 22 328) Located on the pier, they provide updated ferry schedules although the staff can be less than helpful. Open daily 8am-2:30am.

Post Office: (tel. 22 398) To the left of the ferry landing on Ethnegersias Sq., they cash traveler's checks. Open Mon.-Fri. 7:30am-2pm. **Postal Code:** 18010.

OTE: (tel. 22 599) Up Aiakou St. to the right; keep trudging up Aiakou when the street narrows into a walkway. The building has a monstrous rooftop satellite dish. Open Mon.-Fri. 7:30am-3:10pm. **Telephone Code:** 0297.

Banks: National Bank of Greece (tel. 24 438 or 25 697 or 22 632) On the waterfront to the left of the quay at the corner of Peleos St. Cirrus, Plus and Visa cards accepted. Open Mon.-Thurs. 8am-2pm, Fri. 8am-1:30pm.

Tourist Agencies: Colona Tours (tel. 22 334) sells maps (250dr) and books. On the second floor at the corner of Leonardou Lada St. and decorated with "Tourist Office" signs. They might also help with finding a room, but prices are better if you deal directly with the pension owners. English spoken. Open daily 7:30am-11pm.

Bus Station: (tel. 22 787) Buses leave every 50 minutes between 6:15am and 7:15pm for Agia Marina (30min., 300dr), Perdika (20min., 175dr), and Souvala (30min., 250dr).

Ferries: Hourly from Aegina Town to Piraeus (9am-10pm, 1½hr., 965dr). Three boats also land at Agia Marina (1½hr., 965dr). Four boats per day head to: Methana (45min., 900dr), Poros (1½hr., 940dr), Hydra (3 hr., 1200dr), and Spetses (4 hr., 1790dr). Tickets can be purchased from ticket stands (tel. 28 311, 28 312) near the boat landing.

Flying Dolphin: Ticket stand (tel. 24 456, 26 154) next to the port police sells hydrofoil tickets to Piraeus (10 per day, 2050dr), Poros (2 per day, 45min., 2770dr) via Methana (½hr., 1720dr), Ermione (2 per day, ½hr., 1430dr), Porto Heli (1 per day, 45min., 3290dr), and other destinations like Kythera and Nauplion. Schedules from Aegina are inconsistent, and posted time tables are rarely in English.

Bike/Moped Rental: Available from many vendors. (Bikes 500dr per hour, 1500dr per day, 7000dr per week; mopeds 3000dr per day.) **Stratos Rental** (tel. 22 809), at Ethnegersias Square past the bus station, on the corner of Kazantzaki, rents mopeds for 5000dr per day, 20,000dr per week (open Mon.-Fri. 8:30am-7pm, Sat.-Sun. 8:30am-8pm). Be careful—the island's roads are notorious for blind curves, absurdly fast drivers, and, hence, totaled motorbikes.

Pharmacy: (tel. 25 317), 19 Sp. Rodi St. The second street inland parallel to the quay. Open Mon.-Fri. 7:30am-1:30pm, 5-8:30pm.

Hospital: (tel. 22 251), on Nosokomiou St. Above Aegina Town and beyond the OTE. English-speaking doctor available.

ACCOMMODATIONS

The island fills up fast with family vacationers, so you may have trouble finding a place to stay. The high season norm is 5000dr for singles, 7000dr for doubles. To find rooms, ask at the hotels or look for "Rooms to Let" signs. Pensions are sprinkled

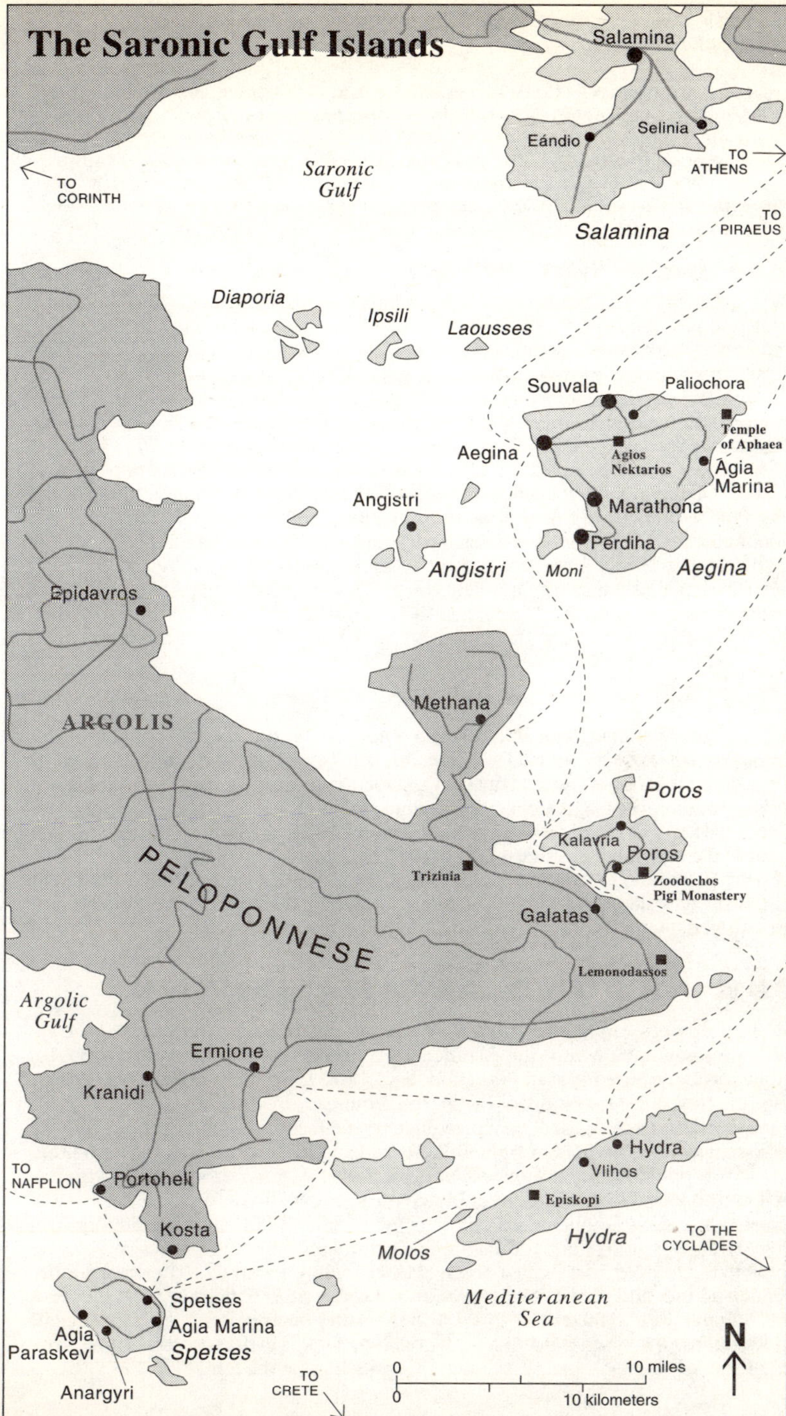
The Saronic Gulf Islands
Salamina
Selinia
Eándio
TO ATHENS
TO PIRAEUS
TO CORINTH
Saronic Gulf
Salamina
Diaporia
Ipsili
Laousses
Souvala
Paliochora
Temple of Aphaea
Aegina
Agios Nektarios
Agia Marina
Angistri
Marathona
Perdiha
Angistri
Moni
Aegina
Epidavros
Methana
ARGOLIS
Poros
Kalavria
Poros
Zoodochos Pigi Monastery
Trizinia
PELOPONNESE
Galatas
Lemonodassos
Argolic Gulf
Ermione
Kranidi
Hydra
Vlihos
Episkopi
TO NAFPLION
Portoheli
Kosta
Molos
Hydra
TO THE CYCLADES
Spetses
Agia Marina
Agia Paraskevi
Spetses
Mediterranean Sea
Anargyri
TO CRETE
0
10 miles
0
10 kilometers
N

generously throughout the streets a few blocks inland from the port and tend to have the lowest prices.

Hotel Artemis, (tel. 25 195), Leonardou Lada St., above the tourist police. Friendly management offers simple but spotless rooms, all with bath (singles 5000dr, doubles 7000dr).
Hotel Xenon Pavlou, (tel. 22 795) Behind the church on the far right of the quay, it has comfortable rooms with balconies (singles 6500dr, doubles 9000dr).
Pension, 16 Kiverniou St. Clean, newly renovated rooms, all with bath. One single has a kitchenette (singles 6000dr, doubles 7000dr, triples 9000dr).

FOOD AND ENTERTAINMENT

There are many no-frills *taverna* along P. Irioti St., which runs parallel to the waterfront one block inland along the right side of the harbor. Menus and prices are somewhat standardized (octopus 800dr, *kalamari* 800dr) so stroll and choose. One popular restaurant is **Vostitsano's** (tel. 23 995 or 26 555), with entrees from 1000 to 1800dr. The portions are small, but the *retsina* (a potent Greek wine) is cheap enough that, eventually, meals look twice as large (400dr for ½L). For tasty sweets after dinner, **Leousis** (tel. 26 306) on the waterfront is excellent (*kataifi*, 350dr).

The **Retro Music Bar** (tel. 22 437), next to the post office, caters to a mellow crowd. (Nightspots open 8pm-3am; drinks 900-1300dr.) The outdoor **cinema,** up Aiakou St., often shows American films (1000dr; summer only). There are two indoor cinemas in the winter, **Anissis** and **Titina.** Check the signs on the fence near the museum for more information about evening events. At night, Agia Marina falls under the spell of a haze of club lights and a dissonant refrain of bar music. Head past the tourist traps to the **Disco-Club LED**, downhill to the left off the main road, where you can watch Greek men show off their *mangia* (manliness) as they dance to the lustful strains of *zeimbekika* music

SIGHTS

Aegina Town's archaeological fame rests tenuously on the last half-column of the **Temple of Apollo.** The 8m tall Doric column dates to 460 BC and stands on *Kolona* hill, a short walk out of town to the north. (Open Tues.-Sun. 8:30am-3pm; admission 400dr, students free). The archaeological museum is closed with no re-opening date scheduled. The underground church of **Faneromeni**, a 15-min. walk inland just south of the town, houses a rare icon of the Virgin Mary. The night before construction was to begin on a site above Faneromeni, locals say the architect had a vision in which he was instructed to dig instead. The man discovered the church and unearthed the icon (modest dress, small donation recommended).

■■■ AROUND AEGINA ISLAND

On the road between Aegina and Agia Marina, in the middle of the island, is the village of **Paleochora,** where the islanders once took refuge from invasions. Paleochora was once "the town of 300 churches." Only 15 of these remain, some with inspiring frescoes. Modest dress (no shorts) required.

Two km from Agia Marina, on a prominent peak, rest the magnificent 5th century BC remains of the **Temple of Aphaia**. Aphaia, daughter of Zeus, was a nymph-huntress worshipped solely on Aegina as a protector of women. Her temple, which is built on the foundation of an earlier 6th-century temple, boasts a rare and spectacular set of standing double-tiered columns (admission 600dr, students 500dr). The Agia Marina bus stops right at the temple. Determined and fit classicists can bicycle uphill to the temple from Aegina Town (11km, 14km via Souvala). The coastal route is much gentler and affords gorgeous views of rocky shores and other islands. From Agia Marina, walk to the end of town with the water on your right and then straight up Kolokotroni St. until it becomes a wooded trail—this is the footpath to the Temple of Aphaia. At night, peacocks roam the quiet hills by the temple.

POROS ΠΟΡΟΣ

Only a sliver of water separates the sinewy hills of the mainland from this tiny isle. The approach by boat from the Peloponnese unveils the red-roofed town and the windmill-laden lemon groves which make Poros memorable. A mere three hours from Piraeus, Poros is actually two small, lush islands—Kalavria and Sphaeria—cut by a canal. Its name, meaning "passage," refers to the channel that forms its border.

The arcane Kalavrian League, a seven-city council, met in Poros to ward off hostile naval powers and order the building of the Temple of Poseidon in the sixth century BC. Three hundred years later, the great orator Demosthenes, who improved his diction by speaking with marbles in his mouth, killed himself beside its columns. Poros was sparsely populated for most of modern history until Greeks arrived from Turkey in the forced population exchange of the 1920s.

■■■ POROS TOWN

Poros Town occupies most of tiny Sphaeria, while woods extend over rugged Kalavria. Less crowded than Aegina, Poros still overflows on the weekends. You can find serenity and spectacular views by climbing the narrow passageways that lead to the top of Poros Town and the hills beyond, away from the crowded waterfront.

ORIENTATION AND PRACTICAL INFORMATION

Ferries (3hr., 1540dr), flying dolphins (1hr., 2980dr), and hovercraft ferries (1hr., 1970dr) leave Piraeus for Poros several times per day. En route, the boats stop in **Methana,** on a volcanic peninsula of the Peloponnese, known since antiquity for its therapeutic springs. In Poros Town, hydrofoils dock at the main landing in the center of town, while car ferries dock either there or a dozen blocks to the left (facing inland) on the northwest side of town. The quay is the center of activity, with tourist agencies to the left, restaurants and souvenir shops in the center, and discos and bars to the far right.

Tourist Police: (tel. 22 256), on Agiou Nikolaou St., 100m to the right of the main ferry landing. Can also help you find a room. Open 24 hr.

Post Office: Occupies the first square to the right along the water. Open Mon.-Fri. 7:30am-2pm. **Postal Code:** 18020.

OTE: 30 Kalomiri, off the alleyway on the wharf. Open Mon.-Fri. 7:30am-3:10pm. **Telephone Code:** 0298.

Bank: The **National Bank of Greece** stands 175m right of the landing on 68 Agiou Nikolaou St. Open Mon.-Thurs. 8am-2pm, Fri. 8am-1:30pm.

Tourist Agencies: Family Tours, 14 Iroon St. (tel. 22 549 or 24 281). English-speaking staff provides general information, sells maps (300dr), changes money, and finds rooms. Open Mon.-Fri. 8:30am-10pm. **Lela Tour** (tel. 24 439 or 24 780) does all that, and has pay showers to boot. Open daily 8am-10pm.

Ferries: To Piraeus (6 per day, 3 hr., 1540dr) stopping in Methana (45 min., 720dr) and Aegina (1½hr., 780dr). Ferries also run to Spetses (usually 2 per day, 2½hr., 1400dr). Small boat ferries to the far right of the quay go to the mainland (Galatas) every 10 min. (8am-8pm, 80dr). Inquire at the **port police** (tel. 22 274) for updated schedules. They are available 24 hr. Tickets can usually be bought across from the ferry when it docks.

Flying Dolphin: (tel. 23 423) Runs to Piraeus and other destinations (including Nauplion, Kyparissia and Kythera). Hydrofoils are 3 times as fast and twice as expensive as ferries. Ticket office open daily, 6:30am-10:30pm.

Bike/Moped Rental: Numerous places rent bikes, mopeds, and motorcycles at similar prices (bicycle 400dr, mountain bike 550dr, medium-sized mopeds 950-1500dr, large mopeds and motorcycles 2500-3500dr). **Stelios's** (tel. 23 026) and **Kosta's** (tel. 23 565) are among the few shops that rent mountain bikes. Stelios's is open daily 8:30am-8:30pm.

Laundromats: Suzi's Launderette Service is to the right of the OTE when facing inland.Wash and dry 1800 dr. Open daily 9am-2pm.

International Press: (tel. 25 205) Along the waterfront near George's Café, sells books and magazines in English, French, German, Italian, Spanish, Dutch, and Swedish. Open daily 8:30am-midnight.

Pharmacy: (tel. 24 793 or 22 241) In the open plaza on Iroon Square.

ACCOMMODATIONS

Most of the low-priced pensions and rooms for rent in Poros are clean, but private baths and singles are extremely rare. Travel agencies can often find rooms (singles with bath from 4000dr., doubles with bath from 6000dr). Most of the rooms are a 10-mi. walk out of town by Askeli beach. Shop around for prices before agreeing to see a room. Many pensions flank the Hotel Latsis 12 blocks to the left of the main pier. In high season, call ahead to secure weekend accommodations. Rooms offered by **Nikos Douros** (tel. 24 721; doubles 7700dr) and his brother **George Douros** (tel. 22 532; doubles 7700dr, triples 9200dr, all with bath) are a safe bet.

FOOD AND ENTERTAINMENT

Poros Town has many of the best restaurants in the Saronic Gulf. For reasonably priced seafood and meats, try **Lagoudera** (tel. 22 389; open 8am-midnight; entrees 700-1500dr), on the wharf. In the square to the right of Takis, the atmospheric **Seven Brothers** (tel. 22 446; open 9am-1pm, 6pm-1am) has large portions of well-prepared food (from 900dr) and live music on occasion. Another fraternal establishment, **Three Brothers** (tel. 23 972; open 7am-midnight), offers boisterously Greek atmosphere (entrees from 900-2000dr). **Zorba's** is conveniently located near the Askeli beach rooms, about ½km up the road to the left of the wharf (facing inland). The *mousaka* is a safe bet. **George's Cafe** (tel. 22 508) opens at 6am for an early breakfast (1000dr for coffee and bread or pastry). It is located in the center of the quay. Several **grocery stores** lie far to the right of the main landing; there is also one past Askeli Beach which sells fresh bread and tasty cheese. Look for the "off-license" signs. You can find delectable goodies a short walk to the left of the harbor. Try the *baklava* (250dr) at **Spithouris** (tel. 25 844; open 9am-11:30pm), and munch on home-made *kataifi* (200dr) at **Vessala** (tel. 25 890).

At the rooftop **Diana movie theater** (tel. 25 204; to the left of Lela Tours), you can sit in a lawn chair and watch American and British movies you missed six months ago (adults 1000dr, children 700dr). If you're itching to groove, try the Greek dancing at **Kavos,** at the far right along the waterfront. **Corali,** a high-tech disco, is next door. Around the big bend, **Sirocco,** the most popular disco, boasts a wonderful view of the Gulf. All nightclubs open around 8:30pm and go to 5 or 6am. There is a 1500dr cover on Saturdays only and drinks range from 800dr to 1200dr.

SIGHTS

In Poros Town itself, the **archaeological museum,** one block before the church along the water, is small but has some interesting inscriptions and photographs of the ruins at Troizen. (Open Mon.-Sat. 9am-2pm; free.)

The main sight is the18th-century **Monastery of Zoodochos Pigis** (Virgin of the Life-Giving Spring), which is nestled in an overgrown glade 6km from Poros Town. Since as early as 200 BC, monks have been quaffing the monastery's blessed, curative waters. Inside you'll find a spectacular gold-inlaid altarpiece depicting scenes from the lives of Jesus and the Apostles, as well as St. Barbara and St. Nikolas. Proper dress is required; men wearing shorts and women wearing pants are forbidden to enter. A few skirt-like coverings are available at the door. (Open daily 8am-4pm.) It's a scenic bus ride from the stop next to the main port in town (every 20min. 7am-11pm, 20min., 150dr). Along the route to the monastery is **Askeli,** a secluded beach.

Unless you're a Greek history maven, the main incentive to visit the knee-deep rubble of the sixth-century BC **Temple of Poseidon** atop the mountain is the panoramic view of the gulf. The Athenian statesman Demosthenes took sanctuary from his Macedonian enemies here in 322 BC. Ignoring the temple's tradition of sanctuary, the Macedonians gave him only a few moments reprieve to write a farewell letter to his family. His captors mocked his cowardice as he sat chewing his pen, but the crafty orator died as they waited, having dipped the end of his quill in poison.

■■■ AROUND POROS ISLAND

Boats run between the Peloponnese and the harbor of Poros (5min., 70dr). Take the *caïque* across the channel to **Galatas** on the Peloponnese for the sunny beaches of **Aliki** (the nicer but farther of the two) and **Plaka,** both quite a distance to the left as you walk along the shore. Aliki is a pleasant bike ride from Galatas town center. Ride east towards Plaka beach and take a left on the dirt road 100m after Plaka. There is also a small aquasports center here. A 10-minute walk from both leads to the enormous lemon grove of **Lemonodassos;** you can also take a taxi (5min., 600dr) to the bottom of the grove. Follow signs to the Taverna for a cool glass of fresh lemonade and a view of windmills and the 30,000 lemon trees that peer onto the sea. Tents crop up behind Plaka and Aliki Beaches, but camping is officially forbidden and police are strict. Official camping can be found at **Camping Kyrangelo** (tel. 24 520), 2km northwest of Galatas (1000dr per person).

Most visitors to the island miss the surrounding Peloponnesian countryside and the best **cycling routes** around, which begin in Galatas going northwest away from the lemon groves. Bicycles can be rented along the quay; try **Manos Pensiones** (tel. 22 100; bicycles 1200dr per day, mopeds from 2500dr per day). The terrain is flat and the fields range from cultivated flowers to apricot groves. You won't ever be far from a cold drink, especially if you pedal down the 3km turn-off by the carnation fields of **Trizinia,** the site of ancient Troizen. Buses run here from Galatas; schedules vary almost daily (call 22 480). Back on the main road, it's 10km from Galatas to the turn-off for Nauplion. Before the bakery in Kaloni is a sign for the long, tranquil **Agios Georgios Beach.**

Neorion Beach is accessible by boat (150dr), foot, or bike. Take the road from the left of the pier about 3km and turn left at the Neorion sign over the canal bridge. **Canali Beach** and its equally rocky neighbor lie just to the right of the bridge.

HYDRA (IDRA, ΥΔΡΑ)

Hydra at first seems to be merely a snazzy version of the typical Greek port town, with its neo-classical houses nestled quietly among steep, limestone hills and a small but bustling harbor. The uneasy knowledge that Hydra is unlike almost anywhere else you've been may come gradually, as the absence of rumbling cars, mopeds and even bicycles sinks in. On the island you'll find donkeys, boats bearing the sign "Taxi," and steep roads and steps. The only automobile is a lonely garbage truck. Once famous for producing great naval generals, Hydra "the well-watered" is now the lush island home of many Greek artists, some of whom display their work along the water. Even more peaceful are the backstreets where the only disturbance is the occasional bray of an irritable donkey. Or take an inexpensive boat from Hydra's port to far-off peaceful beaches.

ORIENTATION AND PRACTICAL INFORMATION

Most tourist agencies and accommodations on Hydra are centered around the pleasant but chic waterfront area accentuated by the clock tower. The crescent-shaped main street wraps around the harbor, adjacent to smaller alleys.

Tourist Police: Miaouli St., (tel. 52 205) Walk along the wharf and turn left after the clock tower.
Port Police: (tel. 52 279 or 52 205) located in the left-hand corner of the harbor.

Post Office: (tel. 52 262), in the alley parallel to Economa St.—there are signs along the quay. Open Mon.-Fri. 7:30am-2pm. **Postal Code:** 18040.

OTE: (tel. 52 262) Opposite the tourist police. Open Mon.-Fri. 7:30am-3:10pm. **Telephone Code:** 0298.

Banks: The **National Bank of Greece** overlooks the harbor between Tompazi St. and Miaouli St. Open Mon.-Thurs. 8am-2pm, Fri. 8am-1:30pm.

Tourist Agencies: Saitis Tours (tel. 52 184), located on the quay 200m before the clock tower, sells a map of Hydra (500dr) and gives a free *Holidays in Hydra* guide. Open 9am-9pm summer only. Or try **Greek Island Tours** (tel. 53 036), just off the quay on the street before the bank. Open 9:30am-9:30pm.

Ferries: Hydra is accessible for daytrips from Poros, Porto Heli, or Spetses. Ferries run twice a day, both trips departing in the afternoon, to Poros (1½hr., 755dr), Portoheli (1¾ hr., 790dr). The second ferry heads to Methana (2hr.,1155dr), Aegina (3hr., 1185dr), and Piraeus (4hr., 1690dr). There is also a ferry to Spetses at 11:30am (1hr., 790dr). The ticket office is located up the first alley to the right of the boat landing.

Flying Dolphins: More frequent than ferries. To Poros (7 per day, ½hr., 985dr), Methana (1 per day, 45min., 1835dr), Ermione (7 per day, ½hr., 1330dr), Porto Heli (10 per day, 45min., 1530dr). Tickets are sold by the Flying Dolphin ticket office (tel. 52 019; open 9am-6pm), on Em. Tombaz St. Go left 100m before the clock tower and look for the blue sign.

Hospital: (tel. 53 150 or 53 151) Next to the town hall by the wharf.

ACCOMMODATIONS

Hydra has the most expensive accommodations in the Saronic Gulf. Singles are practically nonexistent and doubles cost at least 6500dr. Also, it can be almost impossible to find a place without reservations, especially on summer weekends. **Greek Island Tours,** (tel. 24 255 or 24 074), on the waterfront, books rooms on Spetses if Hydra is full. If you are told all rooms on the island are full, head to the right corner of the harbor, down the alley to the left of the Pirate's Bar. **Sophia Hotel,** (tel. 52 313) on the harbor, at the center of the wharf, is one of the cheapest in town. Sophia has only six rooms so reservations are recommended for weekends. (Singles 5500dr, doubles 6600dr; open April-Oct.) **Pension Othon,** (tel. 53 305) is only 15 minutes up the street on which Sophia is located. Othon features immaculate doubles and serene atmosphere (doubles 7000dr). Call ahead and the manager will help you find your way there.

FOOD AND ENTERTAINMENT

Food prices on Hydra vary widely. *Souvlaki* (250dr) joints coexist alongside more posh establishments. The **Art Café,** in the westernmost corner of the harbor, is relatively affordable and serves enormous cheese toast. Ice cream for 280dr, and sandwiches, pizzas, and pies 300-400dr. In more upscale restaurants, know what you're paying before you order and beware of minimum orders. **Restaurant Lulu** (tel. 52 018), straight up from the dock on the same road as Sophia's Hotel, is a bargain. Food is served in small but very tasty portions. (Salads 400-700dr, *mousaka* 1000dr, veal dishes 1100dr.) **Captain George's** (tel. 53 660) has generous portions of the best fish around for 1200-2200dr. Sometimes the Captain provides live Greek music. Follow signs up the street from the hydrofoil office. **The Garden** (tel. 52 329), also up the street from the hydrofoil office, has a wide selection of reasonably priced food (entrees 1000-1800dr). Its quiet garden is pleasantly removed from the waterfront. Just up the street from the OTE, try **Anemoni** (tel. 53 136) for an after-dinner treat of Greek pastries (300dr).

Hydra's clubs all have overpriced cocktails (1000dr), but die-hard dancers won't want to miss the scene. Check out **Disco Kavos Lagoudera,** or **Disco Heaven** (up the whitewashed stairs) on the western edge of the harbor. If you're feeling more lethargic, sit outside at the **Pirate Bar** on the water and watch the world, clad in sequined bra tops, go by (mixed drinks 1000dr).

SIGHTS

Taxes were not levied on Hydra's arid land for most of the Turkish occupation. With few natural resources and a growing refugee population from the Peloponnese, Balkans, and Turkey, Hydra's inhabitants turned to managing other areas' exports, and its merchant princes became shipping magnates. Hydriots grew prosperous by dodging pirates and naval blockades during the late 18th and early 19th centuries, and emerged in the 1820s as financial and naval leaders in the revolt against the Turks. **Koundouriotis,** whose house is on a hill to the west of the harbor, was one of the many Hydriot leaders in the War of Independence. To get to his house, walk up the narrow alley to the right of the Pirate Bar, which becomes Lignou St. Take the second alley on your right, turn right and go straight (and up) following the scenic path until you reach a small church in a shady pine grove. Koundouriotis's home is opposite it. The view of the harbor is superb, but the house itself is usually locked. It may open during high season; check with the tourist police. The houses of **Votsis** and **Economou,** two Hydriots who contributed to the island's naval fame, are closer to the crest of the hill, right on Voulgari St. There are more houses and mansions; most are locked, but they're fun to find. The home of Greek Admiral Iakovos Tombazis is now an **art school** (tel. 52 291), one block up from the harbor's right corner, that has exhibits, but is only open in July and August.

The **Ecclesiastical Church,** built in 1806, bears the clock tower that dominates the wharf. Its peaceful courtyard seems completely removed from the bustling waterfront, and the beautiful icons make this chapel an interesting, calming stopping place. (100dr donation requested—free postcard in return.) Also interesting are the frescoes at the **Church of St. John** in the Platia Kamina. Modest dress required at both churches. East of the harbor, set off by winding, anchor-flanked stairs, is the **Pilot School** of the Greek Merchant Marine, with paintings, models, and class pictures circa 1930. (Open variably 8am-10pm; free.)

A short hike (1hr.) trudges down A. Miaouli St. from the waterfront (the road takes you out of town) uphill to the **monastery** of Prophitis Ilias, and, on a lower peak overlooking the harbor, the **nunnery** of Efpraxia. (Both open 9am-5pm; modest dress, *bien sûr.*) While the nuns at Efpraxia do beautiful embroidery work, Ilias is the prettier of the two and the monk may be willing to show you around. To return to the harbor, climb down the monastery steps and follow the passageways down through town. Another hike is to **Episkopi,** a deserted monastery an hour's walk west from Ilias along goat paths that take you through beautiful uninhabited countryside. The Greek word for footpath is *monopati;* use it when asking for directions to return to town. Cut down to the north coast towards the right of the main harbor. The beach at **Vlihos** is a 40-minute walk from town along the coast.

These are long, hilly walks; bring water and leave early in the morning. If you feel too hot to walk up and down Hydra's hills or fight crowds on the waterfront, take a swim. On the right of the harbor (facing inland) are three levels of flat rock perfect for sunbathing. Swim to your right (facing inland) into purple caves; watch out for children jumping off rocks above. If you want to fit in with other sunbathers, leave your top at home. The beaches on Hydra are rocky ledges a short walk west from town. When the water is calm, small *caïques* run regularly to pretty **Palamida** and neighboring beaches on the west side. Take food and drink with you; there's no place to buy it there. **Mira Mare Beach,** at Mandraki, is easier to reach, either by half-hour walk along the water from the east end of town, or by 15-minute boat ride (300dr). This beach is less attractive than others and dominated by a new water-sports center. Don't take water taxis—even their lowest fares are expensive (3000dr).

SPETSES ΣΠΕΤΣΕΣ

Ancient *Pitiusa*, or Pinetree Island, Spetses is a floating pine forest bordered by white and blue houses. The combination of picturesque villages, tile mosaics, and rocky beaches has made the island a playground for wealthy Greeks. A particular favorite among British tourists, Spetses offers a variety of moods: its café-,disco-, and tourist-filled waterfront supplies excitement, while its quieter interior provides the same serenity that prompted John Fowles to write *The Magus* during his stay here. Spetses was settled just in time to make a significant contribution to the Greek War of Independence of 1821. It was the first island to take part in the revolution, an event commemorated annually by ceremonies held in the Panayia Armata chapel near Agia Marina. Spetses was also home to the fiery heroine Bouboulina, captain of her own ship during the war. She is immortalized in a statue on the waterfront of Spetses Town.

■■■ SPETSES TOWN

The vast majority of Spetsiots live in Spetses Town, which is centered along the waterfront. Today, Spetses' population of 3,500 is composed of locals, tourists (in season), hippies who came and never left, and wealthy Athenians who own vacation homes to the right of the main harbor. Jet-setters also dock their yachts in Spetses' Old Harbor to take advantage of the island's nightlife, proving that Spetses has charms to soothe the savage millionaire as well as the tame backpacker.

ORIENTATION AND PRACTICAL INFORMATION

Restaurants and shops form a 2km line on either side of the port. Facing away from the water, the old harbor is a 20-minute walk left of the boat landing.

Police: Follow the alley to the right of Café Argyris to get to the station. The police, who double as the **tourist police,** are supposedly open 24 hr. (tel. 73 100).

Port Police: (tel. 72 245) Two main cafés, Remetzo and Argyris, are on either side of the kiosk in front of the boat landing where the water taxis park. The port police office is above the left one. They post ferry and hydrofoil schedules.

Post Office: (tel. 72 228) Past the port police, on the road parallel to the waterfront. Open Mon.-Fri. 7:30am-2pm. **Postal Code:** 18050.

OTE: (tel. 72 199) A short walk to the right, on the right side of the Star Hotel. Open Mon.-Fri.7:30am-3pm. **Telephone Code:** 0298.

Banks: The **National Bank of Greece** (tel. 72 286) is left of the OTE. Open Mon.-Thurs. 7:30am-2pm, Fri. 7:30am-1:30pm. Other banks open Mon.-Fri. 7:30am-2pm.

Tourist Agencies: There are several tourist agencies to the left of the boat landing, around the corner. English speaking **Pine Island Tours** (tel. 72 314, 72 594; in front of the café on the right; open Easter-Sept. 9am-9pm) offers free maps. The kiosks also stock maps of the island (400dr).

Ferries: Depart Spetses for Piraeus daily at 2:45pm (Wed. and Sat. also at 1:30pm; 4½hr; 2185dr). Two serve Hydra (1½hr, 790dr), Poros (2hr, 1400dr), Methana (2½hr, 1420dr), and Aegina (3hr, 1780dr). Purchase tickets at **Alasia Travel** (tel. 74 098, 74 130; open 8am-9pm in high season, 10am-noon in low), or **Maledon Tours** (tel. 74 497 or 74 498). Small ferries leave for **Kosta** from in front of **Remetzo's Cafe** (4 per day, 15min., 200dr). In rough weather they leave from the Posseidonion dock, or from the old harbor.

Flying Dolphin: The **ticket office** (tel. 73 141) is next to Pine Island Tours. **Hydrofoils** and **catamarans** go to Piraeus (5-7 per day high season, 3 per day low; 2hr.; 4250dr).

Bike Rental: Michael Alexander's Bicycles, (tel. 73 074), on the right side of the Shell Station, to the left of Pine Island Tours (open Easter-Nov., 9:30am-1pm and 4-6pm). Bicycles 500dr per hour, 1500dr per day. Mopeds 3000-3500dr per day.
First Aid: Call 72 472.

ACCOMMODATIONS

Often crowded, Spetses is a relatively expensive island to stay on. Hotels are plentiful and very visible, but the larger ones overflow with tour groups. Look for something smaller, like the rooms offered by travel agencies in town. **Pine Island Travel and Tourism** offers doubles with bathrooms at 8000dr, singles for 5500dr. On its outer wall is an information sign with advice about nightlife, eating, water use, and the important detail that *topless sunbathing is illegal on Spetses*. Yet this law is as well-heeded as the law requiring helmets when riding mopeds. On the waterfront to the left of the boat landing (facing inland) **Alasia Travel** (tel. 74 098 or 74 130; open 8am-9pm in high season) has singles at 8000dr and doubles at 10,000dr. Next to it is **Maledon Tours** (tel 74 497 or 74 498), which has similar offerings. **Villa Christina,** (tel. 72 218, 74 228, open April-Oct.) has comfortable rooms off a flower-filled courtyard. Singles 8000dr (6000dr low season), doubles for 10,000dr. Prices are roughly 2000dr less in off-season. In August, call ahead. To get there walk between the newsstand and Pine Island Tours, take the first right and follow it to the Palm Tree Café. Jog left and then right. A narrow walkway faces the church bell tower. Follow this to the top. The walk takes less than 10 min, but the manager will pick you up from the ferry if you call ahead. **Hotel Dapia,** (tel. 73 426 or 73 427) offers generous rooms and is centrally located near the harbor (doubles 8000dr, triples 11,000dr).

FOOD AND ENTERTAINMENT

Restaurants, *taverna* and cafés abound in Spetses. Stop at **Stelios** (tel. 73 748), along the wharf past Takis, for traditional Greek fare (entrees 1100-2500dr), or at **Galera** (tel. 73 488; entrees 900-2500dr). If you're up for a 15-minute walk along the coast there are a number of excellent restaurants (which are well-loved by locals) along the road in the opposite direction from the old harbor. **Patralis Tavern** serves scrumptious fish at reasonable prices (fish à la Spetses 1500dr). Look for specials. Their home-made *retsina* is a must (400dr per ½L). Catch it early in the season, before the barrels dry. **Politis** (tel. 72 248), a coffee and pastry shop on the waterfront before the National Bank, serves full English breakfast (1100dr). **Argyris,** near the boat dock, has tasty coffee (350dr) and *amigdaloto,* the island's signature almond cookie (2500dr per kilo). Most restaurants close from 4pm to 6pm, but you'll find plenty of groceries and supermarkets.

Spetses gathers for drinks at the **Socrates** bar (beers 500dr, drinks 900dr), **Anchor II** (beer 500dr, drinks 900dr), and **Galera** (drinks 400-1500dr). Most bars open at 9pm. Devoted seekers of nightlife continue on to other bars in the new harbor or the pulsating **Club Fever** (tel. 73 718), which hosts increasingly popular all-you-can-drink nights (3000dr at the door). Trendy young Athenians can be found in bars along the more sophisticated Old Harbor (*Palio Limani*).

For a mellow evening visit one of Spetses' two open-air cinemas. **Ciné Marina,** near the tourist police, often shows English language films (1500dr), as does **Ciné Titania,** near the post office (tel. 72 090 to reserve; 1000dr).

SIGHTS

The **Anargyrios and Korgialenios College** (high school) is a 25-minute walk from town, to the right (facing inland), past the Posseidonian Hotel. John Fowles taught here from 1951-2 and memorialized both the institution and the island in his novel *The Magus.* It's a gorgeous old building, now closed, mainly worth seeing if you are a big Fowles fan, enjoy walking, or happen to be across the way at Kaiki Beach. (Ask the guard if you can enter through the gate.) For a beautiful walk, especially at dusk, go left past Takis and continue along the stone path between the water and the high, whitewashed stone walls to the old harbor, which is quieter and has fewer tourist shops than the new port. *Spetsai,* by Andrew Thomas, is a helpful book that includes the island's history and walk suggestions.

A walk into the heart of the village takes you to the crumbling-but-cute late 19th-century **mansion of Hadjiyanni Mexi,** Spetses' first governor. The imposing structure affords a great view of the island and houses coins, costumes, mastheads, folk art, religious artifacts and a casket containing the remains of Bouboulina. The building itself is worth seeing, with an old island fireplace, stained glass windows, and carved wooden doors. Follow signs to get there; beware of speeding mopeds. (Open Tues.-Sun. 8:30am-3pm; free) The **house of Lascarina Bouboulina** is next to the park near the Dapia (700dr adults, 300dr children). Mme. Bouboulina was a ship's captain in the Greek War of Independence; her heroic exploits are celebrated on Spetses with a mock naval battle in which a small boat is blown up. The celebration takes place the first Saturday after Sept. 8. The **monastery of Agios Nikolas** stands opposite a square of traditional Spetsiot mosaics in the Old Harbor. Among its treasures is a plaque commemorating Napoleon's nephew, who was pickled in a barrel of rum stored in a monastic cell at Agios Nikolas from 1827-32. You may want to rent a moped or car to get to the monastery; the walk is arduous. While there, have a free sample of the nuns' homemade yogurt, also available for sale. Modest dress is required.

The water in Spetses is clean and clear, but **Paradise** beach and some of the town beaches are crowded and litter-strewn. Check the town beaches on the waterfront heading towards Old Harbor; they are cleaner early in the season. Watch for **sea urchins,** which plague Spetses' beaches and prick bare feet. The road past the tourist police leads to the island's main summit. The bumpy track takes you several km into the hills through sweet-smelling pines to the panorama of the Peloponnese and its train of islands. There's a chapel on the way with picnic tables. From here, trails of similar length descend to the beaches of **Vrelos, Anargyri,** and **Agriopetres.** Vrelos is the nicest, with **nude sunbathing** to boot. A good plan is to take the bus to Anargyri (1-3 times a day from the bus stop by the town beach), or take the bus to Kaiki beach (a.k.a. College beach), Blueberry Hill Cove and the Vrelos beach coves. This bus leaves from the Posseidonion Hotel (to the right of the New Harbor, behind the Bouboulina statue; 4-6 per day; 150dr). It stops just before Zegoria beach, which has a taverna; the coves have no facilities. **Kaiki Beach,** opposite the Anargyrios and Korgialenios College of John Fowles fame, has a bar, a restaurant, and plenty of **watersports.** Buy a return ticket and keep your stub. **Motorboats** leave the harbor (9:30-11:30am, returning from the beaches at about 4pm, 1000dr). Anargyri is 30 minutes away. **Sea taxis** cost a fortune (7000dr for Anargyri). Since only registered cars are allowed on the island, overland transportation is provided by horse-drawn carriages, which usually won't travel past Kastelli Beach or Agia Marina. Spetses has three taxis.

■■■ AROUND SPETSES ISLAND

Kosta, across the water on the Peloponnese, has the only broad, sand beach in the area. A car ferry runs between Spetses and the tiny town of Kosta on the Peloponnese (at least 4 per day, 200dr); small boats make the same trip more often, but charge more.

From Kosta you can catch a bus to the resort of **Porto Heli** (160dr) and its Classical cemetery, or to **Kranidi** (200dr). If there overnight, stay at the **Hotel Porto** (tel. 51 410), to the right of the Flying Dolphin office (doubles with bath 6500-7000dr).

The bus stop in Kosta lies left of the boat landing, on the road between the hotel and restaurant. **Camping Kosta** (tel. 51 571) charges 750dr, 650dr off-season. Boats to Spetses leave continually as they fill up with people, making Kosta an inexpensive base for visiting Spetses by day and other areas on the Peloponnese as well.

CYPRUS ΚΥΠΡΟΣ

US$1 = C£0.44	**C£1 = US$2.26**
CDN$1 = C£0.33	**C£1 = CDN$3.07**
UK£1 = C£0.69	**C£1 = UK£1.45**
IR£1 = C£0.70	**C£1 = IR£1.43**
AUS$1 = C£0.33	**C£1 = AUS$3.07**
NZ$1 = C£0.29	**C£1 = NZ$3.45**
SAR1 = C£0.12	**C£1 = SAR8.26**

Note: Throughout this section, Cyprus pounds will be indicated by £.

ESSENTIALS

Cyprus' history is preserved in the tangible remains of its complex past, in its temples, well-maintained Roman mosaics, remote monasteries, and crusader castles. The land abounds in natural beauty. From the sandy beaches of Agia Napa to the Kyrenia range to the cool, quasi-Alpine air of Platres, the island caters to diverse travelers and remains generally clean, pleasant and grime-free even in its most industrial cities. The people of Cyprus are friendly and hospitable, even more so in recent years, when tourism, especially among Brits and Arabs, has become one of the island's most important industries. Almost all residents speak English, and most signs are in both English and Greek in the south and in Turkish and English in the north. Cyprus is more expensive than Greece, but does have some budget options.

■■■ GETTING THERE

The third largest island in the Mediterranean after Sicily and Sardinia, Cyprus lies 64km from Turkey, 160km from Israel and Lebanon, and 480km from the nearest Greek islands. The Republic of Cyprus is accessible by airplane or boat from Europe and the Middle East. Seemingly thousands of boat agencies connect Limassol to almost every imaginable place. Among your possible destinations/points of origin are Larnaka; Rhodes; Piraeus; Iraklion, Crete; Haifa, Israel; and Port Said, Egypt. To reach the north, take a ferry from Mersin, Alanya, or Taşucu, Turkey.

Salamis Tours, 28th Octovriou Ave., P.O. Box 531, Limassol (tel. (05) 355555). In Piraeus, inquire at **Afroessa Lines S.A.,** 1 Charilaou Trikoupi St. (tel. 418 3777); in Rhodes, **Red Sea Travel**, 11-13 Amerikis St. (tel. 22 460). Travel to Piraeus and the Greek Islands. (High-season price, £71).

Louis Shipping Ltd., 63B Gladstone St., Limassol (tel. (05) 363161). In Piraeus, inquire at 11 Mavrokorstatou (tel. 429 1423, -4; fax 429 1445). To Piraeus and the islands.

Vergina Lines, 3B Olympion St., Honey Court 7, Limassol, (tel. (05) 343978). In Piraeus, inquire at **Stability Line,** 11 Sachtouri St. (tel. 413 2392). In Port Said, **Mena Tours,** P.O. Box 517 (tel. 22 57 42). In Israel, (tel. 67 44 44). Five-day cabin cruises to Piraeus and the Greek islands (double £210 per person, quad £200 per person); and Israel and Egypt (double £130 per person, quad £120 per person).

For a list of available agencies, ask for the Cyprus Tourist Organization's *Information Paper Unit 2,* at tourist offices in Nicosia, Larnaka, Limassol, and Paphos.

By air, Cyprus is accessible from Greece and other European and Middle Eastern countries on **Olympic Airlines** (U.S. tel. (800) 223-1226), **Egypt Air** (U.S. tel. (212)

315-0900), **Cyprus Airways** (U.S. tel. (212) 714-2310), and other commercial lines. Student fare from either Olympic (ages 12-28) or Cyprus Airways (ages 12-24) is 20,900dr one-way from Athens to Larnaka; you will need to show a letter from your university or an ISIC. Otherwise, airfare from Athens to Cyprus is cheaper if purchased round-trip, as one-way tickets are only available in business class. International airports are in Larnaka and Paphos.

■■■ ONCE THERE

TRANSPORTATION

A reliable highway system serves much of Cyprus, but use caution on the winding mountain roads. Cars drive on the left side of the road in the south and on the right in the north. Turks, however, may impound cars brought from the south. There are cars with steering wheels on the left and the right on both sides of the island. The south also has several British rotaries, which are particularly intimidating for American drivers. Transportation is widely nonexistent after 7pm. Service (shared) **taxis** run regularly Monday through Friday (until evening) between Limassol, Paphos, Larnaka, and Nicosia. Service taxis, most of which are converted Mercedes limousines, will pick you up and drop you off wherever you want in the city (£1.50-2 between the 4 major cities). Service taxis cost twice as much as the buses and are sometimes a harrowing ride, but their speed and frequency make them a good deal. If possible, choose the front passenger seat because drivers sometimes cram many people in the back. **Hitching** is not common, and neither locals nor tourists give rides.

Buses to the **Troodos Mountains** travel once daily from both Nicosia and Limassol. There is no direct bus connection from Paphos to Nicosia or Larnaka; you must pass through Limassol. Bus service throughout Cyprus is less frequent in the winter. There is one island-wide **bus schedule** available at tourist offices with all info and prices for buses and service and private taxis. It is accurate and well worth picking up—you're clearly not in Greece anymore. Cypriot law requires seatbelts in front seats. All Cypriot rental cars have manual transmission, and rates are standardized; the cheapest small cars should cost no more than £17 per day, small motorbikes £5, and larger motorcycles £7-8. To drive in Cyprus you need an international driver's license, or a national driver's license from your home country. You can obtain a temporary Cypriot driver's license, good for 6 months, from district police stations if you provide photographs and £1. Even though most dealers rent 50cc two-seaters, if two adults are riding a small bike, the police may stop and fine you.

CROSSING THE GREEN LINE

Crossing the infamous Green Line **from the south** is relatively easy, if you follow the strict regulations. Don't even try to get information about northern Nicosia on the Greek-Cypriot side. Greek-Cypriots have not crossed the line in more than 20 years. You will not be permitted to cross the line if you are a Greek citizen or if you are of Greek descent. Head for the **Ledra Palace Checkpoint** (tel. 361722) between the Greek-Cypriot and Turkish walls. This former hotel, its interior gutted and its exterior marred by bullet holes, stands on neutral territory and houses UN troops.

Before entering this area, you must show your passport and register on the Greek Cypriot side. If you don't know exactly where to go, don't worry—they'll stop you. After checking in, you take a 5-min. walk through the UN wasteland. Ledra will be on your left, and unless you are specifically instructed to go there, there's no reason to stop. You will show your passport again on the Turkish side and fill out a general information form in order to receive a special visitor's visa (£1). They will not stamp your passport. *Do not let them stamp your passport.* If they stamp your passport, you will not be readmitted to Greek Cyprus. They will, however, give you a form to be stamped by someone at another window. Hold on to this form—you will need it to cross back at the end of your visit. If your travels originate from the north, and

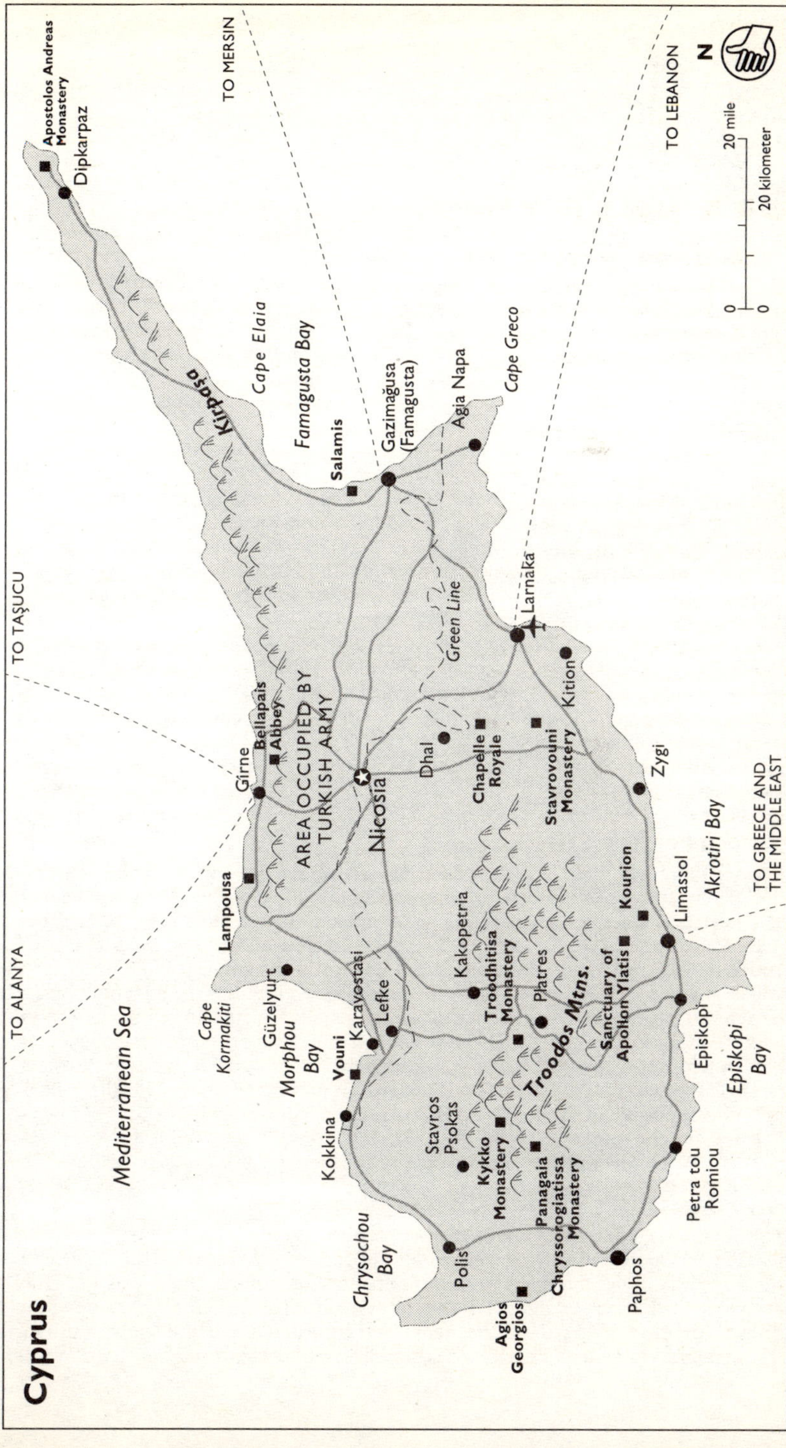
Cyprus
Apostolos Andreas Monastery
Dipkarpaz
TO MERSIN
Kirpaşa
Cape Elaia
Famagusta Bay
Salamis
Gazimağusa (Famagusta)
Agia Napa
Cape Greco
TO LEBANON
N
20 mile
20 kilometer
0
0
TO TAŞUCU
Larnaka
Green Line
Kition
Bellapais Abbey
AREA OCCUPIED BY TURKISH ARMY
Girne
Nicosia
Dhal
Chapelle Royale
Stavrovouni Monastery
Zygi
TO ALANYA
Lampousa
Kakopetria
Troodhitisa Monastery
Platres
Kourion
Limassol
Akrotiri Bay
TO GREECE AND THE MIDDLE EAST
Mediterranean Sea
Cape Kormakiti
Güzelyurt
Morphou Bay
Karavostasi
Lefke
Vouni
Troodos Mtns.
Sanctuary of Apollon Ylatis
Episkopi
Episkopi Bay
Kokkina
Stavros Psokas
Kykko Monastery
Panagaia Chryssorogiatissa Monastery
Petra tou Romiou
Chrysochou Bay
Polis
Paphos
Agios Georgios

you have a Turkish stamp in your passport, you can never enter the south. Northern authorities may stamp a separate piece of paper if you ask.

Some friendly reminders: 1) You may enter Northern Cyprus between 8am and 1pm, but must return by 5pm. No exceptions. 2) Cars are not allowed—you must cross by foot. 3) As in other areas of Nicosia and Cyprus, do *not* take pictures of anything that has to do with the military or police. 4) As you will be forewarned on the Greek side, you are not allowed to buy anything on the Turkish side. If you wish to purchase food, you must exchange your Cypriot pounds for Turkish lira. Also, you cannot bring items from the south to the north—they will be confiscated. 5) Finally, if you have a problem, ask the UN soldiers with the baby blue berets for assistance.

Crossing the line **from the north** is impossible. The quickest way to get to South Nicosia, therefore, is to first fly to London, and then to the south. This trick will only work if you don't have a Northern Cyprus stamp on your passport. A cheaper, and much longer, way is to go by seabus (or ferry) to Taşucu in Turkey, take a bus from there to Marmaris, from there a ferry to Rhodes, and finally a ferry to Southern Cyprus. Travel time—about two days. To be safe, ask the Turkish authorities not to stamp your passport, as a Taşucu stamp gives away that you've been to Northern Cyprus (though this isn't always a problem).

It's Not Easy Being Green

In 1953, a British colonial official, green pencil in hand, partitioned a map of Nicosia between the two battling ethnicities. Following the 1974 Turkish invasion, the northern third of the island became the Turkish Federated State of Cyprus, and the crayon division, later dubbed the **"Green Line,"** or the **"Attila Line"** in the north, came to separate the Turkish section from the Republic of Cyprus. The Green Line extends 180km from coast to coast and, at points, spans several kilometers in width. Patrolled on either side by Greek Cypriot National Guard or Turkish Cypriot troops, in addition to the UN peacekeeping force, the Green Line cannot be crossed by any ethnic Greek or Turk. The border occasionally closes due to political problems. In early August, a group of Greek nationalists may try to break through the line in a motorcycle cavalcade to "take" the north. Don't fret; this happens every year and is always publicized well in advance; the border is shut on this day.

TOURIST ORGANIZATIONS

Cyprus' extremely helpful and efficient **tourist offices** provide invaluable information. There are offices in Limassol, Nicosia, Larnaka, Paphos, Agia Napa, and Platres. The main office is the **Cyprus Tourism Organization,** P.O. Box 4535, 19 Limassol Ave., Nicosia CY 1390 (tel. (2) 337715); in the **U.S.,** 13 E. 40th St., New York, NY 10016 (tel. (212) 683-5280). In general, head for the CTO offices immediately after you arrive in each town for excellent free maps, as well as information about buses, museums, and cultural activities, and a terrific publication called *The Cyprus Traveller's Handbook* (also free). Tourist officials generally speak English, Greek, German, and French, among other languages. In the north, there are tourist offices in Famagusta, Girne, and Nicosia. The office in Nicosia is located just past the Ledra Palace. In both the north and south, emergency treatment at hospitals is free for foreigners. Doctors are cheap; visits average $12-15. The *Cyprus Today,* published every Friday, lists all the night pharmacies on duty in Northern Cyprus for the coming week.

GOVERNMENT

The government of the Republic of Cyprus is based on the Constitution of 1960 that was devised by conservative governments in London, Athens, and Ankara. The constitution was never intended to be a permanent document and it was not truly designed for the Cypriot people. Rather, it was meant as a compromise among the British, Greek, and Turkish governments over control of the island. Now in use for 35 years, the document's curious beginnings created a government that remains deeply divided between its two communities. For example, the president is always a Greek-Cypriot and the vice-president a Turkish-Cypriot. They govern their respective municipalities and are elected by separate elections, but both retain the right of veto. Civil service, police, and parliament posts were divided along a controversial 70:30 split meant to mirror the population. For a bill to pass in the 100-member parliament, it not only requires an overall majority, but also a majority within both communities. So, theoretically, 16 Turkish-Cypriot representatives could oppose a measure that was favored by the remainder and the bill would fail. This dysfunctional government, in case you were wondering, meets in Geneva.

The Turkish Republic of Northern Cyprus (KKTC) came into existence on Nov. 15, 1983. The president is Rauf Denktaş, and his picture, like Atatürk's, graces the walls of many hotels and restaurants. Northern Cyprus has a parliamentary democracy based on the British system. The official language is Turkish and the official currency is the same as Turkey's—the Turkish lira. The roughly 150,000 residents of Northern Cyprus are mostly Turkish Cypriot, but 40,000 of these are Turks who emigrated from the mainland. Several hundred British and German expatriates also reside in the north, but their presence is most noticeable during the summer, when a lot of Brits who own holiday homes come and stay for the season. Roughly half the population speaks English, and many older residents speak Greek.

SIESTAS, HOLIDAYS, AND FESTIVALS

In the summer, most stores, offices, and banks close for **siesta** at 1pm, and reopen from 4 to 7pm, except on Wednesdays and Saturdays, when they invariably stay closed all afternoon. On Sundays, most places, notably museums, reduce their hours or close entirely. Southern Cyprus closes down on the major Greek **holidays:** New Year's Day, Epiphany (Jan. 6), Green Monday (Feb. 26), Cypriot National Day (April 1), Orthodox Good Friday (April 12), Orthodox Easter (April 14-15), Pentecost (June 3), Assumption Day (Aug. 15), Independence Day (Oct. 1), Christmas Eve, Christmas Day, and Boxing Day (Dec. 26). Greek national holidays, on March 25 and October 28, are also honored in the south. Northern Cyprus' major public and religious holidays are: New Year's Day, Children's Day (April 23), Labor Day (May 1), Youth and Sports Day (May 19), Peace and Freedom Day (July 20), Communal Resistance Day (Aug. 1), Victory Day (Aug. 30), Turkish National Day (Oct. 29), Independence Day (Nov. 15), and Christmas Day. During the 12 days between Christmas and Epiphany (*Phota*), evil spirits supposedly visit Cyprus. On the eve of their departure, women throw pancakes and sausages off the roofs of their homes to ensure that the werewolves will leave content, without causing any last-minute atrocities.

Some villages in Cyprus hold **festivals** on the feast day of their patron saint. Some of the most important festivals, such as the feast of the Dormition of the Virgin Mary, are held on August 15 at several villages that consider the Virgin Mary (*Panagia*) their patroness. At these events, peddlers from all over gather in the village for folk dancing, poetry, and music. A general list of the year's activities can be obtained by writing to the Cyprus Tourism Organization (see p. 376). Once in Cyprus, you can obtain a copy of *This Month's Principal Events* from any tourist information office.

■■■ KEEPING IN TOUCH

Post offices are open Monday through Friday from 7:30am to 1:30pm (1pm in the summer). Some have afternoon hours from 3:30-5:30pm (summer 4-6pm). *Poste Restante* is available only in Nicosia, Larnaka, Paphos, and Limassol (10¢ per piece). When sending a letter from the south, make sure your envelope or card is affixed with the 1¢ **refugee stamp**—mail will go nowhere without it.

Cyprus has offical postal codes for the North, but your best bet may be to send letters via Turkey using the postal code **Mersin 10, Turkey.** A sample address is: Dome Hotel, Girne, Northern Cyprus, Mersin 10, Turkey. The KKTC has its own stamps, which are accepted internationally.

Southern Cyprus has a fairly good **telephone company (CYTA).** Direct overseas calls can be made from nearly all public phones if you have enough change. For international calls, **telecards,** sold at banks and newspaper stands, are more convenient; they work in special phones in the south and come in denominations of £2, 3, 5, and 10. To make a collect call, it is cheapest to directly dial an international operator in the destination country: you are charged only one unit. Otherwise, you must go to a CYTA office or a private phone, which in hotels may carry a 10% surcharge.

For telephone purposes, the North functions as a part of Turkey. To call **from abroad,** dial 90 (Turkey) as the country code, followed by 392, the area code for the North. Until the changeover to the mainland Turkish phone system, all numbers had 5 digits. Now they have 7—the same 5 as before, along with two others at the front. All Girne numbers now start with 81; Lefkoşa 22; Famagusta 36. For example, a Girne number listed as 45678 in old literature is now 814 5678. Often, only the last 5 digits are quoted. The North has no city codes.

The **country codes** from the South and North are the same: **Australia** 0061, **Canada** 001, **Ireland** 00353, **New Zealand** 0064, **South Africa** 0027, **U.K.** 0044, and **U.S.** 001. For example, to call the U.S. from Cyprus, dial 001 before the number. To call the South from the U.S., dial 011, then 357, followed by the area code (without the zero) and finally the local number. For **info** on numbers in the South, dial 192. To reach an **international operator** in the U.S., dial 080-90-000 (MCI), 080-90-010 (AT&T), or 080-90-001 (SPRINT). For the U.K., dial 080-90-044 (BT) or 080-90-004 (MERCURY). International operators are also directly available in Australia (080-90-061) and Canada (080-90-012). From the South **ambulance, fire, or police** dial 199.

■■■ ACCOMMODATIONS AND FOOD

Cheap, clean hotels are rare. In general, prices for accommodations drop during off-season to about 20% less than the rates quoted in this book. Nicosia, Troodos, Paphos, and Larnaka all have **HI youth hostels,** and Stavros tis Psokas has a loosely affiliated **forest station.** Although Cyprus has only a few formal campgrounds, you may sleep on beaches and in forests. Choose your site discreetly and leave it as clean as you found it. Be careful if you camp unofficially; women should be especially wary and never camp alone. In the Troodos area, try staying in the monasteries; they're free, but you should leave a donation. Because of complaints from hotels, monasteries are starting to accept only Orthodox guests.

Cypriot food is similar to Greek and Middle Eastern cuisine. Try *meze,* a platter of about a dozen appetizers for two to four people, available in either meat or fish varieties. The exact composition varies between restaurants, but it can include olives, tomatoes, tahini, hummus, and small portions of *souvlaki* and octopus. *Kleftiko,* also popular, is lamb roasted in clay ovens over charcoal. Cypriot *kebap* is similar to Greek *souvlaki,* but the sandwich is larger, the meat less greasy, and it includes tomatoes, cucumbers, onions, and parsley. At £1 each, a *kebap* is probably the cheapest meal you can have. *Sheftalia* (grilled ground meat with onions) is also served in pita pockets. At festivals and street fairs, Cypriots enjoy *soujoukko,* strips of jellied nuts dipped in hot grape juice that resemble a rubber hose. Vegetarians might have to subsist on traditional Greek salad, olives, *hallonui* (a type of cheese made only in Cyprus), or hummus and tahini. *Trahana,* a soup made with yogurt and wheat, is ideal. *Lokurdas,* a sweet fried dough, is a popular dessert.

■■■ HISTORY

ANCIENT CYPRUS

The remains of round stone dwellings indicate settlement on Cyprus as early as Neolithic times, dating back to roughly 7000 BC. The first settlers most likely originated from the nearby Syropalestinian coast. Cyprus first achieved local importance at the onset of the **Bronze Age** due to its wealth of copper ore. Linguists are unsure whether *Kypros,* from which the word "copper" is derived, first referred to the island or the metal itself. The Bronze Age witnessed an increase in Cyprus' trade and cultural exchange with neighboring countries.

The most dramatic change in island culture was fostered by the arrival of the Mycenaeans from the Peloponnese in the **Middle Bronze Age,** initiating a Hellenic tradition that has carried over to the present. The most obvious of these cultural influences can be seen in the pottery of the era, often depicting mythological scenes and bestiaries. From roughly 1400 to the mid-12th century BC, **Mycenaean** traders visited the island regularly, spreading the use of the Greek language and introducing written notation for commerce. The arrival of **Phoenician** traders and colonists in the first millennium BC introduced a fresh cultural impulse to the island. The Phoenicians shared political control with the Greeks until the arrival of the **Assyrians** in the 7th century BC, who dominated the island for 100 years. After the waning of Assyrian power, the Egyptians briefly took hold of the island, but soon were overthrown by the Persian king. There was significant resistance to Persian rule by the native Cypriots, notably in the efforts of pro-Hellenic Evagoras I of Salamis, who forced Persians out of Salamis and fostered Greek culture within his kingdom.

As Persian expansion stagnated, **Alexander the Great** absorbed Cyprus into his growing empire. In 295 BC, following Alexander's death, Ptolemy claimed Cyprus for Egypt. Under the succession of Ptolemies, Cyprus prospered; while cultural and religious institutions remained unchanged, the Greek alphabet came to replace the local syllabic script. Two centuries later, in 58 BC, Rome took advantage of Ptolemy's declining fortunes by annexing Cyprus. Christianity was introduced to the island in 45 AD by the apostle Paul and the Cypriot apostle Barnabas. The spread of the Christian religion continued for three centuries thereafter, and, with the conversion of the Roman governor in 46 AD, Cyprus became the first country in the world to be ruled by a Christian.

BYZANTINE RULE TO THE OTTOMAN EMPIRE

When Constantinople was proclaimed the capital of the eastern half of the divided Roman empire, the stage was set for the synthesis of Roman civic thought, Greek philosophy, and the Greek Orthodox tradition. During these centuries, Cyprus passed through many dark periods—two devastating earthquakes in 332 and 342, a forty-year drought that severely scarred the island, and fierce Arab raids in the 7th century that once again proved the island's vulnerability to foreign attack. At the same time, however, many new towns were founded, and established towns expanded significantly. In 1191, **Richard the Lionheart,** en route to the Crusades in Jerusalem, quickly overran the island, which proved indispensable in provisioning the Christian armies. After robbing the island of its treasures, King Richard sold Cyprus to the **Knights Templar.** Soon after, when the Templars found they could not maintain the island, they passed responsibility on to Guy de Lusignan, a minor French noble who had been involved in the Crusades.

The **Lusignan Dynasty** (1192-1489) ruled through a feudalist system of class privileges and hierarchy that oppressed the lower classes and suppressed Cypriot culture and Greek Orthodox Christianity. Despite French subjugation of the locals, the Lusignan era left a legacy of impressive Gothic architecture in the form of churches, cathedrals, and castles. As setbacks in Palestine forced the Crusaders into full retreat, the Lusignans invited Crusader families to set up camp on the island. By the late 13th century, Cyprus had become the wealthiest island in the eastern Mediterranean. Yet in 1489 the **Venetians,** profiting from the Lusignans' dynastic intricacies, annexed the island. They remodeled and strengthened Cypriot military defenses, but were still no match for the Ottoman Empire. In 1570, following a two-month siege, Nicosia surrendered to the Turks. The fall of Famagusta one year later marked the beginning of the **Ottoman period** in Cyprus.

Cypriots welcomed the Ottoman abolition of feudalism, although the peasants who acquired land under this new system were taxed heavily. The Orthodox Church flourished in this period. Under the Ottomans there was no separation of church and state, and the native Church of Cyprus served as a powerful administrative machine for the sultan. As the Empire weakened in the 19th century, Britain found itself defending Turkish territories in the face of Russian expansionism. In July of 1878, British forces landed peacefully at Larnaka and assumed control of Cyprus as a second military base. **Britain** entered into an arrangement with Turkey in which the island's excess revenue was used to pay off Turkish war loans. Although Cypriots did not enjoy political self-determination under the British, they benefited from the construction of many public works—roads, bridges, drinking and irrigation water supplies, a railway line, schools, and hospitals.

CYPRUS IN THE 20TH CENTURY

When Turkey joined the Central Powers at the start of WWI, Britain immediately annulled their previous agreement and annexed the island, and, in 1925, Cyprus formally became a British Crown Colony. Under British rule, cries for **enosis,** or union with Greece, grew increasingly strong, leading to the violent uprising in 1931 that avalanched into atrocities between ethnic Greeks and Turks. The British responded to the 1931 riot with stringent measures intended to repress nationalistic movements. During these years, the Pan-Cyprian Federation of Labor (PEO), encompassing both left-wing Greeks and Turks, continued to oppose colonial rule from the underground. When political meetings were once again allowed after 1941, the Progressive Party of the Working People (AKEL), a communist organization that still strongly influences Cypriot life, was founded. In the municipal elections of 1943, AKEL gained control of two major cities, after which they began to support strikes and agitate for Cypriot rights under the British regime.

In 1954, **General George Grivas,** in conjunction with **Archbishop Makarios**, founded the EOKA (National Organization of Cypriot Fighters), an underground *enosist* movement. When the United Nations vetoed the Greeks' appeal to grant Cyprus self-determination in 1955, General Grivas and the EOKA initiated a round of riots and guerilla warfare aimed at the British government. In response to increased EOKA activity, the underground, anti-Greek forces of Volkan (Volcano), under the leadership of **Rauf Denktaş,** founded the TMT (Turkish Resistance Organization). TMT was a paramilitary organization designed to fight the *enosists* and to push for **taksim,** or partition of the island between Greece and Turkey. Weary of the perpetual violence but unconvinced by the viability of either *enosis* or *taksim,* Britain, along with the foreign ministers of Greece and Turkey, agreed in 1959, to establish an independent Cypriot republic. On August 16, 1960, Cyprus was granted independence and became a member of the U.N. and the British commonwealth.

The new **constitution** stipulated that a Greek Cypriot president and a Turkish Cypriot vice-president were to be appointed through popular election and that the Greek to Turkish ratio in the House of Representatives would be 70:30. In 1959, Archbishop Makarios became the republic's first president, and **Fazıl Küçük,** leader of the Turkish Cypriot community, was elected to the vice presidency without opposition. In 1963, Makarios proposed thirteen amendments to the constitution, intended to facilitate bicommunal life, which included the abolition of the president's and vice-president's veto power and the introduction of majority rule. When the Turkish government threatened to use military force if these amendments were implemented, renewed violence broke out between the EOKA and TMT, resulting in the division of Nicosia along the Green Line. In February 1964, the U.N. dispatched UNFICYP (U.N. Forces in Cyprus), a temporary peace-keeping force that since then has been renewed indefinitely.

In 1968, Makarios and Küçük were both re-elected by an overwhelming majority, although in the years following they were subject to several coup plots, notably one by former ally General Grivas who returned to Cyprus in 1971 to found the militant EOKA-B and to revitalize the call for *enosis.* Intermittent violence suddenly exploded into an international affair in 1974 when the Greek Cypriot National Guard, assisted by the military **junta** in Greece, overthrew Archbishop Makarios and replaced him with **Nikos Sampson,** a notorious EOKA gunman who favored immediate *enosis.* Five days later, ostensibly moving to prevent the National Guard from attacking Turkish Cypriots, the Turkish army invaded Cyprus from the north, conquering 37% of the island. Early in 1975, the North declared itself the Turkish Federated State of Cyprus (TFSC), officialy partitioning the island.

In November 1983, Turkish-occupied Cyprus proclaimed itself independent as the **Turkish Republic of Northern Cyprus (TRNC).** Though only Turkey has recognized the new state, the TRNC has established trading relations in Europe and with several Arab states. Led by Rauf Denktaş, the TRNC lags far behind the Republic of Cyprus economically but is generally supported by Turkish Cypriots who, in recent years, have been joined by thousands of settlers from mainland Turkey. In 1992, the decision was made to scale down UNFICYP significantly, leaving Cypriots to resolve their situation without much international intervention.

Through the latest presidential election (1993), **Glafkos Clerides,** former head of the conservative Democratic Rally (DISY), became head of the Republic of Cyprus. The re-election of Denktaş in the North aids the resumption of the negotiation process, and, in conjunction with the recent involvement of the United States, resolution seems possible in the near future. After his election, Denktaş promised that 1995-96 would be years of "peace and settlement," although he is under pressure from Turkish nationalists not to compromise. Both Turkey and Greece are eager to win the favor of the United States and the European Union. Greek officials are hopeful that talks for the Republic of Cyprus' acceptance into the European Union, contingent on accord with Turkey, can begin by late 1998 or 1999.

> All divisions in the Cyprus chapter are geographical, not political.

CENTRAL AND WESTERN CYPRUS

■■■ LIMASSOL (LEMESOS) ΛΕΜΕΣΟΣ

The island's second-largest city and port of entry for most passenger ferries, Limassol is the industrial center of Cyprus, complete with a decaying downtown area and ungainly merchant ships anchored offshore. Despite the Cyprus Tourism Organization's promise that "there's always a good reason" to "make Limassol your destination for any season," this port town is not a cordial introduction to an otherwise striking island. Rapid growth and a lack of urban planning have nurtured an endless row of hotels stretching east along the coast, and the new four-lane highway only intensifies the sense of urban blight. Moreover, the city shuts down almost completely on weekends and in order to eat, you may have to head for the touristy and expensive seafront restaurants. Still, the city's palm-tree-lined waterfront promenade is attractive and, even at its worst, Limassol still retains some appeal.

ORIENTATION AND PRACTICAL INFORMATION

Centrally situated in Cyprus' south coast and fairly equidistant from other major cities in Southern Cyprus (50-70km), Limassol is the hub for bus and taxi services.

The **new port,** where passenger boats arrive, is 5km southwest of the town center. To your right, as you enter the arrivals terminal, is a **tourist desk,** with excellent free city maps. Buses #1 and #30 run between the port and downtown Limassol (every 30min., Sat. every hr., 35¢). After ships arrive, buses wait outside the customs building. Otherwise, the stop is right outside the port gates. To get to the port, catch bus #1 or #30 at the bus station near the Anexartisias St. market. A taxi to town costs roughly £2.50. If you're headed directly for another major town, call the appropriate service taxi, and you'll be picked up at the port at no extra charge.

Cyprus Tourism Organization Office: 15 Spiro Araouzos St. (tel. 362756). On the waterfront 1 block east of the castle. The extremely capable and helpful staff can answer all questions, suggest daytrips, and provide maps, bus schedules, and general information for the entire island. Open Mon.-Fri. 8:15am-2:15pm, Mon. and Thurs. 4-6:30pm, Sat. 8:15am-1:15pm. A small office at the **port** (tel. 343868) is open immediately following arrivals. Nearby office in **Dassoudi Beach,** 35 George I Potamos Yermassoyias (tel. 323211), opposite the Park Beach Hotel. Same hours as the Limassol office; reduced hours in winter.

Police: (tel. 330411). At Gladstone and Leondios St. next to the hospital.

Post Office: Main office, (tel. 330190) on Gladstone St., next to the central police station. Open May-Sept. Mon.-Tues. and Thurs.-Fri. 7:30am-1:30pm and 4-6pm, Wed. 7:30am-1:30pm, Sat. 9-11am. **Postal Code:** 3900.

CYTA: On the corner of Markos Botsaris and Athinon St. Phones also in the store next to the tourist office. The phone takes 10¢ and 20¢ pieces. (Open daily 7am-7:30pm.) Guesthouses Ikaros, Excelsior, and the Continental Hotel also have international phones. **Telephone Code:** 05.

Tourist Agency: Amathous, 2 Syntagma Sq. (tel. 362145), near the tourist office on the water. A large chain that sells most plane and boat tickets. Open Mon.-Fri. 8am-1pm and 4-6:30pm.

American Express: 130 Spiro Araouzos St. (tel. 362045), in the offices of **A. L. Mantovani and Sons.** Open for AmEx transactions Mon.-Tues. and Thurs.-Fri. 9am-noon and 3:30-6:30pm.

Buses: KEMEK terminal (tel. 363241), corner of Irenis and Enosis St. Heads to Nicosia (Mon.-Fri. 4 per day, £1.25, Sat. 3 per day), Paphos (Mon.-Sat. 1 per day, £1.25), Larnaka (Mon.-Fri. 4 per day, Sat. 2 per day, £1.10). **Kyriakos,** 21 Thessalonikis St., (tel. 364114) heads to and from Platres (Mon.-Fri. 1 per day, £1.50).

City Buses: Andreas Themistokles St., near Anexartisias St. Bus #1 goes to the new port, #6 and #30 go east along the coast (35¢; most don't run on Sun.).

Service Taxis: Karydas, 129 Spiro Araouzos St. (tel. 362061). **Kypros/Akropolis,** 49 Spiro Araouzos St. (tel. 363979). **Kyriakos,** 21 Thessalonikis St. (tel. 364114). **Makris,** 166 Hellas St. (tel. 365550). Karydas, Kypros/Akropolis, and Kyriakos run frequent taxis to Nicosia (£2). Akropolis and Makris run taxis to Larnaka (£1.70). All the companies except Akropolis go to Paphos (every hr., £1.70). Less frequent service Sept.-May. The taxis only run 6am-4:30pm; plan accordingly or you might end up sleeping with the goats on a mountaintop.

Bike and Moped Rentals: Agencies cluster on the shore road, near the luxury hotels at the eastern edge of town. A motorcycle license is required for rentals, but most agents will take you to the police station, where, if you've forgotten your license, you can be issued a temporary Cypriot license (£1). Motorbikes £4.50 per day. For long term rentals, you'll find lower rates in Polis.

Laundromat: (tel. 368293), Kaningos St. off Markarios Ave., near the Archaeological Museum. Leave laundry for same-day pick-up or do it yourself. Wash £1.80, dry 75¢. Open Mon.-Tues. and Thurs.-Fri. 7:30am-1pm and 3-6:30pm.

Bookstores: Bookworld, 156 St. Andrew St. (tel. 376448). Open Mon.-Tues. and Thurs.-Fri. 9am-1pm and 4-7pm; Wed. and Sat. 9am-1pm.

Pharmacy: Call 192 for the current list of all-night pharmacies.

Hospital: (tel. 330156). On Leondios St.

ACCOMMODATIONS

In Limassol, you get what you pay for: budget accommodations, clustered near the bus station, are cheap but low-quality, and prostitution is common in the area. Those traveling alone, particularly women, may want to stick to a starred hotel or one of the nicer guest houses listed below.

Guest House Luxor, 101 Agios Andreas St. (tel. 362265), on a pleasant pedestrian shopping street. Attractive rooms, cupboard-like showers, and a lovely outdoor garden. Singles £5, doubles £8, w/ bath £10. Cash only.

Guest House Ikaros, 61 Eleftherias St. (tel. 354348). *Twin Peaks* comes to Limassol. Tapestries, fish tanks, animal skins, and chandeliers. Bring your camera. Inter-

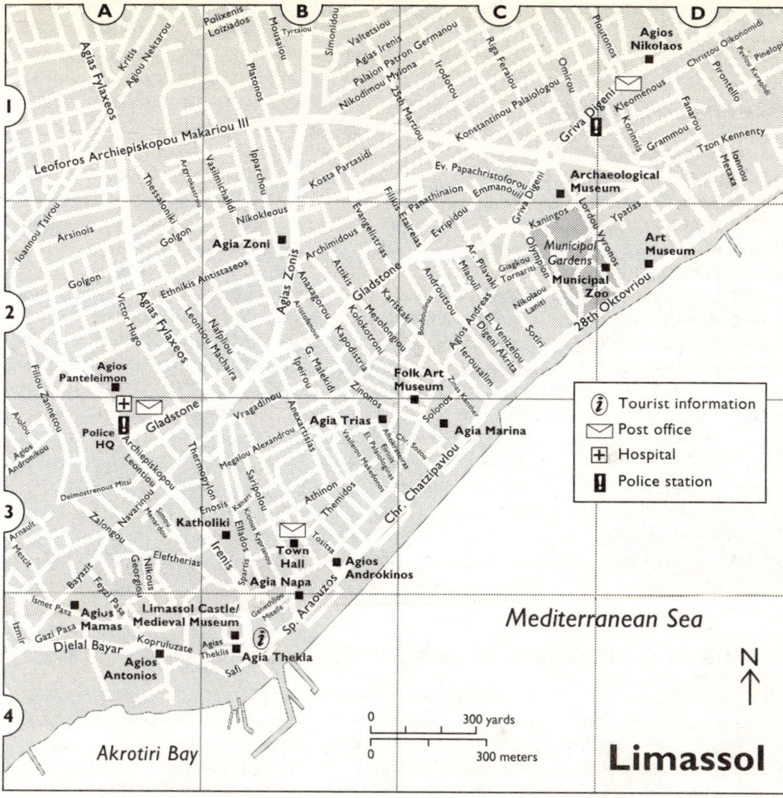

national phone. Singles £5, doubles £10. Showers included. Call to reserve in high season.

Continental Hotel, 137 Spiro Araouzos St. (tel. 362530). 2-star hotel. Pleasant and clean, but a little schmancy for the backpacker. Singles £16, doubles £26, triples £27. Breakfast included. Air conditioning £2 per day.

FOOD, ENTERTAINMENT, AND SIGHTS

Restaurant fare in Limassol is mediocre. Many of the restaurants on the waterfront and in the town center cater to rich, undiscerning tourists: glossy, plastic-coated menus advertise uninspired food at imaginative prices. For real, non-mystery-meat foods, hit a market (unless, of course, it's a Wed. or Sat. afternoon). The bars along the coast near Dassoudi Beach are about as hip as Ringo Starr. At night, *the* place to be is **Whisper's** nightclub (tel. 326464) on Nicosia Old Road.

The **Limassol Castle** is the only building of historical significance in Limassol proper. This 12th-century Frankish structure, where Richard married his Queen Berengaria in 1191, was destroyed by earthquakes and Genoese assaults; the only traces of the old Byzantine fort are in the western wall of the compact building. In the early 14th century, the Knights Templar fortified the castle's walls and covered the Gothic windows. Later, the Knights of St. John converted the great Western Hall into a Gothic church and the chapel into a series of prison cells. The Turks claimed the castle in 1570, and the capacious West Hall was used as a prison under the British regime until 1940. The castle has finally retired to an unruffled existence as the **Cyprus Medieval Museum** (tel. 330419; open Mon.-Fri. 7:30am-5pm, Sat. 9am-5pm; off-season Mon.-Sat. 7:30am-5pm; admission 50¢.) The **Archaeological Museum** (tel. 330132), on the corner of Kaningos and Vyronos, contains an assortment of funerary *stelae,* jewelry, statues, and terra-cotta figurines (once used as stand-ins for Bronze Age Cypriots who were too hung over to do the temple thing on Sun. mornings). (Open Mon.-Fri. 7:30am-5pm, Sat. 9am-5pm, Sun. 10am-1pm; admission 50¢.) On Byron St., closer to the sea, are the **public gardens** and town **zoo,** the largest in Cyprus. (Open daily 9am-noon and 3-6pm; reduced hours in off-season; admission 50¢.) The public gardens are the site of the annual **wine festival** in early September. The **folk art museum,** 253 Agios Andreas St. (tel. 362303), one block east (left facing the water) of the intersection of Zenon and Agios Andreas, houses 19th- and 20th-century embroidery, costumes, etc. (Open Mon.-Wed. and Fri. 8:30am-1:30pm and 3-5:30pm, Thurs. 8:30am-1:30pm; reduced hours in off-season; admission 30¢.)

Visit Limassol's **Reptile House** (tel. 372770) at the Old Port, which showcases snakes, lizards, crocodiles, Republicans, tortoises, and, oddly, a lone monkey. (Open daily 9am-7pm or earlier; admission 50¢-£1.) The city's long stone beach does not inspire ecstasy, but a new breakwater has made the area more pleasant for swimming. **Dassoudi Beach,** 3km east of town, is far better. Take bus #6 or #30 from the market on Kanaris St. (every 15min., 35¢). The ebullient **Ladies Mile Beach** at the new port is also popular (take bus #1). At the end of June, actors from around the world congregate in Limassol for the **Shakespeare Festival.** A two-week **International Art Festival** is held in the zoo gardens during the first half of July. If you arrive in early September, you can attain divine euphoria at the **Wine-Fest. Carnival,** 50 days before Orthodox Easter (usually in Feb.), is celebrated more intensely in Limassol than in any other Cypriot town, with various parades and balls. Details are available at the tourist office and in *This Month's Principal Events*.

■ NEAR LIMASSOL: AKROTIRI PENNINSULA

The **Kolossi Castle,** a square-shaped, three-story structure roughly 9km west of Limassol, played a crucial role during the Crusades. Both the Knights Templar and the Knights of the Order of St. John briefly made the castle their headquarters. When the latter knights moved to Rhodes in 1310, Kolossi–garnering wealth from the surrounding vineyards–remained their richest overseas possession. (Open daily 7:30am-5pm; admission 50¢.) To reach Kolossi, take bus #16 from the urban bus station in Limassol (every 20min., 35¢).

Outside the British sovereign base of Akrotiri, the small resort town of **Pissouri** frolics year-round with Her Majesty's military men. Built on a cliff with the standard enticing views, Pissouri hosts several bars and *tavernas.* The **Bunch of Grapes Inn** (tel. (052) 21275) has a restaurant and rooms. (Doubles £25, breakfast included.)

The remarkably well-preserved ruins of **Kourion** (Curium in Latin), 12km west of Limassol, lie within the British Sovereign Base Area, which includes all of the Akrotiri Peninsula. First settled during the Neolithic Period, Kourion was colonized by Achaïans from Argos in the Peloponnese during the 14th and 13th centuries BC. It became famous for its sanctuary to Apollo (8th century BC) and its stadium (2nd century AD), both located west of the main settlement. In the 4th century AD, Kourion was leveled by the same earthquake that destroyed several other Cypriot coastal cities. The city was rebuilt in the 5th century, only to be burned in the mid-7th century during an Arab raid.

Begin your tour at the impressive **amphitheater,** used for the **Shakespeare Festival** in June, occasional concerts and theatrical productions during the summer, and weekend theater in September. Limassol's tourist bureau can fill you in. The earliest structure on the site, a small theater built in the 2nd century BC, was enlarged with limestone blocks in the first century AD. During Greek and Roman times, the theater was used for drama, but by the 3rd century AD, civilization had progressed and the odeum became an arena for bloody animal fights and professional wrestling.

Across the road from the basilica lie a group of ruins under excavation. In the north corner is a large Hellenistic building and a water reservoir used until the 7th century AD. In the southwest corner is a row of Corinthian columns, all that remains of the **Forum,** a marketplace dating from the end of the 2nd century AD.

Farther northwest are the remains of the **House of Gladiators** and its mosaic gladiator pin-ups. Don't fall into one of the nearby cisterns. The **House of Achilles** faces the highway at the end of the excavation site. The house is fenced off, but you can get the key at the ticket office, or climb in through the narrow path that follows the fence along the road. (Site open daily 7:30am-7:30pm; Oct.-May 7:30am-5pm; admission 50¢.) Visit the nearby **Museum of Kourion** in Episkopi village for a clear explanation of the artifacts. (Open Mon., Wed., and Fri. 7:30am-2:30pm; Thurs. 7:30am-2:30pm and 3-6pm; admission 50¢.)

Buses leave Limassol Castle bound for Kourion (6 per day, returning at 11:50am, 2:50 and 4:50pm, 50¢). If you're mopeding to Kourion, go via Episkopi village. There are no signs for Kourion until you're within a couple of kilometers of the site, so bring a good map. Don't take the highway—the lanes keep changing and ending abruptly, and traffic is heavy. Without a helmet, it's madness. Remember, Cypriots drive on the *left* side of the road; if you can't keep this in mind, don't bike.

■■■ TROODOS MOUNTAINS
ΤΡΟΟΔΟΣ

In this serene mountain range, isolated villages nestled amidst cool, pine-covered hills, halfway between Nicosia and Limassol, provide refuge from sun-baked coastal cities. Tiny hamlets mingle with astounding Byzantine churches while remote monasteries and forests of flat-topped pines ward off the summer heat. In towns like Kakopetria, the rush of water from the mill and the twittering birds add sound to a day of cool relaxation. Hikers and campers in particular will find a small paradise here. What is usually a peaceful and rejuvenating natural experience in June and early July, however, can turn frustrating and costly in August when crowds descend, especially on weekends. From January to March, Mt. Olympus, the highest point in Cyprus (1951m), is host to hundreds of skiers.

Public transportation to the area and between the villages runs infrequently. One **bus** per day heads here from Nicosia and Limassol. The best way to get around is to rent some wheels. Some hitch, but we don't recommend it. The bohemian way to see this area is to leave your things in one of the coastal towns and travel around for a few days with only the map from the tourist office and a few essentials, like a black turtleneck and Jack Kerouac's *On the Road.* In the mountains, only Platres has motorbike rentals. You can play it safe by renting in Limassol, Paphos, Polis, or Nicosia. Remember that the mountain roads are tortuous, winding, bumpy, and sometimes steep. You could also rent a car in one of the major cities.

PLATRES

Platres will most likely be your first stop in the Troodos region, as it is the most accessible by public transportation. **Zingas Bus** (tel. (02) 463154) in Nicosia heads to Platres at 12:15pm and returns at 6am (Mon.-Fri., £1.50 each way). From Limassol, **Kyriakos** (tel. 364114) leaves at 11:30am and returns at 7am (Mon.-Fri., £1.50 each way). A private **taxi** from either city costs £15-20.

Platres is divided into the **pano** (upper) and **kato** (lower) sections. Kato Platres, 20min. downhill from Pano Platres, remains unharrowed by tourism. If you want to stay in Kato Platres, try the florid yet tidy **Kapakioti** (tel. 421202; £8 per person). Otherwise, all tourist facilities have formed a clique in Pano Platres: the **tourist office** (tel. 421316) is left of the parking lot in the main square. (Open Mon.-Fri. 9am-3pm, Sat. 9am-2pm.) The **post office** sits to the left of the tourist office. (Open Mon.-Fri. 8-10am, Wed. 3-5pm; winter Mon.-Fri. 3-5pm.) The **telephone office** is next to the post office (open Mon.-Sat. 7:30am-1:30pm). The **Bank of Cyprus** is across from the Splendid Hotel. (Open Mon.-Fri. 8am-12:30pm and Mon. 3-5:30pm.) The **hospital** (tel. 421324) is just below Pano Platres and houses the **pharmacy.** The **police** (tel. 421351) are across from the Splendid Hotel in a converted military chapel. Platres' **telephone code** is 05. **Postal code** is 4815 in Kato and 4820 in Pano Platres.

Next to the parking lot is the conveniently located **Splendid Hotel** (tel. 421425), which would be more aptly named the Pretty Darn Nice Hotel. All rooms have balconies and showers, and some have toilets. (Singles £10-12, doubles £12-14 per person, family rooms for 3-4 people £1.75.) Paul, the manager, also rents flats a few minutes out of town. Inquire at the hotel.

A large **grocery store** and a **fruit market** are just past the Pafsilypon Hotel. North of Platres on the road to Troodos, **Psilo Dentro** (Tall Tree; tel. 421350) serves sumptuous trout from its fish farm. (Trout £4.20, fish *meze* £6 per person; open for lunch only until 4 or 5 pm.) The urbane (if they come to Platres) step out at **Andy's Disco** (tel. 421122), near the square. (No cover; small beer 50¢; open 10pm-2am.)

Near Platres is the cordial lace and wine village of **Omodos,** with a beautiful long central square, next to the famous **Monastery of the Holy Cross.** Ask for a tour of the **folk museum** in the monastery and the restored **wine press** (*linos*). You can buy a bottle of local, dry wine (£1.70) or the fiery *tsipoura,* a Cypriot whiskey. As you return to Kato Platres, follow the signposts to get to the red-tiled village of **Phini** and revive. The **Pilavakion Museum** (tel. 421508) focuses on *pitharia* (large, red, ceramic jars), wine-making equipment, and the notable "Pithari Sauna" used in traditional Cypriot obstetrics to avoid post-pregnancy stretch marks. (No regular hours; if you wish to visit, call ahead; admission £1.)

TROODOS

Though just 8km north of Platres, **Troodos** is accessible by **bus** only from **Clarios Bus Co.** in Nicosia (Mon.-Fri. at 11:30am, returning to Nicosia at 6:30am the next day, £1.10). Private **taxi** from Nicosia costs roughly £17. Taxi fare from Platres is roughly £5 or you can try hiking it (at least 1hr.). Troodos village is an easily-missed group of hotels, restaurants, and tourist facilities. The **police** (tel. 421623), just outside of town, offer **CYTA** information, but do not operate all year, and sometimes might not be there at all. For more reliable services, head to Platres or Limassol.

Roughly 400m from the center of town on the Troodos Kakopetria road squats the recently re-opened **youth hostel** (tel. 422400), offering clean and quiet rooms with communal kitchen facilities (hostel management not available 10am-3pm; £4). Another cheap place to stay is the **Troodos campground** (tel. 422249), 2km north of the main square in a pine forest (£1 per person). The campsite provides washing facilities, a minimarket, a small bar/restaurant, and a first aid station. The **Jubilee Hotel Bar** (tel. 421647), just outside of town, is a favorite haunt of British expatriates. The sign for horseback riding is on the right driving into town from Platres. Trust the horse; he's going the right way. (£5 per hour.)

Three self-guided **nature trails** originate in the Troodos area. The first is 8½km long and goes from the Troodos post office to Chromion, passing by various villages. A 3km trail leaves from the coffee shop in Troodos Sq. and finishes at a divine lookout point. Shorter but even more captivating is the 2km path that follows a stream from the Presidential Palace in Troodos and finishes at Kaledonia Falls near Platres (roughly 45min.). Noteworthy trees and plants are labeled on the way. The tourist office has a pamphlet outlining the trails. It's helpful to get a guidebook and look on the map for starting points. Ask at a hotel for advice.

KAKOPETRIA AND ENVIRONS

Picturesque **Kakopetria,** literally "bad rock," on the main road from Troodos to Nicosia, is the most popular town in the northern part of the mountains. According to local legend, the large rock perched on the hillside was supposed to bring good luck to newlyweds. That is, until one day, the "bad rock" rolled over and crushed a couple. The government is preserving the oldest section of the village: the shady, cobblestone roads and mudbrick houses overlook a river and soothing water mill. In the rest of the village, slick new pubs and "rustic" hotels cater to vacationers.

The **Bank of Cyprus** is in the main square (open Mon.-Fri. 8:15am-12:30pm), near the **post office** (open Mon.-Wed. and Fri. 7:30am-1:30pm, Thurs. 7:30am-1:30pm and 3-6pm). The **police station** (tel. 922420, -255) is just up the street from the bank. A **pharmacy** (tel. 2020; open 9:30am-9pm) is below the Rialto Hotel, and the **doctor** (tel. 3077) practices a few doors down. The **Rialto Hotel** (tel. (02) 922438) charges £43 per double, w/breakfast. Clean rooms await at the **Hekali** (tel. (02) 922501; £18 per person w/breakfast.) The **Kifissia Hotel** (tel. (02) 922421) has calming views of the small river. (£10 per person; English breakfast included.) Kakopetria and its smaller neighbor **Galata** have five Byzantine churches between them; the most beautiful is **Agios Nikolaos tis Stegis,** roughly 4km southwest of Kakopetria on a dirt road. The interior of this 14th-century church is painted with strikingly unique frescoes like the Virgin Mary breast-feeding Jesus. While more common among Roman Catholic scenes, such icons are exceedingly rare for Greek Orthodox. (Open Tues.-Sat. 9am-4pm, Sun. 11am-4pm.) **Buses** to Kakopetria travel from **Clarios Bus Co.** (tel. (02) 453234 in Nicosia; Mon.-Sat. 12-14 per day, Sun. 2 per day in the summer; £1.10). Don't miss the opportunity to have a delicious dinner with a spectacular view of the Old Village at **Maryland at the Mill** (tel. 922536), located appropriately at the town's mill.

After a walk through the **Old Village,** down a cold brew (90¢) at the **Village Pub.** (Open 10am-midnight.) There are several cheap *kebap* houses in the square, and the **Village Cellar,** a tastefully restored house, is renowned for its *tavas* (lamb and onions, £3) and fresh trout.

Sixteen kilometers northeast of Kakopetria, the teensy Byzantine church at **Asinou** (*Panayia Porviotissa*) contains some of the most excellent mural paintings on the island. The church and original frescoes hail from the 12th century, but new frescoes were added and old ones restored after the church was tampered with by Turks in the 14th and 16th centuries. Today, the church is used for religious purposes only twice a year on feast days of the Virgin, to whom it is dedicated. To visit the church, find the priest in the nearby village of **Nikitare** (ask in the village cafés). Roughly 16km southeast of Kakopetria, the church of **Panagiatou Arakou** is another repository of elaborate 12th-century frescoes, including Christ Pantokrator (on the inside of the dome). South of the church is the comely vineyard village of **Agros,** with simple overnight accommodations (the only rooms in the vicinity).

Eight monks and myriad animals make their home in the modern **Troodhitissa Monastery,** 5km from Platres on the Prodromos-Platres road. Dedicated to the Virgin Mary, the original monastery was built in 1250 to house one of her miracle-working icons; the name Troodhitissa literally means "she who is resident of Mt. Troodos." During the chaos of the iconoclastic movement of the 8th century, a monk hid an icon of the Virgin Mary in Troodos, where a miraculous pillar of fire protected it. More than 100 years later, a sign revealed the site of the monastery, which still stands today. (Open daily 6am-noon and 2-8pm.)

Between Troodos and Prodromos soars **Mt. Olympus** (6401 ft.), the highest peak on the island, now topped with radar stations and observation towers. From here you can get a amazing view of the entire island. From January through March you can alternate sunbathing in Limassol with skiing on the north face of the mountain.

PRODROMOS

Approximately 3 buildings comprise Prodomos, which seems more a tribute to ascetism than to tourism. Ten kilometers northwest of the town of Troodos, **Prodromos** is the second-highest hill resort in the area (after Troodos). Relax at the nearby **Stephos Café** before heading on to **Pedoulas,** a small village to the north of Prodromos, featuring the Church of Archangel Michael, which has mural paintings dating from 1474. Up the street from the church is the **CYTA** and the **police** (tel. (02) 952648), who can answer most tourist questions. Across the street is the miniscule **post office. Postal Code** 4840; **Telephone Code:** 0295.

Kykko Monastery, in the northwest part of the mountains, 14km from Pedoulas and 33km from Troodos, enjoys more wealth and prestige than any other monastery on the island. Founded in the early 12th century when a hermit—after curing the Byzantine Emperor's daughter—was given the Apostle Luke's own Icon of the Virgin Mary, the monastery has burned down numerous times, but the celebrated icon has survived intact. As the icon is though too holy to be viewed directly, it is completely ensconced in mother of pearl and silver casing. After entering the monastery's palatial courtyard, you may think you've wandered into a large luxury hotel; the monastery, whose present buildings date from the early 19th century, is somewhat unmonasteryish, with 400 beds for visitors, a tourist pavilion, and shops.

Kykko gained new fame this century as a communication and supply center during the Cypriot struggle and as the monastic home of Archbishop Makarios III. Only 1½km away were the headquarters of the first military leader of the struggle, "Digh-enis" (General George Grivas). **Makarios' tomb** is just 2km farther in the high hills west of the monastery. The site, guarded at all times by two Greek Cypriot soldiers, is partially open to the east. Makarios requested the opening so that on the day Cyprus was reunited, sunlight would enter his tomb and he could celebrate with his people. Just above the tomb is a path leading up to an icon of the Virgin, called the *throni* (small throne). The bushes alongside the path are laden with scraps of clothing placed there by sick children hoping to be cured. A supermarket, an extortionistic tourist pavilion, and several sweet shops are nearer to the monastery.

■■■ PAPHOS ΠΑΦΟΣ

When the Ptolemies, Greek kings of Egypt, conquered Cyprus, they made Paphos their capital. The city grew fabulously wealthy and developed into a cosmopolitan, commercial center. Paphos maintained its exalted position under Cato and the Roman conquerors, but a 4th-century earthquake halted its supremacy. The Cypriot capital, with the accompanying political and social prestige, moved to Salamis (now in the occupied area near Famagusta). Paphos remained a small village until the Turkish occupation rendered almost all of North Cyprus' tourist areas inaccessible. Since 1974, Paphos has ballooned with luxury hotels and restaurants. Still, it remains a comfortable and manageable city, with all the standard-issue features of Cyprus at its best: archaeological discoveries, gorgeous mosaics, fabulous restaurants, and, in the surrounding countryside, sublime beaches and isolated villages.

ORIENTATION AND PRACTICAL INFORMATION

The city of Paphos is divided into two sections; the upper **Ktima Paphos** (also known as "Paphos"), centered around Kennedy Sq., and the lower **Kato Paphos,** roughly 1km to the south. Formed in the 8th century AD when the townspeople fled inland to evade Arab assaults from the sea, Ktima Paphos is now home to most of the city's shops, budget hotels, and services, while luxury hotels and holiday villas jam Kato Paphos, also the hub of Paphos' nightlife. Everything listed is in Ktima Paphos, unless otherwise noted.

Cyprus Tourist Organization: 3 Gladstone St. (tel. 232841), across from Iris Travel. Helpful staff can provide every scrap of practical information on the region, including excellent free maps. Open Mon.-Fri. 8:15am-2:15pm, and Mon.-Tues. and Thurs.-Fri. 4-6:30pm, Sat. 8:15am-1:15pm. Fewer hours in winter.

Police: (tel. 240140), Grivas Digenes Ave. in Kennedy Sq., opposite the defunct Paphos Palace Hotel.

Post Office: Nikodhimou Mylona St. (tel. 240223), in the District Administration Bldg. Open Mon.-Tues. and Thurs.-Fri. 7:30am-1:30pm and 4-6pm, Wed. 7:30am-1:30pm, Sat. 9-11am. **Postal Code:** 8900. The post office in **Kato Paphos** is on Ag. Antoniou St. (tel. 240226). **Postal Code:** 8903.

CYTA: (tel. 230228) Grivas Digenes Ave. Open daily 7:30am-7:30pm, but may close early. **Telephone Code:** 06.

Banks: Hellenic Bank, 86 Makarios Ave. (tel. 235035). Open Mon.-Fri. 8:30am-12:30pm; in July-Aug. morning service only. **Barclay's Bank,** (tel. 233316)

Kennedy Sq. at Diogenis (next to the defunct Paphos Palace Hotel). Open Mon.-Fri. 8:30am-noon, Tues. and Thurs.-Fri. 3-6pm.

Budget Travel: Iris Travel, 10A Gladstone St. (tel. 237585), opposite the tourist office. Airline tickets (student discounts), and special 4-wheel trips (from £12) and excursions. They also rent cars (Suzuki 700 or Subaru Jeeps £13-25 plus insurance £3), and apartments (from £5 per person). Open Mon.-Fri. 8am-1pm and 4-7pm, Sat. 8am-1pm. Reduced hours in winter.

Airport: C.T.O. (tel. 422833). Opens when flights arrive. Exchange facilities. Private taxis from city center £4, from Kato Paphos £5. No bus service.

Buses: Nea Amoroza Co. (tel. 221114) runs minibuses to Polis (Mon.-Fri. 10 per day, Sat. 6 per day, 75¢). A few go as far as Pomes. Minibuses leave from the easy-to-miss station at 79 Pallikaridi St., across from the ESSO station. **KEMEK** (tel. 234255) runs buses to Limassol from the Mitropolis Bldg., off Thermopylon St. (2 per day, £1.05). Change buses in Limassol for Nicosia or Larnaka. **Excursion buses** make 2 daily round-trips to Palaepaphos Museum and the birthplace of Aphrodite (£1). Bus #30 makes stops at most larger hotels.

City Buses: Municipal buses run between Ktima Paphos and Kato Paphos (31 per day, Sun. 14 per day, 30¢). Catch it in Ktima Paphos just up the road from the post office; in Kato Paphos, at any of the yellow benches lining the road to town. Buses also go to Coral Bay (20 per day, 40¢). Schedules in the tourist office.

Service Taxis: Kyriakos/Karydas, 9 E. Pallikaridi St. (tel. 232459). **Kypros,** 134 Archbishop Makarios III Ave. (tel. 237722); **Makris,** 19 E. Pallikarides St. (tel. 232538), in Kennedy Sq. All companies go to Limassol (£1.75-2); you can change there for Larnaka or Nicosia.

Moped Rental: Mopeds can be rented from several shops in Kato or Ktima Paphos. Prices range £2.50-5. Ask at the youth hostel for information.

Laundromat: Sun Rise, Alkminis and Posidonos St. in Kato Paphos (tel. 234018). Wash and dry £3. Free pick-up in town. Open Mon.-Sat. 9am-1pm and 4-7pm.

International Bookstore: Axel Bookshop, 62-64 Archbishop Makarios III Ave. (tel. 232404). English-language books about Cyprus and a fair selection of English novels. Open Mon.-Sat. 8am-1pm and 4-7pm. Kiosks in Kennedy Sq. sell international newspapers and the English *Cyprus Mail* and *Cyprus Weekly.*

Hospital: Neophytos Nicolaides St. (tel. 240111). Free first aid. English spoken.

Police Emergency: Call 199.

ACCOMMODATIONS

Finding inexpensive accommodations in Paphos is a chore. Solo travelers should stick to the youth hostel; groups might try renting an apartment. The following are in Ktima (upper) Paphos, unless otherwise noted. Prices are higher, but the nightlife is more high-powered, in Kato Paphos.

Youth Hostel (HI), 37 Eleftheriou Venizelou Ave. (tel. 232588), on a quiet residential street northeast of the town center. From the square, follow Pallikaridi to Venizelou; make a right onto Venizelou and follow it a good long way (roughly a 25min. walk from town). The clean, friendly hostel is smothered with pithy advice: "To leave lasting footprints on the sands of time, wear work shoes!" £3.50 per night. Sheets 50¢. Hot showers. Open year-round.

Hotel Trianon, 99 Archbishop Makarios III Ave. (tel. 232193). Toned-down exterior in keeping with the older interior. Doubles £8.

Kiniras Hotel, 91 Archbishop Makarios III Ave. (tel. 241604). Costly, but classy and clean. Singles £15, doubles £28. A/C available at £2 per day. Guests receive a 20% discount on car rentals. Breakfast included.

Pyramos Hotel, 4 Agias Anastasias St. (tel. 235161), in Kato Paphos. Often booked with British tour groups. Singles £16, doubles £24. Breakfast included.

Zenon Gardens Yeroskipou Camping (tel. 242277), east of the tourist beach on the sea, 3km from Paphos Harbor. Minimarket, restaurant, kitchen. Limited shady pitches. £2 per pitch, £2 per 3 people, £1 per small tent. Open March-Oct.

FOOD AND ENTERTAINMENT

While most restaurants in Kato Paphos are geared to pound-laden foreigners, there are some wonderfully cheap options. With an eerie view of the harbor-side ruins, **Hondros,** 96 Pavlou St. (tel. 234256), is one of the oldest restaurants in the area, founded long before the town's tourist boom. Sit under the bamboo-covered terrace beneath the grapevines and eat lamb *kleftiko* off the spit (£3.75), or *mousaka* (£2.50). (Open 11am-4pm and 7pm-midnight.) In Ktima Paphos, bask in the courtyard of **Trianon,** a restaurant on Archbishop Makarios III Ave. (Stuffed vine leaves £2.50). Or try **Feta's Corner,** (tel. 237822) at the beginning of Archbishop Makarios III (lunch from £3). **Peggy's Miranda Café** in Kennedy Sq. serves continental breakfast (£2). You can swap books here. (Open Mon.-Tues. and Thurs.-Fri. 7am-6:30pm, Wed. morning and all day Sun.) Sugar-starved travelers may enjoy the **Athens** sweet shop, 47 Evagora Pallekaride (tel. 232613).

The two most popular **beaches** stretch along **Yeroskipou** and **Coral Bay.** Yeroskipou is a tourist beach with showers and snack bars, while Coral Bay is sandier, a bit less crowded, and frequented mostly by locals. To Yeroskipou, take bus #11 from Ktima Paphos (every 20-25min., 40¢); to Coral Bay, bus #15 from Yeroskipou (every 20min., 35¢). Nightlife in Coral Bay is the most energetic in Western Cyprus.

SIGHTS

Paphos has more interesting sights per square inch than any other city in Cyprus. (We measured and counted.) Like the rest of Cyprus, it lacks student discounts.

Kato Paphos

The mosaic floors of the **House of Dionysus,** the **House of Theseus,** and the **House of Aion** are the city's most dazzling ancient spots. Discovered accidentally in 1962 by a farmer plowing his fields, and subsequently excavated by a Polish expedition, the largely intact mosaics covered 14 rooms of the House of Dionysus, an expansive Roman villa. The floors depict scenes from mythology and daily life with vibrance, sensitivity, and subtle use of color and shading. The colors are the stones' natural hues. The villa's pervasive wine theme led some archaeologists to conclude that it belonged to a vineyard owner or wine merchant (or a drunkard). Even the abstract designs contain images of cups. Inscriptions here and there exhort "In Vino Veritas." To get there, take Sophias Vembo St., off A. Pavlou Ave. (Open daily 7:30am-7:30pm; reduced hours during off-season; admission to all three houses £1.)

Farther towards the water rests the **House of Theseus,** dating from the 2nd to the 6th century AD. The ruins reveal a luxurious building complete with marble statues, a vast courtyard with marble columns, mosaic floors, and a bath complex. The two mosaics of Theseus and Achilles are accessible by walkways. To the north of the mosaics, you'll find the remnants of an *agora* beside the remains of a limestone Roman **odeon**—a small, roofed semi-circular theater. Constructed in the 2nd century AD, the odeon accommodates 3000 spectators and is periodically used for performances. (Open 7:30am-6:30pm; winter 7:30am-5pm; free; contact the tourist office for performance information.)

The musty **Catacombs of Agia Solomoni,** along the road between Ktima and Kato Paphos (to your left as you go from Ktima to Kato Paphos, opposite Apollo Hotel), include a chapel with deteriorating Byzantine frescoes. Dedicated to St. Solomoni (Hannah), mother of seven children who were tortured to death for their faith during the persecution of Jews in Palestine (168 BC), the chapel sits on the site of the old synagogue of Paphos. Part of the deepest chamber is filled with lucent water, which you may not notice until you're drenched in it. A tree with handkerchiefs draped from its branches marks the entrance to the catacombs on A. Pavlos Ave.; the tree is said to cure the illnesses of those who tie a cloth to it. (24 hr.; free.) At **St. Paul's Pillar,** near Chryssopolitissa Church, St. Paul was allegedly whipped for preaching Christianity. Built in the late 7th century on a hill overlooking the harbor, the **Byzantine Castle** (*Saranda Kolones* or 40 Columns) was intended to protect inhabitants from Arab pirates. To get there take Sophia Vembo St., off A. Pavlou Ave.

When an earthquake destroyed it in 1222, the Lusignans built the **Paphos Fort** at the end of the pier. The fort was used and rebuilt by Venetians and later by Turks. (Open Mon.-Fri. 7:30am-2:30pm, Thurs. 3-6pm, Sat.-Sun. 9am-5pm; admission 50¢.)

Ktima Paphos

The **Archaeological Museum** on Grivas Digenes Ave. (tel. 240215) houses a fine array of Bronze Age pottery, tools, classical sculpture, statues, and artifacts from the House of Dionysus and the House of Theseus. (Open Mon.-Fri. 7:30am-2:30pm and 3-5pm, Thurs. 7:30am-2:30pm and 3-6pm., Sat-Sun. 10am-1pm; admission 50¢.)

Don't miss the worthwhile **Ethnographic Museum,** 1 Exo Vrysi St. (tel. 232010), south of the town center in the 100-year old Eliades residence. Admission (£1) includes a guided tour in English conducted by Mrs. Eliades. The garden vaunts a 3rd-century BC Hellenistic tomb, Christian catacombs, and *kleftiko* ovens. (Open Mon.-Fri. 9am-1pm and 2-5pm, Sat. 9am-1pm, Sun. 10am-1pm; admission 50¢.)

The **Byzantine Museum,** #26 25th Martiou St. (tel. 232092), has icons and religious relics from local monasteries and churches. (Open Mon.-Fri. 9am-12:30pm and 2-5pm, Sat. 9am-12:30pm; reduced hours in winter; admission 50¢.)

West of Ktima Paphos, a signposted road runs 1km to the Paleokastra, or **Tombs of the Kings**—a misnomer, since those interred in these stone tombs were not royalty but upwardly mobile local aristocracy. The larger tombs consist of an open court encircled by burial chambers, with Doric columns carved out of the underground rock and stairways leading down to the interiors. The tombs, dating from the Hellenistic and Roman periods, were also used as hideouts by early Christians fleeing persecution. To the north of the tombs within the circular asphalt road lies **Paleoeklisia** (literally "old church") with fragments of Byzantine frescoes. (Tombs and church open daily 7:30am-5:00pm; close at sunset Oct.-May; admission 50 ¢.)

■ NEAR PAPHOS

The area around Paphos conceals some of Cyprus's greatest treasures. Seventeen kilometers southeast of Paphos, adjacent to the modern village of **Kouklia,** lie the ruins of the great **Temple of Aphrodite** and **Paleopaphos** (Old Paphos), once the capital of a kingdom encompassing nearly half of Cyprus. The temple itself was the religious center of the island and a destination for pilgrimages from all parts of the Roman world. Constructed in the 12th century BC, it thrived until the 4th century AD, when the anti-pagan edicts of Emperor Theodosius and a series of earthquakes reduced it to inconspicuous rubble. The scant remains—merely piles of rocks—make little sense without a guide. Buy *A Brief History and Description of Old Paphos,* published by the Cyprus Department of Antiquities and available at most museums (45¢). The **Archaeological Museum** at the site houses an unpretentious collection of pottery and inscriptions. The **Epigraphic Museum** next door has a variety of carved stones which represent aspects of life in the once-grand capital. The sites are most easily seen with the excursion buses (see Practical Information, p. 388). Another way to get to Kouklia is to take a shared taxi for Limassol and ask the driver to drop you off. Renting a moped is not advisable, as there is heavy traffic on the road leading there. (Museums and temple open Mon.-Fri. 7:30am-5pm; Sat.-Sun. 9am-4pm; admission to ruins, city and museums 50¢.)

The **Monastery of Agios Neophytos,** with painted caves and buildings, lies 9km north of Paphos, near Coral Bay Beach. The monastery houses icons and Byzantine frescoes, and affords exquisite sea vistas. Roughly 100m from the monastery complex is a ravine with a winter stream and three contiguous rock caves carved out by Neophytos and covered with beautiful 12th-century frescoes. You can get here by taking the bus to Tala (Mon.-Fri. 6 per day, Sat.-Sun. 4 per day; admission 25¢; inquire at the CTO for further information) and then walk to the monastery. Bring a flashlight. (Open 7:30am-noon; 3pm-dusk.)

Archbishop Makarios III was born in the mountain village of **Pano Panayia,** 38km northeast of Paphos, where he stayed until entering the Kykko Monastery. A monument to Cyprus's most revered figure stands in the town square, and the small house where Makarios was born has been converted into a museum. (Open daily 9am-noon and 1-5pm; free.) One kilometer southeast from Pano Panayia and 40km from Paphos is **Chryssorogiatissa Monastery,** the most picturesquely situated monastery in Cyprus. According to legend, Ignatius found one of three icons of the Virgin Mary painted by St. Luke on the beach at Paphos. The Virgin told him to build a monastery in her honor, and he did, though the current structure dates from 1770. A fire destroyed much of the monastery in 1967, but its collection of 18th-century icons and frescoes is still intact. Four buses per day (last at 4pm) run to Panayia from Pervola station, returning to Paphos the next morning at 6am and 7:15am (40¢).

■■■ POLIS ΠΟΛΙΣ

Polis' minimalist name simply means "town," though Polis is far from pedestrian. Aphrodite, who came to Polis to bathe, was one of this coastal resort's first visitors. The goddess of beauty no longer bathes alone. Tourism has gained a foothold in Polis, which is smaller, cheaper, and more relaxed than Paphos, 37km to the south. Accessible by minibus and taxi, Polis is a popular Cypriot base for budget travel.

Orientation and Practical Information Polis boasts some stellar examples of traditional Cypriot mountain architecture—large rounded wooden doors and stone masonry. At the end of the convoluted main street is the *platia,* or square, where several **travel agencies** offer information. The **police** (tel. 321451) roost one block from the square in the direction of the beach. Around the *platia* you'll find three **banks** (open Mon.-Fri. 8:30am-noon; reduced hours in off-season; the **Popular Bank** in the *platia* is the only one with Mon. afternoon service). The **post office** (tel. 321539; open Mon.-Fri. 7:30am-noon, Mon.-Wed. and Fri. 1-2pm, Thurs. 3-5pm) and **Kyriakos Taxi** (tel. 321101) are also on the *platia*. **Pegasus Video** (tel. 321374) rents mopeds for £4 a day, for a minimum of 2 days. Two **pharmacies** (tel. 321253) and (tel. 321167) are down the street from the post office. The well-staffed **hospital** (tel. 321431) is on the way to the campsite. The **telephone code** for the area is 06. The **postal code** is 8905.

Accommodations Freelance campers pitch tents on bluffs above the shore to the west, and along the road to the Baths of Aphrodite. No one seems to care as long as the sites are kept clean. Several restaurants along this stretch provide free or almost-free camping and the use of facilities to customers. Carrying on the Polis tradition of simple names, **Campground** (tel. 321526) lies 1km from the town center, in a fragrant eucalyptus grove by the sea. (£1.50 per tent pitch, £1 per person. Open March-Oct.) The **Akamas Hotel** (tel. 321330), down the curvy main street, has clean, breezy rooms and a quiet courtyard. (Singles £8, doubles £10.) Also with a courtyard, the **Lemon Garden** (tel. 321443), past the *platia* to the right, provides tasty meals (£4-6), and doubles with kitchen facilities for £14. They also rent **mountain bicycles** (£1.50-4) and sells **fishing/diving equipment.** Look for inexpensive private rooms down the hill from the Bank of Cyprus, or inquire at a café. You should be able to get a room for £5 per person. Rooms-to-let also line the road to the beach. On the right before the turn-off for the Vomos Taverna, **Mrs. Evlalia** (tel. 321580) rents six bright, clean rooms, with access to a kitchen (£5 per bed).

Food and Entertainment **Vomos Taverna** serves snacks by the beach. In town, **Arsinoe** (tel. 321590), across from the church, is run by a fisherman's family and serves their daily catch. (Open 8am-1pm and 7pm-1am. Swordfish £3.50, fish *meze* £4.50.) Nearby, the informal **Kebap House** sells scrumptious *souvlaki* for £1.20. There's a beachside disco, but a more appealing option is to wander over to **Brunnen,** which is located a little before the Akamas Hotel and down some steps. Marios, a Famagustan refugee, has turned this dilapidated Turkish house into a colorful, sprawling **garden bar.** (Large beer 80¢, wine 60¢; breakfast served; open 9:30am-2pm and 5pm-2am.)

Sights 10km west of Polis are the **Baths of Aphrodite,** a shady pool carved out of limestone by natural springs, so named because Aphrodite came here to cleanse herself after her nocturnal exploits. According to legend, whoever bathes in the pool stays forever young. Some mortals splash away heedlessly, but bathing is prohibited. The pool of **Fontana Amorosa,** 8km away to the northwest, can be reached by foot or a sturdy off-road vehicle, through a picturesque but narrow trail overlooking the sea. The amorous pool is reportedly where Aphrodite married Akamas, the son of Theseus.

■■■ AROUND POLIS REGION

The road from Polis to the Baths of Aphrodite leads past pristine **beaches** and some cheap lodgings. One kilometer out of Polis, the friendly **Tamamouna** family (tel. 321269) offers excellence all around. (Singles £5, doubles £10.) Where the road turns to gravel, **CO-MA-NE** (tel. 321042, -310; fax 322171) rents doubles for £15 in Lachi and apartments for 2-3 people in Polis for £24. Inquire at their office in Polis' *platia.* The port of **Lachi,** 2km west of Polis, has a decent selection of coastline, hotels, and fish. Below the **Baths of Aphrodite tourist pavilion,** 1km west, is a long sand beach. Beyond it is **Ttakkas Bay,** a cove many Cypriots consider the best beach on this part of the coast. **Ttakkas Bay Restaurant,** above the beach, has fresh fish and a terrace with a view. (Fish *meze* £4; open 9am-midnight.) The turn-off for the beach is marked "Ttakkas Bay Restaurant Aphrodite Area Refugee."

The coastline and **beaches** east of Polis are just as lovely as those to the west. Between Polis and Kato Pirgos, roughly 65km to the east, there are no rooms to let, no seaside *tavernas,* and no freelance camping—only placid farming villages and deserted stretches of sand. Touring the area is difficult without wheels. **Minibuses** from Paphos pass through Polis (Mon.-Fri. 10 per day 6:30am-7pm, Sat. 5 per day 9am-4pm; £1). Two **buses** from Kato Pirgos also stop here. Some minibuses from Paphos continue on to Pomos. Passing cars are rare, but those that come by usually stop. The second half of the journey is treacherous for mopeds; rent a car.

The coastline east of Polis is visible from the slender band of asphalt optimistically dubbed the "main road;" just find a beach that suits your tastes. Some of the beaches close to Polis are littered with garbage, so head 5-10km out of town before breaking out the cocoa butter. The road runs west along the coast, through banana plantations and tobacco fields, to **Pomos,** a quiet village with a few tavernas and a pebble beach. A few miles beyond Pomos is the village of **Pahiammos** (Thick Sand). Between Pahiammos and Kato Pirgos, roughly 10km west, lies the village of **Kokkina** (Red), a small enclave occupied by the Turks. To prevent an entrance into Turkish territory, the road to Kato Pirgos veers off into the parched mountains for a circuitous 25km detour (45min. by car). In **Kato Pirgos,** there are several places to stay. Inquire in the coffee shop about renting rooms. There are also a few hotels.

■■■ NICOSIA (LEFKOSIA) ΛΕΥΚΩΣΙΑ

Landlocked Nicosia, the capital of the Republic of Cyprus, sits astride the "Green Line," the border that separates the Republic of Cyprus from the area in the north occupied by Turkey. The presence of Greek Cypriot and Turkish border patrols, as well as a significant number of United Nations troops, serves as a reminder that bitterness lies below the serene, peaceful surface. Many tourists bypass Nicosia for the sun and sand in other regions of Cyprus, but a visit to this city is essential for anyone interested in Cyprus' political situation or in ethnic strife in general. Greek Cypriots call their city Lefkosia, but the use of Nicosia is common and inoffensive.

The city has taken measures to restore the old *Laiki Yitonia,* the pedestrian shopping district, where the cobblestone streets are crammed full of shops and restaurants, making a pleasant refuge from the hot, traffic-choked streets. The recent proliferation of museums and monuments reflects the town's eagerness to maintain its spirit and cultural heritage. Nicosia seems geared more towards bureaucrats than backpackers; Larnaka may be a better base from which to explore the East coast.

Built on the site of ancient Ledra during the Roman occupation, Nicosia prospered under the Lusignan dynasty. When Lusignan power waned, Venetians took over (1489), and, in 1567, built huge walls to ward off Turkish cannons. Monomaniacal, they razed all buildings outside the walls that were in their line of fire, including the Lusignan abbey of St. Domenico. The fortifications were effective for a time, but three years later Turks concentrated their effort, gained victory in seven weeks, and presided over the city for several hundred years, until the British took over in 1878. When Cyprus gained independence in 1960, Nicosia became its capital.

ORIENTATION AND PRACTICAL INFORMATION

The easiest way to orient yourself in Nicosia is to refer to the ominous Green Line running east-west at the north end of the city. The line halves the **Old City** within its circular Venetian walls. When you walk down the streets slashed in half by the border, you are confronted by sheet metal barriers or white and blue dividers. At several points on the Green Line, and at points throughout the city, signs forbid the taking of photos; they mean it. The southern (lower) part of Nicosia within the Walls (as the Old City is officially known) contains most budget accommodations, museums, and sights. From **Eleftherias Square,** Evagoras St. heads southwest into the **New City.** Intersecting Evagoras are Archbishop Makarios III Ave., Diagoras St., and Th. Dervis St. (which leads away from the city to the youth hostel), where the banks, embassies, and travel agencies are located. The New City is much busier than the old, and is the center of Nicosia's nightlife. Be sure to obtain one of the superb **maps** (free) from the tourist office.

Tourist Office: 35 Aristokypros St. (tel. 444264), in the *Laiki Yitonia,* within the city walls. Entering Eleftherias Sq., turn right and follow signs from the post office. Route maps, a complete list of village buses, and free copies of *Nicosia: This Month.* A 2-hr. combination bus and walking tour of Nicosia leaves here Mon. and Thurs. at 10am. A tour through the old suburb of Kaimakli leaves Mon. at 10am. Sponsored by the Municipality of Nicosia, the tours are conducted in English free of charge. Open Mon.-Fri. 8:30am-4pm, Sat. 8:30am-2pm.

Police: (tel. 302090). At Paphos Gate, near the British Council. **Police Emergency:** Dial 199.

Post Office: Main Office (tel. 303231), Constantinos Paleologos Ave. just east of Eleftherias Sq. within the walls. Open Mon.-Tues. and Thurs.-Fri. 7:30am-1:30pm and 3-6pm, Sat. 9-11am; reduced hours in winter. Smaller offices on Dhigenis St., Palace St., and Loukis Akitas Ave. (tel. 302076). Open Mon.-Fri. 7:30am-1:30pm, Wed. also 3-6pm. **Postal Code:** 1900.

CYTA: Egypt Ave. (tel. 470261). Open 7am-7:15pm. Dial 196 for telegrams. Telecards sold. Telecard machines in office. **Telephone Code:** 02.

Banks: Bank of Cyprus, 86-88-90 Phaneromeni St. (tel. 477774). Offers **currency exchange.** Open Mon.-Fri. 8:30am-12:30pm, Tues.-Fri. also 4-7pm (3-6pm in winter). Another branch in *Laiki Yitonia* (tel. 461082) on Drakos St.

Embassies: Australian High Commission, 4 Annis Comninis St. (tel. 473001), corner of Stassinou Ave. Open in summer Mon.-Fri. 8am-3pm. **Egypt,** 3 Leoforos Aigyptou (tel. 465144, -5; fax 462287). Open Mon.-Fri. 8am-2pm. **Greece,** 8 Lordou Vyronos (tel. 442880; fax 473990). Open Mon.-Fri. 9am-noon. **Israel,** 4 I. Grypari St. (tel. 445195, -6). Open Mon.-Fri. 8am-4pm. **Lebanon,** 1 Vas. Olgas (tel. 442216; fax 467662). Open Mon.-Sat. 8:30am-1:30pm. **Syria,** at Androkleous and Thoukydidou St. (tel. 474481, -2; fax 446963). Visas in 24 hr. or less; bring 2 photos. Open Mon.-Fri. 8am-2pm, Sat. 8am-1pm. **U.K. High Commission,** Alexanderou Palli St. (tel. 473131; fax 367198), west of the old city. Open Mon. and Thurs.-Fri. 7:30am-2pm, Tues. 7:30am-1pm and 2-5:30pm. **U.N. Headquarters**

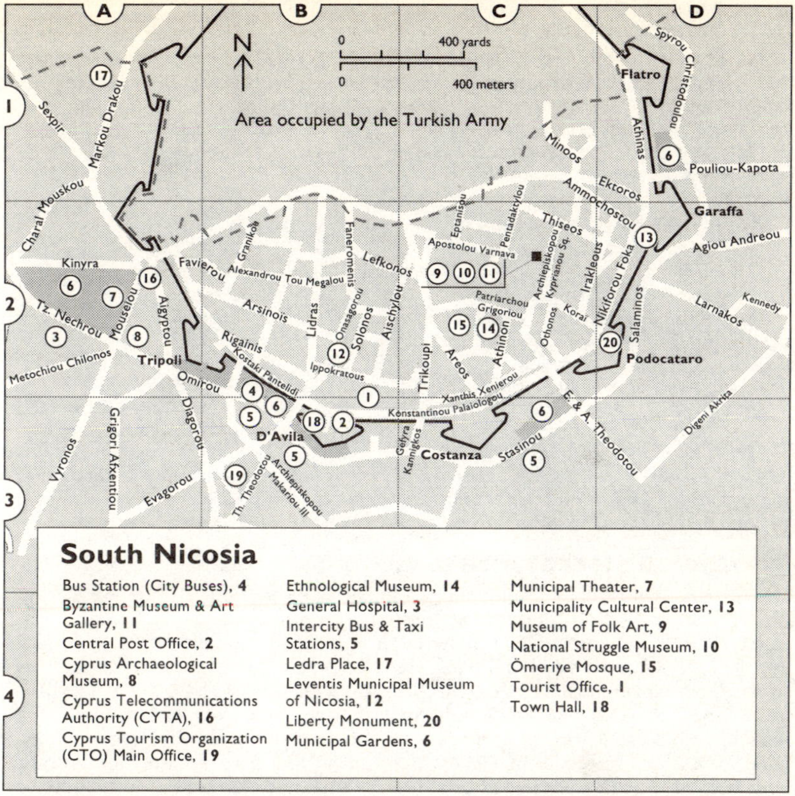

(tel. 359000), on the road to the Nicosia Airport. **U.S.,** Metochiou and Ploutarchou (tel. 476100; fax 465944). Open Mon.-Fri. 8am-2:30pm.

American Express: 35-37 Evagoras Ave. (tel. 443777), in the offices of **A.L. Mantovani and Sons.** 1-2% commission for cashing personal checks. No checks cashed on Sat. Open Mon.-Fri. 8am-12:45pm and 3:15-6:30pm, Sat. 9am-noon.

Buses: KEMEK and **Kallenos Station,** 34 Leonides St. (tel. 463989). To Limassol (3-4 per day, £1.25), Larnaka (4-7 per day, £1.10), and Platres (5 per week, £1.50). **EMAN** bus stop, 50m east of the post office. **City buses** (tel. 473414) leave from Solomos Sq., the first square to the west of Eleftherias for city and suburban areas 5:30am-7pm. The tourist office has a list of routes.

Service Taxis: Makris (tel. 466201); **Akropolis** (tel. 472525); **Kypros** (tel. 464811); and **Kyriakos** (tel. 444114). All are on Stassinos Ave., which runs east along the city walls from Eleftherias Sq. **Karydas,** 8 Homer Ave. (tel. 462269), is nearby. All run to Limassol (£2.15) and continue on to Paphos (additional £2); Makris, Akropolis, and Kyriakos lines also travel to Larnaka (£2).

International Bookstores: Philippides & Son, 10 Paleologos Ave. (tel. 462984.) Huge stock of English books upstairs. **The United States Information Service,** 33B Homer Ave. (tel. 473143), is around the corner from the museum, next to the Dept. of Antiquities. Current issues of the *New York Times* and other periodicals.

British Council: 3 Museum Ave. (tel. 442152), 2 doors down from the museum. Library with books, records, and tapes. Lectures, movies, and cultural events. Open Mon.-Tues. and Fri. 7:30am-1:30pm, Wed. 7:30am-2pm, Thurs. 3-5:30pm, Sat. 9am-noon; off-season afternoon hours, 3:30-5:30pm.

Hospital: (tel. 451111). Between Hilon and Homer St., near municipal gardens.

ACCOMMODATIONS

Unfortunately, flats are not a sensible option in Nicosia. They are more expensive here than in Larnaka and only offered by real estate agents to visitors who are planning a stay of at least a few weeks. Most of Nicosia's budget accommodations are within the city walls and are at least tolerably clean. If you don't like the room you're shown, ask to see another one—the degree of cleanliness and comfort tends to vary widely at most places.

Youth Hostel (HI), 1 Hadjidaki St. (tel. 444808 or 442027), 700m from Eleftherias Sq. Clean with a communal kitchen and friendly atmosphere. Very popular with young folk from the Middle East. American manager loves to speak Americanese. Hot water all day. £4 per person, showers included. Sheets £1.

Tony's Furnished Flats, 13 Solon St. (tel. 466752), at *Laiki Yitonia*. Look for a sign on the 2nd floor. In the heart of the neighborhood near the tourist office. Tidy rooms with fan, radio, and telephone; some with fridge and TV. Singles £10, doubles w/shower £17, triples £24, quads £28; breakfast included.

Sans Rival, 7C Solon St. (tel. 474383), a few doors down from Tony's. Characterless (avec rival). All rooms with sink and fan, wooden floors, and a balcony. Singles £8, doubles £13; breakfast £2.

Royal Hotel, 17 Euripides St. (tel. 463245), on a sidestreet off Ledra, at the corner of Euripides and Aeschylus. Clean; some rooms with private showers (a shower and drain in corner). All rooms w/fan and breakfast. Singles £8.50, doubles £14.

FOOD AND ENTERTAINMENT

There's an abundance of dining choices in Nicosia, but the best ones are hard to find. The touristy restaurants around *Laiki Yitonia,* while not among the select few, serve Cypriot and continental cuisine in clean, cool surroundings with traditional music. The **Byzantine** (tel. 477085), just one block from the tourist office, has wood-beamed ceilings, Byzantine arches, and a shaded courtyard. Try a Cyprus salad for £2.25. (Open for lunch until 5pm.) For authentically delicious food, try a light dinner at **Estiatorio,** 40 Arsinoes St., in the heart of the old city near the Green Line. (*Stifado* £2, meatballs £1.75.) **Matheos** (tel. 475846), a small, traditional restaurant behind the Phaneromeni church (near a small mosque) offers good food for low prices. Try stuffed vine leaves *(koupepia) for* £2.25 or *pilaf* for £1.50. Otherwise, buy your own provisions at the **municipal market** at Dhigenis Akritas and Kalipolis St. Every Wed., a colorful streetside **produce market** sets up shop along Constantinos Paleologos Ave., east of Eleftherias Sq. (Open 7am-1pm and 4-6pm.) The area east of the complex of museums within the old city has a number of restaurants where you can buy tasty, inexpensive Cypriot food for roughly £2. The chickpea dishes are delectable. Vegetarians can find solace at **Fytro Health Foods,** 11 Chytri St. (tel. 461466). For true Nicosian ambience, try **Berlin II Café** (also known as Check Point Charlie), on the corner of Lefkon St. Savor your *kebap* with salad and pita (£2.25) in the shade of the blue and white Green Line.

SIGHTS

Sadly, many find the Green Line to be Nicosia's main attraction. The only spot on the border where photography is permitted is on Ledra St., where the military has erected a makeshift shrine to the north. Remember that this is a military zone and that taking pictures is a serious offence. Visit the **Cyprus Museum** (tel. 302189) and its collection of life-size terra-cotta models of ancient Cypriots, complete with piles of bones, exquisite pottery, and thought-provoking paraphernalia. (Open Mon.-Sat. 9am-5pm, Sun. 10am-1pm; admission £1.) In the same courtyard is the **Folk Art Museum** (tel. 463205), in the old Archbishopric, a former 15th-century Gothic monastery. (Open Mon.-Fri. 8:30am-1pm, 2-4pm; Sat. 8:30am-1pm; admission 50¢.) For more morbid fun, visit the neighboring **National Struggle Museum** (tel. 302465). Founded in 1961 by the Greek Communal Chamber of Cyprus, the museum contains photographs, documents, and other relics from the struggle for *enosis* (union of Cyprus with Greece). (Open Mon.-Fri. 7:30am-2:30pm and 3-5:30pm, Sat. 7:30am-1:30pm; admission 25¢.) For a vivid interpretation of Cypriot culture, don't miss Nicosia's newest attraction, the **Leventis Municipal Museum** (tel. 451475), located on Hippocratis St. in the *Laiki Yitonia*. The exhibit chronicles the history of Nicosia, beginning with the modern city, and takes you back through time to 3000 BC. (Open Tues.-Sun. 10am-4:30pm; free.)

Down Korais St. from the Archbishopric stands another reminder of the Cypriot struggle for freedom, a marble monument depicting 14 Cypriots—each representing a period of the island's history—being released from jail by soldiers and overseen by a religious figure. Nearby, along the Venetian Walls at the end of Theseus St., is the recently restored **Famagusta Gate,** which served as the main entrance to the medieval city. Built in 1567, it now hosts plays, concerts, and lectures. (Open Mon.-Fri. 8am-1pm and 4-6pm; admission free.) Get a free copy of *Nicosia: This Month* at the tourist office for a schedule of events.

The House of Hadjigeorgiakis Kornesios, known as **Konak Mansion** for short, at 18 Patriarch Gregory St., stands around the corner from the Archbishopric complex. A famous dragoman (an interpreter for Ottoman Turks and Greeks) lived in this luxurious, 18th-century structure (tel. 302447; open Mon.-Fri. 8am-2pm, Sat. 9am-1pm; admission 50¢). One of the only Turkish baths outside of Turkey, the historic **Omerye** (properly Ömeriye) **Hamam** is just in from the Podocataro Bastion; look for the nearby minaret. (Women on Wed. and Fri. only; open 10am-12:30pm and 1:30-3:30pm; admission £2.) The colorful **botanical garden** is next to the archaeological museum and behind the Garden Café (open daily 8am-10pm). Its aviaries showcase most of the island's indigenous species (free). The **Cyprus Jewellers Museum,** 7-9 Odos Praxipou, is across the street from the tourist office. It is miniscule, but merits a look. Its 18th to 20th-century collection includes gold and silver plates, spoons, and jewelry hand crafted in the filigree and skaleta techniques. Note the traditional forks and spoons, made according to village customs and used for devouring sweetened fruits drowned in syrup. (Open daily 10am-4:30pm; free.)

EASTERN CYPRUS

■■■ LARNAKA ΛΑΡΝΑΚΑ

The modern city of Larnaka (pop. 60,000) was built over the ruins of ancient Kition, making it one of the oldest continually inhabited cities in the world. In the north of town a segment of the ancient city walls and some Bronze Age temples remain, but the city is curiously indifferent to its history. Instead, Larnaka has become a tourist center that offers visitors a long beach bordered by numerous cafés and restaurants. Quieter and cleaner than Limassol, sunny Larnaka charms visitors with its subtle beauty and friendly demeanor. Larnaka is a bit less expensive than neighboring Agia Napa, but accommodations are just as scarce in summer.

ORIENTATION AND PRACTICAL INFORMATION

Athinon Avenue, also known as the "Palm Tree Promenade," runs along the waterfront and is Larnaka's most noticeable attraction. In the summer, hordes of barefoot young Cypriots and sandal-clad foreigners from every corner of the globe fill its outdoor cafés, restaurants, pubs, and beach. Major renovations on the street are nearing completion. The Promenade, however, already bursts with charm, adorned with tall, French-style lamp posts. **Plateia Vasileos Pavlou** is located one block west of the north end of Athinon Avenue and holds most facilities.

Cyprus Tourism Organization Office: (tel. 654322). Helpful staff will tell you everything you wanted to know about Cyprus but were afraid to ask. Open Mon.-

Sat. 8:15am-2:30pm, also Mon. and Thurs. (or Tues. and Fri.) 4-6:30pm. Call before you go as hours may vary. **Airport branch** (tel. 643000) open 24 hr.

Police: (tel. 630200). On Archbishop Makarios III Ave., just one block north of the tourist office. Open 24 hr.

Post Office: (tel. 630181). Pl. Vasileos Pavlou. Open Mon.-Fri. 7:30am-1:30pm and 3-6pm (4-7pm in July and Aug.), Sat. 9-11am. Reduced hours in off-season. **Postal code:** 6900. A small post office in **St. Lazarus Sq.** (tel. 630182) is open Mon.-Fri. 8am-1:30pm, Thurs. 3-6pm. In July and Aug., open Mon. and Fri. only 7:30am-1:30pm. **Postal code:** 6902.

CYTA: 7-9 Z Pierides (tel. 640257). Follow Lordou Vyronos toward the seafront. Office is on the right, before you reach Zinonos Kitieos. **Telegram service** available. **Phone cards** for local and international calls available in £3, 5, or 10 amounts. Telecard phones located around the corner and throughout the city. Phone cards can also be purchased at *peripteros* (kiosks) or most hotel lobbies. Open Mon.-Fri. 7:30am-7pm, Sat. 7:30am-1pm (closed Sun.). To make an overseas collect call to countries other than the U.S., use the **telephones** on Armenikis Ekklesias St. near the Armenian church. **Telephone code:** 04.

American Express (tel. 652024), Stassinou St., in the office of **A.L. Mantovani and Sons,** across the street from the C.T.O. Open Mon.-Fri. 8am-1pm and 3:30-7pm, Sat. 9am-noon; reduced hours in off-season.

Airport: All flights into Cyprus land at the Larnaka airport. Upon arrival, the #19 city bus runs into town (14 per day, 6:20am-7pm, until 5:45pm in winter; 40¢). Otherwise, grab a taxi, which should cost roughly £2.

Buses: Leave from Athinon Ave., by the marina on the seafront. Look for a sandwich board on the sidewalk listing the schedule. Stop by the C.T.O. for your very own copy of up-to-date bus schedules. **Kallenos Buses** (tel. 654890, -50) venture to Nicosia (Mon.-Fri. 7 per day, 6:30am-4pm, Sat. 4 per day until 1pm; £1.10) and Limassol (Mon.-Fri. 4 per day until 4pm, Sat. 3 per day until 1pm; £1.20). No Kallenos buses on Sun. **EMAN** buses to Agia Napa leave from the same spot (Mon.-Sat. 8:30am-5:30pm, Sun. 4 per day 8:30am-4:30pm; £1). **P.E.A.L.** (tel. 650477; fax 654977) buses leave from St. Lazarus Sq. and stop at St. Helenis, Artemidos Ave., Meneou, Kiti, and Tersefanou (13-14 per day 6:20am-5:45pm; in the summer, one 7pm bus available; 40¢).

Taxis: Makris (tel. 652929), King Paul St., across from the Sun Hall Hotel; **Akropolis** (tel. 655555), at the corner of Archbishop Markarios III Ave., opposite the police station; and **Kyriakos,** 2C Hermes (Ermou) St. (tel. 655100). All run service taxis to Limassol (Mon.-Fri. 6am-4:45pm although sometimes as late as 6pm, roughly every ½hr., £2), and to Nicosia (£1.70). **Service taxis** also run from Nicosia to Limassol (£2.10). Service taxis will pick up and drop off anywhere in the city. Just call ahead (anywhere from a day to the nearest ½hr.). Private taxis between cities are outrageously expensive; stick to service. On Sun., the companies alternate, running until early afternoon. Prices might be slightly higher on Sun. (by roughly 50¢). Alternatively, rent a moped or car from the many companies on Leoforos Archbishop Markarios III, otherwise known as Makarios Ave.

Car Rental: Thaco Rent-A-Car, 1 Gladstonos St. (tel. 626871 or 632386 after hours; fax 657473). Rent a wide range of compact cars and sedans. Prices start at £14 per day with unlimited mileage. Minimum age is 25.

ACCOMMODATIONS

The town's hotels and pensions tend to fall into three distinct categories—luxury hotels full of British package tours, flats, and dives (with the exception of the friendly Youth Hostel). Cleaner, cooler, and more aesthetically pleasing than the dives, flats are hip alternatives to regular hotels in Larnaka. Prices tend to be £5-7 less in the off-season.

Youth Hostel (HI) (tel. 621188), Nikolaou Rossou St. in St. Lazarus Sq. Occupies a converted Turkish mosque and has cleanish rooms. Communal kitchen. £3.

Petrou Bros. Holiday Apartments, 1 Armenikis Ekklisias St. (tel 650600, -1; fax 655122), head south from the C.T.O. and make a right at the Armenian Church. Call ahead. Front lobby moonlights as a bar and TV room. Hospitable staff speaks fluent English. Laundry service (£1.25 per kilo) and video rentals (£1 per video) available. Elevator. Breakfast £1. 1-, 2-, and 3-bedroom suites for 2, 4, and 6 people respectively. Double £15, quad £25, 6 person 30£; extra bed (cot) £2.

Harry's Hotel, 2 Thermopylon St. (tel. 654453), near Marina Pier, the second left inland from the tourist office. Common room upstairs with rag-tag couches of yesteryear, TV, fridge, and common bath/shower. Bar and arrangement of plants and sticks that may be a garden in its next lifetime. Itsy-bitsy, almost clean singles (£8, £9 w/breakfast) and equally tiny doubles (£13, £15 w/breakfast).

Pavion Hotel, 11 Faneromeni St., St. Lazarus Sq. (tel. 656688), offers clean but musty singles for £11, doubles for £16. Breakfast is included.

FOOD AND ENTERTAINMENT

Most of Larnaka's restaurants and bars are on the waterfront. Larnaka also offers an array of international cuisines: Chinese, Lebanese, Italian, French, and Indian. Many restaurants are spread throughout the city. Contact the C.T.O. for more information.

Mauri Helona (The Black Turtle) is one of the town's most interesting *tavernas*. In an old house at the beginning of Yehmet Ali St., at St. Lazarus Sq., it offers *mezedes* and has a cute logo—a turtle schlepping a jug of booze. On Fri. and Sat. nights, a small group of singers and musicians gathers until midnight, singing old Greek songs accompanied by an accordion.

Megalos Pefkos, at the southern end of the harbor by the fortress, has relatively inexpensive fish (swordfish £3.75, Cyprus *meze* £4.50, fish *meze* £5.75).

Midnight Sun, on the south end of Athens Ave., is a popular fast-food café (24 hr.).

The Hobo Pub (tel. 624993), located next to the Pizza Hut, near the north end of Leoforos Athinon, has a pleasant rooftop restaurant and good chicken kebap.

The Gilli Café (tel. 664909), on the corner of Leoforos Grigori Afxentiou and Lordou Vyronos, offers both vegetarian and meat dishes. Mix-your-own cold salads bar (small salad £1, large £2). Pizza, chicken burgers, and desserts served during the day at reasonable prices. Only salads and sandwiches available at night. Sit down or take away.

1900 Art Cafe, 6 Stasinou St. (tel. 653027). Run by a painter and journalist, the café aspires to the exchange of intellectual and artistic ideas over carafes of local wine (£2). Assorted teas, coffees, Greek and Cypriot pastries, and traditional dishes available. Try the *milopita* (apple pie); it's their specialty. Greek book shop on the cozy second floor. Bar, fireplace, and display of local artists' works on the second floor as well. Café open 7am-2pm and 5pm-midnight.

Elitor: The Patisserie, 35 Gr. Afxentiou Ave. (tel. 656929, -7097). Delectable *baklava,* pastries, and *kouriabiedes* (powdery almond cookies). Also sells flowers.

Sweet and Salty, Z. Pierides St. (tel. 620560). Houses small but "sweet" collection of goods from bakeries around Larnaka. Chocolates, *baklava,* Cypriot pastries, cool and hot drinks. Try a sesame-coated, cheese-filled round bread for breakfast (35¢). Ask to have it heated up for a very yummy treat!

SIGHTS

The ancient city of **Kition** is the most historically significant spot, although most of it now lies underneath Larnaka. Settled in the early 13th century BC and abandoned by the end of the century, Kition was rebuilt in 1200 BC by refugees from the Peloponnese, who brought their thriving Mycenaean culture. The city was damaged in wars against the Phoenicians and Egyptians (4th century BC) and leveled by earthquake and fire in 280 BC. The city ruins reveal part of the ancient Cyclopean wall, a large **Temple of Astarte,** goddess of fertility, and four small temples. To get there, follow Kimon St. to the Chryssopolitissa Church, cross in front of the church, and go straight on Sakellariou St. Take the first right to Loizou Filippou St., go left, and take the first right again. (Open Mon.-Wed. and Fri. 7:30am-2:30pm, Thurs. 7:30am-2:30pm and 3-6pm; admission 50¢.)

The **Kition Archaeological Site** lies approximately 500m northeast of the District Archaeological Museum. The small collection includes objects from Neolithic to Roman times. (Open Mon.-Fri. 7:30am-2:30pm, Thurs. 7:30am-2:30pm and 3-6pm.

Admission 50¢.) The newly renovated **Larnaka District Archaeological Museum** (tel. 630169) boasts Neolithic to historic finds from the Larnaka District. (Mon.-Fri. 7:30am-2:30pm, Thurs. 7:30am-2:30pm and 3-6pm; admission 50¢.) The private **Pierides Foundation Museum** (tel. 651345), on Zinonos St. next to Barclay's Bank, is the former home of Demetrios Pierides (1811-1895), a cultured man and collector of Cypriot artifacts. The museum is Larnaka's tiny version of the Parisian Louvre. Prehistoric Cypriot idols are displayed in china chests. Cypro-Geometric pots take the place of end tables, and antique maps of Cyprus hang in lieu of wallpaper. Artifacts abound from 3000 years of Cypriot culture, including Byzantine and traditional folk. (Mon.-Sat. 9am-1pm and 4-7pm; reduced hours in off-season; admission £1.)

At the north end of Athenon Ave. is **Larnaka's Marina,** upon which couples and families warm up for their nightly stroll among the palm trees. A **Museum of Marine Life** will be open as of October 1995. Inquire at the C.T.O. for more information. The **Municipal Museum of Natural History,** where 5000 Cypriot insects are individually labeled and pinned to styrofoam showcases, attracts those with an open mind. Three kinds of extinct snakes have been stuffed, other local animal species are stuffed and arrayed in panoramic displays. Outside there are live versions: turkeys, buzzards, hamsters, canaries, seagulls, and a peacock. A park for all ages and a playground for children less than 10 surrounds this museum.

At the south end of the port, a small **medieval fortress** peers over the water's edge. Constructed by Venetians in the 15th century and rebuilt by Turks in 1625, the fort contains a small collection of finds and photographs from Kition and other excavations in the area. (Open Mon.-Fri. 7:30am-7:30pm; reduced hours in off-season; admission 50¢.) The first left north of the fortress leads to the **Church of St. Lazarus,** built over the saint's tomb. Jesus Christ reportedly resurrected Lazarus, four days dead, in Israel. The resuscitated Lazarus came to Cyprus, became the island's first bishop, and lived in Kition another 30 years before dying again. Lazarus's remains were stolen from Constantinople, but appeared later in Marseilles. The church here was originally built in the 9th century, but it has been burnt and rebuilt several times since then. You can visit the tomb of St. Lazarus by descending a flight of steps near the iconostasis. The church's belfry was constructed in 1857. In the courtyard there's a small museum that houses ecclesiastical art. Modest dress required. (Open daily 8am-12:30pm and 3:30-6:30pm; low season daily 8am-12:30pm and 2:30-5pm; free. Greek Orthodox services Sun. 6, 10, or 11am. Museum open Mon.-Tues. and Thurs.-Fri. 8:30am-1pm and 3-5:30pm, Wed. and Sat. 8:30am-1pm; admission 25¢.)

For a brief encounter with Larnaka's classy, artsy scene, visit the **Art Gallery of Maria Pyrgou,** 5 Stadiou St. (tel. 623993), behind the local market. Once a month (except Aug.), Pyrgou exhibits works of well-known Cypriot, Greek, and European artists in an enchanting 120-year-old traditional Cypriot building. For info on current exhibitions, inquire at the 1900 Art Café (tel. 653027). Gallery open daily 5-8pm.

One of Larnaka's biggest attractions is its **town beach** (a dismal mixture of packed dirt, cigarette butts, and ogling men), which manages to satisfy the vacationers who bake there. The bustling beach also offers **watersports:** canoes (£3 per hr.), pedalboats (£5 per hr.), sailboards (£4 per hr.), waterskis (£5 per ride), water ski lessons (£6), jet skis (£10 per 15 min.), mini boats (£7 per 15 min., £12 per 30min.), or ubiqui-popular banana boats (£3 per person). Beautiful, less crowded beaches are farther northeast on the way to Agia Napa.

■ NEAR LARNAKA

Built at the edge of a salt lake and surrounded by palm trees, the **Hala Sultan Tekke Mosque** is said to be the fourth (or so) holiest Muslim pilgrimage site after Mecca, Medina, and Jerusalem. Also called the Tekke of Umm Haram, the mosque was constructed during the Arab invasion of Cyprus (647 AD) and rebuilt in 1816, over the site where Umm Haram (Mohammed's maternal aunt) fell off a mule and broke her neck. Three gargantuan stones—reputed to have been quarried in Mecca—surround her grave in back of the mosque. The horizontal one supposedly hovered in the air for many centuries, until it lowered itself for fear of injuring the faithful. Bus #6, bound for Kiti, leaves St. Lazarus Sq. (12 per day, 8am-7pm, in winter last bus at 5:45pm, 15min., 30¢), and travels west to the Hala Sultan Tekke Mosque. Ask the driver to stop at the mosque, otherwise you will end up in Kiti. To be dropped at the turnoff, tell the bus driver you're going to "Tekke." From there, walk along the paved road for 1km. (Open daily 7:30am-7:30pm; closes early in winter; free.) The mosque is next to the **Larnaka Salt Lake.** In winter, the lake is covered with pink flamingos, but in the summer, it dries up and the flamingos hop away. Legend claims that the lake was created one day when St. Lazarus turned an old woman's vineyard into a barren salt lake as punishment for her lack of hospitality.

The same bus that goes to the mosque continues on to the village of **Kiti** (25min. from Larnaka), where you can visit the church of **Panayia Angeloktisti** (Built by the Angels). Again, ask the driver to stop there. This church was built in the 11th century, but it contains a section dating from several hundred years earlier. The mosaic in the central apse, representing the Virgin Mary with Christ surrounded by the Archangels Michael and Gabriel, is one of the more important works of art on the island. The narthex of the church was built in the 14th century by the Gibelet family—one of the most prominent Latin noble families of medieval Cyprus. (Open Mon.-Fri. 8am-4pm, Sat. 10am-4pm, Sun. 9am-noon and 2-4pm.)

Forty kilometers from Larnaka and 9km off the main Nicosia-Limassol road is **Stavrovouni Monastery.** According to tradition, the monastery was constructed by order of St. Eleni in 327 BC on a site called Olympus, which a pagan temple had occupied. At the time, Eleni, mother of the Roman Emperor Constantine, was returning from Palestine, where she happened to find the Holy Cross. She presented a fragment to the monastery, which keeps it in the church's iconostasis. Although their founder was female, the monks do not allow women into the monastery. (Open sunrise-noon and 3pm-sunset.) There are no buses to Stavrovouni, but go to the village of Kornos and walk up to the peak. A private taxi costs roughly £25.

Thirty-two kilometers from Larnaka is the Neolithic settlement of **Choirokoitia** (Open Mon.-Fri. 7:30am-5pm, Sat.-Sun. 9am-5pm; admission 50¢.) Forty kilometers from Larnaka is the **Traditional Museum of Embroidery and Silversmithing** (open Mon.-Sat. 10am-4pm; admission 50¢).

■■■ AGIA NAPA ΑΓΙΑ ΝΑΠΑ

Twenty years ago, Agia Napa was a quiet farming and fishing village. Most tourists went to Famagusta, 16km to the north, allowing Agia Napa's ruined monastery and white sandy beaches to lie peacefully vacant. But when Turkey occupied Famagusta in 1974, Agia Napa was gussied up almost overnight into a tourist center replete with marble and brass glitz, all the while absorbing a large refugee community from North Cyprus. Over the years, Agia Napa has developed a raucous nightlife popular among Cypriots and foreigners.

Orientation and Practical Information Agia Napa's center is home to banks, restaurants, and tourist shops. The **post office** is on Dionysiou Solomou St. (Open Mon.-Fri. 7:30am-1:30pm, Sat. 9-11am.) The **C.T.O.** (tel. 721796; open Mon.-Fri. 8:30am-2:30pm, also Mon. and Thurs. 3-6pm; reduced hours in off-season) is now on Leoforos Kryou Nerou. The **bus station, Hellenic Bank** (tel. 721488, fax 722636; open Mon.-Fri. 8:30am-12:30pm, Mon. 3:15-4:45pm, and Tues., Thurs., Fri., 3:30-6:30pm, reduced hours in winter) and a Cyprus Air representative, **AirTour-Cyprus,** 18B Dionysiou Solomou St. (tel. 722133; fax 722134; summer 8am-5pm, Wed. and Sat. until 1:30pm; hours reduced in winter) are on Leoforos Archbishop Markarios III. AirTours also rents bikes—50cc one- or two-seaters £5 per day. **Postal Code:** 5330; **Telephone Code:** 03.

Buses make the 41km trip from Athens Ave. in Larnaka to the **EMAN station,** opposite the Leros Hotel in Agia Napa. (Mon.-Sat. 9 per day, 8:30am-5:30pm; Sun. 4

per day, 8:30am-4:30pm; returning to Larnaka Mon.-Sat. 10 per day, 6:30am-5pm, Sun. 4 per day, 9am-4pm; one-way £1.)

Accommodations Roughly one in every two buildings in town is a luxury hotel full of European box-lunch tours, so inexpensive accommodations are elusive and, in Aug., nearly nonexistent. Call ahead. The **HI Youth Hostel,** 23 Dionysiou Solomou St. (tel. 723433), is converted from old tourist apartments so you and your buddies can have your own pseudo-pad for the night. Communal kitchen and payphone, pool table, and very friendly atmosphere. 6-12 beds and one bathroom per apartment (60-70 beds total); £4-5 per night, sheets included. No curfew. Cheapish rooms cluster at the edge of town. From the bus stop, go up the road to Paralimni until you have to turn. Go left and then right at the Four Seasons Supermarket. Head uphill; at the top you'll find **Xenis Rooms** (tel. 721086), which have fans and fridges. Common kitchen. (Doubles £10.) Three km from town, the **campground** (tel. 721946) is near beautiful but crowded **Nissi Beach** (£2.50 per tent, £1.50 per person). On the Protaras public beach, next to the Flamingo Beach restaurant, is **Costas Camping,** with shady pitches and cold showers. If Costas isn't around, pitch your tent and pay when he returns (£2 per person) or leave your things in Agia Napa, rent a motorbike, and scan the outskirts for a place to stay.

Food and Entertainment **Raven's Rook,** above the Hellenic Bank and near the tourist office, serves meals in a pleasant rooftop garden (tuna salad £2.60, kebap £3.65). **The Square Pub & Café,** next to the monastery in the central square, has inexpensive food (green salad £1.50; *mousaka* with salad £2.40). The cheapest take-away kebap in town can be found at **Cross Road,** 14 G. Pappoulis St. (tel. 721282), near Boyles Irish Bar. A bar which claims to be a Hard Rock Café (tel. 722649; open Mon.-Sat. 11am-2am, Sun. 5pm-2am) is across the street from the monastery. If you really want to economize, however, cruise on over to Kokkinos Supermarket in nearby Paralimni villages, which often sells food at wholesale prices.

Agia Napa boasts the most intense nightlife in Cyprus. Discos like **Pizazz, Babylon,** and **Vip's** have recently become legendary, and attract young people from all over Cyprus. All have young Euro crowds, light shows, and £1.60 cocktails. You can visit some of Agia Napa's immensely popular and crowded pubs, like **Cheers Pub** and **Hot Shot Pub,** which are opposite each other near Babylon Disco. Both have happy hours 7-9pm during which all drinks are 80¢ (as opposed to the usual £1.30).

Sights Deserted beaches wallow between Larnaka and Agia Napa, past the army base. Better yet, and closer to Agia Napa, are beaches north and south of **Protaras** (10km from Agia Napa). Opposite the tourist office is the 16th-century Venetian **Monastery of Agia Napa,** whose main attraction is an octagonal marble fountain covered by a dome. The huge sycamore outside the west entrance is famous in Cyprus. Every summer Sunday at 8pm, locals perform Cypriot **folk dances** in the square near the monastery.

Close to Agia Anargyri and 8km east of Agia Napa is **Cape Greco.** You'll find no tourists here, no half-built concrete hotels, no *tavernas,* and no sand—just rocky coves cascading into the magnificent blue sea. The cape has remained undeveloped because of a military radar installation, giving James Bond aspirants the chance to swim off the rocks beneath two realistic radar dishes. Roughly 2km north of Paralimni, a stone's throw away from the green line, is the small village of **Dherinia;** there's not much here, except **Taylor's** on Sotera Rd., a restaurant that serves delicious, cheap fare. (Open noon-11pm.) Several tourist viewpoints nearby look on to the "ghost" of occupied **Famagusta;** construction cranes stand exactly as they did a quarter of a century ago.

NORTHERN CYPRUS

If you talk to Cypriots living in the southern part of the island, they'll sadly admit that some of the most beautiful parts of their homeland are in the northern 37%, inhabited by the Turks since the summer of 1974. Minefields, barbed wire, and thousands of peacekeeping troops separate the country's two halves.

Tourists (excluding Greeks or those of Greek descent) in the South are allowed to cross the border into Turk-inhabited Nicosia (Lefkoşa), provided that they return on the same day by 6pm. But sometimes political conditions, such as demonstrations, prevent this. To get the latest information on border policy, contact a Cyprus Tourism Organization office, the U.N. Headquarters in Nicosia, or the official checkpoint at the Ledra Palace Hotel (see p. 374).

■■■ GİRNE (KYRENIA)

Girne is Northern Cyprus' most beautiful town and its *de facto* capital. The Kyrenia Range forms the town's backdrop. The town's harbor is lined with fish restaurants and bars and dominated by the vast Kyrenia Castle. Girne's highbrow hotels, supermarkets and restaurants make Girne the center of choice for most visitors to this half of the island. Most of the north's attractions are reachable by daytrips.

Residents may speak Turkish, but Girne is proof that Northern Cyprus is very different from Turkey. More so than any of the surrounding towns, it's easy to tell that Girne was once a British colony. The town is wealthier than much of Turkey and upscale supermarkets carry beer from Germany and chocolates from England.

ORIENTATION AND PRACTICAL INFORMATION

Ferries from Turkey arrive at the **new harbor,** 1km as the crow flies from town—but 2km by road. *Dolmuş* will take you to the main square for 75¢; a taxi to most hotels is $3.50. Arriving by boat at the new harbor, go out the port gates on your right and continue down the road for 500m; take a right at the main intersection. This is **Cumhuriyet Caddesi** (Republic St.); walk for 1½km. Just after the post office you will hit a roundabout; this is the "main square." Beyond the roundabout is a dry, modern-art style fountain; behind it, to the left, runs **Hürriyet Caddesi** (Freedom St.), the main street in town, lined with shops and several cheap hotels. The streets to the right off Hürriyet Cad. lead to the seafront; the nearest ones, to the harbor. Arriving overland, you'll be dropped at the **bus station.** Exit the station, turn right, and walk to the International American University (700m). Go left at this main intersection—the roundabout is 800m down the road. From the ferry terminal, *dolmuş* to the roundabout. When available, they cost 70¢; taxis $3.50 From the bus station, you'll probably have to walk.

Tourist Office: On the harbor. Open Mon.-Fri. 7:30am-1:30pm, and Mon. 3:30-6pm. Excellent free map of Northern Cyprus including city maps of Girne, Lefkoşa, and Gazimağusa, but they frequently run out.

Police: (tel. 815 2014, -125). Just off the harbor, behind the Harbor Club.

Post Office: Cumhuriyet Cad., off the main square (first left with your back to the sea). Open Mon.-Fri. 7:30am-2pm and 4-6pm, Sat. 8:30am-12:30pm. Parcel office open Mon., Wed., and Fri. 9:30am-12:30pm. **Postal Code:** 9900.

Telephones: In the main square, beside Cumhuriyet Cad. Accept phonecards only. Although they are identical to Turkish phones, they do not accept Turkish phonecards. You must buy Northern Cyprus phonecards in the *Telekomunikasyon Dairesi* opposite the post office. The local phonecards cost 95¢, $1.90, or $2.80 for 30-, 60-, and 100-unit cards, respectively. **Information:** 192.

Expatriates' Notice Board: In front of the post office. Provides info on local events, apartment rentals, etc. There is a community of several hundred British expatriates around Girne, mostly middle-aged to elderly.

Banks: Banking hours are Mon.-Fri. 8:30am-noon, with some variation between banks. **Exchange offices,** for cash only, are open Mon.-Sat. roughly 9am-8pm. These are scattered along the shopping street which leads from the Atatürk statue (by the sea, beside the Dome Hotel) up to Hürriyet Cad. There are **ATMs** at either end of this street. For fast over-the-counter cash advances on Mastercard or Visa, go to **Vakıfbank,** on the main square (English spoken). A hefty 8% commission is charged. Bring your passport.

Buses: Run hourly to Mağusa (Famagusta), Güzelyurt, and Lefke from the bus station. From the roundabout, walk up the Lefkoşa Rd. (beside Vakıfbank) for roughly 800m—you should pass Shell and Esso petrol stations on the way. **Dolmuş** to Lapta also run from here. To get to Lefkoşa (Nicosia), take a *dolmuş* ($1) from the little car park behind the main taxi stand beside the roundabout; departures several times per hour, depending on the number of passengers. Buses and *dolmuş* run, approximately, from 7:30am to 5pm with restricted service at weekends. Note that many of Northern Cyprus' most interesting attractions cannot be reached by public transport; you must take a tour or (a better bet) rent a car. Compared to Turkey, the buses in Northern Cyprus are described as arthritic.

Ferries: Two daily seabuses to Taşucu in Turkey are your fastest, most comfortable option. Daily departures at 11am and 2:30pm (2½hr.; one way $16.25, round-trip $29.50). Slower, tiny ferries also run to Taşucu—departures at 11am. (6½hr.; one way $14, round-trip $23.25.) Return from Taşucu at 11am and 4pm (seabus), or midnight (ferry). From June-Sept. only there is a seabus 3 times per week to Alanya (5hr., 70DM one-way, 110DM round-trip). The schedule is highly subject to change Buy tickets from Fergün Ferries on the main square.

Taxis: Several firms have taxi stands around town. No meters; all firms should have a printed list of fares. Trips within town, including the new port, officially cost $3.50; $6 for 2-5 miles outside; $8.25 for 5-7 miles outside; $10.50 for $8-10 miles outside. These fares are high; try bargaining them down. Try to agree on a fare before accepting a ride. 8-hr. tours cost roughly $100 per car.

Car Rental: Atlantic (tel. 815 3053), in the Dome Hotel, offer jeeps for $30 per day (insurance $5). Free pick-up from all points in N. Cyprus, including port and airport. For those w/o a driver's license from home, package tours are available from the affiliated agency **Kyrenia Tours.**

International Bookstore: The **Green Jacket Bookshop,** 20 Temmuz St., offers a good selection of English-language fiction and books on Northern Cyprus. British-owned. Roughly 1½km from town. Walk from the square to the end of Hürriyet Cad. and keep going, along the coast road, for 700m—it's on the left. Open Mon.-Fri. 9am-1pm and 4-7pm, Sat. 9am-noon. **BBD** newsagents on Hürriyet Cad., near the square, have a small selection of the major British and German newspapers.

Hospital: (tel. 815 2254). On Cumhuriyet Cad., roughly 100m past the post office. There is a **doctor** (tel. 815 3528) at Hüseyin Cenkler.

ACCOMMODATIONS

Spend some extra bucks for a harborfront hotel, which delivers an exponential increase of comfort and ambience. Hotel prices without breakfast are $2.25 less than those listed. For diehard, fanatical budget travelers, there are several *pansiyon* around town aimed primarily at Turkish army privates and poor Turks on holiday. Bed without breakfast is typically: singles $6, doubles $11.75. They're none too clean—and taking breakfast into account, you save little more than $3.

Finally, no guidebook would be complete without mentioning Girne's major landmark and meeting place, the **Dome Hotel** (tel. 815 2453). This old colonial institution is a faded beauty—or maybe just a gnarled, bucolic, rasping dowager duchess. President Rauf Denktaş was spotted here; British celebrities like Peter Sellers and comedian Spike Milligan allegedly stayed here; King Farouk dropped in for lunch. Even if you don't stay (singles $37.25, doubles $60.50; breakfast included), it will, at the very least, serve as your **public toilet.**

New Bristol Hotel (tel. 815 2321), Hürriyet Cad. Every ex-Brit colony, from Gibraltar to Lagos, has, inexplicably, its own Bristol Hotel. Girne's version offers spacious, comfortable rooms w/A/C and plastic imitation wood lines every wall. Singles $14, doubles $21, breakfast and bath included.

Bingöl Motel (tel. 815 2749), Hürriyet Cad., on the main square. Basic, comfortable *pansiyon*—rooms include private bath. Singles $11.75, doubles $23.25.

Sidelya Hotel (tel. 815 3951), Nasır Güneş Sok. Second right off Hürriyet Cad., coming from the square. Clean, spacious rooms. Terrace has good views of the harbor. Singles $11.75, doubles $23.25.

Hotel British (tel. 815 2240). Overlooking the harbor, one street back. Enjoy its spacious, luxurious, balconied rooms and excellent views of the harbor at the higher levels. A/C, TV, minibar, and private bath. The view of the harbor from the rooftop terrace is one of the most pleasant scenes in North Cyprus. Singles $22, doubles $30. Excellent, English-style breakfast included. The rooms at the back, without balcony, are small and not worth the extra price.

The Ergenekon (tel. 815 4677). On the harbor—entrance at the back, opposite the Hotel British. Not as luxurious as the British, but it has plenty of character. Front rooms have balconies overlooking the harbor—you could waste many hours sitting here; back rooms not really worth it. All rooms named after local sights and have A/C and private shower. Singles $21, doubles $35; w/breakfast.

FOOD AND ENTERTAINMENT

The best restaurants on the harbor make simply exquisite fish dishes, Girne's specialty. Other Cyprus specialties are *meze* (10-20 saucers containing a huge variety of snacks—from hummus and tabouli to grilled meats, beans, stuffed vine leaves, vegetables, etc.) and *mousaka*. For a typical Turkish *lokanta,* go to **Dedem**—steaming hot trays of delicious Turkish fare for $1.25 per dish. (Open for lunch only.) Get there early (1:30pm) because locals descend on this place like a horde of starving locusts. **Saray,** by the seafront, is another good *lokanta*; go up the street from the Atatürk statue; it's on the left. (Open for lunch and dinner; typically $2.50 per dish.) There's a large selection of high-quality restaurants around Girne. The **harbor** is Girne's most atmospheric eating locale. There are several bars here with wicker chairs and cushions, and a number of fish restaurants. **Set** is perhaps the most popular among locals. A variety of stellar fish dishes are $9 each—try the fish on skewers. Next door, **Venedik** serves great fish *kebap* ($9), but the service is aggravatingly slow. The **Harbor Club Downstairs**—not to be confused with the Harbor Club Upstairs, which serves French cuisine—has sensational (though small) *meze* ($3.50), but their other offerings are mediocre.

Opposite the Dome Hotel is **Niazis.** Established in Limassol in 1949, this Cyprus institution moved to Girne in 1974 along with all of Limassol's Turks. For 46 years its specialty has been full *kebap* ($9), a huge *meze,* and a series of grilled meats. These are grilled by a chef over an open flame, in the middle of the restaurant. There are numerous restaurants that serve English food, run by the expatriate community. If delights such as grilled liver and onions, bangers and mash, or fish and chips, eaten in the company of octogenarians, appeals, then these are for you. **The Grapevine,** on the Lefkoşa road (beside the Esso station) offers all of these, along with a good *mousaka* (the only concession to local taste), for $2.75-3.50 each at lunch, double that in the evenings. Out on the coast road, 5km to the west, you'll pass **Planter's,** which proves that good English food is not a contradiction in terms. Its Yorkshire puddings, steak and kidney pies. (roughly $4.75 each) draw a young(ish) crowd.

SIGHTS

The preeminent sight in Girne is the huge medieval **castle** at the harbor's mouth. Built by the Byzantines with material plundered from the ruins of the now nonexistent Roman city, it was fortified by the Lusignans and refortified by the Venetians. In fact, the whole city was enclosed by walls that extended from the castle to the tower on Hürriyet Cad. and to the site of the Greek Archangelos Church. Though these walls have fallen, the castle is in a good state of repair, and it now houses the interesting **Shipwreck Museum.** When you enter the castle after going through the tunnel, make a left through another tunnel to the small Byzantine chapel, the only remaining structure from the Byzantine period. Almost all of the present castle dates from the Lusignans, except for the outside walls and tower, which are Venetian. Notice the Lusignan coat of arms above the doorway arch. Opposite the museum, or on the left side of the courtyard if facing the water, are dungeons with deep pits in the center. The scraps from the royal family's dinner were dumped from above as the prisoners attempted to grab at the flying food; their intended and cruel punishment came when they reached too far and fell into the pit. From the courtyard, notice the row of brown, locked doors on the upper level; these prison cells were last used by the British in the 1950s, to house EOKA terrorists. The Shipwreck Museum, in the courtyard, contains the remains of a ship from the time of Alexander the Great, 2300 years ago. Also, on display is some of the cargo, including 400 wine amphoras and 9000 blackened almonds, the crew's main staple. Level weights were discovered, which suggests that they also fished. The date of construction of the ship was determined by carbon-dating the wood; its age on sinking (80 years) was found by carbon-dating the almonds. A team of 50 from the University of Pennsylvania spent 3 years locating and excavating the ship, from 1967-69. Restoration work began in 1970 and was completed after the division of Cyprus, in 1975. (Castle open daily 8am-1pm and 2-5pm; admission $3, students 25¢.) Walk along the pier afterwards to get an idea of its vastness. There is an interesting **Iron Museum** in the **Archangelos Church,** behind the Hotel British. (Open 9am-1pm and 3-5pm; admission $1.75, students 25¢.) There is also a small **Fine Arts Museum.** Walk from the harbor past the Dome Hotel; it's 1km farther.

■ EAST OF GİRNE: BELLAPAIS

Six kilometers from Girne is Bellapais (Beylerbeyi in Turkish), a tranquil hillside village that contains one of Northern Cyprus' more notable sights, **Bellapais Abbey.** Founded by monks fleeing the Arab sacking of the city in the 13th century, it is a delicately arched Gothic structure. Huge, 30m-high Cypress trees tower above the cloisters. The **Kybele** restaurant in the abbey grounds often blasts out classical music. (Open daily 8am-5pm; admission $2.75, students 25¢.)

Across from the abbey is the **Tree of Idleness.** Alexander Durrell, a British writer, lived in Bellapais during 1953-56 and wrote *Bitter Lemons*. In the book he warns of the tree of idleness and the café lifestyle. A huge restaurant, the **Tree of Idleness Restaurant** has grown up around the tree and serves good food. Take a break, relax, and then stroll over to the souvenir shop which sells "Tree of Idleness" baseball caps. Walk uphill past the restaurant for 5min. to see Durrell's house—marked by a yellow plaque. Three or four buses per day run from Girne to Bellapais. They're infrequent—you may have to walk back to Girne.

Ten kilometers from Girne, off the Lefkoşa road, is **St. Hilarion Castle.** This is one of three castles built for visual communication, the others being **Bufavento** and **Kantara.** All of Cyprus and its coastline could be seen from this trio—an excellent early warning system. It was renovated and made a monastery in the 10th century, but by the 13th had been converted into a castle. To reach it you must drive; it's 5km uphill from the turn-off on the main Girne-Lefkoşa road. There's a military base on the way up, and walking is prohibited. (Take a Girne-Lefkoşa *dolmuş,* get off at the turn-off.) The castle was damaged by a huge fire which swept across the Kyrenia range in the summer of 1995, and was closed for repair. Bufavento is currently in a military zone; open for a couple of hours on Wed. and Sun. only—arrange for an escort who will accompany you to the site; ask at the tourist office for info.

■ WEST OF GİRNE: KARAMAN (KARMI)

This Greek hill village is one of the North's most beautiful. Abandoned by Greeks in 1974, its population now consists entirely of expatriates, primarily British and Germans. This place is quiet, though—you won't see folks walking around. You'll find them instead in the restaurants and pub. Karaman was known as Karmi pre-'74, although the name is still usually used. There are some walking trails around here;

maps and info available at the **Crow's Nest Pub.** The old **Orthodox church** is open to visitors on Sundays 10:30am-12:30pm. There are some uninteresting bronze-age tombs beside **Duckworth House.**

■■■ LEFKOŞA (NORTH NICOSIA)

The Cypriot conflict is best understood, and felt, through a visit to Nicosia, where the Green Line and the military presence serve as constant reminder's of the country's division. The Turkish side is a quiet, dusty backwater where life moves slowly. Few people walk its streets, and most businesses shut down by early afternoon. It is notably poorer than the Girne region or Southern Cyprus. Few people spend the night in dusty old Lefkoşa; its nightlife is nil, the streets empty and locals head to Girne for entertainment. Hotels in Girne are of a much higher standard—best to do Lefkoşa in a daytrip. If you really want to stay here, be warned that Lefkoşa's *pansiyon* generally cater to locals who can't afford apartments and live here instead.

ORIENTATION AND PRACTICAL INFORMATION

Arriving by bus from other parts of Northern Cyprus, you'll be dropped at the **bus station** (*otogar*), 1km from the old city. Take the street perpendicular to the Girne Rd., which runs beside the bus station to get to town—the Hotel Lapathos Nicosia should appear on your right. After 1km you reach the old city walls and **Girne gate.** The tourist office is at the entrance gatehouse. From here, **Girne Caddesi,** the main street runs to the Venetian column adorned main square, **Atatürk Meydanı** and then continues to the **Green Line.**

Arriving from the south, at the **Ledra Palace** crossing, continue 500m up the street until you hit a roundabout with a Turkish victory monolith in the middle. Follow the city walls to the Girne gate. To reach the bus terminal, continue up this street (bearing left at the nearby fork); it is a 15-min. walk.

Tourist Office: At Girne gate. Open Mon.-Fri. 7:30am-2pm, Mon. also 3:30-6pm.

Police: (tel. 227 1311). Girne Cad., close to Atatürk Meydanı.

Post Office: Sarayönü Sok. From the Girne gate, take a left off Atatürk Meydanı. Open Mon. 7:30am-2pm and 3:30-6pm; Tues.-Fri. 7:30am-2pm and 4-6pm; Sat. 8:30am-12:30pm.

Telephones: Pembe Telefon, 30m to the right of the post office, has metered booths; sells phonecards. Open Mon.-Fri. 8am-2pm and 4:30-6pm. **Government Telecommunications Dept**. is on Arif Salim Cad., one third of the way between Girne gate and the bus station, 3 blocks to the left as you walk to the station.

Embassies: Only **Turkey** has a full embassy in Northern Cyprus, at Bedrettin Demirel Cad. (tel. 227 2313). The following countries have "representative offices," which offer a degree of consular services. **Australia** (tel. 227 1115), in the Saray Hotel, open Tues. and Thurs. only 9am-noon. **Germany,** #15 28 Kasım Sok. (tel. 227 5161). **U.K.,** 23 Mehmet Akif Cad. (tel. 227 1938). Staffed by Cypriots. Passports are issued, but you have to pay in Cyprus Pounds. Buy Cyprus pounds at private exchange offices. **U.S.,** 20 Güner Türkmen Sok. (tel. 227 2443).

Currency Exchange: Several change offices along Girne Cad. open Mon.-Fri. roughly 8am-1pm and 2-4pm. **Banks** close at noon. **ATMs** near Atatürk Meydanı.

Flights: Airport is 17km from town. Taxis roughly $20; no meters. Fix a fare in advance. **Cyprus Turkish Airlines,** (owned by Turkish Airlines), has an office on Atatürk Meydanı. Open Mon.-Fri. 7:30am-3pm and 3-6pm. Flights to İstanbul, İzmir, and Ankara $60 one way, $80 round-trip; London (daily) $200 one way, $250 round-trip. **Akdeniz Air** (tel. 228 5827), Girne Cad., is a new local airline with slightly lower prices. Four times per week to İstanbul and London; 1 per week to Ankara and İzmir. Open Mon.-Fri. 8am-6pm, Sat. 9am-2pm. Please be advised that only Turkish airlines deem this airport safe enough to fly here.

Buses: Buses and dolmuş leave from the station, 1km from the center. With Girne gate and Girne Cad. at your back, go right, bearing left at the fork. Hourly buses to Mağusa (Famagusta) ($1.25), Güzelyurt ($1.50), and Lefke ($2.25). *Dolmuş* several per hour to Girne ($1). Services run from 7am-5pm; fewer on weekends. Buses also run to numerous small villages, but only 1 per day in each direction, arriving in Lefkoşa by 7am and leave in the mid-afternoon.

International Language Bookshop: Rüstem Kitabevi, 26 Girne Cad. A Nicosia institution since 1937. From Girne gate, it's 40m past Atatürk Meydanı, on the left. English-language fiction, books on Cyprus, textbooks, and Turkish-language items. Variable opening hours, but will be open 'til at least 1pm weekdays.

Hospital: (tel. 227 1441). On the road to Girne, roughly 700m from the Victory Monument. Look for the Hastanesi sign.

SIGHTS

The **Green Line** is worth a visit; it's an ever-present reminder of the divisions and hatreds that persist on this island. Take a right off Atatürk Meydanı, walk alongside the old British courthouse and down this road for 5min.; any street to your left will bring you to a vista of barbed wire enclosing an area of ruined buildings including a church and rickety watchtower. In places the Green Line is a barbed or chicken wire fence, sometimes screened with oil drums. In other sections, it is a steel barrier or a wall blocking a road. This is a sensitive military area—photography is prohibited. The **Selimiye Mosque/St. Sophia Cathedral** is a bizarre sight; an ancient (1326) cathedral from which two large Islamic minarets soar. The inside is painted pure white. In spite of the carpets and Islamic calligraphy all around, it still feels like a church. From Atatürk Meydanı, with Girne Gate at your back, continue down Girne Cad., looking left for its twin minarets. Beside it is the **Bedesten** (Orthodox Cathedral of St. Nicholas) which dates from the 14th century; it was converted to a covered market and later a barn by the Ottomans; it is now in ruins. The fascinating **Museum of Barbarism** is situated in a suburban house where, in 1963, a woman and her three children were murdered by Greek gunmen as they tried to take refuge in their bathroom. The bathroom remains as it was in 1963, complete with bloodstains. In the rest of the house, photos of Turkish victims of Greek death squads line the walls; there are some photos of destroyed Turkish villages, and a couple which are presented as evidence of Greek Army involvement in atrocities. The museum is not for the faint of heart. (Open Mon. 7:30am-2pm and 3:30-6pm; Tues.-Fri. 7:30am-2pm; free.) To reach it from Girne Gate, with Girne Cad. at your back, go left and follow the city walls (which should be on your let) to the first roundabout. Continue straight here, for 700m then turn right at the second roundabout. The museum is 1.2km along this road, on the right, and is clearly marked. Go to the rooftop terrace of the **Saray Hotel** for excellent views of the whole city; if you entered via North Cyprus, this is the closest you'll get to seeing the Greek side.

Face the Green Line and follow it to your right (you will have to backtrack now and then due to blocked streets) to reach the **Derviş Paşa Museum,** the mansion of a notable Turkish-Cypriot newspaper owner of the last century; it contains a small collection of clothing and household goods (open daily 8am-7pm, in theory; closes around lunchtime; admission $2, w/ISIC 50¢). Exit the museum, go right and take the first right to reach **Arabahmet Mosque.** From this street you can see the spire of a 14th-century Armenian church, located behind the barbed wire of the Green Line. Stroll around this old **Arabahmet** area—you'll see many damaged buildings, which have not been repaired since the inter-communal fighting. The **Mevlevi Tekke,** near the Tourist office, was once an Islamic monastery and is now a small museum, which houses life-size models of whirling dervishes and a minor collection of Islamic artifacts (open Mon. 7:30am-2pm, 3:30-6pm; Tues.-Fri. 7:30am-2pm; admission $2, w/ISIC 25¢.)

■ NEAR LEFKOŞA

The road west of Lefkoşa leads to **Güzelyurt,** which has an interesting, well preserved Greek Orthodox church, and **Lefke,** home to the nation's second university. Güzelyurt and Lefke can be reached by hourly buses from Lefkoşa (until 5pm).

GÜZELYURT

Güzelyurt is a large and none-too-interesting market town. Visit it to see **Ágios Mámas,** a beautiful, perfectly preserved icon-filled Orthodox church. Check out the **Tomb of Mamas,** an Orthodox saint, inside. It is believed that the moisture which occasionally oozes from the tomb is a cure-all for disease and a pacifier of storms. To visit the church you must first pay to enter the **Museum of Archaeology and Natural History** next door; the curator will admit you to the church. The museum itself contains a collection of stuffed animals and birds downstairs and ancient pottery upstairs; look for the two-headed lamb and the lamb with eight legs. Upstairs is the famed black-faced, multi-breasted statue of **Ephesian Artemis** from Salamis, which was recovered from the sea in the 1980s—you'll see this image on numerous postcards and books around Northern Cyprus.

LEFKE

Lefke is a quiet, rural town, a couple of kilometers inland from the sea. There is little to detain the traveler. A couple of kilometers out into the countryside stands Northern Cyprus' second university. Instruction, as in all the local universities, is through English. Lefke is also home to the Sufi holy man, **Sheikh Nazim** (see box below).

Cult-ural Immersion

Devout followers from all over the world make the trek to Lefke to pray at Sheikh Nazim's **Naqshbandi Derga,** an Islamic monastic center. You may join Nazim's pilgrims, who dress in turbans and low-crotch trousers. Visitors can stay as long as they like, and sleep on the floor of the mosque. Many remain for weeks, and, some, for years. Sufis take after **Mevlâna,** whose tomb is in Konya, Turkey (see p. 527). Sufism is a mystic form of Islam, whose rites involve meditation as well as prayer. It is believed that Sheikh Nazim is the last of a "golden chain" of 40 divine secrets that were passed from the Prophet to his Caliphs, along the "golden chain." If you wish to join them for prayer, you will be welcomed regardless of your religion—casual tourists best stay away. To meet the Sheikh, turn left after the Atatürk equestrian statue at the waterfront; take the first right, and then go left along the narrow road just past the mosque. His house is at the end, where the path veers left; enter via the second door to the left. The sheikh may not strike you as being especially insightful or holy, but his followers worship him; they drop to the ground when they see him and kiss his feet. They obey his commands without question. Incidentally, the Sheikh believes Europe is Satanic.

■■■ MAĞUSA (FAMAGUSTA)

Famagusta is a once-great city gone to seed. The old city walls, 8m thick, enclose a near-wasteland of old, ruined churches converted to mosques, large patches of weed-covered ground and, scattered among them, modern, bland blocks of shops and dwellings. This is a result of the sacking of the city by Ottoman invaders in 1571—it was never properly rebuilt. One kilometer south of Famagusta is the fenced-off, ghost city of **Varosha.** A thriving holiday resort until 1974, it is now an uninhabited "dead zone" under military control. Once busy, now crumbling houses, shops, and hotels line its streets, creating a disturbing, Beirut-like vista.

Famagusta was once the world's richest city, *the* trading post between the Christian West and Muslim East. Stories are told of a local merchant who gave huge banquets; his tables were piled with precious stones, intended as gifts to departing guests. Shakespeare's *Othello* is believed to have been set here—the bard's descriptions of a "seaport in Cyprus" match the layout of Famagusta. Nowadays, all this is hard to visualize. Incidentally, the official name you'll see on maps and road signs is **Gazimağusa,** which means "Unconquered Mağusa." This mouthful of a title is shortened in local parlance, and on buses, business cards, etc., to **Mağusa** (occasionally printed G. Mağusa). Varosha's name in Turkish is **Maraş.**

You're not exactly spoiled for choice of accommodations in this town; due to the fact that most people visit Famagusta on daytrips from Girne.

ORIENTATION AND PRACTICAL INFORMATION

Buses drop off on the Lefkoşa road. Turn right along this road; after 250m you'll see the impressive **Victory Monument** in the center of a roundabout. Behind it are the old city walls. The **Rivettina Bastion** juts out of these walls; beside it is the **Land Gate,** a picturesque entry into the old city. Follow the road outside the city walls (**Fevzi Çakmak Blv.**) and, after 500m, you'll pass the tourist office; 400m more and you'll be at the sea. On the left is the **Canbulat Bastion** and Gate, and past it, the Port, where **ferries** from Turkey arrive. The road on the right leads to Varosha.

Tourist Office: Fevzi Çakmak Blv., opposite city wall, between Rivettina and Canbulat bastions. Open Mon. 8am-1pm and 3:30-6pm; Tues.-Fri. 8am-1pm. Friendly English-speaking woman has excellent maps of N. Cyprus and its cities.

Police: İlker Karter Cad. (tel. 366 5310).

Post Office: İlker Karter Cad., the street to the left of the tourist office as you face it; the post office is 300m along, on the left.

Telephones: On Polat Paşa Blv., the street to the right of the tourist office as you face it. Phonecards sold; two cardphones in the lobby.

Buses: To Lefkoşa (hourly 7:30am-5pm, 1hr.,$1.25). Rare village buses head to most points in the region, including Karpaz Peninsula. Buses arrive in Famagusta Mon.-Fri. by 7am, in time for the typical 7:30am start to the working day; return to villages from the station between 2 and 5pm. Only 1 bus per day in each direction; most villages have no accommodations. **Dolmuş** to Lefkoşa leave from the Victory Monument, at a point called İtimat on the left (as your back is to the old city). Once or twice an hour, 7am-5pm or later, $1.75). *Dolmuş* to Girne depart from a point called Kombos, on the Lefkoşa Road, 100m past the roundabout on the left. Hourly, 7am-5pm, $2.

Ferries: Departures from the Port, between the city wall and the sea. To **Mersin,** Turkey. Departures Tues., Thurs., Fri. at 1pm. (8hr.; $25.75 one way, $42 round-trip). Go to the harbor at least 1hr. before departure to allow for customs clearance. Tickets must be bought in advance from **Turkish Maritime Lines** (tel. 366 5786). From Canbulat Bastion, follow the sea to your right (as you face it). Past the roundabout, take the right fork; the *Feribot* office is 25m farther, on your left. The ferry, *Dolphin* of Mağusa, is tiny. Return from Mersin on Mon. and Wed. at 10pm, Thurs. midnight. Faster, cheaper, more comfortable connections to Turkey are available from Girne. There may be ferry service to Haifa, Israel, starting in 1995; check with travel agents or Turkish Maritime Lines.

Hospital (*Hastane*): Polat Paşa Blv. (tel. 366 5328).

SIGHTS

The **city walls,** surrounded by a huge moat, are quite a sight. The result of 20 years' labor by the Venetians in the 16th century, they are among the strongest fortifications ever built. Yet they failed in their task: after a vicious, year-long siege, the city fell to the Ottomans in 1571. Climb to the top of the **Canbulat Bastion** to get an idea of their thickness. **Othello's Tower** dates from the 13th century and is the city's oldest buildings. Formerly known as the **Citadel,** it was renamed by the British and the new name remains, both in English and Turkish. The tower overlooks the port, from which there are good views of the city. At ground level, notice the old medieval hall and the dark passages and shafts; Peter Scaliger, the last of the Veronese ruling family, was imprisoned in one of these for 11 years by the Venetians. (Open approximately 8am-5pm daily; admission $2.75, students 25¢.) The part of the tower which juts out into the port is still a military zone. **St. Nicholas Cathedral/ Lala Mustafa Paşa Mosque** dominates the old city skyline. Built in the 14th century, it was sacked by the Ottomans after the invasion and converted to a mosque; a minaret was added. It was closed for restoration in 1995 and is likely to remain closed for a number of years. The **Church of St. Peter and St. Paul/Sinan Paşa Mosque** is an ancient, primitive stone church/mosque. It was built by a 14th-century merchant on the profits of one business transaction. Across the road is a car park, the site of the **Venetian Governor's Palace;** some bare walls still stand. Back in the main square (Namik Kemal Meydanı), notice the **covered market** next to the Cathedral of St. Nicholas. Facing the Cathedral entrance, go right for a few blocks to reach the **Church of St. George of the Greeks.** Built in the 15th century, it combined Gothic and Byzantine styles. Its roof was destroyed in the Ottoman invasion; cannonball marks can still be seen on some walls. Go farther right until you find a pretty pair of tiny Orthodox churches. Back opposite Othello's Tower, the **Church of St. George of the Latins** is merely an attractive shell. Continue away from Othello's Tower and the sea; you'll pass, on your left, the Twin Chapels of the **Knights Templar** and the **Knights of St. John of Jerusalem**—usually locked. Continue straight to reach the **Nestorian Church,** or **Church of St. George the Exiler,** dating from the 14th century. There are a few more old churches near the city wall to your left as you face the sea; but this is now a military zone and cannot be entered. Be sure not to leave Famagusta without taking a look at **Varosha.** You cannot enter it; it's a military area, but by peering over the wire fence you can get some idea of how this ghost town once looked. This was the Greek section of town (population 40,000) pre-1974; Turks lived in the old city. Varosha's population fled the advancing Turkish army—since then the city has been fenced off. Those who have been to the neighborhood report fully furnished houses, bookshelves crammed with dusty books, half-eaten meals, and unmade beds left by the harried Greeks. Although the fence is easily breached you would be unwise to cross over it; if you're caught, you'll be arrested by the Turkish military.

■ NEAR MAĞUSA

SALAMIS

Salamis is the best-preserved of the nine ancient cities of Cyprus. Legend has it that it was founded in the 11th century BC by **Teucer,** one of the heroes of Homer's *Iliad.* This Greek-speaking metropolis became the richest, most cosmopolitan city on the island. St. Barnabas was a typical citizen, studying in Jerusalem. In 392 AD its name was changed to **Constantine.** It was destroyed by Arab invaders in the 7th century AD, after which Famagusta rose to prominence.

Close to the entrance are the two best-preserved buildings; the **Palaestra** and **Baths,** immediately on your left, give an idea of the city's former greatness. The Palaestra, surrounded by elegant columns, served as an open-air gymnasium. Beside it are the baths—look for the occasional mosaic. Nearby is the **theater,** built in the Roman era. The lower seats are original; those higher up are a 1960s reconstruction. The remainder of the site is in a poor state of preservation; there is little to see. The ruins include a Roman villa, agora, temple of Zeus, and the old city walls. The **Kanpanopetra Basilica** has some interesting mosaics on its floor; from here there are excellent views of Famagusta and Varosha. The gleaming white skyscrapers of Varosha make it look like a boom town. Salamis is 8km from Famagusta; infrequent buses will drop you at the signposted turn-off, 80m from the site entrance; you may have to walk back. Open daily during daylight hours. ($2.75, students 25¢.)

The **Monastery of St. Barnabas** was built in honor of a Cypriot Jew from Salamis, educated in Jerusalem, who returned to Cyprus to spread Christianity; he was, for a time, a companion of St. Paul. Four centuries after being put to death by Jews who regarded him as a traitor, St. Barnabas appeared to the Archbishop of Salamis, revealing the location of his grave and the existence of the Gospel. The Archbishop ordered the opening of the grave and found the perfectly preserved body of Barnabas and the handwritten Gospel. Hence the legend of St. Barnabas; this site marks the location of his tomb. There was an active monastery here until 1977, when the last monks abandoned it and went south. The church is now an icon museum and rooms near the church have been converted into the best archaeological museum in Northern Cyprus. Excellent exhibits of pottery, primarily, and weapons. Finally, 150m from the monastery is the chapel tomb of St. Barnabas—get the key from the custodian. The actual body has since been moved to Jerusalem. (Open daily 8am-6pm, $2.75, students 25¢.) In the **royal tombs,** (1km from monastery to Salamis) which date from the 8th century BC, royalty were buried along with thier possessions, including manservants and horses. Several skeletons of horses are on display, protected by glass, as they were discovered. There is a small museum, showing the site's excavations. (Open 8am-6pm daily; admission $2, students free.)

KARPAZ PENINSULA

The Karpaz is Cyprus' most remote region. Even the 1974 fighting passed it by; as a result Greek-Cypriots still live here. It is a rough, gently sloping, scrub-covered landscape. Outside of the villages, there is no habitation; this is the place to get away from it all. At the base of the peninsula is one of the island's premier sights, **Kantara Castle.** Built by Richard the Lionheart in the 12th century, it was used by the Lusignans and Venetians, and abandoned in the 16th century. The castle is well signposted—from Famagusta, turn off at Boğaz. It can't be reached by public transport.

Entering the peninsula, there are few specific sights; there is a scattering of empty, damaged Greek Orthodox churches, some of which have been converted into mosques. **Yenierenköy** is the second largest village in the peninsula, but has little to interest the visitor other than the peninsula's last **petrol station. Dipkarpaz** is the largest village; its main street has an Orthodox church, mosque, and impressive Atatürk statue. Out of its population of 3,000, about 400 are Greek. The two cafés in the village are ethnically separated; the one with the signs in English is for Greeks. The communities coexist peacefully if not entirely harmoniously. In 1991, however, the marriage of a Greek and Turk led to angry demonstrations. Go right after the Atatürk statue (watch for the **Manastır** and **Blue Sea Hotel** signs) and rattle downhill to the sea; the road soon turns into a dirt track. Fourteen kilometers along this road is the **Apostolos Andreas Monastery,** which is Greek Orthodox and still in use. When you reach the deserted town with the vast square, you're there (it's on your right). To enter the monastery you must have a passport or driving license; details are recorded by the police. Go down the steps to the dark, icon-filled church. The only pilgrims are the Greeks of Dipkarpaz, who make the trek to Sunday service in a procession of battered, 1950s-style buses. (Open daylight hours; free.)

There are hotels between Dipkarpaz and Apostolos Andreas Monastery. Transportation to Karpaz is rare; renting a car may be easier. Hitching in this area is difficult.

TURKEY TÜRKİYE

US$1 =44,552 Turkish Lira (TL)	**10,000 Turkish Lira (TL) = US$0.22**
CDN$1 = 32,830TL	**10,000TL = CDN$0.30**
UK£1 = 71,136TL	**10,000TL = UK£0.14**
IR£1 = 73,266TL	**10,000TL = IR£0.13**
AUS$1 = 32,834TL	**10,000TL = AUS$0.30**
NZ$1 = 30,104TL	**10,000TL = NZ$0.33**
SAR1 = 12,247TL	**10,000TL = SAR0.80**

All prices are quoted in U.S. dollars because inflation in Turkey tends to correspond roughly with the devaluation of the lira.

Cultural contradictions, as much as majestic landscapes and archaeological treasures, fascinate visitors to Turkey. This same land reared Homer, Midas, St. Paul, and Santa Claus. Today there are actually two Turkeys: one sophisticated, the other rustic and parochial. It seems appropriate that Anatolia, the mountainous bridge between Europe and Asia, belongs to a secular state even though it contains the very first church in Christendom and has a Muslim population. Turkey's sophistication is manifested in the cosmopolitan resorts and cities and has been provisionally welcomed into the European Customs Union. Its rustic side encompasses the country's heartland, which remains virtually unaffected by tourism. All too many English-speaking residents of the city shamelessly swindle tourists; the obliging folk in the country, on the other hand, rarely speak English but still care to house and nourish the occasional wayfarer.

Despite the hordes of con-artists, Turkey is affordable as well as interesting; prices are among the lowest in Europe. For men, Turkey is one of *the* ideal budget travel destinations; some compare it to Greece ten years ago, before the influx of tourism there. Unfortunately, restrictive customs that relegate women to a subordinate status persist in parts of the country. In modern-day Turkey, however, fez hats are as scarce as baseball caps, and Camel cigarettes outnumber desert beasts of burden.

ESSENTIALS

■■■ ONCE THERE

Government offices are open Mon.-Fri. 8:30am-12:30pm and 1:30-5:30pm, banks Mon.-Fri. 8:30am-noon and 1:30-5pm. Food stores, bazaars, and pharmacies have longer hours. During the summer, on the west and south coasts, government offices and other businesses close during the afternoons, but shops stay open until 10pm.

Museums and archaeological sites in Turkey are open Tues.-Sun. 9am-5pm. At all state-run museums, students with **ISIC** cards receive 50% off. Entrance to many museums is free with a **GO25** (FIYTO) youth card.

If you are in need of **medical care** in Turkey, an embassy or consulate can provide you with a list of English-speaking doctors, although they're common in most major hospitals. İstanbul has several foreign-run hospitals (see p. 437). Private hospitals generally provide a higher standard of care than public ones. Payment, with cash or a credit card, is expected at the time of treatment. For **emergency medical service** dial **112.** For the **police** dial **155.** If your difficulties are not urgent, go to the nearest tourist office before trying the police; they can ease communication.

Be wary of English-speaking natives who approach you as friends. After befriending you, they'll offer to take you to a shop with "the best prices." Every time you spend a *lira,* your new best friend earns a commission (up to 50%). This scam is known as **hanut.** This also holds for people who approach you in bus stations offering accommodations. Have a hotel or *pansiyon* name in mind and tell the taxi driver that this is where you want to go. The taxi driver will more than likely be working on the same system and tell you that he knows of a better place. You may even be told that the place you want is full or has burned down. Stand firm.

Pensions that call themselves **aile** (family-style) try to maintain a wholesome atmosphere. Even if an establishment advertises 24-hr. hot water, you may have to ask to have the hot water turned on in your room; be forewarned. Always carry toilet paper with you, since many places don't have any; other **toiletries**—including condoms and sanitary pads and usually tampons—are cheap and readily available, though less so in the remote East.

If you have Visa or Mastercard (Access or Eurocard), or even an internationally networked ATM card from your home bank, use **ATMs:** plentiful in Turkey, they will give you the best exchange rate. American Express cardholders can use **Akbank** ATMs; **Pamukbank** ATMs, among others, are connected to the Cirrus network. Remember to keep your currency exchange receipts, as some banks will not change lira back into dollars even with a receipt.

Be careful not to insult Turks or Atatürk while visiting. Turks take their nationalism and their national hero seriously, and expect visitors to pay equal respect.

■■■ GETTING AROUND

Transport in Turkey can be both frustrating and time-consuming, but a little persistence will usually get you where you want to go for a reasonable price. **Turkish Airlines** has direct flights once or twice weekly from İstanbul to Trabzon, Van, Diyarbakır, Erzurum, İzmir, and Ankara. Domestic flights average $80 one-way, but passengers aged 12-24 may receive a discount. In some cities, an airport shuttle bus leaves from the downtown ticket office ½-1½hr. before flights (for an extra charge).

Frequent, modern, and cheap, **buses** run between all sizeable cities. Many lines provide a 10% discount to ISIC-carrying students who ask. You will need to go from booth to booth to piece together a complete schedule; one company may not divulge competitors' schedules. For long trips, try one of the more expensive bus lines. They usually offer larger seats, air conditioning, a toilet, and tea for only about 50% more than ordinary companies. Reputable companies include Varan Tours, Ulusoy, Kamıl Koç, Pamukkale, and Çanakkale Seyahat. Try to buy a seat in advance, but keep in mind that changing your ticket can be difficult. In rural parts of Turkey, it is customary when catching buses simply to flag them down from the roadside without reserving a seat in advance. Try to spot the bus' destination sign in the front window. Drivers, who keep an eye out for potential passengers, stop only if they have an empty seat. A steward hops off to stow your baggage while you board, and then collects your fare.

Extensive **shared taxi** (*dolmuş*) service follows fixed routes between small towns, or within large ones. These are usually vans or minibuses, though occasionally cars are in service as well (in İstanbul an expanded 50s-make station wagon). They leave as soon as they fill up (*dolmuş* means 'stuffed'), and are almost as cheap as municipal buses, which don't exist in some towns. Best of all, you can get on and off anywhere you like.

Despite low fares, **trains** within Turkey are no bargain. They are slow and follow circuitous routes. First-class gets you a slightly more padded seat and much more room (most Turks travel second-class). Since couchettes are available, overnight train trips are preferable to overnight bus trips.

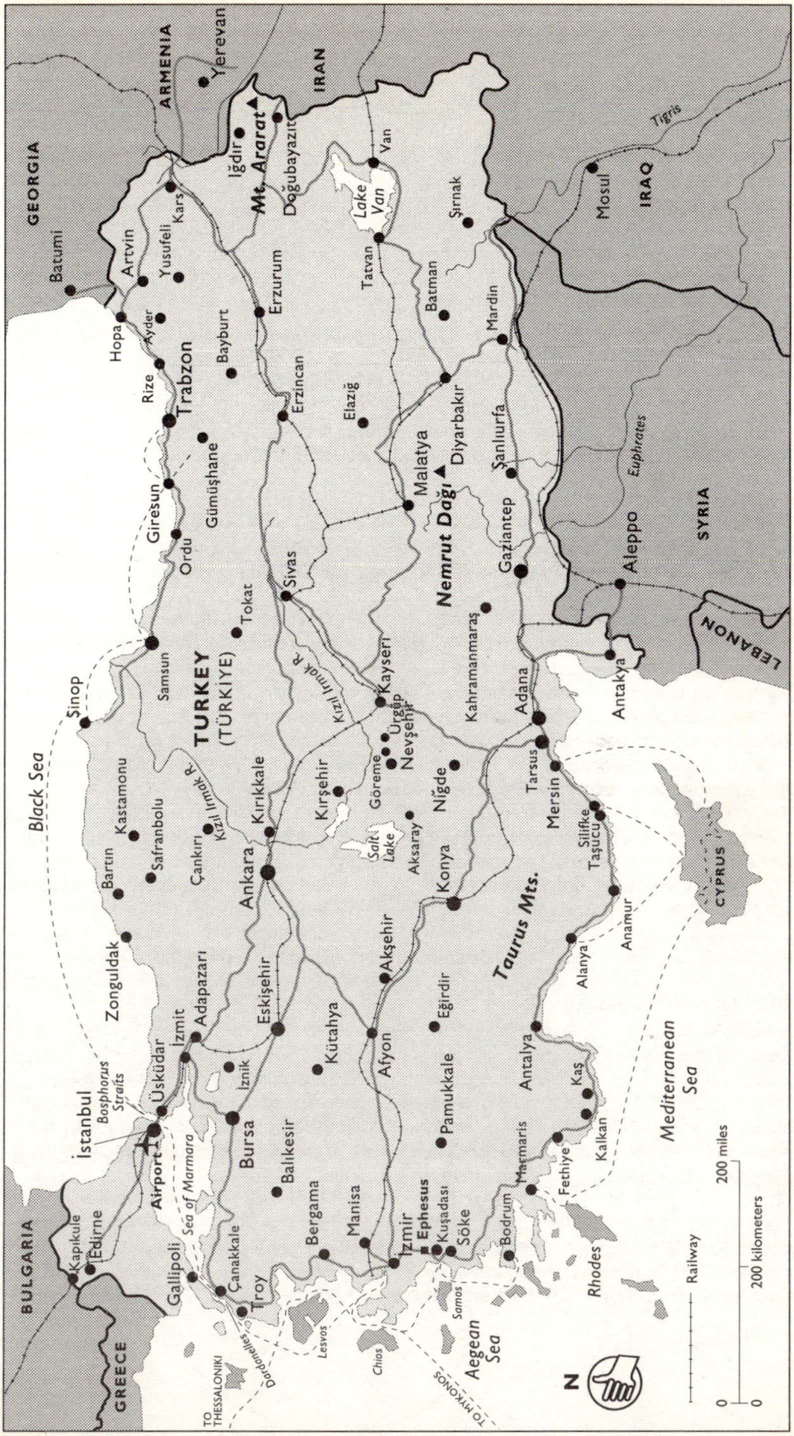
GEORGIA
ARMENIA
IRAN
IRAQ
SYRIA
LEBANON
CYPRUS
BULGARIA
GREECE
TURKEY
(TÜRKIYE)
Black Sea
Mediterranean
Sea
Aegean
Sea
Sea of Marmara
Bosphorus
Straits
Dardanelles
Batumi
Yerevan
Mt. Ararat
Iğdır
Doğubayazit
Van
Lake
Van
Tigris
Mosul
Şirnak
Kars
Artvin
Yusufeli
Hopa
Ayder
Rize
Trabzon
Bayburt
Erzurum
Tatvan
Batman
Mardin
Erzincan
Elazığ
Diyarbakır
Malatya
Nemrut Dağı
Şanlıurfa
Euphrates
Gaziantep
Aleppo
Kahramanmaraş
Antakya
Adana
Tarsus
Mersin
Silifke
Taşucu
Anamur
Alanya
Taurus Mts.
Antalya
Kaş
Kalkan
Fethiye
Marmaris
Bodrum
Rhodes
Giresun
Gümüşhane
Ordu
Sivas
Tokat
Samsun
Sinop
Kayseri
Kızıl Irmak R.
Ürgüp
Nevşehir
Göreme
Niğde
Kırşehir
Kırıkkale
Salt
Lake
Aksaray
Konya
Kastamonu
Safranbolu
Çankırı
Bartın
Ankara
Zonguldak
Adapazarı
İzmit
Eskişehir
Akşehir
Eğirdir
Kütahya
Afyon
Pamukkale
İznik
Üsküdar
İstanbul
Airport
Bursa
Balıkesir
Bergama
Manisa
İzmir
Ephesus
Kuşadası
Söke
Samos
Chios
Lesvos
Troy
Çanakkale
Gallipoli
Edirne
Kapıkule
TO
THESSALONIKI
TO MYKONOS
N
Railway
0
200 miles
0
200 kilometers

Turks drive on the right side of the road; the speed limit is 50kph (31mph) in cities, 90kph (55mph) on the highways. Road signs in English make **driving** somewhat easier. Archaeological and historical sites are indicated by yellow signposts with black writing; village signs have blue. Before taking your own car through Turkey, consider the likely effects poor roads will have on your vehicle. Official tourist literature warns against driving at night. If you get into an accident, you must file a report with the police. The **Turkish Touring and Automobile Association** (TTOK) can provide more information. Major offices include Ankara (tel. (312) 222 8723), Antalya (tel. (242) 247 0699), and İstanbul (tel. (212) 231 4631).

As in Greece, in contests between **pedestrians** and motorists, Turkish drivers take the right of way. They rarely pause for pedestrians, so be alert when crossing the street. Those who decide to **hitchhike** in Turkey generally offer to pay half of what the trip would cost by bus. Hitchers in Turkey signal with a waving hand. *Let's Go* does not recommend hitchhiking as a means of transportation, and urges readers to consider the risks inherent in hitching. Women should never hitch alone.

Ferries do not serve the west coast, but a **Turkish Maritime Lines** (TML) cruise ship sails between İstanbul and İzmir (weekly, 16hr.). In summer, a weekly boat also connects İstanbul and Trabzon. İstanbul has daily service to Bandırma. Larger ports have ship offices; otherwise, just get on the boat and find the purser.

TURKISH BUSES

> Turkish drivers are notorious for recklessness. Anatolia's mountainous terrain and poorly maintained roads aggravate the problem. Even professional drivers for reputable bus lines have a habit of tearing over and around blind curves, much to their passengers' alarm. Road travel remains the most extensive, affordable, and modern way to get around Turkey, but there are risks involved.

For long trips there are always overnight buses; request a window seat in the middle of the bus, away from the driver's radio and behind the overhead window. Every so often a steward will come around spraying cologne; stretch out your palms to receive a squirt, then rub it over your face and neck. If you're thirsty, say *su lütfen* and the steward will bring a straw and plastic pouch of cold water. Every 2-4 hours, the bus will stop at a roadside rest complex where you can stretch your legs, use the toilets (10¢; paper extra), pray, and purchase overpriced cafeteria grub. The driver will announce the duration of the stop in Turkish before you get out, but it might vary by as much as 15min. either way, so keep an eye on your bus. Passengers who get left behind receive neither sympathy nor monetary compensation. If you get stranded, another bus going your way will probably visit the rest complex within a few hours; find the steward on board to buy a ticket for an empty seat.

STREET ADDRESSES

As few Turkish cities follow a grid plan, maps can be difficult to use. To avoid confusion, a three-tiered addressing system is used. First comes the district, or *mahalle.* Then comes the nearest avenue (*cadde* or *bulvar*). Unless the address falls on this avenue, the side street off of it (*sokak, sokağı*) is specified next. Last comes the building's street number, prefixed by "No." A slash after the street number, or the word *kat,* introduces the number of the floor, if applicable. *Mahalle(si)* is abbreviated to **Mah.,** *Cadde(si)* to **Cad.,** *Bulvar(ı)* to **Blv.,** and *Sokak* (or *Sokağı*) to **Sok.** Thus, a complete street address in Turkey might look like *Çiğdem Mah. Atatürk Blv. Söğüt Sok. No. 6/2.* This book, which prints street numbers directly before the streets to which they refer, would list this address as *Çiğdem Mah. Atatürk Blv. 6/2 Söğüt Sok.* It means the second floor of 6 *Söğüt* St., off of *Atatürk* Ave., in the *Çiğdem* District. Few addresses will contain all of these parts. In towns and rural areas, the street names—rarely used by residents—may not appear on maps. Here you will receive nonstandard addresses specifying the desired building's position relative to some visible nearby edifice (e.g., *Süleymaniye Camii Önü,* "in front of Süleyman's Mosque"). In these situations, the following prepositions will come in handy: **önü** (in front of), **arkası** (behind), **üstü** (on top of), **altı** (beneath), **yanı** (beside), and **karşı** (across from).

■■■ KEEPING IN TOUCH

Mail to or from North America can take anywhere from one week to 17 days. **Post offices** (known as **PTT**) are easily recognized by their yellow signs. PTT stands for Post Office, Telegraph, and Telephone. Large post offices in major urban areas are open Monday through Saturday from 8am-midnight, Sunday from 9am-7pm. Major PTTs in İstanbul are open 24 hours. Smaller post offices share the same hours as government offices (Mon.-Fri. 8:30am-12:30pm and 1:30-5:30pm). To send mail Poste Restante, write the person's name, *Postrestant,* and *Merkez Postanesi* (Main Post Office), followed by the town's name; use the postal code if you have it. Picking up letters sometimes costs a small fee. Check under both your first and last name, and have a form of identification handy. Also, specify *Uçak İle* (airmail) when requesting stamps, and write it on your mail (or ask for aerograms). Tell the vendor the mail's destination: *Avustralya, Kanada, Büyük Bretanya* (Great Britain), *İrlanda, Yeni Zelanda* (New Zealand), *Güney Afrika* (South Africa), or *Amerika.*

Turkey has a surprisingly good **phone** system. With few exceptions, even the smallest village is accessible by phone. The numbering system was revised in 1994, so beware of out-of-date listings. Local numbers now all have seven digits, and all area codes have three. (In small towns, all numbers will start with the same three digits, so you may occasionally be given a four-digit phone number.)

When making a **long-distance** call within Turkey, first dial 0, wait for the tone to change to a lower pitch, then dial the area code and the number. Note that the area code and the number always have a total of ten digits. To initiate an international call, first dial 0. When making a **direct international call,** dial 0, wait for the tone, then dial 0 again followed by the country code and the number, without pausing. There are four common phone tones: the dial tone, busy tone, and calling tone, as well as three short beeps followed by one repeated long beep, which means you need to dial again because your call is not going through properly for some reason. Phone cards (*telekart*) are very convenient and can be bought in denominations of 30, 60, or 100 units at PTTs; some kiosks also sell them. Most phones take *telekart;* some take *jeton,* little coin-like tokens also available at PTTs; regular coins are not accepted. *Telekart* are more economical than *jeton* and easier to use, but villages often have a limited supply. Magnetic card public phones are abundant in big cities and resort areas; they have on-screen instructions in English, French, and German. To make calls using MCI (0080011177), AT&T (0080012277), SPRINT (0080014477), etc., a card or *jeton* must be deposited, but the call is free—no credit will be deducted from your card, and your *jeton* will be returned to you. Calling card calls have been known to terminate for no apparent reason.

The cheapest way to make international **collect** (reverse-charge) calls is to contact an operator in the destination country. From *any* (working) payphone, dial: U.S. 0080014477, U.K. 00800441177, Canada 00800331177, Ireland 008003531177, Australia 0800611177, Germany 00800491149, or Japan 00800811177.

Equally pleasant are *kontörlü telefon.* These are phones in the post office; the officer tells you how much you owe at the end of your call. Note that there may be long lines for these phones, especially during the day. Try to use one late at night at one of the 24-hr. PTTs. The same kind of phone is available at some hotels and restaurants, but they may charge you 20-500% more.

LIFE AND TIMES

■■■ HISTORY

ANCIENT TURKEY

Civilization has flourished in what is now Central Turkey since the eighth millennium BC, making it one of the oldest human settlements on earth. This geographical region (historically known as "Anatolia" or "Asia Minor") has long mixed Asian and Western cultures. During the 3rd millennium BC (Bronze Age), an early Hittite nation settled in Central Anatolia. Besides developing techniques for forging iron weapons, the Hittites spoke an Indo-European language considered by scholars to be closely related to modern European languages. Following the massive migration of Greek islanders ("sea peoples") at the end of the 2nd millennium BC, the Hittite empire collapsed. Cyrus extended the Persian empire along the coast of Asia Minor in the 6th century BC, using the region as a base for forays into Greece.

Two centuries later Alexander the Great marched his army into Asia Minor and routed the Persians. Great metropolises emerged after the 2nd century BC, when the coastline became the commercial and political core of the Roman province of Asia Minor. Following the creation of the Eastern Roman Empire in Byzantium (renamed "Constantinople"), Asia Minor prospered, became the center of Greek Orthodox Christian culture, and oversaw a renewed and vigorous empire stretching from the Balkans through Greece to the Levant and Egypt.

Turks began to migrate from their homeland in Central Asia in the second half of the 8th century AD, moving west and establishing independent states in eastern Iran, Afghanistan, and northern India. In the 11th century Seljuk Turks, originally inhabitants of Mongolia, began the most significant Turkish migration, inhabiting the Muslim lands of Iran, Iraq, and Syria, and settling on the plains of central Anatolia. Though Seljuk power was momentarily eclipsed by the pillaging Genghis Khan, the Seljuks were able to maintain their authority for a surprisingly long period. The Byzantine ports along the coast began to lose economic importance as land routes to Asia were monopolized by the various Seljuk fiefdoms in the interior. When Seljuk rule broke down in the 14th century, separate Turkish emirates picked up the pieces. Claiming the northwest corner of Anatolia was Osman, who in time united several fiefdoms to challenge and defeat the Greeks. From such origins grew perhaps the greatest empire in the history of civilization: the *Osmanlı,* or Ottoman.

THE OTTOMAN EMPIRE

From the beginning of the 14th century to the middle of the 15th, Ottoman rulers gradually gnawed away at the Byzantine Empire. In 1453, Constantinople, an Ottoman target since the time of Osman, finally fell to Mehmet the Conqueror. Renamed İstanbul, the city became the heart of a youthful, vigorous Turkish Empire.

The Ottoman Empire incorporated Greece and soon Cyprus into the Muslim/Turkish state apparatus, and penetrated the Balkans as far as Belgrade. Under Selim I (1512-1520), Ottoman armies conquered Syria, Palestine, Egypt, and Arabia. In a feat of military and religious grandeur, the sultan became guardian of the three holy places of Islam: Mecca, Medina, and Jerusalem. Although all power in the empire was vested in a sultan accountable only to God, a number of different individuals actually ruled the territories of the empire. Under the sultans, professional governors (often competing heirs to the sultanate) were sent out to the provinces. The sultans also gave *tımar,* or land grants, to gain the support of Turkish military chiefs. In accordance with Islamic law, monotheistic communities paid the *cizye,* a special head tax, and were on the whole treated well. Orthodox Greek Christians, for example, fared far better under Muslim authority than they did under the crusading Franks. Many Jews, upon their expulsion from Spain in 1492, settled in parts of the empire and took up trade. Despite ruthless counters to occasional rebellions, the early days of the Ottoman Empire brought relative peace and prosperity.

As Ottoman expansion slowed, the military *tımar* holders grew restless, missing the income they had gained from conquests. In order to reestablish military loyalty, Sultan Murad I created the first corps of **janissaries** (from *yeni çeri,* "new army") in the middle of the 14th century. Technically personal slaves of the sultan, these (mostly Christian) sons of subjects were forcibly taken from the provinces and converted to Islam. During their training they were given years of exams and drills and tracked into graduated echelons of the military. Those who made it to the top were assigned duties at the palace under the personal direction of the sultan. The great architect Sinan was a janissary.

When **Süleyman** became Sultan (1520-66), the Ottoman Empire was already considerable, but under him the expanse of the empire was doubled, stretching from the Balkans and Greece north to the Black Sea, west to Iraq, and southward into Africa. Court administration was centralized, and literature, architecture, and decorative arts flourished. Süleyman's military conquests and voluptuous court earned him the title of Magnificent among the Europeans. (It was Süleyman who knocked at the gates of Vienna in 1529.) Süleyman earned the title of *Kanuni* (the Lawgiver) for coalescing the *şeriat* (Islamic jurisprudence) with the *ferman* (court decrees).

Süleyman's most influential wife, **Roxelana,** convinced the Sultan to name his less-than-magnificent son **Selim** as his successor. In order to spend more time carousing in the well-endowed imperial harem, Selim turned virtually all matters of the state over to the Grand Vizier. During the period that followed (a sozzled Selim had drowned in his tub in 1574), palace infighting was rife. Some scholars called this the "rule of the women," as the favorite wives or harem girls of the monomaniacal sultans vied for power. Mothers would order entire families strangled to ensure the throne for their own children. For example, Kösem, a concubine of Sultan Murad (1603-17), scarcely survived banishment to Beyazıt upon the sultan's untimely death, only to return triumphantly to the palace when her sons Murad IV and İbrahim became sultans in rapid succession. Kösem even lived to see her grandson become sultan, but in 1652 she was strangled by order of her daughter-in-law.

Weakness at the top only encouraged abuses by those nearer the bottom. Religious and ethnic minorities, such as the Armenians, Kurds, Greeks, Cypriots, and Jews, were sometimes treated quite harshly. Following a period of devastating inflation caused by the Spanish discovery of American silver, the Ottoman administration became continually weaker. After a series of disastrous military entanglements with Peter the Great and the Venetians, the Ottoman dynasty signed the **Treaty of Karlowitz** on January 26, 1699, thus losing most of Transylvania and Hungary.

END OF AN EMPIRE

After the traumatic loss of Greece in 1832, life did not get any easier for the Ottoman Empire. **Muhammad Ali,** nominally the sultan's governor of Egypt, invaded the Levant. He would have captured İstanbul itself had it not been for the intervention of the European powers. In the mid-19th century, after crushing conservative opposition, the Ottomans instituted a series of administrative reforms collectively known as the *tanzimat.* Besides providing *de jure* religious equality to all, the *tanzimat* attempted to regulate taxation and government conscription, and to establish the private ownership of land. Most peasants, however, were wary that the government's reforms were merely covers for more tax-raising schemes. So they registered their land in the name of wealthy *shaykhs* and landowners, whose great estates thus further accrued. As the Ottoman government became more and more indebted to

British and French bankers, the once fabulous Empire limped in such decrepitude that it was commonly referred to as "the sick man of Europe."

The British, after assuming a "protectorate" over Cyprus in 1878, began fearing that bondholders who had invested in Egypt would not be repaid, so they marched armies into the Nile. Meanwhile, as the self-proclaimed protectors of Greek Orthodox Christians everywhere, the Russians came forth with more extensive claims against the Ottomans, liberating territory in the Crimea. Foreign missionary schools sprang up in the Ottoman Middle East. Arabs, ruled by Turks for more than five centuries, began to blame the Ottomans for the corruption of Islam. Indeed, the Arabs had never recognized the Turks as legitimate protectors of the faith in the first place.

With the advent of the telegraph and steamship, the Ottoman central government was able to reinforce its presence in the remote parts of the empire. As Britain and France vied with Russia for control of the strategic straits of the Bosphorus, the sultans had the opportunity to dive headfirst into the intrigues of European *realpolitik.* Although unrest in the early 1870s prompted the granting of a constitution complete with elected parliament, **Sultan Abdülhamid II** (who ruled 1876-1909) led a pan-Islamic counter-revolution and suspended all democratic reforms.

The 1908 coup of the **"Young Turks,"** a secret organization which had burst from the officer corps, ended Abdülhamid's hold on power. Welcomed at first by most of the ethnic populations, the triumvirate of military officials who controlled the empire soon began to implement a strident plan of Turkification. Traditionally, Islam had been the basis for Ottoman identity, and in accordance with Islamic law minorities had been allowed to open their own schools and keep their own customs. But now the central government decreed that Turkish was to be the national language of the empire for non-Turkish-speaking Muslims and non-Muslims alike.

The government of the Empire sided with the Axis powers in WWI. As British officers led an Arab revolt against the Turks (with the promise of then granting them independence), Turkish officials in the east began to "solve" their ethnic problems. A three-year period witnessed the extermination of more than 1½ million Armenian civilians after Armenian forces sided with the Russian army in an attempt to win their own independence. Officials in the German government expressed dismay at this plan, but no effort was made to interfere. Entire Armenian cities were "disinhabited" under the pretense of a relocation of their inhabitants to the "safer" environs of Mesopotamia. To this day, many Turks are taught in school that this never took place—according to the Turkish government, it was the Armenians who massacred the Turks. A museum in Erzurum exhibits the remains of these "Turkish" victims.

THE TURKISH REPUBLIC

The Ottoman dynasty, however, had breathed its last by siding with the Germans in WWI. After the Allies won, Britain and France divided the Arab provinces, under the auspices of the nascent League of Nations. Plans for the division of Anatolia were drawn up, and Greece invaded in order to capture disputed territory. These two undertakings were stifled by the rise of **Mustafa Kemal,** an Ottoman general who was able to reorganize his army in time to defeat the Greeks. On October 29, 1923, Mustafa Kemal, dubbed **Atatürk** (Father of the Turk), was elected the first president of the newly-established Republic of Turkey. Atatürk turned his back on Ottoman tradition. Equating modernization with rapid Westernization and secularization, Atatürk abolished the Caliphate, outlawed Muslim courts and the veiling of women, decreed that Turkish be written in Latin rather than Arabic script, and, for a time, ordered that the *adhan* (call to prayer) be recited in Turkish rather than classical Arabic. He also gave women the right to vote. These sweeping measures encountered extreme resistance from the religious establishment.

Since the rise of Mustafa Kemal, Turks have been determined in their program to become a part of Europe. The **Republican People's Party** program of 1931 proclaimed the six principles of the modern Turkish state: republicanism, populism, nationalism, statism, secularism, and revolution. Changes were introduced to "re-educate" the public about Turkish achievement, and the government began a systematic campaign to purge foreign-derived words from the Turkish language. Turkification triumphed over the competing systems of Ottomanism and pan-Islamism, if only because it was the only option left.

Shortly before WWII, the increasingly autocratic Kemal died and was replaced by his associate **İsmet İnönü.** Though Nazi Germany's early successes resulted in a popular clamor to join the war on the side of Germany to avenge the humiliation of WWI, the government remained neutral. At the end of the war, with the impending defeat of Germany, Turkey joined the Allies, as the penetration of Soviet power into the south had become a pressing concern. When the Soviets demanded the sharing of control of the Straits and the ceding of large pieces of eastern Anatolia to Soviet Georgia, military and economic aid from the United States was shunted to Turkey. (Today Turkey is still one of the largest recipients of U.S. aid.)

WWII, however, led to the expansion of the Turkish military and fed its role in politics. When a growing professional class demanded increased political participation, the **Democrat Party** (DP) broke off from the old Kemalist Republican People's Party (RPP). Throughout the 50s, the government, dominated mostly by the DP, continually loosened censorship and expanded political rights. However, as the 50s progressed, economic conditions deteriorated almost as fast as relations between the RPP and the DP. When the DP threatened to outlaw the RPP, students participated in widespread demonstrations and the army stepped in and took control.

After the eradication of the DP, the military's ruling **National Unity Committee** made a new constitution. Approved by voters in July, 1961, the constitution established a bicameral parliament which would elect the president jointly. Elections were held in October, and the army soon withdrew from politics. Many former DP members became influential in the new Justice Party (JP), which dominated elections after 1965. In 1970, after right-wing members of the JP split off and reconstituted the old Democratic Party, the army demanded the resignation of the government and assumed *de facto* control.

So You Want To Be A Dervish

Widely regarded as the "intellectuals" of mystical Islam, the Whirling Dervishes wielded great political power from the Seljuk period until 1923, when Atatürk dissolved the order. Their influence at court may partly account for the Ottoman policy of religious toleration toward conquered peoples, especially in the Balkans and Eastern Europe. Atatürk reportedly found the Dervishes' monarchist and politically conservative beliefs to be inconsistent with the reforms he sought to implement. Not long after his death, the government gave in, and now professional Dervishes are free to whirl once a year during a week-long festival held in Konya in mid-December (if that doesn't fit with your plans, you can see genuine dervish dances in İstanbul). The dances, in which the most adept Sufis sometimes make as many as 60 revolutions per minute, are pregnant with symbolism and result from years of repetitive training. In order to learn to spin in one place so fast without losing their balance, aspiring dervishes grip a spike in the ground between their biggest two toes, and whirl by walking their other foot around this post. One arm points down to Earth, the other upwards to Heaven, installing the whirler as a channel unifying the energies from both.

RECENT YEARS

During the 1970s, the government was controlled by a coalition teaming the RPP with a new religious party. Tensions built as economic conditions worsened, and religious opposition to increased Westernization grew. Following the coup in Cyprus which overthrew President Makarios, public opinion in Turkey led to the army's **invasion of northern Cyprus** in July, 1974, as fear that Cyprus would become part of mainland Greece increased. Economic and arms embargoes soon followed and Turkey responded by closing foreign military installations. By the end of the 70s most normal foreign relations resumed.

The military took power again in September, 1980, as the government's control over the interior of the country dissipated. The military dissolved all opposition parties and punished and tortured thousands of opposition leaders. By 1983, the military relinquished most of its hold on power and martial law ceased; elections that year brought the centrist **True Path Party** of **Turgut Özal** to power. Turkish assistance during the Gulf War against Iraq in 1991 proved economically debilitating and led to terrorist attacks against government installations and foreigners. But by cooperating with the United States, Özal may well have claimed a new international role for Turkey, which had lost its traditional strategic position with the end of the Cold War. Boosted economic assistance from the West as well as the Gulf countries seems to have alleviated, for the moment, the threat of further crisis.

In May of 1993 the True Path Party voted **Tansu Çiller,** a woman, as its new leader. However progressive that victory may seem, the 1994 elections saw the emergence of Islamic fundamentalism as a political power at the state and local level; fundamentalists captured the mayoralties of Ankara and İstanbul. In the wake of the Gulf War, **Kurdish separatists** stepped up their terrorist activity, prompting Çiller, in the spring of 1994, to turn the problem over to the military. Traditionally heavy-handed, the military began razing villages suspected of harboring rebels, and thousands of Kurdish villagers fled to the cities. The spring of 1995 has seen the Turkish military determined to destroy the **Kurdistan Workers' Party (PKK),** an unrepresentative Kurdish minority party suspected of using European drug trafficking to finance its terrorist activities. Thus, in an ironic turn of events, Turkey led a brief offensive into the power vacuum of northern Iraq left by the departure of the U.S. forces after the Gulf War. Strong threats of sanctions from the EU may have contributed to this campaign's speedy conclusion.

As the European Economic Community accelerated its drive toward unity, Turkey's role in the global economic arena stood undetermined. In 1987, Turkey applied for full membership, but was rejected in 1989 on the grounds that the completion of a previously defined European market was necessary before any expansion could be considered. Furthermore, the Commission of the European Communities noted Turkey's less than stellar human rights record, high rate of inflation, and control of Northern Cyprus as objections to granting Turkey's membership. (There is also fear that the existing 2 million Turkish workers in Europe will expand exponentially if visas are rendered unnecessary.) In early 1995, Turkey was finally accepted into the European Customs Union, on the condition that the Turkish parliament make hundreds of new laws and changes to the constitution by October. Meanwhile, Turkey has sought economic opportunity in the East, namely in the Muslim former Soviet republics of Kazakhastan, Tajikistan, and Uzbekistan.

■■■ RELIGION

Around 95% of Turks are Muslim. Orthodox Christians of Greek, Armenian, and Syrian backgrounds, and Jews (mainly in İstanbul) compose the remaining population. There's no official state religion, but religion matters enough that every Turkish citizen's national identification card includes a blank for it, filled out at birth by parents. While Atatürk set modern Turkey on a secular course, Islam (*İslam*) plays a key role in the country's history and culture.

The Arabic word *islam* means "submission," and Islam the religion is the faithful submission to God's will. Islam has its roots in the revelations received between 610 and 622 AD by **Muhammad,** who was informed of his prophetic calling by the Angel Gabriel. These revelations, received in Arabic, form the core of Islam and the **Qur'an** (recitation; *Kuran* in Turkish). Muslims believe the Arabic text to be immutable and untranslatable—the words of God embodied in human language. Consequently, the Qur'an appears in Turkey and throughout the Muslim world in Arabic. Muhammad is seen as the "seal of the prophets," the last of a chain of God's messengers which included Judeo-Christian figures such as Abraham, Moses, and Jesus.

Islam continued to grow after the Prophet's death (632), flourishing in the "Age of Conquest." The first four caliphs (*halife*), or successors to the Prophet, known as the Rightly Guided Caliphs, led wars against apostate nomadic tribes, and by the year 642 the Muslims had defeated the Persian empire. By 672, they had reached the walls of Constantinople. The fourth Caliph, Muhammad's nephew and son-in-law Ali, was the catalyst for a major split in the Muslim world; for the first time Muslims fought Muslims. Ali lost power and in 661 was murdered. The *Shi'at Ali* (Partisans of Ali, or Shi'is) believe that Ali, as a blood relative of the Prophet, was the only legitimate successor to Muhammad, thus separating themselves from **Sunni** (orthodox) Islam. **Shi'ism** is not a creed of fundamentalism, but is Islam with a focus on divinely chosen leaders (*imam*) who are descendants of the Prophet. **Sufism** is a mystical movement within Islam that stresses the goal of unity with God. Sufis are organized in orders, with a hierarchy from master to disciple. Most Turkish Muslims are Sunni.

MOSQUES

Any place where Muslims pray is a mosque (*cami, mescit*). The direction facing Mecca, in which all prayer is spoken, is called the *kıble.* It is marked by a niche, the *mihrab.* The *imam* (leader of prayer, not to be confused with the Shi'i leaders) gives a sermon (*hutbe*) at noon prayer on Friday from the *minbar* (pulpit). In larger cities, you may also see a *türbe* (mausoleum) or *medrese* (Qur'anic school).

There are no religious restrictions on non-Muslims entering mosques, but other restrictions may have been adopted for practical reasons in areas with many tourists. Prayer is not a spectator sport, and visitors should stay away during times of worship and always wear modest dress. Men in shorts may be particularly frowned upon. Shoes are usually removed before entering a mosque, and women should cover their heads as a courtesy even if it is not required (technically, men as well as women are supposed to cover their heads in the presence of God).

■■■ ART AND ARCHITECTURE

Sultan Süleyman introduced unprecedented imperial patronage of the arts, his empire's glory finding prolific expression in the mosques, textiles, painted miniatures, and calligraphy of the 16th century. Under Süleyman alone (1520-1566), over 80 major mosques and hundreds of other buildings were constructed in the empire. Most every sultan built and was subsequently buried in a mosque, thereby creating a topographical line of succession along Divan Yolu, İstanbul's processional avenue. The master Sinan served Süleyman and his sons as Chief Court Architect from 1538 to 1588, during which time he created a unified style for all of İstanbul and for much of the empire. Trained first as a carpenter and then as an elite soldier who marched the length of the Empire, Sinan forged an architecture informed by early Islamic and Byzantine styles, but conforming to neither.

LITERATURE

To be Ottoman was, for many centuries, to be part of a palace culture that evolved separately from the cultures of the peoples the empire governed. Ottoman culture was designed to provide a common experience for a ruling class chosen from disparate ethnic, linguistic, and religious backgrounds. Perhaps the most obvious signifier of this cultural otherness was the use of Ottoman Turkish—an ornate combination of Persian, Turkish, and Arabic. Ottoman was the language of choice both for the administration and for literature. The creation of modern Turkish in the 1920s has meant that the literary traditions of the Ottoman administration are lost to all but specialists. Modern Turkish literature looks back not to the early modern period, as is so often the case in Western traditions, but earlier yet to the writings of Türkmen poets such as Celaleddin Rumi and Yunus Emre. Their verses survived the Ottoman centuries relatively unscathed, and interestingly, the Turkish these poets used remains intelligible to a speaker of modern Turkish in a way that Ottoman is not. The *türkü* (modern Turkish folk song), for example, uses language and form that would have been familiar to these late medieval poets. This form of literature survived because of the endurance of the frontier society the Ottomans came from.

DECORATIVE AND PERFORMANCE ARTS

The Ottoman decorative arts amount to a wealth of nature motifs. (Ottoman artists did not always follow the Qur'an's injunction against portraying living beings.) While standard arabesques, inherited from earlier Islamic art, were common, court workshops developed distinctly Ottoman styles as well. The naturalistic ones included flowers and animals, while the *saz* (reed) style, thought to have been inspired by Chinese sketches on porcelain, featured long, self-piercing leaves wound around abstract lotus blossoms. Similar but unrelated was the *rumi* style, which originated in Iran and featured split leaves.

Until the mid-1800s, calligraphy, miniatures, and illuminations were the only formal examples of painting; İznik tiles and colorful *kilim* the most familiar Turkish handicrafts. Music, dance, and theater have become more institutionalized in the past 150 years. Turkish music runs the gamut from folk music (*halk müziği*) to protest music (*özgün*) to popular music (*arabesk* and *taverna*). In 1971, concern over the integrity of Turkey prompted the government to establish the nation's Ministry of Culture. Today, several international arts and music festivals bring performers from all over the world to Ephesus, İstanbul, and other Turkish cities, while the handicrafts of Turkish culture (carpets, meerschaum pipes, knit stockings, and elaborately inlaid wood) continue to be prized.

■■■ LANGUAGE

Once thought to be related to Finnish, Hungarian, and Mongolian, Turkish is today recognized as belonging to a distinct Turkic language group, spoken from Germany to China and comprising Azerbaijani, Kazakh, Khirgiz, Uyghur, and Uzbek. In his effort to forge a secular Turkish identity, in 1928 Atatürk ordered the language written in the Roman alphabet rather than the Arabic script. Furthermore, Atatürk purged Turkish of many of its Arabic and Persian borrowings (the latter evidence of Persian literary influence). While these words continue to be replaced by new Turkish ones, this linguistic cleansing is not absolute; Islamic terminology notwithstanding, words as common as "hello" (*merhaba*) remain of Arabic and Persian origin.

Although you might never have heard anything like Turkish, it is not difficult to master the basics. Pronunciation is entirely phonetic: each letter of the alphabet represents a single sound. There are only six new letters to learn: ş (sh), ç (ch), ğ (silent), ı, ö, and ü, two of which are already familiar to speakers of German. Moreover, grammatical gender does not exist, and Turkish case endings are so regular that you can count the exceptions on your fingers. Body language often matters as much as what is said. When a Turk raises his chin and clicks his tongue, he means "no" (*hayır*); sometimes a shutting or uplifting of the eyes accompanies this motion.

Shaking your head sideways instead means "I don't understand" (*anlamadım*). More intuitively, "yes" (*evet*) may be abbreviated by a sharp downward nod. If a Turk waves a hand up and down at you, palm toward the ground, she is signaling you to come, not bidding you farewell. In Turkey the idle habit of snapping the fingers of one hand and then slapping the top of the other fist is considered obscene.

English is widely spoken wherever tourism is big business—mainly in the major coastal resorts. In the rest of Anatolia, only university students tend to know English. German is probably a more common second language in Turkey as a whole. Buy a phrasebook, such as the *Penguin Turkish Phrasebook* or *Harrap's Turkish Phrasebook.* Langenscheidt has an excellent Turkish-English pocket dictionary. For a pronunciation guide and cursory list of useful phrases, consult the Glossary.

■■■ LEISURE

Many popular Turkish pastimes still take place in all-male enclaves. A favorite is visiting the local *kıraathane* (coffeehouse), where customers sip coffee or tea over games of *tavla* (backgammon). In İstanbul you might still find men smoking *nargile* (hookahs, water pipes). If you purchase a *nargile* as a souvenir, make sure that customs officials do not mistake it for narcotics equipment. Traditional spectator sports include *yağlı güreş* (grease wrestling), *cirit oyunu* (tossing javelins at competitors on horseback), and *deve güreşi* (camel wrestling). Soccer is immensely popular.

THE TURKISH BATH

It's worth your while to visit a **hamam** (Turkish bath) at least once while in Turkey. Because of the Islamic emphasis on cleanliness (pious Muslims perform ablutions before each of the day's five prayers), the baths have been a customary part of daily life since medieval times. Men and women use separate bath houses, or the same place on different days. Enter the bath house, deposit your clothes in a cubicle, don the provided *peştemal* (towel), and proceed to the sauna-like *göbek taşı* (large heated stone). As you sweat, an attendant will give you a rub-down. Following the massage, you can bathe yourself (bring your own shampoo, soap, and towel, or pay to use theirs, and take care not to douse your neighbors since they might have just finished a ritual cleansing) or be bathed. The *kese* (abrasive mitt) they use will strip your excess skin cells. Men should never drop their *peştemal;* cleaning one's lower half is therefore tricky, but not impossible. Visiting the bath in a group can be fun.

■■■ FOOD AND DRINK

It may come as a surprise that such popular Middle Eastern foods as hummus, falafel, and baba ghanoush are practically unknown in Turkey. Like other cuisines from the Balkans to the Persian Gulf, contemporary Turkish cuisine finds its roots in Ottoman kitchens. But Ottoman cooking draws from the nomadic traditions of the Central Asian tribes, and from the many civilizations that swept Asia Minor for thousands of years. An Assyrian cookbook found during recent excavations showed that similar dishes have been served for thousands of years. *Kebap* (kabob), the most famous of these dishes, exemplifies today's simple and hearty Turkish cuisine. This land, which still produces a food surplus, is one of the few places left in the Mediterranean where eating cheaply still entitles you to sample a great variety of dishes.

HOW IT'S DONE

In many restaurants (*lokanta*), guests are shown into the back kitchen and encouraged to order by pointing. The kitchen probably will not display such staples as shepherd's salad, lentil soup, rice pilaf, or yogurt; their availability is understood. Prices, where listed, are by the portion (*porsiyon*), and an excellent way to increase variety while saving money is to order half (*yarım*) or quarter (*çeyrek*) portions, for that fraction of the price. In this way, for example, one can cheaply and guiltlessly sample the sinfully wide variety of *baklava* in a Turkish pastry shop (*pastane*). The same tip applies to street vendors of gyros (*döner kebap*), who tend to be stingy with the meat in thick pocket-bread sandwiches, but who may give more than double the meat for double the price. Turkish restaurants nonetheless offer excellent value for money (filling meals often come to less than $6). Usually, you can't bargain in restaurants, except when ordering fish, because prices are fixed by municipalities. Restaurant food is the notable exception to the rule that the tourist in Turkey should bargain for everything she buys.

When choosing an authentic, out-of-the-way *lokanta,* beware eateries with cloudy water glasses on the table. Successive Turkish patrons of such establishments reuse these glasses without washing them: all they do is wipe off the rims with the colored sheets of paper provided. Although such places may serve safe and particularly cheap food, they probably will not have bottled spring water on hand. Moreover, restaurants that do serve bottled water tend to overprice it. Consequently, tourists who prefer water to soft drinks at meals should buy bottled spring water cheaply at a corner grocery store and bring it along into restaurants.

WHAT'S IN IT

An astonishing variety of simple **meat dishes** forms the heart of Turkish cuisine. Foremost among them, *kebap* means any food broiled or roasted in small pieces. Usually involving lamb or chicken, *kebap* cooking ranges from skewer (*şiş*) or spit (*döner*) broiling, to oven roasting. The result may be served on a plate or as a pocket-bread sandwich, and regional seasonings add personality. *Adana kebap* and *Urfa kebap* are spicy, the former as meatballs and the latter as stew. Originally from Bursa, the popular *İskender kebap* consists of *döner kebap* lamb strips on a mushy bed of yogurt-soaked bread pieces, topped with a tangy tomato sauce. *Kağıt* (paper) *kebap* describes a mixture of lamb and vegetables wrapped and cooked in paper, while *orman* (forest) *kebap* is a mutton and vegetable stew. Other variations on meat stew include *patlıcan kebap* (eggplant stew), *tas kebabı* (goulash), *güveç* (casserole), and *türlü* (generic, occasionally vegetarian stew). After *kebap,* the most pervasive meat form is the medallion-sized, grilled hamburger patty (*köfte*). Frequently mistranslated as "meatballs," these patties receive embellishments like embedded pine nuts (*içli köfte*). They come either skewered and roasted or served in a tomato broth, with potatoes and vegetables. Rarer forms of meat include *bonfile* (sirloin steak), *pirzola* (lamb chop), and *pastırma* (pastrami-like smoked or sun-dried beef). For the brave there are even *kokoreç*—grilled intestines with spices. *Et* is the generic word for meat: lamb is *kuzu,* beef *sığır eti,* veal *dana eti.* Chicken, usually known as *tavuk,* becomes *piliç* when roasted.

More than 8333km of coastline make Turkey's **fish** (*balık*) a specialty. The tastier, most expensive fish are *kılıç* (swordfish) and *kalkan* (turbot). From larger fish one can make a steamed dish called *buğlama.* The tastiest fish are available in early fall. In winter anchovies (*hamsi*) are made into over forty dishes, including one dessert. Turkey also offers *kalamar* (squid), *karides* (shrimp), and *midye* (mussels).

Vegetarians often choose to subsist on Turkey's wide variety of *meze* (appetizers). *İmambayıldı,* a cold concoction of split eggplant, tomatoes, onions, and olive oil, literally means "the priest fainted" (from its delicious taste). *Kabak kızartması* refers to sliced, fried squash in yogurt sauce, and *patlıcan kızartması* is the same dish with eggplant replacing the squash. Easy-to-come-by rice is *pilav. Fasulye* means beans: *(zeytinyağlı) taze fasulye* is green beans, usually in a tomato sauce, and *kuru fasulye* white beans. Unfortunately for vegetarians, the white beans often come stewed in bouillon. One cannot talk about Turkish food without mentioning *dolma*—yes, stuffed, like the taxis. They are sometimes filled with meat and rice and served hot; sometimes made without meat, cooked in olive oil, and served cold; and sometimes prepared using grape leaves rather than hollowed vegetables. *Pilaki* (a cold stew) and *piyaz* (a salad) look alike and share the cold ingredients of dried haricot beans, onions, parsley, and olive oil. *Cacık* consists of chopped cucumber in garlic-flavored yogurt. *Kısır,* a cracked wheat and vegetable salad, resembles tabouli. Shepherd's salad (*çoban salatası*), the quintessential Turkish salad, combines onions, juicy tomatoes, cucumbers, and spicy peppers. Hot sustenance for vegetarians is less plentiful but savory nevertheless. A delicious loose omelette with tomatoes and onions goes by the name of *menemen. Lahmacun* is Arab-style pizza; *pide* is a distant Turkish relative that is longer than *lahmacun*—flat bread served with your choice of eggs, meat, tomatoes, cheese, or spices. The Turkish version of nature burgers, *mercimek köfte,* are made of lentils. *Tost,* often found in fast food stands (*büfe*), can take the form of grilled cheese sandwiches. Pasta (*makarna*), is widely available in cafeterias, is often served with a hot garlic-flavored yogurt sauce. One of Turkey's richest offerings is the bounty of the fresh market (*çarşı*): nuts (*kuru yemiş*), **fruits** (*meyve*), and vegetables (*sebze*). Grapes (*üzüm*), honeydew melon (*kavun*), watermelon (*karpuz*), peaches (*şeftali*), apples (*elma*), pears (*armut*), bananas (*muz*), plums (*erik*), apricots (*kayısı*), cherries (*kiraz*), and figs (*incir*) are all easy to find.

Turkish **tea** (*çay*) claims more drinkers than famous Turkish coffee (*Türk kahvesi*). The *çay,* also known as "rabbit's blood" for its deep reddish color, is served piping hot, along with sugar, in tiny, tulip-shaped glasses. The concave shape of the glasses allows fingers to grasp the rim without getting burned. Expect to be offered free *çay* at any shop you enter. The *kahve,* drunk widely throughout Greece and the Middle East, is served in demitasse cups. You must specify a level of sweetness: *sade* (unsweetened), *orta* (medium-sweet), or *şekerli* (sweet). Impress your friends by inverting the coffee cup on its saucer when finished: the drinker's fortune may be read from the way the grounds have oozed down the cup's interior walls. Western-style decaffeinated coffee (*Nescafé*), cola, lemonade, and milk are also ubiquitous, as is *ayran,* a healthful mixture of yogurt and water, served ice cold with a pinch of salt. Bottled drinks include *meyve suyu* (fruit drink; try cherry or peach nectar); *meyveli gazoz* (a sweet soda); *su* (Turkish designer water); and *maden suyu* (carbonated mineral water, also known as *soda*). Tap water in most larger cities is safe since it is heavily chlorinated, but since this adds nothing to the taste, you might want to buy the widely available bottled water. The water from roadside springs or fountains marked *içilmez* should not be drunk even if you are parched. Food is sometimes less than clean, but squeezing lemon juice over it aids digestion. If you develop a mild stomach ailment, yogurt may replace your body's natural bacteria content. Or try the local remedy, thick Turkish coffee with very little sugar.

Alcohol, though widely available, is frowned upon in the more conservative parts of this Muslim country. Restaurants that post *içkisiz* in their windows have none, while those with *içkili* are taking special pains to announce alcohol's availability. *Bira* (beer) is popular: *Efes Pilsen* and *Tüborg* are the leading brands. The best domestic white wines are *Çankaya, Villa Doluca,* and *Kavaklıdere.* The best red wines are *Yakut* and *Kavaklıdere.* Ice-cold *rakı,* an aniseed liquor with the taste of licorice, is Turkey's national drink. Customarily mixed in equal parts with water, which clouds it, *rakı* has acquired the name "lion's milk." It's similar to Greek *ouzo,* but even stronger. İstanbul's local specialty is *balyoz* (sledge hammer, wrecking ball). Demolition is the appropriate concept here: *balyoz* consists of *rakı,* whiskey, vodka, and gin mixed with orange juice.

There's an endless array of **sweet things**—*baklava,* a flaky pastry jammed with nuts and soaked in honey; *kadayıf,* a shredded-wheat dough filled with nuts and sugar; and *helva,* a crumbly sesame and honey loaf. Of course, there's always Turkish Delight (*lokum*); and Turkish marzipan (*acıbadem kurabiyesi*) is perhaps the best in the world. Mail some home. Most restaurants serve some sort of fresh fruit or melon. *Tavuk göğsü* (chicken pudding), *sütlaç* (rice pudding), and *aşure* (fruit pudding) are all excellent. *Künefe* is a cheese dessert served hot.

But Aren't There Any Bagels?

Hotels often overcharge for traditional Turkish **breakfasts,** which are heavier than Continental breakfasts but lighter than American ones. They consist of tea or coffee, bread from a fresh oval loaf (*ekmek*), cheese (*peynir*), butter (*tereyağ*), and preserves (*reçel*) or honey (*bal*). Sometimes fresh melon (*kavun*) or a hard-boiled egg (*yumurta*) is included as well. A wholesome and even cheaper option is to visit a soup (*çorba*) kitchen, where lentil (*mercimek*) and yogurt-and-barley (*yayla*) flavors are sure to be found, and possibly tripe (*işkembe*) or sheep's trotter (*paça*) as well. A third option is to purchase your breakfast *à la carte* from a pastry shop or open-air market. But Turks don't frequent pastry shops to feast on *baklava* or *kadayıf* for breakfast. *Börek,* a flaky layered pie filled with cheese or mincemeat, has the honor of satisfying Turks' early-morning hunger. Ubiquitous street vendors hawk *simit,* sesame-coated bread rings (10-25¢) that you may think of as the Turkish equivalent of a bagel.

■■■ HOLIDAYS AND FESTIVALS

There are numerous holidays and festivals in Turkey, both religious and secular. Islamic holidays are celebrated with mosque illuminations, prayer, and special food. On national holidays, banks and offices close. The largest holidays of the year, **Şeker Bayramı** and **Kurban Bayramı** (the only religious holidays which are also public holidays), can create the biggest problems. Accommodations become impossible to find, traffic is jammed and dangerous, and prices are 30% higher. Make bus or plane reservations three weeks in advance. Remember, festivals can be *fun.*

Jan. 1: Yılbaşı. New Year's Day.

Jan. 21-March 1: Ramadan (Ramazan). A month-long Islamic holiday during which Muslims abstain from eating, drinking, smoking, and sex between dawn and sunset. Each day's fast is broken with a feast. Only one or two restaurants may be open during the day in the smaller towns and inland, and in such areas it is inappropriate to eat or drink openly during the daytime.

Feb. 28-March 1: Sugar Holiday (Şeker Bayramı). A three-day holiday celebrating the end of Ramazan, an occasion for gift-giving and sweets for children. Eating and drinking in public highly encouraged. Banks and holidays close all three days.

April 23: National Sovereignty and Children's Day (Ulusal Egemenlik ve Çocuk Bayramı). Commemorates the first meeting of the Grand National Assembly in Ankara in 1920. An international children's festival is held in Ankara.

May 1: May Day.

May 10: Festival of Sacrifice (Kurban Bayramı). The most important holiday of the year, this festival recalls Abraham's sacrificial offering of Ismael to God on Mt. Moriah. 2½ million sheep are slaughtered each year in Turkey to honor the faith and piety of Abraham. Banks and offices close for up to a week.

May 19: Youth and Sports Day.

May 27: Constitution Day.

Aug. 30: Victory Day. Anniversary of the final rout of Western invaders, 1922.

Oct. 29: Republic Day (Cumhuriyet Bayramı). Largest civil holiday commemorates Atatürk's proclamation of the Turkish Republic in 1923. Ubiquitous parades.

Nov. 10: Marks the anniversary of Atatürk's death in 1938. At 9:05am (the time of death), all of Turkey stops for a moment of national mourning; horns are blown.

istanbul

In İstanbul, east and west, old and new, rich and poor meet to create a barrage of sensory experiences. Opulent Ottoman architecture, built on an enormous scale, overlooks tiny, winding streets. Thousands of mosques sound the call to prayer five times daily (starting at 4:30am) as crowded, dusty markets filled with street merchants and peddlers sell gold, spices, aphrodisiacs, and more. The city's vast open waterways afford some of the world's most enchanting vistas, while its twisting streets lead to hole-in-the-wall cobblers and subterranean teahouses. Conservative, veiled Muslims share street space with sophisticated Euro-chic travelers. Museums contain astonishing treasures: here you can see the hand of John the Baptist, the hair of the prophet Muhammad, or treasures of art, jewelry, and gold.

HISTORY

Scholars believe that the site of modern İstanbul was settled by **Mycenaeans** as early as the 13th century BC. Evidence, however, is sparse and little more is known about the city's origins. By the 11th century BC, settlers had established various fishing villages here, one of which occupied the exact site of today's **Topkapı Palace.** It was not until the Megarian colonists from Greece landed on the Asian shore of the Bosphorus around 700 BC that the city's known history began.

Byzas, before embarking on his adventure, consulted the ambiguous and infallible Oracle at Delphi, who told him to settle "opposite the Land of the Blind." As Byzas and his crew sailed the Bosphorus, they spotted the Megarian settlement on the Asian shore at Chalcedon (now Kadıköy, one of the two centers of Asian İstanbul). A quick turn to the left, though, and they knew where their new colony would lie. Overcome by the glory of the natural harbor of the Golden Horn on the European shore, they reasoned that the people at Chalcedon must have been blind to ignore this site. This set of colonists settled here in 667 BC and Byzas' younger sister Ramona named the city **Byzantium.** During the following centuries, the city was primarily a pawn in the conflicts of innumerable city-states and empires.

A power struggle within the Roman Empire at the beginning of the 4th century determined the city's fate for the next millennium. The abdication of Diocletian in 305 AD caused a struggle for power between **Constantine,** Emperor of the West, and his rival **Licinius,** of the East. Constantine pursued his nemesis to the city (then called **Augusta Antonina**) and across the Bosphorus to Chrysopolis (Üsküdar), where he defeated Licinius in 324. Constantine consolidated his power here and declared Byzantium to be the "New Rome," capital of his empire in 330. Following the emperor's inauguration, the city came to be known as **Constantinople.**

The spread of Christianity was in large part propagated by Constantine's rise to power. The culmination of this influence is evident in the edicts of the first and second Theodosiuses, who established Christianity as the state religion (380) and forbade all pagan practices throughout the Empire (435). During the first half of the 5th century, **Theodosius II** supervised the construction of several significant edifices: a new, better-fortified set of walls around the city, and the original **Ayasofya** (St. Sofia, Agia Sophia, or the Church of the Holy Wisdom), later burned during riots.

Christianity's final defeat of paganism came in 529 when the emperor **Justinian,** probably at the behest of his religious wife, mandated the closing of all schools of pagan philosophy, including Platonic academies in Athens. Thus the **Byzantine Empire** was ushered in. During this time Christian and Greek influences joined Roman ones. A 532 insurrection (the **Nika Revolt**) by factions in the Hippodrome very nearly achieved its goals; but just as Justinian was on the verge of abdicating and fleeing, his wife convinced him that it was far nobler to stay and fight. Five days of bloodshed followed. Although victorious, Justinian faced a city in ruin; among the destroyed buildings was the Ayasofya. Justinian eventually restored the city to twice its former majesty, but frequent warring, a horrible plague, and hefty taxes devastated much of the population. When **Heraclius** gained power, not just the city but the entire empire was in shambles.

Heraclius, unfazed, set out to rebuild in 610. His success marked the beginning of the heroic **Byzantine period.** Thanks to Heraclius, the empire conquered Armenia, Syria, Egypt, Palestine, and Roman Mesopotamia, and regained its strength. **Basil II,** who reigned from 976 to 1025, watched over a second renaissance for the empire and defended it against attacks by the Arabs and the Bulgars. For his treatment of the latter, Basil earned the sobriquet "Bulgaroctonus" (Bulgar-slayer). To celebrate his final victory, Basil blinded all but ten of 10,000 survivors, and these ten he had the mercy to leave with one functioning eye. This way, they could lead all the others home. The Bulgars never again saw the need to challenge Basil.

Following Basil's death in 1025 the city was faced with numerous other troubles. The **Fourth Crusade** in 1204 resulted in yet another devastation of the city. The Crusaders, attacking from the sea walls in the Golden Horn, plundered the city and maintained control for sixty years. Venice was the lucky recipient of much of the pillaged art, and subsequently, the West began to take a fresh interest in Greek civilization. Following Latin rule, the Empire was seriously debilitated by internal crises of leadership and skirmishes with the Turks, who were steadily making territorial gains. The Byzantine decline was paired with the rise of a new power—the **Ottoman Empire**—in western Asia Minor at the beginning of the 14th century.

By 1451, when **Mehmet II,** known as *Fatih,* or "the Conqueror," came to lead the Ottomans, the Byzantine emperor controlled little besides the coveted capital city: Anatolia and most of the Balkans were already in Ottoman hands. Mehmet immediately began to orchestrate the siege of the city. A victory would not only secure the glory of the Ottoman Empire, but would also cement Mehmet's control over the noble classes. Sparing no expense, his forces finished work on two fortresses on the Bosphorus in 1452 in anticipation of the conquest. *Rumeli Hisarı* and *Anadolu Hisarı* (the Castles of Europe and of Asia respectively) stood on their corresponding sides of the Bosphorus and enabled the Ottomans to control the strategic strait. The Byzantine emperor tried to block the Golden Horn but could not foil Mehmet, who gathered all his boats at a cove and had them transported overland by rollers and slides to the other end of the Gilded Antler during the night. He soon had the unprepared Byzantine defenders in submission. For his final bombardment of the Theodosian city walls, Mehmet insisted on purchasing the largest cannon yet invented. The city fell to the Ottomans in May 1453.

The conqueror Mehmet took to rebuilding and repopulating the city promptly, transforming İstanbul into the exalted administrative, cultural, and commercial cen-

Kingdome Come

The Byzantine **Ayasofya** offered inspiration to Sinan and the Ottoman architects who preceded him. Built by the Emperor Justinian between 532 and 537 AD as the Church of the Holy Wisdom, it was distinguished by a large dome buttressed by two half-domes, and was for 900 years Constantinople's cathedral. Upon the Ottoman conquest in 1453, Mehmet the Conqueror converted the building into a mosque. So ponderous were the height and girth of Ayasofya's central dome that, upon the cathedral's completion, Justinian supposedly proclaimed, "O Solomon, I have surpassed thee!" Sultan Süleyman, whose name meant "Solomon," was well aware of his empire's classical heritage and considered Justinian's gloating a personal challenge. Sinan made Süleyman's ambition a reality. It was Sinan who from 1568 to 1574 built the **Selimiye Mosque** in Edirne, which boasts a central dome the size of Ayasofya's, supported by 8 columns, with 4 axial half-domes and a single half-dome in front. The size of the Selimiye's central dome surpassed even that of Ayasofya, and superior engineering ensured that it didn't collapse, as Ayasofya's original dome did. Thus Sinan surpassed Justinian, Süleyman surpassed Solomon, and Ottoman Classical architecture was born.

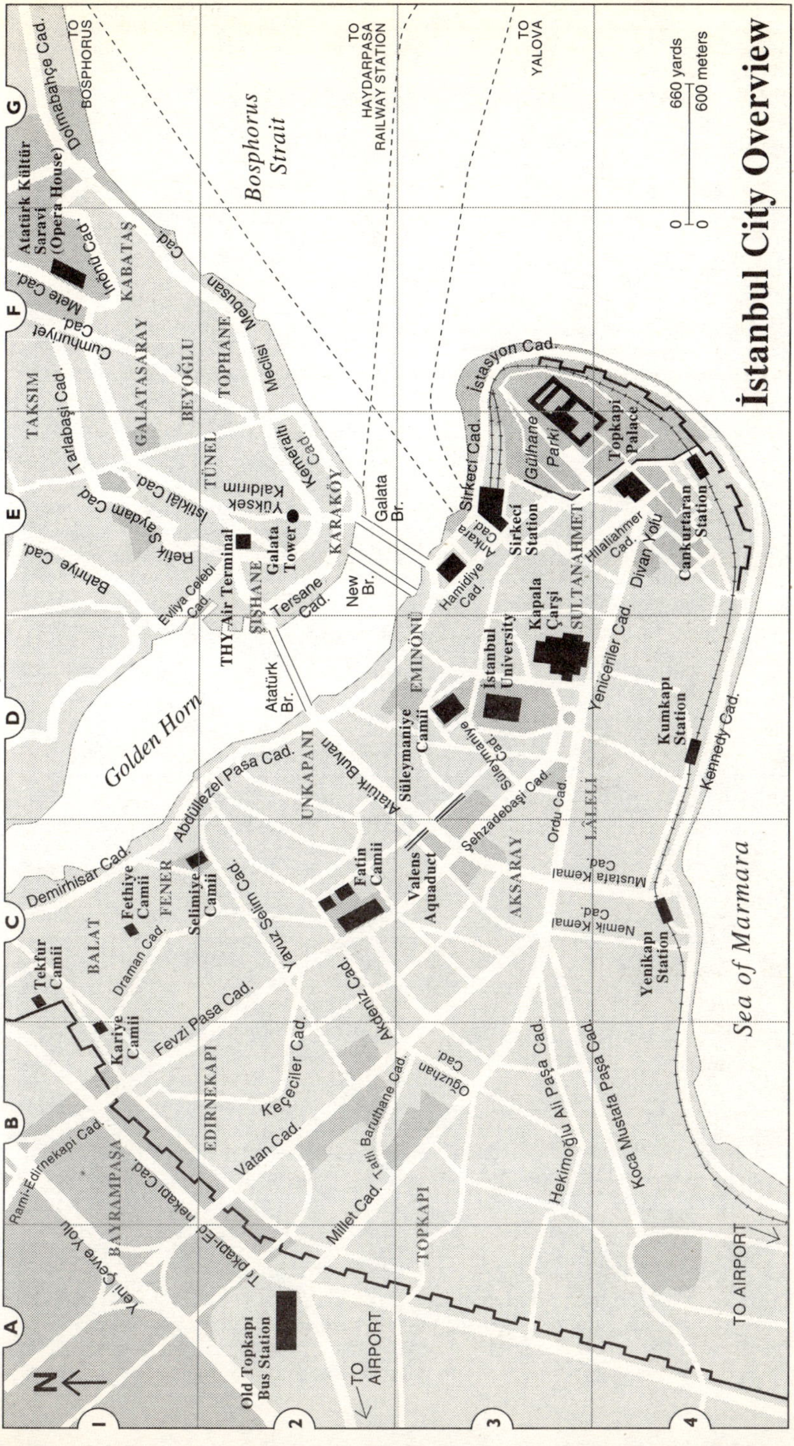
İstanbul City Overview
0
660 yards
0
600 meters
TO BOSPHORUS
TO HAYDARPAŞA RAILWAY STATION
TO YALOVA
Bosphorus Strait
Golden Horn
Sea of Marmara
TO AIRPORT
TO AIRPORT
Old Topkapı Bus Station
Atatürk Kültür Saravi (Opera House)
Dolmabahçe Cad.
İnönü Cad.
Mete Cad.
Cumhuriyet Cad.
KABATAŞ
Cad.
Mebusan
Meclisi
TAKSIM
Tarlabaşi Cad.
GALATASARAY
BEYOĞLU
TOPHANE
TÜNEL
Kemeraltı Cad.
Yüksek Kaldirim
İstiklal Cad.
Sıraselviler Cad.
Refik Saydam Cad.
Bahriye Cad.
Evliya Celebi Cad.
THY Air Terminal
Galata Tower
KARAKÖY
ŞIŞHANE
Tersane Cad.
Galata Br.
New Br.
Atatürk Br.
Sirkeci Cad.
İstasyon Cad.
Gülhane Parkı
Topkapı Palace
Ankara Cad.
Sirkeci Station
Hamidiye Cad.
EMINÖNÜ
Kapala Çarşi
SULTANAHMET
Hilaliahmer Cad.
Divan Yolu
Cankurtaran Station
Istanbul University
Süleymaniye Camii
Süleymaniye Cad.
Yeniceriler Cad.
Kumkapı Station
Kennedy Cad.
UNKAPANI
Abdülezel Paşa Cad.
Atatürk Bulvarı
Şehzadebaşi Cad.
Ordu Cad.
LÂLELI
AKSARAY
Valens Aquaduct
Fatih Camii
Mustafa Kemal Cad.
Nemik Kemal Cad.
Yenikapı Station
Demirhisar Cad.
Fethiye Camii
FENER
Selimiye Camii
BALAT
Draman Cad.
Yavuz Selim Cad.
Tekfur Camii
Kariye Camii
Fevzi Paşa Cad.
EDIRNEKAPI
Akdeniz Cad.
Keçeciler Cad.
Oğuzhan Cad.
Hekimoğlu Ali Paşa Cad.
Koca Mustafa Paşa Cad.
Vatan Cad.
Tatli Baruthane Cad.
Millet Cad.
TOPKAPI
BAYRAMPAŞA
Rami-Edirnekapı Cad.
Topkapi-Edirnekapı Cad.
Yeni Çevre Yolu
A
B
C
D
E
F
G
1
2
3
4
N

ter of his burgeoning empire. The Ottoman Empire witnessed the development of this city into an architectural treasury, best known for its collection of grand imperial mosques. With the expansion of the Ottoman Empire to Eastern Europe, the Middle East, and North Africa, a motley assemblage of people from around the world came to the "Paris of the East." By the 19th century the city's glory was fading but still tangible; the opulent and celebrated *Orient Express,* the first international luxury train, connected İstanbul to Paris.

Despite İstanbul's gloried past, it was Ankara that served as the base for Atatürk's campaign for independence. Atatürk felt the former capital was linked to too many imperial memories and dangerously vulnerable to attack by gunboats. On October 29, 1923, Ankara was officially declared capital of the Turkish Republic. Atatürk's modernization initiatives changed the color of the city, but İstanbul still exudes a confidence that is the product of 16 centuries of world prominence. In 1960 one million people inhabited the city. Today more than fifteen million people live here.

ORIENTATION AND PRACTICAL INFORMATION

İstanbul is the world's only city built on two continents: Asia and Europe. Waterways divide the city into three sections. The **Bosphorus Strait** (Boğaziçi) separates Asia from Europe, and divides İstanbul into European (west) and Asian (east) sections. The Asian side is mostly residential; historical sites, markets, mosques, and museums of the older quarters are situated on the south bank of the **Golden Horn,** an estuary which splits the European half of the city. The modern north bank contains **İstiklâl Caddesi,** the main downtown shopping street, and **Cumhuriyet Caddesi,** lined with airline offices and expensive hotels; both of these lead into **Taksim Square,** the center of the north bank. The **Sirkeci Train Station** lies just east of Eminönü, across from the tram station. Budget travelers converge in **Sultanahmet,** the area around Ayasofya, south of and up the hill from Sirkeci. The main boulevard—leading west from Sultanahmet towards the university, the Grand Bazaar, and Aksaray—changes names from Divan Yolu to Yeniçeriler Cad. to Ordu Cad. (for no other reason, it seems, than to confuse innocent visitors). Shoppers and merchants crowd the district between the **Grand Bazaar,** east of the university just north of Yeniçeriler Cad., and the less touristy **Egyptian Bazaar,** just southeast of Eminönü. The **Kumkapı** district is south of the university and Yeniçeriler Cad. The tourist office provides a free map. In the winding roads, orient yourself using landmarks.

If you come by plane, you'll arrive at either the international or the domestic terminal of **Atatürk Havaalanı** (Atatürk Airport); the two are connected by a free bus (theoretically every 20min., 6am-10pm). If arriving in the international terminal, take the "Havaş" bus to get into town (departs 10min. before the hour, every hour, 5:50am-10:50pm; $2.50). It stops at Aksaray and Şişhane. To get back, however, you can only catch the bus at Şişhane. There are a few campgrounds and one hotel nearby (see Londra Mocamp, page 439). You could also take the bus which leaves from the Domestic Departures Building, stops in Aksaray and Bakırköy, and terminates its run at the THY Airlines Terminal in Şişhane. If you're going to Sultanahmet, get off at Aksaray and take the spiffy new tram five stops along Divan Yolu to Ayasofya in Sultanahmet. When you get off in Aksaray, you'll see two main streets in front of you. Follow the one that forks to the right for roughly 5min. 'til you reach the tram tracks. Then veer right for another couple of minutes to reach the nearest station. Buy a ticket at the little white booth across the road before boarding. Trams traveling to your right, in the direction "Sirkeci," go to Sultanahmet. Public bus #96 and *dolmuş* run to town 8am until 10pm (30¢). The bus stop is on the highway in front of International Arrivals, beyond the parking lot. If you're new to İstanbul, you should use the bus unless you're a masochist who likes life complicated. (You will see how the *dolmuş*—meaning "stuffed" in Turkish—got their name, and how the buses try to outdo them in cramming people in. You'll be deposited, well, God knows where…For the true diehard budget traveler only.) Be wary of occasional rip-offs with the airport taxi service. If you do take an airport taxi, the fare should be $8-12 during the day, 50% more from midnight and 8am. Every taxi has a meter—

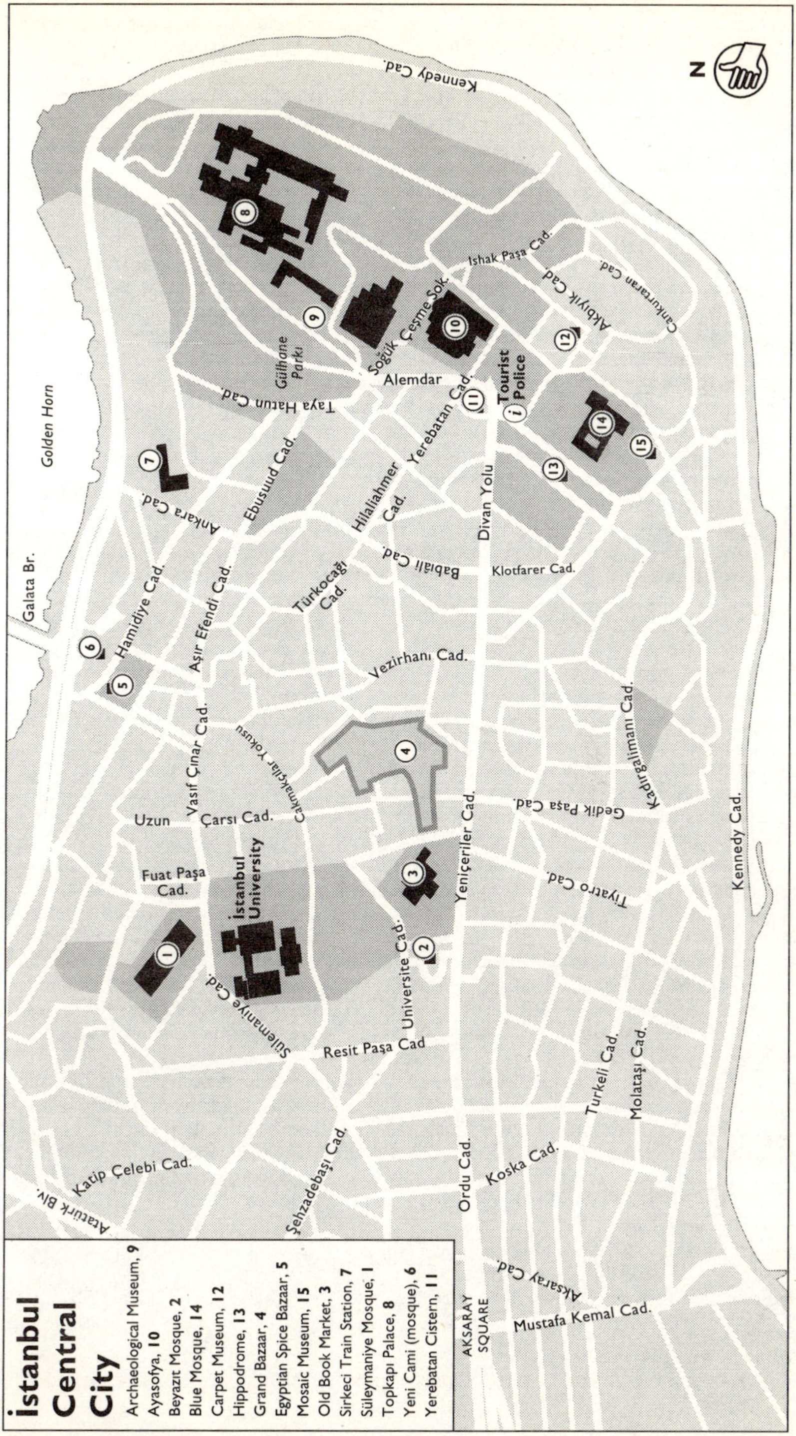
İstanbul Central City
Archaeological Museum, 9
Ayasofya, 10
Beyazıt Mosque, 2
Blue Mosque, 14
Carpet Museum, 12
Hippodrome, 13
Grand Bazaar, 4
Egyptian Spice Bazaar, 5
Mosaic Museum, 15
Old Book Market, 3
Sirkeci Train Station, 7
Süleymaniye Mosque, 1
Topkapı Palace, 8
Yeni Cami (mosque), 6
Yerebatan Cistern, 11
N
Kennedy Cad.
Golden Horn
Galata Br.
Gülhane Parkı
Soğuk Çeşme Sok.
İshak Paşa Cad.
Akbıyık Cad.
Cankurtaran Cad.
Alemdar
Taya Hatun Cad.
Yerebatan Cad.
Tourist Police
Ebusuud Cad.
Ankara Cad.
Hilaliahmer Cad.
Divan Yolu
Babıâli Cad.
Klotfarer Cad.
Türkocağı Cad.
Hamidiye Cad.
Aşır Efendi Cad.
Vezirhanı Cad.
Kadırgalimanı Cad.
Vasıf Çınar Cad.
Çakmakçılar Yokuşu
Uzun Çarsı Cad.
Gedik Paşa Cad.
Fuat Paşa Cad.
İstanbul University
Yeniçeriler Cad.
Tiyatro Cad.
Kennedy Cad.
Üniversite Cad.
Süleımaniye Cad.
Resit Paşa Cad
Turkeli Cad.
Molataşı Cad.
Şehzadebaşı Cad.
Katip Çelebi Cad.
Atatürk Blv.
Ordu Cad.
Koska Cad.
Aksaray Cad.
AKSARAY SQUARE
Mustafa Kemal Cad.

make sure they use it (*taksi meter,* pronounced the same in Turkish; see our warning under Taxis, p. 437.) The tram line to the airport is expected to be complete by late 1995; direct service to Sultanahmet 35¢.

To get to Sultanahmet from the **Sirkeci Train Station,** take the tram two stops or walk for approximately 10min., following the tracks. From the **Haydarpaşa Train Station,** take the ferry to Karaköy (6am-midnight, every 20min., 50¢); walk across the Galata Bridge (the only nearby bridge) to Eminönü, turn left, and walk for 5min. until you see the ornate Sirkeci railway station on your right. Take the tram (2 stops) from outside its entrance (on the right side of the station); buy a ticket (35¢) from the little booth before boarding. Or follow the tram tracks uphill for 10min.

The new intercity **bus terminal** in İstanbul, the **Esenler Otogar,** is several miles from the city. The **metro** (every 5min., 6am-4pm, 35¢) links it and Aksaray station, a 15min. ride away. *Otogar* is the name of the bus terminal's metro stop. From Aksaray metro station, exit, cross the main road (Adnan Menderes Blv.), enter the nearest side street, and walk into its end; the Yusufpaşa train station is in front of you. Catch the tram (direction *Sirkeci*) to Sultanahmet (6 stops, 35¢, buy ticket from the white booth before boarding). The old Topkapı bus station is closed, so beware old maps.

Buses in İstanbul are plentiful and cheap, though confusing for the newcomer. Tickets (35¢) are sold at booths at the larger bus terminals (such as Eminönü and Taksim) at kiosks marked *Planktonluk.* At busy bus stops, they may be sold by street vendors at a market—for roughly 40¢. Stock up on tickets to avoid being stranded in the suburbs without a ticket seller for miles around. Short journeys cost one ticket, longer trips cost two. Service begins at 6am and runs every 5min. or so on major routes. Buses are less frequent after dark and stop completely around 11pm. Numbers and destinations are displayed at the front. For Sultanahmet, which has no bus station of its own, the nearest buses reach Beyazıt (from the north) and Eminönü (from the south and west); both are marked accordingly. One bus leaves from Sultanahmet, however: #210, a double-decker, departs from opposite the back of the tourist office and runs up the European side of the Bosphorus to **Emirgan,** a peaceful village of old Turkish houses. (Emirgan is said to serve excellent Turkish tea.) The ride is scenic and passes several points of interest: **Ortaköy,** a young, liberal, and artsy neighborhood; **Bebek,** a wealthy residential district that includes the prestigious Bosphorus University; and **Rumeli Hisar,** one of the pair of towers that guard the north part of the Straits. (Bus departs approximately every hour, Mon.-Fri. 7am-7pm, Sat.-Sun. 11am-6pm; schedule at the tourist office; two bus tickets each way.) Buses are inevitably slowed by İstanbul's considerable traffic, so if you're not going far, walk. A free map is available from any tourist office.

A **dolmuş** (shared taxi), either a minibus or a vintage Chevrolet or Buick with fins and buffed chrome (lots from 1956), is faster than the bus and generally costs 30¢. *Dolmuş* run on fixed routes, usually between the main bus stops in each quarter (if you ask they'll let you off *en route*). **Hitchhikers** shouldn't really bother and women should *never* hitch alone. Whereas regular public transportation is quite cheap and safe, the availability of drivers is very erratic, and big-city attitudes toward tourists vary widely and dangerously.

The touristy parts of İstanbul have fast-talkers eager to unburden naïve travelers of their money. Anyone who approaches you in a "friendly" manner is trying to sell you something; genuinely friendly Turks are much less brash. Especially avoid people who offer to "help" you buy a carpet—they are helping *themselves* to a commission that can easily be as large as 30-50%. Also, do not exchange money with people on the street—they are most likely passing off fake bills. Most areas of İstanbul are relatively safe even at night, but some districts to avoid after sunset are the **Galata tower; Fatih,** west of the Süleymaniye Cami; and the back streets of **Beyoğlu,** the area north of İstiklâl Cad., a fashionable shopping area by day, but a seething red-light district by night. Women are often targets for street harassment in İstanbul, and while not necessarily "unsafe," getting around alone can be distinctly unpleasant.

Tourist Office: In **Sultanahmet,** 3 Divan Yolu (tel. 518 1802; open daily 9am-5pm), at the north end of the **Hippodrome,** across from the Sultan Pub. In **Taksim,** in the Hilton Hotel Arcade (tel. 233 0592; open Mon.-Sat. 9am-5pm), and near the French Consulate (tel. 245 6876; same hours). In the **Karaköy Maritime Station** (tel. 249 5776; same hours). In the **Sirkeci Train Station** (tel. 511 5888; open Mon.-Sat. 8:30am-5:30pm). In **Atatürk Airport** (tel. 663 0793; open 24hr.). Tourist offices supply superb country and city maps—for free!

Tourist Police: In Sultanahmet, at the beginning of Yerebatan Cad., behind the obelisk in the park across from the tourist office (24-hr. hotline tel. 527 4503 or 528 5369). Open daily 9am-6pm. Helpful. If you lose your passport, go first to your consulate to get a citizen certificate, then to the tourist police.

Travel Offices: Gençtur, 15/3 Yerebatan Cad., 2nd floor (tel. 520 5274, -5), right in the center of Sultanahmet. Very helpful. Sells ISIC ($7) and GO25 ($6), and provides a free poste restante service (holds mail for 4-5 months). Organizes workcamps in villages. Open Mon.-Fri. 9:30am-noon and 1-5pm, Sat. 9:30am-1pm. **Seventur Travel Shop,** 2-C Alemdar Cad. (tel. 512 4183). Follow the Sirkeci tram tracks; it's roughly a 1-min. walk past Ayasofya, on the right. Sells ISIC and youth ID cards, keeps luggage in the office while you look for hotels, and provides free Poste Restante service (holds mail for 1yr.). They issue reliable plane and bus tickets (some agencies have been known to sell bogus tickets). Seventur provides a shuttle to the airport ($3, midnight-6am $4). Check the schedule in the office. Open Sun.-Fri. 9am-6pm, Sat. 9am-1pm. For information on traveling to countries in the Middle East, check travel agencies on Ordu Cad. near the university, or the tourist office on Divan Yolu.

Consulates: All issue visas 10am-noon. **U.S.,** 104-108 Meşrutiyet Cad., Tepebaşı (tel. 251 3602). **U.K.,** 34 Meşrutiyet Cad., Beyoğlu/Tepebaşı (tel. 293 7545). **Ireland** (honorary), Cumhuriyet Cad., Mobil Altı, Elmadağ (tel. 246 6025). **Australia,** 58 Tepecik Yolu, Etiler (tel. 257 7050, -1). **Canada,** 107/3 Büyükdere Cad., Gayrettepe (tel. 272 5174). **New Zealand** nationals should get in touch with the embassy in Ankara, at 24/1 Kız Kulesi Sok. (tel. (312) 445 0556). **South Africa,** 106 Büyükdere Cad., Esentepe (tel. 275 4793). **Bulgaria,** 44 Zincirlikuyu Cad., Ulus/Etiler (tel. 269 2216). **Egypt,** 173 Cevatpaşa Cad., Bebek (tel. 263 6030). **Iran,** 1 Ankara Cad., Cağaloğlu (tel. 513 8230, -1). **Jordan,** 119/2 Kalıpçı Sok., Daire 6, Teşvikiye (tel. 230 1221, -2). **Pakistan,** 11 Abide-i Hürriyet Cad., Şişli (tel. 233 5800, -1). **Syria,** Silâhhane Cad., Ralli Apt. #59, Teşvikiye (tel. 232 7110).

Banks: Currency exchange counters open Mon.-Fri. 8:30am-noon and 1:30-5pm. Most don't charge a commission. The exchange booths at the Yeşilköy Airport and the main post office are open 8:30am-8pm. There is a very convenient **ATM** in Sultanahmet, in a little booth opposite the entrance to Ayasofya. There is also one in the international arrivals building at the airport, and three at the entrance to Sirkeci railway station.

American Express: Their headquarters at 57 Abdi İpekçi Cad., 4th floor, is not open to individual card/checkholders, but they do field corporate inquiries and maintain a customer service hotline for lost or stolen cards/traveler's checks (tel. 232 9556, -7 or -8). Individuals should deal directly with agents. **Türk Express,** 91 Cumhuriyet Cad., 2nd floor (tel. 230 1515), up the hill from Taksim Sq. They handle lost checks and cards as well as other business related to American Express. (Open Mon.-Fri. 9am-noon and 1-6pm.) Their office in the **Hilton Hotel lobby,** Cumhuriyet Cad. (tel. 241 0248), deals with lost cards only when Türk Express is closed. (Open daily 8:30am-8pm.) The above offices do not give cash advances or accept wired money; Turkish law requires that this be done through a bank. American Express's agent is **Koç Bank,** 233 Cumhuriyet Cad. Money is wired here without a fee if you accept Turkish *lira;* 1% fee for other currencies. To get a cash advance on your American Express card, you must have a personal check or know your account number and the address of your bank. (Open Mon.-Fri. 8:45am-12:30pm and 1:30-4:30pm; cardholder services until 4pm). Lost traveler's checks are replaced within 24 hr.; they are sent by courier to the customer's hotel. Cards are replaced within the same time frame. Cardholders can use Akbank ATMs all over Turkey for cash advances.

PTT: İstanbul has more than 100 post offices. The most convenient for those staying in Sultanahmet is the little booth opposite the entrance to Ayasofya, which sells stamps; English spoken. The main branch is at 25 Büyük Postane Sok. Count your change carefully here. Stamp, telegram, and currency exchange services open 8:30am-8pm. All PTTs accept packages; if a customs officer is not present, you will be directed to the **Kadıköy, Beyazıt,** or **Tophane** (on Rıhtım Cad.) offices. Packages more than 2kg can be mailed from the **packet service** on the back side of the main PTT. (Open Mon.-Sat. 8:30am-12:30pm and 1:30-5pm.) The branch just off the west end of Taksim Sq. on Cumhuriyet Cad. is efficient for mailing packages or making long-distance calls. (Open Mon.-Fri. 8am-8pm, Sat. 8am-6pm.) There is a 24-hr. international telephone office in the building, but it does not arrange collect (reverse-charge) calls. (For more info on making collect calls, see Keeping in Touch on page 417.) Pay phones are scattered throughout the city; **international calls** can be made from all. **Telephone Codes** are 212 (European side) and 216 (Asian side); required between sides of the Bosphorus.

Flights: Atatürk Airport is 30km from the city. It has a terminal for domestic flights and one for international flights, roughly 800m apart, connected by bus (every 20min., 6am-10pm). Take a *Havaş* bus from either terminal to the city (10min. before the hr., 5:50am-10:50pm; 30min.; $2.50). The bus stops at Aksaray, where you can catch the tram to Sultanahmet, and at Şişhane. The tram connection from the airport to downtown is expected to be operating by late 1995; this will take you directly to Sultanahmet for 35¢. Be wary of the airport taxis (see warning under Taxis, p. 437).

Trains: Haydarpaşa Station (high-DAHR-pah-shah), on the Asian side (tel. (216) 336 0475, -2063). A convenient ferry connects the station to Karaköy pier #7, on the European side (every 20min. roughly 6am-midnight; schedule posted on the pier; 50¢). The pier is halfway between the Galata Bridge and the Karaköy tourist office, where rail tickets for Anatolia can be purchased in advance at the **TCDD** (Turkish Republic State Railway) office upstairs. The office accepts couchette (*kuşet*) reservations for Ankara (2 days in advance if possible—see Ankara, p. 520). Tickets are also available at Sirkeci station. Trains also service Edirne (2 per day, $3). Europe-bound trains leave from **Sirkeci Station** (seer-KAY-jee; tel. 527 0050, -1), in Eminönü (downhill toward the Golden Horn from Sultanahmet). To Sofia, Bulgaria (2 per day, $33), Athens (1 per day, $64), and Munich, Germany (1 per day, $221). Call ahead to verify these schedules; do not rely simply on this listing, as schedules change often and without warning.

Buses: Intercity buses leave from the new **Esenler Otobüs Terminalı** (*otogar*) in Esenler, several miles from downtown. To get there from Sultanahmet, take the tram 6 stops to **Yusufpaşa** (one stop beyond Aksaray). Before pulling in to Yusufpaşa station, you will pass an overhead motorway bridge; just past it, on your right, is the broad Adnan Menderes Blv., which contains **Aksaray Metro station** (roughly a 1-min. walk from Yusufpaşa train station). Take the metro to *Otogar* (15min., 35¢); you will be deposited in the middle of a huge hexagonal structure. There are 168 offices here, serving destinations as diverse as Mecca, Munich, Bucharest, and Amman. Hundreds—maybe thousands—of buses leave here daily for virtually every point in Turkey. All bus companies should have offices at the *otogar;* they may also have offices in Sultanahmet. The following are reputable: **Varan Tours** (tel. 658 0277) is Turkey's most well-known and is licensed to operate throughout Western Europe; **Ulusoy** (tel. 658 3000) serves Athens and other points in Greece, as well as domestic destinations; **Kamıl Koç** (tel. 658 2000), **Pamukkale** (tel. 658 2222), and **Çanakkale Seyahat** (tel. 658 3640, -1) are also recommended. Most bus companies are authorized to go to Eastern Europe. Unlicensed companies have been known to offer substantial discounts for Western European destinations and then abandon their passengers in Eastern Europe. Frequent buses to Ankara (8hr., $12), Bursa (4hr., $8.25), İzmir (9hr., $14), Bodrum (13hr., $23), and Trabzon (14hr., $24). European services include Athens (2 per week, $62) and Vienna (1 per week, $116). A station across the Bosphorus in **Harem**—accessible by ferry from **Karaköy**—serves Asia.

Ferries (National and International): Turkish Maritime Lines has offices near Pier 7 at Karaköy, just west of the Haydarpaşa ferry terminal: it's the building with blue awnings marked *Denizcilik İşletmeleri.* They sail to İzmir (1 per week, 5:30pm, 21hr., $10-26), Bandırma (4 per week, 9am, 5hr., $6), and Trabzon (1 per week, June-Sept. 2pm, arrives Wed., $17-33). From Bandırma there are connecting trains to İzmir (11hr. total; buy combination boat-train ticket at Sirkeci station). Ferries to Trabzon (and intervening points on the Black Sea coast) depart from Sarayburnu; exiting Sirkeci station, walk for roughly 5min. to the right along the waterfront. These times, prices, and departure points change regularly; confirm them with Turkish Maritime Lines. Although not from İstanbul, Turkish Maritime Lines also serves Venice and North Cyprus. For these longer trips make reservations as far in advance as possible.

Ferries (Local): Ferries constitute a major part of İstanbul's public transport system, and are a sublimely pleasant way to get around. Note that some of the ferries to the north shore of the Golden Horn are commuter ferries; since these leave in the morning and return in the evening, taking an evening ferry out could strand you. The following depart from the Sirkeci area, where piers are clustered around the Galata Bridge. Destinations are written on each pier. Pier 1 serves Üsküdar (every 20min., 6:30am-11pm), Pier 2 serves Kadıköy (every 20min., 7:30am-9pm, 35¢), and Pier 3 sends out separate cruises along the Bosphorus ($4 round-trip) and to the Princes Islands. From Pier 4, the fast, comfortable seabus departs for Kadıköy (roughly every hr., 8am-5pm, 70¢). Pier 5 serves Adalar; Pier 6 Bağlat (past the Galata Bridge). Pier 7, in Kadıköy across the Galata Bridge, serves Haydarpaşa railway station (across the Galata Bridge; every 20min., 6am-midnight). Timetables are posted at each terminal. Buy a *jeton* (token) and insert it in the turnstile to board. Numerous other ferries connect the various İstanbul suburbs. For full details, buy the seasonal timetable *(feribot tarifesi;* 60¢), available at each pier. The seabus timetable is not for sale, but is posted at the seabus terminal.

Taxis: Plentiful in İstanbul. Use of meters is imperative—make sure it's on and don't pay more than it says. (*Taksi meter* is pronounced the same in Turkish.) *Gündüz Tarifesi,* or one light, on the meter indicates the day rate. Two lights indicate the night rate. The night rate, in effect from midnight to 8am, is 50% higher. The starting rate is 35¢ (53¢ after midnight), which rises by 9¢ (13¢) every 200m; waiting time costs 4¢ (6¢) per minute after the first 5 minutes, which are free. Although hailing a taxi on the street is generally reliable, do not take taxis from drivers who approach you in Sultanahmet. Also avoid taxis waiting at the airport. Drivers seldom speak English; if you don't speak Turkish, have your destination written down.

International Bookstores: Aypa Bookstore, 19 Mimar Mehmet Ağa Cad. (tel. 517 4492), behind the Blue Mosque. English and German spoken. (Open daily 6:30am-8pm, winter 7am-7pm.) **İstanbul Kitabığı,** 5 Kabusakal Cad. (tel. 517 6782), up the street from Aypa, has books on İstanbul and Turkey, magazines, and coffee-table books. Also has books in French. Open daily 9am-6:30pm, winter 9am-5pm. **Robinson Crusoe 389,** 389 İstiklâl Cad. (tel. 293 6968, -77; open daily 9am-8pm) is tasteful and upscale, selling books in English, French, and German. **Haşat,** also on İstiklâl Cad., sells magazines and foreign newspapers, including the *New York Times* Sunday edition ($14).

Laundromats: Star Laundry, 18 Akbıyık Cad., next to Star Pension, across from Orient Youth Hostel. Wash and dry $1.25 per kg, minimum 2kg. English-speaking. Open daily 8am-10pm. **Hobby Laundry,** 6/1 Caferiye Sok., part of Yücelt Hostel building. $2 per kg, minimum 2kg. Open daily 9am-6pm. The **Hotel Ema** does laundry for its guests, $2.50 per kg.

Hospitals: American Hospital, Admiral Bristol Hastanesi, Güzelbahçe Sok., Nişantaşı (tel. 231 4050). **German Hospital,** 119 Sıraselaver Cad., Taksim (tel. 293 2150). The German Hospital is more convenient to Sultanahmet. **International Hospital,** 82 İstanbul Cad., Yeşilköy (tel. 574 7801, -2). The International Hospital may soon move to Yeşilyurt (tel. 663 3000). The above are private hospitals, which generally provide a higher standard of care than public ones. Payment with cash or a credit card is expected at the time of treatment.

ACCOMMODATIONS

İstanbul's budget accommodations are concentrated in the **Sultanahmet** district, just steps away from the city's most awe-inspiring sights. Budget prices range from $4 for a cheap single or dorm bed to $20-30 at the middle price range. The side streets around **Sirkeci** railway station provide numerous singles and doubles in the $5-10 range; these are patronized mainly by working-class Turks. **Aksaray** offers dozens of hotels, in every conceivable price range. Its streets are packed with Bulgarian and Romanian businesspeople, who often outnumber the Turks. The Aksaray area resembles an open-air bazaar: merchants, shoppers, and diners at open-air restaurants compete for space in a chaotic and fascinating scene. Watch Bulgarians load several times their bodyweight in merchandise onto ancient buses, to be sold for vast profits in Eastern Europe. Prostitution is on the rise here due to an influx of sex-workers (known as "Natashas") from Romania and the former Soviet republics. A male may receive a knock on his door from a madam; females may be mistaken for prostitutes. The **Taksim** district is home to many of the city's five-star hotels and a smattering of budget lodgings. All of *Let's Go's* recommendations are in Sultanahmet, due to its beauty and convenience. The following are short walks from the Sultanahmet tram stop. Rates rise by roughly 20% in July and August.

Hostels

Yücelt Hostel (HI), 6/1 Caferiye Cad. (tel. 513 6150, -1; fax 512 7628), in the little alley at the left of Ayasofya mosque when you face the mosque's gate. To reach Ayasofya from the Sultanahmet tram stop, follow the tracks downhill toward Sirkeci for a couple of minutes; Ayasofya is the huge, red-tinted mosque on your right. A great place to meet travelers. Attached self-service cafeteria has an impressively loud stereo, played at pre-announced parties. Yücelt is one of only 2 Turkish hostels accredited by HI. Its quiet, picturesque location, clean rooms, and helpful staff make it easy to see why. Free luggage deposit. International telephone. Laundry $1.50 per kg. Transport to airport available. 6-8 person dorm room $4.50, 3-4 person room $5. Doubles $6 per person. Roof $3. Showers included (7:30-10am and 6-9pm). In summer, try to reserve rooms one week in advance. May soon have e-mail.

Orient Youth Hostel, 13 Akbıyık Cad. (tel. 517 9493; fax 518 3894). Near Topkapı Palace. Clean, comfortable, has a cool roof terrace with a small cafeteria. Travel agency, luggage room, and safe on premises. Free bellydancing weekly in summer, every two weeks in winter. Hot water 7am-noon, 5pm-midnight. Doubles, some with balcony, $8. Dorm beds $3. Roof $2 in summer. Laundry service across the street. Orient and the Backpacker's Underground Café are a great source of travel wisdom. Breakfast $1.

Hanedan Hostel, Akbıyık Cad., 3 Adliye Sok. (tel. 516 4869). Friendly, caring management. Pleasant view from terrace. Beautiful cafeteria. An extremely comfortable place to stay. Currency exchange. 24-hr. airport transport available. 24-hr. hot water. Doubles $10, $17.50 w/shower. Dorm beds $4. Roof $2.50. Breakfast $1. Laundry 50¢ per kilo, sun-dried.

Konyalı Youth Hostel, Akbıyık Cad., 15/2 Terbıyık (tel. 518 9468, -8418). Around the corner from Hanedan. Truly budget accommodations. 24-hr. hot water. Doubles $10. Dorm beds $2, $3 w/shower. Roof space also available. Laundry $1 per kilo. Like most other hostels, has travel services (tickets, bus, airport).

Hotels

Hotel Anadolu, Yerebatan Cad. 3 Salkım Söğüt Sok. (tel. 512 1035 or 513 8084). To get to Salkım Söğüt Sok. from the Sultanahmet tram, walk roughly 50m along the tram tracks towards Sirkeci; take a left at the major intersection (Yerebatan Cad.); Salkım Söğüt Sok. will be the first right, roughly 20m up the street. A budget classic. Rudimentary, well-kept rooms, a few with tiny balcony; impressive view of Ayasofya from some. Small terrace outside front door where drinks are served and backgammon played. No water in rooms. Hot and cold showers. Singles $4, doubles $6, triples $9.

Sultan Turist Otel, 3 Terbıyık Sok. (tel. 516 9260; fax 517 1626). Around the corner from Orient Hostel. Turkish pensions don't get any better than the newly-opened Sultan. Immaculate, highly professional, and yet as friendly as any mom and pop establishment. Great views of the Bosphorus from roof restaurant/bar. Meals roughly $3.50 each. Huge TV and VCR with cable in common room, ping-pong, and in-house travel office. Singles $15.75, doubles $20.25, triples $23.50.

Hotel Ema, 18 Salkım Söğüt Sok. (tel. 511 7166 or 512 1463). On the same street as the Hotel Anadolu. A good bet. Very clean; rooftop terrace is a good place to meet other travelers and has impressive views of Ayasofya, Topkapı Palace, and the river; cheap drinks are served here 'til midnight. Management speaks English and French. Dark singles $20, large doubles w/shower and bath $25, triples $35, quads $45. Breakfast included—pay $2.50 less if you opt not to take it. Mastercard and Visa accepted.

Hotel Elit, 14 Salkım Söğüt Sok. (tel. 512 7566 or 526 2549). A couple of doors down from and associated with the Ema, but a bit more basic; dorm beds $4.50, doubles $20, triples $25; shower and toilet included. Free tea. Breakfast, served on the terrace of the Hotel Ema, costs $2.50 extra.

Near the tram stop park is a cluster of roughly 3 parallel streets and a dozen alleys. The following hotels are all located in this area.

Barut's Guest House, 8 Işakpaşa Cad. (tel. 516 0357, -5256). Pleasant, hip little joint (owned by an artist). Lovely terrace overlooking one of İstanbul's oldest mosques (built in 1553) and the Sea of Marmara. Singles $35, doubles $40, triples $50; breakfast included. 10% discount for students.

Alp Guesthouse, Akbıyık Cad. 4 Adliye Sok. (tel. 517 9570 or 518 5728). Yodel on into this family-run guest house with large, spotless rooms, some with excellent views. Mediterranean-style ambience and a friendly, helpful owner. Superb view of the Sea of Marmara and the Asian side of İstanbul from the terrace; occasional barbecues are held here, and drinks are served until 11pm. Singles $35, doubles $40; breakfast $5 extra. All rooms w/shower and bath.

Hotel Side Pension, 20 Utangaç Sok. (tel. 517 6590). A fairly basic little pension, but the third floor walls are lined with beautiful, Ottoman-style tiles. Singles $15, doubles $20 (w/bath). Singles also available for $6.

Ottoman Guest House, Cankurtaran Mah. 6 Tevkifhane Sok. (tel. 518 0790, -2). Take Tevkifhane Sok. across the little park between Ayasofya and the Blue Mosque. Comfortable, very clean, with new furniture and a pleasant terrace. Singles $15, doubles $20, large quad $40; clean shared bath. Bargain for breakfast at no extra cost. Visa and Mastercard accepted.

Hotel Park, Cankurtaran Mah. 26 Utangaç Sok. (tel. 517 6596). A modern hotel in the heart of Sultanahmet. Clean and comfortable—carpets sold in the foyer. Singles $20, w/shower $25; doubles $25, w/shower $40; breakfast included. Mastercard and Visa accepted.

Star Pansiyon, 18 Yeni Akbıyık Cad. (tel. 638 2308). Opposite Orient Youth Hostel. Spartan, no frills. Popular among backpackers. Doubles w/shower $14, roof mattress $2.50.

Yusuf Guest House, 3 Kutlungün Sok. (tel. 516 6878), opposite the Old Prison, toward Topkapı Palace. Basic but clean. Some rooms with showers. Helpful, young management. Dorm beds $4.75, singles $7, doubles $11.

Camping

Londra Mocamp (tel. 560 4200), 1km from the airport, along the noisy and nerve-grating highway to İstanbul. No bus stop; take a taxi. Includes cafeteria, bar, pool, and showers. $3 per person, $2.75 per tent. Two-person bungalows $15.

FOOD

İstanbul's budget dining options are superb. From the sandwich stands in the streets to the elegant seafood restaurants on the Bosphorus, you can expect high quality, kaleidoscopic variety, and reasonable prices. While Sultanahmet may be the best place to stay, it's not the premier eating locale—you'll fare much better in the

Kumkapı district, south of the Grand Bazaar and justly famed for its seafood; or in **Beyoğlu,** where a wide variety of eating establishments awaits around İstiklâl Cad. Besides these clusters, excellent restaurants are scattered all over this city. **Gengelköy** is known for its simple fish restaurants; **Kaanica** is reputed to have the most delicious yogurt in İstanbul; **Ortaköy** has great restaurants with views of the Bosphorus. Some of İstanbul's top restaurants are scattered along the Bosphorus straits, on both the European and Asian sides. Bus #210, a double-decker (hourly 9am-6pm), runs along the European side of the Bosphorus and stops at Gengelköy and Kaanica. For natural diets, two **open-air markets** are centrally located: a general one next to Çiçek Pasajı, in Beyoğlu, and a fruit market next to the *Mısır Çarşısı* (Egyptian Spice Bazaar). The **Egyptian Spice Bazaar** itself sells an astonishing and mouth-watering collection of oriental sweets. For a quick stand-up lunch, the myriad *kebapçı* and *köfteci* will easily fill you up for less than $3. Stop at a *büfe* (snack shop) for *tost* and a soft drink, both for less than $1. Even a complete meal at a cheaper *lokanta* shouldn't run you more than $3.50. But be sure to do most of your eating in İstanbul's restaurants—otherwise you'll miss out on the great cuisine.

Sultanahmet Area

Tourists fill the restaurants of Sultanahmet; many of these places serve bland, international-style food or relatively tasteless Turkish fare in a cafeteria setting. But there are a few exceptions.

Cennet (Heaven), 90 Divan Yolu (tel. 513 1416). On the right as you walk along Divan Yolu from Sultanahmet towards Aksaray, 5min. from the Sultanahmet tram. Specializes in one dish—*gözleme* (Anatolian pancakes). Cheap and delicious. Try the *gözleme mantı* (pancakes stuffed with white cheese, meat, and vegetables in a yogurt sauce; $1.75). The food is cooked in the middle of the restaurant over an open stove by women dressed in traditional peasant clothing. The decor is Turkish, and musicians play at night (when *fes* hats are handed out to all). At peak eating times the place gets overrun with tourists; you may prefer to come when it's quieter. Open 10am-midnight.

Türkistan Aşevi, 36 Tavukhane Sok. (tel. 638 6525, -6). Serves specialties from the Turkish-speaking former Soviet Republic of Turkestan; the food is similar to Turkish. The decor here is exquisite—beautiful Turkish carpets line the floor and walls of this magnificently restored 18th-century Ottoman house. You must take your shoes off on entry, and no alcohol is served. Specialties include *Turkestan manta* (mincemeat cooked in steamed dough), *samsa* (meat wrapped in oven-cooked dough), and yogurt soup, each $1.75. But the best value is the seven-course lunch for $11 or eight-course dinner for $15.

Pandeli Restaurant, 1 Egyptian Spice Bazaar (tel. 522 5534 or 527 3909), a 15-min. walk from Sultanahmet. The Egyptian Spice Bazaar is the little 3-domed, 3-arched structure beside the Mosque, facing the Galata Bridge in Eminönü. Walk through the main archway, then turn 180 degrees; the entrance is on your right. This tile-covered restaurant has been an İstanbul institution for decades. Serves lunch only. Main courses are $5-7, starters $2.50. Try the vine leaves stuffed with rice, or the *yoğurtlu kebap*. Open Mon.-Sat. noon-3pm.

Dârüzziyâfe, 6 Şifahane Cad. (tel. 511 8414, -5). Located in the Süleymaniye Mosque complex designed by Sinan in the 1550s as the mosque's soup kitchen for the poor, as part of the celebration of the centenary of the Muslim conquest of İstanbul. It later became an Ottoman banquet hall, and was converted into a Turkish restaurant in the 1990s. The architecture, which includes a magnificent courtyard, is a sight in itself. A good range of Turkish fare is served. Main courses: $4.50-6. But be warned: tour groups come here. Come between 3-6pm, outside peak hours; open noon-11pm. No alcohol: it's part of a mosque. Beside it is the **İkram Bahçesi,** a Turkish tea garden.

House of Medusa Restaurant, Yerebatan Cad. 19 Muhteremefendi Sok. (tel. 511 4116). Despite the address, this place conveniently fronts onto Yerebatan Cad. Behind a tacky, touristy exterior is a restaurant which serves excellent Turkish cuisine. The stuffed green pepper ($2) and Turkish omelette ($2) should not be missed. *Kebap* ($5-6) are not their strongest point. Good pudding ($2.50). Popular among Turks and tourists alike.

Sultanahmet Köftecisi, 12 Divan Yolu (tel. 511 3960), opposite the tourist office. Catering to locals, this is a real İstanbul eatery. Meatballs ($1.75) are its specialty, as the name suggests. Open daily 11am-midnight. A similar place with the same name operates at 4 Divan Yolu.

Backpacker's Underground Café, opposite the Orient Youth Hostel. The place to meet other backpackers, or grab a beer (80¢) or snack. The atmosphere is, at times, reminiscent of the 60s hippie trail.

Kumkapı Area

Kumkapı is a pleasant square with narrow cobblestone streets extending radially outward. The square and the streets are lined with fish restaurants—there is nothing else here—making the area look like one giant restaurant. Kumkapı is justifiably famous for its seafood. Prices are expensive by İstanbul standards (main courses run $8-12), but it's worth coming here at least once. From the Grand Bazaar, cross Divan Yolu and walk for roughly 5min. down the narrow Tiyatro Cad. to the square. Just before you enter the square, there is a map showing the location of all restaurants. One commendable choice is the **Yengeç Restaurant,** 6 Telli Odalar Sok. (tel. 516 3227); turn right off the square, then right again. Fried and grilled main courses $10-12. Restaurant staff will beckon you into their establishments. This annoying habit doesn't reflect the quality of the food—even the best restaurants do this.

İstiklâl Caddesi

İstiklâl Caddesi is a rather narrow, European-style boulevard, a fashionable street of somewhat faded glory. It is lined with smart boutiques, coffee shops, and foreign language bookshops; and crowded with wealthy shoppers, workers, students—the whole kaleidoscope of İstanbul life. Several major consulates are located here, as well as the city's Catholic cathedral. A 1915 San Francisco tram runs down the middle (from the Tünel station to Taksim Sq., every 10min., 20¢). This district is a center for eating out, and at night it metamorphoses into İstanbul's main nightlife (and red light) area (see warning, p. 441). Roughly halfway between the Tünel and Taksim (on the left as you walk toward Taksim) is the famed **Çiçek Pasajı** (Flower Passage), lined with cheap but classy restaurants. The clientele is mostly Turkish—a good place to escape the tourist hordes. **Huzur Restaurant** (tel. 293 7129; open daily noon-11pm), at the back of the passage, is typical. Main courses cost roughly $3, salads $1.75-2. Their lamb casserole is a delicious stew made of lamb, white cheese, and green peppers—worth dying for (well, killing for at least). At the far end of the fruit market next door is the imposing café **Cumhuriyet Meyhanesi** (Republic Pub), where intellectuals and would-be intellectuals gather in the evenings to eat, drink *rakı,* and solve the world's problems. They claim Atatürk was a regular here: his consumption of strong *rakı* in the upstairs part undoubtedly played a role in his early demise from liver cancer. (Open daily noon-11pm, possibly later.) Delicious coffee in a Euro-Turkish ambience is served in **Café Gramafon,** 3 Tünel Meydanı, to your immediate left as you come out of the Tünel station. (Turkish coffee $1.25, Irish coffee $3, cappuccino $2.) To get to İstiklâl Cad. from Sultanahmet, follow the tram lines to Sirkeci, take a left and follow the water, cross the Galata Bridge (the first bridge you'll see), take a left onto the first major thoroughfare; the Tünel station is then on your immediate right. The Tünel is the world's oldest and shortest subway and will take you to İstiklâl Cad. (every 5min., 8am-9pm, 20¢). From the Tünel it is a 15-min. uphill hike via narrow, confusing streets.

ENTERTAINMENT

A large part of the nightlife in İstanbul consists of excellent restaurants or coffeehouses. West European-style nightlife—bars and nightclubs—is concentrated in the Taksim district, where the action starts at midnight and rages 'til dawn.

Do not club-hop here in a haphazard manner. Some clubs are reputable, but some are run by hustlers who have links with the nearby red light district. The hustlers will charge a lot—perhaps everything you've got—for a single drink. In one well-known scam, a couple of girls sit at your table and order drinks. You get hit for an exorbitant bill even if you haven't ordered anything. The demand for payment is likely to be backed up with an impressive and frightening display of muscle. If you don't have enough money with you, they will take you back to your hotel and take it from your room. Go to clubs which have been specifically recommended, either by *Let's Go* or by trustworthy locals.

The nightclubs are located on İstiklâl Cad., Sıraselviler Cad. (the other main street which runs from Taksim Sq. to the Bosphorus), or in the little side streets which run off them; and all are at the Taksim end. Be sure to try the local specialty, **balyoz** (sledge hammer, wrecking ball). Demolition is the appropriate concept here: *balyoz* consists of *rakı,* whiskey, vodka, and gin mixed with orange juice. Have one, and the next day, you'll feel like you've been poisoned—for, in fact, you have been. **Kemançı** (Violinist), on Sıraselviler Cad., on the left roughly a 1-min. walk from Taksim, is a wild and loud rock bar that frequently hosts live bands. Long hair and tattoos rule. ($4.75 cover charge on weekends includes one drink; *rakı* and beer $2.50.) This is an excellent place to try *balyoz* (4.75). The **Jazz Stop,** on Büyükparmaklıapı, an alley off İstiklâl Cad., to the left, a 2-min. walk from Taksim, offers mellow live music and a sedate, painfully hip crowd (drinks $2.50; no cover charge). The **Yaga Bar,** nearby, is a beautiful pub; no live music, but very 90s. It's on an alley off İstiklâl, a 2-min. walk from Taksim, to the right. The **Carnival Pub,** in the fruit market beside the Flower Passage, is a long, loud, cavernous bar where heavy metal and punk bands play. With the exception of the Carnival Pub, you'll need to be pretty snazzy yourself to get into the above places, so dress up—many get refused. Usually, you'll be the only tourist here. Young Turks also hang out in **Ortaköy** (ferry #22E, 22B, or 25 from Eminönü). At night the bars offer a respite from the tourist-choked thoroughfares of Sultanahmet. You may want to see **bellydancing,** but you'll pay for it—$50 per show, including dinner, is the standard rate. Inquire at the tourist office; locations and names change often.

For a truly authentic **Turkish bath,** it is best to go to the nearby cities of Edirne and Bursa. İstanbul baths, however, can provide a reprieve for the down and dirty. The much-publicized **Cağaloğlu Hamamı** (tel. 522 2424), in Sultanahmet on Yerebatan Cad., is fancy; but avoid it if you are even a little claustrophobic. It now charges between $10 and $20 depending on how much rubbing you want (open daily 8am-10pm). Also try İstanbul's other well-known *hamam,* **Çemberlitaş Bath,** 8 Vezirhanı Cad. (tel. 522 7974), off Divan Yolu. A bath and massage is $10. (Open daily 6am-midnight.) Before indulging in baths, female travelers should know that this Turkish tradition, like many others, is male-oriented—most *hamam* have lesser facilities for women.

SIGHTS

İstanbul's incomparable array of world-famous churches, mosques, palaces, and museums can keep an ardent sightseer busy for weeks. Five or six days of leg-work, however, should be enough to acquaint you with the premier sights. A FIYTO card allows you to enter the major museums for free; ISIC card gets you in for half price.

The **Ayasofya** was built by the Emperor Justinian between 532 and 537 AD. Upstart plebeians destroyed the original building during the Nika Revolt; Justinian undertook construction of a new and improved church in order to cement imperial authority. Converted into a mosque after the Ottoman invasion in 1453, in 1935 it was made a museum by Atatürk. The architecture originally reflected the class structure of Church services. Only the Patriarch was allowed to enter through the center doors. The side galleries separated less perfect souls from the emperor. The Ottomans opened the side galleries, thereby emphasizing the equality of all Muslims in the sight of God. An elaborate marble square in the floor by the altar marks the spot where Byzantine emperors were once crowned. Walk up the stone ramp on the left to the upstairs gallery to observe the remains of the famous wall mosaics of Christ and the archangel Gabriel. (Open Tues.-Sun. 9:30am-5pm. Gallery open Tues.-Sun. 9:30am-noon and 1-4pm; admission $5.25, students $2.75.)

Sultan Ahmet I built the **Blue Mosque** (*Sultanahmet Camii,* or the Mosque of Sultan Ahmet) opposite Ayasofya in a bold, brazen attempt to one-up Justinian. The mosque's formidable silhouette is unforgettable, and the interior, with its blue İznik tiles, is especially powerful. In its day, the mosque was most famous for the controversy over its six minarets—religious leaders didn't want the sultan to match the number of minarets at Mecca. The ever-resourceful Ahmet averted the crisis by providing the money and workers necessary to build a seventh minaret at Mecca. Inside the Blue Mosque, iron bars running across the domes ensure that the whole structure bends in earthquakes—it has withstood 20 so far. You may visit the mosque outside of the five daily prayer times; modest dress and removal of shoes required. Most mosques provide sarongs to cover legs.

From the mid-15th century until the mid-19th century, the **Topkapı Sarayı** (Topkapı Palace) was the nerve center of the Ottoman Empire. The palace, built by Mehmet II, was originally the site of the Ottoman government and the Empire's most exclusive schools. It was also the home of the Sultan and his sizable entourage of wives, eunuchs, and servants. Don't be overwhelmed by the seemingly endless attractions; some punctuate tours inside the palace by sunning on the terraces or reposing in the rose gardens. Not to be missed are the **First Court** and its huge East Asian porcelain collection; and the **Treasury,** which houses an inestimable wealth of diamonds, emeralds, gold, and jade. The latter also contains the spectacular Topkapı Dagger and some of St. John the Baptist's hand bones. Nearby, the **Pavilion of Holy Relics** contains remnants of the prophet Muhammad: his footprint, a lock of hair, a tooth, his original seal, and a letter written by his hand. The swords of the four caliphs are on display in an adjacent room. This is a sacred place to Muslims; men and women pray here. The Harem, with its lush rooms and magnificent İznik-tiled walls, is worth the additional cost. To see it, take a tour (every ½hr. 10am-4pm in English and Turkish; no tour at 12:30pm; admission $2.50). The **Circumcision Chamber,** near the patio throne overlooking the Bosphorus, is beautifully decorated with blue-green İznik tiles. According to Turkish tradition, males were not circumcised at birth (as prescribed by İslam), but after they had come of age. In some of the more rural parts of Turkey, mothers still chastise their sons by threatening to call the dreaded "circumciser." (Palace grounds open daily 9am-5pm; admission $6, w/ISIC $3, w/FIYTO free.) For a more scholarly and historical look at the Topkapı Palace, consult Gülrü Necipoğlu's *Architecture, Ceremonial, and Power: The Topkapı Palace in the 15th and 16th Centuries.* The **Gülhane Park** outside the palace is popular among locals. There's frequently live Turkish music at night: the best artists draw large, loud, adoring crowds. Most of the Gülhane consists of little plastic vending booths (admission 50¢, students 25¢.)

There are several other sights in the nearby area. The enormous **Grand Bazaar** (*Kapalı Çarşı*) is a vast, arched, ornate, colorful, chaotic marketplace which specializes in leather and carpets. You will get lost, but you'll enjoy it. The old part of the Bazaar is a jumble of shops selling hookah pipes, bright baubles, copper filigree shovels, Byzantine-style icons on red velvet, ancient Turkish daggers (made in Taiwan), silver flintlock guns with mother-of-pearl handles, chess sets, and hand puppets, among other treasures. Unfortunately, several warnings are in order. Hawkers prey on tourists. Fake and faulty merchandise is ubiquitous. The summer tourist invasion inflates prices by as much as 300-400%. Beware of glassy, bright *kayseri*—these shoddy imitations of Persian carpets are worthless (worth perhaps $50), though people have been known to pay as much as $1000 for them. The gold is mostly 14-karat, and contrary to rumor, is no more expensive elsewhere in Turkey. In short, it is better here to look than to buy. But if you know what you want, and know what price is reasonable, you may find a deal. To reach the bazaar from Sultanahmet, follow the tram tracks toward Aksaray for approximately 5min. until you see the large mosque on your right. Walk to the mosque, enter its side gate, and walk, with the park on your left, to the bazaar entrance (open Mon.-Sat. 9am-7pm). At the opposite entrance of the bazaar is the **Sahaflar Çarşısı** (used book market). A wide selection of books are sold here, along with Qur'anic inscriptions, artwork, and university texts. The market opens onto a bustling square. Opposite stands the huge, Arabic-style entrance gate of **İstanbul University,** which fronts a pleasant, leafy, well-shaded campus, a haven from the bustle of the city. Its tranquility is spoiled somewhat by the constant presence of riot police, who rest languidly in the shade, helmets at their feet, ready for action. The University is a hotbed of political strife which, on occasion, turns violent. The campus contains **Beyazıt Camii,** the oldest standing mosque in İstanbul.

Trace the university walls to the left until the **Süleymaniye** mosque complex. Together with the **Şehzade Mehmet** (a few blocks southwest, completed 1548) and the **Selimiye** (in the city of Edirne, completed 1574), the Süleymaniye (completed 1557) is one of the three masterpieces of Sinan, who served as Chief Court Architect under Ottoman sultans Süleyman the Magnificent and his son, Selim. The name "Sinan" remains venerated in Turkey today, for it was he who almost single-handedly codified Ottoman Classical architecture, a style so influential that generations of architects began imitating it shortly after the master's death (see Art & Architecture, page 423). The huge Süleymaniye complex—which includes a mosque, seven *medrese* (religious schools), an *imaret* (charitable soup kitchen), and the *türbe* (tombs) of Süleyman and his wife Haseki Hürrem—was intended as a center for Islamic higher education. It is said that there are buried treasures in the minarets. To the east of the mosque reposes a majestic courtyard; to the west a graveyard where Süleyman and Haseki Hürrem rest peacefully in opulent *türbe* drenched in İznik tile and diamond. (Tombs open Tues.-Sun. 9am-4:30pm; 75¢ "donation" buys admission.)

A 20-min. walk northwest from the graveyard leads to the **Fatih** (Conqueror) mosque, the imperial mosque complex of Sultan Mehmet II, who appears notorious in European history books for seizing Constantinople in 1453, converting the Ayasofya into a mosque, and designing the Topkapı Palace. The Fatih, nearly a century older than that of Süleyman, remains impressive nonetheless. The people of Fatih have a reputation for Islamic fundamentalism: here you will see many women covered from head to toe in the *chador,* and bearded men in Islamic dress. The atmosphere differs markedly from the rest of İstanbul: some Turks liken it to Iran. The mosque itself is usually crowded; the rest of the complex serves as a meeting and recreation area for the community. Back at the Süleymaniye, walk downhill toward Eminönü or Sirkeci. This 10-min. walk will lead you through the milling, heaving **market quarter.** About halfway down, there are numerous shops selling pistols and shotguns. When you come within 200m of the Golden Horn, you will pass the Rüstem Paşa mosque, whose famous interior, almost entirely inlaid with İznik tiles, compensates for a humble exterior. Shortly thereafter is the 17th-century **Yeni Cami** (New Mosque), whose steps afford a shaded resting place. In front stretches the **Galata Bridge;** beside Yeni Cami sits the **Egyptian Spice Bazaar.** Egyptians once dominated the spice trade in İstanbul; this is where they held shop. This feast for all the senses is much less touristy than the Grand Bazaar, and does not sell leather or carpets. Instead, it is crammed with a mind-boggling array of sticky sweets (free samples): numerous varieties of Turkish delight, nuts, dates, honey cut straight from the hive, aphrodisiacs, spices, and gold.

There are a few more sights back in the heart of Sultanahmet. The **Yerebatan Cistern** is a vast underground cavern where shallow water eerily reflects the 336 columns—one carved with Medusa's head. Wooden walkways allow you to wander among the columns, while atmospheric lighting and classical music in the background create an other-worldly effect. Underground waterways originally connected the cistern to the Topkapı Palace, but the passage was blocked to stop the traffic in stolen goods and abducted women. (Admission $2.50, w/ISIC $1.25, no

FIYTO reduction; open daily 9am-5pm.) Two pleasant, candle-lit, albeit expensive subterranean coffee shops provide for your relaxation here (coffee $1.50). In the nearby **Sultanahmet** (Blue Mosque) **complex,** visit the tomb of Sultan Ahmet I, which, like other imperial *türbe,* houses the sarcophagi of the sultan and his immediate family. (*Türbe* open Wed.-Sun. 9am-4:30pm; 75¢ "donation" buys admission). To your right as you leave the Blue Mosque are the **Carpet** and **Kilim Museums,** with carpets and woven *kilim* (flat-woven mats) from all over the Muslim world (open Tues.-Sun. 9am-4pm). This is definitely worth visiting if you are at all interested in picking up a carpet or *kilim* of your own. Keep in mind, though, that the finer tapestries cost 50-100% more in İstanbul than in the Anatolian provinces. In any case, there are probably enough rugs to fray your cultural fiber along the road to the **Mosaic Museum.** Inauspiciously located in the gallery of shops below the mosque, the museum features mosaics dating from the 6th century, when the entire area was part of the Byzantine Imperial Palace. But this is not one of İstanbul's more impressive sights; the collection of mosaics is small and in poor repair. (Open Wed.-Mon. 8:30am-8pm; admission $1.25.)

On the other side of the Blue Mosque is the ancient **Hippodrome,** a park where Byzantine emperors once presided over chariot races and circuses. The tranquility of the park today is misleading; long ago it was the site of violent uprisings and demonstrations. In 532 AD, 30,000 people were massacred here as Justinian's troops put an end to the riots that had leveled much of Constantinople. In the Hippodrome stands the granite **Egyptian Obelisk,** the upper part of an obelisk from the 15th century BC which was brought to Constantinople in 390 AD, and the helical **Serpentine Column,** taken from the Temple of Apollo at Delphi. The coarse column of unknown origin at the end of the Hippodrome was coated with bronze plates until obstreperous members of the Fourth Crusade tore off the metal.

Across from the Hippodrome, next to İstanbul's legal administration buildings, stands the 16th-century **İbrahim Paşa Palace.** The magnificent building houses a museum of Turkish and Islamic art featuring tiles, Qur'ans, and a fine carpet collection. The courtyard houses a picturesque teahouse. (Open Tues.-Sun. 10am-5pm.)

Walking back to Divan Yolu along Klodfarer Cad., you'll pass a small park opposite the Halı Hotel. Underneath lies the 5th-century **Binbirdirek Cistern.** Knock on the door of the shack to ask for a flashlight-guided tour (tip the guide roughly $2; don't let them charge you much more). Huge carved columns, crumbling steps, and one or two shafts of light piercing the darkness; but not as aesthetically spectacular as the **Yerebatan Cistern.**

Through a gate marked "Archaeological Museum," downhill from the Topkapı Palace, is a museum complex. The **Çinili Köşk** (Tiled Pavilion), once a petite pleasure retreat belonging to the Topkapı Palace, today houses the Tile Museum. Replete with yellows, blues, and greens, the building's own tiles constitute one of Turkey's best remaining examples of the Tabrizi Persian style, which the Ottomans increasingly avoided in favor of tiles with white backgrounds and naturalistic floral patterns. The **Museum of the Ancient Orient** (with English labels) has an interesting buffet of Hittite, Babylonian, Sumerian, Assyrian, and Egyptian artifacts. Among them are a tablet on which part of the Hammurabi Code is inscribed along with even older laws, and another with a peace treaty between a Hittite ruler and the Egyptian Pharaoh Ramses II. The **Archaeological Museum** displays a prize-winning collection of early Greek, Hellenistic, and Roman marbles and bronzes, including a famous sarcophagus with carvings of Alexander the Great. (All 3 museums open May-Sept. daily 9am-5pm, except the Çinili Köşk, which is closed Mon. and Fri.; admission $1.25.) The park on the ramparts of the Topkapı Palace, overlooks the Bosphorus and Golden Horn and offers a respite from İstanbul's sweltering streets.

Across the Galata Bridge, the 62m-high **Galata Tower,** built by the Emperor Justinian in 528 AD and rebuilt in 1348 by the Genoese as a low-tech spy satellite for observing the old city, still serves its purpose today. The tower was also the take-off site for the first intercontinental flight, executed in a Da Vinci-style hang glider. The view shouldn't be missed. After hours, the tower degenerates into a pricey nightclub. To get to the Galata Tower, cross the Galata Bridge and walk up the narrow, little alley 500m. The tower is on your left. But it's easier to take the Tünel from here up to İstiklâl Cad. and walk down that same alley. Right along the Bosphorus, **Dolmabahçe Palace** was the home of sultans from 1856 until the demise of the Ottoman Empire after WWI. Goose-stepping soldiers guard the royal dock and the memory of Atatürk, who died in the palace on November 10, 1938, at 9:05am (all the clocks were halted at that moment). Pseudo-French architecture reflects the sultan's pretensions of grandeur, even during the decline of the empire. Be sure to see the collection of imperial treasures, including the famous **Spoonmaker's Diamond** and an emerald the size of a cabbage. (Open Tues.-Sun. 9:30am-4pm; admission $5.) From Eminönü, take the ferry to Beşiktaş (50¢) or bus #58. The number of visitors per day is limited, so go early.

Round out your tour with other sights scattered around the city, including **Askeri Müze** (the Soldiers' Museum; tel. 140 6255; open 9am-5pm), in **Harbiye** on the European side. This is a 10-year-old boy's paradise—swords and armor and other implements of war, from all the different cultures that have inhabited Asia Minor over the last few millennia. **Beylerbeyi Sarayı** (tel. 321 9320; open 9am-4pm), in Beylerbeyi, on the Asian side, was the rococo-style summer palace of the Ottoman sultans. **Rumeli Hisarı** (Thrace Castle), next to the second Bosphorus bridge on the European side, was an integral part of the Ottoman defense system. In times of war a huge link chain was stretched from this fort to its mate, **Anadolu Hisarı** (Anatolia Castle), across the Bosphorus on the Asian side. A link of the chain is on exhibit in the Soldiers' Museum. The fortress is composed of several high towers around a central courtyard. The view of the Bosphorus from atop the walls is spectacular.

A mandatory stop for Byzantine-art connoisseurs is the impeccably preserved **Kariye Camii,** a long way up Fevzipaşa Cad., near the Edirne Gate (accessible by *dolmuş,* bus #58 from Eminönü, or any bus in the direction *Edirnekapı*). Having undergone the transition from Byzantine church to mosque, and from mosque to museum, the building showcases superb 14th-century frescoes and mosaics. The insouciance, realism, and expressiveness of this strain of late Byzantine art influenced Giotto and other early Italian painters. (Open Wed.-Mon. 9:30am-4:30pm.) From here you can see the ruined **Theodosian Land Walls,** which stretch from the Golden Horn to the Sea of Marmara. The sole character ever to have surmounted these looming, 5th-century AD ramparts was Mehmet the Conqueror, in 1453.

Another İstanbul highlight is a **Bosphorus cruise.** Boats leave from Pier #3, beside the Galata Bridge in Eminönü. (Winter daily at 10:30am; spring and autumn at 10:30am and 12:30pm; summer Mon.-Fri. at 10:30am, 12:30, and 2:30 pm, Sat.-Sun. 10, 11am, noon, 1:30, and 3pm; $4.) When the ferry makes its final stop on the Asian side, disembark and treat yourself to fish *kebap,* mussels, or fried *kalamari* for $2-5 from the street vendors. Then walk up the hill for beautiful views of the Black Sea. Double-decker bus #210 also runs hourly from behind the tourist office to points along the European side of the Bosphorus; cost is two bus tickets each way.

The **TV tower** at Çamlıca Hill is İstanbul's highest point and offers views of the entire city and Bosphorus straits. There is a beautifully decorated Turkish café here: classical Ottoman music is played, and waiters wear traditional 19th-century costumes. Especially at sunset, the best skyline views can be seen at **Salacak,** another home of excellent cafés and tea shops. Take the bus from Üsküdar, ferry to Çamlıca. The **Chamber of Florence Nightingale** in the Military Hospital in Haydarpaşa is open to the public. The **English Cemetery** in the Selimiye Barracks (one of the world's largest) is a beautifully maintained military cemetery for British soldiers who fell in the 1854 Crimean War against Russia.

Bağdat Cad. (Baghdad Ave.) in Kadıköy on the Asian side is a place of Euro-chic (ferry from Piers 3 and 7, every 20min., 50¢). **Ortaköy** is a liberal place, favored by artists and young people; a church, synagogue, and mosque here are representative of a secular Turkey. It is somewhat avant-garde and Bohemian. **Gengelköy** has excellent, cheap, and simple fish restaurants. **Anadoluhisarı** has small, waterside restaurants and cafés. **Kaanica** is reputed to have the most delicious yogurt in all of

Turkey. **Emirgan** is a peaceful village of old-style Turkish houses and excellent Turkish tea. An 1843 castle is nearby. Bus #210 heads to Kaanica, Emirgan and Anadoluhisarı. İstiklâl Cad., the heart of modern İstanbul, also deserves some time.

Doing Some Hash 'Round Midnight

Based on a true story, the classic 70s flick *Midnight Express*, about an American drug smuggler snagged, imprisoned, and tortured by Turkish police, has done more to shape Americans' conception of Turkey than any promotional pamphlet. At the time of its release, the country's tourist officials were upset about the image attributed to Turkey, but in true Western style, they have capitalized on the publicity. The old prison where the author of *Midnight Express* served time is now being converted into a five-star hotel. It's close to the Ayasofya, but you may not recognize it unless you too were caught walking around İstanbul with a "Class D" substance 20 years ago—the movie is said to have been filmed in Italy for political reasons. The **Pudding Shop,** 6 Divan Yolu, opposite the tourist office, is where the protagonist of Midnight Express scored his infamous bag. You may chalk Midnight Express up to Hollywood magic, but getting caught with drugs in Turkey is a bad idea (see Drugs, p. 8).

■ NEAR İSTANBUL

Eyüp, a popular Muslim pilgrimage site, houses the 15th-century tomb of the eponymous companion of Muhammad who died during an Arab siege of the city in the 7th century. The Golden Horn ferries ride the waves twice hourly from pier #6 in Eminönü, above the Galata Bridge (35min., 40¢), or catch bus #55. You may see regally costumed young boys brought here by their families; the trip is customary for boys before circumcision. Climb the hill above the cemetery for a rare view.

Another ferry line goes to the **Princes Isles,** leaving from Eminönü or Kabataş on the north side. Look for the signs saying Sirkeci Adalar (departs from Eminönü, 6-7 per day, round-trip $3). The ferry stops at four of the nine islands of this minute suburban archipelago on the Sea of Marmara. The area is underdeveloped, has beautiful scenery, and a happy absence of cars. You can tour an island by horse-drawn carriage; be sure to bargain over the fare. Some people prefer the quieter atmospheres of **Burgazada** and **Heybeliada,** but **Büyükada,** the largest and most picturesque of the islands, offers the best swimming (at rocky **Yörükalı beach**) in the İstanbul area (and this, sadly, is not all that great). In Heybeliada, take a horse-carriage to Deçirmen for a picnic (fix the price beforehand).

NORTHWESTERN TURKEY

■■■ SAFRANBOLU

Safranbolu is a treasure. An old, atmospheric, perfectly preserved Turkish town, it contains some of the best examples of early Ottoman architecture in Anatolia. It is also famous for its unique brand of *lokum* (Turkish delight); along with its rival, Afyon, they make the best in Turkey. Still relatively untouristed, Safranbolu, with its narrow, winding streets and houses built of sun-dried brick, is arrestingly beautiful. In 1995, the United Nations declared it a World Heritage Preservation Area.

Orientation and Practical Information Safranbolu has two distinct sections: the beautiful old town, and a dusty new one that consists primarily of two long boulevards lined with five-story apartment buildings and little else of interest.

The heart of old Safranbolu, and its center of transportation, is the main square, **Mehmet Kurtulanı Meydanı.** Local and intercity **buses,** *dolmuş,* and taxis leave from here. Standing in the square, looking toward the old baths, you will notice four streets; on the extreme left, the **Kastamonu road** leads to Hıdırlık Tepesi, a hill from which there is a superb view of the town. To the right of it is **Akın Sok.,** which leads to the old *kervansaray;* to the right of it is **Yukarı Çarşı Sok.,** that contains one of the tourist offices and the Arasna Café-Bar Pansiyon. To the extreme right, **Hasan Dede Sok.** leads past the Tahsinbey Konağı and Paşa Konağı hotels to the old government house, now in ruins; it was built on the site of the town's old castle. These roads are all linked; Safranbolu is small, and most points of interest are within a 5-min. walk. Behind, to the left, **Hilmi Bayramgil Sok.** runs to the new town.

There are two rival tourist offices in Safranbolu. On the main square, the office of the privately owned **Safranbolu Culture and Tourism Association** (*Kültür ve Turizm Vakfım*), Çeşme Mah. 1 Arasta Sok. (tel. 712 1047), supplies maps and information on sights and accommodations. This opens daily at roughly 8am. Its closing time depends on the number of tourists in town; it can vary from 4 to 9pm. The government-run **Tourism Information Office** (*Turizm Danışma Müdürlüğü*), 7 Arasta Çarşısı (tel. 712 3863), provides similar services. Go down Yukarı Çarşı Sok., take the first left after the Aşiyan Otantik Café, then take an immediate right into the little shopping arcade; it's on the right. **Postal Code:** 67710; **Telephone Code:** 372.

There is a telephone in the main square of the old town, and another in the arcade opposite the tourist office; both take phonecards. In the new town, there is one functional phone at the roundabout. There is another on the main road, halfway between the two parts of town, on the right as you go toward the new town. It is best not to use hotel reception phones, as they can be very expensive. The tiny **PTT** office is at 26 Cincinam Sok., a few doors down from the *kervansaray.* (Open Mon.-Fri. 8:30am-12:30pm and 1:30-5:30pm, Sat. 8:30am-12:30pm.) Safranbolu is served by the Güven, Ulusoy, and Avrupa bus companies, which serve Ankara (5 per day, 3hr., $6), İstanbul (4 per day, 7hr., $9.50), İzmir (1 per day, 12hr., $16.25), Adana (1 per day, 13hr., $14), İskenderun (1 per day, 12hr., $16.25), Rize (1 per day, $19.75), Trabzon (1 per day, $17.50), and Samsun (1 per day, $11.75). Officially, all **buses** arrive at **Karabük,** the less-than-lovely steel manufacturing town 10km away. These companies continue into Safranbolu. Numerous other companies serve Karabük, from which you can catch a frequent minibus to Safranbolu; city buses also make the journey every hour Mon.-Sat., and every two hours on Sun. (25¢). A **taxi** from the bus station to old Safranbolu will cost $8-9; taxis are metered, and have the same rates as other Turkish cities. The **Ulusoy** office (tel. 712 4567, in Karabük (372) 424 2434) is in the new town; coming from the old town, turn right at the roundabout; it's roughly 15m down the street, on your right. The **Avrupa** office (tel. 712 4315) is 50m farther along, on your left. These companies offer a pick-up service in Safranbolu only; call and ask, but no English spoken. However, you *will* need to converse in Turkish in order to make use of this service. Try to get tourist office personnel to make the call, or just to go to an office and buy a ticket.

Accommodations **Havuzlu Konak,** 18 Beybağ Sok. (tel. 725 2883), is a luxurious, restored Ottoman villa. Rooms have delicate lace bedspreads, Ottoman couches, and brass tables; bathrooms are larger than single rooms in most pensions. Its café/breakfast room has couches running its length, brass tables, and a large reflecting pool. The atmosphere is very oriental—you will feel like a minor sultan if you stay here. Reservations are recommended, and essential for Saturday, when it fills with middle-class Turks on weekend trips. Singles $25, doubles $35. Stop in for a spot of *çay* even if you can't afford to stay; it is well worth a look. Several places cater to travelers on a tighter budget; and the overall standards in this town are high. **Aşiyan Pensiyon,** 4A Eski Hamam Sok. (tel. 712 3412), walk to the end of Yukarı Çarşı Sok. (the street containing the private tourist office and Arasna Café-Bar), then turn right; the pension is roughly 10m up Eski Hamam Sok., to the right. The unmarked, large white house has a bar downstairs. In a partially restored old Safranbolu house, with courteous management and five large rooms, some with inspiring views of the old town cost $7 per single, $12 per double, breakfast included; shared bathroom; hot showers. The floors are covered in kilims; ceilings are ornate and made of wood, with unique Safranbolu carvings. The **Arasna Café-Bar Pansiyon** has four rooms and offers similar rooms, but without the views. $8.50 per person includes breakfast. Some rooms are restored originals; some less authentic. Nevertheless, this place is classy and comfortable, and has an excellent bar. It's hard to miss the signs for the **Çarşı Pansiyon,** 1 Bozkurt Sok., where you can choose between standard pension rooms with shared bath and Turkish-style, floor-tossed mattresses in rooms with private bath, all for $6 per person. Breakfast $1.

There are some accommodations in the charmless new town—while they're pretty good, the ones in the old town are better. Stay in these if the ones in the old town are full. The **Konak Pansiyon,** 4 Sağlık Sok. (tel. 725 2485), well signposted on the main road between the old and new towns, is clean and comfortable. It is in a modern family home. Singles $11.75, doubles $18.75. The two-star **Hotel Ür** (tel. 712 1086, -2215), just off the roundabout in the new town, offers modern, comfortable rooms for $23 per single, $30 per double—it could be anywhere.

Food For food, don't miss **Kadıoğlu,** on the main square. Their specialty is *kuzu kebabı,* lamb baked in spices ($3). **Konak restaurant,** in the middle of the shopping arcade, is a pleasant place for *çay* or *ayran:* the decor is superb.

The local Turkish delight specialty is *fındıklı lokum,* a yellow delight with a hazelnut in the middle and covered with coconut sawdust. Many other varieties exist. An excellent shop is **İmren,** 1 Arasna Çarşısı, in the little shopping arcade, behind the Aşiyan Café and a couple of doors down from the government-run tourist office (open daily 8am-8pm). **Özkan Lokumlar,** on the street to the left of the private tourist office, roughly 10m down on the right, is an ancient shop, with a mini-factory behind it. Stick your head in to see how Turkish delight is made—you'll be rewarded with odd looks and may be placated with a free sample. In the new town, close to the roundabout, there are about half a dozen Turkish delight shops. Look for the word *Lokum* or *Lokumları.* You can buy delights at $3 per kilo.

Sights In Safranbolu, the town itself is the main sight, but there are also a couple of places not to be missed. The **Kaymakamlar Evi** (governor's residence), a restored house, is the local museum. Enter through the courtyard, where the animals were kept. Various tools and utensils are on display here, including wooden cone frustums. These were filled with yogurt and water to make *ayran;* the mixture had to be beaten with a ladle for two hours or more. On the next floor up are the winter living quarters—above them, the summer quarters, which have higher ceilings. These floors were heavily insulated from each other with sand between floorboards and ceiling. Each room was a home for a family. Mattresses were pulled out from under the couches at night. Some of the cupboards had secret hiding places for valuables. From the market (at the back of the *kervansaray*) walk up the alley beside the T.C. Zakaat Bankası; the museum is the white building on the right. After wandering through the town's narrow streets, stroll up to **Hıdırlık Tepesi,** a lookout point at the town ramparts with excellent views. Walk uphill along the snaking Kastamonu road for 5-10min., then take the paved path on your right to the official-looking building with the Turkish flag. Here are a shop and **public bathrooms.**

■ NEAR SAFRANBOLU

There are several places of interest near Safranbolu. **Bağlar** was the summer residence of Safranbolu's citizens. The houses here are similar but larger, and have gardens. Buses run from the old town's main square roughly every ½hr. **Yörük** village, a smaller version of Safranbolu only 15km away, cooks up some of the best *gözleme* (Anatolian pancakes) in Anatolia. To get there, take a minibus from the main square to **Konarı,** from which it's roughly a 20-min. walk. For **Kastamonu,** there's one bus per day leaving the main square at 7:30am, returning to Safranbolu about 5pm. Hourly or every 1½hr. from the new town.

■■■ EDİRNE

Edirne is a beautiful, peaceful medieval Islamic town that contains some of Turkey's best examples of Ottoman architecture. Located only a few kilometers from the Greek and Bulgarian borders, it remains quintessentially Turkish.

The quiet city of today conceals an eventful past. Named Hadrianopolis after the Roman Emperor Hadrian in the second century AD, the city witnessed the catastrophic defeat of the Roman army by the Goths two centuries later. The Ottomans took control of the city and made it the capital of their empire from 1363 until soon after the fall of Constantinople in 1453. In the Empire's final days, the city was occupied no less than four times as Bulgaria, Greece, Russia, and Turkey struggled for control of the Balkans. Today, Edirne serves as a pleasant resting point for travelers *en route* to İstanbul and other points in the East. The city, situated near the junction of the Tunca and Meriç rivers, houses mosques and baths designed by the famous architect Sinan, including his masterpiece the **Selimiye Camii.** Edirne's large museums, bridges, bazaars, and several *kervansaray* also help maintain its dignity.

ORIENTATION AND PRACTICAL INFORMATION

Edirne is centered around the triangle-shaped **Hürriyet Meydanı** (Freedom Square), which is bounded by the Eski Cami (Old Mosque), Kervansaray Hotel, and a row of shops. *Dolmuş* from the bus station drop you here. Right behind the Old Mosque runs **Talat Paşa Cad.,** the main east-west thoroughfare. Walk from Hürriyet Meydanı to Talat Paşa Cad., take a left, and walk for roughly one minute; the first intersection, on your left, is **Saraçlar Cad.,** the town's main shopping street. Keep going to the next intersection; the tourist office is on the corner. This street, (on the left) Maarif Cad., is home to a good selection of cheap hotels. On your right you will have noticed the beautiful Selimiye Mosque overlooking a park. Walk up the road to the left of the park and you will see on your left the main local bus and *dolmuş* terminal. To the left of the Selimiye Mosque is the Üç Şerefeli Cami (Mosque with Three Galleries). Keep walking for roughly 5min. along Talat Paşa Cad., past the tourist office, to the outskirts of town and the river. To reach the beautiful Beyazıt Mosque, take a right onto the little path beside the river. Walking back along Talat Paşa Cad. in the opposite direction, the town's main intercity bus station (*otogar*) is a 20-min. walk; it's on the right, signposted *otogar*. The Bulgarian embassy is on the right, halfway between the Old Mosque and the *otogar*.

Tourist Office: 17 Talat Paşa Cad. (tel. 213 9208). Roughly 200m west of the Eski Cami. Open daily 9am-6pm, Sept.-May Mon.-Sat. 8:30am-5pm. Staff is helpful and provide free maps.

PTT: 17 Saraçlar Cad. It has **telephones** and 24-hr. **currency exchange.** They are supposed to cash traveler's checks Mon.-Fri. 8:30am-5pm, but it might be better to try a local bank (9am-noon, 3-5pm), as the PTT has been known to refuse to help travelers. **Telephone Code:** 284.

Bulgarian Consulate (Bulgaristan Başkonsolosluğu): 31 Talat Paşa Asfaldı (tel. 225 1069). Roughly 1km southeast of Eski Cami, on the road to İstanbul. The consulate is on your left. Normally visas take a week to issue, and are priced: tourist $31.50, transit $21, double transit $42. Express visas—issued the same day—cost tourist $46.50 and transit $31.50. Multiple entry: 3 months $42, 6 months $73.25, 1 year $105. Visas allow a 30-day stay. Foreigners should get express visas; if you leave your passport at the embassy for a week, you may have difficulty checking into hotels and changing traveler's checks. Both of these transactions require a passport. Open Mon.-Fri. 9am-noon.

Trains: Two train stations serve Edirne, one on the road to İstanbul (tel. 225 1155 or 212 0914), and one in **Kapıkule** (tel. 238 2312), within walking distance of the Bulgarian border. To get to Kapıkule, take a *dolmuş* from in front of Rüstempaşa Kervansaray Otel (every 10min., $1), or a bus (hourly until 6pm) from the local bus station. Kapıkule is the last stop. There is one train per day to İstanbul (8am, 7hr., $2; unless you're broke, take the bus) and Thessaloniki (5:55am, 12hr., $9.50; board at the Kapıkule border station), two per day to Sofia (8hr., $19) and Budapest ($100), and one per day to Europe (arriving from Munich early in the morning and leaving late at night). Buy your ticket only at the Kapıkule station.

Buses: When you arrive at the *otogar*, walk across the street to take a *dolmuş* into Edirne. *Dolmuş* (7am-midnight) run regularly between the depot near the mosques, and the **bus station** (*terminal*), a few km from the center along the road to İstanbul (30¢). Buses depart for İstanbul (every ½hr., 3hr., $6), and Keşan (5 per day, 1½hr., $4). Buses also run to Bursa (2 per day, Nov.-March 1 per night, $9.50) and Ankara (2 per evening, 10hr., $20).

Pharmacies: Most of these are located on Saraçlar Cad.

ACCOMMODATIONS

There are plenty of cheap options scattered along Maarif Cad., the little street to the right of the tourist office, 2 blocks from Hürriyet Meydanı.

Hotel Kervansaray (tel. 225 2195, -6119, -0462), runs the length of Hürriyet Meydanı. Built in the 1550s as an overnight resting place for camel caravans *en route* from Europe to the East, this architectural gem contains two vast courtyards and lined with Turkish/Islamic arches. Rooms are whitewashed and have thick wooden doors; small but comfortable. Recently renovated, they come w/bath, toilet paper, TV, phone, and carpet. The call to prayer from the three nearby mosques resonates through the corridors and rooms, including one at 4:30am. But prayer is better than sleep, you heathen barbarian, you. A uniquely Turkish experience. Singles $17.50, doubles $29, triples $35, breakfast included.

Efe Hotel, 13 Maarif Cad. (tel. 213 6166, -466). Spotless rooms include modern bathrooms and TV. Singles $14, doubles $20, triples $32.50, and quads $32.50.

Hotel Aksaray (tel. 212 6035 or 225 3901), a couple of doors down from Efe Hotel. Cheaper and much more basic. Small and plain rooms. Singles $6; doubles $9.50, w/bath $11.75; triples $11.75, w/bath $14.

Hotel Konak, 6 Maarif Cad. (tel. 225 1348), is even more basic. Grim, cell-like singles cost only $3.50; larger, brighter doubles cost $5.25.

Fifi Camping (tel. 235 7908), on the main İstanbul road, 9km from the center of town. Served by its own private minibus. Camping fee $4 per person, tent rental $2, cars $2, caravans $4. Rooms w/balcony $30. This complex has its own restaurant, bar, and pool. Hotels in town are just as cheap and more convenient.

FOOD AND ENTERTAINMENT

Do not leave Edirne without taking *çay* at **Sera** teahouse. No matter which way you turn, you'll have superb views, the best Edirne has to offer. Look one way to see the glorious Selimiye Camii; turn around for the Eski Camii. These scenes, combined with the sound of the café's fountain and a glass of sweet Turkish *çay,* result in an experience which is quite sublime—drink it in at night, when the Selimiye Camii is floodlit. *Çay* (small 17¢, large 35¢) comes in a small Turkish *çay* glass on a tiny steel tray, or in an ordinary cup. *Ayran* 35¢, soft drinks 50¢, *tost* 29-35¢. Sera is in the park between Selimiye Camii and Eski Cami, closer to the latter. Another excellent *çay bahçesi* (tea garden) is **Café Antik,** which takes up most of Hürriyet Meydanı. Sip *çay* and watch most of Edirne go by. Prices and selections identical with Sera; however, Café Antik has a much wider selection of tasty snacks. (*Karışık sandviç* 40¢, cheeseburger 70¢, *tost* 30¢, ice cream 70¢.)

For more substantial fare, head to **Gati Restaurant,** on Talat Paşa Cad. a few doors past the tourist office (if walking away from Eski Cami). Excellent mixed grill—*köfte* and grilled liver, the local specialty, with rice and fries ($2.50; side dishes 60¢, *Efes* brand beer 60¢). The windows stretch from floor to ceiling, so you can gaze up Talat Paşa Cad. at the domes and minarets of Selimiye and Eski mosques while you eat. **Vatan Restaurant,** on Kıyın Cad., is across the road from Selimiye Camii. (Stand with Eski Cami to your back; then it's on the road that runs along the right-hand side of Selimiye Camii.) This place is informal and packed with students—just grab a seat at the communal tables. (Tasty stew dishes, which change daily, cost 50¢ each;

soup also 50¢; rice 25¢.) As in most Turkish restaurants, the food in these restaurants is on display behind a counter—just point to what you want. The **Park Hotel Restaurant** on Maarif Cad. serves excellent *köfte* and *kebap,* the house specialty ($2.50). The **Café M** is a student restaurant, and a good place to go for a coffee. It's on Saraçlar Cad., on the upper floor of the Vakıf İş Hanı building.

For dessert, there are quite a few **sweetshops** along Saraçlar Cad. One of the best for sweets (and worst for service) is **Roma Pastanesi,** at no. 99 (50m down from the PTT away from the mosques, on opposite side), which offers sticky, gooey treats to satisfy the most demanding sweet tooths. ($3.50 per kilo, or roughly 14¢ per sweet.) A local specialty is *badem ezmesi* (marzipan).

SIGHTS

Edirne's enchants with its Islamic medieval architecture, primarily its mosques. The city's main sight is the **Selimiye Camii,** completed in 1579 by the great Ottoman architect Sinan. This remarkable work of genius, which includes 71-m minarets and 999 windows, is the town's symbol, and can be seen towering above Edirne from several kilometers away. While the exterior is impressive, it is the interior that truly astounds on first entry. It is vast in size, and ornately decorated from dome to floor. With this dome, which rivals the Ayasofya in size, Sinan showed the world that the Muslim Ottomans were not to be architecturally outdone by the Christian Byzantines. Climb to the surrounding balcony—views are best from there. The mosque is approached through an ancient shopping arcade; at the end of this, a small stone staircase (marked "Cami Giriş" and "Moschee Eingang") leads up to the courtyard.

The **Üç Şerefeli Cami** nearby was completed in 1447. Another work of architectural genius, its main feature is its four beautiful minarets, each with a different but complementary design. Unfortunately, there is little to see inside: its interior is undergoing restoration expected to last until the year 2000. The nearby **Eski Cami**—completed 1415—is quite distinct from the others architecturally: instead of one large dome, it has a series of small ones. Its interior is also undergoing restoration, but part of it is still in use and can be visited.

Edirne's other major sight is the **Beyazıt Complex,** a charitably endowed, spiritual and physical welfare facility a couple of kilometers from the center of town. The centerpiece is the **Beyazıt Camii,** a beautiful, single-domed mosque surrounded by multi-domed buildings which were designed to be schools, storehouses, and asylums. (No longer in use, these buildings are locked; the mosque is usually open, though.) To get there, walk along Talat Paşa Cad. until the river, but don't cross the bridge. Turn right and walk along the dirt path that runs parallel to the river. After roughly a 10min. walk there is a bridge below on your left. Cross it, and walk 3-4min. more, until the mosque. This is a beautiful walk through pleasant countryside. For the entire journey you will see, on your right-hand side, the domes and minarets of Selimiye and Eski mosques rising out of the city, and on your left, the Beyazıt mosque, partly obscured by trees. On the way are two of Edirne's historic stone bridges. When you finally clear those trees and see the entire structure for the first time, the walk will seem worthwhile (Although *dolmuş* serve the mosque, they are infrequent and complicated to use.)

Back in the center of town, there are some other sights worth a quick look. The **Bedesten,** on Hürriyet Meydanı, is a half-millennium-old covered market. Now it contains a number of boutiques which would appeal to flea market cronies—cheap shirts, plastic toys, etc. Kent Spor sells Turkish soccer league shirts—be the first on your block to wear the colors of Edirne's soccer team! On the other side of Hürriyet Meydanı is the **Rüstem Paşa Kervansaray.** This multi-domed structure, designed in the style of the Eski Cami, was built as a resting place for medieval caravan trains. Its thick walls and two vast courtyards allowed the camels and their cargo to rest in safety. Two-thirds of it now serves as a university residence. The remainder is a hotel (see Hotel Kervansaray, page 451). Near the Selimiye Camii are two museums of minor interest. The **Ethnography Museum** exhibits clothing, carpets, and medieval armor. (Open Tues.-Sun. 10am-noon and 1-5pm; admission 60¢.) The **Turkish and**

Islamic Art Museum, which similarly exhibits examples of Ottoman architecture, Qur'ans, weapons, and glasswork, has the same hours and admission prices. The low prices, superior service, and inspiring architecture may beckon you to sprawl out in reverie at one of Edirne's Turkish baths. Try Sinan's 16th-century **Sokollu Hamamı** (tel. 225 2193), beside the Üç Şerefeli Cami. You'll see the minarets from the tourist office. (Open daily 6am-11pm for men, 9am-6pm for women, $2, with massage $3.50.) Edirne is also famed for its arched Ottoman bridges; there are a couple on the walk to the Beyazıt Mosque. Turkey's annual **grease wrestling** (*yağlı güreş*) tourney happens in Edirne in the last week of June.

■■■ BURSA

Nestled in the shadow of the 2000m-high slopes of Mt. Uludağ, (literally "Great Mountain," or Mt. Olympus) Bursa is a city of fascinating contrasts. Perhaps due to a tradition of gay singers from the city, some natives mockingly call it "Bursa the gay." But along with Konya, Bursa is one of Turkey's two holy cities of pilgrimage. While many of the 14th century mosques and tombs are still frequented, Bursa has become an industrial center with a wealthy resort area. Mt. Uludağ, which gives the city its traditional moniker "Green Bursa," is home to Turkey's leading ski resort.

Osman, the founder of the *Osmanı* (Ottoman) dynasty, besieged Bursa for nearly a decade; after his death in 1326, his son, Orhan Bey, came to power. Orhan made Bursa the capital of the blooming empire until Edirne usurped that distinction 75 years later. Despite the collapse of the Ottomans and the ascendancy of industry in Bursa, the well-preserved monuments from Orhan's reign that are scattered throughout the city and the thermal baths in the **Çekirge** (Grasshopper) district remain great attractions.

ORIENTATION AND PRACTICAL INFORMATION

To get to the center of town, take a *dolmuş* marked "Heykel" from the bus station (25¢) and get off at **Ulu Cami** (Great Mosque).

Tourist Office: To get to the **main tourist office** (tel. 221 2359) go to the Ulu Cami side of Atatürk Caddesi, walk towards the *heykel* (a huge statue of Atatürk), pass the big fountain, and go down the stairs on your left. The staff is helpful, but the map they distribute is not. Open Mon.-Sat. 8:30am-noon, 1:30-5:30pm; Oct.-May Mon.-Fri. 8:30am-noon, 1-5pm. A tourist office in the bus station keeps the same hours. On weekends, use the office on Atatürk Cad. As you walk away from the *heykel,* it lies about 100m before Ulu Cami. Open Sat.-Sun. 8am-5pm.

PTT: Across the street from Ulu Cami. Offers **currency exchange** and cashes traveler's checks. Some English spoken. Open Mon.-Sat. 8:30am-noon and 1:30-5pm. **Postal code:** 16300. **Telephone code:** 224.

Buses: Depart for Bursa from İstanbul's Esenler Bus Station (every ½hr., 4 hr., $7). **Kamıl Koç** is generally safe and reliable, as are **Ulusoy** and **Varan.** Routes connect Bursa to Ankara, İzmir, and other big cities (every ½hr.). *Dolmuş* to the bus stations are marked "Garaj" and depart from Atatürk Cad.

Ferries: Bursa is accessible by express ferry from Karaköy in İstanbul (Mon.-Fri. 5 per day, $3.50). On weekends the express ferry launches from Kartal on İstanbul's Asian coast. A slow ferry leads to Bursa from Kabataş in İstanbul (8 per day, $2). Early ferries (8:30 or 9am) beat the crowds. The ferries land in Yalova, where you can hop on a *dolmuş* or bus to Bursa (every ½hr., $2). The entire trip takes roughly 3½ hr. There is also seabus service (5 times per day on weekdays, 8 on weekends) to Yalova and Bostancı.

Pharmacy: On the corner of Atatürk Blv. and İnönü Cad.

Hospital: Private (tel. 220 1040) on İnönü Cad. (left from the clocktower). **State** (tel. 220 0020) can be reached via *dolmuş* from Atatürk Blv.

Emergency: Dial 177.

ACCOMMODATIONS

Otel Bilgiç, 30 Başak Cad. (tel. 220 3190). The third right on Atatürk Blv. from the post office. Even rooms without showers have toilets of their own. 24-hr. hot water. Carpeted singles $9.50, w/bath $13.50; doubles $9.50, w/bath $12.50.

Hotel Can, 73 İnönü Cad. (tel. 226 6384 or 221 95 12). With your back to the main PTT, head right up Atatürk Blv. to the clock and statue, then turn left. It's across from the Mobil gas station. Dark, clean, no frills, spacious rooms. Amiable management may be willing to bargain. Try to avoid rooms on the noisy street side. Singles $5.50, w/bath $6.50; doubles $8, w/bath $10.30; triples $9.60, w/ bath $14.50.

Otel Özendim, 135 Garaj Karşısı (tel. 254 9471). Directly across from the depot. In the noisy and distant area around the bus station. Clean but utilitarian rooms. Dorm beds $1.50, singles $6, doubles $9.50, triples $10.50, quads $11.50. Shower 75¢. Bath $1.

Hotel Uğur, 27 Tahtakale Cad. (tel. 221 1989). From the main PTT, go left up Atatürk Blv. and take the fifth left up Kazımbaykal Cad. English is not spoken but rustic, small rooms off a traditional courtyard are well-kept by friendly management. Singles $3.75, doubles $4.50, triples $5, quads $5.50. Bath $1, shower 65¢—sorry, only cold water.

Otel Deniz, 19 Tahtakale Cad. (tel. 22 9238). More expensive, but also more comfortable. Small, quiet rooms around a pleasant courtyard. Hot showers on demand make up for the aging decor and linoleum floors. Singles $4, doubles $6.30. Shower included.

FOOD AND ENTERTAINMENT

Bursa is home to the mushy, tangy *İskender kebap,* a popular yogurt, tomato and lamb dish. Numerous restaurants named "*İskender kebap*" that specialize in the dish are clustered in the area between the Atatürk statue and the Green Mosque. **Kebapçı İskender,** 7 Ünlü Cad. (tel. 221 4615), at the corner of Atatürk Blv. and İnönü Cad., claims to have invented the *İskender kebap.* (One portion $4; open 11am-10pm.) **Bursa Kebapçısı,** down the street from the tourist office, by the Orhan Gazi Mosque, is also well-known but more expensive. Many small and cheaper restaurants are scattered throughout the area and are similarly priced (full meal $3.50). Locals highly recommend **Gümüş Kebapçı** (tel. 220 3401), on Gümüşçeken Cad., a block down from Atatürk Blv. (Kebap $2.50. Open 9am-9:30pm). Picnickers can stock up in the **market** on Tahtakale near the budget hotels. Bursa's **Kültür Parkı** (take a *dolmuş* from Heykel, 30¢) has decent restaurants and is one of the few places to serve alcohol in this conservative city. Concerts, movies, or theater are occasional attractions. The **Arap Şükrü** district, near Altıparmak Cad., is next to the park and features fish restaurants, bars and pubs.

SIGHTS

The city's layout was determined largely during its reign as capital of the Ottoman empire. Accordingly, the mosques date back to the 14th and early 15th centuries. The famous **Yeşil Cami** (Green Mosque) and **Yeşil Türbe** (Green Mausoleum) in the east actually seem blue to many. Spangled inside and out in rich turquoise, cobalt, and occasionally green İznik tiles, the structures are truly sights to behold. Before the capital was moved to Edirne in 1402, the mosque served both religious and administrative functions for the Empire, as well as occasionally housing the sultan and his family. Across the way, finely carved wooden doors and small stained glass windows accentuate Yeşil Türbe's handsome turquoise interior. The large postcard stand on the tomb of Mehmet I and his children is a more recent enhancement. To get there, walk along Atatürk Cad. past the clock to Namazgah Cad., then turn left onto Yeşil Cad. after the small bridge. There are more than 15 mosques and tombs in Bursa, each with it's own design and history. The **Turkish and Islamic Art Museum,** including the **Ethnographic Museum,** is near the small bridge. It includes collections of 16th-century ivory and inlaid mother-of-pearl boxes, costumes and instruments of the dervishes, and silver Qur'an covers.

Built in Seljuk style, the architecture common before the conquest of Constantinople, the **Ulu Cami** (Great Mosque) diverges from designs common in İstanbul that were influenced by the Ayasofya. Rectangular layout and numerous supporting columns are characteristic of the style, and scholars believe that the nearby intricately carved wooden *minbar* (pulpit) represents an astrological chart. The mosque was built by Beyazıt to commemorate his victory in Nikopolis in 1396. It is said that Beyazıt vowed to build 20 mosques if he won the war; but once victorious, he built just the Ulu Cami with 20 domes (a lousy trick to play on God). While the Ulu Cami was under construction, two builders, Hacivat and Karagöz, so entertained fellow workers with jokes and stories that progress became delayed. To speed things up, Mehmet I had them executed, then in a fit of remorse immortalized them in puppet form. The Punch and Judy of Turkey, Hacivat and Karagöz can be seen on puppet stages throughout the country today. A modified form of the shadow puppets, called *Kargiozis*, is also popular in Greece.

In June and September, you can witness the silk production for which Bursa is famous. The brilliantly dyed and patterned silk, *ipek*, can be purchased in the **Kapalı Çarşı (Bazaar)** or in **Koza Han,** by the tourist office, for $4-20 per square meter; you can also buy the silkworm cocoons themselves.

The **Karagöz Antique Shop,** in Eski Aynalı Çarşı, down the hill from the tourist office, is full of genuine handicrafts for all budgets. The owner puts up little Karagöz shows in his shop and also provides guided tours to authentic Turkish villages, handicraft shops, and silk factories. He does not like to talk about money, but he expects you to pay or buy something in return for the entertainment. The **Eski Kaplıca** (Old Springs) **bathing complex,** Çekirge Meydanı, Kervansaray-Termal (tel. 233 9300), was built by Justinian in the 6th century. Take the Çekirge *dolmuş* and get off at the luxurious Kervansaray Hotel. Eski Kaplıca will be on the right when you face the hotel (open daily 7:30am-11pm; entrance to baths costs men $5 and women $3, rubbing and massage $2.50 each). After a long day of travel, ask for the "rubbing" and have at least one layer of dead skin exfoliated with a special cloth. Just past the Kültürparkı and down the hill to the right, a short *dolmuş* ride will take you to **Yeni Kaplıca** (New Springs), 6 Yeni Kaplıca Cad. (tel. 236 6968; fax 235 0536), a bathing complex built for Süleyman the Magnificent in 1555. Three adjacent baths (one per sex and one for families), fed by natural thermal springs, feature cavernous bathing pools. (Men $4.50 for first class bath, $3.25 for second class; women $2.25. Open daily 8am-10pm.)

To reach the **Uludağ cable car** station, take a *dolmuş* marked "Televiewer" (30¢) from the Kafkaf pastry shop on Atatürk Blv., two blocks past the statue. The cable car runs to the mid-station (every hr. on the hr., 9am-9pm, round-trip $1.75), and from the mid-station to a small, scenic town perched at the peak of the 2000m high mountain (every hr. on the ½hr., 20min., $2.65 there and $5.00 back). Be prepared for the cooler climate, sudden changes of weather, and high-priced hotels.

Turk-uoise

Visitors to Turkey are perplexed to find mosques named "Green Mosque" scattered around the country, even though their prevalent color is turquoise, not green. This confusion stems from the Turkish language, which has uses the same word (*yeşil*) for both green and turquoise. In fact, the very existence of the distinction in English is due to the French. As one of the first European allies of the Ottoman Empire, the French coined the word *turquoise* after their name for Turkey, *la Turquie*. It is rare good fortune for newcomers to İstanbul that the *Sultanahmet Camii* is known in English as the Blue rather than Green Mosque.

■■■ İZNİK

"The history of İznik," as the tourist office brochures aptly put it, "is very old." İznik was first constructed in 316 BC by Antigonius, one of Alexander the Great's generals, and was named Antigonia. In 310 BC, another of these generals, Lysimachus, defeated Antigonius and renamed the city after his wife Nicaea. The Romans later invaded and built walls, theaters, and laid out the city's Hellenistic grid plan. Under the Byzantine empire, Nicaea hosted the First Ecumenical Council in 325 AD. Pressured by the Emperor Constantine, the assembly of bishops accepted the Nicene Creed, which stated that God and Christ were one. Six more councils convened throughout Asia Minor to clear up debates. The last Council, called to resolve the issue of iconoclasm in 787 AD, returned to Nicaea and met in the Ayasofya church. After a brief flirtation with the Crusaders and the Seljuks, İznik fell under Ottoman rule in 1331. A porcelain industry developed and thus began the production of the renowned blue İznik tiles, like those which line the interior of the Blue Mosque in İstanbul. Today, İznik is a sleepy town, except for two months in the summer when vacationers fill the few lakeside motels and tea gardens. The ruins here are in no way monumental, but the verdant hills and orchards and soothing waters of Lake İznik will engage you for a day or two. İznik makes a good daytrip from Bursa.

ORIENTATION AND PRACTICAL INFORMATION

Kılıçaslan Cad. and Atatürk Cad. separate İznik into quarters and meet in the center at the Ayasofya church. The lake is at the west end of town, and much of the city is enclosed by ancient walls.

Tourist Office: (tel. 757 1454; fax 757 1933). With your back to the bus station, walk three blocks to the right, turn left onto Kılıçaslan Cad., ascend a flight of stairs, and follow the signs. Open daily, 8:30am-noon and 1-5:30pm, in winter officially Mon.-Fri. although sometimes also Sat.-Sun. when there's demand.

PTT: South of the tourist office on Kılıçaslan Cad. (With your back to the tourist office, turn left onto Kılıçaslan Cad.) Offers **currency exchange** and cashes traveler's checks. Open daily 8:30am-12:30pm, 1:30-5:30pm. **Telephone code:** 224.

Buses: *Dolmuş* and buses serve Bursa (hourly from 6:55am until dusk, 1½hr., $1). One daily bus each to Ankara and İstanbul. *Dolmuş* run to **Yalova** (hourly through mid-afternoon, $1.50). Or hop off the bus to İstanbul at Yalova ($1).

Ferries: Leave from nearby Yalova (58km) for İstanbul.

ACCOMMODATIONS

Frankfurt Pension and Café, M. Kemalpaşa Mah., 18 Sahil Yolu (tel. 757 3029 or 757 1937). Right on the beach (turn right at the end of Kılıçaslan). Clean rooms, with a kindly, solicitous manager who speaks German. The kitchen/lounge on the first floor is very light and airy (bonus: TV). Singles $10, w/ shower $12; doubles $20, w/ shower $24; triples $30, w/ shower $36. Breakfast included.

Burcum Motel, Kemalpaşa Mah., 20 Sahil Yolu (tel. 757 1011). On the same part of the lake. Similarly clean rooms and terraces facing the lake. All rooms have a shower and toilet (even paper). 24-hr. hot water during full occupancy, otherwise available 7:30pm-11am. Singles $15; doubles $20. Breakfast included. You may want to forgo breakfast and pay less. 10% group discount.

Murat Pension, Spandau Blv. (tel. 757 3300). Farther up along the lake. Not as scenic as some other pensions, but cheaper, with 24-hr. hot water. Hall showers. Kitchen on each floor. Pool table in café. Singles $5, doubles $10, triples $15, quads $20. Breakfast $2.50.

Çamlık Motel/Restaurant, 1 Sahil Yolu (tel. 757 1362; fax 757 1630). On the beach in the other direction. Travel stickers decorate the window. All rooms have working showers. Spectacular view from roof. Singles $7, doubles $14, triples $17. Breakfast included.

FOOD AND ENTERTAINMENT

Inexpensive prices and breathtaking location make for ideal dining at the restaurants by the lake. The management and waiters of the **Dallas** do not speak English, but their simple, delicious food makes it worth a trip (chicken dinner, $3.50). Enjoy a gelato after dinner at **Lambada Café** for a trifling 30¢. The **Kırık Çatal Restaurant,** 200m down the street from Dallas, is a little more expensive, but the food is also a little better. Languish on the shady patio as you gaze at the lake. In town, locals suggest **Çiçek Izgara,** 147 Kılıçaslan Cad. (tel. 757 5575), up the street away from the lake (kebap and coke for less than $1). Open 8am-10pm. The cafés across the street from Ayasofya are also quite pleasant.

SIGHTS

The **Ayasofya** (Saint Sophia or Church of the Holy Wisdom) at the town's central intersection was built as a church in the 4th century by the Byzantines. Osman, the founder of the Ottoman dynasty, converted the Ayasofya into a mosque in 1331. Chief Court Architect Mimar Sinan renovated the building during the reign of Süleyman the Magnificent (1520-1566). Decrepit and surprisingly small, this is nevertheless an attractive site. The few pieces of religious art are small and captivating. Notable features include the mosaic floor and a mural of the Virgin Mary and Jesus. (Open daily 9am-noon, 1-5pm. Admission $1.25, 75¢ with ISIC.) The aging **Murat Hamamı** (Turkish bath), just south of the Ayasofya, still offers baths in the company of very amiable patrons who do not speak a word of English. (Open daily 8am-1pm for men, 1pm-5pm for women. Bath $1.50, children $1. Scrub $1. Massage $1.25.) The **Yeşil Cami** (Green Mosque), located near the tourist office in one of the quieter areas of town, was built by architect Hacı Musa in 1378. The green bricks that decorate the minaret were precursors of the celebrated İznik tiles. The pale marble structure rises from the center of a lush park filled with rose bushes and fallen columns. The shade and quiet there make the park a perfect place to have lunch and read in the afternoon sunlight.

Murat I constructed the **Nilüfer Hatun İmareti** (charitable foundation), across the street from the mosque, to honor his mother, the first Christian wife of an Ottoman sultan. The museum now housed in this magnificent building displays many artifacts excavated in İznik and briefly traces the history of İsnik tile-making (admission $1.25, students 60¢). In the winter, museum officials have the keys to all of the following: the Ayasofya; a 4th-century underground baptismal **spring;** and a **catacomb,** intricately decorated with Byzantine murals, 4km out of town (Taxi to catacomb $5. $2 donation expected at the museum). The Roman Theater, the mosques around town, and the four major and 12 minor **gates** of the city walls are all worth a visit.

İznik's *faience* industry has not yet died. Shops along the main street sell earthenware tiles and plates decorated with opaque, colored glazes, starting at $10. Today's tilemakers occasionally let visitors watch the tilemaking process. Ask someone to show you the easy-to-find *fırın* (kiln), or follow the signs leading from the street that feeds into the bus station parking lot (no parking for tourists).

Aegean Coast

Fabulous classical ruins and a sinuous coastline that conceals sublime beaches have helped transform Turkey's once tranquil Aegean Coast into an increasingly popular destination. Carpet shops and discos are slowly edging out traditional Turkish bazaars and teahouses. The Aegean Coast's natural beauty and five millennia of history are captivating, but you may have to search a bit to find traditional settlements, if that's what you seek.

The Aegean Coast's first foreign visitors were the ancient Greeks, who established ports in the area. As Alexander the Great and subsequent Hellenic rulers pushed the Aegean empire eastward, ports became nerve centers of commerce along the major trade routes of the ancient world, growing even as Greek civilization declined. Today, Hellenistic ruins—especially extensive at Pergamon, Ephesus, Aphrodisias, and Hierapolis—stand as weathered testaments to the coast's classical heritage.

Scholarship followed commerce to Asia Minor. Thriving trade necessitated exposure to Eastern cultures and languages. Western philosophy, mathematics, and science—particularly in the teachings of Heraclitus of Ephesus and in the works of Thales, Anaximander, Anaximenes, and Anaxagoras, all scholars in the Ionian school of Miletus—emerged from Hellenic civilization. The Apostle Paul's proselytizing mission started the transmission of Christianity, which culminated in Emperor Constantine's conversion in 323 and the subsequent birth of the Holy Roman Empire. Islam has been the major religion here for the last 600 years, but a sizable Orthodox Christian population survived until the 1923 exchange of populations with Greece. Christian pilgrims continue to flock to the seven churches of Asia Minor referred to in *Revelations:* Pergamon, Thyatira, Smyrna, Sardis, Philadelphia, Laodicea, and Ephesus.

No legal barriers prevent tourists from traveling from the Greek islands to Turkey, though some travelers have reported complications and exorbitant port taxes.

ÇANAKKALE

ORIENTATION AND PRACTICAL INFORMATION

Inexpensive accommodations and frequent bus connections to nearby sights and to other cities make **Çanakkale** an easy base from which to explore Gallipoli and Troy. Because of its proximity to the site of the disastrous WWI battle, Çanakkale is particularly hospitable to New Zealanders and Australians, many of whose troops were slaughtered at Gallipoli, or Gelibolu. Turkish hotel and restaurant managers often mumble Australianisms like "G'day" and "No worries."

Tourist Office: 67 Iskele Meydanı (tel. 217 1187). From the bus station, take a left out the main doors, then take the next right onto Demircioğlu Cad. (following the "feribot" sign), and continue onto the docks. The clock tower and the **tourist office** will be on your left just before the shore. (If you arrive by ferry, the office is straight ahead to your right.) Open Mon.-Fri. 8:30am-noon, 1:30-5:30pm.

Tourist Agencies: Down Under Travel Agency, İsmetpaşa Mah., 14 Atatürk Cad., Eceabat 17900 (tel. 814 2431; fax 814 2430), based on the European side in nearby Eceabat 7km from the Gelibolu battlegrounds, offers a bargain tour of Gallipoli for $6.25. The 30-year old **Troyanzac Travel Agency** (tel. 217 5849; fax 217 5847), to the right of the clock tower, offers car rental, private guides, hotel reservations, and general information as well as half-day guided tours of Gallipoli (4hr., $15) and Troy (3hr., $15). **Anatur** (tel. 217 5482; fax 217 2906) makes hotel reservations, sells bus and airplane tickets, rents cars, and provides tours to Gallipoli (5hr., $15), Troy (2½hr.), and Cape Helles (10hr.).

Postal Code: 17100. **Telephone code**: 286.

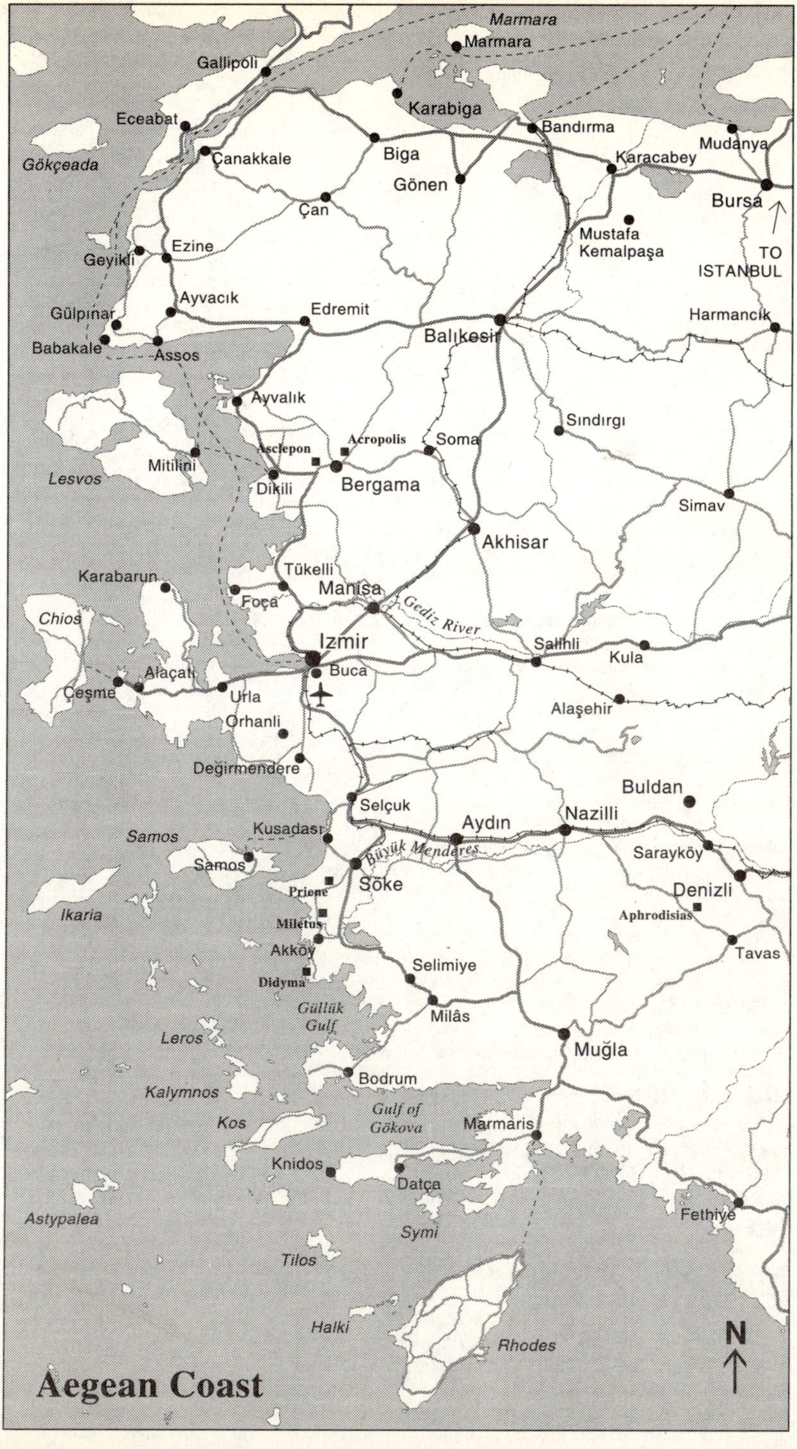
Marmara
Marmara
Gallipoli
Karabiga
Eceabat
Bandırma
Mudanya
Gökçeada
Çanakkale
Biga
Karacabey
Gönen
Bursa
Çan
Mustafa Kemalpaşa
TO ISTANBUL
Ezine
Geyikli
Ayvacık
Edremit
Gülpınar
Harmancık
Balıkesir
Babakale
Assos
Ayvalık
Sındırgı
Acropolis
Soma
Asclepon
Mitilini
Lesvos
Dikili
Bergama
Simav
Akhisar
Karabarun
Tükelli
Manisa
Foça
Chios
Gediz River
Izmir
Salihli
Kula
Alaçatı
Buca
Çeşme
Urla
Alaşehir
Orhanli
Değirmendere
Buldan
Selçuk
Nazilli
Kusadası
Aydın
Samos
Büyük Menderes
Sarayköy
Samos
Priene
Söke
Denizli
Ikaria
Aphrodisias
Miletus
Akköy
Tavas
Selimiye
Didyma
Güllük Gulf
Milâs
Leros
Muğla
Bodrum
Kalymnos
Gulf of Gökova
Kos
Marmaris
Knidos
Datça
Fethiye
Astypalea
Symi
Tilos
Halki
Rhodes
N
Aegean Coast

Buses: Arrive every 1-2 hr. from Bursa (5½hr., $6.25), Edirne (stops at Eceabat for ferry to Çanakkale, 4hr., $6.25), İstanbul (5hr., $9), Bergama (4hr., $6.25), Ayvalık (3½hr., $5), Ankara ($15), and İzmir (5hr., $7.50). Buses leave more frequently in the morning; inquire early as to times. Frequent *dolmuş* run to Çanakkale (45min., $1.20).

Ferries: To Eceabat (every hr., in winter every 2hr., 50¢). Be careful not to take the smaller ferry to Kilitbahir; ask which one is going where. In Eceabat you can hire a taxi (officially $23, but drivers bargain) to tour the battlefields of Gelibolu.

ACCOMMODATIONS

The tourist business here can be quite competitive, and while this situation can give the traveler a better bargaining position when settling on prices, it also lends itself to some cutthroat business practices. If you're curious, competition is one of the first things hotel managers talk about. Use discretion when choosing accommodations and when dealing with pushy proprietors. That said, you can find many budget accommodations in the area surrounding the clock tower.

Yellow Rose, 5 Yeni Sokak, around a corner about 50m from the clock tower. Pension featuring an outdoor garden-café with fountain, laundry facilities, and large wall-papered rooms. Hot showers. The film "Gallipoli," with Mel Gibson, is shown every night for those who plan to tour the site. Singles $5, doubles $10, triples $15.

Hotel Efes, Kemalpaşa Mah. Aralık Sok. (tel. 217 3256). One block from the clock tower. Simple, colorful, and airy rooms with negotiable prices surrounded by a rose-filled garden with a fountain. Some baths with hand-held showers. Toilet paper may be missing. Helpful manager is the sister of the manager of Yellow Rose. Singles $5, doubles $10, triples $11.25. Breakfast $1.25.

Hotel Konak, 14 Fetvane Sok. (tel. 217 1150 or 217 1578). Behind the clock tower to the left. Spacious, dark rooms. Manager gives discount if the hot water runs out. Singles $5, w/ shower $6; doubles $9, w/ shower $10; triples $11.25, w/ shower $13.50. If you have a room w/o bath, hot showers cost $1.25.

Kervansaray Otel, 13 Fetvane Sok. (217 81 92). Across from Konak. A gracefully timeworn structure with a stone fountain in the courtyard. Hand-pump showers. Run by a brother of the proprietors of Yellow Rose and Efes. Some English spoken. Same prices as Konak, but airy atmosphere. Breakfast $1.50.

Anzac Hotel, 8 Saat Kulesi Meydanı (tel. 217 7777; fax 217 20 18). Near the clock tower. Not to be confused with the Anzac House. Carpets, bathtubs, and toilets "sanitized for your protection." Some rooms include TV or refrigerator. Singles $20, doubles $30, triples $40. Bargaining may be fruitful.

Çanakkale Öğrenci Yurdu, on Atatürk Cad. (tel. 217 2966; fax 217 2906). From the bus station, head left and walk for 10-15min. Just past the archaeological museum. Rents beds ($5) in plain, single-sex dormitories to ID-carrying students. To arrange accommodations, ask for the *müdür* (director). Hotel closes for renovations about once a year; call ahead to make sure that it is open. Men's building only open during the summer. Possible group discount.

FOOD AND ENTERTAINMENT

For fresh seafood, go to the restaurants on the quay. Try **Yeni Entelektüel Restaurant** for fresh *lüfer* (bluefish), salad, and a beer ($5). A block or two inland, cheaper restaurants abound. **Yalova Liman Restaurant** is only a brief walk upstairs within 100m of the main pier. Dine on fried mussels and beer for only $2. Its atmosphere, while relaxed, is more formal than prices would suggest. The rooftop terrace affords an inspiring view of the Dardanelles. (Open daily noon-midnight.) To stay away from more pricey harborside restaurants, waltz your Matilda over to the **Aussi/Kiwi Restaurant,** 32 Yalı Cad. (tel. 212 17 22). Take the street to the right of the clock tower and meet Kemal, the amiable manager. A mecca for backpackers of all nationalities, the A/K sells *şiş kebap*, vegetables, and a Coke for under $4. (Open 8am-2am, in winter 8am-midnight.) For a good meal at a reasonable price, also try **Intepe**

Seyir Yeri Aile Kır Lokantası (Observation Point Family-Style Country Restaurant), on İzmir Cad. halfway between Çanakkale and Troy (tel. 223 33 32; 15 minutes by *dolmuş*). The view of the sunset over the Dardanelles is breathtaking.

SIGHTS

The town has only a smattering of sights. The **archaeological museum,** with artifacts from Troy, features a fantastic statue of Hadrian, busts of Augustus, and archaeological finds from the pre-Hellenic, Hellenic, and Roman periods (open Mon.-Sat. 8am-5pm; admission $1.25, 65¢ with ISIC). There's also a **fortress** with a vintage World War I cannon and warship to commemorate the Gallipoli battle. **Çimenlik Kalesi (Grassy Castle),** the castle-turned-naval museum, lies 200m past the clock tower (open Fri.-Sun. and Tue.-Wed. 8:30am-noon and 1:30-5pm; 25¢). The Aegean Coast's northernmost resort, Çanakkale faces the narrowest point of the Dardanelles, which in large part explains why the British chose to mount their disastrous WWI campaign here. Just in case you were wondering, ANZAC, the word that crops up in the names of various establishments in town, stands for the Australian and New Zealand Army Corps, many of whose soldiers fell here during WWI.

About 55km southwest of Çanakkale lie the famed waters of the **Kestanbol thermal springs** (tel. 658 84 28), reachable by *dolmuş* or taxi. The waters supposedly have curative properties for people with skin, heart, and circulation problems.

■ NEAR ÇANAKKALE

GALLIPOLI

Across the Dardanelles on the European side lies the battlefield of **Gallipoli,** known as Gelibolu in Turkey. In 1915-16, seeing an opportunity to secure the Balkan front, Winston Churchill proposed that Britain use its superior naval forces to launch an attack on the Dardanelles. The navy would then conquer Constantinople, driving Turkey out of the war, and open communications with Russia. The navy was bombarded at the narrowest part of the strait, so the British navy turned its forces to the peninsula. The British high command sent wave after wave of Australian, New Zealander, and British troops against the highly fortified Turkish positions here, with brutal losses. This battle launched its hero, Atatürk, on a rapid rise to his status as Turkish founding father. Each year thousands of Australians and New Zealanders make pilgrimages to war cemeteries here, where 22,000 Allied dead lie buried. There is a special dawn ceremony at the cove.

To explore the battlefields systematically, you can take a guided tour. Relaxed and exceptionally affordable tours come from the newly established Down Under Travel Agency, based in nearby Eceabat. $6.25 covers transportation, lunch, and a showing of "Gallipoli." The tour guide T.J., whose nickname derives from his resemblance to Tom Jones, gives excellent Anglo-Australian language guidance. You can make reservations at the Aussie/Kiwi Restaurant. The Troyanzac Travel Agency (not to be confused with Yılmaz Tours) sends tours at 10am and 3pm (only 10am in winter). If not enough people show, the tour is sometimes dropped. Bargain with Hüseyin, the theatrical guide. Or try Anatur, which provides an excellent English-speaking tour guide. The tour begins the night before with showings of "Gallipoli" and a documentary, "The Fatal Shore." Breakfast, tea, and transportation are included. In 1996, Anatur may begin renting bikes ($5-6 per day) for touring Gallipoli. It is usually cheaper to take a tour than to shuttle around in taxis. Nevertheless, the proprietor of **Türkmen Carpet** (in the clock tower square in Çanakkale) can make arrangements with drivers.

The **Kabatepe Museum** (tel. 814 1297. Open 5-6 days per week 8:30am-12:30pm and 1:30-5:30pm; in winter 8am-noon and 1-5pm; admission 50¢, free for tour groups), is accessible by *dolmuş* from Eceabat and located in the **National Park** (tel. 814 1128; open daily 8:30am-5:30pm; admission 15¢), where in July 1994 a bushfire destroyed 4049 hectares. Fortunately, a massive cleanup effort has rendered the landscape green once again. From there it's a 4km walk to **Anzac Cove,** and a 7km hike uphill to the **Lone Pine Monument,** an Australian memorial and cemetery.

TROY

Truva lies 32km south of Çanakkale. The site slept, forgotten, until Heinrich Schliemann, a German-born American millionaire-turned-amateur archaeologist, decided to prove that the Homeric myths were not pure fiction. Staking out the most promising site along the coast, he hired local workers and began excavating. To the astonishment of fellow archaeologists, Schliemann uncovered the ancient city.

People raised on stories of the Trojan War should not expect imposing ruins; the city Homer wrote about came tumbling down 3000 years ago. But the remaining Bronze Age fortifications, given their age, are remarkably well-preserved. The tacky wooden horse that assures you that you've reached Troy is, however, a new addition. Nine distinct strata, each containing the remains of a city from a different period, have been identified and dubbed Troy I through Troy IX. An illustrated explanation of each stratum is available in the Excavation House (on your right after you enter and pass the horse). Troy I dates from 3200 BC. The city of Homer's *Iliad* is now believed to be Troy VI, *not,* ironically, Troy II, the city Schliemann excavated (Open 8am-8pm, off season 8am-5pm. Admission $1, students 50¢.)

Take a *dolmuş* from the station in Çanakkale, and arrange for the *dolmuş* to wait for an hour or two while you explore the ruins. If you want more time to explore, other *dolmuş* are easy to come by. If you must stay, the **Hotel Hisarlık** (tel. 283 1026 or 283 1992) rents very nice rooms with a hot shower, toilet paper, and a common balcony, but they aren't cheap (24-hr. hot water. Single $10, doubles w/showers $20, triples w/showers $24). The proprietor also gives tours and runs a café and a gift shop. For a cultural experience, go to **Pansiyon Varol** (tel. 283 1071), in the center of the village. It is enriched by a teahouse and surrounded by the homey smell of manure. The affable proprietor, who speaks German but not English, will let you camp for free in the garden or terrace, then shower for $1. Doubles $10 per person, including shower and breakfast.

■■■ AYVALIK

Ayvalık's red rooftops and the turquoise waters of the Aegean form a pleasant juxtaposition that lends itself to the ineffable calm of the town. A wealthy Greek settlement until the 1923 exchange of populations, this small fishing village is reminiscent of a Greek town and, appropriately, it still makes its living from oil-production. A mere 30km from the Greek island of Lesvos, Ayvalık features pleasant beaches and eclectic seafood. The town is situated in the Gulf of Edremit, surrounded by 25 outlying islands, pine woods, and olive groves.

ORIENTATION AND PRACTICAL INFORMATION

İnönü Cad., the main road, runs parallel to the coastline and turns into Atatürk Cad. after the bazaar area. The only other main street is Sefa Cad., which runs parallel to İnönü Cad. and Atatürk Cad.

Tourist Office: (tel. 312 2753). In Cumhuriyet Meydanı (Republic Square), on the docks, in the center of town. Open daily 9am-1pm, 3-7:15pm.

Police: İnönü Cad. (tel. 312 1010).

Tours: Both **Ayvalık Tours** (tel. 312 27 40) and **Yeni İstanbul Tours** (tel. 312 6002) offer tours of Lesvos ($40 one-way, $55 round-trip).

Currency Exchange: Günaydın Döviz, across from the Ekonomi Hotel, exchanges currency and cashes traveler's checks.

PTT: İnönü Cad. (tel. 312 1003). Open 8:30am-11pm. **Traveler's checks** cashed 8:30am-5:30pm. **Postal code:** 10400. **Telephone code:** 266.

Buses: *Dolmuş* pass along the highway every ½hr. bound for the bus terminal, on İnönü Cad. next to the Türkiye İş Bankası, about 2mi. south of the tourist office.

Easy service to Çanakkale (roughly every hr., 3½hr., $5) and İzmir (roughly every hr., 1½hr., $3.25). Minibuses run to **Sarmısaklı (Garlicky) beach** and **Altınova (Golden Meadow) beach** every 15min. (40¢), leaving from across the street from the tourist office.

Ferries: To Lesvos (3 per week; $40, not including a steep port tax of 4000dr).

Pharmacies: In the bazaar off İnönü Cad. near Ekonomi Hotel.

ACCOMMODATIONS

Taksiyarhis Pansiyon, (tel. 312 1494) İsmetpaşa Mah., 71 Mareşal Kaçmak Cad. Hidden among the twisting alleyways near Taksiyarhis Church. From Republic Square, go up the second street across from the PTT. Or ask for directions to the church, about 500m off İnönü Cad. Unquestionably a jewel among Ayvalık's hotels, it is quiet, out of the way of the hectic tourist scene, and blessed with breathtaking views of the sea and surrounding neighborhood. Enjoy the traditional Turkish decor and in-house Turkish bath. 24-hr. hot water. Hot showers on first floor, cold on second. Bike rental and laundry service available. Singles $5, doubles $10, triples $15. Breakfast $2.

Ekonomi Hotel, 38-40 İnönü Cad., 80m from the tourist office. Walking to the bus station, it's on the right inside a shopping arcade. Clean, carpeted rooms come with shower, toilet paper, and 24-hr. hot water. Rooms in the back are quieter than in front. Laundry $3.75 per load. Singles $9, doubles $15.50, triples $22, quads $29. Breakfast included. Groups of 20 get 20% off.

Yurtotel (tel. 312 2109), also near İnönü Cad., at Republic Square. Clean-ish rooms with shower and toilet. Second-floor terrace, above the bus stop, has a view of the water. Singles $2.50, w/ bath $4; doubles $5, w/ bath $10; triples w/ bath $15; quads w/ bath $20.

FOOD AND ENTERTAINMENT

Ayvalık may be quiet, but it is blessed with seaside restaurants and quality seafood. **Kardeşler (Brothers) Kebapçı** (tel. 312 18 57; open 8am-2am), has two branches. The first, 3 blocks inland at 42 İnönü Cad., sits across the street from the Emlak Bankası on İnönü Cad. and serves mainly *kebap* ($2.50) and *pide*. The second, well-situated on the sea at 7 Sahil Boyu, offers delectable fish. **Se & Do,** near the seaside Brothers in the direction of the customs office, is sparkling clean, with huge meals (salad; bread; drinks; *kebap*, squid, fish, or shrimp; melon; and coffee) for $6.25. Tourists also rave about **Dayım Ocakbaşı,** across from the Ekonomi Hotel, which has kebaps ($2.50-4), pide ($2), and salad ($1.25). Cheaper places can be found in the bazaar off İnönü Cad. along with pastry shops, barbers, and pharmacies.

SIGHTS

Aya Nikola (Çınarlı Cami) boasts beautiful Old and New Testament frescoes (open 9am-noon and 1-11pm). Several 19th-century Byzantine churches, that have since been converted into mosques, house many of the city's treasures. The **Taksiyarhis church** houses portraits painted on fish skins. Another church, on **Alibey Adası** (Sir Ali's Island), has remnants of frescoes on the walls. Although graffiti has slightly tainted the frescoes, they are in remarkably good condition. For a panoramic view of **Sarmısaklı** and Alibey, visit the **Devil's Dinner Table** (Şeytan Sofrası), which is not a restaurant. From far away, this large rock actually looks like a table. Ordinarily, *dolmuş* (30¢) depart at sunset for the best viewing, wait 45min., and then return. However they do not run if there are too few tourists. Sarmıskalı, 6km south of Ayvalık, is a growing, pricey resort town. Although hotels are expensive, the sandy beach is one of the finest in Turkey.

■■■ PERGAMON (BERGAMA)

Pergamon's archaeological sights, towering 330m above the city, are extensive and impressive, but don't let them distract you from the striking juxtaposition of 150-

year-old Greek houses and thousand-year-old ruins in Bergama. The deep-bedded Caicus River that flows through the city adds to Bergama's quiet charm.

ORIENTATION AND PRACTICAL INFORMATION

The ruins of Pergamon gaze across the river at the pleasant, modern city of **Bergama.** The city's main road winds its way to the ancient ruins.

Tourist Office: (tel. 632 1862). From the new main bus station, go right onto the main road and walk 1km. Open daily 8:30am-7pm, Oct.-March Mon.-Sat. 8:30am-5:30pm. It's in Cumhuriyet Meydanı, on the left coming from the bus station. If you reach the bust of Atatürk, you've passed it.

Police: (tel. 632 7001). Across and up the street from the PTT.

PTT: İzmir Cad. (tel. 632 3996). No English spoken. Offers **currency exchange** during business hours. Open Mon.-Fri. 8:30am-12:30pm, 1:30-5:30pm. **Telephone code:** 232.

Buses: Two terminals (*garaj*) serve Bergama. The old terminal, near the Basilica, runs buses to İzmir, İstanbul, Ankara, and Soma. The new terminal, across from the park on İzmir Cad., runs buses to the same major cities as well as minibuses to Ayvalık. Buses run to Bursa (1 every evening, 6½hr., $9), İzmir (every hr., 1½ hr., $2), İstanbul (1-2 per day, 10hr., $12.50), and Ankara (1 per day running overnight, 8hr., $11). Keep in mind that it's a short ride to İzmir, where there are many more connections. When arriving, try to take a bus that trundles directly into Bergama; most buses from İzmir to Çanakkale drop you at the turn-off 7km away. Frequent *dolmuş* service to town is available ($1.50). If you arrive at night, you may have to spend $3 on a taxi into town. The center of town is to the right as you exit the station.

ACCOMMODATIONS

Pergamon Pension (tel. 633 2395). Heading from the bus station, pass the PTT and you'll see a fork; bear right—the pension's on the left. A 150-year-old Greek-style mansion with high ceilings, a café, and a Turkish bath on the premises. Superior location and comfort. All rooms have toilets. $7.50 per person. Breakfast $2.50.

Pension Athena (tel. 633 3420). In a restored Ottoman house. "Not the best, but we're trying to get there." Hidden and a little bit run down, this nonetheless pleasant pension offers 24-hr. hot water, living-room cable TV, and a café. Breakfast $2. Dinner of 2 dishes, salad, and drink $3 in July-Sept. Generally $5 per person negotiable, depending on number of people and placement. Bathless singles $5, w/ shower $7.

Sayın Pension, Zafer Mah., 12 İzmir Cad. (tel. 633 2405). Near the bus station outside of town. Turn left as you leave the bus station; it's up the street on the right. Immaculate, carpeted rooms, which include mirror and desk, are simple and well-lit. Some rooms lack showers, but there's 24-hr. hot water and toilet paper. Eight-story building with no elevator. Singles $6.25, w/ shower $7.50. Prices are negotiable. Breakfast $1.75. Dinner $2.50.

Berksoy camping (tel. 633 2595), **Kleopatra Kamping,** and **Karavan camping** (tel. 633 3902) lie 2km beyond the tourist office on the main road. Guests have access to electricity, water, a kitchen, and a **pool** (non-guests may swim for $1).

FOOD AND ENTERTAINMENT

Relax under the shelter of luxuriant vines at **Meydan Restaurant** (tel. 633 1793), on the right side of the main street about 500m after Pergamon Pension as you walk from the station. (Full meal $3.50; open 7am-2am, off-season 7am-midnight.) **Sağlam İşletmecilik,** 3 İstiklal Meydanı (tel. 633 20 46), off the main road as you veer left to follow the signs to Pension Athena, has fantastic *kaşarlı kiremitte,* a hot dish of eggplant, tomatoes, peppers, onions, cheese, and bread ($2.50; open 7am-11pm or midnight). Diagonally across the street, **Sarmaşık (Ivy) Lokantası** (tel. 632 27 41), on İzmir Cad., serves great food at reasonable prices (full meal around $4; open 6am-10pm). Sample the *baklava* at one of the many *pastane*.

SIGHTS

Pergamon's long history of fame and wealth began when Piletarus, a regional commander, seized the treasury he had been entrusted to keep and set himself up as king. Its ruins, loping over more than 30,000 acres, are located on two principal sites: the **Acropolis,** which looms majestically above the town, and the **Asclepion** (medical center), lying in the valley below. Under the direction of Galen, the most famous physician of the Roman Empire, Pergamon became the center of the cult of Asclepius, the Greek demi-god of healing and eponym of the Asclepion, which was both a temple and place of healing. Allegedly, no patient left here unhealed, though undoubtedly many were rushed out the back door in the throes of death. An impressive portion of the Asclepion remains, including a marble colonnade, a theater, and healing rooms. The ruins of a huge gymnasium, a Roman circus, several temples, and the lavishly frescoed **House of Attalus** also lie scattered about. The most notable attraction is the mammoth **amphitheater,** capable of seating 10,000 spectators.

In ancient times, only the library in Alexandria surpassed Pergamon's, which contained more than 200,000 volumes. When the Alexandrians attempted to eclipse the Pergamon book bonanza by limiting the flow of papyrus from the Nile, Pergamon scholars invented parchment from goat hide. The plot thickened: when the library's Egyptian rival went up in flames, Marc Antony plundered Pergamon's shelves and presented the pilfered collection to Cleopatra. Most of the **Altar of Zeus** graces the Pergamon Museum—in Berlin. On your way up to the **Royal Palaces** write down a wish and tie it onto a branch of the "wishing tree" on your left.

There are no buses to the ruins; walk, or, if too much *nargile* (water pipe) smoking has debilitated your lungs, take a taxi ($12 for full tour, $5 to the first site). If you take a taxi it's best to be dropped off at the Acropolis, and then to walk down through the rest of the ruins. To reach the Acropolis, follow the main road past the **Kızıl Avlu,** or Red Basilica, which was originally built as a second-century temple to the Egyptian God Serapis and converted into a basilica during the Byzantine Empire. Turn left off the road and walk towards the first ruins, the Lower Agora. Here you'll find a footpath that winds among the ruins to the summit. The hike to the top of the Acropolis can be exhausting, especially on hot days. The Asclepion is on the other side of town, 3km past the tourist office; following the signs. (Do not take photos of the military base along the Asclepion; it is illegal, and armed soldiers take this law seriously.) The **Archaeological and Ethnographic Museum** displays artifacts from Pergamon as well as a collection of traditional Turkish crafts. (The Acropolis, Asclepion, and Basilica are all open daily 8:30am-7pm, Oct.-April daily 8:30am-5:30pm. The museum is open year-round 8:30am-5:30pm. Admission to Acropolis and Asclepion $2.50 each, students $1.25. Admission to Archaeological Museum and Basilica $2.50 each, students $1.25).

■■■ İZMİR

Of the original Hellenistic city-states along the Aegean coast of Asia Minor, only **Smyrna,** now Turkish **İzmir,** survived the catastrophes that befell the region. From the rubble of Smyrna's past, İzmir (pop. 2 million) has risen to become Turkey's third largest city and second largest port. Now a western city with wide boulevards and plazas around an arc-shaped waterfront, İzmir is a sticky industrial wasteland in some places and fascinatingly lush in others. A stroll through the twisting alleyways in one of İzmir's residential districts may be enchanting, but the exhaust fumes on the major boulevards will surely put to rest any thoughts of a Turkish wonderland.

The tumult of modern buildings in İzmir's downtown is marked on the north and south ends by monuments to the city's most prominent personages. Alexander's **Kadifekale** (Velvet Fortress) remains intact and menacing on the waterfront next to NATO headquarters, and an equestrian statue of Atatürk fearlessly leads a regiment of office buildings. The domes of small mosques, unexpected amidst tenements and towers, attest to the traditional lifestyle that persists amidst the concrete. The Ottoman-style clock tower in Konak Square, donated by the Sultan Abdülhamid, serves as the city trademark. Historically fascinating, İzmir nonetheless offers little in the way of conventional sight-seeing. Many of İzmir's cultural attractions were destroyed by the retreating Greek army in 1923; the rest are relatively inaccessible to non-Turkish-speakers who spend only a few days here. But if you want to experience an authentic Turkish town and don't have time to travel east, İzmir is the place to go. In this respect, İzmir resembles Naples, Italy, for both have a nasty industrial atmosphere, represent an intercultural crossroads, and display an intriguingly authentic culture that is largely inaccessible to tourists.

Smyrna first came into its own in the 9th century BC and thrived before Lydians from Sardis destroyed the town in 600 BC. In 334 BC, Alexander the Great conquered and then refounded Smyrna atop Mt. Pagus, now called the Kadifekale. During the Roman and Byzantine periods, the port of Smyrna grew prosperous and cosmopolitan. The diversion of the River Hermes prevented Smyrna's harbor from silting, thereby rescuing it from the landlocked fate of its neighbors. In 1535, Süleyman the Magnificent signed a treaty with France that brought trade to Smyrna. The constant influx of Christian and Jewish merchants during this time earned the city the moniker "Infidel Smyrna." After World War I, Greece, enticed by the vision of a born-again Byzantine Empire, attacked Turkey. Mustafa Kemal, soon to be Kemal Atatürk, expelled the invaders with an impromptu army and regained the ashes of Smyrna in the final battle of the Turkish War of Independence on Sept. 9, 1922.

ORIENTATION AND PRACTICAL INFORMATION

İzmir's principal boulevards radiate from rotaries, called *meydan.* **Cumhuriyet Meydanı,** on the waterfront, is the city's financial center, home to several banks, travel agencies, and consulates. An astounding number of budget hotels and cheap restaurants, along with several bus company offices and the Alsançak **train station,** are located around **9 Eylül Meydanı,** the center of the Basmane district. From **Yeni Garaj,** the bus station, take municipal bus #50, 53, 56, 249, 250, or 260 to Basmane/Çankaya. Remember to buy your tickets (70¢) at the kiosk before you board. To get back to the bus station, take a bus from Basmane to **Konak Square** (3 stops, Konak being the last), from which you can take bus #50, 56, or 60 to Yeni Garaj. Konak, 10 blocks south of Cumhuriyet Meydanı along the coastal **Atatürk Cad.,** is the center for metropolitan buses and *dolmuş.* Finding your way can be difficult, and street signs are hard to come by, so it's best to make the tourist office your first stop.

Tourist Office: 1/1c Gaziosmanpaşa Blv. (tel. 484 2147; fax. 489 9278). The tallest landmark near it is the Hilton Hotel. (It doesn't cost anything to use it as a landmark.) Take a Basmane-bound bus and get off near 9 Eylül Meydanı, recognizable by the Kültürpark, a complex with entertainment facilities. Look for the big "ETF" over the entrance. From 9 Eylül Meydanı, head down Gazi Blv. (facing away from the Kültürpark, it's the third spoke to your right). Go down this street until the rotary with Gaziosmanpaşa Blv. Turn right and continue almost to the water. The tourist office is on your right, under the Hotel Efes. Open Mon.-Fri. 8:30am-7pm, Sat.-Sun. 9am-5pm; reduced hours in off-season. Small tourist information and complaint office in the **bus station** (open daily 8am-noon and 12:30-8pm).

Police: Dial 155 (special "foreigners" department of the police at 489 0500).

Tourist Police: Call 421 1476 or 422 3461.

PTT: Past the tourist office, on Cumhuriyet Meydanı. Full phone facilities (open 24 hr.) and **traveler's check** and **currency exchange** services (open 8:30am-5:30pm). **Telephone code:** 232. **Postal code:** 35.

American Express: Shares office space with **Pamfilya Turizm,** 270 Atatürk Cad. (tel. 422 4753). Open Mon.-Fri. 8:30am-5:30pm, Sat. 8:30am-noon.

Consulates: Turkish-American Association, 23 Şehit Nevres Blv. (tel. 421 8873; open Mon.-Fri. 8:30am-6pm) performs duties of the **American and British Consulate,** #49 1442 Sok., Alsançak (tel. 463 5151), near the main train station.

Buses: To İstanbul (every ½hr., 9hr., $12), Bursa (6hr., $7), Çanakkale (6hr., $7), Bodrum (4hr., $7), Kuşadası (2hr., $3), Selçuk (1hr., $1.50), and Ankara (8½hr.,

$12) to name a few. Buses to Sardis (Sart), 95km from İzmir, also depart from Yeni Garaj, take the bus to Salihli and ask to be let off at Sardis. For buses to Çeşme and other points west, go to the bus lot at **Üçkuyular,** southwest of the center. From Basmane, take a public bus to Konak, then take #4, 216, 217, 245, or 276. Ask where to get off (accomplished by saying "Burası Üçkuyular mı?" to the person next to you). From Yeni Garaj, take bus #249 or 250 directly to Üçkuyular. Buses run to Çeşme (every ½hr., 6am-8pm). The bus companies and travel agencies near the tourist office often have shuttles to both bus stations.

Ferries: One ferry per week goes to İstanbul (Sun., 19hr., $15 and up).

Medical Emergency: Call 112.

ACCOMMODATIONS

Look in the Basmane area: the small streets between Fevzipaşa Bulvarı and Anafartalar Caddesi are loaded with cheap hotels. Beware of taxi drivers in İzmir: some work on commission and insist on driving you to hotels of *their* choice. Hotels here exemplify the credo that you get what you pay for. More expensive places can be found near the tourist office.

Otel Saray, 635 Anafartalar Cad. (tel. 483 6946). Go straight up Gaziosmanpaşa Blv. from the tourist office and make a left on Anafartalar Cad.; Otel Saray is up the street on the left. Clean, airy rooms and pleasant atrium make Saray seem like a transplanted Miami Beach resort (thong bikinis not recommended). Due to its proximity to numerous mosques, calls to prayer may arrest your attention. 24-hr. hot water. Singles $4.75, doubles $9.50, triples $14.25.

Yıldız Palas Hotel, #50 1296 Sok. (tel. 425 1518). One block north of Anafartalar Cad and the train station. Small and quiet; rooms have pleasant views. Clean, utilitarian rooms, none with shower. Singles $4, doubles $7.25, triples $10.75; double bed $6.75.

Bilen Palas Otel, #68 1369 Sok. (tel. 483 9246). Right off 9 Eylül Meydanı. Spacious and clean, with pleasant views and odors; unfortunately, it also has Turkish-style "pit" toilets. Singles $4.75, doubles $9.50, triples $12; shower included. Laundry 65¢.

Otel Özcan, #3 1368 Sok. (tel. 483 5052). Cool, quiet, spacious, and carpeted rooms but the showers are small and have low water pressure. Singles $5.25, w/shower and toilet $6; doubles $9.50, w/same $11; triples $14.25, w/same $19.25; quads w/same $25.75.

FOOD AND ENTERTAINMENT

Decent, inexpensive Turkish restaurants saturate Anafartalar Cad. **Şark Lokantası** (tel. 489 4706), some 4 blocks toward the water beyond Otel Saray, is always jammed by locals at mealtime. (Mixed plate and Coke $2. Open 6am-10pm.) Since you're in Basmane, you might as well try **Basmane Kebap Salonu,** 1571A Fevzipaşa Blv. (tel. 425 5019). Fevzipaşa Blv. is the street that dead-ends into the train station. A small, tidy place, the Salon serves full meals for about $5. (Open 11am-midnight.) For Eastern Turkish cuisine, head to **Urfa Lokantası,** 854 Anafartalar Cad. (tel. 484 3408), across from the police station. (Take the second radial on your left from the Kültürpark entrance and walk past the train station.) At least one unctuous, voluble waiter serves filling meals for about $2; open 24 hr. You can also try a *börek* (see Food, page 425) from one of the abundant *börekçi* along the roads. Gay travelers may appreciate the following welcoming, but somewhat seedy, Turkish baths. **Tevfik Paşa Hamamı,** 501 Anafartalar Cad. (tel. 433 0945 or 484 0326; bath $2.25, scrub $1.50, massage $7.25), and **Yeni Sark Hamamı,** 39c Gaziosmanpaşa Blv. (tel. 425 3785; open daily 6am-10pm; bath, scrub, and massage each $1.75).

SIGHTS

İzmir's **agora** was built in the 4th century BC by Alexander, destroyed by an earthquake in 178 AD, and rebuilt by Emperor Marcus Aurelius soon after. The uninspiring remains are accessible from Anafartalar Cad. Walk south along 941 Sok. from the

Otel Saray. (Open daily 8:30am-5pm. Admission $2.50, students 60¢.) Above the city at Mt. Pagos is the most enduring of Alexander's legacies, the Kadifekale, originally built in the 4th century BC but repeatedly restored and altered by various conquerors. (24 hr.; free.) The park within the walls of Kadifekale is at once vaguely unsavory and intriguing. The view of the city is spectacular, scores of women weaving colorful blankets sit on the lawn, and droves of children scamper about, hassling tourists for money and kicking the occasional dead pigeon. Coming here at night is not advised. Bus #33 from Konak ascends the mountain and affords a thrilling panorama of the bay. If you stroll along Anafartalar Cad. from its beginning at the Basmane station, you'll pass remnants of a less industrialized Turkey: *çay salonu* (teahouses), men smoking *nargile* (water pipes), children and vendors filling the air with their cries, and colorful streets that eventually turn into İzmir's full-fledged **bazaar.** (Open Mon.-Sat. 8:30am-7pm.) İzmir's **archaeological museum** displays the statues of Poseidon and Demeter among various other antiquities. (Open Tues.-Sun. 8:30am-5pm. Admission $2.50, students $1.25.) Next door, there is an **Ethnographical Museum.** (Open Tues.-Sun. 8:30am-5pm; admission $1.25, students 60¢.) The city's cultural center holds a huge **international trade fair** in Kültürpark. İzmir's **international festival** in late June and early July brings classical and folk music concerts to İzmir, Çeşme, and Ephesus ($6-9, depending on event).

■ NEAR İZMİR: SARDIS (SART)

Sardis was the capital of the Lydian Empire, dominant over Aegean Ionia from 680-547 BC. The Lydians embraced and embellished the existing Hellenic culture, giving the world dice, balls, and coin minting. The expression "rich as Croesus" refers to the Lydian King Croesus, once the wealthiest man in the world. When he consulted the oracle at Delphi, it prophesied that if he crossed the river Halys, a powerful empire would be destroyed. Eager to fulfill the prophecy, Croesus promptly rushed his troops across the river, where the Persians trounced him.

Visit Sardis easily from İzmir, or make an ambitious daytrip from Kuşadası. Take one of the frequent **buses** to **Salihli** and ask to be let off at Sardis, or Sart in modern Turkish parlance (every ½hr., 1½hr., $2). Buses leave from the eastern end of the İzmir train station (away from the bus company booths) and drop you off on the highway amid a few teahouses. Most of the ancient city occupies the left side of the highway, 100m from the bus stop. Trains between İzmir and Sart take 3 hr.

The entrance to the ruins leads to the **Marble Way,** lined by a row of **Byzantine shops.** From the end of the Marble Way, turn left to enter the **synagogue,** which houses splendid mosaic floors. The imposing columns of the **gymnasium** shadow a **swimming pool** where fuming Lydians once cooled themselves. Go up the street that slips between two teahouses on the other side of the road, and follow it 1km uphill to the **Temple of Artemis.** Alexander the Great commissioned this temple, one of the largest in antiquity. Only a few columns remain, but their scrolled capitals are exquisite. Along the way to the temple, you'll pass an ancient Lydian gold refinery and a dome from a 12th-century Byzantine basilica built atop a 5th-century church. (Ruins open sunrise-sunset; admission $2.50.)

■■■ ÇEŞME

Çeşme, a small seaside village, is an oasis amidst the barren dustbowl in which it resides. Only one hour west of İzmir, Çeşme has recently gained popularity as a resort town. Although Çeşme was once renowned for its abundant thermal springs, visitors today prize its proximity to the Greek island of Chios and to the Aegean, as well as its cool, dry climate.

Orientation and Practical Information From the bus stop, continue down the main road to the water for the main **tourist office,** 8 İskele Meydanı (tel. 712 6653; open Mon.-Fri. 8:30am-7pm, Sat.-Sun. 9am-noon and 1-5pm; reduced hours in off-season). Next door is the **police** station (tel. 712 6627). Continuing to the right along the shore you'll find the **PTT** (open 8am-midnight, Oct.-May 8am-7pm). For the **bus station,** walk 300m in the opposite direction from the tourist office and turn left before the small bridge. Buses, which are particularly crowded on weekeends, leave roughly every ½hr. from the Üçkuyular bus lot in İzmir (see İzmir listing on page 465). The last bus to İzmir is at 9pm (6pm in winter; $2), but late buses are often booked. You can reserve your seat at the bus station. In Çeşme, the bus stops next to a private **accommodations service** (open summer daily 8am-10pm), but rooms they find are not necessarily the cheapest available. A boat links Çeşme and Chios (1hr.). **Ertürk Ferryboat,** 6/7 Beyazıt Meydanı (tel. 712 6768) goes daily (July-April, 1 per week; May-June 3-4 per week. One-way $25, same-day return $30, open round-trip $35). **Postal Code:** 35930; **Telephone Code:** 232.

Accommodations Çeşme abounds with pensions, most of which charge roughly $15 for doubles in high season. Several rooms cluster along Bağlar Sok., which runs diagonally inland south from the tourist office, and along Müftü Sok., which intersects it on the left. Ask at the tourist office for directions to rooms. The family-run **Adil Pansiyon** (tel. 712 7447), located in a quiet, beautiful area, offers spacious, clean rooms with comfortable beds and floral pattern curtains. None of the management, however, speaks much English. All rooms have toilets, showers, and 24-hr. hot water. (Singles, doubles, and triples $12 per person, negotiable; breakfast and laundry, each $2.50.) **Aras Pension** (tel. 712 7375), by the bus station, has been voted Çeşme's best pension three times and it's easy to see why—clean, light rooms with toilets, showers, and marble-like floors. Many rooms even come with refrigerators, and the management is more professional than in many pensions. It is a little out of the way, however, and the views are not spectacular. (Singles $8.50, doubles $16.75, triples $20, special quad $36. Breakfast extra.) Closer to the castle and the tourist office, **Tarhan Pension,** Musalla Mah. 9 Çarşı Sok. (tel. 712 6599), is clean and even has marble floors. Tarhan is a family-run establishment with 24-hr. hot water. (Singles $12, doubles $14, triples $21.50; breakfast $2.50.) Next door is **Tani Pansiyon,** Musalla Mah., 5 Çarşı Sok. (tel. 712 6238), which is small but swell. It also has 24-hr. hot water, a communal kitchen, and an ocean view. (Singles $10, doubles $13, triples $18; breakfast $2; laundry $2.50.) Like most of the pensions in Çeşme, the nearby **Alim Pansiyon** is a bit pricey but very comfortable. Half the rooms have balconies that overlook a small orchard. All rooms have 2 beds as well as private bath, so singles may be unavailable in high season. (Singles $7.50, doubles $15; breakfast $2.50.) Closer to the water, right across from the string of restaurants, **Ufuk Pansiyon,** Eylül Mah. 52 Hürriyet Cad. (tel. 712 6597) has a terrace with a water view, and one shower, two toilets, and three rooms per floor. Very simple accommodations. Ask to be on the second floor, which has a nice common room. (All rooms are $11 doubles; no single-person discount.) A few **campsites** dot the peninsula: the **V-Kamp** (tel. 727 2224) in Paşalimanı, for example. **Tursite Camping** (tel. 722 1221), Başvuru, has a motel, bar, and private beach (camping $5 per person). Freelance camping is forbidden.

Food and Entertainment Numerous restaurants border the seaside at the center of town. Sample the delicious *İskender kebap* at **Sahil Café and Restaurant,** on the seashore about 300m towards the town center from the tourist office. (Kebap, salad, and cola $5.) The **Körfez Restaurant, Bar, and Disco,** 12 Yalı Cad. (tel. 712 0191), on the shore about 400m toward the center of town from the tourist office, is the center of the city's nightlife. During the day, Körfez serves pizza, hamburgers, and hot dogs, but at 10pm the eatery subsides to a pulsating disco that grooves until the wee hours of the morning. The restaurant may be a little too pricey for the budget traveler, but groups receive a 10% discount, and tourists are sometimes allowed into the nightclub without paying the cover charge. ($5 cover charge includes one double drink; lunch also about $5.)

Revelers with private transportation head to **Ilıca.** Located along the Çeşme-Ilıca highway, **Disco 9½** (tel. 771 4020) is said to fill up every night during its summer season despite the steep cover ($11). Catch a *dolmuş* in front of the tourist office. If you left your dancing shoes at home, sip beer in the **cafés** lining Çeşme's harbor.

Sights The **castle** across from the tourist office was built in 1508 by Ottoman Sultan Beyazıt II for spying on Chios, 11km away. It now houses a tiny, one-room museum. (Open Tues.-Sun. 8:30am-noon and 1-5:30pm; admission $1.25, students 65¢.) Pleasant **beaches** nearby include **Erythrai, Ildırı, Ilıca,** and **Altınkum.** Ilıca offers hot springs called Yıldız Burnu, as does Sifne, where there is a resort. Alaçatı has windsurfing schools. From the tourist office, a *dolmuş* runs to Ilıca and Alaçatı, another to Ildırı and the ancient Ionian village of Erythrai. In Çeşme, **Beyalık Plajı** (beach) is a 10-min. walk from the center, and the Kerman Hotel has a bantam beach to the far right of the waterfront. *Dolmuş* travel around the peninsula until 11pm with routes to Ilıca (6km, 40¢), Altınkum (until 8pm, 10km, 65¢), and south along the beach (5km). Trips to **Donkey Island** cost $14-18, including lunch.

■■■ KUŞADASI

When luxury cruise liners and day trippers from nearby Samos began adding Kuşadası to their Greek island itineraries, the resourceful fisherfolk and farmers of this formerly somnolent town found ways to bait better business and nurture profit. In summer, Kuşadası seems a bit out of control as its population quintuples, English-style pubs advertise refuge from "stomach bugs," and clothiers hawk winter-weight fur and leather. In the evenings, what seems like a thousand bars fuel a frenetic nightlife. Kuşadası may seem like tourism run amok, but its popularity is deserved; this coastal center is one of the best places from which to visit the Aegean Basin's most luminous classical sites, Ephesus, Priene, Miletus, and Didyma.

ORIENTATION AND PRACTICAL INFORMATION

Most visitors to Kuşadası arrive by boat in the harbor. It is best to pay the port tax ($10) in U.S. dollars to avoid changing because of station commissions and weak exchange rates from other currencies. When you do exchange your money, keep heading downhill to find better rates: the first places you come to make you pay for the convenient location. When disembarking, beware of the aggressive, competitive young hustlers who will try to lure you to their "bargain" rooms and then present you with a much higher price.

The harbor master, the duty-free shop, the fish market, the passport police and the customs office are all in the port area. The bus station is about 2km east of the town center and frequent *dolmuş* connect it with İzmir (2hr.). *Dolmuş* also arrive from Selçuk and nearby smaller towns at a separate *dolmuş* stop about 1½km from the **Information Office.** (There's only one such official office; other booths marked "Information" provide information only about their own excursions.) In the skyline, beyond the tourist office, are the turreted walls of an ancient Seljuk *kervansaray*—now a hotel—where itinerant merchants could once spend a night with their goods protected. The structure's turrets make a good orientation point. Facing the Kervansaray, **Yalı Cad.** runs right and uphill, passing through a grueling covered bazaar. Continue up the hill to where **Aslanlar Cad.** intersects; in both directions, you'll find many cheap pensions, in both directions. Left of the **Kervansaray Hotel** is the broad, pedestrian-only **Barbaros Hayrettin.** The PTT, travel agencies, and banks are also there. At the end of the street is a cubist medieval watchtower turned modern-day police station. Through the watchtower and along **Kahramanlar Cad.,** you'll reach the major artery out of town and, within a kilometer, the bus station. **Atatürk Blv.,** parallel to the coastline, exists so that the denizens of Kuşadası have a place to cruise their mopeds and build their luxury hotels.

Perhaps the most practical information about Kuşadası is that if prices for anything are unlisted, you will most certainly be overcharged. Don't hesitate to bargain.

Tourist Office: On İskele Meydanı in the port (tel. 614 1103). The tourist office, 20m beyond the gangway, is conveniently positioned for those disembarking from a cruise liner. To get there from the bus station, it's best to take a taxi, but if you want to walk, direct your ox-strong legs out of the station to the right, staying on the left side of the street so that you can take the left fork on to **Kahramanlar Cad.** Follow this street to the water (it changes names to **Barbaros Blv.**). The tourist office, which offers listings of campgrounds, bus schedules, maps and non-budget accommodations, is around the corner to the left. Open daily 8am-7:30pm, Sept.-May 8am-noon and 1-5:30pm; reduced hours in off-season.

Tourist Police: (tel. 614 1022) in the watchtower. English-speaking staff is helpful. The **police** headquarters, Hükümet Cad. (tel. 614 5350), find translators in emergencies.

PTT: (tel. 614 1212 or 614 1034). Next to the *kervansaray*, halfway up Barbaros Hayrettin. Services open daily 7am-11pm. Stamps, telegraphs and **long-distance telephones** available 24 hr. **Telephone Code:** 256. **Postal code:** 09400.

Budget Travel: Ekol Travel, 3/1 Liman Çıkmazı (tel. 614 9255 or 614 5591; fax 614 2644). Cheap flights, ferry tickets, temporary baggage storage, room finding, message board, car rentals, and emergency help. Will bend over backwards to assist you; also to sell you *something.* English spoken. 15% discount on ferry tickets with *Let's Go.* Open Mon.-Sat. 8:30am-9pm (until 7:30pm in off-season). **Worldspan,** 9-1 Kıbrıs Mah. Buyral Sok. 15% student discount to Samos. Daily cruises in 14m boat along the shore ($16.75 covers meal and beverages). Car rental, English-speaking doctors, and travel insurance available. Free legal advice. Honorary consulate for Australia and New Zealand. Winter hours 9am-5pm.

Banks: Booths on the waterfront offer **currency exchange.** Open daily 8am-10pm. **ATM** access 9am-11pm.

Buses: To İzmir (every ½hr., 2hr., $2.50), Denizli (8 per day, 3 in winter, $5), İstanbul (3 per day, $14.50), Pamukkale (4 per day, 4hr., $6), Bodrum (3 per day, 3hr., $5), and Ankara (3 per day, $14.50). In off-season, there are no connections to Pamukkale or Bodrum. For Pamukkale, catch the bus leaving from Denizli, and for Bodrum, the one departing from Söke. The bus line **Hakaki Koç** offers *Let's Go* readers a 20% discount. **Dolmuş** depart from the corner of Adnan Menderes Cad. and Canadan Tehran Cad. to Ephesus, Selçuk, Söke, or Aydın every ½hr., 7am-8pm. Less frequent service to neighboring villages, including Davutlar and Güzelcamlı. *Dolmuş* run roughly every 15min. from the bus station through town and to **Kadınlar Plajı** (Beach of Women). For Priene, Miletus, or Didyma, you must make connections in Söke.

Ferries: One-way ferry fares to Samos, Greece, are fixed by the government at rates 25% higher on the Turkish side: $30, same-day round-trip $35, open round-trip $50. **Ekol Travel** undercuts the official rate: $27, same-day round-trip $31, open round-trip $50. Flash your guide and ask for your 15% discount. Port taxes are included in the price of the ticket for the country in which it was bought. Turkish boats leave daily in summer at 8:30am, returning at 5pm; off-season, ferries run only when boats fill to capacity (roughly 2 per week). From Greece, you're permitted to take only a Greek boat. For the morning ferry, you must buy a ticket and show your passport at a travel agency at least ½hr. before. (See Samos, page 333.)

Rentals: Toya-Sun Rent-A-Car, 60 Atatürk Blv. (tel. 614 6849). Scooters, cars, and sexy jeeps ($20, $59, and $85 per day, respectively). International driver's license required, plus 2yr. experience with license for cars and jeeps. All-insured unlimited mileage. Must be 18 to rent scooter; no license required.

Bookstore: Kuydaş Kitabevi, 8/B İnönü Blv. (tel. 614 1828). Also on Bahar Sok., just off Barbaros Hayrettin. Sells newspapers, guidebooks, stationery, and pulp novels—in English, French, and German. Open daily 7am-midnight.

Hospital: Atatürk Blv. (tel. 614 1026 or 614 1614), on the waterfront at the northern edge of town.

ACCOMMODATIONS

Rooms here are cheap compared to those in Greece, but expensive by Turkish standards. Finding a room is rarely a problem, and pensions, like those which line smaller streets like Aslanlar Cad., are generally cheapest. The high season rates listed here can often be haggled down. Women should avoid some of the cheapest places.

Hülya Pension, 39 İleri Sok. (tel. 614 2075). Just down the street from Hotel Rose. Clean, well-lit, and comfortable. Communal kitchen. Laundry $1. Singles $3, w/ shower $4; doubles $6, w/shower $8; triples $9, w/shower $12. Excellent more-than-you-can-eat Turkish dinner $3.

Hotel Rose (Salman's Pension), 7 Aslanlar Cad. (tel. 612 2588). Salman (a.k.a. Sammy) Kurt will offer you all sorts of deals on shopping and travel (buses leaving from the front door; tours of Pamukkale, Ephesus, and other sites). Half-price Turkish baths. Comfortable rooms, sociable atmosphere, graffiti-decorated bar and lounge, international telephone, book exchange, 24-hr. hot water, laundry ($2), and roof terrace for dining. Hyperfriendly staff and atmosphere make it easy to overlook a little grunge. Popular with backpackers. 15% discount for *Let's Go* readers. Roof $2, dorm beds $3.75, private rooms $4.75 per person; breakfast $2, dinner $4.75.

Hotel Ada, 12 Aslanlar Cad. All the comforts of a classy hotel in moderate cleanliness. Some rooms with balconies and showers. 24-hr. hot water. Singles $7.25, doubles $14.25, triples $21.50, quads $28.50, roof $6, breakfast included 8-10am; laundry $1.25.

Camping: Önder (tel. 614 2413) and **Yat Camping** (tel. 614 1333), 2km north of town on Atatürk Blv. Take a Selçuk *dolmuş* or walk. Both have good facilities, including laundry and swimming pools. Both campsites cost $2.25 per person and stay open all year, although attached restaurants and rooms close during the winter. Tents are $2 (Önder) or $1.25 (Yat) extra. At Yat, caravans $2.75 per person, cars $1.25, electricity 25¢ per kilowatt.

FOOD AND ENTERTAINMENT

The countless small restaurants in Kuşadası differ only in the extent to which they overcharge tourists. A good way to gauge is by the price of the *şiş kebap:* anything more than $3.50 is a rip-off. There are many cheap, decent joints along Kahramanlar Cad. and its alley tributaries. If you want to meet backpackers, try Pub Lane, where the nectar rarely stops flowing. Sammy, the owner of Hotel Rose, owns a **kebap house** (tel. 612 6042; kebap $1.50) down the street from his hotel. Run by his wife, Hatiçe, it serves free tea and provides a 10% discount to *Let's Go* readers and to guests. (Open 8am-midnight.) Waterfront eating is expensive, but the **Güverçinada Cafeteria** (open 8am-midnight, sometimes until 3:30am) on **Pigeon Island** is a reasonable option. High on the rocks, it absorbs glorious sunsets and features hot *pide* ($2) and Italian pizza ($4), as well as *döner kebap* ($3.75) and other dishes. Lovely tea gardens flourish above.

The **Grand Bazaar** and **Barbaros Hayrettin** are among the most expensive shopping infernos in the country. Nonetheless, as the merchants will never tire of reminding you, it doesn't cost anything to browse. Connected by a slender causeway to Kuşadası, the picturesque Pigeon Island is a tiny fortified islet on which cooing tourists have replaced the birds. (Kuşadası literally means "bird island;" Güverçinada," pigeon island.") Three kilometers beyond Pigeon Island (*dolmuş* 50¢), **Kadınlar Plajı** is a slightly better place to take in the sun than the meager beaches that line the coast in either direction. Vastly superior are sandy **Karovaplajı** and **Yavansu Plajı;** take any *dolmuş* marked "Davutlar" for roughly 7km. Better yet, take a *dolmuş* marked "Güzelcamlı" and "Milli Park" to the National Park, just south of Kuşadası. The best **beach** is at the end of the *dolmuş* line. Meander down to the far end and scale some rocks to find a strip of sand all to yourself. Be careful; the rocks may be slippery.

■■■ EPHESUS (EFES)

For a wholesale archaeological fix, search no farther than Ephesus. The findings here are not just your standard ancient heap, but the remains of one of the most important cities of the Roman Empire. The ruins from the Roman and early Christian era are so extensive and well preserved that one need not struggle to imagine the daily interaction of the 250,000 people who lived here nearly two millennia ago. As a strategic coastal gateway to the Eastern world, this Ionian refuge grew to be the second largest city in the Roman Empire, site of a Christian shrine, and one of the seven (or so) wonders of the ancient world.

HISTORY

The origins of Ephesus are shrouded in myth. Legend has it that the city was founded in a manner prescribed by the Delphic Oracle, which foretold that the appropriate site would be disclosed by a fish and a wild boar. The city's location had to be changed several times due to the continual recession of the harbor waters. Today, the ruins of the ancient port lie 10km inland from the coast.

Ephesians were reluctant to move, particularly because they sought to remain near the colossal **Temple of Artemis.** The pioneer budget traveler Pausanias deemed this structure the "most wondrous of the seven ancient wonders" and "the most beautiful work ever created by humankind." The first major structure built entirely of marble, and the largest edifice in the ancient Greek world, the Temple of Artemis was four times as big as the Parthenon in Athens. Remarkably, this massive monument was actually built twice. The temple was set afire during the reign of Mad King Hesostratos in 356 BC on the night of Alexander the Great's birth. According to legend, the arsonist Erostratus succeeded only because Artemis—watching over Alexander's birth at the time—was absent. Fittingly, Alexander himself restored the temple to its original dimensions and aura. Offerings by hundreds of thousands of pilgrims each year enabled the temple to grow so wealthy that it became the world's first bank. Today, little remains of the magnificent structure. Plundering Goths sacked the sanctuary in the 3rd century AD, followed by the Byzantines. You can see some of the original columns at the Ayasofya in İstanbul (See İstanbul on page 429.)

Ephesus reached its zenith after 129 BC when the Romans established the province of Asia and Ephesus as its capital. It was second only to Alexandria in population, with more than 250,000 inhabitants. The ruins one sees today date primarily from this period. Saint Paul, recognizing the significance of the metropolis, arrived in 50 AD and converted a small group of Ephesians to the new religion. Some perceived this development of Christianity as a threat to the glory of Cybele (mother goddess of Anatolia) and Artemis, and forced Paul and his followers to depart. Ephesus, however, eventually became the center of Christianity in the Roman Empire.

Heraclitus of Ephesus, commenting on the ephemeral nature of life, remarked that one can never step into the same river twice. If you do, he said, you will drown in misfortune. This wisdom proved prescient. As the neighboring river Cayster emptied into the Aegean, it choked Ephesus's harbor with silt, transforming it into a marshy morass. By the 6th century AD, the recession of the sea had sealed the city's fate. The swamps became infested with malaria-carrying mosquitoes, which in turn triggered a tremendous epidemic that resulted in over 200,000 deaths.

ORIENTATION AND PRACTICAL INFORMATION

Disregard ominous signs at the travel agencies on Samos and in Kuşadası which insist that guided tours of Ephesus are "highly recommended." The tours are expensive (about $24 per day) and guides tend to rush you through the 2000-acre site (open daily 8am-7pm; admission $6, students $3). Visit on your own with the aid of a good guidebook to Ephesus. One can be found for about $5 in Kuşadası's souvenir shops or at the entrance to the site. Bring a water bottle—it gets toasty and the refreshment stands at the site overcharge shamelessly.

To get to Ephesus from the Kuşadası bus station, take a *dolmuş* to Selçuk, and tell the driver you want to get off at Ephesus. From the Selçuk train station, take any *dolmuş* towards Kuşadası. It should drop you at the Tusan motel (the first Tusan, of which there are two). Walk 1km uphill along a narrow road to the main Ephesus gate, where you pay admission. Once inside, you can latch onto one of the many tours in your mother tongue. Next to the entrance are **toilets** (15¢), a **post office** with orphaned guidebooks, and several expensive restaurants with chewy Turkish ice cream (if it's authentic, you can stretch it close to a meter).

The *dolmuş* that return to Kuşadası are sometimes full; go to Selçuk first if you want to be sure to get a seat. You should stop in Selçuk anyway to supplement your exploration of Ephesus with a visit to the impressive **Ephesus Museum** (see Selçuk on page 475). In the first or second week of May, the annual **Festival of Ephesus** presents drama, music, and folklore events in the new Selçuk amphitheater.

SIGHTS

If you don't take a guided tour, you'll approach the ruins from the road between Kuşadası and Selçuk; your first glimpse of the site will be the outskirts of the ancient city. The most important of these remains is the **Vedius Gymnasium** to the left as you proceed down the road to the main entrance. On the west end of the gymnasium courtyard (the main entrance is at the north end of the site) are **public lavatories** and a source of potable but warm **water.** Farther on unfold the contours of an enormous **stadium** (the seats were removed to build the Byzantine city walls). Just before the main entrance stand the ruins of the **Double Church** (Church of Councils) where the notorious Ecumenical Council of Churches met in 431 AD.

Once you pass through the main entrance, you probably won't be able to keep yourself from heading straight to the center of the site and marveling at **Arcadian Street,** a magnificent, colonnaded marble avenue. Like the present-day tourist drag in Kuşadası, Arcadian was lined with shops and extended to the harbor, where visitors disembarked and trading ships docked with cargo from the Far East. The street liquifies into a small marsh, but many of the original columns have survived.

Once at the far end of the avenue, turn around for a dazzling view of the **Grand Theater** (open daily 8:30am-6:30pm, winter until 5:30pm; $6). With seating for 24,000 and remarkable acoustics, the amphitheater dominates the entire site from an elevated setting, carved into the side of Mt. Pion. In ancient times, the Ephesians celebrated the Festival of Artemis every April; singing and dancing, the denizens marched 89 golden idols of the goddess to the Grand Theater.

Running before the theater is the slightly elevated **Marble Road,** which once led all the way to the Temple of Artemis. Peek down one of the small holes in the road for a glimpse of the scented sewage system. The **Commercial Agora,** the main plaza of the city, stretches nearby. In the center of the colonnaded square stood a huge horologium, a combination sundial and water clock. Marble Rd. leads past the agora to the **Library of Celsus.** Almost entirely reconstructed by Viennese archaeologists, its elaborately carved marble façade suggests the luxury of ancient Ephesus.

Across from the library at the corner of Marble Rd. and Curetes St. are the vestiges of the **brothel** dedicated to the love-goddess Aphrodite. Romantic commerce took place by candlelight in the small, windowless side rooms. There is a secret passage from the library to the brothel. At the end of the brothel, farthest from the Grand Theater, is a sacred pump whose water supposedly made sterile women fertile. Here was found the statue of Priapus, god of fertility, now displayed in the Ephesus Museum in Selçuk. Just between the brothel and the library is the **world's first known advertisement:** a picture of a foot and a square containing an inscription. Supposedly, if cryptically, it was an ad for the brothel.

Uphill, the imposing ruins of the **Temple of Hadrian** dominate the left side of the road. Renovation shows off the intricately carved façade. The marble archway contains friezes depicting the mythical creation of the city of Ephesus; a bust of the goddess Cybele adorns the keystone. Beyond the temple and adjoining the rear of the brothel are the **Baths of Scholastikia.** Across from the Temple of Hadrian burrow the yet unearthed **Terrace Houses** (closed for restoration in summer 1995 with no reopening date) that extend up the hill. They once housed the wealthiest and most prominent families of the city, who lavished the interiors with superbly preserved frescoes and mosaics. A visit here merits the extra entrance fee, though the attendant is not always there to collect it (closed noon-1:30pm; admission 80¢).

Farther up the hill lie the ruins of the exquisite **Fountain of Trajan.** Various fragments found here have been piled piecemeal to reconstruct the original structure. The statue of the Emperor Trajan that stood before the fountain has been completely destroyed—except for the base, whose fascination factor is abysmally low.

If you make a left after the hill of Trajan's fountain, before the main road, you'll come to the site of the **Grotto of the Seven Sleepers.** According to Christian tradition, seven men fleeing persecution in the 3rd century AD hid in these caves. When they awoke, one of them went to buy bread and discovered that he and the group had been sleeping for 209 years. The story is more interesting than the site.

■■■ SELÇUK

The authentic "Turkishness" of Selçuk, for which the town has been deemed preferable to Kuşadası, has become aggressive and commodified. It is a tourist town. Although it is now encrusted with innumerable carpet shops, souvenir dens, and lame kebapçı with aggressive maîtres-d', flashes of the town's captivating history still glitter in places. Selçuk is smaller, less anonymous, and more beautiful than Kuşadası, and it is easy to escape the commercial fervor of the town center at the archaeological sights that lie in the breathtaking landscape that surrounds the town. On Saturdays in summer, locals as well as tourists flock to the huge **Open Air Market,** which features fresh fruit, cheeses, vegetables, tea, spices, and clothing.

ORIENTATION AND PRACTICAL INFORMATION

The main thoroughfare is the İzmir-Aydın road, yet another **Atatürk Cad.** The road from Kuşadası and Ephesus, **Sahabettindede Cad.,** intersects Atatürk Cad., forming the main crossroads of the town. The **Tourist Information Office,** Atatürk Mah. Agora Çarşısı, 35-6 Mirza Karşısı (tel. 892 6328), at the southwest corner, provides free maps. (Open Mon.-Fri. 8:30am-5:30pm, Sat.-Sun. 9am-5pm, in winter Mon.-Fri. 8:30am-5:30pm.) The **hospital** (tel. 892 7036) lies on the southeast corner of the intersection. With your back toward the tourist office, walk 4 blocks left on Atatürk Cad. to the center of town, a small square with a fountain across from the ruins. Behind it along **Cengiz Topal Cad.** are the **PTT** (open 24 hr., in winter 8:30am-midnight), the **police** (tel. 892 6016), **banks, restaurants, public baths,** and the **train station.** The **bus station** from which the Kuşadası *dolmuş* (until midnight, 90¢) departs is at the northwest corner of the crossroads. Buses from İzmir also come here (1½hr., $1.75). Catch a minibus back to İzmir (every ½hr., $1.50) at the bus station, or a larger bus back to İzmir on the street in front of the bus station. Stand on the opposite side and signal to the driver. (Buses every ½hr., 1½hr., $1.50.) Most **bookstores** sell English-language material. **Pharmacies** are scattered around the town center. Selçuk's **telephone code** is 232; the **postal code** is 35920.

ACCOMMODATIONS

One business practice that Selçuk's pension owners have adopted with increasing frequency over the past few years is to hire people on commission to either seduce or badger travelers into staying at their establishments. It is a good idea to keep a few things in mind with regard to this problem. First, although this is not always the case, often the least well-established places resort to picking up customers this way. Second, since these hustlers work on commission, they will not stop short of lying, nagging, or swearing at you if you don't come with them. Third, some hustlers will even try to convince you to buy a rug as well as stay in their pension. Be prepared for several pension owners to accost you as you disembark from the bus. The best strategy is to have a specific pension in mind and stick to it. In some cases, hustlers pose as officials from the pension where you intend to stay, but lead you to their place instead. Take advice from the official tourist office and other travelers. In the language of this region's young Mamet-esque salesmen, "friend" can usually be translated as "prey." Don't be afraid to tell the bus station importuners that you want to look around before choosing. Since the whole village goes into slumber mode after sunset, the main reason for staying in Selçuk is to arrive at the ruins early the next morning.

Tuncay Pension, İsabel Mah., 3 Ay Sok. (tel. 892 6260). Walking north from the bus stop, take the fourth left. Then the first right and right again. Large, carpeted, and hygienic rooms, some without bathrooms. Clean hall baths. Free service to Ephesus, 24-hr. hot water, laundry service ($2.50 per load), out-of-the-way common kitchen, and small collection of books on Ephesus and novels for loan. Terrace with view of the castle. Tuncay, the affable Americanized owner, is a Selçuk native and speaks English well. Barbecue a couple of times per week. $6 per person in high season. Singles, doubles, triples, and quads available. Breakfast $2.50.

Pansiyon Karahan, 9 I. Okul Sok. (tel. 892 2575). Second right after the bus station heading north. Hotel-like luxury for pension prices. Free service to Ephesus, beaches, and the harbor. Big, immaculately clean, carpeted rooms, all with clean showers, toilets, balconies, secure locks, towels, and comfortable beds. Safe for valuables. $7.25 per person negotiable. Breakfast $2.50. The management arranges boats to Samos (One-way $30; round-trip $35; round-trip open ticket $55. 10% student discount). Open year-round; make summer reservations about one week in advance.

Barim Pansiyon I, Müze Arkası Sok. (tel. 892 69 23). Behind the museum off Turgutreis Cad., Barim is enriched with *kilim,* colorful artifacts, and nesting storks. Carpeted and quite clean, it offers outstanding decor—a bit like Tahiti, with grass mats on the floor and straw gazebos in the courtyard. Cool and quiet. 24-hr. hot water, but no bathrooms in rooms, and no English spoken. $7.25 per person; breakfast $2.50.

Australian New Zealand Pension, 7 Prof. Miltner Sok. (tel. 892 6050), behind the museum (follow the signs). Pleasant courtyard, friendly management, bar filled with rug, sofa, and cushion. The owner lived in Australia for 16 years. Chill with experienced backpackers in the nomadic tent and lounge on the roof. Clientele mainly English-speaking, all ages. Grilled dinner every other night. Free service to Ephesus and the beach. Offers mountain camping packages ($20 per day covers tents, food, transport, and guide) and transport to Samos (one-way $30, round trip $35, open-return round trip $55; 10% student discount). $6 per person, dorm beds $3.50; laundry $1.75; breakfast $1.50. Discounts for trekking groups.

Pansiyon Kirhan (tel. 892 2257), behind the museum. An old Ottoman home with 4 comfortable, carpeted rooms to let. Garden, fireplaces, and 24-hr. hot water. $6 per person; breakfast $2.50; laundry $2.50.

Garden and Camping, 4 İsabey Mah. Kalealtı (tel. 892 6165), behind St. John's Basilica. An idyllic location, away from the noise and bustle of the city center, offers a beautiful view of the basilica. Very friendly management. Electricity, wheelchair-accessible showers and toilets, playground, and reflecting pool. Competitive hustlers at the bus station may tell you the managers are dead; they are alive and well, running one of the friendliest establishments in town. $2.50 per person or tent, $5 per caravan; laundry facilities available; open year-round. 10% discount for students and groups of 10 or more. (On an unpaved side street—women may feel uncomfortable walking at night.)

Victoria Hotel, Atatürk Mah., 4 Cengiz Topel Cad. (tel. 892 3203; fax 892 3204), across from the PTT. Views of the town and the storks nesting in the Roman aqueduct. Lobby and separate TV room. Attached café. Elevator. 24-hr. hot water. All rooms come with bathroom, shower, towels, telephone, closet, and desk. Normally $20 per person, this 2-star hotel offers 5 or more students a 20% discount.

Anzac and Artemis Pension, İsabey Mah., 21 Ak Sok. (tel. 891 5716). Behind the statue of Artemis on the main road. Newly opened pension offers clean rooms, a sun-drenched roof bar with a comfortable rug and cushion corner, English books, and a common kitchen. Free service to Ephesus. English-speaking management. Some rooms with balconies; only 2 rooms with private bath and toilet. 24-hr. hot water. $6 per person, all-you-can-eat breakfast $2.50 (with vegemite for Australians yearning for home cooking), laundry $2.50 per kilo.

FOOD AND ENTERTAINMENT

Restaurants are expensive in Selçuk. The **Özdamar Restaurant** (tel. 892 4097), on Cengiz Cad., has sidewalk tables steps away from the pretty fountain, with a view of the pretty castle up the pretty hill, but it also costs a pretty penny. (*Kebap* $1.10. Vegetarian dishes $1. Open 8am-midnight.) The **Mine Restaurant,** across from the Karahan Pension, is also quite good, if a little pricey (full meal $6). Bar-wise, check out the **Ekselans Bar and Café,** 18/a 1. Okol Sok. (tel. 851 5266), which advertises that it's "sympathetic to Greenpeace;" the owner might sit you down to talk Turkish politics. A very mellow time is to be had in the dark upstairs room.

SIGHTS

Selçuk's few, fascinating archaeological sights have been overshadowed by the towering majesty of its neighbor, Ephesus. Taken alone, however, these sights represent a great reason to visit the town. The colossal and comparatively unadvertised **Basilica of Saint John** ($2.50, students $1.25) is a good place to escape the frenzied consumerism (that is, once you've slipped past the unctuous rug dealers and twinkly card stands near the basilica's entrance). The 6th-century church was constructed under the Byzantine emperor Justinian, on the supposed site of St. John's grave. It was built on such an immense scale that, if reconstructed, it would remain the world's 7th-largest cathedral today. Its stately, if somewhat sparse, remains are characterized by a strange combination of Roman imperial grandeur and early Christian grace and weightiness. The cathedral's idiosyncratic character is made even stranger by an 8th-century wall built around it by invading Arabs, who used materials taken from the 1st-century gymnasium of Ephesus, a stadium where the Romans gleefully watched lions tear Christians to bits. The underwhelming and comparatively over-advertised **House of the Virgin Mary** lies 100m off the road from Ephesus to Mt. Bülbül. About 5 years after the death of Christ, St. John is said to have accompanied the Virgin Mary to Ephesus, where they lived in a small house on the slopes of Mt. Bülbül. The site lay forgotten for centuries until 1892, when the archaeologist Katerina Emmerikin discovered a 7th-century church that was built over the original house. Later that year, Archbishop Timoni of İzmir accepted it as the site of the Virgin's home. The stunning **İsa Bey mosque** lies at the foot of the hill on which the Basilica of St. John and the Ayasoluk castle stand. It was built in 1375 on the orders of Aydınoğlu İsa Bey, and features columns taken from Ephesus, which the Ephesians in turn had pilfered from Aswan, Egypt. The mosque represents a transition between Selçuk and Ottoman styles. Restored in 1975, the mosque has regained much of the august simplicity that 600 years of wear and tear had eroded. The **Temple of Artemis,** one of the seven wonders of the ancient world, used to be the largest temple on the planet; however, it is now as disappointing as it was once awesome. A lone reconstructed column now twists toward the heavens from a bog that roughly approximates the area of the temple's foundation. The ducks, geese, and lizards that caper among the sites's cracked marble blocks are as good a reason to visit the Artemision as the column (for the history of the temple, see Ephesus on page 472). Selçuk's **Ephesus Museum** (open daily 8:30am-noon and 1-6pm; $3.50, students $1.75) is the home of most of the archaeological finds unearthed in the region since WWII (those discovered before then are in Vienna). The **statue of Priapus,** the randy little rascal that decorates postcards at nearly every stand in Turkey, is among the treasures you'll find here. The famous multi-breasted statue of Artemis, as well as exquisite busts of Eros, Athena, Socrates, the emperors Tiberius, Marcus Aurelius, and Hadrian make this one of the most important collections of ancient art in the world.

■ NEAR SELÇUK

Priene, Miletus, and Didyma lie in a tidy row south of Kuşadası. Perch on the slopes of Mt. Mycale to view Priene, practice a soliloquy in the amphitheater of Miletus, and await a revelation from Apollo at Didyma. With an early start and a modicum of efficiency, you can reach all three sites in a daytrip. But you may prefer to explore the ruins in two leisurely days, as the largest site, Miletus, deserves extra time. Less well preserved but interesting to mystery cult buffs are the ruins at Priene, the Delphi of the Ionian cities. You'll only need an hour or so to visit the monumental temple at Didyma. It's possible to take an organized day tour of all three sites from Kuşadası (or more expensively from Bodrum) for roughly $25 per person. Check at the tourist office. You can try to catch an unguided tour from Selçuk ($9 for 1hr. at each site and 2hr. at Golden Beach), but these tours are often cancelled if not enough people show up by 9:30am. Otherwise, visit all the sites from Kuşadası through a series of *dolmuş* rides.

For a daytrip, a good strategy is to use **Söke** (reached by *dolmuş* from Kuşadası) as a base, and return there to make bus connections. This way is least confusing, and—since Söke functions as a hub for minibuses—guarantees a number of *dolmuş* to each site (every 20min., 50¢-$1.50). Another option is to go to Didyma first and then work your way back north. Go to Söke from Kuşadası, then pick up a second *dolmuş* to Didim (its Turkish name), where the temple of Didyma is located. To get to Miletus from Didyma, you can easily catch a *dolmuş* to **Akköy;** from there you must hitch or take a taxi the 7km north to Miletus. To get to Priene, either continue hitching north from Miletus or go back to Akköy; from there take one *dolmuş* to Söke, and another to the small town of Güllübahçe at the foot of the Priene ruins. While in Güllübahçe, visit the **Şelâle Restaurant** (tel. 547 1009; open 8am-10pm; entrees $3.25, *kebap* $4, beer 65¢), where a waterfall from an ancient, moss-covered aqueduct cascades into a reflecting pool within splashing distance of the tables. Taxis usually wait at every site. (All open daily 8:30am-7:30pm, off-season daily 8:30am-5pm. The Miletus and Priene ruins aren't fenced off; admission to each 70¢, students 35¢.)

The small town of **Didim** offers inexpensive pensions. The **Orakle Pansiyon** (tel. (256) 813 1585), overlooking the temple, is the cheapest (singles $11.25, doubles $15.75, triples $22.50; breakfast $1.10), and has satisfactory rooms with a spectacular view of the temple. There's not much to do in town, however, so you might want to stay 5km south at **Altınkum,** a beautiful beach town with a few sleeping options. To the right along the beach you can stay at the **Saray Motel** (tel. (256) 813 1994), with balconies and a patio right on the beach, and clean rooms w/bath (singles $13.50, doubles $18, triples w/bath $24.75; breakfast included). For **camping** around Didim, try the fenced-off **Orman Bakanlığı,** the last campsite when going to Didim from Akköy. There are a number of **campsites** ($4 per person), some with restaurants, at Lake Bafa, east of Akköy.

PRİENE

Priene grew to prominence as a member of the Ionian Confederation of cities in the region of Smyrna (modern İzmir). The confederation controlled the Aegean coast after the decline of the Hittite empire, but Priene lingered in the shadow of its neighboring economic rival, Miletus. The city's population never exceeded 5000 and while its neighbors excelled in commerce, Priene devoted its resources to religion, art, and sport. The city's ruins, on a plateau before the sheer walls of Mt. Mycale, overlook the contortions of the River Meander.

Dolmuş stop by a café; to reach the site from there, follow the road that struggles up the slope and forks off to the right of the road to Miletus and Didyma. First you'll encounter the massive ancient walls that circumscribe the ruined metropolis that was constructed upon the terraced slope of the mountain. From the main entrance, a path leads to what was once the main avenue of ancient Priene. The west side of the block (facing downhill) begins with the **Prytaneum,** the vaulted hearth of the city's sacred flame. Brought to Priene from Athens by the first settlers, the flame was extinguished only when the city was invaded, and rekindled upon liberation. After the Prytaneum is the unmistakable **Bouleterion,** or Senate House, a Selçuk, well-preserved, elegant square auditorium. The interior chamber was equipped with a huge marble altar on which sacrifices were offered both at the opening and closing of the sessions. Only the foundation of this altar remains.

More substantial congregations convened just up the hill at the handsome **theater.** The front row retains five **thrones** of honor with dignified bases carved in the shape of lions' paws. Farther along the upper terrace at the city's acme, the **Temple of Athena** transports you back to the heyday of Hellenistic architecture. Alexander the Great financed the project and Pytheos, the architect whose *chef d'œuvre* is the Mausoleum of Halicarnassus (one of the seven wonders of the ancient world), designed the structure. The temple retains largely intact front steps and interior floors. Descend from the temple to visit the vast remains of the private houses of Priene, an unusual example of Ionian domestic architecture.

Heading back towards the entrance of the site, you'll pass through the spacious **agora.** Women were allowed here only if accompanied by a man, either husband or slave. At the center, a public temple once hosted official ceremonies and sacrifices. Beyond the agora is the 3rd-century BC **Temple of Olympic Zeus.** Downhill on the lip of the plateau stand the **Stadium** and **Gymnasium,** with the names of many young athletes inscribed in the walls. On either side of the main hall were small rooms for bathing and exercise.

MILETUS (MİLET)

Now surrounded by arid plains, Miletus once sat upon a thin strip of land surrounded by four separate harbors. Envied for its prosperity and its strategic coastal location, the city was destroyed and resettled more than once. Miletus suffered the same fate as its Ionian confederates: the silting of its harbor and waters by neighboring rivers caused its decline. For centuries, Miletus was a hotbed of commercial and cultural development. In the 5th century BC, the Milesian alphabet was adopted as the standard Greek script. Miletus later became the headquarters of the Ionian school of philosophers, which included Thales, Anaximander, and Anaximenes. The city's leadership, however, eventually faltered in 499 BC, when Miletus headed an unsuccessful Ionian revolt against the Persian army. The Persians retaliated by wiping out the entire population of the city, massacring the men and selling the women and children into slavery.

The site's main attraction is the **theater,** clearly visible from the Priene-Didyma highway. The strikingly well-preserved structure dates from Hellenistic times, though most of the visible portion was constructed by Romans. The theater, which could seat 15,000, was originally positioned at the water's edge.

During all but the summer months, the remaining portions of Miletus are marshy. To the right of the theater as you enter the site is a Selçuk **Kervansaray** (perennially under restoration). Facing the theater, the footpath meandering to your right leads you to the mephistophelian **Faustina Baths** (behind the theater), erected by Faustina, wife of the Roman Emperor Marcus Aurelius. To the left of the baths are the **North** and **South Agoras.** Next to the baths is the **Delphinium,** or sanctuary of Apollo Delphinus. The temple was first constructed to honor Apollo, who transformed himself into a dolphin and led the Cretans to Miletus. All of the temple's priests were sailors. If nothing else, visit the abandoned 15th-century **İlyas Bey Cami,** the peculiar dome-shaped structure just beyond the baths. Weeds sprouting atop its tiled dome make it look like a huge nest. The family of storks who have made their home here appear extremely content with their modish abode. The interior offers refuge from the heat as well as an exquisitely decorated *mihrab.* Roughly ½km before the main entrance stands a small **Archaeological Museum.** (Open daily 9am-6pm; admission 70¢, students 35¢.)

DIDYMA (DİDİM)

Ancient Didyma was the site of a sacred sanctuary to Apollo and of an oracle that brought in most of the city's fame and wealth. The first Didyma oracles date from about 600 BC. Roughly 100 years later, the sanctuary was destroyed by the Persians when they plundered Miletus. The temple lay deserted until Alexander the Great's arrival, which inspired the arid sacred spring miraculously to flow anew. The present sanctuary was begun during the 2nd and 1st centuries BC. Work continued until the 2nd century AD, but the original plans, like those for Alexander's empire, proved too ambitious and were never completed. Nevertheless, the awesome scale and elegance of the structure make it well worth visiting.

The **sanctuary** at Didyma ranked as the third-largest sacred structure in the ancient Hellenic world after its neighbors to the north, the Temple of Artemis at Ephesus and the Temple of Hera on Samos. Since virtually nothing remains of either of the latter two buildings, the sanctuary at Didyma stands alone as the best surviving example of such colossal temple architecture. It was built to last—many of its individual marble slabs weigh more than one ton. During the Roman period, the unfinished temple attracted pilgrims from all over ancient Greece. A church was constructed on the site in 385 AD after Emperor Theodosius I outlawed the solicitation of pagan oracles. The sacred road that ran from Miletus to Didyma ended at the temple gates; the statues which once lined the final stretch were relocated to the British Museum in 1858 and have been replaced by souvenir shops.

Inside the main gate rests a bas-relief of a giant **Medusa head,** once part of an ornate frieze that girded the temple's exterior, and now star of countless brochures. The building's full magnitude is apparent only when you climb up the stairway to the main façade. Still, you are seeing only a fraction of the original: all that remains of the more than 100 magnificent columns are the bases and lower sections. To transport such immensely cumbersome chunks of marble, the Greeks constructed long shafts of stone leading to the temple site, lubricated them with soap, and then slid the building materials over the slippery surface.

In front of the temple trickles the spring that the priestesses supposedly tapped when receiving prophecies from Apollo. Climb the steps to enter the forecourt. Through the **Hall of Twelve Columns** is the **Hall of Two Columns,** where visitors waited to hear the pronouncements. From here, 22 steps lead down to the **audition.**

In the southeast corner of the courtyard are traces of another **sacred fountain,** as well as the foundations of a **naiskos,** a tiny temple that housed a venerated bronze statue of Apollo. The temple, which served as the site of the oracle, appears to have been erected in 300 BC, before the larger edifice was begun.

■■■ PAMUKKALE (HIERAPOLIS)

Whether as Pamukkale (Cotton Castle) or ancient Hierapolis (Holy City), this village has been drawing the weary and the curious to its thermal springs for more than 23 centuries. The Turkish name refers to the extraordinary surface of the snow-white cliffs, shaped over millennia by the accumulation of calcium deposited by mineral springs. Legend has it that the formations are actually solidified cotton (the area's principal crop) that was left out to dry by giants. Dripping slowly down a vast mountainside, mineral-rich water foams and collects in bowls that terrace the decline, spilling over petrified cascades of stalactites into milky pools below. The site of ancient Hierapolis and the accompanying museums are overshadowed by the springs, but are nevertheless fascinating.

Orientation and Practical Information The bus stops in **Pamukkale Köyü,** the central square, or near the bus-company offices up a curving street. The tourist complex, uphill from the train station, has a **PTT** (open daily 8:30am-7pm) and a **first aid center** behind the Roman Baths. A small **tourist office** (tel. 272 2077) is at the end of the row of shops and cafés near the main site entrance. (Open in summer daily 8am-7pm.) **Postal Code:** 20100; **Telephone Code:** 258.

As you stand in the central square with your back to the tourist map/billboard, the road to the tourist complex starts off straight ahead and to the right, then curves around to the left past bus company offices and up the hill. Go up this hill to reach the tourist office and PTT. Technically, you've then entered the site, and you might be asked to pay the site fee just to get to the PTT. Argue loudly and quickly in English and they'll most likely let you in for free.

Most direct buses that run to Pamukkale leave from Selçuk or Kuşadası (5-6 per day, 4½hr, $4.50). Frequent *dolmuş* and minibuses run between Pamukkale and the regional capital, Denizli, which has extensive service to all major Turkish cities. Less expensive and less comfortable—unless you get an overnight couchette—are the direct trains that travel from İzmir and İstanbul to Denizli. *Dolmuş* and minibuses to Pamukkale leave from the Denizli bus station, roughly 100m south of the train station. Buses run twice hourly between İzmir and Denizli via Selçuk. From Pamukkale, there are infrequent **buses** to Bodrum (3 per day, 4-5hr., $5.50), İzmir (every hr., 5hr., $11.25), Selçuk and Kuşadası (1-2 per day, 4-5hr., $4.50), Marmaris (4 per day, 5hr., $5.50), Fethiye (5 per day, 4½hr., $5.50), and Cappadocia ($11.25).

Accommodations Logistically, Pamukkale presents travelers with a dilemma. Were it closer to the coast, it would make a great daytrip from Kuşadası or Marmaris. Unfortunately, it takes a good 4hr. to get there by bus, so most daytrippers end up spending almost twice as long in transit as they do at the site. Probably the best solution is to spend the night and see the few sights thoroughly, rather than rush the trip and return to the coast sunburnt and exhausted. If you stay, beware of bus station hustlers. They, together with smoke-filled buses, are what tourists complain about most in Turkey. Ignore them and go straight to your pre-planned destination.

The motels in the tourist complex are all expensive; but relatively inexpensive pensions, often with small pools, crowd the village below. Many of the pensions in the village also allow camping on their property and use of their pools. The **Kervansaray Pension** (tel. 272 2209) combines aesthetic appeal, professionalism, and friendliness to a degree rarely achieved by pensions. It offers clean, carpeted rooms with showers and telephones and pretty views from its roof terrace restaurant. ($7 per person, w/breakfast $9.25; regular and vegetarian dinners $7.) To get here from the map/billboard, turn right and take a left after roughly 90m (you'll see the pension from here). On the main road near the center of town, the **Mustafa Motel** (tel. 272 1240) has clean rooms, many w/shower and toilet, and a two-tiered café with views of the springs ($5 per person). **Halley Pension** (tel. 272 2372), in the center of town, is directly across from the map/billboard. Its quiet, sterile, recently renovated rooms have the same conditions as the manager's brother's place, **Özlem Pension,** across the street. ($5 per person; laundry $4.50 per load; breakfast $2.25; dinner $5.50.) **Aspawa Otel** (tel. 272 2094), past Kervansaray Pension off the main road, has an inviting pool; clean, carpeted rooms, all with bath and fans; 24-hr. hot water. ($5 per person; winter heating $1.25 extra; breakfast $2.25; laundry $2.25; free taxi service to baths.)

Food and Entertainment Most of the pensions in town serve lunch and dinner, but if you want to eat out, the **Pamukkale Pizzeria and Restaurant,** down the hill from the Mustafa Motel, serves great pizzas for $2.25-3.50. (Beer $1.25.)

Sights The warm baths at Pamukkale bubble with oxygen. There are two series of terraces situated on either side of the main road down into the village. Elegant, shallow pools located in front of the Tusan Motel (nearest the highway) gradually become deeper farther down the slope. The deepest, most intricately shaped, and most popular terraces are directly behind the nameless restaurant-café facing the main parking lot. On weekends locals flock to bathe in the flat, fan-like pools. Near the entrance to the tourist complex, seek out a place away from the zealots who crowd the pools and attempt to submerge their entire bodies in the six inches of available spring water. Three large motels have been built among the thermal springs and ancient ruins. The motels—demonstrating the foresight characteristic of the Turkish tourist industry—diverted the mineral-rich waters into their own pools, robbing the cliffs of their calcium supply. The government, responding to pressure from residents and environmental groups, recently decided to close the motels and restrict car access to the cliffs. (Admission $4, students $2.50.)

Between the motels soar the colossal vaulted archways of the **Hierapolis City Baths.** The visible portions of this 1st-century structure are all that remain of one of Asia Minor's greatest ancient tourist industries: hygienia. The springs of Hierapolis were particularly popular among vacationing Romans. After an earthquake leveled the spa in 17 AD, Hierapolis was promptly rebuilt, and it reached its heyday during the 2nd-3rd centuries AD. The city bath's glossy marble interior has now been converted into a mediocre **Archaeological Museum.** (Open Tues.-Sun. 9am-5pm; admission $1.75, students 70¢.) Carved into the side of the mountain, the monstrous **Grand Theater** dominates the vista of Hierapolis. Almost all of the seating area for 25,000 is intact, and the various ornately sculpted decorative elements adorning the façade and stage area are well preserved. In front of the theater are the remains of the 3rd-century AD **Temple of Apollo.** Behind the temple stands the **Nymphaeum,** or Monumental Fountain. Nearby is the famous **Plutonium,** a pit that emits poisonous carbonic acid gas, a substance ancients believed could kill all living creatures except priests and pit-toilet-experienced backpackers. The Turks call it *Cin Deliği* (Devil's Hole). Farther to the right lies a hot-water spring. If you continue on the footpath, you'll reach the 6th-century **Christian basilica.**

Down the road to Karahayıt is the north **city gate** on the right, and the ruins of a 5th-century Christian basilica dedicated to St. Philip, who was martyred here in 80 AD. Outside the gate is the **Necropolis,** with more than 1200 tombs and sarcophagi. People who wished to be buried here believed that proximity to the hot springs and vapor-emitting cracks would ease their trip to the Underworld. Among the tombs lies the **Martyrium,** an octagonal 5th-century edifice believed to have been erected upon the site where St. Philip was martyred in 80 AD.

Do not leave Pamukkale without a savory dip in the **sacred fountain** at the Pamukkale Motel (75m after the archaeological museum). Warm, fizzy waters bubble at the spring's source, now blocked off to prevent divers from disappearing into its depths. On the pool's floor rest remains of Roman columns, toppled by the earthquake that opened the source. (Open to the public daily 9am-9pm; $3.50 per hr.)

■■■ APHRODİSİAS

In antiquity, Greeks made pilgrimages here to pay respects to Aphrodite and ask for her blessing. The village evolved into a metropolis, however, only after King Attalos III bequeathed Pergamon to the hated Romans, spurring a massive exodus to this land of divine beauty and love. Aphrodisias was famed for its sculpture; crafted from the fine white and bluish-gray marble of nearby quarries, the finest statues in the Roman Empire were often marked with an imprint from the celebrated Aphrodisian school. Aphrodisias was also an important think tank of Asia Minor. With the ascendancy of Christianity, temples were converted to churches, and the city's name became Stavropolis (City of the Cross).

While the remnants of Aphrodisias have been scrutinized for decades, archaeologists believe that a great deal remains to be discovered. The ruins unearthed to date include a well-preserved Roman stadium and *odeon,* as well as a temple, an *agora,* a palace, and some thermal baths. Although getting to Aphrodisias is a hassle, the site is less overwhelming (and 100 times less crowded) than Ephesus, and the carefully preserved ruins make it worthwhile. Optimistic archaeologists believe Aphrodisias will outshine Ephesus in 50 years.

The highlight of a visit to Aphrodisias is the ancient **stadium,** the most well-preserved ever excavated. Even the marble blocks that once marked the starting line for foot races are still in place in the central arena, whose seating capacity was 30,000. The area in front of the theater was under restoration in the summer of 1995. The looming structure at the bottom of the hill is **Hadrian's Bath,** equipped with a sauna, frigidarium, and changing rooms. To the right, the **Temple of Aphrodite** marks the site of ancient venereal veneration. Although only a portion of its 40-

column spiral-fluted Corinthian colonnade remains, the temple retains its elegance. Dating from the 1st century AD, the shrine originally housed a famous statue of Aphrodite, similar in appearance to the many-breasted Artemis of Ephesus. So far, only copies of the original have been unearthed. With its extraordinary blue marble stage, the **odeon,** just to the south, was the council chamber for the town's elected officials. The nine columns nearby were resurrected as part of a building christened the **Bishop's Palace** by archaeologists, owing to a large number of religious artifacts and statues unearthed on its premises. Some of the original marble floors remain intact. Among the highlights of the site's must-see museum are megastatues of Aphrodite and a satyr carrying the child Dionysus. (Museum and ruins open daily 8am-5pm; admission to ruins and museum each $2.75, students $1.75.)

Getting to Aphrodisias is a challenge. The easiest way to see the ruins is to take a daytrip from Pamukkale. **Buses** leave daily at 10am and return at 5pm (2hr., round-trip $11.25). Some travelers take a bus or *dolmuş* from Denizli, Nazilli, or Kuşadası/Selçuk to the small town of Karacasu, and hitch from there. Buses on the Denizli-Muğla route pass through Tavas, 30km from Aphrodisias. Few hitch from Tavas since cars rarely pass along this road. **Telephone Code:** 256.

Across the highway from the turn-off to Aphrodisias, 300m down the road is **Chez Mestan** (tel. 448 8046, -132), très chic with comfortable rooms, free coffee and laundry. (Singles $6.75, doubles w/showers $11.25, 10% student discount. If all 14 beds are full, they may put you up in the adjacent carpet store for $4.50.)

■■■ BODRUM

Ensconced in the serpentine coastline of the Arcadian Bodrum Peninsula, Bodrum is understandably the favorite retreat of many Turkish jet-setters, intellectuals, and artists. But for all of Bodrum's fashionable sophistication, there really is not that much to see. The only noteworthy sights are the scanty remains of the mausoleum of Halicarnassus, one of the seven wonders of the ancient world, and the solid crusader fortress (the *kale*) which guards the harbor. Still, Bodrum's glorious beaches, rip-roaring nightlife, and flocks of deeply tanned tourists entertain.

Bodrum was built upon the ancient city of Halicarnassus, a powerful port town and capital of ancient Caria. (The Carians were an Anatolian people who lived in this area around 1200 BC, prior to the Greek invasion.) Halicarnassus was known for its succession of female rulers, who succeeded their fathers, husbands, or brothers. One ruler, Artemesia I, led a fleet against the Athenians in their war with Persia in 480 BC; her story is related in the *Persian Wars* by Herodotus, another native of Halicarnassus. In 377 BC, the famous Mausolus of Cairo came to power and made Halicarnassus his capital. Work on his tomb began during his reign, and was completed under his wife's direction following his death in 353 BC. The tomb provided the inspiration for the modern word "mausoleum." Roughly 25 years later, Alexander the Great razed Halicarnassus, ending its period of prominence.

Until 1925, Bodrum was a small fishing village of less than 2000 people. Then, the British-educated Cevat Şakir Kabaağaç (known as "the fisherman of Halicarnassus") settled here in political exile and began to write short stories about Bodrum and the surrounding area. A community of intellectuals flourished until tourists began to frequent Bodrum in the 1970s. A decade later, the town became one of the premier destinations for package tours from England and Germany. Pensions and motels now cover the hillsides around the town. The Turkish intellectual and European package-tour communities lead separate lives in Bodrum; but the city has an atmosphere rare among resort towns combining sophistication and a thrilling nightlife.

ORIENTATION AND PRACTICAL INFORMATION

Streets in Bodrum are poorly marked. The city's most prominent and easily recognizable landmark is the centrally located fortress, the *kale,* from which several streets emanate. Some cheap pensions lie along the bank to the right of the *kale* as you face inland. Breakwaters almost completely enclose the other port, which forms the older, more picturesque half of town. Ferries and most yacht cruises depart from this harbor.

The main thoroughfare along the waterfront starts from the castle and runs along the enclosed left harbor: it begins as **Karantina Caddesi,** becomes **Belediye Meydanı** after the mosque, changes to **Neyzen Tevfik Caddesi** along most of the harbor, and ends at the **Yat Limanı** (yacht harbor). Going right from the castle, Kasaphane Cad. becomes Kumbahçe Mahallesi, then changes to the main commercial drag of **Cumhuriyet Caddesi,** and ends by the Halikarnas Hotel as **Paşa Tarlası.** Extending inland from the castle towards the bus station, **Kale Caddesi** is Bodrum's main shopping strip; it becomes **Cevat Şâkir Caddesi,** which runs past the post office and the bus station, from which all inter-city buses, taxis, and *dolmuş* depart.

Tourist Office: 12 Eylül Meydanı (tel. 316 1091; fax 316 7694), at the foot of the castle. Rooms listings and lousy maps, but helpful staff. Better maps available at the bookstore. Bus info. Open in summer daily 8am-7pm; Nov.-March Mon.-Fri. 8am-noon, 1-5pm.

PTT: (tel. 316 1212, -560), on Cevat Şâkir Cad., 4 blocks from the bus station along the road to the harbor. **Poste restante.** Open Mon.-Fri. 9am-5pm. Another PTT at the ferry landing. International telephones also next to the castle. 24 hr. In summer, expect long lines. **Postal Code:** 48400; **Telephone Code:** 252.

Tourist Agencies: Karya Tours, at the ferryboat landing (tel. 316 1914). Coordinate ferries to Kos and the Datça Peninsula, and daily excursion to Pamukkale ($27) and Ephesus ($27). Open daily 8am-9:30pm. **Apak Tours,** on Cevat Şâkir Cad., down the road from the bus station, towards the water on the left, also offers boat excursions and day-trips.

Currency Exchange: Available at the PTT 24 hr. There are many currency exchange booths by the harbor on Kale Cad., most of which do not charge commissions. Also in banks, which close at 5:30pm.

Buses: Cevat Şâkir Cad. Buses hourly to Marmaris (3hr., $3.50) and every ½hr. to İzmir (4hr., $5.50). Night buses to İstanbul (starting at 6pm, 4 per evening, 14hr., $22.25) and Ankara (2 per evening, 14hr., $22.25). Three buses per day to Pamukkale (6hr., $5.50). Frequent *dolmuş* and minibus service (every 15min. in high season, 30-60¢) to Gümbet, Bitez, Turgut Reis, Gümüşlük, and Gundoğan.

Ferries: Tickets sold through any travel agent. **Bodrum Ferryboat Association** offices in the bus station (tel. 316 0882; fax 313 0205). Boats to Kos leave at 9am and return at 4:30pm. (3-7 per week, 1½hr., $20, same-day round-trip $27, open round-trip $40. Greek port tax $16 (4000dr), paid only on open ticket.) Ferry to Datça Peninsula, 8km from Datça and 80km from Marmaris (2 per day, 2hr., $7.75, same day round-trip $11.25).

International Bookstores: İleri Kitabevi, Kale Cad., 6 Dr. Alimbey Cad. (tel. 316 3069). Tapes and a small selection of English-language books. Open daily 9am-1am. More good English books at the bookstands on Cumhuriyet Cad. across from the 06 Lokantası (open 24 hr. in summer). You can find *Time, Newsweek,* and other magazines near the Belediye Mosque, and English-language newspapers at many corner newspaper stands.

Hospital: Turgutreis Cad. (tel. 316 0880, -1 or -2), past the mausoleum ruins.

Police: 12 Eylül Meydanı (tel. 316 1218), next to tourist office at the foot of the castle. Main branch (tel. 316 1004) left on the main highway up Cevat Şâkir Cad.

ACCOMMODATIONS

Rooms become scarce during the summer; reservations are essential. Pensions are a better bet than hotels; there are hundreds of them and they're inexpensive—for Bodrum. Most rooms are $9-11 per person. Prices are 20-40% less in off-season. If you're traveling alone, it may be a good idea to find a roommate, as pensions rarely have singles. Often rooms are available in private homes called *ev pansiyon.* Look for signs that read *Oda Var* or *Boş Oda Var.*

Uslu Pension (tel. 313 0665), on the very lively Cumhuriyet Cad. (next to Şirin Büfe Döner). Rooms as clean and white as a hospital's, but more tastefully decorated. The café next door will deliver breakfast if you ask in advance. Friendly management. $5.50 per person, $11.25 in high season.

Yenilmez Pansiyon (tel. 316 2520). Walk along Neyzen Tevfik Cad. (the road along the water to the right as you face the harbor) away from the tourist office. Turn right at the alley flanked by Unicar. Run by a friendly family. Clean, spacious rooms w/bath and shower. Kitchen facilities available. Mosquito-netted windows. Quiet, with the green Azize Park next door. $5.50 per person.

Bahçeli Ağar Pansiyon, 4 Yat Limanı Sok. (tel. 316 1648). Roughly 1½km from the city center, 2½km from the main nightlife drag. Turn right at 802 Neyzen Tevfik Cad. just before a red, white, and green canopied Italian restaurant across from the marina. A sparkling clean, family-run pension with spacious rooms, vine-covered patio, and common kitchen. Mosquito-netted windows. Some rooms w/ bath and balcony. $9 per person; breakfast $2.25. No singles, but one person can lodge in a double for $11.25.

Polyanna Pension (tel. 316 1528). On Ortanca Sok., just before the Halikarnas Disco end of Cumhuriyet Cad. If coming from the tourist office, turn left off Cumhuriyet Cad. at the White House Restaurant. Very clean rooms w/showers, arrayed around a soaring atrium. All rooms are doubles or triples. At the center of Bodrum's nightlife. Popular among Aussies, Kiwis, English, and Americans. $13.50 per person. Breakfast $2.25. Open all year.

Toker Pension (tel. 316 1874). Take Neyzen Tevfik Cad. from the center, and turn right on Gerence Sok. after 2 blocks. Cleanish rooms with a big-tubbed hallway bath. TV in the airy linoleum lounge. Serves cheap drinks. Will help with travel arrangements. $10 per person.

Camping: Within Bodrum itself it is impossible, as all the campsites have folded (as of summer 1995). Hopeful campers can take the very short *dolmuş* ride (from the bus station) to **Gümbet,** the next cove west.

FOOD AND ENTERTAINMENT

Bodrum is not bashful about being an expensive resort. But *lira* are well spent here; the port is famous throughout Turkey for its seafood, especially octopus and squid. For the cheapest provisions, stock up at the fruit and vegetable stands on Cevat Şâkir Cad. near the bus station, or at the big **market** that comes periodically on the other side of the station. Along Cumhuriyet Cad., before the harbor, there are a number of *kebap* salons, *dönerci* (purveyors of *döner*), stands that offer fried mussels, and the usual *pide* and *şiş.* One place to try is **06 Lokanta,** 156 Cumhuriyet Cad. (tel. 316 6863). It's the local tourist meeting place, with *meze* ($1-2; open 24 hr.). Numerous pizza, Chinese food, and ice cream places crowd around the harbor.

For nightlife in Bodrum, the **Halicarnassus Disco,** Z. Müren Cad. at the end of Cumhuriyet Cad., 1½km from the center of town, should be your destination (it's marked on the tourist map). Perhaps the only chance in life you'll get to see elderly French women, bisexual Italian models, preppy American college students, and Turkish teenyboppers sharing the same dance floor. The $11.25 cover charge is allegedly necessary to recoup the $1.2 million plus poured into constructing this pseudo-Roman marble theater. (The stage is the dance floor; open until 5am.) One of the more happening nightspots is the **Red Lion Bar,** on Cumhuriyet Cad. before Halicarnas Disco. Central location and lack of a cover charge attract multitudes of multicolored and polylingual thrill-seekers. Follow the cacophonous roar of the music from the Red Lion and the two adjacent bars. The **Hadi Gari,** Cumhuriyet Cad., is a Turkish bar with nominal dancing and the locals' hangout of choice. Pleasant pubs suffice for relaxing and listening to music. Most bars are visible from the street and full of tourists. Others, frequented by Turks who make their summer residence in Bodrum, are more discreet. If you can shoulder the $5 first-drink charge (later drinks $1.75), visit the **Mavi Bar,** near the end of Cumhuriyet Cad, on the left before you get to Halicarnassus. This rather Turkish hangout features floor cushions, *kilim,* and musicians famous throughout Turkey. (Open until 5am.)

SIGHTS

Rising from the azure waters of the harbor, the **Kale** epitomizes a typical medieval fortress' squat austerity. It was constructed over the ruins of the ancient acropolis by the Knights of St. John during the 15th and 16th centuries AD. The castle towers, built by knights of different nations, have been unimaginatively dubbed the English, German, French, and Italian towers. Looming nearby are the stubby yet handsome **Harbor Tower** and the sinister-looking battlement christened the **Snake Tower.** Be sure to visit the castle's famous torture chamber, whose entrance bears the inscription *Inde Deus Abest* (Where God Is Absent). A string of lurid red lights illuminates the passage to this ancient house of horrors, where canned moans and shrieks and anguished mannequins enhance the morbid atmosphere. Despite the castle's immense proportions and extensive fortifications, only 10 years after its completion in 1513, Sultan Süleyman the Magnificent overpowered the knights and forced them to retreat to Malta.

The castle houses Bodrum's **Museum of Underwater Archaeology,** a bizarre assortment of shipwreck flotsam from sites along the surrounding Turkish coastline. The museum itself, which consists mainly of some broken remnants back-lit for eerie effect, is the foremost of its kind in the world. A Byzantine courtyard in the central portion of the castle houses the **Bronze Age Hall,** which contains finds from a 1200 BC shipwreck. Huge jars found on board date from 1600 BC, and their artwork strongly suggests the existence of an ancient trade route between Crete and the Asia Minor coast. The museum also exhibits *cam* (glassware) recovered from a variety of ancient and medieval wrecks. (Castle open Tues.-Sun. 8am-5pm; admission $1.25, students 60¢. Museum open Tues.-Sun. 8am-noon and 1-5pm; museum entry included in castle entry fee.)

The ruins of ancient **Halicarnassus** are Bodrum's better known, if less picturesque, attraction. Most of the remains were either destroyed or buried underneath the modern town of Bodrum. The city walls are visible at points, as are the meager remains of the **theater** on Kıbrıs Schitler Cad., on the main road uphill from and parallel to the left harbor. The most famous of the ruins, the once wondrous **mausoleum,** consisted of a rectangular foundation and stone pedestal upon which the sepulchral chamber rested, supported by 36 Ionic columns. The 50m-high mausoleum, covered with a pythonic pyramidal roof, was crowned by a statue of Mausolus driving a chariot drawn by four horses. To get to the mausoleum, turn onto Saray Sok. from Neyzen Tevfik Cad. It will be on your right at the end of the street. (Open Tues.-Sun. 8am-noon and 1:30-5:30pm; admission $1.25, students 60¢.)

■ NEAR BODRUM

Bodrum's popularity among Turks stems largely from its location at the head of the enchanting **Bodrum Peninsula.** After a day of swimming and sunning, linger over dinner or partake of Bodrum's rousing nightlife. A few of the beaches on the south coast of the peninsula are accessible only by tour boats, which leave from the front of the castle (daily 9-11am, returning 5-6pm). Known as *mavi yolculuk* (blue journeys), these tours are fine alternatives to all the archaic splendor of the ruins and to the Teutonic masses plaguing the beaches around the city. Itineraries for the tours vary widely (check the tour schedule at the dock). Some popular destinations are **Kara Island,** the village of **Akyarlar,** and the beaches at **Baradakçı, Çapa Tatil, Kargı Bay, Bağla,** and **Karaincir.** Boat tours cost roughly $11.25 per person for the day, $16.75 with lunch. In summer, boats leave daily from the castle and head to tranquil **Orak Island** (same prices). These are some of the best swimming spots on the peninsula: pristine and uncrowded. There are no cheap accommodations at these places, so daytrips are your best bet.

Three kilometers out of Bodrum is the crowded and chaotic **Gümbet Beach.** Pensions are expensive, but **Zetaş Camping** (tel. 316 2231) falls within budget range (tent 70¢, car 70¢, caravan $1.25, electricity $1.25, person $3.50). Zetaş has a market, an upscale beach restaurant, squeaky-clean bathrooms and showers, and a kitchen. If you arrive after midnight, enter through the beach; the gate near the *dolmuş* stop will be locked. Farther up this road towards the main *dolmuş* stop is the **Gültekin Pansiyon,** 23 Adnan Menderes Cad. (tel. 316 4106), which offers carpeted rooms w/bath, shower, and 24-hr. hot water. (Person $9; breakfast $3.50.)

Less spoiled than the overpopulated south coast, the north end of the peninsula has rocky beaches and deep water. **Gölköy** and **Türkbükü,** once peaceful fishing villages, now host a large number of Turkish tourists and their yachts. Both offer affordable pensions. A few old windmills dot **Yalıkavak,** at the northwest end of the peninsula, where many even smaller villages, each with a few pensions, are scattered. The best way to find a place to hole up is to walk the beach and look for pensions there. Camp in Yalıkavak at **Yalı Camping** (tel. 385 4142), across Belediye beach at the harbor. Facilities are clean; helpful owner ($2.75 per person).

Because the beach at **Bitez** is narrow, seaside bars have built pontooned docks over the water, where you can order drinks while you sunbathe. The beach around the next large cove from Gümbet is peaceful but has no cheap accommodations. *Dolmuş* from the Bodrum bus station travel to both these beaches. The most accessible point on the west coast of the peninsula, **Turgut Reis,** is 18km away from Bodrum. It's a one-dimensional beach-eat-sleep tourist town, but it has the widest beach on the peninsula. The stretch of coast, however, is usually crowded with sunbathers, and the town is less appealing than villages to the north. There are a number of pensions in town, but they tend to fill up quickly in July and August. They line the street parallel to the beach to the right of the bus stop as you face the sea. **Ferah Pansiyon** (tel. 383 3030) offers clean, cool, eclectically decorated rooms with bath. There is a rooftop terrace with an amazing view; also 24-hr. hot water. There are few English-speakers here. (Singles $9, doubles $13.50, triples $16.75.) The newly painted **Çeylen Pansiyon** (tel. 382 2376) boasts beautiful views and clean rooms w/ showers (person $7.75). From Turgut Reis, *dolmuş* run south along the coast to the crowded beaches at Akyarlar and Karaincir.

Words cannot do justice to the inspiring beauty of **Gümüşlük,** a tiny seaside paradise at the west tip of the Bodrum Peninsula. The Turkish name means "silvery," referring to ancient silver mines that were discovered in the area. Near the beach lie the ruins of ancient Mindos, a 4th-century BC port impregnable even to Alexander the Great. The site consists of the impressive city wall, 3m thick, and a Roman basilica. Gümüşlük's sparkling vistas, cool sea breezes, and relaxed atmosphere make it a great place to escape the frenetic hedonism of Bodrum. **Telephone Code:** 252.

Rooms in Gümüşlük are scarce in high season, as groups usually reserve pensions and villas far in advance. The friendly **Anka Pansiyon** (tel. 394 3193), on the main road halfway between the village and the shore, is new and has pleasant rooms; the 10-min. walk from the beach is the drawback (go up the road towards the PTT). It has a cool pool table, though, as well as laundry and a terrace. Rooms w/bath and breakfast ($11 per person). A little closer to the water on this road, **Deniz Pension** (tel. 394 3149) is a converted village house with multilingual management (Turkish, English, French, and German). Some rooms have private bath ($11 per person).

Mediterranean Coast

Extending from the edges of Greece to the Syrian border, Turkey's Mediterranean coast is alternately chic, garish, and remote. Pine forests, hidden coves, and sandy beaches lie on the stretch between Fethiye and Antalya. Accommodations along the west segment of the Mediterranean coast are generally inexpensive, and excellent seafood abounds. Farther east, broad swatches of sand and concrete dotted with castles and ruins mark the stretch of overcrowded shoreline that tourist propaganda calls the "Turquoise Coast."

During the first and second millennia BC, the area around Fethiye and Kaş formed the Kingdom of Lycia. The Lycians, who reveled in fancy burial rites and funerary monuments, are not remembered for much else. Rock tombs are carved into cliff-sides all along the coast, and Lycian sarcophagi litter the countryside; some are even perched on off-shore islands. The most significant of the Lycian cities that punctuate the coast are the ruins of Xanthos and Patara.

The best boat connection between the Greek islands and Turkey's Mediterranean shores is the ferry between Rhodes and Marmaris, which leaves daily in summer. Allow enough time to explore farther east, and west to the enchanting Datça Peninsula. Distances on maps are deceiving: beyond Fethiye, the road winds through mountain terrain and becomes as slow as it is scenic. Boats run regularly between Northern Cyprus and the ports of Taşucu and Mersin. Travel from these ports to the Republic of Cyprus is impossible. Antalya has an international airport with cheap domestic flights to major Turkish cities.

MARMARiS COAST

MARMARiS

Incongruously metropolitan for the region, Marmaris nonetheless displays palm trees and canopied side streets. Ignore the shops full of camera film and neon shorts, and enjoy the urbane cafés that line the harbor and the wooded mountains that form their backdrop. The town offers the pleasures of sun and sand without the rustic inconvenience that plagues many other resorts; the only danger is occasional overcrowding. Located at a hub of Turkey's Aegean minibus network, Marmaris is only a short ferry ride from Rhodes and makes a perfect point of departure.

ORIENTATION AND PRACTICAL INFORMATION

You're never more than three blocks from the sea in Marmaris—one flailing stretch of hotels, restaurants, and cafés hugs the shoreline. **Kordon Caddesi,** which becomes **Atatürk Caddesi** at the statue, runs along the waterfront. The tourist office, castle, and marina are at the east end of the waterfront (to the left facing the water). From the bus station, cross the bridge over a channel of water and then follow along the coast to reach the tourist office, a handy landmark. Sometimes buses deposit passengers at the dusty *dolmuş* stop. From this stop, head to the water and turn left along the waterfront for 200m to find the tourist office.

Tourist Office: 2 İskele Meydanı on Kordon Cad. (tel. 412 1035, -7277). They speak English and provide maps. Open daily 8am-7:30pm, Mon.-Fri. in winter.

Police: (tel. 412 1494; main office 412 1872). At the corner of Kordon and Fevzipaşa Cad., 3 blocks along the waterfront from the tourist office. No English spoken. In case of **emergency** call 155 or 156. The **passport police** (tel. 412 1696) are behind the new marina to the left of the tourist office as you face the water.

PTT: Fevzipaşa Cad. Three blocks along the waterfront towards the town center and 1 block inland from the tourist office. Open 24 hr. **Currency exchange** 8:30am-11pm. **Telephone Code:** 252.

Buses: Follow the waterfront east (to the left facing the water), turn 1 block inland next to the marina, cross the bridge, and turn left. Buses to İzmir (hourly, 5hr., $6), Datça (4 per day, 2hr., $2.50), Fethiye (hourly, 3hr., $3.50), Bodrum (9 per day, 3hr., $3.50), and İstanbul (5 per day, 13hr., $16.50). It's easiest to buy tickets at the bus line offices across from the town *dolmuş* stop (under the Pepsi sign). Shuttles run to the bus station 15min. before departure.

Ferries: To Rhodes (Mon.-Sat. 8:30 or 9am; $35, port tax $5 per port entered). Passports must be given to the agency the night before departure. Tickets available at any travel agency; there are many along the waterfront. In winter, call 2 or 3 days before departure to ensure that the scheduled ferry is leaving. There is also a hydrofoil for roughly the same price (May-Sept. 9am, 50min.). The ferry dock is beyond the marina, away from the city center. It's a long walk; take a taxi ($2).

Hospital: 167 Hatipirimi Sok. (tel. 412 1029). Five blocks along the water away from the city center and the tourist office, then right onto İsmet Kamil Öner Sok. and up 2 blocks. Private hospital with English-speaking staff.

ACCOMMODATIONS

Marmaris has quite a few reasonably priced pensions and hotels, most of which are booked in July and August. Arrive early in the day to secure a room.

Interyouth Hostel (HI), Tepe Mah. #45 42nd Sok. (tel. 412 3687, -7823; fax 455 3278). At the *center* of town. This is the hostel affiliated with Hostelling International. An impostor on the outskirts, at Kemeraltı Mah. 14 İyiliktaş Mevkii, has a huge Interyouth Hostel sign on it but is in fact called Aşem Motel. No one there speaks English, and it is frequented primarily by Turkish construction workers. To get to the Tepe Mah. establishment from the city center, walk 1 block to the left facing the water, then turn left into the bazaar at the Garanti bank; the hostel is on your right. International phone, MTV, and boat excursions ($21 for hostel guests, $23.25 for others, lunch included). Breakfast in the terrace bar ($2.50), occasional barbecues ($2.75). French, English, and Swedish spoken. Friendly manager lived in New York for 12 years. Dorm beds $4.75, double-bedded singles/doubles $11.75. Laundry $4.75 per load. 10% discount for ISIC, IYH, and GO25 cards.

Kordon Pansiyon, 8 Kemalpaşa Sok. (tel. 412 4762). From the PTT, walk to the end of the block away from the water, turn left, and walk 1 more block. Offers clean-enough carpeted rooms, some with balconies. Hall bathrooms with tubs. $6 per person, laundry $4.75.

Maltepe Pansiyon (tel. 412 1629). Facing the water, walk away from the centrum to the right, turning right at the Maksim 5 disco. Follow this road around and cross the footbridge. Fifteen years old, this was the second pension to open in Marmaris. Clean, airy rooms, a shady garden, free laundry service for small loads, and a common kitchen. Quiet and out of the way, but only 200m from the beach. Rooms per person $3.50-4, w/shower $5 per person; roof $2.50.

Hotel Lahti, 34 Tepe Mah. Sok. (tel. 412 2996). From the post office, follow Fevzipaşa Cad. for 5 blocks away from the water—right, then left, then right, then left, and then right again. This modern building is clean, well-lit, and cool. $11.75 per person, showers and breakfast included.

Camping: A few campsites around the west side of the bay. Every 5-10min., the "İçmeler" *dolmuş* drives around the bay, and will stop at the campgrounds if you ask. **Berk Camping** (tel. 412 4171), 4km from the center, is by the water.

FOOD AND ENTERTAINMENT

Resist the temptation to eat along the waterfront; instead, investigate the inland streets. Cheap meals are scarce in Marmaris, but most places serve *kebap* ($3.50). At **Öz 49,** 200m inland from the PTT, a good full meal runs $3.50. If you're staying at the Tepe Mah. youth hostel, mention it to the waiter for a discount. Restaurants crowd the covered bazaar inland from the post office or the waterfront cafés. To meet other tourists, head to the Kuşadası-style row of pubs behind the tourist office. For dancing, the **Greenhouse** disco is popular. Tepe Mah. guests can get a whopping 25% discount at **B-52 Bar,** near the Greenhouse.

SIGHTS

Marmaris itself has little to offer besides a large town beach and a **fortress,** built in 1522 by Süleyman the Magnificent as a military base for his successful campaign against the Crusaders of Rhodes. The alleyways hugging the castle-walk form the oldest and most picturesque section of the city. (Open Mon.-Fri. 8am-12:30pm, 1:30-5pm; admission $1.25, students 60¢.) Only 1½km away, **Günnücek National Park** features a small beach and picnic tables set against a forest fragrant with rare frankincense trees. To reach the park, follow the coastal road past the marina and out of town, across the small wooden footbridge.

While there is a **beach** in Marmaris proper, the better beaches and scenery around Marmaris are accessible only by boat (an exception is the pretty **İçmeler beach,** reachable by *dolmuş*). Serving the bay, *dolmuş moto* (*dolmuş* boats) depart from the harbor along Kordon Cad. every morning for a variety of destinations. The drivers are casual about the itineraries, and destinations vary according to their moods. Full-day tours cost roughly $8 per person. Most boats make a tour that stops at **Paradise Island Beach** and then the **Akvaryum,** the Turkish version of an aquarium. You're free to go diving when the boat anchors. The tour also visits some phosphorous caves, and then the popular **Turunç Beach,** across the bay from Marmaris. Flanking Turunç to the north and south respectively are the **Gölenye Springs,** whose waters reputedly cure intestinal ailments, and the less crowded **Kumlu Buk Beach,** near the scanty remains of an old fortress. Both are convenient to get to by boat. Most of the mouth of the Bay of Marmaris is sealed off by the heavily wooded **Nimara Peninsula.** Along the far end of the peninsula are the fluorescent phosphorous caves near **Alkoya Point,** another favorite destination for Marmaris' excursion boats. Between the peninsula and the mainland is the tiny uninhabited village of **Keçi,** which offers a good view of the surrounding coastline. The fine sand beaches of **Kleopatras Island** are a good daytrip, reachable by minibus ($16.25, book through a travel agency), or take a bus going toward Muğla, get off at the Sedir turnoff, and walk the last 6km. Then take a *dolmuş moto* to the island ($11.75 per boat).

■ AROUND THE COAST

DATÇA PENINSULA

Jutting out from the coastline at Marmaris, the slim Datça Peninsula extends 120km into the sea, only a short distance from the Greek island of Symi. Cleaved by indigo fjords, the land becomes increasingly appealing farther out. A picturesque, but at times terrifying bus ride on winding roads leads through the peninsula's jagged landscape to drop you at the quiet town of **Datça,** a favorite vacation spot for Turks.

The English-speaking staff at the **tourist office** (tel. 712 3163; fax 712 3546; open Mon.-Fri. 8am-9pm) has a pamphlet on the city and can help arrange a taxi to Knidos. To get there, exit the bus station heading towards the water, turn right, then make another right at the rotary to reach Atatürk Blv. (a.k.a. Yalı Cad.). Within 1km you'll hit the PTT, the tourist office (behind a business complex), and the police. The tourist office also has a smaller summer office (open May-Oct. daily 8am-7pm) down the road on the left (take the left prong of the fork in the road) across from the Pamukkale Bus ticket office, where you can catch a shuttle to the bus station. To call the **police,** dial 712 3792 or, in case of emergency, 155. On the other side of the tourist office stands the **PTT** (open 8am-midnight). Banks **exchange currency** (open Mon.-Fri. 8am-5pm; exchange stops at 4:30pm). **Pir-Pak Laundry** (tel. 712 2040; open 8am-10pm) is at the end of Yalı Cad. past the taxi stand. **Postal Code:** 48900; **Telephone Code:** 252.

Buses travel to Marmaris every 2hr. ($2.25). There is also a ferry from Bodrum (summer only, departs daily at 9am and 5pm; one way $7.75, round-trip $12.25).

Another boat returns to Bodrum from Datça at 9am ($7.75; a service bus runs from the ticket office to the dock at 8:30am). Tickets are available at most travel agencies in Bodrum. Buy tickets at the **Deniz Ticket Office** (open 8am-midnight), behind the summer tourist office outpost on Yalı Cad.

As is usual, rooms are hard to come by in July and August. There are mosquitoes aplenty in Datça, so stock up on repellent or tablets. **Antalyalı Pension** (tel. 712 3812) is centrally located and easy to find (on Yalı Cad., the main road). From the bus station, pass the PTT and take the left fork; the pension is on the right. Rooms are spacious, all w/showers and toilets ($6.75 per person). **Deniz Motel and Restaurant** (tel. 712 3038) sits farther up the road, left past the tourist office. All rooms have shower and toilet, balconies, closets, telephones, and good beds. (Singles $9, doubles $13.50, triples $17.75.) On the right side farther down the road, past the taxi stand, the **Umut Pansiyon** (tel. 712 1117) offers a great location, 24-hr. hot water, and a marvelous balcony, but smallish rooms ($11.75 per person). Behind and above Umut, rooms in **Huzur Pansiyon** (tel. 712 3364; fax 712 3919) are furnished with tables, chairs, and closets. Most rooms have balconies, sea views, and clean bathrooms with toilet paper. ($6.75 per person; breakfast $1.75; 24-hr. hot water.) **Ilıca Camping** (tel. 712 3400), on the beach beyond the harbor (turn right at the taxi station), has a restaurant and two-person bungalows with private baths ($5.50 per person). Camping costs $2.75 per person; breakfast $2.25.

Fresh wild boar is sometimes the main dish at Ilıca's occasional cookouts, served in the Camping's restaurant. The self-proclaimed cheapest food in town is at **Deniz Lokantası,** around the corner from the summer tourist office. (Full meals $3.50, max; open daily 7am-4am.) For fabulous Turkish pastry, try **Nokta Pastanesi,** up the hill from the taxi stand on Yalı Cad. (open daily 7am-3am). A dozen restaurants at the harbor specialize in fish; similar prices (*kalamar* $5, mussels $5).

Knidos, which was built in honor of Apollo, was once a wealthy port city, one of the original six cities of the Dorian League. A pair of **theaters** and **temples** dedicated to Dionysus and Demeter languish above the east harbor. Outside this area are two remote medieval fortresses surrounded by the ancient necropolis of Knidos. One of the artistic and intellectual centers of the ancient Hellenic world, it was the home of Sostratos, designer of the Pharos lighthouse at Alexandria, and of the astronomer Eudoxos, who first calculated the earth's circumference. The city was renowned in antiquity for its **statue of Aphrodite.** Created by Praxiteles, the work scandalized Hellenic society, which had confined its art to the naked male form.

Because Knidos is a government-regulated archaeological zone, pensions and restaurants are forbidden to operate. **Boat tours** leave for Knidos from Bodrum and Marmaris during the summer (ask at the tourist offices). From Datça take one of the boat tours that leave at 9am from the yacht harbor ($11.25 per person), or a taxi (tour $33-45 per carload, negotiable).

CAUNOS AND DALYAN

The road from Marmaris to Fethiye passes by clear, placid Lake Köyceğiz, connected to the sea by a river that outlines a stretch of lush, green marsh. Along this river are the ruins of the ancient Carian harbor city of Caunos, where archaeologists are turning up new structures as fast as they can dig. Aside from the ruins, the area has an alluring landscape of tree-tufted mountains tumbling into swampy waters. The ruins are accessible only by boat from the nearby town of Dalyan. It's a 10-min. walk up the hill to the ruins. From the boat, look at the cliff above the river to glimpse the rock tombs, which date from the 4th century BC.

As you come up the hill in Caunos, the precariously perched **Kale** (castle) looms above. From the base of the mountain, climb (though not easily) the lofty **theater** for a panorama of the ruins and the distant beach. Facing the theater, the ruins of the **basilica** are on your left, and the ancient harbor of Caunos holds the remains of several **temples** and a recently excavated **fountain.** Many people come to Dalyan with quixotic hopes of seeing the endangered **Caretta caretta** (Loggerhead Turtle, see p. 311), which lays its eggs on nearby İztuzu Beach. It is *impossible* to see the turtle in Dalyan—the shy creatures appear only at night, when the beach is closed. (It's open 8am-8pm daily.) Environmentalists have struggled to prevent luxury hotels and tourist development from destroying the turtles' nesting ground. For the turtles' sake, please don't visit the beach at night, don't hire speedboats (they destroy the reed beds), and don't litter or stick an umbrella into the beach.

Stretched along the reedy river, the village of Dalyan stays cool in summer, but hosts the annual conventions of the Voracious Mosquitoes' Union. Make sure you've got bug repellent, or better yet, that your pension has electrified anti-mosquito tablets (most do), lest you wake up looking like a bad case of the mumps.

The **PTT** is the tall white building in the center of town (open 8am-midnight). **Currency exchange** is available at the PTT 11am-11pm. To the left of the PTT as you face the river is the **tourist office** (open daily 9am-noon and 1:30-7:30pm). Next door is the **conservation info office** (open July-Sept. daily 9:30am-noon and 4-8:30pm). Stop in to say hello and see pictures of turtles. Between these two buildings, the **Dalyan Boat Cooperative** (tel. 284 2094; fax 284 3255) arranges public and private boat trips. (10am public boat to beach $2.25 per person, returns every hr. 1-6pm.) *Dolmuş motolarι* run to the baths, springs, ruins, and Turtle Beach $4.50. (Departs 10:30am and returns 6pm; boat rental with customized itineraries $27.) To get to Dalyan from Marmaris, take a *dolmuş* or **bus** to Ortaca (2hr., $2.25), then a *dolmuş* to Dalyan (15min., 50¢). **Postal Code:** 48840; **Telephone Code:** 252.

Finding a room here should be as simple as finding one of 109 signs; there seem to be more pensions than inhabitants. Most of the pensions are to the left of the central plaza if you're facing the river. Coming from the center (with the *dolmuş* station, PTT, and tourist office) follow the main road so that the river is on your right. Three hundred meters ahead you'll hit an intersection. Turn left and proceed roughly 50m to **Kristal Pansiyon** (tel. 284 2263, -3153), on the left, which offers palatial rooms with beds fit for monarchs. All windows are mosquito-netted and the bathrooms are impeccably clean. ($5.50 per person.) Farther up the main street, **Sahil Pansiyon** (tel. 284 2187) also has clean baths and mosquito netting, plus some suites and a patio. No English spoken. (Doubles $15.50, triples $22.25; free laundry and breakfast included). The **Albatross Pension** (tel. 284 3287, -8), closer to the center of town, has an attached bar and clean rooms, all but two of which have private bath ($7.75 per person; breakfast $2.25; English spoken). Campers should head along the main street out past Caretta Restaurant to the signless **Dalyan Camping** (tel. 284 4157). Look for tents on the water ($2.25 per person, caravans $6.75, electricity $1.25, bungalows $11.25, breakfast $2.25). If you're trying to decide whether to camp out, note that pensions generally have mosquito netting.

The **Mediterranean Fruit Bar,** on the main road back toward town (with the river on your left), is an oasis. Enjoy dozens of freshly squeezed juices and shakes from exotic fruits, picked from their photo-album menu, squeezed with expertise while you watch. (Full meal $5.50-7.) Between Sahil Pansiyon and Dalyan Camping, **Caretta Restaurant** (tel. 284 3039) boasts menus in French, English, and German. New and on the water, its attentive staff serves steak, soup, *meze,* and beer for $5. (Open 8:30am-midnight.) If you're looking for fish, try *kefal* (mullet). Beware of chic (i.e., expensive) restaurants along the river.

FETHİYE COAST

■■■ FETHİYE

Telmessos, the ancient Lycian city founded on Fethiye's site in the 4th century BC, was known for its astrologists, mystagogues, palm readers, and oracles. Little of the old city's spirit is said to remain, but in 1958, when Fethiye was devastated by an earthquake, the Necropolis of Telmessos miraculously survived. Now Fethiye is a tumble of concrete buildings lining dusty streets: a small, quotidian port town that, aside from a few ruins, is of little interest. The town is near many interesting sights, however, and Ölüdeniz (14km away) is one of the Mediterranean's best beaches.

Orientation and Practical Information Buses drop off at the station 5km outside of town. Theoretically, the bus companies offer shuttles from there into town, but you may have to take a taxi. Head to the tourist office; they have listings of reputable accommodations divided by price range. If you arrive late at night and want to go directly to a hotel, tell the taxi your destination and ignore any "suggestions" he might have, as this may be a commission scam. If you come by *dolmuş*, you'll be dropped off on **Çarşı Caddesi,** a street swamped by pension signs. (The *dolmuş* to Ölüdeniz leaves from here.) Çarşı Cad. veers right into **Atatürk Caddesi,** the main avenue running parallel to the harbor. **Banks, pharmacies, grocery stores,** and most of the town's shops can be found on this street. The **tourist office** (tel. 612 1975; fax 614 1527; open daily 8am-noon and 1:30-5:30pm in summer), on the waterfront at the large pier where cruise ships dock, is to the left as you face the water from the intersections of Çarşı Cad. and Atatürk Cad. (There's an equestrian statue in this intersection.) You can **exchange currency** at the PTT, or at any of the local **banks** (open Mon.-Fri. 8am-noon; currency exchange stops at 4pm). Make a right onto Atatürk from Çarşı and walk a few blocks. The **police** (tel. 614 1040; emergency 155), **PTT** (open 24 hr.; for letters 8am-noon, 1:30-5pm), and **hospital** (tel. 614 1499) are several blocks to the right of the tourist office as you face the water (10-min. walk). To get back to the **bus station,** your best bet is to go to a bus company office and catch a service bus. **Kamıl Koç** (tel. 614 1973) is here on this stretch of Atatürk Cad. **Pamukkale Turizm** (tel. 614 2855) is back around the corner on Çarşı Cad., on the left side as you head from Atatürk Cad. to the water. To get to the **bazaar,** turn right at the Atatürk-Çarşı junction, head along Atatürk (with the water on your left) 500m, then walk inland 1 block. Tuesday is market day. English-language tapes and a few books are sold at **Net Imagine,** 18 Atatürk Cad. (tel. 614 4846), left of the equestrian statue as you face the water, past the Garanti Bank. **Postal Code:** 48300; **Telephone Code:** 252.

Accommodations Several pensions line Çarşı Cad. between its *dolmuş* stop and the intersection with Atatürk Cad. (The beachfront establishments are more expensive.) **Holiday Pansiyon,** 91 Çarşı Cad. (tel. 614 1696), the closest to the *dolmuş* stop, has clean, wood-adorned rooms; most with balconies. ($11.25 per person, breakfast $2.25, laundry roughly $4.50 depending on amount.) Farther toward the water, the pink and blue **Otel Yılmaz,** 48 Çarşı Cad. (tel. 614 1131), is on the left as the road curves around to the right. The rooms are small and clean enough. Eight rooms have private baths with pit toilets. (Singles $4.50, doubles $9, triples $13.50.) Following the road around, you'll eventually reach a steep flight of stairs on the left, across from the Pamukkale bus office. At the top of the staircase is **Ulgen Pansiyon,** Çarşı Cad., Paspater, #83 Merdiven (tel. 614 3491), with a refrigerator for the use of guests and a pleasant vine-covered terrace with sea view. The management of this backpacker-oriented establishment is friendly and helpful, which makes up for the place's small inconveniences, like the stacks of paraphernalia blocking the hallways. (Singles $3.50, w/shower $4.50; doubles $6.75, w/shower $9; breakfast $1.75; free tea, coffee, and grapes.) On the other side of town is the immaculate and pleasingly decorated **Olimpyat Pansion** (tel. 614 3444), on Dolgus Sahası Cad., which has helpful English-speaking management. (Singles $9, doubles $13.50, triples $17.75; breakfast $2.25; laundry available.)

Food and Entertainment Gourmets should make their way to the upscale restaurants on the water and Atatürk Cad. There is less costly fare along Çarşı Cad. **Meğri Lokantası** (tel. 614 4046), a few doors from the Pamukkale office and across the street from Pizza Pepino, has A/C and a large, tasty selection of meat and veggie dishes. (*Döner* $3.50, chicken *şiş* $5.50, veggie casserole $4.50; open 8am-11pm.)

Sights The road from the north into Fethiye ascends steep hillsides thick with pine trees, crickets, and pungent sap. In ancient times, this region, isolated from the rest of Asia Minor, insulated Lycian culture. Believed to be the descendants of the pre-Hittite Anatolian peoples, the Lycians remained independent until their quixotic stand against Cyrus' Persian armies in 545 BC. The city of tombs that remains, the **Necropolis of Telmessos,** is the most significant vestige of Lycian culture (admission $1.25). The façades of the cliff-hewn tombs resemble Greek temples down to the pediments, porticos, and cornices. The tombs themselves are thought to be replicas of Lycian homes. Connected to the road by several flights of steps just off Kaya Cad. (off Atatürk Cad.) is the **Tomb of Amyntas,** identifiable by a 4th-century BC inscription on the left-hand column. Climb the 150 steps to the tomb to find a tiny chamber beyond the opening. You can enter the other tombs as well, though to reach them you must clamber around the rocks. From the necropolis, the remains of the **Fethiye Tower,** and several islands sprinkled about the Bay of Fethiye, can be seen. The **Archaeological Museum,** one block down from the hospital toward the bus station, contains Lycian artifacts from neighboring digs. (Open June-Sept. Tues.-Sat. 8am-5:30pm; admission $1.25, students 60¢.)

Fethiye's main beach, **Çalış,** 5km to the north, is a relatively uncrowded crescent of sand extending over several kilometers. *Dolmuş motoları* (*dolmuş* boats; every 10-20min., 20min., 90¢) depart from the harbor (look for the sign or call 613 2376); *dolmuş* from the main *dolmuş* station (route goes around town; 15min., 23¢); or *dolmuş* from Atatürk Cad. near the water (route goes along the coast; roughly every 15min., 15min., 45¢) leave for the beach during high season. Boats run from the pier (near 12-island tour boats) to the beaches on the isle of **Sövalye** (every ½hr., $1). Twelve kilometers farther to the north are the beaches of **Günlük Bay** and **Katrancı Bay,** which are less frequented than Çalış (minibuses every 10min. from the minibus station behind the mosque, 80¢). Frequent minibuses run from the main *dolmuş* station to **Ölüdeniz** (20min., 90¢); **Saklıkent** (35min., $1.25); and **Kaya Village** (20min., 90¢). For those who want to explore the region on their own, **Light Tours** rents cars for $75-225 per day with unlimited mileage. Hertz-affiliate **Turem Travel,** 6 Atatürk Cad. (tel. 614 6787; fax 614 3029; open 8:30am-11pm), also rents cars ($60 per day). They also rent motorbikes ($24 per day and up) and scooters ($19 per day). Another option is **First Rent-a-Car** (tel. 614 9312; fax 614 2593), up the street from the tourist office and opposite the marina.

■■■ ÖLÜDENİZ

Posters of the partially enclosed lagoon at Ölüdeniz hang on the walls of almost every Turkish hotel or tourist office. Poised only 14km from Fethiye, this seaside town gets its share of visitors. Thankfully, the lagoon's serenity counters the bustle.

Orientation and Practical Information Even from the east, Ölüdeniz is reached via Fethiye. During the summer, *dolmuş* depart from the main minibus station (every 10-15min., 7:30am-11:30pm). The *dolmuş* to Ölüdeniz stop at a vast pebble beach. This is not Ölüdeniz—Ölüdeniz and most of its good (and cheap) hotels stand farther right, facing the water. To the left there is a string of bars, campgrounds, and restaurants. People who choose to hitch walk 2km to the main turn-off. There is no official tourist office, but the **Tourism Cooperative** (tel. 616 6950, -2; open 9am-midnight), just up the Fethiye road from where it runs into the beach, helps with rooms and arranges boat trips and parasailing excursions.

The town, if it can be called that, has **grocery stores** and a **PTT** (open April-Oct. daily 9am-10pm) 50m to the right from the entrance to the lagoon. The phones in the PTT have been unreliable in the past, but there are several phone booths scattered around town. **Change money** at some of the larger campsites and at the grocery store behind Derya Camping and to the right. **English-language newspapers** and magazines can be found at the newsstands along the beach. Take care of everything else in Fethiye. **Postal Code:** 48300; **Telephone Code:** 252.

Accommodations Up the hill from the beach (5min. dolmuş ride; 30¢), the town of **Hisarönü** (your *dolmuş* might stop there on the way to Ölüdeniz) is growing in popularity because of its cheaper pensions. Most who stay in Ölüdeniz camp along the beach. Some campsites have bungalow-like buildings that are actually full-fledged motel rooms with furniture and private baths. Taxi drivers sometimes drive prospective customers into a campsite and deliver them to the proprietors. Insist on looking around before committing yourself. From the *dolmuş* stop, walk to the right (facing the water) 200m to the fork in the road. The national park is on your left, and on your right is the road to the campgrounds. **Ölüdeniz Camping** (tel. 616 6024) is roughly 300m north from the exit (to the right as you face the water), past the municipal beach; not to be confused with Ölüdeniz Pension on the exit road. Distant from the center of activity, but set at the edge of the lagoon (you only have to pay the entrance fee once), with a small beach, market, café, and restaurant. (Person $1.25, caravans $4.50, electricity $4.50, double bungalow $9, triple $11.25; breakfast $2.25; meals roughly $3.50; beer 90¢. Ask about paragliding.) The **Kum-Tur Motel** (tel. 616 6026), 200m to the left of the exit road, offers ill-lit but passable rooms in a central but overcrowded location. It has a restaurant, 24-hr. hot water, and friendly staff. (Singles $9, doubles $13.25, triples $17.75; breakfast $2.25.) Near Ölüdeniz Camping, backpacker-oriented **Asmali Camping** (tel. 616 6176) offers campers some grass and shade as well as bungalows of two distinctly different quality levels. It also has a café/restaurant and a private beach. (Person $1.25; Type A bungalows $5.50 per person, Type B $3.50 per person; breakfast $1.75, *kebap* $2.75, beer $1.25, laundry $11.25.) **Deniz Camping** (tel. 616 6012; fax 616 6008), to the left of the exit road facing the water, offers a shady campsite and central location. The ebullient Anthia Gurkan, an Englishwoman who speaks perfect Turkish, is an experienced travel guide who can reserve plane and bus tickets for you as well as arrange trekking and paragliding adventures. (Person $2.25, tent $2.25, caravans $4.50, single bungalow $6.75, double $10.) **Han Camping,** between the exit road and Deniz Camping, has a small bar/restaurant and a sandy campground. Smallish bungalows are clean. (Person $3.50, caravans $4.50, treehouses $2.25 per person, double bungalows $9, breakfast $1.75, beer 90¢, laundry $2.25.)

Food and Entertainment Eating inexpensively here is a task. Most people eat at the campground cafeterias, where the food is good but pricey (*şiş* $3.50, beer $1.25). **Dippy Dolly's Pancake House,** to the left from the exit road (as you face the water), serves gourmet confections; enjoy an English-language periodical while you dine (roughly $3.50). At night, drink, mingle, and dance all night at the **Buzz Bar** (tel. 616 6012; open 7:30am-2am) above Deniz Camping. It also serves Turkish ($2.25) and English ($4.50) breakfasts. The **Big Blue Bar Café,** in an upscale fenced-off development to the left of the exit road facing the water, charges a hefty cover, but the bar's pool alone makes it worth the lira.

Sights Some claim that the tranquil circle of the **blue lagoon,** at the tip of the beach, is where the movie of the same name was filmed. They are probably incorrect, but this idyllic bit of land does fill with Speedo-clad beach creatures of another type from dawn to dusk. Although Ölüdeniz looks quite a bit more inviting in tourist office aerial photos than it does from up close, its fine sands and tranquil inland lagoon make it one of the Turkish Riviera's best swimming holes. A quiet dip in these crystal waters, especially on weekday mornings and evenings when it is least crowded, is pure bliss. (Potable water, bathrooms, and showers are available at the site, which is accessible by a 20-min. walk from the exit road or a 25¢-*dolmuş*.)

Kaya and Agia Nikola Island were thriving Greek Christian communities until they were dispersed by the local Muslim population. Two popular excursions from Ölüdeniz visit the remains of these villages. The larger of the pair is **Kaya,** 10km away and accessible only by a dirt road. A more popular destination, tiny **Agia Nikola Island** has great swimming, a spine-tingling view of the coast, and the remains of a Byzantine basilica. **Explora Travel** (tel. 616 6890; fax 616 6274; open

April-Oct. 8am-1pm and 6-11pm), on the main street next to Han Camping, books boat trips to Agia Nikola Island and **Butterfly Valley** for $13.25, lunch included. Visitors to the Butterfly Valley in particular bring reports of having found paradise on Earth. Boats leave from the main anchorage at roughly 10:30am and return at 6pm. Explora also offers a comprehensive jeep safari to **Saklıkent,** the ancient city of **Tlos, Patara Beach,** and trout farms for $39 per person, lunch included.

XANTHOS

Eighty-five kilometers from Ölüdeniz and 22km from Kalkan rest the ruins of the ancient Lycian capital of Xanthos. Lycian rock tombs pepper this attractive site, perched above the Eşen (formerly Xanthos) River. Unwilling to surrender during a revolt against the Persians, the Lycians gathered their women, children, and valuables into Xanthos for a final stand. When all hope was lost, they set the city on fire, and fought until their last soldier died. In the 2nd century BC, the city tried desperately to resist Rhodes. Years later, the Romans fortified Xanthos in return for its peoples' support during the Roman invasion of Anatolia; most of the ruins in Xanthos are from this period. Check out the **Roman City Gate,** dedicated to Emperor Vespasian, and the **Roman Theater.** From the theater you can see the remains of the **Roman Acropolis** and a **Byzantine church.** Nearby are the **agora** and a **Byzantine basilica.** The **Xanthian Obelisk** near the agora bears an inscription which describes the Lycian-Athenian battles of the Peloponnesian Wars. At the end of the theater stands the 6th-century BC Lycian **Tomb of the Harpies,** decorated with a plaster cast of the mythological creatures being summoned to destroy invading armies. The original frieze is in the British Museum. To get to Xanthos, take any *dolmuş* running between Fethiye and Kalkan or Kaş, get off at the village of Kınık, and follow the signs to the site (Fethiye-Kınık 1½hr., $1.75; Kalkan-Kınık 1hr., $1.25). The bus from Xanthos to Patara costs 70¢.

Ten kilometers southwest of Xanthos are the ancient ruins of **Letoon,** which date from the Roman and early Byzantine periods. Myth has it that Letoon, a Lycian religious sanctuary, was the place where the nymph Leto, mother of Zeus' children Artemis and Apollo, fled Hera's wrath. At the site there are three temples each to Leto, Apollo, and Artemis, a function-hall, and a pool. Scholars hope that an inscription found on the Leto Temple in Lycian, Greek, and Aramaic (now in the Fethiye Archaeological Museum; see p. 494) will prove as valuable in deciphering Lycian as the Rosetta Stone was in decoding hieroglyphics. There is no guard, no information booth, and no light. Don't go after sunset.

PATARA

Twenty kilometers farther south (17km west of Kalkan) is the old Lycian port city of Patara. Choked with sand and brush, Patara's imposing ruins lie isolated among a series of seaside hills. Until its harbor silted up, the city was the seat of the Roman governor to Lycia and the site of an oracle to Apollo. Given the size and unwieldiness of the site, most tourists are drawn instead to Patara's vast sand beach, one of the finest in Turkey. The **Mettius Modestus** triumphal arch, built in 100 AD, rests on the right of the road to the beach. A **necropolis** with numerous sarcophagi surrounds the gate. Along the path from the gateway to the sea lie the ruins of Roman baths, a Christian basilica, the **Baths of Vespasian,** and a theater. Farther back from the beach on the road are two pricey restaurants, one with bathrooms and showers.

To get to Patara, take any bus going from Fethiye to Kalkan, and get off at the turnoff ($1.75). Ask the driver for Patara. From there it's 6km to the beach. From Kalkan, *dolmuş* leave every ½hr. and come back at 4 or 5pm ($1.25). From the town, you can walk or take a taxi (roughly $2.25) the last 1.5km to the ruins and beach. Minibuses go directly to the beach every morning around 10am from Kalkan and Kaş. From the beach, regular minibus service travels to surrounding cities (hourly to Kalkan and Kaş until 6:30pm; to Fethiye 5 per day until 5pm). Taxis from Kınık to Kalkan cost roughly $6.75. **Telephone Code:** 242.

Apart from the ruins and nearby beach, the town of Patara consists of little more than pensions, restaurants, and gift shops. **St. Nikolas Pansiyon** (tel. 843 5024, -154), on the main road at the center of town, offers clean, cool rooms with fans, tables, chairs, and balconies. It has a spacious, vine-covered terrace where they serve breakfast and occasionally dinner. All rooms w/bath. (Singles $6.75, doubles $13.50, triples $19.) A little farther from the beach on the main road is **Flower Pansiyon** (tel. 843 5164, -034; fax 843 5078), a friendly establishment with carpeted, lavishly mosquito-netted rooms with balconies. (Singles $7.75, doubles $13.50, triples $17.75; breakfast and laundry service included.) **Rose Pension,** owned by the brother of Flower Pension's proprietor, is 100m away and offers all of the same. All three establishments run boat and canoe trips to the islands and Blue Cave, with dinner included, for $16-20. Patara has no official campsites, but ask about pitching a tent next to one of the restaurants or pensions in town. A large part of the beach is a **Caretta-caretta** sea turtle territory; sleeping there is *strictly* forbidden.

Despite various myths to the contrary, **Santa Claus** actually grew up right here by the sunny Mediterranean. Born in Patara in the 4th century, St. Nikolaus was famed for his annual gift-giving expeditions. After Santa became Bishop of nearby Myra, he was martyred there. You can visit his birthplace and then check out his church and grave at Myra near the village of Demre. The **Archaeological Museum** in Antalya houses St. Nick's relics—a few bits of bone that his 11th-century kidnappers dropped in their haste to get away.

Santa Claus Sure Was One Hip Cat

Next December 25th, when you're roasting chestnuts and frolicking 'neath the mistletoe, spare a moment of reflection for that good-natured Turk, the master-of-elves-and-toys, who travels around the world in one night to fill your stocking with goodies (even *Let's Go* can't rival that daytrip). On the very day of his birth in Patara in 270 AD, Saint Nicholas, or Claus as his close friends called him, is said to have stood up and folded his newborn hands in thankful prayer. Claus' good deeds were many. In one of his travels, he came across a landlord who had not only murdered three young boys, but had pickled their little bodies. A hopeless do-gooder, Saint Nick brought the boys back to life and converted the ruthless innkeeper. Despite these and other amazing deeds, his fame did not spread across Europe until the 13th and 14th centuries, at which time the Dutch coined the white-bearded *Sinterklaas*. The idea of Santa Claus as a bearer of gifts came into being when Nicholas, in another act of kindness, dropped a bag of gold into the window of a poor Turkish family while they were sleeping. These days, jolly old Saint Nick's belly might not be jiggling like jelly nor his cheeks quite so rosy since the Roman Catholic Church took away his sainthood in 1969 and excised his feast day from the church calendar, claiming that his miraculous works and acts of piety were nothing but old wives' tales. Bah humbug.

KAŞ COAST

■■■ KALKAN

Kalkan is a quintessential Turkish fishing village. A graceful stone breakwater encloses its harbor, and austere stone houses with wooden balconies huddle around the quay. The outside world has shown its appreciation by making the city a popular vacation stop (especially for Italians and French), and Kalkan's narrow, winding streets are crammed with clothing stores and ceramics boutiques. Advertisements hawking donkey rides and boat trips beckon at every corner. Still, Kalkan's small scale and impressive setting on steep hills overlooking the bay make it a welcome change from larger cities along the coast.

Kalkan proper does not have much of a beach; just a bunch of rocks on the left of the harbor. Past this, however, the landscape improves. A short climb leads to a tiny, often-deserted pebble beach. Three kilometers along the road to Kaş, beneath a small metal bridge, lies the lovely sandy beach of **Kapıtaş.** The best beaches, however, line the coast between Kalkan and Fethiye, especially around Patara.

Orientation and Practical Information Kalkan, on the main road between Fethiye and Kaş, is serviced by **buses** running roughly every ½hr. between the two ports (1½hr. from Fethiye, $2.25; 45min. from Kaş, $1.25). The highway between the two cities hugs the coast every inch of the way, revealing glimpses of distant isles. Before continuing down the coast, do a little star-gazing; according to Herodotus, nearby Halicarnassus is "where the moon and stars are observed nearest in the world." Buses stop at the top of the village on **Kalkan Caddesi.** The **PTT** (open daily 8am-midnight) stands half a block down the street. **Currency exchange** is available at the PTT. **Postal Code:** 07960; **Telephone Code:** 242.

Accommodations Rooms above the bus stop in Kalkan are cheaper than those in the center of town. Down the hill from the bus stop, to the left when the road forks, resides **Çelik Pansiyon,** 9 Yalı Boyu (tel. 844 2126). All rooms are immaculately clean and carpeted; the terrace offers gorgeous views of the harbor. (Singles $9, doubles $13.50, triples $19; breakfast included.) **Holiday Pansiyon,** 33 Süleyman Yılmaz Cad. (tel. 844 3154), at the northeast corner of town, is a family-run establishment in one of the quietest and most idyllic spots in Kalkan. All rooms in the main pension are clean and have private bathrooms and showers. There is also room for 10 guests in a beautiful 150-year-old wood-floored house next to the pension. (Doubles $15.50, triples $19; laundry $2.25; breakfast $2.25.) Up the stairs between the Kamil Koç office and the PTT is **Öz Pansiyon** (tel. 844 3444; fax 844 3152). Don't let the exterior put you off; the rooms within are clean, spacious, and all have private bathrooms. The two-tiered terrace with hanging grapevines has a sea view. (Singles $5.50, doubles $12.25, triples $14.50; breakfast included.)

Food Eat cheaply and well at the centrally located **Köşk Restaurant** (tel. 844 3046; open daily 9am-1am), which lays a sumptuous table of *meze* for $2.25 per plate. There are several restaurants along the waterfront that charge a bit more (roughly $5.50 for a full meal) for even more sumptuous fare. **Pandora Restaurant,** at the east end of this strip of restaurants, is particularly good. **Belgin's Kitchen** (tel. 844 3614; open 10am-1am) is across the small amphitheater from Köşk Restaurant. Belgin has created an authentic atmosphere here, complete with rugs, copper plates, floor tables, whitewashed walls, and live Turkish music. Full meals go for roughly $4.50. Vegetarians try the **Jolly Roger** (tel. 844 3284; open 9:30am-1am), down the hill on the extreme right of the fork near the bus stop; look for the "Scottish Spoken Here" sign. (Before you get used to the waitress' heavy brogue, you might wonder whether English is spoken here as well.) "Roger" offers at least three veggie options, along with plentiful meat dishes. (Full meal $4.50.)

■■■ KAŞ

If you take the square root of Bodrum, add a quantum of Kalkan, and multiply all of the above by sleepy seaside languor, you get Kaş, a luscious little quark of civilization sandwiched between the sea and mountains. The serpentine road from Kalkan to Kaş passes by glittering inlets dotted with patches of pebble beach. The town itself is replete with inexpensive, hospitable places to stay, excellent restaurants, and enjoyable bars. An uninhabited peninsula curves around from one side of the town's harbor, creating a calm, rock-lined lagoon ideal for swimming. Explore the mountainous, ruin-strewn countryside, take a boat trip around the coast, dance to a cacophonous hodge-podge of Turkish and American pop music in a bar, or wallow on the waterfront, cocktail in hand.

ORIENTATION AND PRACTICAL INFORMATION

Most of the town's activity centers around the small harbor along the main street, **Cumhuriyet Caddesi.** At its west end near the mosque, its name changes to **Hastane Caddesi.** Here it is intersected by **Elmalı Caddesi,** which heads uphill to the bus station. At its east end near the statue of Atatürk, Cumhuriyet is intersected by **Çukurbağlı Caddesi,** which leads to the PTT. From the Atatürk statue, Hükümet Cad. goes above the harbor to two beaches. The street going up the hill behind the tourist office—the one with most of the souvenir shops—is **Uzun Çarşı Caddesi.**

Tourist Office: 5 Cumhuriyet Meydanı (tel. 836 1238). To your left as you face the back of the Atatürk statue. English-speaking staff might refer you to pensions and hold your bags while you look at rooms. Area maps are sold at bookstores. Open daily 8am-noon and 1-7pm, Oct.-April until 5pm.

PTT: Çukurbağlı Cad. (tel. 836 1430). Walk down Elmalı Cad. from the bus station, then turn left before the Hacı Baba Restaurant. Walk 200m through the parking lot and the PTT will be on the left. Open daily 8:30am-10:30pm. **Currency exchange** desk open 8:30am-5pm. **Postal Code:** 07580; **Telephone Code:** 242.

Tourist Agencies: Nearly all agencies offer tours to Kekova (departure 10am, return 6pm; $9, lunch not included). Tour prices vary slightly, so shop around before purchasing a ticket. Beware of tour packages to locations (i.e. Myra) that may be cancelled at the last minute because of insufficient interest. **Kahramanlar Tourism and Yachting** (tel. 836 1062; fax 836 2402), on Cumhuriyet beyond the mosque, offers numerous options. Buses and cruises and cars (oh my!). **Simena Tours,** 1 Elmalı Cad. (tel. 836 1416), down the street from the bus station, can book airline tickets in addition to the regular stock of tours to Kalkan, Demre, Patara, Xanthos, Saklıkent, Kekova, and Dalyan. Open daily 8am-8pm.

Buses: Leave from station at the end of Elmalı Cad. Go to Antalya (hourly 7am-7pm, 4hr., $5), Fethiye (hourly 2¼hr., $3.50), Marmaris (1-2 per day, 6hr., $5.50), and İzmir (2 per day at 9:30am and 9:30pm, 9hr., $9).

Laundromat: Three on street with Kısmet Pansiyon; all charge roughly $6.75.

International Bookstore: It is easier to find **used English books** in Kaş than in many other towns on the Turkish seaside. There is a small used book emporium a few meters up the hill from the Red Point Bar with an ambience and a bespectacled owner straight out of a Spielberg movie. **Smiley's Restaurant** has a surprisingly large book exchange, and the **Kaş Bayii** convenience store, between the Atatürk statue and the mosque, sells and trades books as well. **The Merhaba Café,** between the PTT and the Hotel Turquoise, carries English-language newspapers and has a few pulp fiction novels.

Hospital: Hastane Cad. (tel. 836 1185). From the tourist office, 500m past the mosque, before the campground. For English-speaking health service, call the town's polyclinic at 836 1014.

Police: (tel. 836 1024, emergencies 155). 200m to the left of the tourist office, as you face the water.

ACCOMMODATIONS

The search for inexpensive accommodations in July and August will test your haggling and shopping skills. The pensions in Kaş are usually very clean and pleasant, but they tend to jack their prices up 20-40% in high season.

Yalı Pension and Hotel, 50 Hastane Cad. (tel. 836 1870). One block to the right of the mosque as you face the water. The hotel is on the right and the pension across the street. Both offer spacious rooms with carpets, couches, and balconies. The Hotel has a terrace with a marvelous view of the sea. Singles $9, doubles $13, triples $16.75; breakfast $1.75.

Hotel Turquoise (tel. 836 1800), in the narrow street behind the statue (Askerlik Şubesi Yanı Sok.). Large, turquoise rooms with huge bathrooms. International telephone service, in-house Turkish textile boutique, and a terrace/bar with a sea view. Singles $9, doubles $17.75, triples $24.50; breakfast included. Flash your *Let's Go* book and get a 10% discount.

Kısmet Pansiyon, 17 İlkokul Sok. (tel. 836 1879). From the bus station, follow the directions to the PTT onto Çukurbağlı Cad. Make a left one block after the Benetton store onto Postane Sok. Kısmet is at the top of the street. Bar and reception are on the roof, oddly enough. Beautiful roof patio with amazing view. Large, carpeted rooms. Singles $6.75, doubles $13.50, triples $16.75; breakfast included.

Mini Pansiyon (tel. 836 1038, -888), next to Kısmet Pansiyon. All rooms are clean, tiled, and have private bathrooms. Singles $6.75, doubles $10, triples $14.50; breakfast $1.75, laundry $3.50.

Aka Pension, 50 Çukurbağlı Cad. (tel. 836 1110), 200m from the bus station. All rooms w/shower and bath. Mike, the English owner, was a tour guide in Turkey for 8 years before opening the Aka. He still leads trekking excursions into the hills surrounding Kaş. Mosquito repellent devices available. Singles $7.75, doubles $11.25. Turkish breakfast $1.75, English breakfast $2.25 (served on roof terrace), laundry $5.50 per load.

Kaş Camping (tel. 836 1050, -2438), on Hastahane Cad. 100m past the amphitheater, or 500m past the mosque walking from behind the Atatürk statue. One of the prettier campsites you'll come across in this region. Sea view, hills, shade, and grass. Hot water is somewhat unreliable. Person $2.25, double bungalows $6.75, caravans $5.50 (electricity included), breakfast $1.75.

FOOD AND ENTERTAINMENT

There's a fruit and vegetable **market** halfway between the bus station and the harbor, one block above the mosque on Elmalı Cad. Friday is market day. For breakfast, try the **Hacı Babi Pastanesi** (tel. 836 2330), on Elmalı Cad., next to the vegetable market. Locals and tourists alike gather here to chat over plates of primo pastries and junk food. $4.50 will buy you enough sugar, sodium, and cholesterol to make your heart valves flutter with joy. (Open 6:30am-1am.) The continental breakfast set might want to head on over to the laid-back **Moonlight Bar,** across from Kısmet Pension. Turkish *brekkie* goes for $1.75. (Open 8am-1am.) **Çınar Lokantası** (tel. 836 2128), between the PTT and Otel Turquoise on Çukurbağlı Cad., offers pleasant atmosphere but is a tad crowded. (*Kebap* $3; open daily 8am-midnight.) Another option is **Smiley's Restaurant** (tel. 836 2812), behind the tourist office. The energetic owner İsmail, a.k.a. Smiley, certainly lives up to his name. He started as a waiter and slowly worked his way up to become the manager of one of the most popular restaurants in town. (Vegetarian specials $3.50-4.50, *kebap* $3.50. Backpackers can cook in the kitchen for free in winter. *Let's Go* readers get 10% off. Also check out the burgeoning book exchange here.) **Eriş Restaurant,** Cumhuriyet Meydanı 13 Ortança Sok. (tel. 836 1057), next door to Smiley's. Fancier and pricier than the restaurants along the harbor, but worth it. Founded in 1955. Has all kinds of *kebap,* steak, seafood, pizza, and spaghetti. (Full meal roughly $5.50.)

For good music and dancing, try **Mavi Bar** (tel. 836 1834), on the harbor by the tourist office. (Open 4pm-3:30am; beer $1.25.) The perpetually jam-packed **Red Point Bar** (tel. 836 1605), on the same street as the laundromats, offers much of the same. (Open 6pm-3:30am; beer $1.25.) For a more romantic evening, hit **Elit Bar,** which has live music and a cozy atmosphere. From the start of the pier, take a right and pass between the teahouses on the shore. (Open 7pm-3:30am; beer $1.50.)

SIGHTS

The two beaches of Kaş lie in coves surrounded by rocky cliffs and covered with smooth stones. It takes considerable effort to scramble over the stones, but it's worth it. The entrance to **Küçük Çakil Plajı** (Little Pebble Beach) is at the top of the hill on Hükümet Cad., to your left as you face the harbor (200m left as you exit the tourist office). More determined sunbathers and swimmers frequent **Büyük Çakil Plajı** (Big Pebble Beach), 15min. down the road.

Kaş has several historic sights in or near the town. Most impressive is the **Hellenistic Theater,** just past the hospital on Hastane Cad. as you leave town. The only intact ancient structure in Kaş, the theater rests on a solitary, elevated perch, overlooking the sea and the Greek island Kastelorizo. Climb to the topmost level to admire the landscape and test the resonating acoustics. You can spend the night in the theater (bring a sleeping bag), but don't count on sleeping much: rowdy young people crowd in after the bars close at 3am and sing and play guitar for most of the night. Follow the footpath behind the theater roughly 50m to the 4th-century BC **necropolis.** Back in town, there's a free-standing **monumental tomb,** also from the 4th century BC, up Uzun Çarşı Cad. behind the tourist office.

If you're lucky enough to be in Kaş on July 1, attend the **sea festival** on the harbor. Kaşians celebrate the bounty of the sea by picking up unsuspecting passersby and throwing them into the water, clothes and all. Swimming races are also held.

■ NEAR KAŞ

The farming community of **Demre,** an hour's bus ride east of Kaş ($1.50) on the road to Antalya, sits on a smooth, fertile plain sandwiched between the mountains and the sea. The town itself is unattractive, but several interesting sites are nearby; a long afternoon should take care of them. A short walk from the bus stop brings you to the **Tomb of St. Nikolas,** or **Santa Claus,** housed in a well-preserved 4th-century Byzantine basilica (follow signs for *Aya Nicola*). The saint is better known to Turks as Noel Baba. Remembered for his acts of charity, he came to be seen as a protector of sailors and children. In 1087, thieves plundered Santa's tomb, escaping to Bari, Italy, with his bones and a funny red cap. Today, the burial chapel in the basilica houses his simple marble **sarcophagus,** located in a small niche immediately to your right as you enter. The entrance to the partially ruined basilica is covered with faded 4th-century frescoes of the saints. St. Nikolas is pictured on the wall above his sarcophagus. Each December 6, the saint's birthday is celebrated with a commemorative three-day festival and symposium. (Basilica open Tues.-Sun. 8am-7pm; admission $1.25, students 60¢.) If you stay the night, consider **Şahin Hotel** (tel. 871 5686), on Müze Cad., a few blocks to the left as you leave the bus station. The clean, spacious rooms have 24-hr. hot water. There is also a restaurant and a shady terrace. ($5.50 per person, breakfast included.) **Telephone Code:** 242.

The main attraction around Kaş is **Kekova,** a partially submerged Lycian city roughly 2hr. east. **Excursion boats** visit Byzantine ruins, Kekova, and two fishing villages which flaunt a cliff honeycombed with Lycian tombs and a hill crowned with a half-ruined castle. Both towns are surrounded by a dozen Lycian sarcophagi, some leaning on the village homes. (Tours $9.)

The **Blue Caves,** 15km from Kaş, home to the Mediterranean's only **seal colony,** are worth a visit. Try to swim in the mornings, before the sea becomes rough. Nearby, 2km after Kalkan, is **Doves Cave,** which can be reached only by swimming. Opposite this grotto, the wide **Güvercinlik Cave** spouts a cold underwater stream. The resort of **Kemer,** roughly 80km closer to Antalya, has long stretches of fine beach and some restaurants that will make you think you're in fish paradise.

■■■ OLİMPOS

It's hard to say whether Indiana Jones or Han Solo would feel more at home in this remote outpost. The heavenly village of Olimpos, ensconced in a lush, jagged, rocky ravine, is so alien and ragged that it may be difficult to find a stranger place in this galaxy. Whispers from the village's crickets and winds that whip in off the sea twist the daily Muslim prayers into ghostly echoing wails. Enchanting Olimpos is a backpacker's town, and one of the few true budget destinations on the Turkish Riviera.

Originally a powerful Lycian port city, Olimpos was subsequently overwhelmed by Greek, Roman, and Byzantine invaders, each of whom left their mark on the town's architecture. As late as the 12th century, Venetian and Genovese crusaders used the city as a rest point as they hacked their way to the holy land. At its height, the ancient city was home to more than 30,000 inhabitants. By the 15th century, however, Olimpos was deserted.

Orientation and Practical Information To get to Olimpos from Kaş, take the Antalya bus and ask to be let off at Olimpos, roughly 3hr. into the trip. From Antalya, take the Kaş bus and ask to be let off at Olimpos (1hr. from Antalya). From the highway, take a taxi to the village ($6.75, negotiable; try to form groups). The village consists of a single road, so it's easy to get around. **Telephone Code:** 242.

Accommodations The latest craze to sweep through town is some pension owners' strange fascination with treehouses. Most rooms in town belong to standard, if somewhat ramshackle, pensions, but campsites and treehouses also exist.

The perks and services Kadir offers at **Kadir Pension** (tel. 892 1110; fax 825 7209) make the price worthwhile. For $5.50 travelers get treehouse accommodations a fabulous vegetarian meal (fresh fish and *kebap* available) or a Turkish omelette breakfast. Kadir also offers trips to the Chimaera for $1.50, and secluded mountain ruins. Ask about nighttime spearfishing safaris as well; the pension is on the right roughly 300m after the first pension in town. External showers and toilets. 24-hr. hot water. Pension rooms w/shower and toilet $9 per person. Kadir's other rooms offer similar services. **Yörük** (Nomad) **Camping** (call Kadir pension for info) is run by two English gentlemen named Guy and Dean, who guide Kadir's trekking excursions. Treehouse accommodations, dinner, and breakfast $5.50. Yörük has international telephones, laundry, 24-hr. hot water, common baths, and toilets. **Gypsy Pension** (tel. 892 1223), past both Yörük and Kadir, is new and cheap. Pension rooms are $2.25 per night. Dinner runs $1.25-2.25, and breakfast is $2.25.

Food, Entertainment, and Sights Inexpensive good food, convivial atmosphere, and a marvelous beach is all the entertainment Olimpos offers. Boat trips to the Chimaera and the mountain city ($5.50), as well as trekking, will satisfy your thirst for adventure. The area's archaeological and natural attractions are also enjoyable. Moving towards the sea, the pensions thin out and ancient ruins choked with Amazonian vines become more frequent. It's easy to get distracted on the pathways that veer off the road to the beach. Crabs, frogs, multicolored birds, lizards, and butterflies dart among the sun-dappled ruins, and many of the well-trodden pathways lead to muddy dead ends. Beware of frail footbridges, but don't be daunted—the sights only get better. (Admission to the ancient city and beach $1.25, students 60¢; keep your ticket, and you only have to pay once for your entire stay.)

In antiquity, Vulcan, god of the forge, was Olimpos' patron deity, due to the town's proximity to the **Chimaera,** a perpetual flame springing from a mountainside roughly 7km away. The ancients thought that this flame was the breath of the Chimaera, a mythical beast that was part lion, part goat, and part serpent. Geologists have yet to come up with a better explanation. In past centuries, the flame was even brighter than it is today, and, according to ancient reports, ships navigated by it. A Byzantine church now stands near the site (nighttime tractor tours cost $1.50). The city of Olimpos has only been partially excavated, so the ruins are, in most places, shrouded in vines, shrubs, and flowering bougainvillias. To the left of the beach road, over a small creek, a pathway leads to an ancient mausoleum with two **Greek-inscribed sarcophagi.** The wear and tear of the centuries shows on this structure. Follow the path farther and to the left, to the better-preserved **mosaic house,** an exquisite 5th-century edifice, parts of whose domes and pavement remain intact. The floors of the house were entirely covered with intricate tilework, until an earthquake diverted the course of a stream and flooded the building with 1m of water. On the other side of the road to the beach, across the river, is a decrepit **theater** and numerous **medieval walls** which have been damaged by the river and forest. Several better-preserved and restored sarcophagi lie at the entrance to the beach.

ANTALYA GULF COAST

■■■ ANTALYA

Antalya is Turkey's premier tourist resort. Daily airbuses bring in hordes of tourists from London, Munich, and Amsterdam. Antalya is a city of modern white buildings perched atop a cliff. Behind it and stretching along the bay's edge, are the towering, jagged Taurus Mountains. Tourism has been good to Antalya; it is wealthy, sophisticated, and cosmopolitan. This capital of the Turkish Riviera, although very touristy, never descends to the tackiness of Spain's Costa del Sol. You won't find bratwurst here, or fish and chips; it is closer to the sophistication of the French Riviera. Sophistication is a mixed blessing. People are less friendly here than in inland Turkey, prices are higher, and there is sometimes a "special" price for foreigners—which, in case you were wondering, isn't lower.

ORIENTATION AND PRACTICAL INFORMATION

Antalya's bus station is on the corner of **Adnan Menderes Bulvarı** and **Kazım Özalp Caddesi.** Exit from one of the bus station's gates on Adnan Menderes Blvd. and take the first left onto Kazım Özalp Cad. After roughly 100m this street turns into a pedestrian zone. Note that there are several exit gates—make sure you're exiting onto Adnan Menderes. One kilometer farther, at the end of the street, is the intersection with Cumhuriyet Cad. (Republic St.). You will see the red, pointed **Fluted Minaret** (Yivli Minare) on your right and the **clock tower** in front. To the right of the clock tower, a little street runs downhill into the old city. To reach most of our accommodations, it is easier *not* to enter the old city at this point; instead, go left on Cumhuriyet Cad. Take the first major intersection (150m along) to the right; you are now on the plainly marked Atatürk Cad., the city's main street, which is lined with high-class boutiques and leather shops. Roughly 150m down the street, on the right, is the triple-arched, Roman, Hadrian's Gate. Go through it and take the first left; you are now on **Hesapçı Sok.** This old street runs for about 1½km, past the **Truncated Minaret** (Kesik Minare) to the Hıdırlık Tower on the seafront, at which there are magnificent views of the city, the Gulf of Antalya, and the rugged Taurus Mountains. Most accommodations are scattered along this street.

Tourist Offices: (tel. 241 1747). The main tourist office is in a mansion in the old city; it's a challenge to find it. Enter the old city beside the clock tower and walk under the "Welcome" arch. When the road ends 800m after, go left at the Türk Evi Otel. Keep going straight. Eventually the road narrows and goes uphill. The tourist office is on your right, opposite the Aspen Hotel. English-speaking staff. Open Mon.-Fri. 8:30am-5:30pm. The new city's tourist office (tel. 247 0541, -2) is on Cumhuriyet Cad. Open Mon.-Fri. 8am-6pm, Sat.-Sun. 9am-5pm.

Tourist Police: In the harbor, in the little street to the left of the Atatürk bust.

PTT: The main branch (open daily 9am-5pm for stamps and currency exchange, 24 hr. for phonecalls) sits a block down Anafartalar Cad., on the left from the Selekler Çarşısı. Another is located on the harbor (open 8am-6pm). Currency exchange is available at both PTTs. Smaller branch at İsmet Paşa Cad., the continuation of Atatürk Cad. past Cumhuriyet Cad. Open 9am-10pm. **Telephone Code:** 242.

Honorary Consulates: U.K., Kızılsaray Mah. Dolaplıdere Cad. Pırıltı Sitesi, 1st floor (tel. 247 7000). **Northern Cyprus,** Kışla Mah. 35th Sok. Dörteldemir Apt. 11 (tel. 248 9847).

American Express: Full services offered by their agents **Pamfilya,** #57 30th Ağustos Cad. (tel. 243 1500), near the water at the far end. For international cash transfers go to **Koç Bank,** on Atatürk Cad. opposite the Hadrian Gate—with the gate to your back, look right. **Akbank ATM** for AmEx cards on Kazım Özalp Cad., halfway between the clock tower and the bus station.

ATMs: Several scattered around the intersection of Cumhuriyet and Atatürk Cad.

Flights: Cumhuriyet Cad. (tel. 243 4381, -2). Offices in the same building as smaller tourist office. Open Mon.-Fri. 8:30am-7pm, Sat.-Sun. 8:30am-5:30pm. Direct flights to İstanbul ($65), Ankara ($55), London Stansted (1 per week), Amman (2 per week), and Lefkoşa (2 per week). Other connections via İstanbul and Ankara.

Trains: TCDD provides a bus service to Burdur (2hr.) to connect with its train to İstanbul. Through service from Antalya to İstanbul costs $12.

Buses: Leave from the station at the intersection of Adnan Menderes Blv. and Kazım Özalp Cad., 1km north of the clock tower. A new station is under construction on the far edges of the city. Buses to İstanbul (10 per day, 15hr., $20), Ankara (12 per day, 12hr., $16), İzmir (5 per day, 12hr., $16), Rize (2 per day, 30hr., $27), Adana (15 per day, 12hr., $16) via Alanya (2hr.), Anamur (6hr.), Taşucu (8hr.), Mersin (10hr.) and Göreme/Ürgüp/Nevşehir (3 per day, 12hr., $16). If you plan to take a taxi from the bus station, beware of the drivers at the station, many of whom work on commission for hotels. The best strategy is to walk 100m from the station to one of the side streets and hail a less eager cabbie. Main terminal for city buses is at Meydan, at the intersection of Aspendos Blv. and İbni Sina Cad., 5km from the city center (on the road to the airport).

Dolmuş: *Dolmuş* stop at the big blue signs marked "D." Running to the Museum and Konyaaltı Beach (take *dolmuş* from Konyaaltı Blv.) and to Lale Beach (from the Doğu Garaj (East Station) (35¢). To get to Doğu Garaj from Atatürk Cad., take a right onto Cumhuriyet Cad. Walk one long block to the Start Hotel, then go right; you'll see the *dolmuş* clustered around. The Lale *dolmuş* leaves from 100m down this street, on the right. (The former garage is now a bazaar; *dolmuş* now leave from the streets around it.)

Ferries: Turkish Maritime Lines (tel. 241 1120) serves Venice May-Oct. Departs each Wed. and returns Sat.

Car Rental: Numerous pensions and agencies in the old city rent cars for $35 per day with unlimited mileage, insurance included.

Laundromat: Yıkama Laundry, 28 Tabakhane Sok. (tel. 241 1174), beside the Anı Pansiyon. Wash'n'dry $6. **Ünal Laundry,** 43 Hesapçı Sok. (tel. 248 9372), beside the Truncated Minaret. Wash'n'dry $7. Both open 8am-10pm. Most hotels and pensions do your laundry for a similar fee.

English Bookstore: Owl Bookshop, Barbaros Mah. 21 Akarçeşme Sok. (tel. 243 5718). Just off Hesapçı Sok.—well highlighted. Roughly ½km down, as you walk from new town, on the left. Large selection of new and secondhand books in English. Open daily approx. 10am-1pm and 3-7pm.

Hospital: Özel Antalya Kliniği, Işıklar Cad., Apt. No. 55/2 (tel. 243 6651; fax 243 3159). 24-hr., service includes ambulance and hotel visits. Some English spoken. From Cumhuriyet Cad., walk down Atatürk Cad. to the end. Bear left at the park, staying on the main road. The clinic is roughly 1km down, on the left.

ACCOMMODATIONS

Stay in **Kaleiçi,** the old city, with its twisting alleys and half-timbered Ottoman houses. There are about 200 hotels and pensions in this area. All price ranges are represented, but most are at the lower end. Although historic and well-preserved, the old city is touristy; it is filled with pensions, restaurants, and carpet shops. Unless otherwise stated, prices include private shower and breakfast. Bargaining may be fruitful. The concept of a fixed price hasn't fully taken root.

Sabah Pansiyon, Kaleiçi Kılınçaslan Mah. 60 Hesapçı Sok. (tel. 247 5345, -6). A popular backpackers' hangout. Pleasant courtyard/meeting area. Singles $6, doubles $22, w/breakfast. Roof, couch, or floor $3. Camping $2.50 per person.

Ninova Pension, Barbaros Mah. 9 Hamit Efendi Sok. (tel. 248 6114). A touch of luxury in a beautifully restored historic house. Wooden ceilings and floors in large rooms which are as clean as could be. Singles $15, doubles $25.

Anı Pansiyon, 26 Tabakhane Sok., Hesapçı Sok. (tel. 247 0056). Another historic home restored to a high degree of comfort. Low Turkish table and mats upstairs for you to hang out. Proprietor is a charming old woman. Service is impeccable. Comfortable rooms are smaller than at Ninova. Singles $15, doubles $25.

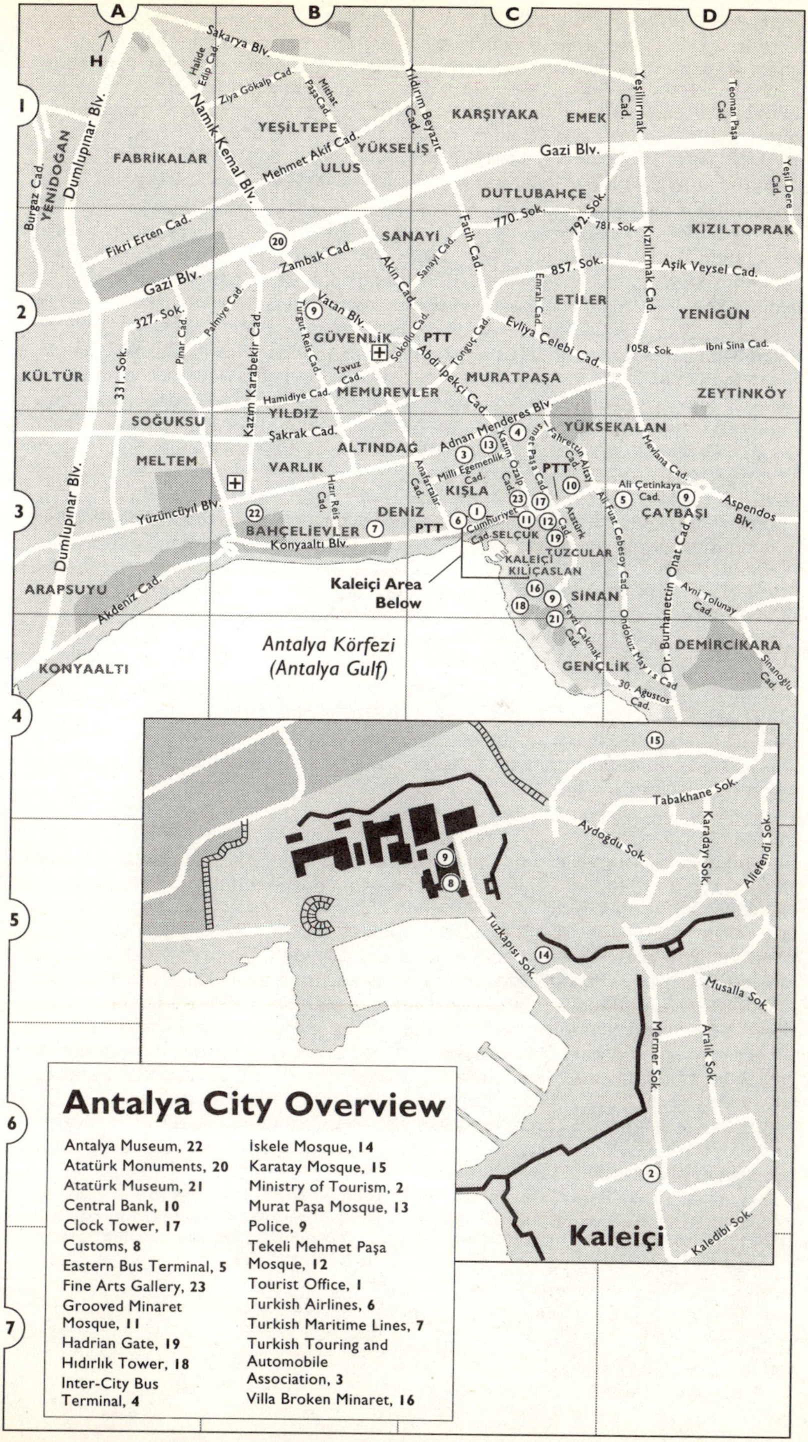

Antalya City Overview

Antalya Museum, 22
Atatürk Monuments, 20
Atatürk Museum, 21
Central Bank, 10
Clock Tower, 17
Customs, 8
Eastern Bus Terminal, 5
Fine Arts Gallery, 23
Grooved Minaret Mosque, 11
Hadrian Gate, 19
Hıdırlık Tower, 18
Inter-City Bus Terminal, 4
İskele Mosque, 14
Karatay Mosque, 15
Ministry of Tourism, 2
Murat Paşa Mosque, 13
Police, 9
Tekeli Mehmet Paşa Mosque, 12
Tourist Office, 1
Turkish Airlines, 6
Turkish Maritime Lines, 7
Turkish Touring and Automobile Association, 3
Villa Broken Minaret, 16

Garden Pansiyon, Kılınçaslan Mah. 16 Zafer Sok. (tel. 247 1930). Basic little pension with a slightly wild garden. Singles $10, w/bath $15; doubles $15.

Sen Kaptan Otel/Pansiyon, Kılınçaslan Mah. 65 Hesapçı Sok. (tel. 248 6690). Restored house with a huge shaded garden, from which the Hıdırlık Tower can be seen. Singles $12, doubles $24.

FOOD AND ENTERTAINMENT

Be sure not to miss the **Tophane Çay Bahçesi** (Battlements Tea Garden), on top of the rampart walls, overlooking the harbor. Enter from the park on Cumhuriyet Cad. Half the city comes here to sit, chat, and relax. (Cold drinks 75¢, snacks 75¢-$1.25.) For dinner, be careful you don't pay "tourist price." Try the **Topçu,** 21 Özalp Cad., roughly 50m from the clock tower, in the pedestrian street which leads to the bus station. This hole-in-the-wall has been a local institution for decades; it's a workers' café with gourmet food. Veggie fans will enjoy *piyaz* and *cacık* ($5 each). There are three main eating areas, all in close proximity. **Eski Sebzeciler İçi Sokak** (The Old Inner Street of the Greengrocers) is a narrow, covered alleyway lined with cheap outdoor *kebap* restaurants. It's the place to try the local specialty, *tandır kebap*—mutton roasted in a clay pot. Another food area is the Old City. Here you can wander past dozens upon dozens of restaurants serving Turkish specialties. The outdoor **Favorit Restaurant,** 19 Uzun Çarşı Sok., 100m past the "Welcome to the Old City" sign (on the left), serves, as its specialty, *Ali Nazik kebap*—delicious grilled chopped lamb served in a thick sauce of garlic and aubergine ($4.75). Wander down to the harbor, the third major eating area. Here, at the base of the old city ramparts, are dozens of crowded, happy, boisterous fish restaurants.

There is not shortage of nightlife in Antalya. **Club 29** in the harbor has a highbrow crowd. ($8 cover weekends, $6 weekdays.) **Olympos,** in the 5-star Falez Hotel near Konyaaltı Beach, includes a laser system, bistro, video bar, and occasional live music. **Cinemas** generally show English-language films with Turkish subtitles. There is **Oscar,** Zafer Sok. in the old city; **Ulusoy,** Kazım Özalp Cad., towards the bus terminal; and **Cultür,** Atatürk Cad., near Police Station and park. (Students w/ISIC get 50% off.) Antalya is known for its spectacular waterfalls (*düdenler*). The upper falls, accessible by *dolmuş* (30min., 30¢), tumble 11km to the north; the less spectacular lower falls are by Lara Beach.

SIGHTS

The **Antalya Museum** is among Turkey's most impressive. Exhibits range from prehistoric times to the Turkish Republic, featuring the first money, artifacts from the Archaic era, and finds from Perge, Aspendos, and Side. (Open Tues.-Sun. 9am-6pm; admission $4, students $2.) It is situated roughly 2½km from town along Cumhuriyet Blv., which changes its name to Konyaaltı Blv. on the way. Take any *dolmuş* labeled *Konyaaltı/Liman* heading to your left (with your back to the sea) along Cumhuriyet/Konyaaltı Blv.; they stop at the large "D" signs. Get off before it heads downhill to the beach. The museum is signposted.

Near the intersection of Cumhuriyet Cad. and the old city entrance, you'll see the red-tinted **Yivli Minare** (Fluted Minaret), dating from the 13th century and virtually the symbol of the city, as well as the nearby clock tower. Down Atatürk Cad., on the right, stands **Hadrian's Gate,** built in 130 AD to commemorate the visit of the emperor Hadrian. Enter this gate to the old city; about halfway down Hesapçı Sok. is the **Kesik Minare** (Truncated or Broken Minaret)—the ruined mosque beside it was transformed from a Byzantine church by the Seljuks. The structure was actually built as a Roman temple before it was converted into a three-nave basilica in the 4th century AD. At the far end of Hesapçı Sok. is the **Hıdırlık Tower,** believed to have been built as a lighthouse in the 2nd century AD. To its left is the city park. The views from here—the Gulf of Antalya, the city, the mountains—are magnificent. It's the best place to watch the sunset. Founded as Attaleia in the 2nd century BC by King Attalos II of Pergamon, Antalya is still partially surrounded by walls built by Greeks and later by Byzantines and Seljuks. You will catch glimpses of these as you stroll. Back on Cumhuriyet Blv., take a stroll to the harbor, flanked by ramparts.

■■■ TAŞUCU

The scenic road from Anamur to Taşucu is punctuated by pine forests and cliffs plunging onto sandy beaches. A deserted beach lies between Anamur and Taşucu, right before Yabişli and after Sıphalı. Taşucu offers the fastest, cheapest, and most comfortable connections to Northern Cyprus—and little else. Nevertheless, if you have to wait a few hours, or spend the night, you'll find it's quite a pleasant place.

Orientation and Practical Information Numerous hotels and restaurants cater to those in transit. The town's main square, complete with Atatürk statue, is next to the harbor. Here is contained the **PTT** (open daily 8am-7pm; no exchange services Sat.-Sun.) and four ferry boat offices, which sell tickets for the seabus and ferry trip to Girne (Kyrenia). **Fergün** (tel. 741 2323) sells tickets for the fast, comfortable seabus (departures 11am and 2:30pm daily, 2½hr., one-way $16.25, round-trip $29.50). **Ertürk** (tel. 741 4033) sells tickets for the ferry (for those who prefer sitting up all night), which departs Sun.-Thus. (one-way $12.75, round-trip $23.25). Add to your ticket price the $2 Taşucu port tax (each time you enter or leave) and an $8.50 Girne tax (applicable only on departures from Girne, as in a round-trip). Schedules are liable to change. Intercity Antalya-Adana **buses** stop in Taşucu but usually on the highway, not at the station. **Telephone Code:** 324.

Accommodations From the highway, it's a 2-min. walk to the sea. Go left to find many *pansiyon,* all featuring clean, sunny rooms at similar prices. All rooms in **Tuğran Pansiyon** (tel. 741 4493) have balcony, shower, and toilet. (Singles $10, doubles $14; breakfast $3.) Two more possibilities lie farther down the road. **Holmi Pansiyon** (tel. 741 2321), offers balconied rooms w/bath. (Singles $15, doubles $20, w/breakfast.) The older **Barış Pansiyon** (tel. 741 4381) is next door (singles $10, doubles $15). Just 8km from Taşucu in Boğsak is **Gürbüzler Camping** (tel. 741 6001). Sandless **Akçakıl Camping** is 6km closer to Taşucu (tel. 741 4451; doubles w/bath $14; camping $2.50 per person, breakfast $3.50). There are no buses to Boğsak, so many hitchhike or take a taxi (about $3.50) from Taşucu.

■■■ ADANA

Adana, Turkey's fourth largest city, is named after the god of weather, Adanus, for good reason. The city has pleasant balmy, Mediterranean climate and fertile countryside surrounds the region. Contemporary Adana is modern and has gained wealth from suppling cotton to the Turkish textile industry and *Adana kebap,* a tasty, spicy beef *şiş,* to Turkey's hungry mouths. Adana is surprisingly Western, due to the nearby U.S. military base at İncirlik.

Orientation and Practical Information Adana is a large city with few street signs. As you may have guessed, that's not a good combination. The main street is the E-5 highway, which runs from the center of town past the bus station and along the Mediterranean coast. In town, the landmarks on the E-5 are the big Akbank building, the overpass, and the towering minarets of the new Merkez Camii (Central Mosque), beside the river. With your back to the bus station, take a right at the Akbank onto Atatürk Cad. The **tourist office** (tel. 359 1994) is 10m ahead. The friendly staff speaks English and will supply you with maps (Open Mon.-Fri. 8am-noon and 1-5pm.). Continue along Atatürk Cad. and take the first right into İnönü Cad. to reach many hotels. Past İnönü Cad., Atatürk Cad. changes its name to Saydam Cad.; a 10-min. walk along here leads to the Atatürk statue. beyond the Atatürk statue, down a side street to your left, is the main **PTT** (24 hr.). Turn left at the Akbank building onto Atatürk Cad. At the end, turn right to reach the railway station (20min.). Opposite the station on İstasyon Cad. is a PTT (Open 24 hr., exchange services 8am-5pm). There is a small PTT on İnönü Cad. (open 8am-5pm).

Daily **trains** to Eskişehir (10:50am), Diyarbakır (3:50pm), İstanbul (Haydarpaşa) (11:30pm), Ankara (7:30pm), Kayseri (5:30pm), Elazığ (8am), Gaziantep (6:50am).

To get to the **THY Airlines** office, 1 Stadyum Cad. (tel. 454 1545; open Mon.-Fri. 8:30am-5:30pm, Sat. 8:30am-noon) make a left out of the tourist office, walk straight and make the first right after the second traffic circle. They don't have service buses to the airport, but around the corner from the big Çetinkaya building, catch a *dolmuş* to the airport. From the tourist office, turn right on İnönü Cad. and then left on Zia Paşa Cad. before the Öz Hotel. Past the museum and at the end of the block, across from Hotel Kaza, is the *dolmuş* stop. Take one that says "Havaalanı" (airport).

To get to the center of town from the inappropriately-named **Merkez Otogar** (central bus station), located 5km away along the E-5, cross the road and take an E-5 *dolmuş*. Be sure to cross the road; destination plates read *Barkal* in both directions. (every 5min., 25¢). The *dolmuş* depart the E-5 roughly 1km short of the Akbank, one block short of the overpass. Get off here and head for **Kurtulus Meydani** (Kurtulus Square), across from İnönü Cad. **Taxis** are metered ($5-6). The larger bus companies offer free service to their central offices, clustered around the Akbank on the E-5. It's easiest to buy your ticket in advance from the offices on the E-5. Free service buses will then carry you to the station, 45min.-1hr. before departure. There is a small **dolmuş station** on the E-5, by the river and opposite the Central Mosque, with services to local towns and villages. *Dolmuş* to Antakya also depart from here (hourly, 3½hr., $1.50), but run along the E-5 first—you can hail them at the Akbank building. *Dolmuş* to Mersin depart from the E-5, near the Akbank.

Currency exchange bureaux (Döviz) cluster around Saydam Cad., the extension of Atatürk Cad., as you exit the tourist office to the right. **Akbank** has an **ATM** and accepts AmEx. For cash transactions, go to **Koçbank,** located on the E-5, 100m past Akbank towards the river, on the right.To get to the **U.S. consulate** (tel. 453 9106) make a left out of the tourist office and pass through three traffic circles. It's on the corner of the Atatürk Park. Foreign-language **newspapers** are sold at **Yolgeçen Kitabevi** on Atatürk Blv. near the railway station; pick up day-old copies of *USA Today* and the *International Herald Tribune.* **Telephone Code:** 322.

Accommodations Unless you're broke, don't stay in the cheapest hotels, as Adana's worst are pretty bad. An exception is the **Otel Mercan,** 5 Ocak Meydanı, Melekgirmez Çarşısı (tel. 351 2603), which is clean and quite plush for a hotel in its class; all rooms have private bath. Facing the Atatürk statue, look right—you can't miss it. (Singles $7, doubles $11.75.) **Otel Duygu,** 14 İnönü Cad. (tel. 359 3916), is clean and comfortable with private shower and TV in each room; some rooms have balconies. (Singles $14, doubles $23.25; breakfast $1.75.) The **İpek Palas,** 103 İnönü Cad. (tel. 351 8741), is similar, as are its prices. Desperadoes may want to head next door to **Hotel Gümüş,** 101 İnönü Cad. (tel. 351 4175), with minimalist, waterless rooms. (Singles $4.75, doubles $8.25.)

Food, Entertainment, and Sights To try Adana's spicy namesake *kebap,* go to **Yeni Onbaşlar,** on Atatürk Cad. opposite the tourist office (open 11am-10:30pm), which, along with its staff, looks like it hasn't been renovated since the 50s—and that's part of its charm. **Limanı Lokantası,** in the arcade opposite the tourist office, serves standard *lokanta* fare (open 6am-9pm).

Walk along the E-5 towards the river to start your tour of the sights. You'll pass the huge **Merkez Camii** (Central Mosque), the "biggest mosque in the Middle East" which is larger than the Taj Mahal. It is still under construction; ask any local when it's likely to be finished—they'll shrug as only the Mediterranean people can (See construction of subway in Athens). Just before it, the **Archaeological Museum** includes Hittite sculptures, Roman jewelry, and bronze-age pottery (open Tues.-Sun. 8am-noon and 1:30-5pm; admission $1.25). Turn right and follow the river; you'll soon pass a small **Atatürk Museum** (open Tues.-Sun. 8am-noon and 1:30-5pm, admission 60¢); in 5min. you'll be at the **Roman bridge,** built by Hadrian. Continue past it for 5min.; go right at the government building to reach the **clock tower.** On the right before the clock tower is a park and just beyond it, the **Ulu Camii** (Great Mosque), built in 1541. The park is well-shaded, with palm trees and views of the minaret; it's a pleasant place to linger awhile. Past the clock tower is the **Bedesten,** a crumbling, but bustling 16th-century market. Continue on to reach **Yağ Camii** (Butter Mosque), an unusual structure dating from 1501. Follow the road to the right; 50m past the Atatürk statue, to the right down some narrow streets, is a Catholic church, home to the city's small community of Christians. Just off İnönü Cad. (follow the sign) is a small **Ethnographic Museum** (open Tues.-Sun. 8am-noon and 1:30-4pm; admission $1.25). Outside of town is a dam and huge man-made **lake**—it's none too beautiful, but pleasant tea gardens and restaurants are scattered along its shore. There are innumerable benches, over which the municipality has thoughtfully erected sunscreens Take a white *dolmuş,* marked "Cemal Paşa" on top and "Göl" on the destination board, from opposite the tourist office (every 10min., 25¢). The *dolmuş* will take you all over Adana before stopping at the lake.

■■■ ANTAKYA (HATAY)

In Antakya, site of the ancient city of Antioch, the heat and tourist levels subside considerably. The formidable Nur Mountains, that separate Antakya from the rest of Turkey, at one time isolated the city from the end of WWI. Consequently, this area was a part of Syria until 1939, and still retains a considerable Syrian influence. If you're continuing on to Syria, this is a good starting point.

As ancient Antioch, the city was one of the most powerful in the Mediterranean. It was the third largest city in the Roman Empire, after Rome and Alexandria. Seleucus, a general under Alexander the Great, founded the city in 300 BC and ruled over much of Asia from here. The population swelled to half a million and Antioch became famous for its liberality and debauchery. During Roman rule, the Apostle Peter settled here and gathered the first Christian congregation in a grotto now outside of town; he chose Antioch to curb its excesses.

After a series of earthquakes, the desperate denizens changed the city's name to Theopolis (City of God) in hope that the powers that be would recognize their repentance. The city's importance, both strategic and commercial, made it a prime target for conquest. By the time the Turks got hold of it, Sassanians, Arabs, Byzantines, Crusaders, and Mamluks had all marauded through, and Antioch's glory had been reduced to ruins. A glance at the city's crumbling walls along the surrounding mountain ridge will give you an idea of city's size in ancient time, compared to the population of 150,000 that live here today.

Orientation and Practical Information You'll probably arrive at the bus station, 1km from the center. Nearly all **buses** pass through İskenderun (every 10min., 1hr., $1), and many through Gaziantep (every ½hr., 3½hr., $3.25). They serve Mersin (3 per day, 4hr., $3.75), Urfa (1 per day, 6hr., $9), Kayseri (2 per day, 8hr., $12), Ankara (10 per day, 11hr., $12), Antalya (2 per day, 11hr., $15), İzmir (3 per day, 16hr., $16), Samsun (2 per day, 16hr., $16), İstanbul (9 per day, 17hr., $16), Trabzon (2 per day, 22hr., $19), and Kars (1 per day, 22hr., $25).

Buses to points east (Urfa, Diyarbakır, etc.) leave around 8pm and arrive in the early hours, around 3 or 4am. To avoid this, take one of the regular *dolmuş* from the bus station to **Gaziantep** (3hr., $3.50; change here for hourly connections. Buses head to Aleppo (3 per day, $14) and Damascus in Syria (11am and noon, $21); and to Amman, Jordan (5 per week, $29). Daily departures to major cities in Saudi Arabia (Mecca, Riyadh, Medina, and Jeddah) as well as to Brayda and H. Bartin. Get your visas ahead of time in İstanbul or Ankara.

Exit the bus station, turn left and left again onto Istiklal Cad. Continue past the Türkiye İş Bankası and Pamukbank ATM until the river (700m). Cross the second bridge into the square with the Atatürk statue, without which we'd all be lost.

The **Archaeological Museum** and the **PTT** (24 hr.) keep Atatürk company. Walk roughly 5min. down Atatürk Cad. (to the right of the PTT) to reach the **tourist office** (tel. 216 0160; open Mon.-Fri. 8am-noon and 1:30-5:30pm) in the park on the opposite side of the circle. Blue inner-city **buses** (10¢) leave from the center, in front of the Hotel Kent. These buses leave every 20min., 6am-9pm. **English-language books** and newspapers can be found at **Ferah Koll. Şti.** (open daily 7am-9pm), just past Restaurant Nuri. **Postal Code:** 31050; **Telephone Code:** 326.

Accommodations Head for the **Hotel Saray,** across the river from the square at 3 Hürriyet Cad. (tel. 214 9001). Management offers brand-new rooms with private bath and desk. (Singles $10.50, doubles $15.25; breakfast included.) The minaret of the Ulu Camii next door will awaken you at prayer time. The huge, hulking factory-like structure of the **Hotel Güney,** 8 İstiklal Sok. (tel. 214 9713) offers old but clean rooms (Singles $8.25, doubles w/shower $14) Back rooms have good views. Heading into town from the bus station, take a left at the fork beside Ata Taxi, into the little alley off Istiklal Cad. Cheap, clean, waterless and minimalist rooms can be found in **Jasmin Hotel,** 14 Istiklal Cad. (tel. 212 7171). (Singles $6, doubles $11.75).

Food and Entertainment The Hatay region has several local specialties. *İçli köfte,* often referred to as *oruk,* is a hot and spicy meatball covered in thick pastry. *Ekşi aşı* is a variation on this, covered in tomato sauce. For dessert, *künefe* (or *peynirli kadayıf*) is a large *baklava*-style pastry stuffed with white cheese. It is not easy to get a taste of these regional treats, as Antakya's eateries are simple (though good) *lokanta* and *kebapçı,* and you must hop on a *dolmuş* in order to get to the gourmet center of **Harbiye** (see Sights below). In town, go to **Restaurant Nuri,** 9 Hürriyet Cad., a cheap, authentic, delicious *lokanta* (open daily 5am-1:30am, entrees $1.25). The **Saray Restaurant** (under the hotel of the same name) is similar and almost as good. **Sultan Sofrası,** 18 İstiklal Cad., a *lokanta* with white tablecloths and waiters, occasionally serves local specialties. Large restaurants serve gourmet local and Turkish specialties at low prices. Harbiye specialties *ızgara tavuuk* (grilled chicken) and *şiş tavuk* (chicken on a skewer) are done in a unique style. You'll get all the local specialties at **Hidro Tesisleri** (tel. 231 4006) on the main street opposite the gorge, where the *dolmuş* pulls in off the Antakya road. (*Oruk* $2.50, *ızgara tavuk* $3.75, *peynirli kadayıf* $1.50.) Try the thick gooey ice cream at **Dedem Dondurma** on Atatürk Cad., opposite the Büyük Antakya Oteli.

Sights **Sen Piyer Kilisesi** (St. Peter's Church) is the world's first Christian church. Founded by the Apostle Peter, who preached here along with Paul and Barnabas, the original congregation coined the word "Christianity" to describe their new religion. Although the Christian community here is now tiny, it has never left Antakya, and liturgy is still given here. To get to the church from the bus station, turn left and then make an immediate right onto Istiklal Cad. Follow it one block to the twin gas stations and take a right, continuing 1.2km until you see a sign on the right. The church is 250m from the sign. Inner city bus #6 will drop you off near the sign. (Church open Tues.-Sun. 8am-noon and 1:30-5:30pm; free.) The hillside near the church has been a holy spot since pagan times and is riddled with the remains of caves, tunnels, and parts of Antioch's city walls. A path zigzags up from the church to the Hellenistic **fire altar** to Haron, god of earthquakes. Antakya's **Archaeological Museum** is renowned for its superb collection of Roman mosaics, the second-largest in the world. Dating typically from the 2nd-4th centuries AD, many of these relics from nearby Daphne represent scenes from Roman mythology. (Open Tues.-Sun. 8:30am-noon and 1:30-5pm; admission $2.50, students $1.25.)

Harbiye, ancient Daphne, with its attractive wooded gorge has been an excursion spot since Roman times. Legend has it that Antony and Cleopatra were married here. Nowadays it is regarded by locals as the region's premier eating locale. Harbiye is 10km from Antakya and *dolmuş* run roughly every 10min. (25¢ each way). From the bus station, go left then right onto Istiklal Cad. At the dual petrol stations, *dolmuş* run along the road to your right. Hail them from anywhere; they are posted "Harbiye." Should you wish to stay here, there are numerous cheap hotels.

Black Sea Coast

The Black Sea Coast has long been overlooked by the majority of Turkey's tourists because of its short summer season. Cool breezes and heavy rainfall nourish this region's forests and thickly cultivated farmland that are more reminiscent of the Northwest United States than a Middle Eastern country.

Despite the isolation fostered by adjacent mountain ranges, trading posts such as Sinop, Trabzon, and Amisus (now Samsun) have become commercial centers. They first exported local products and later profited from the silk route trade when Arab invasions blocked the southern passage. The region still supports itself by the export of tea, cherries, and other crops that were the major produce of ancient times. In recent years commerce with Georgia and other former Soviet republics has brought added prosperity. The Black Sea Coast is bountiful and unspoiled and, though the tourism industry is not developed, travel is easy, and the soft lushness of the countryside profoundly beautiful.

TRABZON

From its hilltop vantage point over the Black Sea, Trabzon has seen empires rise and fall, preserving a little of each in its architecture and lifestyle. Founded by the ancient Greeks as the port Trapezus, the city is best known as a trade center which attracted merchants from all over the world. Though important in the Greek and Roman periods, Trabzon reached its heyday after Alexis Comneni came to the city in 1204, fleeing Constantinople while the Crusaders sacked it. Comneni dubbed the city Trebizond and made it the capital of his empire. The dynasty he founded became the longest and one of the wealthiest in Greek history; its rulers lived off the profits of trade and nearby silver mines. The kingdom held out against the Turks until 1461, even longer than Constantinople, postponing its demise by diplomatically marrying off its daughters, reputedly the most beautiful women in the world.

An industrial region of more than 1.4 million inhabitants, present-day Trabzon has lost much of its romantic appeal as a stronghold of exotic princes. With the influx of impoverished immigrants from the Eastern Bloc came innumerable sex-workers; women traveling alone may be mistaken for prostitutes. A sultry atmosphere traps a rich stink in the city's center, which rains wash away from time to time, leaving the air crystal clear—for a day or so. Trabzon is greener than the cities on the Aegean and Mediterranean, its population, an ethnic bouillabaisse of Turks, Russians, Georgians, and other ex-Soviets. Trabzon may either repulse or bewitch you with its fascinating history, industrial squalor, verdant beauty, and post-Cold War seediness.

ORIENTATION AND PRACTICAL INFORMATION

Tourist Office: (tel. 321 4659). In the southeast corner of the main square's park. Has maps as well as the dates of the huge highland festivals of late June and late July. Open Mon.-Sat. 8am-5:30pm, Mon.-Fri. 8am-noon and 1-5pm in winter.

PTT: Located halfway down Maraş Cad., the street directly west of the main square. Open 24 hr. **Telephone Code:** 462. **Postal Code:** 61000.

Tourist Agencies: Afacan Tour, 40 İskele Cad. (tel. 321 5804), 200m northeast of the main square, can get visas for Georgia ($40 for 1 month, $110 for 3 months) and Russia ($45 for 1 month, $60 for 2 months), as well as schedules of ships (7-15hr., $30-100) and planes (Mon., Wed., Fri., $100) to Sochi. Buses to Georgia and other adventuresome destinations. Afacan Tour also operates daily tours of Trabzon and Sümela ($4); weekend tours of Uzungöl ($11.25) and Ayder ($11.25) including lunch; ski trips to Zigama (groups of 5 or more, $11.25 per person, ski rental $4.50 per day); and trekking expeditions in the Kaçkars and near Uzungöl.

Consulates: Those interested in traveling to Georgia, Russia, or Iran are probably best off working through a travel agency,; applying directly to the consulate is a cheaper, less predictable method. The **Georgian Consulate** (tel. 326 2226) is across the street from Saktur. Visas to Georgia cost $30 for the first month and $19 for each additional month. Visa window open Mon.-Fri. 10am-1pm and 3-6pm. The **Consulate of the Russian Federation** (tel. 326 2600), on Aranfil Cad. roughly 200m southeast of the main square, is open Tues. and Thurs. 9am-noon and 3-5pm. Russian visa requests are somewhat more complex; unless you have an invitation from a Russian, go to a travel agency. The **Iranian Consulate** (tel. 322 4851) is on Boztepe Cad., roughly 1km southwest of the main square.

Flights: THY flies to Ankara (2 per day, 1hr., $36, students $25) and İstanbul (4 per day, 2hr., $47, students $35). Buses leave from the THY office (tel. 321 1680, -3446), at the southwest corner of the main square.

Buses: Run from the *otogar* 3km east of the main square to Artvin (5 per day, 4½hr., $6), Samsun (hourly, 6hr., $5.50), Sinop (daily, 8½hr., $9), Zonguldak (4 per day, 18hr., $17), Konya (daily, 16hr., $15.50), Van (3 per day, 18hr., $22), Urfa (daily, 18hr., $9), Antakya (daily, 24hr., $17), and Hopa (hourly 7am-7pm, 3hr., $3.50). "Coffee, tea, or...cola?" is the only question in the minds of travelers on the A/C luxury services of **METRO bus lines,** which heads to Erzurum (daily, 6hr., $6.75), Ankara (2 per day, 12hr., $11), İstanbul (3 per day, 18hr., $20, students $15.50), Antalya (daily, 20hr., $22, students $20), and Adana (daily, 17hr., $20, students $18). Depart from the *otogar,* reachable from the main square via taxi *dolmuş* marked *Otogar* or *Tıp Fak* (50¢). The main way to get back along the Black Sea coast in either direction, or even inland as far as Artvin or Yusufeli, is by short-distance coastal *dolmuş.* For Artvin, for example, one changes in Hopa.

Ferries: From June-Sept., **Turkish Maritime Lines** (TML) traces the Black Sea Coast from İstanbul to Trabzon. It leaves İstanbul Mon. at 2pm, stops at Sinop, Samsun, and Giresun, and arrives at Trabzon Wed. at 9:30am. The return voyage leaves Trabzon Wed. at 3pm and arrives in İstanbul Fri. at 1:30pm. Try to purchase tickets a week in advance at the **TML office** (tel. 321 7096). Open Mon.-Fri. 8am-noon and 1-5pm, next to the tourist office. Depending on the placement and luxury level of your accommodations, tickets run $15-34. Students ½-off.

English Bookstores: Dilay Kitabevi, 10-13 Uzun Sok. (tel. 321 4134). Near the main square. A small selection of books (Penguin Classics $3-7). Open daily 8am-8pm. **Derya Kitap-Kırtasiye Pazarlama,** 127 Uzun Sok. (tel. 321 1821), has a few English books. Owner wrote a scholarly history of the Sumela Monastery, which you can find at card stands at the site.

Hospital: Call 223 4041.

ACCOMMODATIONS

It's difficult to find a decent, quiet hotel here. Most of the cheaper hotels cluster around **İskele Caddesi,** which runs northeast off the main square. They offer cheerless, basic rooms, and many have degenerated into semi-brothels. Since the opening of the Georgian border up the coast, Trabzon is swarming with Russian tourists and shoppers. They fill every hotel and are not shy about socializing well into the night. The secret to a restful stay is to seek out *aile oteli* (family hotels), places that stake their reputations on their healthy atmosphere for children.

Otel Anıl, 10 Güzelhisar Cad. (tel. 321 9566), is a real find. Spic-and-span, carpeted rooms w/bath, TV, telephones, and Western toilets. Singles $9, doubles $15.50, triples $20; breakfast $1.25; laundry 90¢ per pair of pants.

Otel Toros, 3/a Gençoğlu Sok. (tel. 321 1212), a couple of streets directly north of the east part of the main square, offers clean, carpeted, if somewhat dark rooms. Hall baths are spacious and clean. Free use of kitchen; laundry $2.25 per load. Singles $4.50; doubles $9, w/bath $11.25.

Gözde Aile Oteli, 7 Salih Yazıcı Sok. (tel. 321 9579), manageable, with showers but no toilets in most rooms. Breakfast and meals available in nearby restaurant. Doubles $9, triples $13.50, quads $17.75.

Hotel Benli (tel. 321 1750), 100m east of the main square's south edge. Offers clean, cool, quiet, and comparatively odor-free rooms with telephones. Sky-blue walls and a plush lounge. Has outworn the luxury status it enjoyed at its opening in 1958, but price and charm make up for bathless rooms and basic toilets. Singles $5.50, doubles $9, triples $13.50.

FOOD AND ENTERTAINMENT

Trabzon's local cuisine is an exotic melange of fresh Black Sea fish and corn, potatoes, and peas from the fertile highlands south of the city. Vegetarians can feast on a well-boiled corn-on-the-cob, sold on many street corners for $1.25, or sample the $1 salad bar of **Tad Pizza and Burger** (tel. 321 1238; open daily 11am-9:30pm), on the northeast corner of the main square. West of the square (1½km) along Maraş Cad. you'll stumble upon the **fruit and vegetable market** (open daily 6:30am-9pm), and downhill west of the Luna Park on the shore you'll find the **fish market** (open daily 7am-dinnertime). Several wholesome restaurants with modern decor await along Uzun Sok. (Long Street), a shopping avenue that lives up to its name, west of the square's south edge. **Uludağ Kebap Salonu** (tel. 321 4120; open daily 7am-10pm), at #43; and **Gelik Lokantası** (tel. 326 2445; open daily 7am-11pm), another 1km along at #84; both serve the range of dishes you expect from a *lokanta,* in an exemplary state of cleanliness. Nearly unknown to tourists is *mantı,* a delicious pasta dish like tortellini served in yogurt and seasoned with garlic, mint, and hot pepper. You can try this traditional family favorite for $1.75 at **Kilim Mantı Salonu,** 46 Uzun Sok. (open Mon.-Sat. 9am-9pm). For dessert, **Beton Helva,** 21 Uzun Sok. (tel. 321 2550), has 45¢ blocks of *helva,* a sesame seed confection like gritty fudge, and 45¢ glasses of clear grape cider to wash it down. Another curiosity is *aşure,* a fruity oriental pudding, available at Tad Pizza and Burger for only 70¢ per bowl.

Catch the undersea atmosphere at **Blue Sea Bar,** Kemerkaya Mah. Mektep Sok. 51A Sahil Cad. (tel. 322 2733), across the highway from the shore; it's one of the cooler places in town. (Open daily 11am-1am; beer $1.25.) Trabzon's long seaside terrace makes for a pleasant stroll; at the west end lies the amusement park, featuring rides and a video arcade (admission to the park 15¢; once inside you pay for individual rides as well). Squeaky clean rejuvenation can be had for $3.50, including **scrub and massage,** at Sekiz Direkli Hamam, Pazarkapı Mah. (tel. 322 1012; open daily 6am-11pm for both sexes except Thurs. 8am-5pm, reserved for women only). Constructed by the Seljuks circa 1073 BC and used until 1916, it was renovated 7 years ago with marble and wood paneling. Worth the 2km walk west following Maraş Cad. from the main square to where it turns downhill (follow the signs from there). A taxi costs roughly $2.25 from the tourist office.

SIGHTS

The oldest extant Christian structure in Trabzon is the tiny 7th-century **St. Anne Church.** Head west from the square on Maraş Cad.—it's behind a cluster of newsstands and trees on your left, just before the mosque. At the top of the hill behind the town is **Atatürk Köşkü,** one of Atatürk's villas built at the turn of the century by a rich Greek. Though Atatürk stayed here only two nights in his life, the popular villa is now a museum fat with photographs and paintings of the "Father Turk." Take any *dolmuş* marked "Atatürk Köşkü" from the main square. (Open 8am-noon and 1:30-7pm, in winter 8am-noon and 1-5pm; admission 45¢, students 23¢.)

Romantically set in a rose and oleander garden overlooking the Black Sea, the lovely 13th-century **Aya Sofya** church was once part of a monastery. Now a museum, it features fine frescoes and carvings. From the lower end of the square, take a *dolmuş* marked *Aya Sofya* (25¢). (Open daily 8am-noon and 1:30-5:30pm; admission $1.25, students 65¢.) Within the walls of the old city is the **Ortahisar Cami,** formerly Panagia Chrisokefalos Church, the main basilica of medieval Trebizond. Due north of Ortahisar Cami, on Amasya Sok., is the house where Süleyman the Magnificent, the 16th-century Ottoman sultan, was born. A statue of the turbaned "Grand Turk" stands guard at the newly restored building.

Behind the town rises the hill of **Boztepe.** Check out the remains of the Panagia Theoskepastos convent, and 2.5km farther back into the hills, the Armenian monastery at Kaymaklı with frescoes almost as impressive as those at Aya Sofya. *Dolmuş* to

Rize, for factory-fresh tea, and **Akçaabat,** renowned for its *köfte,* leave frequently from the shore-hugging highway. The most dramatic tourist attraction in the area, however, and one of the most fascinating Byzantine sites anywhere, is the **Sümela Monastery,** 47km southeast of Trabzon, set among lush forested mountains. Established in 385 AD, this cliffside monastery reached its zenith in the late Middle Ages, when it had 72 rooms and an immense library. Monks lived here until the population exchange between Greece and Turkey in 1923. The monastery has been neglected since, although restoration has recently been undertaken. Fire, rain, and vandals have done extensive damage to this sublime retreat over the past 72 years. Nevertheless, Sümela is well worth the taxing pilgrimage through the cloud forest it takes to get there. The inspiring beauty of the site and the richness of its history distinguish Sümela as part of the ancient Trabzon that enchanted 19th-century travelers. (Open daily 8am-5:30pm, in winter closed Sun.; admission $2.50, students $1.25.) To get there, take a tour with Afacan Tour on İskele Cad. (departs 11am, $4) or Ulusoy Turizm, 50m uphill from the tourist office on the right (departs 11am, $3.75). For more flexibility, take a taxi for roughly $30.

■■■ EAST OF TRABZON

The towns along this segment of the Black Sea coast are interesting more for their cultural makeup and serene damp atmosphere than for the few historical monuments they house. Most are small, quiet port and industrial towns. The primordial wildlands to the south, a sultry velvet of dense jungle and mist softening the jagged landscape, are even more deeply entrenched in the past. *Yayla,* or highland campgrounds, dapple the mountains, where natives of this region gather from as far away as Holland and Germany to relax and renew their cultural ties. Farther inland, people maintain autonomous, centuries-old traditions, manners, and dress styles from central Anatolia. The best places for campers to find an uncultivated spot are along the beach, by the highway, on *yayla,* or along riverbanks.

UZUNGÖL

Uzungöl, a pristine trout-filled lake (600m x 400m x 9m) hemmed in by steep, fir-packed mountains, is 98km out of Trabzon via Of and Çaykara. The slow and lumpy 20km from Çaykara follow a whitewater stream past hillsides of terraced corn and hazelnut trees. Discover the lake as soon as the trademark twin yellow minarets poke into view, and continue 3km upstream by a small dam and out to *yayla.* Between the lake and the dam, a handful of new hotel and restaurant complexes has sprung up to accommodate Turkish families, who come as much for the famous trout and rice pudding as for the scenery. Alcohol is not sold in Uzungöl. Campers stake their tents for free in the ground upstream from the dam. Some hotels have free campgrounds. Indoor accommodations tend to be on the expensive side. Perhaps the best bargain is the little **Uzungöl Pansiyon** (tel. 656 6129), on the main road in the village itself. ($4.50 per person w/bath; breakfast $1; free laundry.) **Gülalioğlu Restaurant** is clean and offers plates of standard fare. Most hotels take $9-16 per person for brand-new wood-walled rooms with bath, but they don't have singles. Open all year, the **Sezgin Motel** (tel. 656 6175) is typical and well-kept with carpeted rooms for 2-4 people. ($10 per person, breakfast included.) Its **restaurant** across the road (open daily May-Oct. 7am-midnight) grills delicious red-spotted trout from their farm ($3.50 per plate of 2 fish), to be followed by fresh rice pudding (70¢; fixed meal $5.50). The cozy 3-bedroom bungalows at **Orman İşletme Tesisleri** (tel. 656 6010) make superb bonding spots for up to 8 people ($16; try to make reservations a week in advance). **Postal Code:** 61450; **Telephone Code:** 462.

Minibuses leave from Trabzon for Çaykara (hourly 7:30am-5:30pm, $1.50), from the office of **Çaykara Tur** (tel. 322 5509), behind Trabzon's Russian bazaar. From Çaykara several *dolmuş* run to Uzungöl ($1.25). On weekends, all-day tours from Afacan Tour and other travel agencies ($11.25) are a hassle-free alternative.

RİZE

A nondescript but characteristically languid way station on the seaside highway, Rize is accessible by Pamukkale Turizm bus (passing every 20min. until 8pm, $1.50) or frequent *dolmuş* ($2.25), both of which leave from the coastal highway. The bus drops off 2km west of the town center; from there take a *dolmuş* (marked *şehir merkezi*) into town for 45¢. Rize is the tea capital of Turkey, and the tea here is distinctly better than in most other parts of the country. At the top of the hills south of town are the Ministry of Agriculture's special tea labs, greenhouses, and tea garden (open daily 10am-5pm). Fresh-brewed tea is accompanied by a view of the sea, flowers, and trees galore, labeled by species. Palm trees draped with honeysuckle vines line the last stretch of the 800m road from the central mosque (near the PTT) up to the gardens. Rize's **tourist office** (tel. 213 0408; open Mon.-Fri. 8:30am-5:30pm) is located on the fourth floor of the Özel İdare Tesisleri, a building on the shore on the east side of town, behind the highway. They offer a brochure and general info, though possibly no English. The **PTT** is on the main square near the Atatürk statue; it's hard to miss, especially with its brick roof and lattice woodwork façade. There is a **Turkish Airlines office** (tel. 213 0591; open Mon.-Fri. 8:30am-5:30pm) on Cumhuriyet Cad. **Telephone Code:** 464; **Postal Code:** 53100.

Budget rooms abound in Rize. **Otel Efes** (tel. 217 7555), two blocks up Atatürk Cad. across from Akbank, is sparkling clean. (Singles $9, doubles $15.50, triples $22.25; all w/bath and TV.) For a sea view, try **Otel Turist,** 26 Atatürk Cad. (tel. 217 2009), east of the Otel Efes. Rooms are large, clean, and well-furnished, most with bath, balcony, and TV. (Singles $10, doubles $20, triples $28, 20% student discount.) For a cheap, excellent meal, try **Bekiroğlu Restaurant,** 161 Cumhuriyet Cad. (tel. 217 1380), near Otel Efes (*kebap* $1.75). In Çayeli (18km out of Rize, coastal *dolmuş* 45¢), try the local specialty: cooked dry beans with meatballs.

Buses leave from the *otogar,* 1km northwest of the town center. There are daily buses to Yusufeli (5hr., $6.75), Kars (9hr., $11.25), Erzurum (9hr., $10), Van (14hr., $16.75), Zonguldak (17hr., $20), and İzmir (23hr., $24.50). More frequent buses go to Artvin (2 per day, 6hr., $5.50), Gaziantep (3 per day, 20hr., $22.25), Antalya (2 per day, 22hr., $24.50), Ankara (2 per day, 14hr., $14.50), Mersin (2 per day, 22hr., $22.25), Bursa (2 per day, 18hr., $42.25), İstanbul (4 per day, 18hr., $42.50), and Samsun (5 per day, 7hr., $9). Most destinations between Trabzon and Hopa are best left to highway *dolmuş* (under $3.50), but if you want to reach Trabzon in better time, with more space, and for less money, wait for the Pamukkale Turizm buses ($2.25) that pass down the coastal highway every 20min., 8am-8pm.

AYDER

Forty kilometers east of Rize in the Hemşin Valley of the Kaçkar range is the mountain resort of Ayder. Pronounced "I dare," it's a popular base for hiking. The organic, timbered houses of this mist-shrouded village look as if they naturally sprouted from the mountainside. On the forested far side of the valley, a slender brook cascades over crags fed by the melting snow at the mountain's peak, and joins a roaring stream on the valley floor. The ebullience and colorful dress of the native Hemşin people are as good a reason to visit Ayder as the towering majesty of the site.

Mail should be addressed to Ayder Kaplıcaları, Çamlıhemşin, RİZE 53760. Ayder has a tiny **PTT** booth at the center of town, near the Ayder Hilton, whose telephone seems perpetually out of order (open 9am-5pm). Believe it or not, the attendant in the booth at the gate 4km before the town is entitled to a 45¢ admission fee—if he bothers to collect it. Bring along a rainworthy jacket to beat the evening chill. For trekking info, contact either Kardelen Pansiyon or Pirikoğlu. The booths of two rival **minibus** companies face each other across a bend in the main road. Buses run to Çamlıhemşin (10 per day, ½hr., 70¢), Pazar (13 per day, 1hr., $1.50), and Rize (4 per day, 1½hr., $2.25). To go to Hopa, catch the Pazar bus and connect from there. Early-morning minibuses run up to the *yayla* of Avusor (5km, $1.50), Lower Kavron (7km, $2.25), and Upper Kavron (12km, $2.25). Avusor's annual **festival** falls on Aug. 5; Kavron's happens Aug. 15. **Telephone Code:** 464.

You have a choice between whitewashed stone rooms and wood ones, completely covered in dark planks. Because of the proximity of the springs, few hotels have any sort of shower. Most charge the standard price of $4.50 per person, of which 65¢ is easily haggled away. **Otel Altıparmak** (tel. 657 2062), next to the springs facility, has small, new rooms with balconies and good beds. (Singles $6.75, doubles $9, triples $10.) For rooms with bath, **Otel Ayder** (tel 657 2039, -40), the big, white, institutional building at the lower end of the main road, has six doubles. The rooms are clean almost to the point of sterility. Warm beds fit for royalty guard against nighttime chill. (Singles $5.50, doubles w/bath $11.25; open June-Sept.) In the center of town is the ironically named **Ayder Hilton Hotel** (tel. 657 2024). Rooms are clean, but nothing more. ($4.50 per person; breakfast $1.25, meals $3.50, laundry free.) Camping is free beyond the *yayla* and cluster of buildings above it. That's also where you'll find the **Kardelen Pansion** (tel. 657 2107), the secluded den of Muhammet Önçırak, mountain man and tour guide extraordinaire. Before ascending into the Kaçkars, consult the military issue map hanging on his wall. (5 draughty rooms are available June-Aug.; $4.50 per person, group discounts). For a wholesome meal, try **Pirikoğlu Lokantası** (tel. 657 2021; open May-Oct. 6am-11pm; full meal $3.50). The owner is a good source of mountain info.

Çağlayan Restaurant (tel. 657 2065), next door, serves alcohol and often features live folk music in the evenings. Ayder is a good place to try *muhlama,* a melted mix of cheese, butter, and corn flour that looks like mashed potatoes and behaves like fondue for bread dipping. There are hot (very hot) **springs** housed in a squat, steaming edifice completed only a few years ago. A dip in the marble bathing pools is an exhausting pleasure; as blood charges through every capillary in your body, you'll come to believe the legends about these waters' curative effects. (Open April-Oct. daily 7am-8pm; admission $1.50.)

The Hemşin

Travelers in Ayder and the nearby valley may be astonished to discover the Hemşin, an outgoing, merry, sometimes outrageous people that are distinctly different from the often solemn Central Anatolians. The Hemşin are descendants either from a 10th-century Turkish tribe from the original migration or from Heptacomete Christian or pagan tribesmen that spoke a dialect of Armenian. Hemşin are said to have come from Georgia in recent times, and to have lived isolated in the mountains until roughly 150 years ago. Intrepid and independent, they are known for their hospitality, revelry, and jovial drinking of *rakı.* Although many Hemşin have moved to large cities and opened sweetshops for which they are famed, roughly 15,000 still live in the Hemşin Valley. Hemşin women wear brightly colored silk turbans imported from India, perhaps because the valley was once a stop on the silk road. The women's garb stands in stark contrast to the men, who wear dark, drab colors. To attempt to understand the Hemşin mentality, visit one of their *yayla,* or summer villages. These tightly bunched shanty towns are inhabited during summer months by Hemşin who come from as far as Holland and Germany to get in touch with their homeland.

HOPA

The highway continues along the coast from Ayder for roughly 60km, finally turning inland at **Hopa. Otel Köşk,** 21 Ortahopa Cad. (tel. 351 3501), is relaxing and meticulously clean; most rooms have bathrooms. (Singles $9, doubles $15.50, triples $20; breakfast $1.25). **Otel Cihan** (tel. 351 4897), across the street, is even more upscale, with a view of the sea from the upper floors. (Singles $15.50, doubles $22.25, triples $26.75 w/ bath, TV, and phone.) Consider **Otel Huzur,** 25 Cumhuriyet Cad. (tel. 351 4095), on the waterfront. Simple, clean, mostly bathless rooms with good beds and some sea views. Hall baths have Western-style toilets, rare in this region. (Singles $6.75, doubles $9, triples $13.50.) West of the hotel, near the bridge, **Beslen Lokantası** (tel. 351 4957) offers an array of cheap, fresh, and finely prepared dishes (full meal $4.50). Check out the Russian Bazaar (*rus pazarı*) between the coastal highway and the sea. **Postal Code:** 08600; **Telephone Code:** 466.

Nearby there's not much to see besides the Georgian border, 30km northeast in **Sarp,** on a seamless, partly wooded mountainside. The tea plants and houses look the same on both sides of the border. If you want to see it, however, Sarp is accessible by taxi ($11.25), *dolmuş* ($1.25 and up), and minibus ($1.25), all of which depart from the parking lot outside Hopa's PTT. The rough, winding road to Sarp passes Kemal Paşa (*dolmuş* 60¢), a small town whose gravel beach and tea factory see few visitors. The best way to get acquainted with Georgian people and products is to visit the Russian Bazaars in Black Sea towns. If you wish to visit Georgia itself, see Trabzon (p. 511) for info on visas. Travel at your own risk, however; there is a strong Georgian mafia, and muggings are frequent due to widespread poverty.

Hopa's *dolmuş* and **bus stations** lie west of the bridge into town. *Dolmuş* and buses travel to Borçka (every ½hr., 1hr., 90¢), Artvin (every ½hr., 1½hr., $1.75), Yusufeli (every ½hr., 3hr., $4), Erzurum (every ½hr., 6hr., $4.50), Kars (daily, 8hr., $7), Van (3 per day, 12hr., $11.25), Ankara (3 per day, 16hr., $15.50), Adana (daily, 18hr., $22.25), İstanbul (daily, 20hr., $22.25), İzmir (daily, 24hr., $22.25), and Antalya (daily, 26hr., $26.75). For longer trips consider **METRO Turizm's** luxury buses.

■■■ ARTVİN

Chiseled into the mountain pass is the eerily tranquil town of Artvin, which offers panoramic views of a largely deforested valley. The 15th-century citadel overlooking the highway, which both Georgians and the English sought to control within the last hundred years, receives few tourists since Turkish soldiers still use it. Never mind, though—the nameless road that ribbons 5km up the mountainside to central Artvin puts the tower in its place; the view only gets better.

Orientation and Practical Information In vertical terms, the town occupies the space bounded by the hospital above and bus station below. But the bus station itself is perched 4km up the serpentine road from the valley floor where you get dropped off. To reach it, wait for the municipal bus (roughly every 20min., 55¢) or hop on one of the frequent shuttles. They all go to the center, a main street called İnönü Cad.—home to hotels, restaurants, a *dolmuş* lot, a 24-hr. **PTT,** and a tea garden. There is a small **tourist office** (tel. 212 3071) in Cami Meydanı, to the right of İnönü Cad. as you walk uphill. It has maps and brochures, and can call an English-speaker. **Postal Code:** 08000; **Telephone Code:** 466.

Minibuses travel to Hopa (7 per day, 1½hr., $1.50), Rize (roughly every ¾hr. until 5pm, 6hr., $4.50), Kars (daily, 4hr., $5.50), Erzurum (4 per day, 4hr., $5), Tortum (4 per day, $3.50), Trabzon (7 per day, 5hr., $5), Samsun (4 per day, 10hr., $9.25), Ankara (4 per day, 18hr., $14.50), and İstanbul (1 per day, 22hr., $18). **METRO Turizm** offers A/C and beverage service to larger cities for nearly the same prices.

Accommodations Many of Artvin's hotels feature low prices and good locations, but are also frequented by prostitutes. A trio of clean, cordial, and untainted budget hotels hides down the stairs on the left side of İnönü Cad. as you walk uphill towards the *dolmuş* stop. The **Kaçkar Oteli** (tel. 212 3397) has carpets and showers in every room. Hall bathrooms have Western-style toilets. (Singles $6.75, doubles $11.25, triples $16.75; free use of washing machine.) **Otel Güven** (tel. 212 1118), next door, offers large rooms, some with panoramic views. Hot water is unreliable, and showers cost $1.25 each, but the management speaks English. (Singles $4.50, doubles $7.50, triples $10.) Another door down is **Otel Uğrak** (tel. 212 6505), with well-lit, carpeted rooms, excellent hall showers, and free laundry. (Singles $5, doubles $7.50, triples $9.50.) There's plenty of free **camping** nestled among the evergreens in the highland park of **Kafkasör,** practically a vertical extension of Artvin. A municipal bus makes the ½-hr. climb for 70¢ daily at 8:30am and 5pm, with an extra midday service Sat.-Sun. Non-campers can enjoy half of one of 10 divided cabins, each with clean sheets, shower, and toilet, for $10. (Call 212 6807 for reservations; 1-4 persons per half-cabin; open all year.) In the evening, **Çağdaş Gazinosu** presents live music after 8pm. (Open all year daily 9am-midnight.)

Food and Entertainment Munch on the multifarious treats at the restaurant in **Hotel Karahan** (tel. 212 1800), on the fourth floor of the main street's shopping center. (*Kebap* and cola $3.) Watering hole for Artvin's elite, the **Hanedan Restaurant** (tel. 212 7222; open 8am-11pm), across the street, has a glossy, black bar and a porch with an excellent view of the valley (*kebap* and beer $2.75). Bar and view also come with excellent food at **Nazar Restoran** (tel. 212 1709; open 10am-midnight), at the lower end of İnönü Cad. (*kebap* and beer $2.50). It's decorated with bizarre posters and features a delicious tray of *meze*.

Artvin is close to many *yayla* that locals visit in summer. The plateau of **Kafkasör,** 11km from Artvin, hosts an annual **festival** on the third weekend of June. Traditional dances and other performances take place, but the main events are **bullfights.** The bulls "wrestle" each other like the camels in Manisa, near İzmir. The winner's owner is rewarded and honored. The bull gets nothing. Artvin's Ottoman **hamam** is just down the street (tel. 212 1158; open daily for both sexes 6am-10pm; bath $1.50, massage $1.50, scrub $1).

■■■ YUSUFELİ

The small town of Yusufeli, stretching along the Barhal River, is fast becoming the **whitewater rafting** capital of Turkey. Too dangerous to raft before June, the famous Çoruh River, site of a 1993 rafting championship, passes only 6km away. The Ministry of Tourism plans to open an official fenced-in campground on the bank of the Çoruh (8km out of town). It was still under construction in the summer of 1995. Yusufeli's dry south side on the Kaçkar range makes it an ideal trekking center. Most hotels occupy the upstream end of İnönü Cad., the main street, which passes the **otogar** lot (bus station), **pharmacies,** decent alcohol-free restaurants, and eventually the **PTT** (open daily 7:30am-5pm) at the downstream end of town. The local **hospital** can be reached at 811 2015. **Postal Code:** 08800; **Telephone Code:** 466.

Otel Keleş (tel. 811 2305), on the corner of İnönü Cad. and Halit Paşa Cad., features quality mattresses in modern, carpeted rooms with shared bath. ($2.25 per person; free laundry.) The **Hotel Barhal** (tel. 811 3151), Asma Köprübaşı Cad., on the second floor by the water, stands out for its private baths and river view. (Singles $3.50, doubles $4.50, triples $6.75.) Its perpetually glum-looking owner, Sıralı Aydın, also happens to be a comic playwright and president of the local **rafting club,** which rents six- and eight-person rafts, paddles, life preservers, and helmets at reasonable, negotiable prices. The **Hotel Çiçek Palas,** 30 Halit Paşa Cad. (tel. 811 2393), off İnönü Cad., offers clean, concrete-floored rooms, good beds, shared baths, and free use of the stove ($3.50 per person). Özkan Şahin, a sprightly, English-speaking **mountain guide** (tel. 811 2187), is often outside the Çiçek Palas. Campers should cross the bridge next to the Hotel Barhal, turn right, then right again at the T in the road, then left to find **Greenpeace Camping** (open June-Sept.; $1-2 per campsite), with a secluded campsite, a cold shower, laundry, and pit toilets. One of the cleanest and most popular meeting places for tourists and outdoorspeople is **Çınar Lokantası** (tel. 811 2365; open daily 10am-11pm), overlooking the river beneath the Hotel Barhal. Its offerings include grilled meat and delicious trout, *rakı,* and vegetarian *meze* like *piyaz, pilaki,* and potato salad (full meal $3). Blue inside and out, the **Mavi Köşk Restorant** (tel. 811 2329; open daily 8am-1am), downhill from Hotel Barhal off İnönü Cad. to the right on the second floor, is a clean establishment that has good food with a well-stocked bar (full meal $3.50).

■ THE ÇORUH VALLEY

Yusufeli makes an excellent base for exploring the Çoruh Valley, home to half a dozen 10th-century **Georgian churches.** Begun by Georgians in 730 AD and finished three centuries later, the **İşhan** church (35km from Yusufeli) was enhanced by a Byzantine dome in 1200 AD before its stewardship passed back into Georgian hands. It contains portraits of angels on a blue field inside the dome and a variety of pillar capitals, and on the south face (in the window, up and to the right) a carved lion struggles with a serpent. The pilgrimage to İşhan is doubly worthwhile if only for the road's spectacular mountainscapes of tilted strata and ravine-wrinkled cliffs. The façade of the airy **Öşk Vank** (a.k.a. Çamlıyamaç, 50km from Yusufeli) church has been preserved marvelously and features carvings of angels, patrons, and animals. Inside above the entrance you'll find a colorful band of frescoed faces next to the image of a church that might be Öşk Vank itself. Of the three other churches, which resemble each other in style and height, **Dörtkilise** (a.k.a. Tekkale, 13km from Yusufeli) is the most accessible. Only 12km high, it features arches as its central theme. From **Tekkale Village** (6km from Yusufeli), a rough, walkable road follows the stream for another 7km to a steep bank 50m below Dörtkilise (Four Churches), whose name refers to four churches that once stood nearby. The ground outside makes good, free camping. Before ascending the Kaçkars, consider staying in Tekkale Village's little-known country pension, **Dörtkilise Resting Camp.**

There's little chance of hitchhiking to the **Barhal** church (a.k.a. Altıparmak, 33km from Yusufeli), now a locked mosque whose main attractions are a few exterior carvings of small crosses, a lion, and a bird. Peek through the slats of the shed left of the entrance in order to spy a finger-tall carving of a human (above and to the right of a semi-circular design above a window left of the entrance). As Barhal makes an excellent starting point for long hikes through the Kaçkars, you may wish to spend the night there. A scenic wooden porch poised over a wide stretch of Barhal River rapids is the selling point of **Özyurt Pansiyon ve Restaurant** (tel. 826 2005), which has clean, carpeted rooms with shared bath for $3 per person. (Washing machine at guests' disposal. Omelette 70¢) Note: *fishing is forbidden* upstream of Sarıgöl Village, halfway between Barhal and Yusufeli. Part rubble, part locked mosque, and the farthest away, the **Haho** church (a.k.a. Bağbaşı, 65km from Yusufeli) offers little to repay your traveling pains. One side displays a well-preserved eagle, and the dome is pretty, but that's about it. If you travel south towards Haho, you'll pass the pea-green **Tortum Lake,** supposedly formed 630 years ago when the peak of Mt. Hars collapsed into the Çoruh River valley. Locals claim there's a mosque on the lake floor and remnants of an inundated village. The Çoruh's real treat here, however, is **Tortum Falls,** a natural 50m cascade that the government turned into a hydroelectric plant in the 1950s. The **Şelale Tesisleri** restaurant owns a breathtaking view except mid-June through August, when the dam diverts the water.

The falls are easily reached because the Erzurum highway passes within 1km. Tell the driver "Şelale" and sit back to enjoy the view—warped faces of mountain strata like one huge, prehistoric hunk of *baklava* that was ripped by time. A daily *dolmuş* departs from Yusufeli for each of the three nearby church villages in the afternoon, but doesn't return until morning. Some may want to tour by **taxi.** İşhan ($18), Öşk Vank ($33), Dörtkilise ($6), Barhal ($45), and Haho ($33). From the village of Uzundere, you can catch cheaper taxis to Öşk Vank and Haho. Daily **buses** depart Yusufeli for Uzundere (2 per day, 1½hr., $1.25), Tortum (2 per day, 2hr., $2.25), Erzurum (2 per day, 3hr., $3.50), Artvin (5 per day, 1½hr., $2), Hopa (4 per day, 3hr., $3.50), Rize (4 per day, 4hr., $4.50), Trabzon (3 per day, 5hr., $6.75), Kars (1 per day, 4hr., $3.50), Ankara (2 per day, 16hr., $13.50), Bursa (1 per day, 23hr., $20), and İstanbul (2 per day, 23hr., $20).

Central Anatolia

The high, dry mountain ranges of Central Anatolia form Turkey's bread basket. On top of the mountains' wide plateaus rest some of the most authentic and hospitable villages that this country has to offer. While the Aegean and Mediterranean Coasts have been affected by tourism, and the Black Sea Coast is suffused with an Eastern European atmosphere; it is in the sparse, but accessible, mountains of Central Anatolia that traditional Turkey is best seen by foreigners.

ANKARA

The former city of Angora, this backward settlement was famous for its wool and little else. That is, until Atatürk declared Ankara Turkey's capital in the 1920s. He brought Europeans to design a modern, European-style city of wide boulevards and parks. To a large extent, however, provincial Anatolia is still found here, balanced atop a number of dramatic hills which rise from the surrounding plains. In the Citadel, the way of life remains largely unchanged. The new capital has grown up just to the south, with its main axis, Atatürk Blv., vertically joining the two. Although it lacks the charm of İstanbul, Ankara peers into the soul of modern Turkey. In parts it is quite plush, full of luxury apartments, boutiques, and nightclubs; at other points, it is run-down and dusty, its architecture reminiscent of Eastern Europe. The weather can be windy and miserable much of the year, and the air choked with diesel fumes anytime, but catch Ankara on a sunny day and you might find it more engaging than its mediocre reputation may suggest.

ORIENTATION AND PRACTICAL INFORMATION

The city's main street is **Atatürk Bulvarı,** which runs north-south. At its north end lies the run-down **Ulus,** centered on the equestrian statue of Atatürk at Ulus Sq. Most of the sights are here, as are most of the cheap hotels. A couple of kilometers south is **Kızılay,** a clean, up-scale market area. It contains crowded pedestrian precincts lined with bars, cafés, and restaurants. The University of Ankara is nearby, and the students lend it a youthful, cosmopolitan air. It is also a residential and shopping area. Some mid-range hotels are established here. Two or three kilometers south of Kızılay are ensconced the wealthy residential areas of **Kavaklıdere** and **Çankaya,** home to most embassies and five-star hotels. Frequent buses run the length of Atatürk Blv. Bus #391 runs from the main gate of the Citadel (*Hisar*), in the north, as far south as the Atatürk Tower via Atatürk Blv., connecting these areas. The bus terminal (*otogar*) is 5km west of Kızılay, in **Söğütözü.** The railway station (*gar*) is 1½km southwest of Ulus Sq.

Tourist Offices: Main office at 121 Gazi Mustafa Kemal Blv. (tel. 488 7007 or 231 5572). From the train station's main platform, descend the stairs into the shop-lined tunnel to Tandoğan (marked Tandoğan Kapalı Çarşı). At the end of the tunnel turn left onto Gazi Mustafa Kemal Blv.; the plainly labeled "Tourist Office" will be on the right side of the street after the PTT. Most employees speak only one foreign language. An English-speaker is available at most times. Free city and country maps. Come here to file a complaint with the **tourist police;** the tourist office will serve as your interpreter. Open Mon.-Fri. 8:30am-6:30pm, Sat.-Sun. 9am-5pm; reduced hours in off-season. Another office, at the **airport** (tel. 398 0348), stays open 24 hr.

PTT: On Atatürk Bulvarı in Kızılay and in Ulus. Both open 24 hr. In the train station, open daily 7am-11pm. Poste Restante open Mon.-Sat. 8:30am-5:30pm. Many others scattered around the city; open Mon.-Fri. 8:30am-6:30pm, Sat. 8:30am-12:30pm. **Telephones** at every PTT as well as at the bus and train stations, and scattered throughout the city. **Telephone Code:** 312.

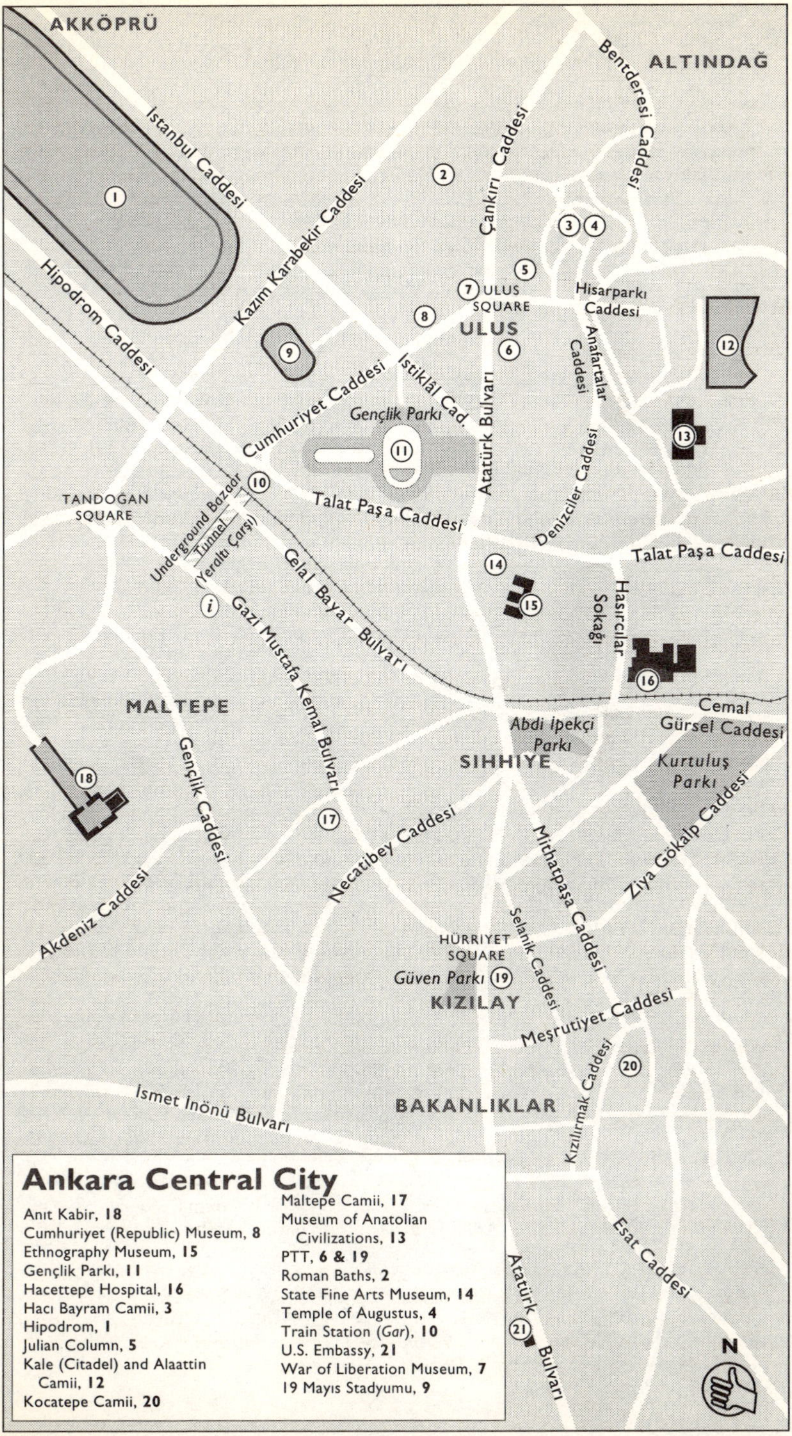

Ankara Central City

Anıt Kabir, **18**
Cumhuriyet (Republic) Museum, **8**
Ethnography Museum, **15**
Gençlik Parkı, **11**
Hacettepe Hospital, **16**
Hacı Bayram Camii, **3**
Hipodrom, **1**
Julian Column, **5**
Kale (Citadel) and Alaattin Camii, **12**
Kocatepe Camii, **20**
Maltepe Camii, **17**
Museum of Anatolian Civilizations, **13**
PTT, **6 & 19**
Roman Baths, **2**
State Fine Arts Museum, **14**
Temple of Augustus, **4**
Train Station (*Gar*), **10**
U.S. Embassy, **21**
War of Liberation Museum, **7**
19 Mayıs Stadyumu, **9**

Embassies: Nearly all embassies in Ankara are south of Hürriyet Sq., along Atatürk Blv. Ankara makes a convenient base for securing visas for Eastern Europe, the Middle East, the former Soviet republics, and Central Asia. **Afghanistan,** 88 Cinnah Cad. (tel. 438 1121). **Albania,** 89 Nenehatun Cad. (tel. 446 6527). **Australia,** 83 Nenehatun Cad. (tel. 446 1180). **Azerbaijan,** 20 Cemal Nadir Sok., Çelikler Apt. (tel. 441 2621). **Bulgaria,** 124 Atatürk Cad. (tel. 425 7455). **Canada,** 75 Nenehatun Cad. (tel. 436 1275). **Czech Republic,** 100 Köroğlu Cad. (tel. 446 1244). **Egypt,** 126 Atatürk Blv. (tel. 426 1026). **Georgia,** 28 Ulubey Sok. (tel. 447 1720). **Germany,** 114 Atatürk Blv. (tel. 426 5465; for visas call 468 5906). **Great Britain,** 46A Şehit Ersun Cad. (tel. 468 6230). **Greece,** 9-11 Zia Ül-Rahman Cad. (tel. 436 8860). **Hungary,** 10 Gazi Mustafa Kemal Blv. (tel. 418 6257). **Iran,** 10 Tahran Cad. (tel. 427 4320). **Israel,** 85 Mahatma Gandi Cad. (tel. 446 3605). **Jordan,** 54/10-12 Cinnah Cad. (tel. 440 2054). **Kazakhstan,** 6 Ebüzzıya Tevfik Sok. (tel. 441 2301). **Kyrgyzstan,** 11 Boyabat Sok., Eren Apt. (tel. 446 8408). **Lebanon,** 44 Kızkulesi Sok. (tel. 446 7487). **Former Yugoslav Republic of Macedonia,** 30/2 Filistin Sok. (tel. 446 9204). **New Zealand,** 13/4 İran Cad. (tel. 467 9056). **Northern Cyprus,** 20 Rabat Sok. (tel. 437 6031). **Oman,** 63 Mahatma Gandi Cad. (tel. 447 0630). **Pakistan,** 37 Iran Cad. (tel. 427 1410, -4). **Palestine,** 45 Filistin Sok. (tel. 436 0823). **Poland,** 241 Atatürk Blv. (tel. 426 1694). **Romania,** 4 Bükreş Sok. (tel. 427 1241). **Russia,** 5 Karyağdı Sok. (tel. 439 2122). **Slovakia,** 245 Atatürk Blv. (tel. 426 5887). **South Africa,** 27 Filistin Sok. (tel. 446 4056). **Syria,** 7 Abdullah Devdet Sok. (tel. 440 9657). **Turkmenistan,** 22 Rabat Sok. (tel. 446 8563). **Ukraine,** 9 Cemal Kadir Sok. (tel. 440 6815). **U.S.,** 110 Atatürk Blv. (tel. 468 6110; fax 467 0019). **Uzbekistan,** 14 Ahmet Rasim Sok. (tel. 439 2740). **Former Yugoslavia,** 47 Paris Cad. (tel. 426 0354).

Banks: All large banks have similar **currency exchange** rates. Slightly better rates are available at the change offices (*döviz*) scattered along Atatürk Blv. in Kızılay. Banks are everywhere. **Vakıf Bank** has an office on the north side of Ulus Sq., and 2 branches on Mustafa Kemal Blv., in Maltepe. Avoid commissions by using ATMs.

American Express: Head office at 88/1 Cinnah Cad. (tel. 441 5205), but this doesn't deal directly with the public. Go to Amex's agents, **Türk Express,** 9/4 Cinnah Cad. **Koç Bank,** 58 Atatürk Blv. (tel. 418 1804) processes Amex's cash transactions. The Koç Bank emblem is a ram. Open Mon.-Fri. 9am-4pm.

ATMs: Pamukbank's 24-hr. machine at the train station accepts Cirrus and PLUS cards, as well as Visa, Eurocard, and Mastercard. There are other Pamukbank machines half a block south of McDonald's on Atatürk Bulvarı in Kızılay. **Türkiye İş Bankası** ATMs are scattered around town, but they only take credit cards.

Flights: *Havaş* buses leave from Hipodrom Cad. (next to the train station) and head to the airport, **Esenboğa,** hourly ($3.50). **Turkish Airlines (THY)** offers direct flights to İstanbul (hourly 6am-10pm, 1hr.), at least 2 per day to Adana, Diyarbakır, Erzurum, İzmir, and Trabzon (1hr.), and at least 1 per day to Malatya and Van (1½hr.). All domestic flights $54 or less; students (14-24) get 25% off. Try to buy tickets two days in advance, because the flights fill up. The THY office is at 231 Atatürk Blv. in Kavaklıdere. Open Mon.-Sat. 8:30am-7:30pm, Sun. 8:30am-5:30pm. This is a new office; if someone directs you anywhere else, they are wrong. It is often more convenient and reliable to buy tickets from one of the private travel agencies visible between Kızılay and Bakanlıklar.

Trains: Built in 1937, Ankara's railway station retains the flavor of the era. Nighttime departures from its crowded platforms capture the romantic spirit of rail travel. Slightly faster blue trains (*Mavi Tren*) serve İstanbul (1 per day, 8hr., $6.50) and İzmir (1 per day, 13hr., $6.50). Normal trains also serve İstanbul (5 per day depart 8am-10:30pm; 7¼hr. during the day, 9½hr. overnight; $5.50) and İzmir (1 per day, 15hr., $5.50), as well as Adana (1 per day, 12¼hr., $4.50), Kars (1 per day, 33¼hr.), Kayseri (1 per day, 7½hr., $2.75), Malatya (1-2 per day, 18½-20hr., $4.75), Sivas (2-3 per day, 11½-14hr., $3.75), and Tatvan (3 per week, 31¾hr.). For overnight trains, make couchette reservations the day before. Overnight trains are more comfortable than overnight buses. On Turkish timetables, İstanbul appears as "Haydarpaşa", İzmir as "Basmane".

Buses: The bus terminal (*Otogar*), in Söğütözü 5km west of Kızılay, is connected to all points in the city by local buses, *dolmuş,* and taxis. *Dolmuş* (50¢) run when full to Ulus; their drop-off point is Hisarpark Cad., in the middle of the cheap hotel area. A taxi for the same trip should cost about $5. City buses make the trip for 25¢. As with İstanbul, scores of companies connect Ankara with nearly every point in Turkey, and buses depart around the clock. Buses (usually 1 per hr.) go to all Turkish cities of significant size: Konya (15 per day, 3hr., $6), İstanbul (8hr., $12), İzmir (8½hr., $12), Kuşadası (3 per day, $14.50), Bodrum (2 per evening, 14hr., $22.25), Trabzon (2 per day, 12hr., $11) Schedules change; call ahead.

City Buses: Ankara has a furiously busy, beehive-like bus system. Buses come in three flavors: red, green, and blue. Red and green buses are government-run, blue ones private. Red buses run on gasoline, green on natural gas. Buy tickets for red and green buses (25¢) from booths near major bus stops, or some street vendors. On the blue buses, you pay the conductor once on board, and he gives change. The fare is also 25¢. The conductor is situated at a little desk halfway down the bus. *Dolmuş* within the city cost 30-50¢, depending on distance.

Laundromat: There is a centrally located self-service launderette in the Beğendik shopping mall under the Kocatepe mosque. Go up the escalator to the second floor ("first" floor to Turks), and take a right; pass through the exit at the end of the corridor and turn left. Wash'n'dry $2.75. If lost, ask anyone for *çamaşırhane.*

English Bookstores: ABC Bookshop, 1 Selanik Cad. (tel. 434 3842), Kızılay, 2 blocks north and ½ block east of the main square. Good selection of English books. Open daily 9am-7pm. The **American Association Library,** 20 Cinnah Cad. (tel. 126 9499), houses a large collection of English literature. Open Mon.-Fri. 1-6pm; closed in Aug. Cinnah Cad. branches off from Atatürk Blv. south of Bakanlıklar. Take any bus marked *Kavaklıdere* from the stop across the Ulus PTT.

Hospital: Bayındır Tıp Merkezi, Kızılırmak Mah. #3-3A 28th Sok. (tel. 287 9000), is one of Ankara's best private hospitals. English spoken. **Numune,** Talatpaşa Blv., Samanpazarı (tel. 310 3030), and **Ankara Üniversitesi Tıp Fakültesi,** Tıp Fakültesi Cad., Dikimevi (tel. 319 2160), are the two biggest university hospitals.

ACCOMMODATIONS

The two main accommodations centers, Kızılay and Ulus. Kızılay will make your memories of Ankara a lot better. This is a clean, upmarket residential area of pleasant, modern architecture which is also the city's main shopping district and home to most of its nightlife. Naturally, you will pay more. Ulus, 2km north, is the old part of Ankara. Close to most of the sights but somewhat grim and dusty, it contains a couple dozen of the city's cheapest hotels. For camping, see Boğazkale on p. 527.

Kızılay

Otel Ertan, 70 Selanik Cad. (tel. 418 4084). Going south along Atatürk Blv., take the fourth left after McDonald's, then the third right onto Selanik Cad. Decent rooms w/showers, and a garden in front. Very peaceful, yet close to the Kızılay nightlife. Singles $10.50, doubles $16.25.

Ulus

To get from the train station to Ulus and its budget hotels, walk straight out along **Cumhuriyet Bulvarı** (a park on your right, a soccer stadium on your left). It's roughly a 20-min. walk; take a taxi if you have a lot of baggage. Continue straight until you reach the equestrian statue, which stands at the center of Ulus, facing west. Continue uphill east on Hisarpark Cad. There are hotels off to either side. The following places are clean, reasonably quiet, and better than some grim alternatives.

Hisar Oteli and Hamam, 6 Hisarpark Cad. (tel. 311 9889 or 310 8128). Rooms at the front suffer a little from street noise, but have nice views of the little houses of old Ankara perched on the hills. Fourth-floor singles are large and have balconies. Cold showers only, but you can use the *hamam* next door for $2.50. Singles $3.50, doubles $7, triples $10.50.

Otel Şan, 8 Şan Sok. (tel. 311 0943). From the equestrian statue, follow Hisarpark Cad. toward the Citadel and turn right on Anafartalar Cad. Şan Sok. will be the fourth street on your left. A somewhat old-fashioned hotel, it has a 1920s feel.

Clean and quiet. Showers, kept locked for most of the day, cost roughly $1.50 extra. Singles $6, doubles $8.25.

Otel Taşçıoğlu, 2 Etizafer Sok. (tel. 310 7410). Around the corner from the Otel Ulus, visible from Hisarpark Cad. (the second left after the statue). The grim exterior masks a rather charming cheap hotel. Lounge and corridors are pleasantly decorated. Rooms are very small but clean. Hot showers $1.75 extra. Availability of showers is restricted. Singles $4.75, doubles $9.50.

Hotel Kale, Anafartalar Cad. 13 Alataş Sok. (tel. 311 3393 or 310 3521). A few doors down from the Otel Şan. A brand-new, clean, and pleasant hotel. All rooms have private shower. Singles $9.25, doubles $16.25; breakfast $1.75.

FOOD

The main eating neighborhoods are Kızılay (mid-range restaurants and cafés), Gençlik Park (cheap), the Citadel (upmarket-expensive by Turkish standards), and Kavaklıdere (expensive). If restaurant life does not suit your wallet, you'll be placated at the many **supermarkets.** The largest are **Gıma,** on Anafartalar Cad. in Ulus; **Beğendik,** under the Kocatepe mosque in Kızılay (at the south end of Mithat Paşa Cad.); and **Migros,** designated by the *MMM* symbol, on Celalbayar Blv. in Maltepe. Mere steps south and to the right of the Atatürk Tower, **Hoşdere Caddesi** lays claim to many good restaurants, as does the little side street one block south of it.

The Citadel

Several restaurants offer traditional Turkish food. To get to them, do not enter the Citadel via the steps at Hisarpark Cad.; the Citadel is a confusing labyrinth, and you're unlikely to find them. Instead, enter via the gate just uphill from the Museum of Anatolian Civilizations; the restaurants are clustered around the main square just inside the gate. All the restaurants around here are high-class, but reasonably priced.

Kale Washington, right on the square, on your left, offers tasty fare; food is served on an open-air, canopied terrace. *İmambayıldı* (stuffed aubergine) $2, main courses roughly $4.75.

Kavaklıdere

There are many upscale restaurants here. Several line Noktalı Sok., the road leading uphill on the right of the Sheraton Hotel; $5-7 will get you a main course. These are favored by workers from the nearby embassies. Nevertheless, the occasional truly excellent *kebap* place also exists. Hoşdere Cad., steps south and to the right of the Atatürk Tower, is another street of good restaurants.

Dürümland, 9/B Filistin Sok. Take the first left off Noktalı Sok. after the Sheraton; Dürümland is roughly 20m down the street to your left. Offers some of the best *döner kebap* you'll taste anywhere ($1.75).

Kızılay

These streets are crowded with cafés and restaurants; locals throng here for food.

Düveroğlu, 18 Selanik Cad., serves up delicious *İskender kebap* for $2.25. Open daily 10am-1am.

Coffee Shop, 1 Selanik Cad., in the basement of the ABC Bookshop. Great coffee, great classical and jazz music. Could be a good place to meet Ankara students. Closing at 7pm, this place is best in the mid-afternoon.

Cafe M, 40 Selanik Cad., beside Yusuf Cad. Everyone even vaguely collegiate or youthful seems to head here; it's always crowded.

Ulus

Çiçek Lokantası, 12 Çankırı Cad. Atatürk Blv. becomes Çankırı Cad. north of the equestrian statue. Established in 1932, this white tablecloth restaurant boasts an indoor fountain, and classic black-and-white photos decorate the walls. You will be taken to the kitchen and shown their selection of dishes ($1.50 each), two or three of which make a good meal. Open daily 7am-10pm.

ENTERTAINMENT

Kızılay

When they roll up the sidewalks at dusk in Ulus, head south to Kızılay for the evening. Some of Kızılay's streets have been turned into pedestrian zones; these crowded streets are lined with bars and cafés. The tree-lined **Yüksel Sok.,** one block south of Kızılay on the left, is crowded with students from Ankara University and the many private and professional schools in the area. To the right is the café-laden **Selanik Sok.,** which runs parallel to Atatürk Blv. Pub life is centered on two streets: **İnkilâp Sok.** and **Bayındır Sok.,** two and three blocks to the left, respectively, of Kızılay Sq. as you look south. Bayındır is the livelier. Try **Büyük Ekspress** at no. 11, an always-crowded joint, popular with students, where the beer and conversation flow freely. On the corner of Bayındır and Sakarya Cad. (one block south) is the tiny but happening **Blues Bar,** where they play loud Western music. It's on the second floor of a corner building—you'll hear it before you see it. Take a left on this street (Sakarya Cad.), i.e. walk away from Atatürk Blv., for one block until you reach the **Z-Pub,** another crowded spot where Turkish music is the style. Back on Bayındır, **Major, Nuans,** and **Atesta** are similar. They usually play Turkish music, as does **Forza.** At the far end of Selanik Cad., just past the Ertan Hotel and close to the Kocatepe Mosque, **Brothers Bar** has a very large, young, yuppie crowd, and Turkish music is played. A few doors down, there is a good view of the mosque from quieter, more hip **Tenedo Cafe,** at no. 67. Kızılay starts to quiet down at roughly 10pm during the week, except for some of the bars mentioned above.

Kavaklıdere

A couple of kilometers south of Kızılay, Kavaklıdere offers much more upscale, less crowded entertainment. Bars are not crammed together as in Kızılay; they are spread out through this residential area and can be hard to find.

A stroll through Gençlik Park makes a pleasant evening walk. This park is crammed with cheap restaurants; there's an amusement park and a lake with pleasure boats. Although lone travelers occasionally visit, it's primarily a family scene. The **opera,** located at the Ulus side of the park, may have some performances. If a long day of sightseeing has left you weary and, after returning to your hotel, you've found the shower locked, check out one of the several city **baths. Karaceby Hamamı,** 101 Talat Paşa Blv., Siteler (tel. 311 8447) offers standard bath services. (Open daily for men 6:30am-10:30pm, for women 8am-7pm; basic fee $2.50.) **Ankara Hamamı,** 166 Talatpaşa Cad., Cecebi; and **Marmara Hamamı,** 17 Denizciler Cad. (tel. 324 2527), in Ulus; scrub scrubworthy and scrubbable alike. From the equestrian statue in Ulus Sq., ascend Hisarparkı Cad. towards the citadel, turn right on Anafartalar Cad., then follow Anafartalar 'til it ends at Denizciler. (Open daily 5am-10pm for men; women's bath open 6:30am-7pm. Bath $2, massage $1.)

SIGHTS

Anıt Kabir, Atatürk's mausoleum, is nearly a kilometer long and built on a monumental scale. As you exit the tourist office, walk left (northwest) up Gazi Mustafa Kemal Blv. until you reach Tandoğan Sq. As you approach the square, notice the next major street to your left exiting the traffic circle. This street, Anıt Cad., leads south to the sprawling grounds containing the mausoleum. The walk takes 10min. On your right you will see an unmarked entrance guarded by two soldiers; beyond it a road leading uphill. It doesn't look like the kind of place you can enter, but you can. The walk from the gate to the mausoleum entrance takes another 10min. On a hot day, take a taxi ($1.80) from Ulus. At its entrance stand statues of 3 Turkish men and women representing all Turks; one of the women has her face covered to mask the ingrained sorrow caused by Atatürk's death. The broad path from these to the mausoleum is lined with 24 lions. The lions symbolize power; they are arranged in pairs according to the Hittite custom. The atmosphere outside is formal and solemn. Soldiers in ceremonial uniform stand on guard. The mausoleum itself is huge and contains **Atatürk's sarcophagus.** An adjacent museum contains some of his belongings. There are photos here showing cloud formations shaped like his profile taken after his death, suggesting that his power extends to the supernatural world.

The **Ethnographic Museum,** roughly 1km south of Ulus off Atatürk Blv., contains a beautiful collection of clothing, calligraphy, ironwork, and woodwork, including some carvings from mosques. (Open Tues.-Sun. 9:30am-12:30pm and 1:30-5:30pm; admission $3.) Beside it, the **Museum of Sculptures and Paintings** is also good, but it can be skipped if time is short. (Open Tues.-Sun. 9am-noon and 1-5pm; free.) Lying at the feet of the Citadel, the **Museum of Anatolian Civilizations** is one of Turkey's most famous. Walk to the top of Hisarpark Cad., turn right at the Citadel steps (without ascending them), and follow the Citadel boundaries until you get there. Its setting is unique—a restored 15th-century Ottoman *han* (inn) and *bedesten* (covered bazaar). It houses a collection of astoundingly old artifacts which traces the history of Anatolia from the dawn of civilization. The exhibits are not as well-labeled as they could be; the illustrated catalogue ($8) explains all. Expensive guides can be hired for a 1-hr. tour; $20 for a group of 4 or more; $15 for 1-3 persons; fix the price in advance. (Open Tues.-Sun. 8:30am-5:30pm; admission $3.)

The pure white **Kocatepe Mosque,** completed in 1987, shines as one of the world's largest and most beautiful. Billed as a 16th-century mosque utilizing 20th-century technology, it continues the architectural dialogue between the buildings of Sinan, the famous Ottoman architect who codified the Ottoman Classical style of architecture under Süleyman the Magnificent. Its four columns are reminiscent of Sinan's Selimiye Mosque in Edirne, and the central dome and half-domes recall the Blue Mosque (Sultanahmet Camii; by Sinan's successor) in İstanbul. Don't miss the stunning interior; you can't fail to notice the gold sphere, surrounded by smaller spheres, which hang from the ceiling. The mosque also contains a model of the mosque at Medina—a present of King Fahd of Saudi Arabia to the people of Turkey in 1993. The mosque's courtyard is covered in glass. Underneath it is the large Beğendik supermarket and shopping mall, ultra-modern and air-conditioned. It is traditional for mosques to pay upkeep by renting space for merchants, but the Kocatepe takes the practice into the modern age. It's an unusual sight, a bizarre juxtaposition of God and mammon. A couple of kilometers farther south soars the Ataküle Observation Tower. Bus #391 runs from the Citadel and Ulus to the tower, via Kızılay and Kavaklıdere; bus #613 from Ulus only. From its observation deck, you can literally see all of Ankara (admission 50¢).

There are some Roman ruins in Ankara, though they're in a poor state of preservation; thus they aren't worth a lot of your time. They include the Roman Baths, a 5-min. walk up Çankırı Cad. from the equestrian statue; the Column of Julian is nearby, as is the **Temple of Augustus,** built in 25 BC over the site of earlier temples to Cybele (an Anatolian fertility goddess) and to the Phrygian moon god; it was later converted into a Byzantine church. Nearby are the 15th-century **Hacı Bayram Mosque,** the old **Parliament** (where Turkey was proclaimed an independent republic), and the **zoo** (Atatürk Orman Çiftliği) in an expansive, tree-filled park.

■ NEAR ANKARA

The ruins of **Hattuşaş,** the once-glorious Hittite capital, lie roughly 200km from Ankara, 30km off the highway to Samsun. The first people to smelt iron, the Indo-European Hittites conquered Anatolia around 2200 BC. United under a central authority at Hattuşaş, the Hittites vied with the Egyptians for control of the fertile lands and trade routes of Mesopotamia. The western Sea People razed Hattuşaş shortly after 1200 BC, but archaeologists have unearthed enough of the ruins to provide a fair representation of the city. The road following the 6km wall that encircles Hattuşaş first passes by the **Büyük Mabed** (Great Temple) of the Weather God of

Hatti and the Sun Goddess of Arinna. A drawbridge over two pools of water granted the only entrance to the original temple. The big, green rock there was a wedding gift from the King of Egypt to his son-in-law, the King of the Hittites. Continuing up the hill and to the right, the road passes the **Aslanlıkapı** (Lion's Gate; the original lions are now in the museum in Ankara) and the **Yerkapı** (Earth Gate). The two sphinxes from the Earth Gate are now in İstanbul and Berlin, and no longer overlook the 70m-long tunnel, built under the south fortifications and used for surprise attacks. The figure carved in relief on the **Kralkapı** (King's Gate) just down the hill is the Hittite war god. The **Büyük Kale** (Great Citadel) rounds out the tour. The small **museum** in the village of **Boğazkale,** 1km from the site, gives a sense of the area's history. (Open daily 8am-6pm; admission to museum and ruins $1.75, to ruins alone 80¢.) Your admission ticket is also valid for **Yazılıkaya,** an open-air temple with 100 of the 1000 or so gods of the Hittite pantheon represented in bas-relief.

To get to Hattuşaş, take a bus to Sungurlu (2½hr., $4 from Ankara; frequent buses along the Ankara-Samsun route). The bus drops off either on the main highway or in the center of town. To get back to Ankara, flag a bus down on the highway. There are *dolmuş* to Boğazkale that leave from the center of Sungurlu. (Ask someone other than a taxi driver.) Often local taxis function as *dolmuş.* (Bargain with the driver; $2 is a good price.) Otherwise, a private taxi costs $10 for a one-way ride to Boğazkale, $15-20 for a full tour of the ruins. Traffic on the road to Boğazkale is very light, so hitching may be a problem. Walking through the ruins—which include the world's first library—takes about half a day.

A quiet hillside village crowned by Yazılıkaya, **Boğazkale** makes a great escape from tumultuous Ankara. The closest you can stay to Yazılıkaya is the **Kaleburg Motel** (tel. (364) 452 2189), perhaps the best summer bargain. All the rooms have balconies and clean bathrooms, and guests can show the proprietor their *Let's Go* guide for a free Turkish breakfast. (Roughly $6 per person, in doubles.) All four establishments offer restaurants, private baths, and hot showers. Two establishments greet travelers on the entrance road. **Attila** (tel. (364) 452 2101) boasts a swimming pool (fee $1), refilled daily, and **campsites** ($1 per person; bring your own tent). **Aşıkoğlu** (tel. (364) 452 2004) has a restaurant and comfortable rooms across from the museum. At $10 per person, the rooms are no bargain, but breakfast is included. Climbing uphill to the village center is worth it for the views and cheaper prices. **Başkent Pansiyon** (tel. (364) 452 2037) which looks out over the entrance to Hattuşaş, has singles, doubles, and triples for $7 per person. Campers will appreciate the particularly clean toilets and showers ($3.50 per site).

■■■ KONYA

In the 13th century, one of the greatest and most well-loved Islamic philosophers, Celâleddin Rumi, known to his followers as Mevlâna (our master) came from his birthplace in Balkh, Afghanistan, and settled in Konya. After his death, some of his disciples founded a Sufi order which later became known for its "whirling dervishes," who sought to achieve ecstasy and unity with God through controlled trance-like spinning (see box on p. 409). Today, Muslims often stop in Konya to visit Mevlâna's tomb before embarking on the pilgrimage to Mecca. Konya retains intense spirituality despite rapid industrialization; you'll notice most of the older men wearing the traditional Muslim hats called *derviş*. But Konya's history dates far beyond the days of the Mevlâna. In Roman times, St. Paul favored Konya (then called Iconium) with a visit, and sparked the city's transformation into a significant Christian center. In the 11th century, the Seljuks swept through Asia Minor, gaining a formidable reputation in the West and priming the area for later Ottoman conquests. They made Konya Turkey's first capital and replaced its churches with the greatest mosques of the era, most of which survive today. If you are respectful of Konya's religious traditions, you'll find its residents amiable and welcoming; hospitality toward visitors is one of the sect's main principles. You will also experience a different type of "hospitality" from its numerous street carpet hustlers, who will try to lure you to their shops with offers of tea. If you want to buy a carpet, go alone; these middle men get a 30% commission (added on to your price).

ORIENTATION AND PRACTICAL INFORMATION

Konya's main street is roughly 1km long and runs between the turquoise conical-towered **Mevlâna tomb** and the circular **Alâaddin Bulvarı,** which runs around the **Alâaddin Tepesi** (Alâaddin Hill) park. The ½km closest to the Mevlâna tomb is called Mevlâna Cad.; the other half is Alâaddin Cad. Konya's sights, hotels, and restaurants are clustered within this small area, and finding your way around is easy. The **bus station** (*otogar*) is 3km from town. Frequent trams head from there to Alâaddin Bulvarı (25¢—ask for Mevlâna). The **railway station** is 2km from the center; when you exit, you'll see the road to town, whose start is marked by a roundabout, to your right. Walk along this street; you'll pass Atatürk Stadium and, after 600m, the Atatürk statue. Take the second left onto Atatürk Blv. after the statue; Alâaddin Blv. is roughly 500m farther on. Bear right on Alâaddin Blv.; Alâaddin Cad. is the first major right. *Dolmuş* also run the route. To get back to the railway station, take a minibus *dolmuş* marked İstasyon or Gar. Bus #4 to Meram also passes nearby. To get back to the bus station, take any *dolmuş* marked *Otogar.*

Tourist Office: 21 Mevlâna Cad., across the street from the Mevlâna Müze. Free maps. Take their accommodation and carpet shop advice with a grain of salt; they get commissions for this. Open Mon.-Fri. 8am-noon and 1:30-5:30pm.

PTT: On Alâaddin Cad. Open 24 hr. Another PTT at the bus station. (Open daily 7am-11pm.) Central **Postal Code:** 42000; **Telephone Code:** 332.

Buses: Run to Silifke (7 per day, 3hr., $6), Ankara (15 per day, 3hr., $6), İzmir (10 per day, 8hr., $10.50), and Aksaray (11 per day, 2½hr., $4). Nighttime buses run to İstanbul ($11) and Nevşehir/Göreme (3 per day, 4hr., $7.75).

Pharmacy (*Eczane*): These are scattered all over town, in the streets off Alâaddin/Mevlâna Cad. Look for the word *eczane* (pronounced "ehj-zah-nay") The night pharmacy (*nöbetçi*) is supposedly posted in all pharmacy windows.

Hospital (*Hastane*): Sağlık Hastanesi, Hastane Cad., Iktap Sok. (tel. 233 8204 or 235 6795), is located in the city center. Clean and comfortable. Reception doesn't speak English, but the doctor does.

ACCOMMODATIONS

Finding rooms in Konya is no problem. Many are clustered in small alleys along the main drag. The cheapies are comparatively expensive by Turkish standards.

Aziziye Oteli (tel. 352 2287), across from the Aziziye Mosque. One of the cheapest in town. Reasonably clean rooms, most with private shower (pit toilets down the corridor). Broad, atmospheric corridors lined with rooms which have frosted-glass doors. Singles $4.75, doubles $8.25. Because of its prices, the clientele are primarily working-class Turkish men—single women may feel uneasy.

Otel Çeşme, İstanbul Cad. 35 Akifpaşa Sok. (tel. 351 2426). Well-kept rooms w/ bath, fake bricks, and stained glass. Singles $8.25, doubles $11.75, triples $17.50.

Yeni Köşk, Yeni Aziziye Cad. 28 Kadılar Sok. (tel. 352 0671). A couple of blocks off Mevlâna Cad. on a wide street. Quieter than the other hotels. The well-scrubbed rooms all have showers. There is a safe on the premises. Singles $9.50, doubles $14, triples $24, quads $32; breakfast $2.50.

Otel Yasin, İstanbul Cad. 25 Yusufağa (tel. 351 1624). Welcomes travelers with its red street-front and extensively wood-paneled lobby. All but 2 of the 18 rooms have private baths. Singles $9.50, doubles $12.25, triples $16.75. Rooms w/o showers cost $1.25 less; but showers cost an extra $2 each.

FOOD AND ENTERTAINMENT

The local specialty is *fırın kebap,* a chunk of oven-roasted lamb. With the tourist office on your left and the Mevlâna in front of you, go right roughly 100m passing by the left-hand side of the Balıkçı Otel; then right again just before the third roundabout (the one in front of Mevlâna being the first roundabout). A bare brick wall and tacky plastic Pepsi sign conceal a 150-year-old **Konya house** which serves some of the best food you'll have in Turkey. Its specialties are sebzeli *çöp kebap* (*kebap* with aubergine, $1.75), *çöp şiş* (some of the best *şiş kebap* you've ever had, $2.25), and *etli yaprak sarması* (vine leaves stuffed with meat and dipped in yogurt, $1.25). If you want some Western-style coffee, **Ankara Pastanesi,** on Alâaddin Cad., serves a delicious, frothy Nescafé. Coming from the Mevlâna, it's a little past the post office, on your left. **Dergah,** 17 Mevlâna Müze Karşısı (facing the Mevlâna, take the street to your right), serves a decent version ($2.50). The **Sema** restaurant on İstanbul Cad., under the Otel Çeşme, specializes in *döner kebap;* it is a fine gourmet version ($2).

If after a long day of walking around, your back begins to ache, head to the **Şems Mah.,** 7 Serfettin Cad. (tel. 353 0093). It is in a newly restored ancient building, beside the Selimiye Mosque, just steps from Alâaddin Cad. (Entry $2.50, complete bath'n'massage $6; tip $2-4 (or nothing), depending on service.)

SIGHTS

The interior of the **Mevlâna Tekke** is among Turkey's more spectacular sights. Inside the complex, originally a type of monastery, are the tomb the Mevlâna and other dervishes, as well as a fascinating museum with hand-written Qur'ans, carpets, dervish garments, and ornate metalwork. (Open Mon. 10am-6pm, Tues.-Sun. 9am-6pm; admission 60¢, students 15¢.) Konya's other major attractions are tame by comparison. They are situated on or around **Alâaddin Tepesi** (which also contains a park and some pleasant tea gardens). Supposedly, this mound contains layers of civilizations stretching back to the Bronze Age. **Alâaddin Camii,** near the hilltop, is an early 13th-century mosque in the Syrian Seljuk style. The mosque re-opened in the summer of 1995 after 11 years of restoration; it is now quite modern inside. Here, the Seljuks studied astrology in the reflection of the night sky off the pool in the main chamber. Nearby, on Alâaddin Blv., is the **Karatay Medresesi**—Museum of Tiles. The interior itself is a great example of Seljuk tilework (open Tues.-Sun. 9am-noon and 1:30-5:30pm; admission 60¢). Also on Alâaddin Blv. is the **İnce Minare Medresesi,** or Academy of the Slender Minaret. It contains primarily Seljuk and Ottoman stone carvings. (Open Tues.-Sun. 9am-noon and 1:30-5:30pm; admission 60¢.) In those two museums, the buildings are of greater interest than the collections.

Hard to find several blocks south of the hill is the **Archaeological Museum,** which features an outstanding 3rd-century sarcophagus illustrating the labors of Hercules. (Open Tues.-Sun. 9am-noon and 1:30-5pm; admission $1.25, students 60¢). On Atatürk Blv., just off Alâaddin Blv. (the first major left if you're coming from Alâaddin Cad.), you'll find **Atatürk house**—a small museum of the great man's personal effects. (Open Tues.-Sun. 9am-4pm; admission 60¢.) The **Aziziye Mosque,** a 5-min. walk from the Mevlâna (back along Mevlâna Cad., off the main street to the left) is 18th-century Baroque, unusual for Turkey. The windows are larger than the door for extra light, and the dome is self-supporting (without columns). Its two minarets, with rows of columns around their tops, are unique in Turkey. Konya's little bazaar is between the Aziziye Mosque and the PTT. There is an **underground gold bazaar;** about halfway along Mevlâna Cad., you'll see the steps, covered by a glass shelter, leading down. You could also explore the older residential streets east of Mevlâna.

■ NEAR KONYA

Every ½hr., bus #64 leaves from the municipal bus stop (on Alâaddin Cad., across from the PTT) for isolated **Sille,** 8km away. Huddled in a small valley, the village faces a cliff into which numerous small rock dwellings have been carved; a mini-Cappadocia. Sille has a 4th-century church, **Aya Elena Kilisesi,** decorated by more recent frescoes. (Supposedly open Tues.-Sun. 9am-4pm, but hours vary; admission 50¢.) The two caves beside it were used as dwellings.

Çatalhöyük (near the town of Çümra 50km south of Konya) is one of the world's oldest known settlements, dating back to the 8th millennium BC. An advanced

Neolithic community, Çatalhöyük vies with Jericho for the coveted title of "world's first city." Its famous cave drawings and artifacts have been moved to the Ankara museum and to Holland; little remains on site but a few crumbling walls. The tour isn't worthwhile, but the guidebook on sale at the Mevlâna is. Take a **bus** from Eski Garaj (Old Bus Station) to Çümra (45min.), then a taxi the remaining distance (roughly $20 round-trip, or take a taxi the whole way for $30-45).

A Dizzying Poet

Celaleddin Mevlâna Rumi, founder of the order of the Dervishes and perhaps the greatest of all the Persian mystic poets, made his home in 13th century Konya. Revered both as a poet and a prophet, Rumi is said to have used his spiritual powers to repulse the invasion of Hulegu Khan's Mongol hordes in 1256. For 700 years, the passionate elegance of his verses has inspired readers from İstanbul to Samarkand, to Muslim India, Arabia, and Africa. He is not widely known in the West, but English literature has felt his impact through translations made by early 19th century Orientalists. The prayer-like rhythm of verses such as this one have ravished poets from Goethe to Ginsberg:

Through Love all that is bitter will be sweet.
Through Love all that is copper will be gold.
Through Love all dregs will turn to purest wine;
Through Love all pain will turn to medicine.
Through Love the dead will become alive,
Through Love the king does turn into a slave.

Westerners interested in Sufi-Muslim worship can get a taste of it in its most impassioned form in Rumi, translations of whose poetry are available in the U.S. *I Am Wind, You Are Fire* by Annemarie Schimmel is an excellent introduction to the life and writings of Rumi. Coleman Barks is renowned for his translations.

■■■ EĞİRDİR

Eğirdir rests along a peninsula that juts into the middle of a large, azure lake, surrounded by the Central Taurus mountains. At the peninsula's tip are great views, numerous pensions, delicious fish restraunts, and soft sandy beaches. Discovered by tourists only a decade ago, this fishing town has installed Western amenities but manages to shield its natural serenity from extravagant tourism.

ORIENTATION AND PRACTICAL INFORMATION

Here in Eğirdir the Seljuks built the world's only walk-through minaret, poised atop an archway in the town center. The archway leads east past municipal headquarters to King Croesus' crumbling fortress, with a sign proclaiming EĞİRDİR. Beyond the fortress, a dusty road threads to the shore across from two small islands. The closer one, little more than a tea garden, is called **Canada** (pronounced *JAHN-ah-dah*), which in Turkish means "adorable island." The larger **Yeşilada** (Green Island) looks a lot like Canada, with rocky shores and verdure, but in addition hosts half the pensions in Eğirdir. Northwest of the archway, **2nd Sahil Yolu** hugs the lakeshore for several kilometers, passing banks, the post office, the tourist office, and two beaches before it brings you to the usually idle train station. 2nd Sahil Yolu runs west and north along the lakeshore. **Yenimahalle** road begins beside the bus station 100m south of the archway and follows more lakeside past the modern hospital. Due west of the archway lies Eğirdir's permanent market place.

Tourist Office: #13 2nd Sahil Yolu (tel. 312 2098). From the bus station gate (a map stands outside), walk straight and follow the road as it curves to the left.

Open Mon.-Fri. 8:30am-noon and 1:30-6pm, sometimes weekends. English, French, and German spoken by staff seldom on duty simultaneously.

PTT: 2nd Sahil Yolu (tel. 311 4591), on the way to the tourist office. Information and Poste Restante open 24 hr., other services Mon.-Fri. 8:30am-noon and 1:30pm-5:30pm. **Postal Code:** 32500; **Telephone Code:** 246.

Trains: (tel. 311 4694). 2km west of town center, off 2nd Sahil Yolu. Open daily 6am-noon and 5pm-7pm. One train leaves for İstanbul at 6pm (12hr.). For Ankara, change in Eskişehir. For İzmir (10hr.), change in Isparta (Tues., Thurs., and Sat.).

Buses: (tel. 311 4036). Just south of the town center. Buses leave daily for Afyon (5 per day, 3hr., $5), Antalya (7 per day, 3hr., $5), Konya (8 per day, 3½hr., $5), Nevşehir (4 per day, 6hr., $11), İzmir (6 per day, 7hr., $10), Ankara (4 per day, 7hr., $9), and İstanbul (1 per day, 10hr., $13). Transport to the city center by *dolmuş* (10¢) or taxi ($2). **Local Buses** (15¢) leave 7am-10pm hourly from behind the mosque, across the street from the bus station.

Luggage deposit: Open roughly 6am-8pm (30¢) at the bus station.

Hospital (*Hastane*): **Sağlık Ocağı,** Güney Sahil Yolu (tel. 311 4855).

Pharmacy: Roughly a dozen between the walk-through minaret and the fortress. The night pharmacy (*nöbetçi*) is supposed to be posted in all pharmacy windows.

ACCOMMODATIONS

Eğirdir offers the complete range of lodging from hotels through pensions and campsites. The hotels tend to be upscale and impersonal but don't have to break your pocketbook. Often the last places to fill up, they make a welcome refuge in a pinch. Yeşilada is the best place to stay, offering tranquility and lakeside views away from the bustle of town. Unless otherwise stated, all rooms have private showers. Note that on your arrival in Eğirdir, you will be besieged by pension staff trying to hustle you into their pensions. They may not take "no" for an answer—at first.

Yeşilada Pension (tel. 311 4413). On your left just as you reach Yeşilada. Offers three marble-finish balcony rooms with great views. Next door, the **Big Apple Pension** is nearly identical, but also offers rooms *sans* view. Singles $10, doubles $15 in both places; breakfast $2.50 extra.

ADAC Pension (tel./fax 312 3074) stands next door. Named after the German motor touring organization, this is a little older. Roof terrace; one room as private balcony. Singles $6, doubles $12, breakfast included. Cheap tours to the National Park and Canyon ($7). Free rowboat for use of guests; free bus station pick-up/drop-off. Good English spoken.

Halley's Pansion (312 3625). Take the right fork upon reaching Yeşilada—150m up. The second oldest pension in town, this is very popular with backpackers. None too plush, but a good meeting place. Two rooms with balcony. Excellent views from rooftop terrace. Singles $8.25, doubles $11.75, triples $15.25. Tours to national park $21. Owners may cook fish fresh from the stream for lunch. Free rowboat for use. English spoken. Free bus station pick-up/drop-off.

Altınkum Plaj Camping, rent a tent ($1.25) and have access to the camp's electricity and showers. Eğirdir's best beach is here; admission 15¢ for non-campsite dwellers. Changing rooms 50¢, parking $1. Roughly 2km past the tourist office; bear right at major junction sign. Taxis from center $1.50.

FOOD AND SIGHTS

Living in close proximity to such a huge body of water means, of course, that the people of Eğirdir make a mean fish—carp, bass, crayfish, and perch are the local specialties. The pensions of Yeşilada have a limited selection—usually fried perch—cooked with varying degrees of skill. The **Sunshine Restaurant,** at the far end of Yeşilada, should not be missed; its tables are so close to the lake's edge that if you consume too much *rakı* with your meal, you could topple in. (Meal $4-5.)

Eğirdir will not disappoint nature-lovers and adventurers. 27km to the east lies **Zindan,** a 1½km-long cave which served the Romans as an open-air temple dedicated to Eurymedon; bring a flashlight. Forty kilometers southeast from Eğirdir stand the **Adada ruins,** consisting of an ancient (1st century BC) temple's fallen columns, sarcophagi, and amphitheater. Only 25km south of town, **Kovada National Park** teams with wildlife and draws butterfly collectors in the spring. Avid walkers can follow a popular stretch of the **King's Road** by which Lydian rulers once made their way from Ephesus to Babylon.

CAPPADOCIA

The strange grandeur of the ancient province of Cappadocia is sure to make a lasting impression. Volcanic formations shape a striking landscape of cone-shaped monoliths (fittingly called *peribaca,* meaning "fairy chimneys" in Turkish) grouped in valleys and along ridges. The region lies between three volcanoes—Hasan Dağı near Aksaray, Erciyes Dağı near Kayseri, and Melendiz Dağı near Niğde—which once deposited a thick layer of volcanic ash here, subsequently hardening to form a soft rock called *tufa,* or tuff. This rock is so soft that you can carve through it with a coin, and in some places even with your fingers. In areas where heavy, harder boulders compress the *tufa,* it escaped erosion. These columns of uneroded *tufa* are today's fairy chimneys. For 2000 years, until the Greek Christian inhabitants were forced to leave in the 1923 population exchange, people in this area carved houses, churches, and entire cities out of the same rock. The central area of the province is defined by the triangle formed by the city of Nevşehir and the small towns of Avanos and Ürgüp, 300km southeast of Ankara.

Most visitors with only a day or two visit the **fairy chimneys** around Göreme and the spectacular **Open-Air Museum,** which contains several frescoed churches carved into the rock; the **underground cities** at Derinkuyu and Kaymaklı; and the heavenly **Ihlara Valley.** The region also contains farming villages, Byzantine chapels, and underground habitations that could occupy a visitor indefinitely. Of the several towns you can stay in, Göreme is perhaps the most appealing. It is a town of fairy chimneys and traditional dwellings, though in recent years it has become more highly developed. Ürgüp is the other main tourist town. Although it is built around bizarre rock formations, it lacks fairy chimneys and is not so "Cappadocian" in appearance or atmosphere. It is a sophisticated town of Greek architecture; in parts, you won't even notice the rock formations. Göreme is patronized primarily by backpackers, Ürgüp primarily by package tour groups.

GETTING AROUND

Transportation in the region includes minibuses, guided tours, and mountain bike, moped, or car rental; there are numerous agencies in Ürgüp and Göreme (car rental is exorbitant here—$70 per day). Biking is an exhilarating way to tackle the area's rudimentary roads. Cycling also allows you flexibility in visiting sites, which are sometimes far apart from one another. Though it is touristy in parts, Cappadocia remains largely rural and conservative; foreigners should expect to be stared at, no matter how appropriately they dress. Freelance camping in the rocks is strictly forbidden. The valley is accessible by **moped** or (if you're fit—hills are steep) mountain **bike. Rentals** are pricey: bikes go for $2.50 per hour, $15 per day; mopeds $5 per hour, $35 per day; cars $75 per day, including unlimited mileage and insurance. These are the official prices agreed upon by agencies in Göreme; but some will undercut substantially to get your business (up to 50% for mountain bikes and mopeds). In summer (June-Sept.), an hourly **minibus** (50¢) links Göreme and Ürgüp: its course is Ürgüp-Göreme (via the Open-Air Museum) to Zelve-Avanos and back. It departs daily from Ürgüp (main *otogar*) at 20min. past the hour, 8:20am-6:20pm. In the same direction it leaves Göreme (opposite PTT) at 30min. past the hour, Zelve (main entrance) 40min. past, and arrives in Avanos at ten to the hour. It leaves Avanos at 20 min. past, reaching Zelve on the ½hr., departing Göreme (PTT) at 40min. past and arriving in Ürgüp 10min. later. If there are a lot of tourists, it may start running in mid-April, but there have been relatively few tourists for several years now. Outside of these months you have to backtrack to Nevşehir by half-hourly minibus (25¢) from the Göreme bus station, or by the Avanos-Nevşehir bus (catch from outside PTT, same side of the road; a quarter to and a quarter past the hour Mon.-Fri. 7am-6pm, Sat. 7am-5pm; 50¢). From Nevşehir, catch a minibus to Ürgüp every ½hr., 7am-6pm, 50¢). Get off at either Nevşehir's tourist office or its bus station, and catch the onward connection from the same place.

Göreme, Nevşehir, and Ürgüp share the same long-distance **bus schedule,** because Cappadocia is a relatively small region served by only two intercity bus companies, Nevtur and Göreme. Although some Cappadocia-bound buses terminate in Nevşehir, many carry on to Göreme, Ürgüp, and Avanos as well. Frequent destinations include Ankara (5 per day, 5hr., $7), İstanbul (2 per day, 12hr., $14.50), Konya (3 per day, 4hr., $6.25), Adana (2 per day, 5hr., $6.25), Mersin (2 per day, 5hr., $6.25), and Antalya (2 per day, 11hr., $12.25). One daily bus serves Side (13hr., $12.50), Alanya (14hr., $14.25), Fethiye (15hr., $15.50), İzmir (12hr., $14.50), Pamukkale (11hr., $12.25), Marmaris (15hr., $16.75), Muğla (12hr., $15.75), Eskişehir (8hr., $11), Bodrum (14hr., $16.75), Kuşadası (13hr., $15.75), Selçuk (13hr., $15.75), and Aydın (12hr., $12). For connections to Eastern Turkey, take the bus from Ürgüp to Kayseri (hourly until mid-afternoon, 2hr., $2).

■■■ GÖREME

Göreme has a distinctly Cappadocian appearance, with dozens of cone-shaped rocks, roughly a hundred feet high, into which cave-houses have been carved. Many are still inhabited; some have been turned into hotels. Among the cones, there are numerous traditional Turkish rural dwellings. Tourism, however, has changed the face of Göreme; more than sixty pensions have sprung up in the last few years. The main square is full of restaurants and tour agencies and more pensions are springing up in its narrow back streets. Göreme is a convenient base for exploring rock-hewn churches and the beautiful Rose Valley; tours run to places farther afield.

Orientation and Practical Information With the bus terminal to your right—lengthways—behind you, to your right runs the road to the mosque. Directly in front of you is the main road; take the first major intersection right (roughly 100m away) to get to the Open-Air Museum. The PTT is on the main road, at this junction, on your left. Downstairs by the entrance to the Open-Air Museum, in the handicrafts building, there is a **post office** (open daily 9am-5pm) and two **banks** (open daily 8:30am-4pm or later) that cash traveler's checks and give Visa (only) cash advances. The post office also changes money. Göreme's bus station is in the main square, and contains the private, hotel-run **tourist office,** which gives info on rooms. The various tour agencies in town are also a good source of free information. The **PTT** (open daily 8:30am-12:30pm and 1:30-5:30pm) is in the center of town. Göreme is small, and it's easy to find your way around. **Telephone Code:** 384.

Accommodations Göreme's pension owners have collectively settled on a price scale: singles $7, w/bath $9.50; doubles $9.50, w/bath $14; dorm beds $3.50. This agreement notwithstanding, occasional undercutting or overcharging persists. To get to the **Melek Otel** (tel./fax 271 2643), take a right off the main street, just before the Hard Duck Café and Tardelli Pizza Restaurant. Set in a handsomely restored Ottoman house, the Melek has a wide variety of rooms, including some caves. (Singles $9.50, doubles $14.) **Paradise Pansiyon** (tel. 271 2248), on the road to the Open-Air Museum, has one fairy chimney room; the others are clustered around a courtyard, where a youth-hostel atmosphere reigns. (Dorms $3.50, w/bath $6; singles $7; doubles $9.50.) Next door, **Peri Pansiyon** (tel. 271 2136) has several rooms in fairy chimneys. (Singles $4.75, doubles $9.50.) To reach **The Ottoman House** (tel. 271 2616), the most opulent of the budget accommodations, walk toward the mosque and take the first right immediately after the bus station (it's the road with the dried-up riverbed in the middle). The hotel is 100m up, on the left.

The lobby is drenched in marble and rooms are very comfortable. The *Harem* bar downstairs is lined with carpets. (Singles $15, doubles $20.) Campers should head to **Göreme Dilek Camping** (tel. 271 2396), across from Peri Pansiyon. The campsite and pool are nestled between undeniably phallic rock structures. (Site $4, tent rental w/site $7, caravan $9; non-resident pool use $2.50.)

Food and Entertainment The **Mehmet Paşa,** in the mansion of the former governor of Cappadocia, serves delicious main courses at good prices. Eat on the terrace (great views) or in the historic governor's visitors' rooms. The room on the right is the *Salemlik,* or men's room, where affairs of state were discussed. On the left is the *Haremlik,* or women's room, where the wall paintings depict flowers, pots, and washing utensils. Take the first right on the road to the mosque, then go left. You can look at the rooms for free even if you don't eat here. (*Köfte* with rice $2.50; spicy Turkish soup with herbs $1.25.) The **Orient** (tel. 271 1346), opposite the Yüksel Motel, will entertain your appetite for $4-6 per main course, including vegetarian dishes; decent *saç tava* $4. Typical rock valley breakfast items include pancakes with syrup, French toast, yogurt with honey ($1.25), and *menemen,* a Turkish classic (a loose, two-egg omelette of tomatoes, peppers, and spices—only $1.75). The **Rock Valley Pension** has a decent restaurant (full meal $5).

Sights The **Rose Valley,** which runs from Göreme to Çavuşin (4km away), makes for a wonderful hike through eerie landscapes of fairy chimneys and bizarre multi-colored rock formations. Tour groups don't come here; you'll have the place to yourself. It is possible to spend a day or more peeking into its man-made caves and rock churches, seeking more wonderful vistas and views. From Göreme, take the first left on the road to the Open-Air Museum; walk for roughly 5min., then go right. You'll be rewarded at this point with your first magnificent vista. Descend into the valley from here. There are several paths through it, but you'll certainly wander off them and get lost from time to time. Eventually you'll end up in the village of **Çavuşin;** the Avanos-Nevşehir bus (every ½hr.) or the Avanos-Zelve-Göreme-Ürgüp minibus (hourly; both June-Sept. only; 50¢) will take you back to Göreme up until 6pm; after that, a taxi from Çavuşin costs roughly $4. The sun is in the best position for photos in the mid- to late afternoon. You could also take a bus to Çavuşin and walk back to Göreme. From the main road's bus stop, walk into Çavuşin past the town square and take the right-hand fork, which leads to the valley's main path; be sure to leave this path from time to time and head deeper into the valley.

In town, notice the large fairy chimney with the Turkish flag on top, between the bus station and the huge carpet emporium on the mosque road. It is believed to have been used as a **Roman burial ground.** The most impressive concentration of sights in the region is at the **Open-Air Museum,** 1km out of Göreme on the Ürgüp road. The churches here are carved into caves and fairy chimneys. The walls were originally covered in frescoes; you can still see their remnants. The churches are the legacy of Cappadocian Christianity under the Byzantine Empire. In the 4th century, St. Basil founded one of the first Christian monasteries here, setting down religious tenets that greatly influenced the teachings of St. Benedict and subsequently the Western monastic movement. The monks of Cappadocia built most of the churches in Göreme between the 4th and 10th centuries, and inhabited the area until the formation of the modern Turkish Republic, when all Anatolian Greeks were relocated in exchange for the Turks living in Greece. The church in the hill before the main entrance to the museum is known as **Tokalı Kilise,** which means Church of the Buckle. Inside the museum are five churches: **Sandal** (Sandal Church), **Yılanlı** (Church of the Serpents), **Barbara, Elmalı** (Church of the Apple, currently closed), and **Karanlık** (the Dark Church, closed for renovations for the last 12 years). Be sure to visit Sandal, and Elmalı if they are open; both contain superb frescoes. (Museum ticket sales open April-Oct. daily 8am-7pm; once in the site you can wander until 1hr. before sunset; admission $3, students $1.50.) The former **residence of the Paşa**

of Göreme has been opened to the public and its frescoed walls and ceilings restored to their 19th-century splendor.

Guided tours of Cappadocia's major sites are available from several agencies in town. Depending on whether they include museum fees, tours are $15-30, and are excellent if you want to see a lot quickly. Although the agencies have a price agreement, they often undercut one another, and all give student discounts of roughly 20%. The most expensive tours are not necessarily the best. Most tours do the loop of Göreme, Üçhisar, Pigeon Valley, Derinkuyu, Ihlara, Ağrıkarahan, Kervansaray, Göreme. Some go off the main road between Derinkuyu and Ihlara to take in **Güzelyurt** (well worth a visit) and the **Crater Lake**—a volcanic crater filled with water.

■ NEAR GÖREME

ÇAVUŞIN

The road north from Göreme to Avanos leads past Çavuşin, known for the ancient hilltop **Church of St. John the Baptist** (free admission), formerly a regional pilgrimage site. Its origin is unknown, but it is believed to date from early Christian times. The section to your left as you face the altar contains tombs. Don't walk right to the edge here to see the view; it's unsafe. To reach the church, take the Göreme-Avanos **bus** or minibus and get off at Çavuşin; it's clearly marked. Walk into town past the main square, and take the left fork. Go left and up the hill after the Walnut Restaurant, keeping left at forks; the church is at the end of the path. This part of Çavuşin is kind of bizarre; lots of empty, brown, well-preserved Greek mansions create a post-nuclear holocaust effect. The Çavuşin Church, on the main road beside the turn-off to the village (look for the steps leading up to the rock face) has some well-preserved frescoes. (Open daily 8am-7pm; admission $1.25.)

AVANOS

The potters of Avanos have been throwing the red, iron-rich Cappadocian clay since time began. There are roughly a hundred workshops around the area, all with similar prices. There is everything here from high art to American kitsch (there's more of the latter). Avanos itself is a pleasant, European-style town; its main square contains several pleasant cafés. Above the square are whitewashed Greek buildings—it looks like a village on a Greek island. French is widely spoken in Avanos, and restaurant and pension signs are mainly in French. The **Kızılırmak** (Red River), Turkey's largest, flows through the town. It is from here that the potters take the red clay for their work. At times, the river turns a deep red color. There is a wooden footbridge, below the square and beside the mosque, which vibrates as you cross it.

Buses from Göreme run to Avanos every ½hr., (Mon.-Fri. 7am-6pm, Sat. 7am-5pm.) They leave across the road from the Göreme PTT a quarter to and a quarter past the hour (25¢). During high season you can also take the Ürgüp-Göreme-Zelve-Avanos minibus. Get off at the first stop in Avanos which contains the **tourist office.** Walk in the direction of continuation of the bus; across the bridge, turn right; you're now on the main street; the square is 250m farther. Just past the square, on the right, is the **PTT.** If you turn left at the bridge, you'll shortly come upon the town **hamam**—the words "Alaadin Hamam" proclaim its existence in Las Vegas neon.

■■■ ÜRGÜP

In Ürgüp, pretty Greek houses coagulate around bizarre rock formations. Its atmosphere is as different from Göreme as possible. Sophisticated, and West European, it has half a dozen ATMs, international car rental agencies, and even a Benetton.

Orientation and Practical Information The Ürgüp **tourist office** (tel. 341 4059), is on Kayseri Cad. Inside the garden, it provides maps of the region, extensive bus schedules, and helps arrange tours. (Open daily 8:30am-8pm or later,

Oct.-March Mon.-Fri. 8am-5pm.) Next door is the town's **museum** (open April-Oct. daily 8:30am-6pm; admission $2.50, students $1.25). From the bus station, go right, then follow the signs. **Telephone Code:** 384.

Accommodations To get to most accommodations, go left from the bus station, and walk about 20m or so to the main square. Our directions all originate from the Atatürk statue. 150m up the road to the right of, and behind, the Atatürk statue, sits the **Born Hotel** (tel. 341 4756). One of the cheapest places in town, it is a pleasant, basic little pension with ancient wooden staircases and atmospheric rooms. (Singles $4.75, doubles $9.50; breakfast $1.75.) **Pension Sun** (tel. 341 4493), directly behind the Atatürk statue, manages to contain a large cave (cave rooms available). The views of Ürgüp from the terrace are unbeatable. If you ask in the morning, the family will prepare you a delicious Turkish dinner ($3.50). (Rooms $8-12 per person.) **Hotel Asia Minor** (tel. 341 4645), the beautiful Greek mansion with reproductions of rock-church frescoes on the lobby walls, is located 75m up the road to the left, behind the Atatürk statue. Beautiful Greek mansion with reproductions of rock-church frescoes on the lobby walls. Every room is different—some are quite ornate, others plain. Some very small rooms are available; they may give a $1 per person discount on these. (Singles $9.50, doubles w/bath $16.25.) Yet another typical Ürgüp Greek mansion is the **Türkerler Otel** (341 3354). This one has a swimming pool in front, which actually detracts from its appearance. ($7 per person.) **Camping** is also available here (person and tent $3.50, caravan $6).

Food and Entertainment Stuffed in the courtyard of an antique inn, the **Sofa Restaurant** serves delicious Turkish fare. *Saç tava* is a Cappadocian specialty—chopped lamb, tomato, and onion served on a sizzling hot plate, with a flame blazing underneath—and this place serves an excellent version of it ($5). Or try ***kiremit kebap,*** which is unique to Ürgüp—diced lamb with onion, tomato, mushroom, and cheese baked in a clay bowl which retains all the lamb juices ($5).

Cappadocia is a major wine-producing region; the industry is centered around Ürgüp. In town, the renowned **Turasan winery,** 100m past the Hotel Hanedan, offers free tours and tasting. For a group of 5 or more, most travel agencies in town will arrange an impromptu tour for roughly $10 per person. Several specialist wine shops around the main square offer free tastings of a variety of Cappadocian wines.

ORTAHİSAR

The village of Ortahisar coagulates around a tall castle hewn from volcanic rock. From the top of the 50m fortress, there's a tremendous view of rock formations and river valleys. (Open daily 8am-sundown; admission 30¢, students 15¢.) Hike around the area south of Ortahisar to see scores of abandoned rock dwellings and rock churches, the best of which have 10th- and 11th-century frescoes, "modern" religious art by Cappadocian standards. Buses leave Ürgüp hourly, 8am-5pm (35¢).

NEVŞEHİR

Although Nevşehir is not especially interesting, it remains the region's transportation hub. Don't stay here if you have time to go on to Göreme or Ürgüp, which have nearly as many bus connections; Nevşehir is dusty and noisy and lacks the uniqueness of other locations in the valley.

There is one main street in Nevşehir, **Atatürk Bulvarı.** To get here from the bus station, while standing in the main (upper level) bus/car park, with the terminal at your back, you'll see **Lale Caddesi** running uphill on your right. Walk up Lale Cad. for roughly 10min. until you reach Atatürk Blv. If you turn left at the intersection, you'll see the tourist office, and beside it, the **state hospital.** The staff at the **tourist office** (tel. 213 3659), at the intersection of Atatürk Blv. and Lale Cad., has maps and brochures. (Open Mon.-Fri. 8am-5:30pm, Sat.-Sun. 9:30am-5:30pm; off-season Mon.-Fri. 8am-5pm, Sat.-Sun. 9:30am-5pm; may close as early as 3pm if there are few tourists.) *Dolmuş* leave from outside the tourist office for most parts of Cappadocia;

they also stop at the main station (every ½hr., 7am-7pm, off-season 7am-5pm). Atatürk Blv. has everything you need: restaurants, shops, a Cappadocian tea garden, several **ATMs,** and a 24-hr. **PTT. Telephone Code:** 384.

KAYMAKLI AND DERİNKUYU

In the villages of Kaymaklı and Derinkuyu, inauspicious passages lead to two of Cappadocia's most spectacular sites. Two stark but well-preserved **underground cities,** thought to be more than 3000 years old, lurk beneath the ground in an endless warren of tunnels, rooms, stairwells, and hallways. Throughout centuries of political uncertainty, Christians fled from their villages to the underground cities at times of imminent attack. It is estimated that five to ten thousand people lived here, for up to 6 months at a time. Strict, military-style discipline was imposed and some pillars have holes drilled at the top, for chaining transgressors due for torture. It was forbidden for anyone to leave—for any reason—while the cities were occupied, lest their departure give away the location. Strangely enough, no toilets have been found in Derinkuyu, though some have been found at Kaymaklı.

The first levels of these cities are believed to have been built by the Hittites c. 2000 BC, either for storage or to escape attack from enemies. Most of the cities were constructed by Christians between 1300 and 1800 years ago. The size and complexity of Kaymaklı—five levels of elaborate passages burrowing down 35m—are mind-boggling, yet Derinkuyu is almost twice as large, with a depth of 120m and 5-6km long escape tunnels (now blocked). One of the Derinkuyu passages is even believed to lead back to Kaymaklı. The cities are south of Nevşehir, on the road to Niğde; Kaymaklı is 20km away, Derinkuyu 29km. Derinkuyu, with eight levels excavated so far, is slightly more impressive and offers sizable public rooms and halls, good lighting, and relatively easy access, but you might find the dark, narrow, often unmarked passages of Kaymaklı even more enthralling. In both cities, the tunnels were built low and tortuous to hamper the progress of invaders. Though marked with arrows, the tunnels form a potentially confounding maze, and if you explore extensively you'll almost certainly get lost. Red arrows lead down, blue arrows up. Both cities have unexplored tunnels which are out of bounds, and thus tempting, but be careful—some contain traps (such as sudden drops) to deter potential invaders. Don't wander too far off the beaten track. *Dolmuş* run to Nevşehir every ½hr. ($2; for a **bus** schedule see p. 533.) Both sites are open daily 8:30am-7pm, in off-season until 5pm. Admission costs $2.50, students $1.25. As with all state museums, a FIYTO card will get you in free. Bring a sweater; the deeper tunnels can be dank.

■■■ IHLARA

The Ihlara Valley, provider of *liras* to Aksaray, is a true garden paradise hidden in a narrow gorge that the Melendiz River cuts through the treeless Cappadocian plateau. You won't even imagine it's there until you literally come up to the edge. For centuries thousands of Greek Christians found this valley an agreeable refuge for sedentary life while their nomadic Turkish neighbors grazed their flocks over the grassy plains above. Although the valley is still somewhat off the beaten track, it becomes more mainstream every year. Eight years ago there were no pensions and no public transport. Now there are half-dozen pensions and a cliffside restaurant.

GETTING THERE

Getting to Ihlara independently is relatively painless; 3 buses per day run to **Aksaray.** The eccentric bus schedule, however, means that it can't be hiked in a daytrip, or even with a single overnight in Ihlara; a two-night stay is necessary. Buses depart Mon.-Sat. from Aksaray's bus station at 11am, 3 and 5:30pm, and arrive the main square of Ihlara village one hour later. In the other direction, buses depart Ihlara at 7 and 7:30am, and 1pm (50¢ each way). Your best option, therefore, is to take the 3 or 5:30pm bus from Aksaray, settle into your pension and have a meal, hike the valley the next day, and leave the following morning. Five daily minibuses connect

Aksaray to Nevşehir's bus station (1hr., $2). You can also charter a private *dolmuş* in Göreme's station for $35 to take you to Ihlara and back (8 or 10 passengers). Some of Ihlara's hotels also provide this service for the same price.

On a bus from Aksaray, 10km south from the last turn-off to Ihlara, you'll pass the town of **Selime** beside huge rock cones similar to those at Göreme, pockmarked with the windows and doors of former troglodyte habitations. Selime marks the north end of the Ihlara Valley; hikers sometimes enter here, or at the village of **Yaprakhisar,** around a bend in the road. Ten minutes later, the bus will stop to let passengers off at the main handful of Ihlara's pensions, then continue 1km downhill to the main square of the village.

With the exception of the Star Motel, all pensions reside roughly 1km uphill from the square; the bus stops there before heading down to the square. Except for the excellent restaurant (full lunch $3.50) at the official entrance to the gorge, little food is served outside the pensions. **Postal Code:** 68570; **Telephone Code:** 382.

ACCOMMODATIONS

All accommodations in Ihlara charge per person, not per room. The Akar and Famille pensions offer private *dolmuş* service from Aksaray and will run you to Selime in the morning, from which you can hike through the valley to Ihlara village.

Star Motel (tel. 453 7429). Conveniently located on the main square and beside the river. Formerly the River View Hotel. Clean and basic, some rooms have balconies overlooking the fast-moving river, whose sound will lull you to sleep at night and greet you the next morning. $6 per person.

Pansion Akar (tel. 453 7018), has clean, comfortable rooms with balconies and private baths; those at the back have views of Mt. Hasan. $7 per person.

Pansion Anatolia is more basic, but clean. Its rooms are large—some singles have balconies. $6 per person.

Pension Famille, where French is spoken rather than English, offers comfortable rooms in a family home. $6 per person.

HIKING THE VALLEY

The Ihlara Valley properly consists of 14km of the north-south course of the Melendiz River, from Selime to Ihlara village. Most people visit the valley on guided tours from Göreme or Ürgüp; these take tourists on a walk from its "official entrance," near Ihlara's pension cluster, to **Belisırma,** 3km north, where there's a restaurant and a **campsite.** What makes the Ihlara entrance "official" is the admission fee ($2.50, students $1.25), which is only charged to people entering at that point. In reality you have lots of flexibility in visiting the valley. Walking itineraries of 7, 10, and 14km along the valley floor are also easily planned. Hikers often explore the valley by taking a *dolmuş* shuttle to Yaprakhisar or Selime and following the river course 7 or 10km, respectively, south back to the official valley entrance. The path, which is flat and well-worn for most of the way, involves a few scrambles among the boulders north of Belisırma. The full 14km route also begins in Selime but continues 3-4km past the official entrance, looping around to where the valley ends and Ihlara village begins. To do this hike in the opposite direction, you can enter the valley near Ihlara village. Take the path which runs beside the Anatolia Pension; enter beside a waterfall. (Entry free; ticket office is under construction.)

If walking from Selime, take the 7 or 7:30am bus from Ihlara to Aksaray and get off at Selime. Ask the locals to point you to the valley entrance (*vadi girişi*). Walk back at your leisure. The views are best in this, the downstream, direction. In the other direction, try to time your arrival in Selime to catch the 5:30pm Aksaray-Ihlara bus (be in Selime by 6pm). If you miss it, you can stay the night in Selime.

The advantage of the **official valley entrance** (unmarked from below) is that it allows tourists to see the highlights of the valley without a hike. There, hundreds of steps painstakingly built up the side of the valley wall both provide peerless views and lead directly to the richer churches (signposted, always open, and free of charge). To reach the official entrance from Ihlara's main square, go up the hill towards Aksaray for roughly 1km and take the first main intersection to your right (it's signposted *Ihlara Valley*). From there it's another 2km to the entrance, a conspicuously hotel-like building on your left. Now, like the tour groups, you can buy your ticket, go down the steps, turn left, and walk 3km to get to Belisırma. The walk will take you through beautiful, unspoiled scenery and several frescoed rock churches. You may even spy children spearfishing, or villagers herding livestock. Walking from Ihlara to Belisırma, most of the churches will be to your left.

The popular **Sümbüllü** and **Ağaçaltı Churches** flank the official entrance stairs at the valley floor. The Sümbüllü is noteworthy for its rock facade and five deep, arched bays separated by pillars. Spectacular blue and white angels ring the Christ figure on the well-preserved dome of the Ağaçaltı. Another 30m south (to the right after descending the entrance stairs, away from Belisırma) past the Ağaçaltı lies the **Pürenliseki Church,** whose faded walls contain the many martyrs of Sivas. The **Kokar Church,** 70m farther along, celebrates biblical stories with colorful frescoes and ornate, geometrical ceiling crosses. Also worth seeing is the **Yılanlı Church** (Church of the Serpent), which gets its name from a display of Satan's serpents. To reach it, backtrack from the Kokar to the steps at the official valley entrance and cross the wooden bridge. The church lies 100m to your left, up the concrete steps. Inside you'll also find saintly arches framing the geometrically decorated altar.

■ AKSARAY

The main reason to visit Aksaray is to catch public transport on to Ihlara. While it's not a destination in its own right, it is a pleasant place to spend a couple of hours.

Orientation and Practical Information For orientation's sake, you're lucky to be dropped off at the **bus station** in town. *Dolmuş* from Nevşehir drop you there, but intercity Nevşehir-Konya buses instead deposit you at a Mobil station on the ring road, 2½km out from the center. Taxis ($1.50) are hassle-free. Ask someone to point the way to the *merkez* (town center); after 500m you should pass soccer fields on your left. From the bus station, take the exit beside the Pension Çakmak, turn left, and follow the main road 20m to the **main square,** which contains several attractive government buildings and a statue of Atatürk. To reach the tourist office from this square, take the first left—pass the mosque on your left—and walk down this shopping street until it forks. In front of you you'll see an İmar Bankası. Above it, to the left, is a tiny green sign which reads "Tourist Office." Enter by a side door, to the left of and past the bank; the tourist office is on the second floor. You'll be ushered into the Director of Tourism's office, as only he speaks English.

Accommodations The **Aksaray Pansion** (tel. 212 4133) offers clean, large, waterless rooms. Although they vary in size and ambience (some in front have balconies), all cost the same. (Singles $6, doubles $10.50, triples $14, quads $18.75.) A couple of doors down is the **Hitit Pansion** (tel. 213 1996), where shoes come off at the door and Turkish carpets and couches decorate the lounge. Waterless rooms cost the same as at the Aksaray. From the bus station, exit by the Pension Çakmak, cross the road, and continue down the road opposite; this pair of *pansiyon* are on the first left. There is a comfortable one-star hotel on the main square, **Yuvam Otel** (tel. 213 2875). (Singles $11.75, doubles $14, 2-room suites $18.75.)

Food Aksaray is not one of Turkey's culinary capitals. One of your best bets is the **Çeşme Lokantası.** With the tourist office and bank at your back, take the right fork; it's 25m down this street, on the right. (Main courses $1.25-2.25.)

Eastern Turkey

Traces of Eastern Turkey's rich past, which has witnessed the rise and fall of empires, are strewn across its plush countryside: the bewitching Armenian churches at Akdamar and Ani, the transfixing scenery of Kars and Hakkâri, the magical waters of Lake Van, the bizarre heads at Nemrut Dağı, and the exquisite palace at Doğubeyazıt, all make spending time in this region worthwhile. Beyond these majestic relics, the beauty of this region lies in the otherworldly nature of the countryside. The starkly flat, deep green pastures extend for miles, flung open to the pale sky, an effect heightened by the mountains that rise precipitously on each side.

Weather here fluctuates between climatic extremes. The lower cities—Gaziantep, Urfa, Diyarbakır, and Mardi—are hot as *cehennem* in summer: daytime temperatures often rise above 43°C (110°F). Conversely, in winter deep snows periodically cut off much of the mountainous east end of Turkey. You are more likely to find people who speak German than English in eastern Turkey, but most of the tourist offices have staff members who can speak some English. Just about every town large enough to stop in has a bank, but you should carry dollars and small denominations of traveler's checks just in case. Some caveats are in order if you decide to travel here. Locals are truly friendly, but women travelers are frequently hassled by local males. Don't get discouraged—try to ignore amorous stares and other indignities. The farther east you travel, the slower the pace, and the more intangibly distant the industrial age. You'll find prices lower here, but tourist amenities such as information offices are scarce, and travel is more difficult than in the west. Travel in the east is more of an adventure than that in the Turkey's cosmopolitan coastal areas.

Less-than-sanitary restaurants and hotels can pose a major problem in the more remote parts of eastern Turkey. Avoid the cheapest places, and don't eat dishes made with ground meat. Lemon juice is not especially reliable as a disinfectant, and *eşki,* a potion concocted by some restaurants, is useless. If you want to avoid meat altogether, ask for dishes which are *et yok* (without meat). Transportation can also pose difficulties. If you get off a bus between two stops, it might be impossible to find another one later.

Since August 1984, the PKK (Kurdish Worker's Party), a Marxist guerilla organization, has been fighting for an independent Kurdish state. The conflict is ongoing; and though violence is rarely directed against tourists, bombs and fighting do pose a threat. For this reason *Let's Go* does not recommend travel into some parts of eastern Turkey: PKK activity is concentrated in the southeast corner of the country, roughly the region east of Urfa and Nemrut Dağı and south of Erzurum and Kars. If you travel in this area, exercise extreme caution. Try to travel by large buses and by train, and only during daylight hours. Do not enter this area if your travel documents identify you as a a member of the military or employed by a government agency.

■■■ KÂHTA

Most visitors to Kâhta see it only as a convenient base from which to visit Nemrut Dağı, ruins of the Commagene empire at Mt. Nemrod. Any closer limits your PTT access; any farther means waking up before 2am to avoid missing the mountain sunrise at 5. Kâhta is typical of the southeast in its vast surrounding fields of grain and tobacco, profusion of traditional men in şalvar (low-crotch baggy trousers), saddle-seat coffeehouses, and scarcity of *döner kebap* and ATM machines. There is a fresh-water lake, a byproduct of the huge Atatürk Dam on the Euphrates between Adıyaman and Urfa. During the day, *dolmuş* pass every 15min. along Mustafa Kemal Cad., the main street, to reach the lake which is slowly being developed with *lokanta* and tea gardens. The lake lies 5km east of town across the former Diyarbakır road, home to one of Turkey's loneliest gas stations.

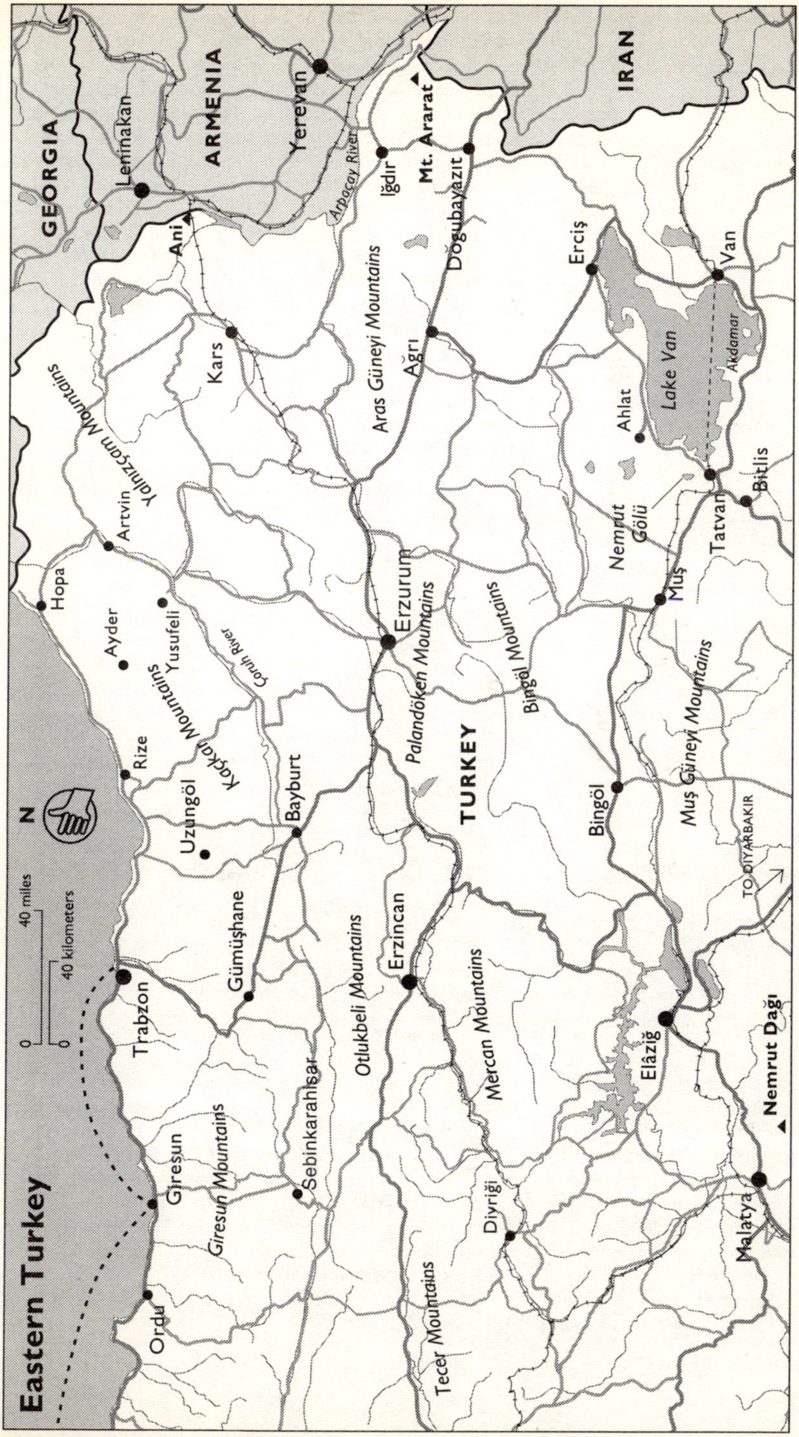
Eastern Turkey
0 40 miles
0 40 kilometers
N
GEORGIA
ARMENIA
IRAN
TURKEY
Leninakan
Yerevan
Arpaçay River
Iğdır
Mt. Ararat
Doğubayazıt
Ani
Kars
Aras Güneyi Mountains
Ağrı
Erciş
Van
Lake Van
Akdamar
Ahlat
Bitlis
Tatvan
Nemrut Gölü
Muş
Muş Güneyi Mountains
Yalnızçam Mountains
Artvin
Hopa
Ayder
Yusufeli
Çoruh River
Kaçkar Mountains
Rize
Uzungöl
Bayburt
Erzurum
Palandöken Mountains
Bingöl Mountains
Bingöl
TO DIYARBAKIR
Trabzon
Gümüşhane
Erzincan
Otlukbeli Mountains
Mercan Mountains
Elâzığ
Nemrut Dağı
Giresun
Giresun Mountains
Sebinkarahisar
Ordu
Divriği
Tecer Mountains
Malatya

Orientation and Practical Information Most major cities have at least one bus per day servicing Kâhta. There was a time when, upon disembarking from your bus in Kâhta, you would be greeted by a slick posse of local drivers clamoring to get you onto buses for Mt. Nemrod. Although hustling has subsided somewhat, be prepared to face hard-sell *dolmuş* drivers. Don't be bullied into taking a tour you don't want, and be skeptical when someone tells you that bus service doesn't exist to a certain town. The **tourist office** is receptive to complaints about tourist harassment, and can verify fishy info. They also publish a list of price ceilings for hotels and tours of the mountain. To get there, zero in on M. Kemal Cad., which runs east-west through the center of town. The tourist office is set back from the corner of M. Kemal Cad. and the road to Mt. Nemrod. For the **PTT,** turn right just before the M. Kemal Cad. fruit stands, pass a white minaret on your right, continue for the better part of 1km to reach the PTT sign, and take a final right downhill for 100m. Kâhta's 3 **banks,** which cash traveler's checks at similar rates, lie in the vicinity of the PTT. (On weekends in high season, the Marc O'Polo clothing shop across from the tourist office occasionally cashes traveler's checks.) One block east of the tourist office is Kâhta's **bus station**, outside of which sits a column of *dolmuş*. The Kâhta-based **Gülaras** bus company services K. Maraş (3hr.), Kayseri (8hr.), Ankara (11½hr.), and İstanbul (19hr.). Their competitor, **Adıyaman Ünal,** sends buses daily from Adıyaman to Diyarbakır (4hr.), Kayseri (7hr.), Mersin (12hr.), Samsun (13hr.), Antalya (8hr.), İzmir (18hr.), İstanbul (18hr.); and Trabzon (19hr.). Every 20min. 6am-6:30pm *dolmuş* leave for Urfa (1½hr.) from across the street from Adıyaman's bus terminal. Alternatively, despite what you may be told, several daily *dolmuş* go directly from Kâhta to Urfa. **Postal Code:** 02400; **Telephone Code:** 416.

Accommodations Rooms in Kâhta are clustered around the west end of M. Kemal Cad. **Nemrut Tur Motel** (tel. 725 6880), on M. Kemal Cad. at the entrance to town (Adiyaman side) is a pricer option. Budget travelers may opt for **Mezopotamya Pansion** (tel. 725 5112). A livelier alternative is **Kommagene Pansion** (tel. 715 1092); walk 250m towards the town center and take the first left. Campers will appreciate the grassy space and facilities of **Zeus Camping** (tel. 725 5695), next to Mezopotamya Pansion. Most establishments in Kâhta accept tourists from April-Sept., a few March-Nov. On the mountain, **Karadut Village** offers fields for camping. Non-campers can stay on the mountain at **Karadut Motel,** 12km from the summit.

■■■ NEMRUT DAĞI (MT. NEMROD)

Through the summer of 1990, one thousand sightseers per day flocked to this isolated mountain to marvel at the massive stone heads of Antiochus, Apollo, Hercules, and Zeus that toppled from the summit burial mound, which dates from before 70 AD. Three years later, only 130 visitors made the trip, leaving a select few to admire "the eighth wonder of the ancient world."

This wonder is the ruined burial monument erected by Antiochus I, ruler of the ancient kingdom of Commagene, in his own honor. The Commagene regime was apparently a splinter of the Seleucids of Antioch, and later was incorporated into the Roman Empire. Antiochus I, who ascended to the throne in 63 BC, was ruler of Commagene before the annexation, and it is only because of him that Commagene has any renown as an independent kingdom. He had himself and his family interred under colossal burial mounds on Mt. Nimrod, and the site was crowned with monumental statues representing the members of the Roman pantheon and one of Antiochus himself. The huge burial mounds on the summit and the immense stone likenesses of Antiochus and various gods are extraordinary not just in their sheer grandeur but in the awesome conceit that made them possible. The western Mt. Nemrut is—with the possible exception of the Great Pyramid at Giza—the greatest material testament to a single ego the world will ever see.

Orientation and Practical Information Tourist agencies in both Kâhta and Adıyaman offer several different package excursions for visiting Nemrut Dağı and other nearby sites. The most important variable is the time you arrive at Nemrut Dağı itself. For some, the stunning sunrise over the eastern mountains justifies waking up at 2am, while others are satisfied with catching the sunset from Mt. Nemrut, which allows you to return to Kâhta or Adıyaman at 10pm. Those who thrive on moderation can miss both. Regardless of when you go, however, take along a jacket and some form of headwear; mountains winds can chill you and even burn ears and noses. Your other major decision is whether to include Arsameia, the ancient Commagene capital and Karakuş, site of Antiochus' wife's burial mound in your itinerary, or to take in only Antiochus' monument. **Tours** are available by either taxi or minibus. A full schedule of prices and options is available from the tourist offices in Kâhta and Adıyaman. Tour prices run $10-25 per person. Longer tours usually go to Nemrut Dağı's summit first, and then to the other sights. This order is unfortunate because Arsameia and Karakuş are an anticlimactic following the excess of Nemrut Dağı. The sunset tour, which ends at Nemrut Dağı, may be preferable.

Sights Departing from Kâhta, the first relic of the Commagene kingdom that one encounters is the burial mound (*tumulus*) at **Karakuş.** One of the few facts known about Antiochus' legacy is that his wife and sister are buried under this mound; possibly other women of royal blood lie here as well. Next to the tumulus are columns with carved animal reliefs, including one of a black eagle that gives the site its name (*karakuş* is Turkish for "black bird"). The larger tours stop at the **Roman Bridge,** also known as the Cenderes Bridge, completed in 211 BC and still in use.

Arsameia, the next stop on the way to Nemrut Dağı, was founded by Mithridates I, the first Commagene king. There you can see the good-as-new, 5m-high relief depicting King Mithridates shaking hands with an anatomically correct Hercules, and a tablet bearing a Greek inscription that will be variously translated for you by different guides. (One local theory: the tablet advises visitors to Mithridates' burial site to wash before approaching.) The site also includes several caves, which house a cistern, more of Mithridates' remains. There is also a very impressive tunnel, which descends into the bowels of the earth, connecting with a fortress on a neighboring mountain. You can explore roughly 300m in before hitting a blockade. (Site admission $1, students 50¢).

Nemrut Dağı itself is what you've come for. As you visited Karakuş and Arsameia you were climbing the mountain itself; a final 15-min. hike uphill from the parking lot brings you to the summit, location of Antiochus' tumulus and its attendant statuary. (Admission to site $3, students $1.50; FIYTO 60¢ park entry fee.) There is a little café at the carpark with tea, soft drinks, souvenirs and postcards. Two terraces flank the summit, known as the East and West Terraces; the great stone heads you see here originally sat atop colossal bodies, but the last head tumbled from its body after a 1957 earthquake. The colossi weigh up to 6000kg; the heads easily stand taller than a man. Some have been identified as representations of the gods Zeus, Apollo, and Tyche, the hero/demi-god Hercules, and totem-figures of a lion and an eagle. In addition to these, there is a statue of Antiochus himself, an implicit claim to godhead that is hardly surprising given the grandiose context of the entire monument. There are more and better-preserved stone heads and reliefs on the Western Terrace. A path of crushed stone connects the two terraces.

■■■ URFA (ŞANLIURFA)

Urfa, one of the world's oldest cities, has seen great civilizations come and go for 7000 years. It has been called Uras by the Hittites, Ruhua by the Assyrians, Edessa by the Greeks, Al-Refa by the Arabs, but it is Turkish Urfa that will greet you today. Abgar Ukoma, King of Osrohene (which existed in the region from 132 BC-242 AD), became one of the first rulers in the ancient Near East to accept Chrisitianity. He invited Jesus to speak in Urfa, who was unable to come but sent a letter (no doubt written by an intern) in which he blessed the city. Since then, Urfa has been known as the "Blessed City" by Christians and the "City of Prophets" by Muslims.

The modern city nourishes the peaceful lives of three peoples—Turks, Arabs, and Kurds—in equal proportions. In the covered bazaar, master craftsmen beat sheet copper into burnished ornamental trays, sooty child apprentices weld stovepipes, and backgammon players sit on saddle-seats as they sip their tea. In contrast to this traditional way of life, the high-tech wonder of the Atatürk Dam, which controls the flow of the Euphrates, has been constructed near Urfa; it is the world's fourth largest dam. In 1986, the city fathers changed the town's name to Şanlıurfa (Glorious Urfa), to commemorate its role in the Turkey's 1921 War of Independence. This piece of one-upmanship put Urfa on a par with its neighbors Antep and Maraş, which earlier had been renamed Gaziantep (Heroic Antep) and Kahramanmaraş (Heroic Maraş). Locals scorn the changes, however, and still use the old names.

Orientation and Practical Information The main street is Atatürk Cad., which runs roughly north to south. Just off it, at the midpoint is the **tourist office,** 3 Asfalt Yol (tel. 215 7610; open Mon.-Fri. 8am-noon and 1:30-5:30pm), which supplies maps. At the street's south end, you'll find the bazaar (open Mon.-Sat. during daylight hours). Continue past it to the right to reach the major sights of Abraham's cave, Gölbaşı (fish ponds), and the fortress. At the north end is a traffic circle which marks the intersection of Atatürk Cad. with the highways to Mardin, Diyarbakir and Gaziantep. Along Atatürk Cad. you'll find hotels, restaurants and services (including ATMs).**THY** (tel. 215 3344) flies to Ankara, Istanbul, and Izmir. THY offices are on Atatürk Cad., across the road from the tourist office. Inquire about the airport bus service. The 24-hr. **PTT** (tel. 313 6600; special services open Mon.-Sat. 8am-noon and 1:30-5:30pm) is a 2-min. walk south of the tourist office. The local **hospital** (tel. 313 1220) is at the top of the hill after you turn west off Atatürk Cad. at the obelisk. **Postal Code:** 63200; **Telephone Code:** 414.

The bus station (*otogar*) is 1km from town. Take the main exit (on the left as you face the terminal), then take the first left (you'll see the fortress) and first left again. *Dolmuş* serve the station as do **taxis** (unmetered, establish price in advance).

From Atatürk Cad., city **buses** (15¢) and *dolmuş* (20¢) run all over town. Ten buses per day go to Biricik ($1.50), Siverek ($1.50), Gaziantep (2hr., $2.50), and Adana (5hr., $4.50). Others service K. Maraş (3 per day, 3½hr., $3), Diyarbakır (3 per day, 2½hr., $3), Tarsus (8 per day, $5), Mardin (4 per day, 2hr., $3), Antalya (3 per day, 14hr., $13), Antakya (1 per day, 6hr., $6.50), Ankara (6 per day, 12hr., $12), İstanbul (5 per day, 18hr., $17), İzmir (5 per day, 17hr., $16), Kars (2 per day, $17), Kayseri (2 per day, $8), Konya (8 per day, 14hr., $12), Sivas (3 per day, $8), Trabzon (1 per day, $17), and Van (3 per day, 10hr., $10). Minibuses bound for Adıyaman (hourly 7am-7pm, $2) leave from an alley near the Abraham complex, and pass within 1km of **Atatürk Barajı,** the dam. Bus prices were due to double at the end of summer 1995; exchange rates tend to smooth out differences, but expect the dollar prices to rise by as much as 50%.

Accommodations **Hotel Altay** (tel. 215 1917) is across from the tourist office; take a right onto Atatürk just past the PTT and walk roughly 500m. It's on your left. Hotel Altay is the cleanest and most pleasant of this town's budget options. Its rooms feature fans, towels, and a basin. Toilets down the hall, come in your choice of Eastern or Western. (Singles $7, w/shower $8.25; doubles $10.50, w/shower $12.75.) Get a room with a shower, as there is no public shower. Very friendly staff, some of whom speak excellent English. **Lala Oteli,** 11 Köprübaşı Kışla (tel. 313 1642), is cheaper and more basic than Altay. (Singles $4.75, w/shower $6; doubles $8.25, w/shower $9.25; triples $10.50.) Make a left onto Atatürk from the tourist office, then take your first left.

Food and Entertainment Urfa's specialties are *patlıcanlı kebap* (aubergine and meatball on a skewer) and *domatesli kebap* (meatball and tomato on a skewer). Usually both are served together for $2-3. You'll see them in *kebapçı* all over town. Urfa's finest dining is at **Urfa Sofrası** on the Mardin Rd., famous for its *kaburga* (lamb chops, served with rice $3.25). Even such staples as *mercimek çorbası* (lentil soup) are exceptionally delicious. As in most of Eastern Turkey, menus are in Turkish and little English is spoken. To get here, take a right at the Atatürk Cad. traffic circle; it's 250m away on the left, a 25-min. walk from the tourist office. Down by Gölbasi, **Göl Lokanta** serves *patlıcanlı* and *domatesli kebap* ($2.50 for the pair). This is also an excellent place to relax in the shade and sip *ayran* (60¢ per steel jug). Other decent restaurants can be found in the north half of Atatürk Cad. Try a bowl of the local ice cream, a thick, gummy mixture, at **Kilim Pastanesi,** 33 Atatürk Cad. (near the traffic circle, open daily 8am-midnight; 50¢ a serving). Also try the local sweet of *kadayıf,* here or in nearby **Gökçin Pastanesi.**

Sights There's at least a full day's worth of sightseeing to do in Urfa. **Abraham's** dim **cave,** the birthplace of the prophet, is beneath the fortress; enter the gate with the ornate Arabic calligraphy. While there, check out the mosque with detailed İznik tiles. At the nearby **Gölbaşı** (Lakeside), you'll find mosques, minarets, arches, parks and pools filled with sacred carp, descended from the time of Abraham. An upward gaze will reveal the dual **Corinthian columns** (242 BC) from which Nemrut shot firebrands at Abraham, as well as the 9th-century **citadel** (open daily 7am-10pm, winter hours 8am-5pm; admission $1.25), accessible by stone tunnel stairs in the hillside. The **archaeological museum** (tel. 313 1588; open daily 8:30am-noon and 1:30-5pm; admission $1.25, students 60¢) houses everything from reliefs to jewelry, and on the second floor you'll find Christian icons surviving from the **Ancient Church of the Twelve Apostles** (now the Fırfırlı Cami). As you face north, go left at the obelisk; the church will be 200m on right. Three kilometers south of the bazaar is **Eyyüp Peygamber,** which contains the cave where the prophet Job lived for seven years while his body was being consumed by worms. (Suggested donation $1; open daylight hours). Located in the mosque complex with the small sign *Hz. Eyyüp Peygamber Camii Dernek Başkanlığı*. Take an "Eyyübiye" *dolmuş* from Atatürk Cad., across the road from the tourist office (every 5min. or less, 20¢). The **Ulu Camii** (Great Mosque, donations appreciated) has a beautiful courtyard and Byzantine belltower (now a minaret); the interior of the mosque disappoints. The **Fine Arts Gallery** is more of an art school than a gallery, but deserves a brief visit because it is layed out like one of Urfa's Ottoman houses. One hallmark is the "bearded arch," which ripples upward to a sharp point, like an upside-down beard. (Open Mon.-Sat. 8am-noon and 1:30-5:30pm; July-Aug. Mon.-Fri.; admission free.) Be sure to wander around the medieval streets of Urfa, across Atatürk Cad. from the Ulu Camii. Step in here and you'll feel you've stepped back 1000 years or more; women in *chadors* and men in Kurdish dress walk its narrow, dusty streets.

Goodness, Gracious, Great Balls of Fire

The prophet Abraham was secretly born in a cave in Urfa at the time of King Nemrut's decree that all children should be put to death. Having escaped the wrath of Nemrut's decree, Abraham, now 10, was seized with monotheistic fervor and, in a fit of pre-pubescent rage, began smashing the city's pagan idols. Nemrut, upset with Abraham's tantrum, made a giant slingshot with the two pillars on the hill, from which he rained firebrands down on Abraham below. God, looking on, took pity on the unfortunate lad and called on nature to protect him: "O fire, be gentle to Abraham and keep him and the fuel safe and cool." A rose garden sprang up around Abraham, the fire became water, and the burning wood turned into fish in the ponds. The pillars, carp, and cave remain for tourists to this day. You can feed the sacred carp for 30¢ (no fishing even if you have a Messiah complex).

■■■ KARS

The poverty and homeliness of Kars, an industrial crossroads that weathers long, brutal winters and blistering summers each year, contrast sharply with the hauntingly ragged, fertile, yellow-green steppe that surrounds Kars in all directions. Sod-roofed hovels and pre-industrial cattle farmers dot the landscape within view of the highway that approaches the town. Because of nagging worries about Kurdish Workers Party (PKK) separatists, the military presence is particularly strong in this region; the army frequently stops buses to check travel documents and may even frisk men. None of this detracts, however, from Kars' old town charm. Horse-drawn carts drive alongside automobiles, and vendors shop their varied wares on irregularly paved streets. In the town center, a few anomalously stately 19th-century buildings are nearly submerged in the welter of smog and hastily built dwellings that came with industrial development. The fabulous Armenian ruins at **Anı,** 48km east of Kars, are the single (but excellent) reason to visit the town. Kars offers little spectacular in the way of food and entertainment; its own sights are limited to the museum and the castle, whose fortifications make a nice place for a picnic.

ORIENTATION AND PRACTICAL INFORMATION

South to north, Kars ranges rectilinearly from the railroad to the castle ridge. **Atatürk Caddesi** leads the way past classy shops north to the 274-year-old stone bridge at the foot of the castle. **Faik Bey Caddesi** also counts as a main street for the numerous cheap hotels, restaurants, and corner grocery stores that line its longer, east-west course. When you arrive at the **otogar** 4km east of town, it pays to wait for the big, light-blue and white municipal shuttle to the center (every 20min. 6am-5pm, 25¢); otherwise share a taxi (roughly $2.25, depending on the hotel).

Tourist Office: 239 Ordu Cad. (tel. 223 2300, -8452). South of where Ordu crosses Faik Bey Cad. Helpful staffers secure routine permissions, tickets, and taxi service for your excursion to Ani, and provide comprehensive color brochures on Kars. Open daily 8am-5:30pm, in winter Mon.-Fri. 8am-noon and 1:30-5:30pm.

PTT: Postal Code: 36100; **Telephone Code:** 474.

ATM: At the Akbank on the corner of Kazımpaşa Cad. uphill (west) from the Hotel Yılmaz. 24 hr. Banks did not cash traveler's checks in the summer of 1995.

Flights: THY flies once daily to Ankara at 11am ($67, students $50), and indirect service to İstanbul costs $89 (students $67). Make reservations at the ticket office, 815 Atatürk Cad. (tel. 223 1511; open daily 7:30am-8pm), from which a 90¢ airport bus leaves daily at 9:15am (a taxi costs $3.50).

Trains: The station lies on the south edge of town, roughly 1km east of the center. A bus leaves Kars each morning at 7am bound for Erzurum (5hr., $1.50), Erzincan (9hr., $2.75), Sivas (16hr., $4.50), Kayseri (20hr., $5.50), Ankara (31hr., $7.25), Eskişehir (36hr., $8.75), and İstanbul (40hr., $10). (Note that İstanbul is listed by its station name of "Haydarpaşa" in Anatolian train schedules.)

Buses: Pass partway along Faik Bey Cad. before heading northeast to the *dolmuş* lot. From the distant *otogar,* aged buses make cheap daily runs to Adana (18hr., $13.50), İzmir (24hr., $15.50), Aydın (26hr., $17.75), Hatay (24hr., $15.50), and Artvin (4hr., $5.50). More frequent buses go to Erzurum (hourly 8am-4pm, 3hr., $3.50), and Ankara (5 per day, 17hr., $11.25). Four daily buses run to Hopa (4½hr., $6.75), Rize (6hr., $7.75), Trabzon (7hr., $9), and İstanbul (40hr., $10).

ACCOMMODATIONS

Otel Temel, 4/A Kazımpaşa Cad. (tel. 222 1276), one block east and one block north of the Akbank. Frequented by Turks and travelers alike. Spacious tea salon for lounging on the first floor. All rooms are clean and carpeted, and have telephones, private baths w/Western-style toilets, closets, and good beds. Singles $5.50, doubles $10, triples $13.50.

Hotel Kervansaray, 204 Faik Bey Cad. (tel. 223 1990), is centrally located and in one of the safest parts of town. The light blue walls and spartan character of the place make it feel a little like an army hospital. Basic rooms include fresh sheets and comforters. Singles $4, w/bath $5; doubles $6.75, w/bath $7.50; triples $10, w/bath $11.

FOOD AND ENTERTAINMENT

Breakfast in Kars is a delight thanks to fresh local cheeses and honey. Party-colored tables and a cheerfully tacky decor characterize **Salon Sema Piknik,** 9 Faik Bey Cad. (tel. 223 2118, -7320), east of Atatürk Cad. (A la carte breakfast $1-2.50, depending on what you get; full meal $3; open daily 6am-10pm; no alcohol served.) The **Grand Manolya Restaurant and Pastane,** 68 Atatürk Cad. (tel. 223 1731), serves a wide range of food and drink on the second floor of its dessertery. (Open daily 8am-midnight; *kebap* $1.75, large beer $1.50.) Similar food for similar prices can be found in **Café Kristal** (tel. 223 2267), next door, but in a slightly more formal atmosphere.

Nightlife, which hardly exists in Kars, is best sought in the restaurants that stay open late and serve alcohol. Try the lively **Otogar Restaurant,** Kazım Karabaçır İşhane (tel. 212 0273; open daily 9am-11pm), roughly 200m east of the Akbank, on the second floor. Eat, shoot pool, and bop to the sounds of Turkish pop. (Open daily 9am-11pm; *kebap* $1.50, large beer 70¢.)

SIGHTS

In good weather, consider picnicking on the **castle's** grassy fortifications, and enjoy a panoramic view of the city and mountains beyond. The castle, originally built by the Seljuks in 1152, was razed by Tamerlane in 1386 and rebuilt in 1579 by Sultan Murat III. (Open daily 8am-noon, 1-5:30pm; free.) **Kars Museum** (tel. 223 2453; open daily 8am-noon, 1:30-5:30pm; admission $2.25, students $1.25), on Ardahan Cad. at the southeast edge of town, contains mostly pottery and regional black-and-white photographs. Its treasures include a dinosaur bone, local *kilim,* and ornately carved wooden doors from a Russian Orthodox Church (now Fethiye Camii).

■■■ ANİ

Despite the harsh climate of the earthquake- and thunder-ridden northeast, Armenian religious monuments of one thousand years miraculously survive at Ani, 48km east of Kars. The Armenians pioneered unprecedented height in their churches by employing a combination of locally abundant sandstone and hard volcanic rock. Their achievement is definitely worth your while if your plans include Artvin or Erzurum, the regional capitals nearest to Kars.

Orientation and Practical Information Ani is a triangular plateau wedged southward between the deep courses of the Alaçay and Arpaçay Rivers, on the west and east, respectively. Armenia lies visibly on the east bank of the Arpaçay, and the terrain rises as you move south towards the Turkish-flag-topped citadel, where a red- and white-striped pole on its east side advertises the beginning of No Man's Land. Access to the plateau is gained by the **Aslan Kapısı** (Lion's Gate), in the middle of the 2500m long, 8m- to 10m-high north walls (972 AD).

Because the sight abuts Armenia, you need special permission to visit it; tourists collect at the Kars tourist office, where friendly staff help with the brief application for permission and arrange a shared taxi. The cabbie ferries them to the Kars museum, the *only* place to buy tickets to the ruins (open daily 7am-6pm; $2.25, students $1.25). (All three places open daily in summer.) A cheaper alternative to taking a taxi is **Ani Tour,** 9 Eski Otogar (tel. 223 7766), which offers daily tours of the site for $6.75 per person, provided that at least four people show up. The only municipal bus to the site does not return until the morning after, and it is illegal for foreigners to spend the night within 15km of the Armenian border.

A guard in Ocaklı will retain your approved application, and an attendant will take your ticket as you enter the ruins. The ride from Kars to Ani lasts 1hr., and since you'll want to spend at least 2hr. exploring the plateau, figure a longer waiting period into the taxi price ($22-45, including 2-hr. wait at Ani). Refreshments are not likely to be available at Ani for another two years, so bring plenty of water. You'll also want bug repellent or a fan to combat the gnats. Try to set off in the morning by 9 or 10am to avoid getting caught in the occasional mid-afternoon thundershowers.

Sights Ani flourished under the Armenians until 1064, when Alpaslan—a Seljuk Turk—conquered the city on his historic entry into Anatolia. As the first Turkish *conquistador,* he is responsible for several "firsts" that Ani boasts. Once through the **Aslan Kapısı,** which takes its name from a lion relief emblematic of the first Seljuk tribe to occupy the region, glance back to see an Armenian cross above the entrance. On the wall inside to the right of that gate stands the inconspicuous **Ejderha Tower,** a 12th-century medical center counted as the first Turkish hospital in Anatolia. From the gate a stone-lined path leads east (left); this is the beginning of the clockwise route that hits most of the worthwhile sights. The first church you come to is the **Pircht Church** (Church of our Redeemer), half rubble since lightning struck it in 1957. On the west side you'll find a characteristic Armenian cross, and far above hovers a carving of an angel. Between the Aslan Kapısı and Pircht Church, the way overlooks valley **caves** inhabited from 3000 years ago up to the turn of the century, at least in summer. Downhill lies the **Tigran Honentz Church** (1215), dedicated to St. Gregory, featuring frescoes from the Bible and Armenian apocrypha. On the Arpaçay River face is a small, 12-sectioned, semicircular sundial as well as animal reliefs, which hide between the archtops like oversized animal crackers.

As you climb back onto the plateau, you'll pass what would resemble a burial mound if it weren't for the stone-delineated parking spaces in front—the mound actually serves as a military helipad. Next comes the **Cathedral of the Virgin Mary** (built 939-1001), the largest Christian building in Ani. It was designed by Titridates, who made a name for himself by restoring İstanbul's Ayasofya after earthquake damage. A passage on the left of the altar space leads upstairs to a private room; bring a flashlight to avoid a nasty fall. (To the north of the cathedral, although not really on the way, slumber the half-excavated foundations of the bigger of the town's two *hamam.*) Continuing west from the cathedral, **Menuçehr Camii** (1072) is supposedly the first Seljuk mosque in Anatolia. Its octagonal minaret is unusually inscribed with Allah's name, as if the rather church-like structure would otherwise be mistaken for one of its Christian neighbors. The riverbank here affords a view of the ruined **stone bridge** which marks Ani's place on the Silk Road and farther down the off-limits **Convent of the Virgins.** Southernmost on the plateau, the 4th-century **citadel,** which claims the best views of both Ani and the Armenian border, has naturally attracted soldiers, occasionally posted there to prevent tourists from wandering farther south. If you get to the top, scan south for a glimpse of the forbidden **Kızkalesi Church** on the riverbank.

Northwest of the Menuçehr Camii stands the **Polatoğlu Church,** which, despite having lost its frescoes, at least boasts some Armenian graffiti from the late 19th century. Northeast rests the former **Church of the Apostles,** a complete cultural melange since Seljuk conquerors enlarged it into a *kervansaray* with a characteristic Seljuk façade. The last of the rotunda-style churches, **Gagik Church** (1001) is back to the northwest, with little to offer but a wealth of toppled columns. The **Seljuk Palace,** northwest again, is fascinating for its three floors overlooking the Alaçay River valley, and its geometric stonework. Be careful of the holes in the middle of the floor. Whistle out into the cave-lined valley for an echo. You can walk around the side of the palace down to the bottom level, where you'll hear the squeaks of a small bat population. On the outside of the city walls to the north, a large raised **Rock Church** stands on the hillside. Your tour is now complete. If you have energy left for wandering, consider working your way back east to the ancient center of town, where the main street will guide you north back to the Aslan Kapısı.

GLOSSARY

GREEK

The table of the Greek alphabet (only 24 letters) below will help you decipher signs. The left column gives you the names of the letters in Greek, the middle column shows the printed lower case and capital letters, and the right column provides the approximate pronunciations of the letters.

alpha	α Α	*a* as in cat
beta	β Β	*v* as in voluminous
gamma	γ Γ	before vowels, *y* as in yo-yo; otherwise a hard *g* as in garter pronounced in the back of the throat
delta	δ Δ	*th* as in bother
epsilon	ε Ε	*e* as in hell
zeta	ζ Ζ	*z* as in zealous
eta	η Η	*ee* or *ea* as in creep
theta	θ Θ	*th* as in theater
iota	ι Ι	*ee* as in treat
kappa	κ Κ	*k* as in kettle
lambda	λ Λ	*l* as in larceny
mu	μ Μ	*m* as in mathematics
nu	ν Ν	*n* as in nascent
ksi	ξ Ξ	*x* as in ducks
omicron	ο Ο	*o* as in Robert
pi	π Π	*p* as in partake
rho	ρ Ρ	*r* as in raven
sigma	σ Σ	*s* in Sue
tau	τ Τ	*t* as in tawdry
upsilon	υ Υ	*ee* as in flee
phi	φ Φ	*f* as in fail
xi	χ Χ	*ch* as in the Scottish *loch*
psi	ψ Ψ	*ps* as in quips
omega	ω Ω	*o* as in ought

GREETINGS AND COURTESIES

In the phrases below, note that "dh" is pronounced like "th" in "the," and that "ch" is pronounced like "ch" in the Scottish "loch."

Good morning	ΚΑΛΗΜΕΡΑ	kah-lee-ME-rah
Good evening	ΚΑΛΗΣΠΕΡΑ	kah-lee-SPE-rah
Good night	ΚΑΛΗΝΥΧΤΑ	kah-lee-NEE-khtah
yes	ΝΑΙ	NEH
no	ΟΧΙ	OH-khee
please/you're welcome	ΠΑΡΑΚΑΛΩ	pah-rah-kah-LO
thank you (very much)	ΕΥΧΑΡΙΣΤΩ	ef-khah-ree-STO (po-LEE)
excuse me	ΣΥΓΓΝΩΜΗ	seeg-NO-mee
hello (polite,plural form)	ΓΕΙΑ ΣΑΣ	YAH-sas
hello (familiar form)	ΓΕΙΑ ΣΟΥ	YAH-soo
OK	ΕΝΤΑΞΕΙ	en-DAHK-see
What is your name?	ΠΩΣ ΣΕ ΛΕΝΕ	pos-se-LEH-neh
My name is ...	ΜΕ ΛΕΝΕ	me-LEH-neh ...

Mr./Sir	ΚΥΡΙΟΣ	kee-REE-os
Ms./Madam	ΚΥΡΙΑ	kee-REE-ah

WHERE?

Where is ... ?	ΠΟΥ ΕΙΝΑΙ	pou-EE-neh ... ?
I'm going to ...	ΠΗΓΑΙΝΩ ΓΙΑ	pee-YEH-no yah ...
When do we leave?	ΤΙ ΩΡΑ ΦΕΥΓΟΥΜΕ	tee O-rah FEV-goo-meh?
restaurant	ΕΣΤΙΑΤΟΡΙΟ	es-tee-ah-TO-ree-o
post office	ΤΑΧΥΔΡΟΜΕΙΟ	ta-khee-dhro-MEE-o
market	ΑΓΟΡΑ	ah-go-RAH
museum	ΜΟΥΣΕΙΟ	mou-SEE-o
pharmacy	ΦΑΡΜΑΚΕΙΟ	fahr-mah-KEE-o
bank	ΤΡΑΠΕΖΑ	TRAH-peh-zah
church	ΕΚΚΛΗΣΙΑ	eh-klee-SEE-ah
hotel	ΞΕΝΟΔΟΧΕΙΟ	kse-no-dho-HEE-o
room	ΔΩΜΑΤΙΟ	dho-MAH-teeo
suitcase	ΒΑΛΙΤΣΑ	vah-LEE-tsah
airport	ΑΕΡΟΔΡΟΜΙΟ	ah-e-ro-DHRO-mee-o
airplane	ΑΕΡΟΠΛΑΝΟ	ah-e-ro-PLAH-no
train	ΤΡΑΙΝΟ	TREH-no
bus	ΛΕΩΦΟΡΕΙΟ	leh-o-fo-REE-o
ferry	ΠΛΟΙΟ	PLEE-o
ticket	ΕΙΣΙΤΗΡΙΟ	ee-see-TEE-ree-o
doctor	ΓΙΑΤΡΟΣ	yah-TROS
right	ΔΕΞΙΑ	dhek-see-AH
left	ΑΡΙΣΤΕΡΑ	ah-rees-teh-RAH
here, there	ΕΔΩ, ΕΚΕΙ	eh-DHO, eh-KEE
open, closed	ΑΝΟΙΧΤΟ, ΚΛΕΙΣΤΩ	ah-nee-KTO, klee-STO

HOW MUCH?

How much?	ΠΟΣΟ ΚΑΝΕΙ	PO-so KAH-nee
I need	ΧΡΕΙΑΖΟΜΑΙ	khree-AH-zo-meh
I want	ΘΕΛΩ	THEH-lo
I would like ...	ΘΑ ΗΘΕΛΑ	thah EE-the-lah ...
I will buy this one	ΘΑ ΑΓΟΡΑΣΩ ΑΥΤΟ	thah ah-go-RAH-so ahf-TO
Do you have?	ΕΧΕΤΕ	Eh-khe-teh
Can I see a room?	ΜΠΟΡΩ ΝΑ ΔΩ ΕΝΑ ΔΩΜΑΤΙΟ	bo-RO nah-DHO E-nah dho-MAH-tee-o
bill	ΛΟΓΑΡΙΑΣΜΟ	lo-gahr-yah-SMO
newspaper	ΕΦΗΜΕΡΙΔΑ	eh-fee-meh-REE-dha
water	ΝΕΡΟ	ne-RO
good	ΚΑΛΟ	kah-LO
cheap	ΦΤΗΝΟ	ftee-NO
expensive	ΑΚΡΙΒΟ	ah-kree-VO

WHEN?

What time is it?	ΤΙ ΩΡΑ ΕΙΝΑΙ	tee O-rah EE-neh?
first	ΠΡΩΤΟ	PRO-to
last	ΤΕΛΕΥΤΑΙΟ	teh-lef-TEH-o
one	ΕΝΑ	Eh-nah
two	ΔΥΟ	DHEE-o
three	ΤΡΙΑ	TREE-ah
four	ΤΕΣΣΕΡΑ	TES-ser-ah
five	ΠΕΝΤΕ	PEN-dheh

six	ΕΞΙ	E-ksee
seven	ΕΠΤΑ	ep-TAH
eight	ΟΧΤΩ	okh-TO
nine	ΕΝΝΙΑ	en-YAH
ten	ΔΕΚΑ	DHEH-kah
eleven	ΕΝΔΕΚΑ	EN-dheh-kah
twelve	ΔΩΔΕΚΑ	DHO-dheh-kah
morning	ΠΡΩΙ	pro-EE
evening	ΒΡΑΔΥ	VRAH-dhee
tonight	ΑΠΟΨΕ	ah-PO-pseh
yesterday	ΧΘΕΣ	ekh-THES
today	ΣΗΜΕΡΑ	SEE-meh-rah
tomorrow	ΑΥΡΙΟ	AH-vree-o

PROBLEMS

Do you speak English?	ΜΙΛΑΣ ΑΓΓΛΙΚΑ?	mee-LAHS ahn-glee-KAH?
I don't speak Greek	ΔΕΝ ΜΙΛΑΩ ΕΛΛΗΝΙΚΑ	dhen mee-LAHO el-leen-ee-KAH
I don't understand	ΔΕΝ ΚΑΤΑΛΑΒΑΙΝΩ	dhen kah-tah-lah-VEH-no
I am lost	ΧΑΘΗΚΑ	HA-thee-ka
I am ill	ΕΙΜΑΙ ΑΡΡΩΣΤΟΣ	EE-meh AH-ross-toss
Help!	ΒΟΗΘΕΙΑ	vo-EE-thee-ah

TURKISH

Be aware that certain letters and combinations of letters in Turkish are pronounced differently from English. Turkish is a phonetic language: each letter has only one sound, and this is always pronounced distinctly. Words are usually lightly accented on the last syllable; special vowels, consonants, and combinations include:

Turkish	**English**
c	*j* as in juxtapose
ç	*ch* as in cheapen
ğ	lengthens adjacent vowels
ı	(no dot on the "i") *i* as in fir
i	*ee* as in creed, but shorter
j	*zh* as in pleasure, or *j* as in French *jadis*
ö	*ö* as in German *könig,* or *eu* as in French *deux*
ş	*sh* as in shave
u	*oo* as in boot
â	dipthong of *ea,* or faint *ya*
ü	*ew* as in lewd
ay	*eye* as in wry
ey	*ay* as in may
oy	*oy* as in soy
uy	*oo-ee* as in hooey

GREETINGS AND COURTESIES

good morning	*günaydın*	gewn eye-DUHN
good evening	*iyi akşamlar*	ee-YEE ahk-sham-LAR
good night	*iyi geceler*	ee-YEE geh-jeh-LEHR
yes, no	*evet, hayır*	EH-vet, HIGH-yuhr
please	*lütfen*	LEWT-fen
thank you (formal)	*teşekkürler*	tay-shayk-kewr-LEHR
thank you (informal)	*sağol*	SAA-ohl
you're welcome	*bir şey değil*	beer shay DEE-yeel
pardon me	*affedersiniz*	ahf-feh-DEHR-see-neez
hello	*merhaba*	MEHR-hah-bah
good bye (said by a guest)	*allaha ısmarladık*	aw-LAH-huss-small-duck
good bye (said by a host)	*güle güle*	gew-LAY-gew-lay
beautiful, good	*güzel*	gew-ZEHL
okay	*pekiyi*	PEHK-ee-yee
What is your name?	*İsminiz ne?*	ees-meen-eez NEH
My name is ...	*İsmim ...*	ees-MEEM
Mr./Sir	*Bay*	Bye
Ms/Madam	*Bayan*	Bye-AHN

WHERE?

Where is... ?	*...nerede?*	...NEHR-eh-deh
I'm traveling to...	*...ya seyahat ediyorum*	...ya say-yah-HAHT eh-dee-OHR-room
How near is it?	*Ne kadar yakın?*	NEH-kah-dahr yah-KUN
post office	*postane*	post-aaaah-NEH
museum	*müze*	mew-ZEH
hotel	*otel*	oh-TEL
room	*yer, oda*	OH-da
toilet	*tuvalet*	too-vah-LET
airport	*hava alanı*	hah-VAH-ah-lahn-uh
bus	*otobüs*	oh-toh-BOOS
doctor	*doktor*	dohk-TOHR
grocery	*bakkal*	bahk-KAHL
pharmacy	*eczane*	ej-zaaaah-NEH
bank	*banka*	BAHN-kah
police	*polis*	poh-LEES
left, right	*sol, sağ*	sohl, saah
passport	*pasaport*	pahs-ah-PORT
train	*tren*	trehn
ticket	*bilet*	bee-LET
here, there	*burada, orada*	BOOR-ah-dah, OHR-ah-dah
open, closed	*açık, kapalı*	ah-CHUHK, kah-pah-LUH

HOW MUCH?

How much is it?	*Kaç para?* or *Ne kadar?*	KACH-pah-rah NEH-kah-dar
I want ...	*...istiyorum*	ees-tee-YOH-room...
a double room	*iki kişilik oda*	ee-KEE kee-shee-leek OH-dah
a twin-bedded room	*çift yataklı oda*	CHEEFT yah-tahk-LUH OH-dah
I do not want any.	*Yok.*	YOHK
cheap, expensive	*ucuz, pahalı*	oo-JOOZ, pah-hah-LUH

bill	*hesap*	hessahp
water	*su*	soo

WHEN?

What time is it?	*Saat kaç?*	SAH-aht kahch
yesterday	*dün*	dewn
today	*bugün*	boo-GEWN
tomorrow	*yarın*	YAHR-uhn

NUMBERS

zero	*sıfır*	SUF-fuhr
quarter	*çeyrek*	chay-REK
half a...	*yarım...*	yahr-UHM
one	*bir*	beer
...and a half	*...buçuk*	boo-CHOOK
two	*iki*	ee-KEE
three	*üç*	ewch
four	*dört*	duhrt
five	*beş*	besh
six	*altı*	ahl-TUH
seven	*yedi*	yeh-DEE
eight	*sekiz*	seh-KEEZ
nine	*dokuz*	DOH-kooz
ten	*on*	ohn
eleven	*on bir*	OHN-bir
twelve	*on iki*	OHN-ee-kee
thirteen	*on üç*	OHN-ewch
twenty	*yirmi*	yeer-MEE
thirty	*otuz*	OH-tooz
forty	*kırk*	kirk
fifty	*elli*	ehl-LEE
sixty	*altmış*	ahlt-MUSH
seventy	*yetmiş*	yet-MEESH
eighty	*seksen*	sehk-SEN
ninety	*doksan*	dohk-SAHN
hundred	*yüz*	yewz
thousand	*bin*	been
million	*milyon*	meel-YOHN

The days of the week: *Pazar* (Sun.), *Pazartesi* (Mon.), *Salı (Tues.), Çarşamba* (Wed.), *Perşembe* (Thurs.), *Cuma* (Fri.), and *Cumartesi* (Sat.).

PROBLEMS

I don't understand.	*Anlamadım.*	ahn-LAH-mah-duhm
Do you speak English?	*İngilizçe biliyor musunuz?*	EEN-ghee-leez-jeh bee-lee-YOHR-moo-soo-nooz
I don't speak Turkish.	*Türkçe bilmiyorum.*	TEWRK-cheh BEEHL-mee-yohr-oom
I'm lost!	*Yolumu kaybettim!*	YOHL-loo-moo KIGH-bet-tim
I am ill.	*Hastayım.*	hahs-TAH-yuhm
Help!	*İmdat!*	im-DAHT

INDEX